INTERNATIONAL HANDBOOK ON TEACHING AND LEARNING ECONOMICS

T0327562

International Handbook on Teaching and Learning Economics

Edited by

Gail M. Hoyt

Professor of Economics, University of Kentucky, USA

KimMarie McGoldrick

Joseph A. Jennings Chair in Business, Professor of Economics, University of Richmond, USA

Edward Elgar
Cheltenham, UK • Northampton, MA, USA

Published by
Edward Elgar Publishing Limited
The Lypiatts
15 Lansdown Road
Cheltenham
Glos GL50 2JA
UK

Edward Elgar Publishing, Inc.
William Pratt House
9 Dewey Court
Northampton
Massachusetts 01060
USA

A catalogue record for this book
is available from the British Library

Library of Congress Control Number: 2011934812

ISBN 978 1 84844 968 8 (cased)
ISBN 978 1 78100 193 6 (paperback)

Typeset by Servis Filmsetting Ltd, Stockport, Cheshire

Contents

Section B   Technology

Section C   Assessment

Section D   Contextual Techniques

Section E   Elementary, Secondary Economic Education

PART III   RESEARCH

Section A   Principles Courses

PART V   INSTITUTIONAL / ADMINISTRATIVE

Section A   Faculty Development: Mentoring, Evaluation, Documentation and Resources

Section B   Undergraduate Education

Section C   The Characteristics of Economics Graduate Students

Section D   International Economic Education

PART VI   INITIATIVES FOR TEACHING ENHANCEMENT

Section A   Private, Corporate and Government Funding for Economic Education

Section B   An Introduction to Economic Education Organizations in the US and Beyond

Section C   Economics Teaching Workshops: Past, Present, Future

Figures

Tables

Contributors

Peter von Allmen is a Professor in the Department of Economics at Skidmore College. Previously, he was also Professor of Economics at Moravian College, and a Fellow of the American Council on Education. He received his BA from the College of Wooster and Ph.D. from Temple University. His primary research area is the economics of sports, focused primarily on compensation schemes, incentives and monopsony power. He has also published in the areas of family labor supply and post-secondary pedagogy. Professor von Allmen is the co-author of two textbooks: *The Economics of Sports* (with Michael Leeds), now in its fourth edition, and *Economics* (with Michael Leeds and Richard Schiming).

William T. Alpert, Associate Professor of Economics, University of Connecticut is co-founding managing partner of FIDES, Philanthropic Management and Advisory Services, LLC. Formerly Senior Program Officer of the William H. Donner Foundation, he publishes in labor economics. He is Executive Director of the Connecticut Council on Economic Education and Director of the Center for Economic Education at the University. He serves on several not-for-profit boards of directors. Alpert previously taught at Lehigh University (1981–3), Washington University, St Louis (1977–81), and Columbia University (1973–7). Alpert earned his Ph.D., M. Phil., and MA degrees (Economics) Columbia University and AB from Lehigh University.

Carlos Asarta is an Assistant Professor of Practice in Economics at the University of Nebraska-Lincoln. His scholarly work focuses on the areas of economic education, assessment and economic literacy. Dr. Asarta is the recipient of several teaching and research awards, including the ASUN Outstanding Educator of the Year (2009) and the Bauermeister Award (2009) for outstanding research. He is a Research Associate with the National Center for Research in Economic Education, Professor with the Foundation for Teaching Economics, Chair of the University Teaching Council and an active Associate of the Nebraska Council on Economic Education.

Joann Bangs is an Associate Professor of Economics at St. Catherine University in St. Paul, Minnesota. She also teaches in St. Catherine's Master of Arts in Organizational Leadership and Doctor of Nurse Practitioner programs. She earned her Ph.D. in economics from the University of Minnesota. Her published papers in economics education include, "Thinking on the Margin: A Classroom Experiment" (*American Journal of Business Education*, 2009) and "Extending Learning Beyond the Exam: Multiple Choice Tests" (*Journal of College Teaching and Learning*, 2008). Her working paper, "Teaching Perfect and Imperfect Competition with Context-Rich Problems", is available on the Social Science Research Network.

Daniel Barbezat is Professor of Economics at Amherst College and has been teaching economic history courses at Amherst since 1988. In addition, he has also taught at Northwestern University, Yale University and Harvard University. In 2004, he was awarded the Economic History Association's Jonathan R. T. Hughes Prize for

Excellence in Teaching. He has published research concerning the International Steel Cartel of the 1920s and 1930s, the pre-history of the European Union and the economics of the European Union. Currently, he is working on the impact of mindfulness on economic decision making and is working on a book entitled *Wanting*.

Robin L. Bartlett received her AB from Western College for Women in Oxford, Ohio and her MS and Ph.D. in Economics from Michigan State University. She is the JPMorgan Chase Professor of Economics and was the Laura C. Harris Chair in Women's Studies (1996–8) at Denison University in Granville, Ohio. In 1998, she received the Carnegie Foundation for the Advancement of Teaching and the Council for the Advancement and Support of Education (CASE) Ohio Professor of the Year Award. She edited *Introducing Race and Gender into Economics* (Routledge, 1997). Bartlett served on the American Economic Association's Committee on Economic Education (1989–94).

Mary Ellen Benedict is a Distinguished Teaching Professor at Bowling Green State University. She received her Ph.D. from the Heinz College at Carnegie Mellon University in 1991. Dr Benedict has published in the fields of economics education, unionization in higher education, wage differentials, and income inequality. She also has won university and national teaching and advising awards for her work with undergraduate and graduate students.

Roger D. Blair is the Walter J. Matherly Professor of Economics at the University of Florida where he has taught for 40 years. He is the co-author of *Antitrust Economics, Law and Economics of Vertical Integration and Control, Monopsony in Law and Economics*, and Volume IIA of *Antitrust Law*. In addition, he has published dozens of articles on various issues in antitrust. He has served as an antitrust economics expert in over 50 lawsuits.

Francine D. Blau is Frances Perkins Professor of Industrial and Labor Relations and Labor Economics at Cornell University and a Research Associate of the National Bureau of Economic Research. She has written extensively on gender issues and inequality. She received the Carolyn Shaw Bell Award from the American Economic Association Committee on the Status of Women in the Economics Profession in 2001 and the IZA Prize for outstanding academic achievement in the field of labor economics in 2010. She is co-author, with Marianne Ferber and Anne Winkler, of *The Economics of Women, Men, and Work*, currently in its sixth edition.

Cecil E. Bohanon is a Professor of Economics at Ball State University. He obtained his BA from Wilmington College (Ohio) and his Ph.D. from Virginia Tech. He has published over 25 refereed professional articles, notes and comments and over 70 popular articles, policy monographs and newspaper editorials. His research interests include public choice, applied microeconomics, and economic education. He was a 2007 winner of the Stavros Teaching Award in Economics Education. In 2009 he was a Virginia Ball Fellow directing the student produced Emmy award-winning film *Increasing the Odds*.

William Bosshardt is an associate professor of economics and director of the Center for Economic Education at Florida Atlantic University. He is currently the reviews editor for the *International Review of Economics Education* and associate editor of the *American Economist*. He has published in a number of journals, including the *Review of Economics and Statistics*, the *American Economic Review*, the *Journal of Economic Education*, and *Economic Inquiry*.

Stephen Buckles currently teaches large and small classes in the Department of Economics at Vanderbilt University. He served as President of the (now) Council on Economic Education in New York. He taught at the University of Missouri – Columbia and headed the Center for Economic Education there. He has worked in the design and development of the National Assessment of Educational Progress Economics exams. He chaired the College Board's initial Economics Advanced Placement Committee. He received the Henry H. Villard Research Award for his research in economic education. His teaching has been recognized with awards from the University of Missouri, the Southern Economics Association, and Vanderbilt.

Joseph Calhoun is a Lecturer in the Economics Department and Assistant Director of the Stavros Center for Economic Education at Florida State University. His teaching focus is on introductory economics, with annual enrollment over 2,000 students. To enhance student learning, he is a heavy user of technology both in and outside the classroom. He is also well known for showing video clips to illustrate concepts. He has presented teaching ideas and technology at several national conferences. He is also responsible for training new graduate students for their initial teaching responsibilities. His Ph.D. is from the University of Georgia.

James F. Casey is Associate Professor of Economics and Environmental Studies at Washington and Lee University. His research and teaching interests lie at the intersection of development and environmental economics. He has studied and conducted research in Central America and the Caribbean for over 14 years. He has published articles in numerous economics and interdisciplinary journals, including: the *Journal of Post-Keynesian Economics,* the *Journal of Sustainable Tourism, Ecological Economics,* the *International Journal of Sustainable Development,* and *Problemas de Desarrollo.* Casey is the founder and President of *General Development Initiative, Inc.*: a non-profit organization involved in microfinance initiatives, poverty reduction, and sustainable development, worldwide.

Avi J. Cohen is Professor of Economics at York University and a Senior Research Fellow at Duke University's Center for the History of Political Economy. He has a Ph.D. from Stanford University, is a past President of the History of Economics Society and works in the history of economics, economic history and economic education. He is the author of *Economics for Life: Smart Choices for You, Smart Choices for All?* (Pearson Canada, 2010, 2011), textbooks aimed at educating citizens. He is the winner of numerous teaching awards, including Canada's most prestigious national award for educational leadership, the 3M Teaching Fellowship.

Patrick Conway is Bowman and Gordon Gray Professor of Economics at the University of North Carolina (UNC) at Chapel Hill, where he has taught courses in introductory, international, development and macroeconomics. He was awarded UNC's William C. Friday Award for excellence in teaching, and was inducted into the Order of the Golden

Fleece and the Frank Porter Graham Honor Society. He received the Pew Faculty Fellowship at Harvard University for his work with the case method. He has conducted teaching workshops on using cases for the American Economic Association, the World Bank, the International Finance Corporation, and university economics departments.

Joab N. Corey is a lecturer in the Department of Economics and a member of the Excellence in Economics Education faculty in the Stavros Center for the Advancement of Free Enterprise and Economic Education at Florida State University. He specializes in teaching large section principles of economics and introduction to economics classes, where he uses interactive class demonstrations, video clips, pop-culture examples, student-designed economic T-shirts, and occasional acrobatics to create an enthusiastic student learning environment. He received his bachelor's, master's, and Ph.D. in Economics from West Virginia University, where his teaching efforts were inspired by Professor Russell Sobel.

Dean Croushore is Professor of Economics and Rigsby Fellow at the University of Richmond and chair of the Economics department. He came to the University of Richmond in 2003 after 14 years as an economist at the Federal Reserve Bank of Philadelphia. Dr. Croushore is a leading expert in the field of real-time data analysis, which studies the implications of data revisions on forecasting, monetary policy, and macroeconomic research. Dr. Croushore's publications include articles in many leading economics journals. He is author of *M&B,* published by Cengage, and co-author with Andrew Abel and Ben Bernanke of *Macroeconomics,* seventh edition.

Peter Davies is Professor of Education Policy Research at the University of Birmingham, UK. He is joint editor of the *International Review of Economics Education* and serves on the editorial boards of *Education,* the *Journal of Social Science Education*, and *Teaching Business and Economics.* He is co-author (with Jacek Brant) of *Economics, Business and Enterprise: Teaching School Subjects 11–19* and (with Nick Adnett) of *Markets for Schooling: An Economic Analysis,* both published by Routledge. His research interests are divided between economics education and economic analysis of secondary and higher education.

David H. Dean is currently an Associate Professor of Economics at the University of Richmond and Co-Director of the Bureau of Disability Economics Research, which assesses the effectiveness of return-to-work programs for persons with disabilities. He became involved in exploring the economics curricula at other schools while re-designing the economics major requirements at Richmond. This work led to a publication in 2001 in the *Journal of Economic Education* which examined the character of the economics curriculum at liberal arts and business schools. His more recent interest is in the development of capstone courses within the major.

Stephen B. DeLoach is currently Professor of Economics at Elon University where he has worked since 1996. He has published a number of articles on pedagogy in journals like the *Journal of Economic Education* and *Contemporary Economic Policy*. He has contributed a number of modules on undergraduate research and mentoring that reside on the Starting Point: Teaching and Learning in Economics website. Since 1998, Steve has served as faculty co-advisor for *Issues in Political Economy*, an undergraduate research journal in economics, and has co-organized undergraduate research sessions at the Eastern Economics Association conference annually since 1998.

Robert C. Dolan is Professor of Economics in the Robins School of Business at the University of Richmond. His publications have appeared in numerous academic journals, including the *Review of Economics and Statistics,* the *Journal of Human Resources,* and the *Journal of Economic Education.* His research in the economics of education has been funded by the National Science Foundation. Dr. Dolan has held the Joseph Jennings Chair in Business, the David Meade White Distinguished Teaching Fellowship, and has received several university awards for teaching.

Alan Duhs recently retired as a Senior Lecturer at the University of Queensland, where he taught economics for many years. He is the winner of teaching excellence awards and was a founding editor of the *Australasian Journal of Economics Education.* His research areas include economic development, economic philosophy, higher education and applied microeconomics. He has published in such journals as the *Journal of Economic Issues, Economic Record, International Journal of Social Economics, Indian Journal of Quantitative Economics, Australian Journal of Education, Journal of Tertiary Education Administration, Australian Psychologist,* and *Review of Development Economics.*

Christine Piette Durrance is an Assistant Professor at the University of North Carolina at Chapel Hill in the Department of Public Policy. She teaches an undergraduate elective on business and competition policy. She is a co-author of Volume IIA of *Antitrust Law* and has published a number of papers on antitrust law and economics topics. Additionally, she has written on empirical health economics and policy issues.

Kenneth G. Elzinga is the Robert C. Taylor Professor of Economics at the University of Virginia where he has served on the faculty since 1967. During his career, he has received numerous teaching awards. An expert in antitrust economics, he has testified in several precedent-setting antitrust cases, including three Supreme Court decisions. The author of more than seventy academic publications, Mr. Elzinga also is known for his mystery novels (under the pen name Marshall Jevons), in which economic analysis is used to solve the crimes. Mr. Elzinga's BA is from Kalamazoo College and Ph.D. from Michigan State University.

Tisha Emerson, Associate Professor of Economics at Baylor University in Waco, Texas, studies the efficacy of active learning pedagogical strategies in promoting student achievement – with particular interest in classroom experiments. Her work in economic education has been published in the *Southern Economic Journal*, the *Journal of Economic Education*, and the *International Review of Economics Education*. Tisha served on the staff of the AEA's Teaching Innovations Program and was a contributor to Starting Point's classroom experiments module. She currently serves on the AEA's Committee on Economic Education, and is an Associate Editor for the *Journal of Economic Education*.

Ross B. Emmett is Professor of Political Economy and Political Theory & Constitutional Democracy, James Madison College, Michigan State University. He recently released a volume of collected essays, *Frank Knight and the Chicago School in American Economics* with Routledge, and is the editor of the *Elgar Companion to the Chicago School of*

Economics, released by Edward Elgar in 2010. He co-edits *Research in the History of Economic Thought and Methodology* with Jeff Biddle and Marianne Johnson.

Deborah M. Figart is Professor of Education and Economics at The Richard Stockton College of New Jersey. She is also Director of the Stockton Center for Economic & Financial Literacy and Vice-Chair of the New Jersey Coalition for Financial Education. She develops and teaches educational and professional training for students, teachers, and adults. Figart has published numerous books and articles on economics topics related to the labor market: pay equity, discrimination, working time, job evaluation, emotional labor, career ladders, employment policies, and poverty. From 2006–7, she served as President of the Association for Social Economics.

Price Fishback is the Thomas R. Brown Professor of Economics at the University of Arizona, where he has won several teaching awards. He has served as the primary advisor on the dissertation committees for over 60 Ph.D. students. His research on historical labor markets and government programs has appeared in three books and in dozens of journal articles and book chapters. Price organized the writing of *Government and the American Economy: A New History*, which is used as supplemental reading in a number of economic history courses. He currently serves as a co-editor of the *Journal of Economic History.*

Christopher L. Foote is a senior economist and policy advisor at the Federal Reserve Bank of Boston. After receiving an economics Ph.D. from the University of Michigan in 1996, Foote taught at Harvard University, where he was responsible for the economics department's largest section of intermediate macro. In 2002, Foote accepted a position as a senior staff economist for macro at the Council of Economic Advisers, serving as the CEA's chief economist in early 2003. Later that year, Foote moved to the Boston Fed, and he has taught intermediate macro at Harvard as a visitor since 2008.

Robert H. Frank is a Cornell economist and a columnist for *The New York Times.* He also co-directs the Paduano Seminar in business ethics at NYU's Stern School. His books, which include *Choosing the Right Pond, Passions Within Reason, The Winner-Take-All Society* (with Philip Cook), *Principles of Economics* (with Ben Bernanke), *Luxury Fever, The Economic Naturalist,* and *The Darwin Economy,* have been translated into 22 languages. He received the 2004 Leontief Prize for Advancing the Frontiers of Economic Thought, the Cornell Johnson School's Stephen Russell Distinguished Teaching Award in 2004 and 2010, and its Apple Distinguished Teaching Award in 2005.

Luke M. Froeb is the William Oehmig Associate Professor of Entrepreneurship and Free Enterprise at Vanderbilt University. After receiving his Ph.D. in econometrics from the University of Wisconsin, Professor Froeb taught at Tulane University, worked in the Antitrust Division of the US Department of Justice, and worked at the University of Chicago Law School before moving to Vanderbilt. In 2003, he was appointed Chief Economist to the Federal Trade Commission. In 2005, Professor Froeb returned to Vanderbilt and was voted Outstanding Professor of the executive MBA program for three years running. Southwestern originally published his textbook, *Managerial Economics: A Problem-Solving Approach* in 2007, with a second edition in 2010.

Robert F. Garnett, Jr. is Professor of Economics at Texas Christian University. He serves on the editorial boards of *Studies in Emergent Order* and the *International Journal of Pluralism and Economics Education* and as a contributing editor to *Conversations on Philanthropy*. His current work examines the goals and methods of liberal learning in undergraduate economics education, the virtues of pluralism in economic inquiry, and the relationship between commercial and philanthropic forms of economic cooperation.

William L. Goffe is a Professor at SUNY Oswego. He received his Ph.D. from the University of North Carolina at Chapel Hill. Early in his career he carried out research in computational economics and how economists use the Internet, while in recent years he has become interested in economic education. He has published in the *Journal of Econometrics*, the *Journal of Economic Perspectives*, and the *Journal of Economic Education*. He currently uses both peer instruction and team-based learning in his courses. He is currently an Associate Editor of the *Journal of Economic Education*.

Arthur H. Goldsmith is the Jackson T. Stephens Professor of Economics at Washington and Lee University. His research combines insights from economics, psychology, sociology, and history to explore questions regarding wages, employment, unemployment, psychological well-being, access to health-care, and educational accumulation. He has published articles in a number of the profession's leading journals, including: the *Journal of Economic Literature*, the *Journal of Economic Perspectives*, the *Journal of Human Resources*, *Economic Inquiry*, the *Southern Economic Journal*, and the *Journal of Economic Behavior and Organization*. Professor Goldsmith serves on the editorial board of the *Journal of Economic Psychology*, and the *Journal of Socio-Economics*.

Allen C. Goodman attended The University of Michigan (AB) and Yale University (Ph.D.). Before coming to Wayne State University in 1986, Professor Goodman taught at Lawrence University and at The Johns Hopkins University. He specializes in health economics and housing economics, and he has published over 75 articles and 3 books. He has had three major proposals funded through NIH, and he has served on other grants from the BCBSM (Michigan) and the Robert Wood Johnson Foundations. Since 1993, he has co-authored *The Economics of Health and Health Care* with Sherman Folland and Miron Stano (sixth edition, 2010).

Rae Jean B. Goodman, Professor of Economics at the US Naval Academy, was appointed Director of Teaching and Learning in 1996. As the Director, she has led faculty workshops for new and experienced faculty, consulted with faculty on teaching issues, and organized workshops by external presenters on teaching evaluation, teaching portfolios, and teaching techniques. She organized three workshops for economics faculty in the Baltimore-Washington area under the AEA-sponsored Regional Workshop Program and served on the AEA Committee on Economic Education. She co-authored the third edition of *Advanced Placement Economics* for the National Council on Economic Education, participated in a Starting Point workshop, and published in the *Journal of Economics and Finance*.

Steven A. Greenlaw is Professor of Economics at the University of Mary Washington in Fredericksburg, VA. He earned his Ph.D. in economics from the State University of New York at Binghamton in 1987. Steve has conducted research on economic education since

1991. He has given numerous conference presentations in this area, and has published pedagogical papers in a variety of journals, including the *Journal of Economic Education, Contemporary Economic Policy*, and the *International Review of Economic Education*. In 2005, his book, *Doing economics: A Guide to Understanding and Carrying Out Economic Research*, was published by Houghton-Mifflin (now Cengage).

Paul W. Grimes is Professor of Economics and Dean of the Kelce College of Business at Pittsburg State University in Kansas and Professor Emeritus of Economics at Mississippi State University. He has a long record of service in the field of economic education – in terms of both research and program delivery. In 2005, Professor Grimes was recognized for his economic education research with the Henry H. Villard Award presented by the National Council on Economic Education. In 2009 he served as president of the National Association of Economic Educators. He is the editor-in-chief of the *American Economist*.

Wayne A. Grove is a Professor of economics and department chair at Le Moyne College in Syracuse, NY. He conducts research on college student learning (e.g. "Incentives and Student Learning: A Natural Experiment with Economics Problem Sets," with Wasserman, *American Economic Review*, 2006), labor market issues regarding higher education, and responsibility attribution of public policy outcomes. Recent articles topics include: the role of noncognitive attributes and workplace preferences for the gender wage gap (*Journal of Human Resources*), the determinants of career success for economics Ph.D.s (*American Economic Review*), and estimated returns to areas of study in MBA programs (*Economic Inquiry*).

Ross Guest is Professor of Economics at Griffith University (Australia), an Adjunct Professor with the Australia and New Zealand School of Government (ANZSOG), a Teaching Fellow with the Australian Learning and Teaching Council (ALTC), and Co-Editor of the *International Review of Economics Education*. He has been teaching university economics for twenty years and taught secondary school economics for ten years. His primary research field is population economics, for which he has received four grants from the Australian Research Council and was an invited participant at the Prime Minister's 2020 Summit in 2008.

James D. Gwartney holds the Gus A. Stavros Eminent Scholar Chair at Florida State University, where he directs the Stavros Center for the Advancement of Free Enterprise and Economic Education. He is the co-author of *Economics: Private and Public Choice*, 13th edition (Cengage South-Western Press, 2010) and an economics primer, *Common Sense Economics: What Everyone Should Know About Wealth and Prosperity*, second edition (St. Martin's Press, 2010). He is also the co-author of the annual report, *Economic Freedom of the World*, which provides data on the consistency of institutions and policies with economic freedom for 141 countries.

Timothy C. Haab is a Professor and Chair in the Department of Agricultural, Environmental and Development Economics at The Ohio State University. He received a BS in Economics from the University of Maryland, Baltimore County (UMBC) in 1991 and a Ph.D. from the University of Maryland, College Park in 1995. His research and teaching focus on nonmarket valuation and econometrics. A previous co-editor of the *Journal of Environmental Economics and Management,* Tim spends his spare time coaching his kids' sports teams in the hopes they turn out to be better athletes than him (not a high hurdle).

W. Lee Hansen, Economics Professor Emeritus, UW-Madison, received his BA and MA from UW-Madison and his Ph.D. in Political Economy from Johns Hopkins University. He has been a Senior Staff Economist for the President's Council of Economic Advisers, Postdoctoral Fellow in Economics – University of Chicago, Guggenheim Fellow, and Fulbright Scholar – University of Sydney. He is recognized widely for his teaching and research in economic education, having received the Marvin Bower Award from the Council on Economic Education and Leavey Award for Excellence in Private Enterprise Education. He is currently writing a book about his "expected proficiencies" approach to the economics major.

Joseph E. Harrington, Jr. is Professor of Economics at Johns Hopkins University, and the author of *Games, Strategies, and Decision Making.* Revealing his love for applying game theory wherever it can enlighten, his research has appeared in leading journals in economics, management science, political science, psychology, and sociology. He is most well-known for his research on cartels and collusion which has been presented before competition authorities throughout the world, including those of the European Union, Japan, South Africa, and the United States, and he has given keynote lectures at many venues, including the European Association for Research in Industrial Economics.

Denise Hazlett, Professor of Economics at Whitman College in Walla Walla, Washington, specializes in designing classroom experiments. She served as a staff member for the American Economic Association's Teaching Innovation Program, providing training and mentoring for professors as they used experiments in their classes. The National Science Foundation gave her a grant to produce six hand-run experiments for macroeconomics courses. She worked with Aplia to computerize two of those experiments.

Barry T. Hirsch is the W.J. Usery Chair of the American Workplace and Professor of Economics, Andrew Young School of Policy Studies, Georgia State University. He is an applied labor economist whose research focuses on wage determination. His work includes the study of unions, survey nonresponse, discrimination, area wage differentials, and labor markets in airlines, trucking, and nursing. Hirsch is past president of the Southern Economic Association. He received his Ph.D. from the University of Virginia.

John Hoag came to Bowling Green State University in 1972 as a fresh Ph.D. from the University of Kansas. Except for the year 1980–81, when he was a Senior Engineer at the Jet Propulsion Laboratory in Pasadena, CA, he has remained at Bowling Green. He was promoted to Professor in 1982 and has been Chair since 1993. He has written an introductory text, and a mathematical economics text, as well as a number of papers in economic education. His undergraduate work was at Purdue, and he has a Master's degree from Minnesota.

Charles A. Holt is the A. Willis Robertson Professor of Political Economy and Chair of the Department of Economics at the University of Virginia. He is the director of the Experimental Economics Lab at Virginia, and his publications include over a hundred articles in academic journals, focused on game theory, auctions, experimental economics, and the teaching of economics. He has written and edited several books on topics in experimental economics, and was the founding co-editor of the journal, *Experimental Economics*. He has previously served as President of the Economic Science Foundation, the Southern Economic Association, and the Society of Economic Educators.

Jessica S. Howell is the Executive Director of Policy Research for the College Board's Advocacy & Policy Center. Prior to joining the College Board in 2011, Dr. Howell was Associate Professor of Economics at California State University, Sacramento. Engaged in quantitative research on pressing education policy issues, she has focused on access and success throughout the educational pipeline for traditionally underserved students. Current research projects focus on intersegmental alignment, early information about college readiness, and degree completion. Dr. Howell received her bachelor's degree in economics from James Madison University and her master's and Ph.D. in economics from the University of Virginia.

Gail M. Hoyt is Professor of Economics at the University of Kentucky where she serves as Director of Undergraduate Studies and as a teaching assistant coordinator, providing teacher training to graduate students. Gail has won various teaching awards and in 2005 was named a "Great Teacher in Economics," by the Stavros Center for Economics Education. Her publications and presentations in the area of economic education emphasize pedagogy in large lecture settings, interactive learning techniques, and graduate student training in economics Ph.D. programs. She coordinates a regional teaching workshop and has participated in NSF funded initiatives such as the Teaching Innovation Program and the Starting Point Project. She currently serves on the AEA's Committee on Economic Education and has served as President of the Society of Economic Educators.

Brad R. Humphreys is a Professor of Economics at the University of Alberta, and the Chair in the Economics of Gaming. He previously was on the faculty at the University of Illinois at Urbana-Champaign. He holds a Ph.D. in economics from the Johns Hopkins University. His research on the economics of gambling, the economic impact of professional sports, and the economics of intercollegiate athletics has been published in academic journals in economics, including the *Journal of Urban Economics,* the *Journal of Policy Analysis and Management*, and the *Journal of Economic Behavior and Organization*. He is Editor-in-Chief of *Contemporary Economic Policy*.

Jennifer Imazeki is Professor of Economics at San Diego State University where she teaches courses in applied microeconomics and data analysis. She has a BA from Pomona College and an MA and Ph.D. from the University of Wisconsin-Madison, all in economics. Her research focuses on the economics of K-12 education, including school finance reform, adequacy, and teacher labor markets. She has worked on several projects to encourage active learning in economics, particularly using technology, and writes a blog about teaching economics.

Elizabeth J. Jensen is a Professor of Economics at Hamilton College. Her teaching specialties are Industrial Organization, American Economic History, and Antitrust and

Regulation. Much of Jensen's recent research focuses on issues related to undergraduate education, including the relationship between application status and academic performance in college and the determinants of student interest in continuing in economics. She is also the co-author of one of the leading undergraduate industrial organization textbooks. Jensen has been honored twice by Hamilton College for her teaching and currently holds the Christian A. Johnson Professorship for Excellence in Teaching.

Mary Mathewes Kassis is an Associate Professor of Economics and Director of Assessment in the Richards College of Business at the University of West Georgia. Her research interests include economic education, labor economics, and regional economics. Dr. Kassis received her BA in Economics and Political Science from Agnes Scott College and a Ph.D. in Economics from Georgia State University.

Peter E. Kennedy received his BA from Queen's University in 1965 and Ph.D. from the University of Wisconsin-Madison in 1968. Apart from visiting positions at Cornell, Wisconsin, the London School of Economics, Singapore, Deakin, Cape Town, Canterbury, Curtin, Adelaide, Otago, and EERC (Ukraine), he was on faculty at Simon Fraser University for forty years. Recipient of four awards for excellence in teaching, and the Villard award for research in economic education, he is best known for his textbooks *A Guide to Econometrics* and *Macroeconomic Essentials for Media Interpretation.* He was an associate editor of the *International Journal of Forecasting* and of *Economics Bulletin*, and associate editor of the *Journal of Economic Education* for over twenty years, with responsibility for editing its research section. Sadly, Peter passed away on August 30, 2010. He will be missed and his contributions to economic education long appreciated.

Michael A. Leeds is Professor of Economics at Temple University. While trained as a labor economist, he is best known for his teaching and research in sports economics. His work has appeared in such journals as the *Social Science Quarterly*, *Economic Inquiry*, and the *Journal of Sports Economics.* Along with Peter von Allmen, he is co-author of *The Economics of Sports* and a Principles of Economics textbook. His recent research includes work on how bonus payments to college football coaches affect the academic progress of their players and the determinants of charitable activity by married couples.

Lynne Y. Lewis is a Professor of Economics at Bates College in Maine. Her research focuses on the economics of water resources and she has worked on transboundary water allocation, tradable emissions programs for water quality and valuation issues related to urban rivers. Currently she is working on projects related to estimating the economic impacts of river restoration and dam removal. She co-authors the popular textbooks, *Environmental and Natural Resource Economics* and *Environmental Economics and Policy* with Tom Tietenberg. She is on the Board of Maine Audubon and the Research Advisory Board of the Senator George Mitchell Center for the Environment and Watershed Research.

Jane S. Lopus is Professor of Economics and Director of the Center for Economic Education at California State University, East Bay. She holds an undergraduate degree from the University of Michigan, Ann Arbor, and a Ph.D. from the University of California, Davis. Through the Council for Economic Education, she has conducted seminars and workshops in 15 former communist and developing countries to train teachers to teach market-based economics. She was named the Cal State East Bay Outstanding Professor in 2006 and has received national awards for both research and leadership in economic education from the National Association of Economic Educators.

Michael A. MacDowell is the President of Misericordia University, where he occasionally teaches Economics. He is also the Managing Director of the Calvin K. Kazanjian Economics Foundation, Inc. He was President of the Council for Economic Education from 1977 to 1989. He has served as Vice President and Associate Professor of Economics at Hartwick College and held a Visiting Chair in Economics Education at Florida State University. MacDowell has published a number of articles and a book on economic education.

Mark Maier, Professor of Economics at Glendale Community College (California), is co-author (with S. Simkins) of *Just-in-Time-Teaching Across the Disciplines*, *Introducing Economics* (with J. Nelson) and author of *The Data Game* and *City Unions*. He is co-principal investigator for the National Science Foundation (NSF) project "Starting Point: Teaching and Learning Economics" and principal investigator for the NSF project "Adapting Effective Outreach and Workshop Practices to Improve Community College Economics Instruction." He has published widely on the adaptation to economics of research-based pedagogies, including just-in-time teaching, interactive lecture demonstrations, context-rich problems, and structured small group work.

Dirk Mateer is a Senior Lecturer in Economics at Penn State University. His economic education research has appeared in the *Journal of Economic Education*, as well as other journals and focuses on media-enriched learning. He is the author of *Economics in the Movies*. Dirk is also an award-winning instructor. Most notably, he has been featured in the "Great Teachers in Economics" series put out by the Stavros Economic Education Center. He was also the inaugural winner of the Economic Communicator Contest sponsored by the Association of Private Enterprise Education.

William A. McEachern won the University of Connecticut's Excellence in Undergraduate Teaching Award in 2000. His research has appeared in a variety of journals, in research monographs, and in edited volumes. Professor McEachern's principles of economics textbook, *Economics: A Contemporary Introduction* (South-Western, Cengage Learning), is now in a ninth edition. For more than two decades, he has been writing his newsletter, "The Teaching Economist" (www.cengage.com/economics/mceachern/theteachingeconomist/). He graduated with honors from Holy Cross College, served three years as a US Army officer, and earned an MA and Ph.D. from the University of Virginia. He can be reached at william.mceachern@uconn.edu.

KimMarie McGoldrick is Professor of Economics and holds the Joseph A. Jennings Chair in Business at the University of Richmond. Her pedagogic research has appeared in numerous academic journals, including the *Journal of Economic Education* and the *International Review of Economic Education*, covering topics including service-learning, cooperative learning, cheating in the classroom, economics as liberal education, and developing critical inquiry skills. Along with Mark Maier and Scott Simkins, she has developed *Starting Point: Teaching and Learning Economics*, an economics pedagogical portal funded by the National Science Foundation. She currently serves as an

Associate Editor of the *Journal of Economic Education* and on the American Economic Association's Committee on Economic Education. Dr. McGoldrick has received several university, disciplinary, and statewide teaching awards.

Daniel P. McMillen has a joint appointment in the Department of Economics and the Institute of Government and Public Affairs at the University of Illinois. He also is a visiting fellow at the Lincoln Institute of Land Policy and a consultant at the Federal Reserve Bank of Chicago. He has previously been a member of the economics departments at the University of Oregon, Santa Clara University, Tulane University, and the University of Illinois at Chicago. McMillen received his Ph.D. in Economics from Northwestern University in 1987. He has been co-editor of *Regional Science and Urban Economics* since 2007.

Helen Meyers has been president of SC Economics since 2003. Her classroom experience includes first grade, middle school reading, high school special education, and head teacher on Child and Adolescent Psychiatry at Palmetto Health Baptist. She has worked in public relations at Palmetto Health and as vice president of Junior Achievement of Central South Carolina. She is also a former president of the National Association of Economic Educators and the SC Jump$tart Coalition. Meyers has a Bachelor of Science degree in elementary/special education from Western Illinois University and a Master's of Education from Southern Illinois University.

Joshua D. Miller is a graduate student and researcher in Transportation Technology and Policy at the University of California at Davis. His current research focuses on the effect of consumer attitudes and preferences on transportation mode choice. He graduated with honors from Vassar College in 2010 with a BA in Economics. Joshua's previous research includes performing a cost-benefit analysis of increased bus service in the Los Angeles Metropolitan Area; evaluating an EPA program to reduce vehicle greenhouse gas emissions; developing an energy efficiency, conservation, and generation plan for Yolo County Housing authority; and evaluating potential benefits of unbundling television programming.

Ewald Mittelstaedt is Assistant Professor at the Chair of Economic Education at TU Dortmund University of Technology, Germany. His dissertation thesis was about the economics of school improvement, with a focus on intellectual capital reporting. He currently functions as an Adjunct Professor in Economic Education at the University of Education, Freiburg, Germany and as a speaker of the junior research group of the German Association of Economic Education (DeGOEB). He is involved in major research projects concerning financial literacy, ICTs in higher education and the economics of complex systems, funded by the European Council.

Franklin G. Mixon, Jr. is a Visiting Professor of Economics at Columbus State University. He has been involved in the field of economic education for 20 years. Mixon has published articles in various economics education journals, such as the *Journal of Economic Education* and *International Review of Economics Education*, and he currently serves on the editorial board of the *Journal of Economics & Finance Education*. He is the editor/co-editor of two published volumes on economic education, *Shaping the Learning Curve* (*i*Universe, Inc., 2005) and *Expanding Teaching and Learning Horizons in Economic Education* (Nova Science, Inc., 2009).

Walter Nicholson (Ph.D., Economics, Massachusetts Institute of Technology) is the Ward H. Patton Professor of Economics at Amherst College. His research interests focus on the economics of unemployment and the evaluation of programs to combat it. He has published widely on such topics as the duration of unemployment, programs to promote re-employment, and short-time compensation programs. Dr. Nicholson is a Senior Fellow at Mathematica Policy Research, a consultant to the US Departments of Labor, Health and Human Services and the Canadian Department of Human Resources Development. He is also the author of two widely used textbooks on microeconomics.

Pamela Nickless is a Professor of Economics at the University of North Carolina at Asheville. In addition to teaching undergraduates for nearly forty years, she has taught economic education workshops to teachers since the 1980s. In 2008, she received the Jonathon Hughes Prize for Excellence in Teaching Economic History from the Economic History Association.

Onsurang Norrbin is the Director of International Economic Education and a lecturer in the Department of Economics at Florida State University. She has received both a department and a university teaching award at Florida State University. Prior to joining FSU, she was an Assistant Professor of Economics at Samford University and at Newman University. Onsurang earned her BA at Thammasat University in Thailand. In the following year she moved to the US and earned her MS from Wichita State University and a Ph.D. in Economics from the Florida State University.

Stefan C. Norrbin is a Professor of Economics and the Director of the Applied Master's program in Economics at Florida State University. Stefan's professional experience includes working as a consultant at McKinsey & Co., an Assistant Professor at the University of Alabama, a Visiting Professor at the University of Hawaii and department chair at Samford University. Stefan has published over 45 articles, in journals such as: *Journal of Political Economy*, *Journal of Monetary Economics* and *Journal of International Economics*. He has received several university teaching awards. Stefan received an AB from Brown University, and an MS and Ph.D. from Arizona State University.

Edgar O. Olsen is a professor of economics and public policy at the University of Virginia. He has taught undergraduate and graduate public economics for more than 35 years, has published papers on public policy in leading professional journals such as the *American Economic Review, Journal of Political Economy,* and *Journal of Public Economics,* and wrote the chapter on low-income housing programs in a National Bureau of Economic Research volume on means-tested transfers in the United States.

Ann L. Owen is the Henry Platt Bristol Professor of Economics at Hamilton College. She has published widely on long-run growth, income distribution, and sustainable consumption choices. The recipient of a college-wide teaching award, Owen also has an established expertise as an educator, having published several articles on pedagogy in the economics classroom, presented in many venues on economics education, and written textbook supplements that facilitate innovative teaching methods. Prior to joining Hamilton College in 1997, Owen was an economist at the Federal Reserve Board. She has a Ph.D. in Economics from Brown University and an MBA from Babson College.

Lynn Paringer is Professor of Economics at California State University, East Bay and a certified financial planner™ with Prime Wealth Management in Berkeley, CA. Lynn has an undergraduate, master's degree and a Ph.D. in economics from the University of Wisconsin, Madison. Lynn has served as a principal investigator on numerous grants in the field of health services research and public health policy and has published articles on the impact of health insurance on access to care and the quality of care received. Lynn was a Fulbright Fellow at the Prague School of Economics and teaches in domestic and international MBA programs.

Elizabeth Perry-Sizemore is Assistant Dean at Randolph College (founded as Randolph-Macon Woman's College), where she is also Associate Professor and Chair of the Department of Economics and Business. She is the past director of Randolph's competitive and college-wide Student/Faculty Summer Research Program. She is an elected Social Sciences Councilor with the Council on Undergraduate Research and a faculty advisor to the online student-refereed journal *Illinois Wesleyan Undergraduate Economic Review* (*IWUER*). She is the author of the undergraduate research module of the online pedagogic portal Starting Point: Teaching and Learning Economics.

Inna Pomorina has been a researcher with the Economics Network since 2000. Before joining the centre she worked as a Senior Lecturer at St. Petersburg University of Finance and Economy and as a visiting lecturer at the University of the West of England. She conducts regular surveys of students, lecturers, graduates and employers to research the current state of teaching and learning in Economics in the UK. They inform the Network's support role and give a voice to the HE Economics community. Inna disseminates the results at various conferences and workshops in UK, USA, Australia and Russia.

Jack Reardon is Professor of Economics in the School of Business at Hamline University. He also lectures regularly at USTC in Hefei, China; Visva-Bharati University in Santiniketan, India, Dr. Gaur Hari Singhania Institute of Management and Research in Kanpur, India and Mansfield College (Oxford University). He is founding editor of the *International Journal of Pluralism and Economics Education* (Inderscience). His most recent book is *The Handbook of Pluralist Economics Education* (Routledge, 2009) and he is currently writing a book on economics education in developing countries.

Ken Rebeck is Associate Professor of Economics at St. Cloud State University and a Research Associate with the National Center for Research in Economic Education. He earned his BA degree from California State University, San Bernardino and his Ph.D. from the University of Nebraska-Lincoln, both in economics. He has published articles in various journals, including the *Journal of Economic Education*, *American Economic Review* and the *Journal of Consumer Affairs*. He has helped revise and norm four national economics tests, including the Test of Economic Literacy and the Test of Understanding in College Economics, and co-authored the examiner's manuals accompanying each.

Robert P. Rebelein is an Associate Professor of Economics at Vassar College in Poughkeepsie, NY. He regularly teaches Introductory Macroeconomics and Public Finance and has taught for over 20 years at large public universities and small private liberal arts colleges. In 2008 and 2009 he was a presenter for the Teaching Innovations Program in Economics. His current research examines the aggregate and distributional effects of alternative health care reform policies. His previous research includes evaluations of the effects of large government budget deficits, studies of the EITC and the AMT, of pharmaceutical pricing practices, and of firm location decisions.

Marla Ripoll is an Associate Professor of Economics at the University of Pittsburgh. Her research interests are in growth and development, including technology creation and diffusion, inequality, schooling and demographics. Her work has appeared in various journals, including the *Journal of Monetary Economics*, the *International Economic Review*, and the *Review of Economics and Statistics*. Her favorite course to teach is growth and development because it relates to her research, and it reflects her initial interest in pursuing economics as an undergraduate in Colombia, her country of origin. She was awarded the 2004 Tina and David Bellet Arts and Sciences Teaching Excellence Award, and the 2009 Chancellor's Distinguished Teaching Award.

Raymond Robertson is Professor of Economics at Macalester College. His research and teaching focus on the union of international, labor, development economics, and econometrics. He has published in the *American Economic Review*, the *Review of Economics and Statistics*, the *Journal of International Economics*, *Review of International Economics*, and others. He is a non-resident fellow at the Center for Global Development and a member of the State Department's Advisory Committee on International Economic Policy (ACIEP). He received his Ph.D. from the University of Texas after spending a year in Mexico as a Fulbright Scholar.

Michael K. Salemi is Professor and Chair of Economics at the University of North Carolina – Chapel Hill (UNC–CH). Salemi is the author of more than fifty published articles in macroeconomics, domestic and international monetary theory, and economic education. Salemi was chair of the AEA Committee on Economic Education and CO-PI for the NSF-funded Teaching Innovations Program. He was awarded the Bowman and Gordon Gray Professorship for Excellence in Undergraduate Instruction by UNC-CH in 1987 and again in 2004, the Bower Medal by the National Council on Economic Education in 1998, and the Villard Research Award by the Association of Economic Educators in 2001.

Sue Lynn Sasser is Professor of Economics at the University of Central Oklahoma and has been actively involved in economic education for about 25 years. Most recently, she has served as Director of the UCO Center for Economic Education and is the past Executive Director of the Oklahoma Council on Economic Education. She is also a former president of the National Association of Economic Educators and the Oklahoma Jump$tart Coalition. In 2009, Dr. Sasser received the Friend of the Family Award from the American Association of Family and Consumer Sciences, and she has won several awards for curriculum development.

Phillip Saunders is Professor Emeritus of Economics at Indiana University, Bloomington, where he received two distinguished teaching awards and served as the director of the IU Center on Economic Education from 1970 until his retirement in 1998. He was the first recipient of the Henry H. Villard Research Award from the National Association of Economic Educators and the Joint Council on Economic Education in 1986. Saunders served as the Chief Consultant for the Pittsburgh Public Schools' Developmental

Economic Education Program (1964–8) and three Agency for Instructional Television/ Technology series: Trade-Offs (1976–8), Give and Take (1981–2), and Tax Whys: Understanding Taxes (1985, 1988, 1993). He received the Distinguished Service Award from the NAEE and the National Council on Economic Education in 1995.

Aaron Schiff is a director at Covec, an economics consultancy. He has published papers on the economics of networks, and developed and taught a course in Internet economics at the University of Auckland.

Geoffrey Schneider is Professor of Economics and Director of the Teaching and Learning Center at Bucknell University. Schneider received a BA from Northwestern University and a Ph.D. from the University of North Carolina, Chapel Hill. He has co-authored two books and authored or co-authored articles in the *Journal of Economic Issues*, the *Review of Social Economy*, the *Review of Radical Political Economics,* the *Forum for Social Economics,* and *Feminist Economics.* He is an award-winning teacher, author of several articles on pedagogy, and guest editor of special issues of the *Forum for Social Economics* on Teaching Heterodox Economics.

Jean Shackelford is Presidential Professor of Economics at Bucknell University in Lewisburg, Pennsylvania, US. She is a founder, past-president and past executive secretary-treasurer of the International Association for Feminist Economics. She has served as an Associate Editor and is currently on the Editorial Board for *Feminist Economics.* She is an associate of the Bucknell Institute for Public Policy and is a co-author of *Economics: A Tool for Critically Understanding Society*, an economic principles text now in its ninth edition. Her current research is in the areas of the history of economic thought and pedagogy in economics.

John J. Siegfried is Professor of Economics Emeritus at Vanderbilt University, and has been Secretary-Treasurer of the American Economic Association (AEA) since 1997. He served on the Vanderbilt faculty for 38 years after earning his Ph.D. at the University of Wisconsin in 1972. He has held visiting appointments at Simon Fraser University, the University of Leeds, the University of Adelaide, the Federal Trade Commission, and the President's Council of Economic Advisers. He does research on antitrust, the economics of higher education, sports economics, and teaching economics. He has been president of the Southern Economic Association and the Midwest Economics Association.

Scott Simkins is the director of the Academy for Teaching and Learning and Associate Professor of Economics at North Carolina A&T State University, Greensboro, NC. He earned his Ph.D. in economics from the University of Iowa in 1988. His research focuses on the adaptation of pedagogical innovations across disciplines. He has co-led multiple National Science Foundation projects focused on pedagogical innovation in economics, most recently the development of the web-based Starting Point: Teaching and Learning Economics pedagogic portal. He is also the co-editor (with Mark Maier) of *Just-in-Time Teaching: Across the Disciplines, Across the Academy*, from Stylus Publishing (2009).

John Sloman has been Director of the Economics Network since 1999. He was formerly Head of School of Economics at the University of the West of England. He is the author of several widely used economics textbooks, including the best-selling textbook in the UK, *Economics* (now in its seventh edition) and the second-best selling textbook, *Essentials of Economics* (now in its fifth edition). These are also widely used around the world, with translations into many languages. He is a member of the Conference of Heads of Departments of Economics Steering Group and is on the Council of the Scottish Economic Society.

Wendy A. Stock is a Professor of Economics and Head of the Department of Agricultural Economics and Economics at Montana State University. She holds Ph.D. and MA degrees in economics from Michigan State University and a BA in economics from Weber State University. She has published numerous research articles, has presented her work at various locations across the United States, and holds several research and teaching awards. She currently teaches ECON 101 – The Economic Way of Thinking to several hundred students each semester, and has just completed a 101-level textbook, *Social Issues and Economic Thinking*, forthcoming from Wiley Publishers.

Thomas S. Ulen is Swanlund Chair Emeritus, University of Illinois at Urbana-Champaign and Professor Emeritus of Law, College of Law at the University of Illinois. He studied at the University of Oxford and then received a Ph.D. in economics from Stanford. He holds an honorary degree from the Katholieke Universiteit Leuven, Belgium. His textbook with Robert D. Cooter, *Law and Economics*, is now in its sixth edition and has been translated into Chinese, Japanese, Italian, Spanish, French, Slovenian, and Russian. He is also a co-author of *Empirical Methods in Law* (2010). He is working on books on the role of law in economic growth and on behavioral law and economics.

Michelle Albert Vachris is Professor of Economics and BB&T Professor for the Study of Capitalism at Christopher Newport University (CNU). She earned a BA in Economics from the College of William and Mary and an MA and Ph.D. in Economics from George Mason University. Before arriving at CNU, she was an economist with the US Bureau of Labor Statistics in the International Price Program. She has since served as a consultant on international statistics for the International Monetary Fund. She is a past president of the Virginia Association of Economists. Dr. Vachris pursues research concerning economic freedom, public choice, and teaching pedagogy.

William Waller is Professor of Economics at Hobart and William Smith Colleges. His Ph.D. in economics is from the University of New Mexico. He is past president of the Association for Evolutionary Economics and the Association for Institutional Thought. He has been a trustee of the Association for Social Economics and on the editorial board of the *Journal of Economic Issues*. He has co-edited three books. His articles on institutionalist methodology, feminist economics, public policy, and Thorstein Veblen are published in *Journal of Economic Issues, Review of Social Economy, History of Political Economy, Review of Institutional Thought* and many edited collections.

William Walstad is John T. and Mable M. Hay Professor of Economics at the University of Nebraska-Lincoln and editor of the *Journal of Economic Education*. From 2004–10, he was the Principal Investigator for the Teaching Innovations Program (TIP) in economics. This faculty teaching project was funded by the National Science Foundation and the results were reported in: *Teaching Innovation in Economics: Strategies and Applications for Interactive Instruction* (Edward Elgar, 2010). From 2000–06, Bill chaired the Committee on Economic Education of the American Economic Association. He served as project leader to develop the Test of Understanding in College Economics (fourth edition).

James C. Ward received a bachelor's degree from Princeton University, and is currently enrolled in the MBA program at Vanderbilt, where he worked as a teaching assistant in Professor Froeb's Managerial Economics class. Before business school, Jim worked in the finance division of Fannie Mae.

John C. Whitehead is a professor in the Department of Economics at Appalachian State University. He received his BA from Centre College and his MA and Ph.D. from the University of Kentucky. His current teaching includes microeconomics and benefit-cost analysis. John's research interests include nonmarket environmental valuation and he is an associate editor at *Marine Resource Economics* and the *Journal of Environmental Management*. His best year was 2008 when he was presented with the Distinguished Economist Award by the Kentucky Economic Association and Player with the Best Attitude award in the Noon-Time Faculty-Staff Basketball Game. His webpage is john-whitehead.blogs.com.

Claudia Wiepcke is Professor and Head of Department in Economic Education at the University of Education Schwäbisch-Gmünd, Germany. Her dissertation thesis was about ICTs and their evaluation in economics education, with a focus on gender mainstreaming. For the last five years she has taught on the teacher education program: economics in secondary school. Her lectures address classroom experiments, cultural diversity and business German as a foreign language. In recent empirical studies, Claudia has thoroughly investigated diagnostics and the development of economic learning standards.

Jonathan B. Wight is Professor of Economics and International Studies at the University of Richmond. Current research centers on the intersection of ethics and economics, with a focus on Adam Smith's moral foundations of capitalism. He is the author of the economic novel, *Saving Adam Smith: A Tale of Wealth, Transformation and Virtue* (2002) and *Teaching the Ethical Foundations of Economics* (2007, with John Morton) and numerous journal articles. He received the University of Richmond's Distinguished Educator Award in 2002 and the Robins School of Business Outstanding Teaching Award in 1997.

Anne E. Winkler is Professor of Economics and Public Policy Administration at the University of Missouri – St. Louis. Her research focuses on the interrelationships between gender, family, and labor market outcomes. She is co-author, with Francine D. Blau and Marianne A. Ferber, of *The Economics of Women, Men, and Work*, currently in its sixth edition. She received the Chancellor's Award for Excellence in Teaching from the University of Missouri – St. Louis in 2005. She is a research fellow at IZA (the Institute for the Study of Labor), an affiliate at the National Poverty Center, and an editorial board member of *Social Science Quarterly* and the *Journal of Labor Research*.

Jeffrey M. Wooldridge is University Distinguished Professor of Economics at Michigan State University, where he has taught since 1991. He taught at the Massachusetts Institute of Technology from 1986 to 1991. Wooldridge received his doctorate in economics in 1986 from the University of California, San Diego. Wooldridge is the author of the textbooks *Introductory Econometrics: A Modern Approach* and *Econometric Analysis of Cross Section and Panel Data*. He is a fellow of the Econometric Society and has served on several editorial boards, including as editor of the *Journal of Business and Economic Statistics* and as co-editor of *Economics Letters*.

Stephen Wu is an Associate Professor of Economics at Hamilton College and holds degrees from Brown University and Princeton University. He conducts research on subjective well-being, higher education, and health economics and has published in scholarly journals, including the *Journal of Financial Economics, Journal of Health Economics, Journal of Human Resources, Review of Economics and Statistics*, and *Science*. He is a recipient of the Association of Princeton Graduate Alumni Teaching Prize, the Alpha Delta Phi Great Professor Award and the Dean's Scholarly Achievement Award at Hamilton College. He is currently writing an introductory economics textbook.

Andrea L. Ziegert is Associate Professor of Economics at Denison University in Granville, OH. Andrea's interest in pedagogy began with a study of personality temperament and learning in economics. This study led to an interest in service-learning. As Director of Curricular Service-Learning at Denison University, she was responsible for faculty and course development. With co-author KimMarie McGoldrick she edited *Putting the Invisible Hand to Work: Concepts and Models for Service-Learning in Economics*, and has published works on the state of service-learning research. Of interest to economic educators and service-learning researchers, her current interests include student learning outcomes, and faculty motivation to adopt service-learning.

James P. Ziliak holds the Carol Martin Gatton Endowed Chair in Microeconomics and is Founding Director of the Center for Poverty Research at the University of Kentucky. He is research affiliate with the National Poverty Center at the University of Michigan and with the Institute for Research on Poverty at the University of Wisconsin. He served as Assistant and Associate Professor of Economics at the University of Oregon, and held visiting positions at Brookings Institution, University College London, University of Michigan, and University of Wisconsin. His research expertise is in the areas of labor economics and tax and transfer policy.

Preface

There is an old adage – "If they aren't learning, you aren't teaching." In June of 2011, at the American Economic Association's inaugural teaching conference at Stanford, keynote speaker and Nobel Laureate, Vernon Smith, added his own slant on this adage. "If YOU aren't learning, you aren't teaching." While the motivation for creating this handbook is multi-faceted, these adages, in tandem, convey the primary goal of the *Handbook*. This comprehensive collection of work is designed to enhance student learning in economics by helping economic educators, both new and seasoned, learn more about course content, pedagogic techniques, and the scholarship of the teaching enterprise.

Economic educators reside in many settings, including the K-12 arena, community colleges, liberal arts colleges, research universities, and online universities. This book is intended to be of benefit to all of these educators and contributes to building the economic education community. It is also our hope that it helps ease the isolation that some educators may feel as a result of being a member of a small department at their institution or because discussions with their colleagues emphasize research activities over teaching.

We seek to enhance economic education by assembling a group of economic educators to offer advice on best practice in terms of teaching, pedagogic research, and specific course content. Much of the advice these experts provide is grounded in scholarship and comes from years of experience and trial and error. We also address the administrative support aspect of teaching by providing advice on activities that enhance teaching and learning outcomes, including peer review, mentoring, evaluation, and teaching workshops. We are hopeful that this volume will assist in the scholarship of teaching and learning as authors provide evidence of effective practices, describe how future research can broaden our understanding of how students learn economics or anticipate how advances in a field may motivate changes in what we teach.

In a broader sense, we paint a picture of the wide (although not exhaustive) array of techniques available that might provide knowledge and courage to instructors to try new techniques, teach new courses or engage in studies that investigate and measure the effectiveness of a pedagogical technique applied to the economic classroom. Additionally, we hope that assembling this collective body of knowledge will foster cooperation and collaboration between all of the different economic education efforts (across organizations, countries, perspectives, etc.) as we move toward a common goal of helping more people know more about economics.

We felt it was crucial for the volume to begin with a chronicle of the history of economic education, demonstrating the foundation on which economic education as we know it rests. We are indebted to those who made great strides to promote economic education, the depth and breadth of their influence, and their guiding vision that has provided clear and constant direction. We hope that this volume in some way pays tribute to ground breakers and leaders like G.L. Bach, Robin L. Bartlett, William E. Becker,

David Colander, Rendig Fels, W. Lee Hansen, Ben W. Lewis, Michael K. Salemi, Phillip Saunders, John Siegfried, Henry Villard, William Walstad, Michael Watts, and others too numerous to mention. We dedicate this *Handbook* to all of these visionaries, who realized the important role of economic education in the advancement of the discipline.

We would like to thank all of our contributing authors for their generous participation in this project. They come from varied backgrounds in terms of types of institutions, class sizes, and areas of interest. Collectively they bring powerful institutional memory and teaching wisdom that comes from hundreds of years of combined teaching experience and interactions with thousands of students. We would also like to extend our gratitude to the countless economists who have offered invaluable advice and recommendations for contributors and topics for this volume, especially the faculty in the Department of Economics at the University of Kentucky. We would also like to extend our gratitude to the many economic educators who, while not contributing directly to this volume through authoring a chapter, have advised authors. A special thank you goes to Tricia Fanney, at the University of Richmond, who provided immeasurable administrative support at all stages of this project. Finally, we would be remiss if we did not thank our families (Andy, Ginny, Bill, and Carol), who put up with many long evenings and weekend hours of work as we endeavored to bring this project to fruition.

So to the new and experienced teacher alike, it is our fondest wish that this volume can serve as a trusted guidebook for navigating the landscape of economic education. May you gain from the wisdom of the travelers who have come before, but also find purchase for your own contribution to this worthwhile endeavor as an able teacher and scholar of economics.

Gail M. Hoyt
KimMarie McGoldrick
June 2011

Foreword

This comprehensive *Handbook* has it all for anyone interested in economic education. The 76 chapters cover a broad range of topics on teaching, research, and economic content. Economics professors, as well as graduate student instructors, will find it to be a valuable resource for their teaching. Researchers in economic education will discover it to be a useful guide for conducting research in economic education. Administrators in economics departments will want to access it when they seek information on economic education that helps them make decisions about economics instruction and the economics major.

KimMarie McGoldrick and Gail Hoyt, the capable editors of this volume, have organized the diverse content material into six manageable parts for the reader. The opening part of the book describes the history of economic education to give readers the necessary perspective on past developments. The second part, a main focus of the book, is devoted to teaching. In particular, it discusses many classroom and contextual techniques for teaching, the contribution that technology can make to enhancing instruction, and assessment methods that are valuable for measuring student understanding and achievement, both within courses and in the economics major.

The third part, another area of major emphasis, turns to research on economic education. Here the reader learns about the principles of economics course and textbooks. The section also provides insights into factors that affect student performance, behaviors, and teaching evaluations in economics courses. The section ends with several chapters on the scholarship of teaching and learning in economics.

An impressive set of 30 chapters on content topics in economics constitutes the fourth part of the book. These chapters cover the traditional content, such as principles of microeconomics and macroeconomics, intermediate microeconomics and macroeconomics, money and banking, econometrics, public economics, labor economics, international trade, game theory, and experimental economics. They also include less traditional or less widely taught topics in the economics curricula of most departments, such as health economics, law and economics, sports economics, poverty economics, feminist economics, and antitrust economics.

The last two parts of the book make additional contributions. The fifth part looks at institutional or administrative matters related to economics instruction. These matters include the development and mentoring of economics faculty, the structure of the undergraduate major in economics, and the characteristics of graduate students in economics. While the book focuses almost exclusively on economic education in the United States, an international dimension is added with chapters on economic education in three other nations – the United Kingdom, Australia, and Germany. The book concludes with a final part describing organizations and initiatives that support teaching and research in economic education.

Economics is a challenging and complex subject to teach to students. This *Handbook* makes that task less daunting and more rewarding by giving economics instructors the knowledge and information they need to enhance their teaching and improve student learning. Researchers and administrators also will benefit from the insights they gain from reading chapters in this book. The editors of this volume, as well as the many chapter contributors, are to be thanked for what they have done to enrich our understanding of economic education.

William Walstad
University of Nebraska-Lincoln

PART I

A HISTORY OF ECONOMIC EDUCATION

1 A history of economic education
Phillip Saunders[1]

Professional economists and professional educators are not the only sources of economics education, but in this chapter I will focus on the efforts of these groups to help students and others understand how the economy works and how to analyze and make decisions on issues of personal and public economic policy. In doing this, I will focus on the activities of the American Economic Association (AEA), which was founded in 1885, the Joint Council on Economic Education (JCEE), which was founded in 1949, and the National Association of Economic Educators (NAEE), which was founded in 1980.[2] I will also focus almost exclusively on developments in the United States. Others have published articles and books on economics education in other countries; and I have little to add to this literature which, in general, deals with developments more recent than most of those described in this chapter.[3]

AMERICAN ECONOMIC ASSOCIATION[4]

Official certification or accreditation of individuals, courses, or programs is sometimes undertaken by professional organizations in other disciplines, but the American Economic Association (AEA) has explicitly and consistently avoided this practice. Despite the lack of official endorsements, however, A. W. Coats has noted: "From its inception the AEA has demonstrated an intermittent interest in the improvement of economics teaching both at the high school and the college level, and of course some of its publication activities have been designed to raise the general public's knowledge of economic affairs" (Coats, 1985, p. 1720). During the 59-year period between its first annual meeting in 1886 and the appointment of its first Committee on Undergraduate Teaching of Economics and the Training of Economists in 1944, the AEA devoted some time at 14 of its annual meetings to roundtable discussions on the problems of general economic education. Three of these roundtables, in 1895, 1918, and 1921, were specifically devoted to economics and the secondary schools (Leamer, 1950a).[5]

Activities and Recommendations of the Taylor and Bowen Committees

In April 1944 the AEA Executive Committee appointed Professor Horace Taylor of Columbia University as Chairman of a five-person "parent" committee to consider possible improvements in undergraduate teaching of economics and the training of economists. Despite this rather strong orientation toward college and graduate level economics, one of the parent committee's 11 subcommittees was appointed in the area of "The Teaching of Economics in the Schools," with S. Howard Patterson of the University of Pennsylvania as the subcommittee chairman. This subcommittee, along with two other subcommittees, however, did not issue a report when the findings of the

Taylor Committee were published as a special 226-page supplement to the December 1950 *American Economic Review* (Taylor, 1950). In addition to recommending the publication of its findings, the Taylor Committee made four other recommendations to the AEA Executive Committee. Of these, only the recommendation to appoint a committee to study and report on graduate training in economics was approved. The other three recommendations to create a standing committee on education in economics, to become an associational affiliate of the National Council for the Social Studies, and to appoint a committee to explore conditions of study and teaching of economics in the schools were not approved. These actions clearly demonstrated the Executive Committee's reluctance to move beyond the AEA's traditional position of simply holding roundtable discussions and publishing papers in the *Papers and Proceedings (P&P)* volumes of the *American Economic Review (AER)*.

The decision to undertake a study of graduate training in economics came only after considerable debate of a report by a four-person ad hoc committee appointed to study the matter. Once approved, a grant was obtained from the Rockefeller Foundation and Howard R. Bowen was appointed to carry out the study with the assistance of an advisory committee consisting of G. L. Bach, Milton Friedman, I. L. Sharfman, and J. J. Spengler. After it was published as a special supplement to the *American Economic Review* in September 1953 (Bowen, 1953), the Bowen report and its recommendations served as the basis for a roundtable discussion at the AEA's annual meeting later that year; and a six-person Ad Hoc Committee on Implementation of the Bowen Report consisting of G. L. Bach, Robert D. Calkins, Robert A. Gordon, John K. Galbraith, Albert G. Hart, and O. J. Brownlee was established in 1954, but later dismissed with appreciation after its members could not come to agreement on several points.

The Taylor and Bowen Committees were significant because they demonstrated that the AEA Executive Committee could appoint a committee and publish its results without an official endorsement of its conclusions or the need to get complete agreement on specific content or recommendations. The Bowen Committee had the added significance of obtaining outside grant funding for its activities. This procedure was later used in connection with other economic education activities, particularly the appointment of the National Task Force on Economic Education in association with the Committee on Economic Development (CED) in 1960. The work of this Task Force, the legacy of which is still with us today, is by far the most significant set of activities in economics education at the pre-college level ever undertaken by professional economists in this country.

Before turning to the Task Force and its activities, however, it is worthwhile to trace the AEA's evolving position on a standing committee on economics education after the Taylor Committee's initial recommendation to establish such a committee was not approved.

The Ad Hoc Committee on Economics in Teacher Education and the First Standing Committee on Economic Education

In 1952, G. Derwood Baker, then the Director of the Joint Council on Economic Education (JCEE), extended an invitation to then AEA Secretary, James Washington

Bell, to have the Association cooperate formally with a newly formed JCEE Commission on Economics in Teacher Education through an officially appointed AEA committee. After a lengthy discussion, Bell accepted membership on the Commission and attended an exploratory meeting. He then recommended that the AEA Executive Committee appoint an Ad Hoc Committee on Economics in Teacher Education, and three members were appointed: Ben W. Lewis, Chairman, Horace Taylor, and Archibald McIsaac. This committee made three reports to the AEA Executive Committee. In its last report in 1955, it recommended that its activities and its membership be expanded, and that it be reconstituted as a Standing Committee on Economic Education. This recommendation was adopted, and Clark C. Bloom and Floyd A. Bond were added to Lewis, McIsaac and Taylor to make a five-man committee.[6] At its meetings in December 1956, the AEA Executive Committee voted to accept an invitation of the JCEE to name three representatives of the AEA as members of the Board of Trustees of the Joint Council. Ben W. Lewis, Clark C. Bloom, and Lester V. Chandler were subsequently named to fill these positions.

The AEA's new Standing Committee cooperated with the JCEE in obtaining a grant from the Ford Foundation for the purpose of compiling a register of economists interested in economic education. The register was compiled by Dean Eugene Swearington of Oklahoma State University. The Committee was also successful in obtaining a grant from the Ford Foundation to study textbooks used in the secondary schools in American History, Social Studies, and Economics. The study was conducted by a subcommittee led by Paul Olson of the University of Iowa. Following the precedents of the Taylor and Bowen committees, the Standing Committee's textbook study was published as a special supplement to the March 1963 *American Economic Review* ("Economics in the Schools", 1963) after Professor Olson had presented an earlier paper on his committee's preliminary findings (Olson, 1961).

The National Task Force on Economic Education

The AEA's Committee on Economic Education provided a panel of names from which the membership of the National Task Force on Economic Education was chosen by AEA president, Theodore W. Schultz in 1960. G. L. Bach was named Chairman of the Task Force, Floyd A. Bond was named Executive Secretary, and Lester V. Chandler, Robert A. Gordon, Ben W. Lewis, and Paul A. Samuelson were the other economists appointed to serve. Arno Bellack of Columbia Teachers College and M. L. Frankel, who succeeded G. Derwood Baker as Director of the JCEE in 1955, were appointed as consulting members.[7]

The Task Force began an unprecedented series of activities almost immediately, and the minutes of the AEA Executive Committee meeting held in St. Louis on December 27 and 30, 1960, state:

> The Task Force recommended that the AEA agree to co-sponsor the Continental Classroom TV program, either in 1961–62 or 1962–63. It was voted (by a show of hands, five to one, others not voting) that the AEA co-sponsor the Continental Classroom under the following conditions: (1) that the Executive Committee have a veto over the personnel conducting the program; (2) that the program be postponed to 1962–63; (3) that detailed supervision by the AEA be effected through its members on the National Task Force. (Bell, 1961, p. 603)

As its work progressed, the Task Force inevitably assumed some of the duties previously undertaken by the AEA's Standing Committee on Economic Education, but the two groups filed separate reports in 1961 and 1962. The cornerstone of the Task Force's work was its report *Economic Education in the Schools* (described below), which served as a topic of discussion at the AEA's annual meetings in December 1962. In addition to the Continental Classroom TV program, which was broadcast as College of the Air's *The American Economy* television course over CBS and PBS stations in 1962–3 and repeated over many public television stations in 1963–4, there were two other activities that were a direct result of the Task Force's work: one that led to the publication of a report entitled *Study Materials for Economic Education in the Schools* in October, 1961; and the other that led to the publication of a *Test of Economic Understanding* in 1964. Each of these four major activities merits further description.

Economic Education in the Schools: Report of the National Task Force on Economic Education was an attempt "to describe the minimum understanding of economics essential for good citizenship and attainable by high school students" (Committee for Economic Development, 1961, p. 4). It was neither a textbook nor a lesson plan but more of a checklist of major concepts, issues, institutions, and subject matter aimed at helping students develop the ability to reason about economic problems. The Task Force also emphasized: "The most important step toward understanding in economics – as in other branches of knowledge – is the replacement of emotional, unreasoned judgments by objective, rational analysis" (p. 14) and it outlined a four-step decision-making model first presented in a publication of the Brookings Institution (Robinson, Morton and Calderwood, 1956). Through a grant provided by the Committee for Economic Development, a copy of the Task Force *Report* was sent to every high school in the United States and to a large number of leading educational officials, businesspeople, and others interested in economic education. A brief summary of the *Report* was sent to a still wider group, including school board members. The Task Force Chairman estimated "a total of about 150,000 copies was distributed" (Bach, 1963, p. 720).

The American Economy television course was co-sponsored by the Task Force, AEA, JCEE, and Learning Resources Institute. It consisted of 160 half-hour lessons, 32 of which dealt with methods of instruction aimed at teachers who were encouraged to take the course for credit at one of 388 cooperating colleges and universities. Most of the 128 economics content lessons were taught by John R. Coleman of Carnegie Institute of Technology, with the advice and assistance of the Task Force and some 40 leading economists and public officials who appeared as guests on individual programs. A full description of the course appeared in the September, 1962 *American Economic Review* ("College of the Air's 'The American Economy,'" 1962, pp. 940–45). A *Television Study Guide* was published (Coleman and Alexander, 1962), and Professor Coleman presented a paper at the 1962 AEA annual meetings describing the course and the challenges of teaching by television (Coleman, 1963). The Task Force Chairman estimated a daily viewing audience of between 1,000,000 and 1,250,000 in 1962–3, and noted: "This is far more than have watched any of the preceding nation-wide education television programs" (Bach, 1963, p. 721).

Two short articles evaluating the effectiveness of "The American Economy" TV series were published in 1964 (McConnell and Felton, 1964 and Saunders, 1964). These articles, both of which found that the TV course was successful in achieving its objectives, were significant in that they appeared in a regular, refereed issue of the *AER* rather than in an un-refereed *P&P* volume or a special supplement to a regular issue of the *AER*. The Saunders article was also the first published article in economic education to employ a multiple regression technique of statistical analysis. This technique later became the standard method employed in many subsequent research projects, including the lead article in the June 1965 issue of the *AER* (Bach and Saunders, 1965) and a shorter follow-up article a year later (Bach and Saunders, 1966).

Study Materials for Economic Education in the Schools (Joint Council on Economic Education, 1961) was the product of a Materials Evaluation Committee appointed by the Task Force and the JCEE. The committee was chaired by Lewis E. Wagner, and its members were selected with the advice of several major professional associations in addition to the Task Force. Using the general framework of the Task Force *Report*, this committee spent the summer of 1961 reviewing some 7,000 pamphlets and other non-textbook teaching materials offered to secondary schools in economics, and they developed an annotated list of 91 supplementary teaching items classified under 21 subject headings to help teachers find materials that they could integrate into their classroom instruction. The JCEE subsequently revised and updated this report on several occasions.

The Test of Economic Understanding (TEU) was developed by a third distinguished professional group under the chairmanship of John Stalnaker, President of the National Merit Scholarship Corporation. Known as the Committee for Measurement of Economic Understanding, this committee developed two 50-item sets of multiple-choice questions designed to measure the type of economic understanding outlined in the Task Force *Report*. The test and an accompanying *Interpretative Manual and Discussion Guide* were published in 1964 (Science Research Associates, 1964). Major revisions of the TEU, which was acquired by the JCEE and renamed the Test of Economic Literacy (TEL), occurred in 1979 (Soper, 1979), 1987 (Soper and Walstad, 1987), and 2001 (Walstad and Rebeck, 2001).

Despite the ultimate success and widespread impact of its efforts, the AEA's association with the National Task Force was not unanimously approved. The five-to-one vote of the AEA Executive Committee, with the many abstentions, as noted above concerning "The American Economy" TV series, gives some indication of the reservations some people may have had. The minutes of the March 1961 AEA Executive Committee describe the vote to nominate a panel from which the JCEE could appoint an Advisory Committee for its guidance in preparing education materials, noting "approval of this matter was not unanimous" (Bell, 1962, p. 538). George Stigler expressed his personal reservations more directly when he reviewed the Task Force *Report* at the December 1962 AEA meetings. He noted:

> Although the American Economic Association explicitly does not endorse the report, it chose the economists and hence certified to their competence and distinction. No other body concerned with economic education has had such professional status, nor is an equally authoritative body likely to appear in this decade. The report will therefore command an audience of unusual size and deference among high school and college teachers.
>
> This unusual status is, I believe, unfortunate. The economists composing the Task Force are leaders in American economics, of unquestionable competence and integrity. But they do not monopolize these virtues, and their special mode of selection serves to give their views

an eminence which is incompatible with the doctrine of free competition (free discussion) in education and scientific work. (Stigler, 1963, pp. 653–4)

Despite the criticism of Stigler and others, the impact of the Task Force *Report* and its associated activities opened new vistas of what might be possible in the way of action-oriented programs in the broad area of economics education. This led to suggestions, later carried out, that the activities of the Task Force and the AEA's Standing Committee on Economic Education be combined in a new, reconstituted AEA Committee on Economic Education.

The Present Standing Committee on Economic Education (CEE): The G. L. Bach Years

A new six-person standing committee was appointed in 1964 consisting of G. L. Bach, Chairman, Robert A. Gordon, Ben W. Lewis, Marshall R. Colberg, Rendigs Fels, and Emanuel T. Weiler. Lewis, Bach, and Fels were also named as members of a special advisory committee to the JCEE. As part of its mandate (Bell, 1961, p. 603), the new CEE was commissioned to arrange one session on economic education at each AEA annual meeting, and the proceedings of this session have been published in the *AER: P&P* volumes each year since 1967.[8]

Under Bach's leadership, the CEE developed an action-oriented, project-centered agenda. In addition to advising the JCEE in a variety of areas, the CEE was instrumental in: obtaining a grant from the Kazanjian Foundation to finance publication of reports on experiments in the teaching of introductory college economics (Haley, 1967a and 1967b);[9] developing a Test of Understanding College Economics (TUCE) to parallel the Test of Economic Understanding previously developed for use in high schools; and in launching a new *Journal of Economic Education (JEE)* in 1969. The TUCE and JEE marked milestones of the same lasting significance as the publication of the Task Force *Report*.

The Test of Understanding in College Economics (TUCE)

Under the leadership of Rendigs Fels of Vanderbilt University, a blue ribbon committee of distinguished economists was created to prepare a standardized test for use in the college-level introductory economics course. In addition to Fels, the TUCE committee, which included two future Nobel Laureates, consisted of G. L. Bach, William G. Bowen, George J. Stigler, Bernard F. Haley, Robert A. Gordon, and Paul A. Samuelson, as well as Paul L. Dressel as Executive Director and John M. Stalnaker as consultant. When published, the TUCE consisted of two versions of a microeconomics test and two versions of a macroeconomics test. Each version contained 33 multiple-choice questions – 132 different questions in all. Fels wrote the introduction and Dressel described the specifications of the tests in the TUCE *Manual* (Fels and Dressel, 1968), and two papers describing the tests were presented at AEA annual meetings (Fels, 1967; Welsh and Fels, 1969).

In addition to identifying key content categories for each test, the TUCE committee broke new ground in specifying an equal number of questions in three cognitive categories: recognition and understanding; simple application; and complex application. This emphasis on questions that required respondents to go beyond rote memory and recall and *use* economic reasoning was a conscious attempt to discourage the teaching of economics as a list of terms and a set of facts. Subsequent editions of the TUCE (Saunders, 1981; Saunders, Fels and Welsh, 1981; and Saunders 1991a and 1991b) refined the content and cognitive categories and reduced the number of questions, but the basic emphasis of the original TUCE committee on *using and applying* economics remained strong.[10] The most recent revision of the TUCE occurred in 2007 (Walstad, Watts, and Rebeck, 2007).

Journal of Economic Education (*JEE*)

The AEA CEE served as the first editorial board of the new *Journal of Economic Education* when it was created in 1969. The *JEE's* first editor was Henry Villard of the City University of New York, who was a member of the CEE at the time of his appointment. Villard served as editor of the *JEE* until 1982.

First published by the Joint Council on Economic Education as a semi-annual journal, the publication of the *JEE* was assumed by the Helen Dwight Reid Educational Foundation in 1982, and Donald W. Paden of the University of Illinois succeeded Henry Villard as editor. Beginning with the Winter 1983 issue, the *JEE* became a quarterly journal and its focus was broadened with the appointment of Associate Editors for sections on research, content articles in economics, teaching and innovations in instruction, and professional information and book reviews. Kalman Goldberg of Bradley University, who had previously been the Associate Editor for the content articles section, replaced Paden as editor of the *JEE* in 1986, and he served until 1990. With the Summer issue of 1990 (Vol. 21, No. 3), William E. Becker of Indiana University, who had previously served eight years as the Associate Editor of the research section, began 20 years of service as the *JEE* editor until he retired in 2009 and was replaced by William B. Walstad of the University of Nebraska. Beginning with Walstad's editorship, the Taylor & Francis Group replaced the Helen Dwight Reid Educational Foundation as the publisher of the *JEE,* and the journal now bears their Routledge imprint.

The launching of the *JEE*, along with the publication of the TEU and the TUCE and the publication of the AEA committee's annual session in the *AER: P&P*, all combined to stimulate a significant increase in published research in economics education. In his presidential address to the Southern Economic Association in 1968, Rendigs Fels reviewed eight studies that had been conducted up to that time that met his standards of "hard" research that leads to a cumulative literature (Fels, 1969). Ten years later a survey published by Siegfried and Fels in the *Journal of Economic Literature*, which limited itself to the teaching of college economics, cited 179 articles and books (Siegfried and Fels, 1979). Later, Becker, Highsmith, Kennedy, and Walstad (1991) noted that, while the number of research articles on college economics stabilized in the 1980s, research articles on pre-college economic education increased from about 50 in the 1970s to about 250 in the 1980s.[11]

Not content to rest on the accomplishments of the CEE to date, Bach followed his earlier challenge to the profession (Bach, 1961) with an ambitious "Agenda for Improving the Teaching of Economics" at the 1972 AEA annual meetings (Bach, 1973). In this agenda he indicated that the CEE had obtained a substantial grant from the Sloan Foundation to inaugurate a program to train Ph.D. candidates to become better teachers of college economics. As it eventually evolved through a close working relationship of the CEE with Arthur L. Welsh of the JCEE, this program became known as the Teacher Training Program (TTP), and supplemental funding was received from other sources in addition to the Sloan Foundation.

The Teacher Training Program led to the publication of a *Resource Manual* (Saunders, Welsh and Hansen, 1978; Hansen, Saunders and Welsh, 1980) and a series of national workshops for college and university professors and graduate students were held at Indiana University in 1973 and 1979, the University of Wisconsin in 1980, the University of North Carolina in 1982, and the University of Colorado in 1983. Later, publication of *The Principles of Economics Course: A Handbook for Instructors* (Saunders and Walstad, 1990) replaced the *Resource Manual* and stimulated interest in a new round of six TTP workshops between 1992 and 1994 (Salemi, Saunders and Walstad, 1996). These workshops were partially financed by the Lilly Endowment and were held at Harvard and Northwestern in 1992, North Carolina and Stanford in 1993, and Temple and Colorado in 1994. Experience with these workshops led to a revision of the *Handbook* (Walstad and Saunders, 1998), with new chapters on active learning and the teaching of intermediate and advanced undergraduate courses.

The Present Standing Committee on Economic Education (CEE): The Post-Bach Era

G. L. Bach's long service as the first chair of the AEA's current Committee on Economic Education ended in 1977. He was followed as chair by Allen C. Kelley of Duke University (1977–83), W. Lee Hansen of the University of Wisconsin (1983–88), John J. Siegfried of Vanderbilt University (1988–94), Michael K. Salemi of the University of North Carolina (1995–2000), William B. Walstad of the University of Nebraska (2001–06), and Michael Watts of Purdue University (2007–). Bach's successors have continued, refined, and expanded the type of action-oriented, project-centered activities initiated under his leadership. As elaborated below, the number of CEE-sponsored paper sessions devoted to economic education at the AEA annual meetings has expanded far beyond the one session whose papers are published in the *AER: P&P*. Papers from other sessions have often been published in the *Journal of Economic Education*, and on some occasions the *P&P* papers have been published in the *JEE* in expanded form along with comments from discussants that were not included in the *P&P*. In 2002, the AEA CEE also began working with the *JEE* to provide an electronic journal for working papers in economic education. The resulting *Economics Research Network Educator* or *ERN Educator* is part of the Social Science Research Network (SSRN).

In addition to the expansion of activities at the AEA annual meetings, the CEE has initiated activities and received grants in several important areas, ranging from the development of a high school Advanced Placement Program in economics through a conference on college principles textbooks to cooperation with the AEA's Commission on Graduate Education in Economics (COGEE).[12] These include studies of the undergraduate economics major, projects to increase the quantity and quality of economics education research, and the expansion of college and university teacher training activities in ways that led to a new, five-year Teaching Innovations Program (TIP). Each of these areas is discussed below.

Studies of the undergraduate economics major
The first grant to study the undergraduate economics major was received from the Sloan Foundation in 1979. John J. Siegfried led a project that resulted in two publications in the *AER: P&P* (Siegfried and Wilkerson, 1982; Siegfried and Raymond, 1984). Later, W. Lee Hansen published two important papers on "What Knowledge is Most Worth Knowing – For Economics Majors" (Hansen, 1986) and "Expected Proficiencies for Undergraduate Economics Majors" (Hansen, 2001). Hansen's "expected proficiencies" have since taken on a life of their own; and they have stimulated several studies and recommendations, most of which are discussed in Hansen (2009) and cited in his chapter later in this *Handbook.*

In the late 1980s the CEE cooperated with the Association of American Colleges (AAC) in a further study of the economics major financed by the Fund for the Improvement of Postsecondary Education and the Ford Foundation. A report of a six-member task force chaired by John J. Siegfried was presented at the AEA meetings in December 1990 and an expanded version of the report was published in the Summer 1991 issue of *The Journal of Economic Education* (Siegfried, Bartlett, Hansen, Kelley, McCloskey, and Tietenberg, 1991a and 1991b). Based on a survey of 126 college and universities, this task force gave the economics major at these schools a grade of B-, but argued that we could do better by adopting their recommendations in the areas of foundation requirements, a breadth requirement, a depth dimension, and a capstone experience.

As a result of increased interest in the economics major, the AEA now annually tracks the number of bachelor's degrees conferred in economics. In 2007 a grant was received from the Teagle Foundation to address the role of the undergraduate economics major in liberal education. David Colander of Middlebury College and KimMarie McGoldrick of the University of Richmond served as co-directors of this project. Conferences were held at Middlebury College in May 2007 and at the University of Richmond in October 2007 to discuss preliminary versions of their report. A short version of the final report was presented at the 2009 AEA meetings (Colander and McGoldrick, 2009a), and an edited volume with a longer version of the report and responses from a large number of economists was published later that year (Colander and McGoldrick, 2009b).

Encouraging research in economics education
The CEE's first set of summer workshops to encourage research in economics education was a cooperative project with the JCEE financed by the General Electric Education Foundation. These workshops, which were aimed at directors of JCEE-affiliated centers for economic education, were held at Carnegie-Mellon University in the summers of 1969 and 1970 and led to the publication of a volume of research papers (Welsh, 1972). A similar project aimed at attracting younger economists into research on economics education was financed by a grant from the Pew Trust in the late 1980s. In seminars held at Princeton University in the summers of 1987 and 1988, the participants were introduced to the norming data from the second edition of the *TEL* (Soper and Walstad, 1987), a database resulting from a national survey conducted in 1986–7 (Baumol and Highsmith, 1988), and an edited volume on *Econometric Modeling in Economic Education Research* (Becker and Walstad, 1987). Participants in these workshops later presented some of their work at the AEA meetings in 1988 and 1989 and in a special Summer, 1991 issue of *The Journal of Economic Education.*

A third research projects conference sponsored by the CEE with funding from the AEA was held in San Antonio in May 2000. The purpose of the conferences was to "jump-start" new research projects, and plans for five new initiatives emerged (Salemi, Siegfried, Sosin, Walstad, Watts, 2001). Subsequent funding was received from the Kazanjian Foundation, the Mellon Foundation, the Ford Foundation, and the Spencer Foundation for three of these projects dealing with the use of technology in economics instruction (Sosin, Blecha, Agarwal, Bartlett, and Daniel, 2004), the long-term effects of learning economics (Allgood, Bosshardt, van der Klaauw, and Watts, 2004), and Ph.D. education in Economics (Stock, Finegan, Siegfried, 2009).[13] A fourth initiative to expand college and university teacher training activities led to several grants described in more detail below.

The two most recent CEE research projects are econometric training modules and a national conference dedicated to economic education. The training modules were developed as the Online Handbook for the use of Contemporary Econometrics in Economic Education Research by William E. Becker, with funds provided by the US Department of Education to the Council on Economic Education (formerly JCEE). There are four modules in the Online Handbook, each of which includes data sets and programs written in LIMDEP, STATA, and SAS, specific to the modules topic, including data management and heteroskedasticity issues, endogenous regressors, instrumental variables, two-stage estimates, panel data, and sample selection issues.[14] Additionally, the first national conference on Teaching Economics and Research in Economic Education took place at Stanford University, June 1–3, 2011.[15]

Expanding college and university teacher training activities

Building on the favorable response to TTP workshops described above, the AEA CEE received funding from the Kazanjian Foundation for two new initiatives. Beginning in January 1996, Michael Salemi and William Walstad started what has since become a yearly series of one-day, multi-session teaching methods workshops at the AEA annual meetings. In 2000, a three-year grant provided matching funds to colleges and universities to sponsor regional workshops to improve the teaching of economics (Goodman, Maier, Moore, 2003). Over the life of the grant, 24 workshops with 817 participants were conducted. One lasting result of the regional workshops (and Phase 3 of the TIP program described below) was a large increase in the participation in the scholarship of teaching and learning in economics. To accommodate this increase, one of the AEA annual meeting workshop sessions has been converted into a poster session allowing multiple presentations on a wide variety of topics. The contents of the poster sessions, which have ranged from six presentations in 2004 to 27 presentations in 2008 and 2009, are listed in the annual reports of the CEE published in the *AER: P&P*.[16]

Beginning in 2005, the AEA CEE launched a major new Teaching Innovations Program (TIP) with a $675,000, five-year grant from the National Science Foundation. Co-directed by Michael Salemi and William Walstad, this program contained three phases. Phase 1, which ended in 2009, featured ten workshops (two per year) on interactive teaching strategies, held in various locations throughout the country. Phase 2, which ran until May 2010, involved on-line instruction for faculty members after they attended one of the Phase 1 workshops. Seven on-line modules were developed on assessment, case studies, classroom experiments, context-rich problems, cooperative learning, discussion, and interactive strategies for large classes. Participants who completed two of the seven on-line modules received a Certificate of Achievement from the AEA CEE. Phase 3, which began in 2006, provided opportunities for participants to present their own work at meetings of the AEA, SEA, and WEA. Michael Watts' May 2010 report of the AEA CEE (2010a, p. 699) indicated that a total of 338 economists attended one of the 10 Phase 1 workshops, and an appended TIP report (p. 703) indicated that 68 participants had completed two Phase 2 modules and qualified for a Certificate of Achievement. Phase 3 of the program also facilitated the development of an edited volume that contains 11 chapters contributed by both staff and participants describing the program and specific pedagogic techniques (Salemi and Walstad, 2010).

Other Economic Education Activities

There have been other significant economic education activities in addition to the programs sponsored by the AEA CEE. The television course *Economics U$A*, produced by the Annenberg Foundation and the Corporation for Public Broadcasting, was first aired during the 1986–7 academic year (Mansfield and Behravesh, 1986). This program contained 28 half-hour lessons evenly divided between 14 macroeconomic topics and 14 microeconomic topics. Before "distance learning" became a widely used term, *Economics U$A* was designed to be a telecourse to be used by colleges and universities to provide economics instruction to students unable to attend classes on campus. Grimes, Krehbiel, Nielsen, and Niss, whose article in *The Journal of Economic Education* is the best published evaluation of this program, stated: "Nearly one hundred institutions used the course for this purpose during the first semester it was available (fall 1986). Nationally, almost 1,600 students enrolled in *Economics U$A* Classes during the first semester" (Grimes, Krehbiel, Nielsen, and Niss, 1989, p. 140). Based on a carefully designed study in the institutional context of Western Illinois University, these authors found that *Economics U$A* was successful in increasing economic understanding but, consistent with other studies with television courses, it was not successful in generating a positive change in attitude toward the discipline.

In addition to the college teaching materials mentioned above, Becker and Watts have published two compilations of papers that have been widely used in teacher training workshops (Becker and Watts, 1998; Becker and Watts, 2005). The first of these was cited (along with Walstad and Saunders, 1998) as one of "the two best books on the subject" by Kenneth Elzinga in his invited address to the Southern Economics Association (Elzinga, 2001, p. 255).

Looking back over 60 years, it is clear that the AEA Committee on Economic Education has come a long way since the initial reluctance of the Association's Executive Committees to appoint a standing committee in this area. Indeed, it is not too much to say that the modern economics education movement stands on the shoulders of three giants whose pioneering work in the 1950s and 1960s established unprecedented and unduplicated landmarks in the history of economic education. These three are Ben W. Lewis of Oberlin College, G. L. Bach of Carnegie Institute of Technology (later Stanford University), and Rendigs Fels of Vanderbilt University. The quality of their work and their professional standing made interest, involvement, and research in the teaching of economics an important and respectable part of the economics profession. They are gone now, but their legacy lives on in the work of the next generation of economic education leaders whose work is mentioned and cited in this chapter. The AEA Membership Directory began listing the Teaching of Economics as a field of specialization in 1978, and the National Association of Economic Educators was founded in 1980. A search of the AEA's Membership Directory in 2010 revealed that 256 economists listed JEL Code A2 "Economic Education and Teaching of Economics" as their primary field of specialization, and there are now master's degree programs in economic education at Ashland University, the University of Delaware, and the University of Nebraska-Lincoln. Delaware and Nebraska also have Ph.D. programs in economic education.

JOINT COUNCIL ON ECONOMIC EDUCATION (JCEE)

The Joint Council on Economic Education was incorporated in January 1949 as an independent, non-profit, non-partisan educational organization to encourage, improve, coordinate and serve the economics education movement. The somewhat unusual use of "Joint" in the name of the organization was explained by its first Director, G. Derwood Baker of New York University, as the result of decisions made at the end of a three-week workshop held on the campus of the Riverdale School for Boys in New York City in the Summer of 1948. This workshop brought together a highly selected group of educators and economists from city and state school systems, universities, research foundations, governmental agencies, business and labor organizations. At the conclusion of the workshop there was unanimous agreement that the participants "had merely broken ground" and that further collaborative efforts of the various groups involved was needed (Baker, 1950, p. 394). An Interim Committee on Economic Education was formed. The Executive Board of this Interim Committee consulted with representatives of other educational organizations and with business and labor leaders before formally establishing and incorporating the JCEE in January 1949. When it was formally incorporated, the JCEE by-laws required representation on its governing body from business, labor, agriculture, education, and economic research organizations. Baker later wrote: "The substantial influence of the Joint Council on Economic Education has been achieved by adhering to well-conceived guiding principles which have assured objectivity and full representation of opinion from professional, business, labor, and farm organizations" (Baker, 1960, p. 401).

Baker retired and was succeeded by M. L. Frankel in 1955. Frankel's title was later changed from Director to President, and he led the Council for 23 years until he retired in 1977. Frankel's professional background was Social Studies Education, but a hallmark of his leadership was maintaining close ties with the AEA Committee on Economic Education and having professional economists of the stature of G. L. Bach, Rendigs Fels, and Ben Lewis on the JCEE Board of Directors. Lawrence Senesh, who was hired in 1952, was the first economist on the JCEE staff. His title was changed to Assistant Director in 1953, and he continued in that capacity until he left to become the first Professor of Economic Education in the United States at Purdue University in 1957.[17]

From its inception, the JCEE placed a heavy emphasis on pre-college teacher training and in-service workshops led by affiliated state councils on economic education. At the time of the publication of the Task Force *Report* in 1961, 29 state councils and one in

Puerto Rico were identified with the statement that they, along with the national head-quarters, "were established to provide advice and assistance to school officials, teachers and others interested in the teaching of economics in the schools"(Committee for Economic Development, 1961, p. 79).

Developmental Economic Education Program (DEEP)

Publication of the Task Force *Report* led the JCEE to establish a process called the Developmental Economic Education Program (DEEP) under the overall coordination of S. Stowell Symmes, its Director of Curriculum, who was hired to implement the program. The aim of the DEEP process was to bring about curriculum change and increase economic understanding through a partnership involving school districts, teachers, administrators, universities, and volunteers and funders from foundations, businesses and labor organizations.[18] Michael Watts (1991) analyzed the first 27 years of the DEEP process in three phases: experimental development (1964–7); cooperating school enrollment (1968–83); and expansion and enhancement (1984–90). The key publication of the first phase was a two-part document: *Teacher's Guide to Developmental Economic Education Program, Part 1: Economic Ideas and Concepts* (JCEE, 1964a); and *Teacher's Guide to Developmental Economic Education Program, Part 2: Suggestions for Grade Placement and Development of Economic Ideas and Concepts* (JCEE, 1964b). Part 1 was written by James D. Calderwood of the University of Southern California to further develop and explain the basic economic concepts in the Task Force *Report*. Part 2 had four sections dealing with the elementary level (written by Ila M. Nixon, Lawrence Senesh, and Dorothy Coles Wass); the junior high level (written by James D. Calderwood, Edwin Fenton, and Edythe Gaines); the senior high level (written by John E. Maher, John P. McIntyre, Roy A. Price, and Stowell Symmes); and business education (written by Robert L. Darcy, Percy L. Guyton, David Meyers, and Roman F. Warmke). As the years passed, these teacher guides were replaced by other documents dealing with economic content and the scope and sequence placement of basic economic concepts in the schools, and the JCEE developed a variety of print and audio visual materials and tests to train and aid teachers in grades K-12.

Master Curriculum Guide

A key development in the second stage of the DEEP process was the publication of a two-part *Master Curriculum Guide in Economics for the Nation's Schools*. Part I, *A Framework for Teaching Economics: Basic Concepts* was published in 1977 (Hansen, Bach, Calderwood, and Saunders, 1977) and revised in 1984 (Saunders, Bach, Calderwood, and Hansen with Stein, 1984). Part II of the Guide, *Strategies for Teaching Economics*, generated a series of six publications dealing with teaching economics at various grade levels and in various subject matter courses.[19] The main themes of the various strategies volumes were integrated into a single document in 1988 as *Economics: What and When, Scope and Sequence Guidelines, K-12* (Gilliard, Caldwell, Dalgaard, Highsmith, Reinke, and Watts with Leet, Malone, and Ellington, 1988). When the Joint Council on Economic Education changed its name to the National Council on Economic Education in 1992, the DEEP project was renamed the *EconomicsAmerica* program, and Parts I and II of the Master Curriculum Guide were merged into a single document (Saunders and Gilliard, eds 1995). The EconomicsAmerica edition of *A Framework for Teaching Economics: Basic Concepts* was also translated into Russian and other languages for use with international programs in the newly independent states of the former Soviet Union.

The 1977 edition of the *Framework* elaborated and refined the two main themes of the 1961 Task Force *Report*. With regard to "the minimum understanding of economics essential for good citizenship and attainable by high school students" (Committee for Economic Development, 1961, p. 4), the *Framework* identified and concisely explained 24 key concepts fundamental to developing economic understanding. With regard to "the replacement of emotional, unreasoned judgments by objective, rational analysis" (Committee for Economic Development, 1961, p. 14), the *Framework* explicitly presented and illustrated the application of a six-step decision-making model to replace the four-step model described in the Task Force *Report*. The *Framework* also emphasized the importance of economic institutions and introduced seven key measurement tools and seven broad social goals to be taken into account in evaluating economic actions and policies. The 1984 edition of the *Framework* reduced the number of key economic concepts to 22 and further refined the explanation of these concepts. It expanded and elaborated the sections dealing with measurement tools and broad social goals, and it also added a section on the grade placement of the 22 basic concepts. Perhaps the most significant contribution of the 1984 *Framework,* however, was the explanation and explicit application of a five-step decision-making grid. This grid, which modified the six-step decision-making model in the 1977 edition, was first developed and used in the *Trade-Offs* series described below. The decision-making grid encourages a systematic, reasoned approach to evaluating various alternatives with respect to specific criteria by listing alternatives in vertical rows and criteria or goals at the top of horizontal columns. The intersections of the rows and columns in this grid create boxes or "cells" which match up each alternative with each criterion. Evaluation marks such as pluses or minuses or some form of numeric evaluation scale can be placed in the cells to indicate how each alternative, including a "do nothing" alternative, helps meet each goal or criterion. Often in personal and social decision-making situations no single alternative meets all of the goals or criteria, and not all criteria are regarded as equally important. But, even in situations where goals conflict and evaluations differ, the systematic use of a decision-making grid can prove helpful in clarifying the issues and making the evaluation process a more reasoned one.

Michael A. MacDowell from the Illinois Council on Economic Education succeeded M. L. Frankel as President of the JCEE in 1977, and he presided over the enrollment and expansion phases of the DEEP program until he was succeeded by Stephen Buckles in 1989. As the DEEP program expanded, the number of state councils on economic education increased to include all 50 states, and there was a dramatic increase in the number of college and university centers for economic education from one in 1956 (Martin, 1981, p. 74) to 273 in 1990 (Walstad, 1992, p. 2045).[20] Like the JCEE, the state councils were organized as independent non-profit, non-partisan educational organizations to raise funds and enroll schools in the DEEP process. The centers, which were located in college and university departments of economics or schools of education, offered the in-service and pre-service workshops and course work needed to train the expanding number of teachers using JCEE materials in their classrooms. A *Guidebook* was developed by the JCEE to aid in these efforts (Suglia and Martin, 1990).

Voluntary National Content Standards

In 1991, JCEE President Buckles initiated an effort to have economics added to the list of subject areas included in the federal National Assessment of Educational Progress (NAEP). In 1994 Congress passed the Goals 2000 Educate America Act which added economics to the list of nine subject matter areas included, but the first national assessment of economics under this program did not take place until 2006 (Buckles and Walstad, 2008). Another national assessment of economics is scheduled for 2012 if funding is available to finance the project at that time.

Robert Duvall succeeded Buckles as President of the renamed NCEE in 1995 and assembled a coalition of organizations to develop a set of content "standards" similar to those used by other NAEP disciplines specified in the 1994 legislation. The coalition included representatives from the NCEE and its network of affiliated councils and centers, the National Association of Economic Educators, the Foundation for Teaching Economics, and the AEA Committee on Economic Education. The writing committee consisted of John Siegfried (chair), Bonnie Meszaros (who was also the overall project director), James Charkins, Nancy Hanlon, Robert Highsmith, Donna McCredie, Robert Smith, Mary Suiter, Gary Walton, Michael Watts, and Donald Wentworth. Prior to the publication of the final document, the work of the writing committee was reviewed by an official Review Committee for the National Voluntary Standards. The Review Committee was chaired by Michael Salemi and actively involved five other distinguished economists: William Baumol, Sandra Darity, Claudia Goldin, Paul Krugman, and John Taylor.

The document *Voluntary National Content Standards in Economics* was published in 1997 (National Council on Economic Education, 1997). As explained in articles by the Chair of the writing committee and the Project Director, the standards are generalizations or "what economists usually call 'principles.' They are, in fact, the fundamental propositions of economics" (Siegfried and Meszaros, 1997, p. 247; Siegfried and Meszaros, 1998, p. 139). There are 20 economics content standards. Each standard is accompanied by a rationale for its inclusion, and includes a set of benchmarks divided into grades 4, 8, and 12 achievement levels. As this chapter is being written, a revised version of the 1997 *Standards* is in press, and Paul Grimes' chapter later in this volume examines the 2010 *Standards* in more detail. It might be noted here, however, that by focusing almost exclusively on content, the parallel emphasis on rational decision-making that was in the Task Force *Report* and the 1977 and 1984 *Framework* documents has been significantly reduced. In discussing the 1984 edition of the *Framework*, John Sumansky, who was at that time the JCEE Program Director, noted: "In effect the 'reasoning model' has been raised to equality with the analytical tools" (Sumansky, 1986, p. 58). This is no longer the case, and the decision-making grid which proved to be useful in *Trade-Offs* and other programs described below appears to be fading from Council on Economic Education materials.[21]

Economic Education in Grades K-12

Over the last 20 years there have been comprehensive survey articles on the teaching of economics in the high schools (Becker, Green and Rosen, 1990; Walstad, 1992 and 2001;

Watts, 2005). Paul Grimes' chapter later in this *Handbook* brings this material up to date, so there is no need to repeat that discussion here. At the pre-high school level, however, it should be noted that a Basic Economics Test (BET) was developed to measure economic understanding of upper elementary grade students (Chizmar and Halinski, 1981; Walstad and Robson, 1990; Walstad, Rebeck and Butters, 2010a) and a Test of Economic Knowledge (TEK) (Walstad and Soper, 1987; Walstad, Rebeck and Butters, 2010b) was developed to replace an earlier Junior High School Test of Economics (Schur, 1974). Other historical developments in teaching economics at pre-high school grade levels that should be mentioned include the work of Lawrence Senesh with the Our Working World set of materials (Senesh, 1973)[22] and Marilyn Kourilsky's work with the Kinder Economy (Kourilsky, 1977) and Mini-Society (Kourilsky, 1983). Perhaps the most influential pre-high school project in the history of economics education, however, was the *Trade-Offs* educational TV/film/video series released in 1978.

Trade-offs

This series of fifteen 20-minute color programs was developed cooperatively by the JCEE, the Canadian Foundation for Economic Education, the Agency for Instructional Television, and a consortium of 53 state and provincial education and broadcasting agencies, with Phillip Saunders of Indiana University serving as the Chief Consultant for the project. Children aged 9 to 13 years old were the target age group for this series, and each program dramatized young people in activities typical of students in this age group as they reasoned their way through the economic aspects of various situations they were likely to encounter in their everyday lives. In documenting his statement that "film-makers have demonstrated the power of their medium to transmit scientific information about the economy in an interesting and accurate manner . . .", Lawrence S. Moss (1979, p. 1013) cited 32 programs. Eleven of these programs were from the *Trade-Offs* series. Several other studies documented the success of *Trade-Offs* in educating fourth to sixth grade students (Walstad, 1980; Agency for Instructional Television, 1981; Chizmar and Halinski, 1983; Chizmar and McCarney, 1984; Martin and Bender, 1985).

June Gilliard, the JCEE Director of Curriculum at the time, stated: "*Trade-Offs* represented several 'firsts' for the Joint Council. It was the Joint Council's first video/film series, the first comprehensive and sequentially developed instructional program, the first program to present and systematically apply an explicit model for economic decision making, and the first Joint Council consortium effort" (Gilliard, 1991, pp. 285–6). The scope of the *Trade-Offs* consortium, the fact that the programs were widely shown on PBS stations, and the fact that state councils on economic education used or adapted the *Guide to Trade-Offs* (Meszaros and Saunders, 1978) materials for hundreds of teacher training workshops made this project the closest we have ever come to having a nation-wide curriculum in economic education. Changes in clothing styles and inflation in prices eventually dated the *Trade-Offs* films and videos, however, and the series has not been replicated.

The early success of *Trade-Offs* led to other cooperative ventures with the Canadian Foundation for Economic Education and AIT, which changed its name to the Agency for Instructional Technology in 1982. A second consortium with state and provincial education agencies was formed to produce a series of twelve 15-minute programs for students in grades 8–10 called *Give & Take* (Freeman and Saunders, 1982). Like the *Trade-Offs* series, *Give & Take* was carefully evaluated and found to be successful with teachers and students (Agency for Instructional Technology, 1986; Chizmar, McCarney, Halinski and Racich, 1985). A third consortium was formed to produce five 15-minute video programs for seven- to ten-year-old students called *Econ and Me* (Jackson, 1989). The JCEE and AIT also worked with the US Internal Revenue Service to produce a series of at first six and later nine television and video programs for high school students on *Understanding Taxes* (Watts, 1984; Watts, Buckles and Freeman, 1984; Saunders, 1988). The very expensive development costs of these TV/video projects, changes in technology, and the increasingly intense competition for educational reform funds following the publication of *A Nation at Risk* (National Commission on Excellence in Education, 1983), however, have made it impossible to update these projects before they outlived their usefulness.[23]

Mission Focus

The departure of Robert Highsmith from the NCEE staff and the appointment of Robert F. Duvall as President and CEO of the NCEE in 1995 marked a reduction in the Council's support for college-level economics instruction and a broadening of its focus in other areas. The Council's traditional focus on economic literacy as spelled out in the Task Force *Report*, the Master Curriculum Guide's *Framework* documents, and the *Voluntary National Content Standards* continues in its *EconomicsAmerica* program. An impressive set of material at various grade levels has been developed for use in US schools and, thanks to the work of James Marlin of the University of Nebraska in the 1990s, the entire library of the Council's curriculum materials for teachers is now available in an interactive format on a *Virtual Economics* CD-ROM.

Beginning with a series of grants from the US Department of Education in 1995, the Council for Economic Education now also has an active *EconomicsInternational* program with its own set of translated materials, focusing on basic economic literacy in transition and developing economies, as well as a focus on building understanding of the global economy in the United States. Two of the main programs of *EconomicsInternational* are a Trainer of Trainers program that includes four one-week sessions for teacher-educators conducted over an academic year, and Teacher Workshops that are six-day programs for classroom teachers. These programs began with the transitioning economies of the former Soviet Union and Central and Eastern Europe, but have switched to developing economies in Latin America, Indonesia, and the Middle East (Egypt and Jordan) in recent years.

The primary motivation for changing the name of the organization from the National Council on Economic Education to the Council for Economic Education in 2009 was to emphasize its international outreach and leadership in promoting economic literacy through *EconomicsInternational*, but other recent programs have also broadened the organization's focus. A $3.5 million grant from the Ewing Marion Kauffman Foundation was received in 2006 to develop and encourage entrepreneurship education programs; and, beginning in the late 1990s, the NCEE began to broaden its focus to include financial literacy. A national Symposium on Economic and Financial Literacy was organized and conducted with the Federal Reserve Bank of Minneapolis in May

2002 and subsequent "summit" conferences on Economic and Financial Literacy were held in Washington, DC in 2005 and 2007. A complete set of K-12 materials and tests, largely financed by the Bank of America Foundation, is now part of the Council for Economic Education's *Financial Fitness for Life* curriculum; and one of the last acts of Duvall's presidency before he was succeeded by Nan Morrison in 2010 was the creation of a new HSBC National Center for Economic and Financial Education in 2009. HSBC North American Holdings is a financial services company, and the current Council for Economic Education website states: "Underwritten by a generous lead grant from HSBC-North America, the new HSCB National Center for Economic and Financial Education will magnify the Council for Economic Education's cause by promoting the importance of K-12 economic, financial, and entrepreneurship education in the United States and internationally."[24, 25]

To increase student interest and encourage more schools to offer courses in economics, the Council for Economic Education also offers the National Economics Challenge. This program is a state, regional, and national competition for high school students who compete in teams for a chance to win prizes and a trip to New York City to compete in the national finals. Many state councils and teachers also use the Stock Market Game (SMG), a Foundation for Investor Education Program that provides students with an opportunity to invest a hypothetical $100,000 in a stock market portfolio over a period of time. In addition to student interest, two recent articles indicate that participation in the SMG also increases student test performance (Grimes, Millea and Thomas, 2008; Harter and Harter, 2010).

THE NATIONAL ASSOCIATION OF ECONOMIC EDUCATORS

As the number of state councils and college and university centers on economic education began to increase during the enrollment and expansion phases of the DEEP program, there was increasing pressure to formalize and professionalize the relationship of this "network" of organizations affiliated with the JCEE. This was done with the creation of the National Association of Economic Educators (NAEE) in 1980.

In keeping with the increasing specialization that was occurring in most academic disciplines, and given the shift in the primary interest of the AEA CEE to the undergraduate economics major and the college-level TTP noted above, the NAEE made its primary goal the improvement of economic education in grades K-12. It works closely with the Council on Economic Education in planning, implementing, and evaluating the activities and programs conducted through the network of affiliated councils and centers. The NAEE also provides opportunities for the professional growth and recognition of its members through conferences, publications, and awards.

Joint meetings of the Council on Economic Education and the NAEE have been held annually since 1980, and the NAEE now has a Conference Committee along with an Executive Committee and standing committees for Professional Development, Publications, Research, Technology, and Awards and Professional Recognition. The Association's current awards and the years in which they were initiated are: Henry Villard Research Award (1986); John C. Schramm Leadership Award (1986); Bessie B. Moore Service Award (1987); Rising Star (formerly Rookie of the Year) Award (1998);

Patricia Elder (named in 2010) International Award (2001); and Abbe Jean Kehler Technology Award (2009). Over the years some NAEE center directors have also served on the AEA CEE. In 2001 former NAEE President William Walstad of the University of Nebraska became the first person from the "network" to be appointed as Chair of the AEA CEE. In 2007, he was followed by another former NAEE President, Michael Watts of Purdue University.

CONCLUDING OBSERVATIONS

The story of economic education over the past 60 years is one of expansion at both the college and pre-college levels. It is also a story of increased specialization. In commenting on the state of economic education a little over ten years ago, Salemi and Siegfried stated: "During the last 50 years, AEA leaders have largely ceded questions on teaching to specialists" (Salemi and Siegfried, 1999, p. 355). This remains the case, although several distinguished economists whose primary field of specialization is not economic education have served and continue to serve on the editorial board of *The Journal of Economic Education*. The guarantee of publication of one session in the *AER: Papers and Proceedings* and the prospect of publishing an expanded version of this session or another session in *The Journal of Economic Education* has also played a role in inducing prominent economists to serve on the AEA CEE.

While the expansion of interest and activity in economic education has been impressively broad, it has also been somewhat thin. At most colleges and universities, even those with a NAEE-affiliated center for economic education, there is often only one person specializing in economic education. When these people resign or retire, they are not always replaced with individuals with similar specializations or interests. This may become an increasing problem as many of the current leaders in economic education got their start as graduate students or young assistant professors during the "boom" that followed the Task Force activity in the late 1960s and early 1970s. As this cohort reaches retirement age, the task of replacing them is likely to be a significant challenge. There are also some signs of increased specialization within the NAEE network that may weaken ties with college and university campuses. In early years, the state councils were often located on the same campuses as one of the affiliated centers for economic education. Subsequent demands for fundraising and other promotional activities have resulted in some state councils now being led by individuals whose background has not been in academia, and some state council offices have moved to non-campus locations.

There are other persistent challenges to the economic education movement. Reflecting on his work with the Task Force, Paul Samuelson noted the perpetual struggle for space in the pre-college curriculum and stated: "Each morning, the rock has to be rolled up the hill again" (Samuelson, 1987, p. 107). The problem of economics instruction for pre-service and in-service teachers also persists. The number of schools participating in the *EconomicsAmerica* program and the number of teachers infusing economics content into their history, social studies or business education courses continues to fluctuate with turnover in school administrators and teachers. If all teachers were required to take more economics before they graduate from college, turnover would cause less of a problem and in-service workshops could be delivered more efficiently.[26]

The response to the AEA CEE's TTP and TIP programs indicates that the improvement of teaching by economists at the college level has progressed further than the economics training of pre-college teachers, but challenges at the college and university level also remain. Few of the recommendations made by Salemi and Siegfried in 1999 have been adopted, and the teaching of economics at two-year colleges remains largely unexplored. Keeping materials and tests up to date is always a challenge; and, outside the use of some essay questions on advanced placement exams, the challenge of developing widely usable, valid, reliable, and efficient methods of assessment that go beyond the multiple choice and questionnaire format remains unmet at both the pre-college and college level.

Someone enlisting in the economic education movement today finds a structure and opportunities that could hardly have been imagined when the Taylor Committee was appointed in 1944. The chapters that follow in this *Handbook* should prove very helpful to those who choose to follow in the footsteps of the economists and educators who have gone before.

NOTES

1. I want to thank the following people who, in addition to the editors of this *Handbook*, provided information or offered helpful comments on an earlier draft of this chapter: Stephen Buckles, Barbara Devita, Patricia Elder, Paul Grimes, Lee Hansen, Robert Highsmith, David Martin, Bonnie Meszaros, Jim O'Neill, Michael Salemi, John Siegfried, Stowell Symmes, William Walstad, and Michael Watts. Even with all of this help, the usual caveat applies.
2. The Joint Council on Economic Education changed its name to the National Council on Economic Education in 1992 and to the Council for Economic Education in 2009. In discussing the activities and publications of this organization, this chapter will use the name or acronym at the time of the activities or publications cited. To avoid confusion with the AEA's Committee on Economic Education for which the acronym CEE is used, however, the Council for Economic Education's name will be spelled out in full.
3. William B. Walstad's edited book *An International Perspective on Economic Education* (Walstad, 1994) has chapters on economic education in the United Kingdom (Whitehead, pp. 137–55), Canada (Myatt and Waddell, pp. 157–67), Japan (Ellington and Uozumi, pp. 169–81), German-speaking countries (Beck and Krumm, pp. 183–201), Korea (Kim, pp. 203–18), Australia (McKenna, pp. 219–32), Russia (Rushing, pp. 233–54), Eastern Europe (Vredeveld and Ispirodonova, pp. 255–72), and China (Shen and Shen, pp. 273–89).

    A more recent edited book by Michael Watts and William Walstad, *Reforming Economics and Economics Teaching in Transition Economies: From Marx to Markets in the Classroom* (Watts and Walstad, 2002), has chapters on economic education in Belarus (Kovzik, Kovalenko, Chepikov, and Watts, pp. 117–30), Bulgaria (Phipps, Vredeveld, and Voikova, pp. 131–43), Kyrgyzstan (Grunloh and Aksenenko, pp. 144–60), Latvia (Biske and Cobb, pp. 161–75), Poland (Brant, Lines, and Szczurkowska, pp. 176–91), Romania (Lopus and Stoicescu, pp. 192–206), Russia (McKinnon and Ravitchev, pp. 207–19) and Ukraine (Dick, Melnyk, and Odorzynski, pp. 220–32).

    Even more recently, a series of papers on economic education in Australia (Round and Shanahan, 2010), England (Davies and Durden, 2010), Japan (Yamaoka, Asano, and Abe, 2010), and Korea (Hahn and Jang, 2010), was published and summarized in the *Journal of Economic Education* (Watts and Walstad, 2010); and some chapters later in this *Handbook* report on economic education activities in countries outside the United States.
4. A considerably more detailed account of the AEA's slowly evolving position on economic education, particularly pre-college economic education, which quotes from the minutes of several meetings of the AEA Executive Committee, is found in Saunders (1992). Appendix I of this account lists the reports of various AEA committees dealing with economic education, published in the *Proceedings* section of the *American Economic Review: Papers and Proceedings (P&P)* for the years 1950–90. Appendix II lists the papers and discussions published in the *Papers* section of the P&P for the same years.
5. Leamer's article presents a very comprehensive description and analysis of the materials published on the

teaching of economics prior to 1950, and it is full of interesting observations and insights that summarize his lengthy bibliography, published in the same supplement to the December 1950 *American Economic Review* (Leamer, 1950b). Hinshaw and Siegfried (1991) have also published an interesting article that describes in some detail papers presented at AEA meetings prior to World War II; and Chapter 2 of David Martin's unpublished doctoral dissertation (Martin, 1981) contains quotations from some early AEA meetings, including a 1918 Report of the Committee on Economics in Secondary Schools (Towne, Virtue, and Clow, 1918).

6. The creation of this first Standing Committee on Economic Education was a tribute to the extended and persistent efforts of Chairman Lewis, of whom G. L. Bach later said: "For over a decade, he has been 'Mr. Economic Education' to economists and to educators in the secondary schools. No one has done more to further humane and effective economics teaching" (Bach, 1969, p. 601). A year after the creation of the Committee in 1955, Lewis presented a very influential paper at the 1956 AEA annual meeting entitled "Economic Understanding: Why and What" (Lewis, 1957). A sixth member, Clark L. Allen, was also added to the Standing Committee in 1957.

7. In the preface to the Task Force *Report*, which was published in September 1961, Donald K. David, Chairman of the Committee for Economic Development which financed the study, and 1960 AEA President Schultz noted: "The Task Force is a distinguished one. Its economist members, at the time of appointment, included the president-elect of the American Economic Association, its two vice presidents, a member of its executive committee, and the chairman of its Committee on Economic Education. All five are distinguished authors and teachers. The two members from the field of education are similarly experienced in the teaching of economics and social studies at the high school level" (Committee for Economic Development, 1961, p. 4).

8. As noted below, in more recent years, the AEA Committee has sponsored several other sessions and activities at the AEA annual meetings in addition to the session designated for publication in the *AER: P&P*.

9. The CEE later played a key role in helping the JCEE obtain a grant from the Sloan Foundation to follow up the Haley reports by sponsoring four projects offering alternative approaches to teaching the college introductory courses at Oklahoma State University (Leftwich and Sharp, 1974b), Vanderbilt University (Fels, 1974), Florida State University (Tuckman and Tuckman, 1975), and Indiana University (Saunders, 1975). Each of these projects was reported as a Special Issue of the *Journal of Economic Education*, and all four projects were evaluated in a paper by Allen C. Kelly (1977). Three of the projects also led to the publication of commercial course materials (Leftwich and Sharp, 1974a; Fels and Uhler, 1976; Saunders, 1977a and 1977b).

10. In addition to two 30-item versions of a microeconomics test and a macroeconomics test, the second edition of TUCE also had two 30-item versions of "hybrid" macro/micro tests. A Hybrid TUCE (Saunders and Welsh, 1975) was used in a major study of the lasting effects of college introductory economics courses (Saunders, 1980).

11. These reviews were followed by two others (Becker, 1997; Siegfried and Walstad, 1998) that indicated that articles on economic education have now appeared in several other journals in addition to the *JEE* and *AER*. Using articles published from 1991 through April 2005, Lo, Wong and Mixon listed the top ten journals based on adjusted citations per page as: *Journal of Economic Literature, Review of Economics and Statistics, American Economic Review, Economic Inquiry, Economic Journal, Journal of Economic Perspectives, Applied Economics*, and *Journal of Finance* (Lo, Wong, and Mixon, 2008, p. 898).

12. AEA CEE Chairs Allen Kelly and Lee Hansen worked with the JCEE in persuading the College Board to develop an Advanced Placement Test in Economics. This program was first implemented during the 1988–9 academic year (Buckles and Morton, 1988) and continues to the present (Morton 2003a; Morton 2003b; Morton, 2003c). With funding from the Lilly Endowment and several publishing companies, the AEA CEE also co-sponsored a conference on the state of economics principles textbooks with the *Journal of Economic Education* in September 1987 (Bartlett and Weidenaar, 1988), and it cooperated with the independent AEA Commission on Graduate Education in Economics (COGEE), which sponsored a session at the December 1989 AEA meetings. Former CEE Chair Lee Hansen served as the Executive Secretary of the COGEE. His report (Hansen, 1991) was published with the Commission's final report in *The Journal of Economic Literature* in 1991 (Krueger, Arrow, Blanchard, Blinder, Goldin, Leamer, Lucas, Panzar, Penner, Schultz, Stiglitz, and Summers, 1991).

13. William Walstad's 2002 CEE report noted: "The total of $673,000 in secured funding for these three research projects is an impressive outcome for the initial outlay of $26,000 by the AEA to fund the organizing conference in May 2000" (Walstad, 2002, p. 515).

14. All modules are freely available on the AEA CEE's website <http://www.vanderbilt.edu/AEA/AEACEE/ Econometrics_Handbook/index.htm>.

15. Information about this conference is also available on the AEA CEE's website <http://www.vanderbilt. edu/AEA/AEACEE/Conference/index.htm>.

16. Beginning in 2009, reports for all AEA standing committees are no longer published in the printed *AER Papers & Proceedings* volume. They are now posted on an AEA Web page.

17. Theodore Boyden and Percy Guyton followed Senesh as economists on the JCEE staff, but the longest serving and most influential economics Ph.D. to serve on the JCEE staff was Arthur. L. Welsh. Welsh was hired from the University of Iowa in 1966 to direct the JCEE's College and University Program, and he left with the title of Vice President and Senior Economist in 1984 to become a Professor of Economics at Penn State University. The last economics Ph.D. to serve an extended period on the JCEE/NCEE's full-time staff was Robert Highsmith, whose title was Director of Research from 1984–89 and Director of Programs and Research from 1989 until his departure in 1994. Both of these economists worked closely with the AEA CEE and played a key role in several CEE projects. Welsh wrote the proposal to the General Electric Education Foundation that led to the first research workshops for directors of JCEE-affiliated centers for economic education. He co-directed these workshops and edited the papers that resulted in a volume published by the JCEE (Welsh, 1972). In addition to his key role in revising the TUCE and initiating the TTP mentioned above, Welsh also edited the four special issues of the *Journal of Economic Education* that appeared in 1974 and 1975. Welsh also negotiated the arrangement with the Helen Dwight Reid Educational Foundation to assume publication of the *JEE* in 1982. Highsmith led the effort to construct the database that was used in the 1987 and 1988 Princeton research workshops mentioned above and participated in the preparation of the special research issue of the *Journal of Economic Education* that followed (Buckles and Highsmith, 1990).

18. A more detailed explanation of the DEEP process was provided by Walstad and Soper in the introduction to their edited volume *Effective Economic Education in the Schools*. They noted:

    DEEP basically embodies three principles intended to achieve *effective* economic education in the schools. First, DEEP requires a commitment on the part of a school district to provide economics instruction from the elementary through the secondary grades. The district commitment is voluntary, but enrolling in DEEP means that the administrators, teachers, and parents in a community recognize the need for students to receive a nonpartisan education in economics. Second, DEEP is a cooperative and flexible model of curriculum change. It involves a partnership among college and university economic educators and school personnel working on needs identified in the school district, such as the revision of the curriculum, and on the dissemination or development of new instructional materials. Third, and most critical to the success of DEEP, is teacher education in economics. Economics is a challenging subject, and it must be taught well for students to improve their understanding. That means that teachers must have a mastery of basic economic concepts and how to teach the subject to students. DEEP improves the economic education of teachers through in-service courses or workshops, which are often sponsored cooperatively by school districts, college and university centers for economic education, and state councils on economic education. (Walstad and Soper, 1991, p. 11).

19. The six strategies volumes, their authors, and the year of their publication by the JCEE were: *Strategies for Teaching Economics: Primary Level (grades 1–3)* (Davison, 1977); *Strategies for Teaching Economics: Intermediate Level (grades 4–6)* (Kourilsky, 1978); *Strategies for Teaching Economics: Basic Business and Consumer Education (secondary)* (Niss, Breneke, and Clow, 1979); *Strategies for Teaching Economics: United States History (secondary)* (O'Neill, 1980a); *Strategies for Teaching Economics: World Studies (secondary)* (O'Neill, 1980b); *Strategies for Teaching Economics Junior High Level (grades 7–9)* (Banaszak and Clawson, 1981).

20. The first center for economic education in the United States was established at the University of Illinois in 1956. This center was directed by Lewis E. Wagner, who, as mentioned above, later chaired the Task Force's Materials Evaluation Committee.

21. The second of the twenty 2010 content standards states: "Effective decision making requires comparing the additional cost of alternatives with the additional benefits. Many choices involve doing a little more or a little less of something: few choices are 'all or nothing' decisions" (Council for Economic Education, 2010, p. 5). The benchmarks for grades 4, 8, and 12 elaborate on this statement, but don't compare with the more extensive explanation and applications of the decision-making grid in the 1984 *Framework*. It should also be noted that in his comments on the 1997 *Standards*, W. Lee Hansen stated: "The almost exclusive focus on *principles-based* standards in economics ignores the need for an explicit *skill* standard" (Hansen, 1998, p. 152; emphasis in original) and "The tested value of the reasoned approach leads to the conclusion that it could easily have been elevated to the status of a skill standard. . . . In short, a skills standard needs to be added to the economics content standards" (Hansen, 1998, p. 153). It does not appear that Hansen's advice has been followed in the 2010 edition of the *Standards*; and this may be the result of an apparent mandate to focus narrowly on only *content* standards.

22. Senesh was awarded an honorary doctorate by Purdue University in 1977, and his work and legacy is described in some detail in Harrington and Rueff (2000).

23. Mike Watts has observed: "The new technologies that 'replaced' the film series – most notably computer

CDs and videos – are very rarely designed or used to show to an entire class. They are more often put up on work stations that individual students or small groups may use, often as a supplementary assignment rather than the main lesson. Ironically, in some ways, we're back to more focus on textbook and print lessons/activities, which are never used as widely and don't have the visual impact or other pedagogical advantages, etc., but they are cheaper" (Watts, 2010b, p. 3).

24. <http://www.councilforeconed.org/nationalcenter/info.php>, accessed April 25, 2011.

25. The creation of the HSBC National Center marks the first time that a named center for economic education is not located on a college or university campus. Some concerns about this apparently arose in preliminary discussions with the AEA CEE. The minutes of the CEE meeting on January 5, 2008 state:

> Mike Watts asked NCEE for clarification on the NCEE's commitment to an academic, non-profit organizational structure for its program delivery network, which he views as a necessary condition for the continuing special relationship that NCEE and the AEA CEE have enjoyed since the 1950s. Bob Duvall asked MacDonald to report NCEE's continued commitment to an academic delivery network, and asked that the minutes of this meeting include that statement. That message was well received and not unexpected, but it was also noted that the relationship between NCEE and the AEA CEE has changed substantially over time. <http://www.vanderbilt.edu/AEA/AEACEE/minutes/minutes08.htm>

For the record it should be noted that what is now the Council for Economic Education continues to support the *Journal of Economic Education* and, as indicated above, has allocated some of its US Department of Education Excellence in Economic Education grants to finance William Becker's development of the AEA CEE's econometric training modules.

26. In 1983 the JCEE appointed a special 13-member Committee on Teacher Education chaired by Henry Hermanowicz, who was Dean of the College of Education at Penn State University at that time. Economists Lee Hansen (Wisconsin) and James Tobin (Yale) played a leading role in this committee's work (Hermanowicz, 1991, p. 73). When the committee's report was published (JCEE, 1985 and Hermanowicz, 1991), it recommended that: all future teachers be required to take one basic course in economics, or preferably a principles sequence; all prospective teachers of social studies, business education, and home economics courses be required to take at least three semester courses in economics, including a principles sequence and an advanced course; teachers who specialize in teaching economics in secondary schools should complete at least six semester courses; and teachers of advanced placement or honors courses in economics should take at least ten courses or the equivalent of an economics major. Walstad's review in 2001, however, indicates that state certification requirements fall far short of these recommendations.

REFERENCES

Agency for Instructional Television (1981), *Trade-Offs: What the Research is Saying*, Research Report 82, Bloomington, IN: Agency for Instructional Television.

Agency for Instructional Technology (1986), *Give & Take: What the Research is Saying*, Research Report 95, Bloomington, IN: Agency for Instructional Technology.

Allgood, S., W. Bosshardt, W. van der Klaauw and M. Watts (2004), "What students remember and say about college economics years later", *American Economic Review: Papers & Proceedings*, **94** (2), 259–65.

Bach, G. L. (1961), "Economics in the high schools: the responsibility of the profession", *American Economic Review: Papers and Proceedings*, **51** (2), 579–86.

Bach, G. L. (1963), "Report of the national task force on economic education", *American Economic Review: Papers and Proceedings*, **53** (2), 720–21.

Bach, G. L. (1969), "Report of the committee on economic education", *American Economic Review: Papers and Proceedings*, **59** (2), 600–601.

Bach, G. L. (1973), "An agenda for improving the teaching of economics", *American Economic Review: Papers and Proceedings*, **63** (2), 303–8.

Bach, G. L. and P. Saunders (1965), "Economic education: aspirations and achievements", *American Economic Review*, **55** (3), 329–56.

Bach, G. L. and P. Saunders (1966), "Lasting effects of economics courses at different types of institutions", *American Economic Review*, **56** (3), 505–11.

Baker, G. D. (1950), "The joint council on economic education", *Journal of Educational Psychology*, **23** (7), 389–96.

Baker, G. D. (1960), "Economic education", in C. W. Harris (ed.), *Encyclopedia of Educational Research* (3rd edition), New York: Macmillan, pp. 398–403.

Banaszak, R. A. and E. U. Clawson (1981), *Strategies for Teaching Economics: Junior High Level (grades 7–9)*, New York: Joint Council on Economic Education.

Bartlett, R. and D. J. Weidenaar (1988), "An introduction to the proceedings of the 1987 invitational conference on the principles of economics textbook", *Journal of Economic Education*, **19** (2), 109–12.

Baumol, W. J. and R. J. Highsmith (1988), "Variables affecting success in economic education: preliminary findings from a new database", *American Economic Review: Papers and Proceedings*, **78** (2), 257–62.

Becker, W. E. (1997), "Teaching economics to undergraduates", *Journal of Economic Literature*, **35** (3), 1347–73.

Becker, W. E. and W. B. Walstad (1987), *Econometric Modeling in Economic Education Research*, Boston, MA: Kluwer-Nijhoff.

Becker, W. E. and M. Watts (eds) (1998), *Teaching Economics to Undergraduates: Alternatives to Chalk and Talk*, Cheltenham, UK and Lyme, USA: Edward Elgar.

Becker, W. E., W. Green and S. Rosen (1990), "Research on high school economic education", *Journal of Economic Education*, **21** (3), 231–45.

Becker, W. E., M. Watts and S. Becker (eds), (2005), *Teaching Economics: More Alternatives to Chalk and Talk*, Cheltenham, UK and Northampton, MA, USA: Edward Elgar.

Becker, W. E., R. Highsmith, P. Kennedy and W. Walstad (1991), "An agenda for research on economic education in colleges and universities", *Journal of Economic Education*, **22** (3), 241–50.

Bell, J. W. (1961), "Report of the secretary for the year 1960", *American Economic Review: Papers and Proceedings*, **51** (2), 597–616.

Bell, J. W. (1962) "Report of the secretary for the year 1961", *American Economic Review: Papers and Proceedings*, **52** (2), 536–52.

Bowen, H. R. (1953), "Graduate education in economics", *American Economic Review*, **43** (4) Part 2, i–223.

Buckles, S. and R. Highsmith (1990), "Preface to special research issue", *Journal of Economic Education*, **21**(3), 229–30.

Buckles, S. and J. S. Morton (1988), "The effects of advanced placement on introductory economics courses", *American Economic Review: Papers and Proceedings*, **78** (2), 263–8.

Buckles, S. and W. B. Walstad (2008), "The national assessment of educational progress in economics: test framework, content specifications and results", *Journal of Economic Education*, **39** (1), 100–106.

Chizmar, J. F. and R. S. Halinski (1981), *Basic Economics Test (Grades 4–6): Examiner's Manual*, New York: Joint Council on Economic Education.

Chizmar, J. F. and R. S. Halinski (1983), "Performance on the Basic Economics Test (BET) and 'Trade-Offs'", *Journal of Economic Education*, **14** (1), 18–29.

Chizmar, J. F. and B. J. McCarney (1984), "An evaluation of a 'Trade-Offs' implementation using canonical estimation of joint educational production functions", *The Journal of Economic Education*, **15** (1), 11–20.

Chizmar, J. F., B. J. McCarney, R. S. Halinski and M. J. Racich (1985), "'Give & Take' economics achievement and basic skills development", *The Journal of Economic Education*, **16** (2), 99–115.

Coats, A. W. (1985), "The American economic association and the economics profession", *Journal of Economic Literature*, **23** (4), 1697–727.

Colander, D. and K. McGoldrick (2009a), "The economics major as part of a liberal education: the Teagle Report", *American Economic Review: Papers and Proceedings*, **99** (2), 611–23.

Colander, D. and K. McGoldrick (eds) (2009b), *Educating Economists: The Teagle Discussion on Reevaluating the Undergraduate Economics Major*, Cheltenham, UK and Northampton, MA, USA: Edward Elgar Publishing.

Coleman, J. R. (1963), "Economic literacy: what role for television?", *American Economic Review: Papers and Proceedings*, **53** (2), 645–52.

Coleman, J. R. and K. O. Alexander (1962), *Television Study Guide for The American Economy*, New York: McGraw-Hill Book Co.

"College of the Air's 'The American economy'" (1962), *American Economic Review*, **52** (4), 940–45.

Committee for Economic Development (1961), *Economic Education in the Schools: Report of the National Task Force on Economic Education*, New York: Committee for Economic Development.

Council for Economic Education (2010), *Voluntary National Content Standards in Economics, 2nd Edition*, New York: Council for Economic Education.

Davies, P. and G. Durden (2010), "Economic education in schools and universities in England", *Journal of Economic Education*, **41** (4), 413–24.

Davison, D. G. (1977), *Strategies for Teaching Economics: Primary Level (Grades 1–3)*, New York: Joint Council on Economic Education.

"Economics in the schools: a report by a special textbook study committee of the committee on economic education of the American Economic Association" (1963), *American Economic Review*, **53** (1), Part 2, i–27.

Elzinga, K. G. (2001), "Fifteen theses on classroom teaching", *Southern Economic Journal*, **68** (2), 249–57.

Fels, R. (1967), "A new test of understanding in college economics", *American Economic Review, Papers and Proceedings,* **57** (2), 660–66.

Fels, R. (1969), "Hard research on a soft subject: hypothesis-testing in economic education", *Southern Economic Journal,* **36** (3), 1–9.

Fels, R. (1974), "The Vanderbilt-JCEE experimental course in elementary economics", *Journal of Economic Education,* **6** (Special Issue No. 2), 1–95.

Fels, R. and P. L. Dressel (1968), *Manual: Test of Understanding in College Economics,* New York: The Psychological Corporation.

Fels, R. and R. G. Uhler (eds) (1976), *Casebook of Economic Problems and Policies: Practice in Thinking,* St. Paul, MN: West Publishing Co.

Freeman, V. and P. Saunders (1982), *A Guide to Give & Take,* Bloomington, IN: Agency for Instructional Technology.

Gilliard, J. G. (1991), "Future requirements for programs and materials", in W. B. Walstad and J. C. Soper (eds), *Effective Economic Education in the Schools,* Washington, DC: National Education Association and Joint Council on Economic Education, pp. 283–94.

Gilliard, J. G., J. Caldwell, B. R. Dalgard, R. J. Highsmith, R. Reinke and M. Watts with D. R. Leet, M. G. Malone and L. Ellington (1988), *Economics What and When – Scope and Sequence Guidelines, K-12,* New York: Joint Council on Economic Education.

Goodman, R. J., M. Maier and R. L. Moore (2003), "Regional workshops to improve the teaching skills of economics faculty", *American Economic Review: Papers and Proceedings,* **93** (2), 460–62.

Grimes, P. W., T. L. Krehbiel, J. E. Nielsen and J. F. Niss (1989), "The effectiveness of economics USA on learning and attitudes", *Journal of Economic Education,* **20** (2), 139–52.

Grimes, P. W., M. J. Millea and K. Thomas (2008), "District level mandates and high school student's understanding of economics", *The Journal of Economics and Economic Education Research,* **9** (2), 3–16.

Hahn, J. and K. Jang (2010), "Economic education in Korea: current status and changes", *Journal of Economic Education,* **41** (4), 436–47.

Haley, B. F. (1967a), "Experiments in the teaching of basic economics", *American Economic Review: Papers and Proceedings,* **57** (2), 642–51.

Haley, B. F. (1967b), *Experiments in the Teaching of Basic Economics,* New York: Joint Council on Economic Education.

Hansen, W. L. (1986), "What knowledge is most worth knowing – for economics majors", *American Economic Review: Papers and Proceedings,* **76** (2), 149–52.

Hansen, W. L. (1991), "The education and training of economics doctorates: major findings of the Executive Secretary of the American Economic Association's Commission on Graduate Education in Economics", *Journal of Economic Literature,* **29** (3), 1054–94.

Hansen, W. L. (1998), "Principles-based standards: on the voluntary national content standards in economics", *Journal of Economic Education,* **29** (2), 150–56.

Hansen, W. L. (2001), "Expected proficiencies for undergraduate economics majors", *Journal of Economic Education,* **32** (3), 231–42.

Hansen, W. L. (2009), "Reinvigorating liberal education with an expected proficiencies approach to the academic major", in D. Colander and K. McGoldrick (eds), *Educating Economists: The Teagle Discussion on Reevaluating the Undergraduate Economics Major,* Cheltenham, UK and Northampton, MA, USA: Edward Elgar Publishing, pp. 107–25.

Hansen, W. L., P. Saunders and A. L. Welsh (1980), "Teacher training programs in college economics: their development, current status and future prospects", *Journal of Economic Education,* **11** (2), 1–9.

Hansen, W. L., G. L. Bach, J. D. Calderwood and P. Saunders (1977), *A Framework for Teaching Economics: Basic Concepts,* New York: Joint Council on Economic Education.

Harrington, P. and J. Rueff (2000), *Lawrence Senesh: His Life and His Legacy,* West Lafayette, IN: Purdue University.

Harter, C. and J. F. R. Harter (2010), "Is financial literacy improved by participating in a stock market game?", *Journal for Economic Educators,* **10** (1), 21–32.

Hermanowicz, H. J. (1991), "Recommendations for teacher education in the context of the reform movement", in W. B. Walstad and J. C. Soper (eds), *Effective Economic Education in the Schools,* Washington, DC: National Education Association and Joint Council on Economic Education, pp. 70–80.

Hinshaw, C. E. and J. J. Siegfried (1991), "The role of the American Economic Association in economic education: a brief history", *Journal of Economic Education,* **22** (4), 373–81.

Jackson, P. (1989), *A Teacher's Guide to Econ and Me,* Bloomington, IN: Agency for Instructional Technology.

Joint Council on Economic Education (1961), *Study Materials for Economic Education in the Schools: Report of the Materials Evaluation Committee,* New York: Joint Council on Economic Education.

Joint Council on Economic Education (1964a), *Teacher's Guide to Developmental Economic Education Program, Part One: Economic Ideas and Concepts,* New York: Joint Council on Economic Education.

Joint Council on Economic Education (1964b), *Teacher's Guide to Developmental Economic Education Program, Part Two: Suggestions for Grade Placement and Development of Economic Ideas and Concepts*, New York: Joint Council on Economic Education.

Joint Council on Economic Education (1985), *Economic Education for Future Elementary and Secondary Teachers: Basic Recommendations*, New York: Joint Council on Economic Education.

Kelly, A. C. (1977), "Teaching principles of economics: the joint council experimental economics course project", *American Economic Review: Papers and Proceedings*, **67** (2), 105–9.

Kourilsky, M. L. (1977), "The kinder economy: a case study of kindergarten pupils' acquisition of economic concepts", *The Elementary School Journal*, **77** (3), 182–91.

Kourilsky, M. L. (1978), *Strategies for Teaching Economics: Intermediate Level (Grades 4–6)*, New York: Joint Council on Economic Education.

Kourilsky, M. L. (1983), *Mini-Society: Experiencing Real-World Economics in the Elementary School Classroom*, Menlo Park, CA: Addison-Wesley Publishing Company.

Krueger, A. O., K. J. Arrow, O. J. Blanchard, A. S. Blinder, C. Goldin, E. E. Leamer, R. Lucas, J. Panzar, R. G. Penner, T. P. Schultz, J. E. Stiglitz, and L. H. Summers (1991), "Report of the commission on graduate education in economics", *Journal of Economic Literature*, **29** (3), 1035–53.

Leamer, L. E. (1950a), "A brief history of economics in general education", *American Economic Review*, **40** (5), Part 2, 18–33.

Leamer, L. E. (1950b), "A selected bibliography on economics in general education", *American Economic Review*, **40** (5), Part 2, 202–13.

Leftwich, R. H. and A. M. Sharp (1974a), *Economics of Social Issues*, Dallas, TX: Business Publications, Inc.

Leftwich, R. H. and A. M. Sharp (1974b), "Syllabus for an 'Issues Approach' to teaching economic principles", *Journal of Economic Education*, **6** (Special Issue No. 1), 1–32.

Lewis, B. W. (1957), "Economic understanding: why and what", *American Economic Review: Papers and Proceedings*, **47** (2), 653–70.

Lo, M., M. C. S. Wong and F. G. Mixon (2008), "Ranking economics journals, economics departments, and economists using teaching-focused research productivity", *Southern Economics Journal*, **74** (3), 894–906.

Mansfield, E. and N. Behravesh (1986), *Economics U$A*, New York: W. W. Norton.

Martin, D. A. and D. S. Bender (1985), "'Trade-Offs', field dependence/independence and sex-based economics comprehension differences", *Journal of Economic Education*, **16** (1), 62–70.

Martin, D. V. (1981), "A conflict model content analysis of the supplementary materials most frequently used in teaching economics in Georgia's public high schools", Atlanta, GA: Unpublished Doctoral Dissertation, Georgia State University.

McConnell, C. R. and J. R. Felton (1964), "A controlled evaluation of 'The American Economy'", *American Economic Review*, **54** (4), 403–7.

Meszaros, B. and P. Saunders (1978), *A Guide to Trade-Offs*, Bloomington, IN: Agency for Instructional Television.

Morton, J. (2003a), *Advanced Placement Economics: Macroeconomic Student Activities* (3rd edition), New York: Council on Economic Education.

Morton, J. (2003b), *Advanced Placement Economics: Microeconomic Student Activities* (3rd edition), New York: Council on Economic Education.

Morton, J. (2003c), *Advanced Placement Economics: Teacher Resource Manual* (3rd edition), New York: Council on Economic Education.

Moss, L. S. (1979), "Film and the transmission of economic knowledge: a report", *Journal of Economic Literature*, **17** (3), 1005–2019.

National Commission on Excellence in Education (1983), *A Nation at Risk: The Imperative for Educational Reform*, Washington, DC: US Government Printing Office.

National Council on Economic Education (1997), *Voluntary National Content Standards in Economics*, New York: National Council on Economic Education.

Niss, J. F., J. S. Breneke and J. E. Clow (1979), *Strategies for Teaching Economics: Basic Business and Consumer Education (Secondary)*, New York: Joint Council on Economic Education.

Olson, P. R. (1961), "This is economics in the schools", *American Economic Review: Papers and Proceedings*, **51** (2), 564–70.

O'Neill, J. B. (1980a), *Strategies for Teaching Economics: World Studies (Secondary)*, New York: Joint Council on Economic Education.

O'Neill, J. B. (1980b), *Strategies for Teaching Economics: United States History (Secondary)*, New York: Joint Council on Economic Education.

Robinson, M. A., H. C. Morton and J. D. Calderwood (1956), *Introduction to Economic Reasoning*, Washington, DC: The Brookings Institution.

Round, D. K. and M. P. Shanahan (2010), "The economics degree in Australia: down but not out?", *Journal of Economic Education,* **41** (4), 425–35.

Salemi, M. K. and J. J. Siegfried (1999), "The state of economic education", *American Economic Review: Papers and Proceedings,* **89** (2), 355–61.

Salemi, M. K. and W. B. Walstad (2010), *Teaching Innovations in Economics: Strategies and Applications for Interactive Instruction,* Cheltenham, UK and Northampton, MA, USA: Edward Elgar.

Salemi, M. K., P. Saunders and W. B. Walstad (1996), "Teacher training programs in economics: past, present, and future", *American Economic Review: Papers and Proceedings,* **86** (2), 460–64.

Salemi, M. K., J. J. Siegfried, K. Sosin, W. B. Walstad and M. Watts (2001), "Research in economic education: five new initiatives", *American Economic Review: Papers and Proceedings,* **91** (2), 440–45.

Samuelson, P. A. (1987), "How economics has changed", *Journal of Economic Education,* **18** (2), 107–10.

Saunders, P. (1964), "The effectiveness of 'The American Economy' in training secondary school teachers", *American Economic Review,* **54** (4), 396–403.

Saunders, P. (1975), "Experimental course development in introductory economics at Indiana University", *Journal of Economic Education,* **6** (Special Issue No. 4), 1–128.

Saunders, P. (1977a), *Introduction to Macroeconomics: Student Workbook,* Columbus, OH: Collegiate Publishing, Inc.

Saunders, P. (1977b), *Introduction to Microeconomics: Student Workbook,* Columbus, OH: Collegiate Publishing, Inc.

Saunders, P. (1980), "The lasting effects of introductory economics courses", *Journal of Economic Education,* **12** (1), 1–14.

Saunders, P. (1981), *Revised Test of Understanding in College Economics: Interpretive Manual,* New York: National Council on Economic Education.

Saunders, P. (1988), A *Teacher's Guide to Understanding Taxes,* Bloomington, IN: Agency for Instructional Technology.

Saunders, P. (1991a), *Test of Understanding of College Economics: Examiner's Manual (Third Edition),* New York: National Council on Economic Education.

Saunders, P. (1991b), "The third edition of the test of understanding college economics", *American Economic Review: Papers and Proceedings,* **81** (2), 32–7.

Saunders, P. (1992), "The official position of the American Economic Association on economics education" in J. S. Brenneke (ed.), *An Economy at Risk: Does Anyone Care?* Atlanta, GA: Georgia State University Business Press, pp. 35–76.

Saunders, P. and J. Gilliard (eds), (1995), *A Framework for Teaching Basic Economic Concepts, with Scope and sequence Guidelines, K-12,* New York: National Council on Economic Education.

Saunders, P. and W. B. Walstad (eds) (1990), *The Principles of Economics Course: A Handbook for Instructors,* New York: McGraw-Hill.

Saunders, P. and A. L. Welsh (1975), "The hybrid TUCE: origin, data, and limitations", *Journal of Economic Education,* **7** (1), 13–19.

Saunders, P., R. Fels and A. L. Welsh, (1981), "The revised test of understanding of college economics", *American Economic Review: Papers and Proceedings,* **71** (2), 190–94.

Saunders, P., A. L. Welsh and W. L. Hansen (1978), *Resource Manual for Teacher Training Programs in Economics,* New York: Joint Council on Economic Education.

Saunders, P., G. L. Bach, J. D. Calderwood and W. L. Hansen with H. Stein (1984), *A Framework for Teaching the Basic Concepts* (2nd edition), New York: Joint Council on Economic Education.

Schur, L. (1974), *Junior High School Test of Economics: Interpretive Manual and Rationale,* New York: Joint Council on Economic Education.

Science Research Associates (1964), *Test of Economic Understanding: Interpretive Manual and Discussion Guide,* Chicago: Science Research Associates.

Senesh, L. (1973), *Our Working World (A six-level basal series),* Chicago: Science Research Associates.

Siegfried, J. J. and R. Fels (1979), "Research on teaching college economics: a survey", *Journal of Economic Literature,* **17** (3), 923–69.

Siegfried, J. J. and B. T. Meszaros (1997), "National voluntary content standards for pre-college economics education", *American Economic Review: Papers and Proceedings,* **87** (2), 247–53.

Siegfried, J. J. and B. T. Meszaros (1998), "Voluntary economics content standards for America's schools: rationale and development", *Journal of Economic Education,* **29** (2), 139–49.

Siegfried, J. J. and J. E. Raymond (1984), "A profile of senior economics majors in the United States", *American Economic Review: Papers & Proceedings,* **74** (2), 19–25.

Siegfried, J. J. and W. Walstad (1990), "Research on teaching college economics", in P. Saunders and W. B. Walstad (eds), *The Principles of Economics Course: A Handbook for Instructors,* New York: McGraw-Hill, pp. 270–86.

Siegfried, J. J. and W. B. Walstad (1998), "Research on teaching college economics", in W. B. Walstad and

P. Saunders (eds), *Teaching Undergraduate Economics: A Handbook for Instructors*, New York: McGraw-Hill, pp. 141–66.

Siegfried, J. J. and J. T. Wilkerson (1982), "The economics curriculum in the United States: 1980", *The American Economic Review: Papers and Proceedings*, **72** (2), 125–38.

Siegfried, J. J., R. L. Bartlett, W. L. Hansen, A. C. Kelley, D. N. McCloskey, and T. H. Tietenberg (1991a), "The economics major: can and should we do better than a B–", *American Economic Review: Papers & Proceedings*, **81** (2), 20–25.

Siegfried, J. J., R. L. Bartlet, W. L. Hansen, A. C. Kelley, D. N. McCloskey and T. H. Tietenberg (1991b), "The status and prospects of the economics major", *Journal of Economic Education*, **22** (3), 197–224.

Soper, J. C. (1979), *The Test of Economic Literacy: Discussion Guide and Rationale*, New York: Joint Council on Economic Education.

Soper, J. C. and W. B. Walstad (1987), *The Test of Economic Literacy: Examiner's Manual* (2nd edition), New York: Joint Council on Economic Education.

Sosin, K., B. L. Blecha, R. Agarwal, R. Bartlett and J. I. Daniel (2004), "Efficiency in the use of technology in economic education: some preliminary results", *American Economic Review: Papers & Proceedings*, **94** (2), 253–8.

Stigler, G. J. (1963), "Elementary economic education", *American Economic Review: Papers and Proceedings*, **53** (2), 653–9.

Stock, W. A. and W. L. Hansen (2004), "Ph.D. program learning and job demands: how close is the match?", *American Economic Review: Papers & Proceedings*, **94** (2), 266–71.

Stock, W. A., T. A. Finegan, and J. J. Siegfried (2009), "Can you earn a Ph.D. in economics in five years?", *Economics of Education Review*, **28** (5), 523–37.

Suglia, A. and D. V. Martin (1990), *Developing Managerial and Technical Proficiency: A Guidebook of the Affiliated State Councils on Economic Education*, New York: Joint Council on Economic Education.

Sumansky, J. M. (1986), "The evolution of economic education thought as revealed through a history of the *Master Curriculum Guide in Economics: Framework for Teaching the Basic Concepts, revised 1984*", in S. Hodkinson and D. J. Whitehead (eds), *Economics Education: Research and Development Issues*, London and New York: Longmans, pp. 48–63.

Taylor, H. (ed.) (1950), "The teaching of undergraduate economics: report of the committee on the undergraduate teaching of economics and the training of economists", *American Economic Review*, **40** (5), Part 2, i–226.

Towne, E. T., G. O. Virtue and F. R. Clow (1918), "Report of the committee on economics in secondary schools", *American Economic Review: Papers & Proceedings*, **8**, 308–12.

Tuckman, H. and B. Tuckman (1975), "Toward a more effective economic principles class", *Journal of Economic Education*, **6** (Special Issue No. 3), 1–72.

Walstad, W. B. (1980), "The impact of 'Trade-Offs' and teacher training on economic understanding and attitudes", *Journal of Economic Education*, **12** (1), 41–8.

Walstad, W. B. (1992), "Economics instruction in high schools", *Journal of Economic Literature*, **30** (4), 2019–51.

Walstad, W. B. (ed.) (1994), *An International Perspective on Economic Education*, Boston/Dordrecht/London: Kluwer Academic Publishers.

Walstad, W. B. (2001), "Economic education in U.S. high schools", *Journal of Economic Perspectives*, **15** (3), 195–210.

Walstad, W. B. (2002), "Report of the committee on economic education", *American Economic Review: Papers & Proceedings*, **90** (2), 514–15.

Walstad, W. B. and K. Rebeck (2001), *Test of Economic Literacy: Third Edition*, New York: National Council on Economic Education.

Walstad, W. B. and D. Robson (1990), *Basic Economics Test Second Edition: Examiner's Manual*, New York: Joint Council on Economic Education.

Walstad, W. B. and P. Saunders (eds) (1998), *Teaching Undergraduate Economics: A Handbook for Instructors*, New York: McGraw-Hill.

Walstad, W. B. and J. C. Soper (1987), *The Test of Economic Knowledge: Examiner's Manual*, New York: Joint Council on Economic Education.

Walstad, W. B. and J. C. Soper (1991), "Effective economic education: an introduction", in W. B. Walstad and J. C. Soper (eds), *Effective Economic Education in the Schools*, Washington, DC: National Education Association and Joint Council on Economic Education, pp. 11–23.

Walstad, W. B., K. Rebeck and R. B. Butters (2010a), *Basic Economics Test (Third Edition): Examiners Manual*, New York: Council for Economic Education.

Walstad, W. B., K. Rebeck and R. B. Butters (2010b), *Test of Economic Knowledege (Second Edition) Examiners Manual*, New York: Council for Economic Education.

Walstad, W. B., M. Watts and K. Rebeck (2007), *Test of Understanding of College Economics: Examiner's Manual (Fourth Edition)*, New York: National Council on Economic Education.

Watts, M. (1984), *A Guide to Tax Whys: Understanding Taxes*, Washington, DC: Internal Revenue Service/ Bloomington, IN: Agency for Instructional Technology/ New York: Joint Council on Economic Education.

Watts, M. (1991), "Research on DEEP: the first 25 years", in W. B. Walstad and J. C. Soper (eds), *Effective Economic Education in the Schools*, Washington, DC: National Education Association and Joint Council on Economic Education, pp. 81–98.

Watts, M. (2005), "What works: a review of research on outcomes and effective program delivery in precollege economic education", http://www.councilforeconed.org/eee/research/WhatWorks.pdf, accessed April 25, 2011.

Watts, M. (2010a), "Report of the Committee on Economic Education for 2009", *American Economic Review*, **100** (2), Online Supplement, May 2010, pp. 699–703.

Watts, M. (2010b), September 13, 2010 e-mail to Phillip Saunders, 1–4.

Watts, M. and W. B. Walstad (eds) (2002), *Reforming Economics and Economics Teaching in the Transition Economies: From Marx to Markets in the Classroom*, Cheltenham, UK and Northampton, MA, USA: Edward Elgar.

Watts, M. and W. B. Walstad (2010), "Economic education in an international context", *Journal of Economic Education*, **41**(4), 410–12.

Watts, M., S. Buckles and V. Freeman (1984), *A Workshop Leader's Handbook to Accompany Tax Whys: Understanding Taxes*, Washington, DC: Internal Revenue Service/Bloomington, IN: Agency for Instructional Technology/New York: Joint Council on Economic Education.

Welsh, A. L. (ed.) (1972), *Research Papers in Economic Education*, New York: Joint Council on Economic Education.

Welsh, A. L. and R. Fels (1969), "Performance on the new test of understanding in college economics", *American Economic Review: Papers and Proceedings*, **59** (2), 224–9.

Yamaoka, M., T. Asano and S. Abe (2010), "The present state of economic education in Japan", *Journal of Economic Education*, **41** (4), 448–60.

PART II

TEACHING

Section A

Techniques

2 Case use in economics instruction
Patrick Conway

This chapter presents the unique comparative advantage of case use in an instructional curriculum. Cases are pedagogical tools with specific content, and this chapter provides a definition, describes the five characteristics of a "star quality" case, and discusses appropriate placement of cases in the syllabus. Cases are effective in stimulating all types of student learning, but they are especially effective in challenging students to develop higher-order mastery of economic concepts (as defined, for example, in Bloom et al., 1956). Three reasons for this comparative advantage are enumerated: cases promote greater learning by bringing real-world problem-solving into the classroom; cases promote discussion and debate, activities that encourage higher-order student learning; and cases facilitate formative assessment (including self-assessment) in real time and thus promote learning. Evidence in favor of all these claims is presented, and guidance on incorporating cases in the classroom is presented. This leads to a simple conclusion: case use in economic instruction challenges the students to learn. It is especially useful in challenging them to apply theoretical constructs in real-life situations, and as such is a potent tool in encouraging "learning by doing."

WHAT ARE CASES?[1]

Case use has become standard in curricula at graduate schools of business: Harvard Business School provides some of the first and best-known examples.[2] Hansen (in Christensen, Hansen and Moore, 1987, p. 7) summarizes a case as "an edited version of a real and thought-provoking event which occurred in some teacher's professional experience." Boehrer (1994, p. 14) offers a related definition: "A teaching case is essentially a story, a brief account, for example, of a crisis in foreign policy decision-making. Like any story, a case presents a conflict, typically the tension between alternative courses of action that bring different viewpoints, interests, and values into contention and that must be resolved by a decision."

After considering these and other definitions, I suggest the following operationalization. A case is:

- A group of source materials on a single subject,
- Drawn from real experience,
- That places the participants in a decision-making analytical role.

This group of source materials may be a short written summary. It could also include an image, a video, a collection of news articles, a cloud of tweets, or any other representation of real events.

Why this definition? Most importantly, it makes precise the difference between a case and a case study. Case studies are summaries of individual historical events that provide background information, analysis or synthesis of that information, and an evaluation drawn by the author. A case study would seem to satisfy the Hansen and Boehrer definitions, but it would have limited use in facilitating learning. If the goal of the course is to stimulate the ability to analyze, synthesize and evaluate, the case study does all the work for the student – the analysis, synthesis and evaluation are all presented there. The case, by contrast, presents the background information and the substantive dilemma. The participants then use that information to create their own analysis (or synthesis, or evaluation). As my definition states, "it places the participant in a decision-making analytical role."

The advantage of using cases in the classroom is similar to the advantage of "learning by doing" over "learning by observing." Most economists have experienced the conversation with the student who explained, "I understood it when you said it in class, but I didn't understand it anymore when asked about it on the test." New developments in the science of learning (an excellent source is Bransford et al., 2000, chapter 1) emphasize the importance of helping people recognize when they understand and when they need more information. In the pursuit of active learning, the student who does the analysis is more likely to recognize the important components of the process than the student who simply reads the analysis in a case study.

Not all cases are created equal. Lynn (1999) proposes five key characteristics for a successful case – characteristics he calls the "five points of a star-quality case." They are:

- Poses problem or decision that has no obvious answer;
- Requires reader to use information provided in the case;
- Provides enough information for successful analysis/synthesis/evaluation;
- Challenges reader to think and to analyze in reaching a solution to the problem;
- Identifies actors who must solve the problem.

A case with these characteristics will provide the raw materials for learning by doing.

There are three primary sources of cases. First, there are case libraries managed by business and professional schools. The appendix lists a few of the major sources for English-language cases, both in the United States and in other countries. These cases are typically well-crafted, and often are provided with "instructor's notes" to assist in integrating the case into the instructor's syllabus. These cases are on average more detailed and require more thought than typically demanded of introductory undergraduates in economics, but I have had a great deal of success in using them in my upper-level undergraduate classes. Second, there are collections of cases available from other case instructors. On my website, for example, are a number of cases that I have created for undergraduate classes.[3] The Starting Point: Teaching and Learning Economics pedagogical portal website offers an assortment of cases written by economists for use in economics classes.[4] Third, the instructor can create cases. This can be as simple as a case that uses a baseball card, a $20 bill, and a short written narrative (as outlined below). For more advanced classes, the descriptive information from published case studies and essays can be combined with short narratives to create "star quality" cases.

THE COMPARATIVE ADVANTAGE OF CASES

Case use is a comparative-advantage technique when my pedagogical goal is for the student to demonstrate higher-order mastery of the concept to be taught in that class.[5] This section illustrates how using cases can attain this goal. The following section will address why it works. To provide concrete examples of the technique, I will begin by describing two cases I use in my undergraduate classes. The first is designed for introductory students, while the second is designed for upper-level students.

Example 1: For Introductory Students

Consider the scenario in which the instructor has begun a discussion of money in an introductory economics course and his/her pedagogical goal is to have the students get beyond definitions of the three characteristics of money (unit of account, medium of exchange, and store of value) to higher-order levels of mastery. To achieve this, the students must be able to distinguish money from another asset with regard to each of these three characteristics. The case "Time is Money, but What About Baseball Cards?" reproduced in Box 2.1 is a vehicle to achieve this.[6] The case document can be distributed during the previous class – or it is short enough that it can be distributed the day of the

---

BOX 2.1   TIME IS MONEY, BUT WHAT ABOUT BASEBALL CARDS?

George is continually amazed at how expensive it is to attend the university. Even though his parents paid for the meal plan, getting to know his classmates is an expensive proposition. Between the movies and the designer coffees, he manages to exhaust his budget by the 15th of every month.

Now, he's come up with an ingenious solution to this problem. He has started an auto detailing business on the side. He charges $20 per car to wash and vacuum the interior, and he's found that if he works on five cars per month, he can make it to the end of the month with cash in pocket and social schedule unhindered. Saving isn't in his game plan yet, and he still hasn't started worrying about taxes . . .

Today's job was no picnic: a Ford Expedition that looked as if it had been driven through the La Brea Tar Pits. When George finished, the owner made him an intriguing offer.

"Since you did such a great job I'll give you a choice. You can have this $20 bill. Alternatively, I'll give you this 1968 Roberto Clemente Topps baseball card #150. It's in mint condition, see? One just like it sold on eBay for $23.55 last week."

George is an eBay fan, and he remembers that auction – it did sell for $23.55. In fact, the same card sold last year for $19.75.

The Expedition owner is waiting, cash in one hand and baseball card in the other. Which should George take?

case class and have students read it in class. (I usually bring a $20 bill and the baseball card as props.)

Given the pedagogical goal, the case is star quality. George faces a payment choice – baseball card or cash? – that has no obvious best answer. To create an answer, the student must use the information provided in the case. While the text is short, it still includes enough information for successful analysis and evaluation. The problem posed is complex enough that the students must think and analyze before responding. Finally, the case identifies the decision-maker (George), and puts the students in the shoes of the decision-maker (by, for example, having students determine if they would take the card instead of cash).

I can incorporate a range of possible active-learning techniques (discussion, role play, small-group work) in the class period. The students have already learned the concept of substitutes in the microeconomics part of the course, and so the exercise in this case is an opportunity to transfer that knowledge to the concept of money. There is vibrant discussion, typically a strong disagreement among students, and a good opportunity for the instructor to observe how well the students can analyze the differences between money and this (not so) near-money.

Example 2: For More Advanced Students

When teaching an upper-level economic development course, the instructor often wants the students to learn and apply the concepts of negative externality and the tragedy of the commons. The pedagogical goal can be to have students successfully apply social-cost pricing and the logic of the Coase Theorem to a specific example. I have had a great deal of success in the past in distributing a published essay to the students and "covering" it with a memo that sets the parameters of the case.

The essay is "Requiem for a Dying Sea," written by Don Hinrichsen and published in the magazine, *People and the Planet*, in 1995. It tells the story of the desertification of the Aral Sea in Central Asia in descriptive detail. The essay alone is not star quality. It has relevant information about the ecological and health outcomes from the shrinkage of the Aral Sea, and there is no unambiguous solution, but it lacks the other three points of the star-quality case. To provide those, I write a cover memo[7] that defines the actor to make the decision (students acting as members of the Environmental and Natural Resource Department), defines the choice to be made (should river water continue to flow to agriculture, or should it be redirected into the Aral Sea?), and requires the students to use the facts of the essay in their analysis. I distribute the six-page essay and memo at the end of the preceding class. The memo includes three guiding questions for students to answer as they read the essay and prepare for the case-use class:

(1) What is the scarce resource here?
(2) What is the current price of that scarce resource?
(3) How are the social costs and benefits distributed geographically?

The structure of the case is well-suited to active-learning activities: I exploit the notion of a multilateral conference to assign role-play responsibilities to various students. Once the students recognize that water is misallocated by the current allocation scheme and that the effective price of water to its users in the current scheme is zero, they can then take the short step to the assignment of property rights and the market-pricing of water as potential solutions. This is an allocation mechanism that will create winners and losers, and there are excellent opportunities for each actor to calculate gains and losses for him or herself from the new policy. The students can then debate whether the Coase Theorem will apply in this instance by changing the allocation of property rights and considering any changes in outcome.

How do these Cases Help the Students Achieve Higher-order Mastery?

While cases are effective in stimulating student learning at Bloom's (1956) lower-level mastery levels, the comparative advantage of case use is evident when the instructor wishes students to demonstrate higher-order mastery.

There are five steps in preparing for a case session (and any active-learning session). First, the instructor defines an explicit pedagogical goal. Case sessions are not just about "letting students talk:" goals motivate the development of a case to enhance specific content comprehension. Second, cases are more effectively implemented when the instructor "reverse engineers" the class period. What should the students achieve by the end of the class period? What logical steps must they take to reach that achievement? This defines the flow of a lesson plan. Third, how should the instructor prepare the students for the case session? (Specific questions in this vein include when to distribute the case or whether to distribute discussion questions to focus students' reading of the case.) Fourth, the lesson plan is correlated with specific learning activities for the classroom. Finally, a plan for summarizing the students' learning in the session is identified: how is learning shared and documented at the end of the class? Instructor's Notes in the internet supplement to this chapter describe the specific implementation of these steps for the two example cases.

In the Baseball-card case, my pedagogical goal is student understanding of the "definition of money." Given the difficulties students typically have in subsequent macroeconomics classes if they do not have a higher-order mastery of the concept, I chose to design an in-class task for the students to analyze the use of money. The Baseball-card case was an effective way to facilitate this. Rather than simply memorizing the three characteristics of money (unit of account, means of exchange, store of value), the students analyzed two assets (currency and baseball card) for the degree to which each embodies those three characteristics. They also combined their understanding of the nature of these two assets with the concept of "substitutes" learned in microeconomics. This established a more nuanced understanding of money than was previously common and stood the students in good stead for their subsequent macroeconomics classes.

The Aral Sea case has the grounding pedagogical goal that students demonstrate higher-order mastery of the externality concept. The "Requiem for a Dying Sea" article paired with a written memo created for the purpose made up a star-quality case for achieving this goal. Student engagement with the case led them to apply the concept of externality to water use, analyze the effects of this externality on downstream populations, synthesize the concept of externality with the previously learned concept of property rights, and evaluate alternative policies to internalize the external costs of excessive water use upstream. The students demonstrated this mastery in their work with one another in the class; if some students were not as advanced as others, the leading students tutored the lagging students.

For both of these examples, I discovered through written tests and formative assessments that (1) a greater proportion of the class could apply the relevant concepts effectively in new circumstances, (2) a greater proportion of the class could use the concepts effectively in analysis, (3) a greater proportion could combine these concepts with others (synthesize) and draw logical conclusions, and (4) a greater proportion retained higher-order mastery of these concepts longer than I observed in classes where cases were not used. I am aware of no statistical tests of the importance of case use to higher-order mastery in economics. Yamarick (2007) provides a persuasive regression-based test of group-based instruction that affirms the positive effect of that related strategy on performance in microeconomics classes. Instructors in the sciences have been more active at testing the importance of cases specifically for student achievement of higher-order mastery. Mayo (2004) reports a statistical test of case-based instruction in achieving higher-order mastery of psychology: students using case-based instruction performed significantly better on both comprehension and application of course concepts. Dori et al. (2003) concluded that performance of non-science majors in biotechnology classes was significantly better for higher-order thinking skills when cases were incorporated in the curriculum. In a non-statistical evaluation, Carlson and Velenchik (2006) provide examples of effective cases.

WHY DO CASES WORK SO WELL?

Cases Enhance Enthusiasm for Learning

There is a hallowed set of statistics first published by Stice (1987, p. 293) in a test of Kolb's learning cycle theory that is often used to justify active-learning methods in the classroom. He found that when students in engineering were tested 60 days later on material presented in class the average student retains

- 10 percent of what s/he reads
- 20 percent of what s/he hears
- 30 percent of what s/he sees
- 50 percent of what s/he sees and hears
- 70 percent of what s/he says
- 80 percent of what s/he says and does

This represents a powerful argument for active-learning strategies (including case use) in the classroom. There is a corollary, however, that is no doubt equally true: the student retains

- Zero percent of what s/he ignores

There is a time-honored technique for inducing attention by students – the instructor announces that the material will be on an examination. This works well for "performance-oriented" students, and less well for "learning-oriented" students. The difference is simple: "Students who are learning-oriented like new challenges; those who are performance-oriented are more worried about making errors than about learning" (Bransford et al., 2000, p. 6). By contrast, "Learners of all ages are more motivated when they can see the usefulness of what they are learning and when they can use that information to do something that has an impact on others" (ibid., p. 6). I call this motivational characteristic of learning the Bransford buzz. The best learning tools generate this buzz.

Cases can be excellent learning tools for this reason. As the earlier definition described, star-quality cases are drawn from real-world experience, showing students that learning from this case will have real-world applications. The Baseball-card case generates Bransford buzz by including a number of concepts that are important to students' everyday life: cash, budgeting, eBay. It challenges them to think about the abstract notion of money in a real and personal context, and that makes it hard for them to ignore. The Aral Sea case generates the Bransford buzz: the students learn about a tragedy, analyze why it occurred, and also devise a workable mechanism that could have allowed the residents of that region to avoid the economic and health disaster that ensued. In my experience, students are on board and engaged for both these cases from the beginning to the end – there is no lost learning due to boredom or inattention.

Within the economics literature, Whiting (1996) reports that a case-like activity (simulating a Federal Open Market Committee meeting in the classroom) had a positive impact on student interest in macroeconomics. Carlson and Velenchik (2006) cite the enthusiasm of students about the use of cases as a major benefit of case use in teaching economics. Active-learning techniques (not specifically, but including, case use) also have a Bransford buzz effect. Jensen and Owen (2001) find that collaborative learning in general encouraged more students to become economics majors and students to take more economics courses. When Yamarick (2007) explained his statistically significant results on performance in his microeconomics classes, he cited "the novelty of working in small groups sparked greater interest in the material" (p. 275).[8] Springer, Stanne and Donavan (1999, p. 21) conclude from a meta-analysis of pedagogical studies in science, mathematics, engineering and technology (SMET) that these techniques are effective in promoting "more favorable attitudes towards learning, and increased persistence through SMET courses and programs."

Cases Facilitate Discussion, Debate and Shared Learning

Attaining lower-level mastery as characterized by Bloom et al. (1956) is a task done by individuals, as anyone who has memorized definitions for an economics exam will attest. There is a one-to-one mapping from concept to definition, the mapping is laid out explicitly in the textbook, and a student working alone can achieve complete mastery with enough effort. Complete higher-level mastery is more difficult to achieve through independent study: there is a jigsaw puzzle of connections among the relevant economic concepts, and generally no "picture on the box" to aid the students in putting the pieces together. Collaborative work among students is an effective methodology in general for creating a shared and complete higher-level mastery of the concept in question. While it is apparently seldom used in economics instruction (Watts and Becker, 2008), it is more widely applied in engineering courses (see, for example, Brawner et al., 2002).

Discussion and debate facilitate learning, and especially higher-order learning. Salemi and Hansen (2005, chapter 1) provide a detailed and persuasive argument for its use, as does the discussion chapter of this *Handbook* by the same authors. Case use provides a structure for this discussion and debate that maximizes the potential for collaborative work while minimizing the potentially negative effects of competing to win. Kahn (1981) observed that the traditional university seminar will at times become a "free for all," with students one-upping one another to appear smartest, or at least smarter than average. This undercuts the collaborative nature of the exercise necessary to achieve shared mastery. McCormick and Kahn (1987) proposed an alternative structure for this collaborative activity: the "barn raising." The class assembles to complete a defined project. Each student brings a contribution, and the group works to fit them all together into the group product. There's a subtle but important difference between this and the "free for all:" rather than search for what's wrong in a fellow student's statement, students search for the part that is right. Cases are excellent vehicles for discussion, have the pedagogical advantages identified by Salemi and Hansen (2005), and in addition they facilitate "barn raising" (as opposed to "free for all") discussions. There is an explicit task to be completed at the heart of each star-quality case. The individual to complete the task is described in the case, with the students typically in the role of advisers. This encourages collaborative discussion.

The two example cases illustrate these points. In the "Baseball-card" case, the decision-forcing feature creates much scope for discussion. The group product is a set of recommendations for George in the form: "If xxx is true, then George should take the cash." For example, "If the time and shipping cost of trading on eBay is greater than $3.55, then George should take the cash." Each student can contribute his or her own statement that can be written on the board. Each statement becomes the focus of discussion, leading ultimately to an analysis of the role of transactions costs, uncertainty, time preference and other factors relevant to the decision. The focus is not "What would you do?," which leads to competition. It is "What should George do?," because that encourages collaboration.

In the Aral Sea case, the actor (James Bond) is tasked to create a summary of social costs and benefits of the current water allocation scheme. This summary list is the puzzle to be assembled. The students, through discussion, can create that list using the information from the reading. Each student enjoys the opportunity to bring a piece to the puzzle. The question of "What do you think?" is translated to "What should James think?", and students are much less shy in telling James Bond what to do. There is the follow-on responsibility built into the case of creating a new water-allocation mechanism. This can be facilitated through role play, with students taking roles of representatives of the World Bank or Central Asian governments, evaluating proposals using these perspectives. Velenchik (1995) and Carlson and Velenchik (2006) provide other descriptions of the facility with which cases can be used to encourage and structure shared learning.

Cases Facilitate Assessment, Including Self-assessment[9]

Instructors are painfully familiar with tests to determine what students have learned. These summative assessments provide a definitive measure of what has been learned, but they often come too late to improve the process of learning. Learning theorists acknowledge

the importance of summative assessments, but place much more importance on formative assessment. This is "the use of assessments (usually administered in the context of
the classroom) as sources of feedback to improve teaching and learning" (Bransford et
al., 2000, p. 140). These assessments serve to demonstrate, both to the learner and to the
teacher, the depth of understanding at that point in time on the part of the learner.

Case exercises distributed through the syllabus provide important formative assessment opportunities for both instructor and student. For example, the Baseball-card case
is placed in an introductory course just after study of the three characteristics of money.
Lower-level mastery of these characteristics can be checked through directed questions
(for example, What is the "unit of account" characteristic of money?). The case also provides a context for formative assessment of higher-order mastery (for example, Can you
find money used as the "unit of account" in this case?). As the students work through the
case, they recognize (a) what they have already learned, (b) what they haven't learned,
and (c) what they've previously learned that isn't so. Through their contributions, the
instructor knows this too. This is valuable information in devising reviews, follow-on
activities or individual exercises for the lagging student.

In the Aral Sea case, students contribute twice. First, they generate lists of social costs
and benefits that the World Bank will provide to the water-allocation conference. This
allows students and instructor to assess understanding of concepts through application
and evaluation (of the relative importance of various social costs). When students are
then asked to create a new water-allocation mechanism, they synthesize their knowledge
of social costs with their prior understanding of the role of property rights in allocation
incentives. The instructor observes this process, and can judge in real time the degree to
which the desired higher-order mastery has been attained.

It's important to recognize that cases can be used for summative assessment as well;
in fact, they create an excellent structure for framing questions challenging the students'
higher-order mastery of the material. Short essays just after case classes can use facts
from the case to test higher-order mastery. The students complete these essays individually, using insights derived from the collaborative case analysis in class. Follow-up questions on examinations require students to use case details to demonstrate higher-order
mastery of an economic concept (for example, externality). Assessment activities help
the students recognize that higher-order mastery skills are important skills to develop.

CONCLUSION

Using cases in economics instruction is effective at facilitating higher-order learning.
Although it is a teaching technique, it also creates a classroom environment in which
active learning can flourish. Using cases in the classroom will be especially effective when
the instructor's goal is to promote higher-order mastery.

Cases bring the real world into the classroom, and put the students in the role of
economic decision-maker. Instructors may have as a goal that students think like economists, but our pedagogic methods often do not include opportunities outside of examinations for students to demonstrate this. There is no better way to assess whether a student
can think like an economist than to give a decision-making role in a situation requiring
higher-order mastery of economic concepts. Further, from the student's perspective,

working with a case in class is "learning by doing:" acting like an economist in a low-stakes environment with the instructor and fellow students as mentors.

John Dewey spoke for many of our students when he said "School should be less about preparation for life and more about life itself."[10] We present simple theoretical paradigms, but students want real-world significance. Using cases in instruction meets both objectives: the instructor can structure the activity to illuminate theoretical paradigms, while the students can see the life-relevance of what they are doing.

NOTES

1. This section is drawn from Conway et al. (2010).
2. Christensen and Hansen (1987) provides a good summary of that usage.
3. For examples, please visit http://www.unc.edu/home/pconway/teaching.html (accessed 9 June 2011).
4. Found at http://serc.carleton.edu/sp/library/cases/ (accessed 9 June 2011).
5. The term "higher-order mastery" refers to an advanced level of complexity and nuance in the understanding expected of students. It is based upon the taxonomy introduced in Bloom et al. (1956) and often referred to thereafter as "Bloom's taxonomy" in the pedagogical literature. For this chapter, it is sufficient to define "lower-order mastery" as the student's ability to recognize and provide a basic definition of a concept. "Higher-order mastery," by contrast, is the ability to apply the concept in new situations, to identify the presence and importance of that concept in an environment when ceteris paribus does not hold. We can take the concept of "minimum wage" as an example: lower-order mastery will consist of an ability to define the minimum wage, while higher-order mastery will include an ability to apply this in determining labor market outcomes, to recognize the isomorphism with price floors in other markets, and to evaluate whether a minimum wage will be welfare improving or reducing for workers and employers.
6. The internet supplement is found at http://www.unc.edu/home/pconway/CaseTraining/handbook_cases.pdf (accessed 9 June 2011).
7. This cover memo is included in the website supplement to this chapter.
8. See also Chapter 4 on cooperative learning in this *Handbook*.
9. See as well Chapter 16 on assessment in this *Handbook*.
10. As cited by Bransford et al. (2000, p. 77). The spirit of the quote, though not the exact wording, is found in Dewey (1897, Article Two.)

REFERENCES

Becker, W. and M. Watts (2001), "Teaching economics at the start of the 21st century: still chalk-and-talk", *American Economic Review*, **91** (2), 446–51.

Bloom, B., M. Engelhart, E. Furst, W. Hill and D. Krathwohl (1956), *Taxonomy of Educational Objectives Handbook I: Cognitive Domain*, New York: David McKay.

Boehrer, J. (1994), "On teaching a case", *International Studies Notes*, **19** (2), 1420.

Bransford, J., A. Brown and R. Cocking (eds) (2000), *How People Learn*, Washington, DC: National Academy Press.

Brawner, C., R. Felder, R. Allen and R. Brent (2002), "A survey of faculty teaching practices and involvement in faculty development activities", *Journal of Engineering Education*, **91** (4), 393–6.

Carlson, J. and A. Velenchik (2006), "Using the case method in the economics classroom", in W. Becker, S. Becker and M. Watts, *Teaching Economics: More Alternatives to Chalk and Talk*, Cheltenham, UK and Northampton, MA, USA: Edward Elgar, chapter 4.

Christensen, C. and A. Hansen (1987), *Teaching and the Case Method*, Cambridge, MA: Harvard Business School.

Christensen, C., A. Hansen and J. Moore (1987), *Teaching and the Case Method: Instructor's Guide*, Cambridge, MA: Harvard Business School.

Conway, P., A. Davis, M. Hartmann and D. Stimel (2010), "Case use in economics instruction", in M. Salemi and W. Walstad, *Discussing Economics*, Cheltenham, UK and Northampton, MA, USA: Edward Elgar, chapter 9.

Dewey, J. (1897). "My Pedagogic Credo", *School Journal*, **54**, 77–80.
Dori, Y., R. Tal and M. Tsaushu (2003), "Teaching biotechnology through case studies – can we improve higher order thinking skills of nonscience majors?', *Science Education*, **87** (6), 767–93.
Hinrichsen, D. (1995), "Requiem for a dying sea", *People and the Planet*, currently reprinted at http://jdainternational.org/Resources/sea.PDF.
Jensen, E. and A. Owen (2001), "Pedagogy, gender and interest in economics", *Journal of Economic Education*, **34** (4), 323–43.
Kahn, M. (1981), "The seminar: an experiment in humanistic education", *Journal of Humanistic Psychology*, **21** (2), 119–27.
Lynn, L. (1999), *Teaching and Learning with Cases: A Guidebook*, Washington, DC: Sage Press.
Mayo, J. (2004), "Using case-based instruction to bridge the gap between theory and practice in psychology of adjustment", *Journal of Constructivist Psychology*, **17** (2), 137–46.
McCormick, D. and M. Kahn (1987), "Barn raising: collaborative group process in seminars", *EXCHANGE*, **7** (4), 16–20, reprinted as Tomorrow's Professor Message 746.
Salemi, M. and W. Hansen (2005), *Discussing Economics*, Cheltenham, UK and Northampton, MA, USA: Edward Elgar.
Springer, L., M. Stanne and S. Donavan (1999), "Undergraduates in science, mathematics, engineering and technology: a meta-analysis", *Review of Educational Research*, **69** (1), 21–51.
Stice, J. (1987), *Developing Critical Thinking and Problem-solving Abilities*, New Directions in Learning and Teaching Series, No. 30, San Francisco, CA: Jossey-Bass.
Velenchik, A. (1995), "The case method as a strategy for teaching policy analysis to undergraduates", *Journal of Economic Education*, **26** (1), 29–38.
Watts, M. and W. Becker (2008), "A little more than chalk and talk: results from a third national survey of teaching methods in undergraduate economics courses", *Journal of Economic Education*, **39** (3), 273–86.
Whiting, C. (2006), "Data-based active learning in the principles of macroeconomics course: a mock FOMC meeting", *Journal of Economic Education*, **37** (2), 171–7.
Yamarick, S. (2007), "Does cooperative learning improve student learning outcomes?", *Journal of Economic Education*, **38** (3), 259–77.

APPENDIX: SOURCES FOR CASES IN ECONOMICS

World Bank Economic Development Institute
   http://www.worldbank.org/html/edi/cases/caseindex.html
   Some of the cases are in fact available for downloading directly from that page.
The Electronic Hallway
   http://www.hallway.org/
Harvard Business School Publishing
   http://www.hbsp.harvard.edu/groups/cases/index/html
Pew Case Studies in International Affairs
   http://www.georgetown.edu/sfs/programs/isd/files/cases/pew.html
National Center for Case Study Teaching in the Sciences
   http://ublib.buffalo.edu/libraries/projects/cases/case.html

Internet Supplement to this Chapter

http://www.unc.edu/home/pconway/CaseTraining/handbook_cases.pdf

3 Teaching with context-rich problems
Joann Bangs

A strong desire of many instructors is to help our students to think like economists. Context-rich problems are one active learning technique that is designed specifically with this goal in mind. How better to get students to think like economists than to give them practice at doing exactly that task? Context-rich problems help by putting students in realistic scenarios so they can practice applying economic concepts.

WHAT ARE CONTEXT-RICH PROBLEMS?

To see the difference between a traditional problem and a context-rich problem consider the following two examples. Let's begin with a traditional problem:

> A discount bond matures in five years. It has a face value of $10,000. If interest rates are 2%, what is the present value of this bond?

Reshaping this problem into a context-rich problem leads to:

> You and your sister just inherited a discount bond. The bond has a face value of $10,000 and matures in five years. You would like to hold onto the bond until maturity, but your sister wants her money now. She offers to sell you her half of the bond, but only if you give her a fair price. What is a fair price to offer her? How can you convince your sister it is a fair price?

The first and most important characteristic to note about this context-rich problem is that the problem places the student in a *realistic scenario*, generally facilitated by having the context-rich problem start with "you." Notice that the situation in the context-rich problem is one in which the students can easily see themselves. The realistic nature of the context-rich problem helps to answer the frequent student question: "why would I ever need to know this stuff?" by putting the student in a scenario that is believable to them. Typically a realistic scenario uses situations such as events happening in the community, at your university, in a small business, or decisions that a new employee or an intern might be asked to work on.

The above context-rich problem incorporates an additional common characteristic: *lack of an explicit target*. Real-world situations rarely include directives such as "calculate present value," but traditional problems often do just that. In contrast, context-rich problems require students to think critically like an economist by first identifying the relevant concept (present value) in order to be able to solve the problem.

Like many situations students face, context-rich problems often *do not provide complete information or include excess information.* The context-rich problem above does not provide complete information. The students are not told what interest rate should

Table 3.1   Car wash example: costs of production

Number of car washes sold per day	Total cost for labor and supplies
1	$10.67
2	$12.67
3	$16.00
4	$20.67
5	$26.67
6	$34.00
7	$42.67
8	$52.67
9	$64.00
10	$76.67
11	$90.67
12	$106.00
13	$122.67
14	$140.67
15	$160.00
16	$180.67
17	$202.67
18	$226.00
19	$250.67
20	$276.67

be used to calculate the present value. Rather, they must use their knowledge of current interest rates, or expand their knowledge if it is incomplete, to select the appropriate interest rate. In contrast, including excess information mirrors the difficulty of real-world decisions where all of the available information must be evaluated to determine which information is relevant to the decision. As an example, consider the following context-rich problem that focuses on profit maximization in a perfectly competitive market:

Your family recently began operating a car wash at a beach resort. There are many other car washes at this beach resort. You have observed that the customers care only about finding the cheapest price for car washes; they do not care which company they use. Your family purchased the equipment and the building for the car wash. They used $1,000 of their savings towards this purchase. To cover the rest of this expense, they took out a small business loan. The cost of the loan comes to $15 per day for the next three years. The business must hire labor and purchase cleaning solutions, car wax, etc. to operate the car wash. After some research you have figured out that the cost for labor and supplies is as shown in Table 3.1.

When the beach resort is in-season, you have observed that you can charge a price of $14.00 per car wash. When the resort is off-season, the demand for car washes is much lower. You are only able to charge a price of $4.67 per car wash. Right now the resort is in-season. Currently you are selling 17 car washes per day. Your family wants your advice. What should your family do now? Why? What should they do in the off-season? Why?

To solve this problem, students need to determine the profit-maximizing level of output, both for the in-season and the off-season. Next, the students must check whether or not the business would be better off shutting down in either season. The problem includes information about the family spending some of their savings to purchase the business. While that information is likely to be known to a person in this scenario, that spending is a sunk cost and therefore irrelevant to the question of how much they should produce to maximize profits.

WHY SHOULD WE USE CONTEXT-RICH PROBLEMS?

Evidence suggests that we learn best when we learn in context. Consider, for example, the process by which students learn new vocabulary words. A 1987 study by Miller and Gildea (as reported in Brown, Collins and Duguid, 1989) finds that by simply reading, talking and listening (i.e. learning in context) an average 17-year-old is able to learn about 5,000 words a year. On the other hand, students tend to learn a mere 100 to 200 words a year though the traditional vocabulary teaching method of getting a diction-ary definition and example sentences. Furthermore, the traditional process frequently ends with the students using the new vocabulary words incorrectly. They simply do not understand the context needed for the words. Brown et al. (1989) compare this experi-ence to acquiring tools (buying hammers, screwdrivers, etc.), but having no idea how to use them. Context-rich problems can help students move past rote memorization of economic vocabulary and concepts to implementing these tools correctly.

Learning in context is not a new idea. The process of apprenticeship is a classic example of learning in context. The master begins by modeling the process for the apprentice. Next the master coaches the apprentice as s/he begins to do the work, starting first with simple parts of the process before moving on to more complex parts. Finally coaching fades over time as the apprentice slowly learns to do the work independently. Brown et al. (1989) suggest a process they label as cognitive apprenticeship to bring learning in context into the classroom. Context-rich problems are a tool that can assist in the cognitive apprenticeship process (model, coach, fade). Instructors begin by mod-eling the way economics can be used, demonstrating their thought process while solving a complex context-rich problem for students. Then, as students work on their own context-rich problems, instructors coach the students through the process (in concert with cooperative learning techniques,[1] students can coach each other). The process begins with relatively simple context-rich problems before moving on to more complex context-rich problems as the students gradually learn the process of applying economic concepts independently (fading).

Although this is an emerging practice in economics, context-rich problems have been used for a number of years in physics education with the goal of improving students' problem-solving skills. For example, Heller, Keith and Anderson (1992) and Heller and Hollabaugh (1992) apply the cognitive apprenticeship approach to investigate the impact of context-rich problems in a cooperative learning environment. They begin by dedicat-ing class time to modeling a problem-solving strategy for the students which includes discussion of relevant physics concepts applicable to the present problem. Students are presented with a grading scheme to encourage the use of the problem-solving strategy.

Next, the authors observe groups of students solving both traditional textbook problems and context-rich problems. Groups solving traditional textbook problems express frustration at having to use the more comprehensive problem-solving strategy because it forces them to write out more information than they feel is needed to solve the problem. Rather than discussing what physics concepts were appropriate, they instead simply look for formulas that use the information given in the problem. However, despite the fact that the students often are not successful at solving the traditional textbook problems with their formula search method, they do not seem to see their lack of success as an indication that they should try an alternative strategy.

The students working on traditional textbook problems in Heller and Hollabaugh's (1992) study were following what Chi, Feltovich and Glaser (1981) label as novice-like problem solving. Chi et al. (1981) note that experts generally begin work on a problem by considering what information is needed to solve it. In contrast, novices tend to look for formulas that use the information given. Heller and Hollabaugh (1992) conclude that their students' use of novice-like problem solving is a result of traditional textbook problems eliminating the need to make problem-solving decisions. Students learn from experience that all information included in the problem is needed to solve the problem, and none of the required information is missing. Finally, students learn that the last sentence of the problem typically tells them exactly what the target outcome is.

Alternatively, students assigned context-rich problems are much more likely to use an expert-like approach in their problem-solving process. These students spend time engaged in discussions about physics concepts instead of searching for formulas. The design of context-rich problems helps discourage novice problem solving by forcing the students to make decisions, beginning with figuring out which information is needed, which information is missing and how they might resolve information gaps. In other words, they follow the expert-like problem solving described by Chi et al. (1981) by asking themselves what is required to solve the problem. Not surprisingly, students assigned the context-rich problems are much more satisfied with the problem-solving process they have been shown. When faced with the need to make decisions, these students find value in the expert-like problem-solving process.

HOW CAN WE USE CONTEXT-RICH PROBLEMS IN THE CLASSROOM?

Students accustomed to working with traditional plug and chug sort of problems will likely need help in getting started. Making use of the cognitive apprenticeship model, begin by modeling a problem-solving approach. Heller, Keith and Anderson (1992) suggest the following problem-solving strategy:

1. Visualize the problem
2. Describe in terms appropriate for the discipline
3. Plan a solution
4. Execute a plan
5. Check and evaluate

Next, instructors should include a period of coaching as students begin to work with their own context-rich problems. Coaching can come in the form of prompting students to follow the problem-solving strategy as they work on context-rich problems, for example, asking the students, "What do you need to know to be able to make a decision?" The context-rich problems can also be designed to provide their own coaching, by incorporating an explicit target, or prompts within the problem. Students can also coach each other. A fairly simple method to facilitate student coaching is to use a think-pair-share approach[2] with context-rich problems. Students are first provided with class time to work independently on the context-rich problem. They are then paired and sequentially share answers before discussing differences and coming to a final solution. Student pairs can be asked to share their answer with the class, generating further discussion.

Building students' problem-solving skills requires careful consideration of the degree of difficulty that is right for the students. Context-rich problems are likely to be more successful if the problem is at a lower level of difficulty. As students become more familiar with the process of solving context-rich problems, more difficult problems can be introduced. The level of difficulty can also be elevated if students are provided with more time or work in groups.

The level of difficulty for a context-rich problem is determined by the degree to which some of the characteristics of context-rich problems are included. Difficulty can be increased by leaving out needed information as the omission forces students to consider where they should go to find the required information. Second, the level of difficulty can be increased by including irrelevant information. The real world often provides plenty of information that will not be useful in our decision making. Including information that someone in the situation described by the context-rich problem is likely to have forces the student to evaluate the usefulness of each piece of information provided. Difficulty can also be increased by requiring more than one key concept to be used to solve the problem. For example, the car wash problem presented above requires students to use concepts of marginal costs, profit maximization, the shut-down condition and conditions for exiting the industry. Finally a lack of an explicit target increases difficulty. Rather than telling the students what they need to do to solve the problem, the context-rich problem can be finished with a more open-ended question such as "What should you do?" The lack of an explicit target forces the student to decide what needs to be done in order to answer the question.

As noted in Maier, Bangs, Blunch and Peterson (2010), context-rich problems can be incorporated with other active learning techniques. The context-rich problems can be the basis around which a cooperative learning exercise is structured, such as in the think-pair-share exercise described above. Context-rich problems have also been incorporated as the basis of the final evaluation of student learning following a cooperative learning round table exercise in Rhoads (2009). Using context-rich problems with more than one possible solution in concert with just-in-time teaching[3] can lead to rich classroom discussions. A variety of responses gathered prior to class through a course management system can be shown to the class to spark a discussion of the strengths and weaknesses of the different responses.

WRITING CONTEXT-RICH PROBLEMS

When writing context-rich problems, it is best to start by focusing on learning goals rather than on course content. As Bain (2004) notes, the most effective teachers tend to focus on what they would like their students to be able to do rather than the facts they want them to know. This idea is very similar to the goal of teaching students to "think like an economist." In other words, start with the learning objective so the focus is on *how* students should think rather than on *what* the students should think about. As an example, a learning objective might be: Students will be able to apply economic theory on price discrimination to real-world settings. The following context-rich problem will help students to meet this learning objective:

> You have been hired to be a consultant on pricing strategies for two different companies. Both of the companies have similar customer bases in that their customers fall into two well-defined groups: college students and young well-paid professionals. The first company is a trendy bar. The bar is currently seeing many young well-paid professionals as customers, but rather fewer college students. The bar has run a marketing campaign to attract more college students, but that only caused a small increase in the number of those customers. The second company is an electronics store selling items such as MP3 players. This company is also currently seeing many young well-paid professionals as customers, but rather fewer college students. The electronics store has also run a marketing campaign to attract more college students, but that also only caused a small increase in the number of those customers. Both of these companies want to know if they could make some changes in their pricing strategy to increase their sales to college students and thereby increase their overall profits. Prepare a report for each company. Each report should be one-half page in length. In each report, make a recommendation to the company detailing what they must do to follow your recommendation and explain why they should follow your recommendation.

The next step is to provide a context that is realistic to the students. Create a scenario that students can easily seem themselves in, and that will require them to make decisions. The following are common prompts that can be used to develop context-rich problems:

- You are . . . (in some everyday situation) and need to figure out . . .
- You are on vacation and observe/notice . . . and wonder . . .
- You are watching TV or reading an article about . . . and wonder . . .
- Because of your knowledge of economics, your friend asks you to help him/her . . .
- You have a summer job with a company that . . . . Because of your knowledge of economics, your boss asks you to . . .

However, context-rich problems do not need to be limited to the common scenarios listed above. Unusual settings can also be helpful in writing context-rich problems. Consider the following context-rich problem:

> Your neighbor is writing a novel. The two main characters in her novel run competing restaurants in a small town. They own the only two restaurants in this small town and are engaged in cutthroat competition with each other. Because your neighbor knows you are taking an economics class, she wants your help. What advice do you have to give your neighbor to make the competition in her novel both interesting and plausible? Prepare a one-page plot outline to give to your neighbor. As you prepare the plot outline, remember that she asked for your help because you are taking an economics class.

Unusual scenarios give the student the opportunity to find creative ways to display their knowledge and understanding of economic concepts.

The final step in writing context-rich problems is to create the appropriate level of difficulty. The level of difficulty can be increased in a number of ways. The context-rich problem can incorporate *missing information*. Any information that students would be able to find on their own in the time they are given to solve the problem is a possible candidate for missing information. Similarly, *excess information* increases difficulty. To be effective, the excess information needs to be related to the problem, but not actually necessary to make a decision. In the car wash problem presented above, the needed information is costs. However, the sunk cost of the savings, while similar in nature to the needed information, is not needed to make a decision.

Requiring *more than one concept* to be used increases difficulty by adding more steps to the process. In the car wash problem presented above, students must recognize the need to have the correct level of output in order to maximize profits. They must examine the context in which the business operates to understand that the firm operates in a perfectly competitive market. They must determine how to use the cost information they are given to calculate marginal costs. Finally, they must consider the possibility of shutting down production.

The *lack of an explicit target* is the feature that likely adds the most difficulty to a context-rich problem. The bond pricing problem would be significantly easier if students were instead asked to explain why half of the present value is a fair price. However, the lack of an explicit target can be taken too far. The problem must contain some clues to guide the student to the right path. In the car wash problem, students are asked to give advice on what should be done now and in the off-season. Putting forth the idea of in-season versus off-season gives the students more direction than if the problem simply asked the students to generically give advice, but yet does not go so far as an explicit target, such as asking students to help the family figure out the best production level in both seasons.

CHALLENGES TO USING CONTEXT-RICH PROBLEMS

Time can be a challenge to incorporating context-rich problems into the classroom. Instructors should expect to spend more time initially on writing context-rich problems than they are accustomed to spending on preparing traditional problems. However, with practice, the time needed to create context-rich problems is reduced.[4] Time must also be set aside to model problem solving and to coach students as they begin to work on context-rich problems. Given the evidence on the power of teaching in context, this time is likely to be well spent.

Instructors should expect to encounter a certain amount of frustration from students when they are first introduced to context-rich problems. This frustration can be minimized by taking care to use context-rich problems with an appropriate level of difficulty. However, some amount of frustration is likely to remain. Explaining to students the purpose of context-rich problems is helpful. When students understand how the features of context-rich problems, such as missing and excess information, actually help to better prepare them for life after college, they tend to be more willing to work through the frustration.

Context-rich problems can be created for any type of class, but it can be more challenging to create realistic scenarios in macroeconomics rather than microeconomics courses. When we think of macro decisions – such as fiscal and monetary policy decisions – we lose plausibility if we set up the problem to have the student take on the role of President of the United States or the Chairman of the Federal Reserve. Making use of unusual settings can be particularly helpful in macroeconomics courses. Scenarios can be created where the student might need to explain information from current events to a family member or friend. The following context-rich problem is an example giving students a realistic situation in which they would need to be able to understand and explain Ricardian equivalence:

> Walking down the street one day, you see a college classmate speaking to a group of people gathered on a street corner. Walking closer, you hear that your friend is protesting the high level of government debt accumulated to this point. His principal arguments are that government indebtedness is preventing our country from doing what needs to be done socially, and that the increasing level of debt will eventually bankrupt us as a nation. Suddenly, he sees you in the audience, and says, "Look, there is my friend from college who is an economics major. This person has studied the matter closely, and can provide an expert's opinion on the matter." All eyes turn to you, and the crowd falls silent. You clear your throat, and begin talking. Write a short, five-minute presentation detailing what you would say to this crowd.[5]

Another challenge in using context-rich problems is that students may generate unexpected answers which can be difficult to grade. For example, in the bond pricing context-rich problem above, an expected answer includes the student determination of an appropriate interest rate to use, a calculation of the present value of the bond and dividing the bond value between the two parties. However, a student could reasonably give an answer such as "looking the price of the bond up in the newspaper and giving his sister half that price." While that is a very reasonable response, it doesn't offer the opportunity to assess their ability to apply present value. Giving students guidelines (such as a grading rubric) about what is expected of them when they complete context-rich problems can help to minimize these occurrences. It is also helpful to use prompts within the problem to help students understand how much information to include in their answer. Consider the following context-rich problem used in a Money and Banking course:

> You work for an organization that raises funds by issuing municipal bonds. You have just been informed that there is a bill before Congress to start taxing the interest earned on municipal bonds. Your boss (who has taken principles of economics classes, but no other economics class) is wondering how your organization would be affected if this bill is passed. Write a brief memo to your boss to explain the effect.

Notice how students are given an indication of the type of knowledge they can assume (principles level) in their answer and what must be explained to their boss. They are also given an indication of the length and format for the response. Note that providing prompts for the student differs from incorporating an explicit target. Prompts give students guidance, whereas explicit targets tell the students what must be done.

CONCLUSION

As with any teaching technique, context-rich problems must be evaluated as to whether or not they help our students meet stated learning objectives. Context-rich problems are particularly useful in helping students to meet learning objectives that focus on problem solving and real-world applications. Learning scenarios research suggests that learning that lasts necessitates students' demonstration of their ability to transfer information to new contexts (Bransford, Brown and Cocking, 2000). Students require practice to master this skill and the context-rich problem is a tool educators can employ to facilitate this process.

NOTES

1. For more information on cooperative learning techniques, see Chapter 4 in this volume.
2. Think-pair-share is a technique that is further described in Chapter 4 in this volume.
3. For more information on just-in-time teaching, see Chapter 9 in this volume.
4. Examples of ready to use context-rich problems are available at the economic pedagogic portal, Starting Point: Teaching and Learning Economics, http://serc.carleton.edu/econ/context_rich/examples.html (assessed 9 June 2011).
5. This context-rich problem was written by Brian Peterson (Central College) and is included here with his permission.

REFERENCES

Bain, K. (2004), *What the Best College Teachers Do*, London, UK and Cambridge, MA: Harvard University Press.
Bransford, J., A. Brown and R. Cocking (eds) (2000), *How People Learn: Brain, Mind, Experience, and School*, Washington, DC: National Academy Press.
Brown, J., A. Collins and P. Duguid (1989), "Situated cognition and the culture of learning", *Educational Researcher*, **18** (1), 32–42.
Chi, M.T.H., P.J. Feltovich and R. Glaser (1981), "Categorization and representation of physics problems by experts and novices", *Cognitive Science*, **5** (2), 121–52.
Heller, P. and M. Hollabaugh (1992), "Teaching problem solving through cooperative grouping. Part 2: Designing problems and structuring groups", *American Journal of Physics*, **60** (7), 637–44.
Heller, P., R. Keith and S. Anderson (1992), "Teaching problem solving through cooperative grouping. Part 1: Group versus individual problem solving", *American Journal of Physics*, **60** (7), 627–36.
Maier, M., N. Blunch, J. Bangs and B. Peterson (2010), "Context-rich problems in economics", in M. Salemi and W. Walstad (eds), *Teaching Innovations in Economics: Strategies and Applications for Interactive Instruction*, Cheltenham, UK and Northampton, MA: Edward Elgar, pp. 170–89.
Rhoads, J. K. (2009), "Cooperative learning in a health economics course: 2008 U.S. presidential campaign and health care reform", cee.econ.uic.edu/workingpapers.html, accessed 14 March 2010.

4 Using cooperative learning exercises in economics
KimMarie McGoldrick

Cooperative learning entails the purposeful use of small groups to achieve enhanced learning outcomes. Research describing positive outcomes associated with this pedagogic technique suggests that successful implementation necessitates both careful choice of the cooperative learning format and incorporation of key supporting structures. Examples involving economic content are used to demonstrate these and other stages of exercise development, as well as the versatility of cooperative learning exercises which can vary by topic coverage, class size, and integration with other pedagogies. Available resources that support faculty in their development of cooperative learning techniques for a wide range of economics courses are discussed, as well as future directions for research.

RESEARCH ON COOPERATIVE LEARNING OUTCOMES

Cooperative learning is "one of the most thoroughly researched of all instructional methods", in part because of the many forms it can take (Slavin, 1990, p. 52). Students participating in cooperative learning exercises have "higher achievement, higher-level reasoning, more frequent generation of new ideas and solutions, and greater transfer of what is learned from one situation to another" (Barkley, Cross and Major, 2005, pp. 17–18). Students develop a greater understanding of material and demonstrate greater recall when cooperative learning groups are heterogeneous (different races, genders, learning styles) (Wenzel, 2000). Enhanced learning outcomes associated with cooperative learning are commonly linked to increased student engagement. Students who participate in cooperative learning exercises demonstrate a greater willingness to ask the instructor questions, both in and outside of class (Slavin, 1996). Johnson et al (1998) note that students like courses and subject matter to a greater extent when exposed via cooperative learning. This cooperative environment also helps students make friends and increases their self-esteem. It should not be surprising, then, that retention is greater in classes with cooperative learning as compared to lecture-based courses (Williamson and Rowe, 2002).

While much of the existing literature on cooperative learning in economics provides descriptive narratives guiding implementation and providing examples associated with specific courses or topics (see, for example, Bartlett, 1995; Maier and Keenan, 1994; Maier, McGoldrick, and Simkins, 2010; McGoldrick, Rebelein, Rhoads, and Stockly, 2010), two recent studies provide initial evidence that positive impacts on learning hold for economics as well.[1] Marburger (2005) compared the performance of two cohorts of principles of microeconomics students, one taught via traditional lecture techniques and the other participating in an otherwise identical course that incorporated cooperative learning exercises, which substituted for lecture content. Results indicate no significant difference in the impact of cooperative learning on outcomes measured using multiple choice questions, but significant differences did exist for questions that required analysis. Yamarik (2007) used a similar treatment/control group process to test the efficacy of cooperative learning in an intermediate macroeconomics course. Exercises were constructed following the key elements of successful cooperative learning (Johnson, Johnson, and Smith, 1998) and using base groups which met in and outside of class over the entire semester. Results suggest that students in the cooperative learning class performed better on examinations. Yamarik argues that this gain in examination scores can be linked to greater instructor–student interaction, greater likelihood of students studying in groups, and enhanced interest in economics.

In order to achieve enhanced learning gains, the development of cooperative learning exercises follow a process not unlike that followed in many active learning exercises, which involves choosing a cooperative learning format, integrating key structures, forming groups and motivating productive functioning, concluding the exercise, and evaluating outcomes.

CHOOSING A COOPERATIVE LEARNING FORMAT

In addition to being one of the most researched pedagogic methods, cooperative learning is also one of the most developed in that there are dozens of potential exercise formats and hundreds of variations and combinations of these from which to choose or adapt.[2] Identifying learning and content objectives facilitates the choice among loosely defined categories of cooperative learning exercises and provides a basis for post-exercise assessment. Barkley, Cross, and Major (2005) describe a number of popular cooperative learning formats, associate each with a common skill or learning objective focus, and organize these formats into categories of discussion, reciprocal teaching, graphic organizers, writing, and problem solving.

The most well-known cooperative learning format, *think-pair-share*, relies upon student discussion to brainstorm ideas, communicate knowledge, and practice using the language of the discipline. The think-pair-share exercise typically begins with students thinking independently about a problem or question. Students then pair up with another student and, taking turns, share their thoughts. Students experience a low threat environment in which to share their initial solutions and have the opportunity to re-evaluate after hearing their partners' reflections before participating in the larger class discussion. There are many permutations of the think-pair-share format, generated by differences in exercise goals and process. A think-pair-share exercise may focus on helping students get started on a problem (identifying key economic concepts within a complex word problem) or grounding abstract concepts in real-world experiences (brainstorming for examples of economics concepts in students' everyday lives). The think-pair-share format may incorporate written as well as oral components, and can vary in time use from a few minutes to more lengthy exercises. For example, this format can be designed as a note-taking pair exercise to address the common problem of introductory students struggling to effectively understand and use the language of economics.

Think-pair-share format – income and substitution effects   In a Principles of Microeconomics course, after introducing the income and substitution effects associated with a price change of a

Table 4.1   Categories of cooperative learning exercises

Category	Associated Skills/ Learning Objectives	Cooperative Learning Format
Discussion	Formulate ideas Practice communication Develop listening skills	**Think-pair-share** Buzz groups Three-step interview
Reciprocal Teaching	Demonstrate understanding of material Receive feedback on clarity of exposition Provide alternative explanation of material	**Note-taking pairs** **Learning cell** **Jigsaw**
Graphic Organizers	Enhances pattern discovery Relationships are explicitly represented Visual displays that organize and classify information	Group grid Sequence chains
Writing	Students demonstrate clarity of thought Process of organizing information is developed Synthesis of information is demonstrated	**Round table** Dyadic essays Peer editing
Problem Solving	Develop strategies Understand applications Critical analysis of solutions	**Send-a-problem** **Structured problem solving** Analytical teams

Note: Bold designates format discussed in chapter.

Source: Adopted from Barkley, Cross, and Major, 2005.

normal good, students are asked to pair with a neighbor. The first student is assigned the task of describing the income effect associated with the price change, using their notes as a guide, while the second student listens and compares this explanation to their own notes and asks questions of clarification. Roles reverse as the second student explains the substitution effect. After this exchange, the instructor can ask if there are any remaining questions before moving on to the more complicated inferior good case.

Faculty who want students to demonstrate clarity of thought as well as organization and synthesis of information may choose the *round table* format within the writing category of cooperative learning exercises. In general, this format requires student groups to respond to a question in a round robin format. The first student begins the response with a written point or two. The student describes these out loud and then passes the question to the next student who repeats the process. After all students have responded, the group evaluates responses, reorders, and refines, until their listing is complete.

Round table format – labor market issues   In a Labor Economics course, students are required to hand in two content-rich articles on topical labor market issues. The instructor then uploads copies of selected articles for students to read prior to class. In class, students are placed in groups, assigned a specific article and begin responding in round robin format to the question "What are the key economic issues raised in this article?" Each student is required to state (and record in writing) one issue before the next student takes his/her turn. (Note that students may identify the main issues quickly in this format, but students are encouraged to note some of the finer points of the article as well.) When time is called (after at least one complete round), students switch to working as a collective to evaluate their list in light of economic theory. Specifically, they are required to identify the associated theory and determine whether the statements made in the article are consistent with that theory.

In economics, Hansen (1986, 2001, 2006) has developed a taxonomy based on proficiencies that suggest that, by the time students have completed the economics major, they should be "effectively equipped to use their knowledge and skills" (1986, p. 231). Students should be able to access existing knowledge, display command of existing knowledge, interpret existing knowledge, interpret and manipulate economic data, apply existing knowledge, ask pertinent and penetrating questions, and create new knowledge. The first proficiency represents what is commonly known as foundational knowledge, whereas the remaining proficiencies describe other dimensions of learning.

Cooperative learning exercises can be developed for any one or a combination of Hansen's proficiencies. The note-taking pair (*think-pair-share*) example described above is consistent with evaluating the extent of students' command of existing knowledge. The *round table* example requires students to interpret existing knowledge (the article) and apply existing knowledge (the theory). The *jigsaw* technique, associated with the reciprocal teaching category, can assist students in interpreting and manipulating data. This cooperative learning format begins when a complicated problem is broken into manageable topical components. Instead of students tackling the whole problem, they are divided into expert groups on each topic and they master a single topic together. After mastery, students are reorganized into problem groups consisting of one representative from each topic group. The problem group now combines the pieces of the puzzle to tackle the original complicated problem.

Jigsaw format – The Economic Report of the President Students in a Principles of Macroeconomics course are divided into expert groups associated with sections of the Economic Report of the President, such as national income, employment and wages, production, prices, money stock, government finance, and international. Each group is required to evaluate and make a summary statement about the state of the economy based on their topic (report section). Once students have developed expertise on their assigned component, groups are reformulated to include one member from each expert group. In round robin fashion, students provide a summary of their topic based on the expert group discussion. As a collective, students are then required to provide an assessment of the state of the economy, taking into account each of the topics mastered in expert groups. The key output for this second grouping is a synthesis of information across topics and not simply a restatement of each individual topic in the resulting summary.

KEY STRUCTURES

While the wide range of potential formats for cooperative learning is an appealing feature, the common *structures* of cooperative learning formats ultimately drive their success. In a review of cooperative learning outcomes, Slavin (1990) notes that more effective cooperative-learning classes stress key structural components, including group and individual accountability. While structures can be described in a variety of ways,

Kagan (1992) presents four key elements commonly referred to by the acronym *PIES* that typify a 'structure.'

- *Positive interdependence* is achieved when individual and group successes are positively correlated (p. 4). Individuals are motivated to contribute to the group because their success is enhanced when the group achieves its goals. Interdependence is typically described in terms of the output goal (individual contributions are integrated into a single group product), the learning goal (that each group member can independently explain the collective group product), resources (a single copy of the task description is provided to the group or each member is provided with a subset of assignment components or necessary information), or roles (assigned to individuals to assist in the functioning of the collective group) (Smith and Waller, 1997, p. 202).
- *Individual (and group) accountability* ensures that evaluation of success reinforces the individual contribution as well as collective functioning. While it is typical to assess individual achievement, the degree to which the group has achieved its goal has been shown to positively impact individual outcomes (Webb, 1983, 1991). Ultimately, responsibility and evaluation occurs at the individual level.
- *Equal participation* ensures that all group members are engaged and participate in the activity. This key element relates specifically to the interactions that occur in groups during the cooperative learning exercise (Smith, 1996, pp. 74–6).
- *Simultaneous interaction* occurs when more than one participant is active as multiple groups tackle the assignment at the same time.

The wide range of cooperative learning formats allow for various methods to integrate these key structures, enhancing the probability of achieving successes demonstrated by research.

The free-rider problem is probably the most commonly cited issue associated with group work, for both students and faculty. However, both positive interdependence and individual accountability structures help to minimize, if not completely eliminate, this negative aspect. As suggested above, positive interdependence can be promoted through output goals, learning goals, resources, or roles. In an innovative application in which the free-rider problem is tackled head on, Bartlett (1995) enforces a common learning goal on the cooperative learning groups. By adding the element of chance to the demonstration of learning, through either a flip of a coin or the roll of a die determining which group member will take an exam, the group is collectively motivated to enhance the learning of its weakest member.

While random choice of who takes an evaluative assignment for the group focuses on the final stage of the cooperative learning exercise to eliminate the free-rider problem, individual accountability at initial stages has a similar effect. For example, Rebelein (in McGoldrick, Rebelein, Rhoads, and Stockly, 2010) describes the use of a *learning cell* in which Principles of Macroeconomics students read assigned newspaper articles and formulate three types of questions demonstrating identification of facts, evaluation of information or connections to other aspects of the course. Questions are submitted to the instructor prior to the cooperative learning exercise. This "ticket to participate" ensures that students not only read the articles in preparation for the exercise but also develop some level of comprehension which is applied when groups use their collective under-standing to generate answers for questions authored by their classmates.

Topics which have multiple intersecting factors are especially well suited to the *group grid* cooperative learning format. In a Principles of Microeconomics course, this can be used to create a summary table describing changes in equilibrium price and quantity associated with supply and demand changes. A grid table that represents a set of cat-egories (columns) and pieces of information or conditions (rows) is distributed to each group and students fill out the table based on the intersection of categories and condi-tions. In the case of market equilibrium changes, the columns might represent conditions associated with supply (no change, an increase or a decrease), whereas the rows would represent demand (no change, an increase or a decrease). The intersection of a row and column results in a cell within which students demonstrate their understanding of the market outcomes associated with the respective changes in supply and demand. Students first independently generate both graphical and intuitive explanations of a number of the assigned cells within the grid and then are grouped together to compare and contrast their solutions. This process can simultaneously enhance positive interdependence and equal participation when each group member serves as leader for one cell, while the other group members provide reflective feedback leading to solutions which are more comprehensive.

GROUP FORMATION AND FUNCTIONING

The extent to which key structures are incorporated can be enhanced with careful con-sideration of group formation and functioning. Three types of groups are associated with cooperative learning exercises, the choice of which depends on the characteristics of the exercise to be implemented. Informal groups can be formed on the fly, address a single concept, absorb few resources (time and preparation) and typically the pairings are not repeated. Formal groups necessitate careful formation as the associated exercises require greater time commitment (developing and implementing) and cover more complex topics. And while membership is consistent during an exercise, it can change across exer-cises. Base groups require even more careful formation as the same group reconvenes several times over the semester and covers multiple topics.

In addition to the importance of choosing a group type that correlates with stated objectives, research indicates that composition and size are important determinants of cooperative learning exercise effectiveness. Groups that are heterogeneous, in terms of academic ability and individual characteristics such as gender and ethnicity, seem to gen-erate "more elaborative thinking, more frequent giving and receiving of explanations, and greater perspective taking in discussing material . . . all of which increase the depth of understanding, the quality of reasoning, and the accuracy of long-term retention" (Johnson, Johnson and Smith, 1991, pp. 60–61). Large groups require more resources (including time), and complications associated with organization of effort can bog down group processing. However, groups that are too small can be dominated by one member or lack diversity of perspective, leading to less rich discussion. Barkley, Cross and Major (2005, pp. 45–50) describe processes for constructing groups through random selec-tion techniques, relying on odd-even number assignments, counting off, and the draw of playing cards. They also explain instructor-driven selection processes that employ student sign-ups and data sheets as well as information about student test scores and learning styles.

Group functioning reinforces many of the key elements of cooperative learning exercises when members are assigned individual roles. Common roles to assign to students include facilitator, recorder, reporter, and time keeper. For larger groups, the instructor might add the roles of summarizer or coach. Assigning specific roles helps smooth group operation as students are encouraged to participate, make positive contributions, and maintain focus on the task at hand.

CONCLUDING THE EXERCISE AND EVALUATING OUTCOMES[3]

If the instructor provides students with a predetermined "quiet signal", such as flickering classroom lights or raising their hand, this can effectively facilitate the end of the group work but not the exercise. Key structural components of cooperative learning exercises, such as positive interdependence and accountability, are frequently facilitated by the subsequent "reporting out" process. It is at this time that the work of the group is made public, further enhancing learning opportunities for the whole class. Accountability may also be enhanced during cooperative learning exercises by announcing follow-up assessment practices.

Reporting out activities can immediately follow the exercise or be delayed until the start of the next class meeting. Reporting out can also call upon an informal format such as conversational sharing or a more formal format such as a written or oral report. The products of the activity can also be graded at the individual or group level and by the instructor, peers, the students themselves, or not graded at all. In this phase of the cooperative learning exercise, regardless of the "reporting out" format, students are engaged in a discussion that summarizes learning as they share their work and receive additional feedback. Although potential closure techniques are too numerous to be described in detail here,[4] consider the following example of a commonly used reporting out process. The gallery walk requires group output to be represented visually, on poster board, using summarization techniques such as outlines or concept maps (Millis and Cottell, 1998). One randomly selected group member is designated to represent the group as other members move from display to display, asking questions and clarifying their understanding of the group-generated outcomes. This process promotes positive interdependence because group members do not know which of them will be chosen to represent the group. Students are provided with immediate, in-class feedback on their work via a method that is informal and not graded.

Grading issues typically arise in most active learning exercises and cooperative learning has its own challenges in this respect. Instructors need not explicitly evaluate all activities if there is a clear indication of the degree to which activities contribute to learning and thus to grades achieved through other avenues such as quizzes and exams. However, some instructors may choose to grade cooperative learning exercises when first introduced, especially if students are unconvinced regarding the long-run learning value of the activity and immediate feedback seems preferable. Students can be assessed individually using traditional formats such as worksheets completed during the exercise, a follow-up homework assignment, or a quiz in a subsequent class period. To achieve positive interdependence and promote synergistic group work, instructors might provide bonus points to all members of a group if individually they all meet some minimum standard level of performance. As mentioned earlier, Bartlett (1995) suggests randomly choosing an individual from each group to be evaluated and the grade earned by that one student is the grade then earned by everyone in the group. While all of the afore-mentioned grading processes assume the instructor as the evaluating authority, the key to cooperative learning success relies heavily on the workings of groups, implying a role for students in the evaluation of their peers.

VERSATILITY OF COOPERATIVE LEARNING TECHNIQUES

Although the examples presented thus far focus primarily on introductory courses with small enrollments, the wide range of techniques allows cooperative learning exercises to be developed across a wide range of environments. Cooperative learning is versatile in that it can be designed for small and large classes, introductory to capstone courses, brick and mortar campus classes or distance learning environments, and a host of other categorical descriptions, as well as in combination with other pedagogic techniques or as components of larger projects.

While not all cooperative learning formats can be easily adapted to the large class setting, with minor modifications many are indeed transferable. Buckles and Hoyt (2006) suggest that the jigsaw, structured problem solving and think-pair-share formats can be used to enhance instruction in large classes. For example, *structured problem solving* begins when students form groups of three to four to work on a problem. The difference between this cooperative format and other problem solving exercises is that the groups first come to a consensus on a plan or series of steps to answer the problem which ultimately guides the presentation of the solution by a randomly chosen member of the group. The modification required in moving from small to large classes is relegated to the reporting out process in which a select number of groups share their work rather than all groups.[5]

Applicability of cooperative learning exercises goes beyond introductory courses. Consider, for example, a senior level research/capstone course in which students must develop an effective question on which to base their research. Greenlaw (2006, pp. 14–18) suggests that an effective economic question has well-defined components: problem-oriented, analytical, interesting, significant, amenable to economic analysis, and feasible. *Peer editing* provides a process through which students receive constructive feedback on the extent to which their developed question meets these stated criteria:

> After deciding on a topic for their research project, students are required to prepare and justify two effective economic questions based on provided guidelines. Students are placed into groups of four and their questions are distributed to other group members. Initially, each student individually evaluates justifications and provides suggestions for improvement. When the individual evaluation process is complete, the group process begins as each reviewer reads an economic question and justification and the group provides reflective comments based on their individual evaluations. The group as a collective helps the author revise their question so that it satisfies the criteria for an effective economic question.

Some course constructs provide natural challenges for implementing cooperative learning exercises, such as those conducted in a distance learning environment. Stockly (in McGoldrick, Rebelein, Rhoads, and Stockly, 2010) demonstrates that such barriers are not insurmountable as she describes a *send-a-problem* exercise in an Intermediate Macroeconomics course conducted simultaneously in a brick and mortar classroom and two remote sites. The traditional classroom send-a-problem exercise begins as students are divided into groups, with each receiving a different problem attached to an envelope. Student groups are directed to solve the problem (using group processing that ensures equal participation) and, after a period of time, they are asked to place their answer in the envelope. Groups exchange envelopes, receiving a new problem to solve and the process repeats. After a series of rounds, groups are asked to open the envelope and evaluate and synthesize the answers provided by other groups. They compile a final answer that is shared with the class as a whole. In the case of the send-a-problem conducted in this distance learning environment, each remote site was designated as a group in addition to the classroom groups. Problems were sent via fax machine and the presentation of final round answers was facilitated using remote access cameras.

Not only are cooperative learning exercises versatile in their applicability to a wide range of class settings, but also through implementation methods for a single format. For example, Maier, McGoldrick, and Simkins (2010) demonstrate a variety of methods associated with the *send-a-problem* format, including using the final round to have students focus on the process of problem solving by comparing methods used by different groups in previous rounds. Alternatively, each round of the send-a-problem can be used to incrementally solve multi-step problems as students build upon previous groups' answers. Likewise, the think-pair-share technique can be implemented as note-taking pairs, to generate lists, solve simple problems, or analyze competing perspectives.

The versatility of cooperative learning exercises also generates positive spillover effects when instructors use them in combination with other pedagogic techniques. Maier, McGoldrick, and Simkins (2011) describe the synergistic nature of cooperative learning and other pedagogies including experiments, just-in-time-teaching (JiTT), context-rich problems, peer instruction, service-learning, and undergraduate research. They demonstrate how learning can be enhanced when pedagogies are combined, using the key structures of cooperative learning to introduce or enhance group work associated with these other techniques.

RESOURCES

The wealth of research on cooperative learning techniques also suggests an abundance of supporting resources. In economics, there is one comprehensive, centralized source emerging. Starting Point: Teaching and Learning Economics[6] is an economics pedagogic portal that seeks to introduce economists to innovative teaching strategies developed both within and beyond the discipline of economics. Starting Point also provides instructors with the tools to begin integrating and assessing cooperative learning strategies in their own classrooms and offers a platform that promotes the sharing of teaching innovations and ideas among instructors. The cooperative learning module on this site includes resources that encourage faculty to learn more about the pedagogic technique (what it is, why use it, and how to implement it), as well as locate and contribute to a growing library of teaching examples. Each example contains:

- A description of the example and a complete set of teaching materials needed for implementation, such as handouts, data and instructions for students
- Teaching notes and tips for the instructor
- Context for how this activity has been used, including the type of course and at what point in the course
- Measurable goals for student learning and assessment information that describes how the instructor can measure students' achievement of specified learning goals
- Author attribution and contact information
- References and links to other resources supporting the example

CONCLUDING THOUGHTS

Cooperative learning is more than group work. It is a well-defined learning process with key structures which generate positive impacts on learning outcomes, student interest, and retention. There is a growing economics literature that provides advice and examples for incorporating various forms of cooperative learning, yet there is considerably less evidence of its effectiveness in economics. Future research on this pedagogic practice should focus on demonstrating that specific formats of cooperative learning (think-pair-share, send-a-problem, jigsaw, etc.) implemented across a range of institutional settings (public or private, large or small class sizes) confer the same positive impacts demonstrated in other disciplines.

NOTES

1. Further evidence that cooperative learning groups were found to significantly improve performance in macroeconomics classes, at both the introductory and intermediate levels, is provided by Cohn (1999) and Johnston et al. (2000).
2. In addition to cooperative learning formats described herein, economic specific examples are also presented in Bartlett (1998), Keenan and Maier (2004), McGoldrick, Rebelein, Rhoads, and Stockly (2010), and Maier, McGoldrick, and Simkins (2010).
3. This section draws from the discussion of these issues in McGoldrick et al. (2010).
4. For examples, see Barkley, Cross and Major (2005, pp. 79–80); Millis and Cottell (1998, pp. 105–9); Kagan (1992, pp. 12:5–12:6).
5. For more on how to integrate pedagogic practices in larger classes, see Chapter 10, "Making the Large Enrollment Course Interactive and Engaging", in this volume.
6. http://serc.carleton.edu/econ/index.html (accessed 10 April 2011).

REFERENCES

Barkley, E. F., K. P. Cross and C. H. Major (2005), *Collaborative Learning Techniques: A Handbook for College Faculty*, San Francisco: Jossey-Bass.

Bartlett, R. L. (1995), "A flip of the coin – a roll of the die: An answer to the free-rider problem in economic education", *Journal of Economic Education*, **26** (2), 131–9.
Bartlett, R. (1998), "Making cooperative learning work in economics classes", in W. E. Becker, M. Watts and S. R. Becker (eds), *Teaching Economics to Undergraduates: Alternatives to Chalk and Talk*, Cheltenham, UK and Lyme, USA: Edward Elgar, pp. 11–34.
Buckles, S. and G. Hoyt (2006), "Using active learning techniques in large lecture classes", in W. E. Becker, M. Watts and S. R. Becker (eds), *Teaching Economics: More Alternatives to Chalk and Talk*, Cheltenham, UK and Northampton, MA, USA: Edward Elgar, pp. 75–88.
Cohn, C. (1999), "Cooperative learning in a macroeconomics course: A team simulation", *College Teaching*, **47** (2), 51–4.
Greenlaw, S. A. (2006), *Doing Economics: A Guide to Understanding and Carrying Out Economic Research*, Boston, MA: Houghton Mifflin Company.
Hansen, W. L. (1986), "What knowledge is most worth knowing – for economics majors?", *American Economic Review*, **76** (2), 149–52.
Hansen, W. L. (2001), "Expected proficiencies for undergraduate economics majors", *Journal of Economic Education*, **32** (3), 231–42.
Hansen, W. L. (2006), "A proficiency-based economics course examinations", Presented at the Midwest Economic Association Meetings, March.
Johnson, D. W., R. T. Johnson and K. A. Smith (1991), *Cooperative Learning: Increasing College Faculty Instructional Productivity*, ASHE-ERIC Higher Education Report No. 4, Washington, DC: The George Washington University, School of Education and Human Development.
Johnson, D. W., R. T. Johnson and K. A. Smith (1998), "Cooperative learning returns to college: What evidence is there that it works?", *Change*, **20** (4), 26–35.
Johnston, C. G., R. H. James, J. N. Lye and I. M. McDonald (2000), "An evaluation of the introduction of collaborative problem-solving for learning economics", *Journal of Economic Education*, **31** (1), 13–29.
Kagan, S. (1992), *Cooperative Learning*, San Juan Capistrano, CA: Resources for Teachers, Inc.
Keenan, D. and M. Maier (2004), *Economics Live! Learning Economics the Collaborative Way* (4th edition), Boston, MA: McGraw-Hill.
Maier, M. and D. Keenan (1994), "Teaching tools: Cooperative learning in economics", *Economic Inquiry*, **32** (2), 358–61.
Maier, M., K. McGoldrick and S. Simkins (2010), "Implementing cooperative learning in introductory economics courses", in B. Millis (ed.), *Cooperative Learning in Higher Education, Across the Disciplines, Across the Academy*, Sterling, VA: Stylus Press, pp. 157–80.
Maier, M., K. McGoldrick and S. Simkins (2011), "Cooperative learning and disciplinary-based pedagogical innovations: Taking advantage of complementarities", in J. Cooper and P. Robinson (eds), *Small Group Learning in Higher Education: Research and Practice*, Stillwater, OK: New Forums.
Marburger, D. R. (2005), "Comparing student performance using cooperative learning", *International Review of Economics Education*, **4** (1), 46–57.
McGoldrick, K., R. Rebelein, J. Rhoads and S. Stockly (2010), "Making cooperative learning effective for economics", in M. Salemi and W. Walstad (eds), *Teaching Innovations in Economics*, Cheltenham, UK and Northampton, MA, USA: Edward Elgar, pp. 65–94.
Millis, B. J. and P. G. Cottell, Jr. (1998), *Cooperative Learning for Higher Education Faculty*, Phoenix, AZ: American Council on Education and Oryx Press.
Slavin, R. E. (1990), *Cooperative Learning: Theory, Research and Practice*, Boston, MA: Allyn and Bacon.
Slavin, R. E. (1996), *Education for All*, Exton, PA: Swets and Zeitlinger.
Smith, K. A. (1996), "Cooperative learning: Making 'Group Work' work", in T. E. Sutherland and C. C. Bonwell (eds), *Using Active Learning in College Classes: A Range of Options for Faculty. New Directions for Teaching and Learning, No 67*, San Francisco: Jossey-Bass, pp. 71–82.
Smith, K. A. and A. A. Waller (1997), "Cooperative learning for new college teachers", in W.E. Campbell and K. A. Smith (eds), *New Paradigms for College Teaching*, Edina, MN: Interaction Book Company, pp. 183–209.
Webb, N. (1983), "Predicting learning from student interaction: Defining the interaction variable", *Educational Psychologist*, **18**, 33–41.
Webb, N. (1991), "Task-related verbal interaction and mathematics learning in small groups", *Journal of Research in Mathematics Education*, **22**, 366–89.
Wenzel, T. (2000), "Cooperative student activities as learning devices", *Analytical Chemistry*, **72**, 293–6.
Williamson, V. M. and M. W. Rowe (2002), "Group problem-solving versus lecture in college-level quantitative analysis: The good, the bad, and the ugly", *Journal of Chemical Education*, **79** (9), 1131–4.
Yamarik, S. (2007), "Does cooperative learning improve student learning outcomes?", *Journal of Economic Education*, **38** (3), 259–77.

5 Improving classroom discussion in economics courses

W. Lee Hansen and Michael K. Salemi

Most economics faculty members, when asked what they hope students take away from their courses, aside from content knowledge, mention higher-order cognitive skills. They talk about critical thinking, about the ability to evaluate an argument, analyze an economic problem or issue, and apply what they are learning. Most of all, they want their students to think like an economist.

Despite these lofty goals, instructors rarely devote any substantial class time to honing the thinking of students through organized classroom discussion. Instructors may fail to appreciate the effectiveness of classroom discussion for both developing these skills and revealing whether students acquire these skills. Many faculty members who do appreciate the value of discussion may fail to understand how to organize and lead effective discussions.

This chapter demonstrates how instructors can make discussion an integral part of their instructional approach. With careful preparation and some practice, almost any instructor can lead discussions that will help students acquire and develop the thinking skills we, as economics instructors, want them to acquire. We draw heavily on experience with the Great Books Foundation "shared inquiry" discussion approach.

"TWO-WAY TALK" IN THE CLASSROOM

The first step is to set out a hierarchy of non-lecture teaching techniques that can be called "two-way talk" (Hansen and Salemi, 1998, p. 208) between instructors and students and also among students themselves. Traditional lectures represent "one-way talk" as instructors talk while students listen and try to understand what is said. In this setting, they are given no opportunity to "talk" or formulate responses of their own.

Several types of two-way talk can be part of a teaching plan. Instructors can initiate questions and field responses during their lectures, a technique useful in checking on student understanding and in breaking lectures into smaller chunks. Or students can pose questions and receive answers without prompting from the instructor; while the initiative would seem to lie with the students, it is the instructor who controls the amount of time devoted to questions by being more or less receptive to them. Alternatively, instructors can have students engage in recitation or "drill" activities; though useful as a method of checking on what students know, the focus is on their providing "correct" responses to the instructor's questions. A more venturesome approach calls for students to work on a question or problem as part of a small group and then "report" the group's results or conclusions to the class as a whole. Finally, instructors and students can participate in a formal discussion of some reading assignment for the purpose of gaining a deeper understanding of what the author is saying and exercising their power to think.

Using two-way talk techniques involves important tradeoffs between breadth and depth. Though more content can be covered with lectures, discussions ultimately facilitate a deeper understanding of covered content. Through lecture, instructors can guarantee that concepts are presented clearly and accurately. Through two-way talk, students process a more extensive but lower quality stream of information and gain facility in evaluating the use of economic concepts by others and in applying economics concepts in the construction of their own responses. Two-way talk may leave some students confused initially, but, in our view, resolving confusion is a necessary step to real learning. Some students may not understand their colleagues' questions or responses. Others may be swayed by weak or even incorrect arguments. Along the way, however, students learn to judge the merits of an argument and to take responsibility for their own understanding.

Why use two-way talk in the classroom? Two-way talk gives students practice doing in class what we say we want them to be able to do in life. It requires students and instructors to think, to think in a more focused way, to frame their own answers to questions, and to interpret written material pertinent to course content. Discussion of the kind being presented here is beneficial because it forces students to switch from passive to active mode, and it requires them to apply course concepts themselves rather than simply recognizing a correct application when it is presented. A successful discussion requires students to resolve the ambiguity inherent in an idea-rich reading. Discussion requires reading material rich enough so that several, sometimes many, potential interpretations and many answers exist to questions that can be asked about the material. During discussion, students strive to produce their own answers and interpretations, as well as understanding and evaluating the interpretations and opinions of their colleagues.

Good discussion is exciting, especially if the reading material is interesting and relevant. Students are stimulated by the realization that they alone will interpret and evaluate the material. The instructor will not provide the "right answers" at the end of class. The only answers are those that students produce through their interaction with the material and with the comments and observations of other students during the discussion. Discussion offers a means for instructors to promote an appreciation of the relevance and vitality of economics, while at the same time sharpening the higher-order thinking skills of their students. The first sections of this chapter explain the elements that underlie effective discussion. The last section offers tips on other types of two-way talk teaching strategies.

INTEGRATING DISCUSSION INTO THE COURSE PLAN

Discussion is an appropriate teaching strategy only when an instructor's course goals go beyond memorization of key terms and manipulation of equations. The syllabus for a discussion-oriented course should spell out that students are expected to develop higher-level thinking skills, to develop an appreciation of the importance and relevance of the course material and to understand why discussion is an important part of the strategy for accomplishing these goals.

Students should be informed that because discussion is an essential element of teaching and learning, it does "count" in assessing student performance. Students may believe that making such an assessment is difficult to do fairly, and it may even make some students reticent about contributing. The instructor can counter these concerns by making it clear that widespread participation is essential in contributing to the class's understanding of the material and that everyone will be given opportunities to participate. To lend further weight to the importance of discussion, the instructor may want to indicate that questions taken up in discussion are appropriate subject matter for examination essays.

SELECTION OF DISCUSSION MATERIAL

Effective discussion requires that instructors select appropriate reading material. A test of appropriateness is whether an instructor can answer "yes" to four questions.

Does the material contain a sufficient number of ideas to warrant discussion?   To test whether a particular piece is sufficiently rich, the instructor should try to write several interpretive questions about it. What constitutes an interpretive question is taken up later in this chapter. For now, suffice it to say that these questions should be interesting, should require that students interpret what the author has written, and should support more than one reasonable answer.

Is the material self-contained?   The reading selection should be able to stand on its own so there is no need to look up key terms or examine supplementary information. Everyone should be able to come to the discussion equally well prepared, and the only reference necessary during the discussion is the selection itself. Of course, the selection can build on knowledge, lectures, and other readings already covered in the course.

Is the material reasonably well written?   Reading selections that are poorly written and organized will cause the discussion to get bogged down in efforts to determine what the author said. Well-written materials permit the discussion to focus on what the author meant. To qualify, the material need not apply economic logic faultlessly. While straightening out a confused or incorrect presentation of economic ideas is a good discussion outcome, discussion should focus on intellectual rather than stylistic confusion.

Is the material interesting to both the instructor and the students?   It is essential that the instructor find the reading material interesting because instructor enthusiasm for the material is an important source of motivation for students. One check on whether students are likely to find the material interesting is for the instructor to ask whether students think it takes up important issues, offers new insights, or helps resolve some puzzle.

Instructors may believe that textbooks are a source of material suitable for discussion. That is not the case because textbook authors have taken pains to provide only correct answers to the questions textbooks present. With the disappearance of books of readings, popular several decades ago, instructors must look elsewhere. The most obvious source is the financial press, particularly the *Wall Street Journal, New York Times* and the *Financial Times*. The *Journal* regularly includes feature articles on various aspects of the US and world economies, as well as editorials on economic policy, many of which are rich enough to support discussion. Also useful are business and economic periodicals oriented to the general public, including *Challenge, Business Week, Fortune*, and *The Economist;* all of them regularly publish articles suitable for discussion. More and more general periodicals, among them the *New Yorker, New Republic*, the *National Interest*, the *American Prospect, Commentary*, and *Foreign Affairs*, publish articles on economics that are good for classroom discussion. Then, there is the *Journal of Economic Perspectives* and the general articles in the *Journal of Economic Education*. Finally, most regional Federal Reserve Banks publish periodic reviews that include articles on issues of current interest; frequently these articles are appropriate for discussion in upper division courses and occasionally they may be suitable for discussion in a principles course.

A final source of discussion material is the body of classic economic writings. Adam Smith's seventh chapter of *The Wealth of Nations* (1776), "On the Natural and Market Price of Commodities," is in many respects a far more interesting and challenging treatment of prices and markets than modern textbooks provide. John Stuart Mill's twelfth chapter from *Principles of Political Economy* (1848), "Of Popular Remedies for Low Wages," gives useful insights pertinent to recent debates and research on the impact of minimum wage laws. Of more recent but not current vintage, R. A. Radford's classic article, "The Economic Organization of a P.O.W. Camp" in *Economica* (1945) offers a fascinating description of how during World War II markets for the exchange of goods and services evolved within German prisoner of war camps. Readings such as these provide first-rate material for classroom discussion. For guidance on discussing both classical and contemporary economic readings, the reader can refer to Salemi and Hansen (2005).

PREPARING DISCUSSION QUESTIONS

Good questions are the necessary starting point of successful discussions. But what is a good discussion question? To answer that question it is useful to classify discussion questions in two ways: by the type of answer the question seeks to elicit and by the role of the question in advancing the progress of the discussion. The two-way classification is summarized in the matrix shown in Table 5.1. Across the top of the matrix are listed the three types of questions: interpretive, factual, and evaluative. These are discussed first.

Table 5.1   Two-way discussion question classification matrix

| | | Question Types | | |
		Interpretive	Factual	Evaluative
Question Roles	Basic	Yes	No	No
	Supporting	Yes	Yes	No
	Follow Up	Yes	Yes	No
	Concluding	Possibly	No	Yes

Interpretive questions   Interpretive questions ask participants to explore what the author means. In contrast to factual questions, interpretive questions require participants to tap their higher-order cognitive skills and, together with the evidence reported in the reading, formulate a response. Interpretive questions are the backbone of successful discussions precisely because they require students to practice using higher-order skills. The essential characteristic of a good interpretive question is that it does not have a single right answer. If students perceive that a question has a "right answer" or that the discussion leader is looking for a particular answer, they will often switch from an active to a passive mode and wait for someone to give that answer. A good interpretive question exploits the richness of the reading selection in the sense that different participants, using evidence from the same reading, can provide what seem to be reasonable, yet different, responses.

By asking good interpretive questions, the discussion leader accomplishes two objectives. First, the leader transfers responsibility for critical thinking to students. Second, the leader makes the discussion more challenging. The challenge comes not only in sifting through the evidence to come up with a response but also in evaluating the responses provided by other participants.

How can a discussion leader write good interpretive questions? Good interpretive questions remind participants that they are to respond using evidence from the reading. To maintain this focus, it is useful to pose the question in the form "Why, according to the author . . .?" A good interpretive question must also admit to several possible answers. To make sure that it does, the discussion leader should carefully examine the reading selection to ensure that the requisite ambiguity is present. If that ambiguity is not present, the question does not qualify as an interpretive question and should be discarded. The most successful interpretive questions are usually those for which the answers without further contemplation are least clear to the instructor.

By way of an example, here is a good interpretive question about the Radford article: "Explain why Radford believes the exchange system in the POW camp operated effectively?" Some students might cite "unity of the market and the prevalence of a single price" (p. 191) as evidence in the affirmative. Others might point to the existence of monopoly profits. Still others might mention the ascendance of cigarettes as a numeraire. The fact that multiple answers emerge provides the challenge of the interpretive question.

Factual questions   Factual questions ask for specific information that can be found in the reading. The "facts" of the reading are the words used by the author. Sometimes these "facts" may differ from the facts as they are understood by the participants. In discussion, however, it is necessary to focus on the facts as the author presents them. In effect, factual questions all are versions of the question "What did the author say about . . .?" Once again, it is important that the reading be self-contained so that no outside facts are required to understand the article.

Evaluative questions   Evaluative questions ask for a judgment. They invite participants to consider the material in terms of their own experience and to determine whether they agree or disagree with the author's point of view. While an evaluative question requires participants to relate the material to their own experiences, participants should base their answers on the reading and discussion of the reading that occurred. An evaluative question is not an invitation to provide unsupported opinions. It is, however, an invitation to use one's own values in answering.

A good evaluative question about the Radford article is: "Do you believe the ranking Allied officer in the POW camp should have allowed this exchange system to develop and operate?" One participant might answer that the system was efficient and for that reason alone was enough to make the exchange system a good idea. Another might argue that it was not fair that the lesser-skilled traders ended up with fewer goods. Still another might argue that the system gave the prisoners too much individual freedom and was therefore bad for camp discipline. Again, differences in the responses provide an opportunity for students to understand why they answered as they did, and perhaps give them a chance to alter their view.

QUESTION ROLES

While the different types of questions discussed above help explore the meaning of a reading selection, questions can also be classified by the role they play in facilitating discussion.

Basic questions   A basic question is one the discussion leader uses to lead off a discussion. It is a question that can lead to an extended discussion of what the leader considers to be some of the main ideas in the reading. It is neither factual nor evaluative. Rather, it concerns an important issue in the reading, and it should stimulate discussion. Participants, in turn, should find a basic question interesting and should not perceive it to be rhetorical. For the Radford article, a good basic question is: "Why did a market system arise in the POW camp?"

Supporting questions   A supporting question is one the discussion leader uses to organize discussion of the basic question. The particular approach the discussion leader opts to use depends on the nature of the basic question and ultimately on the reading material itself. If the basic question addresses a complex issue in the reading, the leader might use supporting questions to break the basic question into smaller parts. If the basic question hinges on a particular concept used by the author, the leader might use a supporting question to ask participants what the author means by that concept. If some facts in the reading bear on the basic question, the leader might use supporting questions to bring those facts forward. Thus, supporting questions, such as those that follow, are used to help move the discussion toward answering a basic question, for example, "What impact did the Red Cross parcels have on the camp market?" or "Why didn't camp officials take action to prevent the market system from evolving and subsequently flourishing?"

Follow-up questions   A follow-up question is one that probes the response to either a basic or supporting question. It is used by the leader to elicit additional responses from the participants. The following scenario illustrates how a leader might use a follow-up question. The leader starts with the basic question: "Does Radford believe that the exchange system in the POW camp operated effectively?" One student responds that the system was not effective because it was not fair. At this point, the leader has several follow-up options. The student might be asked what he or she means by "fair" or what evidence indicates the system was not fair. Or other students might be asked whether they agree that the system was not fair. Obviously, responses will differ and this provides an opportunity to call on students to explain their responses.

Using follow-up questions is the most effective strategy a leader has to ensure that responsibility for advancing and evaluating arguments in the discussion remains with the students. Because they prefer clear answers, students will often try to transfer that responsibility back to the discussion leader by asking a direct question, such as: "What is the right definition of 'fair' in the context of the Radford article?" The leader should then use follow-up questions to deflect that responsibility back to the participants by asking "What do you think it is?"

Follow-up questions serve as a useful tool for the leader to direct "traffic" during a discussion. A good leader listens actively, looking for connections between the responses offered by participants. Follow-up questions are used to make those connections apparent to the participants and to explore their meaning, for example: "How does your notion of fairness differ from that of Ms. Smith's?" Thus, follow-up questions provide a way for the leader to get the participants to talk to one another. Whether or not to ask a follow-up question and what kind of follow-up questions to ask are decisions the leader must make spontaneously.

Concluding questions   A concluding question is used by discussion leaders to bring a line of discussion to a close. There comes a time in the discussion when the leader perceives that participants have done as much as they can to address the issues raised by a basic question. At that point, the leader uses concluding questions to move on to another basic question or to end the entire discussion. One might ask participants to provide an overview of the discussion. Another might ask participants directly whether the issues are sufficiently resolved. Still another might ask them to make judgments about the arguments that have been raised. In all cases, students rather than the leader wrap up the discussion.

QUESTION CLUSTERS

A question cluster is a collection of questions prepared by the discussion leader to address a main idea or ideas in a reading selection. Writing question clusters is the best way, first, to decide whether a reading is suitable for discussion and, second, to prepare to lead that discussion. A good question cluster satisfies three criteria. First, it addresses an important and interesting idea in the reading. Second, it includes basic, supportive, follow-up, and concluding questions. Third, it uses the right type of question for each question role.

Both interpretive and evaluative questions play important roles in a discussion. By interpreting a reading, participants develop the higher-order cognitive skills that we want them to have and come to a deeper understanding of the reading. By evaluating a reading, participants use their deeper understanding to create an informed opinion about it. Evaluating a reading is another important source of motivation and signals to the participants that their informed opinions are important.

A good question cluster combines the several types of questions discussed earlier and the roles these questions play. In effect, they represent a strategy for exploring the reading's meaning. A cluster of questions for the Radford article follows.

- *Basic question*   What, according to Radford, accounts for the development of an exchange system in the POW camp?

- *Supporting questions*   Can the development of the system be explained by the equality or lack of equality in the distribution of supplies?
- Were prisoners generally unhappy with their particular allotment of supplies and thereby motivated to develop an exchange system?
- Which force does Radford think was most important in accounting for the evolution of the exchange system?
- Does Radford believe that differences in preferences gave rise to exchange?
- Does Radford believe that prisoners might have developed an exchange system because they were used to living in an exchange economy?

- *Concluding question*   What weights would you assign to the various forces Radford notes as having contributed to the development of the exchange system?

MUTUAL RESPONSIBILITIES

Discussion can be exciting and rewarding for both the leader and the participants provided all agree to fulfill their responsibilities.

For the leader, three responsibilities stand out. First, it is essential that the leader prepare question clusters in advance. It takes some work to identify in the readings those ideas that are suitable for discussion. It requires still more work to write a good interpretive question that can function as the basic question for the discussion and to devise supportive questions that will break the discussion down into "bite-sized" parts. Only after the leader has prepared question clusters will it be fully clear that an article is suitable for discussion. Second, the leader must listen intently to the participants. The leader is responsible for helping the participants develop critical skills and for identifying the connections among the responses they contribute. To do this, the leader must first hear what each participant is saying. Third, the leader should focus on asking questions. In the course of a discussion, the participants will often "invite" the leader to provide "the right answer" or to take charge in some other way. The leader must not succumb to these temptations. Instead, the leader should ask questions that help the participants arrive at their own answers.

For participants, three responsibilities stand out. First, participants must read the material carefully before the discussion. They must read actively rather than passively, making notes on points they think are important or do not understand. Students who have not read the material may still participate but will have to read the material quickly while the discussion proceeds and enter it later. Second, participants should strive to back up their interpretations and judgments with evidence from the reading. A well-supported view is more valuable both to the participant who contributed it and to other participants. Participants should strive always to be ready to answer the follow-up question "Why?" Third, participants should listen carefully to what their colleagues are saying. It is as important to understand and evaluate the arguments of others as it is to frame one's own contributions. Discussion is a dialogue that requires thinking, talking, and listening.

GROUND RULES FOR EFFECTIVE DISCUSSION

To this point, the focus has been on how to prepare for a discussion. We now turn attention to the mechanics of leading a discussion effectively. What follows is a list of tips we have found that work.

Ensuring student preparation   Because students so often assume that scanning a reading assignment is adequate, they need to be pushed to read and study the assignment. This goal can be realized by requiring students to write a concise (e.g. 100 word) summary of the reading and bring it with them to class to be turned in. A more challenging assignment asks them prepare and write three questions, a factual, an interpretative, and an evaluative question, along with their written responses to each question, to be turned in at the end of the class; these student-generated questions can be used to help guide the discussion. Assignments such as these have the added benefit of making writing an integral part of the discussion experience.

Refreshing student recollections   Because several days may have elapsed since students read the reading selection, they may need a bit of time to refresh their memories of the selection. As they arrive for class, they are urged to review the reading; in some cases, the first two minutes of the class can profitably be devoted to their brushing up on the reading. This simple technique greatly enhances the quality of the discussion; an added advantage is that students find it difficult to claim they do not remember.

Seating arrangements   The ideal seating arrangement is a circle. This shape permits participants to face each other and encourages their interactions with each other rather than with the instructor alone. If circular seating is impossible, a U-shaped seating arrangement, with the leader at the open end of the U is a good substitute. This means that classes which feature discussion should, whenever possible, be scheduled in rooms with movable chairs and tables.

A seating chart   Use of a seating chart helps facilitate the discussion. It enables the leader to more easily call on students by name and keep a brief record of who participated and any special contribution they might have made. Calling on students by name helps build a sense of community among the students, helps them learn the names of the other students, increases the motivation of students to participate in the discussion, and fosters connections among the students through posing questions such as "Mr. Allen, how does your idea bear on the point that Mr. Smith made earlier?"

Encouraging participation   Interesting readings and good questions will stimulate participation. But the style of the discussion leader can also encourage participation. This suggests that the leader should not appear to judge participants' contributions. Rather, the leader should ask follow-up questions when the meaning of a student's contribution is not clear. This is not to say that "anything goes." But the objectives of discussion are far better accomplished when criticism of a contribution originates with the participants rather than with the leader. The leader should thus appear receptive and interested in what participants have to say. The leader can encourage participation by referring to insightful contributions made earlier by participants. ("Ms. Smith, Mr. Jones' point seems to fit in with what you were saying earlier. What is your reaction?").

Directing questions to participants   Whether the discussion leader should pose questions directly to participants or call on volunteers to respond remains controversial. Our view is that directing questions to particular students is both acceptable and desirable. By directing questions the leader is able to break through the extended silence that often occurs in classroom discussions and to reinforce the responsibility of participants to be prepared for discussion. Direct questioning may make some students uncomfortable. A good way to remedy this problem is to give students the right to pass but to come back to them later and offer them another opportunity to contribute.

Involving all participants   The hardest task for the leader once the discussion begins is to involve everyone in the discussion. Some participants are natural volunteers, and they usually dominate the discussion. While the leader need not attempt to ensure that participation is equally divided among all participants, it is important that everyone who is prepared to contribute to the discussion has a chance to do so. In our experience, valuable ideas often come from students who are naturally quiet. Using a seating chart, calling on students by name, and directing questions to specific students are all practices that can be used to help engage all participants.

Cementing student learning   One technique for ensuring that students take something away from discussions of the kind described here is to call on them in the final five minutes of the class to summarize what they learned from the discussion. Not only does this give students another opportunity to put their thoughts in writing but it develops their ability to synthesize their learning.

THE EFFICACY OF DISCUSSION

Relatively little firm evidence exists on the impact of discussion on student learning in economics. Madden (2010a) reports on the connection between higher-order mastery of economic concepts and the use of the discussion technique in a history of thought course. Madden combined discussion with pre- and post-discussion writing assignments in which students constructed written responses to discussion questions. She graded the written responses using a rubric that counted valid arguments and finds that, for the great majority of students, the quality of post-discussion essays was significantly and substantially higher than the quality of pre-discussion essays. She also reports survey results indicating that students judged discussion to be a valuable learning activity.

Madden (2010b) extends her research to the principles of economics course. She finds that principles students give lower rankings to discussion than they give to other techniques. She also finds, by investigating student explanations of what they have learned, that students learned better from discussion than from the techniques that they preferred.

O'Sullivan (2010) reports on the relative efficacy of structured discussion, unstructured discussion and lecture. O'Sullivan divided students in her intermediate macroeconomics courses into three recitation sections, each reading Mankiw (2006). Students in the structured discussion section used the technique described in this chapter to discuss Mankiw. Students in the unstructured discussion section used an informal approach to discussion in which the instructor posed only general questions about the article. Students in the lecture section received a lecture about the Mankiw article. O'Sullivan finds that the use of structured discussion led to many more student interventions and much more student-to-student interaction than either of the other techniques.

The formal results described above confirm our own experiences that students deepen their understanding of economics when they discuss rich economic readings using the inquiry-based approach that we describe.

REFERENCES

Hansen, W. L. and M. K. Salemi (1998), "Improving classroom discussion in economics courses", in W. B. Walstad and P. Saunders (eds), *Teaching Undergraduate Economics: A Handbook for Instructors*, New York: Irwin McGraw-Hill, pp. 207–26.

Madden, K. (2010a), "Engaged learning with the inquiry-based question cluster discussion strategy: Student outcomes in a history of economic thought course", *Southern Economic Journal*, 77 (1), 224–39.

Madden, K. (2010b), "Classroom discussion: Comparison of structured discussion of Adam Smith with other active learning strategies", in M. K. Salemi and W. B. Walstad (eds), *Teaching Innovations in Economics: Strategies and Applications for Interactive Instruction*, Cheltenham, UK and Northampton, MA, USA: Edward Elgar Publishing, pp. 121–8.

Mankiw, N. G. (2006), "The macroeconomist as scientist and engineer", *Journal of Economic Perspectives*, 20 (4), 29–46.

Mill, J. S. (1848), *Principles of Political Economy* (7th edition), trans. W. J. Ashley (ed.), London: Longmans, Green and Co., 1909.

O'Sullivan, R. (2010), "Classroom discussion: Student participation during unstructured discussion, structured discussion, and lecture", in M. K. Salemi and W. B. Walstad (eds), *Teaching Innovations in Economics: Strategies and Applications for Interactive Instruction*, Cheltenham, UK and Northampton, MA, USA: Edward Elgar Publishing, pp. 128–36.

Radford, R. A. (1945), "The economic organization of a P.O.W. camp", *Economica*, XII (48), 189–201.

Salemi, M. K. and W. L. Hansen (2005), *Discussing Economics: A Classroom Guide to Preparing Discussion Questions and Leading Discussions,* Cheltenham, UK and Northampton, MA, USA: Edward Elgar.

Smith, A. (1776), *An Inquiry into the Nature and Causes of the Wealth of Nations*, Edwain Cannan (ed.), New York: The Modern Library, Random House, 1937.

6 Let experience be the guide: experiential education in economics

KimMarie McGoldrick and Andrea L. Ziegert

Imagine a project in an environmental economics course designed to expose students to the economic implications of biofuel production, motivated by a proposed local ethanol plant project. One group of students conducts research on the production of ethanol, evaluating costs and benefits of producing biofuel using alternative inputs (switch grass, corn, sugar beets, etc.). Another group of students considers the political economy of ethanol, researching government incentives to communities and agribusiness pursuing ethanol production. A third group prepares mini case studies of communities near established ethanol plants to detail resulting economic impacts. Across town, two students interview the Director of the Department of Economic Development to learn about local economic challenges, and to discuss potential consequences associated with construction and operation of an ethanol plant in their community. Finally, a group of students meets with grass roots community activists to document concerns regarding construction of the ethanol plant: fears of decreased property values, increases in pollution and transportation costs in and around the community. The work completed by each student group is combined into a comprehensive report presented to community members. Their instructor has grounded the project in a form of experiential education, service-learning, which links course content and service to the community through well-defined classroom learning objectives.

Experiential education is a pedagogic practice that supports learning through experience. This is related to, but distinct from, experiential learning which describes the associated student learning process. Experiential education literature focuses primarily on how pedagogic practices (such as the service-learning project described above) help students master discipline-specific content via reflection on primary experiences (as when students interact with constituents in the community) (Jarvis, 1995: 75). However, it also implies a process of teaching, one that engages students in a direct encounter to apply knowledge and skills in an educationally relevant setting (as demonstrated through a report to community members). Thus, experiential education is both a means to an end and an end in and of itself. In this chapter, we expound on this characterization of experiential education and make an argument for its use. We then describe a range of experiential education methods, provide examples, and discuss key features of effective implementation.

Experience alone is not enough to generate learning; students must practice inductive reasoning *using* their experience as a basis for engagement in the knowledge acquisition process. Bowen (2005: 4–7) defines four different but related meanings of engagement that support the content and process associated with experiential education. The first, and most fundamental, meaning of engagement describes the learning process as students practice metacognition. This form of engagement is most commonly associated with a variety of active learning techniques in which experiences come in the form of in-class activities designed to assist students in acquiring new knowledge and skills. It also requires that learning not stop with content mastery; rather, this form of engagement suggests purposeful reflection on the process of acquiring this newfound knowledge.

Experiential education can also focus on engagement with the object of study (the second meaning) using disciplinary content to better understand the world. Laboratory or field experiences, in which students engage with the world outside classroom walls, are prominent examples. A third, and related, form of engagement is with the context of study. Students who engage with social and civic contexts through an experience often make use of a multidisciplinary approach which provides for more breadth and holistic learning. By understanding context, students prioritize future learning and better anticipate consequences of acting on their knowledge (Bowen, 2005: 6). Finally, the fourth meaning suggests that student experience can provide opportunities to engage with the human condition as a way to better understand others and themselves. This type of engagement, pursued through activities such as community-based learning, asks students to consider how socio-culture shapes experiences and thus their learning.

The service-learning vignette above illustrates Bowen's four forms of engagement: students engage with the learning process when they identify knowledge necessary to evaluate the consequences of ethanol plant construction or develop arguments in favor or against ethanol production; they engage with object and context when considering the political and economic contexts of adopting ethanol; and they engage with the human condition when they isolate the impacts of an ethanol plant on community values, incomes, and living conditions.

Bowen concludes that, taking into account the various meanings of engagement, engaged learners are "those who complement and interpret what they learn from others with direct knowledge based on personal experience, who develop appropriately complex understandings situated in relevant contexts, and who recognize learning's moral implications and consequences" (p. 7). The most important contribution of engagement is "the focus it brings to the learner's personal relationship to learning" (p. 7), a necessary component of learning that lasts. While experiential learning in its purist form does not require the intervention of an instructor, experiential education describes how faculty can facilitate student engagement, deepening student learning and better preparing them for a lifetime of learning experiences.

The well-known Kolb (1984) model describes the learning by experience process. Students move through a learning cycle composed of four stages: (1) engaging in a concrete experience; (2) observing and reflecting upon experiences; (3) forming generalizations and abstract concepts; and (4) testing these concepts in new situations. Associated learning can begin with any stage and takes place throughout the process. This cycle is a developmental model of learning that moves students beyond rote memorization and dualistic thinking. It requires students to use experience and reflection as the context for analysis and synthesis. Students observe, develop and test theories, and integrate current and past learning. In short, Kolb's model provides theoretical grounding for experiential education practices and demonstrates how experiential learning can promote learning for understanding. This deep approach to learning is demonstrated when students "transform factual information into useable knowledge" (Bransford et al., 2000: 16) which necessitates critical thinking skills, integration of knowledge over time and subjects, theoretical application to practical situations and higher order skills of analysis and synthesis (Biggs, 1999; Entwistle, 1981; Prosser and Trigwell, 1999; Ramsden, 2003). Deep learning takes place when students *use* principles learned in the classroom, developing an understanding of *how* and *when* knowledge is applied in different contexts. Many educators adopt experiential learning pedagogies to deepen student learning.

HOW DOES EXPERIENTIAL LEARNING MANIFEST ITSELF IN FORMAL EDUCATION SETTINGS?

Experiential learning, and therefore structures through which instructors can promote such learning (i.e. experiential education), comes in many different forms. Faculty may be inclined to think that experiential learning occurs outside the classroom, but this does not have to be the case. Experiential learning can occur within the classroom, when special attention is paid to the engagement process, moving beyond exercises that promote rote memorization. In this section, we describe an inclusive, but by no means exhaustive, set of pedagogic practices, conducted within and beyond the classroom walls, which supports both the means and ends of experiential education. As a framework for discussion, we ground the skill development process in forms of engagement described above.

In-Class

Economists are likely to be most familiar with classroom experiments as a form of in-class experiential education.[1] This active learning pedagogy engages students in the learning process, as they become participants in a scenario and practice economic thinking to make decisions based upon the presented context. Post-experiment exercises reinforce the learning process when students transfer knowledge to new situations. As a pedagogic practice, experiments increase student learning, interest in the discipline, and course enjoyment (Durham, McKinnon, and Schulman, 2007). Although simulations and games can differ from experiments, in that they attempt to demonstrate outcomes associated with real-world environments rather than test particular theories, they are similar since each promotes inductive reasoning associated with experiential learning (see for example, Koontz et al. 1995).

Experiential education that occurs in the classroom, however, is not limited to role-based activity often associated with experiments. Experiences subsequently used by students to ground the knowledge acquisition process can come in many forms, engaging students in the context of study or learning about the knowledge acquisition process. Presenting students with the task of developing structured formats to tackle economic problems, for example, is the basis of experiential education pedagogies such as cooperative learning, problem-based learning, and interactive lecture demonstrations.

While the reader should refer to Chapter 4 in this volume on cooperative learning for more information about this pedagogic practice and its effectiveness, consider the structured problem-solving format as an example of cooperative learning that is consistent with tenets of experiential education. Structured problem solving motivates students to be purposeful in their knowledge acquisition as they develop an organized process for problem solving. As students tackle the problem at hand, they reflect on the steps necessary to formulate a solution (learning about learning), which can later be applied in new situations (context of study). The experience of solving problems in a purposeful manner leads to "higher achievement, higher-level reasoning, more frequent generation of new ideas and solutions, and greater transfer of what is learned from one situation to another" (Barkley, Cross and Major, 2005, pp. 17–18).

Problem-based learning[2] builds on cooperative learning structures by introducing ill-structured problems to the problem-solving process, reinforcing student engagement with the learning process and context. Textbook problems are typically well-structured problems; they guide students to use a specific method which generates a single answer. In stark contrast, ill-structured problems require students to identify potential processes to be used and often generate multiple solutions, more accurately reflecting real-world problems. Problem-based learning motivates self-directed learning as students are challenged to apply their knowledge in new ways with each problem, learning how to learn in the process. Consider the following problem (Garnett and McGoldrick, 2011):

> Although U.S. universities typically charge identical tuition and fees for all students, this practice is not universal. Public universities often charge differential fees for in-state and out-of-state students, for example. Some public institutions also charge differential tuition for different undergraduate degrees or majors.
>
> Currently, your institution adheres to a single tuition pricing structure. However, the Board of Trustees has asked your President to reconsider this pricing structure and to provide a report, either justifying the single tuition policy or proposing a differential tuition scheme. In order to gather critical data and conduct analysis to inform his recommendation, the President creates a university committee to examine the question of uniform vs. differential pricing. As a member of this committee, chosen because of your economics training, you are asked to provide a sub-report describing the University's pricing policy options. In order to provide the President with a balanced report, you are told to develop strong rationales for both the single and differential tuition policies.

Solving this, or any, ill-structured problem involves a number of steps (Forsythe, 2010). First, students must verbalize their understanding of the problem and identify relevant issues and essential information required. "There are many potential paths by which the student may address the core concept of multi-product pricing, each dependent upon which analytical tools (supply and demand, elasticity, marginal cost, and so on) they choose to use in developing their arguments" (Garnett and McGoldrick, 2011: 16). The second step involves student research to obtain needed information. In terms of this example, "the student will also need to think carefully about what additional information about the institution, students, government and society they might need to consider or what realistic assumptions will need to be made in order to present cogent arguments" (Garnett and McGoldrick, 2011: 16). The final step of the process applies student research to develop a solution. Because this problem does not lend itself to any one target outcome, students will need to apply the information they gather in determining what models they will use in their report to the university President.

Although much of the evidence on effectiveness of problem-based learning is relegated to medical education, students report greater problem-solving skills and self-directed learning than conventionally taught students, an outcome which is sustained long after graduation (Schmidt, Vermeulen and van der Molen, 2006).

Experiential education in the form of Interactive Lecture Demonstrations[3] is designed to address commonly held misconceptions. They begin "by identifying a core concept about which students are confused and then ask students to refine their thinking through guided small group work that includes three steps: predicting the outcome of an interactive demonstration, carrying out the demonstration, and reflecting on the results" (Maier, McGoldrick, and Simkins, 2011: 144). The problem-solving process uses an experience (demonstration) in direct conjunction with student expectations (prediction) to motivate better understanding of key concepts through subsequent reflection. Students are engaged in the learning process as they compare their prior understanding with outcomes of the demonstration. They are challenged to evaluate disconnects between predictions and outcomes and evaluate the extent to which context matters. Stockley (undated) describes an interactive lecture demonstration for an introductory macroeconomics class studying federal budget deficits. The instructor begins by asking students to identify presidential administrations since 1969 and *predict* which administration had the largest budget deficit. Second, students *demonstrate* which administration had the largest deficit by reviewing Congressional Budget Office (CBO) nominal budget data. Students then rank CBO budget data measured as a percentage of GDP. In the final step, students *reflect* upon their alternative rankings to decide which measure is best when comparing budget deficits over time. As suggested by Mazur et al. (2004) "Learning is enhanced . . . by increasing student engagement; students who predict the demonstration outcome before seeing it, however, display significantly greater understanding" (p. 835).

Out-of-Class

Perhaps the most well-known out-of-classroom experiential learning opportunities are associated with internships (or similarly constructed field experiences or co-ops). These short-term professional experiences directly relate to a student's major or career goals as they engage with both context and object of study within a professional environment under guidance and supervision of an expert. Participants explore career options and gain a better understanding of their own strengths and weaknesses as they reflect on internship experiences and integrate classroom knowledge as they develop professional skills. Internship experiences have potential benefits related to post-graduation career progress and satisfaction. Students who graduate with work-related internship experiences are more likely to receive full-time job offers, have higher levels of responsibility on the job, have higher pay, and report higher job satisfaction than graduates who lack internship experience (Hallett et al., undated; Jagacinski et al., 1986; Kysor and Pierce, 2000; Schuurman et al., 2005).

While internships focus on skill development via explicit linkages with formal employment positions, community-based learning provides an alternative avenue for learning through engagement with community members and issues. Learning is facilitated through academically grounded projects developed in partnership with community members that engage students with the human dimension, providing a social and civic context to frame experiences. Upon reflection, students connect classroom content to community-based experiences and engage with the learning process and object of study. Because the tenets of community-based learning incorporate multiple facets of engagement, it is more likely to stimulate learning that lasts. Service-learning and public scholarship are two pedagogical practices that exemplify community-based learning.

Service-learning is a flexible pedagogy that enables students to integrate disciplinary study with community service activities. Students can engage with their community through a variety of activities spanning the continuum from a single engagement making up a small portion of a course to an experience that serves as the basis for the entire course. Economists have used service-learning for more than a decade and resources exist providing examples and guidance on how to structure such experiences (McGoldrick and Ziegert, 2002). For example, service-learning can engage college students in the learning process as they use economic knowledge gained in the classroom to teach basic economic literacy to youngsters in their community (McGoldrick, Battle, and Gallagher, 2000), the economics of race and gender to local high school students (Lopez, 2009), or financial literacy to adults (Govekar and Govekar, 2008). Alternatively, courses can draw on service experiences as the context in which students apply economic theory to help them understand the economics of poverty (Simmons, 2003), develop meaningful projects to demonstrate their mastery of research methods and econometrics (Hoyt, 2002), or appreciate the economic impact of organizations on women in the community (McGoldrick, 1998).

On a more elaborate scale, entire courses can be developed around the service-learning experience. Mungaray et al. (2008) describe a course in which students work as consultants on a project requiring data collection, processing, and analysis, culminating in a report on the performance of a micro-enterprise in Mexico. Brooks and Schramm (2007) demonstrate how service-learning activities can reach beyond a single course, thereby becoming institutionalized within a university setting. Their overarching project investigated the local economic impact of the University of Vermont using a sequence of four semester-long courses. By sequencing the service-learning courses around a common topic, each course built on previous coursework so that student engagement broadened and deepened with each successive course.

Public scholarship, an emerging form of community-based learning, is less well known in economics. It is a pedagogical process that combines research, education, and service into a set of integrated experiences which provide benefits to faculty, students, and community members. Public scholarship can be distinguished from service-learning experiences in that it "combines experiential learning with the purposeful integration of social theory in the process of engagement of both faculty and students" (McGoldrick and Peterson, 2009: 229–30). As a result, students are motivated to critically examine economics premises and illustrate social dimensions of economic problems. McGoldrick and Peterson (2009) describe the integration of public scholarship into a Women in the Economy course at two widely disparate academic institutions. They suggest that public scholarship practices cannot simply be added on to a course; rather, public scholarship provides a framework to reconsider both the content and process of teaching in light of institutional and environmental conditions and constraints. By explicitly combining teaching, research and service in the development of experiences, student engagement is holistic, including the learning process, object and context of study, and the human condition.

Because community-based pedagogies provide students with a wide variety of experiences and multiple forms of engagement, they deepen student learning. Schwartz and

Bransford (1998) find that students are better motivated to learn when they believe their learning can make a difference in their communities. Community-based education enables students to simultaneously make a difference in their communities and learn the habits and skills of an engaged citizen. As described in Ziegert and McGoldrick (2008: 42–3):

> In a review of nearly 150 service-learning research projects, Eyler, Giles, Stenson, and Gray (2001) summarize evidence that service-learning has a positive impact on student social responsibility and citizenship skills, appreciation of diversity, and personal identity, self-efficacy and growth. In addition, Battistoni (2002) lists political knowledge, critical thinking skills, communication skills, public problem solving skills, civic judgment, creativity and imagination, community/coalition building, and organization analysis as the skills of civic engagement. Thus, service-learning motivates a deep approach to learning as students use their education to benefit their communities, developing a wide range of skills in the process.

EFFECTIVE IMPLEMENTATION

Experiential pedagogic practices are most effective when learning experiences are carefully planned. In this section, we briefly review a process for designing courses, with special attention to experiential education applications.[4]

Wiggins (1989) coined the descriptor *backwards design* to emphasize the focus of course design on the process of generating specific outcomes: ". . . the challenge is to focus first on the desired learnings from which appropriate teaching will logically follow" (Wiggins and McTighe, 2005: 14). Backwards design shifts the focus from inputs (texts, readings, activities, etc.) to outputs (skills) and thus directly addresses the question of how to create experiences which generate a deep approach to learning (p. 15). A backwards course design process to support deep learning in an experiential course involves four basic steps: identifying desired learning outcomes; developing appropriate assessment procedures; selecting effective teaching, learning and reflection strategies; and developing resources to support experiential learning.

The first step in effective course design is identifying desired learning outcomes (Gronland, 1995; Saunders, 1998). Objectives are especially critical for experiential learning because they help structure expected learning so participants are not swamped by overwhelming information that often accompanies experiences. One avenue for developing experiential learning objectives focuses on both process and outcomes. Fink (2003) identifies six synergistic categories of "significant learning" within which learning outcomes can be defined: foundational knowledge (learning key information), application (expanding ways of thinking), integration (making connections), human dimension (learning about oneself and others), caring (revealing interests and values), and learning how to learn (understanding the learning process). Because these categories are also consistent with forms of engaged learning, developing objectives that cut across categories enhances the likelihood that experiential learning generates learning that lasts. For example, learning goals for the service-learning vignette at the beginning of this chapter might include understanding methods of valuing environmental and community costs and benefits of building an ethanol plant. Students need to combine basic economics with their understanding of the needs and values of their community to generate useful estimates.

The second step in the course design process uses learning goals to guide development of appropriate assessment procedures. This process begins when generating answers to basic questions, including: "How will the instructor recognize that the learning goal is achieved? What form of assessment is best suited to measuring the gains associated with constructed learning goals? At what point will learning be assessed?" (Jacoby, as cited in Bart, 2010).With respect to experiential learning, assessment should go beyond *what* the student is learning (engagement with the context or object of study) to include considerations of the learning *process* through engagement with learning about learning and the human condition. Complementing summative assessment activities with carefully constructed formative assessment activities provides one avenue for promoting a deep approach to learning and ultimately evaluating the extent to which such learning occurs. For example, students working on the ethanol project might keep a journal describing their experience and links between classroom content and research or discussions with community members. Throughout the service-learning experience, the professor can comment on these connections, providing opportunities for formative feedback. Instructors provide summative feedback when they evaluate students' economic analysis of the proposed impacts of the ethanol plant in the final report to community leaders.

It is only after identifying learning goals and developing assessment practices that one can turn to the third step: selecting effective experiential teaching and learning strategies. In fact, it is during this third step of the course design process that the instructor builds a bridge between expectations and measurement of outcomes using experiences. While this step begins with the identification of a specific pedagogical technique (cooperative learning, service-learning, etc.) it also entails addressing what students will do (learning activities) and what the instructor will do (teaching activities) to generate a deep approach to learning (Fink, 2003: 103). At this stage of the course design process, instructors consider which combination of experiential education techniques and academic content best helps students achieve learning goals. Are in-class or out-of-class experiences most appropriate? If community-based learning practices are chosen, which community partner(s) or community issue(s) best serve learning goals?

In order to develop teaching and learning strategies that achieve objectives, one must go beyond a surface interpretation of experiential learning as a series of experiences that move students from observation to participation and include opportunities for students to reflect on learning process and progress (Fink, 2003: 104). Reflection is a key component of the third step in course design for it enables learners to make sense of past experiences in order to affect and understand future experiences (Daudelin, 1996). Through reflection, students integrate course content with experiential learning components of the course. They reflect upon the learning process, consider the object and context of their experiences, and come to a deeper understanding of the human condition. Eyler (2001) notes that effective reflection occurs at all stages of the service-learning experience. For example, before the experience, students working on the ethanol project reflect upon their goals and expectations, explore hopes and fears, and review relevant academic content. During the learning experience, they document their experience and explore connections between their experiences and course context. And after the experience, they synthesize what they have learned and draw conclusions. Silcox (1993) discusses different reflective techniques to foster a variety of student skills, including cognitive learning, critical thinking skills, leadership and civic engagement skills, and student personal growth.

Because students working on the ethanol project are assigned to groups conducting what might seem to them to be independent projects, in-class reflection is an important part of the learning process. As individual groups report their successes and challenges, other students offer feedback and all class members have multiple opportunities to draw connections between each group's work and to knowledge learned in the course.

The fourth and final course design step involves developing resources to support experiential learning activities. First, a carefully constructed course syllabus provides students with rationales for experiential pedagogies, identifies student roles and responsibilities, includes readings, course materials, and reflective activities, and discusses how experiential learning is assessed. If community-based learning strategies are used, good practice suggests that community partners are included in the development of the project and that they review the syllabus. Discussing the ethanol plant evaluation project with key community members in advance helps the instructor to identify community needs (potentially focusing student research areas) and additional community contacts (student resources). Additionally, instructors need to be prepared to manage the learning process, identifying key resources for both in-class and out-of-class learning experiences. For students participating in the service-learning project, for example, this would entail defining community partner roles and responsibilities and managing student transportation and safety issues.

CONCLUDING COMMENTS

Preparing students for active participation in the world after graduation is a key motivation for incorporating experience into the learning process. Experiential education is a pedagogic practice that demonstrates the value of economic tools and the importance of our discipline. Whether these experiences occur within the classroom via problem-based learning or interactive lectures, or out-of-class through internships or service-learning, this pedagogic practice has the potential to demonstrate the compelling power of economics to change lives.

NOTES

1. See the Experiments entry in Chapter 7 of this volume for more information about this pedagogic practice.
2. One popular form of problem-based learning grounds the learning process in a context-rich problem, described in Chapter 3 of this volume.
3. For more information about Interactive Lecture Demonstrations see http://serc.carleton.edu/introgeo/demonstrations/index.html (accessed February 11, 2011).
4. Ziegert and McGoldrick (2008) provide a detailed discussion of implementation issues associated with integrating service-learning into economics classes.

REFERENCES

Barkley, E.F., K.P. Cross, and C.H. Major (2005), *Collaborative Learning Techniques: A Handbook for College Faculty*, San Francisco: Jossey-Bass.
Bart, M. (April 21, 2010), "Six steps to designing effective service-learning courses", *Faculty Focus: Focused*

on *Today's Higher Education Professional*, Madison: Magna Publications, http://www.facultyfocus.com/articles/curriculum-development/six-steps-to-designing-effective-service-learning-courses/, accessed March 4, 2011.

Battistoni, R.M. (2002), *Civic Engagement Across the Curriculum: A Resource Book for Service Learning Faculty in all Disciplines*, Providence, RI: Campus Compact.

Biggs, J. (1999), *Teaching for Quality Learning at University*, Buckingham: SHRE and Open University Press.

Bowen, S. (2005), "Engaged learning: Are we all on the same page?", *Peer Review*, 7 (2), 4–7.

Bransford, J., A.L. Brown, and R.R. Cocking (2000), *How People Learn: Brain, Mind, Experience, and School*, Washington, DC: National Academy.

Brooks, N. and R. Schramm (2007), "Integrating economics research, education and service", *Journal of Economic Education*, 38 (1), 36–43.

Daudelin, M.W. (1996), "Learning from experience through reflection", *Organizational Dynamics*, 24 (30), 36–48.

Durham, Y., T. McKinnon, and C. Schulman (2007), "Classroom experiments: Not just fun and games", *Economic Inquiry*, 45 (1), 162–78.

Entwistle, N.J. (1981), *Styles of Learning and Teaching*, Chichester: Wiley.

Eyler, J. (2001), "Creating Your Reflection Map", in M. Canada (ed.), *Service Learning: Practical Advice and Models*, San Francisco: Jossey-Bass.

Eyler, J., D.E. Giles, Jr., C. Stenson, and C. Gray (2001), *At a Glance: What We Know about the Effect of Service-Learning on Colleges Students, Faculty, Institutions, and Communities, 1993–2001*, 3rd edition, Corporation for National Service, Learn and Serve America National Service Learning Clearinghouse, St Paul, MN: University of Minnesota.

Fink, L.D. (2003), *Creating Significant Learning Experiences: An Integrated Approach to Designing College Courses*, San Francisco: Jossey-Bass.

Forsythe, F. (2010), "Problem-based learning", 2nd edition, *The Handbook for Economics Lecturers*, http://www.economicsnetwork.ac.uk/handbook/pbl, accessed February 7, 2011.

Garnett, R. and K. McGoldrick (2011), "Big think: a model for critical inquiry in economics courses", presented at the 2011 ASSA meetings.

Govekar, P. and M. Govekar (2008), "Service learning and volunteering: Does the course matter?", *Journal of the North American Management Society*, 3 (1), 13–23.

Gronlund, N.E. (1995), *How to Write and Use Instructional Objectives*, 5th edition, Englewood Cliffs, NJ: Merrill/Prentice-Hall.

Hallett, M., R. Roberts, and D. Jaffee (undated), "Community based transformational learning", http://consensus.fsu.edu/bog-fcrc/pdfs2/UNF_QEProposal_CommunityBasedTrans.pdf, accessed May 15, 2010.

Hoyt, G.M. (2002), "Regression analysis for the community: an application of service-learning in a business and economics statistics course", in M. McGoldrick and A. Ziegert (eds), *Putting the Invisible Hand to Work: Concepts and Models for Service Learning in Economics*, Ann Arbor, MI: The University of Michigan Press.

Jagacinski, C.M., W.K. LeBold, K.W. Linden, and K.D. Shell (1986), "The relationship between undergraduate work experience and job placement of engineers", *Engineering Education*, 76 (4), 232–6.

Jarvis, P. (1995), *Adult and Continuing Education. Theory and Practice*, 2nd edition, London: Routledge.

Kolb, D.A. (1984), "Experiential learning: Experience as the source of learning and development", *Journal of Business Ethics*, 15 (1), 45–57.

Koontz, S.R., D.S. Peel, J.N. Trapp, and C.E. Ward (1995), "Augmenting agricultural economics and agribusiness education with experiential learning", *Review of Agricultural Economics*, 17 (3), 267–74.

Kysor, D.V. and M.A. Pierce (2000), "Does intern/co-op experience translate into career progress and satisfaction?", *Journal of Career Planning & Employment*, 60 (2), 25–31.

Lopez, M. (2009), "Incorporating service-learning into the economics curriculum", *Review of Black Political Economy*, 26 (2), 137–49.

Maier, M., K. McGoldrick and S. Simkins (2011), "Cooperative learning and disciple-based pedagogical innovations: taking advantage of complementarities", in J. Cooper and P. Robinson (eds), *Small Group Learning in Higher Education: Research and Practice*, Stillwater, OK: New Forums.

Mazur, E., A.P. Fagen, C.H. Crouch and J.P. Callan (2004), "Classroom demonstrations: Learning tools or entertainment?", *American Journal of Physics*, 72 (6), 835–8.

McGoldrick, K. (1998), "Service-learning in economics: A detailed application", *The Journal of Economic Education*, 24 (4), 365–76.

McGoldrick, K. and J. Peterson (2009), "Public scholarship and economics: Engaging students in the democratic process", *Forum for Social Economics*, 7 (2), 229–45.

McGoldrick, K., A. Battle and S. Gallagher (2000), "Service-learning and the economics course: Theory and practice", *The American Economist*, 44 (1), 43–52.

McGoldrick, M. and A. Ziegert (eds) (2002), *Putting the Invisible Hand to Work: Concepts and Models for Service Learning in Economics*, Ann Arbor, MI: The University of Michigan Press.

Mungaray, A., M. Ramirez-Urquidy, D. Texis and N. Ramirez (2008), "Learning economics by servicing: A Mexican experience of service-learning in microenterprises", *International Review of Economics Education*, **7** (2), 19–38.

Prosser, M. and K. Trigwell (1999), *Understanding Learning and Teaching, on Deep and Surface Learning*, Buckingham: Society for Research into Higher Education & Open University Press, Chapter 4.

Ramsden, P. (2003), *Learning to Teach in Higher Education*, 2nd edition, London and New York: Routledge.

Saunders, P. (1998), "Learning theory and instructional objectives", in W. Walstad and P. Saunders (eds) *Teaching Undergraduate Economics: A Handbook for Instructors*, Boston, MA: Irwin McGraw-Hill, pp. 85–108.

Schmidt, H.G., L. Vermeulen and H.T. van der Molen (2006), "Longterm effects of problem-based learning: A comparison of competencies acquired by graduates of a problem-based and a conventional medical school", *Medical Education*, **40** (6), 562–7.

Schuurman, M.K., R.N. Pangborn and R.D. McClintic (2005), "The influence of workplace experience during college on early post graduation careers of undergraduate engineering students", Proceedings of the 2005 WEPAN/NAMEPA Joint Conference. Las Vegas, NV, April 10–13, 2005.

Schwartz, D.L. and J.D. Bransford (1998) "A time for telling", *Cognition and Instruction*, **16** (4), 495–522.

Silcox, H.C. (1993), *How to Guide Reflection: Adding Cognitive Learning to Community Service Programs*, Levittown, NY: Institute for Global Education and Service-Learning.

Simmons, K. (2003), "Teaching economics of poverty using a service-learning approach", Social Science Research Network Electronic Paper Collection, http://ssrn.com/abstract=457201.

Stockley, S. (undated), "Which US President generated the highest budget deficit?" http://serc.carleton.edu/econ/demonstrations/examples/budgetdeficits.html, accessed February 1, 2011.

Wiggins, J. (1989), *Educative Assessment: Designing Assessments to Inform and Improve Student Performance*, San Francisco: Jossey-Bass.

Wiggins, J. and G. McTighe (2005), *Understanding by Design*, 2nd edition, Alexandria, VA: Association for Supervision and Curriculum Development.

Ziegert, A. and K. McGoldrick (2008), "When service is good for economics: Linking the classroom and community through service-learning", *International Review of Economics Education*, **7** (2), 39–56.

7 Classroom experiments
Tisha Emerson and Denise Hazlett

WHAT IS A CLASSROOM ECONOMICS EXPERIMENT?

Relatively recently, economists have begun to employ experimental methods – both in research and teaching. Research experiments help economists test the validity of theories and the efficacy of new market mechanisms. Classroom experiments help instructors illustrate concepts and engage students in the learning process, making economic theory easier for students to understand.

Classroom experiments are one of a variety of active learning techniques intended to promote higher-order thinking. A classroom experiment asks students to make economic decisions in a controlled environment. These decisions create data for analysis and discussion. When well designed and implemented, experiments help students discover important concepts for themselves. That discovery leads students to take greater ownership of their new-found knowledge, generating higher levels of engagement with the subject and potentially longer-term retention of the material.

Experiments covering a wide range of concepts are readily available for classroom use. Some sources include Parker (1995), Bergstrom and Miller (2000), Holt (2006), Holt's VeconLab,[1] Aplia,[2] EconPort,[3] indexed experiments in Delemester and Brauer (2000), and economic education journals. Experiments are most frequently employed in principles courses, with many level-appropriate experiments available. More complex experiments and variations of simple ones are available for use in upper-level courses. Most experiments can be run by hand, i.e. using paper and pencil, with face-to-face interactions that students typically enjoy. There are also computerized versions available for many experiments (VeconLab and Aplia are particularly user-friendly sources). Computerized experiments allow for automated data collection and use outside of class time (with either synchronous or asynchronous student interaction). Experiments can often be adapted for a wide range of class sizes. The three experiments described in the next section are illustrative of the variety of experiments and topic coverage available.

EXAMPLES

Double Oral Auction Experiment

The double oral auction experiment demonstrates how prices convey information in a competitive economy. The instructor assigns students the roles of potential sellers and buyers of a hypothetical good. Students begin the experiment knowing only the production cost or consumption value that the instructor has assigned to them. People sometimes refer to this set-up as the pit market experiment because the instructor typically designates a section of the classroom where students mingle to negotiate their trades.

In this trading pit, students call out offers to sell or buy at prices they specify. As they trade and observe other trades, students begin to see how a decentralized economy uses prices to signal decisions about production and distribution. The instructor typically runs several trading rounds, allowing students to note that prices converge despite the initial chaos. The instructor records trades, displaying this information for everyone to see during the experiment and distributing it afterwards for the debriefing and analysis.

The workhorse of classroom experiments, the double oral auction, provides a concrete example of a competitive market. It demonstrates the concepts of market clearing, convergence to equilibrium and gains from trade. The trading experience and the follow-up analysis bring these abstract concepts into sharp focus. In the analysis, students begin to understand how the competitive model can make reliable predictions about behavior. They start with building supply and demand curves from information the instructor distributes (after the experiment) about every buyer's willingness to pay and every seller's cost of production. Using these curves, students find the price and quantity that theory predicts will prevail in equilibrium. They compare these equilibrium predictions to actual prices and quantities in various rounds of the experiment. They similarly calculate consumer and producer surpluses predicted by theory and compare those to experimental results.

The economics education literature describes many extensions of this experiment, including price controls, taxes, subsidies, and other shifts in demand or supply. In a 45-minute class the instructor typically runs several rounds, including some of these extensions. One class session early in the term can give students background for concepts they will use throughout the course. The experiment complements lectures, providing experience that makes students the experts in subsequent discussions. For example, the results from a price-ceiling round offer a starting point for a later lecture on rent controls, with the supply and demand curves from the experiment providing the theoretical structure behind the discussion.

The literature describes how to run and debrief many experiments that use the double oral auction market mechanism, covering a wealth of topics. Gillette (1996) presents a demand-shift extension for a health economics course. Here, a third party offers to pay 80 percent of the price in a market for health care services. Hazlett (2008) uses a credit market where inflation variability causes a wealth transfer between borrowers and lenders. The experiment shows how inflation uncertainty can prevent the credit market from efficiently allocating funds. In Hazlett (2003), most students take the roles of banks that lend and borrow in a federal funds market. The other students run a Federal Open Market Committee Trading Desk, using open market operations to change the amount of excess reserves in the banks, thereby changing the federal funds rate. Hazlett and Ganje (1999) develop a market for foreign exchange where students take the roles of importers and exporters. Their government maintains an official foreign exchange market at an overvalued rate, driving the traders to start a parallel foreign exchange market. The effects of unemployment compensation are illustrated in Hazlett (2004), where students take the roles of employers and workers negotiating wage contracts in markets for skilled and unskilled labor. The government offers workers progressively greater amounts of unemployment compensation, which raises the unemployment rate among the unskilled and narrows the distribution of income between skilled and unskilled.

The double oral auction experiment proves robust as well as versatile. Instructors can try variations on the fly, including some suggested by students. For instance, students may be tempted to collude, organizing themselves into a cartel of buyers or sellers. It works to let them, even to allow them, to step outside of the classroom to do their colluding. When the collusive agreement breaks down after a round or two, students become more firmly convinced of the usefulness of the competitive model.

The basic experiment works in classes of eight or more students. In a hand-run experiment, i.e. with students trading face-to-face rather than over a computer network, the instructor typically starts class by passing out instructions, record-keeping sheets, and private information slips that establish a person's production cost or consumption value. During the experiment, the instructor stands by a blackboard or a computer with projector, ready for students to come and report their trades.[4] Between rounds part-way through the experiment, some instructors pass out new production costs and consumption values so that the high-cost sellers and low-value buyers who were priced out of the market get new roles enabling them to trade. Passing out the new roles also allows the instructor to shift demand or supply (or both), generating a new equilibrium.

When run online, with students entering their offers via computers, the experiment is called a double auction. Holt's freely available VeconLab, and Aplia's commercial teaching resources, both offer browser access to a double auction run on their servers.

With some modifications, the hand-run experiment works even in very large classes. The standard set-up poses problems in large-enrollment courses due to the lack of room for a trading pit, long queues to report trades, and excessive time spent passing out paperwork reassigning roles. To solve these problems, Vazquez-Cognet (in Vazquez-Cognet et al., 2010) redesigned the double oral auction for his class of 500 students. In his version, students negotiate in the general area of their seats, sometimes standing on those seats. He limits rounds to one minute and prices to increments of 25 cents. He uses a show of hands for reporting trades, rather than having students come to the front of the room. After each round, he asks sellers to raise their hands when he calls out the price range that includes the trade they made. He counts the number of hands in each price range and displays that number for all to see.

Vazquez-Cognet notes that, after the chaos of the first trading round, students expect reported prices to range widely. Instead, a mass of hands goes up in a narrow price range. Through this exercise, students see chaos resolved into order more dramatically than if they looked at a list of trades, the way reporting occurs in the standard set-up. Vazquez-Cognet finds fast convergence to equilibrium in very large classes. Because of that fast convergence he has time to add extensions and an in-class follow-up, all within 45 minutes. He even reassigns roles with an announcement that speedily converts low-value buyers into low-cost sellers, and high-cost sellers into high-value buyers. He notes that, after the excitement of hundreds of people trading, and ten calmer minutes of students answering debriefing questions in pairs, the last few minutes of general discussion draw out students who have never before spoken in a large class.

Production Experiment

Variations of an experiment illustrating production and cost concepts can be found in Neral and Ray (1995), Bergstrom and Miller (2000, chapter 10), and Vazquez-Cognet

(2008). In the production experiment, students are presented with the opportunity to produce a simple good (for instance, widgets,[5] paper airplanes, or solutions to mathematical problems). The instructor assigns all students to small production groups, generally consisting of one to four students. Each group is provided with a single unit of some fixed input (typically some type of capital – a stapler, pen, folder, calculator, etc.). Groups engage in production of the specified output for a fixed period of time. Then the level of the variable input (labor) and total output (product) of each group is recorded. After each production round, groups are slowly consolidated so that the number of students (the labor input) in each group increases, while the available capital input remains at one unit per group.

At the end of the experiment, students have production data. Specifically, students have output levels for various levels of labor input. In the debriefing following the experiment, students use this data to study concepts including total, average, and marginal products of labor; diminishing marginal product; total, average, and marginal cost; and fixed versus variable inputs. In reflecting on their production experience and working with the data, students develop a better understanding of production and cost concepts. For example, as bottlenecks arise at the point of the fixed input, students get a clearer idea of the source of diminishing marginal product. This experiment helps students gain a firmer grasp of the distinction between fixed and variable inputs, and between average and marginal products. Further, students are far more engaged and interested in costs associated with their own production than in an abstract cost example concocted by their professor.

The production experiment is relatively simple to implement. It can easily be run and debriefed in a 50–75 minute class period. By way of materials, little more than pens, paper, and a small amount of capital (depending on the variation of the experiment – staplers, folders, etc.) is required. The experiment works with a range of class sizes from relatively small (ten students) to very large classes. An option in larger classes is to have some students participate in production while the others watch (perhaps with some serving as quality control inspectors) and have the entire class participate in the debriefing. Alternatively, Vazquez-Cognet's (2008) version (in which students produce solutions to mathematical problems using varying amounts of labor and a fixed amount of capital – a calculator) allows participation by all of the students in a very large class. Generally, having all students participate maintains student interest better than having a subset participate while others watch.

As with most experiments, for students to fully appreciate the concepts illustrated in this experiment, it is imperative that all students participate in the debriefing and that follow-up exercises be assigned either in class or as homework. For examples of these exercises, see Bergstrom and Miller (2000) or Vazquez-Cognet (2008).

Investment Coordination Experiment

Hazlett (2007) describes a hand-run experiment that helps students see how uncertainty about future economic performance can cause a recession. Each student represents a firm that makes decisions about whether to invest to expand its operations. Groups of four firms play a repeated game in which each firm privately chooses either a high or low level of investment spending. An aggregate economy consists of a group of four firms, e.g. a class of 40 students would have ten such economies. After each round of decisions, students observe the investment levels of the other firms in their economy and of the firms in the other economies around the classroom.

Before they make any decisions, students see a table showing how their profit depends on the investment decision made by all of the firms in their economy. They can see that when others in their economy invest at a low level, they would be best off also investing at a low level. Choosing instead a high level would be tantamount to expanding productive capacity at a time when low incomes (due to low investment by the other firms) prevent customers from buying their firm's extra production. Similarly, when others in their economy invest at a high level, they would be best off also investing at a high level. That high investment allows their firm to take advantage of high incomes (due to high investment by the other firms) that create demand for their extra production. An outcome with every firm in the economy investing at a high level generates the greatest possible profits for all. An outcome with every firm investing at a low level generates modest profit for all. The worst outcome for any firm would be to invest at a high level when all the other firms in its economy invest at a low level.

Students see that when firms anticipate an expansion, their confidently high levels of investment cause an expansion. Likewise, when firms fear a recession, their conservatively low levels of investment cause a recession. In the debriefing, an instructor who wants to use the language of game theory could note that the outcome where all four firms choose a low level of investment is a bad Nash equilibrium for the one-shot game. That is, this outcome is Pareto inferior to the Nash equilibrium of all four choosing a high level.

In initial rounds, firms cannot communicate with each other. They have to guess what other firms in their economy might do. They form their guesses based on what has happened in the past, especially in their own economy, but also in other economies. For instance, in an economy whose firms have mainly chosen low levels in the past, everyone might be on the verge of losing confidence. At this point, seeing another economy where everyone has invested at a high level could inspire these firms. Each might then choose a high level in hopes that the others in its economy feel similarly inspired.

Once a group has experienced a round with everyone investing at a high level, they tend to maintain high levels in future rounds. They can, however, find their confidence shaken by events that introduce new uncertainty. For instance, the instructor can simulate real-world changes by replacing one of their firms with a firm that has a history of choosing low investment.

Between later rounds, the instructor asks some students to explain their past decisions and describe their confidence in the prospects for their economy. Their answers constitute indirect communication between firms, the kind provided by news stories in the real world. The instructor thus serves the role of a journalist reporting on and propagating waves of pessimism or optimism among the business community. Later yet, the instructor allows direct communication between firms, during which almost all firms immediately agree to choose a high level of investment.

In the debriefing, the class considers the self-fulfilling nature of expectations. They discuss what policy makers might do to prevent expectations of a recession from becoming self-fulfilling. The experiment works in classes of eight or more and takes about 45 minutes to run and debrief.

HOW BEST TO IMPLEMENT CLASSROOM EXPERIMENTS

To create a valuable learning experience, the instructor chooses an experiment that promotes deep understanding of an important concept, an understanding that students would not get from an explanation, or would not remember without a hands-on example. Effective experiments engage students in making decisions, holding their attention while not confusing them with unnecessary complexity. Students must be motivated to arrive in time to hear all of the instructions, plus have a chance to ask clarifying questions. To minimize frustration, students must understand the instructions or else they make random decisions that muddy the results. Sometimes, however, it takes a round of experience before the instructions click for all students.

In an experiment like the double oral auction, the instructor wants to give students an incentive to maximize their gains from trade, encouraging them to behave as they would in a real-life profit-maximizing situation. The instructor could motivate students with course credit, extra credit, money, or even candy awarded in proportion to their gains from trade. Some instructors simply give course credit for on-task participation and count on the joy of participation and the typical competitive nature of students to motivate sellers and buyers to seek out the best price.

Experts often recommend running an experiment before lecturing on the theory the experiment demonstrates (Holt, 1996; Noussair and Walker, 1998; Bergstrom and Miller, 2000). Students seem to become more convinced of the predictive power of theory when they discover it for themselves. For instance, when participating in a double oral auction before hearing a lecture on price controls, sellers generally greet the announcement of a price floor with enthusiasm. Disillusionment with minimum prices develops rather quickly as producers realize they cannot sell as many units as they would like at the elevated price.

If at all possible, instructors should arrange for every student to participate. Active participation rather than passive observation gives students better insight. Plus, participation offers more fun.

The role of the instructor should be to facilitate the experiment. This role entails watching out for and helping confused students, but not announcing what the instructor expects to happen or telling students what actions to take. If an instructor suggests, for example, that buyers offer higher prices, students might doubt the power of a market to find the equilibrium without this intervention.

Instructors should not lie to participants. For instance, an instructor who tells students they will receive payoffs according to their choices in a prisoner's dilemma game must distribute the payoffs as promised. Distributing in any other way would cost the instructor credibility. Without that credibility, students might not believe the instructions in future experiments and instead act in a manner that appears random.

Finally, debriefing asks students to put their economic knowledge to use and analyze the results. While an explanation from the instructor might seem a more efficient way to conduct the analysis, it risks circumventing the learning process. Instead, the instructor should plan follow-up questions that guide students through the analysis in a written assignment, in small groups, or in a general discussion.

EVIDENCE ON THE EFFICACY OF CLASSROOM EXPERIMENTS AS A PEDAGOGICAL TOOL

Several studies have addressed the efficacy of classroom experiments as a pedagogical technique. Gremmen and Potters (1997) and Frank (1997) investigate the effect of a single experiment and find that students' participation in the experiment improves their understanding of the specific topic illustrated. Other studies take a more comprehensive pedagogical approach to experiments, utilizing multiple experiments throughout a course. Cardell et al. (1996) find no significant effect on student achievement from the four experiments they employ. Emerson and Taylor (2004), Dickie (2006), Ball et al. (2006), and Durham et al. (2007), however, all find that students realize significantly higher levels of achievement (measured by either the Test of Understanding in College Economics or course work performance) when exposed to a curriculum making extensive use of experiments (between seven and eleven experiments). The positive effect of classroom experiments on student achievement is documented in micro (Emerson and Taylor; Dickie; Ball et al.; Durham et al.) and macroeconomic (Durham et al.) principles courses in classes ranging in size from 20 to 120 students and for both hand-run (Emerson and Taylor; Dickie; Durham et al.) and computerized (Ball et al.) experiments.[6]

Evidence suggests that some students gain more than others from participation in experiments. Emerson and Taylor (2007) use the Myers-Briggs (Personality) Type Indicator (MBTI) to distinguish across student personality types in their sample. They find that the experimental approach appears to benefit students with "intuitive" personality types (as measured on the sensing/intuitive dimension of the MBTI), while it is neutral with respect to most other dimensions. That is, students who tend to be more abstract thinkers (intuitive types) may derive greater benefit from the experimental pedagogy than more concrete and factual thinkers (sensing types). Durham et al. find that the magnitude of the experimental effect varies by learning style. Specifically, multimodal and kinesthetic learners gain significantly more from the experimental approach than do other types. While evidence suggests that classroom experiments are better suited to some personality types and learning styles, more investigation into the role of personality type and learning styles and their combined effect with classroom experiments is needed.

In addition to higher levels of student achievement, there is also evidence (both formal and anecdotal) that students (and instructors) enjoy experiments. Ball et al. find that student evaluations of instructors are significantly higher in microeconomic principles courses where students participated in experiments than in the same course where students only discussed the results of experiments. Durham et al. find that students exposed to an experimental pedagogy have significant, positive increases in their attitudes towards their principles courses compared to those in courses using chalk-and-talk. Abundant anecdotal evidence suggests that students and professors alike enjoy a pedagogical approach involving classroom experiments. To the extent that experiments positively influence students' attitudes towards economics and their economics courses, the experiments are likely to lead to a better overall classroom experience for all involved.

While positive achievement and attitudinal effects support the use of classroom experiments as a pedagogical tool, questions remain. As economists well know, incentives matter. The question with classroom experiments is how to incentivize students to behave as they would in real-world situations; otherwise students may make random choices that generate unclear results. To address the motivation issue, some instructors use grade incentives (course grades or extra credit), while others use prizes (money or candy). Dickie finds that grade incentives tied to student performance in experiments do not increase learning beyond that of a control group who received no incentive. Debate remains as to the best approach.

Little is known about longer-term, post-course, effects of experiments. Durham et al. find evidence that students exposed to experiments perform better in an exam measuring their retention (administered in an upper division business class in a subsequent semester). No other studies have addressed whether differences exist in long-term retention. Further, limited evidence suggests that exposure to classroom experiments does not lead to a difference in the number of majors or upper-division economics classes taken by students in general. However, some students (males and students who took economics in high school) take more upper-division economics courses when exposed to experiments in micro principles (Emerson and Taylor, 2010). The minimal effects on selection of major and subsequent courses are not terribly surprising given the limited influence that the pedagogy in any one course may have. To the extent that some programs adopt classroom experiments (or active learning in general) across the curriculum, it would be interesting to investigate whether there are any significant effects on students' course and major selection.

NOTES

1. http://www.people.virginia.edu/~cah2k/programs.html (accessed 21 June 2010).
2. http://aplia.com (accessed 21 June 2010).
3. http://www.econport.org/econport/request?page=web_experiments (accessed 21 June 2010).
4. Murphy (2004) offers a freely available, downloadable program for instructors running the experiment by hand. His program displays trades, stores and plots results, plots the supply and demand curves, and even tracks individual gains from trade.
5. In the Neral and Ray (1995) incarnation of the production experiment, a widget is defined as a piece of paper folded into fourths and then stapled.
6. While not all papers specify which experiments were employed in their studies, the experiments frequently covered topics including demand and supply (often using the double oral auction experiment outlined in example one), price controls, taxes, monopolies and cartels, production and costs, externalities or public goods, comparative advantage, and the prisoners' dilemma. Emerson and Taylor (2004) and Dickie (2006) identify the topic and the experiment source for all of the experiments administered in their studies. Cardell et al. (1996), Ball et al. (2006), and Durham et al. (2007) identify the topics covered by the experiments implemented in the course of their investigations, but not the source of the experiments.

REFERENCES

Ball, S., C. Eckel and C. Rojas (2006), "Technology improves learning in large principles of economics classes: Using our WITS", *American Economic Review,* **96** (2), 442–6.

Bergstrom, T. and J. Miller (2000), *Experiments with Economic Principles* (2nd ed.), Boston, MA: Irwin McGraw-Hill.

Cardell, N. S., R. Fort, W. Joerding, F. Inaba, D. Lamoreaux, R. Rosenman, E. Stromsdorfer and R. Bartlett (1996), "Laboratory-based experimental and demonstration initiatives in teaching undergraduate economics", *American Economic Review Papers and Proceedings,* **86** (2), 454–9.

Delemester, G. and J. Brauer (2000), "Games economics play: Noncomputerized classroom games", *Journal of Economic Education,* Online Section, **31** (4), 406.

Dickie, M. (2006), "Do classroom experiments increase learning in introductory microeconomics?", *Journal of Economic Education,* **37** (3), 267–88.

Durham, Y., T. McKinnon and C. Schulman (2007), "Classroom experiments: Not just fun and games", *Economic Inquiry,* **45** (1), 162–78.

Emerson, T. and B. Taylor (2004), "Comparing student achievement across experimental and lecture-oriented sections of a principles of microeconomics course", *Southern Economic Journal,* **70** (3), 672–93.

Emerson, T. and B. Taylor (2007), "Interactions between personality type and the experimental methods", *Journal of Economic Education,* **38** (1), 18–35.

Emerson, T. and B. Taylor (2010), "Do classroom experiments affect the number of economics enrollments and majors?: A study of students in the United States", *International Review of Economics Education,* **9** (2), 42–58.

Frank, B. (1997), "The impact of classroom experiments on the learning of economics: An empirical investigation", *Economic Inquiry,* **35** (4), 763–9.

Gillette, D. (1996), "Double-oral auctions and health care", Working Paper, Truman State University.

Gremmen, H. and J. Potters (1997), "Assessing the efficacy of gaming in economic education", *Journal of Economic Education,* **28** (4), 291–303.

Hazlett, D. (2003), "A classroom Federal funds rate experiment", Working Paper, Whitman College, http://people.whitman.edu/~hazlett/econ, accessed 30 January 2011.

Hazlett, D. (2004), "A classroom unemployment compensation experiment", *Southern Economic Journal,* **70** (3), 694–704.

Hazlett, D. (2007), "A classroom investment coordination experiment", *International Review of Economic Education,* **6** (1), 63–76.

Hazlett, D. (2008), "A classroom inflation uncertainty experiment", *International Review of Economic Education,* **7** (1), 47–61.

Hazlett, D. and J. Ganje (1999), "An experiment with official and parallel foreign exchange markets in a developing country", *Journal of Economic Education,* **30** (4), 392–401.

Holt, C. (1996), "Classroom games: Trading in a pit market", *Journal of Economic Perspectives,* **10** (1), 193–203.

Holt, C. (2006), *Markets, Games, & Strategic Behavior,* Boston, MA: Addison Wesley.

Murphy, J. (2004), "A simple program to conduct a hand-run double auction in the classroom", *Journal of Economic Education,* Online Section **35** (2), 212.

Neral, J. and M. Ray (1995), "Experiential learning in the undergraduate classroom: Two exercises", *Economic Inquiry,* **33** (1), 170–74.

Noussair, C. and J. Walker (1998), "Student decision making as active learning: Experimental economics in the classroom", in W. E. Becker and M. Watts (eds), *Teaching Economics to Undergraduates: Alternatives to Chalk and Talk,* Cheltenham, UK and Northampton, MA, USA: Edward Elgar, pp. 49–77.

Parker, J. (1995), "Using laboratory experiments to teach introductory economics," Working Paper, Reed College, http://academic.reed.edu/economics/faculty/parker/exp.html, accessed 30 January 2011.

Vazquez-Cognet, J. (2008), "The production of mathematical problems: A diminishing marginal returns experiment", *International Review of Economics Education,* **7** (1), 103–16.

Vazquez-Cognet, J. J., D. Hazlett, K. A. Paulson Gjerde and J. A. Smith (2010), "Conducting experiments in the economics classroom", in M. K. Salemi and W. B. Walstad (eds), *Teaching Innovations in Economics: Strategies and Applications for Interactive Instruction,* Cheltenham, UK and Northampton, MA, USA: Edward Elgar, pp. 95–119.

8 Interactive lecture demonstrations: adapting a physics education pedagogy for use in the economics classroom
Mark Maier

The Interactive Lecture Demonstration (ILD) is a classroom pedagogy first developed for college physics courses, but adaptable to a wide range of disciplines, including economics.[1] The approach uses a carefully scripted activity to engage students with a core concept *before* the instructor presents a traditional lecture. In this way, ILDs reverse the traditional approach in which the lecture precedes the activity. Instead, the activity, a classroom experiment, a survey, a simulation, or an analysis of secondary data, creates a "time for telling" that research shows can improve student learning in the subsequent, more traditional, directed instruction. What further differentiates Interactive Lecture Demonstrations from traditional classroom demonstrations is careful adherence to a three-step process in which students first predict the outcome, then experience the demonstration (usually as a small group activity), and finally reflect on what they have learned. This combination of steps has been shown to lead to learning that lasts beyond the course and that can be transferred to new situations.

Example of an ILD to teach the demand curve   The instructor announces a classroom auction of a good such as a college logo t-shirt. Prediction step: Students are asked to select which of five diagrams will most accurately describe the demand curve for the auctioned item (linear down, non-linear down, linear up, non-linear up, or U-shaped). Experience step: The instructor asks students to record their reservation prices in a Vickery-style auction.[2] Working in small groups, students use the reservation prices to create a demand schedule and a demand curve. Reflection step: Students then compare their prediction with the auction's demand curve and use economic principles to explain its shape (Salemi, 2009; Starting Point, 2010).

ORIGINS IN PHYSICS EDUCATION RESEARCH

Since the 1980s physics education research has produced insights about student learning, in particular students' failure to achieve sustained and transferable understanding of core concepts.[3] For example, the films *A Private Universe* and *Minds of Our Own* show Harvard students in their graduation gowns with embarrassing lapses in scientific understanding, mistakenly stating: "it is hotter [in summer] when the earth gets nearer to the sun", when, in fact, the earth's tilt causes the seasons, and tree wood forms when matter "is sucked up from the ground" when, in fact, photosynthesis uses elements from the air (Harvard-Smithsonian Center for Astrophysics, 1997). Similar and more rigorous evidence in physics education research reveals that traditionally taught students often retain their pre-course misconceptions about core concepts when they leave the classroom – even when they were able to provide the correct answer on traditional knowledge assessments such as quizzes and tests (Mazur, 1997; McDermott, 1991; Halloun and Hestenes, 1985).

In response to such insights, physics educators have investigated how pedagogy can transform novice thinking so that students think more like experts (McDermott and Redish 1999). One of the most successful resulting new teaching techniques is the Interactive Lecture Demonstration. First developed by Ronald Thornton (Tufts University), Patricia Laws (Dickinson College) and David Sokoloff (University of Oregon), ILDs are now well-tested and widely used in college physics classrooms (Sokoloff and Thornton, 1997; University of Maryland Physics Education Research Group, 2010; Redish, 2003). A version of ILDs also exists in the K-12 literature, called "predict/observe/explain" (Palmer, 1995; Liew, Chong-Wah and D.F. Treagust, 1998) and a similar pedagogy has been introduced in chemistry instruction (Edwired, 2010) and advocated as best practice with classroom response systems (Bruff, 2009).

Example from physics   While studying electric currents, students are shown a simple circuit with two light bulbs and one battery. Prediction step: Will the bulbs burn brighter if they are linked in series or in parallel circuits? Students make a prediction, explaining their answer to a partner. Experience step: Then students conduct an experiment using actual batteries and bulbs. Reflection step: students revise their predictions using their understanding of voltage differences to explain the results (Sokoloff and Thornton, 1997: 265).

EVIDENCE OF STUDENT LEARNING

Physics education researchers report significantly improved student learning in courses using ILDs in comparison with courses offered in a standard lecture or lecture/laboratory format classes. The evidence comes from an assessment tool called "concept inventories" (Concept Inventory Central, 2010) that has been shown to measure students' conceptual understanding, not simply student ability to repeat what they read or hear in class. In a wide variety of institutions and for different levels of skill preparation, students in courses using ILDs show 28 percent – 90 percent greater conceptual understanding than students in traditional courses (Thornton, 2008; Sharma et al., 2010).

Other research studies, using videotapes of student conversations during ILDs, show a fourfold increase in "sense-making" (concept-related talk as opposed to logistical or off-task conversation) during ILDs in comparison to traditional laboratory experiments. Researchers found that students exposed to concepts using ILDs combined with Peer Instruction and Physics Tutorials were more likely to identify the answer "a scientist would give", as also the one that "makes the most intuitive sense"; without ILDs, students often could provide the correct scientific answer, but found it unintuitive. Finally, student favorable attitudes about physics typically showed a *decline* by 5–10 percent after taking a traditional physics course, but showed a 30 percent *increase* when taught using ILD, Peer Instruction and Physics Tutorial pedagogies (Redish and Hammer, 2009).

Each ILD step – predict, experience and reflect – also has independent support in the education literature. Research on physics in-class demonstrations shows that "students who predict the demonstration outcome before seeing it display significantly greater understanding" (Crouch et al., 2004: 835). This finding is explained by research on learning that demonstrates students better retain and use new ideas if they first are able to explicitly state their prior understanding (Bransford et al., 2000; Redish, 2003). Research by educational psychologists also supports the demonstration step as a lead-in to more traditional direct instruction such as a lecture. Students are more receptive to new ideas presented in direct instruction if preceded by a case study (and two contrasting case studies are even more effective). The demonstration creates a "time for telling" in which students are engaged with and motivated to focus on the concept being taught (Schwartz and Bransford, 1998). Finally, the reflection step helps students store new ideas in longer-term memory because they spend time thinking about their own thinking, explicitly identifying what has changed in their understanding. Reflection is also important because it is a vehicle by which students practice newly learned concepts in different contexts; otherwise students may connect the concept with one specific situation, missing its general applicability (Bransford et al., 2000; Redish, 2003).

USING ILDs IN ECONOMICS INSTRUCTION

Application of ILDs to economics begins with identification of appropriate classroom demonstrations, the core of the ILD approach. In economics there are a wide range of activities that can serve as a demonstration, including classroom experiments, classroom surveys, data analysis and simulations.

Classroom Experiments

Economics instructors have access to an extensive set of classroom experiments, developed for a wide range of applications from in-class paper and pencil activities to extensive online programs.[4] During an experiment, students interact in assigned roles such as employer and employee or buyer and seller to determine economic outcomes. The added value of using ILDs in conjunction with the experiment is the incorporation of the prediction and reflection steps that are not always included. By adding the prediction step, student attention is focused at the outset on the main concept to be learned rather than the experiment's potentially distracting procedural steps. The reflection step motivates students to think explicitly about their initial hypotheses and revise their initial understanding based on outcomes of the experiment. In this way students are primed for subsequent direct instruction in which economic concepts are presented to explain experimental results.

Example   In the double oral auction, students take on roles as suppliers and demanders, buying and selling in a series of rounds. This simulated market almost always moves to an equilibrium price that maximizes the number of transactions. Prior to running the experiment, students make a prediction, choosing from three sets of distributions for prices – movement toward bimodality, movement toward an even distribution, or movement toward one price. The reflection step structures student evaluation of what occurred in the experiment, comparing it to what they expected and deriving models to explain the results. Why did the price move to equilibrium? When will this occur and when will it not?

Classroom Surveys

Data collected by students surveying other students in the classroom is well-suited to the ILD approach. Aggregate survey results are not known in advance and thus can lead to an engaging prediction step in which students anticipate their classmates' responses. In the experience step, everyone is involved because information is collected from all students. The reflection step focuses student attention on the economic concept being studied, based on actual data collected right in the classroom.

Example   Working in small groups, students are assigned a good or service such as "a guaranteed parking spot on campus" or "copies of last year's notes for the course". The group predicts the price elasticity of demand for this good or service and then conducts a survey of a small sample of their classmates, asking about quantity demanded at two prices. The group calculates price elasticity of demand, compares it to other elasticities presented in the textbook, and explains its relative elasticity.

Example   Prior to a survey of household income, students predict the Gini coefficient for the class: will it be higher or lower than the Gini coefficient for all US households? Then, based on data collected in a confidential survey, students calculate income shares by quintile, draw a Lorenz curve and estimate the Gini coefficient for the class. Finally, students compare and evaluate their predictions and the estimated Gini coefficient.

Data Analysis

ILDs using data from secondary sources can help students appreciate the value of evidence for confirming or refuting commonly held beliefs. Data analysis can be relatively straightforward, asking students to graph or otherwise manipulate a given set of data, while more sophisticated data analysis may require students to obtain relevant data on their own using internet or library sources. The ILD format models economics research practice by requiring students to form a hypothesis (the prediction step), test it with data (the experience step), and then interpret the results (the reflection step).

Example   Ask students what happened to real GDP/capita during their lifetime based on a series of graphs showing alternative patterns over twenty years: constant growth, cyclical growth, cyclical decline, and cyclical stability. After students make a prediction, they graph real GDP/capita for the last twenty years, revealing a long-term increase in real GDP/capita. In the reflection step, students explain why most people (likely including themselves) underestimate economic growth.

Example   Has the unemployment rate increased for women and for minorities relative to white males? After students predict the answers, they use US Bureau of Labor

Statistics data to analyze unemployment rates by race, ethnicity and gender over time. Because the project requires students to identify both changes over the business cycle as well as longer-term trends, the reflection step should include analysis of multiple factors.

Simulations

Computer and paper-and-pencil simulation activities are available for classroom use in which students learn about economic behavior much in the way professional economists do with more sophisticated models. For example, there are simulations available for classroom use that model tax policy, national budget decisions, environmental policies, and even sport franchises.[5] As in the case of classroom experiments, simulations benefit from the ILD approach because it focuses student attention on core concepts to be learned. Before using the simulation, students are asked to make a prediction, explicitly stating the economic theory that leads to this conclusion. The simulation then offers concrete results that must be interpreted as confirming or refuting the initial prediction in the reflection step.

Example   What is the impact of a change in an excise tax on the distribution of after-tax income? Students make a prediction about the potential regressive or progressive impact. Using a computer model, students input changes in gasoline, alcohol or tobacco taxes to see the impact on different income groups. The results are analyzed in terms of both the regressivity of the taxes and the relative impact of the tax compared with other taxes.[6]

ILD PROCEDURES

Economics instructors can learn from best practices established for each step in the Interactive Lecture Demonstration. Physics education researchers recommend that before students make a prediction the instructor clearly indicates what will take place in the demonstration, usually showing all the steps in the demonstration, without, of course, revealing the outcome. Furthermore, students are encouraged to be as precise as possible about their prediction, for example choosing from a selection of numbers or diagrams, rather than simply predicting "less" or "more". After students record their individual predictions for the demonstration, they discuss their prediction rationale with a classmate, changing the prediction if they like. Finally, with neither praise nor criticism from the instructor, some or all predictions are reported to the class.

   In physics ILDs, the demonstration step usually is conducted by students working in small groups unless time or resource constraints require the instructor to conduct the demonstration in front of the class.[7] Students will be more engaged if they are involved in the demonstration; however, if it is expedient for instructor to conduct the demonstration, student engagement can occur as they analyze the ILD in small groups. For example, after a whole class survey, small groups analyze the data, or after a classroom experiment, small groups explore relevant economic models.[8]

   In the rush to wrap up a topic or end a class meeting, it may be tempting to skip the reflection step. However, research on learning shows that it is important for students to think explicitly about what they have learned, making connections to what they knew before, and identifying what specifically has changed in their thinking. After the demonstration is complete, students can consider ways in which the demonstration challenged their prior beliefs (or not), and how the new results can be explained. Sufficient time should be allotted for such reflection either as a whole-class discussion, pair work, or individually written short papers. Often the ILD will challenge students' preconceptions. For example, in the real GDP/capita ILD described above, students typically underestimate real GDP growth. It is important not only for students to identify the correct empirical results (what was the average real GDP growth?), but also to understand why they, and indeed many other citizens, misconceive the actual situation. Consequently, the reflection step begins by asking students why the original position seemed logical, introspection often best stated as "why do most people believe. . ." to avoid personalizing the student's apparent error. Reflection along these lines can reveal what was in fact partially correct about the original position. When students underestimate GDP growth, it may be an accurate description of the short-run situation, as in the case of a recent recession, or it may be the case that living standards have stagnated for households familiar to the students, even though there were increases in overall GDP per capita. Thus the goal of the reflection step is to help students construct a more sophisticated mental model, one that research on learning suggests requires reconciling previous thinking with new insights.

The reflection step can build in other pedagogical techniques, such as classroom assessment questions: "What was the most important point made in class today?" or "What unanswered question do you still have?" (Angelo and Cross, 1993) or writing across the curriculum prompts such as "Although most people believe . . . because . . ., in fact . . ." (Graff and Birkenstein, 2009). The instructor also can create a short video in which an educated individual, perhaps a college administrator or faculty member, answers a question incorrectly about the concept under study. After watching the film, students write an essay providing the correct answer and explaining why even well-educated people misunderstand the concept. Finally, the reflection step can ask students to transfer their understanding to a new situation using the context-rich problem approach.[9]

FUTURE WORK

Although education research indicates the importance of the prediction, experience, and reflection ILD steps, little is known about their efficiency in economics. Economic educators would benefit from an evaluation of the prediction step: Does it engage students in the subsequent activity? Does it help students connect subsequent results to their underlying mental model? Does it improve student learning? Or, can the prediction step ruin the "aha" moment, such as when the double-oral auction leads to a single equilibrium price in an unexpectedly fast manner?

The experience step, the core of the ILD process, is built around research-based evidence that students learn more when they are engaged. Existing economics classroom experiments, surveys, data analysis or simulations can be put into the ILD framework by adding prediction and reflection steps. What needs to be studied in greater detail is how specifically to develop effective applications in economics. For example, how important is it for students to conduct the demonstration? The demonstration may be distracting if students' attention is focused on the details of the demonstration set-up and materials, rather than the concept under study. At the same time, when students conduct the demonstration, there is collateral learning, such as how to record data in a meaningful graph, a skill that may be as important as the targeted economic concept. Should the experience step be structured so that it involves collaboration with other students? In math, education research finds that small group work prevented minor errors that distracted students from the larger learning goal (Vidakovic and Martin, 2004; Vidakovic, 1997). Likely such benefits are possible in economics.

By studying the reflection step, economic educators can identify preconceptions that students bring to the course, as well as which experiences help students to improve their understanding (Goffe, 2010). How important is the reflection step for learning economic concepts? Is it more important for some concepts than others? Which types of writing help students focus their emerging mental model? Physics education ILDs sometimes ask students explicitly about the accuracy of competing models, an attempt to help students understand the way in which scientists use the modeling principle (University of Maryland Physics Education Research Group, 2010). Would such direct reference to model building be applicable in economics?

In summary, physics education research provides a valuable basis on which economics educators can build effective new pedagogy using Interactive Lecture Demonstrations. The ILD format of "predict, experience and reflect" is readily adaptable to economics instruction, although much remains to be learned about the ways in which this pedagogy will improve student learning.

NOTES

1. For more information on ILDs and examples of their application in economics, see Interactive Lecture Demonstrations on Starting Point: Teaching and Learning Economics, http://serc.carleton.edu/econ/demonstrations/index.html (accessed 15 May 2011).
2. In a Vickrey auction the highest bidder wins, but the price paid is the second-highest bid.
3. See Chapter 36, "Learning from Physics Education Research: Lessons for Economics Education", in this volume.
4. For a detailed description of experiments, see Chapter 7 in this volume.
5. For more information about how to conduct simulations and for economics examples, see http://serc.carleton.edu/econ/simulations/index.html (accessed 15 May 2011).
6. See http://serc.carleton.edu/sp/library/simulations/examples/example4.html (accessed 15 May 2011).
7. For examples of instructor-led demonstrations see http://ild.uit.tufts.edu/ (accessed 9 July 2010).
8. For recommendations about small group composition, structured written work, reporting out and grading, see Chapter 4 on cooperative learning in this volume.
9. For more information on this technique and examples, see Chapter 3 on context-rich problems in this volume.

REFERENCES

Angelo, T. A and P. Cross (1993), *Classroom Assessment Techniques: A Handbook for College Teachers* (2nd edition), San Francisco: Jossey-Bass Publishers.
Bransford, J. D., A. L. Brown and R. R. Cocking (2000), *How People Learn: Brain, Mind, Experience and School*, Washington, DC: National Academy Press.

Bruff, D. (2009), *Teaching with Classroom Response Systems: Creating Active Learning Environments*, San Francisco: Jossey-Bass.

Concept Inventory Central (2010), https://engineering.purdue.edu/SCI/workshop, accessed 9 July 2010.

Crouch, C., A. P. Fagen, J. P. Callan and E. Mazur (2004), "Classroom demonstrations: Learning tools or entertainment?", *American Journal of Physics*, **72** (6), 835–8.

Edwired (2010), Blog archive, http://edwired.org/?p=587, accessed 9 July 2010.

Goffe, W. (2010), "Initial misconceptions in a macro principles class", http://goffe.oswego.edu/Misconceptions.pdf, accessed 9 July 2010.

Graff, G. and C. Birkenstein (2009), *They Say/I Say: The Moves that Matter in Academic Writing* (2nd edition), New York: WW Norton.

Halloun, I. and D. Hestenes (1985), "The initial knowledge state of college physics students", *American Journal of Physics*, **53** (11), 1043–56.

Harvard-Smithsonian Center for Astrophysics (1997), "A Private Universe, Minds of Our Own", Annenberg Media, available from http://www.learner.org/resources/series28.html, accessed 15 May 2011.

Liew, Chong-Wah and D. F. Treagust (1998), "The effectiveness of predict-observe-explain tasks in diagnosing students' understanding of science and in identifying their levels of achievement", Paper presented at Annual Meeting of the American Educational Research Association (San Diego, CA, 13–17 April), available at: http://www.eric.ed.gov/PDFS/ED420715.pdf, accessed 16 May 2011.

Mazur, E. (1997), *Peer Instruction: A User's Manual, Prentice Hall Series in Educational Innovation*, Upper Saddle River, NJ: Prentice Hall.

McDermott, L. (1991), "Millikan Lecture 1990: What we teach and what is learned – Closing the gap", *American Journal of Physics*, **59** (4), 301–15.

McDermott, L. C. and E. F. Redish (1999), "Resource letter: PER-1: Physics education research", *American Journal of Physics*, **67** (9), 755–67.

Palmer, D. (1995), "The POE in the primary school: An evaluation", *Research in Science Education*, **25** (3), 323–32.

Redish, E. F. (2003), *Teaching Physics with the Physics Suite*, Hoboken, NJ: Wiley.

Redish, E. F. and D. Hammer (2009), "Reinventing college physics for biologists: Explicating an epistemological curriculum", *American Journal of Physics*, **77** (7), 629–42.

Salemi, M. (2009), "Clickenomics: Using a classroom response system to increase student engagement in a large enrollment principles of economics course", *The Journal of Economic Education*, **40** (4), 385–404.

Schwartz, D. L. and J. D. Bransford (1998), "Time for telling", *Cognition & Instruction*, **16** (4), 475–523.

Sharma, M. D., I. Johnston, H. Johnston, K. Varvell, G. Robertson, A. Hopkins, C. Stewart, I. Cooper and R. Thornton (2010), "Use of interactive lecture demonstrations: A ten year study", *Physical Review Special Topics – Physics Education Research*, **6** (2).

Sokoloff, D. R. and R. K. Thornton (1997), "Using interactive lecture demonstrations to create an active learning environment", *The Physics Teacher*, **35** (6), 340.

Starting point: Teaching and learning economics (2010), http://serc.carleton.edu/econ/experiments/index.html, accessed 9 July 2010.

Thornton, R. K. (2008), "Effective learning environments for computer supported instruction in the physics classroom and laboratory", in M. Vicentini and E. Sassi, *Connecting Research in Physics Education with Teacher Education*, International Commission on Physics Education, available at http://web.phys.ksu.edu/icpe/Publications/teach2/Table_of_contents.pdf, accessed 15 May 2011.

University of Maryland Physics Education Research Group (2010), http://www.physics.umd.edu/perg/ILD.htm, accessed 15 May 2011.

Vidakovic, D. (1997), "Learning the concept of inverse functions in a group versus individual environment', in E. Dubinsky, D. M. Mathews and B. E. Reynolds (eds), *Readings in Cooperative Learning for Undergraduate Mathematics*, Washington, DC: Math Association of America, 173–95.

Vidakovic, D. and W. O. Martin (2004), "Small-group searches for mathematical proofs and individual reconstructions of mathematical concepts", *The Journal of Mathematical Behavior*, **23** (4), 465–92.

9 Using Just-in-Time Teaching to promote student learning in economics[1]

Scott Simkins

Just-in-Time Teaching (JiTT) was originally developed in physics by Novak, Patterson, Gavrin, and Christian (1999) and was adapted for use in economics by Simkins and Maier (2004). JiTT is an intentionally designed teaching and learning strategy that helps to structure and focus student studying, encourage preparation for class, and suggest "just-in-time" modifications of in-class activities focused on student learning challenges. As Simkins and Maier (2010) illustrate, JiTT can be used in a wide variety of disciplines and in combination with existing teaching practices.

The JiTT strategy is deceptively simple. Students submit responses to online exercises (typically using course management software) a few hours before class. Instructors then review students' responses prior to class, using those responses to organize and develop in-class activities for the upcoming classroom session. JiTT exercises are generally short and focus on concepts and ideas that will be covered in the next class. In addition, they require students to *do* something in order to complete the exercises, such as read a textbook chapter, an article, or newspaper story; carry out a simulation; solve a problem; draw and manipulate graphs; or obtain and analyze data. As a result, JiTT exercises promote increased time on task while also providing valuable information about students' understanding of course concepts *prior to* class.

USING JiTT – AN EXAMPLE

On the surface, JiTT appears to be simply a structured way to organize and focus students' out-of-class study time. However, when used in an intentional and systematic way, JiTT becomes a powerful teaching and *learning* tool that promotes deep and durable learning. The following example illustrates both the benefit of JiTT exercises in making visible students' thinking and the way in which JiTT responses can be used in class to address confusion that students may have about fundamental economic concepts.

Example of a JiTT exercise This JiTT exercise discusses the role of price changes in moving perfectly competitive markets toward equilibrium. While perfectly competitive markets are rarely found in real life, the concept of prices changing in response to actions by buyers and sellers is a critical, if abstract, building block in economics. The exercise would likely be used near the beginning of a principles-level course and would be assigned prior to discussing this topic in class (along with relevant text material).

Describe the role of the price of a good in moving a perfectly competitive market to equilibrium if there is currently a shortage in this market. To fully answer this question, consider the following two questions:

a.   What will happen to the price of the good in this case? Why?
b.   How does the change in the price of a good provide an incentive for demanders and suppliers to change their behavior in this situation, thus bringing the market to equilibrium? Explain.

Student responses   A sample of actual (unedited) student responses is provided below. The responses were selected because they represent a variety of thought processes that are unclear or simply incorrect. Left unchallenged, these ideas could retard further understanding in the course. A select number of responses are provided to students at the start of the next class period in preparation for a brief discussion and in-class activity designed to target the learning gaps illustrated in the responses. For example:

- The prices will increase because of the shortage of goods available. The change in the price would cause demanders not to purchase as much of the good and the suppliers would not be as willing to provide the good. Therefore moving toward equilibrium is good for both sides.
- The prices of the goods will lower for the markets behind to catch up. They would have to make more product because the demand would be great for that product. That's what they would have to do since they are selling the product so cheap.
- If the market is experiencing a shortage then the market will be forced to raise the prices because they are trying to reach equilibrium. Demanders will have to want more and the supplies will have to supply more in order to bring the market from shortage to equilibrium.
- The shortage of a good would, if viewed on a supply and demand model, cause the supply curve to shift to the left. This would raise the price of that good in the market place. If the demand of a product, good, or service is greater than the supply the prices would be higher. The producers of that good or providers of that service would be wise to make more of the good available to take advantage of the higher prices. The consumer on the other hand would have to decide if the good or service in question was a necessity at that present time. The consumer could either pay the going rate or wait until market conditions were more favorable to the consumer. When the demand decreases the prices would again lower.

Note that the responses are often *partially* correct, as we would expect when students are first introduced to a topic. However, they also provide insights into ways that student thinking is flawed and highlight a need for further in-class discussion and practice on this topic before moving on to new material.

In-class exercise   The responses above could be used for a whole-class discussion or as the basis for a cooperative-learning exercise.[2] Consider, for example, a send-a-problem exercise where each group of three to five students takes one of the JiTT responses above (attached to a folder or envelope) and responds to the question: Where is the error in the reasoning of this response? The group writes a response to this question, places it in the folder, and passes it to the next group; other groups do likewise. This process is repeated three more times, until each group gets a folder with the JiTT response they initially analyzed, along with the four group responses to the in-class question. Each group opens its folder, examines the four responses, and determines the best one. Representative groups are asked to report out their selected reasoning to the entire class. After all four of the JiTT responses have been critiqued, the instructor could follow up with a question asking the groups to consider the case of a market experiencing a surplus, to check on transfer of learning, or alternatively, ask each group to come up with an exemplar answer to the original JiTT question, with the results handed in for grading.

Extension   JiTT exercises also alert instructors to student confusions that might otherwise remain hidden with traditional teaching methods. For example, the following (unedited) student response illustrates the challenge of matching up personal economic experience with abstract models and concepts.

> Whenever there is a shortage in the market, it means that the quantity demand is much greater than quantity supplied. Thus companies will raise the prices of their goods or services. Since it's a shortage, consumers will purchase these goods or services. For example, when the Playstation 2 came out last year, there was a shortage, and it ran about $499.00. Since it was a shortage, consumers were quick to purchase it. After consumers keep purchasing the products, it no longer becomes a shortage. Soon or later the company, due to competition, will lower its prices. Like in the example I gave, after a couple of months the price of the Playstation 2 dropped down to $299.00. When the consumers continued to purchase the products it allows the price to go down to reach equilibrium.

It is likely that this student, faced with the four JiTT responses listed earlier, would remain confused, since what he/she experienced in his/her own life was a *fall* in prices following a period of shortage, the opposite of what standard economic theory would predict in the short run.

However, aware of this student's response, the instructor could indicate how the abstract concept discussed above might differ from behavior actually observed in the marketplace due to differences in time periods, market power of firms, and so on – and might even show this response to illustrate the point. Again, the JiTT exercise makes instructors aware of these thought processes *prior to* discussion in class, allowing these ideas to be explicitly addressed and engaging students actively in the knowledge creation process.

WHY USE JUST-IN-TIME TEACHING?

As the example above suggests, using JiTT changes the classroom environment, compared to traditional lecture presentations. Students see their own work, literally, and quickly realize that their out-of-class efforts will be brought back into the classroom. Students are more engaged in class because the activities they complete are directly related to their own learning challenges, made visible in their JiTT responses. Moreover, the in-class sharing of student responses (without name attribution) sends the message, first, that the instructor is paying attention to their out-of-class work, and second, that wrong answers, when they highlight actual student learning gaps, are beneficial starting points for learning.

JiTT Focuses on Student Learning

JiTT is much more than a teaching technique – it is a powerful *learning* tool, both for the instructor and the student. As physics education researcher McDermott (1991, p. 303) notes, "There are often significant differences between what the instructor thinks students have learned and what students may have actually learned." Anyone who has delivered a carefully crafted lecture on an important concept, only to find that half the students failed a related question on the exam, will recognize the universality of McDermott's claim. Used in an intentional and systematic way, students' JiTT responses provide instructors with valuable information about students' thinking processes and preconceptions, before the test, that can be used in a formative, positive, learning-centered way to address observed learning gaps. Often, the JiTT responses provide surprising insights about student misunderstanding that instructors are completely unaware of. This information allows faculty members to target classroom activities where they will provide the greatest benefits for student learning.

JiTT Motivates Preparation for and Student Learning during Class

A common complaint voiced by faculty members is that students fail to come to class prepared for learning. As a result, instructors lecture on material that students should have read prior to class, leaving little time for application of concepts and skills. JiTT helps to overcome this challenge by promoting a positive learning cycle that encourages both in- and out-of-class effort. Because students' JiTT responses inform the development of in-class activities that directly address their learning difficulties, JiTT motivates students to complete the out-of-class JiTT exercises and actively participate in the ensuing classroom activities. In class, students receive immediate feedback on their understanding of the concepts covered in the JiTT exercises, further enhancing their learning.

JiTT Supports Effective Teaching and Learning Practices

JiTT is consistent with good teaching practices, as summarized in Chickering and Gamson's (1987) well-known and widely cited "Seven Principles for Good Practice in Undergraduate Education". In particular, JiTT:

- *Promotes student-faculty contact* by making students and faculty partners in the knowledge generation process; students' responses to JiTT exercises are the basis for in-class discussion and activities.
- *Encourages cooperative and active learning* by asking students to apply or make sense of new information from assigned readings or activities and then participate in follow-up exercises that encourage collaborative idea sharing and problem solving.
- *Emphasizes time on task* by structuring students' study time and focusing in-class instruction on identified student learning gaps.

- *Promotes prompt feedback* by helping instructors identify gaps in student understanding and immediately address those gaps through targeted in-class activities.
- *Communicates high expectations* by reinforcing the message that learning takes place continuously and is most effective when out-of-class studying is closely linked to in-class activities and instruction.
- *Respects diverse talents and ways of learning* by providing multiple ways for students to learn and connect new information and concepts to their own lives.

In addition, JiTT supports the findings from learning sciences research summarized in Bransford, Brown, and Cocking's (2000) seminal *How People Learn*. As the authors note in the introduction, ". . . views of how effective learning proceeds have shifted from the benefits of diligent drill and practice to focus on students' understanding and application of knowledge" (p. xi). In particular, they highlight five areas critical for improving student learning. JiTT supports each of these by:

- *Uncovering and addressing students' pre/misconceptions*: The mental models students bring with them into our classes can retard learning. JiTT exercises are particularly useful for uncovering student pre/misconceptions, which can then be directly addressed in the follow-up class session through activities that help students discover inconsistencies in their thinking processes.
- *Promoting expert-like performance and learning:* Experts use structured mental models to order and categorize new information; novices tend to focus only on superficial (in other words, surface-level) properties of information and learn primarily through rote memorization. As a result, novice learners often fail to make the conceptual connections that we are trying to teach. JiTT exercises make surface-level thinking visible to instructors in time to develop in-class activities that promote more expert-like thinking.
- *Encouraging the development of transferable knowledge:* For students to develop the ability to transfer knowledge to new situations they must be given the opportunity to apply new knowledge in a variety of situations and contexts. JiTT exercises, along with related in-class activities, can provide students with opportunities to apply course concepts in new and novel ways, helping to build transferable knowledge.
- *Emphasizing formative assessment:* Formative assessment provides students with feedback on their learning in a low-stakes environment. JiTT exercises require students to reflect on the processes needed to solve problems, carry out critical analyses, evaluate information, and synthesize ideas. In-class activities provide opportunities for students to obtain immediate feedback on their learning progress.
- *Helping students become reflective (metacognitive) learners:* To promote life-long learning, we need to help students become self-directed, reflective learners. This requires directed practice that encourages student reflection about the learning process. JiTT exercises typically include at least one question asking students to reflect on learning gaps uncovered in their pre-class preparation; in turn, instructors can use this knowledge to assist students in monitoring and assessing their own learning.

DOES JiTT WORK? – RESEARCH FINDINGS FROM CLASSROOM-BASED RESEARCH

Classroom research has regularly illustrated JiTT's positive impact on students' preparation for class, engagement in the learning process, motivation for learning, and academic achievement (see Simkins and Maier (2010) for examples from a wide variety of disciplines). In economics, Simkins and Maier (2004) find that JiTT has a positive, statistically significant impact on student learning in an introductory economics course, even after controlling for a variety of academic and demographic variables. In addition, their results suggest that JiTT exercises provide an efficient way of helping students improve their learning. Students indicated that JiTT exercises were among the most helpful aids to learning while requiring only a moderate level of effort. On end-of-course evaluations, students noted the following benefits of JiTT:

> The JiTT assignments prepared me for class. It allowed me to read ahead so that I would fully understand what would be covered in class the next period.

> The assignments kept me up to date with the material covered in class. They really made me think outside the classroom of things I'd normally not bother with.

> . . . I also liked the fact that the JiTT assignments were used along with class discussion. Even if you got the JiTT wrong you were still able to learn through the discussion.

THE KEY TO JiTT SUCCESS – DEVELOPING EFFECTIVE JiTT QUESTIONS

Intentionally developing JiTT questions with specific learning goals in mind is the key to achieving success with JiTT. Given JiTT's aim of generating responses that make students' thinking processes visible, JiTT questions are generally open-ended and leave room for multiple explanations. Moreover, they typically ask students to apply new concepts or ideas in ways that cannot simply be looked up in a textbook, facilitating higher-order thinking skills and promoting expert-like thinking. The examples below illustrate how effective JiTT questions can be developed to meet a variety of learning goals based on Bloom's taxonomy, *How People Learn* principles, and expected proficiencies for undergraduate economics majors (Hansen, 2001).

Using Bloom's Taxonomy to Develop JiTT Questions

Bloom's (1956) taxonomy provides a useful guide for developing effective JiTT questions and can be used in conjunction with course-level learning outcomes to systematically enhance students' learning. This taxonomy classifies cognitive learning goals according to their complexity, from low-level to high-level: knowledge, comprehension, application, analysis, synthesis, and evaluation.

For example, to develop comprehension-level thinking skills, you might use the following JiTT exercise:

Describe how the Federal Reserve increases the level of bank deposits (and therefore the money supply) through an open market purchase of government bonds. What role do banks play in this process? How about borrowers? Will these actions necessarily lead to an increase in the money supply and a reduction in interest rates? Why or why not?

The next example illustrates a JiTT exercise focusing on application of economic concepts:

Would you rather earn 10% interest on money in a bank account when the inflation rate is 8%, or 4% interest on money in a bank account when the inflation rate is 1.5%? Explain your choice. Explain why the real rate of interest is a more appropriate measure to use than the nominal interest rate when making your choice.

And, finally, an example of a JiTT exercise at the evaluation level:

The US economy currently produces somewhat less than $10 trillion in real GDP annually. During a typical recession, real GDP declines about 3%.
a. If the economy is currently in a recession, by approximately how much (in $) would you need to increase government spending to bring the economy back to full employment, assuming that we began the recession at potential GDP? Make your case as strongly as you can. Each person's estimate may differ somewhat, but explain how you arrived at your answer.
b. In order to boost government spending by the amount you determined in part a., by how much would you need to boost overall discretionary spending (in percentage terms) from its current level? What programs would you increase spending for? Why (with respect to boosting the economy)? Why might Congress fail to support your proposal?

Using Learning Sciences Principles to Develop JiTT Questions

The learning sciences principles summarized in *How People Learn* (Bransford, Brown, and Cocking, 2000) provide another useful framework for developing effective JiTT questions. Some examples of how this might be accomplished in an economics course follow.

Uncovering and addressing students' pre/misconceptions   Use JiTT exercises to make visible students' views about important economic concepts.

- What percentage of the federal government's current budget is spent on military spending (Note to instructors: Or select another category, such as Social Security, Medicare, "welfare", entitlement spending, etc.). How has this percentage changed over time?
- In what ways does international trade help or hurt workers in the United States?

Developing expert-like thinking processes JiTT questions that help students structure knowledge in organized "chunks" promote expert-like thinking.

- In what ways do government macroeconomic policies for long-term economic growth differ from government macroeconomic policies for short-term economic fluctuations? Be as specific and as complete as you can in your explanation and link the policy actions to their intended economic effect.
- For each of the following events, determine whether it would have its primary effect on aggregate demand or aggregate supply and provide the reason for your choice. How will the event likely affect employment and inflation rates in the economy? Again, explain your reasoning. In addition, provide your own example of an event that would affect aggregate demand or aggregate supply and repeat the process above.

  a. A new technological breakthrough that allows manufacturers to produce computer chips with cheaper raw materials.
  b. An increase in military conflicts in the Middle East that restrict the worldwide supply of crude oil.
  c. New laws are enacted that reduce marginal tax rates for households earning less than $250,000 per year.
  d. New laws are enacted that reduce taxes on corporate profits.
  e. The Federal Reserve raises interest rates.

Promoting metacognition JiTT can also be used to build students' metacognitive skills by including questions like those listed below in every JiTT exercise. The responses to these questions also provide valuable insights into students' thinking processes.

- After completing this exercise, what concepts or ideas are still unclear to you? Please provide a brief explanation.
- In addition to determining the answer to the question, please explain the steps you used to arrive at your answer.

Using the Hansen Proficiencies to Develop JiTT Questions

According to Lee Hansen (1986, 2001, 2006), graduates in economics should be proficient in a variety of skills, which have become known as *Hansen Proficiencies*.[3] JiTT questions can be used to promote these skills, as illustrated in the examples below.

Accessing existing knowledge Find current and recent employment data from the US Bureau of Labor Statistics and use it to determine whether economic conditions in the country are improving or declining.

Displaying command of existing knowledge Democrats and Republicans disagree on whether changing federal spending or changing taxes is the best policy for bringing the US economy out of recession. Briefly describe the competing views and provide a legitimate economic argument supporting each option.

Interpreting existing knowledge   Describe the economic concepts and principles that are used in the accompanying newspaper article/magazine story/commentary.

Interpreting and manipulating economic data   Construct a table listing quarterly data for US civilian non-agricultural employment, real GDP, and the consumer price level over the past six years. Use aggregate demand/aggregate supply analysis to explain the patterns/trends found in the data.

Applying existing knowledge   Use economic concepts discussed in this course to write a letter to the student newspaper suggesting solutions to the ongoing parking shortage on campus.

USING JiTT IN CONJUNCTION WITH OTHER PEDAGOGIES[4]

JiTT does not require dramatic changes in pedagogical practice. JiTT exercises can easily be combined with a variety of teaching strategies that economists are already familiar with, including classroom experiments, cooperative learning, and the case-study method.[5] In each case, JiTT questions can be used to intentionally prepare students for in-class activities and alert instructors to student learning gaps that can be addressed explicitly as part of those activities.

In addition, JiTT can be used in conjunction with a variety of innovative teaching strategies adapted from other disciplines, such as peer instruction, interactive lecture demonstrations, and context-rich problems (Simkins and Maier 2008).[6] In particular, JiTT has been shown to be effective when combined with peer instruction, a pedagogy developed by Eric Mazur at Harvard University to make large-enrollment physics lectures more interactive and improve student learning (see Mazur 1996; Crouch and Mazur 2001; Fagen, Crouch and Mazur 2002; and Crouch, Watkins, Fagen and Mazur 2007). In recent years Mazur has begun using student responses to JiTT exercises to develop the in-class conceptual questions that students answer in pairs (peer instruction) using personal response systems (clickers). Classroom research (Watkins and Mazur 2010) shows that integrating peer instruction with JiTT leads to greater student learning than using peer instruction alone.

SUMMARY

As noted at the start of this chapter, just-in-time teaching is a deceptively simple teaching and learning tool. While on the surface JiTT exercises resemble traditional homework assignments or quizzes, their purpose is different. Student responses to JiTT exercises help to "make student thinking visible . . . (and) change the character of the classroom" (Rhem, 2005, p. 1). Students see how their out-of-class work influences in-class activities aimed at directly addressing their learning challenges. The result is greater engagement in the learning process and improved learning.

JiTT is also a remarkably flexible teaching and learning tool. It can be used in economics to support a wide variety of learning goals, including cognitive thinking processes, disciplinary proficiencies, and research-based teaching and learning practices. The key to effective JiTT implementation is intentionally developing JiTT exercises that are directly linked to these goals and then systematically following up in class with active-learning activities targeting student learning gaps made visible in students' JiTT responses. When used intentionally and systematically in this way, JiTT provides a powerful tool for improving student learning.

NOTES

1. This entry draws on the work presented in Simkins and Maier (2004, 2010) and is supported by National Science Foundation grants DUE 0088303 and DUE 0817382. A wide variety of resources supporting the use of just-in-time teaching are available at Starting Point: Teaching and Learning Economics, http://serc. carleton.edu/econ/index.html (accessed 17 May 2011).
2. For a description of effective exercises, see the Chapter 4 on cooperative learning in this volume.
3. For a detailed description of the proficiencies and their development, see Chapter 17 in this volume on the expected proficiencies approach to the economics major.
4. For additional information about how to combine JiTT with other teaching practices, see Maier and Simkins (2010) and the Just-in-Time Teaching module at Starting Point: Teaching and Learning Economics.
5. For more information about these techniques, see the related chapters in this volume.
6. Context-rich problems and interactive lecture demonstrations are further described in Chapters 3 and 8 in this volume.

REFERENCES

Bloom, B. S. (1956), *Taxonomy of Educational Objectives, Handbook I: The Cognitive Domain*, New York: David McKay Co Inc.
Bransford, J., A. L. Brown and R. R. Cocking (eds) (2000), *How People Learn: Brain, Mind, Experience, and School: Expanded Edition*, National Research Council (US) Committee on Learning Research and Educational Practice, Washington, DC: National Academies Press.
Chickering, A. W. and Z. F. Gamson (1987), "Seven principles for good practice in undergraduate education", *AAHE Bulletin*, **39** (7), 3–7.
Crouch, C. H. and E. Mazur (2001), "Peer instruction: Ten years of experience and results", *American Journal of Physics*, **69** (9), 970–77.
Crouch, C. H., J. Watkins, A. P. Fagen and Eric Mazur (2007), "Peer instruction: Engaging students one-on-one, all at once", in E. F. Redish and P. J. Cooney (eds), *Reviews in Physics Education Research Vol. 1 – Research-Based Reform of University Physics*. College Park, MD: American Association of Physics Teachers, available at: http://www.per-central.org/document/ServeFile.cfm?ID=4990, accessed 17 May 2011.
Fagen, A. P., C. H. Crouch and E. Mazur (2002), "Peer instruction: Results from a range of classrooms", *Physics Teacher*, **40** (4), 206–9.
Hansen, W. L. (1986), "What knowledge is most worth knowing – for economics majors?", *American Economic Review*, **76** (2), 149–52.
Hansen, W. L. (2001), "Expected proficiencies for undergraduate economics majors", *Journal of Economic Education*, **32** (3), 231–42.
Hansen, W. L. (2006), "A Proficiency-Based Economics Course Examination", Paper presented at the Midwest Economic Association Meetings, March 2006.
Maier, M. H. and S. P. Simkins (2010), "Just-in-time teaching in combination with other pedagogical innovations", in S. P. Simkins and M. H. Maier (eds), *Just in Time Teaching: Across the Disciplines, and Across the Academy*, Sterling, VA: Stylus Publishing, pp. 63–78.
Mazur, E. (1996), *Peer Instruction: A User's Manual*, Upper Saddle River, NJ: Prentice-Hall.
McDermott, L. C. (1991), "Millikan Lecture 1990: What we teach and what is learned – closing the gap", *American Journal of Physics*, **59** (4), 301–15.
Novak, G. M., E. T. Patterson, A. D. Gavrin and W. Christian (1999), *Just-in-Time-Teaching: Blending Active Learning with Web Technology*, Upper Saddle River, NJ: Prentice-Hall.

Rhem, J. (2005), "Just-in-time teaching", *National Teaching and Learning Forum Newsletter*, **14** (1), 1–4.

Simkins, S. P. and M. H. Maier (2004), "Using just-in-time teaching techniques in the principles of economics course", *Social Science Computer Review*, **22** (4), 444–56.

Simkins, S. P. and M. H. Maier (2008), "Learning from Physics Education Research: Lessons for Economics Education" (June 27), available at: http://ssrn.com/abstract=1151430, accessed 17 May 2011.

Simkins, S. P. and M. H. Maier (eds) (2010), *Just in Time Teaching: Across the Disciplines, and Across the Academy*, Sterling, VA: Stylus Publishing.

Watkins, J. and E. Mazur (2010), "Just-in-time teaching and peer instruction", in S. P. Simkins and M. H. Maier (eds), *Just in Time Teaching: Across the Disciplines, and Across the Academy*, Sterling, VA: Stylus Publishing, pp. 39–62.

10 Making the large-enrollment course interactive and engaging
Stephen Buckles, Gail M. Hoyt and Jennifer Imazeki

An increase in class size is a common cost-saving response when state budgets tighten and endowments shrink. Yet when conditions improve, classes do not necessarily return to their previous sizes. This chapter provides advice and guidance for economists who find themselves called upon to teach large introductory, intermediate or elective classes, in which creative course design, effective delivery, and self-assessment of teaching techniques become increasingly important.

We define courses as large enrollment when the number of students makes it challenging to get most students directly involved in traditional classroom discussions. Perhaps surprisingly, empirical evidence often shows that there is no or little difference between small and very large classes in knowledge gained or in higher-level skills learned (Kennedy and Siegfried, 1997). However, given the evidence that less than optimal "chalk and talk" types of lecturing still dominate the discipline (Watts and Becker, 2008), we suspect that this lack of difference arises because neither small *nor* large classes take advantage of the best available teaching and learning techniques. In this chapter, we propose that the large-enrollment learning experience can be a productive and engaging one, with proper planning and adaptation.[1] In the following sections, we discuss the importance of organization and preparation of courses, the design of lectures, interactive teaching and active learning techniques, and the use of technology in large lecture courses.

THE IMPORTANCE OF ORGANIZATION AND PREPARATION

Organization and preparation are always important parts of effective teaching and classroom management. However, all of the small problems one encounters in a class of 30 or 40 students become multiplied and much more significant and challenging in larger classes. Without careful thought, these have the potential to reduce classroom time that could be devoted to subject matter and consume large chunks of instructor time outside of the classroom.

Prior to the Start of the Semester

The administrative tasks associated with a large-enrollment course can be daunting, partly because the number of questions, emails, and requests for special treatment increase significantly. Fortunately, these requests can usually be reduced to a manageable scale if the instructor takes time to formulate clear policies about grading, communication, missed assignments and other issues prior to the start of the semester. It is then best to stick to these policies, keeping in mind that this is easier if some flexibility is built in from the beginning. For example, in big classes, set test dates, before the semester starts and then do not change them, even if you are behind or ahead with the material. It is easier to adjust exam questions to fit the different material than to change the test date, as many students will have adapted their schedules accordingly. Even with set test dates, however, there are likely to be many students who have a valid excuse for missing a given exam. In smaller classes, offering make-ups is a relatively easy process, but for administrative ease in a big class, consider offering alternatives to make-ups, such as dropping one exam (assuming there are multiple exams) or moving the weight of the missed exam to the final exam.

All policies should be clearly stated in the syllabus; this document helps set the stage for the semester and is an opportunity to provide details about a number of issues. For example, in addition to specifying required material, be clear about how students can obtain this material and when reading assignments should be completed. Be explicit about when you are and are not available, in person or via email. Explain how grades are calculated and what flexibility you allow or do not. Discussing these issues at the beginning of the term can pre-empt many student requests for information or special treatment later.

Information about the class can also be distributed electronically through a wide range of class management programs, allowing you to post announcements and course material, or make changes during the term as appropriate. Unless you are particularly tech-savvy, it is best to keep it simple and get an introduction to software supported by your institution from the instructional technology staff. It is worth spending time getting advice from other users, learning what the software can and cannot do well, and getting the basic site structure organized before the semester begins.

Another important step in pre-semester preparation is getting comfortable with the classroom itself. The physical size of many large classrooms creates obvious challenges with visibility and sound. Consider how large the writing/font needs to be in order to be seen clearly from every seat, and if you do not have a microphone, verify your voice carries to the back of the room. Most large classrooms have equipment to help with these issues (see technology section below). It may be worthwhile to ask a teaching assistant or a colleague to evaluate your work from the back and side of the classroom to see if your presentation is clear and effective.

During Class

One challenge of a large-enrollment course is that the more bodies there are in a classroom, the more distractions there potentially are, and the more difficult it is to hold students' attention. One student coming in late or leaving early may be a fleeting annoyance, but twenty is a major disruption. Thus, it is important to lay down clear ground rules for each class meeting. Late starts and frivolous introductions encourage late arrivals and chatter, so start promptly and begin each class with substance. Also, use all of the class time to signal that this time is important and scarce, and they should interpret it as such. The exception to this is if you are truly finished and do not have time to introduce a new idea or model. It is better to stop than to begin a new topic with three minutes left. You probably already know how distracting the rattling of books and paper can be; that can be amplified many-fold in a large class, so be clear about ending times.

One reason for increased distractions in a large class is that students feel anonymous, as most students realize it is difficult for an instructor to recognize each student. That anonymity not only makes it easier for students to sit passively and let their minds wander, but they are more likely to engage in behavior that is distracting to others. One way instructors can reduce this anonymity is to make a seating chart, giving every student a home and allowing you to address students by name (and look up names when needed). Another option is simply to move around the classroom and address individual students in different parts of the room. Even without knowing names, students are more likely to pay attention if they know you can see them, and they are more likely to respond to questions if you are in close physical proximity to them.

Large classes can also inhibit questions and discussion because the vast majority of students are reluctant to ask or answer questions in front of such a large audience; it takes a good bit of self-confidence to raise your hand in front of 200 or more of your peers and admit you might not know something. So large-enrollment instructors should not expect many questions from students (or answers to posed questions). Calling on individual students can be a tricky endeavor; some students will be terrified and could be scared away from coming to class or sitting anywhere near where you can see them. It can be less intimidating if the question being asked does not have a "right" or "wrong" answer (for example, brainstorming, opinion polls), or if you give students an opportunity to discuss their answers with classmates first (see below for more on techniques to encourage student participation).

Another issue that large-enrollment instructors must consider and that small-enrollment instructors rarely encounter, is how to return graded assignments. For non-automated assignments and exams, returning papers to a large number of students can be a challenge, and institutions have a variety of guidelines as to what faculty are permitted to do to facilitate returning graded work. Unique numbering systems are often required so that individual students' exams cannot be identified. In that case, exams can be physically returned by setting out exams in order of number, allowing students to pick up their own exams (although students should be cautioned to pick up only their own exam and we note that this strategy may still push the boundaries of what is legal). Teaching assistants can also help, as exams can be divided alphabetically and handed out in various parts of the room by calling out student names. Seven or eight teaching assistants can return 500 exams in about 15 minutes. When only multiple-choice exams are used, results can be posted on a course management system, if available. If answer keys are posted and exams have only objective questions, students may be instructed to pick up their exams from the instructor or teaching assistants outside of class time, if they would still like to have the paper copy of their exam. In our experience, when keys have been provided, the number of students who will actually pick up their exam is fairly small.

DESIGNING A LECTURE

In addition to careful preparation and classroom management, the design of the lecture itself can help students stay focused and engaged. Most people can only concentrate for limited blocks of time; attention spans last 15 to 20 minutes, followed by mental lapses of varying length (Davis, 1993). After the initial 15- to 20-minute cycle, the cycle repeats, but over successively shorter time periods. While this suggests modifying the traditional 50- or 75-minute class lecture, it does not necessarily call for a complete departure from the basic lecture format. Many large-enrollment course instructors still find lectures to be an efficient means of demonstrating analysis and delivering new content. However, modifications in the standard class-long format can increase student engagement and thereby improve learning.

One approach is to break a typical lecture into short segments of between 8- and 15-minute segments, separated by a variety of activities.[2] These activities might include simply telling a story, giving an example, or asking a question. Conducting a think-pair-share exercise, discussing multiple-choice questions or asking students to write out and submit possible essay questions are also good candidates (see below for more discussion of these activities). The key point is that the change in activity resets student attention in preparation for a new lecture segment. As a result, students pay greater attention and learn more.

INTERACTIVE TEACHING TECHNIQUES

Although breaking lectures into shorter segments is likely to help students in classes of all sizes, instructors in larger classes have the added challenge that as class size grows, so does the sense of anonymity and the inclination toward student passivity. Thus, effective instructors of large courses must put forth extra effort to make the class period interactive and engaging. The use of active learning techniques in a large class can engage students who might not otherwise be interested in the discipline and generate different levels and types of thinking. As an added benefit, because the frequent use of such activities generally improves student comfort levels and willingness to participate, full class discussion is often more fruitful after these activities and throughout the semester. While some activities may produce gradable output, instructors can also gain feedback about student understanding by listening to groups as they work.

If an instructor chooses to break a lecture into smaller segments, an *engagement trigger* is a useful tool to facilitate a segment change. An engagement trigger is something that captures student attention, helps to engage students in the classroom experience, and initiates an effective interactive lecture segment. Good options for triggers are things that have evocative visual and audio appeal and that might be of unique interest to students, such as physical props, cartoons, photographs, textual passages read aloud or displayed in some way, and clips from the news, movies, or television. For instance, when teaching the concept of elasticity, many instructors take in a visual prop that is stretchy to motivate the topic. One instructor takes two rubber bands of equal size and shows that when pulled, one stretches further than the other. The prices of two products might change by the same proportion, but while consumers for both products respond, one group of consumers exhibits a more substantial response. Other instructors have been known to rip paper money into pieces in front of class when beginning discussion of why a green piece of paper has value to us. Without fail, this trigger captures student attention. In some contexts, the engagement trigger can stand alone in improving engagement and allowing for a change in format during traditional lectures, but triggers are also a great way to initiate a longer learning activity.

Cooperative learning exercises are a great way to foster interaction,[3] yet instructors of large lectures often fear they will not translate well into the larger setting. Not all learning techniques move easily from the small to large-enrollment class, but many cooperative learning techniques can be very effective in a big class.

One of the most popular cooperative learning techniques that large enrollment instructors use is the *think-pair-share*. These activities only require a short amount of class time and usually need only a small amount of preparation in advance from the instructor. Think-pair-share activities pose a question to students that they must consider alone and then discuss with a neighbor before settling on a final answer (Lyman, 1987). Instructors can ask any type of question, but open-ended questions are more likely to generate discussion and higher-level thinking. Even though the activity is called think-*pair*-share, many instructors use small groups (three or four students). The fluid nature of group formation is probably one of the most appealing features of this technique for the large-enrollment instructor since individual student attendance is often not as consistent in large classes and students may not be as likely to know each other. Students can spontaneously pair up with a classmate sitting nearby and formal group compositions need not be maintained from one class period to the next.

Some think-pair-share activities are short, "quick-response think-pair-share," and sometimes the activities may be longer and more involved, "extended-response think-pair-share" (Hoyt et al., 2010). The quick-response version is best applied for a quick format change or to generate student responses as a basis for class discussion, to motivate a lecture segment, and to obtain feedback about what students know or are thinking. Using quick-response think-pair-shares, it is easy to incorporate more than one think-pair-share activity in a given class period. A more extensive think-pair-share might be in order if the instructor would like students to produce a more substantial written product or engage in policy deliberation or multi-stage problem solving. For instance, an instructor might make the following statement, "if the local high school football team raises the admission price to the games, they will bring in less revenue from ticket sales." Students then engage with a quick-response think-pair-share as students independently decide if they agree or not, and subsequently discuss their answer briefly with a neighbor before wrapping up with some quick class discussion. A more extended version provides students additional discussion time to persuade each other to their point of view and defend their position. A pre- and post-discussion vote (show of hands) can indicate the extent to which a consensus is reached. As a further extension of this exercise, students could be charged with making a policy decision about pricing that incorporates some of the same elements of the ticket price discussion, but they have more time to consider policy options and apply the ideas through writing or discussion.

When instructors use the think-pair-share technique, it is often helpful to have students "role play" by assigning them the role of decision makers regarding a policy, resource allocation, or some other outcome. The context of the role-play exercise allows students to immediately apply content in a relevant, real-world situation, which keeps them fully engaged (Maier et al., 2010). The instructor can initiate role play by offering a scenario to students that includes the role the student must play, the details relevant for decision making in the role, and a task to complete based on the scenario.

Demonstrations and experiments can also be used effectively in the large-enrollment classroom. [4] One way to conduct these activities is to use a subset of students in front of the class. Even though not all students are participating, it can still be engaging for all students to watch and react to the demonstration, particularly if students who do not actually participate in the demonstration are asked to summarize and evaluate what they have seen (Keenan and Maier, 2004). Some more effective activities lend themselves to visual appeal, such as the production of a product which demonstrates diminishing marginal product. The flurry of activity that occurs as students try to produce with increasing amounts of variable inputs, while constrained by a fixed input, keeps the remainder of the class focused on the activity. Some professors also find longer experiments, with some modifications for the larger volume of students, to be effective as well.

Another way to keep students engaged is to hand out partial outlines of your lectures, sometimes called *skeleton notes,* with substantial space between major headings. Providing part of the notes, such as lengthy definitions, complicated formulas, or numeric information, can allow the lecture to move more efficiently (and accurately) and frees students to focus on the meaning of the content, leading to better comprehension. When considering the use of skeleton note handouts, instructors might be concerned about lower attendance and students paying less attention in class. To avoid this potential, care must be taken in constructing the skeleton notes; they should guide and assist students in getting more out of lectures, providing an obvious structure to the lecture, rather than serving as a substitute. They are an interactive tool in the sense that they maintain the focus of students and keep them active in an intellectual dialogue with the instructor as they complete the notes as the lecture progresses. Skeleton notes can be made available to students before class (by email, on a course website or in a course packet), or during class as a handout.

Conceptual multiple-choice questions (or conceptests), originally described by Eric Mazur (1997) for students in large physics classes, are short quizzes used to break up the lecture and reinforce understanding of content.[5] Instructors have modified the conceptual multiple-choice question notion to include a wider range of question formats. Some instructors give one-minute writing assignments or have students solve problems or work through a series of questions alone or in groups (see discussion of personal response devices below). The graded quiz aspect of this interactive technique adds incentives for students to attend, participate, and process the material. This boost to the course incentive structure can be vitally important in the larger class setting.

Practical Advice for Using Interactive Techniques in the Large Enrollment Setting

The effective use of any active learning technique begins with identifying the learning goal or objective of the activity. Using this as the basis for designing the activity will keep it focused and thus far more likely to promote associated learning. Before beginning the activity in class, provide clear instructions, then monitor and interact with students during activities. Go out into the classroom during a lecture; you may be amazed at how students in that section of the classroom suddenly come alive.

Advice for Assessment

Collecting feedback and assigning grades are closure components of interactive techniques. The activities described above lend themselves to providing both summative and formative assessments.[6] Instructors can acquire feedback regarding student understanding from something as informal as walking around and listening to students as they work in groups, to more formal output such as collecting written responses or having students submit answers using clickers (see technology section below). Students might produce products that do not require grading, such as writing one-minute papers, answering short questions, or identifying what they found most confusing in the lecture, or they may solve problems or take quizzes for a component of their grade. Note that one of the big challenges for interactive learning in large classes is to get all students to be truly engaged, and summative assessment increases the likelihood of strong student participation by giving students an incentive. However, that incentive does not necessarily have to require a lot of time and energy on your part. A participation grade can be tied to a short product students produce, or a student can be called upon to share their answer with the entire class. One advantage of collaborative activities is that groups produce a product, thereby reducing grading effort. Also, as the following section describes, current classroom technologies have made it far more feasible and efficient to gather and assess student work in the large-enrollment course.

TECHNOLOGY IN THE LARGE-ENROLLMENT COURSE

The sheer physical size of most large-enrollment classrooms generally necessitates using some basic technical hardware, such as microphones and projectors. But beyond that, technology can also facilitate student interaction and interest in the classroom, allow for content delivery outside the classroom to free up class time for more interaction, and minimize the time instructors must spend assessing large numbers of students.

Presentation Hardware

The larger the classroom, the more difficult it can be for students to see and hear what is going on at the front of the room. Thus, most universities equip large classrooms with an amplification system and some kind of projection system. Beyond these basics, several tools can make the large classroom more engaging. Many large-class instructors use presentation software, such as PowerPoint, for the visual part of their classes; this has the added advantage of allowing for easy creation of skeleton notes (see discussion above). A computer with an internet connection will increase options for engagement triggers, and a document camera can facilitate drawing graphs on the fly or recording notes from classroom discussion. If the classroom is not already equipped with these items, you may be able to connect a tablet PC or laptop with interactive whiteboard software that can be used for similar purposes.[7] If available, consider using multiple overhead projectors or tablet computers to leave up notes, graphs, quotes, examples, giving students more time to read and allowing you to refer back to those items. In addition, a wireless microphone and wireless mouse or presentation controller will facilitate changing projections and images while you move around the room and interact more directly with students.

Interactive Technology

An internet-connected computer is essential for the large classroom because music and videos can be excellent engagement triggers and showing a short clip will grab students' attention much more than simply talking about a scenario. Several websites provide examples of movies,[8] songs[9] and news clips[10] specifically tied to economic concepts.[11]

Technology can also be used to facilitate interactive techniques like think-pair-share and conceptests. In particular, personal response devices ("clickers") allow instructors to quickly and easily gather information from any number of students. Clickers are handheld devices that students can use to respond to a question (generally multiple-choice or numeric); the clickers communicate with a receiver attached to the instructor's computer and the software tallies up the student answers. A common use of clickers is to have students engage in "peer instruction" which is similar to think-pair-share.The instructor asks a question[12] and students respond individually with their clickers, then students discuss their answers with their neighbors and the question is asked again. Clickers can also be used to collect data from in-class simulations; for example, Salemi (2009) explains how he has students use clickers to submit bids in an auction, thus generating willingness-to-pay data to create a demand curve. Bruff (2009) provides an excellent introduction to many of the issues instructors encounter when using clickers, while Salemi (2009, 2010) discusses clickers specifically in an economics context. Hoyt et al. (2010) provide additional examples in economics, including a discussion of how clickers can be adapted to assess open-ended and graphing questions.[13]

Content Delivery Outside Class

One of the challenges of making classes more interactive is the time required for class activities, time that would traditionally be used to "cover" more material. Moving some content delivery outside of the classroom can free up class time without necessarily reducing the amount of material covered. In addition to traditional readings, podcasts can provide students with basic introductions so that class time can then be spent exploring the concepts more deeply. Podcasts are pre-recorded "mini-lectures" (commonly in the audio mp3 file format, but they might also incorporate video or screencasts) that students can download and listen to anywhere. The mobility of podcasts is a big advantage over readings; they also give instructors additional flexibility to discuss material that is not in the readings or that you want to cover differently than your textbook. Richardson (2006) provides a good overview for anyone getting started with podcasting.

A short pre-class quiz on the covered content will ensure that students listen to podcasts or complete assigned readings, and understand the material before coming to class. Most course management systems (such as Blackboard, Moodle, WebCT) have modules that allow instructors to administer online quizzes. In addition, many textbook publishers have test bank software that can be easily integrated with these systems. Alternatively, instructors could use clickers to ask a review question (or questions) at the beginning of class, before beginning more in-depth discussion.[14]

While podcasts can be used to provide students with material before they come to class, lecture capture is a way to make material available to students who miss class or who want additional review.[15] In the broadest sense, lecture capture refers to any recording (audio and/or visual) of what happens in the classroom (Educause, 2008). Many students already engage in a simple version of lecture capture when they bring their own recorders to class; a more formal version is for the instructor to record the lecture and make the recording available to all students, such as through a course management system or a specific educational site like iTunesU. The recordings might be audio alone or could include "screencasts" that capture the slides and other material presented on the computer screen. Lecture capture can be particularly useful for large-enrollment courses, given how easily students may be distracted, and the recordings give them a way to review material.[16]

Assessment

For instructors of large-enrollment courses, perhaps the most useful application of technology is assessment. Assessment can be a time-consuming part of teaching any class, and the idea of assessing large numbers of students, either in or out of class, can be overwhelming. For in-class activities, like think-pair-share or conceptests, clickers make it relatively easy to administer and grade any number of student responses. For out-of-class assignments, one option is to use a course management system. This has the advantage for the students of being free and is an environment they are likely to be familiar with; a big disadvantage for the instructor is that the content generally must be created and formatted by the instructor, although as mentioned earlier, some textbook publishers have test banks that can be integrated with Blackboard or WebCT.

There are also online tools, such as Aplia and MyEconLab (from Pearson Publishing), that provide interactive exercises for students; these can be used in conjunction with various textbooks or alone, and may require students to pay an additional fee. With these sites, assignments are graded automatically and students receive immediate feedback about their responses. In addition to multiple-choice and numeric questions, these sites typically allow students to manipulate graphs and may be able to accommodate simple free-response questions as well. Some programs also provide other resources, such as online experiments, tutorials, and electronic versions of the textbook. See California State University (2009) for a more extensive discussion of the advantages and disadvantages of these programs, as well as a detailed comparison of Aplia and MyEconLab.

It should be acknowledged that, although clickers and web-based programs can make assessment much more manageable, faculty may be concerned that these tools give students many opportunities for cheating. Unfortunately, there has been very little research done on this issue so it is difficult to say how serious the concern should be. One way to reduce the temptation to cheat is to limit these types of assessments to a relatively small percentage of the overall grade.

CONCLUSION

Teaching an effective and engaging large-enrollment course in economics poses unique challenges, but also offers unique rewards. Significant time and attention must be devoted to planning and classroom management, the development of interactive teaching strategies and the effective use of classroom technologies. But when the large-enrollment course is taught well, the teaching economist can promote economic literacy with a large number of students.

NOTES

1. By comparing pre- and post-course test results for 6000 students from high school and university physics courses, Hake (1998) found significantly more improvement in students in courses that used interactive-engagement methods (including classes over 100 students) than in those that did not.
2. Wenzel (1999) reviewed research on college lectures and reported that the longer the lecture, the less of the material ended up in the students' notes. He also reported that a class that used a think-pair-share learning structure for two-three minutes for every 12–18 minutes of lecture remembered more of the lecture material directly after the class and 12 days later than the control class that heard the same lecture without the think-pair-share breaks.
3. For more information, see the Chapter 4 in this volume on cooperative learning.
4. See Chapters 7 and 8 on experiments and interactive lecture demonstrations, respectively.
5. Also see Salemi (2009, 2010) for discussion of conceptests in economics.
6. For more information on assessment techniques, see Chapter 16 "Methods of Assessment in the College Economic Course" in this volume.
7. Interactive whiteboard technology allows the user to "write" on top of whatever is on the screen, using the mouse, so presentations could be annotated in class.
8. www.moviesforecon.com (accessed 5 May 2011)
9. http://divisionoflabour.com/music/ (accessed 5 May 2011); http://www.musicforecon.com/ (accessed 5 May 2011).
10. http://class.ysu.edu/~mfm/ (accessed 5 May 2011).
11. For more information on the use of technology in class, see Chapter 13 on incorporating media and response systems in the economics classroom.
12. Questions intended for peer instruction are generally designed to elicit a mixed answer distribution; for example, by having wrong answers that specifically incorporate common student misconceptions. See Mazur (1997) for more discussion of peer instruction.
13. For more information on the use of technology in class, see Chapter 13 in this volume.
14. For alternative methods of developing questions, see Chapter 9 on just-in-time teaching.
15. This can be a particularly relevant issue for large classes where the sheer number of students makes one-on-one assistance outside of class increasingly difficult. That is, if 10% of students seek your help in a class of 50, you only have to deal with five students; in a class of 500, that same 10% becomes unmanageable.
16. Some faculty may be concerned that students will use the recordings as a substitute, not complement, for attending class; however, multiple studies have found that this is generally not the case (Zhu and Bergom, 2010). Attendance is also less likely to be an issue when classes are interactive and provide an experience students cannot receive elsewhere.

REFERENCES

Bruff, D. (2009), *Teaching with Classroom Response Systems: Creating Active Learning Environments*, San Francisco: Jossey-Bass.

California State University (2009), "Transforming course design in principles of microeconomics", http://teachingcommons.cdl.edu/tcd/. accessed 5 May 2011.

Davis, B. G. (1993), *Tools for Teaching,* San Francisco: Jossey-Bass.

Educause (2008), "Seven things you should know about lecture capture", http://www.educause.edu/ELI/7Thin gsYouShouldKnowAboutLectu/163555, accessed 5 May 2011.

Hake, R. (1998), "Interactive-engagement vs. traditional methods: A six-thousand-student survey of mechanics test data for introductory physics courses", *American Journal of Physics*, **66**, 64–74.

Hoyt, G., J. Imazeki, M. Kassis and D. Vera (2010), "Interactive large enrollment economics classes", in M. K. Salemi and W. B. Walstad (eds), *Teaching Innovations in Economics: Strategies and Applications for Interactive Instruction*, Cheltenham, UK and Northampton, MA, USA: Edward Elgar, pp. 220–42.

Keenan, D. and M. H. Maier (2004), *Economics Live: Learning Economics the Collaborative Way,* fourth edition, New York: McGraw-Hill.

Kennedy, P. E. and J. J. Siegfried (1997), "Class size and achievement in introductory economics: Evidence from the TUCE III data", *Economics of Education Review,* **16** (4), 385–94.

Lyman, F. (1987), "Think-Pair-Share: An expanding teaching technique", *MAA-CIE Cooperative News,* **1**, 1–2.

Maier, M. H., J. Bangs, N. Blunch and B. Peterson (2010), "Context-rich problems in economics", in M. K. Salemi and W. B. Walstad (eds), *Teaching Innovations in Economics: Strategies and Applications for Interactive Instruction,* Cheltenham, UK and Northampton, MA, USA: Edward Elgar, pp. 170–89.

Mazur, E. (1997), *Peer Instruction: A User's Manual,* Upper Saddle River, NJ: Prentice Hall.

Richardson, W. (2006), *Blogs, Wikis, Podcasts and Other Powerful Web Tools for Classrooms,* Thousand Oaks, CA: Corwin Press.

Salemi, M. (2009), "Clickenomics: Using a classroom response system to increase student engagement in the principles of economics course", *Journal of Economic Education,* **40** (4), 385–404.

Salemi, M. (2010), "Presentation on peer instruction at the 2010 Robert Morris Education Conference", http://www.unc.edu/~salemi/Papers/Peer%20Instruction%20with%20Clickers.pdf, accessed 14 January 2011.

Watts, M. and W. Becker (2008), "A little more than chalk and talk: Results from a third national survey of teaching methods in undergraduate economics courses", *Journal of Economic Education* (Summer), 273–86.

Wenzel, T.J. (1999), "The lecture as a learning device", *Analytical Chemistry,* **71**, 817A–819A.

Zhu, E. and I. Bergom (2010), "Lecture capture: A guide for effective use", University of Michigan CRLT Occasional Papers, (27), http://www.crlt.umich.edu/publinks/CRLT_no27.pdf, accessed 1 June 2010.

11 Teaching economics Socratically
Kenneth G. Elzinga

Socratic dialogue is a teaching method that has been around for centuries.[1] It is a pedagogical approach implemented most often today in law schools. Think of the iconic academic movie *The Paper Chase*, where Professor Charles W. Kingsfield, Jr. terrified first year law students with his belligerent questioning. There are very few Professor Kingsfields teaching the subject of economics.[2] Indeed, Socratic teaching in the economics classroom is rare compared to the use of lecture or student recitation.[3]

Teaching Socratically is unusual not only in the economics classroom. Most professors in any field of Arts and Sciences do not teach their classroom material in this manner. Yet it may be that many talented students want to have this kind of classroom experience.[4]

Teaching an *economics* class Socratically is, in two ways, a misnomer. First, Socratic dialogues (classically construed) involve only two people, one asking the questions, and the other trying to respond. Socrates supposedly engaged in this kind of dialogue with various citizens of Athens. Plato formalized the Socratic style when he wrote the *Socratic Dialogues*, in which Socrates asks a question and then reformulates a new question in light of the response. In today's educational setting, virtually all classes in economics have multiple students; they are not one-on-one tutorials.

Second, Socratic teaching is dialectical and philosophical. The dialogues of Socrates dealt with weighty content. For example, someone might say to Socrates, "Courage is the endurance of the soul" or "Wealth does not bring goodness" and that would set Socrates off on a series of questions that might end up with the speaker finally conceding that "Courage is not the endurance of the soul" or that "Goodness causes wealth." This is not to say the topics discussed in an economics classroom are frivolous. But it would be idle to contend that they match up to the moral and epistemological concerns of Socrates.

By teaching Socratically, I mean the *method* Socrates used: that of asking a line of questions, where each question is based upon the response given to the prior question.[5] In this method of teaching, one point of view or proposition is tendered and then subject to such extensive questioning that the point of view or proposition may be modified or even rejected.[6] The Socratic method is one where a student is expected to defend, expand upon, possibly change course, and ultimately illuminate the topic at hand through the process of the questions and answers themselves. In Socratic dialogue, students learn not by professorial exposition but by professorial inquisition.

It is an open question whether the Socratic method teaches *what is true*, by way of sequential questions that expose error; or whether the Socratic method, at its taproot, teaches a very different lesson: *how little we know to be true*. Socrates was considered to be the wisest man around, but this was because he saw the road to truth involving knowing what is not true. In this sense, the American humorist Will Rogers was a contemporary of Socrates: Rogers maintained, "It's not what you don't know that hurts you, it's what you do know that ain't so." Socratic teaching can be thought of as ferreting out what students know that ain't so.

SETTING THE STAGE FOR SOCRATIC METHOD

When I use the Socratic method in a course, I first must teach students what Socratic teaching is, what the ground rules are, and how to do it. Early on in my career, I expected students to know (or to catch on by themselves) how Socratic teaching works. That was a mistake. Now, I present a short lecture on the subject before we begin so they will know what to expect from me and what I expect from them. So let me start by explaining what students are told will be the ground rules of Socratic teaching.

Questions and Answers

I inform them the process begins with my asking a student an initial question and typically there will be more questions to follow with this same student. Most questions I ask will have a bit more depth to them than this one, but let's say, for purposes of illustration, the question is: *When was the Sherman Act passed?*

Students learn that there is a set of four legitimate and proper responses that can be given.

- A direct answer to the question, looking at the teacher, not down at the desk. The teacher asked the question. Not the desk.
- A question back to the teacher requesting clarification of the question put to the student. For example, a student might say, "well there are several pieces of legislation associated with Senator Sherman. Which one did you have in mind?"
- A request for time to think, and then eventually an answer. Forming a response before giving it is an important rhetorical skill for students to acquire. It helps avoid shooting from the hip. Socratic teaching helps develop this skill.
- A simple statement: *"I do not know."* Or, if a student wants to dress that up a bit: "I'm not prepared to answer that question just now. But would you call on me again later?"

Any of these answers is within the ground rules for Socratic dialogue in the classroom. Students must be instructed that there also are improper responses. Socratic dialogue will not flow if responses are out of bounds.

One out-of-bounds response would be: "Well, is the answer 1890?" The professor's question is not to be answered with a question (unless it is a question of clarification). One element of Socratic teaching is to encourage students to develop the courage of their convictions, even if they are mistaken. As an aside, I warn students to avoid "I feel" answers. They may "feel great" in class. But they ought not to *feel* anything about the Court's opinion in *Addyston Pipe and Steel* or about how to calculate a Herfindahl index. If they want a prefatory remark before responding to a question, encourage them to begin with "in my judgment, . . ."; "I am persuaded that . . ." instead of "I feel the Sherman Act was passed in 1890."

Another out-of-bounds response involves using someone else's words other than the student's (such as reading an answer from the course textbook). Students are to answer in their own words and not to read the textbook or assigned reading back to the professor and the class. Socratic teaching is an exercise in teaching students to think and then speak (not look in a book and then read). There may be a time for reading an answer, but it occurs when the responding student claims, "I can clarify this part of my answer by quoting this portion of the text (or assigned reading or some other source)."

Student Responsibilities

Many students find Socratic teaching disconcerting until they become accustomed to it. Conventionally taught students expect their teachers to supply them with answers to questions raised in class. But in Socratic teaching, the professor rarely will say, in response to an answer, "That's correct," "Bingo," or "That's wrong." In pure Socratic dialogue, that does not happen. The professor usually masks or hides his or her position. Some students need time to adjust to this.

Socratic dialogue works best if the students are asked to covenant among themselves that their motivation in correcting or clarifying another student's answer is not to dump on a classmate. It is to keep the record straight, because the professor will not be doing that. The students themselves will illuminate the material by a collective endeavor. If one student says the Sherman Act was passed in 1980, another student should correct the error, if only for the sake of others who do not know the correct answer (and for the sake of the class notes being accurate).

Finally, students who are unaccustomed to Socratic teaching must come to understand that one of the key elements in the success of Socratic dialogue is for them to *listen* to their classmates when they are not the student being called upon. A common tendency is for those students not called upon to breathe an audible sigh of relief. These students need to recognize that their task is, in a sense, more taxing than that of the student who is on the point. Students who get the most from a Socratically taught class are those who learn to listen carefully to their peers, and are always asking: is that a solid answer? What would *I* have said? They have two jobs: to think through how they would have responded had they been called on, *and* to evaluate the answer being given. The student who was called on has only a single task.

Finally, the professor who is teaching Socratically should let students know, after an issue has been discussed thoroughly, whether it is OK to ask if the professor has an opinion and if so what it is. Presumably this is always fair game during a professor's office hours and after class. Some teachers who teach Socratically demur on this at all times in the classroom.

Unlike lecturing, Socratic teaching has a public goods or communal characteristic. Student must be prepared for class. If they are unprepared, it is unlikely that there will be a good class experience. A professor can deliver a lecture before a class of unprepared students – and give a brilliant lecture – and unprepared students can learn from the experience. There is no brilliant Socratic dialogue with totally unprepared students. Indeed, in a Socratic-based classroom, it is fair game not to pursue or continue to question an unprepared class.[7]

Generally, students require a few class periods to adjust to the Socratic method. But once this happens, most students become engaged in the course and its material. They catch on that the professor will not supply the answer after a couple of failed attempts to respond to a question. Students realize that coming to class unprepared leads to a painful experience in front of their peers, whereas knowing the material makes them able to participate in the "game" everyone else is playing. This breeds a responsibility for keeping up to date with course readings and that, in turn, helps students get more out of the class.

PREPARATION FOR THE SOCRATICALLY TAUGHT CLASS

At first glance, a teacher might think that teaching Socratically would be easier than lecturing. After all, there is no lecture outline to develop. One simply asks questions – or so it may appear. Actually, even for experienced users of the Socratic technique, developing the line of questions can take more time than preparing a lecture.

Nobody disputes that a good lecture requires a thorough knowledge of the material. Socratic teaching requires more than a thorough knowledge of the material. To know the right follow-up question to a student's response generally means that the professor must know the level of understanding reflected in that response. Put differently, the right follow-up question rarely can be asked unless the teacher knows a lot about the material embedded in the "Q & A."

Some teachers who use the Socratic method think (implicitly if not explicitly) of Socratic teaching as being like a decision tree. A carefully thought through first question is asked with the expectation that the student-respondent will tender one of a handful of probable responses, call them A, B, C, and D. The teacher has each of these in mind when the initial question is asked. If the student offers response B, the professor also has in mind a follow-up question to that particular response. The pre-determined question is asked with a follow-up question for the expected set of responses. Each of these is considered prior to class (the equivalent, as it were, of preparing a lecture) and will be put in play, based on how the student answers.

There are two main challenges in implementing Socratic dialogue. Here is the first: just as "kids say the darndest things," students do not always offer any of the expected responses. At times, the response may be so "off the wall" that it is not anticipated. At other times, the response may be brilliant, but not expected. In either event, the teacher must be ready with a follow-up question. Usually, experience helps in this regard. Sometimes a classroom Muse will save the day. At other times, the Socratic dialogue flounders rather than flourishes. Socrates may never have had an off day, but mere mortals in the economics classroom will. Just as a lecture can go flat, so can Socratic dialogue. When these awkward teaching moments occur, the teacher using Socratic dialogue can revert to the lesson taught students earlier and say, "may I have a moment to form my next question."[8]

The second problem in Socratic teaching is that most people cannot keep a decision tree in mind that goes on for more than a few branches. But in teaching economics, this generally is not a significant obstacle to Socratic teaching. For most topics in the field of economics, the decision tree need not be a mighty oak with far-flung branches in order to get a particular lesson across.

SOCRATIC TEACHING AND STUDENT NOTES

Socrates expected the full attention of the person he was questioning. There is no evidence that, after each question from Socrates, the student stopped to take notes. Socratic teaching works best in the absence of note-taking. Indeed, note-taking cuts against the grain of Socratic teaching. A student being questioned cannot juggle taking notes on what was just said while thinking about a response to a follow-up question. In like fashion, students to whom the question was not addressed cannot shoulder the task of forming their own response to the question (had they been asked) *and* critique the response of the student responding – *and* take notes.

For these reasons, Socratic teaching works best with a designated note-taker. The student performing this function generally is excused from the Socratic dialogue for that class as he or she takes notes for the entire class. Economists will appreciate this as an application of Adam Smith's specialization and division of labor. The designated note-taker's endeavors become the notes for the class. The student who serves in this capacity is exempt from questions for that day. At the start of class, the note-taker receives instructions and the deadline for submitting that day's notes to the rest of the class.[9] At the end of the course, all students in the class have a set of notes more complete than if they tried to participate in the Socratic dialogue *and* take their own notes.

Most serious students, by the time they enter college or university, are hard-wired to take notes. If they hear something they believe to be important, they want to write it down, even when there is a designated note-taker. Because Socratic dialogue requires such a high degree of attention to the dialogue then going on, students who start to "write something down" may need to be called up short, and reminded that the designated note-taker is fully engaged in the task of compiling a written record of all that is said in class of importance. Most students, after they see the quality of the notes being taken by the "specialist," realize that this method will produce a higher quality set of notes than if they tried to take notes each day for themselves.

GRADING SOCRATIC DIALOGUE

In *The Paper Chase*, students were intimidated by the classroom questioning because they feared humiliation in front of their peers. They also recognized that part of their grade depended upon their classroom performance. In Socratic teaching, because the questioning of students is front-and-center as course pedagogy, most students assume their in-class performance will be graded. But the ministerial aspect of grading Socratic dialogue is problematic. There are essentially three options.

The first is, keep a record of how each student does *during* class. With this approach, when a student is asked a series of questions, before the next student is called upon, the professor stops a moment, records how that student did, then asks questions of another student. The problem with on-the-spot recording is that it affects the chemistry of the class: most every student, particularly the one just called upon in class, wonders what grade was recorded. Recording grades on-the-spot is very distracting to the class (and usually to the professor as well).

The second approach is to record student performance *after* class is dismissed. This enables the Socratic dialogue to move along without interruption. The problem with this approach is being able to reconstruct the quality of each student's responses later, after the professor has gone back to the office or home for the evening.

A third approach is to not grade on classroom performance, at least not explicitly.[10] This solves both problems. The professor may choose to assess classroom performance in letters of recommendation and, if a student is on the margin based on written course metrics, to bump up or bump down the grade in the course based on a general recollection of classroom performance.

SOCRATIC DIALOGUE AND CLASSROOM ATTENDANCE

Because there are network externalities in Socratic teaching that do not exist in straight lectures, it is important that all (or most) students be prepared. Otherwise the dialogue will not yield content that can be summarized and recorded in notes. Most students recognize that their preparation makes them potentially a positive externality in a Socratic classroom, and that a lack of preparation might make them a negative externality. A lack of preparation also raises the probability that students will be embarrassed in the classroom should they be called upon. As a consequence, a student who is not prepared, for whatever reason, may be more apt to cut any class that involves Socratic dialogue. There are two solutions to the externality problem.

The first is to encourage students to attend class, but offer them the option to be excused from being called upon (if they check in with the professor before class starts). There are any number of reasons good students may not be prepared for class discussion on a particular day (a term paper due the next day, an illness, etc.). An excuse from being called upon recognizes the legitimacy, in some circumstances, of not being prepared and encourages the students still to attend class, where the kind of skills mentioned earlier (that are to be developed when *not* called upon) can be developed. Another option is to ask the student who asked to be excused from questioning to serve as the designated note-taker for that day.

SOCRATIC DIALOGUE AND BREAKOUT GROUPS

Adopting Socratic teaching for a particular economics class does not mean Socratic teaching must monopolize the pedagogy for that course. Socratic dialogue lends itself to be blended with breakout groups.[11, 12] This may improve the overall classroom experience because Socratic dialogue can be intense and demanding for both students and teacher alike. In an economics class, a hypothetical problem or issue is put before the class. The parameters of the hypothetical are carefully explained (and put on a board or screen for future reference by the students). Students then go into breakout groups (usually of three to four members) to discuss and find solutions to the hypothetical.[13]

After time has elapsed, the class reconvenes and the professor conventionally asks one person in a group to articulate that group's collective response. The professor may then press that student on the group's response. If the spokesperson for that group seems to go off track, the professor may ask others in the group to chime in. As a variation on the

Socratic theme, the professor may ask other breakout groups (perhaps that have been assigned opposing views) to take over the questioning task.

THE OBJECTIVE OF SOCRATIC DIALOGUES

The conventional wisdom is that Socratic dialogue is fierce, with the professor looking for "gotcha" moments that intimidate students or impress them with the professor's talents. This need not be the case. Socratic teaching need not be a situation where only professors like Charles Kingsfield need apply. It is possible to use Socratic teaching to cajole students through back and forth Q & A, and to push students hard to induce them to be articulate – *and* at the same time for the students to realize that the professor is firmly on their side. Successful coaches have done this for years, pressing their athletes to perform, with the athletes knowing that this is for the good of the team. For years, physicians have prescribed unpleasant remedies for the long-run health of their patients. Socratic teaching may have its parallels to coaching and medicine. John Stuart Mill (1873, p. 45) once wrote: "A pupil from whom nothing is ever demanded which he cannot do, never does all he can." Socratic teaching is a time-proven method to take students into areas they otherwise never would be challenged to go.

NOTES

1. For an introduction to teaching Socratically, see Leal (2004), Nelson (2004), and Krohn (2004). Many readers have become acquainted with Socratic dialogue by the fictional encounter of Aldous Huxley, John F. Kennedy, and C.S. Lewis (all died within a few hours of each other), skillfully crafted by Kreeft (1982), a philosopher.
2. Walter Adams' legendary "Econ 444" class in regulatory policy at Michigan State University would be an exception that proves the rule.
3. Walstad and Saunders (1998, p. 9) report, "Passive instruction seems to be the norm in economics. . ." Becker and Watts (1998, p. 4) conclude, "[v]ery few economists have taken the time or trouble to teach using any method other than traditional lectures presented at the front of the room. . .the vast majority of economists fall into the institutional habit of 'talk and chalk.'" Perhaps today, it might be "talk and PowerPoint."
4. I have had waiting lists of two years for students who want to enroll in my Antitrust Policy class. This is not because most students are eager to learn this particular subject. They want to experience first-hand Socratic teaching but have few options to do so.
5. This is distinct from holding a discussion, which is described in Chapter 5 in this volume.
6. In law school, the initial proposition that begins the Socratic dialogue often is a student's interpretation of an important legal decision that was assigned reading for the class. The student called upon will be asked to summarize some part of the opinion. The student's exegesis of the case provides the jumping-off point for a line of subsequent questions in which the student will be asked to defend or expand upon his or her initial response.
7. I once had a class where the first three or four people I called on were unprepared. I adjourned the class. That group of students, beginning next time, became one of the best that I have taught.
8. A pensive look at this point may give students the impression that their professor is deep in thought, probing for just the right question, the class being unaware that the professor actually is unsure where to go next in the line of questioning.
9. Here is a summary of the note-taker instructions I use: (1) You are to take notes in class today and then type them later this evening. (2) Save the file as a Word document. (3) List: your name, the class date, the time of the class section, and the course title (Econ 420). (4) Tomorrow, email the notes to the class. Trepidant students are welcome to see a copy of exemplary notes from a prior year's class.
10. When I teach Socratically, the student's letter grade for the course is based on a final exam and a research

paper. The incentive to do well in classroom participation is based on wanting to acquire the skill of framing responses to unexpected questions, and (I suppose) the desire not to appear foolish in class before one's peers.

11.   http://www.thefreedictionary.com/break-out+group (accessed 12 January 2011).

12.   Please refer to Chapter 4 in this volume on cooperative learning for tips on effective group work.

13.   A variation on this theme, common in law schools where advocacy is a valued skill, is to assign breakout groups a particular point of view to defend (whether students actually hold that position or not).

REFERENCES

Becker, W. E. and M. Watts (1998), "Teaching Economics: What was, is, and could be", in W.E. Becker and M. Watts (eds), *Teaching Economics to Undergraduates*, Cheltenham, UK and Brookfield, MA, USA: Edward Elgar, pp. 1–10.

Kreeft, P. (1982), *Between Heaven and Hell*, Downers Grove, IL: InterVarsity Press.

Krohn, D. (2004), "Theory and practice of Socratic dialogue", in R. Saran and B. Neisser (eds), *Enquiring Minds: Socratic Dialogue in Education*, Staffordshire, UK: Trentham Books, pp. 15–24.

Leal, F. (2004), "The Socratic method: An introduction to the essay of Nelson", in R. Saran and B. Neisser (eds), *Enquiring Minds: Socratic Dialogue in Education*, Staffordshire, UK: Trentham Books, pp. 121–5.

Mill, J. S. (1873), *Autobiography*, New York, NY: Penguin Books, 1989.

Nelson, L. (2004), "The Socratic method", in R. Saran and B. Neisser (eds), *Enquiring Minds: Socratic Dialogue in Education*, Staffordshire, UK: Trentham Books, pp. 126–65.

Walstad, W. B. and P. Saunders (1998), *Teaching Undergraduate Economics*, Columbus, OH: McGraw-Hill.

12 Writing for learning in economics
Elizabeth Perry-Sizemore and Steven A. Greenlaw

Writing is a powerful tool for enhancing student learning. Research suggests that writing promotes a variety of positive learning attributes, including student engagement (Light, 1992), assimilation of lecture content (Crowe and Youga, 1986), comprehension of core concepts in economics (Wight, 1999) and critical thinking (DeLoach and Greenlaw, 2005). Yet it appears, based on Schaur, Watts, and Becker (2008), that most economics courses do not include writing assignments. This chapter explores how writing affects learning, and the roles that writing can play in the economics curriculum. Writing can be used effectively at all levels of the major, and in large lecture classes as well as small seminars. Writing exercises in economics can assume a wide range of forms, from informal assignments like in-class writing, reflection pieces and blog posts, to formal assignments like critical analyses, research proposals and research papers. This chapter provides suggestions for how economics faculty can manageably create and assess meaningful writing exercises for undergraduates.

WRITING PROMOTES LEARNING

Writing is not just a tool for communicating knowledge – it is also a creative activity, a tool for developing understanding, much like the way one completes a problem set, at times struggling to work out an answer. Writing is a means of discovery (Greenlaw, 2005; Thomson, 2001). Knoblauch and Brannon (1983) argue: "Writing enables new knowledge because it involves precisely that active effort to state relationships which is at the heart of learning. . . . It involves the sustained effort to select and order ideas as patterns of connection, and thereby to generate creative insights" (pp. 467–68). Indeed Jacobsen (1994) declares "strong evidence indicates that students who have writing assignments in their classes learn the material more effectively than those who do not" (p. 32).

Writing can be used to enhance class discussion and improve student understanding of lecture material and core concepts. For example, completing a short writing assignment prior to class requires students to think about the topic in advance, preparing them to contribute to discussion. At the end of class, Crowe and Youga (1986) propose a variation of the "minute paper" exercise, in which students are asked at the end of lecture to briefly summarize their understanding of the major topics presented.

Writing may also improve critical thinking. Field et al. (1985) argue that "being required to explain their economic understanding in writing during the learning phase of the course, rather than merely on the exam when the course is over, encourages students to organize their ideas and reexamine their beliefs" (p. 214). DeLoach and Greenlaw (2005) find that writing in electronic media promotes critical thinking skills in economics. More recently Dynan and Cate (2009) conclude that regular, short, structured writing assignments "improve student performance on lower-order learning assessment (the multiple-choice examination)," but that "structure may be only weakly claimed to enhance the performance of students on higher-order assessments" (p. 82).

Writing teaches students to learn the way experts learn, and in doing so fosters a deep approach to learning. Bain and Zimmerman (2009) distinguish between surface approaches to learning, exemplified when students cram for exams, overloading short-term memory and subsequently retaining little, and deep approaches, where students engage with content in ways that provide lasting understanding. Many students arrive at college better skilled at the former. Writing, because it demands active, thoughtful engagement with ideas, is more likely to develop a deep approach to learning than are passive pedagogies like lecture and reading. This type of engagement with ideas develops a deep approach to learning because it helps students transition from being novice learners to being expert learners. Expert learners understand how a discipline is organized, and as a result, their learning is enhanced by the ability to place new information in the context of that structure (National Research Council, 2000). Novice learners see new information as more or less random data points. By contrast, when experts learn, they quickly categorize new information and plug it into the appropriate part of their mental model of the discipline. In this regard, expert learning strategies provide a framework for a deep approach to learning.

The thinking of experts is organized around what Bransford et al. (1999) call "big ideas," or central concepts in the field. For economists these are the so-called "principles" of economics. Carefully constructed writing assignments help students explore and learn how to use concepts in ways that go beyond rote learning, in ways that mimic how experts learn. Such assignments require students to draw connections and identify relationships, which ultimately enable them to build the mental framework necessary for understanding and applying economic concepts more broadly. Simkins and Maier (2009) argue that

> students need to do economics, but with developmental guidance that encourages them to order ideas, structure their knowledge, and build confidence in their skills. By providing this "scaffolding," students can then be progressively challenged to develop more complex thinking processes that promote the acquisition of new skills and ideas, but with an underlying framework that makes the learning both deep and durable. (p. 85)

Writing is an excellent medium for implementing these learning processes, and as such, helps bridge the gap between novice and expert learning.

In sum, writing can be used as a tool for students to explore and ultimately improve their understanding of economic concepts and relationships, and to apply them in disciplinary appropriate ways. It is important, though, to remember that as economists our goal is not to teach writing, but rather to use writing as a tool for teaching and learning economics. Knoblauch and Brannon (1983) note, "Only the teacher of a particular discipline knows enough about the learning process characteristic of that field, the ways in which information is gathered and organized, the perspectives that apply, the ways in which problems are solved and questions answered, to respond in a manner" appropriate for disciplinary thinking and writing (p. 471). There should be no expectation that an economics instructor be a writing expert, only that he or she be an expert on economic thinking.

CREATING WRITING EXERCISES IN ECONOMICS

There are a wide variety of writing assignments which enhance teaching and learning economics. Writing assignments can be informal or formal, and can vary by genre, audience and purpose. They can be assessed formatively (to promote progress toward learning) or summatively (to judge a student's level of knowledge). Some types of writing assignments are better suited than others to achieving a given learning objective.

Using Writing Assignments to Promote Hansen's Proficiencies

Hansen, in this volume, describes a hierarchy of seven core competencies that economics students should master by the completion of their undergraduate program. These proficiencies can inform the creation of learning objectives which can then guide the instructor in selecting the types of writing exercises to create and how best to assess them.

Short writing assignments can engage students in displaying command of a particular economic concept. For instance, principles students can demonstrate an understanding of opportunity cost by not only defining it in their own words, but identifying and explaining the opportunity cost of a choice they recently made. This exercise motivates students to understand the concept of opportunity cost rather than simply memorize a textbook definition.

Some writing assignments can achieve multiple learning objectives. When students prepare an op-ed essay in which they identify an externality in the local community and recommend and justify a means of dealing with it, they practice accessing, displaying and applying economic knowledge.

Quantitative writing exercises are another way to achieve multiple learning objectives. Such exercises require students to organize and examine data and communicate in writing the conclusions that can be drawn from it. In contrast to word problems with unambiguous answers, quantitative writing exercises require students to deal with ill-structured problems, problems that resemble many real-world problems in that they may be framed in different ways and lack unique answers. These types of problems require individuals to deal with ambiguous data or to carefully compare multiple points of view. Such tasks lead to higher-order learning (King and Kitchener, 1994). For example, students can be asked to collect data for several economic indicators from the last several decades and then make a judgment about which decade had the best economic performance. Greenlaw (n.d.) offers best practices in quantitative writing, as well as a database of specific examples of simple, medium-level and advanced quantitative writing exercises in the discipline.[1]

Research papers, assigned as a component of a course or as the focus of the entire course, can help students create knowledge. McGoldrick (2007) describes the relationship between Hansen's proficiencies and the research process in economics. A complex writing assignment like a research paper can achieve multiple learning objectives and strengthen student understanding and appreciation of what it means to "do economics." Research papers advance students from proposing questions amenable to economic analysis to actually developing and testing hypotheses about them. Learning objectives can help the instructor choose the level of autonomy students have in each step of the research process. For instance, in some cases the instructor may provide the data, while in others the students obtain it themselves. Borg (n.d.) describes a project in which students examine effects of race and ethnicity on a state's high school graduation rates by reviewing literature, forming a hypothesis, determining a methodology, collecting and analyzing data and reporting the results.[2] Perry-Sizemore (n.d.) details ways to facilitate student research and provides a database of examples that use writing to promote learning in undergraduate research experiences.[3]

Choosing the Form of Writing Assignment

After considering learning objectives, writing exercises can be further defined by establishing the audience for and purpose of the writing. Writing exercises can also be designed to be informal or formal, and of a particular genre.

Bean (n.d.) asserts that "[W]riting for different audiences and purposes not only helps students learn to transfer writing skills from one context to another but also deepens engagement with subject matter concepts."[4] Thus, using a variety of assignment types enhances student learning of economics.

Writing can be addressed to oneself (for example, notes about a journal article), the instructor – this is the default students assume when the assignment does not specify the audience – to the students' peers or to an outside audience (for example, policy makers, the general public). Each of these audiences expects and responds best to a different style of writing. When writing to an audience of experts, disciplinary jargon is appropriate. However, when writing to a lay audience the same language may obstruct readers' understanding, and attempting to define the jargon within the text is a delicate exercise – while it can educate, it has the potential to overwhelm and distract from the piece's mission. Here students have to learn to strike a balance.

A writer also writes with a particular purpose in mind. Some writers write to summarize or interpret, others to evaluate or recommend. The writer's goal can be to inform but not persuade, or to inform and persuade. Each of these purposes offers useful assignments for economics.

Learning objectives, audience and purpose can help the instructor determine if a writing exercise should be formal or informal. Formal writing typically involves a process that focuses on a student's own understanding of a particular issue in the discipline and requires her to learn a genre's conventions for organizing and presenting that knowledge to others. By contrast, informal writing can be thought of as exploratory writing – writing for the primary purpose of helping the writer herself discover what it is she knows.

Most formal writing assignments in economics fall into one of Palmini's (1996) four identified genres: research studies, social criticism, policy analyses and business analyses. Formal writing assignments are typically assessed in summative ways, although, as argued below, this need not be the case. Furthermore, formal writing exercises like research papers can include intermediate steps that themselves can be formal and informal writing assignments, assessed in either formative or summative ways (as described below). Examples of formal writing exercises include:

- One page summaries of articles from popular or professional journals
- Research abstracts of professional sources

- Two to five page critical reviews of articles, monographs or books
- Five page summaries of readings or points of view/schools of thought
- White papers
- Business analyses
- Opinion pieces
- Components of a research project: statements of the problem, literature surveys, theoretical analyses, data analyses, empirical analyses
- Research proposals
- Research papers (ten plus pages).

By contrast, informal writing assignments are not usually assessed by the conventions of formal writing, and when they are (as in the case of a rough draft), they are usually assessed in more formative than summative ways. Additionally, it may not even be necessary to collect or review informal writing. Stand-alone informal writing exercises have their own value, as they can shift student awareness from the *product* of writing to the *process* of writing to learn. Informal writing exercises can provide scaffolding for improving both the product and process of more formal writing assignments. There are numerous examples of informal writing exercises:

- *Research journals* require students to record ideas for possible projects, identify why these are interesting and refine them into research questions with testable hypotheses. Although a journal provides scaffolding for a course with an independent research paper, it can also be a free-standing exercise that helps students move closer to understanding disciplinary practice by using the language of and knowledge in the discipline to develop research questions and lines of inquiry.
- *Personal journals* contain entries where students react to what they are learning. They can be spaces for students to challenge the assumptions of a model, make connections between an economic concept and a decision they have made, identify what material they find interesting or challenging and make connections between the course material and "the real world," or the course and extracurricular activities or career aspirations. For example, students can be asked to find and read an article in the popular press which implicitly or explicitly employs an economic theory or model. Students can then identify the model and explain how it is used in the article.
- *Freewrites* are documents composed in a short time period during class in response to an instructor prompt, usually related to something just read and about to be discussed. For instance, prior to class discussion of price discrimination, students can be asked to provide a written description of an instance where a producer might charge two different people different prices for the same good and to explain why such a scenario might exist. Freewrites concentrate students' thoughts prior to class discussion, making discussions more focused and meaningful. Regular freewrites can increase the likelihood that students prepare for and participate in class.

PREPARING STUDENTS

It is important for students to understand both why and how they are to write. Writing is not the same across all disciplines, and students need to be introduced to writing as economists. Presenting writing as a particular process – a medium for thinking through issues and problems that involves carefully considering subject, analysis and presentation – may be a novel idea to some students.

Students benefit from knowing in advance the expectations for each specific assignment. Identifying the exercise as formal or informal writing and specifying the genre help students understand what the assignment involves. Students may have little to no prior experience with informal writing, and experience with formal writing may not be with the genres typical in economics. Most students will know what a letter to the editor is, but they may not know what a policy analysis entails. If an assignment type is new to students, they will need more direction. Providing and discussing a sample assignment with a model answer helps students understand what they are being asked to do.

The importance of process can also be explained. For formal writing, students benefit from the chance to mull over the subject and to write multiple drafts, using each draft as an opportunity to not only edit but to rethink content and approach, to ask themselves, "Are my arguments clear?" and "Is the evidence persuasive?" Failing to start the process early enough to allow time for asking and responding to these questions may compromise the quality of the final product. These habits can be developed using informal writing as well. For instance, weekly research journals can encourage students to return to earlier thoughts, clarifying them and building upon them.

Students also benefit from knowing the assignment's purpose, be it to summarize an article, analyze or evaluate an article, or persuade the audience of a particular point of view. Even informal assignments benefit from an explanation of purpose, whether it be to foster personal reflection, stimulate class discussion or encourage students to pay closer attention to the class or readings. Communicating the chosen learning objectives and the rationale for them can go a long way toward helping students achieve the goals of the assignment.

Students should also be informed whether they are expected to draw and communicate conclusions, and, if so, to understand why doing so enhances their learning. Students find summary easier than evaluation, since with the latter there may be no obvious answer. This makes students uncomfortable since they are acutely aware they might choose "wrong." For some assignments, there is not always one right answer; rather, a reasoned argument is required. Such an assignment can promote student judgment and encourage students to make meaning for themselves of what they learn. By requiring students to grapple with the unknown and to draw conclusions when there may be normative aspects to the evidence at hand, higher-order cognitive skills are promoted.

Students also need to know if and how they will be assessed. Beyond knowing whether assessment is formative or summative and how much weight an assignment receives, when students are asked to draw conclusions and make personal reflections, they may worry about how their work will be received if the instructor doesn't agree with their perspective. In the case of informal journals, students may need to be reassured the instructor is looking for evidence that they are thinking actively, working to interpret knowledge, and considering its relevance outside the classroom – not that they are expected to share the instructor's interests or opinions. Students also need to know the attention that will be given to writing quality. For an informal in-class writing assignment where students are writing for themselves, grammar and spelling may not receive a high level of scrutiny by the instructor. But if a formal research paper is required later, students should be told that writing quality can affect an audience's ability to understand the content of the paper, and communicate how that will be considered in assessment. More generally, when students are given an assignment, they can be provided with a grading rubric, since if they understand more fully how the paper will be evaluated, the quality of the writing is likely to improve.

ASSESSING WRITING

Writing is an excellent tool for both summative and formative assessment. Crowe and Youga (1986) portray writing as "an activity, a process of recording thought while the thinking and learning are occurring and after they are completed – thus reflecting both the 'technique of thinking' and the 'conclusions'" (p. 219). Compare for example the responses on a multiple choice exam to an essay exam: with the former we know what the student thinks, but not why. By responding to the thought processes expressed in student writing, an instructor can guide students to a better understanding of how economic analysis is employed (Petr, 1998, p. 228).

In a summative approach to assessing a paper, the instructor thinks about how well the student has met the goals of the assignment and determines an appropriate grade. Feedback to the student tends to identify the flaws in the paper to justify the grade given. For an assignment with multiple drafts, one hopes the student will incorporate the feedback from early drafts into subsequent ones. Often though, the student simply corrects the flaws identified by the instructor, expecting to obtain a higher grade on the subsequent draft, when she really should take the opportunity to reimagine her argument. If the assignment is limited to the initial draft, ideally the student will incorporate that feedback into subsequent assignments.

Multiple draft assignments also offer excellent opportunities for formative assessment. Instead of criticizing where the draft has fallen short, the instructor can simply ask questions about the paper, leading the writer to clarify what is opaque, and to provide evidence that is lacking. This approach, which has much in common with the way faculty respond to written work by colleagues, is likely to result in greater student learning, since it doesn't merely provide answers. A summative response is still appropriate for the final draft, but inclusion of the formative process can enrich the associated learning process.

How can Economics Teachers Assess Writing Efficiently?

Assessing student writing does not require one to grade the writing per se, just the economics. A common rule of thumb is that if the writing quality distracts from the content, it is appropriate to deduct points because the content is unclear. Providing a model of good writing for students to refer to and pointing out errors of exposition will help students improve their composition. It is not necessary to mark all the errors in the paper – doing so may even be counterproductive from the formative perspective discussed above. It's preferable to simply mark the errors on the first page of an assignment draft, to provide a model for correcting the rest of the paper.

When one takes the perspective that writing is a *learning* tool, one no longer feels the obligation to grade every written product. Consider the case in which students keep a weekly journal. Credit can be given for completion of journal entries, and skimming can reveal whether the student is generally adhering to the assignment's requirements. Larger classes can be divided into groups, with different groups submitting their journals for review on different weeks. Another option is to ask students to select a portfolio of entries, a subset of the total, to submit for a grade. Since this option requires students to reflect on which entries to include, it can reinforce the learning process.

Shorter papers also ease the grading burden and can lead to enhanced learning. Asking students to condense their thinking is good practice, since it makes them think carefully about what is important and worthy of retaining and keeps them from padding to meet some minimum page limit.

A Well-Structured Assignment Makes Assessment Easier

As noted in the previous section, well-structured assignments have clearly stated learning objectives. These, in turn, provide the basis for assessment. For example, if the assignment begins: "Your answer should address the following questions," then the paper content can be skimmed until an answer for each question is encountered, at which point a more careful reading is warranted. If students are required to present an argument supported by evidence, the paper can be browsed until the main assertion of the argument is presented and then read carefully for supporting arguments. If one purpose of the assignment is to show mastery of a particular economic model, graphs can be required to illustrate the analysis. The graph can provide a quick, initial evaluation of student comprehension, while the text should be read more carefully to insure student understanding of the graph's analysis. Note that graphs should illustrate a written argument, not substitute for it.

One way to structure more substantial writing assignments, e.g. research papers, is to divide them into logical components, due sequentially and reviewed or graded consecutively over the term. If multiple drafts are assigned, assessment of initial drafts saves time in evaluating the final version, especially when one retains notes from the earlier drafts.

The Value of Rubrics

Stevens and Levi (2005) define a rubric as "a scoring tool that divides an assignment into its component parts and objectives, and provides a detailed description of what constitutes acceptable and unacceptable levels of performance for each part" (p. 3). Rubrics make grading quicker, easier and more focused. They do this by directing attention to the specific learning goals of the assignment and away from tangents.

The form of a rubric can vary from simple to complex, and can be holistic or analytic. It can be composed of a short list of criteria which one marks plus, check or minus. Alternatively, it can consist of a detailed matrix listing each assessment element and allowing a range of numerical ratings. McGoldrick and Peterson (2011) provide a theoretical discussion of the value of rubrics in teaching economics, and offer several practical and modifiable examples of rubrics for economics assignments.

One strong advantage of rubrics is that the process of designing one focuses the instructor on identifying exactly what he or she is looking for in the assignment. Ideally, rubrics are created while preparing the assignment sheet, so that the assignment sheet is most helpful to students. Greenlaw (2005) provides rubrics for research proposals and papers, and DeLoach (n.d.) provides one for a senior thesis. Both resources focus on higher-level writing assignments, but they suggest ideas applicable to other assignments.

CONCLUSION

Far more than a tool for demonstrating what one knows, writing is a powerful tool for learning economics. Knoblauch and Brannon (1983) characterize writing as a tool of intellectual dialogue between student and teacher, in which the student presents initial thinking to which the teacher responds. "The teacher here is not an examiner, . . . but rather an intellectual guide whose concern is to lead the less knowledgeable toward fruitful lines of inquiry of interest to them both" (p. 471). The techniques described in this chapter can make the costs of assigning writing very manageable. In short, writing is a teaching tool that deserves serious consideration by any economics instructor.

NOTES

1. http://serc.carleton.edu/econ/quantitative_writing/quantitative_wr.html (accessed 16 March 2011).
2. http://serc.carleton.edu/econ/studentresearch/examples/36498.html (accessed 16 March 2011).
3. http://serc.carleton.edu/econ/studentresearch/index.html (accessed 16 March 2011).
4. http://serc.carleton.edu/econ/quantitative_writing/index.html (accessed 16 March 2011).

REFERENCES

Bain, K. and J. Zimmerman (2009), "Understanding great teaching", *Peer Review* (Spring), 9–12.
Bransford, J. D., A. L. Brown and R. R. Cocking (eds), (1999), *How People Learn: Brain, Mind, Experience, and School*, Washington, DC: National Academy Press.
Crowe, D. and J. Youga (1986), "Using writing as a tool for learning economics", *Journal of Economic Education*, **17** (3), 218–22.
DeLoach, S. (n.d.), "Economics Senior Thesis", in Starting Point: Teaching and Learning Economics: Undergraduate Research Module, http://serc.carleton.edu/econ/studentresearch/examples/36324.html, accessed 16 March 2011.
DeLoach, S. and S. A. Greenlaw (2005), "Do electronic discussions create critical thinking spillovers?", *Contemporary Economic Policy*, **23** (1), 149–63.
Dynan, L. and T. Cate (2009), "The impact of writing assignments on student learning: Should writing assignments be structured or unstructured?", *International Review of Economics Education*, **8** (1), 64–86.
Field, W. J., D. R. Wachter and A.V. Catanese (1985), "Alternative ways to teach and learn economics: Writing, quantitative reasoning, and oral communication", *Journal of Economic Education*, **16** (3), 213–17.
Greenlaw, S. A. (2005), *Doing Economics: A Guide to Understanding and Carrying Out Economic Research*, Boston, MA: Houghton Mifflin.
Jacobsen, J. P. (1994), "Incorporating data collection and written reports in microeconomics", *Journal of Economic Education*, **25** (1), 31–43.

King, P. M. and K. S. Kitchener (1994), *Developing Reflective Judgment: Understanding and Promoting Intellectual Growth and Critical Thinking in Adolescents and Adults,* San Francisco, CA: Jossey-Bass.

Knoblauch, C. H. and L. Brannon (1983), "Writing as learning through the curriculum", *College English,* **45** (5), 465–74.

Light, R. J. (1992), *The Harvard Assessment Seminars: Second Report,* Cambridge, MA: Harvard University Graduate School of Education and Kennedy School of Government.

McGoldrick, K. (2007), "Undergraduate Research in Economics", in *Handbook for Economics Lecturers,* http://www.economicsnetwork.ac.uk/handbook/ugresearch/, accessed 16 March 2011.

McGoldrick, K. and B. Peterson (2011), "Assessing Student Learning with Rubrics", presented at the ASSA meetings, Denver.

National Research Council Committee on the Addendum to National Science Education Standards on Scientific Inquiry (2000), *Inquiry and the National Science Education Standards: A Guide for Teaching and Learning,* R. Olsen and S. Loucks-Horsley (eds), Washington, DC: National Academy Press.

Palmini, D. J. (1996), "Using rhetorical cases to teach writing skills and enhance economic learning", *Journal of Economic Education,* **27**(3), 205–16.

Petr, J. L. (1998), "Student writing as a guide to student thinking", in W.B. Walstad and P. Saunders (eds), *Teaching Undergraduate Economics: A Handbook for Instructors,* Boston, MA: Irwin McGraw-Hill, pp. 227–43.

Schaur, G., M. Watts, and W. E. Becker (2008), "Assessment practices and trends in undergraduate economics courses", *American Economic Review,* **98** (2), 552–6.

Simkins, S. and M. Maier (2009), "Using pedagogical change to improve student learning", in D. Colander and K. McGoldrick (eds), *Educating Economists: The Teagle Discussion on Re-evaluating the Undergraduate Economics Major,* Cheltenham, UK and Northampton, MA, USA: Edward Elgar, pp. 83–91.

Stevens, D. and A. Levi (2005), *Introduction to Rubrics: An Assessment Tool to Save Grading Time, Convey Feedback, and Promote Student Learning,* Sterling, VA: Stylus Press.

Thomson, W. (2001), *A Guide for the Young Economist: Writing and Speaking Effectively about Economics,* Cambridge, MA: MIT Press.

Wight, J. B. (1999), "Using electronic data tools in writing assignments", *Journal of Economic Education,* **30** (1), 21–7.

Section B

Technology

13 Incorporating media and response systems in the economics classroom[1]

Joseph Calhoun and Dirk Mateer

The active use of media and technology is having a measurable impact on economic education. Instructors have access to a wide array of media (movies, music, television, and news-related) content that pertains to economics. In addition, technology is increasingly playing a vital role in economic instruction. Classroom response systems ("clickers") and other in-class communication channels are transforming the traditional classroom and allowing for real-time feedback that faculty can use to assess learning. We also discuss the merits of response systems such as Live Question that enable students to post questions and answers during class. In this chapter, we explore sources and uses of media and technology, providing an overview with the hope that readers will feel emboldened to implement or expand these techniques in their own courses.

USING MEDIA TO TEACH

Media provides a unique communication channel that motivates and reinforces learning. The effective use of media can enhance a student's learning experience and complement many traditional approaches to learning by enhancing student retention, motivating interest in the subject matter, and helping to illustrate the relevance of many concepts (Serva and Fuller, 2004). The use of media serves as a scaffold to help transfer knowledge from the instructor to the student, increasing the efficiency of the learning process.

Understanding the learning process is one of the goals of neuroscience research on brain functioning. Researches in the neurosciences have documented differences in functioning between the left and right hemispheres of the brain. The left brain specializes in digital, deductive tasks that characterize oral and written media, while the right brain specializes in iconic, intuitive tasks that characterize visual media, especially the visual and sound characteristics of film (Springer and Deutsch, 1998). Neuroscience, learning sciences research, and media and cognition research point compellingly to using multimedia in a teaching program (Bransford, Brown, and Cocking, 1999).

Media can be used to enhance learning. Short film and television clips, written articles, and blog postings[2] can be viewed to reinforce concepts and spark discussion. Songs and music videos, especially when the lyrics are made available, can be used to the same effect.

Media in Economics

Ben Stein's role as a high school economics teacher in *Ferris Bueller's Day Off* (1986) demonstrates a "dismal" view of the economics profession and the teaching of economics. However, economic education does not have to be the exclusive domain of the lecture model as portrayed in the film and as evidenced by the work of Becker and Watts (2008) who examine the way that economics is taught at the college level and find that the discipline has been slow to adopt innovative approaches to teaching. There are many new and exciting teaching methods available to instructors, none more so than using media (music, news, video and visualizations) to enhance teaching and learning in economics.

To demonstrate the use of media in illustrating economic concepts, our discussion will focus primarily on film clips. Films are a familiar medium to students, enhancing their interest in theories and concepts as they view them in action. Many feature films and television shows have very high production quality, capable of showcasing complex ideas in a short period of time. Students can hone their critical thinking skills by analyzing clips, then applying the theories and concepts to what they are studying. Students can also experience worlds beyond their own, such as what life would be like in other countries, cultures, and unfamiliar environments. Film media also generates both cognitive and affective experiences. It can provoke discussion of economic concepts as well as an assessment of one's values and self if the scenes have strong emotional content. With respect to instructors, a positive consequence of utilizing media is that instructors are encouraged to keep their materials and examples up to date.

An Example – The Hudsucker Proxy

The Hudsucker Proxy (1994) is a period film that chronicles the introduction of the hula hoop, a toy that set off one of the greatest fads in United States history. According to Wham-O, the manufacturer of the hoop, when the toy was first introduced in the late 1950s, over 25 million were sold in four months. In the movie there is a scene that illustrates the difference between a movement along a demand curve and a shift of the entire curve, a subtle point with which many students struggle.

The Hudsucker Corporation has decided to sell the hula hoop for $1.79. In the key scene, we see the toy store owner leaning next to the front door waiting for customers to enter, but business is slow. Next, the movie cuts to the President of the company, played by Tim Robbins, and we see him sitting behind a big desk waiting to hear about how the launch of the hula hoop is going. It does not go well. The price starts to drop, first to $1.59, then to $1.49 and so on down until the hula hoop is "free with any purchase." Even this is not enough to attract consumers. So the toy store owner throws the hula hoops out into the alley behind the store, and one of them rolls across the street and lands at the foot of a boy who is skipping school. He picks up the hula hoop and tries it out. He is a natural. About this time school lets out and a throng of students rounds the corner and sees him playing with the hula hoop. Suddenly everyone wants a hula hoop and there is a run on the toy store. Preferences have changed, and the overall demand has increased. The hula hoop craze is born and we account for this by shifting the entire demand curve to the right. The toy store responds by ordering new hula hoops and raising the price to $3.99, which happens to be the new market price after the increase, or shift, in demand.

The entire scene lasts three minutes and provides a memorable way for students to learn. Since most students have never seen the movie, showing the clip in class provides a fresh reference point that aids learning.

Useful Media Websites for Economics

In this section we group media websites into four categories: music, news, video, and visualizations. We restricted each list to a handful of websites in order to showcase the best examples of each type of media.

Music resources

- *Flash Music for Economics* (Mateer and Rice, 2007). Contains 50 animated songs that provide an economic interpretation of the artist's original lyrics.
- *From ABBA to Zeppelin, Led: using music to teach economics* (Hall, Lawson, and Mateer, 2008). Offers a variety of songs and lyrics that instructors of economics can use.

News resources

- *Media for Microeconomics* (Porter, 2009). A database over 300 citations to audio and video stories about topics covered in principles of microeconomics from major news outlets.
- *Stossel in the Classroom.* Videos by John Stossel (mostly from his reports on ABC News and 20/20, and more recently on Fox Business News) for use in both microeconomics and macroeconomics courses.
- *Freakonomics Radio.* Podcasts from Steven Levitt and Stephen Dubner, authors of *Freakonomics* and *Superfreakonomics.*
- *NBC Learn.* Microeconomic and macroeconomic news footage from NBC news.

Video resources

- *Movies for Economics* (Mateer and Li, 2008). Provides a database of feature films that cover most concepts in principles of economics.
- *Television for Economists* (Ghent, Mateer and Stone, 2011). Provides a database of television episodes that relate to principles-level economics.
- *Economics in the Movies* (Mateer, 2005). Is a collection of 20 streaming videos supplemented by questions designed to test economic understanding for principles of economics.
- *The Economics of Seinfeld* (Ghent, Grant, and Lesica, 2010). This website showcases scenes from *Seinfeld* that are useful in teaching a variety of economic concepts.
- *Teaching Economics with YouTube* (Mateer, 2007). Contains a set of media resources related to economics on YouTube along with a small sample of many of the best student-generated economics uploads.
- *Fear the Boom and the Bust* (EconStories, 2010). This rap anthem compares the ideas of Keynes with Hayek.

Visualization resources

- *Gapminder* (Rosling). This extensive and unique approach to utilizing data increases student interaction with statistical data by producing videos, Flash

presentations and PDF charts showing major global development trends with animated statistics in colorful graphics.
- *GeoFred* (Federal Reserve Bank of St. Louis). This web application allows users to create thematic maps based on a particular set of economic data.

Instructors interested in the latest media resources should also access Starting Point: Teaching and Learning Economics, a portal designed to service economic educators.[3] This website, along with the *Journal of Economic Education* online section, provides an extensive list of media for use in instruction.

Some Cautions about Using Media

One concern that inevitably arises pertains to copyright issues that accompany using this medium in teaching. The use of film scenes, music, and content found on the Internet during class, falls under the fair use exemption in the Federal Copyright Act (Section 110.1, in the Federal Copyright Act, Public Law 94-553, Title 17). The display of copyrighted materials during face-to-face teaching permits the instructor to show entire feature-length films, play music, or use articles so generated under most circumstances. The crucial factor is that the public showing of any media is narrowly defined for educational purposes and the instructor must take steps to ensure that the copyright holder's interests are protected. Placing copyright material on the Internet, even for class purposes, violates the fair use exemption. For this reason, the promulgation of education-related media over the Internet has been severely limited.

In addition, instructors interested in using media oftentimes have additional setup costs (for example, prepositioning a DVD at the start of a scene before class or digitizing media for playback on a computer, along with making sure that the audio-visual equipment is functioning properly beforehand). Furthermore, the content of media scenes (for example, humor, drama, terror, and language) may distract some students from the theories and concepts the scenes portray. Some students may become offended by media with objectionable content.

Finally, utilizing media takes time away from other classroom activities. By using selected media that are short (generally ten minutes or less), the instructor can focus on specific theories or concepts with fewer distractions from content that is unrelated to the learning objectives. As a result, instructors need to decide whether the media makes its point efficiently and with enough effect to warrant the use of class time.

USING CLASSROOM RESPONSE SYSTEMS TO TEACH

A Classroom Response System (CRS) is a technology which enables an instructor to ask questions during class and receive electronic answers from all students (which can be saved to generate grades at a later time). Students commit by submitting their answer via the system, which subsequently generates a histogram displaying the distribution of answers for the entire class. Both the instructor and individual student receive immediate feedback on the extent of concept comprehension in the form of this visual summary.

Questions can be embedded into a PowerPoint presentation or asked as stand-alone questions posed throughout the class period. A CRS is also known by other names such as a Personal Response System, Audience Response System, Student Response System, Electronic Response System, Electronic Voting System, and Classroom Performance System. Most people simply refer to such a system as "clickers" because the transmitter used to send answers looks like a TV remote control.

A Classroom Response System (CRS) is a technology that can be used in conjunction with other learning strategies to enhance student learning. However, simply inserting some questions facilitated by using a CRS into an economics lecture is not likely to produce the desired results. The tool must be carefully combined with an overall pedagogical strategy; CRS is most effective when it is viewed as a *way* of teaching, not just a new technology to add to a class. A Classroom Response System offers many opportunities to combine the technology with other teaching pedagogies, including ConcepTests, Just-In-Time Teaching, Cooperative Learning, Interactive Lectures, Classroom Experiments, and Interactive Lecture Demonstrations. For example, clickers work well as a cooperative learning tool. Students can be directed to discuss the question during the time allotted to answer or can discuss the question after the results histogram is displayed. Instead of the instructor explaining the correct answer, students could explain the answer to their peers. Instructors interested in other pedagogical tools should access Starting Point: Teaching and Learning Economics.[4]

Caldwell (2007, p. 13) summarizes the literature on CRS as, "Most reviews agree that 'ample converging evidence' suggests that clickers generally cause improved student outcomes such as improved exam score or passing rates, student comprehension, and learning and that students like clickers." In economics, Salemi (2009, p. 400) reports results based on a survey conducted over several semesters of his introductory economics class. He finds that "Nearly 90 percent of students recommend their (CRS) continued use and 69 percent agreed or strongly agreed that the course was designed to keep them engaged." Economists are realizing their potential to dramatically alter and improve their classes.

Changing Student Perceptions and the Classroom Culture

A CRS has the potential to change the culture of the classroom. Trees and Jackson (2007, p. 38) suggest "the final effectiveness of the clicker will rest with each student accepting the potential of clickers to positively affect their learning. The success of the clickers is in many ways dependent on social, not technological, factors. Instructors must work to facilitate student acceptance and to frame student perceptions of the technology."

Determining the role a Classroom Response System will play in the classroom environment is a critical decision for instructors. A formal or informal style may be adopted, the technology can be mandatory or optional, and it can be implemented in many different ways. Salemi (2009) proposes the following clicker strategies for the principles course: (1) sampling student opinion, (2) asking "Are you with me?" questions, (3) acquiring economic data from students, (4) peer instruction activities, and (5) games and simulations.

An Example – "Are You with Me?" Questions

One of the most common points of confusion for principles of economics students is the difference between demand and quantity demanded. After a careful presentation of these ideas, an instructor may be inclined to ask, in some form or another, "Does everybody understand the difference?" A CRS question can be a more effective substitute in that it requires students to demonstrate their understanding immediately. Consider the following two CRS questions as examples:

1. When economists say the demand for a product has increased, they mean the
   a) demand curve has shifted to the right.
   b) price of the product has fallen, and consequently, consumers are buying more of it.
   c) cost of producing the product has risen.
   d) amount of the product that consumers are willing to purchase at various prices has decreased.
2. When economists say the quantity demanded of a product has decreased, they mean the
   a) demand curve has shifted to the left.
   b) demand curve has shifted to the right.
   c) price of the product has fallen, and consequently, consumers are buying more of it.
   d) price of the product has risen, and consequently, consumers are buying less of it.

When the distribution of answers is revealed in the histogram, both the instructor and the students will know if they understand. High incorrect response rates suggest that students don't know the difference as well as they should; information which is valuable for the instructor in determining whether he or she should move on to the next topic or engage students in additional reviews of demand and quantity demanded concepts.

Combining media and CRS can prove to be very powerful. Consider the increase in understanding that is likely to occur when the instructor adds these two techniques to a traditional lecture about demand and quantity demanded. After a brief introduction of the concepts, students view the *Hudsucker Proxy* video clip. Then the instructor provides more detail and constructs demand curves. Two CRS questions are added to the end of the discussion to gauge student understanding. The concepts have now come alive in a new way and students' understanding is assessed before moving forward. If a majority of the class correctly answers the questions posed, it can serve as a signal to those who incorrectly answered about the degree of effort they need to put forth in the future.

Technical Issues Associated with a Classroom Response System

Every CRS system has three common features. The first is a receiver which accepts answers or responses from students. It is plugged into a computer via a USB connection. The second is a transmitter or clicker which transmits responses. The older technology, infrared (IR) transmitters, which are line-of-sight devices that transmit a beam of light to the receiver, has given way to radio frequency (RF) devices that transmit a radio signal to the receiver. Third, each system requires software to store and manage the data.

A CRS can be integrated with PowerPoint or used as stand-alone software. Either way, the same questions can be asked and data are collected in the same manner. Most systems allow for two methods to ask questions. The most common is a pre-created question that is typed into the software or PowerPoint slide before class and asked at a predetermined time. Alternatively, instructors can create a question "on the fly" during class, providing flexibility and spontaneous creativity when using the system. Since data is received and stored electronically, answers can be quickly graded. The data can be manipulated in a spreadsheet or exported into files that are readable by most learning management systems such as Blackboard, WebCT, or Angel.

CRS technology can be equally effective in large or small classes, but it is usually associated with large class instruction. As Hoyt et al. (2010) discuss, a clicker question will allow the student to answer a question anonymously in class, engaging students who might be shy or uncomfortable taking risks answering questions in front of their peers. Since their answer is known to the instructor after class, a student must commit to an answer instead of sitting idly and watching others participate.

Challenges and Issues with Using a Classroom Response System

On any given day, instructors employing CRS are likely to hear students make the following claims: "I forgot my clicker," "My clicker isn't working," "I didn't get to answer one of the questions." Absenteeism also generates missing grades and a wealth of excuses. It is best to formalize the consequences of non-participation resulting from those and similar situations and include them in the syllabus and grading policies. A common way to deal with these issues is to implement some kind of "forgiveness" policy so that missing some questions will not harm a student's grade. The following grading policy has been used by an instructor who's been using clickers for several years. Each clicker answer is awarded one point for an incorrect response and three points for a correct response. At the end of the semester, students' earned point totals are summed and divided by the number of points possible. Students earn full credit for the clicker portion of their grade if they earn 75 percent or more of the points possible. For any percentage less than 75 percent, the student earns their percentage multiplied by the clicker portion of the grade. So if a student earned 50 percent of the clicker points, they would earn 50 percent of the clicker portion of their grade. The clicker portion is 15 percent of the total course grade. Thus, a few absences, technical issues, or even incorrect answers will not prevent students from earning full credit for the clicker portion of their overall grade.

Instructors may find that cheating on clicker questions is a problem, especially in large classes. By providing clear definitions of cheating and its consequences on the syllabus, these events can be minimized. While some instructors discourage "chit-chat" or sharing of information when students are answering questions as a way to combat cheating, other instructors use clicker questions to actively encourage student discussions. Reinforcing the learning goals associated with the CRS will help students see the value in answering questions on their own. Another common cheating avenue is when one student has two or more clickers and is answering on behalf of another absentee student. Again, outlining the consequences of this behavior on the syllabus can provide students with incentives to not engage in this practice. The best way to combat cheating is to walk around the room and watch students as they answer. In a large lecture hall, one or more teaching assistants can be assigned to monitor the room with the instructor.

As with any technology, it is prudent to have a backup plan in case the software or computer fails. The simplest policy is to just cancel the clicker points for the day. Trying to collect data manually and enter it into the clicker software is usually not a feasible option, and a makeup policy might be difficult to administer. As with any data, regular backing up of clicker data is important. Lost or corrupted data will be virtually impossible to restore or recreate.

Useful Classroom Response Systems Websites for Economics

This section offers online resources instructors can access to aid in their selection and implementation of a CRS that fits their needs.

CRS manufacturers

These are the current major companies that manufacture response systems. Product details, tutorials, downloads, and contact information are provided on the company web sites. Barber and Njus (2007) and Burnstein and Lederman (2003) offer reviews of the clicker technology available.

- eInstruction Personal Response System: http://einstruction.com/products/assessment/prs/index.html
- eInstruction Classroom Performance System: http://einstruction.com/products/assessment/cps/index.html
- iClicker: http://iclicker.com
- Turning Point: http://www.turningtechnologies.com
- Qwizdom: http://qwizdom.com
- Poll Everywhere is a web- and cell-phone based Classroom Response System, available at http://www.polleverywhere.com/sms-classroom-response-system

"How to" videos, user support, and demonstrations

- Starting Point: Teaching and Learning Economics at the Science Education Resource Center at Carleton College introduces economists to innovative teaching strategies developed both within and beyond the discipline of economics: http://serc.carleton.edu/econ/classresponse/index.html
- One extraordinarily rich resource is a set of high quality videos about using clickers in the classroom from the Science Education Initiative at the University of Colorado and the Carl Wieman Science Education Initiative at the University of British Columbia: http://www.cwsei.ubc.ca/resources/SEI_video.html
- Vanderbilt University's Center for Teaching and Learning has an extensive set of resources about and demonstrations of the use of clickers: http://www.vanderbilt.edu/cft/resources/teaching_resources/technology/crs.htm

- Derek Bruff, the Assistant Director for Vanderbilt University's Center for Teaching and Learning, has a blog about teaching with a classroom response system: http://derekbruff.com/teachingwithcrs/
- EDUCAUSE, a nonprofit association advancing higher education technology, offers research and reports about classroom response systems: http://www.educause.edu/Resources/Browse/ClassroomResponseSystems/28524
- Classroom Clickers is a website comparing classroom response systems and school adoption procedures. Case studies from different institutions are documented: http://www.classroomclickers.com/
- Florida State University's Center for Teaching and Learning has online resources for using clickers and best practice strategies: http://learningforlife.fsu.edu/ctl/explore/bestPractices/prs.cfm
- The University of Wisconsin System clicker project: http://www4.uwm.edu/ltc/srs/
- The University of Wisconsin System Learning Technology Development Council document what four UW system campuses learned while adopting clickers: http://www.uwsa.edu/olit/ltdc/epedagogy/

LIVE QUESTION

Live Question[5] is an educational tool developed at Harvard University and is an example of a promising emerging technology. This free resource allows an instructor to solicit anonymous feedback from students, by logging into an administrative interface that allows students to post questions in real-time during class using a smart device. Student users can then vote on their favorite questions, with those receiving the most votes rising to the top of a queue. Once a particular question is answered, it can be hidden or deleted so that remaining questions are prominently displayed. Live Question is a technology that facilitates horizontal information flow from one student to another instead of the more common student-instructor interaction.

Live Question can be used as a tool to organize interactive review sessions where the material that is covered is determined by the questions and votes that are received. Live Question can also be used during any particular class period to uncover questions about material in a timely manner. In both cases, instructors should be careful to quickly review the posted content before projecting the questions to the entire class. While Live Question is more structured than other social media (such as Twitter and Facebook), its live and informal nature invites a level of familiarity that occasionally produces odd or amusing questions that faculty may not wish to post. To combat this issue, the administrative interface allows faculty to quickly delete these questions to keep attention focused on the content.

This tool is especially effective in large classes where some students are reluctant ask questions and participate in front of their peers. Large classes also provide the scale necessary to create the traction for use. While smart technology is becoming more pervasive – it is not ubiquitous – so, at least for now, smaller classes may not have enough students with smart devices to create a representative sample of student questions.

If you are interested in a more detailed description of how Live Question works, there is a handy description put out by EDUCAUSE titled, "7 Things You Should Know About Live Question Tool."[6]

CONCLUDING THOUGHTS

Informal research and anecdotal evidence suggests students have more fun and enjoy economics more with these new teaching techniques. Media, clickers and Live Question can be effective because they appeal to students' regular lifestyles of watching videos and texting. They are already part of students' cultural norms, therefore students can easily incorporate them into their learning process. Instructors are also realizing benefits. In addition to receiving real-time feedback about class retention and knowledge level, they are changing the culture of their classrooms to make them more interactive, interesting, and fun.

These teaching techniques are not designed to add to the instructor's already full slate of material to cover; they can be used to supplement or augment the material that's already being covered. After gaining some experience, instructors adopting these techniques will find they have only to give up a small amount of class time to implement the methods. The opportunity cost is small compared to the increased benefits of learning and understanding that students will achieve.

NOTES

1. All websites referenced in this chapter were accessed on 9 June 2011.
2. For more information about the use of blogs, see Chapter 15, "Economic Blogs and Economic Education", in this volume.
3. http://serc.carleton.edu/econ/index.html.
4. http://serc.carleton.edu/econ/index.html.
5. http://cyber.law.harvard.edu/questions/chooser.php.
6. http://www.educause.edu/ELI/7ThingsYouShouldKnowAboutLiveQ/170032.

REFERENCES

Barber, M. and D. Njus (2007), "Clicker evolution: Seeking intelligent design", *CBE – Life Sciences Education*, **6** (1), 1–8.
Bransford, J., A. Brown and R. Cocking (1999), *How People Learn: Brain, Mind, Experience, and School*, Washington, DC: National Academy Press.
Burnstein, R. A. and L. M. Lederman (2003), "Comparison of Different Commercial Wireless Keypad Systems", *The Physics Teacher*, **41**, 272–5.
Caldwell, J. E. (2007), "Clickers in the large classroom: Current research and best-practice tips", *Life Sciences Education*, **6** (1), 9–20.
EconStories (2010), http://econstories.tv/2010/06/22/fear-the-boom-and-bust/, accessed April 23, 2011.
Ghent, L. S., A. Grant and G. Lesica (2010), "The economics of Seinfeld", http://yadayadayadaecon.com/, accessed April 23, 2011.
Hall, J., R. Lawson and G. D. Mateer (2008), "From ABBA to Zeppelin, Led: Using music to teach economics", *Journal of Economic Education*, **39** (1), 107.
Hoyt, G., J. Imazeki, M. Kassis and D. Vera (2010), "Interactive Large Enrollment Economics Courses", in Michael K. Salemi and William B. Walstad (eds), *Teaching Innovations in Economics: Strategies and Applications for Interactive Instruction*, Cheltenham, UK and Northampton, MA, USA: Edward Elgar.
Mateer, G. D. (2005), *Economics in the Movies*, Mason, OH: South-Western, Thomson.
Mateer, G. D. (2007), "Teaching Economics with YouTube", http://www.youtube.com/dmateer.
Mateer, G. D. and T. Ferrarini (2009), "YouTube, economic education, and classroom assignments", Presented at the Council for Economic Education.
Mateer, G. D. and H. Li (2008), "Movie scenes for economics", *Journal of Economic Education*, **39** (3), 303.

Mateer, G. D. and A. Rice (2007), "Using music synchronized with lyrics to teach economics", *Perspectives on Economic Education Research*, **3** (1), 53–64.

Mateer, G. D., L. S. Ghent and M. A. Stone (2011), "TV for economics", *Journal of Economic Education*, **42** (2), 207.

Porter, T. S. (2009), "Media for microeconomics", *Journal of Economic Education*, **40** (4), 447.

Rosling, H., "Gapminder", http://www.gapminder.org/, accessed April 23, 2011.

Salemi, M. (2009), "Clickenomics: Using a classroom response system to increase student engagement in a large-enrollment principles of economics course", *Journal of Economic Education*, **40** (4), 385–404.

Serva, M. A. and M. A. Fuller (2004), "Aligning what we do and what we measure in business schools: Incorporating active learning and effective media use in the assessment of instruction", *Journal of Management Education*, **28** (1), 19–38.

Springer, S. P. and G. Deutsch (1998), *Left Brain, Right Brain*, San Francisco: W. H. Freeman.

Trees, A. R. and M. H. Jackson (2007), "The learning environment in clicker classrooms: Student processes of learning and involvement in large university-level courses using student response systems", *Learning, Media, and Technology*, **32** (1), 21–40.

Watts, M. and W. Becker (2008), "A little more than chalk and talk: Results from a third national survey of teaching methods in undergraduate economics courses", *Journal of Economic Education*, **39** (3), 273–86.

14 Distance education: course development and strategies for success
Mary Mathewes Kassis

The use of distance education techniques to deliver course material has grown in post-secondary education. Distance education, where the instructor and student are in different locations, is not a new concept. Correspondence courses, the earliest form of distance education, have existed since the 1800s (Simonson et al., 2006). In recent years, distance education has become primarily associated with online courses that make use of technology to teach classes over the internet. In the 2006–07 academic year, online courses were offered by 61 percent of two-year and four-year post-secondary institutions, resulting in more than 9 million student enrollments (Parsad and Lewis, 2008). Online courses in economics have also been growing. Using survey data, Harmon and Lambrinos (2008) estimate that the number of online economics courses grew 373 percent between 1997 and 2000.[1] Most of the online courses in economics so far have been at the introductory level, although the number of upper-level and graduate online courses appears to be growing as well (Coates and Humphreys, 2003). The expansion of online distance education courses in economics presents both new challenges and new opportunities for faculty and students. This chapter lays out some issues involved in developing and implementing a new online economics course and offers ideas and strategies for instructors who teach online courses.

DEVELOPING AN ONLINE ECONOMICS COURSE

Instructor Training

Many instructors first become interested in distance education when they are asked to teach an online course. Since many college instructors have little or no experience with distance learning, they often need training to get started developing their course. Course management systems vary among schools, so the best place to turn for initial training is your university's distance education office, which often offers faculty training. This training can help faculty learn the basics of building an online course and can also help instructors identify other training resources available at their university. Another source of information for online instructors is the Faculty Focus website,[2] which contains reports with strategies and tips for online instructors and offers online training related to distance learning. If possible, taking an online course as part of the training process can be helpful since it gives instructors experience as online students, which can be useful as they design and teach their online courses.

Communication with Students

One important issue to keep in mind when developing an online course is the importance of organization and clear communication of expectations. It is critical that students understand how to find their assignments and course material and that they are clear on when assignments are due. Although students can email the instructor with questions, it takes time for the instructor to respond and this delay may frustrate the student and put them behind. I find it useful to set up my course with weekly learning modules that generally cover one textbook chapter. A week runs Monday to Sunday, although posting the module by the Friday before the week starts is advantageous because students have two weekends to work on it. Weekly homework assignments are due by Sunday night at 11:45 pm. Every Monday morning, students are emailed a description of the material that will be covered that week and the assignments that are due. In addition, the weekly learning module has an introduction that describes material for the week and a check-list that shows all the relevant assignments (textbook reading, videos, graded assignments, etc.). Modules are presented in outline form and contain links to all material that students need to complete that week's assignments. This learning module approach has worked well to help students understand what is expected, and students seem to appreciate having consistency in the structure of the course material.

Orienting Students

Clear communication is particularly important at the start of the course to make sure students understand the course structure and the syllabus. In most face-to-face classes, at least part of the first class is devoted to a course orientation. In the case of online courses, this orientation is even more critical for student success given the independent nature of their work. One approach would be to hold a face-to-face orientation. At the University of West Georgia, instructors can require students to come to campus twice during an online course, and many faculty choose to hold a mandatory face-to-face orientation (with students being dropped from the course if they miss the orientation without permission from the instructor). The face-to-face orientation is advantageous because instructors can demonstrate how to access course material, and it provides students with the opportunity to ask clarifying questions. Face-to-face orientations have been shown to improve student retention in online courses (Ali and Leeds, 2009). However, a face-to-face orientation may not always be practical since some schools do not allow face-to-face meetings in their online courses and some students may not live close enough to campus to make a face-to-face orientation feasible.

Course orientations may also be conducted online. In my online course, I use the first learning module to explain the structure of the course. An introductory video describes the basic structure of the course and directs students to an orientation module that contains the syllabus and a video explaining how to purchase the online textbook package. Students are also emailed on the first day of class, welcoming them to the course and telling them how to get started. As part of the orientation module, students are required to complete a syllabus quiz and an introductory icebreaker discussion assignment. These graded assignments help students take the orientation module more seriously and make sure they complete the module in a timely manner. A follow-up email is sent to students who do not complete the introductory assignments to make sure there is not a problem and that they are aware of the course requirements. In addition, students are offered an optional face-to-face orientation, but attendance has been low. In general, online orientation can be quite effective and is a reasonable alternative to a face-to-face orientation.

Course Content

Navarro and Shoemaker (2000) suggest that there are four important features that should be included in an online economics course: classroom-like multimedia lecture presentations, a threaded discussion board, a chat room for synchronous interaction, and electronic quizzing with instant feedback. Most course management systems have options for instructors to post documents, PowerPoint slides, and videos, as well as for having class discussion boards and chat sessions with individual students. Assessment options generally support both multiple choice and essay format. Using these features, instructors can design courses with both traditional lecture-style components as well as interactive student activities such as discussions and wikis. In fact, the variety of instructional options available give faculty the ability to develop online courses that students can tailor to their individual learning styles by spending more time on the activities they find most useful (Coates and Humphreys, 2003).[3]

Fortunately for online instructors, the growth of distance education courses has created a new market encouraging textbook publishers to develop internet-based resources that support the development of online course material. Many textbooks now have dedicated webpages containing quizzing, videos and test banks that are compatible with course management systems. Some publishers offer professionally edited video lectures. There are also several interactive online homework programs, including Aplia and MyEconLab, which provide instructors with the ability to assign interactive problems and experiments in their online courses. Many problems require the student to manipulate graphs and the programs offer students feedback, as well as the ability to re-do problems they did incorrectly, a feature that is not possible with many course management systems. These programs can be linked to a wide range of textbooks and can be customized by the instructor.

Videos[4]

In addition to using videos from textbook publishers, instructors can develop their own videos or use videos from other sources. Developing videos can be done relatively simply with narrated PowerPoint slides or via webcams using programs such as Impatica and Camtasia Studio. Another approach is lecture capture. Some instructors choose to film actual classroom lectures to use online, whereas other schools have set up studios where instructors can videotape mock lectures. In addition to instructor-lecture videos, other educational videos and media clips can be used in online courses just as they are in face-to-face courses. Some university libraries have digital collections available online which have videos that can be embedded into online courses. There are also many videos available at no cost on the internet that students can access through a link on the course homepage. These videos can be found by searching the internet or using the search tool in YouTube. For example, YouTube contains news clips from EUtube and the Associated Press. Instructors can also use the Economics Search Engine on the American Economics Association's Resources for Economics on the Internet website[5] to search for videos and other online resources at over 23,000 economics websites. In many cases, videos or movie clips that instructors would use in a face-to-face classroom can be digitized and used in online courses as long as the requirements of copyright laws are met.[6]

DISTANCE EDUCATION CHALLENGES

Student Retention

Distance education poses new challenges for instructors beyond those associated with course development. A major concern on many campuses is the high withdrawal rates in online courses, in some cases estimated at over twice the rate of traditional face-to-face courses (Vachris, 1999). Many schools have been looking for ways to help encourage student retention in online courses. On campuses where online courses are relatively new, students may not have realistic expectations about what an online course entails. Many first-time online students mistakenly believe the course will involve less work and will be easier than face-to-face courses. The reality is that most online courses require more commitment and at least as much work as a traditional course. One avenue for managing student expectations is through the advising process. Academic advisors can work to inform students of the nature of online courses, bringing their expectations in line with those of the instructor. Some schools require students to complete an online module describing the nature of online courses before they are allowed to register for their first distance education course. Student expectations can also be managed during the course orientation process as noted above. Other strategies to encourage retention include using discussion boards as a forum for discussing policies and procedures during the first few weeks of class, having instructors maintain regular contact with students at the beginning of the course, and faculty being willing to help students get assistance with technical problems (Morris and Finnegan, 2008–09). Over time, as students become more familiar with the online course environment, differences in withdrawal rates between face-to-face and online courses are likely to shrink, reflecting student self-selection into the environment that best suits their needs and learning style.

Cheating

Another challenge that online instructors face is cheating, since it may be possible that the person completing assignments is not the student registered for the course. Although some economists have argued that high transactions costs make it unlikely that a student would hire someone to take an online class for them (Vachris, 1999), internet technology has lowered the costs tremendously. An internet advertisement found by an instructor at the University of West Georgia where someone was offering to take an online course for someone else suggests a market for this type of cheating. A less radical, and perhaps more likely scenario, is that students are receiving assistance from other students or using unauthorized materials in completing their graded assignments.

While it is not possible to prevent all cheating in online courses, any more than it is possible in face-to-face courses, there are actions that online instructors can take to deter cheating. Harmon and Lambrinos (2008) found evidence that cheating was more likely if exams were not proctored. Some institutions allow faculty to require proctored exams in online courses. Students generally have the option to take the test on campus or at a proctored testing center off campus. Students are required to show a picture ID when they take the exam to verify that they are enrolled in the course. Although there is an administrative cost to requiring proctored exams, especially when students use off-campus testing centers, it is a good way to limit opportunities for students to cheat.

An approach that makes it difficult for students to cheat on un-proctored online exams is to put a time limit on the assignment and to limit the time window that the assignment is available to students. This makes it harder for students to get help from other students or to simply look up the answers in the textbook or on the internet. Students can also be required to take the exam using a lockdown browser, so they cannot access any other websites during the exam. Other approaches that have been suggested to reduce the incidence of cheating on online exams include password protecting tests, placing time limits on each question, having questions selected randomly from a pool of questions, and having the answer choices randomly ordered (Harmon, Lambrinos and Buffolino, 2008).

Time Costs

Online instructors also face challenges associated with the time commitment involved in developing and teaching online courses. There are significant start-up costs to developing an online course. Navarro (2000) finds that the majority of the online economics instructors he surveyed said that it took at least twice as long to develop an online course as it would take to develop a traditional course. Some schools have used course releases as a way to help compensate faculty who are developing new online courses, while some offer additional financial compensation for initial development of the course.

The extra time commitment does not end after the course is developed. Evidence suggests that the time spent teaching online courses is actually greater than the time spent teaching a traditional course (Navarro, 2000; Vachris, 1999). Unfortunately this is the nature of online courses – the act of teaching is not confined to a specific time window and instructors are teaching throughout the day. One approach to help manage the time demands is to set aside times each day to answer emails in your online course rather than trying to answer them as they come in. Cavanaugh (2006) offers other practical suggestions for managing instructor time in online economics courses: creating a FAQ to address common student questions and including a quiz or other graded incentive to ensure students read it; automatically posting the answers to quiz or homework problems so that students do not need to ask you to explain their grade; and giving students guidelines to make email more efficient, for example giving specific details such as page or problem number when asking questions about course material. Although online courses offer advantages, such as flexible schedules, distance education requires a different type of time commitment of which faculty and administrators need to be aware.

Efficiency

Although the number of economics courses offered online continues to grow, the impact of online teaching techniques on student learning is still not fully understood. Results from research studies comparing student performance in online versus traditional economics courses have been mixed. Navarro and Shoemaker (2000) found that online students perform as well or better than students in traditional courses. However, other studies have found that online students perform worse than traditional students (Brown and Liedholm, 2002; Coates et al., 2004; Anstine and Skidmore, 2005) or that the impact was insignificant or negative (Gratton-Lavoie and Stanley, 2009). Shanahan and Bredon (2006) argue that online students may not perform as well due to the difficulty of designing online courses that promote higher levels of thinking. While the pedagogy in face-to-face economics courses is still "chalk and talk" (Watts and Becker, 2008), the pedagogy in online economics courses appears to involve more active learning. Coates and Humphreys (2003) found that 76 percent of the online economics courses they surveyed used active learning techniques and 78 percent used interactive text-based material. As faculty experience with distance education grows, it seems likely that the mix of pedagogical techniques used in online courses will continue to grow. Rather than trying to replicate the traditional classroom on the internet, the future of distance education will likely be using technology to develop a different style of teaching and learning. Hybrid courses can also be developed that combine online learning with traditional class room teaching to give students the best of both environments.

CONCLUSION

The growing presence of distance education courses in economics is creating both new challenges and new opportunities for faculty. Teaching an online course requires faculty to learn new technology and teaching techniques; however, it also gives instructors the opportunity to use a variety of learning tools that can be adapted to meet the needs of students with different learning styles. Distance education offers colleges the ability to reach out to more non-traditional students who find it difficult to attend face-to-face courses. When online courses are introduced on campus, it is important to manage student expectations so that they understand what taking an online course involves. It is also important to manage faculty and administrator expectations about the time commitment involved in distance education. Distance education has a great deal of potential to meet the needs of students, but much research still needs to be done on the effectiveness of different pedagogical approaches in the online environment.

NOTES

1. This estimate comes from the results of two similar surveys. The economics departments responding to the 1997 survey offered 40 online courses and the departments responding to the 2000 survey offered 189 online courses.
2. www.facultyfocus.com (accessed 9 June 2011).
3. The problem with the variety of instructional options available to online faculty is that training is generally

required to ensure that instructors are aware of and know how to use all features of available course management systems. In addition to training new online faculty, the continual improvements to available technology suggest a need to provide training even for experienced faculty.

4. A discussion of the use of film clips can be found in Chapter 13, "Incorporating Media and Response Systems in the Economics Classroom", this volume.
5. www.rfe.org (accessed 9 June 2011).
6. Simonson et al. (2006) contains a detailed discussion of the copyright laws related to distance education.

REFERENCES

Ali, R. and E. M. Leeds (2009), "The impact of face-to-face orientation on online retention: A pilot study", *Online Journal of Distance Learning Administration*, **XII** (IV).

Anstine, J. and M. Skidmore (2005), "A small sample study of traditional and online courses with sample selection adjustment", *Journal of Economic Education*, **36** (2), 107–27.

Brown, B. W. and C. E. Liedholm (2002), "Can web courses replace the classroom in principles of microeconomics?", *American Economic Review Papers and Proceedings*, **92** (2), 444–8.

Cavanaugh, J. (2006), "Practical strategies for reducing the time spent teaching economics online", *Economics Bulletin*, **1** (2), 1–7.

Coates, D. and B. R. Humphreys (2003), "An inventory of learning at a distance in economics", *Social Science Computer Review*, **21** (2), 196–207.

Coates, D., B. R. Humphreys, J. Kane and M. A. Vachris (2004), "'No Significant Distance' between face-to-face and online instruction: Evidence from principles of economics", *Economics of Education Review*, **23** (5), 533–46.

Gratton-Lavoie, C. and D. Stanley (2009), "Teaching and learning principles of macroeconomics online: An empirical assessment", *Journal of Economic Education*, **40** (1), 3–25.

Harmon, O. R. and J. Lambrinos (2008), "Are online exams an invitation to cheat?", *Journal of Economic Education*, **39** (2), 116–25.

Harmon, O., J. Lambrinos and J. Buffolino (2008), "Is the cheating risk always higher in online instruction compared to face-to-face instruction?", *University of Connecticut, Department of Economics Working Paper*, *2008-14* .

Morris, L. V. and C. L. Finnegan (2008–9), "Best practices in predicting and encouraging student persistence and achievement online", *Journal of College Student Retention*, **10** (1), 55–64.

Navarro, P. (2000), "Economics in the cyberclassroom", *Journal of Economic Perspectives*, **14** (2), 119–32.

Navarro, P. and J. Shoemaker (2000), "Performance and perceptions of distance learners in cyberspace", *American Journal of Distance Education*, **14** (2), 15–35.

Parsad, B. and L. Lewis (2008), *Distance Education at Degree-Granting Postsecondary Institutions: 2006-07* (*NCES 2009-044*), Washington, DC: National Center for Education Statistics, Institute of Education Sciences, US Department of Education.

Shanahan, M. and G. Bredon (2006), "Teaching and Learning Economics at a Distance", in W. E. Becker, M. Watts and S. R. Becker (eds), *Teaching Economics: More Alternatives to Chalk and Talk*, Cheltenham, UK and Northampton, MA, USA: Edward Elgar, pp. 133–50.

Simonson, M., S. Smaldino, M. Albright and S. Zvacek (2006), *Teaching and Learning at a Distance: Foundations of Distance Education* (3rd ed.), Upper Saddle River, NJ: Pearson Education.

Vachris, M. A. (1999), "Teaching principles of economics without 'Chalk and Talk': The experience of CNU online", *Journal of Economic Education*, **30** (3), 292–303.

Watts, M. and W. E. Becker (2008), "A little more than chalk and talk: Results from a third national survey of teaching methods in undergraduate economics courses", *Journal of Economic Education*, **39** (3), 273–86.

15 Economics blogs and economic education[1]
Timothy C. Haab, Aaron Schiff and John C. Whitehead

Gone are the days when teachers and professors were forced to distribute paper hand-outs during class, when student research required a trip to the library and when professors had to require students to purchase a subscription to the *Wall Street Journal* to keep up with current events. The internet, aka web 1.0, has revolutionized teaching, allowing communication with email and posting of electronic syllabi and assignments and links to readings that can be accessed from any networked computer (Goffe and Sosin, 2005). A limitation of web 1.0 technology, however, is that it is a one-way street and professors are the drivers. Static course webpages are useful, but they limit the flow of information.

Dynamic web 2.0 technologies allow teachers, professors and students to interact and more easily share content, discuss and collaborate. Examples of web 2.0 technology include social-networking sites (for example, facebook), video-sharing sites (for example, YouTube), audio-sharing sites (for example, podcasts such as Econtalk[2]), collaborative webpages (for example, wikis such as Welker's Wikinomics[3]) and dynamic webpages (for example, blogs such as Marginal Revolution[4]). Web 2.0 technology promises to further revolutionize economic education by allowing professors and students greater ability to interact outside the classroom (as well as within the classroom). Professors can post video lectures[5] and develop lectures and other assignments along with students using wikis and blogs. Professors and students can communicate using Facebook groups, Facebook chat and Twitter in addition to old-fashioned email. Students can make up for absences with an online discussion or a laboratory experiment using decentralized software (Greenlaw and DeLoach, 2003; Bostian and Holt, 2009). Web 2.0 technology enhances active learning in a radical way (Greenlaw, 2011).

In this chapter we limit our focus to economics blogs.[6] Blogs are direct descendents of static webpages.[7] A blog is a dynamic webpage that is updated hourly, daily, weekly or only occasionally with posts of varying length (Ayres and Sachania, 2009). Posts can range from short comments about news article clippings to long essays about economic issues and current events. Economics blogs may focus on a narrow topic (for example, environmental economics) or discuss broader economic issues.[8] Blogs usually allow comments from readers which ultimately may generate a community of readers. Blogs can be read as a webpage or posts can be downloaded to a computer or mobile device with 'really simple syndication' (RSS). The sum of all blogs is known as the blogosphere; or in economics, the econoblogosphere. Blog posts can occur instantaneously with current events. A blogger can read a newspaper article and comment on it in a blog post within minutes of the newspaper's publication. Through blogging, economics teachers, professors and students have easy access to the unfiltered opinions of some of the top thinkers in economics (DeLong, 2006).

Greenlaw (2011) argues that blogs can be used by students for reflection on a topic, for student discussion and as a research tool. Blogs can be used by teachers and professors as a "learning management system." Ayres and Sachania (2009) describe a number of other ways that blogs can be used in economics courses. The first is for the professor to develop and maintain a class blog as a substitute for a class web page or syllabus. Also, professors can write their own blogs where the more substantive posts can serve as textbook supplements. Greg Mankiw, the author of the popular introductory textbook, has a "blog map" link for his textbook users.[9] His readers can access up-to-date examples of economics principles. The Environmental Economics blog offers "Environmental Economics 101" with primers, data and recommended readings.[10]

In addition, blogs can form the basis of student assignments. Students can be assigned blog posts as reading assignments. Students can be required to write posts for the class blog, compare positions on issues across blogs or write comments on other students' posts.[11] Students can even develop and maintain their own blog which would be ideal for courses with a research project component. The student blog could provide updates on the research process and posts about current events related to the topic.

In the rest of this chapter we describe the "market" for economics blogs with respect to economic education. In the next section we describe the product and market (in other words, the econoblogosphere). Then we describe the supply side (in other words, bloggers) and the demand side (in other words, blog readers) of the market. Finally, we provide a brief conclusion and discussion of economics blogs, teaching and opportunities for future research.

ECONOMICS BLOG MARKET

The econoblogosphere is a well-developed and growing niche of the academic blogosphere. The American Economic Association's Resources for Economists on the Internet[12] lists 73 blogs (in other words, the number of producers). The list of economics blogs at Wikipedia currently stands at 200. The Economics Roundtable,[13] maintained by William Parke of the University of North Carolina, aggregates posts from over 150 economics blogs. The Palgrave Econolog[14] lists 467 economics blogs. Brian Gongol collects and maintains visitation statistics for economics and business blogs.[15] Between June 2006 and March 2008 the number of economics and business blogs increased from 42 to 140. At the time of writing, the number of economics and business blogs included in the Gongol rankings is 166, with another 150 not providing enough data to be ranked.

According to Palgrave Econolog, the number of posts on economics blogs published per week is about 4000. According to Gongol, the average number of page views per blog, which can be interpreted as the equilibrium quantity in the market, ranged from 1700 to 2500 per day over the same time period. The total number of page views over the entire market increased from 80,000 to 350,000. The econoblogosphere is highly concentrated. The four-blog concentration ratio began at 44 percent in June 2006, quickly fell to 33 percent and then steadily rose to 50 percent by March 2008. At the time of writing, the number of daily page views is 454,000, an increase of almost 30 percent over the past 33 months. The four-blog concentration ratio is 52 percent. The ten-blog concentration ratio is 74 percent.

Given the amount of time academics have for blogging and their willingness to share that knowledge through teaching means that economics blogging is heavily influenced by academic economists. Of the top business and economics blogs in the Gongol rankings, a large percentage has primary or significant contributions from academic authors. Currently, the top five academic economics blogs include Marginal Revolution (Tyler Cowen and Alex Tabarrok at George Mason University), Economist's View (Mark Thoma at the University of Oregon), Greg Mankiw's Blog (Greg Mankiw at Harvard University), Overcoming Bias (Robin Hanson at George Mason University) and Carpe Diem (Mark Perry at University of Michigan, Flint).

Mixon and Upadhyaya (2010) use the academic reputation of economics bloggers, as measured by citations of the primary authors' scholarly work, to rank economics blogs.[16] They find that a ranking of economics departments based on the ranking of the blog authors' academic reputation is highly correlated with rankings of departments based on other criteria. Mixon and Upadhyaya (2010, p. 7) conclude that their findings are "consistent with the hypothesis that bloggers of higher scientific quality or credentials attract more attention."

SUPPLY SIDE

Why do bloggers blog? In this section we present some results of a survey of economics bloggers. The objectives of the survey were to assess the characteristics of these bloggers and understand their blogging activities and motivations for blogging (Schiff, 2008). In total, 183 different blogs were included, based on the criteria that most or all of their content be relatively closely related to economics. The common characteristics of all the included blogs are that they cover academic or professional topics, and are generally written by academics or professionals. In total, 104 complete responses are used.

Among survey respondents, about half of economics bloggers were aged under 40, and about 40 percent were between 40 and 60. Only 1 percent were 20 years old or younger, reflecting the fact that most economics blogs are written by professors or professional economists. Over 50 percent had been blogging for more than two years. About 58 percent of bloggers surveyed were employed at an academic institution, while 9 percent were students.

The average number of blog posts written over the past month was 33, with a median of 25. Most bloggers, 54 percent, spend less than 20 hours per month on tasks related to their blog. Fifty percent of their time was spent writing or editing posts and 36 percent spent reading or researching material for posts. Sixty-seven percent have third party advertising on their blogs and 73 percent of bloggers advertise their books, consulting services and other products. However, 52 percent of bloggers consider their payments from blogging to be very inadequate compensation.

Survey respondents were asked to rate ten different motivations for blogging. Public motivations of contributing to debates, public education and research dissemination rate relatively highly, as do the private motivations of fun/entertainment, profile raising and recording thoughts and ideas. Income, improving writing skills and getting reader feedback are relatively minor motivators for most economics bloggers. The drawbacks to blogging include the time required (only 5 percent rate the time required as not important), lack of interest from readers (80 percent), difficulties coming up with new material for posts (65 percent), concerns about adverse reputational effects (60 percent), inappropriate comments from readers (64 percent) and low actual or potential income (56 percent).

To investigate further the supply of economics blogging, we ran regressions on the quantity of blog posts over the past month as reported by survey respondents against a number of variables relating to the blogger's characteristics and motivations. The independent variables include whether the blogger had paid advertising on their blog, whether the blogger advertised other services they sell such as consulting or textbooks on their blog, the importance of advertising revenue as motivation for blogging, other potential revenue, blogger age, length of time blogging and the average amount of time spent writing each blog post. In contrast to the self-reported motivations of bloggers, the regression results suggest that actual and potential advertising revenue are significant drivers of the quantity of posts per month. This may be influenced by a relatively small number of professional bloggers in our data set who get paid to blog. Bloggers who spend less time on each post write more posts per month, which is not surprising. Some bloggers choose to write less frequent but more lengthy posts, while others generate frequent short posts.

DEMAND SIDE

The number of blog readers has also increased significantly over the past few years. In 2007, the *Wall Street Journal*'s "Numbers Guy," Carl Bialik, reported that between 16 percent and 50 percent of US adults were blog readers with varying intensity.[17] We conducted an internet survey of economics blog readers during March 2008. The primary purpose of the survey was to determine how much time users spent reading economics blogs relative to other reading activities and the purpose of that attention to blogs. The basis of our analysis is a convenience sample of 378 voluntary respondents to a call for participation at the (now retired) 26econ blog, the Environmental Economics blog and several other more prominent blogs. As such, it can not be considered representative of the economics blog reader, but the results are suggestive.

Ten percent of the sample identifies themselves as "a teacher or professor," 10 percent are "a non-academic professional economist in the public or private sector" and 48 percent are "some other kind of professional." Twenty-four percent identify themselves as a student. The average age is 34 years, weekly work hours are 29 and average annual personal income is $60 thousand. Eighty-seven percent of economics blog readers are male and 89 percent are white. Most respondents consider themselves politically liberal (36 percent), followed by libertarian (24 percent), independent (14 percent) and conservative (9 percent). Seventy-two percent of respondents live in North America and 21 percent in Europe.

Survey respondents also read multiple economics blogs. Thirty-nine percent read between one and five blogs, 31 percent read between six and ten and 26 percent read eleven or more economics blogs. The most popular blogs written by academic economists are, in order, Marginal Revolution (Tyler Cowen and Alex Tabarrok), Greg Mankiw's Blog, Freakonomics (Steven Levitt and Stephen Dubner), Conscience of a Liberal (Paul Krugman), and Economist's View (Mark Thoma).

Respondents were asked "What is the most important reason that you read economics blogs?" Of the suggested responses over 70 percent of respondents indicated "my own enjoyment/knowledge" and 13 percent indicated "research for my work or writing my own blog." Less than 10 percent use blogs primarily "to get ideas for teaching," "research for a school project," because "it is required by my teacher/professor," "to get information or advice related to investing" or "to identify interesting or important news stories." Eighty-three percent of students are reading economics blogs for their own enjoyment or knowledge while only 66 percent of non-students do so. The differences between students and non-students are statistically significant at the p = 0.05 level. About 75 percent somewhat agree or strongly agree with the statement that it is important for blogs to keep up with current events and news.

Next, respondents were asked "How much time during the past month did you spend reading economics blogs?" The sample was evenly distributed with 21 percent indicating two to five hours, 24 percent indicating five to ten hours, 23 percent indicating ten to twenty hours and 21 percent indicating more than twenty hours. There are no statistically significant differences between students and non-students. When inquiring as to how their time use had changed compared to one year ago, 33 percent and 48 percent of respondents are spending "a little more" or "a lot more" time reading economics blogs. Fifteen percent are spending about the same amount of time. There are statistically significant differences across students and non-students but the practical differences are slight. For example, fifty percent of students are spending a lot more time reading economics blogs compared to 47 percent of non-students who do so.

Finally, respondents were asked "How much time during the past month did you spend reading *all* blogs?" Eleven percent answered two to five hours, 14 percent answered five to ten hours, 26 percent answered ten to twenty hours and 44 percent answered more than twenty hours. Only 32 percent of students are reading all blogs for more than twenty hours, while 48 percent of the non-students are doing so. This difference is statistically significant at the p = 0.05 level. Compared to one year ago, 37 percent and 38 percent of respondents are spending "a little more" and "a lot more" time reading all blogs. There are no statistically significant differences across student and non-student samples.

The increased reading of economics and other blogs has done little to cut into overall reading of economics literature. Fifty-two percent of all respondents state that they are spending about the same amount of time "reading printed economics-related books, magazines and newspapers" now compared to one year ago. Twenty-two percent are reading a little less while 17 percent are reading "a little more." There are no statistically significant differences across students and non-students. Forty-seven percent of those in the sample are reading printed economics-related books, magazines and newspapers about the same as they did a year ago. Twenty-three percent of students are reading a little more compared to 20 percent of non-students. Sixteen percent of students are reading a lot more print economics compared to 6 percent of non-students. These differences are statistically significant at the p = 0.05 level.

The Pearson correlation coefficients on the ranks of responses indicates that the time spent reading economics blogs and all blogs is positively correlated (r = 0.64, p < 0.01). These activities therefore appear to be complements. There is no correlation between time spent reading economics blogs and print economics. These results are similar for student and non-student sub-samples. Comparing time spent from year to year, there is a positive and statistically significant rank correlation between time spent reading economics blogs and time spent reading all blogs ($r = 0.59$, $p < 0.01$). Overall, there is no correlation between time spent reading economics blogs and print economics compared to one year ago. However, for students there is a positive correlation between time spent reading economics blogs and time spent reading print economics compared to one year ago ($r = 0.23$, $p < 0.05$). For students, there appears to be a trend toward complementarity of economics blogs and print economics.

DISCUSSION

While the use of interactive web 2.0 technologies as teaching tools in economics is still relatively new, anecdotal evidence suggests that blogs are increasingly being used for teaching.[18] Blogging might help an economist think more carefully about a particular topic, and in our experience, blog comments provide useful feedback to shape this thinking. To the extent that thinking about economics enhances teaching, then blogging enhances teaching. Blog posts are often short, and blog readers can switch to a competing blog with a mouse-click, so successful bloggers must develop a concise and engaging style of communication which also may enhance teaching. Blogging requires reading; very few bloggers write posts off the top of their heads. Therefore, many bloggers are required to expand their reading, which increases the current event-type material that can be presented in the classroom. Our own experience is that blogging is a good source of ideas for teaching and research.[19]

Our survey results suggest that there is a growing audience for economics bloggers among those in the general public, and especially students with an interest in economics. The student audience is especially attractive for the informal teaching opportunities that blogging presents. However, little is known about the impact of economics blogs and other web 2.0 technologies on teaching effectiveness. To better understand the potential of these technologies in economic education, it would be useful for economics education research to examine the link between blogs and specific learning outcomes. These outcomes could include both objective measures of academic performance as well as subjective measures of student participation and satisfaction. Another interesting avenue for research is to examine the effectiveness of blogs to educate people outside of the formal education system on economic concepts and ideas. For example, regular economics blog readers who do not have formal backgrounds in economics and are not economics students could be tested to assess their level of understanding of economics against a control group of non-blog readers.

NOTES

1. A previous version of this chapter was presented at the 2008 Kentucky Economic Association meetings and the 2011 Allied Social Science Associations meeting. Haab and Whitehead blog at Environmental Economics (www.env-econ.net, accessed 9 June 2011) and Schiff formerly blogged at 26econ (26econ.com, accessed 9 June 2011).
2. http://www.econtalk.org/ (accessed 9 June 2011).
3. http://welkerswikinomics.wetpaint.com/ (accessed 9 June 2011).
4. http://marginalrevolution.com (accessed 9 June 2011).

5. http://www.economistsdoitwithmodels.com/microeconomics-101/ (accessed 9 June 2011).
6. Our own experience is as economics bloggers, as teachers who use blogs and as researchers who have conducted two surveys on economics blogging.
7. In contrast, wikis are websites that any user can edit and can be used for class outlines, class notes and student discussion of course essays and papers (Greenlaw 2011). See Ferris and Wilder (2006) for further discussion about wikis and education.
8. For example, see the list of "Ten Interesting Economics Blogs" on p. 96 of the January–February 2007 volume of *The Milken Institute Review*.
9. http://www.cengage.com/economics/book_content/0324224729_mankiw/map/ (accessed 9 June 2011).
10. http://www.env-econ.net/environmental_economics_1.html (accessed 9 June 2011).
11. http://aguanomics.com/2009/10/here-they-come.html (accessed 9 June 2011).
12. http://rfe.org (accessed 9 June 2011).
13. http://www.rtable.net (accessed 9 June 2011).
14. http://www.econolog.net (accessed 9 June 2011).
15. at http://econdirectory.com (accessed 9 June 2011).
16. Academic citations are notoriously fickle measures of academic quality. Problems of miscounting and double-counting abound. Nevertheless, citations rankings are a useful start for understanding the contributions blogs can make to the understanding of economics by the broader public.
17. See "Counting Bloggers, and Blog Readers," http://blogs.wsj.com/numbersguy/counting-bloggers-and-blog-readers-181/ (accessed 9 June 2011).
18. See Jennifer Imazeki's blog "Economics for Teachers" for a good example of how blogs can support teaching economics even if the blog is not specifically for an economics class.
19. Ayres and Sachania (2009) provide a guide to blogging software options, writing and content management.

REFERENCES

Ayres, P. and B. Sachania (2009), "Using blogs in economics", *Computers in Higher Education Economics Review*, **20**, 32–7.

Bostian, A. A. and C. A. Holt (2009), "Price bubbles with discounting: A web-based classroom experiment", *Journal of Economic Education*, **40** (1), 27–37.

DeLong, J. B. (2006), "The invisible college", *Chronicle of Higher Education Review*, **52** (47), B8.

Ferris, S. P. and H. Wilder (2006), "Uses and potentials of Wikis in the classroom", *Innovate: Journal of Online Education*, **2** (5), http://www.innovateonline.info/index.php?view=article&id=258, accessed 24 May 2011.

Goffe, W. L. and K. Sosin (2005), "Teaching with technology: May you live in interesting times", *Journal of Economic Education*, **36** (3), 278–91.

Greenlaw, S. A. (2011), "Augmenting teaching & learning with social software", *Journal of Economic Education*, **42** (1), 97.

Greenlaw, S. A. and S. B. DeLoach (2003), "Teaching critical thinking with electronic discussion", *Journal of Economic Education*, **34** (1), 36–52.

Mixon, F. G. and K. P. Upadhyaya (2010), "Blogmetrics", *Eastern Economic Journal*, **36**, 1–10.

Schiff, A. (2008), "A Survey of Economics Bloggers", http://ssrn.com/abstract=1080238, accessed 24 May 2011.

Section C

Assessment

16 Methods of assessment in the college economics course
Ken Rebeck and Carlos Asarta

Assessment is a means to an end, not an end in itself. (Miller, Linn and Gronlund, 2009, p. 31)

Assessment is not a panacea; it is a complex activity with many facets, and it is part of the contemporary higher education scene, with all its problems and possibilities. (Walvoord, 2004, p. 10)

The role of assessment evolves over the careers of most economics instructors, but it is likely to undergo the most significant changes within the first few years of teaching. Sole responsibility for teaching a course typically occurs first when the instructor is a graduate student, when time devoted to designing the course must come at the expense of efforts to advance in the program. The initial year as a faculty member after graduate school is often the first time the instructor faces multiple courses to prepare, and, even if the dissertation is finished, pressure will already be felt to publish. These new economics instructors probably devote most of the time and energy they have allocated to their courses to methods of instruction. They want to find and develop examples of concepts to be taught, experiment with alternative forms of conveying the material, and present the material coherently. Assessment of student understanding is simply a chore with a purpose no more important than to produce a reasonable distribution of final grades.

After these new instructors have a few semesters of experience, courses have been taught twice or more, and needed preparation time diminishes or at least becomes more flexible. As workload expectations become clearer, instructors begin to look more deeply into the test results they have seen. Why does half of the class apparently not understand the difference between demand and quantity demanded? Is it the presentation of the material? Is it student effort? Is it a problematic question I continue to use? Thoughtful instructors might then question how important it is that students understand certain concepts; whether or not student understanding of the concept is critical, or even consistent with, the goals of the course. Assessment begins to evolve into something much more than a tool used to assign grades. It becomes the process by which instructors answer these questions.

This chapter discusses assessment of student understanding in the economics classroom. It focuses on college economics courses, but much of it is relevant for high school economics instructors. The chapter begins by defining assessment and describing how both formative and summative assessment are necessary for a comprehensive assessment program. The second section discusses the current state of assessment in US colleges, focusing on what tools are being used, and to what extent instructors are using these tools. The advantages and disadvantages of using multiple-choice and free-response tests are examined in the third section. This section also provides a few tips and resources for instructors attempting to improve the quality of their tests. The fourth section describes three assessment tools that can be used to provide immediate feedback on student understanding. The last section provides a few concluding thoughts.

ASSESSMENT DEFINED

Assessment in the economics course does involve gathering data, often from exams as seen in the next section, to be used to assign grades. But assessment limited to this task leads an instructor to miss tremendous opportunities to improve the course and ultimately advance student achievement over time. A sound assessment *strategy* in an economics course consists of both (1) gathering data to summarize the level of understanding of students, and (2) using this data to evaluate the current effectiveness of the course and make changes to the course to increase student understanding. The second of these components involves identifying areas where the course is thriving, where it might only modestly influence student learning, where it might have a weak or no effect, and areas where the effect it does have does not further the objectives of the course.

This assessment strategy for an economics course can be described in the context of summative and formative assessment. Summative assessment measures and describes the achievement levels of students. It is designed to determine assignment and course grades or for certifying student mastery of the intended learning outcomes (Miller et al., 2009, p. 39). For example, if a student receives a score of 86 out of 100 points on a comprehensive final exam in an instructor's principles of microeconomics course, this provides information on the level of achievement of this student. The instructor can use these test scores to help assign grades, and these grades, in turn, can provide students with feedback on how much they understand relative to how much they were expected to understand. For students, if letter grades are assigned based on a predetermined scale (for example, 80 percent to 89 percent correct receives a "B"), then the instructor is signaling to students their understanding on a criterion-referenced basis – in this case, 86 percent of the material that was expected to be understood was understood. If letter grades are determined by a curve, with the instructor assigning grades by, for example, ranking scores and determining grades with carefully considered yet subjective cutoffs, students are provided a signal of their understanding on a norm-referenced basis. Students glean from their grade their achievement relative to scores achieved by their peers. Using either approach, summative assessment provides students with information about what they have learned. For the instructor, summative assessment provides data used to assign grades, and importantly, information on the effectiveness of the course as it has been implemented and as it relates to course objectives.

Formative assessment is used to produce information that provides feedback to students to help them gauge their performance and to improve their learning process. It is an ongoing process implemented throughout the duration of the course. This information is used to monitor learning progress during instruction (Miller et al., 2009), identify misunderstandings and confusion about certain topics, and correct these misunderstandings before summative assessment takes place. The instructor can modify his or her approach, and if the feedback is immediate, these changes can take place quickly.

In her summary of how expert assessment practitioners have defined assessment, Suskie (2009, p. 4) discusses four steps required of an effective assessment program:

1. Establish clear, measurable expected outcomes of student learning;
2. Ensure that students have sufficient opportunities to achieve those outcomes;
3. Systematically gather, analyze, and interpret evidence to determine how well student learning matches expectations;
4. Use the resulting information to understand and improve student learning.

The inclusion of both summative and formative assessment is clear in her list. Steps one through three establish a foundation for a carefully planned summative assessment of student learning. When these three steps are combined with step four, assessment becomes a process used to reconsider and revise the approach to teaching certain concepts with the goal of improving student learning.

The process of creating an assessment plan begins by stating the learning outcomes for the course that students have a realistic opportunity to achieve in the given setting. Departments of economics often have a written set of goals. These goals might be a nice starting point, but according to Allen (2004), departmental goals are usually too general to guide assessment and planning.[1] Faculty need to develop more specific learning objectives to operationalize these program goals. These learning objectives must describe observable behaviors that faculty can measure.

Miller et al. (2009) suggest criteria to use when preparing goals. We modified their list to more closely match the needs of economics faculty:

1. Do the objectives include all important outcomes of the course?
2. Are the objectives in harmony with the goals of the department?
3. Are the objectives realistic in terms of student abilities and time available?

A few sources provide guidance to help economics instructors with the specifics of creating learning objectives for their economics courses. Saunders (1998) suggests instructors begin with a few general outcomes such as "knows basic terms" and "applies economic principles to new situations." Within these general objectives, he recommends listing specific illustrative behaviors like "uses terms correctly" and "predicts the probable outcome." When applied to specific concepts covered, he argues that these objectives must encompass the conditions in which the student will be able to accomplish the objective, and the criteria used to judge his or her achievement.

In a series of writings, Hansen (1986, 2001) provides a framework for choosing what should be included in these objectives. His "proficiencies approach" identifies what students should be able to do at the end of a course or program. His discussion of six proficiencies (1. access existing knowledge; 2. display command of existing knowledge; 3. interpret existing knowledge; 4. interpret and manipulate economic data; 5. apply existing knowledge; and 6. create new knowledge) will help instructors better focus on what specific outcomes are important, and how to achieve these outcomes.[2]

Evidence of student understanding can be generated with the use of a variety of tools. Formal examinations in the form of instructor-created exams (discussed below) are used extensively in the college economics course (see the next section), and norm-referenced standardized test instruments such as the Test of Understanding of College Economics (TUCE)[3] are available to assess student knowledge and compare it to the achievement of groups of similar students. Non-examination writing assignments, such as student essays, journals and other written work, can also generate valuable information on student learning. Information on student learning can also be captured with the use of classroom simulations and experiments, group work and other activities, many covered elsewhere in this volume. There are also immediate feedback techniques that can be utilized, a few of which we discuss in a later section of this chapter.

Using assessment results to help guide changes to teaching is the last of Suskie's (2009) four ongoing steps. For economics instructors, these changes can be as simple as finding new alternatives to define a concept or seeking new real-world examples of economic relationships, or they can be elaborate changes to approaches to helping students learn topics. The importance of finding and employing alternatives to traditional lectures ("chalk-and-talk") has been stressed by Becker and Watts (2001). An earlier section of this volume provides numerous teaching techniques that economics instructors can employ to improve student learning of economics.

THE CURRENT STATE OF ASSESSMENT IN COLLEGE ECONOMICS COURSES

The results of two studies provide a glimpse into college economics classrooms to identify the relative use of alternative forms of assessment. Both studies used national surveys and identified the use of various assessment techniques for grading purposes, but we cannot ascertain from the survey results to what extent these are used for formative assessment or to alter instructive practices. Nevertheless, the surveys reveal the extent to which examinations are used relative to other assessment tools to determine grades in economics courses. It also reveals the relative use of multiple-choice (fixed-response) items and free-response measures such as essay questions on examinations.

The US 1989–90 national norming of the third edition of the TUCE included a questionnaire given to participating instructors. The TUCE was administered in introductory microeconomics and macroeconomics courses, so the responses cannot be generalized beyond these specific courses. Siegfried et al. (1996) utilized responses to address two questions: What counts toward the final course grade? and What format is used for examinations, and to what extent are these formats used?

Siegfried et al. (1996) found that about 94 percent of the 139 respondents utilized final exams in their courses, and about 94 percent utilized midterm exams.[4] Forty-nine percent also used quizzes. Homework was utilized by 51 percent of the sample and accounted for about 6 percent of course grades. About 11 percent of the sample utilized term papers, and these contributed only about 1.5 percent to course grades. The results suggest that about 90 percent of a randomly selected student's grade in an introductory microeconomics or macroeconomics course in this national norming sample is likely to be determined by his or her performance on examinations and quizzes.[5]

Siegfried et al. (1996) found that nearly all respondents, 96 percent, used multiple-choice items exclusively or in combination with other question types (100 percent of the microeconomics instructors). Utilization of free-response questions was lower; short answer questions were used by 62 percent of respondents and long-answer questions by 26 percent. Twenty-two percent also used true-false questions. These results, combined with the relative weights respondents placed on the different question types, suggest that our randomly selected student will find that 65 percent of his or her course grade will be determined by performance on multiple-choice items.

Watts and Schaur (2011) explore the results from questionnaires sent in 1995, 2000, 2005 and 2010 to college economics faculty inquiring about their teaching and assessment strategies in undergraduate courses. Concerning principles and pre-principles courses, their results show the importance placed on examinations (including quizzes) relative to other forms of assessment. Examinations accounted for 85 percent or more of students' course grades from 1995 to 2005, but dropped roughly 15 percentage points to around 70 percent by 2010. The composition of these exams stayed stable during this period, with multiple-choice questions determining around 57 percent of the exam scores. The only other assessment methods found to determine more than 10 percent of course grades were homework and problem sets, which increased from 10 to 15 percent over these 15 years.

Taking into account all assessment instruments, multiple-choice questions accounted for 50 percent of course grades from 1995 to 2000, then fell to 40 percent by 2005 with the decline in emphasis on examinations. A possible explanation for the greater emphasis on multiple-choice questions found in the Siegfried et al. (1996) study is that the TUCE norming contained a self-selected sample of instructors who volunteered to pretest and posttest with a multiple-choice instrument, while respondents in the Watts and Schaur (2011) study were only asked to fill out a questionnaire.

The Watts and Schaur study also reports results for instructors teaching upper-division courses. Multiple-choice questions were rarely used by upper-division economics instructors, with the one exception being the intermediate theory courses in 2010, where multiple-choice questions accounted for 6 percent of the course grade. Grades in upper division courses are primarily determined by short- and long-answer examinations, problem sets and writing assignments.

MULTIPLE-CHOICE AND FREE-RESPONSE EXAMINATIONS

With the lion's share of an economics student's grade likely determined by examinations, this chapter now turns to the choice between fixed-response exams, specifically multiple-choice exams, and free-response (constructed-response) exams, such as those comprised of short-answer and long-answer questions. The advantages and disadvantages of multiple-choice and free-response exams will be discussed, and a few sources to help guide instructors with the creation of each type of exam will be provided.

Comparing Multiple-Choice and Free-Response Exams

Numerous studies have examined the use of multiple-choice exams and free-response exams, either separately, as complements or as substitutes, when assessing student understanding in economics (see, for example, Becker and Johnston, 1999; Buckles and Siegfried, 2005; Chan and Kennedy, 2002; Walstad, 1987 and 1998; and Walstad and Becker, 1994). A few common themes can be found throughout this literature.

Multiple-choice exams require far less time and effort to grade than do free-response exams. For most faculty, completed machine-scored answer sheets can be taken to the university's testing center and results can be received within an hour. Even if an instructor was to grade such exams by hand, time spent grading would still be less than the time needed to grade free-response exams of about the same length. This *efficiency* in scoring is unquestionably the primary reason for its extensive use in introductory or principles-level economics courses, as noted above, where class sizes are larger on average than in upper-division courses.

Multiple-choice exams can cover a broader range of concepts within the content domain than can free-response exams of the same length. Given the same amount of time, a multiple-choice exam can require students to respond to many items spread across a variety of concepts covered in class, while an exam that requires students to develop and explain an answer is limited in this respect. When exams cover only a portion of the material, as might be the case with a free-response exam, there is a differential benefit across students who had greater comprehension regarding content included in the exam, and those who had a greater level of understanding of concepts not tested. This could be a form of *bias* in the assessment of student learning. Content coverage can become important when the instructor gives only one midterm exam and a final exam. However, if exams are given frequently throughout the term, this bias may not be as severe; free-response exams can approach the content coverage of multiple-choice exams when less material is covered between exams. If the instructor clearly signals to students which material covered is more central to the goals of the course and, in turn, focuses on this material when creating exams, ultimately matching objectives and assessment practices, the content-coverage bias also diminishes.

Multiple-choice exams are more *objective* with regard to grading than free-response exams. Knowing the names of students being graded, grading some examinations while tired and others while refreshed, and the order in which the exams are graded can all be factors leading to less-reliable scores that vary inconsistently across students (Walstad, 1998). The problem with objectivity can be exacerbated by large class sizes and several teaching assistants grading exams.

Free-response exams, such as those containing short- and long-answer questions, essay questions, and problems to be solved with explanations, have advantages over multiple-choice exams in other areas. The thought process of the student can be drawn out and observed much more easily with free-response questions. With multiple-choice items, student guessing can be a major factor influencing both scores on the assessment instrument and in the course. A correctly answered multiple-choice item is not always an accurate signal of student understanding as even the best quality multiple-choice item can be answered correctly by a student who knows nothing about the topic but guesses correctly. But a carefully written free-response item can require both a correct answer (if one exists) and a response that reveals the reasoning that takes place when the student answers the item. This can be important with regard to the assessment process. Written responses can arguably provide better feedback on student understanding when they are used to identify areas of confusion and help guide changes to approaches to enhance student learning.

Free-response tests can also help develop higher levels of student understanding of economics. Some argue that multiple-choice items are limited to assessing understanding at the three lowest levels of Bloom's (1956) taxonomy; multiple-choice items providing insight into cognitive areas no higher than knowledge, comprehension and application.

Buckles and Siegfried (2006) argue that, if written effectively, multiple-choice items can also capture achievement at the level of analysis. Free-response questions, on the other hand, have the potential to capture a student's ability to achieve at the highest levels of Bloom's taxonomy: synthesis and evaluation.

Walstad (2001) provides a framework, utilizing an economic decision-making grid, for instructors to use when deciding upon the assessment instrument that best fits their objectives and constraints. His criteria include ease of construction, economy of scoring, domain coverage, bias in scoring, freedom of student response, guessing problems and tapping into higher cognitive levels. He demonstrates how different weights assigned to criteria will lead to different outcomes, consistent with instructor choices as noted in survey results above. Principles-level economics courses have, on average, larger class sizes than do upper-division courses, and instructors likely place greater relative weight on economy of scoring. Multiple-choice items are used extensively in these courses. When teaching upper-division courses with smaller class sizes, economy of scoring might not be as important to the instructor, leaving cognitive levels tested and other criteria to dominate the decision and leading to the greater use of free-response items.

How different are multiple-choice exams and free-response exams at assessing student understanding of economics? Walstad and Becker (1994) explore the Advanced Placement exams in microeconomics and macroeconomics and find relatively high correlations between the scores earned on the multiple-choice and essay sections of the exams. They concluded that there was little to no difference in what the two types of test questions measure, a finding consistent with prior research. Becker and Johnston (1999) find evidence to the contrary. In a study using data from Australia, they developed and estimated a two-stage least-squares model and found that scores on multiple-choice exams were not good predictors of scores in essay exams, and vice versa.

Creating Quality Exams[6]

Creating valid and reliable instruments for a course's assessment program can be a time-consuming task. Nearly all textbooks for use in principles and intermediate economics courses provide test banks. Standards for quality items are not always followed when creating these test banks, so multiple-choice items and free-response questions taken from test banks should be used with care. An efficient approach might be to enhance existing questions from test banks, and write new questions to cover learning objectives where test bank questions are of poor quality, non-existent, or where higher cognitive levels are not assessed. Sources are available to help guide instructors in creating valid and reliable tests. Among them, Walstad (1998) provides the elements required of sound multiple-choice items for use in economics courses, and in the same edited volume, Welsh and Saunders (1998) provide a detailed description of good practices for creating and grading essay questions in economics. Many well-respected books have been written to help young faculty succeed as academics, often including valuable chapters on test creation (see, for examples, Davis 2009 and McKeachie 2010).

IMMEDIATE-FEEDBACK, FORMATIVE ASSESSMENT TECHNIQUES

Although examinations can provide faculty and students with formative feedback (especially in the case of midterm exams), they are only one limited method. Limiting formative assessment to exams and writing exercises misses other opportunities to gather information that can be used to improve instruction and learning. In this section we describe a few less traditional and quite creative tools that have been used to gather assessment data.

Classroom response systems,[7] such as "clickers," are a unique means of immediate formative assessment which keep students actively responding throughout the class. Salemi (2009) describes in detail the use of classroom clickers in a principles of economics course. These are remote hand-held devices that students can use to respond to an instructor's questions and responses can be instantly tabulated and displayed on the screen for the instructor and class. These responses, similar to the feedback from student keypads in state-of-the-art classrooms, offer instructors and students immediate checks on learning (Becker, 2000, p. 116). Utilized wisely, classroom response systems can provide faculty with a means with which to undertake formative assessment only dreamed of decades ago.

Student understanding can be assessed directly with exams, quizzes or even single knowledge questions, but indirect methods of assessment can also be valuable. *One-minute papers* are a powerful tool for providing instant and continuous feedback on how well students are learning material. In its common form, at the end of a class students are asked to respond to two questions: What is the most important thing you learned today? and What is the muddiest point still remaining at the conclusion of today's class? Instructors can analyze the responses, identify what is working and what concepts are being misunderstood, and adapt instruction accordingly. Chizmar and Ostrosky (1998) describe how to implement the one-minute paper in both traditional classrooms and in classes taught in computer labs. (The latter use suggests instructors might find unique ways to include variants of one-minute papers for formative assessment in today's online courses.) Through personal experience, the authors were convinced of the power of the assessment information provided by one-minute papers. They empirically tested their expectations and found one-minute papers to be effective at improving student learning.

Another form of indirect assessment is "post-then-pre" surveys (Rockwell and Kohn, 1989). Gathering feedback on the amount of learning that takes place during instruction is central to formative assessment. Utilizing knowledge pretests and posttests come at costs to instructors and students in the form of time and effort. One low-cost alternative is to simply ask students in a single survey to report their self-perceived level of understanding before and after instruction takes place. There will be a loss of reliability from direct test questions to self-reported knowledge, but the minimal cost of these surveys make their frequent use practical. A problem that arises with administering such self-perceptions surveys before and after instruction ("pre-then-post") is response-shift bias (Howard and Dailey, 1979). For example, a student might believe she knows something about the incidence of a specific (excise) tax before the topic is covered in class, and respond with a three on a five-point Likert scale (with five suggesting complete understanding) to a question asking for her self-perceived level of knowledge. Instruction takes place and she realizes there is much more to the topic than she originally knew. She now understands that in most cases the buyer and seller share the burden, but she does not grasp the entire analysis. When asked to respond after instruction, she once again reports a three, even though learning did indeed take place. Alternatively, post-then-pre surveys ask her to report, after instruction takes place, her self-perceived knowledge before and after instruction, removing this response-shift bias. Where one-minute papers might generate more detail about what is being learned and what are the various misconceptions, post-then-pre surveys are easier for instructors to quantify, making the documentation of learning straightforward.

CONCLUDING REMARKS

Implementation of a high-quality assessment program is crucial if one wishes to evolve as an economics instructor. Developing, executing and systematically reviewing and revising an assessment plan for every course in an instructor's portfolio will not only generate benefits to students, but to economics faculty required to provide evidence of effective teaching when applying for tenure and promotion. Creating learning outcomes for each economics course taught, establishing a mechanism for gathering evidence on whether or not these outcomes are being met, and documenting how this information has been used to grow as an instructor will offer powerful evidence of effective teaching. The instructor's assessment program can become an important complement to the often-utilized summaries of student evaluations of teaching.

Furthermore, many universities require assessment to take place for degree-granting programs. An understanding of the elements of a quality assessment plan, and familiarity with the tools and techniques that can improve summative and formative assessment, can make an instructor a valuable contributor to the assessment process in his or her department. These benefits to the economics instructor and department are, however, above and beyond the primary purpose of assessment. A comprehensive assessment program generates information to frequently identify whether or not student learning outcomes are being met, and uses this information to provide feedback directly to students regarding their learning successes and failures, and to instructors to revise, modify and improve the course to enhance student learning of economics.

NOTES

1. Additionally, at some institutions where departments are told they must have objectives to assess, these objectives are endogenously determined, with the goal of ease of assessment. Some departments might intentionally develop easily assessed goals that might not otherwise have been the true goals of the department.
2. For more information about this approach, see Chapter 17, "An Expected Proficiencies Approach to the Economics Major", in this volume.
3. The TUCE and other test instruments are described in greater detail in Chapter 29, "Measurement Techniques of Students Performance and Literacy: College and High School", in this volume.
4. These were not the same respondents across final exams and midterm exams. For the instructors administering the TUCE in introductory microeconomics, 94 percent gave final exams and 90 percent gave

midterm exams. For the instructors administering the TUCE in introductory macroeconomics, 94 percent gave final exams and 99 percent gave midterm exams.

5. These principles-level instructors voluntarily administered the TUCE as a pretest and posttest during the norming process of the third edition of the TUCE. A reasonable argument can be made that this is not a representative sample of principles-level teachers. The results reported in Siegfried et al. (1996) are not as generalizable as would be results from a pure random sample.
6. There are certain characteristics of quality test instruments. For a discussion of test validity, reliability and item analysis, see the appendix to Chapter 29 in this volume.
7. This technology is further described in Chapter 13, "Incorporating Media and Response Systems in the Economics Classroom", in this volume.

REFERENCES

Allen, M. J. (2004), *Assessing Academic Programs in Higher Education*, Bolton, MA: Anker Publishing Company, Inc.

Becker, W. E. (2000), "Teaching economics in the 21st century", *Journal of Economic Perspectives*, **14** (1), 109–19.

Becker, W. E. and C. Johnston (1999), "The relationship between multiple choice and essay response questions in assessing economics understanding", *The Economic Record*, **75** (231), 348–57.

Becker, W. E. and M. Watts (2001), "Teaching economics at the start of the 21st century: Still chalk-and-talk", *American Economic Review*, **91** (2), 446–51.

Bloom, B. S. (ed.) (1956), *Taxonomy of Educational Objectives*, New York: David McKay.

Buckles, S. and J. J. Siegfried (2006), "Using multiple-choice questions to evaluate in-depth learning of economics", *Journal of Economic Education*, **37** (1), 48–57.

Chan, N. and P. E. Kennedy (2002), "Are multiple-choice exams easier for economics students? A comparison of multiple-choice and 'equivalent' constructed-response exam questions", *Southern Economic Journal*, **68** (4), 957–71.

Chizmar, J. F. and A. L. Ostrosky (1998), "The one-minute paper: Some empirical findings", *Journal of Economic Education*, **29** (1), 3–10.

Davis, B. G. (2009), *Tools for Teaching* (2nd ed.), San Francisco: Jossey-Bass.

Hansen, W. L. (1986), "What knowledge is most worth knowing for economics majors?", *American Economic Review*, **76** (2), 149–53.

Hansen, W. L. (2001), "Expected proficiencies for undergraduate economics majors", *Journal of Economic Education*, **32** (3), 231–42.

Howard, G. S. and P. R. Dailey (1979), "Response-shift bias: A source of contamination of self-report measures", *Journal of Applied Psychology*, **64** (2), 144–50.

McKeachie, W. J. (2010). *McKeachie's Teaching Tips: Strategies, Research, and Theory for College and University Teachers* (13th ed.), Boston, MA: Houghton Mifflin.

Miller, M. D., R. L. Linn and N. E. Gronlund (2009), *Measurement and Assessment in Teaching* (10th ed.), Upper Saddle River, NJ: Pearson Education, Inc.

Nunnally, J. C. (1982), "Reliability of measurement", in H. E. Meitzel (ed.), *Encyclopedia of Educational Research* (5th ed.), New York: Macmillan, pp. 1589–601.

Rockwell, S. K. and H. Kohn (1989), "Post-then-pre evaluation", *Journal of Extension*, **27** (2), 19–21.

Salemi, M. K. (2009), "Clickenomics: Using a classroom response system to increase student engagement in a large-enrollment principles of economics course", *Journal of Economic Education*, **40** (4), 385–404.

Saunders, P. (1998), "Learning theory and instructional objectives", in W. B. Walstad and P. Saunders (eds), *Teaching Undergraduate Economics: A Handbook for Instructors*, New York: Irwin/McGraw-Hill, pp. 85–108.

Siegfried, J. J., P. Saunders, E. Stinar and H. Zhang (1996), "Teaching tools: How is introductory economics taught in America?", *Economic Inquiry*, **34** (1), 182–92.

Suskie, L. A. (2009), *Assessing Student Learning: A Common Sense Guide* (2nd ed.), San Francisco: Jossey-Bass.

Walstad, W. B. (1987), "Measurement instruments", in W. E. Becker and W. B. Walstad (eds), *Econometric Modeling in Economic Education Research*, Boston, MA: Kluwer-Nisjhoff, pp. 73–98.

Walstad, W. B. (1998), "Multiple choice tests for the economics course", in W. B. Walstad and P. Saunders (eds), *Teaching Undergraduate Economics: A Handbook for Instructors*, New York: Irwin/McGraw-Hill, pp. 287–304.

Walstad, W. B. (2001), "Improving assessment in university economics", *Journal of Economic Education*, **32** (3), 281–94.

Walstad, W. B. and W. E. Becker (1994), "Achievement differences on multiple-choice and essay tests in economics", *American Economic Review*, **84** (2), 193–6.

Walvoord, B. E. (2004), *Assessment Clear and Simple: A Practical Guide for Institutions, Departments, and General Education*, San Francisco: Jossey-Bass.

Watts, M. and G. Schaur (2011), "Teaching and assessment methods in undergraduate economics: A fourth national quinquennial survey", *Journal of Economic Education*, **42** (3), 249–309.

Welsh, A. L. and P. Saunders (1998), "Essay questions and tests", in W. B. Walstad and P. Saunders (eds), *Teaching Undergraduate Economics: A Handbook for Instructors*, New York: Irwin/McGraw-Hill, pp. 305–18.

17 An expected proficiencies approach to the economics major

W. Lee Hansen

WHAT IS IT?

The author's expected proficiencies approach to the economics major focuses on developing in students the capacity by the time they graduate *to demonstrate and subsequently use to good effect* the knowledge and skills they acquired in individual economics courses and sequences of courses in the major (Hansen, 1986).

Proficiency-based courses differ fundamentally from traditionally organized courses. In traditional courses, the focus is on how well students can display their content knowledge, ultimately, in course examinations or papers. In proficiencies-based courses, the focus goes beyond any individual course; it embraces the required sequence of courses students take in their major but also electives. It centers on developing in economics majors by the time they graduate their ability to demonstrate what they can do with the content knowledge they learned. The seven proficiencies are defined as follows:

1. Accessing and organizing existing knowledge
2. Displaying command of existing knowledge
3. Interpreting existing knowledge
4. Interpreting and manipulating quantitative data
5. Applying existing knowledge
6. Creating new knowledge
7. Questing for knowledge and understanding

These proficiencies have two dimensions. The first is a hierarchy in the spirit of ever more complex levels of knowledge and understanding that students are expected to demonstrate (Bloom, 1956). The first six proficiencies within this hierarchy range from the lowest level, how to access information, to the highest level, creating knowledge. The second dimension is represented by the seventh proficiency, a cross-cutting, all-purpose proficiency that does not fit neatly into this hierarchy. It might best be described as "questing for knowledge and understanding," the ability to ask penetrating questions and to engage effectively with others in exploring and discussing economic issues and policies.

What does it mean to be able to demonstrate these proficiencies? Examples of how mastery of these proficiencies can be nurtured and also demonstrated follow (Hansen, 2009):

Accessing existing knowledge Retrieve, assemble, and organize information on particular topics and issues in economics. Locate published research in economics and related fields. Track down economic data and data sources. Find information about the generation, construction, and meaning of economic data.

Displaying command of existing knowledge   Explain key economics theories and concepts, and describe how they can be used. Write a precis or summary of a published journal article. Summarize in a two-minute monologue or a 300-word written statement what is known about the current condition of the economy and the economic outlook. Summarize the principal ideas of an eminent economist; describe the unique contribution of a recent winner of the Nobel Prize in Economic Science. Summarize a current controversy in the economics literature. State succinctly the economic dimensions of a current policy issue.

Interpreting existing knowledge   Explain and evaluate what economic concepts and principles are used in economic analyses published in articles from daily newspapers, weekly news magazines, and academic journals. Describe how these concepts aid in understanding the analyses. Do the same for nontechnical analyses written by economists for general purpose publications. Read and interpret a theoretical analysis, which includes simple mathematical derivations, reported in an economics journal article.

Interpreting and manipulating quantitative data   Explain how to understand and interpret numerical data found in published tables, such as those in the annual Economic Report of the President. Be able to identify patterns and trends in published data, such as those found in the Statistical Abstract of the United States. Construct tables from already available data to illustrate an economic issue. Describe the relationships among several different quantitative measures (e.g. unemployment, prices, and gross domestic product). Explain how to perform and interpret a regression analysis that uses economic data such as might appear in an economics journal article.

Applying existing knowledge   Prepare an organized, clearly written three-page analysis of a current economic problem. Assess in a four-page paper the costs and benefits of an economic policy proposal. Prepare a two-page decision memorandum for your employer that recommends some action on an economic decision faced by the organization. Write a 600-word op-ed essay on some local economic issue.

Creating new knowledge   Identify and formulate a question or series of questions about an economic issue that will facilitate its investigation using the tools of economics. Synthesize the literature on a topic to determine gaps in our existing knowledge and how those gaps might best be filled. Prepare a five-page proposal describing a potentially useful research project and how that project might be undertaken. Complete a research study whose results are presented in a carefully edited 20-page paper or in an undergraduate thesis. Engage in a group research project that prepares a detailed research proposal and/or a finished research paper.

Questing for knowledge and understanding   Demonstrate an understanding of questions that stimulate productive discussion of economic issues and help keep discussions centered on the issue under discussion.[1] Develop a line of questions that probe the meaning or seek to interpret the meaning of a reading selection written by a well-known economist. Show how a questioning approach can get to the heart of substantive issues by focusing, for example, on the equity and efficiency implications of alternative arrangements, policies, and programs (e.g.: What are the benefits? What are the costs? How do the benefits and costs compare? Who pays? Who gains?).

The proficiency-based approach to economics goes an important step beyond the generally accepted goal of helping students learn "to think like an economist" (Siegfried et al., 1991; Siegfried, 2009). Rather its goal is to help students not only "to think like economists" but also "to do what economists do," which is more than simply "thinking."

Readers should note that the proficiencies described above are largely free of content knowledge. Economists already give adequate attention in their teaching and in the range of courses offered in their departments to the content knowledge they generally agree needs to be taught. This includes the central principles, theories, concepts, and factual and institutional material. Given this focus on content, little or no attention is given in the expected proficiencies to content knowledge.

Little systematic information is known about the ability of economics majors to demonstrate mastery of these proficiencies. Some evidence comes from a spring 2006 survey of senior economics majors at the University of Wisconsin-Madison (Hansen, 2006). That survey reveals that relatively few courses in the economics major give attention to any of these proficiencies, and those courses that do give them attention give them only moderate attention. Much more attention is given to them in what might be called "capstone" courses, among them junior and senior thesis seminars, a research methods seminar, and independent study courses. On average, slightly less than 20 percent of the majors rate their mastery of the proficiencies as "excellent." At the other end of the spectrum, 25 percent rate their mastery as only "fair" or "poor." These findings are similar to what other economists tell me they would expect to find for their economics majors.

Though these proficiencies are designed to be mastered during the undergraduate major, they must be embedded in the various courses students take to complete their major. Because courses are taught by individual faculty members, whereas the major and its requirements are determined collectively, by departments, some coordination is required. The first comes in determining what proficiencies are to be emphasized in specific courses. The second comes in ensuring that collectively the courses in the major give appropriate emphasis to all of the proficiencies (Carlson, Cohn, and Ramsey, 2002; Grant, 2005). Inasmuch as instruction takes place in courses, and that is where students learn, much of the discussion that follows describes how the proficiencies approach can be introduced into individual courses.

HOW DOES IT DIFFER FROM THE TRADITIONAL APPROACH?

Helping students master the proficiencies requires a range of teaching strategies. This differs from economists' heavy reliance on the widely used "chalk and talk" lecture approach to teaching (Watts and Becker, 2008). Unfortunately, this mode of teaching, while convenient for instructors, fails to exploit the possibilities for increasing student learning of the content knowledge of economics, not to mention their mastery of the expected proficiencies.

Adoption of the proficiencies-based approach to the economics major requires significant changes in the "educational process." Most important, it alters what goes on in the classroom. Proficiency-based courses require devoting greater attention to the development of students' intellectual skills, among them close reading, writing, speaking, discussing, reasoning, thinking, and creating. These courses do so by actively engaging students' minds in the learning process, as the extended descriptions of the proficiencies make clear. Striving towards increasing mastery of the proficiencies is essential to learning and serves as a valuable aid to students in assessing both the content knowledge they are learning and their mastery of the expected proficiencies.

Proficiency-based courses also alter the "relationship" between instructors and their students. No longer is so much attention centered on course examinations and course grades. For instructors, their efforts shift to helping students develop their mastery of those proficiencies being emphasized in the particular courses they teach. For students, their efforts shift to gaining practice in developing a mastery of the proficiencies by the time they graduate. Instructors continue to concentrate on teaching subject matter or content knowledge, but do so knowing that students must be able to combine their content learning with demonstrations of the broader skills associated with mastery of the expected proficiencies. Students continue to concentrate on learning content knowledge, but do so recognizing they must be able to use that learning to good effect.

In addition, a proficiencies-based approach lengthens the "learning time horizon" for both instructors and students. It shifts attention away from the quarter or semester that ends with the final examination to how each course in the major helps build the proficiencies expected of graduating economics majors. It shifts the focus from how well students can display their content knowledge, ultimately in course final examinations, to how well they can demonstrate mastery of the expected proficiencies acquired through a challenging variety of closely integrated learning activities.

These "activities" can take many forms. They include summarizing and discussing non-textbook reading assignments, completing a variety of writing assignments, making use of quantitative reasoning skills, and applying what is being learned to new problems, issues, and policies. All of these activities can be classified as promoting "active learning" in contrast to the passive, note-taking, memorization routine prevalent in so many economics courses. Particularly important are the skills of writing and discussion (Hansen, 1998).[2]

If students are to master these proficiencies, they must be given opportunities to practice. This means completing particular kinds of assignments more than once, ideally, several times, so that students develop some facility and confidence in undertaking these assignments and in turn build their mastery of the expected proficiencies. As in most human endeavors, students can become proficient only through regular and frequent guided practice. The prospects for student success in proficiencies-based courses will be enhanced if students already possess the basic intellectual skills that are emphasized in the general education core "skill" courses students must take.

Greater accommodation to differences in student *learning styles* occurs naturally in an expected proficiencies regime. The varied learning activities offered play to differences among students in their learning styles. They do so by reducing the advantage to those students who thrive on the "chalk and talk" approach so prevalent in undergraduate instruction.

WHAT DOES IT MEAN FOR INSTRUCTIONAL STRATEGY?

If these proficiencies are accepted as embodying what we want our economics majors to be able to do with what we are teaching them, we must decide what kind of instructional strategy is required to ensure that students can master these proficiencies. It seems obvious that, over the course of a semester, students must be exposed to a wide range of learning activities that reinforce the content knowledge they are being taught and at the same time help them build their mastery of the expected proficiencies.

A useful approach to organizing proficiencies-based courses and the major is to construct a grid organized around the content knowledge and the expected proficiencies (Hansen, 2001). For individual courses the grid can link the various learning activities (rows) to the proficiencies (columns), with each cell describing the details of the specific assignment. Such a grid is essential in determining how the nature, number, variety, and timing of the assignments fit with the flow of content knowledge. A similar grid for the major can sequence the emphasis given to the proficiencies by course level. For example, introductory courses are likely to give greater emphasis to the first three proficiencies, intermediate courses would focus on proficiencies three, four, and five, whereas advanced field courses would focus more heavily on proficiencies four, five, and six. Capstone courses embracing research and thesis writing would focus heavily on proficiencies six and seven. It goes without saying that the seventh proficiency would be emphasized through the full range of undergraduate economics courses.

It must be recognized that incorporating these learning activities into individual courses does require some class time to manage, and that may mean less content knowledge can be "covered" in any given course (Salemi and Siegfried, 1999). But inasmuch as instructors often cram too much content knowledge into their courses, this reallocation of class time could be beneficial. The reason is simple: proficiencies-oriented learning activities help reinforce student mastery of content.

HOW CAN STUDENT MASTERY BE ASSESSED?

Assessing student mastery of the proficiencies poses an important challenge. There is no simple and obvious way of doing this. Ideally, students would be called upon just prior to graduation to orally demonstrate their mastery of the proficiencies in the major (Grant, 2005); for departments with substantial numbers of majors this would be an impossible task. Another possibility is using a capstone course (McGoldrick, 2008), but institutions with large majors would have difficulty generating enough resources to offer such an experience. Alternatively, to the extent students are made responsible for their command of both course knowledge and mastery of the proficiencies, course grades could serve, albeit imperfectly, as a measure of mastery of the proficiencies. For this approach to work, both types of learning would have to be emphasized in a department's courses, and final examination questions would have to be proficiencies-oriented and require written responses.

New ways of assessing student mastery of the proficiencies are being developed at some smaller institutions (Myers et al., 2009a; 2009b). These involve the use of electronic portfolios that pull together the work students have completed in each of their economics courses and in all of their courses in the major. This work provides a basis for departments to assess the effective implementation of their proficiencies approach.

HOW DID THIS APPROACH ORIGINATE?

What motivated my development of this approach? It began when I finally recognized the inadequacies of our majors in demonstrating in practical ways what they were learning. It crystallized as a result of periodic surveys of recently graduated undergraduate economics majors at the University of Wisconsin-Madison that asked students what they learned that was of most value to them in their real-world jobs. Subsequent discussions with undergraduate focus groups helped inform us what our students were learning or not learning. Additional feedback came from informal conversations with students. Not surprisingly, little information of value was obtained from the mandated course evaluation surveys.

The clincher came when I checked the accuracy of my assessment by interviewing a wide range of employers of undergraduate economics majors, in the private, non-profit, federal, state, and local government sectors. The goal was to identify their expectations as to what the economics majors they hired could and should be able to do with the economics knowledge they brought with them. Out of all this emerged the list of expected proficiencies in the economics major, a list that has been fine-tuned by my classroom experience and by helpful suggestions from colleagues.

CONCLUSION

The expected proficiencies approach is making headway in the economics profession (Myers, Nelson and Stratton, 2011) and has been shown to work where it has been implemented (Hansen, 2009). Progress in gaining adoption of this approach has been slow and will probably continue to be slow. This situation may change for the better as pressures mount through accrediting agencies for greater accountability in assessing student learning.

Most economists, because they are heavily oriented to their discipline and its content knowledge, have not rushed to embrace the expected proficiencies approach. The reason is clear: it requires them to view economics as part of a liberal arts education. While every student must meet the "depth" requirement by completing an academic major, that is only one part of what it means to be well educated. There is also the "breadth" requirement that calls for completing certain general education requirements and electives of interest to students. General education courses can begin building student proficiencies; so can the electives students take for breadth.

Firmly embedding these expected proficiencies in the economics major can give the undergraduate learning experience the cohesiveness it so desperately needs. This approach will help both students and faculty members realize that "becoming educated" involves much more than completing prescribed course requirements and amassing sufficient credits to graduate. The expected proficiencies to the major approach provides a crucial link to help integrate what students are learning and thus ensure they can demonstrate mastery of the expected proficiencies both in the economics major and also in their other courses.

NOTES

1. For more information about the formal discussion technique, see Chapter 5, "Improving Classroom Discussion in Economics Courses", in this volume.
2. For more information see Chapter 12, "Writing for Learning in Economics" and Chapter 5 in this volume.

REFERENCES

Bloom, B. S. (ed.) (1956), *Taxonomy of Educational Objectives: The Classification of Educational Goals, Handbook I; Cognitive Domain*, New York: David McKay Company, Inc.

Carlson, J. L., R. L. Cohn and D. D. Ramsey (2002), "Implementing Hansen's proficiencies", *Journal of Economic Education*, **33** (spring), 180–91.

Grant, R. R. (2005), "A small college's adventure with accreditation and assessment", *Perspectives on Economic Education Research*, **1** (l), 60–75.

Hansen, W. L. (1986), "What knowledge is most worth knowing – for economics majors?" *American Economic Review*, **76** (2) (May), 149–52.

Hansen, W. L. (1998), "Integrating the practice of writing into economics instruction", in W. E. Backer and M. Watts (eds), *Teaching Economics to Undergraduates: Alternatives to Chalk and Talk*, Cheltenham, UK and Lyme, USA: Edward Elgar, pp. 79–118.

Hansen, W. L. (2001), "Expected proficiencies for undergraduate economics majors", *Journal of Economic Education*, **32** (summer), 231–42.

Hansen, W. L. (2006), "Economics majors: Their mastery of the expected proficiencies", Unpublished.

Hansen, W. L. (2009), "Reinvigorating liberal education with an expected proficiencies approach to the academic major: An application to economics", in D. Colander and K. McGoldrick (eds), *Educating Economists: The Teagle Discussion on Re-evaluating the Undergraduate Economics Major*, Cheltenham, UK and Northampton, MA, USA: Edward Elgar, pp. 107–25.

McGoldrick, K. (2008), "Doing economics: Enhancing skills through a process-oriented senior research course", *Journal of Economic Education*, **39** (4) 342–56.

Myers, S., M. Nelson and R. Stratton (2009a), "E-portfolios and student research in the assessment of a proficiency-based major", in T. Banta, K. Black and E. Jones (eds), *Designing Effective Assessment: Principles and Profiles of Good Practice*, San Francisco, CA: Jossey-Bass, pp. 95–9.

Myers, S., M. Nelson and R. Stratton (2009b), "Assessing an economics program: Hansen proficiencies, eportfolio and undergraduate research", *International Review of Economics Education*, **8** (1) (June), 195–9.

Myers, S., M. Nelson and R. Stratton (2011), "Assessment of the undergraduate economics major: A national survey", *Journal of Economic Education*, **42** (2), 195–9.

Salemi, M. K. and J. J. Siegfried (1999), "The state of economic education", *American Economic Review*, **89** (2), 355–61.

Siegfried, J. J. (2009), "Really thinking like an economist", in D. Colander and K. McGoldrick (eds), *Educating Economists: The Teagle Discussion on Re-evaluating the Undergraduate Economics Major*, Cheltenham, UK and Northampton, MA, USA: Edward Elgar, pp. 215–33.

Siegfried, J., R. Bartlett, W. Hansen, A. Kelley, D. McCloskey and T. Tietenberg (1991), "The status and prospects of the economic major", *The Journal of Economic Education*, **22** (3), 197–224.

Watts, M. and W. E. Becker (2008), "A little more than chalk and talk: Results from a third national survey of teaching methods in undergraduate economics courses", *Journal of Economic Education*, **39** (3), 273–86.

Section D

Contextual Techniques

18 Ethics and critical thinking
Jonathan B. Wight

This chapter seeks to demonstrate that investigations in positive economics rely on ethical perspectives and practices, and further, that critical thinking requires a wider ethical viewpoint than normative economics generally permits. Positive economics generally relies, for example, on the unsung virtues of the investigator who demonstrates honesty and transparency in the search for truth. Ethical failures in this regard are not uncommon (DeMartino, 2011). But another unstated ethical perspective appears in the worldview from which a researcher sets out to model behavior. Modelers almost always assume that rationality requires that an economic actor undertake an action in pursuit of a goal or end. Hence, positive economics is said to be the analysis of outcomes based on a theoretical understanding of causal relationships (if action X is taken, outcome Y will result). This broad analytical approach is termed *consequentialism*.

A widely recognized form of consequentialism is utilitarianism, from which modern welfare economics evolved. Welfare consequences are examined only in regard to desired outcomes, such as the metric of satisfying consumer preferences. This approach is so thoroughly ingrained that many economic practitioners fail to recognize the judgments involved: first, that outcomes are assumed to be the only value, and second, that only a particular outcome (satisfying preferences) counts in the economic assessment of welfare. In short, while economists may believe they are mainly doing science, they are usually doing far more philosophy than they acknowledge (Hausman and McPherson, 2006).

While traditional calculations of welfare based on market valuations are important, the analysis of public policy demands critical thinking that goes beyond this. Ronald Coase observed that:

> [T]he choice between different social arrangements for the solution of economic problems should be carried out in broader terms than this and that the total effect of these arrangements in all spheres of life should be taken into account. As Frank H. Knight has so often emphasized, problems of welfare economics must ultimately dissolve into a study of aesthetics and morals (1960, p. 43).

To address these points, the following sections provide a review of alternative ethical frameworks that can enrich students' understanding of controversial public policies.

ALTERNATIVE ETHICAL FRAMEWORKS

Despite its allure, the analysis of outcomes is not the only normative approach and in some cases it is insufficient for understanding economic institutions, behaviors and policies. Consequentialism was attacked in the mid-1700s, for example, by Immanuel Kant (1724–1804), who argued on the basis of pure practical reason that we have a duty to treat others as ends in themselves. An examination of the duties of rational agents produces a process for making decisions (Kant, 1785). In Kant's approach, the ends can never justify the means. Kantian philosophers routinely analyze public policies such as climate change, prostitution, selling body parts, sweatshops, and other economic issues using this *duty-based* perspective – which is fundamentally at odds with the neoclassical welfare approach. This does not mean that Kant was opposed to prices, profits, or markets; only that his method of evaluating their appropriateness to society was diametrically different.

Likewise, John Locke's *rights-based* ethical framework begins with the notion that humans have "inalienable" entitlements (life, liberty, and happiness) that cannot be abridged. A "right" is the flip side of a "duty": my right not to be harmed imposes a duty on you not to harm me. No valuable outcome (such as greater economic efficiency) should deprive someone of their rights. The law and economics movement, which presses judges to make legal decisions based on calculations of economic welfare, is fundamentally at odds with a rights-based approach. Thus, in *Kelo v. New London* (2005), the Supreme Court ruled five to four that Suzette Kelo could be forced off her land by powers of eminent domain, even though the City of New London was simply acting as an agent for a private developer who wished to use her land to build expensive condominiums on the waterfront. Economic welfare trumped Kelo's property rights.

Another normative tradition is that of *virtue ethics*. Since Socrates, philosophers have evaluated states of affairs by considering the motives and characters of economic agents. Adam Smith (1723–90) devoted considerable attention to analyzing why intentions mattered to judgment. To most modern economists, motives are irrelevant since only outcomes matter. However, a growing number of philosophers, including economists such as McCloskey (2006) and Sen (1977), are interested in reviving the discussion of virtue ethics. Two dimensions are of particular interest: First, both utilitarian and Kantian ethics start from the premise that moral agents have the will and the self-control to carry out actions that conform to their respective ethical traditions. By contrast, virtue ethics assumes that people need to be taught, encouraged, and even cajoled to control contradictory impulses. Justice is the virtue of acting with a proper balance of interests toward self and others. Proper socialization and moral suasion provide a process that can mold preferences toward virtuous habits – such as toward personal and even civic responsibility (Sandel, 1998).

A second dimension of virtue ethics in Adam Smith is that humans have limited powers of rationality. As a starting point, people will often rely on their instinctive *feelings* – hence the title of Smith's first book, *The Theory of Moral Sentiments* (1759). Moral sentiments provide the building blocks used to create institutions (rules and laws). A good society requires that people develop an internal commitment to obey the rules in society – rather than calculating gain or loss. However, moral sentiments can and do evolve, hence the duties of a citizen are expected to change over time.

The Public Policy of Slavery

Consider how the three ethical approaches can aid a teacher in analyzing the following public policy question: Is slavery a good or bad institution? A consequentialist would focus on the outcomes of slavery. More specifically, an economist would analyze the particular outcome of maximizing the economic surplus, calculating the gains and losses to society of forced labor (assuming that property rights in slaves exist). In a modern cost-benefit analysis, it is not necessary to show that everyone gains from a policy change (the Pareto condition), but only that winners would win more than losers would lose. Using this approach, slavery could be justified on efficiency grounds if people's preferences (measured by willingness to pay) are better satisfied by this institution than without it, given the current distribution of income and wealth.

Kantians would reject the economic efficiency argument as deeply flawed. From a Kantian perspective one would proceed quite differently, by deducing fundamental laws of duty based on treating others with respect. Because Kant says we have a duty not to treat others merely as a means to our own ends, a policy of slavery would be wrong regardless of any beneficial outcomes. Rights-based ethicists would equally object, since owning one's own labor is the most "sacred and inviolable" of all rights (Smith 1981, p. 138). Virtue ethicists would not necessarily be opposed to slavery (slavery was widespread in early times and religious leaders like Jesus noted the appropriate duties of a slave). However, moral sentiments evolve and slavery can be viewed with new eyes. Smith's moral sentiments approach would place an impartial observer in the shoes of a slave and engage the imagination of "fellow-feeling." To Smith, moral imaginings are stimulated by art, music, and literature (Wight, 2006). Thus, after Harriet Beecher Stowe published *Uncle Tom's Cabin* in 1852, the fellow-feelings of free citizens were aroused because they could understand, and empathize with, the feelings of slaves. From this perspective, abolitionists were inspired to end slavery not because of economic calculations of deadweight losses and not because of rational deductions of duty, but because a large number of people had become emotionally outraged at injustice. To Smith, the impetus for changing institutions and public policies arises from the evolution of moral imagination.

This discussion does not diminish the insights of economic analysis, but identifies complementary (and at times contradictory) critical-thinking traditions that enrich a student's comprehension of public policies. Economists regularly argue cases based on efficiency grounds without considering rights, duties, and other claims. However, only 12 percent of the world's people in 2010 enjoyed basic human rights ensured by democratic constitutions or laws.[1] Highly controversial public issues (e.g. same sex partners, the environment, legalizing the sale of organs) generally entail considerations that cross the boundaries of ethical frameworks. The thesis presented below is that it is preferable to engage students from their own starting ethical beliefs and then build intellectual bridges toward the economic way of thinking.

CLASSROOM ACTIVITIES

Rather than lecturing on the three alternative ethical theories, one can simply allow students to uncover these in class activities. Wight and Morton (2007) provide a set of ten active-learning exercises that engage students in economic problem solving with a modest dose of ethical theory. Lessons include the ethical foundations of efficiency, market sales of kidneys, outsourcing in sweatshops, Rawlsian economic justice, and the role of self-interest in economic analysis. An additional lesson, discussed here, is called the "Desert Island" game (Wight, 2009b). On the first day of class, students are randomly placed in groups of four to five and asked to select a leader. Each leader receives a candy bar and is informed that the group is shipwrecked on an island; the leader has five to ten minutes to decide what to do with the candy bar. Based on an analysis of 165 leader decisions over multiple class sections and academic years, principles students show an overwhelming preference for pro-social behavior manifested by cooperation and equal rationing in most cases.[2]

When students are queried as to why they prefer an equal-sharing approach (in over 80 percent of the groups), their responses are often emotionally charged. Many simply assert that in times of crisis, the proper allocation is equitably, and they exhibit vocal clues as to the degree of moral outrage at any other suggestion.[3] Students' reactions generally conform to experimental evidence. When faced with a moral dilemma, humans commonly respond in an instinctively emotional way. Haidt (2001) demonstrates using fMRI scans that moral decisions activate the brain hemisphere where affective cognition takes place; later, when justification is called for, another hemisphere fires to produce logical rationalizations. Primate studies reinforce the notion that some aspects of social interaction are hardwired, such as the emotional desire for fairness (Brosnan and deWaal, 2003).

The Desert Island activity demonstrates that the economic approach to welfare, valuing outcomes on the basis of consumer preferences satisfied, is not intuitively obvious to many students. Indeed it is largely alien to their thinking and feeling about public policies. Students have been socialized within families, churches, clubs, and other groups. Group psychology revolves around multi-layered judgments about fairness and trust that directly affect the group's survival and evolution (Wight, 2009a). While standard economics generally portrays behavior as rationally self-interested (giving rise to free-riders and sub-optimal Prisoners' Dilemma outcomes), experimental evidence finds that people also operate within a more complex web of moral norms, legal rules, and customs (Gintis et al., 2005). Ostrom (2000), for example, describes the properties of successful local governance in common goods as entailing the evolution of rules and norms that give rise to reciprocity and trust and the perception of fairness.

DEFINING ECONOMICS

Lionel Robbins provides this commonly used definition: "Economics is the science which studies human behaviour as a relationship between ends and scarce means which have alternative uses" (1945, p. 16). Robbins himself notes, however, that a discipline cannot be defined in advance but only after the boundaries of investigation have been determined. In proposing the *ends* and *means* definition, Robbins sought to stretch the boundaries of the field beyond the confines of his day, in which economics was limited to explaining only the causes of material welfare. Robbins expands it to include any outcome-directed activity in which there are resource constraints. In light of the three ethical frameworks presented in this chapter, students can be offered an even broader definition:

> Economics involves the systematic examination of the patterns of individual and group behavior used for the provisioning of the socio-economic system.

In addition to prices and markets, this definition encompasses duty and commitment in economic life (Sen, 1977) and the study of cognitive mechanisms that are not consciously controlled, yet likely play a role in economic activity. Zak (2011), a neuroeconomist, provides evidence of an autonomous brain function that controls social behaviors through the release of hormones such as oxytocin (the "moral molecule"). By varying hormone levels, Zak alters the degree of "fellow-feeling" and hence changes behaviors in experimental settings. Hormones and neural networks appear to provide the biological scaffolding for sociability that underlies Adam Smith's conception of moral behavior.

Social modeling thus grapples with interpersonal ethical considerations that are psychologically, philosophically, and biologically intertwined. Smith theorized that humans pursue self-deceptive goals whose ultimate ends are not consciously knowable, even as they serve higher purposes (1759, p. 183). The "invisible hand" arises within this context: "It is this deception which rouses and keeps in continual motion the industry of mankind" (1759, p. 183). For a classroom treatment of this subject, see Wight (2007).

Over the centuries, Smith's philosophy devolved into the separate (and, to a large degree, isolated) disciplines of psychology, philosophy, economics, sociology, political science, and law. In the 1920s, Balliol College at Oxford (where Smith had studied) began reintegrating the study of philosophy, politics, and economics (PPE). Teachers can use the academic novel, *Saving Adam Smith: A Tale of Wealth, Transformation, and Virtue* (Wight, 2002) to explore Smith's moral underpinnings for wealth creation as a pillar of his market philosophy. There are presently more than 50 universities with PPE programs, including Yale, Pennsylvania, Notre Dame, Glasgow, and Richmond.[4] A discussion of ethics is beginning to appear in principles textbooks.[5] A PPE approach can be instituted in many economics classes without substantial opportunity cost.

JUSTIFYING AN ETHICAL FRAMEWORK

As noted above, Kantians use rationality for understanding the appropriate means of acting (rather than for achieving a particular end). And virtue ethicists like Smith explore the emotionally cognitive behaviors that arise from instincts needed for survival in groups. Economists argue that people make rational decisions to achieve the goal of maximizing utility. In reality, people make decisions for complex reasons, not all of which can be understood by a single model. The practice of tipping at highway restaurants, for example, relates to all three approaches: first, because of a rational calculation of reputation-building and future services to be received (economic); second, from logically derived rules for treating others with respect (Kantian); and third, from instinctual fellow-feelings (Smithian). Many other economic behaviors can be modeled in deeper ways than simply connecting means with desired ends.

If there are valid multiple perspectives, how can any one of these be "right"? One approach is to simplify economics to produce a "single, coherent" set of concepts that won't confuse students.[6] Hence, many teachers portray economics as engineering, with non-controversial goals and methods that yield the "right" answers to allocation questions. In his Nobel Prize address, Ronald Coase laments: "What is studied is a system which lives in the minds of economists but not on earth. I have called the result 'blackboard economics'."[7] In addition to being unscientific, "blackboard economics" is antithetical to critical thinking (Nelson, 1989).

A commitment to critical thinking requires that teachers deal with complexity and controversy. When policy issues are discussed, teachers should encourage students to think outside the economists' toolbox. It is not simply that there are additional outcomes (besides preferences) that could be considered, it is also that *non*-outcomes-based ways of thinking are ubiquitous. During emergencies, people instinctively reject markets in favor of rules for sharing derived from duty or virtue ethics. Non-price allocations are also widely used in families, churches, and schools, institutions which are paternalistic and geared toward cultivating virtuous habits in young people.

The moral justification for markets arises from considering the problems that arise within these contexts (Wight, 2009b). Teachers can discuss Bentham's (1789) advocacy of utilitarianism as a result of his growing discontent with policies imposed by authority and precedent. In the 18th century, Enlightenment thinkers contended that the institutions of human society should be examined and debated just like the laws of physical science; public policies should be chosen based on their outcomes rather than simply the tyranny of tradition, or by misguided appeals to duties, rights or virtues. Hence, even after considering the objections of other ethical frameworks, a strong justification for policies based on a consequentialist cost-benefit analysis can be made (Frank, 2008).

CONCLUSION

Outcomes, duties, and virtues are three competing and overlapping ways of conceptualizing how to study the world of choice. By focusing on outcomes, economics teachers make an ethical judgment about how a scientist *should* try to understand the world. For this and other reasons, the demarcation between positive and normative economics is blurred. The study of economic choices rarely is placed in the wider context of goals, commitments, and virtues that comprise the active life of politics, business, and society. This omission is curious and paradoxical, considering that "even in the most market-oriented economy, a majority of transactions do not actually go through markets" (McMillan, 2003, p. 6). The ubiquity of non-price trade in households, governments, and within firms suggests that social costs and trust play important roles in economic life, even if unrecognized. Behavior derives from multiple origins, including expected outcomes, duties and commitments, and conceptions of character. The pluralistic account advocated here expands the scope of inquiry in positive economics and provides a springboard for understanding non-neoclassical approaches to the analysis of public policies.

NOTES

1. The Economist Intelligence Unit, "Democracy index 2010: democracy in retreat," http://graphics.eiu.com/PDF/Democracy_Index_2010_web.pdf (accessed 5 January 2011).
2. This is not an experiment and the "set-up" virtually ensures cooperation; few students want to appear to be unsociable. This is Adam Smith's main point, that humans are highly social creatures and desire approbation.

3. Outcomes do not have to be equal to be equitable. Some group members may be heavier, or exert more energy, and thus "need" more food. Equity in this context means something like, "From each according to ability, to each according to need." Hence, students instinctively act like good communists (Samuelson 1969).
4. Source: http://en.wikipedia.org/wiki/Philosophy,_Politics_and_Economics (accessed 26 April 2010).
5. See, for example, Cowen and Tabarrok (2010) and Goodwin et al. (2005).
6. This is the stated goal of the Council on Economic Education's revision of the Voluntary National Content Standards in Economics. See: http://www.councilforeconed.org/ea/standards/standards_preface.pdf (accessed 5 January 2011).
7. http://nobelprize.org/nobel_prizes/economics/laureates/1991/coase-lecture.html (accessed 5 January 2011).

REFERENCES

Bentham, J. (1789), *Introduction to the Principles of Morals and Legislation,* available at http://www.econlib.org/library/Bentham/bnthPML.html.
Brosnan, S. F. and F. B. M. de Waal (2003), "Monkeys reject unequal pay", *Nature,* **425**, 297–9.
Coase, R. (1960), "The problem of social cost", *Journal of Law and Economics,* **3** (October), 1–44.
Cowen, T. and A. Tabarrok (2010), *Modern Economics: Microeconomics,* New York: Worth Publishers.
DeMartino, G. (2011), *The Economist's Oath: On the Need for and Content of Professional Economic Ethics,* Oxford, UK: Oxford University Press.
Frank, R. H. (2008), "The status of moral emotions in consequentialist moral reasoning", in P. J. Zak (ed.), *Moral Markets: The Critical Role of Values in the Economy,* Princeton, NJ: Princeton University Press, pp. 42–59.
Gintis, H., S. Bowles, R. T. Boyd and E. Fehr (eds) (2005), *Moral Sentiments and Material Interests: The Foundations of Cooperation in Economic Life,* Cambridge, MA: MIT Press.
Goodwin, N., J. A. Nelson, F. Ackerman and T. Weisskopf (2005), *Microeconomics in Context,* Boston, MA: Houghton Mifflin Co.
Haidt, J. (2001), "The emotional dog and its rational tail: A social intuitionist approach to moral judgment", *Psychological Review,* **108** (4), 814–34.
Hausman, D. M. and M. S. McPherson (2006), *Economic Analysis, Moral Philosophy, and Public Policy,* Cambridge: Cambridge University Press.
Kant, I. (1785), *Groundwork of the Metaphysics of Morals,* reprinted in M. Gregor (ed.) (trans) (1998), Cambridge: Cambridge University Press.
McCloskey, D. N. (2006), *The Bourgeoise Virtues: Ethics for an Age of Commerce,* Chicago: University of Chicago Press.
McMillan, J. (2003), *Reinventing the Bazaar: A Natural History of Markets,* New York: W.W. Norton.
Nelson, C. E. (1989), "Skewered on the unicorn's horn: The illusion of tragic tradeoff between content and critical thinking in the teaching of science", in L. W. Crow (ed.), *Enhancing Critical Thinking in the Sciences,* Washington, DC: Society for College Science Teachers, pp. 17–27.
Ostrom, E. (2000), "Collective action and the evolution of social norms", *Journal of Economic Perspectives,* **14** (3) (Summer), 137–58.
Robbins, L. (1932), *An Essay on the Nature and Significance of Economic Science* (2nd edition), (1945), London: Macmillan and Co., http://mises.org/books/robbinsessay2.pdf, accessed 24 April 2010.
Samuelson, P. (1969), "Love", *Newsweek,* reprinted in P. Samuelson (ed.) (1983), *Economics from the Heart: A Samuelson Sampler,* San Diego: Harcourt Brace Jovanovich, pp. 9–11.
Sandel, M. J. (1998), "What money can't buy: The moral limits of markets", *The Tanner Lectures on Human Values,* Oxford University, http://www.tannerlectures.utah.edu/lectures/documents/sandel00.pdf, accessed 11 February 2011.
Sen, A. K. (1977), "Rational fools: A critique of the behavioral foundations of economic theory", *Philosophy & Public Affairs,* **6** (summer), 317–44.
Smith, A. (1759), *The Theory of Moral Sentiments,* D. D. Raphael and A. L. Macfie (eds) (1982), volume I of the *Glasgow Edition of the Works and Correspondence of Adam Smith,* Indianapolis: Liberty Fund Press.
Smith, A. (1776), *An Inquiry into the Nature and Causes of the Wealth of Nations,* R. H. Campbell and A. S. Skinner (eds) (1981), volume II of the *Glasgow edition of the Works and Correspondence of Adam Smith,* Indianapolis: Liberty Fund Press.
Wight, J. B. (2002), *Saving Adam Smith: A Tale of Wealth, Transformation, and Virtue,* Upper Saddle River, NJ: Prentice-Hall.
Wight, J. B. (2006), "Adam Smith's ethics and the 'noble' arts", *Review of Social Economy,* **64** (2), 155–80.

Wight, J. B. (2007), "The treatment of Smith's invisible hand", *The Journal of Economic Education,* **39** (3), 341–58.

Wight, J. B. (2009a), "Adam Smith on instincts, ethics, and informal learning: Proximate mechanisms in multilevel selection", *Review of Social Economy,* **67** (1), 95–113.

Wight, J. B. (2009b), "Sociability and the market", *Forum for Social Economics,* **39** (2/3), 97–110.

Wight, J. B. and J. S. Morton (2007), *Teaching the Ethical Foundations of Economics,* New York: The National Council on Economic Education.

Zak, P. J. (2011), "The physiology of moral sentiments", *Journal of Economic Behavior and Organization,* **77** (1), 53–6.

19 Feminist pedagogy and economics
Jean Shackelford

This chapter will explain the core concepts of feminist pedagogy, describe how it might be implemented in economics, and explore various costs and benefits of this approach. Feminist pedagogy integrates race, class and gender into course content,[1] examines a variety of power relationships, enhances critical thinking skills and emphasizes student-centered learning with the goal of fostering student engagement.

Feminist pedagogy in economics has two primary roots. The first root is feminist theory; the second is a perspective on pedagogy that can be traced from Dewey (1910, 1966) to Freire (1996). Each plays an important role in the construction and development of feminist pedagogy in economics.

FEMINIST PEDAGOGY AND FEMINIST THEORY

Feminist pedagogy was introduced in women's studies courses in the 1980s and quickly spread to other disciplines. Scholarship by Bricker-Jenkins and Hooyman (1987), Maher (1987) and Shrewsbury (1987) outline key components of feminist pedagogy. While feminist pedagogy is employed across disciplines, scholars in women's studies continue to publish the vast majority of research on, and examples of, applications (Crabtree, Sapp and Licona, 2009).

Like feminist theory, feminist pedagogy is contested. There is not a single, monolithic pillar proclaiming: "this is feminist pedagogy." Indeed, there is a multiplicity of feminist pedagogies, suggesting to some, perhaps, that this particular pedagogy is not firmly grounded, or that it is a pedagogy that is continually changing. While feminist pedagogy has many variants, each is firmly grounded in feminist theory, epistemology, and methodology, offering direction, not absolutes.

The understanding of power and power relationships are central to both feminist theory and feminist pedagogy. In a feminist classroom, the understanding of power is played out not only in course content but also in the relationships between teacher and students, resulting in a more student-centered classroom. Like feminist theory, feminist pedagogical approaches are not reductionist or essentialist. Explanations of complex social, economic and scientific systems that are reduced to a few basic ideas or assumptions may preclude more inclusive explanations, questions and research leading to potentially better theory (Harding, 1991). While reductionist theories may indeed facilitate student understanding of the current accepted state of a discipline such as economics, because of their simplicity (even elegance), they preclude more complex, contextual explanations and stifle questions that might generate research leading to theory and policy that is applicable in a wider context. For example, reductionist theories incorporated into most economics texts failed to provide an analysis (or understanding) of the global financial crisis. Reductionist explanations of the crisis may fail to explore the important causes of the crisis and its effects on populations worldwide.

Feminist pedagogy, like feminist theory, avoids essentialism, or defining a group or population, according to a certain set of characteristics (Fuss, 1989). Instead it focuses on a social construction of knowledge recognizing that "fixed traits," particularly when assigned to race, class and gender, may obscure a better understanding of the economy, of society or of developing better theory and policy. For example, child poverty has a multiplicity of faces. An examination of this multiplicity may lead to a better understanding of the causes of child poverty and result in improved policy.

While feminist pedagogy is anchored in feminist theory, it is also a pedagogy rooted in pedagogic traditions that center on engaging students by integrating their experiences into learning environments.

FEMINIST PEDAGOGY AND CRITICAL PEDAGOGIES

The second root of feminist pedagogy in economics derives from educational reformers John Dewey (1859–1952) and Paulo Freire (1921–97). Dewey outlined his views on pedagogy and the role of education in preparing fully informed citizens to actively participate in democratic processes (Dewey, 1910, 1966). Viewing education as necessary for social life, Dewey advocated active student involvement by bringing student experiences into the classroom.[2] To Dewey, teachers are intellectual leaders because of their "wider and deeper" knowledge. His reforms emphasized connecting student experiences and instruction in the learning process. Dewey's goal for the education system was to educate all students as critical learners to become active as informed citizens (Dewey, 1910, 1966).

Like Dewey, Paulo Freire developed a more student-centered pedagogy resulting from his work in Brazil teaching adults to read and write. In *Pedagogy of the Oppressed* (1968), Freire rejected what he called the "banking approach" to education in which teachers make "deposits" into students' empty minds – or accounts – emphasizing instead the integration of students' lived experiences into lessons that result in immediate understanding, meaning and transferability, and at the same time, create a balance between theory and practice. Freire's goal was not simply to teach the mechanics of reading and writing, but to empower students with the tools necessary to critically evaluate their society and their situation in it. And, like the practical pedagogy of Dewey and the critical pedagogy of Freire, feminist pedagogy in economics recognizes the importance of linking student experiences to learning, and applying economic tools, concepts and theories. This student-centered learning produces transferable knowledge essential for an informed citizenry evaluating current and past policies and practices, and participating in private and public decisions.

INTEGRATING FEMINIST PEDAGOGY IN ECONOMICS INTO THE CLASSROOM

From its roots in feminist theory and pedagogies of Dewey and Freire, feminist pedagogy in economics moves toward empowering students in their growth as critical thinkers and creative learners by focusing on student-centered instruction, where process and content transform traditional economics classrooms and institutional structures (Shackelford, 1992). To create feminist pedagogical strategies in an economics classroom, instructors re-evaluate course content and teaching strategies that include power relationships, and classroom approaches, assignments, etc. in order to engage all students.

Feminist Pedagogy in Economics – Course Content

Feminist pedagogy in economics requires that course contents are carefully evaluated and adapted so that they are inclusive of gender, race and class (as well as other identities such as sexual orientation, ethnicity or regional identity). Feminist economist educators recognize that an examination of economic power and power relationships is integral for examining and understanding these topics. Given the nature of the questions raised in economics, traditional text materials are often supplemented or substituted with readings or additional data or cases. For example, introducing the Human Development Index and adding discussions that incorporate the construction and interpretation of data may enhance the understanding of GDP. Inclusion throughout the course is necessary to engage more women and students from diverse backgrounds and identities by presenting them with a more complete representation of their economic reality (Aerni et al., 1999). Aerni et al. (1999), following McIntosh (1983), identified phases in adapting course content. These phases range from adding a few readings in a traditional course to completely integrating topics of race, class and gender seamlessly throughout all topics, concepts and examples so that they are not viewed as special cases or anomalies by some, or not worthy of further interest by others. A complete transformation would integrate race, class and gender issues not only throughout a course but also through the entire economics curriculum. Identifying materials for content challenges instructors wishing to employ feminist pedagogy in their economics classrooms since US texts generally do not devote more than a chapter or section or minor mention to these topics. As the literature on feminist economics expands, a variety of new resources aid instructors to more completely transform content (Schneider and Shackelford, 2001; Aerni and McGoldrick, 1999; Strassmann, 1998).[3] And, as technologies develop, web-based information, videos and visual resources join traditional publications in providing a basis for transforming courses.

Expanded content helps develop a better and more complete understanding of the world and of the strengths and weaknesses of economic tools and theories used to analyze economic problems and events. While instructors may introduce the global financial crisis and resulting Great Recession in the US into their courses to better understand macroeconomic analysis, it is also useful to examine the winners and losers from each, including changes in income distribution and labor force participation, as well as groups and occupations hard hit by unemployment. Thus, inclusive content sets forth traditional and non-traditional contexts for discussion, developing applications and constructing criticism to implement feminist pedagogical strategies in economics courses. Bransford et al. (2000) suggest that students are more likely to "grasp the new concepts and information that they are taught" when their initial understanding or preconceptions of the topic are engaged, "providing a foundation for building new knowledge" (pp. 15–16). Through critical examination of content and context, higher-order thinking constructs enable students to begin assessing and evaluating economic topics. Adapting course content and materials with assignments that focus on using content rather than memorizing it, as well as by re-examining the classroom environment and class attitudes, empowers students to become active learners and creative and critical thinkers (Shackelford, 1992; Lewis, 1995; McGoldrick, 1999).

Feminist Pedagogy in Economics – Student-centered Classrooms and Active Learning Strategies

The second component of creating an inclusive learning environment focuses on active critical engagement (Shackelford, 1992). Traditional economics courses involve mostly passive students, with Freire's lecturer making deposits of information into their empty minds. More recently, a resurgence of Socratic methods[4] – particularly in writing intensive courses – has engaged students a bit more, as instructors ask questions and lead classes in discussion[5] of course materials. While the Socratic classroom can add more activities and class projects soliciting greater responses from students, all too often the instructor remains at the center, coordinating these activities (Stage et al., 1998). Even though more instructors vary their teaching methods, the majority of economics instructors continue to rely on lectures (Becker and Watts, 2008). Moving to a more student-centered, less hierarchical classroom fostering cooperation and community requires a more egalitarian model where students become more responsible for their learning and skill development.[6] Still, even in more student-centered classrooms, instructors cannot fully divest themselves of power over students, since grading and overall responsibility for the integrity of the course cannot be shared.

Over the past decade, economic education literature has emphasized developing and assessing active learning strategies in the teaching/learning process – strategies that may be used to focus classroom activities on students (Meyers and Jones, 1993; McGoldrick, 1999; Shackelford, 2006). One aim of Dewey and Freire's pedagogies was to center learning around students' lived experiences. Feminist pedagogy in economics often integrates techniques of active learning strategies, and integrates transformed content with student-centered projects, cases or service-learning aimed at engaging students' lives with course content. Active learning means that students are integrally engaged in employing higher-order thinking tasks, including analysis, synthesis and assessment. Listening, repeating, and memorizing are insufficient. "They must read, write, discuss, or be engaged in solving problems" (Bonwell and Eison, 1991, p. iii). Indeed, employing active learning is one of the "Seven Principles of Good Practices in Higher Education" outlined by Chickering and Gamson (1991). While assessments comparing active and passive learning strategies have not consistently led to measurable outcomes showing that one is superior to the other, evaluation of these strategies does suggest that active learning promotes development of thinking and writing (Bonwell and Eison, 1991).

BENEFITS AND COSTS OF FEMINIST PEDAGOGY IN ECONOMICS

As with all transformations, there are both benefits and costs. Two primary benefits of utilizing feminist pedagogy in economics classrooms come to mind. First, there is evidence that utilizing a variety of teaching strategies, beyond the lecture, engages a wider, more diverse group of students, and secondly, critical thinking and other skills, fundamental to higher education goals, may be enhanced by implementing feminist pedagogy in economics courses. Additionally, students who are able to integrate new knowledge with their experiences are encouraged to forge directly useful and meaningful links to economic concepts and principles and begin to critically evaluate and assess data, theory, and other forms of economic information (Bransford et al., 2000).

Reaching a Broader Audience

Research examining ways of learning demonstrates that some women learn differently than men (Tobias, 1990; Belenky, Clinchy, Goldberger and Tarule, 1997), and learning styles research indicates that women and students with other cultural differences often respond and learn more effectively from nontraditional strategies.

While the large and growing literature on learning styles has generated theories, assessment devices, and many studies, there are few clear-cut recommendations due to a lack of longitudinal studies. Most studies focus on three interrelated aspects of student learning, including the ways students informally process information, their instructional preferences (including individual and collaborative learning) and their responses to different learning strategies (CIPD, 2010). Some studies address issues linked to gender and learning, finding that *most* females and males learn from the *same* strategies, but there are some differences. Fox and Ronkowski (1997) found that a greater percentage of women than men preferred active experimentation and concrete experience to abstraction, and that a greater percentage of males than females preferred abstraction and experimentation. Since economics courses tend to be abstract, some female students may find themselves at a disadvantage compared with some male students. Guild (1994) found that there are cultural differences in learning styles as well. While there are many studies employing various measuring instruments of learning styles, the common result is that different people learn and process information in different ways. Regardless of which assessment device is used to evaluate learning, the bottom line seems to be that that there are multiple learning strategies and that incorporating more rather than fewer of them into one's course is preferable to relying on one strategy (Coffield et al., 2004). Feminist pedagogy in economics employs a multiplicity of strategies in course assignments and in class activities so that more students will have greater opportunities for learning economics.

Developing Skills

The second benefit of employing feminist pedagogy in economics courses is to engage students in critical and creative thinking skills. In outlining the purposes of higher education, Bok (2006) notes that 90 percent of US faculty members surveyed consider critical thinking as most important (Bok, 2006, pp. 67–8) and presents qualities that critical thinking might encompass. These include "an ability to recognize and define problems clearly, to identify the arguments and interests on all sides of an issue, to gather relevant facts and appreciate their relevance, to perceive as many plausible solutions as possible, and to exercise good judgment in choosing the best of these alternatives after considering the evidence and using inference, analogy and other forms of ordinary reasoning to test the cogency of the arguments" (Bok, 2006, p. 68). Such qualities are more than compatible with the goals of feminist pedagogy as students transform content, gather facts and data, define problems and use evidence to forge and test conclusions in collaborative student-centered classrooms.

Bok's list of higher education purposes also includes the ability to communicate well with audiences; moral reasoning; preparing citizens for the process of democratic self-government; living with diversity; living in a more global society; breadth of interest; and preparing for work (2006, pp. 67–78). While feminist pedagogy may not serve to further *all* of these purposes, the preceding discussion outlines the importance of understanding diversity and the importance of critically evaluating data and policy.

Who Bears the Burden?

And, while there are significant benefits of employing feminist pedagogy in economics both for individual students and for society, the costs are mostly born by individual instructors who must transform course content, classrooms and traditional assignments. Current practice in economics encourages lecturing from a text that is augmented with prepared PowerPoint presentations for each chapter and assessment practices based on a test bank of multiple choice and short answer questions. Using these "out of the box" resources requires far less time and effort than practicing feminist pedagogy. Becker and Watts (1998) suggest that there is evidence that current practices are "established by convenience, custom and inertia rather than efficiency or, especially, by what represents effective teaching practices in today's undergraduate curriculum" (Becker and Watts, 1998, p. 4). When instructors do transform courses with successful student outcomes, departments or universities may not consider or reward these considerable investments in teaching, as Boyer (1990) suggests. Before engaging in alternative pedagogies, instructors should have a clear sense of how their department and the university evaluate teaching and research in tenure and promotion guidelines.

Experimenting with new pedagogies is risky in other ways. Experiments don't always work, and sharing control of one's classroom is at times disquieting as active student-centered pedagogies are unpredictable and, they take more in-class time than lecturing. That may result in fewer topics being covered, a tradeoff that may not be negotiable with economic department colleagues.

CONCLUSION

Employing feminist pedagogy in economics examines power relationships within economics by casting a feminist lens over traditional topics. Feminist pedagogy is inclusive, integrating race, class and gender into economics course content, fostering engagement of all students through transformed content and accommodating a variety of learning styles. Linking student experiences to learning by applying and using economic tools, concepts and theories, students in student-centered environments rehearse skills necessary for critically evaluating the economy and assessing and evaluating their economic position in society. These skills are essential for an informed citizenry evaluating economic policies and public and private decisions.

NOTES

1. For more information about this process, see Chapter 20, "Integrating Race, Gender, and Class", in this volume.
2. For additional information see Chapter 6, "Experiential Education in Economics", in this volume.
3. For more information see Chapter 20 in this volume.
4. For more information about this process, see Chapter 11, "Teaching Economics Socratically", in this volume.
5. For more information about this process, see Chapter 5, "Improving Classroom Discussion in Economics Courses", in this volume.
6. See the Section A – Techniques of Part II – Teaching of this volume for more information.

REFERENCES

Aerni, A. L. and K. McGoldrick (eds) (1999), *Valuing Us All: Feminist Pedagogy and Economics*, Ann Arbor, US: The University of Michigan Press.

Aerni, A. L., R. L. Bartlett, M. Lewis, K. McGoldrick and J. Shackelford (1999), "Toward a Feminist Pedagogy in Economics", *Feminist Economics*, **5** (1), 29–44.

Becker, W. E. and M. Watts (eds) (1998), *Teaching Economics to Undergraduates: Alternatives to Chalk and Talk*, Cheltenham, UK and Northampton, MA, US: Edward Elgar.

Becker, W. E. and M. Watts (2008), "A little more than chalk and talk: Results from a third national survey of teaching methods in undergraduate economics courses", *Journal of Economic Education*, **39** (3), 273–86.

Belenky, M., B. Clinchy, N. Goldberger and J. Tarule (1997), *Women's Ways of Knowing: The Development of Self, Voice, and Mind*, New York, US: Basic Books.

Bok, D. (2006), *Our Underachieving Colleges: A Candid Look at How Much Students Learn and Why They Should Be Learning More*, Princeton, US and Oxford, UK: The Princeton University Press.

Bonwell, C. C. and J. A. Eison (1991), *Active Learning: Creating Excitement in the Classroom*, ASHE-ERIC Higher Education Report No. 1. Washington, DC, US: The George Washington University.

Boyer, E. L. (1990), *Scholarship Reconsidered: Priorities of the Professoriate*, The Carnegie Foundation for the Advancement of Teaching, San Francisco, US: Jossey-Bass.

Bransford, J., A. L. Brown, and R. R. Cocking (2000), *How People Learn: Brain, Mind, Experience, and School*, National Research Council. Washington, DC, US: National Academy Press.

Bricker-Jenkins, M. and N. Hooyman (1987), "Feminist pedagogy in education for social change", *Feminist Teacher*, **2**, 36–42.

Chickering, A. W. and Z. F. Gamson (eds) (1991), *Applying the Seven Principles for Good Practice in Undergraduate Education*, New Directions in Teaching and Learning, No. 47, San Francisco, US: Jossey-Bass.

CIPD Learning Styles (2005), http://www.cipd.co.uk/subjects/lrnanddev/general/lrngstyles.htm, accessed 20 April 2010.

Coffield, F., D. Moseley, E. Hall and K. Ecclestone (2004), "Learning styles and pedagogy in post-16 learning: A systematic and critical review", Learning & skills research centre.

Crabtree, R. D., D. A. Sapp and A. C. Licona (eds) (2009), *Feminist Pedagogy: Looking Backward to Move Forward*, Baltimore, US: The Johns Hopkins University Press.

Dewey, J. (1910), *How We Think*, New York, US: D.C. Heath & Co.

Dewey, J. (1966), *Democracy and Education*, New York, US: The Macmillan Company.

Fox, R. L. and S. A. Ronkowski (1997), "Learning styles of political science students", *PS: Political Science and Politics*, **30** (4), 732–7.

Freire, P. (1996), *Pedagogy of the Oppressed*, New York, US: Continuum.

Fuss, D. (1989), *Essentially Speaking: Feminism, Nature & Difference*, New York, US: Routledge.

Guild, P. (1994), "The Culture/learning style connection", *Economic Leadership*, **5** (8), 16–21.

Harding, S. (1991), *Whose Science? Whose Knowledge? Thinking from Women's Lives*, Ithaca, US: Cornell University Press.

Lewis, M. (1995), "Breaking down the walls, opening up the field", *Journal of Economic Issues,* **29** (2), 555–65.

Maher, F. A. (1987), "Toward a richer theory of feminist pedagogy: A comparison of 'Liberation and Gender' models for teaching and learning", *Journal of Education,* **169** (3), 91–100.

McGoldrick, K. (1999), "The road not taken: Service learning as an example of feminist pedagogy in economics", in A. L. Aerni and K. McGoldrick (eds), *Valuing Us All: Feminist Pedagogy and Economics,* Ann Arbor, US: The University of Michigan Press, pp. 168–83.

McIntosh, P. (1983), "Interactive phases of curricular re-vision: A feminist perspective", Working Paper No. 124. Wellesley College Center for Research on Women.

Meyers, C. and T. B. Jones (1993), *Promoting Active Learning: Strategies for the College Classroom,* San Francisco, US: Jossey-Bass.

Schneider, G. and J. Shackelford (2001), "Economic standards and lists: Proposed antidotes for feminist economists", *Feminist Economics,* **7** (2), 77–89.

Shackelford, J. (1992), "Feminist pedagogy: A means for bringing critical thinking and creativity to the economics classroom", *American Economic Review,* **82** (2), 570–76.

Shackelford, J. (2006), "Practicing feminist pedagogy: Places/spaces/cases for feminist economic education", Unpublished paper presented at the Conference on Feminist Economics, July 7–9, Sydney, Australia.

Shrewsbury, C. M. (1987), "What is feminist pedagogy?", *Women's Studies Quarterly,* **25** (3&4), 6–31.

Stage, F., P. Mujller, J. Kinzie and A. Simmons (1998), "Creating learning centered classrooms. What does learning theory have to say?", Washington, DC, US: George Washington University, Graduate School of Education and Human Development, ERIC Clearinghouse on Higher Education.

Strassmann, D. (1998), "Editorial: Towards a more accountable economics", *Feminist Economics* **4** (2), viii–ix.

Tobias, S. (1990), *They're Not Dumb, They're Different: Stalking the Second Tier,* Tucson, US: Research Corporation.

20 Integrating race, gender and class
Robin L. Bartlett

Integrating race, gender and class into the content of disciplines has progressed from integrating one social construct, such as race, to integrating multiple, intersecting and layered levels of social constructs, such as race, gender and class. The progress across and within disciplines has been uneven, with starts, stops, and turns. Economics is one of the last disciplines to integrate race, gender and class into its core content.

The process of integrating the social constructs of race, gender and class into economics usually proceeds along one of two paths: adding more content related to one or more of these social constructs or examining the existing content from the perspective of a particular social construct. On the first path, the behaviors and economic realities of missing, overlooked and otherwise invisible peoples are added to the content of economics. The materials for inclusion can sometimes be found in very specialized subfields of labor, income inequality and public finance. An additional place to look for more inclusive materials is in other disciplines. For example, in psychology, Hyde (2005) found, using a meta-analysis to test the gender similarities hypothesis, that a few differences in motor abilities, sexual and aggressive behaviors exist and that they vary widely by age and context. The assumed male and female differences, however, such as mathematical, verbal, and writing abilities, were all over inflated, resulting in substantial costs to women in the workforce and in relationships.

An alternative path to explore is to take the accepted economic principles found in traditional introductory or advanced economics textbooks and to consciously examine them from different perspectives or using different lenses. This means taking an economic concept such as growth and examining it from the perspective of people of color, women or people from different socioeconomic classes. For example, a Department of Commerce press release informs introductory macroeconomics students that Gross Domestic Product grew more than expected last quarter. The stock markets on Wall Street soar. This is good news. Yet, the owners of retail stores on Main Street feel the pinch as companies move out of the US to overseas. The exceptional growth means different things for the entrepreneurial as opposed to the working classes.

MAKING COURSE CONTENT MORE INCLUSIVE

Fortunately, others have gone down this path before economists. The ideas that follow are ones that have been developed over the past three decades. This work began with the pioneering efforts of Peggy McIntosh at Wellesley College's Center for Research on Women. During the academic years of 1982–3 and 1983–4, the Center offered four New England Regional Seminars for faculty on integrating the new scholarship on women into the various disciplines. Over the two-year period, each semester a seminar focused on one of the following academic divisions: the arts, humanities, social sciences and sciences. The impact of these seminars on the scholars who participated in them and on their subsequent work has not been studied. McIntosh's model, however, is still used as a framework for incorporating race, gender, and class into the content of disciplines.

The McIntosh Model

In her faculty development seminars, McIntosh (1983) outlined five progressive and interactive phases of a model that systematically integrates what was then called the new scholarship on women into the content of the disciplines. The first phase of her model is called "The Womanless Discipline" phase. In this phase, women are totally absent from the content of the discipline. The canons of the discipline are put forth as if they are gender blind. Theoretical concepts and analytical frameworks are presented as if they are objective, without any kind of bias. The received doctrines, principles, and laws are thought to be universal. It is assumed that, with little modification, they can be effectively used to explain the behaviors and realities of all people, at all times in history, and in all countries around the globe.

In the second phase, designated as "Women Notables," the works and accomplishments of a few distinguished women are highlighted and added to the content of the discipline. These exceptional, probably previously overlooked or even discounted, women are heralded as pioneers in their discipline. These women are also held up as role models. The message is that anyone (male or female) who wants to achieve this status can. At this phase, the canon remains intact.

The third phase is known as "Add Women and Stir." Two things can happen in this phase. The theoretical works and analytical frameworks of the women uncovered or rediscovered in the second phase are discussed alongside the traditional content of the discipline, often relegated to insert boxes on one of the many pages of a chapter in the textbook or consolidated and placed into a special chapter. Alternatively, women's "special interests" or "special issues" are analyzed, using the discipline's traditional tools of analysis. Applying the canon with its accepted theoretical concepts or analytical frameworks to the specific interests and issues of women may reveal similarities and/or differences. When women's behaviors and realities differ from those of their male counterparts, they are often labeled as deviant, problems, or anomalies.

The differences found in the third phase cannot be slid under disciplinary rugs and hence motivate the fourth phase: "Women as Problems, Deviants, and Anomalies." Attempts to improve the theoretical robustness of accepted theories are made by incorporating the behaviors and realities of both men and women into the analyses. Assumptions are modified and the models are expanded to include new variables and new parameters. For accepted theories that cannot be sufficiently modified to explain the observed differences, alternative heterodox explanations may be explored.[1] Heterodox explanations, however, do not always provide better explanations of observed anomalies because they too may suffer from the same biases and preconceived notions of models that are based upon male norms and lenses.

The final phase of the model is "Women as the Discipline or the Discipline Re-visioned." Given that the orthodox and heterodox core concepts and theories of a discipline may not adequately explain the behavior and realities of women, new analytical structures are needed. This phase entails a re-visioning of disciplines and their processes of inquiry. For example, rather than gender being added as a variable in the analysis, women become the subject of analysis. In short, what makes women, women? How do the interlocking systems of political, social and economic institutions that surround women create their identities?

Re-visioning is the most difficult phase of McIntosh's model to implement. To re-vision, a scholar must give up any preconceived notions, schema, analytical frameworks or beliefs about a discipline and the objects of its inquiries and discover anew. For example, what if fear trumps rationality in humans? We are wired like the animals to "fight or flight" when threatened with harm. What happens when the animal brain takes precedence over the rational brain?

Applications of McIntosh's Model

As a white, economically privileged woman, McIntosh (1988, 1990) was surprised when a friend of color said that she would not change places with McIntosh. After much thought, McIntosh realized that her friend did not want to give up her racial culture or identity, but would be willing to give up her circumstances. So, McIntosh developed the notions of male privilege and white privilege.

Male privilege is when the skills or qualities attributed to males are seen as the norm. This occurs when males only see the attributes of the male culture: a male monoculture. People without these attributes are seen as deficient. Men see themselves as being hard-nosed, unemotional, "tough" business decision-makers. Since fewer women either are born with, or acquire, these particular attributes, women are seen as deficient. Hard-nosed, unemotional, tough decision-making is the kind of decision-making that is privileged. Typically business decisions are made in this manner; the way the dominant group, males, make decisions. The possibility that there may be a different, perhaps even better, way of making business decisions outside of this monoculture is not recognized or considered.

McIntosh discusses the concept of white privilege as the unrecognized and unacknowledged privilege that white people have over people of color. White people generally think that people of color would be more than willing to trade places with them. So people of color who do not buy into the white cultural norms and conform are seen as deficient. Most white workers would never think that they got their jobs because they were white. Nor would they think that losing their jobs discredits all white workers. However, according to McIntosh's model of privilege, people of color hired into a predominantly white workforce may think in the back of their minds that they got the job because they were a person of color. They also may carry the burden that, if they fail, other people of color may suffer. White privilege means not having to think about these possibilities.

Labeling groups of individuals as deficient can have devastating consequences. For example, nonnative English-speaking students in public schools may be labeled as deficient because they have trouble learning US history. They are then stigmatized as not as capable as native English-speaking students. Sometimes, they are put in special classes for slower learners who may have very different learning challenges.[2] Interventions are then misdirected. However, students who have learned one language are not deficient in language skills. They simply need to learn another language.

Class privilege exists also, but incorporating class into the disciplinary constructs is difficult because there is no one definition of class. Class is characterized by combinations of economic, social or political power. Those with the most economic, social or political power are defined as the upper classes and those with the least economic, political and social power are the lower classes. Class power, and thus privilege, can originate in claims to economic resources. Marxists define a group's class by its relationship to the means of production (Beer, 1955). Those who own capital are the bourgeoisie and those that sell their labor to the owners of capital are the proletariat. Modern Marxists include another class, the petite bourgeoisie, consisting of managers, artisans and professionals who own their human capital and sell it to those in the other classes. The more capital, physical or human, the more resources a class controls.

In an effort to determine who is poor and who is rich, the US Census Bureau puts income recipients in order from the lowest to the highest values and then divides the population into fifths, or quartiles. In 2009, the poor, in the lowest quartile, received 3.4 percent of all income. The rich, in the highest quartile, received 50.3 percent of all income (DeNavas-Wall et al., 2010). Consequently, the poor have disproportionately less economic and political power than the rich do.

Amott and Matthaei (1996) outlined a socialist-feminist framework within which to define class. Upper-class workers are those who work in primary occupations characterized by career ladders and opportunities for significant remunerative opportunities. These workers tend to be white males. In contrast, lower-class workers are assigned to secondary occupations with minimal skill requirements. In these occupations, career advancement and increased remunerative possibilities rarely exist. These workers tend to be people of color and women. Racial prejudice and gender roles dictate educational opportunities, routing workers into secondary occupations.

Economic power can originate from a variety of social and political institutions. Educational attainment increases economic opportunities and vice versa. Church and religious leaders by virtue of their social positions have tremendous influence over their followers. Edicts and fatwas direct followers' behaviors. Kings and queens have tremendous political power. They make the laws and dole out the resources. In democracies, the people give Congressmen the power. Military dictators, however, expropriate the power. There is no doubt that class, no matter how it is defined, or from where the power is derived, is an important category for analysis.

INTEGRATING RACE, GENDER AND CLASS INTO ECONOMICS

McIntosh's model can be used as a starting point for integrating race, gender and class into economics. The interactive phases allow for a great deal of flexibility in material choices.

Phase I

The first phase, a "Womanless, Raceless and Classless Economics," is economics, as it currently exists. Rational economic man goes about his business, making economic decisions by maximizing his utility or profits given the appropriate constraints. His decisions are made within a competitive market framework. As long as the stringent underlying assumptions of the neoclassical model prevail, the invisible hand of the competitive market gives society the most goods and services at the lowest cost. Everyone earns his/her marginal revenue product. Those who earn more get to buy more. The market solution is the efficient solution.[3]

Since textbooks play such a critical role in dictating the content of the only economics courses most undergraduates will take (Siegfried, 2000), a thorough examination of the integration of race, gender and class in introductory texts is important. In an early study, Feiner and Morgan (1987) found that women were virtually absent from introductory textbooks. In the hundreds of pages reviewed in leading texts, women and minorities were mentioned in 1.3 percent of them. Their qualitative analyses suggest that introductory textbooks are indeed race and gender blind and that white male behavior, both implicitly and explicitly described, is held up as the norm. In later studies, Feiner (1993) and then Robson (2001) found that the inclusion of women and minorities in introductory texts had improved; they could now be found in around 3 percent of the pages.

Phase II

In McIntosh's second phase, "Race, Gender and Class Notables in Economics," the contributions and accomplishments of people of color, women and various classes are highlighted and discussed. However, because of their exemption from the discipline as a result of the first phase, supporting materials are not readily available. Previous economists may have ignored, discounted or completely forgotten the contributions of people of color, women and those with less socio- and eco-political power (Polkinghorn and Thomson, 1998).

For example, very few people know about the contributions of Phyllis Wallace. Wallace was an African American, female economist who grew up in Maryland. After high school, the only state college that she could attend was Morgan State College. At the time, the University of Maryland was white-only. However, the state of Maryland would pay for the education at any institution in the US of a resident black person who wanted to major in a discipline that was not available at Morgan State College but was offered at the University of Maryland. Wallace compared the course offerings of the two schools and decided upon economics as a major so she could go out of state. Maryland sent her to New York University for her undergraduate degree and from there she went to Yale University to earn a Ph.D. in economics. She made several significant contributions to the discipline of economics. Her work focused on black women's labor force participation (Wallace, 1980). She did not study poor black women. Instead, she studied the behaviors and economic realities of black women managers. Her work was one of the first to demonstrate the achievements of black women (Malveaux, 1994).

Molly Orshansky, while working at the Social Security Administration in 1963–4, calculated the first Poverty Threshold measures (Wellis, 2010). In 1965, the Johnson Administration adopted her Poverty Threshold measures for its "War on Poverty." Since then, several commissions have been appointed to develop a better measure of poverty, but Orshansky's method is still in use. Surprisingly though, her Poverty Threshold measures have never been dubbed the Orshansky Poverty Thresholds measures. Yet, other significant empirical relationships are named after their inventors: the Phillips Curve, the Cournot Solution, or Taylor's Rule.

Another notable female economist is Katherine Coman, a development economist who taught at Wellesley College. She attended the University of Michigan and received a BS in Pharmacy, one of the few majors open to women at the time. Even without a Ph.D., she wrote the first article in the first issue of the *American Economic Review*. Without Ph.D.s, the work of many early women economists, who were intimately involved in the creation of the American Economic Association, was ignored.

Phase III

The third phase of the McIntosh model, "Add Race, Gender and Class and Stir into Economics", can be developed in various ways. First, traditional economic content can be supplemented by additional readings. Chapters from readers on race (Conrad et al., 2005), gender (Moe, 2003) or class (Feiner, 1994) can be used to add content on these social constructs. Articles from newspapers or magazines can also serve as another source. Bartlett (1997) demonstrates how to integrate women and minorities into introductory economics.

Second, economic concepts and analysis can be applied to problems that are typically considered to be of "special interest" to people of color, women and classes. For example, should a woman enter the labor force? And if she does, how many hours should she spend working in the market as opposed to working at home? Simple labor supply models can be easily applied to women's economic activities. When they are, many of these analyses appear in specialty topics courses on race, gender and class.

Finally, one can examine a simple empirical relationship from the perspective of people of color, women or class (Bartlett 1985, 1996, 1997). For example, the empirical relationship between inflation and unemployment is known as the Phillips Curve. This empirical relationship is used to illustrate the potential impacts of various macroeconomic policy alternatives on unemployment.

Bartlett and Haus (1997) disaggregated the Phillips Curve by race, gender and class from 1970 to 1990. In terms of gender, the Female Phillips Curve for the period of 1985–90 (the second half of the Reagan Administration) is very similar to that of the Male Phillips Curve. The two curves overlap at around 6.0 percent unemployment and the female curve is slightly steeper. In terms of race, the White Phillips Curve for the period of 1985 to 1990 has a much lower natural rate of unemployment (5 percent versus 12 percent) and a steeper slope than those characteristics of the Black Phillips Curve. Looking at the slope of the Phillips Curve from the black workers' perspective reveals that they disproportionately bore the brunt of the deflationary policies of the Reagan Administration.

In addition, Bartlett and Haus constructed a Class Phillips Curve. Segregating the labor force into primary and secondary workers as described above, they found that the natural rates of unemployment were 3.6 versus 7.5 for the primary and secondary occupations, respectively. The slope of the Phillips Curve for the secondary occupations was greater than that for the primary occupations. The comparison suggests that secondary workers bore more of the unemployment costs for the deflationary policies of the Reagan Administration in the 1980s than did primary workers.

Lage and Treglia (1996) conducted a comprehensive study on the impact of "adding and stirring" women into several sections of introductory microeconomics courses at Miami University in Oxford, Ohio. They found that adding women and stirring improved the performance of all students in the experimental sections as compared to those in control sections. Moreover, female students improved more than male students.

Phase IV

The limitations of the basic economic model when applied to women, people of color or classes as demonstrated in stage three create theoretical anomalies giving rise to the fourth phase: "Race, Gender and Class as Anomalies." In order to account for such differences, scholars may tweak their theories by examining basic assumptions and/or by adding race, gender or class as variables. The simple labor supply model mentioned earlier redefines the trade-offs from work and leisure to market work and nonmarket work. Adding women to the model made it nonsensical to view leisure as the only alternative to market work. Yet, much of the work that women or men do at home cannot be categorized as nonmarket work. Folbre (2001) introduced the concepts of love, obligation and reciprocity, or caring to the model.

Analyzing the intersections of race, class, and gender is important also. For example, Williams and Boushey (2010) try to determine the impact of childcare alternatives on the labor force participation of women. Typically, economic theory would suggest that the lack of childcare alternatives would deter women from working. Their analysis, however, suggests that the working poor have different decision parameters as compared to upper-class women. The missing middle, as she describes those families that are not part of the poor or the upper class, have an entirely different set of constraints. The poor rely on relatives because they cannot afford childcare. The missing middle uses a tag-team approach because the childcare available is substandard. Professionals can afford decent childcare, but are faced with the constraint of typically being required to work well over 60 hours per week. So the answer of how to provide adequate, affordable childcare is multidimensional and complicated by class.

Phase V

When a sufficient number of anomalies occurs, a new vision or model becomes necessary. This is the fifth phase of the McIntosh model, "Economics as Redefined and Restructured by Race, Gender and Class." To redefine and restructure economics, several paths can be followed. First, a more multidisciplinary approach may be proposed. Economists could use models and methodologies from its sister disciplines, such as psychology and neuroscience. Behavioral economics has benefited greatly from both of these disciplinary intersections.

Unfortunately, interdisciplinary studies do not guarantee inclusiveness. Alternative ways of progressing have manifested themselves in economics. Feminist economists (Aerni and McGoldrick, 1999; Faulkner, 1986) tend to focus more on gender. Heterodox economists (Knoedler and Underwood, 2003; Schneider 2009) tend to focus on class as a social construct. Other economists (Saunders, 1995; Tatum, 1992), speaking from their own experiences as people of color, address the importance of the intersection of race and gender.

CONTENT IN CONTEXT

Incorporating race, gender and class into the content of economics does not happen in a vacuum. Inclusive pedagogies (Aerni et al., 1999), positive relationships, and respect facilitate the learning. While these are addressed to various degrees throughout this volume, they are presented here in the context of facilitating the incorporation of race, gender and class into instruction.

Pedagogy

At major universities and colleges in the US, economics is generally taught via the lecture method, regardless of the size of institution or its classes (Becker and Watts, 2001; Watts and Becker 2008). Students sit passively and listen. They take notes as the instructor reviews the standardized material presented in most introductory and advanced economics textbooks. Multiple choice tests or short answer questions in exams test students' understanding of the material (Schaur et al., 2008).

Some students are served well by this approach to learning and the competitive nature of the grading process. They have the requisite note-taking, study and test-taking skills to do well. Other students may find that the form of testing and assignment of grades do not adequately allow them to demonstrate what they have learned. These students become less engaged in the material and the class. Ultimately, these otherwise bright students end up in other disciplines.

Listening is not the most effective strategy for learning and long-term comprehension for most students. Studies have shown that women and people of color or from different cultural backgrounds have different ways of learning based upon their innate abilities, socialization and cultural heritage (Ginorio, 1995). More interactive learning in terms of active and cooperative learning serves not only these students well, but also traditional economics students.

Relationships

Sandler, Silverberg and Hall (1996) document the many ways that the college classroom can be a very "chilly" place for students of color, women and lower classes. Nonverbal and verbal communications between the instructor and the student can build or destroy a student's interest in the subject, involvement in the class and confidence in his/her abilities in an instant. Chilly learning environments do not engage students, or offer an opportunity to challenge the status quo, and thus stifle the process of integrating race, gender and class.

Respect

Student experiences and insights must be taken seriously. They have experienced some of the same economic realities as the instructor, but from a totally different point of view.

The behaviors and economic realities of people of color, women and different classes must be welcomed in the economics classroom. Their multicultural norms, their stories, can be used as text and brought forward to examine economic models. Moreover, economic models can be used to analyze their lives as normative and not deviant.

SUMMARY

Integrating race, gender and class into the content of economics is important and may be what is necessary to reinvigorate the discipline. McIntosh's model is a helpful guide, but those in the classroom, instructors and students, have important roles to play. Without a more diverse economics profession, the discipline and our understanding will be unnecessarily narrow. Economics is an evolving discipline. What is currently mainstream economics, once was marginalized. How it evolves from this point forward depends significantly on those who make a life study of it. If economics pedagogies are not more inclusive, we stand a chance of losing those students with the voices and experiences who have the most to contribute to making economics more universally applicable.

NOTES

1. For more on these perspectives see Chapter 23, "Pluralism in Economics Education" and Chapter 61, "Teaching Political Economy to Undergraduate Students" in this volume.
2. These observations come from personal experiences reported to me by family and friends.
3. Ferber and Nelson (1993, 2003) provide excellent critiques of the assumption and workings of the generally accepted neoclassical model.

REFERENCES

Aerni, A. L. and K. McGoldrick (eds) (1999), *Valuing Us All: Feminist Pedagogy in Economics*, Ann Arbor, MI: University of Michigan Press.

Aerni, A. L., R. L. Bartlett, M. Lewis, K. McGoldrick and J. Shackelford (1999), "Toward a feminist pedagogy in economics", *Feminist Economics*, **5** (1), and in April Laskey Aerni and KimMarie McGoldrick (eds), *Valuing Us All: Feminist Pedagogy in Economics*, Ann Arbor, MI: University of Michigan Press.

Amott, T. and J. Matthaei (1996), *Race, Gender and Work: A Multicultural Economic History of Women in the United States*, Boston, MA: South End Press.

Bartlett, R. L. (1985), "Integrating the new scholarship on women into an introductory economics course", American Economic Association Meetings, New York, 28–30 December.

Bartlett, R. L. (1996), "Discovering diversity in introductory economics", *Journal of Economic Perspectives*, **10** (2), 141–53.

Bartlett, R. L. (ed.) (1997), *Introducing Race and Gender into Economics*, New York: Routledge.

Bartlett, R. L. and P. Haus (1997), "The natural rate of unemployment by race, gender, and class", *Challenge*, **44** (6), 1–14.

Becker, W. E. and M. Watts (2001), "Teaching methods in US undergraduate courses", *Journal of Economic Education*, **32** (3), 269–80.

Beer, S. (1955), *Marx and Engels: The Communist Manifesto*, New York: Appleton-Century-Crofts.

Conrad, C. A., J. Whitehead, P. Mason and J. Stewart (eds) (2005), *African Americans in the U.S. Economy*, Lanham, MD: Rowman & Littlefield Publishers, Inc.

DeNavas-Wall, C., B. D. Proctor and J. C. Smith (2010), "Income, poverty, and health insurance coverage in the United States: 2009", Washington, DC: US Census Bureau, http://www.census.gov/prod/2010pubs/p60-238.pdf, accessed 2 February 2011.

Faulkner, C. (1986), "The feminist challenge to economics", *Frontiers: A Journal of Women's Studies*, **8** (3), 55–61.

Feiner, S. F. (1993), "Integrating economic textbooks and the treatment of issues relating to women and minorities, 1984 and 1991", *Journal of Economic Education*, **24** (2), 145–62.

Feiner, S. F. (1994), *Race and Gender in the American Economy: Views from across the Spectrum*, Englewood Cliffs, NJ: Prentice-Hall.

Feiner, S. F. and B. A. Morgan (1987), "Women and minorities in introductory economics textbooks: 1974 to 1984", *Journal of Economic Education*, **18** (4), 376–92.

Ferber, M. A. and J. A. Nelson (1993), *Beyond Economic Man: Feminist Theory and Economics*, Chicago, IL: University of Chicago Press.

Ferber, M. A. and J. A. Nelson (2003), *Feminist Economics Today: Beyond Economic Man*, Chicago, IL: University of Chicago Press.

Folbre, N. (2001), *The Invisible Heart: Economics and Family Values*, New York: The New Press.

Ginorio, A. B. (1995), *Warming the Climate for Women in Science*, Washington, DC: Association of American Colleges and Universities.

Hyde, J. S. (2005), "The Gender Similarities Hypothesis", *American Psychologist*, **60** (6), 581–92.

Knoedler, J. and D. Underwood (2003), "Teaching the principles of economics: A proposal for a multi-paradigmatic approach", *Journal of Economic Issues*, **37** (3), 697–725.

Lage, M. and M. Treglia (1996), "The impact of integrating scholarship on women into introductory economics: Evidence from one institution", *Journal of Economic Education*, **27** (1), 26–36.

Malveaux, J. (1994), "Tilting against the wind: Reflections on the life and work of Phyllis Ann Wallace", *The American Economic Review*, **84** (2), 93–7.

McIntosh, P. (1983), "Interactive phases of the curricular re-vision: A feminist perspective", Center for Research on Women, Working Paper No. 124, Wellesley College, Wellesley, Massachusetts, USA.

McIntosh, P. (1988), "White privilege and male privilege: A personal account of coming to see correspondences through work in women's studies", Center for Research on Women, Working Paper No. 189, Wellesley College, Wellesley, Massachusetts, USA.

McIntosh, P. (1990), "Interactive phases of curricular and personal re-vision with regard to race", Center for Research on Women, Working Paper No. 219, Wellesley College, Wellesley, Massachusetts, USA.

Moe, K. S. (ed.) (2003), *Women, Family and Work: Writings on the Economics of Gender*, Malden, MA: Blackwell Publishing.

Polkinghorn, B. and D. L. Thomson (1998), *Adam Smith's Daughters: Eight Prominent Women Economists from the Eighteenth Century to the Present*, Cheltenham, UK and Lyme, USA: Edward Elgar.

Robson, D. (2001), "Women and minorities in economics textbooks: Are they being adequately represented?", *Journal of Economic Education*, **32** (2), 186–91.

Sandler, B. R., L. A. Silverberg and R. M. Hall (1996), *The Chilly Classroom Climate: A Guide to Improve the Education of Women*, Washington, DC: National Association of Women in Education.

Saunders, L. (1995), "Race and economics", Remarks, National Science Foundation Workshop on Integrating Race and Gender into the Introductory Economics Course, Wellesley College, Wellesley, Massachusetts, 15–20 June.

Schaur, G., M. Watts and W. E. Becker (2008), "Assessment practices and trends in undergraduate economics courses", *American Economic Review*, **98** (2), 557–634.

Schneider, G. E. (ed.) (2009), *Forum for Social Economics, Special Issue: Teaching Heterodox Economics*, **38** (2–3), Netherlands: Springer.

Siegfried, J. J. (2000), "How many college students are exposed to economics?", *Journal of Economic Education*, **31** (2), 202–4.

Tatum, B. D. (1992), "Talking about race, learning about racism: The application of racial identity development theory in the classroom", *Harvard Educational Review*, **62** (spring), 1–2.

Wallace, P. A. (1980), *Black Women in the Labor Force*, Cambridge, MA: MIT Press.

Watts, M. and W. E. Becker (2008), "A little more than chalk and talk: Results from a third national survey of teaching methods in undergraduate economics courses", *American Economic Review*, **98** (2), 552–6.

Wellis, J. (2000), "How we measure poverty: A history and brief overview", Oregon Center for Public Policy, http://www.ocpp.org/poverty/how.htm, accessed 20 April 2010.

Williams, J. C. and H. Boushey (2010), *The Three Faces of Work-Family Conflict: The Poor; the Professional and the Missing Middle*, Washington, DC: Center for American Progress.

21 Economics and literature: the gains from trade
Cecil E. Bohanon and Michelle Albert Vachris

Economists are tellers of stories and makers of poets, and from recognizing this we can know better what economists do. (McCloskey, 1990, p. 5)

There are mutual benefits from trade, not autarky. Presumably that holds across academic disciplines and markets for ideas. . . (Watts, 2004, p. 11)

Economic scholarship and teaching has never had much interaction with literary scholarship and teaching. This chapter explores the possibility of gains from trade between these two disciplines. First, a survey of both articles in economics journals that analyze works of literature and ones on the use of literature in the teaching of economics is presented. This is followed by an overview of literature written by economists and students for the purpose of teaching and learning economics. The chapter concludes with arguments in favor of incorporating literature into the economics curriculum and a description of how prevalent such activities are at undergraduate colleges and universities.

LITERATURE THROUGH THE ECONOMICS LENS

There has, over the past eight decades, been a persistent trickle of articles in mainstream economics journals on literature. These works of scholarship are, for the most part, unrelated to one another. The themes of these papers are eclectic, but generally focus on broad socio-economic issues. They are not primarily concerned with offering literary illustrations of economic principles for classroom use, yet they offer intriguing insights into the intersection of literature and economics that are of interest to economic educators.

Some articles focus on a single literary work. Thomas Deloney's quasi-novel *Jack of Newbury* [1597] (1953) is used by Kuehn (1940) to corroborate and refine the understanding of actual political events in late 16th century London that influenced the regulation of the weaving trade. Sinclair Lewis's novel *Babbit* [1922] (1992) generated a number of responses from the business community in the decade and a half after its publication, ranging from partial acceptance to outright hostility, as Hines (1967) outlines. Biddle (1985) examines how Mark Twain's *A Connecticut Yankee in King Arthur's Court* [1889] (1963) describes popular economic thinking of Twain's time and is a precursor to later analysis by economists.

Edward Bellamy's novel *Looking Backward* (1889) which outlined the workings of a 21st century socialist utopia, is the subject of articles by both Samuels (1984) and Tilman (1985) who consider the work's accuracy, relevance, insights and impacts. Bogart (1995) also links ideas in Bellamy's novel to the socialist vision found in Schumpeter's *Capitalism, Socialism and Democracy* [1942] (1962). Bohanon and Hutson (2009) describe the economics found in Bradbury's *Fahrenheit 451* [1953] (1993).

Works of juvenile literature have also been the focus of economic scholarship. The meaning of Frank Baum's *Wizard of Oz* [1901] (1991) is the (rare) subject of debate about literature in economics journals. Rockoff (1990) argues that the Baum work is a monetary allegory. For example, Dorothy's silver slippers garnered from the Wicked Witch of the East are a symbol of a bimetallic monetary system. However, Hansen (2002) questions many of Rockoff's conclusions and offers alternative explanations of Baum's work. Further insights on the issues associated with Baum's work are offered by Dighe (2007). Grapard (1995) links Defoe's *Robinson Crusoe* [1719] (2003) to homo economic par excellence and finds it indicative of economists' views on race and gender issues. George Orwell's *Animal Farm* [1945] (1954) is the springboard from which Hamlen (2000) generates a formal model of political economy grounded in the Orwellian notion that "all animals are equal but some are more equal than others" (p. 492). His model, and by extension Orwell's insight, is falsified in household income data from post-reform China. Jonathan Swift's *Gulliver's Travels* [1735] (1977) is the subject of an article by Fernandes (2001), who considers economic themes in the work and how economic reasoning adds to a literary understanding of the work.

Single works of literature also illuminate certain broad economic ideas. A tract by Jonathan Swift [1728] (1964) provides the seeds for supply-side economic analysis according to Bartlett (1992), and Ayn Rand's *Atlas Shrugged* [1957] (2005) illustrates the Public Choice theory of government intervention according to Caplan (2007).

Other economists focus on the body of work of a single author. One of the earliest efforts was Farnum's *Shakespeare's Economics* (1931), which indexes economic references and implicit economic reasoning in the work of the Bard. Neilson (1956a, 1956b, 1956c, 1957a, 1957b, 1957c) also contributes a series of articles on Shakespeare, emphasizing how economic and social conditions of the times influenced his work. Hausknecht (1950) examines the work of H. G. Wells, arguing his work is a precursor of future efforts in social science. Kennedy (1953) considers the novels of Thomas Wolfe as illustrating how economic values corrupt spiritual values. George Orwell's views on capitalism, socialism and technological change are sketched out by Roback (1985). The economic thinking of Alexander Solzhenitsyn is developed by Bohanon (2005), drawing from the Russian author's fiction and non-fictional works.

Yet other economists consider a whole literary genre. Aydelotte (1948) analyzes the thinking of mid-19th century British authors such as Dickens and Thackeray on the economic changes generated by the ongoing industrial revolution, and concludes that the authors were not pre-Marxist. He also argues that novels are useful "not for the history of facts, but for the history of opinions" (p. 43). The President of the Southern Economic Association in 1959 devoted his inaugural address to "American Businessman in the American Novel" (Smith, 1959). He outlines a number of methodological problems with characterizations of literary genres and concludes that no generalization about the portrayal of businessmen in novels is warranted from his reading of 66 novels by 24 authors. Fletcher (1974) considers the novels of Harriet Martineau and Ayn Rand to be "sugar coating for tracts" (p. 368) on economics, a characterization that is hotly contested (at least for Rand) by Ridpath and Lennox (1976). Breit and Elzinga (2002) note the similarities between detective fiction and economic problem solving. Cantor and Cox (2010) use the free market perspective of the Austrian School to examine various works of literature.

Each of the abovementioned works can be, and undoubtedly have been, used for pedagogical purposes. However, in the late 1980s another vein of works about literature emerges that focuses on identifying literary passages that are useful for illustrating economic concepts in a classroom setting. Watts and Smith's seminal article (1989) offered a compendium of examples of economic themes, principles, and concepts that are illustrated in literature, with the explicit purpose of encouraging their use in economics courses. This contribution can be seen as the beginning of a self-conscious literature in economic education on the use of literary works in economic pedagogy. Watts has made additional contributions in this vein (1999, 2002), culminating in *The Literary Book of Economics* (2003). This anthology of literary works is organized according to topics typically found in principles of economics textbooks. Each section is prefaced by introductory remarks that explain the economics lessons found in the passages.

Several pedagogical papers illustrate how to use examples from specific works in the teaching of economics. O'Donnell (1989) discusses how Harriet Martineau's novels were explicitly designed to teach economic principles. Scahill (1998) shows how Chapter 33 of Twain's *Connecticut Yankee* is an apt pedagogical device for explaining the difference between real and nominal values. Kish-Goodling (1998) offers a detailed analysis of how Shakespeare's *Merchant of Venice* can be used to teach monetary economics and in explaining the role of interest rates in the period. Boettke (2005) explains how he uses *Atlas Shrugged* to illustrate economics principles such as the gains from trade, the efficiency of markets, and the importance of innovation.

ECONOMISTS AND STUDENTS AS WRITERS OF LITERATURE

Rather than relying on pre-existing literature as outlined above, some economists have taken up the pen and entered the world of novel writing in order to convey economics in a very user-friendly way. One of the first to do so was the writing team of William Breit and Kenneth Elzinga, writing under the pseudonym Marshall Jevons. Jevons published a series of three murder mystery novels: *Murder at the Margin* (1978), *A Fatal Equilibrium* (1985) and *A Deadly Indifference* (1995). The protagonist in each of these is Henry Spearman, a Harvard economics professor, who uses economic principles to figure out "who-done-it."

Writing under his own name, Russell Roberts has published three novels, each covering a different theme. *The Choice: A Fable of Free Trade and Protectionism* (first published in 1994, now in its third edition, 2006) presents a compelling and easy to understand case for free trade as the ghost of David Ricardo tries to earn his wings "It's a Wonderful Life" style. *The Invisible Heart: An Economic Romance* (2001) introduces readers to public policy issues, including corporate responsibility and product safety, as they follow the romance of two teachers at a private high school: one a free-market economics teacher and the other a market skeptic literature teacher. In *The Price of Everything: A Parable of Possibility and Prosperity* (2008), a university professor mentors a Cuban American student protest organizer and teaches him about economic growth and the unseen order in our price system.

Jonathan B. Wight brings the 18th century writings of Adam Smith to life in *Saving*

Adam Smith: A Tale of Wealth, Transformation and Virtue (2001). Here students are shown that there is more to Smith than the concept of self-interest that is usually highlighted in undergraduate textbooks. Wight uses an adventure story to present an introduction to Smith's moral philosophy.

How can these entertaining books be used in the teaching of economics? Generally they are used to supplement textbooks in principles of economics courses. Breit and Elzinga,[1] as well Roberts,[2] provide online teaching guides. In the case of the Jevons' murder mysteries, students can be assigned the task of trying to use economic principles to solve the mystery before the culprit is revealed in the story and the authors provide guidelines for this assignment (such as no peeking at the last chapter!). The study guides also provide suggested questions for use in tests or class discussions, based on chapters throughout the novels. For example:

> Professor Spearman purchased a glass of iced tea on the boat trip across Pillsbury Sound. Had the iced tea not been accompanied by a wedge of lime, he would have rejected the purchase. What deceptively simple yet complex chain of reasoning led Spearman to make this decision?[3, 4]

While these novels can be used for discussion sessions in a traditional classroom setting, they may also be used to facilitate online discussion group assignments in computer-based courses or as an online supplement to a classroom-based course.[5] The novels can also be used as the basis for essay assignments. For example, in *The Choice*, many examples of trade protection are discussed, and students can be assigned to research and analyze an example from current events that the character Dave Ricardo would frown upon.[6] An assignment using *Saving Adam Smith* might have students write about a normative economic issue of the day.

Whether used for tests, discussions or essay assignments, novels written by economists can be a productive supplement to undergraduate economics courses. Especially at the introductory level, these books can appeal to students outside the economics/business disciplines who might otherwise be intimidated by economics. The use of novels can also allow for more in-depth coverage of topics than is generally found in principles textbooks.

A recent trend in using literature to teach economics is to have students become authors themselves. Goma (2001) describes the use of a creative writing assignment in a principles of economics class. Students are given a scenario and discussion questions and are asked to respond using some sort of creative writing form, such as a short story, a play or a newspaper article. Students respond favorably to the assignment and it makes it easy for non-business/economics majors to relate economics to their primary disciplines. Ziliak (2009) describes the uses of haiku in economics. Since haiku are poems of seventeen syllables arranged in three lines of five, then seven, then five syllables, students face the basic economic problem of scarcity in writing their own haiku. The haiku format itself demonstrates efficiency, according to Ziliak (2009, p. 4), in that haiku "deliver big stories, insights, and meanings about *economics and the economy itself*, in a comparatively small package – that is, at minimum cost." Some haiku end with a touch of irony or a surprise, which can illustrate the law of unintended consequences in economics. In addition to teaching students about economics, the use of haiku can improve the conciseness of their economic writing. Haiku are not just useful in teaching principles of economics, as evidenced by Keisuke Hirano, who provides a set of econometrics haiku, such as

Supply and demand:
without a good instrument,
not identified.[7]

JUSTIFICATIONS FOR USE OF LITERATURE IN ECONOMICS PEDAGOGY

Why should economists be familiar with literature? Or more to the point for this chapter, why should economics teachers use literature? As Watts (1999) points out, the use of literature in the teaching of economics is not without costs, including the diversion of resources away from the offering of more traditional courses and the inefficiencies introduced by the amount of reading it takes to identify and understand economics in literary passages. These costs, however, are outweighed by several benefits of incorporating literature into the economics curriculum.

The fundamental justification is that students learn more economics, retain economic concepts longer and at a deeper level, if literature is used to introduce or reinforce economic concepts. Memorable, interesting and captivating stories are essential for learners, especially at an introductory level.[8] McCloskey (1983, 1990) has argued that *all* knowledge transmission is based on storytelling and that economists would do well to pay attention to the stories they are telling in their diagrammatic and mathematical models. Few students of economics, especially at the introductory level, are likely to be inspired, motivated or convinced by intersecting lines, mathematical equations or robust empirical specifications, and most teachers of economics already "tell stories" in conjunction with the tools of analysis. If economics teachers are compelled to teach economics via narratives, why not use the narratives of those writers whose works have been acclaimed and with which students may already have a familiarity? As the literature review above has shown, a careful examination of literature will yield passages that illustrate key economic concepts. By judiciously sharing those passages with students, economics teachers can be more effective transmitters of economic ideas. As Watts (2003, p. xxii) has argued, ". . .literary passages are wonderfully effective teaching tools both because they are well written and memorable and because they introduce variety in the economics classroom, compared to the typical diet of textbook prose, graphs, tables of numbers, and math." He goes on to point out that this also helps students develop the "ability to explain economic concepts verbally as well as graphically and mathematically. . . ." (p. xxii). Supplementing the typical diet with works of literature is also an effective way to reach students outside the business/economics major who may take principles of economics courses as an elective course or to fulfill a general education requirement.

A secondary justification for the use of literature in economics pedagogy is to promote the interdisciplinary and integrative goals of a liberal education. Consider the following idealized version of such a vision. An undergraduate student in a principles of economics class is exposed to key concepts as the instructor incorporates a number of works of literature. The same student is simultaneously enrolled in an introductory literature class where the same works of literature are covered and the literature instructor makes reference to the same economic principles.

Although such an idealized pedagogy is an unlikely reality, it raises the point that incorporating literature into the economic curriculum can broaden undergraduate economics training consistent with the ideals of a liberal education. As disciplines have become more technical and specialized, undergraduate training has become more narrowly focused on discipline-specific skills. The ability of undergraduates to see and work with the "big picture" and use a variety of tools has waned (see Colander and McGoldrick, 2009). Yet it is often the students with "big picture" skills – those who in Colander's (2009, p. A72) words, "can think, communicate orally, write and solve problems and who are comfortable with quantitative analysis" – who are most valued in the marketplace. Combining economic analysis with literature and writing in economics courses is one method by which to round-out the student's skill set. As Wicksteed (1910) stated over a century ago, "The prophet and the poet may regenerate the world without the economist, but the economist cannot regenerate it without them."[9]

Despite the usual distance between English and Economics Departments,[10] Cowen (2008) argues that economic models and literary novels have more in common than usually imagined. Models and novels complement one another, opening the possibility that the literary analyst and economic model builder can enhance the quality of each other's work by examining one another's analysis. Cowen explains that economic models propose patterns of human activity in formal, often high mathematical, form. They posit that certain exogenous variables (such as price and income) influence certain endogenous behavioral variables (such as consumer purchases). The economic researcher sets the model's initial conditions and then "shocks" the system by allowing some or all of the exogenous variables to change, and examines the outcomes of the exercise. The results that emerge are the logical internal by-product of the structure of the model. Critical analysis of an economic model looks not only at the internal logic of the model, but also seeks empirical verification of the model's implications.

A novel begins at the second step of the process outlined above, with the author describing an initial state of the characters and social setting of the novel. As Cowen (2008, p.11) explains, novels are similar to models that existed in economics "[b]efore the mathematization of the economics profession." Authors then proceed to "shock" the equilibrium in the system by introducing some set of events that create change. The results that emerge are based on the imagination of the author providing either one or a number of potential outcomes. Critical analysis of a novel often attempts to derive the implicit model of the author and assess its plausibility both within the novel and as a general proposition.

Cowen (2008) concludes that although obviously not the same, it is apparent that the two intellectual exercises have notable commonalities, including comparative static analysis and critical analysis to assess plausibility. Therefore, the novelist may provide insight and intuition for the economic modeler, and the economic modeler and her empirical evidence may provide a check on the plausibility and realism of the novel.

HOW PROMINENT IS THE USE OF LITERATURE IN ECONOMICS INSTRUCTION?

There exist a number of special economics courses that have used literature extensively, although we lack data to identify the prevalence of such courses. Indeed, Watts (2004) explains that one of the reasons why he compiled the anthology, *The Literary Book of Economics*, was to facilitate the teaching of courses in economics and literature. Vachris (2007) provides an overview of an interdisciplinary course with a clear economics focus that is built around Watts' anthology and Rand's *Atlas Shrugged*. Hartley (2001) describes an introductory course in economics in which all of the reading material comes from the great books of Western civilization. Since these kinds of courses are typically not intended to prepare students for upper-level study in economics, topics outside the traditional principles syllabus are often explored. Most principles of economics courses focus on positive, as opposed to normative, economics. Much of literature has a normative component, so students can be exposed to some of the more interesting and controversial topics in economics, including fairness in markets and the proper role of government. For example, students could be asked to contrast the views of income inequality presented in Kurt Vonnegut's short story "Harrison Bergeron" [1961] (2009) with that illustrated by an excerpt from *The Octopus* [1901] (1963) by Frank Norris. Both are included in Watts (2003).

Watts and Becker (2008) constructed and administered a survey of methods of undergraduate economics instruction. The survey included a query on the "use of literature, drama and music" (p. 275) in the classroom, asking respondents to indicate whether a particular method was used: never (0), rarely (1), occasionally (2), frequently (3), or always (4). The question was asked in surveys administered in 1995, 2000 and 2005. Responses were classified by type of economics course (introductory, theory, statistical or econometric, upper division) and by institution type (doctoral granting, master's granting, baccalaureate granting).

The most prominent *median* response across school and course types indicates that no reference to literature, drama, or music is likely in a majority of economics courses taught in North America. The *mean* usage ranges from a low of 2 percent to a high of 11 percent across course and institution types. In other words, reference by instructors to literature, drama or music is typically made only two to three times over the course of a semester. The survey also suggests that use of literature, drama and music is somewhat more prominent in economics classes at non-doctoral granting institutions, but shows little variation across types of courses. The data also suggest a minor decline in usage between 1995 and 2005.

CONCLUSIONS

While survey data reveal low levels of inclusion of literature in the teaching and learning of economics at the undergraduate level, this chapter explains the many benefits of doing so. The gains from trade between economics and literature include the ability to foster increased retention and deeper-level understanding of economics concepts by economics and non-economics students alike, to promote the interdisciplinary and integrative goals of a liberal education, and to broaden the economics student's skill set. It should be noted that these gains from trade do not depend on an all-or-nothing approach. Whole courses on economics and literature exist, but economics instructors and students can benefit from even small doses of literature such as the inclusion of a relevant poem or a small creative writing assignment added to an existing course. In addition to incorporating literature into economics instruction, this chapter illustrates that economists can engage in research that finds economics content in classic and current literature and may even inspire economists to become authors of literature, themselves.

There are several current movements in the economics profession that may encourage the exploration of further ties between economics and literature. An important source of the increased interest in the complementarities of the two disciplines is the Liberty Fund which sponsors interdisciplinary conferences in which both economists and literature scholars participate. A notable source of the increased number of economics and literature courses offered is the Moral Foundations of Capitalism program of the Branch Banking & Trust (BB&T) Charitable Foundation that encourages the use of Ayn Rand's *Atlas Shrugged* in the study of free markets at over sixty colleges and universities. While more and more sessions on economics and literature are being added to programs of economics academic conferences, these papers still do not usually find their way into the mainstream journals. It is not clear whether this is because the quality and quantity of submissions are lacking or editors and referees find literature and economics papers uninteresting, or some of both. However, in order to fully capture the gains from trade, it would be useful if the trickle of literature and economics scholarship became a more persistent flow.

NOTES

1. http://marshalljevons.com/how-to-teach.html (accessed 25 April 2011).
2. http://www.invisibleheart.com/books.php (accessed 25 April 2011).
3. For Henry Spearman, then, iced tea and lime wedges are complementary goods.
4. http://marshalljevons.com/how-to-teach.html (accessed 25 April 2011).
5. See Chapter 5 in this volume for a formal approach to facilitating such conversations.
6. See Lisa McNary, "Questions for Students", http://www.invisibleheart.com/Iheart/CQuestions.html (accessed 25 April 2011).
7. http://www.u.arizona.edu/~hirano/haiku.html (accessed 25 April 2011).
8. See the literature on learning behavior, such as Bransford et al. (2000).
9. Book 1, Chapter 3, section 35. http://www.econlib.org/library/Wicksteed/wkCS.html (accessed 28 April 2011).
10. At a cocktail party at a mid-sized Midwestern University, an English professor inquired of an Economics professor, "Do you economists teach Marxist economics?" The Economics professor replied, "Oh no, we let you English professors do that."

REFERENCES

Aydelotte, W. O. (1948), "The England of Marx and Mill as reflected in fiction", *The Journal of Economic History*, **8** (Supplement: The Tasks of Economic History), 42–58.
Bartlett, B. (1992), "Jonathan Swift: Father of supply-side economics?", *History of Political Economy*, **24** (3), 745–8.
Baum, L. F. [1901] (1991), *The Wonderful Wizard of Oz*, edited by William R. Leach., Belmont, CA, US: Wadsworth Pub. Co.

Bellamy, E. (1889), *Looking Backward, 2000–1887*, New York, NY, US: Houghton, Mifflin and Company.
Biddle, J. E. (1985), "Veblen, Twain, and the Connecticut Yankee: A note", *History of Political Economy*, **17** (1), 97–107.
Boettke, P. J. (2005), "Teaching economics through Ayn Rand: How the economy is like a novel and how the novel can teach us about economics", *The Journal of Ayn Rand Studies*, **6** (2), 445–65.
Bogart, W. T. (1995), "Looking backward at feasible socialism: Using Bellamy to teach Schumpeter", *The Journal of Economic Education*, **26** (4), 352–6.
Bohanon, C. E. (2005), "The economics of Alexander Solzhenitsyn", *Laissez- Faire*, **22–3**, 35–49.
Bohanon, C. E. and W. A. Hutson (2009), "The economics of Ray Bradbury's *Fahrenheit 451*", *Laissez-Faire*, **30–31** (March–September), 23–30.
Bradbury, R. [1953] (1993), *Fahrenheit 451*, 40th Anniversary ed., New York, NY, US: Simon & Schuster.
Bransford, J. D., A. L. Brown and R. R. Cocking (2000), *How People Learn: Brain, Mind, Experience, and School: Expanded Edition*, Washington, DC: National Academy Press.
Breit, W. and K. Elzinga (2002), "The economist as detective", *Journal of Economic Education* **33** (4), 367–76.
Cantor, P. and S. Cox (eds) (2010), *Literature and the Economics of Liberty: Spontaneous Order in Culture*, Auburn, AL, US: Ludwig Von Mises Institute.
Caplan, B. (2007), "*Atlas Shrugged* and public choice: The obvious parallels", in E. Younkins (ed.), *Ayn Rand's Atlas Shrugged: A Philosophical and Literary Companion*, Burlington, VT, US and Aldershot, UK: Ashgate, pp. 215–24.
Colander, D. (2009), "Economics is the 'Just Right' liberal-arts major" *The Chronicle of Higher Education*, **A72** (March 6).
Colander, D. and K. McGoldrick (eds) (2009), *Educating Economists: The Teagle Discussion on Reevaluating the Undergraduate Economics Major*, Cheltenham, UK and Northampton, MA, US: Edward Elgar.
Cowen, T. (2008), "Is a novel a model?", in S. J. Peart and D. Levy (eds), *The Street Porter and the Philosopher: Conversations on Analytical Egalitarianism*, Ann Arbor, MI, US: The University of Michigan Press, pp. 319–37.
Defoe, D. [1719] (2003), *Robinson Crusoe,* introduction and notes by L.J. Swingle, 1st ed., New York: Barnes & Noble Classics.
Deloney, T. [1597] (1953), *Jack of Newbury*, in *Elizabethan Fiction*, edited with an introduction and notes by Robert Ashley and Edwin M. Moseley, New York: Rinehart.
Dighe, R. S. (2007), "The Fable of the Allegory: The Wizard of Oz in Economics: Comment" *Journal of Economic Education,* **38** (3), 318–24.
Farnum, H. (1931), *Shakespeare's Economics*, New Haven, CT, US: Yale University Press.
Fernandes, M. (2001), "Economics and literature: An examination of Gulliver's Travels", *Journal of Economic Studies*, **28** (1), 92–105.
Fletcher, M. E. (1974), "Harriet Martineau and Ayn Rand: Economics in the guise of fiction", *American Journal of Economics and Sociology*, **33** (4), 367–79.
Goma, O. D. (2001), "Creative writing in economics", *College Teaching*, **49** (4), 149–52.
Grapard, U. (1995), "Robinson Crusoe: The quintessential economic man?", *Feminist Economics*, **1** (1), 33–52.
Hamlen, Jr., W. A. (2000), "The economics of Animal Farm", *Southern Economic Journal*, **66** (4), 942–56.
Hansen, B. A. (2002), "The fable of the allegory: The Wizard of Oz in economics", *The Journal of Economic Education*, **33** (3), 254–64.
Hartley, J. E. (2001), "The great books and economics", *Journal of Economic Education*, **32** (2), 147–59.
Hausknecht, M. (1950), "H. G. Wells: A modern primitive", *American Journal of Economics and Sociology*, **9** (2), 205–16.
Hines, Jr., T. S. (1967), "Echoes from 'Zenith': Reactions of American businessmen to Babbitt", *The Business History Review*, **41** (2), 123–40.
Hirano, K. "Haiku", http://www.u.arizona.edu/~hirano/haiku.html (accessed 25 April 2011).
Jevons, M. (1978), *Murder at the Margin*, Glen Ridge, NJ, US: T. Horton.
Jevons, M. (1985), *The Fatal Equilibrium*, Cambridge, MA, US: MIT Press.
Jevons, M. (1995), *A Deadly Indifference*, New York, NY, USA: Carroll & Graf Publishers.
Jevons, M. "How to Teach: Murder at the Margin", http://marshalljevons.com/how-to-teach.html (accessed 25 April 2011).
Kennedy, W. (1953), "Economic ideas in contemporary literature: The novels of Thomas Wolfe", *Southern Economic Journal*, **20** (1), 35–50.
Kish-Goodling, D. M. (1998), "Using *The Merchant of Venice* in teaching monetary economics", *The Journal of Economic Education*, **29** (4), 330–39.
Kuehn, G. W. (1940), "The novels of Thomas Deloney as source for 'Climate of Opinion' in sixteenth-century economic history", *The Journal of Political Economy*, **48** (6), 865–75.
Lewis, S. [1922] (1992), *Main Street & Babbitt*, New York, NY, US: Library of America,.
McCloskey, D. N. (1983), "The rhetoric of economics", *Journal of Economic Literature*, **21** (2), 481–517.

McCloskey, D. N. (1990), "Storytelling in economics", in C. Nash (ed.), *Narrative in Culture: The Uses of Storytelling in the Sciences*, London, UK and New York, NY, US: Routledge, pp. 5–22.

McNary, L., "Questions for students", http://www.invisibleheart.com/Iheart/CQuestions.html (accessed 25 April 2011).

Neilson, F. (1956a), "Shakespeare and 'The Tempest'", *American Journal of Economics and Sociology*, 15 (4), 425–36.

Neilson, F. (1956b), "Shakespeare and 'The Tempest II'", *American Journal of Economics and Sociology*, 16 (1), 89–103.

Neilson, F. (1956c), "Shakespeare and 'The Tempest III'", *American Journal of Economics and Sociology*, 16 (2), 177–93.

Neilson, F. (1957a), "Shakespeare and 'The Tempest IV'", *American Journal of Economics and Sociology*, 16 (3), 309–26.

Neilson, F. (1957b), "Shakespeare and 'The Tempest V'", *American Journal of Economics and Sociology*, 16 (4), 421–9.

Neilson, F. (1957c), "Shakespeare and 'The Tempest'", *American Journal of Economics and Sociology*, 17 (1), 43–52.

Norris, F. [1901] (1967) *The Octopus: A Story of California*, foreword by Irvin S. Cobb. Port Washington, NY, US: Kennikat Press.

O'Donnell, M. G. (1989), "A historical note on the use of fiction to teach principles of economics", *The Journal of Economic Education*, 20 (3), 314–20.

Orwell, G. [1945] (1954), *Animal Farm*, illustrated by Joy Batchelor and John Halas, New York, NY, US: Harcourt, Brace.

Rand, A. [1957] (2005), *Atlas Shrugged*, [35th anniversary ed.] Centennial ed., New York: Dutton.

Ridpath, J. B. and J. G. Lennox (1976), "Ayn Rand's novels: Art or tracts? Two additional views", *American Journal of Economics and Sociology*, 35 (2), 213–24.

Roback, J. (1985), "The economic thought of George Orwell", *The American Economic Review*, 75 (2), Papers and Proceedings of the Ninety-Seventh Annual Meeting of the American Economic Association, 127–32.

Roberts, R. D. (2001), *The Invisible Heart: An Economic Romance*, Cambridge, MA, US: MIT Press.

Roberts, R. D. (2006), *The Choice: A Fable of Free Trade and Protectionism* 3rd ed, Upper Saddle River, NJ, US: Pearson Prentice Hall.

Roberts, R. D. (2008), *The Price of Everything: A Parable of Possibility and Prosperity*, Princeton, NJ, US: Princeton University Press.

Roberts, R. D., "A Teacher's Guide for *The Invisible Heart: An Economic Romance*", http://www.invisible heart.com/books.php (accessed 25 April 2011).

Rockoff, H. (1990), "The 'Wizard of Oz' as a monetary allegory", *The Journal of Political Economy*, 98 (4), 739–60.

Samuels, W. J. (1984), "A centenary reconsideration of Bellamy's Looking Backward", *American Journal of Economics and Sociology*, 43 (2), 129–48.

Scahill, E. M. (1998), "A Connecticut Yankee in Estonia", *The Journal of Economic Education*, 29 (4), 340–46.

Schumpeter J. A. [1942] (1962), *Capitalism, Socialism, and Democracy*, 3rd ed., New York: Harper & Row.

Smith, H. R. (1959), "The American businessman in the American novel", *Southern Economic Journal*, 25 (3), 265–302.

Swift, Jonathan [1728] (1964). "An answer to a paper called a Memorial of the Poor Inhabitants, Tradesmen, and Labourers of the Kingdom of Ireland", in *Jonathan Swift: Irish Tracts, 1728–1733*, edited by Herbert Davis, Oxford: Basil Blackwell.

Swift, J. [1735] (1977), *Gulliver's Travels*, edited by Colin McKelvie; illustrated by James Millar, New York, NY, US: St. Martin's Press.

Tilman, R. (1985), "The utopian vision of Edward Bellamy and Thorstein Veblen", *Journal of Economic Issues*, 19 (4), 879–98.

Twain, M. [1889] (1963), *A Connecticut Yankee in King Arthur's Court*, San Francisco, CA, US: Chandler Pub. Co.

Vachris, M. A. (2007), "Economics lessons in literature", *Virginia Economic Journal*, 12 (1), 23–32.

Vonnegut, K. [1961] (2009) "Harrison Bergeron", in *The Riverside Reader*, edited by Joseph F. Trimmer, Heather Milliet, Boston, MA, US: Houghton Mifflin.

Watts, M. (1999), "Using literature and drama in undergraduate economics courses", in W. E. Becker and M. Watts (eds), *Teaching Economics to Undergraduates: Alternatives to Chalk and Talk*, Cheltenham, UK and Northampton, MA, US: Edward Elgar, pp. 185–208.

Watts, M. (2002), "How economists use literature and drama", *The Journal of Economic Education*, 33 (4), 377–86.

Watts, M. (ed.) (2003), *The Literary Book of Economics*, Wilmington, DE, US: Intercollegiate Studies Institute.

Watts, M. (2004), "Economic insights from and about literature, drama, and literary criticism", Presented at a conference on "What We Teach and How We Teach It: Perspectives on Economics from Around the Globe", held at the University of South Australia, 13–16 July.

Watts, M. and W. E. Becker (2008), "A little more than chalk and talk: Results from a third national survey of teaching methods in undergraduate economics courses", *Journal of Economic Education*, **39** (3), 273–86.

Watts, M. and R. F. Smith (1989), "Economics in literature and drama", *Journal of Economic Education*, **20** (3), 291–307.

Wicksteed, P. H. (1910), *The Common Sense of Political Economy, Including a Study of the Human Basis of Economic Law*, London: Macmillan, http://www.econlib.org/library/Wicksteed/wkCS.html, accessed 28 April 2011.

Wight, J. B. (2001), *Saving Adam Smith: A Tale of Wealth, Transformation and Virtue*, Upper Saddle River, NJ, US: Financial Times/Prentice Hall.

Ziliak, S. T. (2009), "Haiku economics: Little teaching aids for big economic pluralists", *International Journal of Pluralism and Economics Education*, **1** (1/2), 108–29.

22 The interdisciplinary approach to teaching economics

Arthur H. Goldsmith and James F. Casey

> The theory of economics does not furnish a body of settled conclusions immediately applicable to policy. It is a method rather than a doctrine, an apparatus of the mind, a technique of thinking which helps the possessor to draw correct conclusions. (Keynes, 1922)

> The most exciting science in the 21st century is likely to evolve among not within traditional disciplines . . . yet the education of scientists has historically been constrained by disciplines, paralleling patterns of science funding. (Sung et al., 2003, p. 1485)

If economics is an apparatus of the mind, then interdisciplinary teaching of economics should be the norm: if only it were so. Many economic educators are suspicious of teaching in an interdisciplinary manner, fearing their classroom will lack precision and that they will be forced to abandon formal models – the hallmark of modern economics. Moreover, they believe it is necessary to be a "jack-of-all-trades" or "expert" in a myriad of disciplines in order to explore issues with economics students in an interdisciplinary fashion. The purpose of this chapter is to allay such fears and make the case that economists who are interdisciplinary educators provide their students with a richer understanding of the contribution economic analysis can make to complex policy issues. Moreover, we clarify what interdisciplinary teaching entails, offer tips on how to be an interdisciplinary educator, and describe two examples of how interdisciplinarity can provide a more enriching discourse with economics students on topics typically covered in standard economics classes.

WHAT IS INTERDISCIPLINARY TEACHING?

Interdisciplinary instruction entails the use and integration of methods and analytical frameworks from more than one academic discipline to examine a theme, issue, question or topic. Interdisciplinary education makes use of disciplinary approaches to examine topics, but pushes beyond the norm of exploring questions from a single discipline by engaging in an analysis that features the integration of ideas from relevant disciplines, leading to a more complete perspective on the issues under investigation.

Economists are increasingly taking into account notions from a host of disciplines when conducting research on a wide range of topics.[1] This development highlights the view that many economic educators are coming to believe that interdisciplinary perspectives are needed to adequately understand complex and multi-faceted issues such as climate change, sources of economic growth, teenage pregnancy, biodiversity loss, new drug development, genetically modified foods, and health care access. Interdisciplinary teaching is different from multi- or cross-disciplinary teaching in that it requires an integration and synthesis of different perspectives rather than a simple consideration of multiple viewpoints.[2]

WHY USE INTERDISCIPLINARY TEACHING IN ECONOMICS?

Improved Economics Instruction

The discipline of economics is a behavioral science primarily concerned with the production of goods and services and the allocation of scarce resources to promote social welfare. Economics educators are expected to help students master the conventional formal economic models used to explore material that is central to the course they are leading. However, they typically face a number of additional objectives in their role as educators, many of which are well served by incorporating and integrating insights from other disciplines. Many economics courses broach questions of concern to policy makers. Therefore, policy makers and educators are charged with helping students develop the skills needed to analyze tradeoffs associated with alternative courses of action. Not surprisingly, the associated questions economics teachers explore with students are also being investigated in other disciplines, but with different analytical frameworks and methodologies. An interdisciplinary approach that fuses knowledge and insights from other disciplines with an economic framework of analysis to form a more inclusive means of examining questions will foster a richer, more productive, discourse. For instance, economic educators are likely to find an interdisciplinary perspective useful when helping students understand causes and consequences of: joblessness, welfare reform, pollution, educational attainment, and access to health care. All of these issues have psychological, sociological, moral, and political dimensions for which a neoclassical market framework may not provide a sufficient means of exploration.

Improved Contribution to Overall Student Education

College administrators believe that economic educators, especially those teaching introductory courses, should assist students in the acquisition of the broad array of skills and talents associated with a liberal education.[3] There is also an emerging viewpoint in higher education (see for instance Fogarty and Pete, 2009) that interdisciplinary instruction is an effective way to engage students and to help them develop knowledge, insights, problem-solving skills, self-confidence, self-efficacy, and a passion for learning that are fundamental general educational goals.[4] For instance, prominent social learning theorists (Bandura, 1977; Gardner, 1983) and education policy researchers (Repko, 2009; Fink, 2003) report that interdisciplinary inquiry leads to gains in cognition and advances a student's capacity to recognize and overcome – when appropriate – preconceptions. Moreover, Fink (2003) asserts that interdisciplinary instruction leads to "significant learning" – learning that is meaningful and has a lasting impact on a student's ability to analyze. Thus, teaching economics in an interdisciplinary fashion allows economists to make a greater contribution to their student's liberal or overall education.

HOW TO TEACH WITH AN INTERDISCIPLINARY APPROACH

Economic educators can provide students with interdisciplinary learning experiences by forming an interdisciplinary teaching team or by broadening their own approach to education. However, in either of these settings, instructors must model for students how to approach issues in an interdisciplinary fashion to help them overcome the standard discipline-based learning structure and learn how to synthesize or integrate insights from a range of disciplines into an interdisciplinary framework of analysis.

The framework adopted for delivery of interdisciplinary learning can be *discipline neutral* or *hierarchical*. A discipline-neutral form of interdisciplinary education places each discipline on equal footing, with their alternative methodologies and frameworks of analysis, to explore questions of interest. The goal for students and faculty is to identify, evaluate, synthesize, and integrate contributions of each discipline. In a hierarchical arrangement, the conventional methodology or analytical framework of the discipline – typically the home discipline of the instructor or the lead member of the interdisciplinary team – becomes the baseline method of inquiry. This analytical paradigm is then extended to account for and integrate insights from other disciplines to foster an interdisciplinary perspective. Given the importance of formal modeling to economic thinking, a hierarchical approach, with economics as the jumping off point, is likely ideal for most economics educators attempting to teach in an interdisciplinary fashion.

Instructors can structure one or more meetings, particular sections of a course, or the entire course as interdisciplinary. The extent to which interdisciplinary perspectives guide the teaching process will depend on instructor expertise, the comfort level of the educator(s), and the nature of the topics being addressed. There is no explicit or implicit requirement that an economics educator wanting to engage in interdisciplinary instruction must do so at all times. An instructor can selectively choose topics they want to approach in an interdisciplinary manner and over time build up a large stock of interdisciplinary lessons which can ultimately serve as the basis for an entire course. Clearly, the intensity of interdisciplinarity adopted will depend on the type of course being led by the economics instructor (i.e. principles of economics, core theory classes, field course, freshman seminar, capstone course in economics) because of differences in goals, academic level, place in the curriculum, and nature of the enrolled students.

The most challenging part of interdisciplinary instruction is moving beyond the examination of an issue from the lens of multiple disciplines, to the synthesis and integration of insights into a more inclusive framework of analysis. Effective design and implementation of interdisciplinary classroom explorations, regardless of the level or type of class, entails four fundamental steps that are easily within the grasp of all economic educators.

1. *Pre-instructional planning* – establishes topics to be examined in an interdisciplinary manner, and allows the educator to identify and acquire the requisite knowledge, as well as develop an action plan to guide the classroom experience.
2. *Introduce the methodology to students* – explain to students the nature of interdisciplinary, in contrast to discipline-based, learning. Impress upon them the importance of integrating insights and approaches from multiple disciplines to form a framework of analysis that will lead to a rich understanding of complex questions.

3. *Take it to the classroom* – demonstrate for students how to engage in interdisciplinary analysis. Using the hierarchal approach, start with a discipline-based examination and then extend the investigation to identify theories and insights from other disciplines and ultimately build them into an integrated approach to examining the issue of interest.
4. *Practice interdisciplinary thinking* – give students assignments that require them to explore questions from an interdisciplinary perspective. Consider initiating this process using groups, so students can collectively practice this approach prior to attempting it individually. Have students mimic the hierarchical approach, by summarizing an issue discussed in class in a discipline-based manner, then bringing insights from another discipline to bear, and finally attempting to synthesize and integrate their analysis. After practicing this method with guidance in class and from peers, ask them to take a fresh topic and examine it in an interdisciplinary manner on their own.

EXAMPLES OF TOPICS WARRANTING AN INTERDISCIPLINARY APPROACH[5]

Economic Growth

Every principles of economics student is introduced to the circular flow model/diagram. The most simplified depiction of the flow of inputs, such as capital equipment, technology, and labor, to firms for a fee and the associated movement of goods and services from firms to households for a price allows students to begin to understand the closed-system nature of an economy – how one person's expenditure becomes another's income. Students typically learn that an economy grows in the near term through the use of additional labor, subject to the law of diminishing returns, and over a longer horizon by adding more capital and technology. Natural scientists often challenge this characterization of the productive process as incomplete and potentially misleading.

Ecologists have argued for decades that the economy does not function on its own or in a bubble separate from the natural world. They assert that there are ecological constraints or planetary boundaries that govern the economy and alter the conventional economic characterization of the link between inputs and output growth. They offer three insights that an interdisciplinary economics educator could incorporate into the circular flow framework. First, natural resources need to be included in any model of economic growth and should be viewed as a potential input to growth, but also a constraint on the process. Second, the production process creates waste which must be assimilated back into the biosphere and the environment may be coming under severe stress due to this inefficiency in the production process. This idea/concept leads directly to the third insight that the contribution of inputs to output is contingent upon the level and status of natural resources. For example, the combination of boats and fishers in the Gulf of Mexico is unable to produce any seafood for a period due to the condition of the Gulf waters as a result of the 2010 British Petroleum (BP) oil leak. Thus, expanding the circular flow framework to account for ecological insights can enrich the understanding of production and growth.[6]

The circular flow framework can be expanded to account for ecological insights by placing economic activity within the biosphere and adding energy and natural resources as inputs and wastes, and pollution as an output. By taking a conventional economic model and incorporating insights from ecology to produce an interdisciplinary framework for exploring economic growth, students are likely to ask a number of questions that would be neglected otherwise, including (1) How big can the economy get before it starts to push up against these planetary boundaries? (2) Where does the pollution go and how might this affect the environment and the productivity of other inputs? (3) How much energy and what amount of natural resources are used to sustain the economic system? and (4) What is the effect of a degraded environment of the economy and the quality of life? Clearly, this interdisciplinary discussion with students will lead to a richer understanding of how economic growth occurs than a more narrow discipline-specific conversation.

The Black–White Wage Gap

The racial gap in wages is a longstanding feature of the US economy. The source and consequences of this phenomenon are covered in most principles of economics classes in the section on poverty and inequality and it is a central theme discussed in every labor economics class. This topic also highlights the value of teaching economics in an interdisciplinary manner.

Conventional, neoclassical, economic theory asserts that firms are led by managers who act rationally – engaging in activities at the point where the additional costs of an action (i.e. the marginal costs) are equivalent to the additional benefits from that action (i.e. the marginal benefits) and seek to maximize profits. Thus, firms are assumed to hire labor to the point where the cost of an additional worker or real wage (W) is equivalent to the output gains generated by that worker, referred to as the marginal product of labor (MP). Moreover, economists typically assume that worker productivity is primarily governed by their level of formal schooling or human capital (H).

$$W = MP(H). \tag{22.1}$$

According to this set of propositions, if black (b) and white (w) workers are equally well educated ($H^w = H^b$), their levels of productivity would be equivalent, $MP^w(H^w = H^b) = MP^b(H^b)$, so they would be paid the same hourly wage.

In order to assess the validity of this hypothesis, i.e. equal pay for workers with equivalent levels of education regardless of racial background, economists have estimated the following model of wage determination:

$$W = \alpha + \beta(H) + \delta(X) + \psi(b) + \varepsilon, \tag{22.2}$$

where H is the level of formal schooling, X is a set of additional factors expected to influence worker productivity, such as workplace experience, age, and marital status, and b identifies workers who are black, and ε is an error term.

The estimated coefficient $\hat{\psi}$ reveals the impact of being black, relative to white, on the wage rate (W) for workers who are otherwise equivalent (i.e. they have the same level of human capital and all elements in X). Countless empirical studies using data from the US provide evidence that $\hat{\psi} < 0$ and is roughly -0.20 or that black workers earn 20 percent less than white workers with apparently equivalent productivity-based characteristics (i.e. H, X). The standard economic explanation for this is that black workers possess poorer quality schooling, so they are less productive than their white peers even when they have accumulated the same level of education. When school quality (Q) is controlled for, estimates of the racial wage gap continue to be negative; however, they decline in magnitude to about 15 percent (i.e. -0.15). Some economists interpret the negative estimate of $\hat{\psi}$ when school quality is accounted for as evidence of discrimination, while others assert that additional factors which favor white workers remain unaccounted for. But, what are these mysterious elements and why do they matter? Posing this question and appealing to insights from other disciplines to help uncover the remaining source of the racial wage gap reveals the power of approaching a topic of interest to economists in an interdisciplinary manner.

Worker productivity may depend on a number of factors that are typically ignored by economists but that are central to the process governing productivity advanced by other disciplines such as sociology or psychology. For instance, sociologists see worker productivity as influenced by human interaction and expect a person's productivity to depend on the talents or human capital of their co-workers (H^{co}). But, they also recognize that the rate at which co-workers share their talents (φ) may depend upon factors such as group identify, trust, comfort, power, and status. In the US, black workers on average have accumulated less formal schooling than white workers, putting them in a position to contribute less to white worker productivity than white workers could contribute to black worker productivity. However, given the historical nature of black–white relations in the US, black workers are often in a subaltern position and white workers in a dominant position in the labor market, resulting in a situation where black workers feel compelled to share their skills to a greater extent with white co-workers than white co-workers share with black co-workers ($\varphi^b > \varphi^w$).[7] Thus, it is possible, in racially mixed worksites, that black workers contribute more to their white peers than they gain from white peers ($\varphi^b H^w > \varphi^w H^b$).

Workplace experience (E) leads to informal learning, a form of human capital that economists expect to influence productivity. However, employers rarely have direct evidence on the quality of prior workplace experience a worker possesses. Thus, they must make an assessment of how much on-the-job learning has occurred due to prior work (π). Psychologists note that persons, including managers, tend to hold stereotypes and there is a tendency to possess more favorable views of those from a group with which they identify. In the US, where most managers are white, psychologists would expect managers to place greater value on the prior workplace experience of white workers than of black workers ($\pi^w > \pi^b$), so white workers would be considered more productive – leading to higher pay – than black workers with equivalent levels of prior workplace experience ($\pi^w E^w > \pi^b E^b$).[8]

Industrial psychologists note that customers (C) can also influence the productivity of workers, especially those with direct customer contact, such as workers involved in sales. The level of rapport (μ) a salesperson develops with their customers is therefore likely to govern their effectiveness as a salesperson.[9] It is possible that white salespersons are able to build greater rapport with white customers than black sales persons

($\mu^w > \mu^b$) which can lead to greater sales on the part of white salesmen ($\mu^w C > \mu^b C$) and thus contribute to the racial wage gap in earnings.[10] Sociologists and psychologists have identified a number of channels that can account for lower rapport with white consumers for black salesmen than white salesmen, including white consumers perhaps being less comfortable interacting with black sales persons or less trusting of black salespersons due to a lack of prior interaction (Pettigrew, 1998 and Wilson and Eckel, 2007), and they may believe they are less knowledgeable (Harrison and Thomas, 2009).

The standard economic model of wage determination can be extended to integrate insights about worker productivity offered by psychologists and sociologists leading to the following characterization of wage determination

$$W = MP(H, X, Q, \phi HC^{co}, \pi E, \eta C)   (22.3)$$

Discussion of the racial wage gap using this interdisciplinary framework is likely to be more informative and enriching than a conversation confined to the more narrow conventional specification of wage determination.

CONCLUSION

Interdisciplinary teaching can help students view economics in a broader way, seeing it as more relevant to their daily lives and helping them to better understand the world around them. Learning to analyze by integrating insights from other disciplines into economic models will be challenging for economics majors and economics educators. However, through this process, students are likely to see economics as a more valuable framework for interpreting diverse information (Powlick, 2009).

NOTES

1. See for instance Bedard and Dhuey (2006), who explore the biological advantages associated with "redshirting" children or delaying their entry into kindergarten, or Berns, Laibson, and Loewenstein (2007) who draw on neuroscience scholarship to examine how persons make decisions about outcomes today: such as marriage, enrolling in school, saving and alternative outcomes at a future date.
2. Cross-disciplinary analysis: examine an issue typically germane to one discipline through the lens of another discipline (i.e. how physicists explore music, sociological perspectives on the purpose of religion). Multi-disciplinary analysis: examine an issue from multiple perspectives, without making a concerted effort to systemically integrate disciplinary perspectives.
3. See Colander and McGoldrick (2009) for a thorough discussion of the challenges economics faces in playing a more central role in the liberal education of college and university students.
4. Gardner (1983) established that students bring multiple forms of intelligence to the learning process and that students are heterogeneous in their learning styles. Thus he believes that drawing on a broad array of frameworks and methodologies will enhance student engagement.
5. For more examples of interdisciplinary teaching in economics, see the economic pedagogic portal Starting Point: Teaching and Learning Economics, http://serc.carleton.edu/econ/index.html (accessed 1 January 2011).
6. See Steffen, Crutzen and McNeill (2007) and Rockstrom et al. (2009) for easily accessible essays by natural scientists that explore these ecological constraints.
7. For a discussion of dominant and subaltern groups and their interaction, see Lewis (1955).

8. Goldsmith, Hamilton, and Darity (2006) offer evidence that managers value prior workplace experience acquired by white workers more than that of black workers, and that they revise their view the longer workers are with their firm, but not to the point where they are treated equally.
9. Becker's (1971, chapter 5) taste for discrimination model can also be extended to explicitly account for a link between customer discrimination and worker productivity or performance.
10. In the US white households possess far more wealth than black households and are thus responsible for a much larger share of total product sales, so racial differences in customer rapport can account for a substantive share of the racial wage gap.

REFERENCES

Bandura, A. (1977), *Social Learning Theory,* New York: General Learning Press.
Becker, G. S. (1971), *The Economics of Discrimination,* Chicago, IL: The University of Chicago Press.
Bedard, K. and E. Dhuey (2006), "The persistence of early childhood maturity: International evidence of long-run age effects", *The Quarterly Journal of Economics,* **121** (4), 1437–72.
Berns, G. S., D. Laibson and G. Loewenstein (2007), "Intertemporal choice – toward an integrative framework", *Trends in Cognitive Sciences,* **11** (11), 482–8.
Colander, D. and K. McGoldrick (2009), *Educating Economists,* Cheltenham, UK and Northhampton, MA, US: Edward Elgar.
Fink, L. D. (2003), *Creating Significant Learning Experiences: An Integrated Approach to Designing College Courses,* San Francisco: Jossey-Bass.
Fogarty, R. J. and B. M. Pete (2009), *How to Integrate the Curricula,* Thousand Oaks, CA: Corwin Press.
Gardner, Howard (1983), *Frames of Mind: The Theory of Multiple Intelligences,* New York: Basic Books.
Goldsmith, A. H., D. Hamilton and W. Darity, Jr. (2006), "Does a foot-in-the-door matter? White-nonwhite differences in the wage return to tenure and prior workplace experience", *Southern Economics Journal,* **73** (2), 267–306.
Harrison, M. S. and K. M. Thomas (2009), "The hidden prejudice in selection: A research investigation on skin color bias", *Journal of Applied Social Psychology,* **39** (1), 134–68.
Keynes, J. M. (1922), "Introduction to Cambridge Economic Handbooks", in D. H. Robertson (ed.), *Money,* New York: Harcourt, Brace, p. v.
Lewis, A. W. (1955), *The Theory of Economic Growth,* London: Unwin Hyman.
Pettigrew, T. (1998), "Intergroup contact theory", *Annual Review of Psychology,* **49**, 65–85.
Powlick, K. M. (2009), "The value of advanced interdisciplinary classes for students of economics: Case study of a 300-level class on gender in the economy", *Forum for Social Economics,* **38** (2–3), 189–200.
Repko, A. F. (2009), "Assessing interdisciplinary learning outcomes", Working Paper, School of Urban and Public Affairs, University of Texas at Arlington, http://www.uta.edu/ints/faculty/REPKO_Outcomes_AEQ.pdf, accessed 20 June 2010.
Rockstrom, J. et al. (2009), "A safe operating space for humanity", *Nature,* **461** (24), 472–5.
Steffen, W., P. J. Crutzen and J. R. McNeill (2007), "The anthropocene: Are humans now overwhelming the great forces of nature?", *Ambio,* **36** (8), 614–21.
Sung, N. S. et al. (2003), "Educating future scientists", *Science,* **301**, 1485.
Wilson, R. K. and C. C. Eckel (2007), "Initiating trust: The conditional effects of skin shade on trust among strangers", Working Paper, Department of Political Science, Rice University.

23 Pluralism in economics education
Robert F. Garnett, Jr. and Jack Reardon

Pluralism has been a rallying cry for openness and broad-mindedness in economics since the early 1980s, when the methodological and epistemological monism of post-World War II economics was challenged by McCloskey (1983) and others (Negru, 2009). In 1992, the *American Economic Review* published a 'Plea for a Pluralistic and Rigorous Economics' (Hodgson, Mäki, and McCloskey 1992, p. xxv), a petition signed by forty-four leading economists, including four Nobel laureates, calling for "a new spirit of pluralism in economics, involving critical conversation and tolerant communication between different approaches" and demanding that this pluralist spirit be "reflected in the character of scientific debate, in the range of contributions in its journals, and in the training and hiring of economists."

The pluralist campaign found vocal allies in economics education. Feminist economists led the way, posing pluralist objections and alternatives to received models of economics education (Bartlett and Feiner, 1992; Shackelford, 1992; Aerni et al. 1999; Lewis, 1999).[1] In 2000 and 2001, the push for pluralism in graduate and undergraduate economics became an international *cause célèbre* when petitions from Ph.D. students and professors in France, the UK, the US, and Italy sparked the formation of the Post-Autistic Economics (PAE) movement (Fullbrook, 2003). This student-led movement called for "a total overhaul of economics and economics teaching," guided by a principled pluralism that "rejects the idea that any school [of thought] could possess final or total solutions, but accepts all as possible means for understanding real-life economic problems" (Fullbrook, 2003, pp. 8–9). The pluralistic ethos of the PAE movement inspired economists across the globe to think anew about the goals and tools of economics education (Groenewegen, 2007; Fullbrook, 2009; Reardon, 2009).

Our task in this chapter is to describe the nature and importance of pluralism in undergraduate economics education. We distinguish pluralist and monist approaches to economics education and situate the former within the classical tradition of liberal education. Liberal education offers a generative framework – a shared language and philosophy – in which economists of all schools can craft pluralistic alternatives to monist texts, courses, and curricula. Against the backdrop of these fundamental ideas, we discuss the types of courses and pedagogies through which instructors have implemented pluralist ideals. Finally, we consider the educational benefits and costs of pluralist education in economics, and strategies for mitigating these costs.

PLURALISM VS. MONISM IN ECONOMICS EDUCATION

Pluralism and monism are each embedded in received approaches to economic science and economics education as distinct views of knowledge and learning (Caldwell, 1988). The monist approach presupposes a scientific consensus about "good economics" – a core of foundational concepts, methods, and propositions that is "accepted by all but a few extreme left-wing and right-wing writers" (Samuelson, 1967, pp. 197–8). The notion of a singular economic way of thinking is a hallmark of Samuelsonian monism. The main task of economics education, from a monist perspective, is to teach the prevailing orthodoxy. For example, the elimination of history of economic thought courses during the 1980s was directly inspired by monist thinking, particularly the arguments of Stigler (1969) and Samuelson (1987), who claimed that all relevant ideas from previous thinkers were embodied in the prevailing mainstream consensus (Boulding, 1971, pp. 556 and 559; see also Negru, 2009).

Pluralists, in contrast, see economics as a polycentric discipline comprised of "not one, but many sciences of economics" (Denis, 2009, p. 7). Through a pluralist lens, reductionist depictions of economics as a "single coherent view" are factually misleading and pedagogically counterproductive. As Ferber argues, "It is difficult, if not impossible, to teach economics effectively while pretending that there is consensus in the discipline about either theory or policy. . . Ignoring these issues deprives students of learning about the most thought-provoking discussions of the profession" (1999, pp. 137–8). Pluralists believe that every undergraduate economics program should introduce students to the intellectual diversity of economic science.

Similar differences can be seen in economists' tacit conceptions of learning itself. In contrast to the monist view of education as a one-way transmission of knowledge from authorities (teachers, textbooks) to novices, pluralist educators emphasize the multiplicity of voices in the educational process (Bartlett and Feiner, 1992, p. 563). Feminists, for example, see student learning as a byproduct of decentralized interactions among many minds (Shackelford, 1992), including the "mind" of the subject matter itself (Palmer, 1999). The implied contrast here is not simply "top-down" monism versus "bottom-up" pluralism. Pluralists recognize that every educational process includes a "top-down" element due to the hierarchical nature of the instructor/student relationship. The pivotal contrast lies in the pluralist commitment to liberal education as an epistemically inclusive enterprise, wherein students and instructors interact not as equals but as partners in the process of inquiry.

To cultivate students' willingness and ability to engage in semi-autonomous inquiry, pluralists believe that the standard goal of "thinking like an economist" should include the liberal art of critical thinking (Thoma, 1993; Garnett and Butler, 2009). In the tradition of Dewey (1933) and Perry (1970), critical thinking is defined as a process of reflective judgment, "making judgments in the context of uncertainty" (Borg and Borg, 2001, p. 20). Pluralists contend that "thinking like an economist" is often confined to analytical thinking: the "complex correct thinking . . . required to solve problems where there is a single right answer" (Nelson, 1997, p. 62; Negru, 2010). To address this educational gap, pluralists suggest that economic educators should supplement analytical exercises, even at the introductory level, with "big think" questions: ill-structured problems that require students to confront analytical and normative ambiguity (Colander and McGoldrick, 2009).

Critics of educational pluralism worry that a premature emphasis on ambiguity or controversy may weaken student motivation and reduce learning. Too much complexity too soon "risks undermining the entire venture . . . with too many qualifications and alternatives [so that] teachers and their students may abandon economics entirely out of frustration born of confusion and uncertainty" (Siegfried and Meszaros, 1997, p. 249). Pluralist educators are acutely aware of these dangers. Yet in their view the greater danger and disservice to their students would be to suppress the fact that economics "contains more than one approach, more than one theory, and more than one proposed solution to every problem it faces" (Freeman, 2009, p. 7).

PLURALIST EDUCATION AS LIBERAL EDUCATION

Long before the PAE movement hoisted the pluralist flag, the Socratic-pluralist goal of teaching students to think for themselves was shared by an array of economics educators (Fels, 1974; Barone, 1991; Moseley et al., 1991; Siegfried et al., 1991; Shackelford, 1992; Ferber, 1999). The common thread linking these diverse endeavors is the project of liberal education. In the words of British economist George Shackle:

> The first task of the University teacher of any liberal art is surely to persuade his students that the most important things he will put before them are questions and not answers. He is going to put up for them a scaffolding, and leave them to build within it. He has to persuade them that they have not come to the University to learn as it were by heart things which are already hard-and-fast and cut-and-dried, but to watch and perhaps help in a process, the driving of a causeway which will be made gradually firmer by the traffic of many minds (Shackle, 1953, p. 18).

Though cherished by a minority of economics educators, the vision of economics as a "liberal art" has never won broad professional support, in part because its leading advocates – mainstream and heterodox – have been unable to sustain collaborative ties across the methodological, ideological, and sociological divisions of our profession.

The recently published volume by Colander and McGoldrick (2009) offers new hope. The diversity of contributors and convergence of themes in this collection suggest that the time may be ripe for new coalitions of mainstream and heterodox educators to rethink undergraduate economics through the lens of liberal education. In addition, the recent shift in the US, UK, and other nations' higher education industries from content- to outcome-based measures of learning offers further reason for optimism. Outcomes-based education systems facilitate the achievement of pluralist educational goals in two ways: (1) making it relatively easy to institute pluralist learning outcomes, since these outcomes generally echo the overarching academic, vocational, and citizenship goals of liberal education (Denis, 2009; Freeman 2009; O'Donnell, 2009; Dow, 2009; Garnett, 2009); and (2) increasing the likelihood of compliance by affording departments and instructors the freedom to devise their own methods for achieving the stated outcomes, based on their unique histories, priorities, and constraints.

PLURALIST ECONOMICS EDUCATION IN PRACTICE

Existing strategies for introducing pluralism into undergraduate economics programs fall into three broad categories. For individual courses, the classic strategy is still the "contending perspectives" model (Barone, 1991) in which students are introduced to the core concepts and methods of various economic paradigms (Moseley et al., 1991; Feiner and Roberts, 1995; Underwood, 2007; O'Donnell, 2009). Such courses can be offered at the introductory, intermediate, or upper level. Their general objectives are to introduce students to theoretical perspectives and arguments beyond those covered in standard texts and to increase students' ability to understand, employ, and assess economic arguments from multiple perspectives.[2]

A second type of pluralist course is the problem-centered "big toolbox" approach (Nelson, 2009). This approach puts economic problems rather than theories in the fore-front and asks students to use concepts from their "toolbox" to analyze these problems. Nelson (2009) finds this an effective method for infusing pluralism and critical thinking into introductory micro- and macroeconomics courses. Similar strategies have been proposed for the introductory microeconomics course (Diduch, 1999; Peterson, 1999; McDonough, 2008; Raveaud, 2009) and for upper-level courses in monetary/macro-economics (Kinsella, 2010; Dow, 2009), labor economics (Champlin and Weins-Tuers, 2009), and international economics (Warnecke, 2009). For example, Champlin and Weins-Tuers (2009) describe a pluralist labor economics course organized around a series of topics (discrimination, labor supply, wage differentials, labor market structure and the concept of labor itself), each of which is explored from multiple perspectives.

A third way to promote pluralist outcomes – to increase students' capacity to engage with economic ideas critically and creatively – is to add complementary courses or learning experiences to standard economics curricula. Hodgson (2002), for example, advocates the addition of a social science literacy course, much as Dow (2009) suggests adding a course on methodology and the history of economic thought. More recently, McGoldrick (1999) and Peterson and McGoldrick (2009) have proposed service-learning as an effective means to achieve pluralistic learning goals (see also Banks, Schneider, and Susman, 2005).

IS PLURALISM WORTH IT?

As vividly conveyed by Earl's account of "the perils of pluralistic teaching" (2002), the common expectation that instructors are supposed to deliver "the present state of knowledge in neatly packaged form" (2002, p. 2) leads some students to resist plural-ist pedagogies. Economics instructors and students often require encouragement and concrete support as they navigate the transition from monistic to pluralistic modes of teaching and learning (Dow, 2009, pp. 53–4). For teachers, the adoption of pluralist pedagogies is likely to create more work and greater fears of failure, at least initially. Gathering appropriate course materials and experimenting with unfamiliar classroom strategies is generally more stressful and time consuming than preparing for lectures, particularly when instructors' own educational backgrounds provide few resources or role models for teaching economics in a pluralistic manner (Colander and McGoldrick, 2009; pp. 3–42; see also Nelson, 1999, p. 178). For students too, pluralist education can create added anxiety and frustration. Perry claims that every step in the process of intel-lectual development "involves not only the joy of realization but also a loss of certainty and an altered sense of self" (Perry, 1989, cited in Kloss, 1994, p. 157). In view of these obstacles, an economist must ask: do the educational benefits of pluralism outweigh the costs?

Due to the relative youth of the pluralist literature, few investigators have attempted to assess the relative merits of pluralist versus monist approaches to economics education. One preliminary study that has already received considerable attention (Mearman et al., forthcoming) reports qualitative data from focus groups at five UK universities. The authors explore student experiences and perceptions of course modules conducted in a pluralist manner. As expected, some students expressed frustration and disappointment about the multiplicity of economic perspectives. One student remarked, "I just find it difficult to say that economics as a body can explain something" (Mearman et al., forthcoming, p. 21). Other students found the emphasis on theoretical differences to be exaggerated or "unnecessary" (*ibid.*, p. 22). O'Donnell (2009) reports similar perceptions based on an end-of-course questionnaire administered to students in a pluralistic intermediate-level course at the University of Sydney, Australia.

With regard to the educational advantages of pluralism, the findings of Mearman et al. (forthcoming) suggest that pluralist modules create increased student interest and engagement (*ibid.*, p. 21), an increased ability to debate or argue a case (*ibid.*, p. 17), "the development of intellectual capacities and practical skills" such as "greater capacity for judgment" (*ibid.*, p. 14), writing skills (*ibid.*, p. 21), and the value of looking at problems from different perspectives (*ibid.*, p. 17). O'Donnell (2009) and Mearman et al. (forthcoming) also underscore the human capital advantages of pluralist courses: how they "make students more employable" (Mearman et al., forthcoming, p. 14) by conferring a broader suite of transferable skills and dispositions than comparable monist courses. Anecdotal evidence suggests that pluralist courses generate broader and deeper learning for instructors too. Warnecke (2009), after attempting a pluralist revision to her international economics course, observes that "the value of teaching from a pluralist perspective is not simply encouragement of critical thinking in students, but in professors as well. It is a mutual learning experience, which is the essence of a university education" (p. 98).

These provisional results suggest that the net advantages of pluralist methods may indeed be positive, especially when institutional and professional resources are available to offset some of the transition costs for instructors and students. Insofar as pluralist education cultivates students' intellectual autonomy, it multiplies their opportunities to achieve "significant learning" (Fink, 2003). In the absence of such opportunities, even high-achieving economics students show a limited ability to apply theoretical principles to real-life personal, professional, and public problems (Salemi and Siegfried, 1999; Hansen, Salemi, and Siegfried, 2002; Katz and Becker, 1999; Walstad and Allgood, 1999). Pluralist revisions of Samuelsonian economics – in other words, the (re)infusion of liberal arts goals and tools into traditional undergraduate courses and curricula – promise to improve these outcomes by enhancing students' capacity for creative, critical thought.

NOTES

1. See also Chapter 19 on "Feminist Pedagogy and Economics", in this volume.
2. A critical dialogue on the pluralist aims and learning outcomes of the contending perspectives model appears in the *International Journal of Pluralism and Economics Education*, **2** (1) (2011).

REFERENCES

Aerni, A. L., R. L. Bartlett, M. Lewis, K. McGoldrick and J. Shackelford (1999), "Toward feminist pedagogy in economics", in A. L. Aerni and K. McGoldrick (eds), *Valuing Us All: Feminist Pedagogy and Economics*, Ann Arbor, MI: University of Michigan Press, pp. 3–18.

Banks, N., G. Schneider and P. Susman (2005), "Paying the bills is not just theory: Service learning about a living wage", *Review of Radical Political Economics*, **37** (3), 346–56.

Barone, C. A. (1991), "Contending perspectives: Curricular reform in economics", *Journal of Economic Education*, **22** (1), 15–26.

Bartlett, R. L. and S. F. Feiner (1992), "Balancing the economics curriculum: Content, method, and pedagogy", *American Economic Review*, **82** (2), 559–64.

Borg, J. R. and M. O. Borg (2001), "Teaching critical thinking in interdisciplinary economics courses", *College Teaching*, **49** (1), 20–29.

Boulding, K. E. (1971), "After Samuelson, who needs Adam Smith?", *History of Political Economy*, **3** (2), 225–37.

Caldwell, B. (1988), "The case for pluralism", in N. de Marchi, *The Popperian Legacy in Economics*, Cambridge: Cambridge University Press, pp. 231–44.

Champlin, D. and B. Wiens-Tuers (2009), "Pluralism in Labor Economics", in J. Reardon (ed.), *Handbook of Pluralist Economics Education*, London: Routledge, pp. 171–80.

Colander, D. and K. McGoldrick (eds) (2009), *Educating Economists: The Teagle Discussion on Re-Evaluating the Undergraduate Economics Major*, Cheltenham, UK and Northampton, MA: Edward Elgar.

Denis, A. (2009), "Editorial: Pluralism in economics education", *International Review of Economics Education* **8** (2), 6–21.

Dewey, J. (1933), *How We Think: A Restatement of the Relation of Reflective Thinking to the Educative Process*, Lexington, MA: Heath.

Diduch, A. M. (1999), "Teaching case studies in the principles of economics classroom: One instructor's experience", in A. L. Aerni and K. McGoldrick (eds), *Valuing Us All: Feminist Pedagogy and Economics*, Ann Arbor, MI: University of Michigan Press, pp. 202–14.

Dow, S. (2009), "History of thought and methodology in pluralist economics education", *International Review of Economics Education*, **8** (2), 41–57.

Earl, P. E. (2002), "The perils of pluralistic teaching and how to reduce them", *Post-Autistic Economics Review*, **11** (January), article 1.

Feiner, S. F. and B. B. Roberts (1995), "Using alternative paradigms to teach about race and gender: A critical thinking approach to introductory economics", *American Economic Review*, **85** (May), 367–71.

Fels, R. (1974), "Developing independent problem-solving ability in elementary economics", *American Economic Review*, **64** (2), 403–7.

Ferber, M. A. (1999), "Guidelines for pre-college economics education: A critique", *Feminist Economics*, **5** (3), 135–42.

Fink, L. D. (2003), *Creating Significant Learning Experiences: An Integrated Approach to Designing College Courses*, San Francisco, CA: Jossey-Bass.

Freeman, A. (2009), "The economists of tomorrow: The case for pluralist subject benchmark statement for economics", *International Review of Economics Education*, **8** (2), 23–40.

Fullbrook, E. (ed.) (2003), *The Crisis in Economics: The Post-Autistic Economics Movement: The First 600 Days*, London: Routledge.

Fullbrook, E. (2009), *Pluralist Economics*, London: Zed Books.

Garnett, R. (2009), "Rethinking the pluralist debate in economics education", *International Review of Economic Education*, **8** (2), 58–71.

Garnett, R. and M. Butler (2009), "Should economics educators care about students' academic freedom?", *International Journal of Pluralism and Economics Education*, **1** (1 and 2), 148–60.

Groenewegen, J. (ed.) (2007), *Teaching Pluralism in Economics*, Cheltenham, UK and Northampton, MA, US: Edward Elgar.

Hansen, W. L., M. K. Salemi and J. J. Siegfried (2002), "Use it or lose it: Teaching literacy in the economics principles course", *American Economic Review*, **92** (2), 463–72.

Hodgson, G. M. (2002), "Visions of mainstream economics: A response to Richard Nelson & Jack Vromen", *Review of Social Economy*, **60** (1), 125–33.

Hodgson, G. M., U. Mäki and D. N. McCloskey (1992), "Plea for a pluralistic and rigorous economics", *American Economic Review*, **82** (May), xxv.

Katz, A. and W. E. Becker (1999), "Technology and the teaching of economics to undergraduates", *Journal of Economic Education*, **30** (3), 194–9.

Kinsella, S. (2010), "Pedagogical approaches to theories of endogenous versus exogenous money", *International Journal of Pluralism and Economics Education*, **1** (3), 276–82.

Kloss, R. J. (1994), "A nudge is best: Helping students through the Perry scheme of intellectual development", *College Teaching,* **42** (4), 151–8.

Lewis, M. (1999), "Breaking down the walls, opening up the field: Situating the economics classroom in the site of social action", in A. L. Aerni and K. McGoldrick (eds), *Valuing Us All: Feminist Pedagogy and Economics*, Ann Arbor, MI: University of Michigan Press, pp. 30–42.

McCloskey, D. N. (1983), "The rhetoric of economics", *Journal of Economic Literature*, **31** (June), 434–61.

McDonough, T. (2008), "Integrating heterodox economics into the orthodox micro course: A pluralist approach", unpublished paper, Department of Economics, National University of Ireland, Galway.

McGoldrick, K. (1999), "The road not taken: Service learning as an example of feminist pedagogy in economics", in A. L. Aerni and K. McGoldrick (eds), *Valuing Us All: Feminist Pedagogy and Economics*, Ann Arbor, MI: University of Michigan Press, pp. 168–83.

Mearman, A., T. Wakely, G. Shoib, and D. Webber (forthcoming), "Does pluralism in economics education make better educated, happier students? A Qualitative Analysis", *International Review of Economic Education*.

Moseley, F., C. Gunn and C. Georges (1991), "Emphasizing controversy in the economics curriculum", *Journal of Economic Education*, **22** (3), 235–40.

Negru, I. (2009), "Reflections on pluralism in economics", *International Journal of Pluralism and Economics Education*, **1** (1 and 2), 7–21.

Negru, I. (2010), "From plurality to pluralism in the teaching of economics: The role of critical thinking", *International Journal of Pluralism and Economics Education*, **1** (3) 185–93.

Nelson, C. E. (1997), "Tools for tampering with teaching's taboos", in W. E. Campbell and K. A. Smith (eds), *New Paradigms for College Teaching*, Edina, MN: Interaction Books, pp. 51–77.

Nelson, C. E. (1999), "On the persistence of unicorns: The trade-off between content and critical thinking revisited", in B. A. Pescosolido and R. Aminzade (eds), *The Social Worlds of Higher Education*, Thousand Oaks, CA: Pine Forge Press, pp. 168–84.

Nelson, J. (2009), "The principles course", in J. Reardon (ed.), *Handbook of Pluralist Economics Education,* London: Routledge, pp. 57–68.

O'Donnell, R. (2009), "Economic pluralism and skill formation: Adding value to students, economies, and societies", in R. Garnett, E. Olsen and M. Starr (eds), *Economic Pluralism*, London: Routledge, pp. 262–77.

Palmer, P. (1999), *The Courage to Teach*, San Francisco, CA: Jossey-Bass.

Perry, Jr., W. G. (1970), *Forms of Intellectual and Ethical Development in the College Years: A Scheme*, New York: Holt, Rinehart and Winston.

Perry, Jr., W. G. (1989), "Notes on scheme", Unpublished notes, Cambridge, MA: Bureau of Study Counsel.

Peterson, J. (1999), "Addressing U.S. poverty in introductory economics courses: Insights from feminist economics", in A. L. Aerni and K. McGoldrick (eds), *Valuing Us All, Feminist Pedagogy and Economics*, Ann Arbor, MI: University of Michigan Press, pp. 75–85.

Peterson, J. and K. McGoldrick (2009), "Pluralism and economics education: A learning theory approach", *International Review of Economics Education*, **8** (2), 72–90.

Raveaud, G. (2009), "A pluralist teaching of economics: Why and how", in R. Garnett, E. Olsen and M. Starr (eds), *Economic Pluralism*, London: Routledge, pp. 250–61.

Reardon, J. (2009), "Introduction and overview", in J. Reardon (ed.), *Handbook of Pluralist Economics Education*, London: Routledge, pp. 3–16.

Salemi, M. K. and J. J. Siegfried (1999), "The state of economic education", *American Economic Review*, **89** (2), 355–61.

Samuelson, P. A. (1967), *Economics*, 7th edition, New York: McGraw-Hill.

Samuelson, P. A. (1987), "Out of the closet: A program for the Whig history of economic science", Keynote Address, History of Economics Society Meetings, Boston, June.

Shackelford, J. (1992), "Feminist pedagogy: A means for bringing critical thinking and creativity to the classroom", *American Economic Review,* **82** (2), 570–76.

Shackle, G. L. S. (1953), *What Makes an Economist?* Liverpool: Liverpool University Press.

Siegfried, J. J. and Meszaros, B. T. (1997), "National voluntary content standards for pre-college economics education", *American Economic Review*, (May), 247–53.

Siegfried, J. J., R. L. Bartlett, W. L. Hansen, A. C. Kelley, D. N. McCloskey and T. H. Tietenberg (1991), "The status and prospects of the economics major", *Journal of Economic Education,* **22** (summer), 197–224.

Stigler, G. (1969), "Does economics have a useful past?" *History of Political Economy*, **1** (3), 217–30.

Thoma, G. A. (1993), "The Perry framework and tactics for teaching critical thinking in economics", *Journal of Economic Education,* **24** (spring), 128–36.

Underwood, D. (2007), "The principles of economics: An American's experience", in J. Groenewegen (ed.), *Teaching Pluralism in Economics*, Cheltenham, UK and Northampton, MA: Edward Elgar, pp. 123–39.

Walstad, W. and S. Allgood (1999), "What do college seniors know about economics?", *American Economic Review*, **89** (2), 350–54.

Warnecke, T. (2009), "Teaching globalization from a feminist pluralist perspective", *International Journal of Pluralism and Economics Education*, **1** (1 and 2), 93–107.

24 Threshold concepts in economics education[1]
Peter Davies

The threshold concept idea (Meyer and Land, 2005) draws on theories of "conceptual change" that include social as well as cognitive dimensions of learning (such as Variation Theory). It is suggested that some conceptual changes within each discipline are distinctive in the way they integrate and transform learners' view of the world.

Threshold concepts should *not* be confused with "key concepts" (Rutherford, 2007), "core concepts" (Lumsden and Attiyeh, 1971), or "basic concepts" (Sumansky, 1986). They are derived from a different theory of learning and therefore have different implications for teaching and learning. The literature on key/basic/core concepts is underpinned by Piagetian theory as developed by Bruner (1960). The fundamental proposition in this approach is that the most important ideas within any discipline can be understood at a number of "developmental" levels. The implication for teaching is that "core concepts" should be identified within a discipline and the teaching of these concepts should provide the spine around which the curriculum should be organized. Students new to a discipline should be introduced to simplified versions of these concepts. Subsequent teaching should periodically "re-visit" these concepts as students are able to understand them in more abstract and sophisticated terms.

The fundamental threshold concept proposition is that the most important ideas in a discipline *cannot* be simplified or made accessible to "novices". Learners new to a field must first develop an *interim* understanding of the way in which the field categorizes experience and the procedures it uses to construct explanations (rather than simplified versions of its most powerful concepts). For example, students have to learn that the ways in which words like "cost" and "investment" are used in economics are different from the ways in which these words are used in everyday language. Students also have to become familiar with the way in which economists use "ceteris paribus" as a procedure in the development of explanations and the ways in which this is represented in comparative statics diagrams. At this interim stage in their learning, it is not possible for students to understand the derivation of the concepts and procedures (such as ceteris paribus) they are being asked to accept and use. It only becomes possible for students to begin to see the "big ideas" (or threshold concepts) in the discipline after they have developed a provisional understanding of a range of more basic economic concepts and procedures.

Davies and Mangan (2007, 2009) differentiate challenges that students face at different stages in their learning. They suggest one kind of conceptual change in which students' everyday understanding is replaced or developed when they learn to use "basic concepts" (such as the distinction between costs and price, short run and long run etc.) in their thinking. Some students may erroneously imagine that this enables them to think like an economist. It does, however, enable them to begin to understand the way in which economists construct their understanding of the world (modeling concepts). Understanding basic and modeling concepts gives students access to the discipline's threshold concepts. Developing an understanding of these integrating ideas transforms students' understanding of basic and modeling concepts. For an "insider" in the discipline, the meaning of the basic and modeling concepts is derived from the threshold concepts which have been developed through the history of thought in the discipline.[2] This is not to imply that students follow the same process in learning that the discipline has followed in its development. Rather, it suggests that it is useful to think of the changes in the structure of understanding that students experience in learning economics, using ideas drawn from the development of the discipline.

However, the process of coming to understand one of these big ideas is likely to be rather gradual, possibly including setbacks and uncertainties. The literature on threshold concepts uses the term "liminal space" to refer to the period during which a learner is coming to terms with a threshold concept. Having "passed through the threshold" the learner is now able to understand in a new way the concepts and procedures they were introduced to earlier. Since the concepts and procedures in a subject are derived from its big ideas, when a learner comes to understand one of these big ideas, their prior learning takes on new meanings for them. Some learners interpret the sense that prior learning has to be completely re-thought as deeply problematic and resist the big idea. This limits their capacity to develop an integrated understanding of economics. But once they do develop an expert understanding of a "big idea", this should improve their understanding of many subsidiary parts of the subject.[3]

The theories of learning in which the idea of threshold concepts is embedded do not favor the distinction between "understanding" and "applying" a concept. This understand/apply distinction is rooted in Bloom et al.'s (1956) *Taxonomy*. In contrast, the threshold concepts literature assumes that any particular phenomenon (such as price) may be understood in a number of different ways. Each of these ways of understanding is referred to as a "conception". Everyday experience leads to the development of naive conceptions of economic phenomena and the first task of teaching is to help students to discard these naive misconceptions in favor of the conception of the phenomenon that is preferred by the discipline. The difference between these two perspectives on the typical sequence of teaching and learning may be summarized thus:

- (Bloomian): blank slate → acquire definitional understanding of concept → learn to apply concept.
- (Conceptual Change): develop naive conception through everyday experience → progress to more sophisticated conception as a result of instruction (equivalent of "acquiring the concept").

According to this latter perspective, there is *no* understanding *without* making sense of particular examples. The concept provides the lens through which the world is viewed.

The remainder of this chapter discusses the meaning of threshold concepts in economics. No attempt is made to identify a definitive list of "threshold concepts" in economics (see, for example, Davies and Mangan, 2007). This is for two reasons. First, the application of threshold concepts is still fairly new and much work on their development has to be done, not least in terms of gathering evidence, to establish the credentials of threshold concepts in relation to learning economics. Second, the usefulness of threshold concepts resides principally in offering a way of thinking about progression of understanding in economics. Some implications for practice are summarized in the conclusion.

A DEFINITION OF THRESHOLD CONCEPTS

Meyer and Land (2005), who introduced the idea of threshold concepts, define them in terms of five characteristics. The following explanation recasts their account slightly by framing it in terms of "conceptual change". That is, there are, within each discipline, some conceptual changes, typically associated with particular concepts, which are distinctive in the way that they:

(i)   *integrate* prior understanding;
(ii)   *transform* a student's sense of belonging to the discipline;
(iii) are *irreversible*, in that once these concepts are understood it is not possible to turn the clock back to a state before this understanding was reached;
(iv)   *mark the boundary* of the discipline as these are concepts which profoundly distinguish the thinking of experts in one discipline from the thinking of experts in another discipline;
(v)   *tend to be troublesome* in that they entail a reconstruction of prior learning, a change in sense of identity in relation to the discipline and may be counter-intuitive.

The distinctiveness of threshold concepts follows largely from the way in which integration and transformation are defined (Davies and Mangan, 2007, 2008).

Integration

In principle, we would expect any conceptual change to involve some *integration* of conceptual understanding. For example, research on students' conceptions of price (e.g. Pang and Marton, 2005; Leiser and Halachmi, 2006) has suggested a progression in conceptions from "price determined by demand" or "price determined by supply" to "price determined by supply and demand". So it is necessary to identify a particular kind of integration which is restricted to conceptual change involving threshold concepts for this to be a definitional characteristic. A first step is to distinguish between types of integration.

The kind of integration described by Pang and Marton and by Leiser and Halachmi will, for convenience, be referred to as *component relations*. This change *could* occur for students who hold different conceptions of costs (underpinning their conception of supply). For example, two students may accurately answer a standard multiple choice question, designed to assess whether they understand the interaction between supply and demand in price determination. They are then presented with a question: "The number of pubs (bars) in a small town falls by forty percent over a period of three years. What do you think is likely to be the effect on the costs experienced by the remaining pubs in the town?" One student responds to the question by only referring to possible effects on the variable costs, whilst the other student refers to possible effects on average variable and average fixed costs. One student makes no connection between their thinking about costs for individual pubs (bars) and their thinking about the shape of the supply curve, whilst the other student does make connections. A change in conception of price to "interaction between supply and demand" which is *accompanied by* a change to a more complex conception of supply will be referred to as *component reconfiguration*.

Finally, it is also possible to describe a type of integration which will be referred to as *theoretical re-framing*. One of the interesting aspects in the literature on conceptions of price is the way in which no distinction has been made between explanations of price in terms of decisions of individual producers and explanations of price in terms of markets. Students' explanations of the price of a bun in a university refectory and explanations of the price of face masks during a SARS epidemic have been categorized in terms of supply and demand, with no reference to the distinction between price making and price taking. In contrast, Davies (2010) cites differences between students' explanations of why the price of fuels and lubricants in the UK rose faster than other prices in the year 2009/10. Whilst some students answered this question in terms of price determination in a market, other students answered it in terms of price determination by a representative firm. In each case, students referred to demand and supply, but they did so whilst using different models of explanation. Students who explained prices in terms of a representative firm assumed that firms always had freedom to "make prices" and did not refer to interaction between equilibrium quantity in related markets. The suggestion here is that whilst some students were able to move fluently between explaining price in terms of markets or individual producers, others were not, and that this difference reflected the theoretical frame in which students' understanding of price was embedded.

The contention here is that conceptual change which involves both theoretical re-framing and component reconfiguration is characteristically found at the moment when students come to an understanding of "threshold concepts" such as general equilibrium.

Transformation

According to the second characteristic of a threshold concept, "transformation", learning is more than a matter of thinking; it is also a matter of identification. This is, of course, suggested by the familiar phrase "learning to think like an economist" (for example, Siegfried et al., 1991). This association between a sense of identity and a way of thinking can be viewed from the standpoint of the philosophies of science put forward by Kuhn (1962) and Lakatos (1970) or from theories of social learning such as "communities of practice" (Lave and Wenger, 1991). The argument here is that progress in learning a subject (like economics) is intrinsically bound up with learning to become part of a community. There are tacit as well as explicit rules and procedures with which a novice needs to become familiar. For example, an undergraduate interviewed by Davies and Mangan (2009) described her experience with graphs in economics:

> . . . People draw them just like in theory and stuff, not like if you are going to apply a graph, you are going to apply it properly with data and stuff, but the way people just plot trends . . . I don't know, I tend not to believe things like that unless I see it, which is probably why I've been searching, why I have searched for like data and things, just to see that that actually happens.

This student expected economists to use graphs in the same way that she had experienced in mathematics and science. She was troubled by the use of graphs as a tool for theoretical exposition and exploration and could not figure out what was going on or why. A sense of alienation which this student expressed elsewhere in this interview may also be inferred from her decision to switch to another subject at the end of her first year. This contrasts with another student at the same university who expressed a strong identification with the subject and the people who practiced it:

> At A level [final years of schooling aged 16–18] I think we all assumed that we all thought like economists and like it was very straightforward whereas now that we have started doing the macro we saw that with A level they had glossed over a lot of things and also at A level there was like just one way of looking at economics whereas now we have been introduced to the different schools of thought. Just making it more interesting I think.

One thing to notice about this statement is that the student expresses an early identification with the subject ("assumed we all thought like economists"). In this, and other interviews reported by Davies and Mangan (2009), there is a strong positive association between this identification with the discipline and students' reporting of a sense of making progress in their learning. However, at the time of the interview, his sense of what it meant to think like an economist had changed and he was now trying to position himself within his perception of economics as a community. He was also quite abrupt in his declaration of how his thinking as an economist distinguished him from others:

> Well for something like maybe Geography or the environment like the green people would say that there should be no pollution at all. Whereas environmental economics would say that there is a sustainable level of pollution and we should pollute up to the point where the costs and benefits equal each other. So I think that economics presents a much more practical way of thinking than some other disciplines.

The critical question for threshold concepts is the extent to which transformations of this kind depend on the way in which a student's conceptual structure is reorganized around threshold concepts. Some indicative evidence is provided by Davies and Mangan (2007). They compared responses from economics lecturers and undergraduates to short, applied problems which were expressed in non-technical language. Although responses from lecturers were no longer than those from students, they used many more economic concepts which were tightly bound together and provided more cautious answers than those offered by students. That is, a key difference between the expert and novice answers was that the experts readily used a framework which enabled them to bring to bear a series of related ideas, whilst students tended to take a rather one-dimensional view. This is consistent with the evidence (Chi et al., 1981) that experts sort physics problems using a "deep structure", whilst novices rely on "surface features" for their categorization. One difficulty with interpreting this evidence is that it compares different individuals' knowledge states, without providing a view of transition from one state to another.

Davies and Mangan (2009) report evidence from student interviews describing their experiences (from school and university) of learning economics, describing critical points in the progress of their understanding of, and identification with, economics. The interviews were conducted with undergraduates attending both research-intensive and teaching-intensive universities in the United Kingdom. Many students referred to their experience studying IS/LM and aggregate supply and demand as critical in their development as undergraduates. They discussed the way in which their understanding (or lack of understanding) had affected them. Some undergraduates were troubled by the way in which teaching had expected them to reconfigure what they thought they already knew (from school) and this had been an alienating experience. Others described themselves as still in transition; knowing they had not yet developed the holistic view that they could see was expected, but still trying to understand. They knew they were not yet insiders, but wanted to be. Still others expressed confidence in their understanding and talked about the way they were using this understanding to interpret events reported in newspapers.

SOME IMPLICATIONS FOR PRACTICE

There are several implications of threshold concepts for the design of curricula and the practice of teaching. The reasoning behind each of these points is explained in Davies and Mangan (2008). Probably the most important implications are:

1. Do *not* try to introduce "simplified versions" of profound ideas to students in the early stages of their learning.
2. Do be explicit about the modeling process in economics – illustrating how, as an economist, you set about framing problems.
3. Do encourage students to expect to reconfigure their understanding of the subject: it is not that they or their teachers "got it wrong" earlier – the process of learning should involve some major re-working.

Teaching which embodies these principles is more likely to help students to develop a powerful and well-structured understanding of the subject.

NOTES

1. I am grateful to Jean Mangan, Jan Meyer, Martin Shanahan, Mike Watts and Ming Fai Pang for helpful comments on earlier drafts of this chapter.
2. That is, threshold concepts may be thought of as a partial application of the ideas developed by Kuhn (1962) and Lakatos (applied to economics in Latsis, 1976) to the process of learning the discipline.
3. Research evidence is needed to test this conjecture. Shanahan et al. (2006) have attempted this with regard to "opportunity" cost and find only a weak relationship between students' performance on opportunity cost multiple choice questions and course grades. However, given the criteria for defining a threshold cost, it seems unlikely that the multiple choice questions they use can be judged as a valid way of testing the hypothesis.

REFERENCES

Bloom, B., M. Englehart, E. Furst,W. Hill and D. Krathwohl (1956), *Taxonomy of Educational Objectives: The Classification of Educational Goals. Handbook I: Cognitive Domain*, New York, Toronto: Longmans, Green.
Bruner, J. (1960), *The Process of Education*, New York: Random House.
Chi, M. T. H., P. J. Feltovich and R. Glaser (1981), "Categorization and representation of physics problems by experts and novices", *Cognitive Science*, **5** (2), 121–52.
Davies, P. (2010), "Transforming knowledge structures: A procedure for developing students' understanding of threshold concepts", Exploring Transformative Dimensions of Threshold Concepts Conference, University of New South Wales, Sydney.
Davies, P. and J. Mangan (2007), "Threshold concepts and the integration of understanding in economics", *Studies in Higher Education*, **32** (6), 711–26.
Davies, P. and J. Mangan (2008), "Embedding threshold concepts: From theory to pedagogical principles to

learning activities", in R. Land, J. H. F. Meyer and J. Smith (eds), *Threshold Concepts in the Disciplines*, Rotterdam: Sense Press, pp. 37–50.

Davies, P. and J. Mangan (2009), "Understanding graphs in economics: An interpretation through threshold concepts", Biennial Conference of the European Association for Learning and Instruction, Amsterdam.

Kuhn, T. (1962), *The Structure of Scientific Revolutions*, Chicago: University of Chicago Press.

Lakatos, I. (1970), "The methodology of scientific research programmes", in I. Lakatos and A. Musgrave (eds), *Criticism and the Growth of Knowledge*, Cambridge: Cambridge University Press.

Latsis, S. J. (ed.) (1976), *Method and Appraisal in Economics*, Cambridge: Cambridge University Press.

Lave, J. and E. Wenger (1991), *Situated Learning: Legitimate Peripheral Participation*, Cambridge: Cambridge University Press.

Leiser, D. and R. B. Halachmi (2006), "Children's understanding of market forces", *Journal of Economic Psychology*, **27** (1), 6–19.

Lumsden, K. and R. Attiyeh (1971), "The core of basic economics", *Economics*, **9** (1), 33–40.

Meyer, J. H. F. and R. Land (2005), "Threshold concepts and troublesome knowledge (2): Epistemological considerations and a conceptual framework for teaching and learning", *Higher Education*, **49** (3), 373–88.

Pang, M. and F. Marton (2005), "Learning theory as teaching resource: Enhancing students' understanding of economic concepts", *Instructional Science*, **33** (2), 159–91.

Rutherford, D. (2007), *Economics: The Key Concepts*, New York: Routledge.

Shanahan, M. P., G. Foster and J. H. F. Meyer (2006), "Operationalising a threshold concept in economics", *International Review of Economics Education*, **5** (2), 29–57.

Siegfried, J. J., R. L. Bartlett, W. L. Hansen, A. C. Kelley, D. N. McCloskey and T. H. Tietenberg (1991), "The status and prospects of the economics major", *Journal of Economic Education*, **22** (3), 197–224.

Sumansky, J. (1986), "The evolution of economic thought as revealed through a history of the Master Curriculum Guide: Framework for teaching the basic concepts", in S. Hodkinson and D. Whitehead (eds), *Economics Education: Research and Development*, London: Addison-Wesley Longman Ltd., pp. 48–63.

Section E

Elementary, Secondary Economic Education

25 Economic education in American elementary and secondary schools

Paul W. Grimes

The prevalence and breadth of economics instruction in American elementary and secondary schools is greater today than at any time in the past. Virtually every state includes specific economics standards in its official public school curriculum and students from kindergarten to twelfth grade are now exposed to economic principles once reserved for serious study by those in college. Furthermore, a significant body of research and national assessments indicate that elementary and secondary students are learning economics, often at levels equal to or greater than other social studies subjects. Even with such good news, economic education advocates argue that the race has not yet been won and that more can, and should, be achieved.

To understand and appreciate the current state of K-12 economic education, a brief glance into the past is instructive. The first major push to create a space for economics in the K-12 curriculum began with the formation of the non-profit Joint Council on Economic Education in the late 1940s.[1] With the Council's support, regional coalitions of academic, business, and labor groups worked to train teachers and develop appropriate curriculum materials. But perhaps the most defining moment of economic education advocacy came in 1960 when the American Economic Association and the Committee on Economic Development formed the National Task Force on Economic Education. The Task Force's recommendations shaped the K-12 economic education landscape over the subsequent decades and remain relevant today (National Task Force on Economic Education, 1961).

The pursuit of the primary goals of the National Task Force on Economic Education's recommendations by economic education advocates eventually resulted in our current environment. Today's curriculum requirements, either through infusion of economics into other subjects or as stand-alone courses, are manifestations of the goal to increase economics instruction. The recommendations to revise the economics curriculum led over time to the formation of the *Voluntary National Content Standards in Economics* (Council for Economic Education, 2010c), which are widely used today by state departments of education as the basis for local curriculum guidelines. The goals of improving teacher education and classroom materials were taken up by the successor organizations of the Joint Council on Economic Education, now known as the Council for Economic Education (CEE), resulting in the formation of a national network of more than 200 university-based centers which provide professional development training for teachers and the dissemination of professionally developed and age-appropriate lesson plans. The results of the goal to involve others in economic education are also seen today as numerous non-profit organizations, including the CEE, receive significant financial support from private businesses and governmental agencies for promoting economic education across the nation.

Even though much has changed in the last fifty years, many of the original 1961 recommendations still speak to the issues that economic educators face today. This chapter examines the current extent of K-12 economics instruction, what is being taught, and how effective economic education advocacy has been at promoting student knowledge and understanding.

THE CURRICULUM

Extent of Instruction

The decentralized and local nature of the American educational system makes it virtually impossible to succinctly characterize the extent and exact content of economics instruction that an average student receives during the elementary and secondary years of schooling. However, we do know that nearly every K-12 public school student is supposed to receive some systematic instruction in economics at some point during his or her studies. One of the defining trends in American education over the past fifty years is the adoption and implementation of standards-based curricula. Curriculum standards explicitly detail what level of knowledge and understanding a student should obtain and demonstrate upon successful completion of a course of study. By 2009, economics standards were part of the official K-12 public school curricula in forty-nine states and the District of Columbia (CEE, 2009). Only Rhode Island failed to incorporate economics as part of the state's official public school curriculum.

Unfortunately, inclusion of economics standards does not mean the same thing in all states. Although forty-nine states have economics standards, only forty states require local school districts to implement those standards. Thus, in nine states, the standards are essentially voluntary guidelines and not mandates. Furthermore, some states provide school districts with the option to teach economics as a separate discipline or to infuse it into other required subjects. Only twenty-one states require local school districts to offer a stand-alone economics course which is compulsory for high school graduation. Such mandates, which first appeared in the 1970s, are generally in states with strong networks of economic education centers affiliated with the CEE (Grimes and Millea, 2003). The number of mandate states has tripled since 1982 when only seven states included an economics course in their graduation requirements (Walstad, 1992). The full effects of economics course mandates have been debated in the research literature (Belfield and Levin, 2004), with at least one possible negative externality being identified. Utilizing a national sample of high school students, Marlin (1991) found that the degree of student learning was positively correlated with teacher attitudes; however, he also found that teacher attitudes were diminished when state authorities mandated inclusion of economics in the curriculum. On the other hand, Grimes and Lee (2000) found that statewide economic education mandates are found in states with relatively higher levels of growth in overall economic output.

Compounding the problem of measuring the extent of economics instruction is the definition of what exactly constitutes economics. In recent years, economics instruction in some locales has come to focus primarily on applications of personal finance. Historically, economic education advocates championed a wide variety of personal finance topics under the umbrella of economic education, but some resistance to this is now apparent as financial lessons crowd out more traditional and broader-based economics lessons. Leading economist and college textbook author Greg Mankiw said, in response to a legislative proposal in California that would require one-half of a high school economics course to be devoted to personal finance, ". . . this law would be a step in the wrong direction. The legislation is akin to requiring high school biology teachers to spend half their time on issues of personal health and nutrition. Personal finance is a useful life skill, but students need a more thorough grounding in other basic economic principles . . ." (Mankiw, 2009). Although some state departments of education recognize the differentiation between economics and personal finance by including separate and specific standards in their official curricula guidelines (Tennyson and Nguyen, 2001), many include personal finance topics under the economics heading.

The CEE routinely conducts a national survey to determine the extent of economics instruction in state K-12 curricula. The requirements in forty-six of the forty-nine states with an economics curriculum are inclusive of both elementary and secondary grade levels. However, only twenty-nine of the forty-four states with personal finance requirements include elementary grades in the finance standards.

Twenty-one states required completion of an economics course for high school graduation in 2009 and thirteen states required a course in personal finance.[2] The states with the strongest curriculum mandates are those that require formal student testing of knowledge and understanding. In 2009, nineteen states tested in economics and only nine in personal finance. Interestingly, the number of states testing in economics in 2009 was four fewer than in 2007 – most likely crowded out by other student testing due to revisions in the No Child Left Behind federal legislation and other mandated testing.

As a result of the movement to include economics as a required course for graduation, the number of students taking economics courses in high school increased dramatically over the past three decades. Table 25.1 provides a comparison of high school economics course enrollment between 1982 and 2000, the latest year that full data are available from the National Center for Education Statistics (NCES). In 1982, a little more than one-quarter of all students earned high school course credit in economics, but by 2000, that number had risen to just less than one-half of all students. Preliminary results from a 2005 survey indicate that the overall percentage was not significantly different from the 2000 results (NCES, 2007a).

Interestingly, Table 25.1 also reveals that relatively larger percentages of Black (54.4), Hispanic (67.3), and Asian (61.0) students earned high school credit in economics when compared to White (45.3) students in 2000. The reason for this is not obvious, but it may reflect the racial and ethnic demographics of states with an economics course mandate, as well as student preferences in those states without a course mandate. In 1982, relatively more students in rural communities took an economics course (30.7 percent versus 28.6 percent in urban and 24.9 percent in suburban areas), but by 2000 rural students were less likely to earn an economics course credit. This is not surprising given that smaller rural school districts in non-mandate states have fewer resources to offer elective courses. Perhaps the most obvious effect of course mandates seen in Table 25.1 is the difference between students in public and private schools by 2000. A full one-half of public school students earned economics credit, while only 37 percent of private school students did so. In many states, private schools are not obligated to offer the prescribed public school

Table 25.1   Percent of high school graduates earning course credit in economics: 1982 and 2000

Characteristic	1982	2000
All Students	27.4	49.2
Student Gender:		
Male	27.5	49.5
Female	27.2	49.0
Student Race/Ethnicity:		
White	27.7	45.3
Black	29.4	54.4
Hispanic	24.3	67.3
Asian/Pacific Islander	16.3	61.0
Native American	27.0	34.4
Curriculum Type:		
Academic	28.9	49.7
Vocational	26.8	36.4
Both	27.2	50.9
Neither	25.4	43.9
Community Type:		
Urban	28.6	50.3
Suburban	24.9	52.3
Rural	30.7	42.0
Region:		
Northeast	18.4	36.6
South	31.5	52.9
Midwest	33.2	34.9
West	22.1	71.8
School Type:		
Public	27.8	50.4
Private	24.1	37.1

Source: National Center for Education Statistics (2007b).

curriculum. For economic education advocates, private schools offer an opportunity to expand their reach.

Walstad (1992) estimated that in 1961, the year that the National Task Force on Economic Education released its Report, only 16 percent of American high school students took an economics course in high school. Fifty years later, the picture looks considerably different. Based on projections, the twenty-one states with an economics high school course mandate will account for more than 60 percent (1,975,965 of 3,225,017) of all high school graduates in 2011 (NCES, 2009). In comparison, states with a personal finance course mandate will produce about twenty-seven percent (886,680 of 3,225,017) of all graduates in that year. Given that many students never take a separate high school course in economics but are exposed to the discipline through infusion in other courses, and that many more were taught basic economic concepts while in elementary school, it is safe to say that the extent of formal economics instruction is broader today than at any time in the past.

Curriculum Content

In addition to the increased extent of economic instruction in elementary and secondary schools over the years, the breadth of content coverage also increased. Again, the movement towards standards-based instruction played a large part in this trend. Most state curriculum standards are very specific in identifying the concepts and principles which students are expected to master for any given grade and subject. Once identified, these concepts and principles form the basis for student testing and assessment of learning. Experience shows that the natural tendency is for the expansion of standards over time – once a concept finds its way into a set of educational standards, it is often difficult to remove. Thus, K-12 teachers often face difficult decisions as to how much classroom time to devote to any given standard.

As discussed earlier, forty-nine states and the District of Columbia have economics standards for their elementary and/or secondary public schools. All of the K-12 economics standards today were influenced by, or explicitly based on, the *Voluntary National Content Standards in Economics* originally developed by the CEE in 1997 and revised in 2010. These recommended standards evolved from earlier works by the CEE to establish a "framework" on which K-12 schools could build a comprehensive and age appropriate economic curriculum (Saunders et al., 1984). The current national standards were developed by a team of prominent economists and educators and include detailed benchmarks for twenty primary content standards. Benchmarks for both knowledge and application of the standards are provided for grades four, eight, and twelve. Table 25.2 provides a listing of the twenty content standards and indicates in which grade level introductory (I) and extended (E) benchmarks are provided.

The extended breadth of content coverage at the elementary and middle school level is apparent when comparing the current standards to the recommended "framework" concepts published in the mid-1980s. Today, sixteen of the twenty content standards have benchmarks for fourth grade students, whereas only nine of twenty-one "framework" concepts were recommended for introduction through fourth grade. Subsequently, at the eighth grade level, today's standards include only four introductory content benchmarks, whereas the "framework" guidelines included ten new concepts. Also telling is the fact that only one standard, concerning fiscal and monetary policies, is now reserved for introduction by the twelfth grade. In fact, when taken as a whole, the national content standards and accompanying benchmarks are remarkably similar to what would be found on most principles of economics course syllabi at the college level.

It is difficult to ascertain to what extent the expansion of content coverage has come at the expense of the *depth* of coverage. To date, economic education researchers have not specifically explored this issue; however, we do know that a growing proportion of secondary school students do study economics at a depth equivalent to an introductory college course. One of the major educational trends in recent years is the expanding provision of college credit for students still in high school through Advanced

Table 25.2   Council for Economic Education's National Content Standards in Economics: 2010

Content Standard	Grade Level		
	K-4	5-8	9-12
1. Productive resources are limited. Therefore, people cannot have all the goods and services they want; as a result, they must choose some things and give up others.	I	E	E
2. Effective decision making requires comparing the additional costs of alternatives with the additional benefits. Many choices involve doing a little more or a little less of something: few choices are "all or nothing" decisions.	I	E	E
3. Different methods can be used to allocate goods and services. People acting individually or collectively must choose which methods to use to allocate different kinds of goods and services.	I	E	E
4. People usually respond predictably to positive and negative incentives.	I	E	E
5. Voluntary exchange occurs only when all participating parties expect to gain. This is true for trade among individuals or organizations within a nation, and among individuals or organizations in different nations.	I	E	E
6. When individuals, regions, and nations specialize in what they can produce at the lowest cost and then trade with others, both production and consumption increase.	I	E	E
7. A market exists when buyers and sellers interact. This interaction determines market prices and thereby allocates scarce goods and services.	I	E	E
8. Prices send signals and provide incentives to buyers and sellers. When supply or demand changes, market prices adjust, affecting incentives.	I	E	E
9. Competition among sellers usually lowers costs and prices, and encourages producers to produce what consumers are willing and able to buy. Competition among buyers increases prices and allocates goods and services to those people who are willing and able to pay the most for them.	I	E	E
10. Institutions evolve and are created to help individuals and groups accomplish their goals. Banks, labor unions, markets, corporations, legal systems, and not-for-profit organizations are examples of important institutions. A different kind of institution, clearly defined and enforced property rights, is essential to a market economy.	I	E	E
11. Money makes it easier to trade, borrow, save, invest, and compare the value of goods and services. The amount of money in the economy affects the overall price level. Inflation is an increase in the overall price level that reduces the value of money.	I	E	E
12. Interest rates, adjusted for inflation, rise and fall to balance the amount saved with the amount borrowed, which affects the allocation of scarce resources between present and future uses.		I	E
13. Income for most people is determined by the market value of the productive resources they sell. What workers earn depends, primarily, on the market value of what they produce.	I	E	E
14. Entrepreneurs take on the calculated risk of starting new businesses, either by embarking on new ventures similar to existing ones or by introducing new innovations. Entrepreneurial innovation is an important source of economic growth.	I	E	E

Table 25.2   (continued)

Content Standard	Grade Level		
	K-4	5-8	9-12
15. Investment in factories, machinery, new technology, and in the health, education, and training of people stimulates economic growth and can raise future standards of living.	I	E	E
16. There is an economic role for government in a market economy whenever the benefits of a government policy outweigh its costs. Governments often provide for national defense, address environmental concerns, define and protect property rights, and attempt to make markets more competitive. Most government policies also have direct or indirect effects on people's incomes.	I	E	E
17. Costs of government policies sometimes exceed benefits. This may occur because of incentives facing voters, government officials, and government employees, because of actions by special interest groups that can impose costs on the general public, or because social goals other than economic efficiency are being pursued.		I	E
18. Fluctuations in a nation's overall levels of income, employment, and prices are determined by the interaction of spending and production decisions made by all households, firms, government agencies, and others in the economy. Recessions occur when overall levels of income and employment decline.		I	E
19. Unemployment imposes costs on individuals and the overall economy. Inflation, both expected and unexpected, also imposes costs on individuals and the overall economy. Unemployment increases during recessions and decreases during recoveries.	I	E	E
20. Federal government budgetary policy and the Federal Reserve System's monetary policy influence the overall levels of employment, output, and prices.			I

Note: I = Introductory; E = Extended.

Source: Council for Economic Education (2010c).

Placement (AP) courses and testing, or through dual enrollment programs with local colleges and universities. While well below the rates seen in subjects such as history, the incidence of students taking AP economics (either macro or micro) rose dramatically in the 1990s. Walstad and Rebeck (2000) report that the incidence of enrollment in an AP economics course increased from 0.4 percent of all high school students to 1.0 percent between 1982 and 1994. By 2006, 16 percent of those students earning high school credit in economics did so by taking an advanced course – either, AP, International Baccalaureate, or honors (NCES, 2009). While we can say with certainty that more students are studying college-level economics earlier in their lives, no data are yet available to determine if this trend ultimately results in a greater accumulation of economics human capital or if there is merely a temporal shift as to when economics human capital is obtained.

Table 25.3   A sample of modern high school economics textbooks

Textbook Title	Author(s)	Publisher
Comprehensive Mainstream		
Economics in Our Times	Roger A. Arnold	Glencoe McGraw-Hill
Economics: Principles and Practices	Gary Clayton	Glencoe McGraw-Hill
Economics: Principles in Action	Arthur O'Sullivan and Steven Sheffrin	Prentice Hall
Economics: Concepts and Choices	Sally Meek, John Morton, and Mark C. Shug	Holt McDougal Publishers
Southwestern Economics	Holten J. Wilson and J. R. Clark	Glencoe McGraw-Hill
The Study of Economics: Principles, Concepts, and Applications	Turley Mings and Matthew Marlin	Dushkin Publishing Group
Specialized Target Markets		
Economics for Christian Schools	Alan J. Carper	Bob Jones University Press
Economics for Everybody	Gerson Antell and Walter Harris	Amsco School Publications
Economics: Institutions and Analysis	Gerson Antell and Walter Harris	Amsco School Publications
Economics: Work and Prosperity	Russell Kirk	A Beka Book
Exploring Economics	Ray Notgrass	Notgrass Company
High School Economics	Laurence G. Christopher	Christopher Productions
JA Economics	Not Identified	Junior Achievement
Pacemaker Economics	Not Identified	Globe Fearon, Incorporated

Source: Derived from Leet and Lopus (2003) with author updates.

Another indication of how high school economics is becoming more like introductory college economics is evident when reviewing high school textbooks. Leet and Lopus (2003) found that a majority of those published by the leading textbook publishers for the mainstream market are written by college professors, several of whom also author college principles of economics textbooks. In fact, some of these books are abridged versions of the authors' college text, augmented for the high school marketplace. Leet and Lopus also found that the majority of these high school textbooks tend to cover all of the CEE's recommended content standards, but do vary with respect to treatment and depth of analytical coverage.

A listing of the textbooks written for the high school economics classroom and available for adoption in 2011 is provided in Table 25.3. Note that the number of books designed for specialized markets exceeds the number of titles issued by the four leading secondary school textbook publishers. This appears to be a recent phenomenon and a reflection of the fragmentation appearing in the educational system. Two of the specialized textbooks are published for inclusion in the curricula of private Christian schools (*Economics for Christian Schools* (Carper, 2009) and *Economics: Work and Prosperity* (Kirk, 2009)), but also marketed to the homeschool market. One textbook is specifically written for homeschoolers (*Exploring Economics* (Notgrass, 2009)). Two economics textbooks are available for low-achieving or special needs students (*Economics for Everybody* (Antell and Harris, 1999) and *Pacemaker Economics* (Globe Fearon, 2001)) and one has been written for the non-traditional adult student market (*Economics: Institutions and Analysis* (Antell and Harris, 1997)). The non-profit Junior Achievement organization sells an economics textbook as a complement to its outreach and mentoring programs. Finally, in response to the escalation of textbook prices, at least one low-priced paperback alternative is being produced for schools seeking to reduce textbook expenditures, *High School Economics* (Christopher, 2010). It is also important to note that a variety of publishers are beginning to publish multimedia "learning kits" that contain videos, computer simulations, and interactive games in lieu of traditional textbooks. These are becoming available for both traditional mainstream classrooms as well as for specialized niche market classrooms.

In addition to traditional textbooks and ancillary student workbooks, many K-12 teachers rely on curriculum guides and lesson plans written and distributed through organizations such as the CEE. This is particularly true for elementary and middle school students. The production and distribution of age-appropriate effective curriculum materials is a hallmark of the CEE and its network of university-based centers. Through the network of economic education centers, the CEE provides local teacher training and support for a wide variety of economics curricula. In addition to materials designed for standalone economics courses and content, the CEE publishes K-12 lessons and teacher guides for infusing economics into a wide variety of subjects, such as mathematics, history, civics, government, environmental studies, children's literature, and others. Most CEE lesson plans are designed with active learning pedagogies and are constructed to keep students engaged in an experiential learning process. The CEE's library of curriculum materials is widely available in electronic format. The digitization of the library, originally funded by the National Science Foundation in the late 1990s, resulted in a CD-ROM (*Virtual Economics*) that was distributed to every school district in the nation. Later private funding resulted in major updates (NCEE, 2005) and additional enhancements are now planned for a future release.

Teachers of economics are supported by a number of other organizations and institutions.[3] Among the most prominent are the Foundation for Teaching Economics, Junior Achievement, The JumpStart Coalition, and the Federal Reserve System. The Federal Reserve Board of Governors charges each of the twelve district banks with a public mandate to support economic and financial literacy in their regions. The Federal Reserve banks are now a major source of classroom materials and lesson plans for K-12 teachers and many of the banks and their branches produce numerous teacher workshops and public programs each year.

The importance of professional development programs for teachers of economics cannot be overstated as adequate initial teacher preparation remains a major and persistent challenge for K-12 schools. State teacher licensing requirements often fail to include coursework in economics, even for high school social studies teachers. Walstad (2001) reported that only half of the states include at least one college course in economics for licensure as a high school social studies teacher, compared to as many as ten history courses being required in some states. Research has consistently showed a strong positive correlation between the number of college courses taken and teacher effectiveness in the economics classroom (for example, see Bosshardt and Watts, 1990, Allgood and Walstad, 1999). Even though many states have instituted content standards in economics, reform of teacher education programs lags far behind. The result is strong demand for economic education workshops for K-12 teachers who are required to instruct students in a complex subject they are ill-prepared to teach.

ASSESSMENT OF ECONOMIC EDUCATION

Economic educators have a strong tradition of K-12 program evaluation and assessment of student learning (Sosin, Dick and Reiser, 1997; Walstad, 2001). New curriculum materials, training programs, and classroom pedagogies are routinely scrutinized under the analytical eyes of research economists. To support these efforts, the CEE publishes three standardized student examinations for the K-12 grades. The *Basic Economics Test* (BET; CEE, 2010a) is designed for use in grades five and six, the *Test of Economic Knowledge* (TEK; CEE 2010b) covers middle school material taught in grades seven through nine, and, the comprehensive *Test of Economic Literacy* (TEL; Walstad and Rebeck, 2001b) is used in grades eleven and twelve. All of these tests were developed by teams of experienced economists and educators, with each test item being keyed to the *Voluntary National Content Standards in Economics* and reflecting a hierarchy of cognitive functioning. The tests are normed using extensive nationwide sampling of schools and students (see, for example, Walstad and Rebeck, 2001a). Together, they provide an opportunity for schools to empirically evaluate the effectiveness of their local economic education efforts, in a way that is not readily available in other social science disciplines.

A major milestone in the formal assessment of economic education was achieved in 2006 when the US Department of Education included economics in the National Assessment of Educational Progress (NAEP) program. NAEP is the primary tool used by American policymakers to monitor the academic achievement of elementary and secondary school students. Eleven thousand-five hundred twelfth grade students, from nearly six hundred public and private schools across the nation, participated in the first NAEP economics examination during the spring of 2006. A summary of the major results is reported in Table 25.4.

Overall, the NAEP results are encouraging but they also highlight a few areas of concern (Buckles and Walstad, 2008). Seventy-nine percent of the sample scored in the "At or Above Basic" category of understanding and forty-two percent scored in the "At or Above Proficient" category. Thus, a significant number of high school students appear to be learning and mastering economic principles. However, as seen in Table 25.4, a gender gap appears in the "Proficient" and "Advanced" levels of understanding. A greater number of male students scored in these categories relative to their female cohorts. (The mean test score for all male students was 152, while the mean for all female students was 148. This was found to be a statistically significant difference.) This result is consistent with previous research finding for high school economics (Heath, 1989) and is an issue yet to be satisfactorily explained or overcome by economic educators. A significant racial and ethnicity gap is also apparent in the NAEP results; Black, Hispanic, and Native American students scored significantly below White and Asian

Table 25.4   National Assessment of Educational Progress: results for economics, 2006

Characteristic	Percent of Students Attaining Achievement Levels			
	Below Basic	At or Above Basic	At or Above Proficient	At Advanced
All Students	21	79	42	3
Student Gender:				
Male	21	79	45	4
Female	21	79	38	2
Student Race/Ethnicity:				
White	13	87	51	4
Black	43	57	16	< 0.5
Hispanic	36	64	21	< 0.5
Asian/Pacific Islander	20	80	44	4
Native American	28	72	26	2
Parents' Education:				
Less than High School	41	59	17	< 0.5
High School Graduate	31	69	27	1
Some College	18	82	39	1
College Graduate	13	87	54	5
Free/Reduced Price Lunch:				
Eligible	38	62	20	1
Not Eligible	16	84	48	4
Not Available	14	86	50	4
School Location:				
Central City	24	76	39	3
Urban Fringe	20	80	44	3
Rural	20	80	40	2
Region:				
Northeast	19	81	46	4
Midwest	17	83	45	3
South	23	77	37	2
West	#	#	#	#

Notes:
Basic = Partial mastery of the knowledge and skills that are fundamental for proficient work at given grade.
Proficient = Solid academic performance; demonstrated competency over challenging subject matter.
Advanced = Superior performance for a given grade.
# Reporting standards not met for region.

Source: National Center for Education Statistics (2009).

students. Although additional research is needed to determine the root sources of these gaps, the preponderance of racial minorities in relatively resource-poor urban center and rural school districts is a likely contributing factor. The effect of restricted resources is also seen in the results for students eligible for the federal free and reduced price lunch program; students eligible for the program were more than twice as likely to be in the "Below Basic" category of understanding relative to those who were not eligible. On the other hand, the positive impact of family human capital is evident in the results when broken down by parents' educational attainment. Five percent of students coming from homes headed by a college graduate scored in the "Advanced" category, while only 1 percent of those from homes headed by a high school graduate did so.

The NAEP economics results compare favorably with the results obtained for other social science disciplines such as history, civics, and geography. The demographic patterns of relative academic achievement noted above are also consistent with those found in these and other subjects that are part of the NAEP program. The second NAEP assessment of economics is scheduled for 2012.

CONCLUSIONS

In summary, the overall state of economic education in American elementary and secondary schools appears healthy and strong. Economics is now firmly rooted in the curricula of most state public education systems through the adoption and implementation content standards and guidelines. About one-half of today's high school graduates have taken either a required or elective course in economics, and a small but growing percentage are taking economics courses for college credit while still in high school. Many of the other half have studied economic concepts and principles through infusion in other subjects throughout their K-12 studies. Teachers of economics are supported by a variety of professional development opportunities and modern curriculum materials produced and provided by the CEE's national network of university-based centers, the Federal Reserve System, and other organizations. A wide variety of textbooks and other instructional materials for high school courses is available, including those for specialized groups of students. Teachers and local school districts also have access to nationally normed and standardized exams to evaluate and assess economic education classes and programs at the elementary, middle, and high school levels. The recent nationwide assessment revealed that the academic achievement of high school students in economics compares favorably with other social study areas. However, the results also showed that all demographic groups are not scoring at the same level and that work needs to be done to eliminate a gender gap and to raise the performance of racial and ethnic minorities. Perhaps the greatest challenge facing economic education today is the continuing need for more training for teachers. In 1961, the National Task Force on Economic Education recommended six college credits in economics for teacher certification; fifty years later, the average licensure requirement is only half of that.

NOTES

1. A description of the historical context in which today's economic education advocacy movement developed is presented in Chapter 1 "History of Economic Education", in this volume.
2. The CEE's website, http.//www.councilforeconed.org (accessed 9 June 2011), provides links to the latest *Survey of the States*. As of 2009, states requiring a high school economics course included: Alabama, Arizona, Arkansas, California, Florida, Georgia, Idaho, Indiana, Louisiana, Michigan, Mississippi,

New Hampshire, New Jersey, New Mexico, New York, North Carolina, South Carolina, South Dakota, Tennessee, Texas, and Virginia. Likewise, states requiring a high school personal finance course included: Arkansas, Georgia, Idaho, Illinois, Louisiana, Maryland, New Jersey, New York, Oklahoma, South Dakota, Tennessee, Utah, and Virginia.
3. For more information, see Chapter 75, "Near and Far: An Introduction to Economic Education Organizations in the US and Beyond", in this volume.

REFERENCES

Allgood, S. and W. B. Walstad (1999), "The longitudinal effects of economic education on teachers and their students", *Journal of Economic Education*, **30** (2), 99–111.

Antell, G. and W. Harris (1997), *Economics: Institutions and Analysis*, New York, NY: Amsco School Publications, Incorporated.

Antell, G. and W. Harris (1999), *Economics for Everybody*, New York, NY: Amsco School Publications, Incorporated.

Arnold, R. A. (2001), *Economics in Our Times*, New York, NY: Glencoe McGraw-Hill, Incorporated.

Belfield, C. R. and H. M. Levin (2004), "Should high school economics courses be compulsory?", *Economics of Education Review*, **23** (4), 351–60.

Bosshardt, W. and M. Watts (1990), "Instructor effects and their determinants in precollege economic education", *Journal of Economic Education*, **21** (3), 265–76.

Buckles, S. and W. B. Walstad (2008), "The national assessment of educational progress in economics: Test framework, content specifications, and results", *Journal of Economic Education*, **39** (1), 100–106.

Carper, A. J. (2009), *Economics for Christian Schools* (3rd ed.), Greenville, SC: Bob Jones University Press.

Christopher, L. G. (2010), *High School Economics*, Portage, MI: Christopher Productions.

Clayton, G. (2004), *Economics: Principles and Practices* (3rd ed.), New York, NY: Glencoe McGraw-Hill, Incorporated.

Council for Economic Education (2009), *Survey of the States*, New York, NY: Council for Economic Education.

Council for Economic Education (2010a), *Basic Economics Test* (3rd ed.), New York, NY: Council for Economic Education.

Council for Economic Education (2010b), *Test of Economic Knowledge* (2nd ed.), New York, NY: Council for Economic Education.

Council for Economic Education (2010c), *Voluntary National Content Standards in Economics, 2nd Edition*, New York: Council for Economic Education.

Globe Fearon (2001), *Pacemaker Economics* (3rd ed.), Lebanon, IN: Globe Fearon, Incorporated.

Grimes, P. W. and D. O. Lee (2000), "Economic education and economic growth", *Atlantic Economic Journal*, **28** (4), 490.

Grimes, P. W. and M. J. Millea (2003), "Economic education as public policy: The determinants of state-level mandates", *Journal of Economics and Economic Education Research*, **4** (2), 3–18.

Heath, J. A. (1989), "An econometric model of the role of gender in economic education", *American Economic Review*, **79** (2), 226–30.

Junior Achievement (2000), *Junior Achievement Economics*, Colorado Springs, CO: Junior Achievement Publications.

Kirk, R. (2009), *Economics: Work and Prosperity*, Pensacola, FL: A Beka Book.

Leet, D. R. and J. S. Lopus (2003), "A review of high school economics textbooks", Social Science Research Network elibrary, http://ssrn.com/abstract=381760, accessed 15 February 2011.

Mankiw, G. (2009), "Redefining high school economics", *Greg Mankiw's Blog: Random Observations for Students of Economics*, 13 April 2009, http://gregmankiw.blogspot.com/ 2009/04/defining-high-school-economics.html, accessed 15 February 2011.

Marlin, J. W. (1991), "State-mandated economic education, teacher attitudes, and student learning", *Journal of Economic Education*, **22** (1), 5–14.

Meek, S., J. Morton and M. C. Shug (2011), *Economics: Concepts and Choices*, Geneva, IL: Holt McDougal Publishers.

Mings, T. and M. Marlin (2000), *The Study of Economics: Principles, Concepts, and Applications* (6th ed.), New York, NY: Dushkin McGraw-Hill, Incorporated.

National Center for Education Statistics (2007a), *America's High School Graduates 2005*, Washington, DC: United States Department of Education.

National Center for Education Statistics (2007b), *The 2000 High School Transcript Study Tabulations:*

Comparative Data on Credits Earned and Demographics for 2000, 1998, 1994, 1990, 1987, 1982 High School Graduates, Washington, DC: United States Department of Education.

National Center for Education Statistics (2009), *Digest of Educational Statistics*, Washington, DC: United States Department of Education.

National Council on Economic Education (2005), *Virtual Economics V. 3*, New York, NY: National Council on Economic Education.

National Task Force on Economic Education (1961), *Economic Education in the Schools*, New York, NY: Committee on Economic Development.

Notgrass, Ray (2009), *Exploring Economics*, Cookeville, TN: The Notgrass Company.

O'Sullivan, A. and S. Sheffrin (2004), *Economics: Principles in Action* (3rd ed.), Upper Saddle River, NJ: Prentice Hall, Incorporated.

Saunders, P., G. L. Bach, J. D. Calderwood and W. L. Hansen with H. Stein (1984), *A Framework for Teaching the Basic Concepts* (2nd ed.), New York, NY: Joint Council on Economic Education.

Sosin, K., J. Dick and M. L. Reiser (1997), "Determinants of achievement of economics concepts by elementary school students", *Journal of Economic Education*, **28** (2), 100–121.

Tennyson, S. and C. Nguyen (2001), "State curriculum mandates and student knowledge of personal finance", *The Journal of Consumer Affairs*, **35** (21), 241–62.

Walstad, W. B. (1992), "Economics instruction in high schools", *Journal of Economic Literature*, **30** (4), 2019–51.

Walstad, W. B. (2001), "Economic education in U.S. high schools", *Journal of Economic Perspectives*, **15** (3), 195–210.

Walstad, W. B. and K. Rebeck (2000), "The status of economics in the high school curriculum", *Journal of Economic Education*, **31** (1), 95–101.

Walstad, W. B. and K. Rebeck (2001a), "Assessing the economic understanding of U.S. high school students", *American Economic Review*, **91** (2), 452–7.

Walstad, W. B. and K. Rebeck (2001b), *Test of Economic Literacy Examiner's Manual* (3rd ed.), New York, NY: National Council on Economic Education.

Wilson, H. and J. R. Clark (1997), *Southwestern Economics*, New York, NY: Glencoe McGraw-Hill, Incorporated.

26 Organizations focused on economic education
Sue Lynn Sasser and Helen Meyers

Several organizations today focus on the mission of promoting economic education, some presenting a broad-based perspective of economics and others with a more focused purpose. The majority of these organizations work either with educators or directly with students in grade K-12. While there may be other groups who provide services at a local level, this chapter will highlight national groups with a rich history of contributing to economic education.

ECONOMIC EDUCATION ORGANIZATIONS

Committee on Economic Education[1]

The Committee on Economic Education is a standing committee of the American Economic Association (AEA); its purpose is to improve the quality of economics education at all levels: pre-college, college, adult, and general education. Formed in 1955, the Committee sponsors research sessions and workshops at the Allied Social Science Association Meetings. It also maintains a partnership with the Council for Economic Education in promoting the quality and quantity of economics education taught in our nation's schools.

The Committee's web site also hosts four Econometrics Training Modules, developed by William E. Becker through a cooperative effort with the Council for Economic Education (see below), which assist in designing empirical projects that will improve the quality of research in economic education. The four modules include Data Management and Heteroskedasticity Issues; Endogenous Regressors with Natural Experiments, Instrumental Variables, and Two-stage Estimators; Panel Data and Sample Selection Issues. Each of the modules is available for free download.

To further support the mission of economic education, the Committee now hosts a conference focused on teaching economics at the collegiate level (both graduate and undergraduate) and research in economic education in K-16.

Council for Economic Education (CEE)[2]

The Council for Economic Education (CEE), formerly known as the National Council on Economic Education, offers a comprehensive K-12 program through a unique delivery model of 200 affiliated state councils, university-based centers, and its new internet campus. These programs include a variety of curriculum and activities related to general economics (micro, macro and international), personal finance and entrepreneurship.

Originally formed as the Joint Council on Economic Education by the AEA in 1949, CEE offers teaching resources across the curriculum, professional development for teachers, student competitions and nationally normed assessment instruments. The Council's mission is to empower individuals "to make informed and responsible choices throughout their lives as consumers, savers, investors, workers, citizens, and participants in our global economy."[3]

CEE's programs annually reach more than 150,000 K-12 educators and over 15 million students in the United States.[4] In addition, CEE is now working in about 40 countries, serving more than 20 million students since 1995 and has translated materials into two dozen languages.[5] The majority of funding for CEE programs, both at the national and state levels, comes from the private sector, including corporations, foundations and individual contributors. While CEE has initiated several online training opportunities for teachers, the majority of its programs are delivered by its network of state councils and university-based centers.

CEE's three core areas include: EconomicsAmerica®, EconomicsInternational® and EconomicsExchange®.[6]

- EconomicsAmerica® is the Council's comprehensive domestic program designed to increase the economic literacy level of students across the United States. The goal is to improve the quantity and quality of economic education taught in classrooms across the United States by equipping teachers with the tools needed to help students understand how the "real" world works. CEE and its affiliates are frequently involved in assisting with the development of both federal and state standards in economics, personal finance and entrepreneurship, as well as assessing the effectiveness of implementing those standards in the classroom. CEE also offers a national Economics Challenge competition for high school students.
- EconomicsInternational®, supported primarily with funding from the US Department of Education and grants from international partners, serves a similar mission by providing educational opportunities for teachers in other countries. While the program was initiated in Eastern European nations transitioning to market economies, it has expanded to include other nations. EconomicsInternational helps provide connections between classrooms in those countries and classrooms in the US. Some initiatives in this area include study tours for teachers from the US to visit teachers and classrooms in other countries, bringing teachers from other countries to visit teachers and classrooms in the US, and curriculum development in international economics.
- EconomicsExchange® is an "economics for life" program providing practical economic and financial literacy skills for employees in the workplace, parents, and other adults.

Additionally, CEE collaborates on other projects to make curriculum resources readily available for classroom teachers. One of the most visible examples of these collaborative efforts is EconEdLink,[7] an online "source of classroom-tested, internet-based, economic lesson materials for K-12 teachers and their students." EconEdLink is a free resource for its users and includes several hundred lessons which can be accessed through a variety of searchable menus. Each lesson includes teacher and student versions, and the lessons are designed for use in a "variety of formats and classroom settings." EconEdLink is part of Thinkfinity, a comprehensive digital learning platform built upon the merger of Verizon

MarcoPolo and the Thinkfinity Literacy Network that provides discipline-specific, standards-based educational resources.

In partnership with the National Association of Economic Educators and the Foundation for Teaching Economics, CEE has produced a set of curriculum standards based on the essential principles of economics, titled *Voluntary National Content Standards in Economics.*[8] Each of the 20 content standards, developed by a panel of economists and economic educators, includes a rationale for its inclusion; benchmarks indicating attainment levels for students in grades 4, 8, and 12; samples of what students can do to enhance or demonstrate their understanding of economics, and correlation of EconomicsAmerica publications to the standards.

CEE also produces a biennial Survey of the States, outlining the growth and development of economic, financial and entrepreneurship education in US schools. The Survey is posted on the Council's web site and is available free of charge. The Council has also convened three National Summits on Economic and Financial Literacy, providing forums to bring together advocates from the public and private sectors who are focused on advancing economic and financial education in common education.

Federal Reserve System[9]

The Federal Reserve Board of Governors and its twelve Federal Reserve banks offer numerous resources and activities for K-12 students and educators, the majority of which are posted on a special web site dedicated to students and teachers. This all-inclusive site has links to videos, simulations, web sites, research and other tools that promote economic and financial literacy. Most of the Fed banks and their branches have full-time staff devoted to economic education as part of their public affairs mission.

In addition to providing an assortment of educational resources, most Fed banks offer teacher workshops on a wide variety of economic and Fed-related topics, ranging from banking and consumer credit to the financial crisis and international trade. The workshops are designed to help teachers gain a deeper understanding of the role of the Fed and monetary policy in the US economy, to explore economic issues and to examine principles of personal financial education. Several Fed banks also offer student-oriented activities, such as bank tours or student competitions, including the Fed Challenge, where teams of high school students portray themselves as members of the Federal Open Market Committee and make policy recommendations, and essay competitions, where students research and write about current topics in economics.

Many of the Federal Reserve Banks also sponsor workshops and conferences for college faculty, including those interested in K-12 education, such as the Midwest Economic Education Conference held annually at the Kansas City Fed.

Foundation for Teaching Economics (FTE)[10]

The Foundation for Teaching Economics (FTE) was established in 1975 to encourage the instruction of the economic way of thinking in high school classrooms. The FTE is a non-profit organization that offers a variety of workshops for high school teachers and students, in both "face to face" and online training environments. Its programs are supported by contributions from individuals, foundations and corporations. One of its premiere programs is the Economics for Leaders which teaches high school students how to use economic reasoning to address public policy issues and improve their leadership skills. Its teacher training includes topics such as The Environment and the Economy, The Economic Demise of the Soviet Union and The Economics of Disasters.

FTE materials cover a wide breadth of content areas that allow teachers to maintain flexible, up-to-date, interactive lessons, correlated to state and national content standards. Most lessons are written by classroom educators and include background materials, as well as a video demonstrating the lesson. Since its beginning, FTE has delivered professional development training to more than 16,000 high school teachers, who have provided classroom instruction in economics to over 25,000,000 students.

Junior Achievement (JA)[11]

One of the oldest organizations committed to economic education for youth, Junior Achievement (JA), was founded in 1919 by Theodore Vail, president of American Telephone & Telegraph; Horace Moses, president of Strathmore Paper Co. and Senator Murray Crane of Massachusetts. JA Worldwide offers experiential programs designed to engage students in learning about workforce readiness, entrepreneurship and financial literacy. Annually, JA Worldwide reaches almost 10 million students in thousands of classrooms and after-school locations throughout the United States and over 100 countries.

JA's programs are divided into elementary, middle school and high school. The elementary programs focus primarily on basic economic principles, while middle school programs target careers. Its high school programs are designed to help students connect their education with the workplace by building the skills needed for citizenship and productive workers.

The traditional JA model involves community volunteers, such as local business people, parents, retirees or college students, to partner with classroom teachers to present lessons one day a week for five to eight weeks. This model is designed to bring real world experiences to the classroom and encourage students to develop their critical thinking skills.

In recent years, JA has expanded its programs to include other specialized projects including JA BizTown and JA BizKids$. JA BizTown takes fifth grade students through a series of classroom lessons before spending the day at a JA BizTown site, where the students work as employees in various businesses. As part of the experience, they are paid for their labor and then learn to manage their own checking accounts. JA BizKid$ is a multi-media initiative that teaches young students similar skills, such as money management and entrepreneurship. Instead of the onsite visit, it features weekly television shows and classroom activities.

JA also conducts a number of national polls, such as the Teen Ethics Survey and Kids and Careers Survey, to gain insight into how teens think about the different issues. One of its most recent projects is developing the Junior Achievement Innovation Initiative (JAII), which brings community leaders together to discuss the current and future needs of students. Their findings and recommendations are frequently used to modify ongoing JA programs and shape the future of its educational offerings.

National Assessment of Educational Progress (NAEP)[12]

The National Assessment of Educational Progress (NAEP) was established in 1969 to provide periodical assessments in reading, mathematics, science, writing, US history, civics, geography and other subjects taught in schools across the United States. Its primary responsibility is to measure the academic achievement of elementary and secondary students, and report those findings to the general public as part of the Nation's Report Card on education. These findings are frequently used to modify teacher training programs, classroom instructional strategies and other assessment models.

In 2006, NAEP carried out its first test of economics and the second round of economics assessment is set to happen in 2012. The economics test is administered to high school seniors, who answer questions on a wide range of content from three areas: market, domestic economics, and international economics.

The Commissioner of Education Statistics, who heads the National Center for Education Statistics in the US Department of Education, is responsible for the NAEP project and works with the National Assessment Government Board on the assessment. Members of the National Assessment Governing Board are appointed by the Secretary of Education and serve as an independent entity within the US Department of Education. Created by Congress in 1988, the 26-member Governing Board is a bipartisan group whose members include governors, state legislators, local and state school officials, educators, business representatives, and members of the general public.

National Association of Economic Educators (NAEE)[13]

The National Association of Economic Educators (NAEE) is the professional organization for economic educators. Started in 1980, NAEE offers its members a variety of opportunities for professional growth and offers one of the few awards programs for outstanding contributions to economic education. It collaborates with the Council for Economic Education to host one of the largest annual conferences for economic educators each fall, which includes classroom teachers, college professors, international educators and others interested in promoting effective classroom instruction. NAEE membership is open to anyone whose responsibilities are specifically designated in economic education or who expresses an interest in the organization's mission.

NAEE annually recognizes outstanding economic educators through its award programs for leadership, service, research, international and technology achievements. In addition, it assists members by providing an online "workbench", containing various resources related to managing effective economic education programs. The organization also provides various opportunities for mentoring inexperienced economic educators, such as "mini-grants" and online training sessions.

SPECIALIZED ORGANIZATIONS

With the increased emphasis on personal financial literacy in the public schools, several other national organizations have been created in recent years to help address these specific concerns. These specialized organizations play an important role in providing educational opportunities for both students and educators.

Jump$tart Coalition for Personal Financial Literacy[14]

The Jump$tart Coalition for Personal Financial Literacy is a national collaboration of organizations dedicated to improving the financial literacy of children and young adults. Its focus is primarily on students from kindergarten through college. Since its founding in 1995, the coalition has become a leading source of "advocacy, research, standards and educational resources" for personal finance. The coalition is probably best known for its national bi-annual survey of high school students which measures their knowledge about personal finance concepts.

Jump$tart does not specifically or exclusively endorse any product or program. Instead, it provides a clearinghouse of personal finance materials on its web site, with free access to all users. It also created and maintains the National Standards in K-12 Personal Finance Education to delineate the personal finance knowledge and skills that should be achieved by the nation's youth.

Jump$tart was originally called the Partnership in Personal Finance and Consumer Credit Consortium and has evolved into an alliance of approximately 180 national organizations and entities from the corporate, non-profit, academic, government and other sectors. It was based on an idea credited to William E. Odom, who was then Chairman and CEO of the Ford Motor Credit Corporation and Chairman of the Council for Economic Education Board of Directors.

National Endowment for Financial Education (NEFE)[15]

The National Endowment for Financial Education (NEFE) is a private, non-profit foundation that focuses on the financial health and well-being of individuals and families by partnering with other organizations that provide financial education to members of the general public. NEFE originally evolved from the College for Financial Planning in Denver, Colorado, becoming an independent entity in 1997.

Its programs primarily target underserved populations, such as youth, low-income individuals and families, and people facing special economic challenges. One of its most noted programs is the NEFE High School Financial Planning Program®, a personal finance curriculum for high school students. It also offers Cash Course®, an online non-commercial resource designed specifically to assist colleges and universities in engaging young adults in financial education.

Securities Industry and Financial Markets Association (SIFMA) Foundation[16]

The Securities Industry and Financial Markets Association (SIFMA) Foundation pro-vides several educational opportunities for students of all ages. The Foundation's signa-ture program is The Stock Market Game™, a classroom simulation for grades 4–12. The Game™, as it is commonly called, started about 30 years ago and now has thousands of students participating in all 50 states, as well as in several countries around the world. In this simulation, students work in teams to build an investment portfolio by buying and selling stocks, bonds and mutual funds. A few years ago, the Foundation expanded its offerings to classroom teachers by developing a new activity called InvestWrite®, a national essay contest focused on long-term saving and investing. A third program, The Capitol Hill Challenge, is also sponsored by the Foundation and involves matching students participating in The Game™ with members of Congress selected by SIFMA to participate. During the semester's competition, the selected members of Congress track the progress of students in their district who are enrolled in The Game™; students from the winning teams are then awarded a trip to Washington, DC to meet their legislator.

SUMMARY

Economic and financial literacy are critical skills for young people growing up in today's complex environment. Engaging students in learning economics and personal finance initiates a lifelong learning process that will assist them in making more informed choices about the use and allocation of society's resources. The organizations described in this chapter provide the tools educators need to empower students with the knowledge to build a solid future for themselves and their families. These tools in turn allow students to establish a framework for making life decisions as consumers, savers, investors, workers, citizens, and participants in our global economy.

NOTES

1. www.vanderbilt.edu/AEA/AEACEE/index.htm (accessed 24 April 2011).
2. www.councilforeconed.org (accessed 20 February 2011).
3. http://www.councilforeconed.org/about/ (accessed 14 June 2011).
4. www.councilforeconed.org/news/story.php?story_id=192 (accessed 14 June 2011).
5. http://www.councilforeconed.org/ (accessed 14 June 2011).
6. http://www.councilforeconed.org/programs/ (accessed 14 June 2011).
7. www.econedlink.org (accessed 10 June 2011).
8. For more information about these Standards (including a detailed list), see Chapter 25, "Economic Education in American Elementary and Secondary Schools" in this volume.
9. www.federalreserveeducation.org/fred/ (accessed 24 April 2011).
10. www.fte.org (accessed 21 February 2011).
11. www.ja.org (accessed 20 February 2011).
12. http://nationsreportcard.gov/ (accessed 21 February 2011).
13. www.naee.net (accessed 24 April 2011).
14. www.jumpstart.org/ (accessed 20 February 2011).
15. www.nefe.org (accessed 26 February 2011).
16. www.sifma.org/Education/SIFMA-Foundation (accessed 26 February 2011).

PART III

RESEARCH

Section A

Principles Courses

27 The purpose, structure and content of the principles of economics course
Geoffrey Schneider

Economists have been wrestling with the purpose, structure, and content of the principles of economics course for more than a century (Brandis, 1985). Recent data indicate some alarming trends that warrant revisiting the principles course: economics is experiencing a declining share of all bachelor's degrees awarded, and has continuing difficulty attracting women to the economics major. As Siegfried (2010, p. 330) reports, the number of economics bachelor degrees awarded increased by 23.7 percent from 1991 to 2009, while the total number of bachelor's degrees awarded in all disciplines grew by 46.4 percent, indicating that economics lost market share among undergraduate majors. In addition, "economics has been attracting a steadily declining share of female undergraduates" – the share of women among economics undergraduate majors has stagnated at about 30 percent, even while the share of women among all college graduates grew from 54.2 to 57.4 percent (Siegfried, 2010, p. 330). With the principles course as the window into the field, it represents a key site for the cultivation of new majors.

There is much common ground in the work of those who have examined the principles course. A regular recommendation for more than a century has been for the principles course to be structured as a less dense, single-semester, broad-based, welcoming, interesting class that devotes less time to models and more time to a core set of fundamental principles and a set of relevant applications of those principles drawn from the world around us. Yet, despite repeated recommendations for this type of restructuring, many principles of economics instructors and most principles texts have continued to adhere to the encyclopedic, model-based, two-semester sequence.

This chapter will describe some of the key issues concerning the purpose, structure and content of the principles course, including the scope of the course, the role of the principles course in the curriculum, the debate over the one-semester versus two-semester principles sequence, and some possible designs for the content of a principles course or sequence. This is followed by a discussion of some alternative forms that the principles course might take.

THE SCOPE OF THE PRINCIPLES COURSE AND STUDENT LEARNING: LESS IS MORE?

Going back as far as 1909, introductory economics courses have been criticized as too broad and too abstract (Brandis, 1985). The American Economic Association's 1950 report on *The Teaching of Undergraduate Economics* complains of "too many objectives" and a "principal stress on theory" in the principles course (Taylor, 1950, p. 5). Similarly, Hansen, Salemi and Siegfried (2002, p. 464) argue that

> The Principles course fails to improve economic literacy of not only those who take it, but also those frightened away by its reputation as a technical course. The course fails because it does not teach students how to apply economics to their personal, professional, and public lives. The cost of jamming many topics into the course is that students never master the basics.

A study by Walstad and Allgood (1999, p. 354) demonstrates "that many college seniors who have taken an economics course still show a lack of understanding of basic economics." This result may be due to the overwhelming nature of the principles course, an idea which is supported by a substantial body of educational research on deep versus shallow approaches to learning. Deeper approaches to learning are characterized by greater focus, more connections to prior knowledge and experience, and repeated application of methods. Whereas, a course with too many applications is likely to lead to a shallow approach to learning via memorization where students perform "an *imitation* of the discipline" rather than gaining lasting facility with the tools of the discipline (Wankat, 2002, pp. 171–2).

This is borne out by Bransford, Brown, and Cocking (2004, p. 20), whose landmark study of student learning concludes that "Superficial coverage of all topics in a subject area must be replaced with in-depth coverage of fewer topics that allows key concepts in that discipline to be understood." Bransford et al. (2004, p. 139) go on to argue that "Ideas are best introduced when students see a need or a reason for their use – this helps them see relevant uses of knowledge to make sense of what they are learning." In order to take advantage of these recent advances in the study of how students learn, the principles course should contain a narrower range of topics, make connections to students' lives and the world around them,[1] involve repeated applications of a narrower set of economic tools, and engage students actively with the material by placing them at the center of the learning process.

THE ROLE OF THE PRINCIPLES COURSE IN THE CURRICULUM: MAJORS OR NON-MAJORS?

What to focus on in the principles course is a matter of negotiating between conflicting goals. Do we want broadly educated students, able to understand economic issues that affect their lives and to vote intelligently, or do we want to prepare students for the major? The focus of textbooks on models seems to indicate an emphasis on the latter. It is difficult to imagine voters being able to make intelligent decisions about candidates espousing various economic arguments without at least one course in economics. Kennedy (2000, p. 81) argues that "a major goal of the Macroeconomics Principles course is to produce students capable of understanding macroeconomics encountered in the media." If we decide to focus on educating the general population on economic issues, we must do more to get a greater number of students into the principles course, which also implies that the course must be welcoming. One way to reach greater numbers of students might be to take Kennedy's argument to heart and to build our principles courses around the economic issues in the news. However, Watts and Becker (2008) report that economists only occasionally (22 percent of the time) use newspapers or other current events materials in their classes. A related issue is whether or not to teach the principles sequence in one or two semesters.

ONE- VS TWO-SEMESTER FORMAT

In the very first issue of the *Journal of Economic Education*, the debate over whether or not to teach a one-semester or a two-semester principles course was addressed (Klos and Trenton, 1969). Although their sample was limited to sections of principles at one university, Klos and Trenton found that students with two semesters of economics demonstrated no greater mastery of economic literacy than students with only one semester. This led them to conclude, like Hansen, Salemi and Siegfried (2002), that a one-semester principles course focusing on a narrow range of material was the best approach:

> The one-semester course should cover much material which is not far removed from the students' experience and incorporate techniques which motivate the beginner to learn more about the subject matter. The introductory semester should then be followed by a course chosen by the student as being nearest to his interest (Klos and Trenton, 1969, p. 54).

However, Paden and Moyer (1971) show that students in a two-semester sequence obtain 10 percent greater content knowledge than those in a one-semester course, which could aid performance in upper-level courses. Thus, economists must accept some small cost in terms of depth of understanding if they choose a one-semester course over a two-semester sequence. Given the unsettled nature of this debate and the tradeoffs that institutions face when selecting an approach, this continues to be a rich opportunity for future study.

The issue of format is critical because of the number of students who do and do not take the introductory economics classes. Estimates of how many college students in the United States take at least one economics course vary. Siegfried (2000) uses a survey of department chairs to estimate that 40 percent of undergraduate students take at least one economics course. He also reports that 78.9 percent of four-year institutions have a two-semester principles sequence, and that 66.2 percent of the students at these institutions who take the first semester continue on to the second. However, using transcript data from a nationally representative sample of students (the Baccalaureate and Beyond study of the US Department of Education), Bosshardt and Watts (2008) estimate that 59.3 percent of all undergraduate students complete at least one course in economics. Unfortunately, for students who did not major in economics or business, only an average of 46.9 percent completed at least one economics course. Thus, the data indicate that economists will teach anywhere from 40 to 59 percent of undergraduate students a principles of economics course.

Given that only 40–59 percent of students start the principles sequence and an additional one-third of those do not take the second course (Siegfried, 2000), this means that only 26–39 percent of students at institutions teaching a two-semester principles course are exposed to a complete range of microeconomic and macroeconomic principles. For a complete introduction to economics, students should be exposed to both microeconomic and macroeconomic material.

If economists were to adopt the goal of fostering basic economic literacy in many if not most undergraduate students, then it is clear from the information above that they should choose a one-semester principles course including both microeconomics and macroeconomics. For those institutions desiring to give depth to students who will continue in economics, a second principles course building on the first one could follow (see Hansen, Salemi and Siegfried, 2002). This way, students taking only one economics course would get enough economics to help them understand the world around them, while students continuing in economics could still get the depth they need.

CONTENT: THE FOCUS OF THE PRINCIPLES COURSE

Mainstream economists have proposed various themes to form the core of the principles course: (1) thinking like an economist, (2) cultivating economic literacy, (3) a "Social Issues" approach, and (4) a historical approach. There can, of course, be substantial overlap between these approaches.

The notion of teaching introductory students to "think like an economist" appears throughout most standard texts, as well as in the literature on teaching economics. However, as we shall see below, the definition of thinking like an economist is subject to debate, and once defined, the realization of this goal can be quite difficult to achieve. The original definition of this approach can be found in Siegfried et al. (1991, p. 21):

> Thinking like an economist involves using chains of deductive reasoning in conjunction with simplified models (such as supply and demand, benefit-cost analysis, and comparative advantage) to illuminate economic phenomena . . ., identifying and evaluating tradeoffs in the context of constraints, distinguishing positive from normative analysis, and tracing behavioral implications of change while abstracting from aspects of reality. It . . . involves describing redistributive implications of change, amassing data to evaluate economic events, and testing hypotheses about how consumers and producers make choices and how the economy works. Finally, thinking like an economist involves examining many problems through the filter of efficiency – coping with limited resources.

Most texts and many instructors have interpreted thinking like an economist to mean studying a wide variety of basic economic models. As noted above, this encyclopedic approach to teaching principles is inconsistent with research on student learning.

Interestingly, Siegfried et al. (1991, p. 21) go on to state that, "Thinking like an economist requires creative skills too." Yet one may argue that the creative aspect of economic analysis is lacking in principles courses. Models are often presented in simplified or reduced formats, abstracting away from the nuanced, creative aspect of applying economic models to the real world. Unfortunately, this may give students an incomplete perspective on what thinking like an economist really means.

As reported by Strober, Cook and Fuller (1997), and as probably experienced by anyone who has taught a lot of undergraduate economics courses, students may be able to use economic models in simplified textbook or classroom examples, but they have substantial difficulty applying these tools to real-world problems and issues. A course that selects teaching students to think like an economist as a primary goal would likely benefit from spending some time teaching the limitations and creative applications of economic models. Instructors could emphasize the *art* of applying economic analysis to messy, real-world situations.

As one method of teaching students the art of applying economic analysis, Becker (2000) suggests adding some newsworthy, contemporary applications of economics to introductory courses, such as nominal versus real interest rates, technological change and economic growth, expectations and risk, switching costs and lock-ins, innovation-versus price-based competition, and network economies and externalities. This should help to breathe life and relevance into the principles course, while helping students wrestle with the complexity of real-world applications.

Colander and McGoldrick note another problematic aspect of how many instructors teach students to think like economists: they do not incorporate advances in economic theory and modeling into their principles courses. The result is that,

> It is as if introductory economics is being taught in a time warp. . . . [T]he economic way of thinking is changing. It is more inductive than previously; it uses laboratory, natural and field experiments to test assumptions and models, and is based more on game theory and strategic reasoning than on deductive calculus subject to strict agent rationality assumptions. . . . [S]ince all these approaches are part of the modern economic way of thinking, it would seem that the issues they raise should be presented if the "economic way of thinking" is actually the focus of the introductory courses (Colander and McGoldrick, 2009, p. 32).

Thus, it is not at all clear that the instructors are teaching students to think like a modern economist if they focus on older models while neglecting current research.

An approach to principles that is similar to thinking like an economist is the notion of concentrating on economic literacy. In stark contrast to the encyclopedic approach, the economic literacy approach involves focusing on a discrete set of key topics. Hansen, Salemi and Siegfried (2002) have argued for a focus on economic literacy, by which they mean teaching the standards developed by the Council for Economic Education (hereafter CEE Standards).[2] The CEE Standards that have been argued by some as a basis for economic literacy are listed in Chapter 25 in this volume by Paul Grimes. Siegfried and Meszaros (1997, p. 247) describe these standards as "the fundamental propositions of economics." For this reason, Hansen, Salemi and Siegfried (2002) advocate using the CEE Standards as the core of a one-semester principles course.

To make the principles course more oriented towards a deep approach to learning, Hansen, Salemi and Siegfried (2002) suggest eliminating a number of elements of the standard principles course. They suggest dropping coverage of cost curves, limiting graphs, dropping comparisons of imperfectly competitive industries, limiting computations of elasticity, limiting coverage of national income accounting, dropping formulas for multipliers, and dropping aggregate demand and aggregate supply. Instead, they would "focus on problems, issues, policies, and puzzles" (Hansen, Salemi and Siegfried, 2002, p. 468). The emphasis would be on using fundamental economic concepts to explain important world events covered in leading news publications, and on creating more opportunities for students to practice economics. And, as noted above, Hansen et al. (2002) also promote the development of a second principles course to cover the CEE Standards in greater depth for those students continuing in economics.

From the perspective of student learning and engagement, the CEE Standards approach seems to represent a significant improvement over the encyclopedic, model-based principles course. The shorter list of topics, the opportunity for students to practice and apply a narrower range of tools, and the emphasis on topics and issues more relevant to students' lives should have a substantial payoff in terms of attracting students and deepening learning.

The CEE Standards approach is also more conducive to a course focused on public policy issues of the day, or what Grimes and Nelson (1998) term "social issues pedagogy." By limiting the number of topics and models that must be covered, this frees up time in the principles course to use the narrower range of tools to focus on the major social issues of the day. If a primary goal is to create an educated populace that is well-informed on the major issues, this approach has much to commend it. However, the social issues approach is quite rare in principles courses and "survives primarily in niche courses designed for specific groups of non-majors" (Grimes, 2009, p. 96). Grimes (2009) theorizes that this approach failed to survive due to

> the relative time cost that professors bore when teaching a social issues class. It takes substantially more time and effort to teach an effective social issues course as compared with teaching a traditional principles course. Instructors must know the ever-changing landscape of the social issues that provide the platform to deliver the economics content (p. 96).

The social issues approach could be an excellent method of exposing students to the major economic issues and debates of the day, helping to make students engaged, well-informed citizens. And, it should foster interest in economics by connecting students to the world in which they live.

Similar to the social issues approach, Colander and McGoldrick (2009) advocate structuring the principles course around "big think" questions linked to liberal education goals. This includes "Reconnecting economic analysis to the lives that students currently lead and the issues they will face after college" (Colander and McGoldrick, 2009, p. 33). A practical application of this approach for both introductory micro and macroeconomics is presented by Garnett and McGoldrick (2011).

Another approach that tweaks the principles course in a direction related to the social issues approach is that of incorporating the history of economic ideas. One important issue to acquaint voters with might be the general economic philosophies that economists have adopted over the years, and how contemporary politicians at both ends of the political spectrum reflect those philosophies. With politicians on the right espousing various degrees of libertarianism and supply-side economics, it behooves us to acquaint students with these ideas and how economists tend to view them. Similarly, with politicians on the left advocating greater levels of government intervention and, in Europe and developing countries, greater levels of equality and access to basic needs, the ideas of Keynesian as well as Marxian, Institutionalist, post-Keynesian and Feminist economists are also relevant. A principles course with the goal of creating an educated voter could expose students to the debates economists have had over how to run the economy and how these debates are connected with contemporary political debates. Indeed, with the return of fiscal policy in the United States in the wake of the financial crisis of 2008–10, and with ongoing debates about the role of government in most countries, a section on how economists view the role of government could be a cornerstone of the principles course. Fortunately, there are resources to aid faculty in incorporating these perspectives, such as Heilbroner's *The Worldly Philosophers* (1999), but it would require a shift away from the encyclopedic approach to the principles course.

ALTERNATIVES TO THE CEE STANDARDS

There are some alternatives to the CEE Standards that propose definitions of what it means to think like an economist, and that go further than the social issues approach in seeking to broaden the subject matter that would constitute achieving economic literacy. These alternatives emphasize critical thinking, focus more on the actual economy rather than abstract models, and incorporate debates among professional economists. Some economists have been quite outspoken in their criticisms of the CEE Standards. Ferber (1999) argues that the CEE Standards are overly conceptual and not focused enough on basic facts about the world economy or the institutional setting for the economy being studied. This can potentially limit students' knowledge of how the existing economy actually functions, a crucial element in understanding the world around them. In presenting the Standards as an organizing structure, Siegfried and Meszaros (1997, p. 249) argue that assumptions behind economic theory can frequently be omitted from the principles course, but Ferber (1999) notes the strong possibility that this will create dissonance in students who see the disconnect between the tidy models and the messy real world.

Furthermore, the CEE Standards ignore controversies and debates within the discipline of economics, especially the views of heterodox economists. Being an economist often means being involved in such debates, but in another example of how the CEE Standards oversimplify what it means to think like an economist, the authors chose to exclude economic debates from the subject matter. For example, the CEE Standards continue to promote an oversimplified vision of international trade, arguing that free trade creates a win-win situatation, even though many modern economists focus on the strategic growth considerations that make it possible for some countries to win from trade at the expense of others. Finally, the CEE Standards "show no conern about students who find little in economics as it is taught now that is relevant to the world they know, particularly women and members of minorities, but also young people of working-class background" (Ferber, 1999, p. 140). Given the problems that economics has in attracting women, this latter criticism is particularly important.

One effort to construct a critical thinking approach to the principles course that directly engages some of the concepts in the CEE Standards has been undertaken by Steve Cohn. Cohn has analyzed the key subtexts found in mainstream and heterodox approaches, especially at the principles level. By "subtext," Cohn (2003) is referring to "(1) the tacit and unprovable assumptions about the nature of society and the (2) normative ideas about the goals of economic knowledge that underlie all economic paradigms" (p. 4). Cohn utilizes subtexts to describe some of the key differences between mainstream and heterodox approaches, which helps us to understand why many heterodox economists are dissatisfied with the CEE Standards. His subtexts are outlined in Table 27.1.

In response to the perceived inadequacies of the encyclopedia approach and the CEE Standards approach, especially the lack of attention paid to alternative viewpoints, two groups of heterodox economists have developed lists of alternative principles of economics that could be incorporated into a principles course. Knoedler and Underwood (2003) describe ten Institutionalist principles of economics, reproduced in Table 27.2, and Schneider and Shackelford (2001) outline ten feminist "antidotes" to the CEE Standards, which are listed in Table 27.3. From the alternative lists of principles, and from Cohn's analysis of mainstream and heterodox subtexts, we can see a consensus emerging in the heterodox community regarding the perceived inadequacies in the CEE Standards and the outlines of an alternative. Readers may note the substantial overlap between these heterodox lists, which is an indication of the extent to which a number of heterodox schools seem to have become more unified in their approach to economics.

Table 27.1   Implicit subtexts found in mainstream and heterodox economics

A. Key subtexts found in mainstream, neoclassical principles texts:

1. Neoclassical economics is a scientific theory and as such demands belief in ways similar to modern physics.
2. Market outcomes reflect free choice.
3. People are naturally greedy, with insatiable consumer appetites. Capitalism is successful, in part, because it offers an incentive system that builds on this "human nature."
4. The major purpose of economic theory is to promote economic efficiency and economic growth, as both provide a basis for human happiness.
5. There is no alternative to capitalism. The failure of the former Soviet Union proves that socialism can't work. The message of the 20th century is "let (capitalist) markets work." The onus is on the government to justify "intervention" in the market.

B. Key subtexts found in heterodox economic writings:

1. Economic analysis contains much more subjective and ideological content than acknowledged in neoclassical texts.
2. Markets offer both "free" and "coerced" "choice." Market exchange can not meet the full range of human needs.
3. The link between economic growth and human well-being is much more complicated than implied in neoclassical textbooks and has weakened considerably in the advanced economies.
4. Equity, environmental concerns, and the nature of the non-market economy (for example, the household economy) need increased attention in economic analysis.
5. Capitalist economies need to be embedded in a system of social governance to meet human needs (and for a subset of heterodox theorists: alternatives to capitalism need to be explored).

Source: Cohn, 2003, p. 4.

Table 27.2   Ten [institutionalist] things every principles student should learn

1. Economics is about social provisioning, not merely choices and scarcity.
2. Both scarcity and wants are socially defined and created.
3. Economic systems are human creations; no particular economic system is "natural."
4. Ecological literacy (economy-ecology interface, unity between biophysical first principles and economic sustainability) is essential to understanding the economic process.
5. Valuation is a social process.
6. The government defines the economy; laissez-faire capitalism is an oxymoron.
7. The history of economic thought is critical to the study of "basic principles" of economics.
8. Economic theory ("logical economics") and real-world economics are often very different things.
9. Race, gender and class shape economic processes, outcomes and policies in the real-world economy.
10. There are many types of economists who do not agree on many things. This reflects the fact that economics is not "value free" and ideology shapes our analyses and conclusions as economists.

Source: Knoedler and Underwood, 2003, p. 714.

Table 27.3 Feminist "Antidotes" to the CEE Standards

1. Be wary of definitive lists of the principles of economics – including feminist principles of economics.
2. Remind our students and ourselves that values enter into economic analysis at many different levels.
3. Introduce the household as another locus of economic activity.
4. Non-market activities are important in economics as well.
5. Note how important power relationships are in an economy.
6. Introduce gender, race and ethnicity as important concepts in economics.
7. Describe the complexity of human interactions and how they are affected by a multiplicity of motives.
8. Emphasize the importance of cooperation and caring.
9. Government action *can* improve market outcomes.
10. Expand the scope of economics to include relevant contributions from other disciplines.

Source: Schneider and Shackelford, 2001, various pages.

The implementation of an alternative approach to the structure and content of the principles course that incorporates some of the ideas of heterodox economists has emerged along two distinct lines. Knoedler and Underwood (2003) advocate a "multi-paradigmatic approach" in which mainstream ideas are contrasted with heterodox ideas. Nelson proposes a "broader perspectives and bigger toolbox approach" that "starts with interesting and engaging questions, and then proceeds to draw from a variety of perspectives" (Nelson, 2009, p. 60). Both approaches add heterodox perspectives to the standard material in the principles course, so the main difference is that the multi-paradigmatic approach makes the contrasts between mainstream and heterodox analysis transparent to students, while the broader perspectives approach promotes a pluralistic view and does not always define which economists take which approach. Both approaches broaden the principles course to include the varied perspectives that economists take on key issues.

What emerges from the alternatives to the CEE Standards, as outlined above, is a definition of thinking like an economist that includes recognizing the multiplicity of viewpoints that economists hold. In addition, we see a definition of economic literacy that includes substantial knowledge of the functioning of the institutions and characteristics of the actual economy.

CONCLUSION

If the goals for the principles course include improving students' ability to think like an economist and enhancing economic literacy, economists may want to consider the following options: (1) Economists could discard the encyclopedic approach and focus on a more clearly defined set of topics. (2) The CEE Standards are one approach for mainstream economists to teach students a limited set of tools to begin thinking like an economist, albeit one which is grounded solely in a mainstream perspective. (3) Economists could include more real-world issues, such as readings from the news, articles on contemporary social issues, and material describing the economic philosophies underlying contemporary political positions. (4) Economists could give students some idea of the art of applying economics to the often messy real world. (5) The principles course could be broadened to include multiple perspectives to reflect the debates that exist in economics.

Why present students with an oversimplified vision of economics and economists? Certainly students must start at a basic level. But if our goal is truly to get them to think like economists, they must understand the nuances and qualifications that economists use when applying models to the real world, especially the advances in behavioral economics that have been so important in recent years. And, they must understand the disagreements and the debates that characterize a discipline as unsettled as ours.

NOTES

1. As Patricia Wolfe (2001, p. 135) observes, "Learning is a process of building neural networks." These networks are constructed by making connections to existing neural pathways, and engaging in various types of learning activities to build on existing knowledge. Students will retain more material and adopt a deeper approach to learning if they are able to connect material to existing knowledge and experiences.
2. A description and listing of the CEE Standards are provided in Chapter 25, "Economic Education in American Elementary and Secondary Schools", in this volume. The complete presentation of CEE Standards can be found at http://www.councilforeconed.org/ea/program.php?pid=19 (accessed 3 April 2011).

REFERENCES

Becker, W. E. (2000), "Teaching economics in the 21st century", *Journal of Economic Perspectives,* **14** (1), 109–19.

Bosshardt, W. and M. Watts (2008), "Undergraduate students' coursework in economics", *Journal of Economic Education,* **39** (2), 198–205.

Brandis, R. (1985), "The principles of economics course: A historical perspective", *Journal of Economic Education,* **16** (4), 277–80.

Bransford, J. D., A. L. Brown and R. R. Cocking (2004), *How People Learn: Brain, Mind, Experience and School* (expanded edition), Washington, DC: National Academy Press.

Cohn, S. (2003), "Common ground critiques of Neoclassical principles texts", *Post-Autistic Economics Review,* (18), February 4, http://www.paecon.net/PAEReview/issue18/Cohn18.htm, accessed 12 October 2010.

Colander, D. and K. McGoldrick (2009), "The Teagle Foundation report: The economics major as part of a liberal education", in D. Colander and K. McGoldrick, *Educating Economists: The Teagle Discussion on Re-evaluating the Undergraduate Economics Major,* Cheltenham, UK and Northampton, MA, US: Edward Elgar, pp. 3–39.

Ferber, M. A. (1999), "Guidelines for pre-college economics education: A critique", *Feminist Economics, * **5** (3), 135–42.

Garnett, R. and K. McGoldrick (2011), "Big think: A model for critical inquiry in economics courses", presented at the ASSA meetings, January.

Grimes, P. W. (2009), "Reflections on introductory course structures", in D. Colander and K. McGoldrick, *Educating Economists: The Teagle Discussion on Re-evaluating the Undergraduate Economics Major,* Cheltenham, UK and Northampton, MA, US: Edward Elgar, pp. 95–8.

Grimes, P. W. and P. S. Nelson (1998), "The social issues pedagogy vs. the traditional principles of economics: An empirical examination", *American Economist,* **42** (1), 56–64.

Hansen, W. L., M. K. Salemi and J. J. Siegfried (2002), "Use it or lose it: Teaching literacy in the economics principles course", *American Economic Review,* **92** (2), 463–72.

Heilbroner, R. L. (1999), *The Worldly Philosophers: The Lives, Times and Ideas of the Great Economic Thinkers* (7th edition), New York: Touchstone Press.

Kennedy, P. E. (2000), "Eight reasons why real versus nominal interest rates is the most important concept in macroeconomics principles courses", *American Economic Review*, **90** (2), 81–4.

Klos, J. J. and R. W. Trenton (1969), "One semester or two", *Journal of Economic Education*, **1** (1), 51–5.

Knoedler, J. T. and D. A. Underwood (2003), "Teaching the principles of economics: A proposal for a multi-paradigmatic approach", *Journal of Economic Issues*, **37** (3), 697–724.

National Council on Economic Education (n.d.). "Council for economic education", National Standards: http://www.councilforeconed.org/ea/standards/, accessed 29 August 2010.

Nelson, J. A. (2009), "The principles course", in J. Reardon, *The Handbook of Pluralist Economics Education*, London: Routledge, pp. 57–68.

Paden, D. W. and M. E. Moyer (1971), "Some evidence on the appropriate length of the principles of economics course", *Journal of Economic Education*, **2** (2), 131–7.

Post-Autistic Economics Network (2000), "Open letter from economics students to professors and others responsible for the teaching of this discipline", *Post-Autistic Economics Newsletter* (2), October 3, http://www.paecon.net/PAEReview/wholeissues/issue2.htm accessed 14 October 2010.

Schneider, G. and J. Shackelford (2001), "Economics standards and lists: Proposed antidotes for feminist economists", *Feminist Economics*, **7** (2), 77–89.

Siegfried, J. J. (2000), "How many college students are exposed to economics?", *Journal of Economic Education*, **31** (2), 202–4.

Siegfried, J. J. (2010), "Trends in Undergraduate economics degrees, 1991–2009", *Journal of Economic Education*, **41** (3), 326–30.

Siegfried, J. J. and B. T. Meszaros (1997), "National voluntary content standards for pre-college economics education", *American Economic Review*, **87** (2), 247–53.

Siegfried, J. J., R. L. Bartlett, W. L. Hansen, A. C. Kelley, D. N. McCloskey and T. H. Tietenberg (1991), "The economics major: Can and should we do better than a B-?", *American Economic Review*, **81** (2), 20–25.

Strober, M. H., A. Cook and K. A. Fuller (1997), "Making and correcting errors in student economic analyses: An examination of videotapes", *Journal of Economic Education*, **28** (3), 255–71.

Taylor, H. (1950), "The teaching of undergraduate economics", *American Economic Review*, **40** (December (supplement)), 1–226.

Walstad, W. and S. Allgood (1999), "What do college seniors know about economics?", *American Economic Review*, **89** (2), 350–54.

Wankat, P. C. (2002), *The Effective, Efficient Professor: Teaching Scholarship and Service*, Boston, MA: Allyn and Bacon.

Watts, M. and W. Becker (2008), "A little more than chalk and talk: Results from a third national survey of teaching methods in undergraduate economics courses", *Journal of Economic Education*, **39** (3), 273–86.

Wolfe, P. (2001), *Brain Matters: Translating Research into Classroom Practice*, Alexandria, VA: ASCD.

28 The principles of economics textbook: content coverage and usage[1]

Jane S. Lopus and Lynn Paringer

Faculty members teaching principles of economics today are faced with a wide array of textbooks and supplementary materials from which to choose. While the publishing market has undergone substantial consolidation in the past two decades, the available textbook options have increased. Improved technology and the development of online course management programs are altering both textbook delivery and the nature and delivery of supplements available to instructors and students. Textbook content continues to evolve due to changes in theoretical emphasis in economics and changes in the economy itself. Although there is general consensus on content coverage and point of view, differences among textbooks do exist. This chapter provides an overview of the current principles of economics textbooks. After a brief literature review, we discuss features of today's texts, focusing on those that may interest textbook adopters. We address publishers and market share, organization and structure, level of difficulty, point of view, selected content issues, and pedagogical features. Our discussion focuses on 26 full, two-semester versions of principles of economics textbooks published in 2009 or later. We conclude by discussing the role of online course management programs and the future of the principles textbook.

LITERATURE REVIEW

Although the principles of economics textbook has been the subject of a variety of studies, only one to date (Meinkoth, 1971) investigates the relationship between choice of textbook and student learning. The author compares scores on the Test of Understanding College Economics (TUCE) and attitudes toward economics from students who had used five different textbooks in their principles classes at one university. She finds no significant differences in TUCE scores or attitudes attributable to the different textbooks, and argues for allowing instructors to select their own textbooks.

Several later studies focus on the treatment of specific content in principles of economics textbooks such as fixed and sunk costs (Colander, 2004), consumption possibility frontiers (Olson, 1997), international economics (Lee, 1992), and entrepreneurship (Kent, 1989). Other studies investigate the treatment of women and minorities in principles of economics textbooks (Robson, 2001; Feiner, 1993).

Stiglitz (1988) discusses the market for economics textbooks and offers several criticisms of then-existing textbooks. He views the structure of the principles textbook market to be one of monopolistic competition, resulting in a limited degree of innovation and ". . . too many similar products at the center of the market, (too) few products at the fringes" (Stiglitz, 1988, p. 172). He finds most of the existing books to be clones of

Samuelson's, and that the market forces for imitation lead to a standardization of textbooks that in turn leads to a standardization of principles of economics courses.

In his 1991 Presidential Address to the Southern Economic Association, Kenneth Elzinga discusses the first eleven editions of Paul Samuelson's textbook *Economics* and the impact that this book has had since first published in 1948. Although criticized from both the right and the left (for being too Keynesian and not Marxist enough), the Samuelson textbook is reputed to have been the largest worldwide seller of any textbook in any discipline (Elzinga, 1992, p. 872). New textbooks entered the market, and in 1960 the first edition of McConnell's *Economics* was published. By 1975 McConnell had overtaken Samuelson in annual sales (p. 874), thereby reducing the monopoly position long held by the Samuelson text.

Probably the most recent comprehensive study of principles of economics textbooks is conducted by Walstad, Watts, and Bosshardt (1998). They briefly present the history of principles of economics textbooks from *The Wealth of Nations* through Samuelson's 1948 first edition. They discuss several issues related to textbooks in 1998, including textbook length (averaging about 800 to 900 pages), inadequate coverage or emphasis on certain topics such as international economics, the micro-before-macro debate, and the fact that "solid research on the use of textbooks in the principles course is almost non-existent" (p. 191). A content analysis of seven textbooks using an index of page-counts reveals some differences in emphasis and treatment of newer micro topics, such as risk and uncertainty; however, they find a "surprising degree of consensus" with respect to coverage of macro theory and topics (pp. 198–9).

TEXTBOOKS TODAY

There are many different types of textbooks designed for the principles of economics class available today. Some are designed for one-semester survey courses or courses focusing on economic issues and others are designed for those majoring in specific subjects such as engineering. There are a variety of books available that take heterodox approaches to economics.[2] Many principles of economics textbooks are offered in a variety of formats: as full two-semester versions, as macro and micro splits, in brief editions, in "essentials" editions designed for the survey courses and as electronic editions or e-books. There are also books only available electronically, self-published books, and print and electronic versions where instructors can pick and choose from existing chapters. In this chapter we discuss 26 full two-semester versions of mainstream principles of economics textbooks published in 2009 or later and that were available in June, 2010. We list the 26 textbooks in our study alphabetically and clustered by publisher in Table 28.1.

Publishers and Market Share

The textbook industry has undergone major consolidation over the past two decades, with many former publishing houses being bought out by others. As Table 28.1 indicates, there are four main publishers of traditional principles textbooks today, down from more than ten firms 20 years ago (Sichel, 1988 p. 179).[3] McGraw-Hill, Pearson, and Cengage are the top three in terms of sales (in that order).[4] Worth is smaller, and

Table 28.1   Mainstream principles of economics textbooks (published in 2009 and later)

Publisher/author	Title	Edition/year
BVT		
Dolan	Economics	4th/2010
Cengage Learning		
Arnold	Economics	10th/2011
Baumol/Blinder	Economics: Principles and Policy	11th/2010
Boyes/Melvin	Economics	8th/2011
Gwartney/Stroup/Sobel/ Macpherson	Economics: Private and Public Choice	13th/2011
Hall/Lieberman	Economics: Principles and Applications	5th/2010
Mankiw	Principles of Economics	5th/2009
McEachern	Economics: A Contemporary Introduction	8th/2009
Sexton	Exploring Economics	5th/2011
Taylor/Weerapana	Principles of Economics	6th/2010
Tucker	Economics for Today	7th/2010
Pearson Education		
Bade/Parkin	Foundations of Economics	4th/2009
Case/Fair/Oster	Principles of Economics	9th/2009
Hubbard/O'Brien	Economics	2nd/2009
Miller	Economics Today	15th/2011
Parkin	Economics	9th/2010
O'Sullivan/Sheffrin/Perez	Economics: Principles, Applications and Tools	6th/2010
McGraw-Hill Irwin		
Colander	Economics	8th/2010
Frank/Bernanke	Principles of Economics	4th/2009
McConnell/Brue/Flynn	Economics	18th/2009
Samuelson/Nordhaus	Economics	19th/2010
Schiller	The Economy Today	12th/2010
Slavin	Economics	9th/2009
Worth		
Cowen/Tabarrok	Modern Principles: Economics	1st/2010
Krugman/Wells	Economics	2nd/2010
Stone	Core Economics	1st/2011

the three books on our list published by Worth are either first or second editions. Of the 26 textbooks in Table 28.1, McConnell/Brue/Flynn and Mankiw together represent over 40 percent of total sales, and there is a large gap to other top ten market share textbooks. Because of the dominance of texts authored by McConnell/Brue/Flynn (hereafter McConnell) and Mankiw, we use these as a basis of comparison in the next sections.

Organization and Structure

Although we do not attempt word counts or detailed indexed page counts among textbooks,[5] we note that Mankiw, McConnell, and the other 24 textbooks are generally close in length and have similar organizational formats. Introductory chapters are usually followed by micro and then macro chapters. Most texts are around 800 to 900 pages, although Sexton has over 1000 pages. However, there are differences in approach within the fairly standard structures that may appeal to some textbook adopters. For example, Mankiw includes much more micro in the core introductory chapters than does McConnell. Mankiw and others (for example, Baumol/Blinder, O'Sullivan/Sheffrin/Perez) begin with a list of basic principles and then refer back to the principles throughout the text. McConnell and others (for example, Bade/Parkin, Schiller) include an overview of the US economy as a core chapter.

Level of Difficulty

The principles of economics course is taught to a wide range of students at institutions ranging from community colleges to elite private universities. Consequently, it is likely that some books would be written at higher or lower levels to appeal to different audiences. However, we find that this distinction is not straightforward and that the level of difficulty is likely to be one of perception. For example, some books (for example, Case/Fair/Oster) may be viewed as more difficult because they include more mathematics. But for some students, a mathematical approach makes economic theory easier and more intuitive, rather than more difficult. Other texts (for example, Parkin) may be perceived as being more difficult because of more in-depth analysis of theory. But for some students, the depth of coverage may make theory easier to understand. In phone interviews with representatives of the four major publishers, we found general consensus that most textbooks are aimed at a middle level of difficulty, rather than attempting to be more or less difficult than others. Exceptions include Taylor/Weerapana and Baumol/Blinder, which are generally viewed as being higher level, and Tucker and Slavin, which are viewed as being lower level. Bade/Parkin aims to be at a lower level than Parkin by focusing more on frequent practice of core concepts.

Point of View

With few exceptions, the mainstream principles textbooks today attempt to provide a balanced point of view and do not present the material from a strictly liberal or conservative perspective. Two texts (Gwartney/Stroup/Sobel/MacPherson and Cowen/Tabarrok) offer a perspective that is more public choice oriented than other texts. Colander introduces the student to alternative heterodox approaches (Austrian, institutional, radical, feminist, religious, post-Keynesian) at the beginning of the text and then includes questions from some of these approaches at the end of each chapter. Some texts are viewed as being more policy oriented (Krugman/Wells) or more Keynesian (Baumol/Blinder). Texts today emphasize real-world applications (over widgets), frequently in boxed inserts. Treatment and content of the real-world applications varies, however. For example, Gwartney/Stroup/Sobel/MacPherson includes 14 short chapters at the end of the text applying economic theory to real-world issues; Hubbard/O'Brien emphasizes business applications.

Selected Content Issues

We identified several newer content topics and changes in content emphasis in textbooks today, and checked to see if these topics were included in different textbooks. We found that principles textbooks are increasingly covering consumer and producer surplus earlier and in more detail, and are using these tools to explain market efficiency. Both Mankiw and McConnell do this, as do Krugman/Wells, Case/Fair/Oster, and some others. Other books mention consumer and producer surplus but do not emphasize the tie-in with market efficiency.

We also investigated current coverage of behavioral economics. Both Mankiw and McConnell introduce the topic of behavioral economics, with Mankiw devoting more pages to it than McConnell. A search of index topics in other books indicates that some books include coverage of behavioral economics (for example, Taylor/Weerapana, Hall/Lieberman), whereas others do not. Colander integrates a considerable amount of behavioral economics throughout the text as well as in a chapter entitled "Game Theory, Strategic Decision Making, and Behavioral Economics."

The financial crisis that began in 2007 will no doubt affect the macroeconomic content of principles textbooks. Blinder (2010) discusses the desirability of renewed emphasis on the short run and the Keynesian multiplier model, the problem with using "one-interest-rate" models, and the desired level of complexity for teaching about financial markets in principles classes. Both Mankiw and McConnell have specific chapters on financial economics: two and one, respectively. Several other textbooks also include separate chapters on financial economics, primarily in the macro sections of the texts (for example, Bade/Parkin, Colander, Parkin). Boyes/Melvin includes a chapter on capital markets in the micro section of the text, and Arnold includes a financial economics chapter under a "Practical Economics" section. Dolan includes a chapter on the banking system and regulation and addresses the financial crisis in this context. The sixth edition of Taylor/Weerapana is subtitled "*The Global Financial Crisis Edition*."

The treatment of international economics in principles books has changed from the former standard of having two international chapters at the end of the book. Both Mankiw and McConnell include an international economics chapter as an introductory core chapter and both integrate international topics throughout their textbooks. In addition to the introductory chapters, Mankiw includes a micro chapter and two macro chapters on international economics, whereas McConnell has two macro chapters. Although some books continue to have all of the international chapters at the end of the texts, others, like Mankiw and McConnell, introduce these topics in an introductory core chapter or before the end of the book (for example, Boyes/Melvin, Dolan, Frank/Bernanke).

We find the treatment of mathematics in principles textbooks to be fairly standard. Both Mankiw and McConnell include early chapter appendices to review graphs, as do other textbooks (for example, Samuelson/Nordhaus, Baumol/Blinder). In supply and demand analysis, both focus on plotting supply and demand curves without going into the underlying equations. The overall level of math is that of basic algebra and geometry, which is true to differing degrees in other texts also. Case/Fair/Oster presents a "three tiered approach" to explaining economic concepts: first a story, then a graph, and finally an equation where appropriate.

Pedagogical Features

There is a vast array of pedagogical features available both in textbooks and as supplements.[6] Textbook prefaces generally provide comprehensive overviews of the features both in the texts and available as complements to texts. We find that the features may be divided into four broad categories: in-text features for students, student supplements (both online and in print), instructor supplements (available online, in print, or on CDs) and learning objectives. Although textbooks sometimes have different names for similar features, many pedagogical features are fairly standard across texts.

Most textbooks include in-text features for students, such as end-of-chapter questions and problems and chapter summaries. Other common features include boxed current events and applications, emboldened concepts, case studies, and quizzes. Although most texts make use of boxed inserts, some (for example, Hall/Lieberman, Cowen/Tabarrok, Stone) do not. Hall/Lieberman argues that boxed features are distracting, and Cowen/Tabarrok states that students do not read them and that they interrupt the flow of the text.

Standard student supplements include online and print study guides and textbook websites for students. Study guides generally include chapter summaries and practice questions. Some include other features, such as online flashcards (for example, Mankiw, Dolan) and links to outside resources and readings (for example, Krugman/Wells). For an extra charge, some textbooks (for example, Frank/Bernanke, McConnell) offer links to news videos, narrated PowerPoint slides, and iPod content.

Instructor supplements accompanying textbooks generally include instructor manuals with solutions to student problems, chapter overviews, test banks, and PowerPoint slides. CDs and password-protected websites for instructors frequently include all of the instructor materials. Some instructor resources also include materials to accompany use of clickers or classroom response systems[7] (for example, Miller, McConnell, Bade/Parkin). Others include relatively unique features, such as tips for teaching large classes (Colander) or teaching tips on how to encourage classroom participation (O'Sullivan/Sheffrin/Perez).

Student learning objectives, which state what students should be able to do after reading a chapter, are included in many textbooks (for example, Colander, McConnell) or in instructors' manuals (for example, Mankiw). The inclusion of learning objectives is perhaps due to accreditation requirements at some universities. Reference to the Association to Advance Collegiate Schools of Business (AACSB) assurance-of-learning standards are also included in some texts (McConnell, Case/Fair/Oster, Frank/Bernanke) and, in some cases, text-bank questions may be searched by specific skill (McConnell).

Online Course Management Programs

Probably the most significant innovation in principles of economics textbooks over the past decade is associated with online course management programs, beginning with Aplia. Today the four major publishers all have or are developing their own in-house course management systems. Cengage has Aplia, Pearson has MyEconLab, McGraw Hill has Connect Economics, and Worth is developing the EconPortal, although continuing to work with Aplia.

Aplia was the first widely available course management program for economics. It was developed by Paul Romer at Stanford University in 2000 with the goal of increasing student engagement in learning economics, while not requiring increased effort from professors. Through auto-graded assignments tied to textbooks and accompanied by detailed accessible explanations, students are more actively involved in learning and applying economic theory and concepts. Aplia currently supports 14 subjects in addition to economics and has been used by an estimated 1,000,000 students at 1300 intuitions (www.aplia.com). Aplia was purchased by Cengage in 2009.

Students are able to purchase e-textbooks tied to a course management system for about half the price of a printed textbook. E-books are cheaper to produce, distribute, and update and also enable publishers to avoid the used-textbook market, where they earn no revenues. Although e-textbooks have been in existence for over 20 years, the advent of Aplia and competing programs has greatly changed their use and delivery. Online course management programs work well with e-textbooks, since e-textbooks can link course management program study questions to sections in the text, allowing students to more readily find related material. Students can work problems, use interactive graphs and take practice quizzes and tests that are all linked back to the text, providing a more interactive and dynamic learning experience.

The economics textbook market appears to be moving rapidly in the direction of e-textbooks supplemented by online homework management programs. Major principles of economics texts are currently available as e-books and all have or soon will have connectivity to an online course management program. McGraw-Hill estimates that e-books today represent over 10 percent of textbook revenue, up from less than 1 percent ten years ago.

CONCLUSIONS

We expect that the market for economics textbooks will continue to change and that it will look very different ten years from now given the continuing evolution and expansion of interactive e-books. Whether students object to texts in this format or prefer them to traditional textbooks (in part, due to lower prices) is yet to be seen. The opportunity these resources provide to keep the principles content up to date and relevant should help students of economics to be better prepared to make decisions and analyze real-world phenomena. We hope that the new teaching tools, combined with the modifications and changes in the text materials, will enhance the ability of students to understand and manage the world of tomorrow.

NOTES

1. We would like to thank representatives from Cengage, McGraw-Hill, Pearson and Worth publishers for helpful information.
2. The Heterodox Economics Directory (http://heterodoxnews.com/directory/) contains links to publishers of heterodox economics texts. The Economics Network lists heterodox economics texts by subject (http://www.economicsnetwork.ac.uk/books/HeterodoxEconomics.htm). Both sites accessed 1 March 2010.
3. Other smaller publishers of textbooks do exist. Norton publishes a principles textbook by Joseph

Stiglitz (which does not make our list since it has not been updated since 2006). Firms such as Flatworld Knowledge and Dot.Learn offer different styles of textbooks and textbooks in different formats. There are also less traditional forms of publishing, such as self-publishing. These alternative styles of publishing currently represent a small share of the total market for principles textbooks.

4. We conducted phone interviews with representatives from the four major publishing houses and asked questions relating to consolidation of publishers, market share of existing textbooks, perceived differences in textbooks (including difficulty level and point of view), content trends, innovations, and available supplements. Publishers' representatives told us that although precise market share and sales information is proprietary, publishers purchase sales information from the same source and are willing to share general information.

5. We also do not purport to have read all 26 books on our list.

6. Outlining the pedagogical features for each of the 26 texts would be a major undertaking. For example, the two leading texts, Mankiw and McConnell, each list over 30 pedagogical features for their textbooks.

7. For more information regarding the use of this technology, see Chapter 13, "Incorporating Media and Response Systems in the Economics Classroom" in this volume.

REFERENCES

Aplia: Engage, Prepare, Educate, www.aplia.com, accessed 1 July 2010.

Blinder, A. S. (2010), "Teaching macro principles *after* the financial crisis", Princeton Center for Economic Policy Studies Working Paper No. 207, 1–6.

Colander, D. (2004), "On the treatment of fixed and sunk costs in the principles textbooks", *Journal of Economic Education*, **35** (4), 360–64.

Elzinga, K. G. (1992), "The eleven principles of economics", *Southern Economics Journal*, **58** (4), 861–79.

Feiner, S. F. (1993), "Introductory economics textbooks and the treatment of issues relating to women and minorities, 1984 and 1991", *Journal of Economic Education*, **24** (2), 145–62.

Kent, C. A. (1989), "The treatment of entrepreneurship in principles of economics textbooks", *Journal of Economic Education*, **20** (2), 153–64.

Lee, D. Y. (1992), "Internationalizing the principles of economics course: A survey of textbooks", *Journal of Economic Education*, **23** (1), 79–88.

Meinkoth, M. R. (1971), "Textbooks and the teaching of economic principles", *Journal of Economic Education*, **2** (2), 127–30.

Olson, T. L. (1997), "Construction of consumption possibility frontiers in principles textbooks", *Journal of Economic Education*, **28** (1), 76–81.

Robson, D. (2001), "Women and minorities in economics textbooks: Are they being adequately represented?", *Journal of Economic Education*, **32** (2), 186–91.

Sichel, W. (1988), "Principles of economics textbooks: Innovation and product differentiation – a response", *Journal of Economic Education*, **19** (2), 178–82.

Stiglitz, J. E. (1988), "On the market for principles of economics textbooks: Innovation and product differentiation", *Journal of Economic Education*, **19** (2), 171–7.

Walstad, W. B., M. Watts and W. Bosshardt (1998), "The principles of economics textbook: History, content, and use", in W. B. Walstad and P. Saunders (eds), *Teaching Undergraduate Economics: A Handbook for Instructors*, Boston, MA: Irwin McGraw-Hill, pp. 185–205.

Section B

Measurement Techniques of Student Performance and Literacy: College and High School

-

29 Measurement techniques of student performance and literacy: college and high school

Carlos Asarta and Ken Rebeck

Economic literacy has been identified as a critical input in preparing our youth for their roles as consumers, workers, employers and citizens. While most students are exposed to formal or infused economic training in elementary, secondary and college education, a recent study by Czelusniak (2009) identified a widespread deficient level of economic literacy in the United States. This finding is of particular importance given that an economically literate populace is more likely to understand risks, save and make sound economic decisions (Danes, Huddleston-Casas and Boyce, 1999). As a result, many US States conduct regular economic knowledge assessments of their students and have adopted economic standards in their curriculum. Additionally, the US Department of Education conducted the first comprehensive economics study for twelfth-grade students in 2006.

The use of nationally normed, valid and reliable[1] measures of economic knowledge has provided educators and administrators with tools to gauge the economic understanding of our youth. Fortunately, these instruments have been available for over 40 years and have allowed teachers to track economic knowledge changes over particular courses or over an entire curriculum, as well as providing educators with an opportunity to compare the performance of their students with that of large national samples. Furthermore, these tests have allowed researchers in economic education to identify key determinants in the production of economic knowledge and they continue to be an integral tool for improving economic literacy in the United States and other parts of the world.

In this chapter, we discuss the development and characteristics of two major tests of economic knowledge, the Test of Economic Literacy (TEL) and the Test of Understanding of College Economics (TUCE). We review their national norming results and summarize a select number of studies that have used these instruments as a measure to estimate economic literacy at the pre-college and college levels. Additionally, we document other efforts to measure student performance and literacy in economics at the national level by examining the development and results of *The Standards in Economics Survey* and The National Assessment of Education Progress (NAEP) instrument in Economics. The chapter concludes with a discussion of criticisms for the TEL and TUCE, and final thoughts on the future direction for assessment tools.

THE TEST OF ECONOMIC LITERACY (TEL)

The Test of Economic Literacy (TEL) was created in 1977 by the Joint Council on Economic Education to assist high school teachers, college faculty, administrators and researchers in gauging and improving the economic understanding of students enrolled in economics courses or classes with infused economic content. Currently in its third edition, the TEL (TEL III) (Walstad and Rebeck, 2001a) is a nationally normed, standardized, valid and reliable measure of understanding of basic economics. The alpha reliability coefficient of the TEL is 0.89, indicating a high degree of internal consistency and scores that measure economic knowledge with a high degree of accuracy. The content validity of the test is based on the *Framework for Teaching Basic Economic Concepts* (Saunders and Guillard, 1995) and the *Voluntary National Content Standards in Economics* (NCEE, 1997). The final norming versions of the exam[2] were approved by three national committees, including experienced economics high school teachers, directors of councils and centers for economic education and distinguished university faculty with experience in the development and implementation of economic assessment instruments at the high school level (Walstad and Rebeck, 2001a).

The TEL III was normed at the end of the fall and spring semesters of the 1999–2000 school year. Norming data was collected for 7,261 high school students from 384 classes in 36 states who had completed a course in basic, honors or Advanced Placement (AP) economics. These students were tested in four distinct content categories (fundamental economics, microeconomics, macroeconomics and international economics). The percentage of questions in each content section is: 35 percent in fundamental, 25 percent in microeconomics, 25 percent in macroeconomics and 15 percent in international. A total of 21 economic concepts are represented among the four content areas and cover diverse areas of study, such as scarcity, income distribution, and international growth and stability. The final version of the TEL III consists of two parallel forms (Form A and Form B), each including 40 multiple-choice questions with four answer options. There are several methods available in the Examiner's Manual to equate the raw scores of the two versions and make comparisons among students taking different versions of the test, or for pre- and post-test comparison purposes.[3] However, Form A and Form B share 11 common test items that allow direct comparisons to be made between forms for a limited number of economic topics.

Walstad and Rebeck (2001b) examined the results from the norming of the TEL III and found that taking a course dedicated to economics positively contributes to the economic knowledge of students. Specifically, students in dedicated economics courses outscored students participating in social studies classes with infused economic content by 20 percentage points.

Test scores also indicate that students in both groups tend to score highest in the fundamentals and microeconomics content categories of the test and lowest in the macroeconomics and international content categories. It is difficult to distinguish between student knowledge of the concepts across content categories and the inherent difficulty of the items across these categories when comparing average scores across content areas. Comparing content category scores across groups can, however, suggest the effectiveness of the high school economics course. The largest difference between scores achieved by economics students and those achieved by social studies students was 25 percentage points in the fundamental economics content category. The difference in scores between these two student groups was 19 percentage points for the macroeconomics content category and 17 percentage points for the microeconomics content category. The smallest difference, 14 percentage points, was found in the international economics content category.

The authors further examined the percent correct by specific economic concepts and found that, on average, economics students were more likely than social studies students to correctly answer items covering all concepts. The largest differences, greater than 25 percentage points, were found for the concepts of "scarcity" and "economic systems," both in the fundamental economics category. The smallest differences in average scores, 15 percentage points or less, were found in the "market failures," "monetary policy" and "balance of payments" concepts.

A similar score pattern was found for students in honors and AP courses. These results suggest that there might be different emphases placed on different concepts, or that teachers' knowledge of the concepts and the way they teach them vary across concepts. These results nevertheless provide evidence that the high school economics course increases student knowledge across all concepts covered on the TEL III. Based on their findings, Walstad and Rebeck (2001b) recommended that all high school students take a dedicated course in economics to enhance economic literacy.

The TEL various editions have been used in research studies to assess the impact of economic training on the stock of economic knowledge at the secondary level.[4] Walstad and Soper (1982) used an absolute-level model to measure the stock of economic understanding for high school students at a given time. The authors used the post-TEL I score as a dependent variable and found that, other things equal, the type of course students take has a significant impact on their level of economic knowledge. Specifically, students who completed a course in economics during high school scored significantly better than those students who were not exposed to economic training. Walstad and Soper (1989) corroborated their previous findings, but expanded the types of economic knowledge exposure. They found that students who completed a semester of economics or received economic instruction infused in a social sciences course scored significantly better on the TEL II than those students whose teachers did not include economics in their social studies classes. In contrast, completing a consumer economics course was found to have a negative but insignificant effect on economic knowledge.

A more recent study conducted by Butters and Asarta (2011) used TEL III results collected during the Online EconChallenge competition to assess the economic knowledge of US high school students. Data included 2,149 high school students from 22 states and diverse backgrounds. Participation in the competition was voluntary and students had incentives, in the form of prizes, to perform well on the test. Using an absolute-level model similar to Walstad and Soper (1982), their results corroborate previous research findings that document the relationship between additional economic training and student understanding at the secondary level. Students in AP/honors and other advanced economics courses scored markedly better on the TEL III than students whose education was limited to a traditional economics or social studies class with infused economic content. Specifically, the mean test score for advanced students was 80 percent correct, while the mean score for students in traditional semester and social studies courses was 57 percent correct. Students in the advanced group were most proficient in the macroeconomics content category, with an average score of 82 percent correct. Students in single semester and social studies courses score highest on the fundamentals content category, with an average score of 63 percent. Of particular interest is the ongoing deficit found in student mastery of international economics and monetary policy concepts for both groups of students. Previous explanations for the students' poor performance on these concepts had centered on their placement at the end of the test, implying that fatigue may have played a role. This study's use of the Online EconChallenge eliminated this effect by randomly ordering the questions for each student, and yet the weaker performance remained.

THE TEST OF UNDERSTANDING OF COLLEGE ECONOMICS (TUCE)

The Test of Understanding of College Economics (TUCE) was first made available to economic educators in 1969 and is currently in its fourth edition (TUCE-4). This instrument was created with two goals in mind: to provide a valid and reliable instrument that can be used to assess the economic understanding of students in principles of economics classes and to provide results from a large national sample of students to be used as a benchmark for comparisons. The TUCE-4 (Walstad, Watts and Rebeck, 2007) consists of both a microeconomics and macroeconomics exam. The alpha reliability coefficient of the TUCE-4 is 0.70 for the microeconomics test and 0.77 for the macroeconomics test. The Committee on Economic Education of the American Economic Association and the National Council on Economic Education (NCEE) were in charge of the revision of the TUCE. The content validity of the fourth and final draft of the TUCE-4 was determined by a committee of distinguished college faculty and a national panel of distinguished economists.

The norming of the TUCE-4 took place during the fall semester of 2005. Test scores for 3,255 and 2,789 college students who completed the pre- and post-test in microeconomics and macroeconomics exams, respectively, were used for the norming. Students in the microeconomics sample were enrolled in 43 different institutions and were taught economics by 71 instructors, while those in the macroeconomics group were taught by 62 instructors in 44 different institutions. Each economics test included 30 multiple-choice questions with four answer options. There are six content categories represented in the microeconomics test: the basic economic problem, markets and price discrimination, theories of the firm, factor markets, the role of government in a market economy, and international economics. The macroeconomics test is also divided into six content categories: measuring aggregate economic performance, aggregate supply and demand, money and financial markets, monetary and fiscal policy, policy debates, and international economics. The items of each test were distributed across three cognitive levels: 80 percent of each test required either implicit or explicit application, and 20 percent required recognition and understanding.

TUCE-4 norming results indicate that the exams are challenging for undergraduate students. Pre-test results generate mean test scores in the vicinity of 30 percent correct for both the microeconomics and macroeconomics exams. However, improvements are experienced in post-test mean scores, with students in the microeconomics sample answering about 43 percent of items correctly, and students in the macroeconomics sample answering about 47 percent correctly. These improvements indicate that the TUCE-4 measures overall learning in economics principles courses.

Although the inherent difficulty of individual questions influences the percentage of students correctly answering them, the variation across questions is revealing. The most difficult question on the microeconomics pre-test was related to long-run changes in prices and quantities in competitive markets. This question was answered correctly by only 11 percent of students in the norming sample. The highest percent correct for any question in either the microeconomics pre- or post-test was based on the "prisoner's dilemma," with correct answers provided in the pre- and post-test 56 and 59 percent of the time, respectively. For the macroeconomics version, a question on the composition of the M1 money supply measure was the most challenging in the pre-test, with only 11 percent of students identifying the correct answer. The best post-test result for an individual macroeconomics question was 69 percent of students who correctly identified the change in the price level and real GDP generated by an increase in short-run aggregate demand.

The TUCE has been used in a number of research studies in economic education during the past 40 years and the findings have been summarized and reviewed in the literature (Siegfried and Fels, 1979; Becker and Walstad, 1987; and Siegfried and Walstad, 1998). Additionally, contemporary research studies have used the TUCE instrument to identify determinants of student performance in principles of economics. Ziegert (2000) examined the relationship between personality type and knowledge of economics using standard measures of student achievement (course grades or TUCE scores) and found that personality types affect student performance on the TUCE. Becker and Powers (2001) used the instrument to explore the relationship between class size and student performance in principles courses. Their findings suggest a negative and significant class size effect. Dickie (2006) examined whether classroom experiments and incentives impact learning in principles of microeconomics and report that, after controlling for ability and other student characteristics, experiments increase learning in microeconomics, but grade incentives do not. Thus, the TUCE has been utilized not only for assessing the economic knowledge of college students but also for identifying determinants of student learning.

OTHER EFFORTS TO MEASURE STUDENT PERFORMANCE AND LITERACY IN ECONOMICS

The TEL and TUCE provide the economic education profession with standardized tests for assessment and research. The norming of these assessment instruments provides estimates of the economics understanding of high school and college students, as well as the potential influence of formal economics courses on this knowledge. Two other projects conducted at the national level have sought to estimate high school economic literacy: *The Standards in Economics Survey* conducted in 2005 and the 2006 inclusion of economics in the National Assessment of Educational Progress (NAEP). Although the purpose of neither project was to provide the economics profession with an assessment instrument to be used in the future, their development was similar to the TEL and TUCE, and they have provided further information on the level of economic knowledge of high school students.

The Standards in Economics Survey

The National Council in Economic Education conducted *The Standards in Economics Survey* (Markow and Bagnaschi, 2005) to assess the high school student and adult understanding of basic economics, knowledge of the US economy and familiarity with key economic terms. The instrument was created using the *Voluntary National Content Standards in Economics* (NCEE, 1997) and consisted of 20 test items covering economics and the consumer (five questions), factors pertaining to production (five questions), money, interest and inflation (four questions), and government and trade in economics (six questions). An additional four questions on personal finance were included as part of the instrument. A total of 2,242 US high school students completed the online test in 2005. The study also tested an additional 3,512 adults in 2005. Consistent with the goals of this chapter, we only report the results obtained from the sample of high school students.

The overall mean test score achieved was 53 percent correct. The proportion of students scoring at or above 80 percent correct was about one out of ten students, while six out of ten students, on average, failed the exam. Students who learned economics in a dedicated economics course or a social sciences course with infused economic content scored better on the test. The average score was 50 percent for students without previous economic training and 56 percent for those who had received economic instruction in their high schools. Overall test scores also indicate that the average score increased with grade level. While students in ninth grade were able to correctly answer an average of 49 percent of the questions on the test, tenth graders' average score was 51 percent, and eleventh- and twelfth-grade students received a mean score of 54 and 59 percent, respectively. The proportion of students correctly answering at least 80 percent of questions was highest for students in twelfth grade and lowest for eleventh grade students. The largest percentage of students failing the test within their specific grade level was found in grades nine and ten (Markow and Bagnaschi, 2005).

The range of scores for the test's economics and consumer content category shows that three out of five questions in that section were answered correctly by at least 75 percent of students. For example, 84 percent of students understood that benefits and costs need to be evaluated before purchasing an item. On the other hand, none of the four test items on money, interest rates and inflation was answered correctly by more than 75 percent of students. In fact, only 27 percent of participants were able to identify who in the economy would benefit from unanticipated inflation. Additionally, the impact of lower interest rates on businesses was also challenging for students, since only 38 percent were able to select the correct answer. A similar pattern of understanding was observed in the government and trade in economics questions. About 27 percent of high school participants were able to identify the relationship between higher gross domestic products and the production of goods and services. Equally low was the percent correct (27) found in the pollution abatement question that required the use of marginal analysis. Finally, only 41 percent of students were able to determine the impact of exchange rate changes on the purchase of goods and services (Markow and Bagnaschi, 2005).

The National Assessment of Educational Progress (NAEP)

The National Assessment of Educational Progress (NAEP), also known as the "Nation's Report Card," is a longitudinal assessment report that measures the knowledge of American students in grades 4, 8 and 12 in different areas of study. The National Assessment Governing Board (NAGB) is responsible for NAEP and its members are appointed by the US Secretary of Education. In 2001, NAGB members selected economics for the first time as one of the subject areas for assessment in the United States. As a result, NAGB members and experts in the field of economic education developed the 2006 economics instrument to measure the economic knowledge and skills of twelfth-grade students in US high schools.

The instrument is based on the NAEP *Economics Framework* (NAGB, 2006), which defines economic literacy and attempts to measure it in three different content areas, namely the market economy, the national economy and the international economy. Each content area accounts for approximately 45, 40 and 15 percent, respectively, of the assessment's content and is based on the *Voluntary National Content Standards in Economics* (NCEE, 1997). Benchmarks from each of the 20 Standards were selected and an additional benchmark on the time value of money was included in the assessment.[5] Furthermore, 20 to 30 percent of questions were created to fit personal finance, business and public contexts. Cognitive levels, specifically knowing, applying and reasoning, were also tested and measured as part of the assessment instrument.

In addition to testing the cognitive abilities of students, NAEP collected student, teacher and school data from four different questionnaires. Demographic characteristics were collected for students in addition to the training and background of instructors. Furthermore, school principals reported data on school characteristics, and students with disabilities and English language learners completed an additional questionnaire to put the assessment findings in context.

The NAEP economics instrument was designed for students to spend approximately 60 percent of their time answering multiple-choice questions, 30 percent on short-response and 10 percent on extended-response items. Test items were reviewed by test development contractors, the content area standing committee, state testing officials and curriculum specialists, the NAGB Assessment Subcommittee and the Planning Committee to ensure the validity of the instrument. Multiple-choice questions included four options and were graded electronically. The short- and extended-response items were graded using standardized grading rubrics to ensure that the results were consistent and fair. In addition, scorers were trained by experts and their performance and reliability were monitored throughout the grading process. While NAEP grading guides assign numerical values to represent a student's knowledge on a particular question, these grades are based on a simple three-tier system that classifies knowledge as basic, proficient or advanced.

A diverse group of 11,500 students from 590 public and private high schools completed the economics assessment instrument in 2006. Overall, the average twelfth-grade student in the United States performed at the basic knowledge level. Seventy-nine percent of students fell within the basic knowledge category or higher, while 42 percent scored at the proficient level or higher. Only 3 percent of students were found to score at an advanced level of knowledge. Results from the market economy content area of the test indicate that 72 percent of students were able to describe a benefit and risk associated with abandoning a full-time position to receive further education. On the other hand, only 36 percent were able to correctly approach profit maximization through marginal analysis. With respect to the national economy content, 60 percent of students were able to identify factors that contribute to increases in the national debt, while only 11 percent were able to analyze the impact of unemployment changes on income, spending and production. Sixty-three percent of students were able to determine the impacts of eliminating trade barriers in the international economy content area. Additionally, only 32 percent of students were able to identify the relationship between economic growth and educational achievement (NCES, 2006).

Student, teacher and school questionnaires allowed for further analysis of test scores. An important finding for economic educators and the future of our youth is that most students in the United States were exposed to economic content during their high school education. While 16 percent of students received economic training in Advanced Placement, honors and International Baccalaureate courses, 49 percent had received economic training in a dedicated course. Additionally, the assessment results indicate that 23 percent of participants were exposed to economic content that was infused in other subject areas such as personal finance or government, and only 13 percent of students reported not receiving formal economic training in high school (NCES, 2006).

CRITICISMS

While the use of reliable and valid measures of economic knowledge has been instrumental in measuring basic economic literacy at the pre-college and college levels, a number of criticisms have risen over the years regarding their content coverage, test format, cognitive level and other factors (Walstad and Rebeck, 2001b). For example, Nelson and Sheffrin (1991) argued that some of the test questions in the TEL II, although reliable and valid, were biased towards a Panglossian microeconomic and Keynesian macroeconomic approach. While the potential for bias in this type of tests exists, the review process conducted by different economists, the field testing done with students and the periodical revisions performed by test developers should minimize the potential for such biases (Walstad, 1991). Critics have also focused on the "guessing" nature of these multiple-choice instruments (Becker et al., 1990), while student fatigue towards the last topics covered on the exams was an informal criticism dismissed by Butters and Asarta (2011) using an online portal to randomly select questions from the TEL III instrument. Additionally, another criticism is the use of these norm-referenced tests to evaluate understanding on a criterion-referenced basis (Becker et al., 1990). Walstad (1990) addressed the norm- or criterion-referenced test issue by clearly explaining how the results from norm-referenced tests should be interpreted. Measuring economic knowledge with a single instrument does not capture all the economic understanding that students possess (Walstad and Rebeck, 2001b), but the use of standardized and reliable tests of economic literacy provides reasonably good estimates of economic knowledge and has gained widespread acceptance with instructors and evaluators (Walstad and Buckles, 1983).

CONCLUDING COMMENTS

The use of assessment instruments in economics has been instrumental in gauging the economic understanding and literacy of students in pre-college and college education over the past 40 years. At the pre-college level, tests have allowed educators and administrators to compare the performance of their students to national samples and provide policy recommendations to further increase their economic knowledge. Additionally, results from national samples have allowed researchers to identify determinants in the production of economic education. The use of reliable and valid measures of economic understanding continues to be a key element in assessing and improving the potential of students as consumers, workers, employers and citizens.

This chapter has focused on the techniques used to measure knowledge of economics at the high school and college levels. As with other educational tools, assessment instruments need to be revised periodically to account for new economic conditions and emphasize relevant content areas. Unfortunately, the costs associated with revising the current versions of tests of economic understanding and literacy are not trivial and often require national funding. Additionally, while the revision of existing assessment instruments and the development of new tests are necessary to accurately measure economic literacy and improve student learning (Salemi et al., 2001), the public-good nature of these tests may be the main deterrent to their development (Walstad, 2001).

As the profession focuses on the revision of existing instruments and begins to develop new techniques for assessing economic literacy, it is important to remember that the objective of education is student behavioral change (Becker, 1983). An important component of this change is student understanding of what many educators believe to be fundamental to an economically literate citizen. A distinguished group of economic educators and researchers led by John Siegfried has recently revised the K-12 *Voluntary National Content Standards in Economics* (CEE, 2010), which will be used as the basis for the 2011–12 revision of the TEL. A similar group of prominent economists developed the college principles-level content on which the latest edition of the TUCE was based, and a *separate* group of prominent economists reviewed the test for face and content validity. Development and revision of instruments able to capture student knowledge in economics is the first step in measuring the achievement of efforts to effect change in student behavior, since an understanding of this content is the basis for informed economic decisions.[6]

Even if future knowledge instruments are valid in this respect, this is only the first step in measuring changes in student behavior. There are areas for future improvement of national assessment efforts. It might be reasonable to expect that multiple-choice instruments will continue to dominate because of their cost effectiveness and broader content coverage than free-response questions, but attempts should be made to reach higher levels of cognitive abilities with these multiple-choice tests. The highest cognitive level in Bloom's (1956) taxonomy captured by the TEL III and the TUCE-4 is "application." Buckles and Siegfried (2006), however, argue that multiple-choice test questions are able to capture student achievement at the "analysis" level, Bloom's fourth cognitive level, and provide examples of how this can be accomplished. Development and revision of multiple-choice-based national assessment instruments should involve meaningful attempts to include questions directed at measuring students' abilities at this higher cognitive level.

Similarly, efforts at measuring economic knowledge at the national level using free-response questions should attempt to reach higher cognitive levels. An inspection of free-response example questions from the National Assessment of Educational Progress (NCES, 2006) shows how these questions can capture a student's ability to analyze an economic situation, but also provides a question that captures the understanding of a relationship that could have been easily measured with a multiple-choice item.[7] If costs are going to be incurred to grade free-response questions, both in time grading and potential loss in reliability across graders, these free-response items should be used wisely.

Lastly, norm-referenced instruments measuring the affective domain are needed to provide further evidence toward achievement of economically literate students, and thus the next step toward measuring the ability of high school or college courses to change economic behavior. Walstad (1987) argues that the acceptable practice with respect to measuring economic attitudes toward methods of economics instruction or toward economic issues is to develop one's own instrument. The validity and reliability of these instruments can lead to problems with inference. Since then, the two most commonly used instruments are the *Survey of Economic Attitudes* (Soper and Walstad, 1983), developed for use primarily at the high school level, and all or parts of the Alston, Kearl and Vaughan survey (1992) developed primarily to measure consensus among economists about economic issues. As these instruments and the national sampling results obtained from them become older, their usefulness diminishes. The cost of revising or developing a set of norm-referenced affective instruments will not be trivial, and finding agreement as to the composition of these instruments will not be easy, but the benefit these instruments would provide to the profession would be substantial.

NOTES

1. A reliability, validity and item analysis discussion can be found in the Appendix.
2. The first draft of the TEL III was developed by three national committees and was revised by the test developers. The exam was then field tested with about 900 high school students and 300 college students enrolled in principles of economics courses. The field test results and final reviews from the national committees were used to create the norming versions of the exam.
3. The two methods presented in the Examiner's Manual are "Equipercentiles" and "Linear Equating."
4. William E. Becker, Jr. has developed four research modules to enable researchers to appropriately use statistical methods in empirical education studies. The modules were created through funding from the Excellence in Economic Education grant and in cooperation with the Council for Economic Education and the American Economic Association Committee on Economic Education. The four modules can be found online at: http://www.councilforeconed.org/eee/research/econometrics (accessed May 16, 2011).
5. The following Standards were listed in more than one content area: the economic role of government; government decision-making; investment, productivity and growth; and markets.
6. See Becker (2007) for a critique of the current state of standards-based economic education.
7. For example, one free-response question asks: "How will an increase in real interest rates affect the amount of money that people will borrow? Explain why this will occur." The response rated as "correct" is: "People will borrow less money when interest rates increase because it will be more expensive to do so."

REFERENCES

Alston, R. M., J. R. Kearl and M. B. Vaughan (1992), "Is there a consensus among economists in the 1990s?", *American Economic Review, Papers and Proceedings*, **82** (2), 203–9.
Becker, W. E. (1983), "Economic education research: Part I, issues and questions", *Journal of Economic Education*, **14** (1), 10–17.
Becker, W. E. (2007), "Quit lying and address the controversies: There are no Dogmata, laws, rules or standards in the science of economics", *The American Economist*, **51** (1), 3–14.

Becker, W. E. and J. R. Powers (2001), "Student performance, attrition, and class size given missing student data", *Economics of Education Review*, **20** (4), 377–88.

Becker, W. E. and W. B. Walstad (eds) (1987), *Econometric Modeling in Economic Education Research*, Boston, MA: Kluwer-Nijhoff.

Becker, W. E., W. Green and S. Rosen (1990), "Research on high school economic education", *Journal of Economic Education*, **21** (3), 231–45.

Bloom, B. S. (ed.) (1956), *Taxonomy of Educational Objectives*, New York: David McKay.

Buckles, S. and J. J. Siegfried (2006), "Using multiple-choice questions to evaluate in-depth learning of economics", *Journal of Economic Education*, **37** (1), 48–57.

Butters, R. B. and C. J. Asarta (2011), "A survey of economic understanding in U.S. high schools", *Journal of Economic Education*, **42** (2), 200–205.

Council for Economic Education (CEE) (2010), *Voluntary National Content Standards in Economics, 2nd Edition*, New York: Council on Economic Education.

Czelusniak, S. (2009), "The crisis of economic illiteracy", *The Journal of the James Madison Institute*, http://www.jamesmadison.org/wpcontent/uploads/pdf/materials/Journal_SpringSummer2009_CZELUSNIAC.pdf, accessed August 10, 2010.

Danes, S. M., C. Huddleston-Casas and L. Boyce (1999), "Financial planning curriculum for teens: Impact evaluation", *Financial Counseling and Planning*, **10** (1), 25–37.

Dickie, M. (2006), "Do classroom experiments increase learning in introductory microeconomics?", *Journal of Economic Education*, **37** (3), 267–88.

Markow, D. and K. Bagnaschi (2005), "What American Teens & Adults Know About Economics", Report prepared by Harris Interactive, Inc., for the National Council on Economic Education, http://38.121.131.180/WhatAmericansKnowAboutEconomics_042605–3.pdf, accessed August 10, 2010.

Miller, M. D., R. L. Linn and N. E. Gronlund (2009), *Measurement and Assessment in Teaching* (10th ed.), Upper Saddle River, NJ: Pearson Education, Inc.

National Assessment Governing Board (NAGB) (2006), *Economics Framework for the 2006 National Assessment of Education Progress*, Washington, DC.

National Center for Education Statistics (NCES) (2006), *The Nation's Report Card: Economics 2006 – National Assessment of Educational Progress at Grade 12*, NCES 2007–475.

National Council on Economic Education (NCEE) (1997), *Voluntary National Content Standards in Economics*, New York: National Council on Economic Education.

Nelson, J. A. and S. M. Sheffrin (1991), "Economic literacy or economic ideology?" *The Journal of Economic Perspectives*, **5** (3), 157–65.

Salemi, M. K., J. J. Siegfried, K. Sosin, W. B. Walstad and M. Watts (2001), "Research in economic education: Five new initiatives", *American Economic Review, Papers and Proceedings*, **91** (2), 440–45.

Saunders, P. and J. Guillard (eds) (1995), *A Framework for Teaching the Basic Economic Concepts*, New York: National Council on Economic Education.

Siegfried, J. J. and R. Fels (1979), "Research on teaching college economics: A survey", *Journal of Economic Literature*, **17** (September), 923–69.

Siegfried, J. J. and W. B. Walstad (1998), "Research on teaching college economics", in W. B. Walstad and P. Saunders (eds), *Teaching Undergraduate Economics: A Handbook for Instructors*, New York: McGraw-Hill, pp. 141–66.

Soper, J. C. and W. B. Walstad (1983), "On measuring economic attitudes", *Journal of Economic Education*, **14** (4), 4–17.

Walstad, W. B. (1987), "Measurement Instruments", in W. E. Becker and W. B. Walstad (eds), *Econometric Modeling in Economic Education Research*, Boston: Kluwer-Nijhoff, pp. 73–98.

Walstad, W. B. (1990), "Research on high school economic education: comment", *Journal of Economic Education*, **21** (3), 248–53.

Walstad, W. B. (1991), "A flawed ideological critique", *Journal of Economic Perspectives*, **5** (3), 167–73.

Walstad, W. B. (2001), "Improving assessment in university economics", *Journal of Economic Education*, **32** (3), 281–94.

Walstad, W. B. and S. Buckles (1983), "The new economics tests for the college and pre-college levels: a comment", *Journal of Economic Education*, **14** (2), 17–23.

Walstad, W. B. and K. Rebeck (2001a), *Test of Economic Literacy (Third Edition): Examiner's Manual*, New York: National Council on Economic Education.

Walstad, W. B. and K. Rebeck (2001b), "Assessing the economic understanding of U.S. high school students", *American Economic Review, Papers and Proceedings*, **91** (2), 452–7.

Walstad, W. B. and J. C. Soper (1982), "A model of economic learning in the high schools", *Journal of Economic Education*, **13** (1), 40–54.

Walstad, W. B. and J. C. Soper (1989), "What is high school economics? Factors contributing to student achievement and attitudes", *Journal of Economic Education*, **20** (1), 23–38.

Walstad, W. B., M. Watts and K. Rebeck (2007), *Test of Understanding of College Economics (Fourth Edition): Examiner's Manual*, New York: National Council on Economic Education.
Ziegert, A. L. (2000), "The role of personality temperament and student learning in principles of economics", *Journal of Economic Education,* **31** (4), 307–22.

APPENDIX

Reliability and Validity

The effectiveness of a standardized test instrument is dependent on the quality of the test. Two characteristics are essential for a test to generate information useful for assessment: reliability and validity.

Reliability refers to the consistency with which test scores measure performance. A score obtained by testing a student at one point in time should be roughly equal to the score the student achieves if taking the same test instrument at another point in time, if no factors intervened that would otherwise influence the test scores, including, obviously, changes in knowledge. This stability of test scores over time, one type of reliability, can be estimated with the test-retest method (Miller et al., 2009, p. 110). Students can be tested on consecutive days or from one class meeting to the next.

Internal consistency is also an important characteristic of a reliable standardized exam. A test will have internal consistency if the items on the test work well together measuring the knowledge of the underlying concepts the test covers. (The characteristic of validity, below, deals with whether or not these underlying concepts that make up the test lead to appropriate interpretations for assessment purposes.) For example, if the scores achieved on one half of a test are highly correlated with the scores achieved on the other half of the test across students, then the items in the first half are consistently measuring knowledge of the same underlying concepts as the items on the second half. This approach to measuring internal consistency is called the split-half correlation. The outcome of this measure depends on how the test was split. A more general measure of internal consistency is the alpha reliability coefficient, or the Kuder–Richardson Formula 20 (KR-20). (The latter is equivalent to the former when the items are scored in a dichotomous fashion like "correct" or "incorrect," while the former can be used when items are measured on a scale.) Coefficient alpha values range between zero and one, with higher values reflecting higher reliability, and can be thought of as the average of all possible split-half correlations. Coefficient alpha is reported in the examiner's manuals for the standardized tests discussed in this chapter.

Although scores from a test instrument can be reliable in terms of both stability and internal consistency, if the test does not measure what it is intended to measure – if it is not valid – the test is of no value for assessment. Validity with respect to standardized tests refers to whether or not the test is measuring achievement of an underlying set of knowledge objectives, such as knowledge of macroeconomics at the college introductory level. Two major types of validity are content validity and construct validity.

Content validity can be attained through careful planning of a standardized test instrument. For example, the *Framework for Teaching Basic Economic Concepts* (Saunders and Guillard, 1995) and the *Voluntary National Content Standards in Economics* (NCEE,

1997) provided the content used to develop the high school level Test of Economic Literacy III (TEL III). The TEL III has content validity to the extent that it covers the economic concepts these publications suggest be taught in high schools.

A test with construct validity discriminates students who know more from those who know less about the subject. Construct validity is an important characteristic of an assessment instrument when used to identify whether or not learning is taking place. Each of the assessment instruments discussed in this chapter were shown to provide average scores that varied across students in predictable ways: scores were higher, on average, at the time of the post-test relative to the pre-test, or for students who had taken a formal economics course relative to students who had not.

Miller et al. (2009) provide a clever analogy using a shooting target to explain the importance of both reliability and validity. Shots widely scattered across a target represent unreliable shooting. Shots clumped together but away from the bullseye represent high reliability, but invalid shooting. Only when shots are clumped together within the bullseye does there exist both reliability and validity. Reliability, therefore, is a necessary, but not sufficient, condition for validity (p. 108).

Item Analysis

Each item on a standardized test is evaluated on the basis of certain characteristics. Two reported in most examiners' manuals for multiple-choice tests are the item percent correct and the point-biserial correlation (discrimination coefficient). The former provides information on average understanding of the concept covered by the item. The latter, which ranges from -1 to 1, is the correlation across students between the score on the item (correct or incorrect) and the score achieved on the remaining items on the exam. If this item is positive but close to zero, the item is not very effective at discriminating, and if it is negative, students who had less knowledge about the exam's underlying concepts in total were more likely to correctly answer the item, a clear red flag. Examined together, item percent correct and point-biserial correlations play an important role in determining which items survive the field test and are included in the final assessment instrument without changes, which items require changes, and which items are removed completely from the assessment instrument.

Section C

Factors Influencing Student Performance in Economics

30 Research on the effectiveness of non-traditional pedagogies

Joshua D. Miller and Robert P. Rebelein

The variety of pedagogical techniques available to economics instructors can be broadly classified as either "passive" or "active," characterizing the role of the student in the learning process. The most prevalent method of passive learning is the traditional lecture, in which the instructor presents the material and students sit quietly, often making notes, and attempt to take in the material. This process generally leads only to "surface" learning (in other words, rote memorization with no lasting impact) of the material, but seldom facilitates a deep understanding of the intricacies and nuances of the subject matter (Bransford et al., 2000). Active learning techniques can help students develop a deeper understanding of the material by requiring students to become engaged in the learning process.

A significant body of research examines the effectiveness of different pedagogical techniques in teaching economics. This research reveals that using active learning techniques, such as cooperative learning exercises, classroom experiments, and case studies, can improve student learning outcomes and increase student interest in economics.[1] Despite the demonstrated effectiveness of active learning strategies, lecture is still the dominant teaching strategy used by economics instructors.[2] In a 2005 survey of post-secondary institutions, Watts and Becker (2008) find that the median portion of class time spent lecturing in economics courses is 83 percent, the same percentage found in 1995 and 2000. Watts and Becker also report modest increases in the use of alternative teaching strategies such as classroom experiments and computer-generated displays (for example, PowerPoint), each used in a median of 6 percent of courses in 2005, up from 0 percent in 1995 and 2000. A post-graduation survey of over 2,000 students finds that they are much more likely to report that their economics instructors utilized lectures more (relative to other disciplines) than they are to report that economics instructors utilized alternative teaching strategies (Allgood et al., 2004), suggesting instructors in other disciplines utilize non-lecture teaching strategies more often than do economics instructors.

This chapter reviews research on the effectiveness of several different teaching strategies available to economics instructors. Specifically, it reviews research studying the effectiveness of several non-lecture teaching strategies often recommended by advocates for use by economics instructors: cooperative learning, classroom experiments, case studies, experiential learning, and undergraduate student research. The reader should note that each of these strategies has an entire chapter in this volume dedicated to their description. However, this chapter provides an overview of the effectiveness and thus complements those chapters. We also address two issues arising with increasing frequency in economics courses: technology utilization and distance learning.[3] This chapter also briefly examines research on the training received by economics instructors when beginning their teaching careers in graduate school in order to provide some indication of the future of pedagogic practices in economics. Note that this is not intended to be a comprehensive review of all research on all possible nontraditional teaching strategies; rather, it is intended to provide a sense of the breadth of alternative strategies and the extent to which they have been studied.

COOPERATIVE LEARNING

Cooperative learning requires students to engage with their peers, teaching and learning from each other with guidance from the instructor and to cooperate to complete exercises and assignments.[4] Cooperative learning can take place inside or outside the classroom, and can range from a brief in-class exercise to group research papers and presentations. The benefits associated with cooperative learning include increased motivation through peer accountability, increased opportunity for students to ask and resolve questions about the material, and increased student understanding and retention. The primary cost of cooperative learning is the opportunity cost of time that could otherwise be used to convey more material (although not necessarily more effectively) by lecturing. While instructors do spend time assisting individual students during cooperative learning exercises, most interaction will occur between students. Indeed, well-constructed cooperative learning exercises will actively engage all students in the learning process.

Yamarik (2007) compares student performance across several sections of intermediate macro taught with a cooperative learning component and a control section taught using a traditional lecture style. The cooperative learning component involved students working in permanent groups of three or four throughout the semester and collaborating on problem sets and cooperative assignments – both in and out of class. While Yamarik allows students to have some say in their group assignment, he attempts to ensure heterogeneity of aptitude and demographic characteristics within groups. Results indicate a statistically significant positive effect of cooperative student learning on student performance equal to a 3–4 percent improvement on exam scores, even when controlling for demographic and academic factors. Although students were unaware of the difference between sections during advance registration, some selection bias could have been created by students switching between the cooperative learning sections and the traditional lecture-style section at the beginning of the semester. Two additional sources of bias also may be present in Yamarik's results: first, instructor bias may be present if he were more excited about teaching the cooperative learning course and thus more effective; second, student social attitudes about being in a group may have contributed to greater student effort. However, if cooperative learning did indeed contribute to greater effort, then cooperative learning exercises positively affect student performance, albeit indirectly, by increasing student motivation.

Marburger (2005) studies the effect on student performance of substantially replacing lecture with cooperative learning in principles of microeconomics. The author taught a control section using only lecture and an experimental section using cooperative exercises along with a five-minute debrief at the end of each class period. Marburger finds no significant difference in student performance on a multiple choice exam as a result of replacing lecture with cooperative learning; this result is particularly interesting in that student performance did not significantly decrease as a result of reduced lecture time.

Further, Marburger finds that the cooperative learning class performed significantly better on a policy analysis project that required students to think critically and apply economic theory. These results suggest that the type and measurement of performance matter; multiple choice exams may target foundational knowledge, facts and rote memorization, whereas cooperative learning may improve students' ability to understand and apply economic theories.

Duke and Awokuse (2009) examine the effects of a cooperative learning exercise designed to enhance critical thinking and writing performance by combining student understanding of agricultural and trade policies in developing nations with their respective economic and environmental impacts. The instructors evaluate student performance in one control section and four experimental groups (drawn from separate but related courses), using pre/post writing assignments graded by an outside professor using a standard rubric based on content and style. These one-page policy briefs require students to present an argument that answers a question provided by the instructors and develop two points that support their thesis. Students in the cooperative learning groups complete three additional policy briefs and attend a three-hour colloquium, during which students give oral presentations to small groups and complete peer reviews. The authors find that the additional cooperative colloquium and policy briefs had a positive and statistically significant effect on student performance – an average of one point for each policy brief on a ten-point scale. These findings indicate that cooperative learning exercises can be used to improve student performance, particularly on written assignments that require critical analysis and application of economic theory.

CLASSROOM EXPERIMENTS

Classroom experiments offer instructors the opportunity to demonstrate and reinforce economic concepts by allowing students to apply economic concepts and see the effects of their decisions in interactive situations. Classroom experiments can either supplement or replace traditional lecture presentations. The complexity of classroom experiments can vary widely, and the time needed can range from a few minutes to multiple class periods. Holt (1999) reviews and summarizes many of the issues pertinent to selecting and running classroom experiments. As with cooperative learning, the main opportunity cost of classroom experiments is foregone lecture time. The studies discussed below indicate that benefits to student learning make it worthwhile to incur this cost. Instructors who choose to create their own experiments will experience considerable development cost, but this cost can be avoided by taking advantage of the substantial set of existing experiments.[5]

Studies that examine the effect on student performance of replacing a portion of lectures with classroom experiments consistently find positive impacts, although the results are not always statistically significant. Gremmen and Potters (1997) study this effect by randomly assigning 47 students across three sections of a course to either a control group, taught using only lectures, or an experimental group, taught using an introductory lecture followed by an experiment, using the same amount of time. The authors do not report the specific course studied. The impact on student learning is measured by administering the same multiple choice pre/post-test to each group. The experimental group participated in an international relations experiment in which students play the role of government policy-makers and seek to make decisions that would raise their country's welfare above those of other, competing countries. The authors seek to eliminate bias in their results by switching the instructors of each section every class, altering the sequence of instructors, and not informing the instructors of specific content of the pre/post-tests. Although the experimental and control groups have very similar average scores on the pre-test, the post-test scores of the experimental group improved much more than those of the control group, with the difference being statistically significant despite the small sample size. In addition, a third test a few weeks later showed that the experimental group retained a greater understanding of the material than did the control group, with the difference being statistically significant, indicating that teaching using classroom experiments can result in sustained, positive effects on student learning relative to the traditional lecture method.

Dickie (2006) reports similar findings in a study of 108 microeconomics principles students divided into two experimental sections, each incorporating seven experiments, and a control section taught using only the lecture method. In one of the experimental sections, Dickie employs additional grade incentives for student performance on experiments. In his analysis of student performance, Dickie controls for indicators of student aptitude and other factors, including cumulative GPA, standardized test scores, age, race, gender, and semester hours completed. In order to ensure that academic expectations were consistent across sections, Dickie uses the same textbook and study guide for each section and assigns homework assignments of equal length. Results indicate a significant positive effect of classroom experiments on student test score improvement relative to the impact of plain lecture. In addition, he finds no statistically significant effect of grade incentives on student performance, suggesting instructors could incorporate classroom experiments into their courses without offering additional incentives to encourage participation.[6]

Emerson and Taylor (2004) study the effect of classroom experiments on student performance using a sample of 300 students in nine different sections of microeconomic principles, two of which are experimental and seven of which are controls. The authors take numerous steps to ensure statistically robust results, including: homogeneity of students across classroom sections; use of the Test for Understanding of College Economics (TUCE) for testing on the first and last days of class; controlling for a host of factors regarding student ability (using data on GPA, gender, major, previous semester hours completed, average weekly hours of employment, SAT scores, and whether or not students had taken a high school economics course); and using a set of 11 standard experiments drawn from a principles textbook designed to incorporate classroom experiments (Bergstrom and Miller, 2000).[7] Students in experimental sections improved their TUCE scores (post-pre) by an average of 2.42–2.99 points more than students in control sections, an improvement equivalent to 11.1–12.3 percent of the possible improvement in scores; however, they find few statistically significant differences between experimental and control students in performance on a departmental final exam, student evaluations, or class attrition rates. One characteristic of this study worth noting is that in end-of-course student evaluations, students in experimental sections ranked the most important course components as: experiments, lectures, readings, and homework, while students in control sections ranked the most important components as: homework, readings, lectures, and quizzes. While both groups recognize the need to use economic understanding to enhance their learning, those presented with experiments find them far more effective than homework assignments.

In addition to quantifiable improvements in student performance, classroom experiments have the potential to increase student interest in and engagement with the course material. Yandell (1999) tests the hypothesis that teaching a microeconomics course that incorporates classroom experiments will yield improved student learning. He compares outcomes for 31 students in two sections taught with a traditional lecture format with outcomes for 35 students in two sections that incorporated classroom experiments. In all sections, Yandell taught the same concepts, used the same book and chapter sequence, and administered an identical final exam. The author analyzes differences in student grades and evaluations, controlling for common aptitude indicators such as high school GPA, gender, and SAT scores. Yandell finds that the impact of experiments on student performance was positive, although statistically insignificant. Also interesting are differences in student evaluations, which reveal that the experimental section had statistically significant higher ratings for teaching effectiveness of the instructor, instructor enhancement of student interest, and interest level of class sessions. That is, while students may not have performed better on exams as a result of introducing experiments, students in the experimental sections found their course more interesting than did students in the traditional sections.

CASE STUDIES

Two forms of case studies are used to teach economics. Case studies in textbooks are typically one- or two-page examples illustrating economic concepts in the real world. Although they can help students recognize the ways in which economic decisions are made, this form of case study seldom requires students to critically examine the material and make their own decisions. In contrast, traditional case studies do not provide students with analysis, but present them with information and charge them with performing their own analysis. Carlson and Schodt (1995) define case studies as "narrative accounts of actual, or realistic, situations in which policymakers are confronted with the need to make a decision" (p. 18). Marks and Rukstad (1996) similarly define case studies not as simple examples that illustrate an application of economic theory, but rather as complex, real-world scenarios in which students must interpret and think critically about a substantial amount of information and apply economic concepts as they read about a situation in which an important economic decision was made.[8]

Carlson and Schodt (1995) analyze student evaluations (as opposed to student performance) from economics courses at different institutions to evaluate the efficacy of case studies when used in combination with lectures, problem sets, and exams.[9] In response to a question about how much case studies contributed to what students learned, 39 out of 55 students indicated "substantially" (the highest choice), 14 indicated "somewhat," only two indicated "little," and none indicated that the case studies should have been replaced with lecture. In addition, 39 out of 55 students indicated that case studies were the most useful course component for "learning how to use economics to solve real problems" (p. 22). Carlson and Schodt consider written assignments to be an important component of effective case-method teaching, but cite increased instructor effort and grading time associated with written assignments as a significant cost of implementing case studies.

Marks and Rukstad (1996) build a compelling argument for the use of case studies to teach students to read and evaluate economic data, understand tradeoffs and constraints, deal with ambiguities in data and theories, and ultimately make informed policy decisions. The authors argue that in-depth traditional case studies give relevance to economic principles and teach students information about qualitative tradeoffs within a complex environment that cannot be acquired from a simple knowledge of basic economic principles alone. In particular, they point out that instructors of terminal economics courses may best serve their students by teaching them how to use economic principles to make informed economic decisions in real-world scenarios rather than teaching them how to build advanced economic models.

EXPERIENTIAL LEARNING

Many students can benefit from hands-on pedagogies such as experiential learning.[10] By requiring students to engage directly with the material, these teaching strategies are more likely to lead to deep learning. One form of experiential learning is service-learning, a pedagogy that can take many forms, and can be utilized at all levels of the curriculum, in small or large courses. Service-learning deepens student understanding of concepts taught in the classroom by having students integrate these concepts with work outside the classroom. Ziegert and McGoldrick (2008) observe that "One of the strengths of service-learning is that the embedded learning process promotes student engagement with the material and student ownership over learning is strengthened" (p. 43). Instructors in other disciplines have known about the benefits of service-learning for some time, but use of the technique is somewhat newer to economics. Economics instructors can, however, learn from others' experience.

Markus et al. (1993), in a study of 89 students in an undergraduate political science course at a large research university, find that an assortment of benefits accrue to students engaging in service-learning activities. For example, they find that classroom learning and course grades increased by a statistically significant amount and that students are more likely to report that they "learned to apply principles from [the] course to new situations" (p. 414). The authors conclude that "experiential learning counters the abstractness of much classroom instruction and motivates lasting learning by providing concrete examples of facts and theories" (pp. 416–17). Further, they find non-academic benefits to service-learning, such as "greater awareness of societal problems" and "significant effects [on] students' personal values and orientations" (p. 410).

Studying a sample of 3,450 undergraduates at 42 institutions, Astin and Sax (1998) seek to gauge the effects of community service participation on undergraduate development. Students engage in a variety of community service activities, including tutoring at-risk elementary or secondary school students and volunteering at churches, hospitals or clinics, social or welfare organizations, community centers, etc. The authors find that participating in community service "substantially enhances the student's academic development, life skill development, and sense of civic responsibility" (p. 251).

UNDERGRADUATE STUDENT RESEARCH

Undergraduate student research can also have benefits beyond those available to students from traditional teaching methods. It can be one part of a single course or can span multiple semesters, as might a senior thesis. In a study of 139 undergraduate students, approximately 55 percent of whom participated in an undergraduate research experience and 45 percent of whom did not, Seymour et al. (2004) find that participation in research increases undergraduates' self-confidence (both in general and with regard to the specific discipline), increases their ability to think and work like a scientist, and deepens student understanding of their discipline.[11] These conclusions are based on data collected during interviews of the students and their faculty sponsors. Seymour et al. also include several quotes from students that describe additional gains in areas such as communication skills, relationship with research faculty, and clarification of career objectives.

Hathaway et al. (2002) survey 288 undergraduates at the University of Michigan. Sixty-three percent of students in the sample participated in a research experience and thirty-seven percent did not. They conclude that undergraduate research participation leads to statistically significant increases in student likelihood of pursuing postgraduate education.[12]

DISTANCE LEARNING AND TECHNOLOGY UTILIZATION[13]

The increased use of computers and the internet in the classroom motivates research evaluating the impact of technology and distance learning on student performance. Online courses in economics have a variety of distinct advantages and disadvantages compared to traditional, face-to-face economics courses. Online courses allow students who live in remote locations to take classes without incurring significant travel costs and provide flexibility to working students who might not be able to attend day classes. Depending on the nature of coursework, online classes may allow instructors to teach larger classes, especially if the majority of coursework can be graded automatically or with minimal instructor time (for example, online problem sets or discussion posts). Potential costs associated with distance learning include startup costs for instructors, less personal interaction between students and instructors, fewer opportunities for real-time discussion and active learning, and an increased potential for cheating on exams. While many online instructors give the equivalent of take-home exams to their students, some instructors require students to take exams in a brick-and-mortar setting.

Gratton-Lavoie and Stanley (2009) study learning outcome differences across online and traditional principles of microeconomics classes at California State University, Fullerton. The instructors teach both an online version, in which all course material, including lectures, are delivered online, and a traditional version, in which students have access to a basic course website (containing the same course material as the online course) and lectures are delivered face to face. The instructors seek to eliminate any bias they might introduce by alternating which course they teach every semester and adhering to previously agreed-upon course materials, assignments, and exams. Students freely select whether they take an online or traditional version of the course and comparisons across these two formats reveal significantly different student characteristics. Notably, students in the online course are, on average, older, more likely to be married and have children, and more likely to be female. After controlling for these differences, Gratton-Lavoie and Stanley find no statistically significant effect on student performance of teaching online economics courses versus traditional classroom economics courses. The lack of performance differences provides justification for developing online courses, particularly for students who face barriers to attending traditional brick-and-mortar college courses.

Agarwal and Day (1998) evaluate the degree to which using the internet as a tool for economic education has an effect on student learning and retention of concepts, student perceptions of instructor effectiveness, and student perceptions of and attitudes towards economics. Based on a sample of 210 students (130 in undergraduate macroeconomics, 80 in graduate microeconomics), and defining internet tools as email, a class discussion list, and resources for internet research, Agarwal and Day find that introducing the internet as a learning tool had a positive and statistically significant effect on TUCE scores and student grades in both undergraduate and graduate classes. Their results also indicate that internet use as a component of economic education improves student perception of instructor effectiveness. Lastly, they find that internet tools had a positive effect on graduate student attitudes toward economics, but no significant effect on undergraduate attitudes toward economics.

Sosin et al. (2004) study the effect of technology utilization on student performance using a sample of 67 introductory economics courses with a total of 30 instructors and 3,986 students. The authors measure student performance across courses by comparing pre- and post-course scores on the TUCE. The authors find that extensive electronic technology use had an overall, positive and significant effect on student performance in both microeconomics and macroeconomics courses; however, they find that instructor use of PowerPoint had a significant negative effect on performance. Additionally, they find that, while emailing materials to students had a significant negative effect on macroeconomics student performance and courseware like Blackboard and WebCT had a significant positive effect, these effects were reversed for microeconomics students. These results suggest that differences in the type of material may impact the efficacy of technology utilization.

TEACHER PREPARATION

Most economics instructors get their first teaching experience while in graduate school. Economics departments often employ graduate students as teaching assistants (to grade papers, etc.), as recitation leaders, and as independent instructors of undergraduate courses. Walstad and Becker (2010) summarize survey data collected from 81 PhD-granting economics departments in 2008. Their results indicate that 89 percent of economics graduate students have some form of teaching responsibilities. The survey also inquires about the type of training given to graduate students before putting them in front of a class. Of the departments that use graduate students as instructors, Walstad and Becker report that less than half require the students to attend a noncredit program on teaching and less than one-third require students to attend a for-credit graduate course on teaching. Some departments offer training for graduate instructors themselves, while others rely on university resources such as staff from a teaching and learning center.

Walstad and Becker report that graduate instructors are much more likely to attend internal department programs than they are to attend external programs (87 percent vs 17 percent for for-credit courses and 86 percent vs 70 percent for noncredit programs; pp. 205–6). The authors express surprise that PhD-granting economics departments invest so little in training their graduate instructors, particularly since "most graduate students who earn a PhD are likely to assume significant teaching responsibilities when they secure an academic position" (Walstad and Becker, 2010, p. 208).

In a similar study, McCoy and Milkman (2010) survey 124 recent economics PhDs about the pedagogical training they received in graduate school and how well-prepared they were to teach upon graduation. About 38 percent of respondents reported attending a noncredit teacher training program while in graduate school and less than 12 percent of respondents reported taking a for-credit graduate teaching course.[14] Respondents who had participated in the different programs report similar perceptions of their preparedness for teaching upon graduation. When asked to evaluate student perceptions of their teaching, respondents who had taken a for-credit training course reported receiving higher student evaluations than did respondents who had not received any teacher training in graduate school, a difference that is statistically significant.

CONCLUSION

Active learning strategies are generally found to produce greater student learning, as evidenced by higher test scores and longer retention, with generally modest costs to the instructor. Further, while the strategies have been discussed independently here, Pollock (2006) finds that learning outcomes are highest when instructors use a combination of active learning strategies in lectures and associated recitation sections.[15]

While the research on the effects of replacing or supplementing lectures with cooperative learning exercises, classroom experiments, case studies and other active-learning pedagogies provides substantial evidence of their efficacy, there is room for additional work. Future research should examine larger samples of students, instructors, and courses, more carefully control for non-pedagogical factors, focus on identifying specific benefits associated with individual teaching strategies (or combinations of strategies), and attempt to quantify the learning gains that come with the use of different strategies. In addition, researchers could further explore exactly *why* active learning techniques promote deep learning. Finally, as technology evolves, so will the economics classroom; future research should evaluate the benefits of new technologies that might enhance student learning.

NOTES

1. Siriopoulos and Pomonis (2006) review 40 papers that study the effectiveness of different pedagogies in economics and finance and report that 35 of the 40 strongly recommend significant use of non-lecture techniques to improve student learning.
2. Explanations for this remain an open question. Watts and Becker (2008) suggest there are strong "inertial forces leading most economists to use chalk and talk teaching methods" (p. 285).
3. For more information about distance learning, see Chapter 14 in this volume.

4. Both Hoxby (2000) and Sacerdote (2001) find positive and statistically significant peer group effects on student performance.
5. Greg Delemeester and Jurgen Brauer maintain a list of over 170 non-computerized classroom games currently available for use in college economics courses at http://www.marietta.edu/~delemeeg/games/ (accessed 11 June 2011). The games are organized by topic and are available for introductory macro- and microeconomics, money and banking, labor economics, and other post-principles courses. Charles Holt maintains a similar list of computerized classroom games at http://veconlab.econ.virginia.edu/admin.php (accessed 11 June 2011).
6. The findings of Bastian et al. (1997) support the conclusion that students do not require special incentives (monetary incentives in their experiment) to learn from classroom experiments.
7. See Chapter 29 in this volume, for more information about the TUCE.
8. Carlson and Velenchik (2006) provide a set of guidelines for instructors to follow when utilizing the case method in the classroom. These strategies include allowing for silence to let students think, encouraging students to respond directly to other students, and giving serious thought to what one is trying to teach with a case before using it.
9. One course was an upper-level Development Economics course taught at a selective liberal arts college and the other was an upper-level International Monetary Issues course taught at a large public research institution.
10. Ziegert (2000) finds that a majority of students have a personality that leads them to prefer experience-based learning opportunities; Ziegert and McGoldrick (2008) observe that service-learning better serves such students.
11. Seymour et al. (2004) also lists 53 articles that describe the potential benefits of undergraduate research.
12. The student sample is drawn from students who applied to participate in an undergraduate research program. Selection to the program was randomly determined by lottery so as to eliminate any possible bias due to more-qualified students participating in the research program.
13. See Chapter 14 "Distance Education: Course Development and Strategies for Success" and Chapter 13, "Incorporating Media and Response Systems in the Economics Classroom", in this volume, for additional information on these topics.
14. It is unclear whether there is any overlap between these two groups.
15. Pollock (2006) studies three sections of Physics I at a large public research institution, with each section taught using a different mix of traditional and non-traditional teaching strategies.

REFERENCES

Agarwal, R. and A. E. Day (1998), "The impact of the internet on economic education", *Journal of Economic Education*, **29** (Spring), 99–110.
Allgood, S., W. Bosshardt, W. van der Klaauw and M. Watts (2004), "What students remember and say about college economics years later", *American Economic Review*, **94** (2), 259–65.
Astin, A. W. and L. J. Sax (1998), "How undergraduates are affected by service participation", *Journal of College Student Development*, **39** (3), 251–63.
Bastian, C., L. VanTassell, K. Williams, D. Menkhaus and L. Held (1997), "Active learning with monetary incentives", *Review of Agricultural Economics*, **19** (Fall–Winter), 475–83.
Bergstrom, T. C. and J. H. Miller (2000), *Experiments with Economic Principles: Microeconomics* (second ed.), Burr Ridge, IL: McGraw-Hill Higher Education.
Bransford, J. D., A. L. Brown and R. R. Cocking (eds) (2000), *How People Learn: Brain, Mind, Experience, and School*, Washington, DC: National Academy Press.
Carlson, J. and D. Schodt (1995), "Beyond the lecture: Case teaching and the learning of economic theory", *Journal of Economic Education*, **26** (Winter), 17–28.
Carlson, J. A. and A. Velenchik (2006), "Using the case method in the economics classroom", in W. E. Becker, M. Watts and S. R. Becker (eds), *Teaching Economics: More Alternatives to Chalk and Talk*, Cheltenham, UK and Northampton, MA, US: Edward Elgar, pp. 59–74.
Dickie, M. (2006), "Do classroom experiments increase learning in introductory microeconomics?", *Journal of Economic Education*, **37** (Summer), 267–88.
Duke, J. M. and T. O. Awokuse (2009), "Assessing the effect of bilateral collaborations on learning outcomes", *Review of Agricultural Economics*, **31** (2), (Summer), 344–58.
Emerson, T. L. N. and B. A. Taylor (2004), "Comparing student achievement across experimental and lecture-oriented sections of a principles of microeconomics course", *Southern Economic Journal*, **70** (3), 672–93.

Gratton-Lavoie, C. and D. Stanley (2009), "Teaching and learning principles of microeconomics online: An empirical assessment", *Journal of Economic Education*, **40** (1), (Winter), 3–25.

Gremmen, H. and J. Potters (1997), "Assessing the efficacy of gaming in economic education", *Journal of Economic Education*, **28**, 291–303.

Hathaway, R. S., B. A. Nagda and S. R. Gregerman (2002), "The Relationship of Undergraduate Research Participation to Graduate and Professional Education Pursuit: An Empirical Study", *Journal of College Student Development*, **43** (5), 614–31.

Holt, C. A. (1999), "Teaching economics with classroom experiments: A symposium", *Southern Economic Journal*, **65** (3), 603–10.

Hoxby, C. (2000), *Peer Effects in the Classroom: Learning From Gender and Race Variation*, NBER Working Paper No. 7876, Cambridge, MA: National Bureau of Economic Research.

Marburger, D. R. (2005), "Comparing student performance using cooperative learning", *International Review of Economics Education*, **4** (1), 46–57.

Marks, S. G. and M. G. Rukstad (1996), "Teaching macroeconomics by the case method", *Journal of Economic Education*, **27** (2), 139–47.

Markus, G. B., J. P. F. Howard and D. C. King (1993), "Integrating community service and classroom instruction enhances learning: Results from an experiment", *Educational Evaluation and Policy Analysis*, **15** (4), 410–19.

McCoy, J. P. and M. I. Milkman (2010), "Do recent PhD economists feel prepared to teach economics?", *Journal of Economic Education*, **41** (2), 211–15.

Pollock, S. J. (2006), "Transferring transformations: Learning gains, student attitudes, and the impacts of multiple instructors in large lecture courses," *AIP Conference Proceedings 2005*, **818** (1), 141–4.

Sacerdote, B. (2001), "Peer effects with random assignment: Results for Dartmouth roommates", *Quarterly Journal of Economics*, **116** (2), 681–704.

Seymour, E., A.-B. Hunter, S. L. Laursen and T. Deantoni (2004), "Establishing the benefits of research experiences for undergraduates in the sciences: First findings from a three-year study", *Science Education*, **88** (4), 493–534.

Siriopoulos, C. and G. A. Pomonis (2006), "Alternatives to chalk and talk: Active vs. passive learning – A literature review of the debate", http://ssrn.com/abstract=977283, accessed 10 March 2011.

Sosin, K., B. J. Blecha, R. Agarwal, R. L. Bartlett and J. I. Daniel (2004), "Efficiency in the use of technology in economic education: Some preliminary results", *The American Economic Review*, **94** (2), 253–8.

Walstad, W. B. and W. E. Becker (2010), "Preparing graduate students in economics for teaching: Survey findings and recommendations", *Journal of Economic Education*, **41** (2), 202–10.

Watts, M. and W. E. Becker (2008), "A little more than chalk and talk: Results from a third national survey of teaching methods in undergraduate economics courses", *Journal of Economic Education*, **39** (3), (Summer), 273–86.

Yamarik, S. (2007), "Does cooperative learning improve student learning outcomes?", *Journal of Economic Education*, **38** (3), (Summer), 259–77.

Yandell, D. (1999), "Effects of integration and classroom experiments on student learning and satisfaction", *Proceedings: Economics and the Classroom Conference*, Pocatello, ID: Idaho State University and Prentice-Hall Publishing Company, pp. 4–11.

Ziegert, A. L. (2000), "The role of personality temperament and student learning in principles of economics: Further evidence", *Journal of Economic Education*, **31** (4), 307–22.

Ziegert, A. L. and K. McGoldrick (2008), "When service is good for economics: Linking the classroom and community through service-learning", *International Review of Economics Education*, **7** (2), 39–56.

31 Factors influencing performance in economics: graphs and quantitative usage[1]
Mary Ellen Benedict and John Hoag

THE ROLE OF MATHEMATICS IN THE MAJOR

This chapter presents research regarding the impact of graphical and quantitative skills on performance in economics classes. Mathematical tools are employed in every economics course, including introductory courses provided to non-economic majors. Thus, understanding the association between mathematical ability and economics class performance is important for understanding "how" to teach economics.

Mathematics is deeply entwined with economics, both by history and practice. Many economists had strong quantitative backgrounds, which spilled over into their professional work. Alfred Marshall was a second Wrangler (Keynes, 1951, p. 131), signifying the second best student in the final mathematics exam at Cambridge in his year. While he often eschewed formal mathematics, his sleight of hand with mathematics led Keynes to say that the footnotes (Keynes, 1951, p. 169), where the mathematics was likely to be found, was the best part of Marshall's *Principles*. Keynes himself was 12th Wrangler (Moggridge, 1992, pp. 74–5).

In the 1930s there was powerful movement toward a more mathematical approach from John Hicks and R. G. D. Allen in Britain and Paul Samuelson in the United States, and it was not long before others pushed the mathematical envelope in economics. By the 1960s mathematics was an important staple in graduate education and journal articles were more likely to bristle with equations. Faculty advised students to have at least three semesters of calculus and one of linear algebra before entering graduate school. It is little wonder then that mathematical tools have come more into play in the undergraduate curriculum. Butler et al. (1998, p.186) reported that, in 1980, at research universities and top liberal arts colleges, 26 percent of all economics majors required a calculus course. By 1990, the percentage had risen to 81 percent. Siegfried et al. (1996, p. 185) found that, based on data from 53 universities during the 1990s, over half the students in principles had had some college calculus prior to economics. Mathematics is now an important part of how the major is defined.

For the typical economics major, a minimal level of mathematical comprehension is required, amounting to not less than college algebra. In addition, some mathematical concepts are deeply imbedded in economics, for example, the concept of marginal and the relation of marginal to average (Siegfried et al. 1991, p. 203). At the intermediate level, mathematical tools are used more extensively. Intermediate microeconomics books include sections where differential calculus is used. Furthermore, entire classes are dedicated to the application of mathematical tools in economics, including mathematical economics and econometrics. Mathematics is embedded in the undergraduate economics curriculum via relevance to economic concepts, major requirements, and the existence of specific courses.

THE ROLE OF GRAPHS IN THE ECONOMICS MAJOR

For many students, a course in economics is a course in graphs. Students who have trouble understanding graphs generally have trouble with economics, as demonstrated by Strober and Cook (1992). They developed an experiment where small groups of students were asked to solve a problem and include a graph in their analysis. An evaluation of student effort indicated that they faced many graphing challenges, including an inability to correctly label axes, trouble translating problem facts to a graph, not seeing the graph as a representation of anything useful, and not clearly understanding the role of price on a market graph. While it is difficult to generalize from this exercise, it is illustrative of the problems that students are likely to encounter in an economics classroom.

Cohn and Cohn (1994) reported that many students cannot accurately reproduce graphs, but those with this ability perform better on a post-test on material covered in one lecture, but which was not covered in the text. Cohn et al. (2001) found that unless a student has taken more mathematics, graphs do not improve post-test scores. In a related paper, Cohn et al. (2004) found that students who have trouble with graphs accumulate fewer total points in their economics class. Further, students who think graphs are helpful do not have improved test scores compared to those who do not think graphs are helpful, all else held constant. Hill and Stegner (2003) investigated attributes likely to increase student ability to use graphs. They find that if the student came from a larger city, liked math, had a higher GPA, or had a mother with a bachelor's degree, then the individual was more likely to be able to use graphs.

While the work on how graphs are used in economics and their contribution to learning is not well developed, the literature on how mathematics affects performance in principles level courses has been examined in greater detail.

THE ROLE OF MATHEMATICS IN THE PRINCIPLES LEVEL COURSES

The investigation of the relative importance of mathematics begins with a determination of how performance is measured. With respect to economic knowledge, three methods have been employed in the literature: (1) the difference between the post- or pre-scores on the Test of Understanding College Economics (TUCE), (2) total points accumulated in the class (or the percentage of possible points, and (3) the course letter grade.[2] More problematic, however, is a useful representation of accumulated mathematical skills. Several have been used in the literature, including scores on the mathematics portion of the SAT (or ACT), mathematics courses taken, grades in the mathematics courses, or scores on a mathematics quiz.

The studies using the TUCE as a measure of economic learning have generated mixed results. Gery (1972) found a statistically significant and positive relationship between post-pre TUCE and mathematics SAT scores. However, a later paper by Milkman et al. (1995) found no relationship between post-pre TUCE and total ACT or mathematics classes taken. Using the post-pre difference of a ten-question subset of the TUCE, Schuhmann et al. (2005) found that the quantitative skill (as measured by a mathematics quiz) significantly enhanced economic learning, and that quantitative improvement (post-pre mathematics quiz) led to more economic learning.

Turning to the total points (or percentage of total points) as a measure of economic learning, Ballard and Johnson (2004) found the mathematics portion of the ACT, completing a calculus course, and the student's score on a mathematics quiz have statistically significant positive impacts. Their analysis also indicates poorer performance by students who had taken remedial math. Cohn et al. (1998) found no significant relationship between total points earned and having a calculus class or performance on a mathematics skills quiz.

Using course letter grades, Brasfield et al. (1992) found a positive impact of having taken college mathematics. Hoag and Benedict (2010) found a positive relationship between the course grade and whether the student took college mathematics or took calculus, and the sub-scores on the mathematics ACT test.

UPPER-LEVEL COURSES AND MATHEMATICS PREPARATION

Studies examining the effect of mathematics preparation on upper-level undergraduate courses are sparse and typically focus primarily on intermediate microeconomics or macroeconomics and economic statistics courses. The difficulty in examining the math-performance relationship beyond principles is a result of several factors. Self-selection issues limit data collection and analysis. There are also problems in generalizing from the research because the typically required calculus class has a wide variation in topic coverage across institutions and the degree of calculus integrated varies by type of course and instructor (von Allmen and Brower, 1998). Finally, there may be an endogeneity issue because instructors of upper-level economics courses adjust the expectation bar in their own classes based on the expected level of mathematics skills, thus confounding the ability to examine how mathematics skills affect performance.

Early papers that examined performance in upper-level coursework did not control for mathematics preparation when investigating intermediate microeconomics (Moore, 1978) or macroeconomics (Specter and Mazzeo, 1980). An exception, McConnell and Lamphear (1974) included controls for the hours of statistics and the hours of mathematics (less statistics) prior to students taking an intermediate macroeconomics course. They found a positive but statistically insignificant relationship between performance and both measures of quantitative preparation, even when the measures were weighted by the grades in the mathematics courses. Park and Kerr (1990) found no impact of mathematics preparation on grades earned in a money and banking course. Raimondo et al. (1990) examined the effect of class size in introductory courses on subsequent performance in either intermediate microeconomics or macroeconomics and included a binary control variable if the student completed a required one-semester calculus course prior to taking intermediate-level economics.

The authors found a positive relationship between performance and completion of a calculus course.

The seminal work by Butler, Finegan, and Siegfried (1994, 1998) provided important policy implications about required calculus for economics majors. They examined the performance of 1,099 Vanderbilt University students in intermediate microeconomics and macroeconomics, controlling for self-selection bias and including measures of quantitative performance. They found that a second semester of calculus and the higher the grade one received in the highest level mathematics course taken improved performance in microeconomics. The first semester calculus course did not have a statistically significant impact and students with more hours of mathematics (11 or 12 hours) tended to perform less well in microeconomics compared to those students with less (eight or nine) hours of mathematics. The level of mathematics and grade in the highest level taken had no effect on macroeconomic performance.

Von Allmen (1996) employed an ordered probit to investigate the effect of mathematics preparation on intermediate microeconomics performance. He found that higher grades in calculus increased the probability of receiving higher grades in microeconomics. Further, students required to take a two-semester sequence of calculus due to weak pre-college skills had the same estimated probability distribution of grades as their better prepared or more able counterparts. Unlike Raimondo et al. (1990), von Allmen found that a longer wait time between principles and intermediate microeconomics improved performance in the upper-level course. Von Allmen suggested that intellectual maturity may be the reason for the effect.

Econometrics and business statistics courses have also been a focus of research on the relationship between mathematics preparation and performance. An early paper by Cohn (1972) suggested that taking previous economics or statistics courses does not improve performance in the economic statistics course, but additional hours in mathematics do help performance in the class, especially when the prerequisites for the class are low and the student has taken a substantial number of mathematics courses. Green et al. (2009) examined how a one-time reduction in the mathematics prerequisites for a business statistics course affected performance. Normally, students were required to take a two-semester sequence in business mathematics in order to take the statistics course. Due to changes in the curriculum, there was one semester where a student could skip the second mathematics course (calculus). The authors examined the final grade in the business statistics course as a function of the usual control variables and dummy variables that indicated if the individual took only the pre-calculus course, or higher-level courses, as opposed to the typical two-sequence mathematics set. Results indicated that students with higher-level mathematics courses had higher grades than those with the (normally required) two-semester sequence, and students with only pre-calculus had lower average final grades relative to the other groups. Further, higher grades in the mathematics courses led to enhanced performance in the statistics course.

Green et al. (2009) examined the consequence of changing basic prerequisite mathematics courses for business statistics from a two-semester sequence that included differential and integral calculus in the second course to a sequence that went slower and moved topics from the first to the second course, thus omitting some advanced concepts. Results indicate that students who were prepared more rigorously in math, particularly in calculus, tended to perform better in their business statistics course. In addition, students with higher grades in math, regardless of which sequence they chose, did better in statistics, and those who were weak performers in mathematics had high probabilities of receiving low grades in statistics. Thus, the level of mathematics preparation and success in related classes appear to be important determinants for subsequent economic statistics courses.

CONCLUSION

Our review of mathematics preparation and success in economics generally indicates that mathematics ability does matter in learning economics, despite a complicating factor that the model specification used to test the various hypotheses is quite diverse among the studies reviewed in this chapter. In addition, success in higher-level economics courses requires more mathematical understanding.

At the principles level, graphs seem to be important, but if a student is not capable of understanding graphs, then subsequent success in one's economics class is less likely. Are instructors using graphs because they find them useful when students do not? Substantial work has been done on what the content of principles and the major should be (Siegfried et al. 1991; Colander and McGoldrick, 2010). It could be that if the intention is to prepare students to use economics to understand policy and everyday life, graphs generate more harm than good. However, an alternative argument is that economics helps students see that a variety of mental processes, including graphical analysis, can be useful in understanding the world.

In examining performance in upper-level economics courses, mathematics, particularly previous exposure to calculus, seems to be important for intermediate microeconomics and econometrics, but not for intermediate macroeconomics. It is not entirely clear whether the individual who is good at higher-order mathematics is just better at upper-level economic concepts or if the mathematics preparation matters.

There is an obvious relation between an understanding of calculus and economics. It also seems that some mathematical maturity helps even nonmajors find success in their economics classes. While the connection between economics and mathematics would appear to be why students dread taking economics, students do not cite a lack of mathematical training as their reason for being apprehensive in economics classes (Benedict and Hoag, 2002). Perhaps then it is the teaching methodology. Our discipline had a tradition of "chalk and talk" in the classroom and despite a movement within the discipline to change how one teaches economics, using problem-based solving, case studies, and project work to provide students with "real world" applications (Colander and McGoldrick, 2010), traditional lectures are still employed by a majority of instructors (Watts and Becker, 2008, p. 275).

On a different dimension, the literature leaves unresolved the question of what specific mathematical skills are useful or whether some general maturity is more important. Additionally, future research should explore whether there is some common underlying factor that determines both the student's mathematical ability and propensity to choose economics. It may well be that such an underlying factor matters more than completing more mathematics classes.

NOTES

1. The authors would like to thank Rachel Childers for her excellent research support. The quality of the chapter has been improved by the efforts of the editors. We appreciate their help and support. All remaining errors are the authors' responsibility.
2. For more information about measurement techniques, see Chapter 29 on measurement techniques in this volume.

REFERENCES

Ballard, C. and M. Johnson (2004), "Basic math skills and performance in an introductory economics class", *Journal of Economic Education*, **25** (4), 3–23.
Benedict, M. E. and J. Hoag (2002), "Who's afraid of their economics classes?", *The American Economist*, **46** (2), 31–44.
Brasfield, D., J. McCoy and M. Milkman (1992), "The effect of university mathematics in principles of economics", *Journal of Research and Development in Education*, **25** (4), 240–47.
Butler, J., T. Finegan and J. Siegfried (1994), "Does more calculus improve student learning in intermediate micro and macro economic theory?", *The American Economic Review*, **84** (2), 206–10.
Butler, J., T. Finegan and J. Siegfried (1998), "Does more calculus improve student learning in intermediate micro and macroeconomic theory?", *Journal of Applied Econometrics*, **13** (2), 185–202.
Cohn, E. and S. Cohn (1994), "Graphs and learning in principles of economics", *American Economic Review*, **84** (2), 197–200.
Cohn, E., S. Cohn, D. Balch and J. Bradley (2001), "Do graphs promote learning in principles of economics?", *Journal of Economic Education*, **32** (4), 299–310.
Cohn, E., S. Cohn, D. Balch and J. Bradley (2004), "The relation between student attitudes toward graphs and performance in economics", *The American Economist*, **48** (2), 41–52.
Cohn, E., S. Cohn, R. Hult, D. Blach and J. Bradley (1998), "The effects of mathematics background on student learning in principles of economics", *Journal of Education for Business*, **74** (1), 18–22.
Cohn, S. (1972), "Students' characteristics and performance in economic statistics", *Journal of Economic Education*, **3** (2), 106–11.
Colander, D. and K. McGoldrick (eds) (2010), *Educating Economists: The Teagle Discussion on Re-evaluating the Undergraduate Economics Major*, Cheltenham, UK and Northampton, MA, US: Edward Elgar.
Gery, F. (1972), "Does mathematics matter?", in A. Walsh (ed.) *Research Papers in Economic Education*, New York: Joint Council on Economic Education, pp. 143–57.
Green, J., C. Stone, A. Zegeye and T. Charles (2009), "How much math do students need to succeed in business and economic statistics? An ordered probit analysis", *Journal of Statistics Education*, **17** (3), 27–38.
Hill, C. and T. Stegner (2003), "Which students benefit from graphs in a principles of economics class?", *The American Economist*, **47** (2), 69–77.
Hoag, J. and M. E. Benedict (2010), "What influence does mathematics preparation & performance have on performance in first economics classes?", *Journal of Economics and Economic Education*, **11** (1), 19–42.
Keynes, J. (1951), *Essays in Biography*, New York: W. W. Norton.
McConnell, C. and F. C. Lamphear (1974), "Factors affecting student performance in intermediate macroeconomics", *Nebraska Journal of Economics and Business*, **13** (4), 30–42.
Milkman, M., J. McCoy, D. Brasfield and M. Mitchell (1995), "Some additional evidence on the effect of university math on student performance in principles of economics", *Journal of Research and Development in Education*, **28** (4), 220–29.
Moggridge, D. (1992), *Maynard Keynes: An Economist's Biography*, London and New York: Routledge.
Moore, G. A. (1978), "A note on factors affecting student performance in intermediate microeconomic theory", *Journal of Economic Education*, **10** (1), 51–3.
Park, K. H. and P. M. Kerr (1990), "Determinants of academic performance: A multinomial logit approach", *The Journal of Economic Education*, **21** (2), 101–11.
Raimondo, H., L. Esposito and I. Gershenberg (1990), "Introductory class size and student performance in intermediate theory classes", *Journal of Economic Education*, **21** (4), 369–81.
Schuhmann, P., K. McGoldrick and R. Burrus (2005), "Student quantitative literacy: Importance, measurement, and correlation with economic literacy", *The American Economist*, **49** (4), 49–65.
Siegfried, J., P. Saunders, E. Stinar and H. Zhang (1996), "How is introductory economics taught in America?", *Economic Inquiry*, **34** (1), 182–92.

Siegfried J., R. Bartlett, L. Hansen, A. Kelley, D. McCloskey and T. Tietenberg (1991), "The status and prospects of the economics major", *Journal of Economic Education*, **22** (3), 197–224.

Specter, L. C. and M. Mazzeo (1980), "Probit analysis and economic education", *Journal of Economic Education*, **11** (2), 37–44.

Strober, M. and A. Cook (1992), "Economics, lies and videotapes", *Journal of Economic Education*, **23** (2), 125–51.

von Allmen, P. (1996), "The effect of quantitative prerequisites on performance in intermediate microeconomics", *Journal of Education for Business*, **72** (1), 11–22.

von Allmen, P. and G. Brower (1998), "Calculus and the teaching of intermediate microeconomics: Results from a survey", *Journal of Economic Education*, **29** (3), 277–84.

Watts, M. and Becker (2008), "A little more than chalk and talk: Results from a third national survey of teaching methods in undergraduate economics courses", *Journal of Economic Education*, **39** (3), 273–86.

32 Student characteristics, behavior, and performance in economics classes
Ann L. Owen

What are the characteristics and behavior of students who perform well in economics classes? This is an important question for instructors of economics because the answer helps them to understand outcomes they observe in their classrooms. This chapter reviews a fairly extensive literature that examines student characteristics over which instructors have little influence, such as gender, race, or personality type, as well as behaviors over which instructors may have influence, such as attendance and math preparation.[1]

ENROLLING IN ECONOMICS CLASSES: THE ROLE OF GENDER AND RACE

In order to perform well in an economics class, of course, the students need to first enroll. In examining the characteristics of students who do take economics classes, one that stands out is that the majority of economics majors are male.[2] Although it is difficult to know why some students do not take economics, Dynan and Rouse (1997) examine registrars' data and find that female students are less likely to enroll in introductory economics and that math preparation played an important role in determining the probability of taking introductory economics.

Once students decide to take the principles class, male students are also more likely to continue to take advanced economics classes. Dynan and Rouse (1997) present evidence on this phenomenon using data from Harvard University students, showing that math ability and the grade earned in economics relative to grades in other courses is important in determining the decision to major in economics. Jensen and Owen (2001) corroborate this finding with a broad sample of students from 34 different co-ed liberal arts colleges, showing that female students are less confident in their understanding of economics and also earn lower relative grades in economics. Chizmar (2000) also emphasizes the importance of relative grades, arguing that the probability of continuing for male and female economics majors are similar, once relative grades and economics credit hours are included in the estimation.

The importance of grades as motivation to study economics is also highlighted in Rask and Tiefenthaler (2008), who demonstrate that female students are more sensitive than male students to lower relative grades when deciding to take additional economics courses. Of course, identifying the direction of causation between grades in economics and a desire to take more economics classes is difficult because students might work harder and earn better grades in economics classes if they are interested in the subject and intend to take more similar classes. Owen (2010) addresses this issue and provides more convincing evidence that higher grades cause students to take more economics classes through the use of regression discontinuity analysis. She presents evidence that the decision by female students to major in economics is affected by the letter grade received in introductory economics, even after controlling for course performance via the numerical course average. Owen's study finds no evidence of a similar effect of the feedback embedded in a course letter grade for male students.

GENDER, RACE, AND PERFORMANCE

Once students decide to take economics, however, the evidence is mixed on whether or not female students perform worse than male students in absolute terms (in other words, not relative to the grades they receive in other classes). Anderson, Benjamin and Fuss (1994) provide evidence that female students perform worse than their male counterparts at the introductory level, and Hirschfeld, Moore and Brown (1995) show that this disadvantage exists even among more advanced students, based on the performance of a sample required to take the Economics GRE as a graduation requirement. At the same time, a number of studies have found no male advantage. Watts (1987) examines the economic knowledge of public school students and finds that, once they are exposed to formal economics education, female students perform just as well as male students. Rhine (1989) finds similar results in a different sample of high school students. Some have even found that females have a performance advantage under certain circumstances. Lumsden and Scott (1987) find that females perform better than male students when essay questions are used to evaluate them and Williams, Waldauer and Duggal (1992) find mixed results for male vs female performance, depending on the course (principles, microeconomic theory, macroeconomic theory, or statistics) and the nature of the questions asked (essay, multiple choice, or numerical/spatial).

While the evidence regarding absolute advantage of male economics students over female students is inconclusive, there is much broader agreement that female students perform better in their non-economics classes than in economics classes. Dancer (2003) dispels the notion that math ability is a reason for the gender differences in performance using a comparison of student performance in economics and econometrics classes. She finds that female students actually perform better than male students in econometrics, but not as well as male students in economics classes. Because econometrics requires a direct application of math skills relevant to success as an economist, this finding casts doubt on the importance of math preparation as an explanation for the lower relative performance of female students in economics classes. Greene (1997) combats another stereotype about female students by showing that female students do not perform better than male students on test questions that require verbal reasoning. In fact, Ballard and Johnson (2005) argue that the stereotypes about female performance are themselves responsible for the actual level of performance. They document lower expectations for success in economics among female students than male students even after controlling for family background, academic experience and math preparation. Interestingly, they find that these expectations, which are partly self-fulfilling, are formed even before the students have any exposure to economics at the college level. Nowell and Alston (2007) corroborate these conclusions surveying students in economics and quantitative courses and finding that male students exhibit more overconfidence in their abilities than female students.

While a good deal of the literature on performance of females in economics focuses on the undergraduate experience, there is a segment of this literature that examines the performance of female PhDs. Because the goal of most graduate programs in economics is to create prolific research economists, publication records of economists are indicators of their success in graduate school. Although Broder (1993) finds that female economists have lower rates of publication, Barbezat (2006) explains these differences based on characteristics more likely to be associated with being female. Using detailed survey data from PhDs from top economics programs, Barbezat (2006) decomposes the effect of gender on publications and finds that once job type and type of academic institution are controlled for, the gender gap in number of publications is insignificant. Thus, the raw difference in publications is more likely attributed to other characteristics that are associated with being female than with some inherent difference in the publication abilities of male versus female economists.

There are fewer studies of the impact of race on student performance in economics. However, generally, authors have found that minority students from segregated neighborhoods do not perform as well in college as their white counterparts. Massey (2006) argues that this is a result of the poor quality of high schools in segregated neighborhoods, while Charles, Dinwiddie and Massey (2004) find evidence showing that minority students from segregated neighborhoods experience more family stress, which negatively affects college academic performance. Walstad and Soper (1988) conduct one of the few studies that examine the determinants of economics knowledge and control for race. They examine results from the Test of Economic Literacy taken by high school students who have completed different kinds of high school courses with different economic content.[3] Although they find a negative and significant coefficient on an indicator variable controlling for African-American students, the interpretation of this is limited because they do not explore how race might have affected the economic content of the high school class in which the students enrolled.

PERSONALITY TYPE AND PERFORMANCE

An interesting extension of the work that examines the effects of race and gender on student performance in economics looks at the interaction between race, gender, and personality type. Borg and Shapiro (1996) are the first to examine the effects of personality type on student performance in introductory economics. They use the Myer-Briggs Type Indicator to categorize both the students and the teachers along four dimensions: extroversion/introversion, sensing/intuition, thinking/feeling, and judgment/perception. They link these personality types to different teaching and learning styles and find that in the principles of economics classes, students who are more introverted learners and dependent on structure provided by the instructor have the highest probability of receiving an A and the lowest probability of failing the course. In addition, students that had a personality type that matched their instructor had significantly higher probabilities of receiving an A and lower probabilities of receiving an F. Ziegert (2000) presents further evidence on this issue using a larger sample and alternative measures of performance.

While she corroborates the general finding that personality type affects student performance in economics classes, she does not find evidence that a match between personality type of the instructor and student is a significant factor in explaining student grades.

However, given that personality type may be related to race or gender, some researchers have explored whether or not controlling for personality type can explain gender or race gaps in performance. In both the Ziegert (2000) and the Borg and Shapiro (1996) studies, when personality types are included, gender dummies become insignificant in explaining performance. Following up on this finding, Borg and Stranahan (2002a) interact race and gender dummies with personality type and find significant results, suggesting that race, gender, and personality type interact in complex ways to determine performance in introductory economics. Borg and Stranahan (2002b) corroborate these findings with a sample of students from upper-level economics courses. Swope and Schmitt (2006) use a larger sample from the US Naval Academy and also examine the role of personality in conjunction with race and gender. Once they control for personality type, like others, they find no significant effect of gender on performance in economics classes, but they still find a role for race, with male minority students underperforming relative to other students. However, Boatman, Courtney, and Lee (2008) use a slightly different method for classifying student learning styles and corroborate the earlier conclusions that both ethnicity and gender-based performance differences can be explained by differences in personality traits and learning styles.

ATTENDANCE AND PERFORMANCE

Of course, gender, race, and personality type are all student characteristics that are largely out of the control of the student and instructor. A large body of research examines student characteristics and behaviors that students and instructors are in a better position to influence. For example, much has been written about the effect of attendance on performance in economics classes. Romer (1993) made a seminal contribution in this area, investigating the effect of absenteeism on student learning at three different elite institutions. He documents rampant absenteeism (between 25 percent and 40 percent) at all levels of the economics curriculum and shows that attendance is an important determinant of performance, even after controlling for student GPA and other measures of motivation, such as fraction of problem sets completed. He estimates that the difference in grade between students who have perfect attendance and those who miss one-quarter of the classes is a full letter grade.

Romer's initial findings are supported by others. Durden and Ellis (1995) extend these findings to suggest a non-linear effect of absences, showing that a few absences over the course of a semester do not affect grades, but that once a student has missed five or more classes, grades suffer. Marburger (2001) refines these conclusions further by keeping records on exactly which material was covered on the day students were not in attendance. He finds that students who were not present when a specific topic was covered are more likely to respond incorrectly to an exam question relating to the missed material. Cohn and Johnson (2006) corroborate these findings and also test the hypothesis that low test scores cause poor attendance rather than the other way around. They find no evidence for this idea, strengthening the conclusions of the previous studies. Stanca (2006) is also concerned about the endogeneity of student attendance and assembles panel data by collecting multiple observations on the same students over the course of the semester, matching up attendance records for a specific part of the semester with exam scores on the material covered during that time. Stanca (2006) concludes that, although controlling for unobserved student characteristics through the use of fixed effects estimation lowers the magnitude of the estimated effects, the effects are still quantitatively relevant. The results of the fixed effects estimations suggest that a student with perfect attendance earns a little more than one additional point on each exam compared to the student with average attendance. Importantly, these results suggest that the effect of an extra hour spent in class is substantially higher than that of each extra hour spent in self-study.

Chen and Lin (2008) take this literature in an interesting methodological direction, implementing a randomized experiment to determine the effects of attendance on exam performance. They argue that there may be different types of students for which the impact of attending class differs. Suppose, for example, that one type of student gets a larger benefit from attending class and, therefore, attends class more. In this example, the students who don't attend class receive a smaller benefit. The studies mentioned above based on regression analysis calculate an average effect across all types of students. Rather, Chen and Lin argue, what one really wants to know is what the effect is for both types of students, especially if one wants to draw conclusions about the impact of increasing class attendance for the students with low attendance. To address this issue, they implemented a randomized experiment in which the instructor covered different topics in two different sections of the same public finance course. In other words, the treatment applied to the individuals in the different sections was effectively to force them to skip some topics in lecture. They found that for students with perfect attendance, the marginal effect of attendance on grades was 18 percent, much higher than the average effect. As attendance declined, the marginal effect of attendance did so as well (but remained positive and meaningful), consistent with the idea that students who get the most benefit from attending class are more likely to have better attendance records.[4]

Benedict and Hoag (2004) study a related phenomenon to class attendance – seating location in large lectures. They find that student preferences for seating are related to final course grades, with students who prefer to sit in the back earning lower grades. However, that negative effect can be mitigated by forcing students forward. Therefore, similar to the conclusions of the literature on attendance, they find evidence of both the effect of a student characteristic (for example, seating preference) and of student behavior (for example, seating location).

MATH PREPARATION AND PERFORMANCE

In addition to attendance, students can also influence their performance by taking more math classes prior to taking economics classes.[5] In a 1995 mail survey to intermediate microeconomics professors, von Allmen and Brower (1998) queried respondents about the use of calculus in their classes. Findings indicate that about 40 percent of respondents stated that one semester of calculus was a prerequisite for intermediate microeconomics and that 63 percent indicated it was a requirement for the major. Given the nature of the discipline, these findings may not be surprising; however, the majority of the respondents who required calculus indicated that, although students were "exposed" to calculus in the lectures or textbook, they were not responsible for completing problems using calculus in exams. In spite of this, many studies have found that students who have more math background perform better in economics classes. Butler, Finegan and Siegfried (1994) show that a second semester of calculus improves the grade earned in intermediate microeconomics by a full letter grade, but does not significantly affect the grade earned in intermediate macroeconomics.

Several other studies examine the effects of various aspects of mathematical aptitude on performance in introductory economics classes. Cohn, Cohn, Balch, and Bradley (2004) examine student attitudes towards graphs and performance in a one-semester principles class. They find that about half the students surveyed have difficulty interpreting graphs, yet about 70 percent report that they believe graphs are helpful in understanding economics. Furthermore, they show that students who report having difficulty with graphs earn significantly lower exam scores. Ballard and Johnson (2004) also focus on relatively basic math skills and student performance in introductory economics. They administer a survey to students that includes seven basic math skills (for example, finding the area of a triangle, solving two simultaneous equations, manipulating fractions, etc.). After controlling for a variety of individual characteristics, which include previous math classes, their results indicate that the score on the basic math skills quiz significantly affects test scores.

Lagerlof and Seltzer (2009) point out that many of these studies may be influenced by unobserved heterogeneity of the students. Students who are more motivated to do well in economics courses may also be more likely to take additional math courses or develop math skills. To determine if these results hold up to a random assignment of students into math courses, they took advantage of a change in policy at the University of London that required students to take a remedial math course prior to enrolling in university-level economics courses. They compared the performance of students who were required to take the math course to those who were not, controlling for other individual characteristics, including high school math background. They found that performance in secondary school math classes does predict success in economics. However, in contrast to the conclusions of the previous studies, they find that students who were required to take the remedial math course did not perform better than those who were not. This finding supports a correlation between math ability and performance in economics, but does not support policy interventions that require students to take remedial math courses.

HIGH SCHOOL EXPERIENCES

In addition to taking math classes prior to taking college economics, many students also have some exposure to economics in high school. Walstad and Rebeck (2000) estimate that about half of all high school students are exposed to some economics and that this is part of an increasing trend. They estimate that, in 1982, only 24 percent of high school students received credit for some type of economics courses, but that by 1994, that percentage had increased to 44 percent. However, Lopus and Maxwell (1994) find that students who took high school economics did not perform better than those who did not on either a pre-test or a post-test of college economics. While this result seems counterintuitive, in a follow-up to this study, Lopus (1997) points out that high school economics classes take a variety of approaches, with some focusing on economic institutions, some on business, while others have a significant component that focuses on consumer education. Given this, she argues that it is unreasonable to expect that taking an "economics" class in high school will have the same effect on performance in a college economics class for all students. She finds that students who have taken a high school class that covers macroeconomic or microeconomic concepts perform better on a pre-test of economic concepts given at the beginning of a college principles class. However, only in limited circumstances does this advanced prior knowledge carry through to higher post-test scores. In general, these findings suggest that high school economics may give students an advantage early in the semester, but that the advantage diminishes by the end of the course.

High school experiences also differ in public and private schools. Grimes (1994) examines the impact of public versus private schools on the economic education of high school students. He notes that, although private school students are more likely to be exposed to an economics course than public school students, economics teachers at public schools are more likely to have taken more college credit hours in economics than economics teachers at private schools. Furthermore, public school teachers are more likely to receive support services from an economic education agency. After controlling for sample selection and individual characteristics, he finds that students who attend private school perform significantly worse than their public school counterparts with the same characteristics in tests of economics knowledge. Interestingly, however, these results do not hold for Hispanic and Black students in private schools who perform better than their public school counterparts. All together, these findings suggest that high school experiences vary along important dimensions, including the curriculum and the preparation of the teachers and that these differences affect the learning outcomes of the students.

THE BEST AND WORST STUDENTS

Finally, while most studies of performance examine behavior for the average student in an economics class, a few studies look at the extremes, examining the best and the worst students. Bosshardt (2004) examines students who drop introductory economics classes and finds that students with lower GPAs, lower test scores, and those who are taking both micro and macro principles classes simultaneously, are more likely to drop a course. He identifies students who have these characteristics as being "at risk" of dropping a course. However, there is likely also an unobserved characteristic related to perseverance or life circumstances affecting student choices as well, suggested by his finding that only 16 percent of the "at-risk" students who dropped the course were enrolled at the university in the following year, compared to 58 percent of the students who completed the course but earned lower than a C.

At the other end of the spectrum, Jensen and Owen (2003) examine the performance of "good" students in introductory economics. In a departure from most of the literature, they examine additional measures of performance beyond grades on exams or in classes. Specifically, they also examine the determinants of students' confidence in their ability to understand economics and their belief that economics studies ideas and issues that they find relevant. They use several dimensions of what might be considered "good" students in their analysis: students with high GPAs, students with high SAT scores, students who report that they like to solve problems, and those who like to express their ideas and opinions in class. They find, for many of these "good" students, that interests that they had prior to entering the class play an important role in determining their success in several dimensions. In particular, "good" students who think economics will be important for their careers, as well as those who are considering economics as a possible major, find economics more relevant, receive higher relative grades and are generally more confident in their abilities to do economic analysis. Overall, these results support the idea that attitudes towards economics prior to entering a class are important determinants of the success of these good students and of their continued interest in studying economics.

CONCLUSION

This chapter has reviewed a fairly extensive literature on the influence of student characteristics and behaviors on performance in economics classes. While this literature sheds light on some characteristics and behavior that may help us predict the performance of students, such as good attendance or better math preparation, we can say less about the causal role of these factors in determining performance. More work in this area needs to be done that addresses the endogeneity of student behaviors and the sample selection issues that are unavoidable when we study only those who have enrolled in an economics class or who have chosen to continue in economics.[6] Related to this is the criticism that many studies are necessarily performed on convenience samples at only a small number of institutions.

More broadly, the literature would benefit from expanding the definition of good performance. Few studies look beyond somewhat one-dimensional measures of performance, such as course grades or exam scores. If the ultimate goals of college economics are broader than good grades, then broader measures of success need to be employed. Thus, while the literature does seem vast, many opportunities remain to contribute to it. There is still much work to be done that expands our way of thinking about successful outcomes in economics education.

NOTES

1. For a discussion of research on instructor characteristics, pedagogy and classroom environment see Chapter 33, "Class and Instructor Characteristics", in this volume.
2. For more information about trends in the economics major, see Chapter 68, "The Economics Major in the United States", in this volume.
3. For more information about this and related measures, see Chapter 29 "Measurement Techniques of Student Performance and Literacy: College and High School", in this volume.
4. For more discussion of instructor policies that encourage attendance, see Chapter 33 in this volume.
5. For more detailed analysis of quantitative skills, see Chapter 31, "Graphs and Quantitative Usage", in this volume.

6. For more about these and related econometric issues, see Chapter 35, "Data Resources and Econometric Techniques", in this volume and the Econometrics Training Modules developed by William Becker and the Committee on Economic Education page of the AEA website.

REFERENCES

Anderson, G., D. Benjamin and M. A. Fuss (1994), "The determinants of success in university economics courses", *Journal of Economic Education*, **25**, 99–119.

Ballard, C. and M. Johnson (2004), "Basic math skills and performance in an introductory economics class", *Journal of Economic Education*, **35** (1), 3–23.

Ballard, C. and M. Johnson (2005), "Gender, expectation, and grades in introductory economics at a U.S. university", *Feminist Economics*, **11** (1), 95–122.

Barbezat, D. A. (2006), "Gender differences in research patterns among Ph.D. economists", *Journal of Economic Education*, **37** (3), 359–75.

Benedict, M. E. and J. Hoag (2004), "Seating location in large lectures: Are seating preferences or location related to course performance?", *Journal of Economic Education*, **35** (3), 215–31.

Boatman, K., R. Courtney and W. Lee (2008), "See how they learn: The impact of faculty and student learning styles on student performance in introductory economics", *The American Economist*, **52** (1), 39–48.

Borg, M. O. and S. L. Shapiro (1996), "Personality type and student performance in principles of economics", *Journal of Economic Education*, **27** (1), 3–25.

Borg, M. O. and H. Stranahan (2002a), "The effect of gender and race on student performance in principles of economics: The importance of personality type", *Applied Economics*, **34**, 589–98.

Borg, M. O. and H. Stranahan (2002b), "Personality type and student performance in upper-level economics courses: The importance of race and gender", *Journal of Economic Education*, **33** (1), 3–14.

Bosshardt, W. (2004), "Student drops and failure in principles courses", *Journal of Economic Education*, **35** (2), 111–28.

Broder, I. (1993), "Professional achievements and gender differences among academic economists", *Economic Inquiry*, **31**, 116–27.

Butler, J. S., T. A. Finegan and J. J. Siegfried (1994), "Does more calculus improve student learning in intermediate micro and macro economic theory?", *American Economic Review*, **84** (2), 206–10.

Charles, C. Z., G. Dinwiddie and D. S. Massey (2004), "The continuing consequences of segregation: Family stress and college academic performance", *Social Science Quarterly*, **85** (5), 1353–73.

Chen, J. and T. Lin (2008), "Class attendance and exam performance: A randomized experiment", *Journal of Economic Education*, **39** (3), 213–27.

Chizmar, J. F. (2000), "A discrete-time hazard analysis of the role of gender in persistence in the economics major", *Journal of Economic Education*, **31** (Spring), 107–18.

Cohn, E. and E. Johnson (2006), "Class attendance and performance in principles of economics", *Education Economics*, **14** (2), 211–33.

Cohn, E., S. Cohn, D. C. Balch and J. Bradley, Jr. (2004), "The relation between student attitudes toward graphs and performance in economics", *The American Economist*, **48** (2), 41–52.

Dancer, D. M. (2003), "The gender issues revisited: A case study of student performance in economics and econometrics", *Economic Analysis and Policy*, **33** (1), 73–89.

Durden, G. C. and L. V. Ellis (1995), "The effects of attendance on student learning in principles of economics", *American Economic Review*, **85** (2), 343–6.

Dynan, K. E. and C. E. Rouse (1997), "The underrepresentation of women in economics: A study of undergraduate economics students", *Journal of Economic Education*, **28** (4), 350–68.

Greene, B. (1997), "Verbal abilities, gender and the introductory economics course: A new look at an old assumption", *Journal of Economic Education*, **28** (1), 13–30.

Grimes, P. W. (1994), "Public versus private secondary schools and the production of economics education", *Journal of Economic Education*, **25** (1), 17–30.

Hirschfeld, M., R. L. Moore and E. Brown (1995), "Exploring the gender gap in the GRE subject test in economics", *Journal of Economic Education*, **26** (1), 3–15.

Jensen, E. J. and A. L. Owen (2001), "Pedagogy, gender, and interest in economics", *Journal of Economic Education*, **32**, 323–43.

Jensen, E. J. and A. L. Owen (2003), "Appealing to good students in introductory economics", *Journal of Economic Education*, **34** (4), 299–325.

Lagerlof, J. N. M. and A. J. Seltzer (2009), "The effects of remedial mathematics on the learning of economics: Evidence from a natural experiment", *Journal of Economic Education*, **40** (2), 115–36.

Lopus, J. S. (1997), "Effects of high school economics curriculum on learning in the college principles class", *Journal of Economic Education*, **28** (2), 143–53.

Lopus, J. S. and N. L. Maxwell (1994), "Beyond high school: Does the high school economics curriculum make a difference?", *The American Economist*, **38** (1), 62–9.

Lumsden, K. G. and A. Scott (1987), "The economics student reexamined: Male-female differences in comprehension", *Journal of Economic Education*, **18** (4), 365–75.

Marburger, D. R. (2001), "Absenteeism and undergraduate exam performance", *Journal of Economic Education*, **32** (2), 99–109.

Massey, D. S. (2006), "Social background and academic performance differentials: White and minority students at selective colleges", *American Law and Economics Review*, **8** (2), 390–409.

Nowell, C. and R. M. Alston (2007), "I thought I got an A! Overconfidence across the economics curriculum", *Journal of Economic Education*, **38** (Spring), 131–42.

Owen, A. L. (2010), "Grades, gender and encouragement: A regression discontinuity analysis", *Journal of Economic Education*, **41** (3), 217–34.

Rask, K. and J. Tiefenthaler (2008), "The role of grade sensitivity in explaining the gender imbalance in undergraduate economics", *Economics of Education Review*, **27** (6), 676–87.

Rhine, S. L. (1989), "The effect of state mandates on student performance", *American Economic Review*, **79** (2), 231–5.

Romer, D. (1993), "Do students go to class? Should they?", *Journal of Economic Perspectives*, **7** (3), 167–74.

Stanca, L. (2006), "The effects of attendance on academic performance: Panel data evidence for introductory microeconomics", *Journal of Economic Education*, **37** (3), 251–66.

Swope, K. J. and P. M. Schmitt (2006), "The performance of economics graduates over the entire curriculum: The determinants of success", *Journal of Economic Education*, **37** (4), 387–94.

Von Allmen, P. and G. Brower (1998), "Calculus and the teaching of intermediate microeconomics: Results from a survey", *Journal of Economic Education*, **29** (3), 277–84.

Walstad, W. B. and K. Rebeck (2000), "The status of economics in the high school curriculum", *Journal of Economic Education*, **31** (2), 95–101.

Walstad, W. B. and J. C. Soper (1988), "A report card on the economic literacy of U.S. high school students", *American Economic Review*, **78** (2), 251–6.

Watts, M. (1987), "Student gender and school district differences affecting the stock and flow of economic knowledge", *Review of Economics and Statistics*, **69** (3), 561–6.

Williams, M. L., C. Waldauer and V. G. Duggal (1992), "Gender differences in economic knowledge: An extension of the analysis", *Journal of Economic Education*, **23** (3), 219–31.

Ziegert, A. L. (2000), "The role of personality temperament and student learning in principles of economics: Further evidence", *Journal of Economic Education*, **31** (4), 307–22.

33 Factors influencing student performance in economics: class and instructor characteristics[1]
Wayne A. Grove and Stephen Wu

Of the numerous characteristics that influence student performance in economics classes, this chapter focuses on the role played by the characteristics of the instructor, different course policies, and the nature of the class environment.[2] We begin with a discussion of various instructor characteristics, such as gender, nationality, quality and experience. Next, we highlight the importance of course policies, including graded problem sets and mandatory attendance. Finally, we discuss other elements of the class environment that may influence performance and the study of economics. These elements include class size, seating location, and the mathematical rigor of the class. We write this chapter with two audiences in mind: faculty who wish to improve their students' learning by seeking changes they can influence, and administrators controlling some of the remaining factors that faculty cannot manipulate.

Evaluating the role of class and instructor characteristics on student performance necessitates some discussion of measurement.[3] Many different measures of student achievement matter beyond grades within a particular course; namely, whether the student decides to drop the economics course in question, the extent to which students take additional economics courses, the decision to major or minor in economics, overall attrition in school, and the pursuit of a graduate degree in economics or a related field. The research surveyed uses a number of these measures, though most focus on grades within a particular class.

INSTRUCTOR CHARACTERISTICS

We begin our survey with a discussion of the importance that instructor characteristics play in affecting student outcomes in economics. While this chapter focuses on the discipline of economics, a large body of literature addresses how instructor characteristics affect student outcomes in post-secondary education.

Instructor Gender

One of the big questions facing researchers and academics is the underrepresentation of women undergraduates in certain academic fields, such as math and science. One explanation put forth for this student gender gap is instructor gender.

Within the discipline of economics, a number of studies have analyzed the role of instructor gender on student outcomes, examining effects on both grades in principles of economics courses and further study in economics. Dynan and Rouse (1997) find no effect of instructor gender on the decision to pursue an economics major. Robb and Robb (1999) obtain similar results: instructor gender has no effect on either performance in economics or the decision to continue in economics and this holds true for both men and women. Results by Jensen and Owen (2001) show that instructor gender does not strongly influence the decision to major in economics for students in general, although it does influence students who were not predisposed to continue in economics when they signed up for their first course. Thus, they find that instructors are more likely to "encourage" students of the same gender to take another economics course. McCarty et al. (2006) also show that matching student and instructor gender increases student improvement on the Test of Understanding College Economics (TUCE).[4]

The mixed results found in the economics literature are consistent with the broader higher education literature on the effects of instructor gender on student outcomes. Canes and Rosen (1995) show that the proportion of female faculty in a particular department is not related to students' major choices. However, their study is limited by the fact that they rely on aggregate measures rather than on microdata of the gender of particular instructor/student combinations. Bailey and Rask (2002) use detailed information obtained from student records, transcripts, and faculty records to study the impact that instructors have on the probability that students will pursue particular majors. They find significant "role model" effects: students that take introductory courses from instructors of the same gender are more likely to pursue a major in that department. This effect holds both for men taking courses from male faculty, and for women taking courses from female faculty.

Bettinger and Long (2005) get mixed results on the effects of instructor gender on student course choice. Female students who have a female instructor in introductory mathematics, geology, sociology, or journalism courses are more likely to take an additional course in the respective field. However, in other fields, there are no significant role model effects. Having a female instructor does not increase the likelihood of pursuing additional courses in fields such as engineering, physics, and computer science.

One difficulty of this literature is that some students may self-select into classes that are taught by instructors of the same gender. To address this issue, Carrell et al. (2010) take advantage of a random assignment of students to professors in the US Air Force Academy and find that although instructor gender has little impact on male students, it significantly affects female students' performance in math and science classes, their probability of taking additional math and science courses, and their likelihood of majoring in math, science, or engineering. Hoffman and Oreopoulos (2009b) focus on first-year courses in order to limit selection issues because first-year students cannot easily identify instructors. In contrast to Carrell et al. (2010), they find that having a same-gender instructor only marginally impacts student grades and the likelihood of dropping the course and does not have a significant effect on continuation of further courses within the department or major choice.

Instructor Race/Nationality

Another instructor characteristic that has often been linked to student performance and outcomes in higher education is nationality and/or race. Several papers analyze whether foreign-born instructors have an effect on student outcomes in economics courses. An early study by Watts and Lynch (1989) indicates that teaching assistants at Purdue University that were non-native English speakers had negative learning effects on students in a principles of economics course. Evidence from Borjas (2000) is also consistent with this study. For students in a large intermediate microeconomics class, those assigned to a tutorial section with a foreign-born teaching assistant perform worse than those with an American-born teaching assistant. However, Fleisher et al. (2002) find little evidence that foreign-born teaching assistants adversely affect student performance in a principles course. In fact, their results show that, in some cases, foreign-born TAs have *positive* effects on student grades in an economics course.

There is also research looking at the effect of student-instructor match along racial lines. Bailey and Rask (2002, also discussed above) find that minority students are more likely to continue studying economics when they have a minority faculty member as an instructor at the introductory level. Price (2010) shows that black students are more likely to continue in the fields of science, technology, engineering, or mathematics when they have black instructors at the introductory level. These results are consistent with the broader literature on the effects of having an own race teacher in primary and secondary school. Klopfenstein (2005) finds that increasing the percentage of high school math teachers that are black increases the likelihood that a black geometry student will enroll in a subsequent rigorous math course. There is also research that suggests that teacher perceptions of student performance and effort are strongly affected by racial dynamics (Dee, 2004). Specifically, both white and minority students are likely to be perceived more negatively by a teacher of a different race.

Instructor Quality

Instructor quality is another dimension which may affect college student outcomes. Of course, defining quality is not an easy task, and the literature uses a variety of measurements. Instructor quality is often proxied by indicators such as tenure-track or not, part- or full-time, rank, salary, publication record, etc. The evidence on these effects is mixed. In Ehrenberg and Zhang (2005), the share of faculty employed in part-time or full-time non tenure-track positions is negatively related to graduation rates across a broad set of institutions, based on aggregate data. Bettinger and Long (2010) find that the number of adjunct instructors in a department has either zero or positive effects on student interest in a particular field. The largest positive effects are present in the fields of education, engineering and the sciences. Hoffman and Oreopoulos (2009a) show that instructor traits such as faculty rank, salary and employment status (part- versus full-time) do not have significant effects on student performance. However, they find that subjective course evaluations are strongly linked with grades and future course choices. Students who take courses with instructors who generally receive high teaching evaluations receive higher grades, are less likely to drop the course and more likely to continue taking similar courses in future years.

Two innovative studies attempt to improve our understanding of professor quality impacts by measuring how students in introductory courses perform in subsequent courses that build upon the introductory course. Carrell and West (2010) analyze data from the exceptionally controlled curriculum of the US Air Force Academy (USAFA), where there is a strict course sequence for students that does not depend on performance in previous courses, and where many students take common exams across different sections of the same course. The authors find that professors who "teach to the test" and promote higher grades in their own contemporaneous courses actually have *negative* effects on the grades in future related courses. Students also reward teachers who provide value added to grades in current courses, but give lower evaluations to those who promote more permanent learning, as measured by performance in future courses. In related work, Fleisher et al. (2009) use data for nearly 50,000 enrollments in almost 400 offerings of principles of microeconomics, principles of macroeconomics, and intermediate microeconomics. In this study, learning, measured by future grades, is unrelated to student evaluations (once current grades have been controlled for) even though student evaluations are strongly related to grades.

COURSE POLICIES

Recitation Session

We now turn our focus to various course policies that may affect student learning. Having recitation sessions increases the number of contact hours a student has with an instructor, which may boost student learning. Huynh, Jacho-Chavez and Self (2009) find that introductory economics students who attend a recitation session (induced with grade incentives) improve their final grade by a third of a letter grade. Importantly, to overcome ethical constraints that limit some experimental studies, students were allowed to select into the recitation sessions (for example, the treatment group) rather than being randomly assigned and the authors controlled for student selection on observables with econometric techniques.[5, 6]

Required Homework

A few studies analyze the effect of homework assignments on student performance in economics courses. There are two main reasons that required and graded homework might affect student performance. Required homework may increase the amount of time spent studying material if students would not necessarily complete optional assignments. Also, if students know that assignments count towards their final grade, they may take them more seriously. This may enhance the learning that occurs during the completion of homework. Grove and Wasserman (2006) show that graded homework increases student performance by a third of a letter grade in an introductory economics course, relative to students in a parallel course taught by the same professor in the same semester without graded homework. Freshmen especially experienced this effect, a particularly important result given the high attrition rate among college students. Emerson and Mencken (forthcoming) design a comparable experiment using weekly, online, automated-graded homework assignments (via Aplia) – for one group, the final grade included the online homework grades, whereas for the other group, the online homework grades did not affect the course grade. In this study, students with the homework grade incentive perform about a third of a grade better on the final exam, but not on the TUCE, than the control group.

Mandatory Attendance

Numerous studies report a positive association between class attendance and perform-ance (for example, Marburger, 2006; Romer, 1993; Durden and Ellis, 1995), but to claim causation requires addressing the possible endogeneity between attendance and grades. To address this problem, two recent studies use panel data sets of higher education insti-tutions to take account of the effect of unobservable factors correlated with attendance, such as ability, effort and motivation: Arulampalam et al. (2007) for economics student cohorts at a UK university and Stanca (2006) for introductory economics students at the University of Milan. Stanca (2006) concludes that attendance has a small signifi-cant effect on performance; specifically, a single missed lecture lowered exam grades by half of a percentage point. While also concluding that missing classes leads to poorer performance, Arulampalam et al. (2007) find that absences are most detrimental for better-performing students.

Dobkin, Gil and Marion (2010) address the endogeneity concerns by using a regres-sion discontinuity design to study the effect of a policy of mandatory attendance for all students who score below the median on the first of two exams in three intermediate economics courses. They find that the post-midterm attendance was 36 percentage points higher for the compulsory attendance students just below the median grade, relative to those just above; students who increased attendance that much experienced more than half a standard deviation increase in performance on the final exam.

CLASS CHARACTERISTICS

Class Size

Persistent fiscal pressures encourage assigning more students per class to save money. Ultimately, good policymaking requires a cost-benefit analysis weighing any detrimental student outcomes against the cost savings of larger classes (for example, Krueger and Whitmore's (2001) analysis of Project STAR). Here we review what is known about (1) whether class size affects college students', especially economics students', achievement, (2) if so, by how much, and (3) for which students are the benefits the greatest? Although considerable attention has been paid to the role of class size and student performance in K-12 education, class size varies much more dramatically in higher education, for example, student class size within many institutions varies widely from fewer than ten in seminars to more than 500 for some introductory classes.

In elementary and secondary education, a number of studies that use experimental and quasi-experimental data show strong evidence that larger classes reduce learning (Krueger, 1999; Krueger and Whitmore, 2001; Angrist and Lavy, 2001; Urquiola, 2006), although other studies indicate little effects (Hanushek, 1999; Hoxby, 2000).[7] So, why might class size matter? Lazear (2001) theorizes that student behavior, namely disruptive in nature, links class size and student achievement. In the context of the collegiate class-room, where more self-directed learning occurs, large classes may reduce attentiveness and decrease the time available for individual students during office hours. Larger classes may also leave instructors little alternative to lecturing and to multiple choice exams. On the other hand, there may be mitigating factors that decrease the negative effect of large classes. Students and faculty may compensate for larger classes, altering their behavior by, for example, students' studying more outside of class and instructors specifically preparing for a large class.[8]

Studies of college student learning of economics and class size variation typically evaluate introductory courses and largely find no negative effects on standardized test scores of class sizes greater than 20 students (Kennedy and Siegfried, 1997). Beyond test scores, though, enrollment in large classes is associated with the following negative effects: (1) greater attrition from the course (Becker and Powers, 2001), (2) less enjoyment of the course, controlling for course grades (McConnell and Sosin, 1984; DeCanio, 1986), (3) lower student evaluation of teacher effectiveness (controlling for instructor and course fixed effects – Bedard and Kuhn, 2008), and (4) less subsequent enrollment in economics courses (Maxwell and Lopus, 1995).

Kennedy and Siegfried (1997) evaluate the impact of class size using TUCE III data for 36 introductory microeconomics and 33 introductory macroeconomics classes taught by many different professors at many different institutions of higher education, with class sizes ranging from 14 to 109. They find that, once proper control is made for student ability, class size does not influence achievement. As the authors note, a standardized exam comprised of multiple choice questions provides a limited measure of student achievement. They argue that the lack of class size impact is due either to the fact that faculty fail to teach classes of different sizes differently or that different class sizes affect some students positively and others negatively.

Two recent studies – one including data about economics courses, but both focused on college students generally – find strong negative effects of larger classes. Kokkelenberg et al. (2008), using data for over 760,000 undergraduate observations at a northeast public university, find average grade point declines as class size increases, precipitously up to 20 students and then more gradually beyond that. The negative effect holds for economics courses (and those in other disciplines), controlling for peer effects, student ability, year of student, level of course, gender, and minority status.

Using data for master's students at a leading UK university between 1999 and 2004, Bandiera et al. (2010) estimate class size effects from within-student variation based on their scores on end-of-semester standardized exams. They find large and negative effects only for the smallest and largest classes, but not for intermediary sizes. More precisely, moving a student from a class of ten to a class of 25 students or from 25 to 45 lowers their exam score by around 12.5 percent of within-student standard deviation, whereas moving from a class of 80 to one of 150 caused a further 25 percent drop. Interestingly, the best-performing students are most hurt by increases in class size, the reverse of what largely has been found for elementary and secondary students (see Schanzenbach, 2010).

Other Class Characteristics

In a multi-school study of online versus in-class student learning of principles of economics, Coates et al. (2004) show that selection-corrected TUCE scores were significantly lower for the online course, especially so for first- and second-year students. In Dills and Hernandez-Julian (2008), there is some evidence that college students generally earn higher grades in classes that meet more often. In addition, students appear to perform better in late afternoon classes that they select into. There is even evidence that where you sit in a classroom affects exam performance (Benedict and Hoag, 2004). Specifically, students that are forced to move closer to the front of the classroom tend to receive higher grades, despite their preferences for seats at the back of the classroom.

CONCLUSION

Given the fiscal pressures facing colleges and universities, faculty and administrators should have a clear understanding of the benefits of policy variables, for example class size and pedagogical approaches, on student outcomes. Among academics, economists have the necessary analytic methods to provide comparative cost-benefit analyses of higher education policies to improve student achievement. Thus, what economists and higher education administrators need is a systematic research plan to conduct experimental studies, similar to what we have reported regarding class size, to evaluate the efficacy of different pedagogical approaches and of policy variables, such as online classes, the day and time of classes, and split or single course introductory economics classes.

NOTES

1. For helpful comments, we thank the co-editors of this volume and Elizabeth Jensen.
2. A survey of the relationship between student characteristics, behavior and performance in economics can be found in the chapter bearing that name in this volume.
3. For information on measuring student performance, see Chapter 16, "Methods of Assessment in the College Economics Course", in this volume.
4. For a description of this and related measurements, see Chapter 29, "Measurement Techniques of Student Performance and Literacy: College and High School", in this volume.
5. Econometric techniques especially useful for economic education research are further described in Chapter 35, "Data Resources and Econometric Techniques", in this volume and in "Econometric Training Modules", developed by William Becker: http://www.vanderbilt.edu/AEA/AEACEE/Econometrics_Handbook/index.htm (accessed 11 May 2011).
6. Although Huynh, Jacho-Chavez and Self (2009) argue for the efficacy of cooperative learning which was the pedagogical approach used in the recitation sessions, they actually test attendance versus non-attendance at recitation sessions (not a cooperative learning versus a non-cooperative learning session). Thus, one may interpret their results more broadly as the impact of attending a recitation session.
7. See Schanzenbach (2010) for a brief review of this literature.
8. For more information about how instructors prepare for such classes, see Chapter 10, "Making the Large Enrollment Course Interactive and Engaging", in this volume

REFERENCES

Angrist, J. and V. Lavy (2001), "Does teacher training affect pupil learning? Evidence from matched comparisons in Jerusalem public schools", *Journal of Labor Economics*, **19** (2), 343–69.
Arulampalam, W., R. A. Naylor and J. Smith (2007), "Am I missing something? The effects of absence from class on student performance", mimeo, University of Warwick.
Bailey, E. M. and K. N. Rask (2002), "Are we role models? Major choice in an undergraduate institution", *Journal of Economic Education*, **33** (2), 99–124.
Bandiera, O., V. Larcinese and I. Rasul (2010), "Heterogeneous class size effects: New evidence from a panel of university students", *The Economic Journal*, **120** (549), 1365–98.

Becker, W. and J. Powers (2001), "Student performance, attrition, and class size given missing student data", *Economics of Education Review*, **20** (4), 377–88.

Bedard, K. and P. Kuhn (2008), "Where class size really matters: Class size and student ratings of instructor effectiveness", *Economics of Education Review*, **27** (3), 253–65.

Benedict, M. E. and J. Hoag (2004), "Seating location in large lectures: Are seating preferences or location related to course performance?", *Journal of Economic Education*, **35** (3), 215–31.

Bettinger, E. and B. T. Long (2005), "Do faculty serve as role models? The impact of instructor gender on female students", *American Economic Review*, **95** (4), 152–7.

Bettinger, E. and B. T. Long (2010), "Does cheaper mean better? The impact of using adjunct instructors on student outcomes", *Review of Economics and Statistics*, **92** (3), 598–613.

Borjas, G. (2000), "Foreign born TAs and the academic performance of undergraduates", *American Economic Review: Papers and Proceedings*, **90** (2), 355–9.

Canes, B. and H. Rosen (1995), "Following in her footsteps? Faculty gender composition and women's choices of college majors", *Industrial and Labor Relations Review*, **48** (1), 486–504.

Carrell, S. and J. West (2010), "Does professor quality matter? Evidence from random assignment of students to professors", *Journal of Political Economy*, **118** (3), 409–32.

Carrell, S., M. Page and J. West (2010), "Sex and science: How professor gender perpetuates the gender gap", *Quarterly Journal of Economics*, **125** (3), 1101–44.

Coates, D., B. R. Humphreys, J. Kane and M. A. Vachris (2004), "No significant distance between face-to-face and online instruction: Evidence from principles of economics", *Economics of Education Review*, **23** (5), 533–46.

DeCanio, S. J. (1986), "Student evaluations of teaching: A multinomial logit approach", *Journal of Economic Education*, **16** (3), 165–76.

Dee, T. (2004), "The race connection", *Education Next*, **4** (2), 53–9.

Dills, A. K. and R. Hernandez-Julian (2008), "Course scheduling and academic performance", *Economics of Education Review*, **27** (6), 646–54.

Dobkin, C., R. Gil and J. Marion (2010), "Skipping class in college and exam performance: Evidence from a regression discontinuity classroom experiment", *Economics of Education Review*, **29** (4), 566–75.

Durden, C. and V. Ellis (1995), "The effects of attendance on student learning in principles of economics", *American Economic Review*, **85** (2), 343–6.

Dynan, K. and C. Rouse (1997), "The underrepresentation of women in economics: A study of undergraduate economics students", *Journal of Economic Education*, **28** (4), 350–68.

Ehrenberg, R. and L. Zhang (2005), "Do tenured and tenure-track faculty matter?", *Journal of Human Resources*, **40** (3), 647–59.

Emerson, T. L. and K. D. Mencken (forthcoming), "Homework: To require or not require? Online graded homework and student achievement", *Perspectives in Economic Education Research*.

Fleisher, B., M. Hashimoto and B. Weinberg (2002), "Foreign GTAs can be effective teachers of economics", *Journal of Economic Education*, **33** (4), 299–325.

Grove, W. A. and T. Wasserman (2006), "Incentives and student learning: A natural experiment with economics problem sets", *American Economic Review*, **96** (2), 447–52.

Hanushek, E. (1999), "The evidence on class size", in S. Mayer and P. Peterson (eds), *Earning and Learning: How Schools Matter*, Washington, DC: Brookings Institution Press, pp. 131–68.

Hoffman, F. and P. Oreopoulos (2009a), "Professor qualities and student performance", *Review of Economics and Statistics*, **91** (1), 83–92.

Hoffmann, F. and P. Oreopoulos (2009b), "A professor like me: The influence of instructor gender on university achievement", *Journal of Human Resources*, **44** (2), 479–94.

Hoxby, C. (2000), "The effects of class size on student achievement: New evidence from population variation", *Quarterly Journal of Economics*, **115** (4), 1239–85.

Huynh, K. P., D. T. Jacho-Chavez and J. K. Self (2009), "The efficacy of collaborative learning recitation sessions on student outcomes", *American Economic Review*, **100** (2), 287–91.

Jensen, E. and A. Owen (2001), "Pedagogy, gender, and interest in economics", *Journal of Economic Education*, **32** (4), 323–43.

Kennedy, P. E. and J. J. Siegfried (1997), "Class size and achievement in introductory economics: Evidence from the TUCE III Data", *Economics of Education Review*, **16** (4), 385–94.

Klopfenstein, K. (2005), "Beyond test scores: The impact of black teacher role models on rigorous math-taking", *Contemporary Economic Policy*, **23** (3), 1–13.

Kokkelenberg, E. C., M. Dillon and S. M. Christy (2008), "The effects of class size on student grades at a public university", *Economics of Education Review*, **27** (2), 221–33.

Krueger, A. B. (1999), "Experimental estimates of education production functions", *Quarterly Journal of Economics*, **114** (2), 497–532.

Krueger, A. B. and D. Whitmore (2001), "The effect of attending a small class in the early grades on college-test taking and middle school test results: Evidence from Project STAR", *Economic Journal*, **111** (1992), 1–28.

Lazear, E. P. (2001), "Educational Production", *Quarterly Journal of Economics*, **116** (3), 777–803.

Marburger, D. R. (2006), "Does mandatory attendance improve student performance?", *Journal of Economic Education*, **37** (2), 148–55.

Maxwell, N. and J. Lopus (1995), "Cost effectiveness analysis of large and small classes in the university", *Educational Evaluation and Policy Analysis*, **17** (2), 167–78.

McCarty, C., G. Pagham and D. Bennett (2006), "Determinants of student achievement in principles of economics", *Journal of Economics Educators*, **6** (2), 1–9.

McConnell, C. R. and K. Sosin (1984), "Some determinants of student attitudes toward large classes", *Journal of Economic Education*, **15** (3), 181–90.

Price, J. (2010), "The effect of instructor race and gender on persistence in STEM fields", *Economics of Education Review,* **29** (6), 901–10.

Robb, R. and A. Robb (1999), "Gender and the study of economics: The role of gender of the instructor", *Journal of Economic Education*, **30** (1), 3–19.

Romer, D. (1993), "Do students go to class? Should they?", *Journal of Economic Perspectives*, **7** (3), 167–74.

Schanzenbach, D. (2010), "The economics of class size", in E. Baker, B. McGaw and P. Peterson (eds), *International Encyclopedia of Education*, Amsterdam: Elsevier Publishers, pp. 183–90.

Stanca, L. (2006), "The effects of attendance on academic performance: Panel data evidence for introductory microeconomics", *Journal of Economic Education*, **37** (3), 251–66.

Urquiola, M. (2006), "Identifying class size effects in developing countries: Evidence from rural Bolivia", *The Review of Economics and Statistics*, **88** (1), 171–7.

Watts, M. and G. Lynch (1989), "The principles course revisited", *American Economic Review Papers and Proceedings*, **79** (2), 236–41.

Section D

What Every Economist Should Know about the Evaluation of Teaching: A Review of Literature

34 What every economist should know about the evaluation of teaching: a review of the literature
Stephen B. DeLoach

The subject of teaching evaluations is uniformly controversial within academe. Despite decades of research verifying their reliability, their validity continues to be questioned by researchers and faculty. One reason is that such methods only consider a relatively small number of factors that correlate with "good instruction." Even though these limitations are well-established in the literature and widely acknowledged by faculty, the implementation of alternative or complimentary forms of assessment is far from universal.

What students are capable of assessing does not always coincide with what is required for learning. Evaluation of teaching and evaluation of learning are two different things (Becker and Watts, 1999). Evidence strongly suggests that students can reliably assess factors such as teaching skill, rapport with students, organization, difficulty, and feedback (Paulsen, 2002). They cannot assess subject mastery, curriculum development and course design (Arreola, 2000; Chism, 1999).

The literature also indicates that student evaluations of teaching are biased. Four factors are routinely cited as primary sources for these biases. These include prior interest in subject, expected grades, perceived workload, and reasons for taking course (Marsh, 1987). Interestingly, recent research in economics by Weinberg, Hashimoto and Fleisher (2009) shows that these biases may also have disparate effects on different courses. The implication is that one-sized-fits-all evaluations are inappropriate.

The vast majority of existing methods of evaluating instruction are mandated by administrators and designed at the university level (Becker and Watts, 1999). Nevertheless, it is difficult to argue that good economics instruction is the same as good biology or language instruction. As a result, university-administered student evaluations of teaching are likely to capture only a small portion of what we might believe is relevant for economics. With all the controversy over the use of student evaluations to assess effective teaching, one might think that economics departments have developed more sophisticated instruments to use in assessing instruction. While alternative methods exist, departments have been slow to implement anything but the most superficial of these alternatives.

The purpose of this chapter is to review the current methods used to assess teaching. While evaluations can be used either for summative or formative purposes, the evidence strongly suggests that most departments are primarily concerned with summative feedback. This will be the primary focus of this chapter. Different methods for evaluating teaching are reviewed, including evidence of their prevalence across both economics and the academy in general, with special attention paid to research on the reliability and validity of alternative assessments. This is followed by a description of the use of assessments, including both summative and formative uses. The chapter concludes with some recommendations for the discipline.

REVIEW OF CURRENT METHODS FOR ASSESSING TEACHING

Fundamentally, there are two ways of formally assessing instruction: (1) student end-of-course evaluations; and (2) peer evaluation.[1] The choice of method by departments and universities depends on a number of factors, including the purpose of the evaluation (in other words, annual merit raises, promotion and tenure, etc.), the size of the institution, and the mission of the school or department (in other words, liberal arts colleges, research universities, PhD programs, etc.).

Student Evaluation

The most common method of evaluating teaching, even at liberal arts colleges, is end-of-course student evaluations. These evaluations typically consist of fixed-response questions scored on a Likert scale (Cashin, 1999; Seldin, 1999), complemented by open-ended questions where students can write their opinions of the instructor's relative strengths and weaknesses. In their 1998 survey, Becker and Watts (1999) found that 83 percent of economics departments used fixed-response qualitative measurement instruments with open-ended questions on forms. Areas most often assessed include overall effectiveness, communication skills, organization, and knowledge of material; the least likely are decorum, use of technology, rapport and use of applications and examples.

Research suggests that such evaluations have high inter-rater reliability.[2] Centra (1993) notes that, as long as more than ten students are surveyed, inter-rater reliability is generally high (0.70 and higher). Reliability over time is also good, with inter-rater reliability of at least 0.83 (Marsh and Dunkin, 1997). Reliability, however, is not the same as validity. In general, metrics must meet both criteria to be considered good measures of teaching effectiveness.

One way of assessing validity is how correlated student measures are with other forms of evaluation, referred to as "construct validity" (Marsh, 2007). Here, the evidence appears to support validity. For example Feldman (1989a) finds that students' end-of-course evaluations are correlated with alumni (0.69), instructors (0.29), colleagues (0.55), administrators (0.39), and external, trained evaluators (0.50). Despite the demonstrated construct validity, this still falls short of validating whether student evaluations are correlated with student learning.

Validation of learning experiments typically employs multiple sections of a course. Not surprisingly, a number of tight controls are needed to make these experiments well-designed.[3] Sections must use the same textbook, variation in student enrollment must be controlled (through either randomized assignment or econometric sample selection controls), and consistent pre- and post-tests must be administered. In an analysis of 41 suitably designed studies, Cohen (1987) found that student achievement was positively correlated with factors typically evaluated by students on end-of-course assessments. For example, learning was correlated with student assessments on factors such as course structure (0.55), interaction (0.52), instructor skill (0.50), overall course (0.49), overall instructor (0.45), rapport (0.32), and feedback (0.28).

A great deal of evidence shows measures of teaching effectiveness are biased by a number of factors, including prior interest in the subject, expected grades, perceived workload, and reasons for taking course (Marsh, 1987). However, not all biases are evidence of a lack of validity (Marsh, 2007). In fact, many of the factors affecting student evaluations *should* affect both learning and teacher effectiveness. Examples of these include class size and prior interest in the subject. Not surprisingly, the most controversial bias factor is grades.

A number of studies find evidence that grading leniency increases student end-of-course evaluations, but the effect appears to be relatively small (Marsh 2007). Recent evidence in economics is more damning. In a study from principles sections at Ohio State University from 1995–2004, Weinberg et al. (2009) find that a student's current grade is a significantly positive determinant of evaluation scores. In contrast to earlier studies, Weinberg et al. (2009) find an extremely large effect of grades on evaluations. Interestingly, the grade-induced bias is roughly triple for macroeconomics than for microeconomics courses. Moreover, they find that after controlling for current grade, learning is not significantly correlated with student evaluation scores.

With the growing use of online methods for administering student evaluations, many fear that sample selection bias has further eroded the validity and reliability of student evaluations. However, the existing evidence appears to refute this. The obvious advantage in such systems has to do with the cost and ease of implementation. One unexpected advantage in online evaluations is that students appear to write longer, more detailed comments (Hardy, 2003). The main concern in administering evaluations online is the response rate. As expected, response rates are lower with web-based evaluations than with traditional methods (Hardy, 2003; Avery et al., 2006). While this increases the standard error of point estimates, there is little evidence that mean ratings are significantly affected. In a recent study in a large economics-based public policy school, Avery et al. (2006) found virtually no difference in mean responses to any of the survey questions. They did, however, find evidence that *who responds* differs online. Females and those expecting higher grades were significantly more likely to respond. Their evidence also suggests that response rates increase over time once web-based systems are implemented.

As serious as the concerns over the validity of student evaluations is the criticism that they only assess a limited set of factors related to good teaching (Becker, 2000). Even if valid, they represent a narrow range of factors generally accepted as necessary for effective teaching. According to Cashin (1999), students are in a position to evaluate delivery of instruction, clarity of presentation, availability to students and administrative requirements. They cannot evaluate subject mastery, curriculum development and course design, factors appropriate for peer evaluation (Arreola, 2000; Chism, 1999).

Peer Review

Despite widespread acknowledgment that it is needed, peer review is significantly less prevalent than student-based evaluations of teaching. At a minimum, peer assessment is needed to evaluate course content. Since faculty members' work is valued more highly when it is subjected to rigorous review, peer review should result in the increased importance of teaching in the overall evaluation of faculty (Chism, 1999). The most commonly employed method is direct classroom observation, although the use of teaching portfolios is increasing.

According to Seldin (1999), undergraduate institutions – liberal arts colleges and small universities – are the most likely to use peer review of teaching. Collecting data from liberal arts colleges over a twenty-year period from 1978–98, Seldin (1999) reports that, as early as 1978, nearly half of all liberal arts colleges claimed to require peer review in the form of committee review, even more by the Dean and department chair. However, in 1978 less than 15 percent of liberal arts colleges mandated either classroom visits or review of teaching materials by peers as part of the review process. By 1998 this figure had grown to over 40 percent. Interestingly, nearly 10 percent of colleges also report that analysis of grade distributions is part of the review process. Overall, these findings suggest that the evaluation of teaching is becoming more multifaceted and sophisticated.

Seldin's findings are consistent with what appears to be going on in economics departments as well. White (1995) found that 26 percent of departments required classroom visits and 30 percent reviewed teaching materials; 59 percent used multiple methods, including formal and informal follow-ups. In a later, more comprehensive survey, Becker and Watts (1999) found that 52 percent of Bachelor, 51 percent of Master's, 42 percent of Doctoral, and 37 percent of Research institutions required some form of peer review. While classroom observation was most frequently cited, review of syllabi, exams and other materials were also reported. Becker and Watts (1999) report that department chairs are typically the ones that appoint peer-evaluators. For the most part, this consists of classroom visits, but may also include reviews of syllabi, tests, and other materials. Ironically, White (1995) reports a general reluctance for classroom visits, which are typically only required for junior faculty.

While there is a wealth of research indicating the validity and reliability of student evaluations of teaching, the same is not true for peer review. Not surprisingly, most of the work has focused on classroom observation (Cohen and McKeachie, 1980; Feldman, 1989b). In general, those studies find a notable lack of reliability. However, the reliability of peer review using teaching portfolios appears to show more promise. Root (1987) finds reliability rates of 0.90 using a common faculty committee to assess research, service and teaching based on portfolios assembled by the individual faculty member. Unfortunately such results are not universal (Centra, 1994). Two key factors that account for differences in reliability rates are the selection and training of peer reviewers. For example, Centra (2000) finds that acceptable reliability rates can be obtained when evaluators are not selected by the individual being reviewed. In general, he suggests that small committees, formed for three-year periods, be used to conduct peer reviews. Others argue that reliability rates also increase when the content of portfolios is relatively uniform (Seldin, 1993; Chism, 1999).

Partly because of reliability problems and partly because of faculty antipathy, the focus appears to be turning from classroom observation towards committee review of teaching portfolios. This begs the question of "what to review?" Most argue that portfolios should include a broad range of sample work, syllabi, test, etc. There is universal agreement that peers should receive training that includes methods, standards, and criteria. At a minimum, small committees of between three to six reviewers should be used. Seldin (1999) recommends the following mandatory elements: reflective instructor statement about approach, three years of student evaluations, three years of syllabi for all courses taught, innovative instructional material, and evidence of activities to improve one's teaching.[4]

USE OF ASSESSMENTS

Whether by students or peers, the evaluation of teaching can be used for formative or summative purposes. For evaluations to be used formatively, faculty must value the input of the evaluator and be willing to change behavior.

While theoretically student evaluations can be used for formative purposes, the reality is that they are not. Evidence shows that instructors do not use student evaluations to significantly change their course or their classroom behavior. In a study of 195 teachers over a 13-year period, Marsh and Hocevar (1991) found little change in instructor ratings over time. Ironically, Roche and Marsh (2002) found that student evaluations did change instructor perceptions about their own teaching, as their self-assessments converged with students over time. Thus, student assessments are used by instructors to provide information about the quality of their teaching, but they do not motivate changes in teaching practices. This is precisely why many scholars argue for the importance of alternative systems to complement the use of student evaluations.

Unlike student evaluations, peer evaluation is (theoretically) more likely to result in changes in behavior because the evaluator is qualified to judge the most important aspects of good teaching (Becker, 2000). Because of this, many colleges and universities have established "teaching centers", which, along with supporting scholarship on teaching and learning, typically offer consultation services. Since these centers typically do consultations with faculty directly, such feedback is formative in nature. There is considerable evidence that student evaluations supplemented by professional peer consultations can lead to significant improvements in teaching (Penny and Coe, 2004). One must be cautious in making broad generalizations about the effectiveness of this process as faculty typically self-select into consultations. Also, these groups are not disciplinary experts and thus are limited in the areas of expertise.

The desire to supplement student evaluations helps explain the growing interest in peer evaluation for formative purposes. At the same time, there is little evidence that peer evaluation plays much of a role in summative assessments. Becker and Watts (1999) report that peer assessments were a relatively small part of the overall assessment of teaching used in determining annual merit raises (24, 18, 14, and 11 percent of the teaching assessment at Bachelor, Master's, Doctoral and Research institutions, respectively). Since peer evaluation in economics departments does not appear to be either widespread or highly valued, there is little reason to believe that faculty members have the incentive to respond to potential criticism from their disciplinary peers.

While there is little evidence that faculty use student evaluations for formative purposes, these evaluations do appear to play an important role in summative decisions. In the absence of widespread peer review, any summative assessment of teaching relies predominantly on student evaluations. Moreover, there is evidence that teaching performance is factored into the determination of annual raises, tenure and promotion decisions (Becker and Watts, 1999). Not surprisingly, the relative importance of teaching differs by type of institution. For annual raises, teaching is important for 43 percent of Bachelor, 38 percent of Master's, 37 percent of Doctoral, and 27 percent of Research institutions. The rates are similar for tenure and promotion decisions.

Overall, the evidence suggests that (1) unless used in conjunction with consultation services, faculty do not use student evaluations for formative purposes; (2) peer review in economics departments is not widely used and, when it is, it is not highly valued; (3) summative decisions are being made almost exclusively on the basis of student end-of-course evaluations; and (4) evaluations of teaching play a significant role in decisions regarding annual merit raises, tenure, and promotions.

CONCLUSION

Despite the plea over a decade ago by Becker and Watts (1999) for economics departments to invest time and energy in using peer review of teaching, it appears little has changed. While teaching effectiveness is a major factor in determining raises and promotions at nearly every institution, economics departments appear to be content to leave such decisions in the hands of undergraduate students. While the research shows students can potentially assess some of the characteristics of good teaching, there is strong reason to believe that biases exist in student evaluations. Even if student evaluations are reliable, they cannot validly assess many of the factors that relate to learning. This is the best argument for peer review. Only colleagues have the disciplinary expertise to assess whether course material is appropriate, whether it facilitates learning and academic challenge and whether it meets departmental goals.

This chapter highlights the need for economists to do more rigorous research on the relative validity of different methods of assessing teaching effectiveness. With few exceptions, the literature focuses almost exclusively on student evaluations. Though a trend towards the increased use of peer review appears to be taking place, in economics and across the academy, there has been little research to validate peer review. Moreover, most research on the effectiveness of teaching has been conducted in other disciplines or at institutional levels. But, as Becker and Watts (1999) argue, there is reason to believe that teaching in economics is different, with a unique approach and specific learning outcomes. As the recent evidence from Weinberg et al. (2009) shows, this may even extend to differences across courses. Taken together, considerably more research into the assessment of teaching *in economics* needs to be undertaken.

NOTES

1. There are other methods that are more formative in nature, such as mid-semester evaluations. In addition, many institutions now offer teaching consultations to faculty.
2. There are a number of excellent meta-analyses on the topic. See Centra (1993), Paulsen (2002), and Marsh (2007).
3. For more information about good research design, see Chapter 35, "Data Resources and Econometric Techniques", in this volume.
4. See Chism (1999) for more about how to design and operate peer evaluations systems.

REFERENCES

Arreola, R. (2000), *Developing a Comprehensive Faculty Evaluation System: A Handbook for College Faculty and Administrators on Designing and Operating a Comprehensive Faculty Evaluation System*, Bolton, US. Anker.

Avery, R. J., W.K. Bryan, A. Mathios, H. Kang and D. Bell (2006), "Electronic course evaluations: Does an online delivery system influence student evaluations?", *Journal of Economic Education*, **37** (1), 21–37.

Becker, W.E. (2000), "Teaching economics in the 21st Century", *The Journal of Economic Perspectives*, **14** (1), 109–19.

Becker, W.E. and M. Watts (1999), "The state of economic education: How departments of economics evaluate teaching", *The American Economic Review*, **89** (2), 334–49.

Cashin, W. E. (1999), "Student ratings of teaching: Uses and misuses", in Peter Seldin (ed.), *Current Practices in Evaluating Teaching: A Practical Guide to Improved Faculty Performance and Promotion/Tenure Decisions*, Bolton, US: Anker, pp. 24–44.

Centra, J. A. (1993), *Reflective Faculty Evaluation: Enhancing Teaching and Determining Faculty Effectiveness*, San Francisco, US: Jossey-Bass.

Centra, J. A. (1994), "The use of the teaching portfolio and student evaluations for summative evaluation", *Journal of Higher Education*, **65** (5), 555–70.

Centra, J. A. (2000), "Evaluating the teaching portfolio: A role for colleagues", *New Directions for Teaching and Learning*, **83** (Fall), 87–93.

Chism, N. (1999), *Peer Review of Teaching: A Sourcebook*, Bolton, US: Anker.

Cohen, P. A. (1987), "A Critical Analysis and Reanalysis of the Multi-section Validity Meta-Analysis", Paper presented at the Annual Meeting of the American Educational Research Association (Washington, DC, April 20–24).

Cohen, P. A., and W.J. McKeachie (1980), "The role of colleagues in the evaluation of college teaching", *Improving College and University Teaching*, **28** (4), 147–54.

Feldman, K. A. (1989a), "The association between student ratings of specific instructional dimensions and student achievement", *Research in Higher Education*, **30** (6), 583–645.

Feldman, K. A. (1989b), "Instructional effectiveness of college teachers as judged by teachers themselves, current and former students, colleagues, administrators, and external (neutral) observers", *Research in Higher Education*, **30** (2), 113–35.

Hardy, N. (2003), "Online ratings: Fact and fiction", *New Directions for Teaching and Learning*, **96** (Winter), 31–8.

Marsh, H. W. (1987), "Students' evaluations of university teaching: Research findings, methodological issues, and directions for future research", *International Journal of Educational Research*, **11** (3), 253–388.

Marsh, H. W. (2007), "Students' evaluations of university teaching", in R. P. Perry and J. C. Smarts (eds), *The Scholarship of Teaching and Learning in Higher Education: An Evidence-based Perspective*, Netherlands: Springer, pp. 319–83.

Marsh, H. W. and M. J. Dunkin (1997), "Students' evaluations of university teaching: A multi-dimensional perspective", in R. P. Perry and J. C. Smart (eds), *Effective Teaching in Higher Education: Research and Practice*, New York, US: Agathon Press, pp. 241–320.

Marsh, H. W. and D. Hocevar (1991), "Students' evaluations of teaching effectiveness: the stability of mean ratings of the same teachers over a 13-year period", *Teaching and Teacher Education*, **7** (4), 303–14.

Paulsen, Michael B. (2002), "Evaluating teaching performance", *New Directions for Institutional Research*, **114** (Summer), 5–18.

Penny, A. R. and R. Coe (2004), "Effectiveness of consultation on student ratings feedback: A meta analysis", *Review of Educational Research*, **74** (2), 215–53.

Roche, L. A. and H. W. Marsh (2002), "Teaching self-concept in higher education: Reflecting on multiple dimensions of teaching effectiveness," in N. Hativa and P. Goodyear (eds), *Teacher Thinking, Beliefs and Knowledge in Higher Education*, Dordrecht: Kluwer, pp. 179–218.

Root, L. S. (1987), "Faculty evaluation: Reliability of peer assessments of research, teaching and service", *Research in Higher Education*, **26** (1), 71–84.

Seldin, Peter (1993), *Successful Use of Teaching Portfolios*, Bolton, US: Anker.

Seldin, Peter (1999), *Changing Practices in Evaluating Teaching: A Practical Guide to Improved Faculty Performance and Promotion/Tenure Decisions*, Bolton, US: Anker, pp. 1–24.

Weinberg, Bruce A., Belton M. Fleisher and Masanori Hashimoto (2009), "Evaluating teaching in higher education", *The Journal of Economic Education*, **40** (3), 227–61.

White, Lawrence J. (1995), "Efforts by departments of economics to assess teaching effectiveness: Results of an informal survey", *The Journal of Economic Education*, **26** (1) 81–85.

Section E

Scholarship of Teaching and Learning

35 Data resources and econometric techniques
William Bosshardt and Peter E. Kennedy

Data in economics education are typically cross-section or panel in nature, and almost never have a substantive time series dimension. They appear in a wide variety of forms, however, and span the full range of problems and techniques found in econometrics textbooks. Consequently researchers in this area need to be well-versed in applied econometrics, able to deal with ordered data, count data, duration models, measurement errors, heteroskedasticity, simultaneity, sample selection, clustering, limited dependent variables, panel data, and multicollinearity, to give just a few examples. Fortunately there are plenty of good sources of help in this regard. Econometrics textbooks contain detailed accounts of these standard econometric problems and techniques, and William Becker has provided an exposition of several common econometric techniques employed in economics education, along with extremely valuable appendices showing how to implement them in three popular econometrics software packages.[1]

Because textbooks provide such thorough expositions of econometric techniques, from the elementary to the expert level, it does not make sense for this chapter to present more of the same. Instead, in addition to describing data resources, this chapter discusses good practice when applying econometrics to address research topics in economic education, with particular reference to mistakes that researchers in this area are prone to make.[2] As will be seen, these mistakes are more often elementary errors in logic rather than sophisticated errors involving technical econometric matters; a major lesson from this chapter is that although empirical work in economic education occasionally involves advanced econometric techniques, a more important dimension of work in this area is that it be thought out carefully. Indeed, as articulated by Angrist and Pischke (2009, p. xi), some advanced econometric techniques "are needlessly complex and may even be harmful."

THE GOLD STANDARD

In the economics education literature, the most frequently encountered empirical specification is an "educational production function" in which student performance is written as a function of relevant explanatory variables. Student "performance" is typically the score on an examination, and the most common explanatory variables are characteristics of the student (such as ability and sex), characteristics of the instructor (such as experience and clarity of explanations), and characteristics of the course (such as use of a novel teaching technique). The simplest manifestation of this is a "controlled experiment" investigating the impact of some "treatment" such as a novel teaching technique. One group of students is exposed to the treatment, and an outcome measure of this group is compared with the outcome of a control group. In a controlled experiment the researcher assigns students randomly to the two groups, and ensures that the two groups are treated in identical fashion except for the treatment. The impact of the treatment is assessed by comparing the average outcomes of the two groups.

This experimental design is viewed as a "gold standard" to which research in economic education should aspire,[3] because it allows a researcher to draw conclusions without employing sophisticated econometric techniques that inevitably require assumptions that cloud conclusions. Despite this, more often than not, advanced econometric techniques are employed in published research in this area, because, in most cases, the students have not been assigned to the two groups randomly. The data have not come from a controlled experiment and so are contaminated by problems such as selection bias and other dissimilarities between the two groups. Indeed, the main reason that econometrics evolved as a discipline separate from statistics was because economic data do not in general come from controlled experiments and so special empirical techniques are needed to overcome the resulting non-randomness.

Suppose a researcher wishes to assess the impact of a novel teaching technique and to this end arranges for one class (the control class) to be taught in the usual way and another (the treatment class) to be taught using the new technique. We address several features of this research setup that should guide econometric work, followed by an extended discussion of selection bias problems, which seems to be the most common dilemma faced by researchers in economic education.

The output measure needs to be fully described and defended   If interest focuses on learning of the course material, this measure must not be contaminated by things like marks for attendance or hand-in assignments which do not unequivocally correspond to learning. A best measure here is typically score on a comprehensive final exam.

The output measure must be directly comparable for the two classes   In the example above this means that the two classes must write exactly the same final exam. Without this feature, the experiment fails, and no amount of sophisticated econometrics can save it.

The two classes must be operated identically except for the treatment   The same instructor must teach both classes, using the same textbook, readings and assignments. Failure on this score also means that the experiment fails. Ideally they should be at equally attractive times of the day/week (because attendance differences may contaminate the results), and be in the same semester (because fall semester students are typically not similar to spring semester students). Failure to control these features is not fatal, but requires that conclusions be qualified.

For the "gold standard," assignment of students to the two classes must be done via a process that is essentially equivalent to random assignment   There should be no reason to believe that the students in the treatment class are on the whole different in some important respect from students in the control class, particularly so in regard to unmeasured characteristics. If the data satisfy this requirement, the econometrics simplifies immensely and the results are much more credible. With random assignment, the impact of the treatment is directly measured by the difference between the mean scores of the treatment and control classes, and testing the null hypothesis of no difference can be done via a simple t test.[4]

Two things are required to justify a random assignment assumption First, the average measured characteristics and outcomes of both classes should be reported in a table, along with t tests of their differences, so that readers can see for themselves what differences might exist between the two classes. This should always be done, regardless of whether random assignment is claimed. Second, the nature of the class assignment mechanism should be discussed fully to convince readers that there are no unmeasured differences between the two classes. If, for example, one class filled up early during registration and so the second class was introduced, the students in the first class, compared to the second class, would be more eager, organized and enthusiastic, unmeasured characteristics that would surely affect their performance.[5]

Use regression analysis if measurable differences occur between the two classes If a researcher is confident that there are no unmeasured differences between the two classes, but the table of measured differences indicates that there are measured differences, regression analysis is the appropriate alternative to simply comparing average final exam scores across the two classes. By regressing final exam scores on a treatment dummy and whatever explanatory variables are thought to be of consequence among the measured characteristics,[6] the estimated coefficient on the treatment dummy measures the impact of the treatment, holding constant all those characteristics included as regressors. The inferiority of the regression procedure stems from having to assume a particular functional form for the regression. Typically a linear functional form is employed, but unknown nonlinearities, such as cross-product terms, squared terms and logged values, may be more realistic, and specification search procedures undertaken by the researcher may lead to results favored by the researcher but not most accurately reflecting reality.

DEALING WITH SELECTION PROBLEMS

When assignment has not been random and so there is a possibility that there are unmeasured differences between the control and treatment groups, ordinary regression is problematic. The main culprit is selection bias which can arise in many forms, some examples of which follow. Each example of a research question is followed by a description of the selection issue as well as how researchers have approached the problem.

Does attendance affect performance? Students choose to attend, so using attendance as an explanatory variable will attribute to attendance the influence of unmeasured characteristics associated with attendance, such as conscientiousness, that may be the real reason that students who attend more frequently tend to perform better.

Romer (1993), in a paper addressing the influence of attendance on performance, regresses performance on attendance and an ability variable (GPA). He deals with the selection problem by reporting some "suggestive evidence" to supplement his regression results. He restricts his sample to only those students who completed all the problem sets, reasoning that this would eliminate any role that attendance might have through proxying for interest in the material or focus on academics. He also adds the fraction of problem sets completed as an extra explanatory variable, using similar reasoning. None of these ways is entirely adequate, however, as Romer acknowledges. Marburger (2001) is a more convincing study, exploiting panel data. In this study, N students wrote a final exam consisting of Q multiple-choice questions, so there were NQ panel data observations. Attendance data on students were available, identifying which days a student was absent, and the exam questions were associated with course material dealt with on specific days. Putting in a dummy for each student (fixed effects estimation for these panel data) controlled for unmeasured characteristics of students, circumventing the selection problem. Chen and Lin (2008) create a randomized experiment by covering some topics with class A but not with class B (and covering some other topics with class B but not with class A) and then see how the students did on questions related to this material.

Do students who sit at the front do better?   Students choose where they sit, so using seat selection as an explanatory variable will attribute to seating the influence of unmeasured variables, such as eagerness, that may be the real reason that students who sit at the front tend to perform better.

Benedict and Hoag (2004) investigate the influence of seating choice on student performance. Serendipitously, because of seating constraints, some students were randomly forced to sit at the front of the lecture hall instead of at the back where they stated they preferred to sit. These observations created a "natural experiment" that allowed investigation of the role of seat location.

Should dropouts be ignored?   The treatment by its nature may cause more/fewer marginal students in the treatment group to drop the course than in the control group. By removing these students from the final data the average performance of the treatment group would be over/under estimated.

Becker and Walstad (1990) investigate the impact of a national program for enhancing student learning of economics, while recognizing that not all students at the beginning of the study, those who took the pretest, also took the posttest. They employ the Heckman two-stage method to deal with possible selection bias due to the missing observations, finding a smaller impact of the program than had earlier been reported. Becker and Powers (2001) investigate the influence of missing observations (dropouts, or students not providing data) on estimating the influence of class size. They use the maximum likelihood version of the Heckman procedure[7] to correct for the selection bias caused by larger classes having higher dropout rates, finding that this correction reveals a negative influence of class size, contradicting earlier studies that did not correct for this sample selection phenomenon.

Do special training programs work?   Suppose some (treatment) instructors are chosen to participate in a special teacher training program. The value of the training program could be measured by the difference between the average performances of these instructors' students and those of a control group of instructors. But if the best instructors are selected to experience the training program, the results would be questionable because we would expect these instructors to do a better job in the absence of the program.

Walstad and Rebeck (2001) investigate whether students taught by instructors who had participated in a special seminar program (the treatment group) did better on a common final exam than students in a control group. As recognized by the authors, the results need to be viewed with caution because the participants in the seminar program were selected on merit (rather than via a random process) and so would be expected to be better teachers regardless of their participation in the program. Grimes and Millea (2011) investigate this same issue but with an experiment carefully designed to avoid selection bias.

These examples illustrate several ways in which selection problems are dealt with in the literature. A variable thought to capture the unmeasured characteristic associated with the selection phenomenon could be added as an extra explanatory variable, a randomized assignment could be created in some clever way, a "natural experiment" may have occurred that allows a researcher to escape the selection bias, and a maximum likelihood procedure could be used to "correct" for the selection bias, for example.[8] The strongest message these examples should convey, however, is that it is better for researchers to think out their research design so as to produce data that are not contaminated with selection bias.

Selection bias is by far the most important issue for empirical work in economic education, which is why the discussion above has been so extensive. Space restrictions require that other econometric issues be described very briefly.

Other Estimation Considerations

Use an appropriate estimator　Estimate standard errors using robust methods. If there is an excessive number of zeros, test for overdispersion and use a hurdle or ZIP model rather than a Poisson. If there are no observations at the limit, do not use a Tobit model. Do not use analysis of variance – it is dominated by regression for several good reasons.

Avoid elementary econometric errors　Do not use variables measured on a Likert scale (for example, 1, 2, 3, 4, 5) as explanatory variables – code them as dummies instead. Do not use interaction terms without including the terms separately. Do not deal with multicollinearity by replacing a variable with residuals from regressing it on another variable.

Do not fall into the significance trap　Statistical significance is necessary but not sufficient for concluding that something is of import – the magnitude of coefficient estimates, not just their statistical significance, needs to be assessed.[9] When testing explanatory variables for inclusion in a specification, researchers should use a significance level of about 30 percent rather than the usual 5 percent to avoid type II errors.

Report all specifications　In any event report a full specification as well as your final specification. And follow Kennedy's (2002) tenth commandment – report a sensitivity analysis.

DATA RESOURCES

One of the most difficult tasks a researcher in economic education faces is to obtain appropriate data with which to work. Large-scale efforts to measure economic literacy are usually conducted by the education departments in state/provincial or national governments. Generally, these data are available to qualified researchers upon request, although security of the data is often a sizable hurdle for researchers. One example of a national data set is the National Assessment of Educational Progress (NAEP). This assessment is conducted by the US Department of Education Institute of Educational Statistics and is nationally representative of what US students know in the areas of mathematics, reading, science, writing, the arts, civics, economics, geography, and US history. The economics portion of the assessment was conducted for the first time in 2006; a second assessment is planned for 2012. The assessment included three areas of economics – the national economy, the market economy and the international economy. The assessment tested three cognitive levels – knowing, applying and reasoning. The assessment also includes information on the students and their teachers.

Using the NAEP data requires caution. The NAEP uses a complex assessment design. Researchers must apply appropriate estimation techniques to account for the sampling methods, as well as for the fact that every student was not asked the same set of questions. Initial results from the NAEP are found on the NAEP website and in Walstad and Buckles (2008).[10] This data set will grow in its importance as the data are investigated further and as more assessments are conducted.

Some state or provincial governments require standardized economics examinations of students, along with exams in other disciplines. An example is Georgia which routinely administers End of Course Tests (EOCT) to its students in various subjects, including economics (Economics/Business/Free Enterprise).[11] Clark, Scafidi and Swinton (2011) have used these data in several studies. Other states require testing in economics. The Council for Economic Education releases reports that detail what amount of economics is required to be taught and tested by state.[12] According to the Survey of the States 2009: The State of Economic, Financial and Entrepreneurship Education in our Nation's Schools, 19 states require testing of student knowledge in economics – which is lower than in previous years. The usefulness of the data depends on how comprehensive the testing of economics is in the state tests. In some cases, the economics questions may be embedded in a social studies exam, limiting the use of the data to researchers.

Internationally, few data sources compare economic knowledge across countries. At the tertiary level, the OECD is beginning a project that will (if completed) shed light on comparisons of economic knowledge. The OECD Feasibility Study for the International Assessment of Higher Education Learning Outcomes (AHELO) is "to assess learning outcomes on an international scale by *creating measures* that would be valid for all cultures and languages." The project seeks to measure four strands of learning outcomes. One of the four strands is discipline-specific knowledge. Economics, along with engineering, has been selected for the feasibility study to measure discipline-specific knowledge. One of the major hurdles the project faces is determining exactly which economic concepts should be understood by students worldwide. While this study is years from completion, the results will provide economic educators with interesting cross-country data.[13]

In the meantime, comparisons of economic education data have often centered on information derived from standardized tests created by economic education researchers. A number of tests have been published by the Council for Economic Education.[14] The Test of Understanding in College Economics (TUCE) is appropriate for testing principles level knowledge at the university level. The Test of Economic Literacy (TEL) is designed for high school students. The Test of Economic Knowledge (TEK) is for students in grades 7–9. The Basic Economics Test completes the battery of tests by testing the economic knowledge of elementary level (grades 5–6) students. These tests have served as a public good, allowing researchers to use a common output measure in their studies. The TEL, for example, has been administered by researchers in the US, Japan, New Zealand and South Korea. As more studies are conducted, comparisons of the level of economic education across countries will become possible.

DATA COLLECTION ISSUES

The main problem with many state/provincial or national data sets is that they do not always produce data capable of testing a researcher's specific hypothesis. In this case, researchers are forced to gather their own data. This has the advantage of tailoring the data to the researcher's questions, but requires the researcher to overcome several hurdles.

One such hurdle is that researchers must negotiate a Research Ethics Committee or some equivalent body. As noted in Lopus et al. (2007), many economic education researchers are unaware that they must adhere to regulations of this type, requirements that vary from institution to institution and from country to country. Indeed, it is generally the case that researchers must undertake training to become familiar with the principles behind these requirements. Usually a trade-off exists between the student's right to anonymity and right to select coursework, instructor or instruction methods, and the researcher's desire to set up an experiment that has the results of tests and evaluations as a component of the study. Since the application of these principles varies greatly, it is recommended that researchers work closely with their institution's ethics committee in designing their project.

A second hurdle is that of the registrar's office. Since economic educators are often interested in students' demographics, performance in courses and standardized test scores (such as SAT or ACT), a university's own records can provide a researcher with a valuable source for collecting information about students. In practice, the willingness of the registrar's office to supply these data due to confidentiality reasons varies considerably. If possible, researchers should gather original source data as opposed to relying on self-reported data. Maxwell and Lopus (1994) illustrate the "Lake Wobegon Effect" of students who tend to inflate their poor grades or not report them; substituting information from student surveys as opposed to registrar information can introduce bias into estimations. Haley, Johnson and McGee (2010) suggest that though the effect may exist, it may be relatively small as compared to other mismeasured variables.

A third hurdle that researchers face is data loss. Inevitably, students drop classes,[15] miss exams, and do not answer some questions on surveys. There are two variants of this problem. The first, and more serious, is when the data loss takes the form of a selection bias, as described earlier. It may be, for example, that students who are weaker in some unmeasured way are induced by the treatment to drop a class, biasing the study's results in favor of the treatment group. This problem is usually associated with missing values of the dependent variable, and is dealt with by modeling the decision to drop and estimating using maximum likelihood as noted earlier. A researcher alert to this problem will gather information on variables relevant to the decision to drop, primarily variables related to the opportunity cost of course attendance, such as course load, as measured by number of courses and difficulty of courses, requirements for major, hours worked at a job, distance from school and other demographic variables. Variables that are correlated with dropping, but not necessarily performance, are desirable for this purpose.

The second variant occurs when information is missing on some explanatory variables for some students. One way of dealing with this is to drop all observations with missing values of important explanatory variables. In general, however, a better way is to use a regression to predict the missing values using the other explanatory variables as explanatory variables, and retain all observations by substituting these predictions for the missing values. See Kennedy (2008, pp. 165–6) for more on this. This advice follows the general rule that one should use all the data at one's disposal. There is an important caveat to this, however. A major problem with educational production functions is that the functional form is not known; in practice it is usually approximated by a linear functional form. A way of improving/assessing this linear approximation is to homogenize the data by dropping those observations which are markedly different from the majority of the data and seeing if the results are qualitatively similar. For example, use only data on white sophomores and juniors, taking the course because it is required, with English as a native language, who did not transfer from another institution, who have not previously taken micro, and who don't attend infrequently or rarely. If reasonably large data sets can be obtained in this way, specification problems are less damaging.

A fourth hurdle is measurement error associated with an explanatory variable. The most common way in which this occurs is when a pretest of some kind is administered. There are two main problems here. First, if the students are not given an incentive to take the pretest seriously, such as marks towards their final grade, many will not bother to take care with their answers, rendering this measure without value. Second, any test result embodies measurement error, so that using the pretest score as a regressor creates bias, in this case considerable bias. Because of these issues, in general making use of pretest results is problematic and so not advisable.[16] Should a researcher feel it necessary to use a pretest measure, however, there are three possibilities.

a. If the pretest and posttest are the same test, the difference between the two can be used as the dependent variable. This makes good sense: The point of administering the pretest is to examine the improvement in knowledge. This difference has twice the measurement error variance of the posttest, the price one pays for avoiding the substantive bias that would arise if the pretest were used as a regressor.
b. If a standard test is employed as the pretest, such as TUCE or TEL, the documentation associated with that test should provide the magnitude of the variance of the measurement error. With this knowledge the linear structural relations estimation method or a GMM counterpart could be employed for estimation. See Kennedy (2008, pp. 167–8).
c. If the test is multiple-choice and the answers for each student to each of the questions are known (as opposed to just knowing a total score), the procedure of Salemi and Tauchen (1982) can be employed. Their approach creates a learning model that combines a learning function based on study time and student aptitude with an equation linking student aptitude to demographic information. Estimation of test score outcomes is done with a probit model.

A fifth hurdle is the choice of dependent variable, typically some measure of learning. Ideally, a test that has been shown to be valid and reliable should be employed, but often researchers employ alternative measures such as final course grade or score on their own final exam. In this circumstance, the researcher must explain fully the nature of the alternative measure to confirm that it is not questionable because, for example, it is not comprehensive, it includes marks for peripheral things like attendance, it is "take home", or it counts for very little towards the final grade.

A sixth hurdle concerns what the proper unit of observation should be. Many educational production function studies use a panel data approach with courses taught by instructors. Often, studies that seek to examine instructor characteristics report the total number of students used in their estimations, but fail to acknowledge that the results are based on a handful of instructors. Studies that examine instructor characteristics need to be of a large enough scale that enough variation in instructors exists to have confidence in the results. This limits what can be done at a single university or school – with sizable studies across schools increasing the costs of data gathering considerably.

The bar for data collection in educational production function style studies has increased over the years. Ethics obligations, concern about selection issues, and preference for large-scale studies make publishing in the economics education area challenging. Good preparation will avoid some of the pitfalls we have listed above. Avoiding the pitfalls will lead to methodologically sound papers that contribute significantly to the body of economic education research.

NOTES

1. The handbook is found at http://www.vanderbilt.edu/AEA/AEACEE/Econometrics_Handbook/index. htm (accessed 11 June 2011).
2. These mistakes were identified during the twenty years that the second author served as editor of the research section of the *Journal of Economic Education*.
3. Although not prominent in textbooks, this view is widely recognized by applied econometricians, as evidenced by Angrist and Pischke (2009, p. xii): "we believe that empirical research is most valuable when it uses data to answer specific causal questions, *as if* in a randomized clinical trial." (Emphasis in original.)
4. A qualification is required here. Random assignment could by chance produce ex post an odd distribution of students across the two classes, in which case it would make sense to move to a regression analysis.
5. More generally, following Kennedy's (2002) third commandment, the context of the study needs to be explained in detail. So, for example, if the study is examining the role of graphs in learning, the researcher should describe in great detail how graphs entered the study: Was the textbook graph-oriented? Could the exam questions be answered without graphs? Did the instructor base explanations on graphs or just use them as pictorial aids to story-telling?
6. A measure of student ability must be among these regressors; the literature in economic education suggests that in general, once ability is controlled for, nothing else matters!
7. Kennedy (2008, pp. 270–71) documents the superiority of maximum likelihood estimation in this context.
8. Schlotter, Schwerdt and Woessmann (2009) is a very readable survey of empirical strategies devised to identify causal impacts in the closely related area of economics of education, discussing controlled experiments, lotteries of oversubscribed programs, instrumental variables, regression discontinuities, differences-in-differences, and panel-data techniques.
9. See Ziliak and McCloskey (2004) for an example of their many published complaints about economics research in this regard. This is particularly relevant in economics education because most studies have shown that taking an economics course has a remarkably small impact on test scores, but is statistically significant.

10.   Information about the NAEP is found at www.nationsreportcard.gov (accessed 11 June 2011).
11.   Information about this test is found at http://www.doe.k12.ga.us/ci_testing.aspx, in the end of course testing section of the website (accessed 11 June 2011).
12.   See Chapter 25, "Economic Education in American Elementary and Secondary Schools", in this volume for details.
13.   Information on the project is found at www.oecd.org/edu/ahelo (accessed 11 June 2011).
14.   See the Chapter 25, "Economic Education in American Elementary and Secondary Schools" and Chapter 29, "Measurement Techniques of Student Performance and Literacy: College and High School" in this volume.
15.   Bosshardt (2004) examines the behavior of those who drop principles courses.
16.   The classic reference here is Cronbach and Furby (1970, p. 80): "It appears that investigators who ask questions regarding gain scores would ordinarily be better advised to frame their questions in other ways." This refers to a context in which only two measures are available, the typical case in economic education.

REFERENCES

Angrist, J. and J.-S. Pischke (2009), *Mostly Harmless Econometrics: An Empiricist's Companion*, Princeton, NJ: Princeton University Press.

Becker, W. E. and J. R. Powers (2001), "Student performance, attrition, and class size given missing student data", *Economics of Education Review*, **20** (4), 377–88.

Becker, W. E. and W. B. Walstad (1990), "Data loss from pretest to posttest as a sample selection problem", *Review of Economics and Statistics*, **72** (1), 184–8.

Benedict, M. E. and J. Hoag (2004), "Seating location in large lectures: Are seating preferences or location related to course performance?", *Journal of Economic Education*, **35** (3), 215–31.

Bosshardt, W. (2004) "Student drops and failure in principles courses", *Journal of Economic Education*, **35** (2), 111–28.

Chen, J. and T. F. Lin (2008), "Class attendance and exam performance: A randomized experiment", *Journal of Economic Education*, **39** (3), 213–27.

Clark, C., B. Scafidi and J. R. Swinton (2011), "Do peers influence achievement in high school economics? Evidence from Georgia's economics end of course test", *Journal of Economic Education*, **42** (1), 3–18.

Council for Economic Education (2009), *Survey of the States Economic, Personal Finance and Entrepreneurship Education in our Nation's Schools in 2009*, New York: Council for Economic Education.

Cronbach, L. J. and L. Furby (1970), "How we should measure 'Change' – or should we?", *Psychological Bulletin*, **74** (1), 68–80.

Grimes, P. W. and M. J. Millea (2011), "Economic education in post-Soviet Russia: The effectiveness of the training of trainers program", *Journal of Economic Education*, **42** (2), 99–119.

Haley, M. R., M. Johnson and M. K. McGee (2010), "A framework for reconsidering the Lake Wobegon effect", *Journal of Economic Education*, **41** (2), 95–109.

Kennedy, P. E. (2002), "Sinning in the basement: What are the rules? The Ten Commandments of applied econometrics", *Journal of Economic Surveys*, **16** (4), 569–89.

Kennedy, P. E. (2008), *A Guide to Econometrics* (sixth edition), Oxford: Wiley-Blackwell.

Lopus, J. S., P. W. Grimes, W. E. Becker and R.A. Pearson (2007), "Human subject requirements and economic education researchers", *American Economist*, **51** (2), 49–60.

Marburger, D. (2001), "Absenteeism and undergraduate performance", *Journal of Economic Education*, **32** (2), 99–109.

Maxwell, N. L. and J. S. Lopus (1994), "The Lake Wobegon effect in student self-reported data", *American Economic Review*, **84** (2), 201–5.

OECD, OECD feasibility study for the international assessment of higher education learning outcomes (AHELO), Organisation for Economic Co-operation and Development, n.d., www.oecd.org/edu/ahelo, accessed May 15, 2011.

Romer, D. (1993), "Do students go to class? Should they?", *Journal of Economic Perspectives*, **7** (3), 167–74.

Salemi, M. K. and G. E. Tauchen (1982), "Estimation of nonlinear learning models", *Journal of the American Statistical Association*, **77** (380), 725–31.

Schlotter, M., G. Schwerdt and L. Woessmann (2009), "Econometric methods for causal evaluation of education policies and practices: A non-technical guide", CESifo Working Paper #2877.

Walstad, W. B. and S. Buckles (2008), "The national assessment of educational progress in economics: Findings for general economics", *American Economic Review: Papers and Proceedings*, **98** (2), 541–6.

Walstad, W. B. and K. Rebeck (2001), "Teacher and student understanding in transition economies", *Journal of Economic Education*, **32** (1), 58–67.

Ziliak, S. T. and D. N. McCloskey (2004), "Size matters: The standard error of regressions in the American Economic Review", *Journal of Socio-Economics* **33** (5), 527–46.

36 Learning from physics education research: lessons for economics education[1]
Mark Maier and Scott Simkins

Economics educators have much to learn by examining pedagogical research in other disciplines and exploring its adaptability to economics. In particular, economists can gain valuable insights into ways to improve student learning from educational research conducted in physics, a discipline that has systematically developed a deep body of knowledge on student learning and effective classroom practice. As leaders in discipline-based educational research, physicists have used that knowledge to develop a series of innovative teaching methods, informative assessment techniques, and engaging curricula (McDermott and Redish, 1999; Stokstad, 2001; Wieman, 2007). The lessons learned from physics education research are especially relevant to economics because many of the same challenges are present in both disciplines, most notably the need for students to develop facility with graphical, numerical, and mathematical representations in order to master conceptual knowledge for modeling real world behavior.

LEARNING FROM PHYSICS EDUCATION RESEARCH: THREE DIFFERENCES

Physics education research differs from economics education research in three important ways: (1) broad discipline-level support for research in physics education, (2) an intentional research agenda focused on gaps in student learning, and (3) the centrality of learning-sciences findings in physics education research and pedagogical innovation. These differences yield important insights that can be used to advance both economic education research and practice.

Broad Discipline-level Support for Research in Physics Education

Physics education research benefits from a large and well-established research community supported by a worldwide network of university-based physics education research groups (PERGs). Heron and Meltzer (2005) list more than 50 such groups, whose primary focus is on improving college-level teaching and learning. In a number of cases, entire physics courses and curricula have been developed around the research findings of these groups (see, for example, McDermott et al., 1996; Redish, 2003; Laws, 1997; and Sokoloff et al., 2004; Physics Education Research Group at Colorado, 2010). While the specific research foci of these groups vary, PERGs are connected by a common mission – determining student learning gaps and intentionally developing pedagogical and curricular innovations to address them. In short, PERGs have helped to shape a physics education research agenda, built around well-defined student-learning challenges, that guides the development of a cumulative educational knowledge base in the field.

The situation is quite different in economics. Even though the discipline enjoys a long history of research on economic education (see Becker, 1997), most economic education research has been undertaken by individuals, not discipline-based education research groups, and has been conducted without any intentional link to a systematic discipline-wide research agenda. Thus, despite a growing number of individuals pursuing economic education (Maier, McGoldrick and Simkins, 2011), there has been little impact on actual classroom practice (Watts and Becker, 2008).

Physics education research also benefits from the active leadership of top physicists, including Carl Wieman and Eric Mazur. Wieman, after winning his Nobel Prize in 2001, has dedicated himself to the task of improving science education using research-based teaching methods (Wieman, 2007). Mazur, an internationally recognized laser researcher from Harvard, has been an ardent supporter of interactive classroom-based instructional innovations in science education (Mazur, 2009). The fact that prominent scientists like Wieman and Mazur continue to lead active physics education research groups and conduct physics education research themselves provides high visibility and disciplinary credibility for this work. Similar examples in economics are difficult to identify.

Dissemination opportunities also differ in physics and economics. New discoveries in physics education research are quickly made available to instructors through a variety of discipline-supported journals, including the prestigious *Physical Review* (*Special Topics – Physics Education Research*). In addition, the American Association of Physics Teachers (AAPT) holds semi-annual meetings that feature hundreds of invited and contributed papers focused solely on pedagogical innovations in the field. Dissemination opportunities are more limited in economics. While the *Journal of Economic Education* has published economic education research for over forty years and the American Economic Association's annual meeting includes sessions on economic education, overall there are fewer outlets for publishing and presenting economics education research, relative to physics education, retarding the dissemination of new teaching and learning ideas.[2]

Intentional Research Focused on Student Learning Gaps

Central to physics education research is a consistent, decades-long focus on understanding how students learn physics concepts and the conceptual roadblocks that hinder the development of deep, long-lasting learning. The resulting cumulative body of knowledge informs current teaching practices and serves as a shared foundation for ongoing educational research (Redish, 1999). In particular, physics education research emphasizes understanding the gap between what is taught and what is learned. As McDermott (1991, p. 303) notes:

> What the instructor says or implies and what the student interprets or infers as having been said or implied are not the same. There are often significant differences between what the instructor thinks students have learned in a physics course and what students may have actually learned.

To better understand the factors responsible for this gap, physics education researchers look closely at the actual *process* of learning in individual students (see, for example, Podolefsky and Finkelstein, 2007). The knowledge gained from this micro-level research often leads to innovative new pedagogies, teaching resources, and assessment processes that improve student learning. This process has its foundation in a systematic physics education research protocol made popular by Lillian McDermott (and her University of Washington PERG) that has been used in dozens of projects dating back nearly three decades (McDermott, 1991, p. 305). The key steps include:

1. administering problem-based tests on a core concept and carefully observing students solving these problems to determine student learning gaps;
2. creating new instructional resources and techniques based on insights gained about the learning gaps revealed in the previous step; and
3. testing the effectiveness of the methods and materials in closing the gaps.

To gain a sense of the way that physics education researchers approach their work, consider a study by the University of Washington Physics Education Research Group PERG (see Kautz et al., 2005a and 2005b), representative of a broad body of research focusing on close observation of student learning. Beginning with a concept recognized as fundamental for understanding and using physics – the first law of thermodynamics – researchers interviewed 45 undergraduate students enrolled in an upper-division physics course, students most professors would expect to be able to answer standard physics problems. Surprisingly, interviews revealed that most students could not apply this foundational physics concept to solve a basic applied physics problem.

Based on this initial qualitative inquiry, three new problems targeting this learning gap were written and administered to more than 1000 students in physics courses at four universities. Again, many of the students answered these problems incorrectly, regardless of course type (algebra or calculus based) or timing of assessment (before or after instruction). Responses were categorized to pinpoint the sources of student error and the results were used to design new instructional methods specifically aimed at closing the learning gaps identified in the study. Follow-up testing took place nationwide, providing evidence that the pedagogical approach was effective even when implemented by instructors not involved in physics education research (Pollock and Finkelstein, 2008).

The most similar research in economics education involved analyses of videotapes as students solved problems (Strober and Cook, 1992; Strober, 1997) . Even though these studies did not lead to widespread adoption of a new pedagogy, it is possible to imagine a systematic research protocol modeled after physics education research in which economic educators would develop and test new pedagogies based on close examination of students' inability to use core concepts correctly.

Educational Research Grounded in the Learning Sciences

Much of the research in physics education is grounded in a small set of learning sciences research findings associated with deep and long-lasting learning (see Bransford et al. 1999): identifying and directly addressing student pre/misconceptions (or 'common naïve conceptions' (Redish 2003, pp. 26, 30)); developing students' metacognitive skills; and increasing students' ability to transfer knowledge to new situations. We believe that economists can learn valuable lessons about how students learn economic concepts by devoting greater attention to similar ideas in economics.

Identifying and addressing preconceptions The starting point for nearly all physics education research is identifying how students misperceive core concepts, both before and often after successfully completing a traditional physics course. One of the key reasons for this intellectual disconnect is that students bring their own mental models to our classrooms. These "naïve conceptions" are often resistant to change and retard the development of new knowledge. The result is that students maintain novice views of scientific concepts, even after completing multiple science courses or, sometimes, advanced study in the field (Redish, 2003).[3]

The notion that instructors need to identify and address students' current conceptual understanding in a course prior to developing new knowledge is central to pedagogical and curricular innovations developed in physics education. Most notably, physicists have been at the forefront in developing "concept inventories", short multiple-choice tests designed to reveal persistent student preconceptions. The most famous is the Force Concept Inventory (FCI) (see Halloun and Hestenes 1985a and 1985b; Hestenes, Wells, and Swackhamer, 1992). Concept inventories such as the FCI use semi-realistic situations and everyday speech to develop distracter answers derived from common student preconceptions identified by previous research. Building on their successful use in physics, concept inventories have now been developed in many fields, including astronomy, biology, chemistry, geosciences, mathematics, and statistics (*Concept Inventory Central,* 2008; Richardson, 2004).

The results of concept inventories are often instrumental in promoting pedagogical innovation. Perhaps the most famous example of this involves physicist Eric Mazur, who, upon finding that his Harvard undergraduates were simply "learning 'recipes' or 'problem-solving strategies' . . . without considering the underlying concepts" (Mazur, 1997: 7), revised his lecture-based instructional approach to intentionally address student preconceptions using an innovative set of teaching strategies, incorporating concept tests, peer instruction, and later, just-in-time teaching. Integrating these interactive, structured, and student-focused teaching practices in his large lecture courses has produced measurable gains in student learning (see Mazur, 1997; Crouch and Mazur, 2001; Crouch et al., 2007).

The importance of students' prior experience on learning in economics was recognized by Saunders (1998), but concept inventories like the FCI do not currently exist in economics. Understanding what misconceptions students bring to our economics courses could help us identify and address learning gaps in much the same way that the FCI has done in physics. Research by Goffe (2009) found that the median student believed the US government sets or controls 40 percent of prices, estimated the inflation rate at over 11 percent in 2008, and maintained that real per capita GDP had increased only 25 percent since 1950. To what extent are these types of misconceptions reduced or eliminated through traditional teaching methods? Could other teaching strategies be developed that would be more effective? We currently don't know the answers to these questions, but the results from physics suggest that additional research in this area is worth pursuing. Indeed, some pedagogies developed in physics education to identify preconceptions have been adapted for economics.[4] However, there has been little research in economics attempting to *systematically* identify and catalogue student preconceptions and develop instructional methods to intentionally address them.

One reason for the lack of research on common misconceptions in economics is that, while disciplines like physics have a few generally accepted "key concepts" or principles around which course material and pedagogical innovations are built (for example, the first law of thermodynamics), no such consensus on key principles exists in economics, especially at the introductory level (Hansen, Salemi, and Siegfried, 2002). Nonetheless, concept inventories hold promise as a way to identify student preconceptions that persist even after studying economics – even if economists may not select the same core concepts as most important. Once these preconceptions are identified, pedagogical strategies and curricular materials can be developed to confront students with these preconceptions directly and change their underlying mental models.

Promoting metacognitive skills   Another important area for improving student learning is helping students understand and monitor their own thinking processes (metacognition). As Redish (2003) points out, students are generally unfamiliar with this type of mental activity:

> The key element in the mental model I want my students to use in learning physics appears to me to be *reflection* – thinking about their own thinking. This includes a variety of activities, including evaluating their ideas, checking them against experience, thinking about consistency, deciding what's fundamental that they need to keep and what is peripheral and easily reconstructed, considering what other ideas might be possible and so on. My experience with students in introductory classes – even advanced students – is that they rarely expect to think about their knowledge in these ways. (p. 62)

Metacognition can be enhanced in many ways, including specific classroom assessment techniques, such as the one-minute paper, which has previously been investigated by economic educators (Chizmar and Ostrosky, 1998). However, as emphasized by Bransford et al. (1999), to promote deep and durable learning students must be trained to intentionally reflect on their own thought processes and problem-solving practices, recognize gaps in their understanding, be given multiple opportunities to address those gaps, and asked to explicitly describe their problem-solving processes.

Without the development of these metacognitive skills, including contradictions between student observations and their implicit mental models, student thinking is likely to be surface level and episodic. Many pedagogical innovations in physics education, such as interactive lecture discussions,[5] are specifically designed to build metacognitive skills in students. Similarly designed teaching approaches in economics have been limited (see Grimes, 2002; Allen, 2005).

Developing knowledge transfer skills   Many problems identified by physics education researchers deal with students' inability to transfer knowledge to new contexts. As Mazur (1997) notes, when confronted with a new problem, most students rely on novice-like "plug-and-chug" algorithms rather than the structurally connected and organized knowledge maps of experts. As a result, these students are often unable to transfer basic principles and concepts to environments unlike those in which they were originally presented. Even for those students who are able to transfer knowledge by solving a problem in a new context, they may not carry over this knowledge to learn in a new way that is critical for more advanced study in the discipline (Hammer et al., 2005; Schwartz, Bransford, and Sears, 2005). For example, students might learn how to correctly use

Newton's third law in a variety of contexts but fail to transfer the concept into subsequent learning about multibody problems. Transfer for learning is best accomplished when instructors explicitly require students to connect their understanding to prior knowledge and reflect on their learning processes (Hammer et al., 2005, p. 115).

In economics, the importance of student transfer of disciplinary concepts has been explicitly recognized by Saunders (1998) and is implicit in techniques such as the case method[6] and problem-based learning (Maxwell and Bellisimo, 2005; Carlson and Velenchik, 2006; Smith and Ravitz 2008; and Higher Education Academy Economics Network, 2008). However, unlike in physics, transfer of knowledge was not based on key insights from the learning sciences when developing new classroom teaching practices.[7] Physics education researchers have maintained a steady focus on the transfer issue and have systematically worked to develop teaching resources and practices that directly address this challenge. Similar knowledge transfer studies in economics might look at ways in which students are unable to apply their understanding of price elasticity of demand to other types of elasticity. Alternatively, a study might investigate students' ability to transfer knowledge about compound growth in the value of financial assets to issues of macroeconomic growth.

SUMMARY: LESSONS FOR ECONOMISTS: INTENTIONALITY AND CUMULATIVE KNOWLEDGE-BUILDING

Physics education research is characterized by a systematic approach to uncovering, explaining, and addressing student learning gaps, focusing primarily on students' learning *processes* rather than specific knowledge acquisition. The result of this learning-centered approach is the development of a cumulative knowledge base of *how students learn* physics that drives both educational research and pedagogical innovation. Indeed, a defining characteristic of physics education research is the intentional, long-term process of cumulative knowledge building about not only which pedagogies can improve student learning, but also how and under what conditions.

To be sure, economists build on the work of others, but too often this work is difficult to place in a broader economics education research agenda in the same way that is possible with physics education research. Educational research on economic experiments provides perhaps the best example of a sustained community of researchers working on a common pedagogical framework within economics education (Hazlett, 2006), but even here there has been neither an intentional connection to learning theory nor a systematic, comprehensive building of evidence on what works, how, and when. As is the case with much economic education research, the issues and topics often reflect the interests of individual researchers rather than the intentional focus of the discipline.

Economic education researchers are widely recognized for the development and application of sophisticated statistical tools to assess the impact of instructional innovations on student learning (Becker, 2004), yet this expertise has failed to lead to a systematic process for improving student learning or the development of a cumulative knowledge base on student learning gaps. Physics education research offers a complementary educational research model for building a coherent core body of knowledge explicitly aimed at improving student learning. In physics education, research strategies intentionally focusing discipline-wide attention on addressing students' misconceptions, metacognitive skills, and transfer of knowledge have produced innovative pedagogical strategies, instructional activities, and curricular reforms that have been shown to *broadly* improve student learning in physics, not only in the classrooms where the innovations were developed (Pollock and Finkelstein, 2008). Given this success in physics, it is worth undertaking broad-based research to determine how these teaching tools can best be used in economics to improve student learning in similar dimensions. By looking outside our own discipline for answers to these questions, we are likely to gain valuable insights.

NOTES

1. The authors gratefully acknowledge financial support from the National Science Foundation (DUE #04-11037 and DUE #08-17382). Extensive information on the pedagogical innovations discussed in this chapter is included in the Starting Point: Teaching and Learning Economics pedagogic portal: http://serc.carleton.edu/econ/index.html (accessed 11 June 2011).
2. The first National Conference on Teaching Economics and Research in Economic Education, sponsored by the American Economic Association's Committee on Economic Education, focused solely on economic education research and practice and was held in June, 2011.
3. This point is dramatically illustrated in the PBS video, *A Private Universe* (Harvard-Smithsonian Center for Astrophysics, 1997), where students are asked to explain the causes of the seasons. Even students who have taken multiple science courses maintain the erroneous belief that the earth's proximity to the sun in its annual orbit explains seasonal changes.
4. Two examples include just-in-time teaching and interactive lecture demonstrations. For more information, see Chapters 8 and 9 in this volume and the economic pedagogic portal Starting Point: Teaching and Learning Economics, http://serc.carleton.edu/econ/demonstrations/index.html (accessed 17 May 2011).
5. For more information, see Chapter 8, "Interactive Lecture Demonstrations", in this volume.
6. For more on this technique, see Chapter 2 on case use in this volume.
7. One recent exception is the adaptation of context-rich problems, originally developed in physics, for use in economics. See Chapter 3 on context-rich problems in this volume and at Starting Point: Teaching and Learning Economics, http://serc.carleton.edu/econ/context_rich/index.html (accessed 17 May 2011).

REFERENCES

Allen, D. (2005), "Metacognition and your learning of economics", http://www.economicsnetwork.ac.uk/projects/mini/pdp/report.doc (accessed 17 May 2011).

Becker, W. E. (1997), "Teaching economics to undergraduates", *Journal of Economic Literature*, **35** (3), 1347–73.

Becker, W. E. (2004), "Quantitative research on teaching methods in tertiary education", in W.E. Becker and M.L. Andrews (eds), *The Scholarship of Teaching and Learning in Higher Education*, Bloomington, IN: Indiana University Press, pp. 265–309.

Bransford, J., A. L. Brown, R. R. Cocking and National Research Council (1999), *How People Learn: Brain, Mind, Experience, and School*, Washington, DC: National Academy Press.

Carlson, J. A. and A. D. Velenchik (2006), "Using the case method in the economics classroom", in W. E. Becker, S. R. Becker and M. W. Watts (eds), *Teaching Economics: More Alternatives to Chalk and Talk*, Cheltenham, UK and Northampton, MA, US: Edward Elgar, pp. 59–74.

Chizmar, J. F. and A. L. Ostrosky (1998), "The one-minute paper: Some empirical findings", *The Journal of Economic Education*, **29** (1), 3–10.

Concept Inventory Central (2008), https://engineering.purdue.edu/SCI/workshop (accessed 17 May 2011).

Crouch, C. H. and E. Mazur (2001), "Peer instruction: Ten years of experience and results", *American Journal of Physics*, **69** (9), 970–77.

Crouch, C. H., J. Watkins, A. P. Fagen and Eric Mazur (2007), "Peer instruction: Engaging students one-on-one, all at once", in E. F. Redish and P. J. Cooney (eds), *Reviews in Physics Education Research Vol. 1 – Research-Based Reform of University Physics*, College Park, MD: American Association of Physics

Teachers, available at: http://www.per-central.org/document/ServeFile.cfm?ID=4990 (accessed 17 May 2011).

Goffe, W. L. (2009), "Initial misconceptions in a macro principles class", http://goffe.oswego.edu/Misconceptions.pdf, accessed 17 May 2011.

Grimes, P. W. (2002), "The over confident principles of economics student: An examination of a metacognitive skill", *The Journal of Economic Education*, **33** (1), (Winter), 15–30.

Halloun, I. A. and D. Hestenes (1985a), "The initial knowledge state of college physics students", *American Journal of Physics*, **53** (11), 1043–55.

Halloun, I. A. and D. Hestenes (1985b), "Common sense concepts about motion", *American Journal of Physics*, **53** (11), 1056–65.

Hammer, D., A. Elby, R. E. Scherr and E. Redish (2005), "Resources, framing and transfer", in J. P. Mestre (ed.) *Transfer of Learning from a Modern Multidisciplinary Perspective*, Greenwich, CT: Information Age Publishing, pp. 89–119.

Hansen, W. L., M. K. Salemi and J. J. Siegfried (2002), "Use it or lose it: Teaching literacy in the economics principles course", *American Economic Review*, **92**, 463–72.

Harvard-Smithsonian Center for Astrophysics (1997), "A private universe", Annenberg Media, http://www.learner.org/resources/series28.html, accessed 17 May 2011.

Hazlett, D. (2006), "Using classroom experiments to teach economics", in W. E. Becker, S. R. Becker and M. W. Watts (eds), *Teaching Economics: More Alternatives to Chalk and Talk*, Cheltenham, UK and Northampton, MA, US: Edward Elgar, pp. 21–37.

Heron, P. R. L. and D. E. Meltzer (2005), "The future of physics education research: Intellectual challenges and practical concerns", *American Journal of Physics*, **73** (5), 390–94.

Hestenes, D., M. Wells and G. Swackhamer (1992), "Force concept inventory", *The Physics Teacher*, **30** (3), 141–58.

Higher Education Academy Economics Network (2008), "Reflections: Learning approaches", The Higher Education Academy Economics Network, available at: http://www.economicsnetwork.ac.uk/showcase/approaches.htm (accessed 17 May 2011).

Kautz, C. H., P. R. L. Heron, M. E. Loverude and L. C. McDermott (2005a), "Student understanding of the ideal gas law, Part I: A macroscopic perspective", *American Journal of Physics*, **73** (11), 1055–63.

Kautz, C. H., P. R. L. Heron, P. S. Shaffer and L.C. McDermott (2005b), "Student understanding of the ideal gas law, Part II: A microscopic perspective", *American Journal of Physics*, **73** (11), 1064–71.

Laws, P. W. (1997), *Workshop Physics Activity Guide*, New York: Wiley.

Maier, M. H., K. McGoldrick and S. P. Simkins (2011), "Is there a signature pedagogy in economics?", in N. Chick, A. Haynie and R. Gurung (eds), *Exploring More Signature Pedagogies*, Sterling, VA: Stylus Publishers.

Maxwell, N. and Y. Bellisimo (2005), "Problem-based learning and high school macroeconomics", *Journal of Economic Education*, **36**, 315–31.

Mazur, E. (1997), *Peer Instruction: A User's Manual*, Prentice Hall Series in Educational Innovation, Upper Saddle River, NJ: Prentice Hall.

Mazur, E. (2009), "Farewell lecture?", *Science*, **323** (5910), 50–51.

McDermott, L. C. (1991), "Millikan Lecture 1990: What we teach and what is learned – Closing the gap", *American Journal of Physics*, **59** (4), 301–15.

McDermott, L. C. and Physics Education Research Group, University of Washington (1996), *Physics by Inquiry*, Vol. I and II, New York: John Wiley and Sons.

McDermott, L. C. and E. F. Redish (1999) "Resource letter: PER-1: Physics education research", *American Journal of Physics*, **67** (9), 755–67.

Physics Education Research Group at Colorado (2010), http://www.colorado.edu/physics/EducationIssues/about.htm (accessed 17 May 2011).

Podolefsky, N. S. and N. D. Finkelstein (2007), "Analogical scaffolding and the learning of abstract ideas in physics: Empirical studies", *Physical Review Special Topics – Physics Education Research*, **3** (2), 020104.

Pollock, S. J. and N. D. Finkelstein (2008), "Sustaining educational reforms in introductory physics", *Physical Review Special Topics – Physics Education Research*, **4** (1), 010110.

Redish, E. F. (1999), "Millikan Lecture 1998: Building a science of teaching physics", *American Journal of Physics*, **67** (7), 562–73.

Redish, E. F. (2003), *Teaching Physics with the Physics Suite*, Hoboken, NJ: John Wiley & Sons.

Richardson, J. (2004), "*Concept inventories: Tools for uncovering STEM students' misconceptions*", Paper read at Invention and Impact: Building Excellence in Undergraduate Science, Technology, Engineering, and Mathematics (STEM) Education, at Washington, DC.

Saunders, P. (1998), "Learning theory and instructional objectives", in P. Saunders and W. B. Walstad (eds), *The Principles of Economics Course: A Handbook for Instructors*, New York: Irwin/McGraw-Hill, pp. 62–85.

Schwartz, D. L., J. D. Bransford and D. Sears (2005), "Efficiency and innovation in transfer", in J. P. Mestre (ed.), *Transfer of Learning from a Modern Multidisciplinary Perspective*, Greenwich, CT: Information Age Publishing, pp. 1–51.

Smith, T. and J. Ravitz (2008), "Problem based learning in college economics", *Academic Exchange Quarterly*, **12** (1), 22–8, from Buck Institute: http://www.bie.org/research/study/pbe_college, accessed 17 May 2011.

Sokoloff, D. R., R. K. Thornton and P. W. Laws (2004), *RealTime Physics: Active Learning Laboratories*, Hoboken, NJ: Wiley.

Stokstad, E. (2001), "Reintroducing the intro course", *Science* **293** (5535), 1608–10.

Strober, M. H. (1997), "Making and correcting errors in student economic analyses: An examination of videotapes", *Journal of Economic Education*, **28** (3), 255–71.

Strober, M. H. and A. Cook (1992), "Economics, lies and videotapes", *The Journal of Economic Education*, **23** (2), 125–51.

Watts, M. and W. Becker (2008), "A little more than chalk and talk: Results from a third national survey of teaching methods in undergraduate economics courses", *Journal of Economic Education*, **39** (3), 273–86.

Wieman, C. (2007), "Why not try a scientific approach to science education?", *Change*, **39** (5), 9–15.

37 Journals and beyond: publishing economics education research

Peter Davies and William L. Goffe

The purpose of this chapter is to offer a brief résumé of the scale and scope of possible publication outlets for research in economics education and to briefly discuss some associated issues. We begin with a focus on more traditional journal outlets and then introduce other forms of publication such as blogs and working papers. This chapter addresses questions such as: Does a review of research publication opportunities suggest that there is a healthy level of activity in economics education research? What is the relationship between *economics* and *education* in this research? Is research in economics education developing as a coherent body of work?

JOURNALS

Some economics journals regularly include articles on economics education. For example, a Google Scholar search for 2001–10 on the term "teaching" yields 72 hits in the *Southern Economic Journal* (SEJ), 39 hits in the *Economic Record* and 38 hits in the *American Economist*. A large proportion of these refer to teaching economics and conditions under which this teaching takes place. The editor of the SEJ (Razzolini, 2010) reports that between 2005 and 2009 the SEJ published fourteen articles in the *Journal of Economic Literature* (JEL) category "General Economics and Teaching." One electronic journal (the *Journal of Economics and Economic Education Research*) announces in its title an intention to include articles on economic education as well as economics. Prominent education journals such as *Studies in Higher Education, Higher Education* and *Higher Education Research and Development* have also included papers reporting research in economics education in recent years. However, in the interests of brevity this chapter concentrates on journals which focus specifically on economics education. All these journals are double-blind refereed.

The *Australasian Journal of Economics Education* was launched in 2004 with two issues a year. Although originally published in paper format, it is now an online only journal and articles can be accessed without charge.[1] The journal espouses ten objectives which include giving recognition to issues of economic philosophy, the place of history in teaching economics and interdisciplinary issues. The journal also seeks to establish a link between the teaching of economics in tertiary and secondary education. From 2005 onwards, the two annual issues were published in a combined form, with the number of papers per year being reduced to four to five in the last two years.

The *Computers in Higher Education Economics Review* (CHEER)[2] was launched in 1987, with its most recent volume published in 2008. Previous issues, from volume 9 (1995) onwards, are available on the journal web site, which is hosted by the Economics

Network of the UK's Higher Education Academy (HEA). In 1995 the journal published three issues containing thirteen papers and another thirteen short notes and reports. By 2008 this had fallen to four papers, published in the single issue that year. From 2011 CHEER was incorporated within *International Review of Economics Education* (IREE, described below). As a section within IREE, CHEER now focuses on accounts and evaluations of the innovative use of information technology in economics education worldwide.

The *International Journal of Pluralism and Economics Education* (IJPEE) was launched in 2009. It aims to provide a forum for the "pluralist community"[3] to share and discuss research findings in the field of economics education and ideas for teaching pluralist economics. A substantial first issue (2009) included thirteen articles in three sections: "general articles on pluralism and economics," "incorporating pluralism into the class-room" and "global dialogue on teaching economics." Papers in the first section discussed the need for pluralism within economics education, the second section offered practical teaching examples which could be adopted and adapted, whilst papers in the final section discussed economics education in national contexts from a pluralist perspective. This journal is only published online and there is free access to papers.

The *International Review of Economics Education* (IREE) was launched in 2003 by the HEA's Economics Network.[4] From 2012 it will increase to three issues a year.[5] Initially it included four to five papers in each issue, although more recently this has increased to about seven to eight per issue. The journal has a research in economics education section devoted to systematic empirical evidence and a practice in economics education section which includes examples of specific approaches to teaching economics. A reviews section was added in 2009. There have been special issues in 2009 on "Pluralist Economics Education" and in 2010 on "Experiments in Economics Education."

The *Journal for Economics Educators* invites novel expositions of economic theory and evidence, as well as examples of "high-quality undergraduate research." It is published online[6] by the Tennessee Economics Association. The journal is divided into sub-sections which vary from issue to issue according to the character of the published papers. The number of issues and papers varies substantially from year to year, with no clear trend towards an increasing or decreasing volume of published papers.

The *Journal of Economic Education* (JEE), launched in 1970, is published quarterly in cooperation with the National Council on Economic Education and the Committee on Economic Education of the American Economic Association. The journal has five main sections: research in economic education, economic content, economic instruction, online and features and information. Detailed guidance for authors and a contents listing of previous issues can be accessed via the journal's web site.[7] Most previously published papers can be accessed via the Research Papers in Economics (Repec)[8] site, aside from being available through university library subscriptions for online access. The number of papers published per year has remained within the 31–40 bracket in most recent volumes. The JEE is the only economics education journal included in the Journal Citation Index (JCI) for Economics for 2009, with an impact factor of 0.145.

Perspectives on Economic Education Research (PEER) was launched in 2005 and has published one issue a year. Subscribers gain online access and a hard copy of each issue. The journal concentrates on providing examples and discussion of teaching activities, reflecting the journal's aims: "a broad range of research including pedagogy models, case studies, experiments, active learning strategies, student-oriented issues, and other classroom-based scholarship of high quality and broad interest to economic educators."[9]

BEYOND JOURNALS

The Internet has dramatically increased access to economic education research. Most obviously, what used to require a trip to the library (or requests through interlibrary loan) can now be achieved via keyboard and mouse from anywhere in the world. Working papers are now often available online instead of being distributed among the favoured or the fortunate. Journal access has also been increased through a more subtle mechanism. Many institutions purchase online journal access through consortiums or from vendors that offer journal packages, so institutions that never had access to hard-copy editions now have online access. Finally, RePEc[10] offers searchable indexes to the economics literature.

However, these improvements in access are evolutionary; while useful, improved access will not likely dramatically change scholarly discourse. Revolutionary change may come from new communication mediums that the Internet has spawned. Here, we focus on those that have drawn the most attention to date from economics educators: "informal outlets," listservs, blogs, and online archives. Although it might be tempting to say that these new methods are distinct from journals, both represent a discussion, albeit one that journals manage through high barriers to entry, extensive quality control, and latency that is often measured in years. These new methods are much more accessible to authors and offer instant access to readers (who might also directly engage in the discussion through a response). The content quality of new media might well be lower, but this may be an acceptable tradeoff given their easy access, speed, interactivity, and informality.

Informal Outlets

For lack of a better term, an informal outlet is defined here as something that looks like a journal, but differs in fundamental ways, such as degree of reviewing, degree of rigor, or topics contained therein. Certainly these outlets existed in the past, but they were hindered by distribution issues. The Internet opens up new audiences and possibilities for these informal outlets. While less than a journal in stature, they still convey valuable insights for economics educators. Perhaps the best-known is *The Handbook for Economics Lecturers*[11] from the HEA's Economics Network. It offers a very useful set of guides for all who teach and is a possible outlet for lecturers.

Listservs

Certainly the vast majority of academics understand and use listservs. Listservs are software that allows a group of people to send email to one address, which then resends that email to all members of that group. Thus, by sending and receiving email from that one address, many can easily hold a conversation. Since most listservs are organized by areas of mutual interest, scholarly ones can be a significant resource for those without local colleagues in their field. Although there is no dedicated listserv for economics education research per se, tch-econ[12] is devoted to the teaching of economics, and research-related discussion often arises in the form of calls for papers and discussion of research findings. The potential for research enhancements through this medium is significant, as we hope the following example demonstrates. The analogous listserv in physics, physlrn,[13] facilitates many discussions of specific research questions. The second author recently implemented "Team-Based Learning",[14] and its listserv[15] was an essential aid through the advice received from more experienced TBL users. In a very real way, listservs not only help build communities, they are communities.

Blogs

Blogs are also a well-known feature of today's Internet; in a blog, a writer or writers comment on most anything imaginable.[16] Since many blogs accept reader comments, a spirited discussion may follow a "post." Seemingly less well known is that while one can read blogs as one reads web pages, blogs run with specific software that specialized "newsreaders" can interpret so readers can easily read many blog postings from numerous sites. Thus, rather than going from web page to web page to read new blog entries, one can go to a single page that presents all subscribed blogs to the reader. Common web-based newsreaders include "My Yahoo!" and "Google Reader."

To obtain insights on why economics educators might blog, two of the most consistently prolific were interviewed: Steve Greenlaw[17] and Jennifer Imazeki.[18] Surprisingly, sharing their experiences and insights with others was not a major goal of either; in part, they blog to keep a log of their thoughts on teaching for themselves and to engage themselves by writing about their experiences. Greenlaw reports that he uses his blog to keep track of ideas for potential papers.[19] Both report receiving valuable feedback from their readers, but at times the volume is limited. Greenlaw reports that he has received many offers of speaking engagements due to his blog; in fact, his friend Gardner Campbell refers to an academic's blog as their "real CV." Both Greenlaw and Imazeki acknowledge concerns associated with writing about current classes, but they feel relevant issues can be presented if special care is taken.[20] Neither believes that many, if any, students follow their blogs.

Working Paper Repositories and Announcement Listservs

Working papers have long been a mainstay of serious economics discourse.[21] As above, the Internet has dramatically expanded equitable access to them. This has largely been accomplished with two systems, Social Science Research Network (SSRN) and Research Papers in Economics (RePEc). SSRN is a centralized archive where interested scholars upload their papers, while RePEc is a system of nearly 1,200 archive sites in 70 plus countries that cooperate through a common set of protocols. These sites are typically run by economics departments, research institutions, or government agencies. RePEc software scans their archives and the RePEc services, such as IDEAS[22] and EconPapers,[23] let users search the RePEc database. RePEc covers economic content exclusively and recently passed one million items in its database (primarily working papers and publications), while SSRN is spread across numerous disciplines and hosts about a quarter of a million works.

Both RePEc and SSRN offer announcement listservs for new works in their databases (eJournals for SSRN and New Economics Papers for RePEc). Both have listservs of interest to economics educators: SSRN's Economics Educator: Courses, Cases & Teaching eJournal[24] and RePEc's nep-edu[25] (the latter also covers the economics of education).

To have your working papers announced in either, you must put your paper in the relevant system. It is simple to join SSRN, while with RePEc instructors have two choices. First, your institution might have a RePEc archive; in that case, you would check with your local administrator. If not, then Munich Personal RePEc Archive[26] is the appropriate route as it offers a place for those without a local RePEc archive to place a paper into the RePEc system.

The Future

Clearly, the Internet has changed scholarship, but on a moment's reflection, the impact has been well short of the revolution seen in some industries. Journals play a smaller role in distributing research (online working papers have often taken their place), but they still operate as a filter and as a permanent research archive. Interestingly, for some authors, the Internet offers an outlet distinct from the increasingly arduous peer-review process. As recently as the 1960s, "revise and resubmit" was rare and review times have increased dramatically (Ellison, 2002, 2007). Some of the innovations listed above have had a limited impact to date: the tch-econ listserv averaged less than two messages a day in the first quarter of 2011 and it is quite rare to find a blogging economic educator. Thus, the Internet has largely supplanted existing practices, while truly innovative and widespread services are rare.

Two innovations that might have direct relevance for research in economics education come to mind. First, one could imagine short works devoted to very specific topics, such as how best to teach a specific concept. While still peer-reviewed, by their nature they would be shorter than a traditional journal article. Second, the Internet might reduce the costs of massive collaboration. This would be useful for large studies of teaching techniques, which are largely non-existent in economics. Of course, large studies can improve statistical power. Other disciplines have performed such studies and the results have been very influential. Hake (1998) involved 6,000 students and his striking results have been cited more than 1,300 times (according to Google Scholar in March, 2011). Prather et al. (2009) involved nearly 4,000 students and also found strong results; like Hake, they found traditional lectures led to inferior learning. One could imagine peer-based Internet-enabled collaboration for studies in our discipline rather than top-down projects that are difficult and expensive to coordinate.

CLOSING THOUGHTS

The brief review presented here brings to light the scale of interest in economics education research. Whilst the number of academic journals in all disciplines has been increasing in the last decade, a rise from two to six journals devoted to economic education is a substantial rate of change. This market is experiencing growing pains as some journals (such as CHEER) have had difficulty in maintaining the flow of suitable papers. Nevertheless, more papers were published in specialist economics education journals in 2008 than in 1998 and the trend appears to be upwards. Interest in conducting and publishing economic education research appears strong and the existing range of journals gives authors options for their preferred outlet as well as the opportunity to submit elsewhere if a paper is rejected.

Who is reading these papers? Limited indications are provided by citations, downloads, and web site visits. Mixon and Upadhyaya (2006) used Google Scholar to measure the citations of papers published in the eighteen month period starting January 2003. They found an average rate of citations of about 3.5 per paper in the JEE and about three per paper in IREE. They interpret the near parity of IREE to JEE as indicating the scope for new journals to be successful in entering the market. It should be noted, however, that during this period the JEE published roughly four times as many papers as IREE and Mixon and Upadhyaya's sample period was relatively short. Moreover, the use of Google Scholar captures the impact on the whole academic community, not just economics. Whilst impact of research in economics education beyond the boundaries of the discipline is to be applauded (it is surely helpful for the profession to be seen as innovative and informative in the field of teaching and learning), it is pertinent to focus inquiry on impact within the profession. One source of information that may relate more closely to impact in economics is the rate of downloads of papers through the RePEc service. Each of the specialist economics education journals described above can now be accessed through this service. This ease of access (since the downloading of most of the papers is free) should encourage greater impact of their results. A brief review of downloads in 2009 and the first five months of 2010 for papers published in 2008 is encouraging. Downloads for the JEE over this period ran at an average of around 30 per paper, with IREE at just over sixteen. Downloads for both these journals were higher than for *Applied Economics Letters* which occupies a similar JCI economics ranking to the JEE. However, this measure of impact also has limitations as it may overestimate impact if researchers download the same article multiple times, or it may underestimate impact if researchers can download papers from other sources (not least the web sites of the open access online journals). It is also not clear who is downloading and the purpose for which the paper is being downloaded.

A second issue our review of journals brings to light is the prominence of debate about the nature of economics in the literature on economics education. One new journal, the IJPEE, is specifically targeted at this debate and some of the most highly cited papers across all journals address key themes in this debate. This may well be fuelled, as Becker (for example, 2004) has consistently argued, by a disjunction between a rather monolithic and static conception of the core undergraduate economics curriculum (Reimann, 2004) and a varied and vibrant economics as observed in the research and policy analysis practised by economists.

A third issue is the extent to which research in economics education is developing as a coherent field. Is there agreement over key research questions? Is there consensus over methods? Is there a firm theoretical base for the research being conducted? Is the pattern of citations showing a strong sense of knowledge being accumulated by a community? For recurring questions (such as the extent and causes of gender differences in participation and achievement in economics and the effects of a range of organizational factors such as amount of study time and class size on achievement), evidence has been steadily accumulating as researchers address the same question in different contexts. However, even in these cases there is not a strong sense of a shared theorizing of problems. A fair proportion of valuable empirical evidence has been gathered through "black box" studies which leave room for speculation about model specification. In cases where researchers have appealed to theoretical standpoints on learning and teaching, there is less agreement about which standpoint to accept, with the consequence that studies have tended not to build upon previous results within the context of economics education. For example, Hedges (2008) describes a "Learning Styles" approach to economics teaching. Terregrossa et al. (2009) address the same issues, but also acknowledge recent evaluation of evidence for different theories of learning styles and approaches to learning. Nevertheless, neither of these papers refers to the earlier work such as Shanahan and Meyer (2001).

NOTES

1. Available online at the journal web page found at http://www.uq.edu.au/economics/AJEE/ (accessed 8 June 2010).
2. Available online at http://www.economicsnetwork.ac.uk/cheer/ (accessed 8 June 2008).
3. For more about pluralism and economic education, see Chapter 23 in this volume.
4. For more about this network and economic education more broadly in the UK, see Chapter 71, "Supporting Economics Higher Education in the United Kingdom."
5. Previously available online at http://www.economicsnetwork.ac.uk/iree/ (accessed 8 June 2010). From 2012 available through Science Direct.
6. Available online at http://frank.mtsu.edu/~jee/issues.html (accessed June 8 2010).
7. Currently (June 2010) with Heldref and available online at http://www.heldref.org/pubs/jece/about.html (accessed 8 June 2010). The journal is transferring to Taylor and Francis.
8. This web site provides access to papers and working papers and records levels of downloads and citations. Available online at http://ideas.repec.org/s/jee/journl.html (accessed 8 June 2010).
9. From the journal web site at http://www.isu.edu/peer/ (accessed 8 June 2010).
10. Available online at http://repec.org (accessed 29 June 2010).
11. Available online at http://www.economicsnetwork.ac.uk/handbook/ (accessed 1 July 2010).
12. Available online at http://org.elon.edu/econ/tch-econ/ (accessed 29 June 2010).
13. Available online at http://listserv.boisestate.edu/archives/physlrnr.html (accessed 1 July 2010).
14. Available online at http://teambasedlearning.apsc.ubc.ca/ (accessed 1 July 2010).
15. Available online at http://teambasedlearning.apsc.ubc.ca/ (accessed 1 July 2010).
16. They are among the reasons why magazines and newspapers are under such competitive pressure today.
17. Greenlaw's blog is at http://pedablogy.stevegreenlaw.org (accessed 29 June 2010).
18. Imazeki's blog is at http://economicsforteachers.blogspot.com/ (accessed 30 June 2010).
19. For more about blogs and their use in the classroom, see Chapter 15, "Economic Blogs and Economic Education", in this volume.
20. For those who want to write about a given topic only for themselves, Greenlaw reports that some blog software allows bloggers to restrict access to their posts.
21. In many other disciplines, formal publications still fill this role and pre-publication works rarely circulate.
22. Available online at http://ideas.repec.org (accessed 1 July 2010).
23. Available online at http://econpapers.repec.org (accessed 1 July 2010).
24. Available online at http://ssrn.com/ern/index.html (accessed 30 June 2010).
25. Available online at http://lists.repec.org/mailman/listinfo/nep-edu (accessed 30 June 2010).
26. Available online at http://mpra.repec.org/ (accessed 30 June 2010).

REFERENCES

Becker, W. (2004), "Goodbye old, hello new in teaching economics", *Australasian Journal of Economics Education* **1** (1), 5–17.

Ellison, G. (2002), "The slowdown of the economics publishing process", *Journal of Political Economy*, **110** (5), 947–93.

Ellison, Glenn (2007), "Is peer review in decline?", NBER Working Paper, 13272.

Hake, R. R. (1998), "Interactive-engagement versus traditional methods: A six-thousand-student survey of mechanics test data for introductory physics courses", *Journal of Physics,* **66**, 64–74.

Hedges, M. R. (2008), "Learning styles and introductory economics: A matter of translation", *Australasian Journal of Economics Education*, **5** (1–2), 1–16.

Mixon, F. G. Jnr. and K. P. Upadhyaya (2006), "A citations-based appraisal of new journals in economics education", *International Review of Economics Education*, **7** (1), 36–46.

Prather, E. E., A. L. Rudolph and G. Brissenden (2009), "Teaching and learning astronomy in the 21st Century", *Physics Today*, **62** (10), 41–7.

Razzolini, L. (2010), "Editor's report", *Southern Economic Journal*, **77** (2), 241–3.

Reimann, N. (2004), "First-year teaching and learning environments in economics", *International Review of Economics Education*, **3** (1), 9–38.

Shanahan, M. P. and J. H. F. Meyer (2001), "A student learning inventory for economics based on the students' experience of learning: A preliminary study", *Journal of Economic Education*, **32** (3), 259–67.

Terregrossa, R. A., F. Englander and Z. Wang (2009), "Why learning styles matter for student achievement in college economics", *Journal for Economics Educators*, **9** (1), 16–31.

PART IV

CONTENT

38 Less is more: the perils of trying to cover too much in microeconomic principles
Robert H. Frank

As taught in American colleges and universities, introductory economics courses leave almost no measurable trace on students. When they are given tests that probe their knowledge of basic economic principles six months after taking these courses, they perform no better than others who never took an introductory course at all (Hansen, Salemi, and Siegfried, 2002).

In many professions, clearly substandard performance provokes malpractice lawsuits against. But the instructors of introductory economics courses have never, to my knowledge, been confronted with such lawsuits. Perhaps that is because few people outside of academic economics departments have any appreciable working knowledge of basic economic principles, so almost no one can tell how poorly we train our students. But that does not make our performance any less scandalous. How can a university justify charging thousands of dollars for courses that add no measurable value?

STUDENTS FAIL TO MASTER EVEN BASIC CONCEPTS

Even the most basic economic concepts, such as opportunity cost, do not seem to be getting across. Everyone who ever took an economics course has at least heard of the concept. There is not unanimous agreement on how it should be defined, but for present purposes, we can work with the definition I personally prefer, which is that the opportunity cost of engaging in an activity is the value of everything you must give up to pursue it.

Suppose, for example, that you have won a free ticket to see an Eric Clapton concert tonight, which has no resale value. Bob Dylan is also performing tonight, and his concert is the only other option you are considering. A Dylan ticket would cost you $40, and on any given day you would be willing to pay as much as $50 to see him perform. (In other words, if Dylan tickets were priced above $50, you would pass on his event, even if you had nothing else to do.) For simplicity, assume there is no other cost of seeing either performer. What is your opportunity cost of attending the Clapton concert?

The only thing of value that you must sacrifice to attend the Clapton concert is seeing Dylan. You would miss out on a performance that would have been worth $50 to you, but you would also avoid having to spend $40 for a ticket to the event. The value of what you give up by not seeing Dylan is thus $50 – $40 = $10. In this example, if seeing Clapton is worth at least $10 to you, you should attend his concert. Otherwise you should see Dylan.

Opportunity cost is, by consensus, one of the two or three most important ideas in introductory economics. Yet we now have persuasive evidence that most students do not master this concept in any fundamental way. The economists Paul Ferraro and Laura Taylor recently posed the Clapton/Dylan question to groups of students to see whether they could answer it (Ferraro and Taylor, 2005). They gave their respondents only four choices:

a. $0
b. $10
c. $40
d. $50

As noted, the unambiguously correct answer is $10, the value of what you sacrifice by not attending the Dylan concert. Yet when Ferraro and Taylor posed this question to 270 undergraduates who had previously taken a course in economics, only 7.4 percent of them answered it correctly. Since there were only four choices, students who picked at random would have had a correct response rate of 25 percent. A little bit of knowledge seems to be a dangerous thing here.

When Ferraro and Taylor posed the same question to 88 students who had never taken an economics course, 17.2 percent answered it correctly – more than twice the correct response rate as for former economics students, but still less than chance.

Why did the economics students perform so poorly? The main reason, I suspect, is that because opportunity cost is only one of several hundred concepts that professors throw at them during the typical introductory course, it simply goes by in a blur. Students do not spend much time on it, nor do they use it repeatedly in different contexts. So it never really sinks in.

The evolved human brain apparently relies on a simple rule of thumb to help it cope with what would otherwise be an overwhelming onslaught of information: Unless the same piece of information comes up repeatedly, the best bet is to ignore it. Trying to assimilate and react to the terabytes of information that bombard our senses each day is simply not a feasible option. When a piece of information recurs, however, it is much more likely to be worthy of attention, and the brain begins laying down new circuits to deal with it. So it is not reasonable to expect students to learn basic economic concepts if they are exposed to each one only fleetingly.

But Ferraro and Taylor suggest a different explanation for why introductory courses are so ineffective: the instructors who teach them may not have mastered the basic concepts themselves. After all, they first heard about opportunity cost when it was one of hundreds of concepts that went by in a blur when they took their own first course in microeconomics.

When Ferraro and Taylor examined the leading introductory economics textbooks, they discovered that most did not devote sufficient attention to the opportunity cost concept to enable students to answer the Dylan/Clapton question. When they examined intermediate microeconomics texts, they discovered that the opportunity cost concept received only cursory mention, possibly because authors assumed it had been adequately covered in the introductory course. And when they examined graduate microeconomics texts, they found that the term did not even appear in the indexes of many of them.

To test their hypothesis that instructor knowledge gaps were a contributing factor to poor student performance, Ferraro and Taylor posed the same Clapton/Dylan question to a sample of 199 professional economists at the annual American Economic Association meetings in 2005. Only 21.6 percent chose the correct answer; 25.1 percent thought the opportunity cost of attending the Clapton concert was $0, 25.6 percent thought it was $40, and 27.6 percent thought it was $50.

The opportunity cost concept is undeniably important. It helps explain a host of interesting behavior patterns. Consider, for example, the widely remarked cultural differences between large coastal cities in the United States and smaller cities in the Midwest. Why do residents of Manhattan tend to be rude and impatient, whereas residents of Topeka are more likely to be friendly and courteous?

You could dispute the premise, of course, but most people seem to find it roughly descriptive. If you ask for directions in Topeka, people seem eager to stop and help you; in Manhattan, they may not even make eye contact. Because Manhattan has the highest wage rate and the richest menu of things to do of any city on the planet, the opportunity cost of people's time is very high there. So perhaps it is only to be expected that New Yorkers would be a little quicker to show impatience.

LIMIT TOPIC COVERAGE

The best way to teach introductory microeconomics – or any other subject, for that matter – is to expose students to repeated applications of a short list of the core ideas of the discipline. But whose short list? If we asked a thousand economists to provide their own versions, we would get a thousand different lists. Yet to dwell on their differences would be to miss their essential similarities. Indeed, almost all would contain variants of propositions like these:

- *The Scarcity Principle:* Having more of one good thing usually means having less of another.
- *The Cost-Benefit Principle:* Take no action unless its marginal benefit is at least as great as its marginal cost.
- *The Principle of Comparative Advantage:* Everyone does best when each concentrates on the activity for which he or she is relatively most productive.
- *The Principle of Increasing Opportunity Cost:* Use the resources with the lowest opportunity cost before turning to those with higher opportunity costs.
- *The Equilibrium Principle:* A market in equilibrium leaves no unexploited opportunities for individuals, but may not exploit all gains achievable through collective action.
- *The Efficiency Principle:* Efficiency is an important social goal, because when the economic pie grows larger, everyone can have a larger slice.

My point is not that this is the best short list, but that the introductory micro course will be taught most effectively if it begins with a well-articulated short list of some sort, and then doggedly hammers away at it, illustrating and applying each principle in context after context.

Many introductory economics textbooks, of course, do nothing of the sort. To be sure, versions of the core principles are found in these books, but so is virtually every other economic principle that has surfaced over the last 200 years. The mind-boggling detail of these books – thousand-plus page encyclopedic reference tomes, many of them – could not have been purposely designed to camouflage more effectively the handful of principles that really matter.

Why did this happen? An important factor may have been that adoption decisions are often made by committee. When five busy faculty members meet to consider textbooks, broad philosophical and methodological discussions quickly give way to detailed comparisons of topic coverage. Each committee member, of course, has his or her own favorite set of topics. And from the individual faculty member's perspective, one of the most costly mistakes is to choose a text that omits several of her favorite topics. Choosing such a book means that she will either have to abandon those topics when she teaches the course, or else have to prepare supplementary readings or special handouts in order to cover it. Time is short, and for many, the tenure clock is ticking.

Thus it is no surprise that, given two otherwise equally attractive texts, the one with broader topic coverage has a clear edge. Book publishers know this, of course, and have become understandably reluctant to invest in texts with limited topic coverage. So despite their occasional promises of new, leaner versions, almost all of today's introductory texts follow the encyclopedic format.

At one level, this might seem the most sensible compromise since, after all, professors can always pick and choose from the topics available in the text. Yet, as a practical matter, few of us attempt to fine-tune our assignments in this way. ("In chapter 4, read sections 4.1, 4.3, 4.4–4.6, 4.8, pages 231–33 of section 4.9, pages 245–47 of section 4.11, and sections 4.14–4.16.") In most cases, professors either assign the entire text, or else attempt to cover, in sequence, as many chapters as time permits. On the rare occasion when a professor does take the trouble to assign only excerpts from one of the encyclopedic texts, students invariably complain about having been forced to spend so much for a book that was used so sparingly.

When the dust settles, most students leave the introductory course never having fully grasped the essence of economic fundamentals. Opportunity cost and other basic concepts are more important than, say, the idea that the short-run average cost curve is tangent to the long-run average cost curve at the output level for which capacity is at the optimal level. But students would never realize that from the relative emphasis these topics receive in many of our introductory textbooks.

Intelligent instructors with Ph.D.s in economics may wonder whether so much repetition is really necessary, fearing that they will bore their students by exposing them to yet another application of the opportunity cost concept, or to yet another application showing why sunk costs should not matter. To many, it will seem that the same time would be better spent discussing why the average fixed cost curve is asymptotic to the quantity axis. At some point, it surely is better to move on to the technical properties of the average fixed cost curve. But that point almost surely does not come during the micro principles course. For decades, I have had the privilege of teaching some of the most capable undergraduates in the world. That experience has persuaded me that by attempting less, I end up teaching more.

THE ECONOMIC NATURALIST WRITING ASSIGNMENT

It is important for students not just to be able to apply core economic principles, but also to have an inclination to do so. The most effective strategy I have discovered for achieving that goal is to encourage them to become "economic naturalists." Studying biology enables people to observe and marvel at many details of life that would otherwise have escaped notice. For the naturalist, a walk in a quiet wood is an adventure. In much the same way, studying economics can enable students to see the mundane details of ordinary existence in a sharp new light.

I require my students to submit two short papers (500 words maximum), one due at mid-term, the other at term's end. The title of each paper is supposed to be an interesting question prompted by something they have experienced and observed personally. I call this assignment "the economic naturalist" because it was inspired by the kinds of questions an introductory course in biology enables students to answer. If you know a little evolutionary theory, you can see things you did not notice before. The theory identifies texture and pattern in the world that is stimulating to recognize and think about.

For example, here is a standard Darwinian question: Why are males much bigger than females in most vertebrate species? Bull elephant seals, for instance, can exceed 20 feet long in length and weigh 6000 pounds – as much as a Lincoln Navigator – whereas female elephant seals weigh only 800 to 1200 pounds.

Similar sexual dimorphism is observed in most vertebrate species. The Darwinian explanation is that most vertebrates are polygynous (meaning that males take more than one mate – if they can), and so males must compete for females. Bull elephant seals pummel one another on the beach for hours at a time, until one finally retreats, bloodied and exhausted.

The winners of these battles command nearly exclusive sexual access to harems of as many as one hundred females. This is a Darwinian prize of the first order, and it explains why males are so much bigger. A male with a mutant gene for larger size would be more likely to prevail in fights with other males, which means that this gene would appear with higher frequency in the next generation. In short, the reason males are so large is that small males seldom gain access to females.

A similar explanation accounts for the large tail displays in peacocks. Experiments have demonstrated that peahens prefer peacocks with longer tail feathers, which are thought to be a signal of robust health, since parasite-ridden males cannot maintain a bright, long tail.

For both the large bull elephant seal and the peacock with a long tail display, what is advantageous to males individually is disadvantageous to them as a group. A 6000-pound seal, for example, finds it harder to escape from the great white shark, its principal predator. If bulls could all cut their weight by half, each would be better off. The outcome of each fight would be the same as before, yet all would be better able to escape from predators. Similarly, if peacocks' tail displays were all reduced by half, females would still choose the same males as before, yet all peacocks would be better able to escape from predators. But bull elephant seals are stuck with their massive size and peacocks are stuck with their long tail feathers.

Of course, such evolutionary arms races do not continue indefinitely. At some point, the added vulnerability inherent in larger size or longer tail displays begins to outweigh the benefit of increased access to females. It is that balance of costs and benefits that is reflected in the characteristics of surviving males.

The biologist's narrative is interesting. It coheres. And it seems to be right. Thus if you look at monogamous species, ones in which males and females pair off for life, you do not see sexual dimorphism. This is "the exception that proves the rule" in the old-fashioned sense of the verb "to prove": it tests the rule. Polygyny led to the prediction that males would be bigger. And in its absence, males are not bigger. For example, because the albatross is monogamous, theory predicts that males and females will be roughly the same size, which in fact they are.

THE IMPORTANCE OF NARRATIVE

The biologist's narrative regarding sexual dimorphism has legs. It is easy to remember and satisfying to recount to others. If you can tell such stories and understand why they make sense, you have a far better grasp of biology than if you have simply memorized that birds belong to Class Aves. It is the same with narrative explanations based on principles of economics.

Most introductory microeconomics courses (and my own was no exception in the early days) make little use of narrative. Instead, they inundate students with equations and graphs. Mathematical formalism has been an enormously important source of intellectual progress in economics, but it has not proved an effective vehicle for introducing newcomers to our subject. Except for engineering students and a handful of others with extensive prior training in math, most students who attempt to learn economics primarily through equations and graphs never really grasp that distinctive mind-set known as "thinking like an economist." Most of them spend so much effort trying to make sense of the mathematical details that the intuition behind economic ideas escapes them.

The human brain is a remarkably flexible organ with the capacity to absorb new information in myriad different forms. But information gets into most brains more easily in some forms than others. In most cases, students grasp equations and graphs only with difficulty. But because our species evolved as storytellers, virtually everyone finds it easy to absorb the corresponding ideas in narrative form.

I stumbled onto this insight by chance some twenty years ago when participating in the writing across the disciplines program at Cornell, which was inspired by research showing that one of the best ways to learn about something is to write about it. As Walter Doyle and Kathy Carter, two proponents of the narrative theory of learning, have written, "At its core, the narrative perspective holds that human beings have a universal predisposition to 'story' their experience, that is, to impose a narrative interpretation on information and experience" (2003). Psychologist Jerome Bruner, another narrative learning theorist, observes that children "turn things into stories, and when they try to make sense of their life they use the storied version of their experience as the basis for further reflection. . . . If they don't catch something in a narrative structure, it doesn't get remembered very well, and it doesn't seem to be accessible for further kinds of mulling over" (quoted by Doyle and Carter, 2003).

In short, the human brain's specialty seems to be absorbing information in narrative form. My economic naturalist writing assignment plays directly to this strength. It calls for the title of each student's paper to be a question. For three reasons, I have found it useful to insist that students pose the most interesting questions they can. First, to come up with an interesting question, they must usually consider numerous preliminary questions, and this itself is a useful exercise. Second, students who come up with interesting questions have more fun with the assignment and devote more energy to it. And third, the student who poses an interesting question is more likely to tell others about it. If you cannot actually take an idea outside the classroom and use it, you do not really get it. But once you use it on your own, it is yours forever.

To illustrate, an economic naturalist is someone like Bill Tjoa, a former student who wanted to know, "Why do the keypad buttons on drive-up automatic teller machines have Braille dots?" A plausible answer, he reasoned, is that once the keypad molds have been manufactured, the cost of producing buttons with Braille dots is no higher than the cost of producing smooth ones. Making both types would require separate sets of molds and separate batches of inventory. If the patrons of drive-up machines found buttons with Braille dots harder to use, these extra costs might be worth incurring. But since the dots pose no difficulty for sighted users, the best and cheapest solution is to produce only keypads with dots.

Another of my favorite submissions was by Greg Balet, who asked, "Why do regulators require toddlers to be strapped into safety seats for even a two-block drive to the grocery store, yet permit them to sit untethered on our lap during cross-country airline flights?" Many students, on first hearing this question, respond that it is because if a plane crashes, you are going to die anyway, even if you are strapped in. But Mr. Balet reasoned that the primary rationale for seatbelts in planes was never to enable people to survive a crash, but rather to prevent injury during severe air turbulence. And since severe air turbulence occurs far more frequently than auto accidents, regulators were quicker to require seatbelts in airplanes than in cars.

Mr. Balet concluded that the real explanation for the asymmetry he was trying to explain had to lie on the cost side of the cost-benefit test, rather than the benefit side. If you already have a safety seat set up in the back seat of your car, it is essentially cost-less to strap your child in. But if you are on a full flight from New York to Los Angeles, you would have to buy an extra seat, which might cost you $1000. That cost, he argued, explains why safety seats are not required on airplanes.

In response to my challenge to employ economic principles to cast light on their own experiences, my students have tackled a host of other fascinating questions. Some examples:

Why do brides spend so much money on wedding dresses, while grooms often rent cheap tuxedos, even though grooms could potentially wear their tuxedos on many other occasions and brides will never wear their dresses again? (Jennifer Dulski)

Why do top female models earn so much more than top male models? (Fran Adams)

Why do fast food restaurants often post signs saying, "If you do not receive a receipt, your meal is free?" (Sam Tingleff)

Why does a $500 tuxedo rent for $100 a day, while a $20,000 car rents for $50 a day? (Jon Gotti)

> Why do airline tickets purchased at the last minute sell for premium prices, while Broadway tickets sold at the last minute sell at deep discounts? (Gerasimos Efthimiatos)

Students often struggle to come up with an interesting question in the weeks leading up to their first paper's due date. But as the due date for the second paper approaches, it is quite common for students to ask whether they can do a medley. They have three great questions, they will say, and want permission to write about each one.

Once students realize that they can pose and answer interesting questions on their own, they are hooked. A lifetime trajectory begins in which their mastery of economic principles not only does not decay with each year since completion of the course, but actually grows stronger.

If one of our important goals in the course is to train economic naturalists, it becomes much easier to decide which topics to cover and which to leave out. Other things equal, the more a topic enables students to make sense of their observations and experience, the stronger the case for including it. I find it astonishing that many people receive college degrees without ever once having been exposed to ideas like the prisoner's dilemma or the tragedy of the commons. These and other simple applications of game theory are not only ideal vehicles for illustrating several of the core ideas of economics, but they also have enormous power to explain events in the world.

Some instructors ask how a less-is-more version of the introductory microeconomics course can find time to include such topics, which, after all, do not even make it into some of the encyclopedic texts. The answer is that there is plenty of time, provided we abandon topics like the largely futile attempt to explain why the long-run average cost curve is tangent to the firm's demand curve in the Chamberlain model of monopolistic competition. Abandoning those topics is a small price to pay for the opportunity to learn a general principle that explains, among other things, why urban freeways are too crowded, why whales have been hunted to near extinction, why North Atlantic fisheries are near collapse, why the ozone layer is in danger, why many fail to vote, and why the National Hockey League has a helmet rule.

In addition to focusing on a short list of core principles, it is also useful to focus extra attention on those important concepts that students find most difficult to master. Here we may take useful cues from behavioral economics research showing that people often systematically violate the prescriptions of the rational choice model. For example, the model says that rational persons will ignore sunk costs when making decisions, yet many people are in fact strongly influenced by them. Someone who has purchased a basketball ticket for $50 is more likely to drive through a snowstorm to get to the game than is an equally avid fan who won her ticket in a raffle. A rational ticket holder should weigh the benefit of attending the game against the cost of driving through the storm when deciding whether to make the trip. If the former is larger, she should go, no matter how she came to acquire the ticket.

It is common for people to ignore implicit costs, and they are also likely to focus on average costs and benefits, rather than marginal costs and benefits. And because these tendencies often lead to bad decisions, topics like these merit extra emphasis. Student resources are limited, which underscores the importance of focusing on precisely those issues for which knowing economic theory is most likely to be helpful.

It may seem natural to wonder whether discussing examples of irrational choices might confuse students who are struggling to master the details of the rational choice model. Ironically, however, my experience has been exactly to the contrary. Such examples actually underscore the normative message of the traditional theory. Students who are exposed to them invariably gain a deeper understanding of the basic theoretical principles at issue. Indeed, they often seem to take an almost conspiratorial pride in being able to see through their friends' errors of judgment.

CONCLUDING REMARKS

The world is a more competitive place now than it was when I started teaching in the 1970s. In arena after arena, business as usual is no longer good enough. Baseball players used to drink beer and go fishing during the off season, but they now lift weights and ride exercise bicycles. Assistant professors used to work on their houses on weekends, but the current crop can now be found most weekends at the office. The competition for student attention has grown similarly more intense. There are many tempting courses in the typical college curriculum, and even more tempting diversions outside the classroom. Students are freer than ever to pick and choose.

Yet many of us seem to operate under the illusion that most freshmen arrive with a burning desire to become economics majors. And many of us seem not yet to have recognized that students' cognitive abilities and powers of concentration are scarce resources. To hold our ground we must become not only more selective in what we teach, but also more effective as advocates for our discipline. We must persuade students that we offer something of value.

A well-conceived and well-executed introductory microeconomics course can teach students more about society and human behavior in a single term than virtually any other course in the university. This course can and should be an intellectual adventure of the first order. Not all students who take the kind of course I am advocating will go on to become economics majors. But many will, and even those who do not will leave with a sense of admiration for the power of economic ideas.

Some economists fret that a course like the one I have described would leave students unprepared to tackle the rigorous demands of higher-level courses in the economics major. But that has not been the experience at Cornell. Here and elsewhere, the intermediate microeconomics course essentially starts from scratch, as if students had never taken an introductory course. (In the light of evidence that students learn nothing in typical introductory courses, this should hardly be surprising.) Students who enter the major with a firm intuitive grasp of the most important economic principles are not only well-equipped to meet the demands of upper-level economics courses, they are much more likely to want to take those courses in the first place.

A salesman knows that he gets only one chance to make a good first impression on a potential customer. The principles course is our discipline's one shot at making a good impression on students. By trying to teach them everything we know, we often squander this opportunity.

REFERENCES

Doyle, W. and K. Carter (2003), "Narrative and learning to teach: Implications for teacher-education curriculum", http://faculty.ed.uiuc.edu/westbury/jcs/Vol35/DOYLE.HTM, accessed 15 June 2011.

Ferraro, P. J. and L. O. Taylor (2005), "Do economists recognize an opportunity cost when they see one? A dismal performance from the dismal science", *The B.E. Journals in Economic Analysis and Policy*, **4** (1), Article 7, available at: http://www.bepress.com/bejeap/contributions/vol4/iss1/art7, accessed 15 June 2011.

Hansen, W. L., M. K. Salemi and J. J. Siegfried (2002), "Use it or lose it: Teaching economic literacy", *American Economic Review* (Papers and Proceedings), May, 463–72.

39 Macroeconomic principles are still relevant and still important
William A. McEachern

At the January 2009 meetings of the Allied Social Sciences Association, just four months after the financial crisis, there was great anxiety about the economy. Sessions on the crisis were jam-packed, and many were turned away. My sense at the time was that most attendees wanted to hear comforting words from the sages that all would be well. But there were few such words. It is said that geologists learn more about the nature of the earth's crust from one major upheaval, such as a huge earthquake or volcanic eruption, than from a dozen lesser events. Similarly, extreme brain disorders allow neurologists to compare how the brain works under normal conditions. In that same way, we should eventually learn more about how the economy works from the financial crisis and Great Recession than from the more modest business fluctuations of recent decades. But all that learning will take time, likely years (after all, we are still sorting out the causes and cures of the Great Depression). In the meantime, courses in macroeconomic principles must be taught, and there is still plenty to teach, even if we have not yet fully digested recent events.

Emerson said that the years teach us much that the days never know. What follows are some thoughts on what the years have taught me after three decades and more than ten thousand principles students. I begin with a brief overview of the macroeconomic principles course, propose a few topics to be underscored, suggest several teaching ideas, identify three areas of expanded coverage in the future, and close with some general thoughts about teaching and learning. My intent here is not to lay out the ideal course or to tell colleagues how to teach, but simply to offer more ideas for the course. To have good ideas about teaching macroeconomic principles, we need a lot of ideas. Some of what I have to say will seem obvious, but success is a study of the obvious. And some of it may simply remind you of what you already know or once knew. But according to an adage, none of us is smart enough to remember all we know.

COURSE OVERVIEW[1]

The macro principles course introduces aggregate economic issues, including nominal and real GDP and its components, business cycles, inflation, unemployment, economic growth and productivity, technological change, money and banking, government deficits and debt, fiscal and monetary policies, nominal and real interest rates, exchange rates, trade balances, and economic development. Aggregate supply and aggregate demand usually provide a central framework and unifying element. The course addresses the sources of and remedies for short-run business fluctuations. The focus in the long run is more on economic growth and productivity.

Macroeconomics lumps into four aggregates the 120 million US households, the 32 million businesses, the 90,000 government jurisdictions, and the 200-plus foreign economies. Less attention is paid to the individual entities that make up each aggregate. Macroeconomics examines the forest, not the trees. The assumption is that the forest is different enough from the trees to deserve its own focus, its own field of study. Macroeconomists formulate theories about how the economy works, then test these theories using data on production, prices, employment, and other aggregate measures. The financial crisis and Great Recession have rekindled interest and debate in macroeconomics and added a sense of urgency to what, during a period of "great moderation," was becoming a more settled field.

Lucas and Sargent (1979) argued that economics should not have two incomparable foundations – micro and macro – separated only by Christmas vacation. The push to spell out the micro foundations of macro led to the dynamic stochastic general equilibrium model now taught as part of the macro core in graduate economics programs. This model may be elegant, but its level of abstraction and limited real-world implications make it less useful for macroeconomic principles. The best we can do at the principles level is try to present a model that is logical, internally consistent, understandable, and offers students some idea of how we think the economy works. I want students to think analytically and critically about the economy – well enough to comprehend a newspaper account of economic events and issues. Ultimately, I want them to be better consumers, resource suppliers, and voters. I suggest to students that understanding the macroeconomy is like knowing the weather. The individual may not be able to change it, but at least he or she can adapt to it better.

I use the income-expenditure framework to develop the aggregate demand curve. The short-run aggregate supply curve gets its upward slope from differences between the economy's expected price level and the actual price level. In the long run, the expected price level and actual price level are identical, and this generates a vertical aggregate supply curve at the economy's potential output. Because macroeconomics typically involves a higher level of abstraction than microeconomics, wherever possible, I try to turn the abstract into the concrete to help students learn and remember. For example, to explain how real GDP can exceed the economy's potential in the short run, I remind students of their own study habits. Students normally study a certain amount per week, but during the closing days of the term, most shift into a higher gear to finish research papers and cram for final exams. This pattern exceeds their normal study habits, their normal capacity. In the same way, real GDP can exceed potential output during economic expansions in the short run.

The portion of the course devoted to each macro topic and the analytical approach will likely be reflected in the textbook selected. Lopus and Paringer in this volume summarize the coverage of principles textbooks on the market. I have authored one, now in a ninth edition (McEachern, 2012), and it reflects my philosophy of how to approach this course. But the focus here is on teaching macroeconomic principles not textbook selection.

Another benchmark that sheds light on the relative weights assigned to each macro topic is the fourth, and most recent, version of the Test of Understanding of College Economics, or TUCE-4 (Waldstad and Rebeck, 2008, p. 548). The six macro categories tested by TUCE-4 (and the percentage of questions in each category) are as follows:

measuring aggregate economic performance (13 percent), aggregate supply and aggregate demand (25 percent), money and financial markets (13 percent), monetary and fiscal policies (28 percent), policy debates and applications (10 percent), and international (10 percent). That distribution offers a rough idea of how test developers believe instructors spend their time in the course. Note that "policy debates and applications," topics that occupy much public discourse about macroeconomics, are targeted by only 10 percent of TUCE questions. Policy differences have heated up some because of the financial crisis and Great Recession, but, as Woodford argues, "there are fewer fundamental disagreements now among macroeconomists than in past decades" (2009, p. 267).

SOME TOPICS TO UNDERSCORE

Regardless of the textbook selected, we all tend to give certain topics our own special emphasis. Here are some recommended topics to underscore:

The financial crisis and Great Recession   To help students get some feel for recent developments, the course might include discussions of subprime mortgages, mortgage-backed securities, "too big to fail," moral hazard, the troubled-asset-relief program, the federal stimulus plan, the banking "stress test," and the Dodd-Frank financial legislation. One way to personalize the financial crisis and recession is to ask students how they and their families were affected by these events. But trying to explain the causes of the financial crisis and the impact of the government's response is like peeling an onion. These topics could take over a course. Don't let them. We should not neglect all the macroeconomics we can teach even if we can't yet fully explain recent events.

Automatic fiscal stabilizers   Though some federal programs introduced during the Great Depression were aimed more at income redistribution, they now ensure that consumption fluctuates less than income, thus stabilizing the economy over time. Automatic fiscal stabilizers are the unsung workhorses of fiscal policy. They deserve more credit than they usually get in the macro principles course.

The Fed's balance sheet   This has become more important as a guide to monetary policy. With the first round of quantitative easing, or QE1, the Fed purchased mortgage-backed securities to keep interest rates low and relieve pressure on that securities market. During the second round, or QE2, the Fed purchased treasuries to keep long-term interest rates low. These discretionary monetary policies can be spelled out by tracking the Fed's balance sheet over time. Low interest rates help the banking sector recover, but hurt people who rely on interest income, particularly retirees. The distributional effects of the Fed's policy may be worth discussing. The Fed's decision to hold a press conference after each FOMC meeting should offer still more fodder for the course.

Long-term joblessness   The US Labor Department's Current Population Survey (CPS) now allows respondents to report longer spells of unemployment. Before the change, the CPS accepted spells of up to two years; a response any longer was recorded as two years. Starting with data for January 2011, respondents could report durations of up to five years. This change affects estimates of the average duration of unemployment but not the number unemployed or the median duration of unemployment. Long-term unemployment in 2010 and 2011 was the longest it's been in decades.

Dynamic nature of the economy   Although aggregate measures usually report snapshots of economic activity at a point in time, the economy is better captured as a video. For example, every month employers shed millions of jobs and add millions of jobs. The net result shapes job opportunities, unemployment rates, and the economy's vitality. Between 1970 and 2000 the US economy gained an average of 161,700 jobs a month. Between 2000 and 2010, gains averaged only 19,200 jobs a month, not nearly enough to absorb new entrants to the labor force. As a result, the unemployment rate more than doubled from 4.0 percent in 2000 to 9.6 percent in 2010. You might explore with students why the economy turned from what was viewed as an incredible job machine and envy of the world into a puny job producer.

Productivity growth   The decade from 2000 to 2010 was not good for US job growth, but it was good for US labor productivity growth. An hour of nonfarm work produced 29 percent more in 2010 than in 2000, the best decade of productivity growth since the 1960s. Competition and technological change helped boost productivity. For example, two decades ago, a TV reporter on location would need a camera operator, a sound technician, and a broadcast editor. Now, because of fierce media competition and better equipment, TV reporters typically set up their own cameras, record their own footage, and do their own editing. One person can do what it had taken four to accomplish. The economy may disappoint in the short run, but two centuries of progress offer us some guidance and comfort about the long run. US labor productivity is about 20 times greater now than in 1870. Perhaps you can explain to students that, though the wheels of productivity at times seem to grind slowly, they grind very fine, and the cumulative effect of compounding is powerful.

Technological change and living standards   Technological change has created thousands of new products, and more efficient production methods have lowered many prices over time. Computers, the Internet, cell phones, HDTVs, Blu-ray players, and video cameras have all experienced improved quality and lower prices. For example, the first "portable" video camera, the Ampex VR-3000 Backpack, weighed over 40 pounds and sold for more than $60,000 in 1967 (or more than $400,000 in 2011 dollars). Now, about $100 buys a high-definition video camera that fits in a shirt pocket. Is there any doubt that if 3D TVs are still around in five years, they will cost less? Although most students seem to take the fruits of technological change for granted, economic progress is relatively recent in the long sweep of history. People of Shakespearian England experienced a living standard little better than those of Ancient Greece. Students today, with their smart phones, iPads, and social networks, to name just a few recent developments, may not appreciate what a golden age of discovery and innovation they enjoy. Perhaps you can remind them.

The institutional setting or rules of the game   My macro principles course emphasizes the laws, customs, manners, conventions, and other features of the economy that encourage people to undertake productive activity. A stable political climate and system of well-defined property rights and respected laws are important. People will invest less in human and physical capital if they believe the fruits of their investment could be stolen by thieves, destroyed by civil unrest, blown up by terrorists, or seized by the government. Uncertainty about the rules of the game, such as taxes and regulations, hurts the economy. For example, in 2011 US tax rates on personal income, payrolls, corporations, and estates were expected to change within a year or two. Remaining questions about health-care legislation, yet-to-be-written financial regulations, and massive federal deficits also make some investors and employers wary.

Bring macro estimates to life   Students seem to develop more interest in macroeconomic measures if they have some idea what goes into them. For example, to come up with quarterly GDP estimates, the Bureau of Economic Analysis draws on thousands of data sets. On estimation day, the office is locked down, with windows covered, and phones silenced. Only certain people are allowed in the room. As has been the custom for the last half century, nobody speaks aloud the final estimate for fear that eavesdroppers might be able to exploit the information in financial markets. Once they estimate GDP and its components, they write a press release and lock all but one copy in a safe for distribution to the media the next morning at 8:30 a.m. Eastern Time (an hour before US stock markets open). The single copy not locked away is delivered to the head of the Council of Economic Advisors, who can give the president a heads-up. The consumer price index is estimated under similarly secure conditions. This CSI-like background can heighten student interest in what otherwise might be just a lifeless number.

Compare macro measures across economies   Whenever national measures are introduced, such as unemployment, inflation, growth, productivity, per capita income, tax rates, government spending, government deficits, and government debt, consider comparing US estimates with those for other economies around the world. Students thereby develop more context for the US economy in the world setting.

HAVE SOMETHING WORTH SAYING AND SAY IT WELL

To be a successful teacher in macroeconomic principles, you don't have to do extraordinary things. Just do ordinary things well. The formula is simple: Have something worth saying and say it well. To have something worth saying, we must build up an account from which to draw. We become better teachers when what we say is just the tip of the iceberg of what we know. Economics may be centuries old, but each new day offers fresh evidence that can be used to support or revise evolving economic theories. Data about the macroeconomy abound, and, indeed, can be overwhelming. The challenge is to help students distill this ocean of data into a lake of information, a cup of knowledge, and, perhaps, a drop of wisdom.

The key to saying it well is to generate and sustain student interest. Here are four possible ways to do that: First, when possible, open each class with a hook – a question, a problem, a controversy, an example, a parable, an analogy, a relevant joke, some interesting news, an outrageous statement – something to get their attention. For example, discuss the security precautions taken in estimating the GDP or CPI, note the cost and weight of the first portable video camera and compare that to what's now available, relate some surprising fact about the economy, or ask a provocative question. Once you engage students, keep it going. And be wary about a parade of PowerPoint slides. PowerPoint may help when presenting time series aggregate measures, but, beyond that, student interest and zest for learning drain when lectures are reduced to the routine transmittal of predigested information.

Second, draw on the power of the narrative. Cognitive scientists believe the mind is instinctively programmed to lock onto a story (for example, Willingham, 2009, pp. 51–8). Stories have a privileged position in the brain. We explain macroeconomic theories by telling stories about how we think the economy works. To tell a compelling story, we rely on theories, graphs, supporting data, case studies, anecdotes, parables, and the personal experiences of our students. For example, the aggregate-supply/aggregate-demand framework can help explain the Great Depression, the stagflation of the 1970s, and the Great Recession. This model, or story, has its flaws and its critics, but it is simpler and more powerful than the alternatives.

Enthusiasm is the oil that lubricates the machinery of teaching. Your enthusiasm is a third way to generate and sustain student interest – an enthusiasm for the students, for macroeconomics, and for your ability to deliver the goods. Your presentation should demonstrate an interest in or perhaps even affection for macroeconomics. After all, what course could be more significant and more relevant for our times? An average speaker fired with enthusiasm can be more engaging than can a skilled orator without it. The color and animation of your language in describing the economy convey your enthusiasm, but your nonverbal actions often say more. Direct your nonverbal actions in positive ways. Students are able to sense how enthusiastic and committed you are, and they are judging you all the time. Send the message that you care about them and the material.

Fourth, interest flows from variety – variety in what's presented and the way it's delivered, including theories, facts, statistics, graphs, anecdotes, examples, analogies, humorous stories, questions, opinions, discussions, role-playing, team efforts, online sites, and personal observations from you and from students. Here are some suggestions for more variety in the course:

Unemployment rate for the class   Using a simple show of hands, survey the class and then have students compute unemployment statistics for the group. Ask how many have a job? How many don't have a job but have looked for one in the past month? How many don't have a job and haven't looked for one in the past month? Based on the totals, have each student compute both the labor force participation rate and the unemployment rate. Compare your results to national averages. To discuss discouraged workers, you could also ask about those who want a job but haven't looked for one in the last month. Ask why they have failed to look for a job.

Macro effects on the local economy   You might ask students how they would observe an economic slowdown in the community. Do they notice fewer job postings in newspapers and online or fewer help-wanted signs in store and restaurant windows? With fewer people working, there are fewer job commutes and fewer trips to the mall. This frees up parking spaces, another marker of a slowdown. And because of lighter traffic, accidents decline (US traffic fatalities fell 9 percent in the down year of 2009).

A simple view of money   Students have been around money for so long they take its role in the economy for granted. Since money is nothing more than a sophisticated system of IOUs, students can think of the monetary system as follows. Suppose, in return for a dozen doughnuts, the student gives the baker an IOU promising to supply an hour of unskilled labor. The baker can claim that hour of labor or can trade the IOU for a bag of flour. The IOU circulates as money until someone down the line redeems it for the student's hour of labor. Likewise, the Federal Reserve issues IOUs in the form of Federal Reserve notes, except that ultimately these notes cannot be redeemed for anything of intrinsic value – just more Federal Reserve notes. Why do people accept these pieces of paper? Because they believe that others will (which is reasonable given that every US note issued since 1861 remains legal tender today). That's one reason US dollars are hoarded around the world as a store of value. They all come with a lifetime money-back guarantee, so to speak. Many other nations discourage such hoarding by redesigning their currencies and putting a time limit on the acceptability of the old designs. You might discuss with students how the United States benefits when dollars go abroad and remain there.

Bank failures   The Wall Street Journal offers a handy interactive map of bank failures across the country.[2] Failures increased from only three in 2007 to 157 in 2010. Identify the failures in your area. Ask students why banks fail. Incidentally, the FDIC division that shuts down dead banks had only 219 employees in 2007 but 2,133 by the end of 2010, including more than 50 veterans of the savings-and-loan crisis of the late 1980s who came out of retirement. Still, the 157 failures in 2010 were only about a quarter of the 608 banks that went under in 1989, the worst year of failures during the savings and loan problems. You could discuss why, despite the many more bank failures in the late 1980s, that banking crisis did not do wider damage to the economy. The unemployment rate in 1989 was only 5.3 percent, and there was not even a recession until July of 1990, triggered more by the first war in the Persian Gulf. That recession lasted only eight months, versus 18 months for the Great Recession.

Facebook's happiness index   Happiness indices have been introduced by a few countries around the world as alternatives to GDP as measures of economic welfare. You could discuss the benefits and limitations of such indices. Facebook keeps tabs on national moods via its Gross National Happiness Index, which every day counts "positive" and "negative" words used in each status update, converts them to percentages based on all users that day, then subtracts the negative percent from the positive percent. Facebook has been tracking this measure for 21 countries since September 2007. The results can be observed for each country over time with an amazingly flexible time-series chart.[3] Based on these criteria, US Facebook users seem happier on weekends and holidays than during midweek. Between September 2007 and April 2011, the saddest day for America occurred during the third week of January 2008, the first full month of the US recession, when bitter cold stretched coast to coast. The happiest day was 25 December 2009, the first Christmas after the recession ended.

Weekly review of macro   The Wall Street Journal offers an email service that each Friday highlights several macroeconomic stories appearing in the newspaper that week. For each article, the email provides a link to the article, a summary, classroom applications, some questions, and, in some cases, a small-group assignment. Some articles also come with a video link.[4]

Online videos   Hans Rosling, a Norwegian physician and medical statistician, has developed a four-minute video that demonstrates the economic progress of 200 countries over 200 years. The video shows time-series data in ways that students will enjoy and understand. It required the plotting of 120,000 numbers relating per capita income and average life span over 200 years.[5] For another high quality video, see "The Fight of the Century: Keynes vs. Hayek, Round Two."[6] Many more videos are readily available; a YouTube search for "macroeconomics" on 27 April 2011 turned up 2,300 videos.

FUTURE TRENDS IN THE COURSE

Here are three possible topics that the macro principles course of the future will cover in greater detail:

The world economy   As computers get better and faster, record keeping improves, and governments become more democratic and more transparent, we will get a clearer picture of the world economy as a distinct entity. For example, according to the *World Factbook*,[7] based on purchasing power parity, world GDP declined 0.7 percent in 2009. This is the first drop since 1946. World GDP rebounded to $74.4 trillion in 2010, a growth of 4.6 percent, with the highest growth coming from emerging market economies. The United States, which made up 4.5 percent of the world's population in 2010, accounted for 20 percent of world output.

Sovereign deficits and debt   A major macro policy issue for the coming decade will be how to address high federal deficits and growing debt in the United States and in other economies around the world. Countries such as Greece, Ireland, and Portugal all received rescue packages from the European Union and the International Monetary Fund, yet they continue to struggle, some with violent public responses to belt-tightening measures. For example, Greece had a 2010 federal deficit amounting to 10.5 percent of GDP (about the same as the US) and total federal debt of 143 percent of GDP (more than double the US). The interest rate on its two-year government bonds topped 20 percent (versus 1 percent for the US). Greece, Ireland, and Portugal may serve as canaries in the mineshaft for how all this could play out for larger economies such as the United States, the United Kingdom, and Japan.

Behavioral macroeconomics   Behavioral economists question some assumptions of neoclassical economics, particularly assumptions about unbounded rationality and unbounded willpower. For example, according to the standard life-cycle model of consumption and saving, young people borrow, middle agers pay down debt and save, and older people draw down savings. This pattern is supposed to smooth consumption over a lifetime. But behavioral economists argue that because saving for retirement is both a difficult cognitive problem and a challenging self-control problem, most people save little for retirement. Many low- and middle-income families have essentially no savings. Behavioral economists note that nearly all US household savings are "forced savings" – for example, accumulating home equity by paying the mortgage, participating in pension plans, and paying high withholding taxes to ensure a refund. Behavioral economists are contributing to a range of macroeconomic topics, including bubbles, Keynes's "animal spirits," and the impact of gas prices on inflation perceptions.

SOME GENERAL THOUGHTS ABOUT TEACHING AND LEARNING

According to cognitive scientists, students learn by organizing new information into a coherent mental structure, integrating that information with their prior knowledge, then retrieving that information from memory and transferring it to other situations (Willingham, 2009). Macro principles students show up the first day of class after years of experience with economic choices, economic institutions, and economic events. They have heard and read about inflation, unemployment, recessions, expansions, economic growth, technological change, money, the financial crises, and many other relevant macro topics. Remind them that they have been around the subject matter all their lives, and may know more than they think. Teaching and learning are easier if students begin with something familiar. Begin with what students bring to the party, and then use that material to help build bridges from the familiar to the new.

Our instincts tell us to present material as clearly as possible, but research suggests that this may be misguided. Don't try to lay out everything on a silver platter. Students will think less, and they'll maintain the illusion that the material is easier than it actually is. And don't offer the macro course as just a series of explanations, a series of answers. Presentations need not be exhaustive. Better to offer material in a way that forces students to connect some of the dots, fill in some of the blanks, and draw some of the inferences. For example, many explanations in macroeconomics are symmetrical, such as the effects of higher interest rates versus lower ones, an increase in the money supply versus a decrease, or a tax increase versus a decrease. Consider working through one side of the analysis and then leave it to students to work through the other side. Students find learning more satisfying if they can solve some of the puzzles along the way. Leaving some of the analysis to students also helps us cover more topics in class. At worst, this approach may prompt more class questions, but that's a good thing. Good questions are like gold, and we should do all we can to nurture them. Even an off-the-wall question can help us see a problem with fresh eyes.

Some cognitive scientists recommend offering material with "desirable difficulties" (for example, Bjork and Bjork, 2011, p. 58). Desirable difficulties are challenges introduced during instruction that seem to benefit long-term learning. Teaching that appears to create difficulties for students, such as presenting macro models in different contexts, different formats, with different examples and organization from the textbook, may seem to slow the apparent rate of learning in the short run, but this seems to improve long-term retention and transfer. A more challenging presentation engages them more, and this helps them learn and remember. More generally, the easier we make the course, the less students seem to engage and learn. We take one step forward, they take one step back.

Finally, there is often too much emphasis on differences across students in their abilities to learn, and too little emphasis on differences in their efforts. What students do in the course determines what and how much they learn and under what conditions that knowledge can be recalled and transferred, which, after all, is the point of the macro principles course. Good teaching is an important part of the mix, but what we do in class as instructors matters less than what we ask and expect students to do in the course. The best coaches get the most from their players. The best teachers get the most from their students. We shouldn't confuse inputs with outputs. The day's product is not how well organized our presentation is, but what students take away from the class and what they do for themselves in the course. It's not what we teach, it's what they learn.

NOTES

1. For more information about the structure and content of principles courses, see The Purpose, Structure and Content of the Principles of Economics Course chapter in this volume.
2. http://graphicsweb.wsj.com/documents/Failed-US-Banks.html (accessed 26 April 2011).
3. http://apps.facebook.com/usa_gnh/ (accessed 26 April 2011).
4. Learn more about the program at http://professor.wsj.com/info/2010/07/19/weekly-review/ (accessed 26 April 2011).
5. http://www.youtube.com/watch?v=jbkSRLYSojo (accessed 26 April 2011).
6. http://econstories.tv/2011/04/28/fight-of-the-century-music-video/ (accessed 26 April 2011).
7. https://www.cia.gov/library/publications/the-world-factbook/geos/xx.html (accessed 26 April 2011).

REFERENCES

Bjork, E. L. and R. Bjork (2011), "Making things hard on yourself, but in a good way: Creating desirable difficulties to enhance learning", in M. A. Gernsbacher, D. Pew and L. Hough (eds), *Psychology and the Real World: Essays Illustrating the Fundamental Contributions to Society*, New York: Worth Publishers, pp. 56–64.

Lucas, R. E., Jr. and T. J. Sargent (1979), "After Keynesian economics", *Quarterly Review*, Federal Reserve Bank of Minneapolis (Spring Issue), also available at http://www.minneapolisfed.org/research/qr/qr321.pdf, accessed 14 April 2011.

McEachern, W. A. (2012), *Economics: A Contemporary Introduction* (9th edition), Mason, OH: South-Western Cengage Learning.

Walstad, W. B. and K. Rebeck (2008), "The test of understanding of college economics", *American Economic Review: Papers and Proceedings*, **98** (2), 547–52.

Willingham, D. T. (2009), *Why Don't Students Like School: A Cognitive Scientist Answers Questions about How the Mind Works and What It Means for the Classroom*, San Francisco: Jossey-Bass.

Woodford, M. (2009), "Convergence in macroeconomics: Elements of the new synthesis", *American Economic Journal: Macroeconomics*, **1** (1), 267–79.

40 Teaching non-majors[1]
Deborah M. Figart

Economists' teaching methods have relied heavily, if not exclusively, on "chalk and talk," especially at the introductory level. According to a survey of teaching methods in 1995, 2000, and 2005 by Watts and Becker (2008), instructors made greater use of student-centered learning methods. Though the authors found that the standard lecture format was still the mainstay of instruction, more professors have adopted classroom discussions, cooperative learning, assignments in a computer lab, internet activities, games and simulations, applications to economic and financial news in the press, and even sports, popular fiction, music, and drama. Surprisingly, Watts and Becker found few differences in teaching methods across different types of courses. Writing assignments were more likely to be doled out in upper-division courses, yet writing assignments other than homework and problem sets remained "relatively rare" (p. 284). A scan of the past ten or fifteen volumes of the *Journal for Economic Education* provides excellent examples of assignments and techniques for those teachers who are willing to experiment and deviate from the norm. Websites are proliferating that are devoted to, for example, the applications of Hollywood movies or popular music to economics concepts and ideas.[2]

Economists' pedagogy is slowly changing and helping to retain the interest of potential economics majors. But instructors in academe teach more non-majors than majors; only 2 percent of US undergraduates choose to major in economics (Siegfried and Round, 2001).[3] Economics professors are charged with introducing economics to students in other declared majors. Faculty colleagues and curriculum committees (across institution types) have decided that an understanding of basic economics is crucial to many disciplinary studies. Students also enroll in economics to fulfill a distribution requirement (for example, social sciences) for graduation. And most important of all, economists teach students with a variety of majors and interests who just want to learn more about a critical area of their lives – the economy. At my liberal arts college, for example, an economics course is required for students majoring in social work or preparing to teach social studies. Some of these students struggle mightily with the abstract graphical representations of the theory and wonder how it could apply to their profession and help them in their future career.

Unfortunately, by focusing on the study of "economics" and not "the economy," we run the risk of squeezing much of students' interest and zeal out of them (Figart, 2010a). College-level principles courses emphasize teaching tools to think like an economist (just look in any top-selling textbook, for example) rather than teaching about the real economy (Colander, 2006, ch. 4; Wunder, Kemp, and England, 2009). Students therefore learn the science of economics rather than broad issues related to public policy and how societies sustain themselves and grow, issues that have been the focus of economists, philosophers, and others for centuries. To students, it can appear as if what is taught is algebra and/or calculus rather than what many students expected following high school.

Today's students in colleges and universities, especially in the United States, are more likely to enter principles of economics classes with some background in economics as well as exposure to topics in personal financial literacy. According to the (National) Council on Economic Education's *Survey of the States 2009*, 21 US states require students to take an economics course as a high school graduation requirement and 13 states require students to cover topics in financial literacy. As a result, students have already discussed the economy in social studies and business classes. Contextual lessons in high school, however, frequently emphasize understanding institutions, history, and current events. Students are interested in the economy in which they have to live and work. To borrow Tiemstra's phrase, students are interested in learning about the "history and institutions" of the economy (1999, p. 559), a more interdisciplinary emphasis than what is often stressed.

According to Caviglia-Harris (2003, p. 195), "Economic education research has not focused on interdisciplinary approaches or on the teaching of economics to nonmajors." This chapter aims to remedy the dearth of research in this area.[4] It explores issues related to teaching alternative forms of introductory courses to non-majors, primarily as a key component of a liberal education. While some students may flourish in traditional introductory courses, economics professors have created distinctive courses for non-majors. Questions posed in this chapter address the mission of teaching non-majors: What are we teaching in terms of content? To what extent are we emphasizing abstract theories and associated techniques? Are we teaching interesting topics, and drawing students in? Do we teach what students need to know in order to feel empowered as economic actors and citizens if they never take another economics course?

APPROACHES TO TEACHING INTRODUCTORY ECONOMICS: WHAT ARE OUR GOALS AND OBJECTIVES?

An Economic Issues Course

If a primary goal of teaching non-majors is to make economics more relevant to students with diverse interests, then an economic issues course is an option. Introduction to economic issues is a frequent one-semester, introductory course intended for non-majors. A student who subsequently chooses to study economics further must then proceed to take principles of macro and micro. Publishers have responded to this market with textbook-equivalents on economic issues focused by topic or by theory or paradigm.[5] Faculty can build these courses around a number of issues, selecting topics available in issues textbooks and/or having students vote on additional ones they wish to explore. The course may count toward an economics major, sending the message that the issues approach is "real economics."

Colleges and universities have also offered introductory economics courses that focus on particular economic issues. Such courses can be directly related to a regularly offered department of economics list of courses, or an interdisciplinary freshman (first-year) seminar or an honors program seminar. For example, Caviglia-Harris (2003) describes a model for teaching introductory economics at Salisbury University in Maryland, using environmental issues as the theme. Three faculty members team-taught the course around the topic of temperate and tropical forests. Class time was divided among three key disciplinary approaches: economics, ecology, and philosophy. The economics "module" or segment covered fairly conventional concepts such as supply and demand, opportunity costs, comparative advantage, and market failure. Readings included selected chapters from a principles of economic textbook and an environmental economics textbook. Students found the course challenging and interesting. Though the course provided connections between the three disciplinary approaches, students seemed to be provided with a multidisciplinary perspective as opposed to one that was integrated or interdisciplinary.[6]

A multidisciplinary team-taught course on health issues by an economist and a sociologist at Spelman College in the US is another example of an economic issues course targeted at non-majors. At Spelman, both the economics and sociology departments approved the course, but only the sociology department allowed "Health – Sociological and Economic Perspectives" to be counted as an elective for the major. Institutional barriers were reflected upon by the instructors in the *Journal of Economic Education*:

> The main issue involved in the institutional acceptance of the course was the economics department's insistence that the course be restricted to only satisfy the social science core requirement. . . . The reasons for this may have reflected the traditional hostility of economics to sociology (which manifests itself in the relative lack of pluralism in economics programs compared to sociology programs). Further, the economics faculty may have feared the potential dilution of course enrollment of major electives in the economics department . . . (Wade and Stone, 2010, p. 76)

While serving the goal of reaching non-majors, this policy reflects an implicit devaluing of the issues course versus the core courses counted toward the undergraduate major in economics.

Freedman (2008), from Stevenson University in Maryland, has also designed a team-taught course to introduce economics issues to non-majors who are first-year honors students. She built the course around gender issues. Team-taught with an historian, both professors tried to weave the two disciplines together throughout the course. As the semester progressed, there was greater integration of the disciplines. This outcome was achieved because the instructors did not require a textbook. According to Freedman:

> We did not assign any textbook for the course. Instead, we composed an extensive reading list, and we wanted to make sure that students read and comprehended these assigned readings on a basic level. In addition, we hoped that, by forcing the students to be active participants right from the start, we would be more successful in setting a seminar-type atmosphere from the beginning. (2008, p. 255)

Team-teaching an issues course can be quite expensive for administrative budgets because of faculty workload. It is unlikely that all participating faculty will receive 100 percent workload credit for the course over time. Further, traditional departments can reject the newly created courses as "soft" and inappropriate for their own majors. Thus, such courses tend to only count toward a student's general education requirements.

Another drawback of the economic issues approach to teaching non-majors is elucidated by John Tiemstra from Calvin College in Michigan. Tiemstra (1999) argues that with some economic issues, abstract models still need to be introduced, but doing so seems both ad hoc and disconnected from the other models and issues: ". . . these students are not in fact going on to further work in economics, so they will never get enough practice with abstract economic models to be able to use them effectively, or enough experience to be able to apply them wisely" (p. 560). Without a theoretical grounding, students' positions on issues may be based on unexamined pre/misconceptions rather than a deeper understanding of the assumptions underlying alternative views.[7]

Fact-based Economic Literacy

A common alternative approach to teaching non-majors is an economic literacy course focusing on basic vocabulary and understanding the health of the US and global economies through economic indicators. Rather than theoretical modeling, such courses often emphasize objective economic facts, trends, and statistics. This allows the learner "to understand some of the realities of the economy they live in. From that starting point the student can go on to make decisions about where they envision the economy is going and also make normative suppositions about how the economy should be directed" (Wunder, Kemp, and England, 2009, p. 467).[8]

Naturally, instructors can target a specific audience when using this approach. In 1999, I created a course open to all non-majors, but primarily directed to majors in social work, political science, and social studies certification students in our teacher education program. All three of these populations are required or recommended to take an economics course for their degree. The largest constituency is social work majors. Historically, they were often advised to take introduction to microeconomics because somewhere in week 12 or 13 they might learn about poverty and income inequality!

The approach has been to focus on economic literacy through the study of everyday economic indicators and some alternative theoretical and policy debates about how to improve those indicators. The course description reads:

> This course provides an introduction to the discipline of economics and the subject of how economic life is organized in the United States. Students will first be introduced to the ways in which economists analyze economic and social problems and the basic measures of economic life and well-being. Next we will discuss how economists measure poverty, income distribution, and inequality. We will also examine economic policy. Throughout, considerable attention will be placed on understanding competing interpretations of the role that economic actors, including businesses, households, and the government, play in economic growth and well-being. (Figart 2010b)

In the course, students learn how to utilize government websites to find and analyze economic indicators such as GDP, unemployment, inflation, budget deficits and surpluses, food insecurity, poverty, income distribution and inequality, and the race- and gender-based wage gaps.[9] They develop statistical literacy along with economic literacy, including the ability to write papers using quantitative evidence.

One homework assignment requires students to visit the website of the US Bureau of Labor Statistics to find news releases on unemployment and asks them to answer the following overall questions: How has the economy of the United States been doing in meeting the macroeconomic goal of "full employment?" Have jobs been readily available in the US economy over the past 36 months? Do current measures of employment growth (or decline) differ across demographic groups (race, age, education level, etc.), regions/states of the US, and why? Parallel assignments cover topics including the inflation rate (CPI), GDP, and poverty. An indicator not typically covered in principles of economics, the US Department of Agriculture's annual measure of food security, is also important for non-majors, especially social workers. One project is an essay:

> Two essential elements of provisioning are food and housing. Yet both can be difficult for the working poor to provide for themselves on a regular basis. As we prepare to celebrate the Thanksgiving holiday and take time to appreciate the material goods that we have been fortunate to enjoy, this assignment will focus on those who are less fortunate. Your assignment is to write a short descriptive essay summarizing the problem of food insecurity in the US. Your essay will incorporate quantitative evidence on the extent of food insecurity. Go to the US Department of Agriculture website[10] and look for the links to the section on food security.
> Be sure to address the following questions:
>
> - What is the definition of food security/insecurity?
> - Briefly explain the process the USDA uses to measure food security and insecurity.
> - What was the prevalence of food insecurity and hunger in 2010? (Hint: Look for the PDF file of the reports titled *Household Food Security in the United States.*)
> - From the same report, summarize the level of food security/insecurity by US state, race-ethnicity, household type, and other salient demographic categories. (Figart, 2010b)

In each of the written assignments on economic indicators, students need to evaluate the strengths and weaknesses of the indicator(s) and suggest what the indicator may not be revealing. In a sense, then, a fact-based economic literacy course reveals a process as opposed to a specific outcome; economic statistics are one way of portraying some "facts" about the economy, but those facts are products of a data design and data-collection process that involves human decisions and public policy.

A broader approach to economic literacy is learning about our capitalist economy. Lynn Duggan from Indiana University, who teaches in a labor studies program, has a lengthy course description of an introductory course for non-majors that includes the following:

> This course is an introduction to the current situation of workers and families in the US economy . . .. To do this we need to learn about capitalism – how is it working, and how it could work better? . . .We'll also look at the global context that surrounds the US economy, including the pressures faced by working people in other countries (both those who work for pay and those who do unpaid work). . . .. Our emphasis will be on intuitive understanding, rather than memorization of mathematical formulas. (Duggan, 2010)

In her course, Duggan spends a considerable amount of time trying to have students understand and critically assess how capitalism works within and among economic sectors, and its affect on workplaces, well-being, and public policy. One of two required readings for the course is *Understanding Capitalism* by Bowles, Edwards, and Roosevelt (2005). Professors with similar goals and objectives have assigned *Economics for Everyone: A Short Guide to the Economics of Capitalism* by Stanford (2008).

In the Netherlands, Irene Van Staveren from the International Institute of Social Studies at Erasmus University teaches a similar course using the Stanford book, with more emphasis on economic development for students majoring in interdisciplinary development studies. Van Staveren will often ask her students to enrich their work with examples from their home countries. The objective of the course explains that it is a non-technical introduction to economics:

> This economics course teaches real-world economics, which is a more democratic economics not using high abstract terminology and mathematics. It is closer to the experiences of us all in every day life. This enables all of us to better understand the economy and to participate in debates about the economy and to influence economic policies. (Van Staveren, 2010)

Another choice is to approach teaching economics as a discipline grounded in contending worldviews as a way to engage students' interest, while nurturing their critical instincts. For example, Edward J. O'Boyle, a longtime member of the faculty at Louisiana Tech University describes his one-term principles of economics course for non-business majors: "The general goal of the course is to instruct the beginning student as to how a capitalist economy functions and dysfunctions from both a conventional-economics perspective which underscores economics as the study of things and from a social-economics perspective which focuses on human beings as the subject of economics" (1999, p. 531).

What these course descriptions and assignments have in common is their emphasis on critical thinking, critical reasoning, and interrogating the economy, economic statistics, and economic relationships. They also have in common a learning objective focused on helping students understand economics and the economy through an analysis of economic ideas and/or economic history. Zohreh Emami of Alverno College in Wisconsin echoes that this is a key goal in her general education economics course (Emami, 1999).

Teaching non-majors by building a course around economic literacy necessarily means that the goals and objectives of the course will be different from a standard principles of macroeconomics or microeconomics course. While supply and demand graphs, marginal analysis, cost-benefit analysis, and other tools of economic thinking can serve the goals of advancing liberal education, they can also be taught in a way that reinforces disciplinary boundaries by discouraging students from making connections between method and applications to the economy and society. General education goals may be furthered if an economic literacy course includes writing, critical thinking, and skills such as reading and understanding websites and newspapers. These skills are critical to serving emerging visions of liberal education such as the Liberal Education and America's Promise (LEAP) initiative of the Association of American Colleges and Universities (see AAC&U, 2007; 2010).

Economic Journalism

Another common way to teach non-majors is through story-telling. Susan Feiner from the University of Southern Maine favors this approach. To get students' attention in everyday economic life, faculty members such as Feiner have built courses around journalistic narratives that describe the lived economy. Although these serve as attention-getters, they are also applications of key economic concepts and issues.

For instance, *New York Times* columnist Frank Rich spent a year reporting on and living with people in the top 1 percent of the income distribution. Feiner (2010) suggests that the chapter in *Richistan* on bigger-is-better is compelling because students learn concepts such as conspicuous consumption and how social norms foster "keeping up with the Joneses," as in: "Your yacht is only 250 feet, well mine is bigger." This not only engages students, but allows professors to introduce economics concepts in an applied way. *Richistan* can be supplemented with Shell's book, *Cheap* (2010), on the history of retailing since the 1950s, focusing on themes of consumerism and happiness (Feiner, 2010, 25 August). Non-majors may be better served by discussing emulation of consumption among income levels rather than learning how to differentiate normal goods from inferior goods. They could debate whether to distinguish needs versus wants rather than graphing marginal utility.

There are numerous journalistic accounts of workers and families trying to create a life for themselves and trying to make ends meet. One notable and oft-assigned book in social sciences and freshman seminar courses in the US is the best-selling *Nickel and Dimed* by Ehrenreich. Alternatively, *Cheap Motels and a Hot Plate* (Yates, 2007) chronicles the day-to-day lives of people at the bottom of the economic ladder (low-paid jobs, jobs in more depressed economic communities), supplementing economic statistics with case studies. This "road book" swings through the American southwest, with stops including Santa Fe, New Mexico, Flagstaff, Arizona, and Estes Park, Colorado, and the author narrates striking, moving, and meaningful exchanges on the experiences of people of color and native American Indians, such as:

> More than one million black men and women are in our jails and prisons, about the same number as whites, though the black share of the population is less than one-sixth that of whites. It is more likely that a black person of college age is in prison than in college. There are no economic indicators showing a black (or Hispanic or American Indian) advantage. Black median income, whether for families or individuals, is less than whites, as is wealth. Black wages are lower. Black poverty rates are higher, by wide margins. Black unemployment rates are typically double white rates. All of these indicators show differences between blacks and whites even after variables that might influence them are held constant. (Yates, 2007, pp. 247–8)

One could easily imagine a web-based investigation and writing assignment that requires that students find the most recent specific economic statistics that Yates refers to in this reflection paragraph.

CONCLUSIONS: CRITICAL IDEAS, STARTING WITH THE DEFINITION OF ECONOMICS

Teaching students about the economy in order to prepare them for rich lives as economic actors and citizens is certainly as important as socializing the next generation of economists. When we teach to non-majors, it is important to know who our students are (see also Arvidson, 2008). Are they training to be social workers or social studies teachers? Are the students drawn from different countries and interested in economic development? Are they labor studies students with vast experience in the workplace? Perhaps students in the natural sciences or engineering are urged to take an economics course and are very familiar with and comfortable with algebra and calculus and prefer quantitative tools. All students are not homogeneous.

When we teach, we need to have a vision. We need to set goals and objectives. These are guided by our expertise but should also be grounded in who our students are. Our students are delivered a message about what those goals and objectives are on day #1, not just on the syllabus but in the content delivered in the very first class. The definition of economics is a good place to start. That definition of what we study delivers a message about where we are taking our students while we have them in our classes. There are two contrasting paths, emanating from two contrasting definitions. In my courses, but especially in my course for non-majors, I begin with these two contrasting definitions:

1. Economics studies the efficient allocation of the scarce means of production toward the satisfaction of human wants (from any standard textbook).
2. "Economics is the study of the way people organize themselves to sustain life and enhance its quality" (Goodwin, Nelson, and Harris, 2009, p. 3, inspired by institutional and social economists who maintain that economics studies "the provisioning of human life," the commodities and processes necessary for human survival (Nelson, 2006; Figart, 2007)).

I then relate to my students that we will be tackling concepts and issues that draw upon the latter definition. The second definition focuses on the processes that constitute our economic lives rather than introducing a particular mode of analysis. It defines economics in terms of its subject matter rather than methodology. It does not embed a bias in favor of efficiency over all other possible economic goals. This broader definition of our subject matter engages students in enduring questions central to a liberal education.

What many of the economics principles alternatives to teaching non-majors have in common is the emphasis on critical thinking and critical reasoning, through reading the kinds of non-fiction trade books that we hope a college graduate would continue to read as part of lifelong learning, and writing essays and papers that address complex questions with more than one possible answer. Such assignments resemble assignments in other courses in the liberal arts and are consistent with the argument that economics (and non-majors alike) should encounter more "big think" questions (see Colander and McGoldrick, 2009). What unites the content is that instructors build courses around focusing on the state of the everyday economy and how it affects workers, households and families, sectors, and countries.

These skills are some of the "essential learning outcomes" that the Association of American Colleges & Universities has defined as critical for twenty-first century liberal education (AAC&U, 2010). The first learning outcome focuses on content knowledge that involves "engagement with big questions, both contemporary and enduring." Beyond content knowledge, however, the architects of LEAP (Liberal Education and America's Promise) also emphasize the attainment of "intellectual and practical skills," including inquiry and analysis, critical and creative thinking, written and oral communication, quantitative and information literacy, problem solving, and teamwork. These are to be practiced across the curriculum. AAC&U also emphasizes the need for applied learning, civic engagement, and lifelong learning. Those of us who teach economics need to seriously engage the challenges of providing a liberal education to all of our students. Teaching non-majors about economic life is one way to address these challenges.

NOTES

1. The author would like to thank Susan Feiner, Ellen Mutari, and Martha Starr for comments on a previous draft.
2. See, for instance, Chapter 21 by Bohanon and Vachris in this volume.
3. A nationally representative survey shows that about 60 percent of all undergraduates take at least one course in economics; of non-economics and non-business majors, about 47 percent completed at least one economics course (Bosshardt and Watts, 2008).
4. A related topic is an evaluation of the economics major, itself. That is not covered here, but it is handled well in *Educating Economists: The Teagle Discussion on Re-evaluating the Undergraduate Economics Major* (Colander and McGoldrick, 2009).
5. Popular books assigned have included the *Taking Sides* and *Annual Editions* series (Bonello and Lobo, 2010; Cole, 2009), *Economic Issues and Policy* (Brux, 2011), *Issues in Economics Today* (Guell, 2010), *Current Economic Issues* (Fireside et al., 2009), and the formerly published *Economics Issues Today: Alternative Approaches* (Carson et al., 2005).
6. This approach to economic education is further described in Chapter 22 "The Interdisciplinary Approach to Teaching Economics" in this volume.
7. Grimes (2009) adds that the social issues approach has failed to thrive, or even survive at a majority of institutions.
8. By the phrase "economic literacy," I explicitly mean understanding economic indicators loosely as "facts," and this also includes assessing the strengths and weaknesses of those indicators. This is not a one-to-one correlation with any book that has economic literacy in its title since the book may be an alternative approach to teaching economics principles (see, for example, Weaver, 2011).
9. They also learn the basics of supply and demand and the difference between neoclassical and political economy theories of discrimination. One of the books used is *Unlevel Playing Fields* (Albelda, Drago, and Shulman, 2010).
10. http://www.usda.gov (accessed 14 June 2011).

REFERENCES

Albelda, R., R. Drago and S. Shulman (2010), *Unlevel Playing Fields: Understanding Wage Inequality and Discrimination* (3rd ed.), Boston, MA: Economic Affairs Bureau.

Arvidson, P. S. (2008), *Teaching Nonmajors: Advice for Liberal Arts Professors*, Albany, NY: State University of New York Press.

Association of American Colleges and Universities (2007), *College Learning for the New Global Century*, Washington, DC: AAC&U.

Association of American Colleges and Universities (2010), "Liberal education and America's promise", http://www.aacu.org/leap/vision.cfm, accessed 20 September 2010.

Bonello, F. J. and I. Lobo (2009), *Taking Sides: Clashing Views on Economic Issues*, New York: McGraw-Hill.

Bosshardt, W. and M. Watts (2008), "Undergraduate students' coursework in economics", *Journal of Economic Education*, **39** (2), 198–205.

Bowles, S., R. Edwards and F. Roosevelt (2005), *Understanding Capitalism* (3rd ed.), New York: Oxford University Press.

Brux, J. M. (2011), *Economic Issues and Policy* (5th ed.), Mason, OH: Cengage Learning.

Carson, R. B., W. L. Thomas and J. Hecht (2005), *Economic Issues Today: Alternative Approaches* (5th ed.), Armonk, NY: M.E. Sharpe.

Caviglia-Harris, J. (2003), "Introducing undergraduates to economics in an interdisciplinary setting", *Journal of Economic Education*, **34** (3), 195–203.

Colander, D. (2006), *The Stories Economists Tell: Essays on the Art of Teaching Economics*, New York: McGraw-Hill Irwin.

Colander, D. and K. McGoldrick (2009), *Educating Economists: The Teagle Discussion on Re-evaluating the Undergraduate Economics Major*, Cheltenham, UK and Northampton, MA, USA: Edward Elgar.

Cole, D. (2009), *Annual Editions: Economics* (35th ed.), New York: McGraw Hill.

Council of Economic Education (2009), *Survey of the States: A Report Card*, New York, NY: Council for Economic Education.

Duggan, L. (2010), "Syllabus for L230, labor and the economy", Indiana University School of Social Work, Spring 2009, Bloomington, IN, sent to author on 24 August 2010.

Ehrenreich, B. (2008 [2001]) *Nickel and Dimed: On (Not) Getting By in America*, New York: Henry Holt and Company.

Emami, Z. (1999), "Teaching principles of economics from a social economics perspective", in E. J. O'Boyle (ed.), *Teaching the Social Economics Way of Thinking*, Lewiston, NY: The Edwin Mellen Press, pp. 501–12.

Feiner, S. (2010), Personal email communications, 25 August, 26 August, and 28 August.

Figart, D. M. (2007), "Social responsibility for living standards", *Review of Social Economy*, **65** (4), 391–405.

Figart, D. M. (2010a), "Editorial: Teaching during the global financial crisis", *International Journal of Pluralism and Economics Education*, **1** (3), 236–41.

Figart, D. M. (2010b), "Syllabus for ECON 1120, economics of social welfare, Fall 2010", The Richard Stockton College of New Jersey, Galloway, NJ.

Fireside, D., A. Reuss and C. Sturr (2009), *Current Economic Issues* (13th ed.), Boston, MA: Economic Affairs Bureau.

Freedman, O. (2008), "Sex, class, and history: An experiment in teaching economics in an interdisciplinary setting", *Journal of Economic Education*, **39** (3), 251–59.

Goodwin, N., J. A. Nelson and J. Harris (2009), *Macroeconomics in Context*, Armonk, NY: M.E. Sharpe.

Grimes, P. W. (2009), "Reflections on introductory course structures", in D. Colander and K. McGoldrick (eds), *Educating Economists*, Cheltenham, UK and Northampton, MA, USA: Edward Elgar, pp. 95–8.

Guell, R. (2010), *Issues in Economics Today* (5th ed.), New York: McGraw-Hill.

Nelson, J. (2006), *Economics for Humans*, Chicago: University of Chicago Press.

O'Boyle, E. J. (1999), "The person behind the principles", in E. J. O'Boyle (ed.), *Teaching the Social Economics Way of Thinking*, Lewiston, NY: The Edwin Mellen Press, pp. 531–58.

Rich, F. (2007), *Richistan*, New York: Crown Publishers.

Shell, E. R. (2010), *Cheap: The High Cost of Discount Culture*, New York: Penguin USA.

Siegfried, J. and D. Round (2001), "International trends in economics degrees during the 1990s", *Journal of Economic Education*, **32** (3), 203–18.

Stanford, J. (2008), *Economics for Everyone: A Short Guide to the Economics of Capitalism*, London and Ann Arbor, MI: Pluto Press.

Tiemstra, J. (1999), "A new approach to the general education economics course", in E. J. O'Boyle (ed.), *Teaching the Social Economics Way of Thinking*, Lewiston, NY: The Edwin Mellen Press, pp. 559–69.

Van Staveren, I. (2010), "Syllabus and first lecture/tutorial for ECO 1106", International Institute of Social Sciences, Erasmus University, Rotterdam, The Netherlands, sent to author on 6 September 2010.

Wade, B. H. and J. H. Stone (2010), "Overcoming disciplinary and institutional barriers: An interdisciplinary course in economic and sociological perspectives on health issues", *Journal of Economic Education*, **41** (1), 71–84.

Watts, M. and W. E. Becker (2008), "A little more than chalk and talk: Results from a third national survey of teaching methods in undergraduate economics courses", *Journal of Economic Education*, **39** (3), 273–86.

Weaver, F. S. (2011), *Economic Literacy: Basic Economics with an Attitude*, Lanham, MD: Rowman & Littlefield Publishers, Inc.

Wunder, T. A., T. Kemp and S. England (2009), "Fact based economic education", *Journal of Economic Issues*, **43** (2), 467–75.

Yates, M. (2007), *Cheap Motels and a Hot Plate: An Economist's Travelogue*, New York: Monthly Review Press.

41 Intermediate microeconomics
Walter Nicholson

I was hired by Amherst College in 1968 with the primary purpose of introducing a course in intermediate microeconomics into their economics curriculum. Prior to that time, microeconomic theory had been included as one segment of their industrial organization course (titled "The American Economy") taught by Jim Nelson, a well-known regulatory economist. My curricular mandate was to cover as much of microeconomic theory as I could in one semester while using some calculus (at that time, the Amherst economics department already required all majors to have completed one semester of calculus). After a brief transition period, my course was to be required of all majors. Since 1968 I have taught intermediate microeconomics at least once in most years. In this chapter I will try to draw some useful lessons from this experience. The chapter is organized around four broad questions: What should the goals of an intermediate micro course be? What topics should be covered in intermediate micro? How much mathematics should be used in the course? And how should students (and professors) be assessed? A concluding section then raises some broader issues about the role of intermediate microeconomics in the general economics curriculum.

WHAT SHOULD THE GOALS OF THE INTERMEDIATE MICROECONOMICS COURSE BE?

It is misleadingly simple to state what the main goal of an intermediate microeconomics course should be. As for all courses in economics, the goal should be to aid students in developing the ability to "think like an economist." Two components of the economist's toolkit seem especially salient to the typical intermediate microeconomics curriculum: learning how to define economic concepts correctly and learning how to use economic models.

Defining Concepts Properly

With regard to the proper definition of concepts, consider the following four examples:

Costs   The economist's definition of costs (essentially opportunity cost) has relevance to all areas of economics. It is important to understanding what economic profits are, to correctly analyzing entry and exit decisions, and to thinking correctly about public goods provision. Distinctions among types of costs (variable, fixed, or sunk) are also relevant to a wide variety of economic topics.

Economic efficiency   The notion that resources can be inefficiently allocated and that therefore there may be a "free lunch" (in which everyone is made better off) from reallocations is an important discovery, probably dating from Ricardo's analysis of comparative advantage. But there are many different efficiency concepts in economics and students can be overwhelmed by them. It is therefore important to start with a clear example (certainly comparative advantage is a good one) and then show how other notions of efficiency (for example, p = mc) are related to this basic idea.

Tax incidence   The determination of who ultimately pays a tax is one of the major insights of microeconomic analysis. The truism that "only people pay taxes" is eye-opening for many students and the ability to identify which people pay which taxes can help clarify many contentious political issues that concern them.

Externalities   The distinction between "pecuniary" and "technological" externalities was largely cleared up in the 1950s (see Scitovsky, 1954). The conclusion was that only the latter types of externalities have allocative significance. That is, only technological externalities cause the price system to allocate goods inefficiently. Hence, the Pigovian rationale for taxation (or subsidy) applies only to such technological cases. Even a cursory reading of recent commentary, some of it by very prominent economists, suggests that this lesson has been largely forgotten. A careful coverage in the intermediate microeconomics course can help students differentiate between correct uses of the externality concept and incorrect uses, which are usually some form of pleading by special interests.

Of course these examples are only illustrative of how stressing definitions can help students in the intermediate microeconomics course to begin to "think like economists." But making sure students get such definitions right should be a key aspect of any course.

Using Economic Models Correctly

Learning to use economic models properly is the second key goal of the intermediate microeconomics course for students. The issues in model use might be divided into two categories: (1) How to think about any model; and (2) How to choose the right model for the problem at hand. With regard to the general methodology of models, economists generally do not do a good enough job in differentiating between the exogenous and endogenous variables in them. Confusing the two can lead to all sorts of problems for students. For example, students learn in their introductory economics course that all economic theorizing involves some form of the *ceteris paribus* assumption under which some things are held constant in a model whereas other things are varied. But I doubt that many students know that this distinction applies only to exogenous variables. Typically one exogenous variable is varied in an economic model whereas the others are held constant. So, in consumer theory, we ask how the quantity demanded of orange juice changes when the price of orange juice changes (exogenously), while holding constant things like the price of apple juice, consumer income, or preferences. In this context the *ceteris paribus* assumption clearly makes sense. But students can easily become confused if asked questions such as "shouldn't we also hold the quantity bought of apple juice constant?" This is where the instructor must be adamant – it is only other exogenous variables that are held constant when we speak of "other things" being held

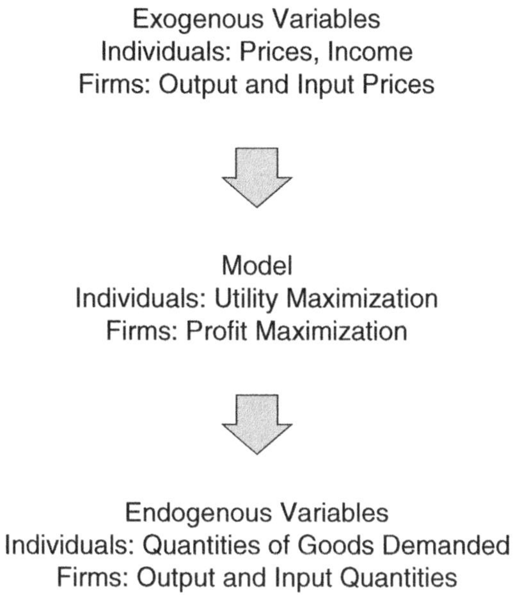

Exogenous Variables
Individuals: Prices, Income
Firms: Output and Input Prices

Model
Individuals: Utility Maximization
Firms: Profit Maximization

Endogenous Variables
Individuals: Quantities of Goods Demanded
Firms: Output and Input Quantities

Figure 41.1   Structure of typical economic models

constant. All of the endogenous variables in a model can change when one or several of the exogenous variables are changed.

It may be helpful to make this distinction by using the schematic graph on Figure 41.1. Exogenous variables feed into any economic model, which then is supposed to spit out endogenous variables. We may only be interested in one or a few of these outcomes (the quantity of orange juice demanded), but it makes no sense to hold any of them constant.

Another way to make the point is with the algebra of simultaneous equations which most students encounter in high school. Consider the two-equation system

$$x + y = 3$$

$$x - y = 1$$

Obviously the solution to this system is $x = 2, y = 1$. But it is surprising how many students will try to answer the question "now suppose x increases by one, how will y change?" This is, of course, a nonsensical question because the values of both x and y are endogenously determined in this model. Only a change in an exogenous variable (such as one of the constants in the equations) would change the values. For example, changing the first equation to $x + y = 4$ changes *both* solutions to $x = 2.5, y = 1.5$. Throughout the intermediate microeconomics course students have to be constantly reminded of such insights if they are to avoid serious confusions about the models they are studying. Consider two examples. First, in partial equilibrium models consumer income is usually treated as exogenous. But in general equilibrium models wages and incomes are endogenous. So, it all depends on what model one is using. Similarly, under the Marshall concept of demand, prices and income are exogenous, utility is endogenous. On the other hand, the Hicks concept treats prices and utility as exogenous, but expenditures are endogenous. Hence, the distinctions shown in Figure 41.1 are quite model-dependent.

Choosing the right economic model for a particular application is difficult even for professional economists. Indeed economists often disagree about whether, say, a perfectly competitive model, a monopoly model, or something in between is right for describing, say, the world market for crude oil. Since intuition in making such choices can probably only be developed over many years of experience, it is generally a mistake to let students make the choice. Instead, they should always be told at the outset of a problem set or a test what kind of model they are to use. That is, they should be asked to assume that one of the models they have studied is appropriate for the situation to be studied. Instructors can, of course, explain why they made this model choice. They can even explain why the model choice may, in fact, be incorrect. Assuming the world crude oil market to be perfectly competitive may be useful in some instances, but it clearly strains credulity when OPEC adjusts production quotas. But explaining such ambiguity in model choice is not helpful for students who are simply trying to learn how a particular model works. Eventually they may gain sufficient intuition to enable them to make model choices on their own. Giving them free rein to choose whatever model they want in a problem set or examination is an invitation to produce a garbled treatment in which elements of various models are combined in nonsensical ways (it also makes grading much more difficult).

WHAT SHOULD BE COVERED?

The number of interesting microeconomic models that might be covered in an intermediate microeconomics course has exploded in recent years. Historically, the standard course covered utility maximization, profit maximization, competitive markets, monopoly, and perhaps a few classes on market failures. Now one must decide how much to include regarding uncertainty, game theory, asymmetric information, labor and capital supply, general equilibrium, and many other topics. As any economist will recognize, the choice is not an easy one because there are trade-offs. Covering a new topic will necessarily mean less time devoted to more standard topics and it is probably inevitable that students will not learn those topics as well. Still, microeconomic theory has made major advances in the past thirty years and it is a mistake not to cover significant amounts of this new material. Three topics seem especially important, primarily because these provide the foundation for further study in many applied fields.

Uncertainty and risk aversion Understanding why individuals are assumed to dislike risk and to be willing to pay something to avoid it are key insights that underlie virtually all aspects of modern finance theory and many other fields. The problem, of course, is that many students have no background in mathematical statistics before encountering this material in intermediate microeconomics. It is inevitable then that one must introduce statistical ideas virtually from scratch. Students usually have no trouble with the concept of expected value (especially for the binomial), but motivating the concept of variance can be problematic, especially given the short time usually available. For that reason, variance should only be introduced formally in an advanced (mathematical) microeconomics course. In the intermediate course, one can make do by using the standard risk aversion graph by comparing the utility from fair bets of increasing size. For more advanced coverage, the Rothschild-Stiglitz (1976) two-state model is especially useful because it makes clear that risk-aversion can best be measured by willingness to depart from equal ex post wealth allocations – a treatment that aligns very nicely with the usual approach taken to consumer theory in which risk aversion can be shown by the curvature of indifference curves. This very useful graph may be a bit too much for the standard intermediate course, however, because it relies on the concept of state-contingent contracts.

Game theory and Nash Equilibrium   The concept of Nash Equilibrium is at the heart of most recent models in industrial organization and related fields. Hence, introducing the idea to students early on is crucial. In addition, understanding the simultaneity inherent in the Nash concept can help students understand notions of equilibrium more generally. Although the Nash concept is most often introduced in conjunction with the Prisoner's Dilemma in a two-by-two payoff matrix, that example does not really give students enough insight about the generality of the idea. Hence, it is important to introduce games with continuous strategies such as the Tragedy of the Commons game. Including such games allows best-response diagrams to be used to illustrate simultaneity in strategic choices. It also permits one to show how changes in exogenous factors can change equilibrium outcomes (note the similarity to supply-demand graphs).

Models of asymmetric information   Forty years ago the standard treatment of imperfect information would be to start and end the discussion with some statements about how it could interfere with the efficiency properties of competitive prices. Today the story must be made more elaborate primarily because students will encounter issues in imperfect information every day in the news and in their daily lives. To introduce this field, instructors can make the customary distinction between "hidden action" models and "hidden type" models and then provide one example of each. A principal-agent application (perhaps owners/managers) provides the best illustration of the first set of models, whereas an adverse selection insurance model (or perhaps the lemons model) is a good illustration of the second type. Introducing these models may have the unfortunate side effect of giving students the impression that this is the end of the story and nothing can be done to ameliorate the allocative problems that asymmetry of information causes. I think that is unfortunate and does a disservice to the vast new field of contract design. Hence, it is important for the instructor to stress that this is just the start of the story. Owners often can design contracts to control managers, and insurance companies (or used car buyers) can gather information and design contracts that mitigate adverse selection.

Of course, there are a number of other concepts that might be added to the intermediate course beyond these three key topics. One possibility is to leave the final two weeks of the semester as a "viewers' choice," asking the students what added subjects they would like to cover. Often their preferred choices focus on either finance or environmental topics. Including a class or two on each of these topics provides a good opportunity to reinforce basic concepts learned earlier in the course.

HOW MUCH MATH SHOULD BE USED IN THE COURSE?

Most economics departments now require students to have a semester of calculus and many look to the intermediate microeconomics course as the primary place where this requirement can be justified. I am ambiguous about this connection. Students with only one semester of calculus know how to differentiate simple functions and they probably know the necessary conditions for a single variable function to reach an optimal value. Unfortunately, such knowledge is of rather little use in microeconomics. In fact, only the marginal revenue/marginal cost condition for profit maximization is a direct application. The fundamental difficulty is that microeconomic theory is about choice and trade-offs and these can only be studied mathematically using multivariable calculus. Hence, the calculus requirement seems either unnecessary (since most topics can be covered graphically) or woefully inadequate. What is one to do?

Perhaps some personal history will help. When I was hired to teach intermediate micr-oeconomics, the understanding was that I would teach a course that justified our depart-ment's calculus requirement. My plan, then, was essentially to teach students with only one semester of calculus something about multivariable calculus (partial derivatives) and about constrained optimization problems (the method of Lagrange). Although I did this for many years, I do not recommend it as a general practice. The mathematics prepara-tion of our students was just too varied for the approach to be successful for the weaker students. Ultimately, Amherst College went to a two-track approach to intermediate microeconomics. The basic track still requires one semester of calculus and uses a few handouts to show how calculus can be used in an otherwise graphically oriented course. Our mathematical track now requires multivariable calculus and I believe this works much better. Not only does the requirement insure that more advanced students have the background they need to be comfortable with partial derivatives, but it also provides a signal informing students about the level to which the course will be pitched.

For those students who can handle the mathematical approach to intermediate micro-economics (about 25–30 percent of the students at Amherst College), this can be very effective. Most importantly, students get a better understanding of basic theoretical results. For example, deriving the Slutsky equation using Cook's (1972) one-line proof is, by far, the best way to teach income and substitution effects. Similarly, using the envelope theorem readily clarifies various notions of how firms' demands for inputs should be treated. An added benefit of this approach is that students now have the tools to read a great deal of the published theoretical work. Without such a background, it is unlikely that an undergraduate student can read any of that literature. For those going to graduate school, encountering this material before arrival can also be extremely helpful.

One lingering concern, of course, is whether students taking the basic track of intermediate microeconomics get a good enough background. For those not pursuing further study in economics, the level of coverage may indeed be adequate – a fundamen-tally graphical approach is probably good enough to give students an appreciation of how markets work that they can use in later courses (and possibly in their life beyond college). But taking the basic course can be a bit of a trap for students who then decide they would like to pursue economics at the graduate level – they will need to do quite a bit of added preparation if the first year of graduate school is not to come as a rude shock to them.

HOW SHOULD STUDENTS AND PROFESSORS BE ASSESSED?

There is no substitute for doing problems as a way of learning microeconomics. On many occasions instructors will have heard students say "I really understand this material, but just can't show it on tests." But even the slightest prod will reveal that they really do not "understand" the material and have convinced themselves otherwise by a cursory reading of the text. Only when students have to grapple with concepts explicitly and try to prove important results can they develop any sort of real understanding.

Assigning weekly problem sets and including them as an important component of students' grades is one approach to having students grapple with this material. Working together on these problem sets can help students generate insights and can also build a nice camaraderie among members of the class. But what invariably happens is that one or two of the best students become "gurus" for the entire class and the rest act as free riders. Such behavior can lead to a rude awakening come exam time, even when the exam questions are only minor modifications of the assigned problems. Hence, unless the free-rider problem can be addressed, cooperation on problem sets is, in general, not a good idea.

A problem-based approach extends to examinations also. It is simply too easy for students (at least students who can write well) to answer essay type questions with the patina of knowledge. Only analytical exercises can detect whether students really understand the material. Of course, some students panic at the first sight of problems on a test. Providing a brief pre-test or quiz that covers the test subject at an elementary level can help ease such fears. Additionally, having a relatively large number of exams (four or five) during each semester can mitigate the effects of any single disaster.

The inclusion of one question on each test that relates to a published paper that students are expected to have read can help foster active engagement with the professional literature. Students can bring a copy of the paper to the test and can be asked to explain how the author derived one of his or her results. This approach works best in more mathematically oriented microeconomics classes. Some excellent papers to use for this purpose are: Hausman's (2003) paper on the CPI (including the appendix), Borcherding and Silberberg (1978) on shipping the good apples out, Locay and Rodriguez (1992) on popcorn pricing in theaters, Liabson (1997) on hyperbolic discounting, Parry and Small (2005) on US and UK gasoline taxes, Borenstein et al. (2002) on the California electricity price spike, and Weitzman (2007) on the global warming debate. Though none of these papers is easy reading, each covers a very interesting topic and uses many of the tools students should learn from a mathematically oriented microeconomics course.

Devising ways to ask about published papers for students without the mathematical preparation is more difficult. Sometimes papers will have nice graphical analyses that students can be asked to read (the body of the Hausman (2003) paper is a good example) and the *Journal of Economic Education* offers a number of such examples on a variety of topics. But generally this approach is less successful than it is for the mathematically inclined students.

Finally, a word about students' assessments of professors teaching of intermediate microeconomics and especially how these are used in tenure processes. At many schools this process consists solely of brief written responses to questionnaires at the end of a course and, perhaps, retrospective letters written by students sometime after they have taken a course. These methods are not especially informative and, in some cases, they can be quite unfair to teachers of courses like microeconomics. Student commentary is often uninformative because most responses are positive, so attention focuses necessarily on the few negative comments received. Because such negative comments are rare, they can simply reflect idiosyncrasies of students or unfortunate one-time student/professor interactions. Such feedback can be unfair to junior faculty teaching intermediate microeconomics, especially in a comparative perspective. Intermediate microeconomics is a required course in most curricula and therefore will necessarily have some enrollment by students who do not want to be there. Intermediate microeconomics classes are often larger than other classes so, again, student opinion may be more negative because of this fact. Finally, it is hard to deny that the content of intermediate microeconomics is not quite as "sexy" as the latest course on film or pop culture. It may not even be as sexy as a course on international finance! For all of these reasons, therefore, faculty members teaching intermediate microeconomics, especially junior faculty members, are at a disadvantage in these standard forms of teaching assessment. Both junior faculty and their senior colleagues should be aware of the problem.

CONCLUSION – THE ROLE OF THE INTERMEDIATE MICROECONOMICS COURSE

The intermediate microeconomics course may be the only place in today's economics curriculum where students are exposed to economic theory in its purest form. It should therefore play a key role in getting students to "think like economists." It is better that they do this sooner, rather than later, in their economics education. Hence, the course should be taken as soon as feasible after completing the introductory course. In fact, for students that enter the economics major with introductory credit from the Advanced Placement or International Baccalaureate programs, this is the first course they should take. Some students may find such an immediate immersion in economic theory too jarring given the other social science courses they have taken. For these students some transitional course may be desirable (for example, a course on Current Economic Problems). But the majority of students will benefit from the development of clearly specified models that they can use elsewhere in the curriculum. Indeed, because of the importance of this course to the entire economics major, a two-semester (or equivalent) required micro sequence could be justified on educational grounds. But the practicalities of such a requirement probably make this innovation impossible for most departments.

In a more controversial vein, I believe most economics faculty members should teach intermediate microeconomics at some point in their careers. (They also should teach econometrics, but that is another story.) In my teaching career I have been astonished by the gaps that some new faculty members have in their understanding of economic theory. There is no better way to correct such misunderstandings than by teaching this material to a group of befuddled students. Personally, I do not believe I ever understood, say, input demand by firms or the mysteries of the constant-relative-risk-aversion utility function until I taught this material in detail. I have no doubt that other new professors' teaching and research would similarly benefit from this opportunity to review essentials.

REFERENCES

Borcherding, T. and E. Silberberg (1978), "Shipping the good apples out: The Alchian-Allen theorem reconsidered", *Journal of Political Economy*, **86** (1), 131–8.

Borenstein, S., J. Bushnell and F. Wolak (2002), "Measuring market inefficiencies in California's restructured wholesale electricity market", *American Economic Review*, **92** (5), 1376–404.

Cook, P. J. (1972), "A 'One Line' proof of the Slutsky equation", *American Economic Review* **62** (1), 139.

Hausman, J. (2003), "Sources of bias and solutions to bias in the Consumer Price Index", *Journal of Economic Perspectives*, **17** (1), 23–44.

Liabson, D. (1997), "Golden eggs and hyperbolic discounting", *Quarterly Journal of Economics*, **112** (2), 443–77.

Locay, L. and A. Rodriguez (1992), "Price discrimination in competitive markets", *Journal of Political Economy*, **100** (5), 954–65.

Parry, I. and K. Small (2005), "Does Britain or the United States have the right gasoline tax?", *American Economic Review*, **95** (4), 1276–89.

Rothschild, M. and J. Stiglitz (1976), "Equilibrium in competitive insurance markets: An essay on the economics of imperfect information", *Quarterly Journal of Economics*, **90** (4), 629–50.

Scitovsky, T. (1954), "Two concepts of external economies", *Journal of Political Economy* **62** (2), 70–82.

Weitzman, M. (2007), "A review of *The Stern Review of the Economics of Climate Change*", *Journal of Economic Literature*, **XLV** (September), 703–24.

42 Intermediate macroeconomics
Christopher L. Foote[1]

Getting the assignment to teach intermediate macro can be both a blessing and a curse. The good news is that intermediate macro explores the same real-world issues that attract many students to economics in the first place. This is especially true at the time of this writing, when the economy has yet to fully recover from the Great Recession of 2008–09. Because intermediate macro also covers economic growth, it tackles global income disparities, a topic of intense interest on college campuses. So what's the catch? Intermediate students typically lack the math background to understand fully optimizing and dynamic models of the macroeconomy. A good intermediate class is therefore an artful blend of real-world data, careful modeling and judicious hand-waving.

Consider the IS curve, a prominent feature of most intermediate texts. This curve shows the combinations of real interest rates and output levels where the goods market is in equilibrium (or, equivalently, where investment equals savings, hence "IS"). The IS curve slopes down because lower interest rates increase investment; the higher investment translates into higher output via the consumption-based Keynesian multiplier. The IS curve is shifted by government purchases and taxes as well as shocks to the autonomous components of consumption and investment. Intermediate texts differ in their characterization of the other major market in the economy – the money market – but the specification of the IS curve is remarkably similar across different books.

The IS curve has many well-known flaws. It depicts a static equilibrium, but investment is a forward-looking variable. The treatment of consumption is primitive, with no formal role for expectations or wealth, and no allowance for lifetime utility maximization. For a macroeconomist trained to view microfoundations as essential, these flaws (among others) can be deflating. And if the professor doesn't like what is being taught, the students won't either.

But in my view, simple modeling devices like the IS curve, which are the stock and trade of intermediate macro, are both useful for students and fun to teach. A tiny fraction of intermediate students will study economics in graduate school. Yet all of them will sort through competing economic viewpoints as they work, save, and invest after graduation. Simple macro models can help them navigate this world, because these models often capture what is most important about current events.[2] The workhorse IS curve, for example, gets across the idea that there is a negative "demand-side" relationship between the real interest rate and current output, which the Fed takes into account when setting interest rates. Modern, micro-founded models also have an IS relationship, which specifies that current output falls when the real interest rate rises. But teaching the formal version requires a lot more math.[3]

In this chapter, I discuss ways to construct an intermediate class that will resonate with students while limiting the angst of the professor. I start by discussing the two fundamental components of the course, long-run growth and short-run fluctuations. I then discuss the impact of the recent credit crisis and recession on intermediate macro. I conclude with suggestions for how to keep students interested and involved in the course.

TEACHING ECONOMIC GROWTH: THE SOLOW MODEL IS JUST THE BEGINNING

Most intermediate macro textbooks now include the Solow Model. Students typically find the math in this model within their reach, but many struggle with it just the same. One reason why relates to a key insight of the Solow Model: the best way to study economic growth is to construct a theoretical variable that settles down to a steady state and then remains constant. In the Solow Model, this variable is the ratio of aggregate capital per effective unit of labor, typically denoted k.

The problem for many students is that k is a theoretical construct with no real-world counterpart. Students have to learn that we do not care about k for its own sake. Rather, we model k because its movements determine the values of other variables that we do care about, such as consumption-per-worker ("living standards"). Until they reach intermediate macro, students generally study static models, such as the workhorse supply and demand diagram. But a formal study of growth requires us to move through time, making sure that investment today is properly incremented to the capital stock tomorrow, which determines output and investment tomorrow, etc. The trick is to turn this dynamic problem into something like a static one. Hence we model the *steady-state* value of k to which the economy eventually settles.[4]

A second reason students struggle with the Solow Model is that its direct empirical content does not exactly resonate with the typical college sophomore. Few students take intermediate macro because they are dying to know why the US capital-output ratio has remained nearly constant for decades. They are more interested in why China is growing so quickly, why Bangladesh is so poor, and whether their living standards will rise as quickly as those of their parents. The Solow Model provides some answers to these questions. China is growing quickly both because it is converging to a new steady state (determined by its high savings rate) and because China started its transformation with a low level of initial capital. Bangladesh is poor in part because of its high population growth rate.[5] But the Solow Model also leaves a lot to the imagination. Steady-state growth rates of living standards are equal to the growth rate of technological progress, which is an exogenous constant of the model. And differing levels of living standards across countries stem in large part from their differing levels of labor-augmenting technology, which is also left unexplained.

These findings need not be anti-climactic. The Solow Model does not have all the answers we might want, but it prevents us from following dead ends and it points us to some promising leads. The model implies that the fundamental determinant of *growth* in living standards is ongoing technological progress – capital accumulation alone is not enough. And when the Solow framework is taken to the data, we find that technology also plays a big role in differences in the *levels* of output-per-worker across countries (Hall and Jones, 1999). The big theoretical and empirical role for technology means that any explanation of cross-country income differences requires us to understand why some countries are so much better at turning inputs into output than others.

At this point, professors with research interests in growth may want to teach formal models of technological progress.[6] I move in another direction, giving students a non-technical outline of three broad schools of thought on why productive efficiency varies around the world. The "geography school" argues that some regions are poor because they are located in inhospitable climates. Empirical support for this theory comes in part from looking at a map: global poverty tends to be concentrated near the Equator, where tropical diseases are endemic. Prominent proponents of the geography view include Jeffrey Sachs, whose work with the UN's Millennium Project has stressed the need for rich countries to address the geographical disadvantages of poor ones.

The "institutions school" argues that the geographical distribution of poor countries is an accident of history. The seminal paper of Acemoglu, Johnson, and Robinson (2001) concedes that poor countries generally have bad climates. But it explains this fact by noting that colonial powers could not establish well-functioning societies and commerce-friendly institutions in colonies where settlers died off quickly.[7] Students are typically interested in the measures of institutional quality that this line of research has spawned – such as the number of procedures needed to officially license a business, how easily the government can appropriate productive investment, and the frequency of corruption. Many of these measures are correlated with economic outcomes, and while correlation does not imply causation, it is fair to say that most economists now view institutional quality as an important determinant of economic performance.

A third, more heterodox approach to global poverty is the "culture school." Arguing that deep-seated characteristics of national cultures generate differences in living standards, this school has antecedents in Max Weber's views on the Protestant Ethic and includes Landes (1999) and Clark (2007) as modern proponents. Two points are an important part of this discussion. First, economists generally like to explain economic behavior without resorting to exogenous differences in preferences, but that doesn't mean such differences are not important in the real world. Second, the discussion of a culture's economic effects is not necessarily an evaluation of that culture. The difference between positive and normative economics is important for both students and professors to keep in mind.

TEACHING BUSINESS CYCLES: SYMPATHY FOR THE LM CURVE

Most intermediate macro texts explain business cycles with a Keynesian framework.[8] For generations, the IS-LM-AS model was the specific way in which intermediate students learned the Keynesian model. In addition to the goods-market IS curve discussed above, this standard model includes an LM curve, which depicts combinations of interest rates and output levels that equilibrate the money market at a given real money supply. Under the usual assumptions that money demand depends negatively on the interest rate and positively on output, the LM curve slopes up in an interest-rate/output graph.

The IS and LM curves combine to form the aggregate demand (AD) block of the classic Keynesian model. They generate a downward-sloping AD curve in an AS-AD diagram with the price level on the vertical axis and output on the horizontal axis. Closing the model is the short-run aggregate supply curve (SRAS). This curve is either flat or slopes up, reflecting the nominal rigidities that allow shifts in aggregate demand to affect output. The bridge between the short and long runs comes by assuming that SRAS shifts down in recession and up in booms, so that output eventually returns to its potential level after any disturbances.

Mastering the IS-LM-AS framework requires a lot from students. One problem stems from the resemblance of the IS-LM graph to a standard supply-and-demand diagram. This resemblance tempts students to apply their hard-won microeconomic intuition. Students must instead be taught that IS-LM delivers an intersection where not one but two markets are in equilibrium (the goods market and the money market). Another problem is that the LM curve is shifted by changes in the money stock, while the real-world Fed conducts monetary policy in terms of a targeted interest rate. The IS and LM curves also depend on different interest rates: the nominal interest rate determines money demand, while the real interest rate determines investment demand.[9] Finally, the IS-LM-AS model is couched in terms of the price level, not the inflation rate. But in the real world, policy discussions usually involve inflation, and the well-known Phillips Curve links inflation, not the price level, to the real economy.

To address these shortcomings, a new way of presenting the Keynesian system has become popular. This system, outlined in Romer (2000) and Taylor (2000), models equilibrium in the money market with a Taylor-type interest-rate rule rather than an LM curve.[10] This rule generates an upward-sloping "MP" curve in interest-rate/output space, as higher levels of output prompt the Fed to raise interest rates to stabilize the economy. Additionally, the MP curve shifts up when inflation rises, as the Fed fights higher inflation with higher interest rates.[11] As in IS-LM, the IS and MP curves underpin a downward-sloping AD curve. But the new AD curve is drawn in a graph with inflation, not the price level, on the vertical axis. Its downward slope reflects the desire of the Fed to fight increases in inflation with higher real interest rates and lower output. The corresponding aggregate supply relation in the new AS-AD graph is a flat inflation-adjustment (IA) curve, whose slope reflects the sluggishness of inflation with respect to changes in aggregate demand. As was the case with the traditional AS curve, however, shifts in the IA curve ensure that output eventually returns to its potential level.[12]

As explained in Romer (2000), the new system will probably seem more intuitive to both students and professors. Most new intermediate books use it. But in my opinion, there are some good reasons to the keep the old LM curve around.[13]

One drawback of the new system is the way it responds to demand shocks in the long run. Consider a permanent increase in government purchases (G). In both the old and new systems, higher G shifts out the IS curve, resulting in an outward shift in AD and higher output. Long-run adjustment then kicks in – the SRAS curve shifts up in the old system, while the IA curve shifts up in the new system. These shifts mean that in both systems, the economy eventually returns to potential output with a higher real interest rate. But the economy has a higher *price level* in the old system and a higher *inflation rate* in the new one.

This discrepancy makes a difference. By predicting a higher price level, the old IS-LM system illustrates a fundamental lesson of intermediate macro: The long run is just the short run plus complete price flexibility. In a classical long-run model, higher G does not raise output, but it does reduce national saving. If the economy is closed, then the result-ant increase in the real interest rate crowds out just enough investment to leave long-run output unchanged. This is exactly what the IS-LM-AS model predicts for an increase in G, once price adjustment is complete. Specifically, after a fiscal expansion, the higher price level implied by IS-LM is consistent with a lower level of real money balances, a higher real interest rate, lower investment, and unchanged output.

The long-run implications of the IS-MP model are more complicated. After price adjustment, the economy has a permanently higher inflation rate, *even though the Fed is supposedly targeting inflation.* The problem here is that, after an increase in G, the basic IS-MP model does not allow the Fed to update its estimate of the equilibrium real interest rate in its interest-rate rule. As a result, the Fed does not increase real interest rates enough in response to the fiscal expansion, and inflation goes up.

One way out of this conundrum is to appeal to realism. Romer (2000) notes that the drop in consumer confidence during the 1990–91 recession appears to have lowered the long-term inflation rate. Another strategy, used by Jones (2011) and Mankiw (2010), is to assume that all demand shocks are temporary, so that the AD curve shifts back to its original level at some future date.[14]

The old IS-LM approach ignores these difficulties by keeping the money stock fixed. This modeling choice allows professors to stress the quantity-theory intuition that inflation is ultimately determined by the rate of money growth, not the Fed's interest-rate rule. Instructors wanting to stress this intuition, or the simple relationship between short-run and long-run effects, may therefore prefer the old system to the new.

The severity of the Great Recession may have also given the LM curve a new lease of life. For the first time in decades, the zero lower bound on nominal interest rates is a real-world policy concern. This bound can be fruitfully explored by noting that the LM curve tends to flatten out at low interest rates. In the resulting "liquidity trap," expansionary monetary policy is ineffective, as the horizontal LM curve simply shifts out across itself. Fiscal expansions, by contrast, are highly effective because IS shifts crowd out little investment spending. This feature of IS-LM explains why many economists were quick to argue for a fiscal expansion in 2008 when the zero lower bound was reached. Of course, a fiscal expansion is not the only way to shift out the IS curve in a liquidity trap. Higher inflation expectations can also do the trick by reducing the real interest rate associated with the zero nominal rate.[15] When the Fed hit the zero lower bound in late 2008, many economists pressed the Fed to commit to higher-than-normal inflation over the medium term for precisely this reason.[16]

As a more general matter, the ability to model "exogenous" movements in expected inflation turns a weakness of the old IS-LM approach into a strength. One of the motivating ideas behind the new IS-MP approach is that the same (real) interest rate should be relevant for both the goods market and the money market. Modeling the money market with a real interest rate rule accomplishes this task. But in the old IS-LM approach, the fact that the money market and the goods market respond to different interest rates allows a discussion of how changes in expected inflation affect output.[17] The expansionary effect of increases in expected inflation can also provide some basic intuition for why some economists prefer price-level targeting over inflation targeting. Inflation tends to fall in a recession, so during the ensuing recovery, the Fed must produce higher-than-normal inflation if the economy is to return to a price-level path. This extra bit of expected inflation coming out of a recession lowers real interest rates and helps support economic growth.[18]

THE IMPACT OF THE GREAT RECESSION ON INTERMEDIATE MACRO

The financial crisis and recession of the late 2000s increased student interest in macro-economics, but for professors, this interest has come at a price – for one thing, there is now a lot more material to cover in intermediate courses. For example, when students learn that the Fed supposedly "printed" billions of dollars in the wake of the Great Recession in an attempt to lower long-term interest rates, they typically want to know the effect of this policy on inflation. Working through the details of the Fed's balance sheet to give them the answer could easily take an entire class period, even when students have already learned about the money multiplier in their principles courses.[19]

Then there are the details of what actually happened as the crisis unfolded. There are now semester-length courses covering the emergence of the housing bubble, the expansion of subprime lending, the development of collateralized debt obligations and other structured-finance products, the rise in credit default swaps and AIG's role in that market, the popping of the housing bubble, the rise in foreclosures, the collapse of Lehman Brothers, and the assorted fiscal and monetary responses to the crisis.[20] The obvious challenge for the professor is to figure out what details students really need to learn.

Course texts can be helpful here, as several new or revised editions feature in-depth treatments of financial markets and financial crises. But at the end of the day, inter-mediate macro teachers must ask themselves two hard questions. First, what specific details of the credit crisis must be understood by an economically literate person in the early 21st century? Second, what are the lasting lessons from the episode? Did the Great Recession teach us something fundamental about the macroeconomy that we didn't know before?

One lesson that will probably work its way into most courses involves financial markets. When teaching the classical long-run model, I have typically noted that the goods-market equilibrium condition ($Y = C + I + G$) implies that investment equals savings, and that it was the job of the financial system to bring that equality about. Then it was on to the next part of the course. In the future, I will spend more time discussing the problem of asymmetric information in financial markets, noting that financial crises are periods in which this information problem is particularly severe. A related point is that the past three decades of monetary economics have stressed the importance of expecta-tions, including the way in which inflation expectations can be anchored by interest-rate rules and formal inflation targets. The focus on expectations helped policymakers tame the Great Inflation of the 1970s, but it may have crowded out work on the links between financial markets and the real economy. This omission is now being addressed in both academic papers and new editions of intermediate texts.[21]

Another potential addition to intermediate courses is an in-depth discussion of asset bubbles. This discussion can be linked to existing material on the q-theory of invest-ment. In a textbook world, the price of a capital asset (for example, a house) is deter-mined by the present-value of its future income stream (such as future rents). Higher expected marginal products, or lower interest rates, cause the price of the asset (essen-tially, q) to increase, which encourages firms to add to the physical capital stock. In a rational, frictionless world, marginal q should be a sufficient statistic for investment.

Everything that managers need to know about the profitability of investment projects is summarized by the ratio of the marginal value of a unit of installed capital to its replacement cost.

During the last 15 years, the real world has fallen short of the q-model's assumptions. The rise in dot-com stock prices in the late 1990s encouraged firms to install high-tech capital, but much of this investment was unprofitable (at least for the original owners). A few years later, residential capital experienced its own boom-bust cycle. Because the housing boom was fueled with borrowed money, the ensuing bust devastated the financial system.

The technology and housing cycles are the latest manifestations of bubble psychology, but they are unlikely to be the last. So students should learn how to formally define bubbles, even though economists do not yet understand how bubbles form, or why they pop.[22] Students should also be warned that in the future, economists will probably disagree over whether a high price for any given asset reflects a bubble or strong fundamentals.[23] Finally, students should understand that bubbles have aggregate consequences. Not only do they affect the allocation of capital, but they also damage financial systems when assets are purchased with borrowed money.

The link between borrowing and asset bubbles relates to another lesson: Credit booms often occur alongside asset booms, but it is hard to know whether easy credit is causing high prices or vice versa. Many analysts claim that the increase in mortgage securitization and other lending innovations in the 2000s encouraged poor underwriting of mortgages, and that these lower standards contributed to higher housing prices. In his treatment of the relationship between credit and asset prices, Mankiw (2010) writes that in the early 2000s,

> interest rates were low, and mortgages were easy to come by. Many households with questionable credit histories – called *subprime* borrowers – were able to get mortgages with small downpayments. Not surprisingly, the housing market boomed. Housing prices rose, and residential investment was strong. A few years later, however, it became clear that the situation had gotten out of hand, as many of these subprime borrowers could not keep up with their mortgage payments. When interest rates rose and credit conditions tightened, housing demand and housing prices began to fall. (p. 541, emphasis in original)

It is true that expanded credit in the early 2000s could have driven housing prices higher. But expectations of ever-rising housing prices could have also loosened credit standards. Any real estate loan is a good loan if the value of the collateral is rising, no matter how risky the borrower. But when collateral values are falling, lenders typically pull in the reins.

This identification problem between expanded lending and higher asset prices is worth covering in class, because it has important implications for public policy. If credit availability really did drive the recent housing cycle, then policymakers should reduce or eliminate incentive misalignments in the financial sector that cause unwarranted credit expansion. But public policy is harder if a housing bubble lowered credit standards instead. In that case, the financial system responded exactly as we would expect given the price signals it received. The policy implication is that society is better off making the financial system robust to large declines in asset prices, given our incomplete knowledge of what determines asset prices in the first place.

STRATEGIES FOR KEEPING STUDENTS INTERESTED

A general rule for keeping macro students plugged in is to bring up the real world whenever possible. Sometimes this is as simple as showing a time-series graph of a variable the first time it appears.[24] I also play up the first Friday of each month as "Labor Market Friday." This is the day that the government releases its Employment Situation report, which includes both the unemployment rate and the growth in nonfarm employment. This report gets a lot of attention in the press, so teaching students to think about it systematically pays big dividends. The same is true of the official statements released after meetings of the Federal Open Market Committee (FOMC). Students particularly enjoy mapping the FOMC's formal language into concepts covered in class.

Another method to maintain student interest is personalization. Professional business writers know that stories about "the Fed" are not nearly as interesting as stories about "the Bernanke Fed." Many prominent economists now stake out positions on economic issues via personal blogs, and I sometimes ask students why a particular economist with a well-known general outlook might prefer one policy over another. The blogs of Paul Krugman, Greg Mankiw, and Gary Becker and Richard Posner can be great sources for discussions of this kind – especially when these economists disagree.

The best assignments in intermediate macro also have close links with the outside world. After the 2010 Haitian earthquake, I asked students to evaluate four newspaper opinion columns that discussed Haitian poverty, using the geography vs. institutions vs. culture material from class. When teaching IS-LM, most of one class period is devoted to discussing facts about particular economic episodes in the context of IS-LM. For example, students are told that oil prices spiked in the fall of 1990, after Saddam Hussein invaded Kuwait. Some students dismiss this shock as related to aggregate supply, not demand, but others reason that the shock might have depressed consumer confidence and spending, which would have shifted the IS curve back, reduced aggregate demand, and slowed the economy. As it turns out, this "consumption shock" story works pretty well in explaining the data (Blanchard, 1993). Newspaper columnists also like to write about inflation, and their arguments can be mapped into the language of the Phillips Curve.

The best thing about teaching intermediate macro is the opportunity for practical analysis like this. Teaching intermediate macro is not for wimps, because achieving the right level of analytical rigor is hard when using simple models. But students need to learn what intermediate macro can teach them. By thinking carefully about what to explore and what to downplay, professors can construct a course that will stick with students long after they graduate.

NOTES

1. The views expressed are those of the author alone, and do not necessarily reflect those of the Federal Reserve Bank of Boston or the Federal Reserve System. In preparing this chapter, I benefitted greatly from discussions with Susanto Basu, Greg Mankiw, Richard Ryan, Robert Triest, and Paul Willen.
2. Krugman (2000) and Romer (2000) also discuss advantages of simple macro models.
3. In formal models with micro-founded IS curves, investment and capital are sometimes omitted. Output is therefore equal to consumption plus government purchases. The IS curve relates current output to the

real interest rate, future output and a government spending shock. As consumers optimize over time, higher real interest rates encourage higher consumption growth. So, holding future output and current government purchases constant, a higher real rate depresses current consumption and output. See Clarida, Galí and Gertler (1999) for an exposition of the baseline New Keynesian model and Estrella and Fuhrer (2002) for a discussion of modern IS-curve dynamics.

4. The difficulty of moving between static and dynamic modes of thought may also explain why students often confuse the concept of a steady state with the Golden Rule (which is the particular steady state at which the level of consumption per worker is maximized).

5. The Solow Model assumes that population growth is exogenous, but fertility is doubtlessly influenced by living standards. Making this clear to students is a good way to repeat the correlation-is-not-causation mantra that should be part of every undergraduate economics course.

6. Jones (2011) includes a chapter on Paul Romer's ideas model, for example.

7. See Albouy (2008) for a critique of Acemoglu, Johnson and Robinson (2001).

8. Notable exceptions include Auerbach and Kotlikoff (1998), Barro (2010), and Williamson (2011).

9. Thus, when the IS-LM block of the model is built, it is common to assume that expected inflation is zero, so that nominal and real interest rates are the same.

10. David Romer has also written a standalone treatment of the new system that is suitable for intermediate courses (Romer 2006). This supplement allows professors who choose a textbook with IS-LM to teach the new method instead.

11. A simpler version of the MP curve is simply a flat line at the Fed's targeted real interest rate, which shifts up if inflation rises. See Romer (2000).

12. Romer (2000) also describes an upward-sloping version of this curve that allows changes in AD to affect inflation as they occur. Notably, because the new AS-AD graph is drawn in terms of inflation and output, this upward-sloping version is an expectations-augmented Phillips Curve, relating inflation, not the price level, to the level of economic activity.

13. For an alternative defense of the LM curve to the one developed here, see Friedman (2004).

14. Most of the short-run model in Mankiw (2010) uses IS-LM. But the new seventh edition of this text includes an additional chapter that uses IS-MP and adds an explicit dynamic structure.

15. Higher inflation expectations shift the IS curve as long as the IS-LM diagram is drawn with the nominal interest rate on the vertical axis. When the diagram is drawn with the real rate on the vertical axis, higher inflation expectations shift the LM curve. The predictions of the model for real rates, nominal rates, and output are of course invariant to how the vertical axis is labeled. But because the zero lower bound applies to the nominal interest rate, using that variable on the vertical axis is easiest for students to understand.

16. If a class discussion is feasible, conducting one on policy choices under the zero lower bound is a good idea. What concrete steps could the Fed take to engineer higher inflation expectations? Would doing so affect the Fed's anti-inflation credibility? Why might economists prefer a reduction in real rates that stimulated private investment, over a fiscal expansion that raised aggregate demand directly?

17. Mankiw (2010) has a wonderful discussion of the Great Depression and 1929–32 deflation that illustrates this point.

18. A good topic for class discussion would be whether the public would applaud the Fed for *raising* interest rates after a temporary positive innovation to inflation, in order to return the price level to its previous path. Also note that while movements in expected inflation can be discussed in an IS-LM diagram, it is difficult to tie these movements rigorously to the AS-AD diagram that is also part of the model. This difficulty returns us to the issue discussed in the Introduction: teaching intermediate macro requires some hand-waving now and then.

19. What the Fed has created is bank reserves, not currency. Currency and reserves are liabilities of the Fed and make up the monetary base, but the link between this base and wider measures of money (the so-called money multiplier) has changed, thanks in part to the Fed's recently acquired ability to pay interest to banks on reserves they hold at the Fed.

20. A good place to look for material on these issues is the *Journal of Economic Perspectives*, which ran symposia related to the crisis in its Winter 2009, Winter 2010, and Winter 2011 issues. Swagel (2009) provides a fascinating insider's account of the crisis, with an emphasis on what policymakers were thinking at the time.

21. A new text by Mishkin (2012) includes chapters on financial systems and financial crises immediately after the discussion of the short-run model. A forthcoming book by R. Glenn Hubbard, Tony O'Brien, and Matt Rafferty places financial-markets material even earlier, right after discussion of macroeconomic data. A new text by Mankiw and Ball (2010) combines material from Mankiw's macro text with Ball's new money-and-banking text. And Jones (2011) embeds a discussion of recent events deep within his short-run treatment; the chapter titled "The Great Recession: A First Look" appears immediately before the chapter on "The IS Curve."

22. Brunnermeier (2008) provides an accessible treatment of bubbles. He writes that bubbles occur when

investors are willing to pay more than an asset's fundamental value, because the investors expect to be able to sell the asset for a higher price later on.

23. For a review of disagreement during the recent housing bubble, see Gerardi et al. (2010).
24. The St. Louis Fed's data repository, FRED (http://research.stlouisfed.org/fred2/, accessed 15 June 2011), can produce almost any graph an intermediate macro professor might want. For ambitious professors who want to make their own graphs, the Stata command "freduse" allows the easy importation of FRED data into Stata. See Drukker (2006).

REFERENCES

Acemoglu, D., S. Johnson and J. A. Robinson (2001), "The colonial origins of comparative development: An empirical investigation", *American Economic Review*, **91** (5), 1369–401.

Albouy, D. Y. (2008), "The colonial origins of comparative development: An investigation of the settler mortality data", NBER Working Paper No. 14130, http://www-personal.umich.edu/~albouy/AJRreinvestigation/AJRrev.pdf, accessed 7 April 2011.

Auerbach, A. J. and L. J. Kotlikoff (1998), *Macroeconomics: An Integrated Approach* (2nd ed.), Cambridge, MA: MIT Press.

Barro, R. J. (2010), *Intermediate Macro*, Mason, OH: South-Western Cengage Learning.

Blanchard, O. (1993), "Consumption and the recession of 1990–1991", *American Economic Review*, **83** (2), 270–74.

Brunnermeier, M. K. (2008), "Bubbles", in S. N. Durlaf and L. E. Blue (eds), *The New Palgrave Dictionary of Economics* (2nd ed.), Basingstoke: Palgrave Macmillan. http://www.dictionaryofeconomics.com/article?id=pde2008_S000278, accessed 7 April 2011.

Clarida, R., J. Galí and M. Gertler (1999), "The science of monetary policy: A New Keynesian perspective", *Journal of Economic Literature*, **37** (4), 1661–707.

Clark, G. (2007), *A Farewell to Alms: A Brief History of the World*, Princeton, NJ: Princeton University Press.

Drukker, D. M. (2006), "Importing Federal Reserve economic data", *The Stata Journal*, **6** (3), 384–6.

Estrella, A. and J. C. Fuhrer (2002), "Dynamic inconsistencies: Counterfactual implications of a class of rational-expectations models", *American Economic Review*, **92** (4), 1013–28.

Friedman, B. M. (2004), "The LM curve: A not-so-fond farewell", in C. Goodlet, D. Longworth and J. Murray (eds), *Macroeconomics, Monetary Policy, and Financial Stability*, Ottawa: Bank of Canada, pp. xiii–xix.

Gerardi, K. S., C. L. Foote and P. S. Willen (2010), "Reasonable people did disagree: Optimism and pessimism about the U.S. housing market before the crash", Federal Reserve Bank of Boston Public Policy Discussion Paper No. 10-5, http://www.bos.frb.org/economic/ppdp/2010/ppdp1005.htm, accessed 7 April 2011.

Hall, R. E. and C. I. Jones (1999), "Why do some countries produce so much more output per worker than others?", *Quarterly Journal of Economics*, **114** (1), 83–116.

Hubbard, R. Glenn., A. P. O'Brien and M. Rafferty (forthcoming), *Macroeconomics*, Upper Saddle River, NJ: Pearson.

Jones, C. I. (2011), *Macroeconomics* (2nd ed.), New York: W. W. Norton.

Krugman, P. (2000), "How complicated does the model have to be?" *Oxford Review of Economic Policy*, **16** (4), 33–42.

Landes, D. S. (1999), *The Wealth and Poverty of Nations: Why Some Are So Rich and Some So Poor*, New York: W. W. Norton.

Mankiw, N. G. (2010), *Macroeconomics* (7th ed.), New York: Worth Publishers.

Mankiw, N. G. and L. Ball (2010), *Macroeconomics and the Financial System*, New York: Worth Publishers.

Mishkin, F. S. (2012), *Macroeconomics: Policy and Practice*, Boston, MA: Addison-Wesley.

Romer, D. (2000), "Keynesian macroeconomics without the LM curve", *Journal of Economic Perspectives*, **14** (2), 149–69.

Romer, D. (2006), "Short-run fluctuations", http://elsa.berkeley.edu/~dromer/papers/text2006.pdf, accessed 7 April 2011.

Swagel, P. (2009), "The financial crisis: An inside view", *Brookings Papers on Economic Activity*, (Spring), 1–68.

Taylor, J. B. (2000), "Teaching modern macroeconomics at the principles level", *American Economic Review*, **90** (2), 90–94.

Williamson, S. D. (2011), *Macroeconomics* (4th ed.), Boston, MA: Addison–Wesley.

43 Teaching undergraduate econometrics
Jeffrey M. Wooldridge

With the advent of fast computers, easy-to-use statistical software, and readily available data sets on the worldwide web, the role of econometrics in undergraduate education has changed markedly over the past 25 years.

In thinking about the role of econometrics in the economics major, there are two separate issues. The first concerns the extent to which econometrics has become a required part of the undergraduate curriculum. A recent, comprehensive study by Johnson, Perry, and Petkus (2010) sheds considerable light on this issue, at least in the United States. These authors compiled undergraduate econometrics requirements for all colleges and universities ranked by *U.S. News & World Report*. For those who think econometrics is a critical component of an economist's training, Johnson, Perry, and Petkus' (2010) findings are somewhat sobering: only about 40 percent of American colleges and universities offering a bachelor's degree in economics require a course in econometrics. At so-called "national" universities the rate is higher, almost 52 percent. But that still means many highly regarded undergraduate economics programs do not require students to learn data analysis beyond basic statistics.[1]

A second aspect of how technological improvements and access to information have changed the role of econometrics in undergraduate education concerns the way in which we actually teach undergraduate econometrics – whether or not a course is compulsory. Although others have written on this topic (see, for example, Kennedy, 1998 and Becker and Greene, 2001), this chapter will focus on related issues. I draw primarily on my experiences teaching at Michigan State University (MSU) and my time as an assistant professor at Massachusetts Institute of Technology (MIT), but also on conversations I have had with others about teaching introductory econometrics. My philosophy on teaching undergraduate econometrics is pretty well captured by my introductory econometrics text (Wooldridge, 2009), but I will condense and summarize it here.

WHAT SHOULD UNDERGRADUATES LEARN IN AN INTRODUCTORY COURSE?

Prior to the availability of cheap computing and easy-to-use econometric software, most econometrics courses were heavy on algebra and light on hands-on empirical work. Now that students can easily upload data into econometrics packages, and have access to a variety of econometric methods, it makes sense for introductory courses to rely more on empirical applications. An important skill that we can give economics students is to critically evaluate empirical research that claims to have some relevance for policy analysis or business decision making. This skill is most successfully developed when students see a variety of applications, and are asked to explore extensions and variations on their own – either through problem sets or class projects.

In terms of particular tools, it is most important that undergraduates have a thorough understanding of multiple regression analysis, including its application in a variety of settings and its limitations. When I teach an introductory course, I usually *only* cover multiple regression.[2] This may seem very narrow, but multiple regression is still the workhorse when it comes to empirical work, and for most students (even professional researchers) it is challenging enough to learn how to intelligently apply multiple regression to answer different kinds of questions using a variety of data structures (cross-section, time series, and structures with cross-section and time-series dimensions). The ceteris paribus nature of regression analysis, understanding various functional forms, learning to interpret regression models with discrete explanatory variables or dependent variables, knowing the potential pitfalls of regression with time-series data – these are all critical topics.

When teaching multiple regression, I emphasize the perspective of the empirical researcher. I use the language, and tailor the assumptions, to what one would find (at least implicitly) when reading applied papers in labor economics, public economics, development economics, macroeconomics, or any other of a variety of fields. It is important to emphasize that the language of the empirical researcher tends to be different from that of a classical treatment of regression analysis. For example, one never sees or hears an empirical researcher discuss whether the explanatory variables in their models are "fixed in repeated samples," even though the majority of introductory econometrics textbooks still approach regression from this perspective. Instead, empirical researchers think in terms of correlation between the unobserved error and the explanatory variables (which can arise for a variety of reasons).

Treatments of econometrics that start with nonrandom regressors in order to facilitate the algebra of the classical linear model tend to treat the possibility of "random regressors" almost as an anomaly. This is a mistake, as we want students thinking early and often about sources of bias in multiple regression estimators. Another way of saying this is that more important than algebra is an understanding of assumptions as they apply in practice, when they are likely to fail, and the consequences of those failures.

PREREQUISITES AND BACKGROUND

All students taking an introductory econometrics course should have taken an introductory statistics course. Ideally, the course is offered in the economics department and covers not just basic statistics but also ways to collect, manipulate, and summarize economic data.[3]

Naturally, the students should know at least college-level algebra. At MSU, we require the students to take a course in calculus before econometrics, although we do not use calculus heavily. The main benefit of being able to use differential calculus is that it simplifies the interpretation of commonly used functional forms.

Over the past 25 years I have talked with instructors at various universities about their approaches to teaching econometrics. I have been struck – and, frankly, baffled – by the many who claim they cannot possibly teach econometrics without calculus. Some have even claimed that they cannot, in good conscience, teach the course without matrix algebra. I must stress that I strongly disagree with the view that introductory econometrics must be taught with high-level math. In fact, I will go so far as to state the opposite:

for most students taking a course in undergraduate econometrics, advanced mathematics takes up valuable time and gets in the way of the interesting material. Students taking introductory econometrics should be trained to critically evaluate others' research and to undertake their own empirical research. Good empirical practice can be taught without resorting to complicated mathematics.

Ironically, the high-level mathematics approach is often used in conjunction with the assumption mentioned earlier, namely, that the explanatory variables are fixed in repeated samples. An instructor who takes this approach is, in effect, signaling to students that realism and practical application should take a back seat to the mathematics.[4]

WHERE SHOULD THE COURSE BEGIN?

One of the more difficult decisions in teaching undergraduate econometrics is where to start the course. Conversations with colleagues reveal an apparent seeming consensus regarding this issue: most begin with a review of basic statistics, with some instructors dedicating a few weeks to this review. I do not prefer to start with a stand-alone statistics review, for several reasons. First, it takes away precious time from topics that will be more useful and interesting to the students. For example, spending two or three weeks reviewing basic statistics is likely to come at the expense of introductory material on regression with time-series data.

If one chooses to review probability and statistics, it raises the difficult question of where to begin and where to end. Should one start with the definition of probability? Should one derive estimators for the classical distributions used in basic statistics, such as the binomial and Poisson? Or, should one just remind students of what a t statistic is, and how it is used? These are questions that are difficult to resolve, and can lead one to spend too much time on review at the expense of much more useful material.

A second reason I prefer to jump right into econometrics is that, whether we like it or not, the typical economics student generally has bad feelings toward statistics. On the first day, I try to convince the students that econometrics is relevant and fun, and perhaps the most useful course they will take. If I then launch into a review of statistics, it gets the students thinking that they are just taking another course in statistics.

The approach I prefer is to integrate the statistical review into the material on econometrics as the course proceeds. It is then clear to the students which concepts from their earlier course are most important, and they can see immediately how these concepts arise in the context of econometrics. For example, when I cover simple regression and need the notion that two random variables are uncorrelated, I can stop briefly at that point and remind students what a correlation coefficient is and why the concept is important. If students are fuzzy on the subject, they can review material commonly included in econometric texts. As another example, when showing students the equations solved by the ordinary least squares (OLS) estimates, stop and remind them how to manipulate the summation operator.

Many concepts from basic statistics – such as computing and using t statistics for testing hypotheses – are no more difficult to describe in the context of multiple regression analysis than in the introductory statistics setting concerning testing hypotheses about the mean from a normal population. At the appropriate point it is helpful to remind students that estimates come with standard errors, and that we must account for the sampling error in estimates when conducting hypotheses tests. These ideas are straightforward in the context of multiple regression. Then, we can proceed to see the variety of applications of *t* testing in the multiple regression setting. For example, we can ask questions such as "Does variable *x* have a ceteris paribus effect on *y*?" or "Is the relationship between *y* and *x* linear?" Knowing how to set up hypotheses tests for these kinds of questions is of great importance, and deserves to be illustrated often. It is also important to understand that the *t* statistic is invalidated by violations of certain multiple regression assumptions, something that is not at all helped by starting with a review of *t* testing in the simple setting of testing hypotheses about the mean from a normal population.

STRUCTURE AND DIFFICULTY LEVEL OF LECTURES

I prefer to spend the entire first lecture – and even part of a second lecture – discussing the nature of econometrics, its scope, and the kinds of data that economists use to empirically answer various questions. Discussing several applications that are likely to grab the students' attention is important. Topics that are of immediate interest to the students and also topics that are of widespread interest are included in this overview. An example of the former is determining whether attending lecture has a causal effect on performance in a course. Such examples make it easy to discuss, in an intuitive way, the important notion of ceteris paribus, and how access to observational (or nonexperimental) data makes a ceteris paribus analysis tricky, but not necessarily impossible. At a large public university such as Michigan State, applications to sports – such as studying whether having successful athletic programs has an effect on academics – are popular.[5] More serious topics, such as the value of a year of schooling, or the effects of class size on student performance, or the effects of capital punishment on murder rates, allow students to see that the econometrics they learn is used to answer very serious questions.[6]

Beginning the course with regression analysis using cross-sectional data is highly recommended for a variety of reasons. Random sampling is familiar to students and it is easy to get them thinking in terms of populations. The key assumptions for OLS to have good properties are population assumptions.[7] In addition, contrary to what some introductory texts lead students to believe, analyzing time-series data with regression methods introduces many complications (for example, trends, seasonality, serial correlation, and the possibility of spurious regression). As mentioned above, it is best to treat time-series regression at the end of the course, where the pitfalls of using time-series data can be more clearly discussed. By this time, students are comfortable with the mechanics and interpretation of OLS and can focus on the special considerations associated with time-series data.

In my coverage of cross-sectional regression, I begin with the simple regression model but try not to get bogged down. Students taking econometrics should understand the notion of an estimator, how estimators can be derived using basic principles, and how they can be evaluated using sampling properties. Simple regression is the natural setting in which to derive the OLS estimates, discuss the algebra of least squares (such as residuals summing to zero), and derive unbiasedness of OLS along with its sampling variance.[8] Once I have moved on to multiple regression, I keep derivations to a minimum. Again,

I want the students to see the motivation for multiple regression and to understand the assumptions under which it works – and what happens when those assumptions fail.

During class, I rotate among lecturing, showing pre-made computer output, and demonstrating regression analysis in real time, projected on a screen. It is rare for a lecture to go by without some demonstration on the computer. Even when discussing statistical properties, it is useful to illustrate the notion of a sampling distribution – including the concepts of unbiasedness and sampling variance – using simulated data, and actually showing the students what happens across several simulations.[9]

As the instructor presents each new concept – R-squared, logarithms, quadratics, dummy variables, interactions, and so on – it is best to use at least one empirical example to illustrate the general discussion. It is through seeing lots of examples that many students learn the material.

Historically, I used a mixed media presentation to teach introductory econometrics. Models, assumptions, and derivations were written in real time on overhead transparencies and then, at the appropriate time, a switch was made to work at a computer console projecting on the screen. I have since created a set of electronic slides (based on my introductory text) that I will probably use next time I teach the course.[10]

I think the jury is out on whether using pre-prepared slides is the most effective way of teaching introductory econometrics. At a minimum, the slides need to be carefully crafted to step through the basic derivations, and to include a sufficient number of graphs. On the plus side, more material can be covered, and the students can spend time listening and making annotations, rather than writing down equations. Another advantage of electronic slides is that it is easy to switch between the slides and econometric software that is used for demonstrations.[11]

Some students may learn the material better by being actively engaged in the note-taking process. If electronic slides are used, some sort of tablet device is preferred so that the instructor can make annotations and comments directly on the slides during lecture – and so can students who either have a hard copy of the slides or also a tablet. Being able to annotate slides makes the lecture more organic: it is easier for the instructor to provide different examples, say, in real time. Of course overhead transparencies also admit annotations and corrections.[12]

COURSE LOGISTICS

In addition to lecture structure and the integration of computer work into the lecture, exams and problem sets bring about other logistical issues that require attention. I have never given multiple choice questions on an econometrics exam, but I am not opposed to the idea – at least for part of the exam. I prefer short answers that require students to interpret an equation, explain a concept, or show they can apply the concepts in slightly unfamiliar circumstances. Included among the short answer questions are "agree/disagree" questions, where students answer whether they agree or disagree with an assertion and then explain why.[13]

In the past, I have included an exam question that requires students to derive properties of simple estimators other than OLS. For example, in a simple regression model with a zero intercept, the ratio of the sample averages is generally unbiased for the slope.

Having the students show the estimator is unbiased, and deriving its sampling variance, are challenging for most of the students. I have moved away from such exam questions, preferring instead to have students work through such questions on problem sets.

I have not attempted to have students undertake computer work in real time during an exam, partly because it would be a logistical nightmare in a large class and partly because the resources are not available. However, exams always include at least one question consisting of computer output that students use to answer several questions about interpreting estimates, obtaining predictions, and testing hypotheses.

At least half of the questions on my problem sets require students to interpret equations, interpret Stata output, or use Stata themselves to answer questions using provided data sets. As the course progresses, the problem sets are tilted more and more heavily to fairly serious applications of multiple regression analysis. Because hands-on work is a very important part of the course, I tend to give a fairly heavy weight to problem sets in computing the final grade (usually of the order of 30 percent).

SPECIFIC COURSE TOPICS

As mentioned above, my main goal in an introductory econometrics course is to teach students a thorough understanding of multiple regression in settings likely to be important to economists. Repetition is important to get students comfortable with interpreting multiple regression equations and output. For many students, being able to use regression to predict can be important for future employment, and so I spend some time on obtaining prediction intervals.

The common functional forms used in economics (for example, those with constant elasticities) are important. Because many applications involve discrete variables, a lot of time can be dedicated to showing various ways that qualitative information can be incorporated into multiple regression. It is worthwhile to spend time allowing interactions among discrete and continuous variables.

I always teach linear regression analysis when the dependent variable is binary – giving rise to the so called "linear probability model" (LPM). Applications where one must explain a binary response, such as a customer defaulting on a loan or a person purchasing a life insurance policy, are common, and yet most students will never take a course on nonlinear models. The LPM has proven to be resilient over the years, for good reasons: it is easy to estimate, easy to interpret, and decades of experience show it often provides a good approximation. Purists who worry about fitted probabilities outside the unit interval are robbing the students of a simple, powerful tool that is well within their ability to grasp.[14]

Given the availability of easy-to-compute standard errors that are robust to any kind of heteroskedasticity, the treatment of heteroskedasticity can be streamlined. Stock and Watson (2011) go so far as to focus primarily on heteroskedasticity-robust inference, choosing to skip the classical linear model assumptions. I understand the attraction of doing so – mainly, it saves on time – but I cannot quite bring myself to bypass finite-sample analysis. It is useful for students to know the assumptions under which t statistics have an exact t distribution and F statistics have an exact F distribution. Further, students can be exposed to the idea that OLS can be justified not just in terms of unbiasedness but also in terms of efficiency (under the Gauss-Markov assumptions, which include homoskedasticity).

When I discuss heteroskedasticity, the primary focus is on using OLS and adjusting standard errors and test statistics so that they are valid for any form of heteroskedasticity, including none. (It is important to emphasize to students that we are still using OLS; we are not using a different estimation method.) After that, it makes sense to spend a little time covering the most straightforward tests for heteroskedasticity: those based on regressing squared residuals on the explanatory variables. My main reason for covering heteroskedasticity tests is that sometimes we are really interested in knowing whether certain factors affect the variability of y. For example, is the variance in college grade point average higher for men or women, or is there no difference? Might smaller class sizes not just affect the average test score but also the variance in test scores?[15]

Covering heteroskedasticity-robust inference requires us to appeal to large-sample properties of OLS – at least implicitly. Intricate asymptotic theory is not something most undergraduates will have the background or patience for, but they should have seen the law of large numbers and central limit theorem in their introductory statistics course. I find that, in no more than 30 minutes, the important large-sample results can be stated and discussed. After a discussion of consistency, it is straightforward to emphasize that relaxing the normality assumption is trivial: our approach to computing test statistics and inference is unchanged; we simply should recognize that our tests, p-values, and confidence intervals are only "approximately" valid.

A special topic that I illustrate via examples is the notion of "outliers." A formal treatment is beyond the scope of introductory courses, but I think it is important to illustrate the sensitivity of OLS to one or a few observations. An example is using a state-level data set to show the effects of capital punishment on murder rates in the United States, where dropping Texas makes a substantive difference. It is hard to know whether Texas is truly an "outlier," but there is no doubt it is an "influential" observation.

In teaching my course, I find one of the hardest tasks is to switch gears with a few weeks remaining and turn to regression with time-series data. Even the thought experiment about the process generating random outcomes is different from cross-sectional analysis. However, exposing students to some examples provides the opportunity to properly warn them that using time-series regression can be tricky.

In addition to covering static and distributed lag examples, I cover simple one-period-ahead forecasting. I try to finish the course with testing and correcting for serial correlation. Similar to the modern way of handling heteroskedasticity, one could cover serial correlation (and heteroskedasticity) robust inference methods for OLS – via the so-called "Newey-West" standard errors (see, for example, Wooldridge, 2009, chapter 12). In the past I have favored generalized least squares, but Cochrane-Orcutt and related procedures are valid only when the explanatory variables are strictly exogenous (see Wooldridge, 2009, chapter 12). Robust inference for OLS is now straightforward in most statistical packages and makes an appealing alternative.

Instructors whose own areas of research are oriented towards empirical microeconomics (especially labor and public finance) may prefer not to teach regression with time-series data at all. In lieu of time-series analysis, a case can be made for teaching the second most important estimation approach used in empirical economics: instrumental variables (IV). Conceptually, it is easy to jump from OLS with cross-sectional data to instrumental variables with cross-sectional data, especially because IV solves a problem that has been discussed throughout the term: possible correlation between one or more explanatory variables and the error term.

Teaching IV estimation to undergraduates does raise some difficulties. Even experienced researchers find it hard to apply IV in a convincing way because instrumental variables are difficult to come by. It is now recognized that IV estimation with questionable instrumental variables is not always "better" than OLS; and it can be a lot worse. Trying to teach undergraduates to use IV methods can be as dangerous as trying to teach them regression with time-series data.

If I were to skip time-series regression, I would probably first spend time on independently pooled cross-sections and two-period panel data structures; each has lots of applications and they entail none of the technical difficulties of studying pure time series. Students will easily understand the notion of using dummy variables to capture aggregate differences across time. Combining that with "control" and "treatment" groups sets up the standard difference-in-differences estimator – a powerful yet simple method students can take with them to evaluate government or business policy. If I still had time to teach basic IV methods, I would do so from the perspective of using eligibility as an instrument for actual participation, a scenario that can lead to a convincing analysis and one that students might confront in the future.

TEACHING CHALLENGING CONCEPTS THROUGH EXAMPLES

As anyone knows who has tried to teach econometrics to undergraduates with wide dispersion in background and interests, it is a difficult task. Ideally, students will understand a general presentation of concepts and then successfully apply them to special cases – without having to see an application in every case. However, my experience is that examples are the best way to get across general points. Things that seem clear to us are not at all clear to most students.

As an example, when covering goodness-of-fit I emphasize that a high R-squared is neither necessary nor sufficient for a multiple regression analysis to provide convincing ceteris paribus estimates; whether the explanatory variables and errors are uncorrelated is quite distinct from whether the explanatory variables explain much of the variation in y. The students can take my word for it, but it is more effective to use an example or two. For this purpose, I have some experimental data sets where I know the explanatory variables were set independently of any observable or unobservable factors. One that is especially useful is a "willingness-to-pay" example, where household heads were presented with randomly chosen prices of two different kinds of apples and asked what their demand would be for each.[16] Multiple regression leads to very plausible estimates of price effects, yet the R-squared from the regression is very low: less than 4 percent. Adding controls for family structure, income, and education level barely moves the R-squared. The fact that the R-squared never increases above 5 percent does not invalidate the estimated price effects. It does mean that the equation is expected to do poorly in predicting an individual's apple demand: most factors, as measured by variance, are unobserved.

As a second example, consider the problem of including interaction terms in multiple regression models. If one is not careful in constructing the interaction terms, the results can seem very strange – especially compared with the model without interactive effects. I emphasize to students that adding an interaction to a model changes the interpretation of the coefficients on the original explanatory variables. In fact, often the coefficients on the level variables in the expanded model are meaningless. Writing down the slopes with respect to each variable when an interaction is included makes the general point, but the students are more impressed by an example. I sometimes use data relating attendance in principles of microeconomics to final exam score. In addition to attendance – which likely suffers from a "self-selection" problem – I have as controls the students' prior GPAs and their achievement test scores (ACT). As it turns out, attendance and prior GPA have a positive, statistically significant interactive effect. And when the interaction is included, the coefficient on the attendance variable goes from positive and statistically significant to negative and statistically significant.[17] The problem is that the new coefficient on attendance measures the effect of attendance for someone with a zero prior GPA – a population that does not even exist. The "problem" is easily resolved by centering prior GPA (usually about its average) before constructing the interaction. This adjusts the coefficient on the attendance variable so that it is the effect for the student at the average GPA. Seeing this done in real time seems to seal the point.

FUTURE TRENDS

It is rare for current research methods in econometrics to filter down to the undergraduate level, largely because cutting-edge econometrics is often specialized and mathematically challenging. For teaching undergraduate econometrics, it is more fruitful to look to various empirical literatures and to business consulting to see the kinds of methods that are applied. In doing so, one is struck by the increasing importance of data structures with both cross-sectional and time-series dimensions. Internet companies, banks, insurance companies, and marketing firms now have access to very large, rich data sets on individuals, and they are looking for employees capable of extracting information from such data sets. If I were to squeeze more material into an introductory course, I would introduce the analysis of pooled cross-sections and panel data methods. We now have very good tools for inferring causality from such data sets and for explaining economic behavior. The econometric methods have become easily accessible in popular econometrics packages. The main challenge for the community of econometrics instructors is deciding how much rigor can be sacrificed in order to cover additional topics.

NOTES

1. In the mid-2000s, I conducted an informal survey of econometrics requirements among the Big Ten universities. Michigan State has always had an econometrics requirement for a degree, but we were facing resource constraints with the number of our majors growing substantially. I was surprised to find out that Michigan State was one of just a few economics degrees in the Big Ten that required students to take introductory econometrics.
2. At MSU, we have a follow-up econometrics course that about 25 to 30 students take per year. Typically

that course covers panel data methods, instrumental variables, limited dependent variable models, and some advanced time series methods.

3. At MSU, we are not currently in this ideal situation: the students take a course from the statistics department and so, when they enroll in econometrics, they probably have less appreciation of why statistics is important for economics than they should.

4. Becker and Greene (2001) also make the point that "chalk and talk" approaches to econometrics, with heavy emphasis on algebra and little on applications, can no longer be justified. I also agree with these authors that using unrealistic, overly simplistic empirical exercises is unlikely to convince students of the value of econometrics.

5. The sports topics tend to appeal more to men than women. One cannot help notice at MSU that enrollment in the economics major is dominated by men. How one should go about making economics more attractive to undergraduate women is worth discussing, but well outside the scope of this chapter.

6. At MSU, all economics majors are required to take a "capstone" course in the form of a senior seminar. Students are required to undertake a serious research project, and most students write empirical papers. Thus, students like to hear about lots of possibilities that they may want to eventually pursue for their senior seminar papers. Some faculty members use part of the senior seminar to teach slightly more advanced econometric methods, with special emphasis on how to use pooled cross-sections and panel data for policy analysis.

7. Fifteen years ago, starting with cross-sectional regression under random sampling, with the focus on the population, was unconventional. Since then, other textbooks – notably, Stock and Watson (2011) – have taken a similar approach.

8. Earlier I mentioned that I stated and interpreted assumptions allowing draws of the explanatory variables to be random outcomes – and I think this is important. However, for derivations of statistical properties, it is helpful to wave one's hands a bit and treat the regressors as nonrandom; this approach is operationally the same as conditioning on the sample outcomes.

9. According to Kennedy (1998), students' poor understanding of the notion of a sampling distribution is a major impediment to the understanding of econometrics.

10. I am happy to make these slides available on request. Although the slides are aligned with my text, they may be useful in providing an outline, and specific examples, for courses based on other texts.

11. In some cases, the software can be integrated into the slides directly. For example, Sweave allows one to imbed R commands in LaTex files, and then output is generated in real time. If, say, some of the data change, the analysis is updated automatically when the LaTex file is recompiled.

12. Some instructors use electronic slides but do not make them available to their students because of worries about class attendance. But there are ways to encourage class attendance even if students have online access to the slides. One should emphasize that the slides are intended only as an outline; many important explanations are given in lecture that do not appear on slides. Also, omitting the real-time computer output from the slides is another way to encourage attendance in lecture. I have never used pop quizzes to ensure good class attendance, but it is possible in introductory econometrics.

13. I am happy to provide sample problem sets and exams on request.

14. A related issue is using linear regression models when the dependent variable is discrete but has quantitative meaning – such as the number of children born to a woman. After all, having another year of schooling cannot reduce the number of children by, say, 0.15. In discussing these kinds of examples, I emphasize that regression allows us to measure the effects of explanatory variables on the *average* outcome on y: give 100 women another year of schooling and they will have, among them, about 15 fewer children.

15. Due to time constraints, I no longer cover weighted least squares (WLS) in my introductory course. In some ways, this is too bad, as WLS can be more efficient than OLS even if we have misspecified the model of heteroskedasticity. And it is easy to make WLS inference just as robust as OLS inference.

16. The data set is called APPLE.RAW. As of 3 September 2011, it can be obtained at the web site http://mit-press.mit.edu/catalog/item/default.asp?ttype=2&tid=11227&xid=13&xcid=16146 (accessed 3 September 2011).

17. This situation can be confusing even to experienced researchers; I have seen cases where the interaction term is dropped, even though it is practically and statistically significant, because it leads to "weird" results.

REFERENCES

Becker, W. E. and W. H. Greene (2001), "Teaching statistics and econometrics to undergraduates", *Journal of Economic Perspectives,* **15**, 169–82.

Johnson, B. K., J. J. Perry and M. Petkus (2010), "The status of econometrics in the economics major: A survey", Working Paper, Centre College Department of Economics.

Kennedy, P. E. (1998), "Teacher undergraduate econometrics: A suggestion for fundamental change", *American Economic Review Papers and Proceedings,* **88**, 487–91.

Stock, J. H. and M. W. Watson (2011), *Introduction to Econometrics* (third edition), Boston, MA: Addison-Wesley/Longman.

Wooldridge, J. M. (2009), *Introductory Econometrics: A Modern Approach* (fourth edition), Mason, OH: South-Western.

44 An interdisciplinary approach to teaching antitrust economics
Roger D. Blair and Christine Piette Durrance

Antitrust Economics is an interdisciplinary course at the interface of microeconomic principles and antitrust law and policy. Many students find this to be a challenging, but interesting, opportunity to apply their economic tools to some high-stakes legal problems. In so doing, the student learns to think like an economist by focusing on social welfare, identifying incentives, and structuring policy to obtain the desired outcome.

In this chapter, we provide some teaching strategies that we have found useful in teaching this material to different audiences. At the University of Florida, the students are primarily advanced undergraduate economics majors with a good deal of background in economics. At the University of North Carolina, the students are largely advanced public policy majors, who have completed an intermediate microeconomics course, while others are business, political science, economics, or other social science majors, not all of whom have studied intermediate microeconomics.

We begin by describing more fully what Antitrust Economics entails, starting with a brief outline of the antitrust laws that govern competition in the United States. Then we turn to the role and importance of economic analysis in understanding and evaluating the judicial decisions that define the law. We next offer some suggestions on how to organize the material, as well as advice on pedagogical approaches that can be tailored to different audiences. We also offer suggestions on textbooks and other teaching materials, and we conclude with some brief closing remarks.

ANTITRUST ECONOMICS

Competition policy in the United States is governed primarily by the Sherman Act of 1890 and the Clayton Act of 1914. These statutes provide broad prohibitions. The Sherman Act prohibits agreements that unreasonably restrain trade and monopolizing conduct. The Clayton Act forbids price discrimination, conditional sales, and mergers that may substantially lessen competition or tend to create a monopoly. The central thrust of these statutes is to promote and protect competition as a means of allocating society's scarce resources.

Due to the broad language in the statutes, judicial decisions interpreting that language add substance to the statutory framework of competition policy. From an economic perspective, these decisions should promote competition, but do not always do so. This is where economic principles can inform the discussion. Economic analysis is used to identify the effects of the business practice in question on price, quantity, and quality in the affected market. In the case of incorrect decisions, in other words, those that fail to promote competition, there is still reason for hope. Incorrect decisions lead to economic inefficiency and, therefore, there are net gains from correcting the precedent. Usually, the resulting economic forces lead to evolution in the precedent and eventually the rules of the game make sense. For example, maximum resale price restraints were once forbidden under *Albrecht v. Herald Company*,[1] but such restraints prevent the exploitation of local monopoly power, which was clearly pro-competitive rather than anticompetitive. The Supreme Court rightly recognized its judicial misstep and corrected it nearly 20 years later in *State Oil Company v. Khan*.[2] In part, the Court's reconsideration of *Albrecht* was driven by economic commentary.

This interplay of antitrust statutes, judicial opinions, and economic analysis is what Antitrust Economics is all about. Depending upon the audience, the material can be geared toward economic analysis or antitrust policy. In order to promote learning as well as active discussion, the most effective classes provide a balance of the economic theory of antitrust economics and the application to public policy.

ORGANIZING THE MATERIAL

Since the antitrust laws are intended to promote competition, a logical starting point is to make the case that competitive markets result in social welfare maximization. In contrast, monopoly (and other forms of imperfect competition) result in allocative inefficiency and social welfare losses. This provides an analytical foundation for the general prohibitions in the Sherman Act and the somewhat more specific prohibitions in the Clayton Act. The resulting problematic business behaviors can be characterized as horizontal and vertical.

We address horizontal problems of monopoly and collusion in the second section of the course. We cover market power first because it follows naturally from the economic case for having antitrust policy, and stress the importance of market definition. Economic models with market power on the selling side (monopoly) are contrasted with market power on the buying side (monopsony). After monopoly, we turn to price-fixing cartels and other forms of collusion (for example, market division and group boycotts), as well as discuss predatory behavior. The troublesome case of oligopoly and tacit collusion follows. This, in turn, leads to an economic case for limiting some horizontal mergers.

Vertical issues fill the remainder of the course. A solid foundation is provided with the theory of vertical integration and vertical mergers. Then a number of contractual forms of vertical integration are presented and analyzed. These include vertical price fixing, tying contracts, customer and territorial limitations, and exclusive dealing.

Difficult Topics

Antitrust economics is a challenging course at the intersection of economics, law, and policy. In our experience, two of the most troublesome topics for most of our students are (1) the dominant firm model and (2) vertical integration. The reasons for the difficulty are somewhat different.

Dominant firm model   Monopoly power, either unilateral or collusive, is the central concern of antitrust. But a textbook monopoly (in other words, a single seller of a product with no close substitutes) is rare indeed. Dominant firms, which are near monopolies, are more common. Standard Oil in 1911, American Tobacco also in 1911, Alcoa in 1945, and even Microsoft more recently, were all charged with monopoly, but none of them controlled 100 percent of industry output.[3] Cartels similarly fail to include every competitor. In order to analyze the competitive effects, the dominant firm model is extremely useful, but it confuses many students for several reasons. First, the dominant firm is aware of the economic consequences of its smaller rivals and decides to accommodate their presence. The smaller rivals appear to act as though they are in a competitive market. Many students seem to struggle with the basic behavioral aspects of this model. It is effective to consider the alternatives available to the firms. The fringe firms are price takers because they are too small to influence the market price. The dominant firm accommodates their presence because crushing them may be too costly and may arouse attention. Second, the model is quite straightforward once we find the residual demand curve that drives the dominant firm's profit-maximizing calculus. But this derivation poses a difficult problem of explanation. Deriving the dominant firm's residual demand proceeds in a sequential fashion, which is not, of course, how the profit-maximizing solution is obtained. It is important to separate the development of the graphical framework from the dominant firm's profit-maximizing calculus. Once this is done, the solution is quite simple as long as the students recognize that the profit-maximizing price is found on the residual demand. Consequently, it is important to be sure that everyone understands the derivation of the residual demand before proceeding to the solution.

Vertical integration   The economic analysis of vertical integration is extremely important because it provides the economic foundation for understanding the competitive significance of vertical mergers and a host of economically equivalent contractual alternatives to vertical integration, such as vertical price controls, tying, exclusive dealing, franchise location restrictions, and the like.

Although there are some notable, historical exceptions (for example, *Brown Shoe*[4]), vertical integration arouses suspicion only in the presence of monopoly power. In a simple two-tier distribution system, the manufacturer, which is a monopolist, sells to its competitively organized distributors, which, in turn, sell to consumers. The manufacturer reacts to the derived demand rather than the final demand. Under competitive conditions, the derived demand is relatively easy to find, but a full understanding is essential if the students are to grasp the competitively neutral effects of vertical integration. Things get much tougher when the structure involves successive monopoly. The derived demand falls out of the downstream monopolist's first-order condition, which looks like a conjuring trick. Students run into problems when they do not understand how to find the derived demand in this context. It is imperative that the instructor emphasize this point because the rest of the analysis is pretty straightforward. The pro-competitive effects of vertical integration in a successive monopoly situation also require some care in explaining.

Student Misconceptions

One misconception that many students share is the notion that the law is arbitrary and devoid of logic. This is not true even though some decisions are "incorrect" from an economic perspective. The economic inefficiency that accompanies bad legal decisions creates an incentive for the law to evolve and thereby correct these decisions. Antitrust laws have evolved over more than 100 years in ways that promote economic efficiency. There are several good examples. First, the per se illegality of simple price fixing and bid rigging, which can be traced to the earliest days of antitrust enforcement, has evolved to capture many horizontal variants: minimum fee schedules, agreements to refrain from competitive bidding, geographic market division, and other restraints on non-price competition. This expansion of the per se rule has generally been sound as it captures conduct that is economically equivalent to simple price fixing. It also economizes on scarce judicial resources, since per se treatment requires no proof of adverse economic effects. If a practice is deemed unlawful per se, its adverse effects are presumed.

Second, the Court's misadventure in *Schwinn*,[5] which made non-price vertical restraints illegal *per se*, attracted considerable academic criticism. It also led the lower courts to find ways to avoid following the unfortunate precedent. Finally, in *Sylvania*,[6] the Court came to its senses and overruled *Schwinn* and *Albrecht*. Similarly, *Dr. Miles*[7] was overruled by *State Oil* and *Leegin*.[8]

Additionally, students are often naïve about the complexity of business behavior. They frequently want to impose one rule on different kinds of anticompetitive conduct. The problem in the actual application of antitrust policy to real cases is that business behavior is indeed complex. Students find the application of per se rules quite transparent, but in some cases struggle when a rule of reason inquiry is warranted and competitive and anticompetitive consequences must be assessed. In *Broadcast Music*,[9] for example, there was an element of price fixing among copyright holders that was inevitable in the blanket licenses issued to Broadway Music, Incorporated. But there was a pro-competitive aspect of the blanket licenses since they assured compensation and provided an incentive for further creative efforts. The case required a balancing of pro-competitive and anticompetitive consequences.

PEDAGOGY

There are, of course, many ways to teach Antitrust Economics. Here we offer some suggestions on pedagogy that we have found helpful in promoting student learning, organized as goals for students, lectures/discussion, assignments, and projects.

Goals for Students of Antitrust

We want our students to accomplish two things in their study of Antitrust Economics. First, with respect to antitrust law and policy, we want our students to acquire a basic understanding of the antitrust statutes and the policy that has been developed through an evolutionary process embedded in the judicial system. By studying Antitrust Economics, our students gain an understanding of the legal process. They also observe the ways in which antitrust precedent changes over time and how economic reasoning influences that change.

Second, we want our students to gain experience in applying economic principles to somewhat complex settings. Gaining some experience by analyzing business practices in an antitrust context is both interesting and challenging, as the following examples demonstrate. The *Socony-Vacuum*[10] case illustrates the economic equivalence of price fixing and output restrictions. The *Goldfarb*[11] case reveals the competitive significance of agreements on minimum fee schedules. *Broadcast Music* requires a balancing of the anticompetitive consequences of blanket licenses for intellectual property that require an agreement on price and the pro-competitive incentives that such licenses create for the future production of intellectual property. The *Staples*[12] decision instructs students that market definition matters a good deal. In this case, the FTC challenged the merger of two office supply super-stores. The relevant market was limited to the segment served by the big box discounters and excluded the vast number of alternative sources of supply.

When it comes to vertical restraints, *State Oil*, which overruled *Albrecht*, illustrates the competitive significance of *maximum* resale price restraints in a successive monopoly agreement. The *Leegin* decision, which overruled the *Dr. Miles* precedent, reveals the economic impacts of *minimum* resale price restraints. Understanding the economic equivalence of vertical integration and various contractual alternatives comes from studying *Sylvania, Kodak,*[13] and *IBM.*[14]

Lectures and Discussion

We have found that one effective way of organizing lectures and discussions is to present the economic theory and then the policy applications by topic. A discussion of a particular business practice and its competitive (or anticompetitive) consequences is followed by a look at the relevant court opinions. We conduct an overview of the relevant cases by topic area, combined with an in-depth look at a few landmark cases that are particularly revealing examples. Use of such examples describes the setting of the particular litigation, the economic issues under dispute, the relevant precedent to consider, the conclusion of the Court, the rationale of the decision, and the resulting precedent that is created or modified.

One of the topics presented, for example, is predatory pricing. We start by reviewing the economics of predatory pricing, when predatory pricing is profitable to the predator, and what requirements must be met in order to prove a predatory pricing claim. We then discuss the economic theory and competitive implications of a predatory pricing scheme by a predator on its prey. Next, we turn to the relevant case law in this area. We review the particulars in several predatory pricing cases, including what the case law tells us about the burden of proof in a predatory pricing case, and how this evidentiary standard has evolved over time.[15] Finally, the class reads one Supreme Court opinion in its entirety, for example, *Brooke Group*,[16] to understand the issues faced by the Court in one specific example of a predatory pricing case. Class discussion and individual student participation are accomplished through use of discussion leaders.

Students are assigned in pairs or groups to be *discussion leaders* for a particular day and Court decision. Specific court opinions are selected in advance for assignment to pairs of discussion leaders; some cases are covered in summary form from the class textbook and subsequent lecture, while others are addressed through discussion leadership. Discussion leaders are responsible for reading the Court's opinion in advance, generating discussion questions for the class, distributing these questions in advance of class, and for leading the class discussion on these and other questions that arise during the class meeting. In order to provide guidance on this assignment, the instructor typically serves as the discussion leader for the first case read in its entirety. For example, the students are assigned to read *Hanover Shoe*[17] and *Illinois Brick*[18] at the beginning of the course. The instructor provides discussion questions to the students on these two cases and facilitates class discussion on these cases and their related question. For every discussion leadership day, all students are expected to have read the Supreme Court decision in its entirety and to come to class prepared to discuss the case and the discussion questions. This has proved to be a useful exercise for the students by engaging them directly in non-lecture format.

Analytical Problems

As with any other economics class, students learn a good deal by working on analytical problems. For this purpose, we assign several problems per week. For the most part, the focus is on stylized situations that may involve reductions in competition. The student must then identify the injured parties and the corresponding welfare losses. These problems often involve mathematical calculations or derivations, graphical analysis, and economic reasoning and justification. These can be individual or group exercises. For example, some analytical problems that we have used in the past include:

(1) Suppose that the demand for a good is given by $P = 100 - 0.1Q$ and the constant marginal and average cost is 40. Answer the following questions: (a) Find the price and output in a competitive market; (b) Find the price and output under monopoly; (c) Calculate the monopoly profits; (d) Compare consumer surplus under competition versus monopoly; (e) Calculate the social welfare loss associated with monopoly; (f) Show all the results in parts (a) through (e) on a graph.
(2) The best quality T-shirts are 100 percent cotton. In an effort to improve profits, the T-shirt manufacturers agreed to reduce quality and produce T-shirts that are 50 percent cotton and 50 percent polyester. They have not agreed on price. Answer the following questions: (a) In the figure below, show the effect of the agreement on the price and quantity of T-shirts in the market. Explain your answer; (b) Are consumers hurt by this agreement if there has been no agreement on price? Explain your answer.

In either case, we always emphasize the application of economic principles to the antitrust policy problem at hand. For example, *Addyston Pipe & Steel*[19] is an example of an early cartel case that has several interesting issues: (1) bid rigging, (2) customer allocation, (3) competition from some distant rivals. In analyzing the court's condemnation of the conspirators, we emphasize the economic rationale, which is the promotion and protection of competition and the impact on social welfare.

Projects

There is benefit to offering students both individual writing assignments as well as group presentations to engage them with antitrust economics and policy in different ways. We feel very strongly that undergraduate students should be given ample experience in effective writing, as well as opportunities for oral presentation of material and discussions in group settings. These skills are important for economics and policy, but of course spill over into all areas of a student's career.

Individual projects
One option is for each student to complete an individual writing assignment. We stress the importance of developing skills in clear and effective writing. Students are offered a choice of several *recent* Supreme Court decisions, complete with questions that should be specifically addressed in the paper. This assignment requires what most papers do – an introduction and conclusion, appropriate spelling and grammar, well-structured paragraphs, and effective communication, and the like. Moreover, it requires the application of knowledge of antitrust economics to a case the students have not yet faced, as well as the identification of relevant elements of the decision. Students must analyze the competitive and anticompetitive issues that arise within the particular business behavior of the case, and understand the Court's decision.

The Supreme Court's *Dagher*[20] decision in 2006, for example, was one recent choice for the individual paper assignment. In this case, gasoline service station owners brought suit against Equilon Enterprises, a joint venture formed by Texaco and Shell oil companies, alleging that the setting of prices by the joint venture constitutes price fixing in violation of Section 1. In their analysis, students were expected to demonstrate an understanding of the basics of the litigation (identification of the plaintiff, defendant, the alleged antitrust violation, and the Court's decision and the basis for that decision), as well as define the nature of a joint venture in general and the purpose of the joint venture in this case. Additionally, students were expected to compare and contrast a joint venture and a price-fixing cartel. Finally, students were required to explain the antitrust treatment of the business behavior described in *Dagher,* justify the rationale for such treatment, and explain any considerations for deterrence. In this, and all other case assignments, students must decide if they agree with the Court's decision and justify that conclusion.

Group project: battle of the experts
Usually, group projects pose serious free-rider problems – lazy students let the more ambitious group members do all or nearly all of the work. This often results in unfair rewards and causes the victims of the free riding to be disgruntled. In addition, there is a significant risk that the group will cheat in some fashion – plagiarism is not uncommon. The project described here, which was developed by David Kaserman, has several virtues. This group project does not permit free riding nor does it permit cheating. At the same time, it is extremely instructive for the participants, as the students assume the roles of the parties involved in the litigation.

Each group has four members. A specific antitrust case can be assigned to the group or can be selected by the group. The group will need the Court's opinion and other supporting materials, such as briefs for the plaintiff and for the defendant, as well as any amicus briefs that may have been filed with the Court. Once the case has been selected and the materials gathered, two of the students will represent the plaintiff and two will represent the defendant. The first student serves as the plaintiff's expert economist and presents the economic argument supporting the plaintiff's case on liability or on damages. A student representing the defendant then cross-examines the plaintiff's expert to challenge his or her economic analysis. The defendant's expert then presents the economic argument to support the defendant's case. That student is then cross-examined by the plaintiff's "lawyer." The instructor must serve as the judge to maintain order as tempers may flare, and to grade the performance. Each student's performance can be judged (in other words, graded) on its own merit.

TEXTBOOKS AND TEACHING MATERIALS

Due to the interdisciplinary nature of antitrust economics, there are few textbooks that address this material from an antitrust economics and policy perspective; however, a fairly wide array of teaching materials exist. Many of these materials are accessible to undergraduates with only the most basic economics background. Some combination of these textbooks and materials can be used to tailor individual courses to the specific needs of the students.

Textbooks

In this section, we describe several books that can be used as textbooks for the kind of antitrust economics course that we teach. A brief description is also provided.

- *Antitrust Economics*, 2nd ed. (2009) by Roger D. Blair and David L. Kaserman, Oxford University Press. This, of course, is our personal favorite for obvious reasons. The level of economic analysis is a bit above the principles level, but the book is self-contained, since all of the economic models are explained as they are encountered. The focus is primarily on the economics of antitrust law and policy. The case law itself is developed briefly to summarize the rules. The judicial reasoning that leads to those rules is not fully developed. This text has a large number of end-of-chapter questions and problems.
- *Competition Policy: Theory and Practice* (2004) by Massimo Motta, Cambridge University Press. This book is organized somewhat differently from Blair and Kaserman, but it presents the material in a rigorous fashion. It has an international flair as it includes references to European cases. The level of the economic analysis is somewhat more sophisticated, but it could be used by the advanced undergraduate.
- *Federal Antitrust Policy: The Law of Competition and Its Practice*, 2nd ed. (2006) by Herbert Hovenkamp, West Publishing. This is not exactly a textbook, but could be used for that purpose. It provides a summary of antitrust law as it has evolved through judicial opinions. It also includes a good deal of basic economic analysis. If not used as a textbook, this book is also a valuable reference for the instructor.
- *Understanding Antitrust and its Economic Implications*, 5th ed. (2009) by E. Thomas Sullivan and Jeffrey L. Harrison, Lexis/Nexis. This book was designed to be used as a supplement to law school courses in antitrust. The economic analysis is good and the antitrust coverage is comprehensive, albeit not deep. With other supplements, it could be used by undergraduates as the main text in an antitrust economics course.

- *Economics of Regulation and Antitrust*, 3rd ed. (2005) by W. Kip Viscusi, John M. Vernon and Joseph Harrington, MIT Press. As the title suggests, this textbook is not confined to antitrust. As a result, the material on antitrust is not as deep as the other books. The economic analysis should be accessible to undergraduates.

Monographs

There are several monographs that can be used as supplements in an antitrust economics course. These cannot be used as the main text, but each can be used to enrich a course as additional student readings or as additional instructor materials. All of the authors are renowned experts in the field.

- *The Antitrust Paradox* (1993) by Robert H. Bork, The Free Press.
- *The Antitrust Enterprise* (2005) by Herbert Hovenkamp, Harvard University Press.
- *Antitrust Law: Economic Theory and Common Law Evolution* (2003), by Keith N. Hylton, Cambridge University Press.
- *Antitrust Law*, 2nd ed. (2001) by Richard A. Posner, University of Chicago Press.

Antitrust Casebooks

These books are destined for use in law school courses in antitrust, but can be useful for an undergraduate course in Antitrust Economics. Casebooks contain excerpts from the most important antitrust opinions, and to varying degrees have economic analyses of the relevant antitrust problems. These excerpts can replace the reading of entire Supreme Court decisions, instead focusing on the most relevant aspects. Alternatively, these casebooks can provide the instructor with additional material and insight for the class lecture and subsequent discussion. There are many choices, but the following are the most prominent.

- *Antitrust Law, Policy and Procedure*, 5th ed. (2003) by E. Thomas Sullivan, Herbert Hovenkamp and Howard Shelanski, Lexis/Nexis.
- *Antitrust Analysis*, 6th ed. (2004) by Phillip Areeda, Louis Kaplow and Aaron Edlin, Aspen Publishers.
- *United States Antitrust Law and Economics* (2008) by Einer Elhauge, Foundation Press.

Full Court Opinions

As we have discussed above, there are times when full opinions are worth pursuing. The Court's decision and other materials can be accessed via LexisNexis Academic through most university libraries. Students can "look up a legal case" by using the citation, name(s) of the parties, or topic of the case. For example, if a student was interested in obtaining the information about a specific case against Standard Oil, e.g., *Standard Oil Company v. United States*, he could use the appropriate citation (221 U.S. 1 (1911)), one of the party's names (for example, Standard Oil), or the keyword in the case (for example, monopolization). Finding court decisions with the correct citation is the most direct way of finding decisions, but the other approaches can work as well.

CONCLUDING REMARKS

Antitrust economics is fun to teach. We approach antitrust economics from an interdisciplinary perspective using a variety of teaching methods including traditional lecture, class discussion leadership, analytic problems, individual writing assignments, and group presentations. Students in successful classes will learn how to do economic analysis and apply this learning to real-world issues. We like teaching this course and have explained how we go about it. Our way is not the only way and we would appreciate your passing along to us any new tricks that you develop.

NOTES

1. *Albrecht v. Herald Co.*, 390 U.S. 145 (1968).
2. *State Oil v. Khan*, 118 S. Ct. 275 (1997).
3. *Standard Oil Company v. United States*, 221 U.S. 1 (1911); *United States v. American Tobacco Company*, 221 U.S. 106 (1911); *United States v. Aluminum Company of America*, 148 F. 2d. 416 (2d Cir. 1945); *United States v. Microsoft*, 253 F. 3d 34 (D.C. Cir. 2001).
4. *Brown Shoe Company, Inc. v. United States*, 370 U.S. 294 (1962).
5. *United States v. Arnold Schwinn & Co.*, 388 U.S. 365 (1967).
6. *Continental T.V., Inc. v. GTE Sylvania, Inc.*, 443 U.S. 36 (1977).
7. *Dr. Miles Medical Co. v. John D. Park & Sons Co.*, 220 U.S. 373 (1911).
8. *Leegin Creative Leather Products, Inc. v. PSKS, Inc.*, 551 U.S. 877 (2007)
9. *Broadcast Music, Inc. v. Columbia Broadcasting System*, 441 U.S. 1 (1979).
10. *United States v. Socony-Vacuum Oil Company*, 310 U.S. 150 (1940).
11. *Goldfarb v. Virginia State Bar*, 421 U.S. 773 (1975).
12. *Federal Trade Commission v. Staples, Inc.*, 970 F. Supp. 1066 (D.D.C. 1997).
13. *Eastman Kodak Co. v. Image Technical Services, Inc.*, 504 U.S. 451 (1992).
14. *International Business Machines Corp. v. United States*, 298 U.S. 131 (1936).
15. *Standard Oil Company v. United States*, 221 U.S. 1 (1911); *United States v. American Tobacco Company*, 221 U.S. 106 (1911); *Matsushita Electric Industrial Co. v. Zenith Radio Corp.*, 475 U.S. 574 (1986).
16. *Brooke Group Ltd. v. Brown & Williamson Tobacco Corp.*, 509 U.S. 940 (1993).
17. *Hanover Shoe v. United Shoe Machinery Corp.*, 392 U.S. 481 (1968).
18. *Illinois Brick Co. v. Illinois*, 431 U.S. 720 (1977).
19. *United States v. Addyston Pipe & Steel Co.*, 85 F. 271 (6th Cir. 1898).
20. *Texaco Inc. v. Dagher*, 547 U.S. 1 (2006).

45 The economics of education: applying economic theory and empirical tools to public policy
Jessica S. Howell

The Economics of Education is an elective that can adeptly combine models and topics from Labor Economics, Public Finance, Econometrics, and Economic Research Methods. As such, it makes for a useful applied microeconomics elective for students who have been interested in any one of these other courses and are seeking combinations of electives that work well together. Perhaps because of the overlap with other applied microeconomics electives and because it is not a field course taught in doctoral economics programs, the Economics of Education is not a particularly common offering in most undergraduate economics programs. In departments that offer concentrations within the major, the Economics of Education makes an excellent addition to concentrations with a public policy focus. Similarly, the course may service non-majors who are in departments with a public policy component. This course also serves as a useful complement to coursework in statistics or research methods, since education data are widely available, making it easy to generate scatter plots and other descriptive charts, run simple regressions, or even elucidate various approaches to causal research design (experiments, quasi-experiments, natural experiments).

The Economics of Education is most commonly taught with Principles of Economics as a prerequisite. These prerequisites enable easy reference to basic concepts (like opportunity cost and externalities) and useful models (supply and demand). Yet, departments exist where the course is taught with no prerequisites and some time is devoted initially to conveying these basic economic principles and models used in the discipline. Anecdotal evidence has led some to hypothesize that initial exposure to the economic way of thinking within the context of a topic with which the student is intimately familiar lays a strong foundation for future coursework in economics.

There are some easily identifiable benefits and costs to the department, instructor and students associated with offering a course on the Economics of Education. The primary cost is that there currently exists no textbook to synthesize the menu of topics an instructor would logically choose to cover. Although there are plenty of accessible books, popular press articles, and even journal articles on the topics covered in the course, instructors generally must put together a course reader or a reading list, cobbling together a variety of sources on each topic. There are three primary benefits associated with the course. First, because all students have first-hand experience in the education market (elementary, secondary, and postsecondary) and understand quite well that their educational choices very likely influence the returns that await them in the labor market, there is a basic level of interest in the topic that usually generates substantial demand for the course. Their first-hand experience also tends to make it easier for students to comprehend readings and data brought to bear on the major topics discussed in the course. Second, in departments with an econometrics requirement, a senior capstone experience, or simply an emphasis on developing students' empirical skill set, the wide availability of education data provides students with ample opportunity to work on straight-forward empirical projects in this course and in future courses. Finally, the knowledge gained in the Economics of Education potentially improves students' financial literacy, which may positively influence their own future educational investment decisions, either in the process of completing their undergraduate training or with regard to graduate study. To the extent that students, even those who are successfully enrolled in college, have not been adequately informed about the returns to education and a variety of education finance issues, this feature of the course may generate nontrivial positive externalities.

COURSE CONTENT AND OBJECTIVES

Many might consider the content of this course to be simply bifurcated into K-12 (kindergarten through the 12th grade year or the end of high school) and higher education issues, as is the case for much of the economics of education research. Although it is quite natural to talk about these two education segments as two modules in the course, it is prudent to begin the course with a clear understanding of why economists have something important to say about the market for education more broadly.

Introduction and Historical Perspective

Economists are interested in the market for education primarily because it is different from many other goods markets in important ways that fall under the umbrella of market failures (credit constraints, externalities, information asymmetries) and this results in the public funding and provision of education. In the early days of the course, care should be taken to define the players in the education market and to provide students with some historical context around the public provision of education in the United States. Claudia Goldin's accessible *Education Next* article, "The Human Capital Century," provides both a solid historical and international perspective for students on the role of education in economic growth (Goldin, 2003).

Following this historical perspective, the instructor can easily segue into presenting time series data on the labor market returns to education. Simple time series graphs on real wages by level of education, disaggregated by gender and race/ethnicity, start a conversation about why people invest in education and how those incentives may have changed over time. A time series graph of the college wage premium – average wages of college graduates over average wages of high school graduates – shows that the return to college declined during the 1970s and then began to steadily climb, beginning in the 1980s. The supply and demand model can be employed to explain how these changes over time were driven by changes in the relative supply of college-educated workers, skill-biased technological changes, and changes in international trade patterns. It is quite easy to find popular press articles that discuss the college wage premium and allude to the underlying shifts in relative supply and demand for college-educated workers.

Once students have some appreciation for how the college wage premium has changed and how the supply and demand model is useful in explaining those changes, the next logical step is to develop a more formal model of the decision to invest in education. The human capital model associated with Becker (1964) and Mincer (1974) enables students to become comfortable with the basics of any investment decision – weighing various costs and benefits and utilizing the tool of discounted present value. Understanding the effect of changes in these various costs and benefits on the predictions of the model is the key to transitioning to a Mincer-style model of educational investment as is commonly covered in Labor Economics (in other words, the wage–schooling locus). This is a good point at which to make sure that students understand how differences in unmeasured ability can bias estimates of the return to schooling in the labor market, which can be both demonstrated graphically in this model as well as discussed conceptually.

Classroom discussions around the human capital model inevitably result in a student pointing out that they are not learning anything in college that is likely to be particularly useful to them in a specific job. This provides a natural segue to discussing the signaling model of educational investment and, more broadly, distinguishing between the private and social returns to education. Students who are in the process of investing in their own four-, five-, or six-year college degree seem to quickly understand that society might benefit from a faster, cheaper, or more efficient way for individuals to signal that they are of high ability to potential employers. In higher level courses or with more advanced students, the concepts of pooling and separating equilibria can be introduced within the context of the signaling model. If time permits in the course, students really enjoy some discussion (complemented with data) on the labor market returns to college selectivity and specific college majors. Because these issues so naturally tie into the basic debate between human capital and signaling theories, this is a good opportunity to ask students to apply what they've learned about the models to one of these two particular issues, about which they likely already have preconceived opinions.

Roughly one-third of the way through the course, students have the proper grounding in some of the reasons why economists are so intrigued with education markets; market failures require public provision, strong ties between educational investments and macroeconomic growth, and a demonstrated connection (albeit through different mechanisms) between individuals' educational investments and their labor market outcomes. The remaining two-thirds of the course can be divided between elementary/secondary education issues and additional topics in postsecondary education.

Elementary and Secondary Education Topics

The portion of the course that is devoted to discussing issues around elementary and secondary education can be tailored to the instructor's interests and knowledge. A natural starting place is an analysis of the effect of resources on student outcomes, which has occupied the minds of many researchers and reveals how little consensus can exist over even the most straight-forward and basic research questions that researchers have tackled for decades. The literature on education production functions is rich with examples of programs, policies, and interventions that involved dedicating more resources in an attempt to improve some measurable student outcome. A prime example is Project STAR in Tennessee, which addressed the effect of reducing class sizes on student test scores. Project STAR was evaluated with an experimental research design, so it also serves as an excellent opportunity to discuss research methods.

Most students will have attended their local public schools. The instructor might spend some time discussing the Tiebout (1956) model and how school quality differences are reflected in differences in home values because people purchase a bundle of local public goods. The local nature of school finance should also be discussed along with some basic overview of landmark cases and laws in school finance (for example, *Serrano v. Priest*, California's Proposition 13, etc.). School choice is another topic that can be explored to the extent of the instructor's or students' level of interest. Discussions of private schools, charter schools, magnate schools, voucher programs, other forms of inter/intra-district choice, and homeschooling will give some students a chance to contribute to classroom discussion by way of their personal experiences, but the instructor can certainly delve deeper into any of these topics by exploring research on the effectiveness of these different schooling models in raising student achievement.

The K-12 segment of the course might also include analyses of how schools and teachers produce education, and what incentives they face to do their jobs well. Potential topics include both federal and state-initiated school accountability programs, teacher labor markets, and teacher effectiveness. Labor market applications of the supply and demand model can be brought to bear on teacher licensure and certification, requirement variations across states, the role of teacher unions, and teacher productivity.

Postsecondary Education Topics

Mimicking the order of content in the K-12 segment of the course, the postsecondary portion of the Economics of Education course might first focus on what colleges produce and how, then discuss higher education financing and student affordability, and wrap up with analyses related to the fact that labor markets provide postsecondary institutions with an accountability framework that is quite different from the accountability measures we have seen develop in K-12.

Colleges and universities, which are predominantly not-for-profit institutions, are very unique in that they produce a service whose value is difficult to determine until long after purchasing decisions are made and they produce this service with complementary inputs that are, in themselves, difficult to quantify – faculty teaching efforts, faculty research efforts, and the students themselves. Students find it interesting to examine the research on peer effects in higher education and are generally surprised to learn more about faculty research endeavors and the ways in which research activities might complement the production of their education. An accessible introduction to these concepts is provided by Winston (1999). This is a natural place in the course to segue into the economics of college admissions, perhaps presenting information on differences in college enrollment by race/ethnicity, income, and type of postsecondary institution chosen. Time permitting, this is also a logical time to present information on selective admissions processes, the costs and benefits associated with early decision/action admissions programs, race-sensitive admissions, and even legacy admissions.

Students' understanding of higher education finance may actually be worse than their understanding of K-12 school finance. It is instructive to make clear the distinction between the *price* of admission (both list and net of financial aid) and the *cost* of educating a student. Providing examples, or having students search for the information online, of a specific institution's state subsidy relative to tuition revenue per enrolled student as well as information on the role of private donations allows students to see that across-the-board subsidies frequently dominate targeted financial aid resources. Because these across-the-board subsidies do not vary by student characteristics, except in the sense that students with different characteristics select different types of postsecondary institutions, this is a natural segue into the financial aid policy, which is more likely to be need-based and highly targeted. The instructor may elect to spend time explaining the details of the whole system – federal aid, institutional aid, and loans – or may simply provide a brief overview and instead focus on the evidence around how financial aid influences student behavior. There is a wealth of research on the effect of Pell Grants, state merit aid programs, and loan debt on a variety of student outcomes (Kane, 1998; Dynarski, 2000).

Although the labor market returns to schooling were likely covered earlier in the course, the very end of the course is a good point to return to this topic. The instructor might discuss differential returns to college major or to graduate degrees, along with some emphasis on how students in the course may evaluate their own post-baccalaureate decisions. This might also be a good point for a more nuanced discussion of selection bias (in selecting a particular type of institution or field of study, for example) and the research that attempts to estimate the return to college that is free of selection bias (Dale and Krueger, 2002). Because employers and graduate programs have the proper incentive to correctly evaluate the skill set and potential of students graduating with various degrees across different types of postsecondary institutions, there are natural market forces that hold higher education accountable for the services sold to students and the education produced. This also raises another natural place to debate the human capital and signaling models of educational investment.

Course Objectives

The basic objective in this course is to have students demonstrate mastery of the basic subjects discussed above. Mastery need not be limited to conceptual discussions of the topics and the various public policy concerns that surround each issue, which is the "education" portion of the course. Mastery really requires that the economist's tools of analysis be brought to bear on the issues discussed. It is imperative that students come away with an understanding of how to analyze the incentives of the market players, the way in which education finance shapes individual and institutional choices, and the role for public policies and programs to alter those incentives, costs and benefits to result in improved student outcomes.

Another possible objective of a course in the Economics of Education might be to correct and elucidate the most common student misconceptions on these topics. Misconceptions might vary widely with the student body demographics or geographic location, but typical topics include list versus net college tuition, the size of the state subsidy per student in public colleges and universities relative to list tuition charged, differences in labor market returns to education and college majors, and state variation in K-12 school choice.

Finally, depending upon the instructor's preferences and the economics major curricular focus, an objective of this course might be to improve student understanding of research design and the role of empirical analysis in providing evidence on important public policy issues. Because students enrolled in the course already have a solid experience-based foundation in the topics covered, it appears to be easier for them to understand the distinction between a research question that seeks evidence of a causal relationship and one that does not. As a result, it may be quite manageable to expose students to research papers that utilize regression, difference-in-differences, regression discontinuity, natural and quasi-experimental design, and randomized control trial experiments. A conceptual understanding of these methods in the context of a particular elective likely provides a solid foundation for more pure methods courses like Econometrics or Economic Research Methods.

PEDAGOGICAL APPROACHES

As in most college courses, the interplay of class size, course level, and prerequisites is important to consider when planning the course. With no prerequisites and opening the course to non-majors, the class is likely to be taught at a lower technical level and could, therefore, be quite large (100+ students). As prerequisites are added and the technical level increases, students benefit substantially from having a smaller class (35–40 students). If the instructor wishes to generate true discussion and debate, particularly over policies, programs, and empirical evidence, an even smaller class size (20–25 students) is recommended. It is also possible to combine these arrangements through the use of teaching assistants running smaller discussion sessions to accompany a larger lecture.

The format of the course, lecture versus seminar for example, is as much about tailoring to the audience as it is to the instructor. Although class size might dictate format, one might also think of the format varying naturally with the topic. Topics with interesting policy debate angles (for example, school choice or the return to college selectivity) are probably better as seminars with a few empirical studies to guide different sides of the debate. A lecture format likely suits the portions of the class that involve explaining the nuts and bolts of the supply and demand model or the human capital model. Pedagogically, having the flexibility to mix these formats throughout the course may be a very successful way to maintain student interest and cater to various learning styles.

Perhaps the biggest pedagogical decision to be made in this course is with regard to the technical level of the course materials utilized. There are some very good popular press pieces that identify challenges in the field and also explain programmatic and policy solutions that have been successfully shown to improve student outcomes (for example, *New York Times*, the *Chronicle of Higher Education*, *Education Next*, etc.). These less-technical sources along with papers from the *Journal of Economic Perspectives* are definitely sufficient to provide an introduction to most issues and enable a discussion of economic ways of analyzing and solving various education problems. Good examples include Goldin and Katz (1999) and Winston (1999).

Yet, a real benefit of the Economics of Education is that it is easier than in other elective courses to harness students' interest and first-hand experience to teach methodological and empirical approaches used by economists that identify correlational and causal relationships in the data. While this requires the incorporation of higher level course materials and journal articles, something that the instructor may prefer not to do all semester long, it is perhaps worthwhile to add more technical materials into the coverage of at least a few topics. For example, Dynarski (2000) is a straight-forward application of differences-in-differences to understanding the causal impact of financial aid on college attendance. Similarly, Mosteller (1995) is a straight-forward demonstration of how a randomized control trial was used to examine the causal effect of class size on student outcomes. These and similar papers are very accessible relative to typical academic journal articles. The instructor can easily find ways to discuss one of these empirical strategies in examining almost any topic that appears in the Economics of Education; thus, at a minimum, students could come away from the course understanding these basic approaches to causal inference and the data required in order to utilize them.

Like many economics elective courses, the assignments, projects, and exams in the Economics of Education should measure students' ability to write effectively, analyze topics both graphically and mathematically, and perhaps their ability to effectively bring data to bear on various topics. It is challenging to find this sort of balance in any course because the homework assignments should give students the opportunity to practice all three tools of analysis. When homework assignments are centered around just two or three topics, those topics may lend themselves to written response discussion-style questions but not graphical problems, or to mathematical examples but not data analysis. The best assignments find a way to combine all three tools for each topic covered in the course. Instructors may find it useful to think of each topic covered in the course as a small empirical paper in which the research question must be clearly stated, an economic model must be used to offer up theoretical evidence on that question, and then empirical evidence must be employed to either refute or support economic theory. If questions on homework assignments and exams cover this mix, then students come away from the course very well-prepared to either read more advanced economic studies or to engage in a small research project of their own.

To be more concrete about these ideas, it is worthwhile to examine which topics naturally lend themselves to a particular tool of analysis. The instructor may find that the first segment of the course provides a good opportunity to have students use the supply and demand model to analyze the effect of various changes in the college-educated labor force and demand for such workers. Data on wages can be utilized to have students get a stronger sense for how substantially the demand and supply of college-educated workers must have changed relative to less well-educated workers at various points in our country's history. Later in the course, when the human capital model is introduced, students may be asked to again use their graphical skills to explain the return to schooling using a wage-schooling locus diagram that is common in most Labor Economics texts. Simple numerical problems in this section may ask students to utilize some hypothetical salaries associated with various education paths and the concept of net present value to determine what educational choices different individuals would make. Students might be asked in a written response question to discuss public policies that might successfully alter the costs or benefits associated with investing in education and encourage more attainment.

In an effort to satisfy varied learning styles, the pedagogical approach may best be varied with the topic being taught. For example, when discussing educational investment decisions, it is very easy to supply half of the class with a reading on human capital theory and the other half with a reading on signaling, and then schedule a debate. Nearly all students can see both sides of the debate, so assigning them to make the case for just one theory focuses their attention. Of course, the theories are not mutually exclusive, and this salient fact will likely fall out of a proper debate. Debate may also be a useful approach when discussing the labor market returns to college quality or specific majors.

A different pedagogical approach may capitalize on the fact that there are almost always education topics being covered in the news. The instructor may introduce a topic and then ask students to find a recent story in the news that relates. A simple writing assignment on what economics brings to bear on the topic may be sufficient or students could complete this task as a part of a semester-long project (such as a news portfolio) designed to train them to be better consumers of information in the popular press. Examples of topics that currently receive quite a bit of press coverage, in large part because there is movement in state and federal policy or interest, include poor alignment between K-12 and higher education segments and the related issue of poor academic preparation (for example, high rates of remedial or developmental course-taking in college, where these courses generally do not involve credits that count toward a degree), stagnant college degree completion rates and the national push, led by President Obama and US Education Secretary Arne Duncan, to substantially increase postsecondary degree and credential achievement in the United States, and international comparisons of student performance and concerns over shortfalls in STEM (Science, Technology, Engineering, and Math) fields. Depending on the location of the college or university, it may be logical to address particular state policies or local issues. Focusing on topics that are particularly timely or particularly relevant to the student body enables the instructor to really customize the Economics of Education in a way that truly engages students in an effective manner.

CONCLUSION

The Economics of Education is an excellent elective to add to any department's curriculum. This course may have large positive externalities for financial literacy around educational decision-making in the United States. Students in this course learn about education as an investment, gain an understanding of the difference between subsidized and unsubsidized loans, see the importance of discounting future payments, are exposed to information about labor market returns to different choices of postsecondary institution and college major, and understand many policies designed to improve students' educational outcomes. As a result, this course not only impacts students' understanding of their own educational investment decisions, but that knowledge potentially spills over to impact the quality of the decision-making by their friends, family, and children.

In addition to the many benefits cited above, an argument can be made that this is an especially relevant and important time to have the Economics of Education available to college and university students. The current emphasis on educational attainment, particularly collegiate credential and degree completion, by the White House, many foundations, and education policy institutes surely indicates that all participants in the education market – schools, colleges, administrators, and state and federal policymakers – will be interested in programs and policies designed to meet these goals. Yet, when the national attention switches to some other goal, the focus of the course is just as easily redirected to maintain timeliness and policy relevance. It is imperative that economics departments, many of which feed students into the graduate programs in law, public policy, and business that create future leaders and public policymakers, expose students to the ways in which the tools of economic analysis are appropriately applied to education markets.

REFERENCES

Becker, G. S. (1964), *Human Capital*, Cambridge, MA: Columbia University Press.

Dale, S. B. and A. B. Krueger (2002), "Estimating the payoff to attending a more selective college: An application of selection on observables and unobservables", *Quarterly Journal of Economics* (November), 1491–527.

Dynarski, S. (2000), "Hope for whom? Financial aid for the middle class and its impact on college attendance", *National Tax Journal*, **53** (2), 629–62.

Goldin, C. (2003), "The human capital century", *Education Next*, **3** (1), 73–8.

Goldin, C. and L. F. Katz (1999), "The shaping of higher education: The formative years in the United States, 1890 to 1940", *Journal of Economic Perspectives*, **13** (1), 37–62.

Kane, T. J. (1998), *The Price of Admission: Rethinking How Americans Pay for College*, Washington, DC: Brookings Institution Press.

Mincer, J. A. (1974), *Schooling, Experience, and Earnings*, Washington, DC: Columbia University Press.

Mosteller, F. (1995), "The Tennessee study of class size in the early school grades", *The Future of Children: Critical Issues for Children and Youths*, **5** (2), 113–27.

Tiebout, C. (1956), "A Pure Theory of Local Expenditures", *Journal of Political Economy*, **64** (5), 416–24.

Winston, G. C. (1999), "Subsidies, hierarchy and peers: The awkward economics of higher education", *Journal of Economic Perspectives*, **13** (1), 13–36.

46 Environmental and natural resource economics: teaching the non-major and major simultaneously
Lynne Y. Lewis

Interest in the field of environmental and natural resource economics has mushroomed in recent years. Policy conversations surrounding carbon taxes and cap-and-trade, for example, have brought this field into the limelight and into daily conversation. Environmental catastrophes such as the Deepwater Horizon oil spill have illustrated the need for and the use of environmental valuation techniques.

Students choosing to take environmental or natural resource economics courses have also changed dramatically. Name recognition of previously obscure economic terms, access to environmental information, consensus on the science behind climate change – all of these things have moved the starting point as students arrive in the classroom with a heightened awareness of the issues. Economics students have more interest in and knowledge about environmental issues and Environmental Studies students are more open to learning about how economic tools can be used to aid in decision-making or to help solve environmental problems in a cost-effective way.

Facebook, Twitter, blogs, YouTube, Wikipedia, etc. have altered the way information flows. Smart phones allow constant access to information. However, available information does not mean unbiased or purely factual information. News commentary/ entertainment shows such as The Daily Show impact the way information is received. Likewise, big news stories such as those on environmental catastrophes receive constant and varied attention, including segments of varying accuracy and quality with respect to the economic impacts.

This chapter presents some of the challenges with teaching environmental and natural resource economics. I begin by providing context through a description of how the field and types of students taking these courses have evolved. Selected course topics and suggestions for how to expose students to environmental economics using a variety of teaching methods are then presented. The chapter concludes with a glimpse at the continuing challenges of the field and teaching the subject to undergraduates.

LITERATURE ON TEACHING ENVIRONMENTAL ECONOMICS

Very little has been written about teaching environmental economics courses. A quick survey of the *Journal of Economic Education* using the keywords "environmental economics" yields 40 articles, only half of which are dedicated exclusively to some aspect of environmental economics, and none of which are dedicated to the teaching of a course. Most involve a single subject or cover specialty subjects like the use of Geographic Information Systems (GIS) in teaching economics (Peterson, 2000). Whitmarsh (1995) introduces computer-assisted instruction for the teaching of fisheries economics and the dynamic processes of biological growth. Alden (1999) discusses the use of role-play for teaching environmental economics. Several articles offer examples of classroom games (Murphy and Cardenas, 2004; Giraud, 2002), for example, and several of the classroom experiments focus on tradable discharge permits (Ando and Harrington, 2006; Walbert and Bierma, 1988; Nguyen, 2009). Caviglia-Harris (2003) introduces a model for teaching economics in an interdisciplinary class using environmental economics content as her example. A similar search of the *Journal of Environmental Education* from 1994 to the present generates no articles on teaching environmental economics, but highlights some articles that discuss topics typically covered such as sustainability, a few book reviews about books on ecological or "eco-" economics and one article on a study of environmental awareness of environmental studies and economics majors (Sherburn and Devlin, 2004).

One of the few journal articles focused on teaching a course on environmental economics dates back to when the field was relatively young. Carter (1972) discusses the then recent and emerging interest in applying economics to environmental problems. The article includes a list of readings for potential teachers, but does not highlight the many complexities and roadblocks associated with teaching the subject. Evolution and growth of the field has increased this complexity, but advances in teaching practices that provide concrete methods for addressing such challenges are lacking in the literature. Christainsen (1988) examines the state of economic education with respect to the natural environment by analysing the prominent textbooks available at the time. He notes, "Environmental and natural resource economics has thus become a tremendously exciting area of study and is now an accepted part of the curriculum at major colleges and universities" (p. 185). Since this time the field has grown from an accepted part to a requirement for many environmental studies and environmental science majors and environmental economics is even a major area of concentration or minor at some institutions.

UNDERGRADUATE ENVIRONMENTAL AND NATURAL RESOURCE ECONOMICS

Environmental and natural resource economics courses are taught at different levels and to different audiences. Larger schools typically have the staff and student demand for separate courses for environmental and natural resources. Smaller schools tend to offer one or the other or a combined one-semester course. Further complicating course offerings is the fact that both environmental and natural resource economics courses can be designed with simply a principles prerequisite or with intermediate and/or econometrics prerequisites. Some have no prerequisites at all. Versions of these courses, especially those with no prerequisites or solely a principles prerequisite, are frequently populated with a very broad array of different majors and learners. Thus, students are likely to have different goals and interests as well as technical backgrounds. This chapter focuses on a semester-long course with a prerequisite of only principles, one populated by both majors and non-majors, but the challenges are similar for courses at other levels.

In the Teagle Foundation report, Colander and McGoldrick (2009) discuss the economics major as part of a liberal education. In one of their recommendations, they articulate, "much of graduate training (in economics) is highly specialized, devoted to creating economic scientists in the same way that natural scientists are devoted to creating natural scientists. Neither is designed to train students in applying policy or the associated broader moral philosophy aspects, yet this is where a majority of students' interests reside" (p. 25). Environmental economics courses are an excellent example of this divergence, since non-majors are drawn to these courses because of a strong interest in policy and ethics.

Environmental Studies majors are frequently encouraged, and often required, to take environmental economics. Environmental Studies students likely have a good grasp of environmental problems, but very little comprehension of or experience with economic theory. They may also come with a bias toward restoration or cleanup as a moral imperative. On the other hand, Economics majors usually have a solid grasp of economic theory and are proficient with graphical and mathematical concepts, but have rarely if ever applied these tools to environmental problem solving. They also tend to be less environmentally literate. They may even feel that the course is biased toward pollution control. (Ironically, Environmental Studies students will think quite the opposite – that economics favors growth and pollution.) A third type of student in these classes takes environmental economics purely for interest in the subject or for a general education requirement. These students come from majors in French or Physics or Psychology or Art History, for example.

This diverse student body makes teaching these courses extremely challenging. Teaching the content exclusively for one group satisfies their goals and interests, while leaving a large constituency frustrated. Providing a balanced approach, while admittedly challenging, ultimately can be the most rewarding. Tapping into the breadth of the Environmental Studies major and the depth of the Economics major yields a powerful combination. Using the strengths and interests of each group to help inform and engage the other will enhance the learning experience of both. One key to success will be in knowing *who* is in the class. A brief first-day survey of background courses and analytical skills will help inform the teaching approach. With courses populated with majors and non-majors, no two courses are identical, and even when teaching two sections in a single semester, student background differences are likely to generate two very different class experiences.

In order to balance major and non-major backgrounds and interests, consider the following components and approaches:

- Illustrate the complexities of environmental problems and environmental policy.
- Introduce economic theory as applied to environmental and natural resource issues.
- Use conceptual models, graphical models *and* mathematical models in teaching.
- Use examples of actual analyses such as benefit-cost – both well done and less than well done.
- Introduce data analysis.
- Teach both breadth and depth.
- Utilize combinations of mathematics, experiments and experiential learning whenever possible.
- Emphasize where economics can help us in decision-making and problem solving.

● Simultaneously highlight the shortcomings of economics for environmental problem solving.

Such goals for teaching can be achieved by addressing a series of broad questions, such as: What is environmental and natural resource economics? What role does economics play in addressing environmental issues and problems? And perhaps, more importantly, what can it not do? In other words, how does economics help us to solve problems? How can we view environmental problems and solutions through an economic lens? And where and why does economics fail in solving problems? Or, more likely, where does it fit within the multiple complexities of decision-making?

Topic coverage is varied dependent on whether the department has the luxury of offering separate courses in environmental and natural resources. A typical course in natural resource economics covers the mechanics of cost-benefit analysis and resource allocation questions. Water, land, agriculture, forests, fisheries and energy are topics through which these mechanics are developed. Environmental economics courses typically cover the economics of pollution control via local and regional pollution, climate change, mobile source pollution and water pollution. Extensions in either course include topics in environmental justice, development and population. A combination course is likely to emphasize tools such as discounting, cost-benefit analysis, cost-effectiveness analysis, and economic incentives through a mix of topics associated with each stand-alone version of the course.

CONNECTING THE ENVIRONMENT AND ECONOMICS – INTERDISCIPLINARITY?

It is certainly not difficult to convey the relevance of environmental economics to undergraduates. Long standing debates regarding off-shore wind projects and climate change and environmental disasters such as the Deepwater Horizon oil spill in 2010 – just to name a few examples – have highlighted the connection and tension between environmental issues and economics, as well as the need for solid economic analysis. Valuation, benefit-cost, cost-effectiveness, cap and trade, carbon taxes, etc. are all important components that deserve classroom attention.[1]

The very nature of environmental problems brings many disciplines into the conversation. Fisheries economics models rely on a biological model and fish catch quotas cannot be set without working together with marine biologists. Climate change issues involve biologists and chemists among others, including economists, who ask questions such as: What is the best level for the cap to be set? Which gases should be controlled? What is the effect of different gases? Developing solutions to environmental issues naturally raises normative and ethical questions including: Who should pay for the damages? Which countries should control emissions? Where do displaced peoples go?

While students are easily engaged by the relevance of topics covered, the interdisciplinary nature of the course makes it challenging to keep students on track with learning the economic models and tools necessary to understand or perform economic analysis, while not dismissing the other important questions. Students are likely to raise questions not directly related to the economics, but very interconnected with the topic being discussed. Typical questions include, "How is carbon dioxide measured?" "Where does mercury come from?" "How do you get the sediment out from behind a dam?" "How do we measure maximum sustained yield?"

The next three subsections provide examples of select topic areas, chosen because they tend to offer many different kinds of teaching opportunities and also illustrate the challenges and complexities of this subject. Entire graduate and undergraduate courses have been devoted to benefit-cost analysis and an entire subfield of environmental economics is devoted to valuation of the environment. Emissions trading is a growing research area. All of these topics tend to be covered in a typical undergraduate course.

Benefit-cost Analysis

Few students taking this course will ultimately become professional economists. However, the likelihood that a student will come across some form of benefit-cost analysis in his/her lifetime is substantially higher. Understanding the mechanics, shortcomings, limitations and appropriateness of chosen benefits and costs is very important. What was the discount rate? What is the lifetime of the project? Were all costs and benefits included? If not, why not and if so, how were they measured? Was sensitivity analysis performed? Who performed the analysis and for whom?

It is quite common for undergraduates to "believe" what they read, so the challenge of teaching them healthy skepticism and how to ask appropriate questions is woven throughout this type of course. Recalling that students are taking this class for different reasons, the benefit-cost analysis facilitates a critical learning process: that what makes up a solid analytical argument (in other words, understanding the fundamentals of the tools used) is as important as being able to perform one. Additionally, since the data used to conduct such analyses can be represented in different fashions to suggest different results, it is important to teach students to learn about who conducts analyses in addition to general data availability and sources.

It is not difficult to impress upon students the relevance and importance of at least a cursory understanding of benefit-cost analysis. Many government agencies require benefit-cost analysis for decision-making; the Federal Energy and Regulatory Commission (FERC) requires benefit-cost analysis for relicensing of dams; the Congressional Budget Office (CBO) and the Office of Management and Budget (OMB) both provide guidelines for economic analysis and discount rates.[2] The US Environmental Protection Agency (EPA) uses benefit-cost analysis to evaluate the effectiveness of policy and, for example, recently issued a summary report of the benefits and costs of the Clean Air Act from 1990–2020 (US EPA, 2011). This document discusses both direct and indirect benefits of the Clean Air Act.[3] Enhancing students' economic literacy using the language and the mechanics of benefit-cost analysis as applied to these or other examples helps make abstract material more accessible to all majors.

One aspect of benefit-cost analysis that deserves attention, especially with mixed background students, is the concept and mathematics of discounting. The time value of money and rates of time preference – explicit or implicit – are not always obvious to all students. Economics majors are likely to have been exposed to discounting. Principles courses may introduce discounting in lectures on bond and stock valuations. Money and banking courses utilize discounting in the context of securities prices as well as when discussing yield to maturity and theories about the term structure of interest rates. Hyperbolic discounting may be used to teach about procrastination and impatience in behavioral economics and in public finance; discounting is important background to learning about what discount rates are suitable to public investments.

Non-majors, on the other hand, are not likely to have any prior experience with discounting. Using examples related to environmental problems will keep majors engaged, while teaching the mechanics to the non-majors. Simple examples in which a resource is allocated over two periods allows for an observation of the effect of the discount rate on allocations across the present and future (Tietenberg and Lewis, 2009). A two-period model also allows for demonstration of the effect of changing the discount rate on resource allocation. It also facilitates discussion of sustainability and intergenerational equity. Additionally the two-period model can be discussed conceptually, drawn graphically and solved mathematically, reaching students with differing learning styles.

Discounting mechanics naturally leads to a discussion of the choice of the discount rate and the social discount rate, or social rate of time preference. There is a relatively active discussion in the literature about appropriate rates of discount for climate change mitigation, and the Stern report and its critics offer great fodder for class readings and classroom debate. What does it mean to discount something that is not expected to happen for 50 or 100 years? What does it mean for the choice of the discount rate if there is great uncertainty in the estimates of costs and benefits? Also, different government agencies advocate different rates of discount for public projects. Why? Does this affect the numbers and types of projects that get chosen? Obviously, the answer is yes and this form of sensitivity analysis becomes an important component of this course.

For example, the US Office of Management and Budget provides guidelines for cost-benefit analysis. One part of their guidelines suggests:

> Analyses should show the sensitivity of the discounted net present value and other outcomes to variations in the discount rate. The importance of these alternative calculations will depend on the specific economic characteristics of the program under analysis. For example, in analyzing a regulatory proposal whose main cost is to reduce business investment, net present value should also be calculated using a higher discount rate than 7 percent. Analyses may include among the reported outcomes the *internal rate of return* implied by the stream of benefits and costs. The internal rate of return is the discount rate that sets the net present value of the program or project to zero. While the internal rate of return does not generally provide an acceptable decision criterion, it does provide useful information, particularly when budgets are constrained or there is uncertainty about the appropriate discount rate (Office of Management and Budget Circular, 1994, Revised, December 2010, A-94).[4]

Other agencies advocate for different rates. Internationally, the World Bank and other lending organizations use much higher rates for projects.

Finally, continuous discounting and continuous compounding represent situations with instantaneous or continuous growth. These concepts are appropriate for biological growth and topics such as forestry and fisheries. The material can be made more challenging with the incorporation of a rate most appropriate for discussions about fisheries or forests.

Valuation of the Environment

The 1989 Exxon Valdez oil spill moved nonmarket valuation, including environmental damage estimation, into a broader debate about methods used for the monetization of environmental goods and services. When the Exxon Valdez tanker spilled 11 million gallons of crude oil into Prince William Sound in Alaska in 1989, the calculation of nonuse (or passive use) values was not a widely researched topic. The spill, and the resulting *Ohio v. US Department of the Interior* case, led to a new ruling that lost passive use values could now be compensated within natural resources damages assessments. Since this time, the estimation of nonuse values has become a rapidly growing research area and damage assessment is now commonplace.

This topic is not without great debate, however. Putting a value on something that is outside the marketplace is so foreign to most people that it deserves special attention in the course. If, as described above, benefit-cost analysis is so widely used, how are the benefits and costs measured? Illustrating to students the value of goods and services within a marketplace is relatively straightforward, such as the value of hydropower from a dam project. But comparing that to the value of an endangered species or a pristine view is conceptually, as well as methodologically, challenging.

The Deepwater Horizon spill and the Exxon Valdez oil spill are just two of many examples of catastrophes for which there are and will be lawsuits. Relevant questions for environmental economics students include: How are losses from beach closures estimated? What about the value of the (for example) Brown Pelican? Should we put a value on these? If we don't, will such losses be neglected in both damage assessments or future analyses of the benefits and costs of offshore drilling or tanker safety measures?

Dedicating substantial classroom time to catastrophes also provides the opportunity to facilitate a more thorough discussion of the estimation of damages. Teaching nonmarket valuation topics includes discussions about methods including contingent valuation, choice experiments, travel cost and hedonic estimation. There are numerous examples and classroom experiments that enhance these discussions, especially related to survey work. Survey biases such as information, hypothetical, payment vehicle biases and the difference between *willingness to accept compensation* (WTA) and *willingness to pay* (WTP) are covered in most textbooks. One interesting classroom exercise is presented in Croson et al. (2005). They present an experiment designed to illustrate one potential reason for the discrepancy between willingness to pay and willingness to accept compensation. They utilize an experiment that asks respondents to assess spill-associated fines under various hypothetical scenarios: an accident, negligence or an intentional dumping. This experiment is relatively simple to replicate in the classroom and the data can be used to test the hypothesis that WTA increases with culpability, as long as the party causing the damage is paying for the repairs. Obvious extensions include culpability associated with the Deepwater Horizon explosion and payments for damages.

When damage cases actually do make it to trial, briefing reports and expert witness summaries can provide enlightening commentary from economists on both sides of the case. For example, the American Trader oil spill evidence summaries make for great course material to supplement a discussion of travel costs and methods used to value recreation sites (Chapman et al., 1998; Dunford, 1999).

Another valuation method, not without its own debate, is benefit transfer and meta-analysis. A benefit transfer takes estimates from a study site and applies them to a policy site using either a point transfer, a function transfer or a structural transfer. Benefit transfer has the advantage of being quick and inexpensive, but the accuracy of estimates deteriorates the further the new context deviates temporally or spatially from the context used to derive the estimates, even if the sites are similar. Benefit transfer relies heavily on the availability of good data. One source of environmental valuation data comes from the Environmental Valuation Reference Inventory (EVRI). EVRI contains numerous valuation studies and data and has been used in many benefits transfer studies and in meta-analysis (the "analysis of analyses").[5] Very few studies have tested the validity of environmental value transfer (benefit transfer) across sites. In those that have, the transfer errors have been sizable. Some literature has focused on the issue of site similarity (Johnston, 2007, provides a nice summary). Most studies agree that an important factor related to transferability is the similarity between sites: both physical similarity and similarity of affected populations.

Trading Pollution Rights: Cap and Trade

Studying how economic incentives can be used for pollution control is a key component of any environmental economics course. It used to be the case that the phrase "cap and trade" was recognized only among those academics who studied resource and environmental economics. This term has become much more commonplace, and if you ask your students about it, it is now very likely they know something about cap and trade. This knowledge, and recognizing the diverse background of students in the course, provides fertile ground for a multi-stage approach to enhancing student learning.

The "right to pollute" as a tradable good is a challenging concept for many students. For example, environmental studies students may become frustrated with the idea of potentially profiting from selling (or owning) a right to pollute. Students often are also uncomfortable with the concept of "efficient allocation of pollution" or optimal level of pollution. Compounding these conceptual challenges is the fact that the theory of "optimal pollution" and trading the rights to pollute relies heavily on graphical analysis and depends on the marginal control costs of the firms involved and the marginal damages to society.

Lewis (2011) presents a three-stage teaching approach that combines theory, a classroom experiment and an experiential learning component using the EPA's sulfur dioxide program for a real-world cap and trade example. The three stages are designed to address different learning styles and satisfy multiple learning objectives, but also to illustrate real-world complexities via both a classroom experiment and participation in a real cap-and-trade auction. This approach also helps students understand the practical aspects of abstract theory in addition to topic-specific issues associated with using economic incentives for pollution control.

The first stage of Lewis' three-stage learning exercise begins with a classroom lecture (or two) on the theory of tradable pollution allowances and another on the EPA's Acid Rain Program. This abstract theoretical perspective is grounded in the second stage, a trading experiment during which all students act as polluters with differing marginal cost of abatement schedules. Each student knows only his or her abatement costs, but not the costs of the other students (firms). Thus, one inherent initial challenge is that students do not know if they are buyers or sellers of pollution rights. For firms with mid-range costs, players may actually have both roles depending on whether or not they are negotiating with a high-cost or low-cost (of abatement) firm.

The objective for participants in the experiment is to come away with lower total costs of abatement than their initial costs and the experiment ultimately illustrates that, over all firms, the pollution reduction goal can be met at lowest cost via trading. In one version of the experiment, the lowest cost firms can actually end up with negative total cost by selling all their allowances and abating all their emissions.[6]

The final stage of this learning exercise is participation in the annual sulfur dioxide (SO_2) allowance auction hosted by the US EPA. As part of the 1990 Clean Air Act Amendments, the US EPA created a system of tradable allowances for SO_2 for coal-burning utilities.[7] As part of the 1990 amendments, utilities previously granted allowance for SO_2 emissions were now allowed to buy and sell these allowances, generating a market-based cap and trade program, with each allowance worth one ton of sulfur dioxide. (For evaluations of the success of this program, see Kruger, 2005; Burtraw and Palmer, 2003; Burtraw et al., 2005.) Utilities may buy and sell allowances from a broker or another utility at any time, usually in 250–500 ton blocks. One interesting feature of this program is that each utility must also "give back" 2.8 percent of its annual allotment to the US EPA, which then auctions off those allowances at the public auction. Utilities may bid to buy these allowances back and other utilities and brokers may also bid on these tons. Allowances are auctioned in increments as small as one ton and as such, any individual or group with an account at the EPA may submit a bid to purchase one ton or more.[8]

Participants in the auction can bid on two types of allowances: spot market allowances and seven-year advance allowances. Spot market allowances are immediately usable; seven-year advance allowances are usable in seven years. Student participation in markets for both types of allowances allows for advancing the classroom discussion theory and analysis to include time preference and futures.[9]

The auction is a sealed bid auction, and since bidders pay their actual bid and not the market clearing price, students have an incentive to bid as close to the market clearing price as possible without underbidding and losing out. Studying the market has numerous classroom discussion opportunities involving energy costs, abatement technology and costs, buyer anticipation of new rules and their impact on price, price variation over time, and auctions.[10] Students appreciate participating in a real market and linking classroom theory with real-world events. Some students will find retiring the allowance after purchase very satisfying as well.

This multi-staged exercise works well because it meets the needs of so many different learning styles of students. The economic theory of pollution control can be covered both graphically and mathematically with varying levels of difficulty. The classroom experiment also helps to cement the concept of achieving pollution reduction at lowest cost. Even the brightest students may think they have a good grasp of the theory, only to find after the exercise begins that they do not fully grasp the goals or even in which direction to trade.[11] Finally, participation in the auction highlights both the relevance and the connection to real-world cap-and-trade programs.

Another option or extension for the final stage of this learning exercise involves using the Regional Greenhouse Gas Initiative as the real-world example. This is the first mandatory carbon cap and trade market in the United States and includes ten Northeast and Mid-Atlantic States. Now in its fourth year, the program offers another set of auctions and prices to study.[12]

CONCLUDING THOUGHTS

Christainsen (1988) predicts that the directions the field of environmental economics takes will depend on the "current controversies and prevailing ideological movements" (p. 195). He suggests that topics such as hazardous waste and global pollution are likely to become prominent issues. He notes that such issues require more dynamic analysis which "leads to difficult theoretical and ethical questions regarding the appropriate discount rate by which future costs and benefits are to be weighed against present costs and benefits" (p. 195). He was not wrong. Numerous articles have emerged in the literature recently with respect to the appropriate choice of the discount rate when we are considering the distant future (climate change). A very heated debate ensued when economist Nicholas Stern from the London School of Economics issued a report that used a discount rate of 0.1 percent to conclude that early and strong action to prevent climate change would outweigh the costs. Other economists disagreed. Nordhaus of Yale University argued for a discount rate of 6 percent and believes that the best economic policy for slowing climate change is to reduce emissions only modestly in the short term and more in the long term. The policy prescription here depends in part on the size of the discount rate used to evaluate costs and benefits. The choice of the discount rate has become an important, if controversial, topic in environmental economics since the allocation of scarce resources across future generations depends, in part, on the rate chosen. Environmental economics is also working to better address many issues that overlap traditional environmental economics textbook chapters, e.g. those on forestry or water. Topics as varied as "sprawl" or "biofuels" or "conservation" or "development and health" may find their way into several sections or book chapters. "Environmental justice" and "ecosystem services" can be stand-alone chapters.

As the field evolves and grows, more schools and types of programs are offering environmental economics courses. Programs in environmental law, public health and policy are now offering environmental economics courses. Courses that combine majors and non-majors are also now quite common.

Environmental problems are complex and inherently interdisciplinary. A common misperception is that economics is the answer to many environmental problems. While economics offers powerful tools to help aid decision-making and offers valuable information to policy makers, it cannot stand alone. This is one of the reasons why courses populated by multiple majors can be so rewarding.

NOTES

1. Blogs such as www.env-econ.net apply economics to current environmental events and these can be good supplements to a course or class. John Whitehead, co-author of this blog (accessed 23 May 2011), also has co-authored a chapter in this volume.

2.   http://www.cbo.gov/doc.cfm?index=601&type=0 and http://www.whitehouse.gov/omb/circulars_a094 (accessed 23 May 2011).
3.   Any of these documents might prove useful as a course supplement or for a class exercise or homework.
4.   http://www.whitehouse.gov/omb/circulars_a094#8 (accessed 23 May 2011).
5.   https://www.evri.ca/Global/Splash.aspx (accessed 23 May 2011).
6.   For another example of a classroom tradable discharge permit game, see Ando and Harrington (2006), for example.
7.   Details can be found at http://www.epa.gov/airmarkets/progsregs/arp/index.html (accessed 23 May 2011).
8.   Opening an account simply requires filing the appropriate forms with the EPA.
9.   One pedagogical advantage of participating in a "futures" market is the ability to utilize and apply the important discounting concepts that are covered in most environmental and natural resource economics classes. However, unlike actual futures markets, these markets require paying now for something you cannot use until a future date (instead of committing to buying something at a future date). Technically, these are implied rates of time preference and not discount rates.
10. Recent rule charges such as the Clean Air Interstate Rule, the Transport Rule and most recently, the Cross-State Air Pollution Rule have resulted in large price variations due in large part to regulatory uncertainty. It will be interesting to follow this market in the future since now some states are subject to new rules with the creation of four new emissions trading markets.
11. Another option for a more sophisticated classroom experiment is for watershed-based trading. Instructors can set up a market for the entire class at www.nutrientnet.org, a World Resource Institute program (accessed 23 May 2011).
12. http://www.rggi.org/home (accessed 23 May 2011).

REFERENCES

Alden, D. (1999), "Experience with scripted role play in environmental economics", *Journal of Economic Education*, **30** (2), (Spring), 127–32.
Ando, A. W. and D. R. Harrington (2006), "Tradable discharge permits: A student-friendly game", *Journal of Economic Education*, **37** (2), (Spring), 187–201.
Burtraw, D., D. Evans, A. J. Krupnik, K. Palmer and R. Toth (2005), "Economics of Pollution Trading for SO2 and NOx", RFF Discussion paper 05–05, available at http://www.rff.org/Publications/Pages/PublicationDetails.aspx?PublicationID=17379, accessed 25 May 2011.
Burtraw, D. and K. Palmer (2003), "The paparrazzi take a look at a living legend: The SO2 Cap-and-Trade Program for power plants in the United States", Resources for the Future, Discussion Paper 03-15.
Carter, W. (1972), "Teaching environmental economics", *Journal of Economic Education*, **4** (1), (Autumn), 36–42.
Caviglia-Harris, J. (2003), "Introducing undergraduates to economics in an interdisciplinary setting", *Journal of Economic Education*, (Summer), 195–203.
Chapman, D. J., W. M. Hanemann and P. Ruud (1998), "The *American Trader* oil spill: A view from the beaches", Association of Environmental and Resource Economists Newsletter.
Christainsen, G. G. (1988), "The natural environment and economic education", *Journal of Economic Education*, **19** (2), 185–97.
Colander, D. and K. McGoldrick (2009), "The Teagle foundation report: The economics major as part of a liberal education", in D. Colander and K. McGoldrick (eds), *Educating Economists*, Cheltenham, UK and Northampton, MA, US: Edward Elgar, pp. 3–39.
Croson, R. J., J. Rachlinski and J. Johnston (2005), "Culpability as an explanation of WTA-WTP discrepancy in contingent valuation", working paper.
Dunford, R. W. (1999), "The *American Trader* oil spill: An alternative view of recreation use damages", Association of Environmental and Resource Economists Newsletter.
Giraud, K. L. (2002), "Classroom games: The allocation of renewable resources under different property rights and regulation schemes", *Journal of Economic Education*, **33** (3), (Summer), 236–53.
Johnston, R. J. (2007), "Choice experiments, site similarity and benefits transfer", *Environmental and Resource Economics*, **38** (3), 331–51.
Kruger, J. (2005), "From SO2 to greenhouse gases: Trends and events shaping future emissions trading programs in the United States", Resources for the Future Discussion Paper 05-20.
Lewis, L. Y. (2011), "A 'Virtual' Field Trip to the Real World of Cap and Trade: Environmental Economics and the EPA SO$_2$ Allowance Auction", forthcoming in *Journal of Economic Education*, **42** (4).

Murphy, J. J. and J. Cardenas (2004), "An experiment on enforcement strategies for managing a local environment resource", *Journal of Economic Education*, **35** (1), (Winter), 47–61.

Nguyen, T. N. (2009), "NutrientNet: An internet-based approach to teaching market-based policy for environmental management", *Journal of Economic Education*, **40** (1), (Winter), 38–54.

Nordhaus, (2007), "A review of the Stern Review on the economics of climate change", *Journal of Economic Literature*, **45** (3) (September), 686–702.

Ohio v. Department of Interior, 880 F.2d 432 (D.C. Cir. 1989).

Office of Management and Budget, "Discount rates for cost-effectiveness, lease purchase and related analysis", OMB Circular A-94 Appendix C, revised December 2010, http://www.whitehouse.gov/omb/memoranda_m00-06, accessed 23 May 2011.

Peterson Jr., K. D. (2000), "Using a geographic information system to teach economics", *Journal of Economic Education*, **31** (2), (Spring), 169–78.

Sherburn, M. and A. S. Devlin (2004), "Academic major, environmental concern, and arboretum use", *Journal of Environmental Education*, **35** (2), (Winter), 23–36.

The Stern Report: http://webarchive.nationalarchives.gov.uk/+/http:/www.hm-treasury.gov.uk/sternreview_index.htm; accessed 25 May 2011.

Tietenberg, T. and L. Lewis (2009), *Environmental and Natural Resource Economics* (8th ed.), Boston, MA: Pearson Education, Addison-Wesley.

US Environmental Protection Agency (2011) "Benefits and costs of the Clean Air Act 1990–2020", Summary Report, USEPA, Office of Air and Radiation, March, available at http://www.epa.gov/cleanairactbenefits/feb11/summaryreport.pdf.

Walbert, M. S. and T. J. Bierma. (1988), "The permits game: Conveying the logic of marketable pollution permits", *Journal of Economic Education*, **19** (4), (Fall), 383–9.

Whitmarsh, D. (1995), "Richer harvests: A CAI approach to teaching fisheries economics", *Journal of Economic Education*, **26** (4), (Fall), 336–51.

47 Teaching experimental economics: reinforcing paradigms and bringing research into the undergraduate classroom
Charles A. Holt[1]

For me, the most motivational career insight has been the realization that teaching and research really can be strong complements. In particular, teaching experimental economics is an ideal forum for bringing current research into the classroom. Undergraduates typically find journal articles to be inaccessible. However, this is generally not the case with papers that report experiments, since a workable "treatment" design necessarily involves selecting special cases of economic models and policy environments.[2] Moreover, carefully selected classroom experiments reinforce a student's understanding of important economic paradigms like the tragedy of the commons, free-riding, adverse selection, and the efficiency properties of competitive markets. Finally, a class format based on experiments, presentations, and reports by teams of students can be used to develop the workplace skills that prospective employers value. This chapter presents a research-oriented perspective on teaching experimental economics, but the insights and tips may be useful for experienced teachers who wish to enhance the active-learning components of more traditional courses.

PARADIGM REINFORCEMENT

The primary value of an economics major is that the traditional analytical courses force students to develop a logical, rigorous way of thinking about economic issues and public policies. Experimental economics complements and underscores the standard "chalk-and-talk" approach to teaching economics, by providing first-hand experiences of market trading, bargaining, bidding, price bubbles, etc. Economic theories like supply and demand work surprisingly well, and because they do, students gain a deeper confidence in the theory they are learning. This confidence is especially valuable for international students or math-science majors who have mainly been exposed to the more abstract, technical side of economics. Conversely, the behavioral focus that results from considering actual human decisions helps students appreciate the limits of the selfishly rational economic "straw man." More precisely, the goal is to help students develop a mature understanding of environments in which predictions based on selfish/rationality models need to be modified or viewed with skepticism.

The standard economics major comprises such a broad collection of topics that students often lose sight of basic insights.[3] A lot of what is meant by "thinking like an economist" is the ability to relate a situation to one of the powerful paradigms that characterize the incentive landscape for broad classes of economic interactions. For example, the issue of property rights came up at a recent NSF workshop on the allocation of bands of broadcast spectrum to be used for wireless communications. The spectrum is typically divided up into licenses based on specified frequency ranges and geographic locations. The initial discussion at the workshop centered on making the spectrum more like "the sea" in which anyone can freely sail around, as opposed to the land where property rights are well defined. This vision was echoed by some of the engineers and computer scientists in the room, but the direction of the discussion changed sharply when someone evoked a powerful visual image of the "mud-pit of the grazing commons."[4] Notably, the only economist who was mentioned by name in the three-day workshop was Ronald Coase, whose ideas about property rights were referenced again and again. A former student who just graduated from Harvard Law School told me that the Coase theorem came up in just about *every one* of her law school courses. Economics majors ought to recognize the power of competitive markets and the costs of rent-seeking, free-riding, asymmetric market power, etc. But often students seem to be shell shocked from overexposure to increasingly technical models that loom large for the doctoral student teaching assistants who do so much of the teaching these days. Carefully selected laboratory experiments can reinforce key paradigms by putting students into the situation being studied.

For example, there is no better way to teach the notion of opportunity cost than to show students that those who did not consider the full opportunity cost earned only a fraction of what the others took in. For example, a classroom exercise can provide students with free "grandfathered" allocations of tradable emissions permits in a simulated market. If these permits can be bought and sold in secondary markets, then the failure to consider the opportunity cost of "free" permits will have a significant downward effect on their earnings (Myers et al., 2010). Experiment-based paradigm reinforcement has also been incorporated into political science and philosophy courses with a "political economy" orientation.[5]

An effective classroom exercise often differs from a research experiment. For example, the norm for research experiments in economics is to use financial or other motivations, but this may not be necessary in class. Students are naturally competitive in market scenarios, so no external motivation is required in the classroom (unless there is a need to deter excessive risk taking). But in situations where fairness, inequity, and reciprocity are important, as would be the case with voluntary contributions, it helps to select one group *ex post* for payment with the throw of a 20-sided die. Students understand if the actual payment fraction is determined "on the fly" to limit the payment amount to several dollars. Another difference from a research environment is the need to strictly limit the number of "rounds" and treatments, in order to save time for subsequent discussion. A quick understanding of the incentive structure is often facilitated by using a more suggestive context (for example "takeovers," "raiders," "contributions," "pollution") than would be acceptable in a typical research experiment.

A well-rounded experimental economics course should include topics that reinforce the key paradigms and insights. My own "top ten" list:

- Market experiments in which buyers and sellers negotiate trades that roughly correspond to the predictions of supply and demand, with the resulting maximization of the gains from trade, as illustrated by the "surplus" areas. This exercise helps correct a common misperception that competitive market theories are only relevant with "large" numbers of buyers and sellers and "good" information about the structure of the market.

- Market experiments in which the inability of buyers to ascertain quality prior to purchase may result in the provision of low-quality products, an inefficient outcome that is analogous to the "lemons effect."
- Voluntary contributions experiments that illustrate how "free-riding" behavior can block the efficient provision of a public good, in the absence of political or economic coordination.
- Common pool resource experiments that illustrate the "tragedy of the commons" that results from excess exploitation of common resources when property rights are not well defined.
- Bilateral bargaining, for example the ultimatum game, in which fairness considerations intrude and prevent efficient agreements. I always point out that the person who makes the take-it-or-leave-it offer in an ultimatum game is like a seller with monopoly power, and that fairness considerations are often of less importance in more competitive market experiments.
- Rent-seeking games in which the real costs of lobbying efforts to obtain a prize or license are a significant fraction of the economic value of the prize. Rent-seeking experiments illustrate the potential inefficiencies of non-market allocations, and can be complemented by auction experiments that tend to result in efficient allocations at lower transactions costs. One key aspect of "thinking like an economist" is to be able to anticipate that behavior will adjust to incentives, so naïve extrapolations may provide biased estimates of the effects of changes in public policy. In the case of rent-seeking games, a reduction in the cost of each unit of lobbying effort expended may not reduce total effort if the amount of effort per person declines, for example reducing the cost of waiting in line may just result in longer lines.
- Coordination games with multiple equilibria, in which strategic decisions often lead to a "bad" equilibrium in which players essentially exert low effort because others are expected to do the same. I always discuss the macroeconomic implications of such games, for example bank runs in which withdrawal is best if others are expected to withdraw, but not withdrawing funds can produce a high-payoff equilibrium (Anderson and Carpenter, 2001). Coordination games are useful in helping students get past the common misconception that all games are prisoner's dilemmas in which players have unilateral incentives to defect from more cooperative decisions.
- Asset markets that reliably generate price "bubbles" relative to the fundamental value of the asset. Such bubbles are more prevalent and striking in cash-rich environments with easy credit (Coppock and Holt, 2010).
- Lottery choice experiments that illustrate the effects of risk aversion, especially in high-stakes environments. Here is an example in which showing students the results of research experiments with high payoffs is a useful complement to class-based exercises.
- A good way to reinforce students' understanding of selection effects is to run an auction for an item that has an unknown value, common to all bidders. Even though individual value estimates may be unbiased, the winning bidder tends to be one who over-estimated the value, and hence overpaid. The resulting selection

effect, known as the "winner's curse," is more of a problem with large numbers of bidders, as can be illustrated by running auctions with bidder pairs and with larger groups, as discussed below in the section on classroom response systems ("clickers").

Each of the above topics is covered in one of the chapters in Holt (2006), and can be implemented by one or more of the web-based (Veconlab) experiments described below. With the exception of the asset market experiment, all of the above listed experiments can also be run "by hand" with props like playing cards, using the instructions provided in the appendix to Holt (2006). Other classroom experiments are published regularly in the *Journal of Economic Education*, the *International Research in Economic Education*, *Perspectives on Economic Education Research*, and the teaching tips section of the *Southern Economic Journal*. A good source of macroeconomic experiments is Denise Hazelet's web page.[6, 7] For a relatively comprehensive list of classroom experiment sources, see the University of Exeter FEELE web page.[8]

POST-EXPERIMENT BRIEFING: HELPING STUDENTS DISCOVER INSIGHTS ON THEIR OWN

The most important tip for a first-time instructor of experimental economics is to engage students in the particular experiment *before* they read about the relevant theory. It is hard to resist the impulse to turn to the blackboard after an experiment and present the underlying economic model, such as supply and demand graphs for a market experiment. It can be much more effective to have a structured set of post-experiment Socratic-style questions to put to students that leads them to the key insight, for instance that an equilibrium price excludes low-value buyers and high-cost sellers in a manner that maximizes total earnings (surplus). For example, the instructor could mention a high price relative to equilibrium, say $8, and ask: "At a price of $8, would there be (more buyers or more sellers) at that price? At that price, would you expect sellers to (raise or lower) prices as a result?" Then the instructor could pick a low price and ask the same questions. This could be followed by a question about how to find a price for which there is neither market pressure to raise prices or to lower them, which can be used to let students discover the notion of an equilibrium price that balances the quantities that sellers wish to supply and with the quantity that buyers wish to demand. The notion of market efficiency can be raised by taking a tally of buyers' unit values and sellers' unit costs after the market trading has occurred, marking those that were actually involved in transactions. Asking students what types of sellers were excluded (those with high costs) and what types of buyers were excluded (those with low values) can yield insight into the role of a clear notion of a going market price. A discussion of surplus maximization can be prefaced by asking what would be the effect of forcing a low value buyer to purchase from a high cost seller.

Many law and business schools have developed a culture that involves questions directed to particular students, with the goal of maintaining attention, enforcing advanced reading, and inducing students to think and communicate "on their feet." In experimental economics, carefully thought-out sequences of questions can guide thinking toward self-discovery of the key insight or theory. To do this well, the instructor needs to consider various directions that the discussion might lead, including incorrect approaches that require supplemental questions to redirect thinking.[9]

In a course that centers around Socratic-style discussions, it is possible to avoid tests and exams, and to use online quizzes or fill-in-the-blank lab reports to ensure that students do the reading immediately after the experiment and prior to the next class. For example, the preceding questions that focused on supply and demand can be used in a workbook format by having the students circle the correct answer in each of the parenthetical phrases. Such lab reports can be done at home after class and are quite easy to grade, especially when the sequence of questions is straightforward; some examples are provided in Holt (2010).[10] The subsequent class discussion is at a higher level, since everyone has participated in the strategic scenario being discussed. The class that I teach is a fourth-year course with an intermediate microeconomics prerequisite, which provides students with the maturity needed to do the readings before class.

CAREER-RELEVANT SKILL BUILDING

An alternative to organizing the course into units and end-of-unit exams is to implement a student-run experiment/presentation pattern, which can foster creative thinking, teamwork, presentation, internet search, and writing skills that are important in the workplace. The key is to assign readings that correspond to single-class-length topics. Some experienced researchers rely on published journal articles, but I have found that it is better to begin with readings of a more uniform pace and difficulty to develop some analytical skills before turning students loose with internet searches. I use the first five chapters of Holt (2006) to establish a historical perspective for the field and to provide basic exposure to methodology issues, statistical analysis, market trading, risky decisions, and Nash equilibrium predictions for simple games of strategy that have been played in class. The remainder of the book consists of short (ten-page) chapters that constitute single-class-size bites. These chapters can be covered selectively in various orders, depending on the interests of the instructor and the students.

I divide the class into three-student teams, each selecting a chapter or a topic that conforms to their interests.[11] Each student group designs an experiment (web-based, paper-based, etc., as described in the next section) to be run at the end of one class, followed by their presentation at the start of the subsequent class. These team projects are important because employers conducting on-campus interviews are accustomed to talking to business and public policy majors who are routinely involved in team projects. The experiment projects provide students with something interesting to talk about, and the experience of team-based work is important since most workplace activities in consulting firms and public agencies are organized in this manner. Student presentations provide the teacher with specific observations that enable letters of recommendation to be both personal and informative. A team of three is a good size for 30-minute presentations, so that each student can speak for about 10 minutes, leaving time for questions from the class. Students are more likely to ask questions of fellow students, and questions are deeper and more exploratory in nature, as opposed to requests for clarification that are often directed to an instructor.

As an example of what a group might come up with, consider a "volunteer's dilemma," a game in which only one "volunteer" is needed to provide a public good. Each person is willing to incur the cost of volunteering if nobody else is expected to volunteer, but since only one volunteer is needed, it makes no sense to volunteer if others are expected to do so. With simultaneous decisions, the equilibrium involves randomization, with lower volunteer rates for large groups and for higher costs of volunteering. In one class, the students working on this topic looked at three treatments in which the group size was increased from two to three to six, with costs being decreased so that the equilibrium prediction was for a volunteer rate of 50 percent in all treatments. The subsequent student presentation began with some background on popular press stories about failures of people to help others in large groups, along with a discussion of psychological theories and alternative game theory predictions. The observed volunteer rates were close to game-theoretic predictions, and deviations were considered from a behavioral perspective, for instance in terms of aversion to payoff inequities. Students in a different class took a more psychological perspective, changing the payoffs in a manner that made losses impossible in the first treatment and possible in the second, while holding the equilibrium volunteer rate constant. The purpose was to investigate possible effects of "loss aversion," which were not observed, although the student presentation stimulated a lively discussion of ways to make losses credible in classroom and laboratory experiments. Notice that students have the opportunity to design a laboratory experiment to test the key implication of basic theory by selecting treatments that discriminate between alternative explanations. This first-hand exposure to the scientific method in a lab environment is something that is rare these days, where basic laboratory science courses have been increasingly replaced by broad survey courses.

Some groups choose topics where the readings are less theoretical, for example the "lemons market" outcome where quality deteriorates when it cannot be observed by buyers prior to purchase. After summarizing quality deterioration in the aggregate, this group identified interesting decision patterns of particular individuals from the class and gave them cute descriptive titles like "K Mart special," "the Dupe," "Bowman's revenge," and so on. This personal approach was much more effective than claims based on data averages. Although grades are not based on humorous add-ins, this group engaged the audience with a graphic of a lemon on each page of the power-point presentation, including a photo of a lemon with wrinkles suggesting a cat's face, a tiny yellow car on a European cobblestone street, and so on.

Former students almost universally mention the importance of concise writing in their careers. Accordingly, each team member is required to identify, review, and critique a pair of laboratory experiment papers related to their presentation topic. The identification phase is facilitated by providing hints about internet searches that begin with "economics experiment" and end with some of the key words that students encounter in the chapter or reading that their group has elected to cover. Having the critique cover more than one paper helps students think through what convinces them and what justifies criticism. I limit these summary/critiques to five individually written pages. It helps students to hand out a set of guidelines for non-fiction writing, with guidelines for simple sentences, well-organized paragraphs, uniform pace, clear flow of ideas, and avoidance of common writing and spelling errors (clichés, "affect" vs. "effect," etc.). It also helps to require students to submit a one-page initial draft, to be sure that they have found an appropriate topic and a selection of papers that actually use experimental methods. This draft should consist of several introductory paragraphs (in prose, not outline form), double spaced so that suggested edits and comments on writing style can be marked in a non-confrontational manner, without having to assign specific grades at this early stage. Another possibility is to hand out a sample single-page draft from a prior class, with instructor edits marked, to provide an example of the tone and degree of formality that is expected.[12] Concrete examples are more effective than bullet lists of hints for writing and structure, which I also distribute (and update each year after grading the final papers).

GETTING OUT OF THE LAB: PLAYING CARDS, WIRELESS LAPTOPS, CLICKERS

I have taught experimental economics in a dedicated research lab with banks of net-worked computers. Such a setting allowed students to experience the feel of a research environment, but reserving such a space can be difficult, and many labs have visual barriers that impede class discussion. The popularity of the course (it often fills in the first half hour of open registration) has motivated me to move it to a regular classroom that holds 40–50 or so students (14 groups of three). I use a seating chart with name cards, so that students can quickly arrange to have one of the group members sign on with a laptop if the experiment is going to be web-based. Students working together tend to discuss strategy and refrain from surfing the internet, perhaps because of the tendency for more serious students to stay focused on the experiment. Grouping also facilitates playing-card and paper-based experiments, since there are fewer cards or paper sheets to collect and process.[13] The wireless network capacities of most classrooms will support 20 or more laptop connections, but it is useful to ask a computer support person in advance. For large classes with hundreds of students, I have used classroom response ("clicker") systems to run experiments. These approaches will be illustrated with specific examples that illustrate the pros and cons of each approach.

The appendix to Holt (2006) provides paper-based instructions and worksheets for hand-run experiments, which are easy for students to adapt and modify, using props like dice and playing cards. For example, voluntary contributions to a public good can be collected by providing each participant with two "red" cards (hearts and diamonds) and two "black" cards (clubs and spades).[14] Each student participant or team plays two cards, and red cards played into a public investment provide $1 for each person in the group, regardless of whether they have contributed a red card or not. In contrast, red cards kept in a private investment earn an amount, say $4 per red card, but only for the person keeping the red card. As long as the number of participants in the group exceeds the private return of $4, the socially optimal outcome is for each person to play both of their red cards, which is not likely to happen. In my experience, contributions are even lower when private returns are variable (such as when the value is the number on the red card, so a nine of diamonds would earn $9 if kept, but only $1 per person if played into the public investment). In a class of 12 students, the contributions rose from five red cards in the first round to 15 in the second round (after some uncontrolled cross-aisle discussion), but the switch to individual-specific "keep values" reduced contributions to three red cards in the third round. I ended the class with the observation that, to avoid free-riding, public goods are often provided with taxes. Their assignment was to design a class experiment in which participants select a tax rate that determines investments in the public good. This design flexibility is one advantage of hand-run experiments, since web-based setups typically offer a limited range of possible setup options.

Alternatively, experiments can be run with web-based programs available from commercial sites like Aplia or Pearson's MyEconlab. The Veconlab software that I have developed has over 50 different programs, each of which has a variety of configuration options.[15] For example, the "Public" link on the admin page takes you to a list of seven public economics experiments, from which you can select "Voluntary Contributions." The first page that follows shows a graph of data from the default, two-treatment setup in which several rounds of a standard voluntary contribution game (described above) are followed by rounds in which participants can incur costs to punish others with low contributions. Such punishments tend to induce high cooperation rates, although the costs of punishment may mitigate the increase in total earnings.

Web-based experiments are invaluable for situations that require ongoing records of cash balances, asset holdings, etc., as is the case for the Bostian and Holt (2009) price bubble experiment. The "Leveraged Asset Market" experiment on the Veconlab site even has the option of letting people enter price predictions several periods in advance, and the resulting data can be distributed to students for analysis of the extent to which expectations are or are not "rational" (Coppock and Holt, 2010). The Veconlab instructor results pages for all experiments contain a "data" link that can be copied into a spreadsheet and emailed to students subsequently. Another nice feature of web-based experiments is that the data are displayed with individual earnings amounts, which can be used to drive home the main points, for example, that correct appreciation of opportunity costs may enhance earnings. Some of the Veconlab programs have the option to provide participants with relative earnings comparisons to induce them to think more carefully. There is also a graph feature that lets the instructor or student team present the data averages sequentially by round, along with theoretical predictions (if available) that can be shown or hidden with the click of a button.

With larger, auditorium-sized classes, commercially available classroom response systems ("clickers") can be used to collect data quickly.[16] For example, Salemi (2009) uses clickers to collect bids on an item (a Banana Slug T-shirt) in a second price auction that helps illustrate the notions of a demand function and consumer surplus. Similarly, I have used clickers to elicit guesses of the number of mini-marshmallows in a translucent freezer (Holt and Bostian, 2011). The resulting numerical guesses are not announced prior to an auction in which students click in bids, on the understanding that the highest bidder will earn the difference between the prize value (one penny per marshmallow) and the person's own bid (but will not get to keep the marshmallows). Even though guesses about the number of marshmallows tend to be biased downward due to the failure to appreciate depth, the highest guesses are associated with the highest bids in a pay-as-bid auction, so that the winning bidder typically ends up paying a lot more than the value of the prize. Such "winner's curse" effects are more severe with a large number of bidders, so clickers are ideal for running this experiment in a large class. Classroom response systems generally permit the data to be exported into a spreadsheet program for ranking and analysis that is the basis of the subsequent class discussion. Clickers also let you record attendance, quiz students on key concepts, and assess reading comprehension prior to class. It is important not to become so fixated on the technology that opportunities for class discussion are limited. For example, an awareness of selection effects is a key aspect of "thinking like an economist," and it is important to let students come up with examples of selection effects in their experience, for example, why average incomes or physical appearances at high school reunions may be misleading.

CLOSING THOUGHTS

Experimental economics is ideally suited for bringing current research into the undergraduate classroom. Carefully selected experiments reinforce a confident and deep understanding of basic paradigms that characterize the economic way of thinking. Experiments can be conducted quickly and easily for class sizes ranging from ten (using cards), to 50 (using one student's wireless laptop per team), to several hundred (using clickers or web-based experiments done from home after class). Current clicker technology limits the information that can be sent back from the instructor to individual students, although I expect this to change with new technology. A second limitation of clickers is that off-the-shelf commercial software only produces bar graphs of answers received, whereas many experiments require the joint analysis of a series of decisions, often from students who have different roles, such as buyers and sellers.[17] Current wireless technology limits the numbers of laptops that can be connected to the web in a single classroom, but that situation is changing as students start using browsers on cell phones or other broadband devices with large color displays.

Team-based experiment designs and presentations in small to medium-sized classes provide students with a chance to develop skills that prospective employers value. Associated workbook or online quiz exercises can be structured to monitor attendance and further incentivize students to keep up with the reading, so that class discussions are deeper and more animated. These classes are enjoyable for students and for instructors too!

NOTES

1. This work was supported in part by the University of Virginia Bankard Fund, the University of Virginia Quantitative Collaborative, and the National Science Foundation (DUE 0737472 and SES 0098400). I would like to thank Rachel Blank, David Cates, Karl Schurter, Ken Elzinga, and the editors of this volume for thoughtful suggestions.
2. Conversely, insights that I've gleaned from classroom experiments have had a major impact on my own research program. For example, the design for the Anderson and Holt (1997) information cascade experiment was worked out and refined in a classroom exercise, Anderson and Holt (1996).
3. Frank (2006) makes a convincing case for a narrower, deeper principles class.
4. Actually, "open access" can be a good policy for very high-frequency transmissions that only travel short distances, like those used for garage door openers, classroom response systems, etc. In contrast, the most valuable spectrum bands are in lower frequencies in which signals have wider ranges, creating congestion and interference.
5. For example, Rick Wilson (Rice) and Catherine Eckel (University of Texas – Dallas) have developed a sequence of classroom experiments for politics courses. Catherine Johnson at the University of Arizona has some experiments that are used in the discussion sections of very large sections of philosophy classes, such as the "trust game:" http://www.teacheconomicfreedom.org/files/johnsontrust-game.pdf (accessed 6 June 2011). Katelyn Sacks uses hand-run versions of some of these same experiments for discussion

sections of an international relations class at the University of Virginia. The new Batten School of Public Leadership and Public Policy at Virginia has targeted much of its initial hiring at social psychologists and behavioral economists who are using classroom experiments to develop an analytical approach to the study of leadership, which complements more traditional case study approaches. Bargaining simulations have a long history of use in business school negotiation courses (Croson, 2005). These classes are so popular that business school administrators sometimes "adjust" interpretations of the high teaching evaluations that are typical in those classes.

6. http://people.whitman.edu/~hazlett/econ/ (accessed 14 June 2011).
7. See also Chapter 7, "Classroom Experiments", in this volume.
8. http://people.exeter.ac.uk/dgbalken/FEELE/links.html (accessed 10 June 2011).
9. See the Chapter 11 by Elzinga in this volume for an excellent guide to the Socratic method. There is, however, no substitute for watching an accomplished teacher engage students and guide the discussion in this manner. I have learned a lot from observing Ken Elzinga, and from sitting in on several antitrust classes taught in law schools.
10. Holt (2010) provides a set of lab reports with a circled-answer or fill-in-blank structure for a series of ten experiments selected to accompany a microeconomics principles class. Grading is also facilitated by providing pre-drawn grids for graphs. I also like to include open-ended questions that let students relate their own experiences to the concepts being discovered. The ten experiments are designed to teach ten key concepts: gains from trade, marginal analysis, market equilibrium, opportunity cost and supply, cost curves, elasticity and monopoly, public goods, rent seeking, congestion and externalities, and games of strategy.
11. An alternative source of materials would be the Plott and Smith (2008) *Handbook of Experimental Economics Results*, which contains over one hundred short chapters on specific sectors of the field, although these readings presume knowledge of game theory, expected utility, and standard economic models.
12. Last year I also passed round a draft of this chapter with handwritten editorial suggestions that I received from my colleague, Ken Elzinga, who is highly respected, even revered, by all economics students at Virginia.
13. Larger classes may require larger groups. John Morgan, who teaches up to 90 Berkeley MBA students at a time, used groups of six or so.
14. For tips on the setup and class discussion, see Holt and Laury (1997).
15. Simply Google "veconlab admin" to get the instructor setup page, or "veconlab login" to get to the page where participants log in after an experiment has been set up. The instructor (or student team) obtains a user name (a sequence of lower case letters) online from the "Get Started" and "Register" links on the admin page. This user name can be used to run one or more experiments, for example my own user name "cah" has "session names" of cah1, cah2, etc. for specific classroom experiments that I have done. Participants enter the session name to be used on the login form, and they receive automatically configured instructions matching the setup parameters that were selected in advance by the instructor or student team.
16. The logistics of using clickers are discussed in the Calhoun and Mateer chapter in this volume. These logistics are not as difficult as most people expect. If you are not comfortable with this kind of technology, then it helps to hire a savvy undergraduate to help you with setup, which is essential in classes involving hundreds of students.
17. In joint work with A. J. Bostian, I am working on solutions to these limitations. A beta version of Veconlab for Clickers will be publicly available on a link from the Veconlab site in late 2011.

REFERENCES

Anderson, L. R. and S. B. Carpenter (2001), "A Classroom Bank Run Experiment", Working Paper, College of William and Mary.

Anderson, L. R. and C. A. Holt (1996), "Classroom Games: Information Cascades", *Journal of Economic Perspectives*, **10** (4), 187–93.

Anderson, L. R. and C. A. Holt (1997), "Information Cascades in the Laboratory", *American Economic Review*, **87**, 847–62.

Becker, W. E. and M. Watts (eds) (1998), *Teaching Economics to Undergraduates: Alternatives to Chalk and Talk*, Cheltenham, UK and Lyme, USA: Edward Elgar.

Bostian, A. J. and C. A. Holt (2009), "Bubbles in an Asset Market", *Journal of Economic Education*, **40** (1), 27–37.

Coppock, L. and C. A. Holt (2010), "Teaching the Crisis: A Leverage Experiment", draft, University of Virginia.

Croson, R. (2005), "An Economist's Guide to Negotiation Experiments", draft, Wharton School, University of Pennsylvania.

Davis, D. D. and C. A. Holt (1993), *Experimental Economics*, Princeton, NJ: Princeton University Press.

Frank, R. H. (2006), "Do We Try to Teach Our Students Too Much?" Discussion Paper, Cornell University, presented to the APPAM Meeting, Park City, Utah.

Holt, C. A. (2006), *Markets, Games, and Strategic Behavior*, Boston, MA: Pearson.

Holt, C. A. (2010), "Ten Laboratory Exercises for Microeconomics", draft manuscript, University of Virginia.

Holt, C. A. and A. J. Bostian (2011), "Classroom Clicker Games: Wisdom of the Crowds and the Winner's Curse", draft, Department of Economics, University of Virginia.

Holt, C. A., and S. K. Laury (1997), "Classroom Games: Voluntary Provision of a Public Good", *Journal of Economic Perspectives*, **11** (4), Fall, 209–15.

Myers, E., C. A. Holt, M. Wråke, S. Mandell, and D. Burtraw (2010), "Teaching Opportunity Cost in an Emissions Permit Experiment", *International Research in Economic Education*, **9** (2), 34–42.

Plott, C. R. and V. L. Smith (2008) *Handbook of Experimental Economics Results, Volumes 1 and 2*, New York: Elsevier Press.

Salemi, M. (2009), "Clickernomics", Discussion Paper, University of North Carolina.

48 Game theory in a liberal arts education
Joseph E. Harrington, Jr.

A redesign of the liberal arts curriculum would first and foremost include a course on statistics and, almost as compelling, a course on game theory. It is left to a statistician to argue the former and, as regards the latter, there are several reasons why game theory should be part of a general college education. First, it intersects with many disciplines including economics, sociology, political science, anthropology, history and biology. Second, it provides a way to understand social situations and to systematically analyze and engage in strategic reasoning, which goes beyond being ubiquitous in society to being a defining feature of society. Third, though it is applied mathematics, game theory – in all its glory and not a dumbed-down version – can be conveyed with a level of mathematics that students will have mastered by their junior year in high school. This is not to say it is easy, but the difficulties are conceptual, not mathematical. Finally, game theory is fun. People routinely engage in strategic reasoning for enjoyment; playing board games, solving puzzles and riddles, discussing strategy in sports and politics, reading mystery novels and the like. While game theory can be presented in a sufficiently technical manner so that such pleasure is abstracted away, it is unnecessary to do so. It was in that spirit that I wrote my undergraduate textbook, *Games, Strategies and Decision Making*. My approach is to convey the principles of game theory in a lighthearted though rigorous manner, with a minimum of mathematical fuss. In short, game theory is fundamental and fun and deserves to be part of a general college education.

COURSE OBJECTIVES

The first and primary course objective is to teach students how to teach themselves when it comes to analyzing a strategic situation. Game theory provides a framework for thinking about strategic issues and it is that framework, more than a catalog of results, that is likely to have a long half-life in students' memories and to have relevance for their future self, whether as a manager, doctor, lawyer, engineer, you name it. The course's emphasis is not on answers per se but rather on the problem-solving process, that is, how one gets an answer. What is to be seared into a student's mind is the logic of a game-theoretic argument, the process by which an answer is derived to a puzzle about human behavior. This is fully consistent with a microeconomics education which promotes a style of reasoning involving a proper appreciation of incentives and equilibrating forces. Game theory, with its drilled-down focus on strategic reasoning, is in that spirit.

A second objective is for students to develop their logical reasoning muscles. The game-theoretic framework is a set of tools, and proper use of those tools requires practice in conducting careful, rigorous, systematic analysis. It is all too easy for people to evaluate and decide based on their gut or an emotional response. While there may well be intelligence embedded in visceral reactions, it is one thing to listen to one's gut and quite another to feel that it obviates the need to engage in logical reasoning. Students should be encouraged to regularly and strenuously exercise their reasoning muscles and hone them for purposes of understanding and deciding.

While students should learn how to generate insight on their own, from having learned a framework and how to use it, the provision of some broadly relevant insight is a third course objective. Science is all about finding commonality, understanding how phenomena are alike because they are driven by the same set of underlying forces, and determining when apparent differences are irrelevant. There is then a fair amount of insight to be conveyed during the course which is applicable to a broad class of situations. Let me provide a few examples.

One of the most significant contributions of game theory is understanding the many cooperative norms and institutions in society, why they occur, where they occur and what allows them to persist. It is valuable to understand the incentive to cooperate (that is, most equilibria to games are Pareto-inefficient because of externalities) and when cooperation can be a stable outcome even though there is a short-run incentive to deviate. Students can learn how sustaining cooperation requires the prospect of future interactions, effective monitoring of choices or outcomes, and the presence of mechanisms to punish.

A second piece of insight concerns signaling. Teaching games of incomplete information is notoriously difficult but it offers some of the most exciting applications. A fundamental insight that signaling games provide is that there can be information in individuals' actions but in order to extract that information you need to understand their incentives, in terms not only of the intrinsic value they attach to an action but also of the temptation to deceive. These incentives can imply that a "good" type of person, in order to distinguish herself from a "bad" type, must take such an extreme action that a bad type wouldn't choose it even if she was inferred to be a good type. This mechanism and its behavioral implications are quite common in society. An example known all too well to college students is the considerable effort expended to build up a list of high school extra-curricular activities designed to impress a college admissions officer.

A third piece of insight comes from analyzing basic games, and then determining whether a particular real-world strategic situation has the rudiments of that game. For example, in learning about and how to apply Nash equilibrium, it is standard to consider some classic games: prisoners' dilemmas, coordination games, battles of the sexes, and out-guessing games (a term to capture situations of pure conflict). Students learn that players have a dominant strategy in a prisoners' dilemma and it leads to a Pareto-inferior outcome; that what players do is secondary to doing the same thing as other players in a coordination game; that players want to coordinate in the battle of the sexes but they differ on what it is they want to coordinate on; and, for an out-guessing game, the desire to do something different from what the other player thinks you're going to do prevents the existence of a stable collection of (pure) strategies. Rarely do people face situations as simple as those classic games suggest, but we often encounter situations for which a simple game captures part of what is going on. For example, in spite of its industry clout, IBM's operating system OS/2 failed partly because it fell prey to a coordination failure; a software developer didn't create an application because it didn't expect other applications to be written and, without many applications, few people would buy OS/2 and, therefore, few applications would be sold. That was one equilibrium, but there was another equilibrium in which software developers did write applications because each expected others to do so.

Along the way to providing a framework for producing insight, developing students' abilities to reason logically, and delivering some kernels of insight, a fourth course objective is to convince students that all this matters. The case should be made that game theory is relevant as both a descriptive and prescriptive tool, and it can shed light on the playful (soccer penalty kicks), the practical (FCC spectrum auctions), the pernicious (preventing nuclear war), and the profound (existence of God). If students are going to be put through the pain of head-aching trains of logical thought, they need to be convinced that it is worth doing.

The fifth and final course objective, which is the primary reason I teach game theory, is to have fun! I want us to revel in clever reasoning that we can't wait to tell our friends (in the card game Concentration, you may want to flip a card that you know will not result in a matched pair), examine an everyday situation with a fresh look to show that something deeper is going on (how price-matching guarantees can stifle rather than promote price competition), or to state a conundrum and then solve it (how people can act racist while not being racists).

TEACHING METHODS

A three-pronged approach is deployed when I teach game theory: motivate (generate enthusiasm), build (gradually develop a concept or piece of insight), and deliver (provide something rewarding at the end of this process).

Motivating Students

If students are to learn then their minds must be focused, and the best way to do that is to get them interested. To spark enthusiasm, I begin with a puzzle. It could be an inexplicable phenomenon (such as why, on occasion, soldiers achieved a truce in the trenches of World War I) or a mystifying claim (price-matching guarantees can be anti-competitive) or describing a strategic situation and asking what one should do (how should you bid at a second-price auction?). As there is a Gatesian-size wealth of game-theoretic applications from which to draw, an example should be appealing to students, either because it is relevant to them (dating dilemmas, team projects), of some importance or significance (brinkmanship, Galileo and the Inquisition), or just cool or intriguing (penalty kicks, *Lord of the Rings*). Of course, an example can be mesmerizing either in the sense of being enthralling or in the sense of putting you into a deep coma, and which applies may vary across students. There is no satisfying everyone with any particular game, which argues for presenting a diverse collection of applications during the course.

This enthusiasm can be amplified by augmenting an intriguing phenomenon or situation with rich context. This can take the form of facts, quotations, anecdotes, empirical and experimental evidence, and multimedia. For historical episodes, one can read actual transcripts of people, whether it is from meetings of the Joint Chiefs of Staff during the Cuban Missile Crisis or the journal entries of World War I soldiers. It could be an anecdote from a film, book, or newspaper – a prisoners' dilemma in the cartoon TV show

Dilbert, chicken in the timing of the release of Dreamworks' *Shark Tale* and Disney's *The Incredibles*, Rock-Paper-Scissors in *The Simpsons*, or a coordination game among East German civil protestors in 1989. These cases can be described or, better yet, presented using video footage.[1] It could be statistics, such as the percentage of times in English Premier League play that players shoot to the left, center, or right on a penalty kick and the frequency with which the goalkeeper dives to his left, right, or remains in the center; and such facts can be complemented with YouTube clips from World Cup play. All this serves to enrich the question being posed: What should the kicker do? What should the keeper do? Even if it is purely for entertainment, it engages students and that is reason enough. Of course, there is not always time in class to cover background material, which is why a textbook with detailed applications and supplemental reading material is instrumental.

Explaining Concepts

The concepts of game theory can be effectively presented at the lowest common denominator among college students, which means, at most, high school algebra. At the same time, it is important to present central concepts regardless of their subtlety or complexity (games of incomplete information and repeated games with non-stage game Nash equilibrium punishments immediately come to mind). To deal with this pedagogical challenge, an incremental approach is used which I refer to as "building an explanation." This may mean (when it is possible) breaking a concept down into its constituent parts, presenting each of those parts, and then putting them together to construct the concept. Or it may involve working with a series of models, going from the simple to the complex, to eventually reach the concept or insight. Or it could mean offering a stripped-down version of the concept, which captures some but not all of its essence, and then gradually enriching it.

Consider two examples in which a concept is broken down into its constituent parts. Prior to ever mentioning Nash equilibrium, we first examine what can be learned from more basic primitives; specifically, the game is common knowledge and the rationality of players is common knowledge. As "rationality is common knowledge" encompasses an infinite hierarchy of assumptions (players are rational, players know players are rational, players know players know players are rational, etc.), it is straightforward to incrementally work towards the ultimate goal of understanding what is implied by rationality being common knowledge. Armed only with the assumption that players are rational, the class is asked what we can infer about behavior. The prisoners' dilemma, in the form of Puccini's opera *Tosca*, is presented and it is quite transparent that assuming only rationality is enough to conclude what Tosca and Scarpia will do. But then another game is introduced, Steven Bram's inventive scenario between man and God on the matter of whether man should believe in God. Here we find that assuming man and God are rational is insufficient to say what will happen. However, if the assumption that man believes God is rational and God believes man is rational is added, then the game can be solved. In this manner we gradually move towards more subtle reasoning. The next setting is a three-player game among athletes who are deciding whether or not to take steroids. Solving it necessitates three levels of knowledge: athletes are rational, athletes believe other athletes are rational, and athletes believe other athletes believe other ath-

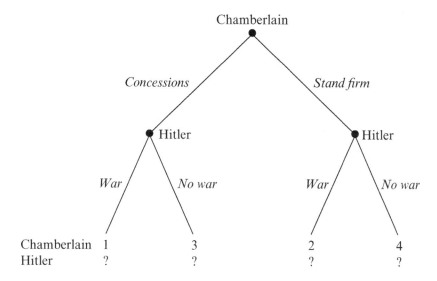

Source: Figure 10.1 from Joseph E. Harrington, Jr., *Games, Strategies and Decision Making* (Worth Publishers, 2009).

Figure 48.1 Modeling the 1938 Munich Agreement as a game of incomplete information

letes are rational. The final step is to define rationality as common knowledge and introduce the iterative deletion of strictly dominated strategies (IDSDS). It is then pointed out how the previous three analyses are all special cases of the IDSDS. Starting simple and special and moving toward complex and general gives students a better chance of reaching that final destination by being able to mentally keep pace with the increasing sophistication of the argument.

Another place where this "breaking down the concept into smaller parts" approach is taken is with one of the most challenging but exciting areas of game theory: games with incomplete information. I originally did not cover this material at the undergraduate level because of its difficulty, but ultimately came around to doing so because private information is integral to so many strategic situations. Again the discussion begins with a particular scenario; here it is the negotiations leading up to the 1938 Munich Agreement between Neville Chamberlain and Adolf Hitler. In deciding whether to propose concessions to Hitler in exchange for a peace agreement, Chamberlain is described as being uncertain of Hitler's ultimate objectives or, in other words, his payoffs. (In the spirit of gradualism, the private information is initially one-sided.) The initial situation presented before students is Figure 48.1. We then ask what possibilities Chamberlain may be considering when it comes to assessing Hitler's intentions, of which we consider two. First, Hitler is *amicable* and the payoffs for Hitler are 3, 4, 2, 1 (reading from left to right); second, he is *belligerent* and the payoffs are 4, 2, 3, 1. At this point, we introduce the Harsanyi trick of "turning back the clock" to when Nature determines Hitler's type. Pictorially, this means attaching the *amicable* and *belligerent* extensive forms together with an initial move by Nature that determines Hitler's type (the interested reader is referred to Figures 10.2 and 10.3 in Harrington, 2009). By gradually constructing a game of incomplete information, students better understand it by observing the components that underlie it.

A second way in which gradualism can be deployed is to work with a series of models before getting to the model that delivers the insight or encompasses the concept. This approach is useful to convey how cooperation can be sustained through repeated interaction. The discussion revolves around the following puzzle: How was it that there were sustained episodes of informal truces in the trenches of World War I? A video clip from the classic film *All Quiet on the Western Front* can be used to provide context by depicting the horror of trench warfare. That carnage is then juxtaposed with cases in which peace "broke out" in some trenches. To provide emphasis, passages are read from soldiers' diaries describing the presence of this truce and how it operated. This then leads us to ask: How do we explain this observed peaceful behavior?

The approach is to construct a plausible model for which an equilibrium has soldiers not trying to kill each other. It starts with a one-shot trench warfare game in which each side decides whether or not to shoot to kill. The game is a prisoners' dilemma and the dominant strategy is to shoot to kill. As we have failed to explain the observed behavior, this leads to an in-class discussion to identify what is missing from our model. Some students will say that payoffs are not as assumed, that these soldiers are pacifists, but then that assumption would fail to explain why, at other times, these same soldiers did try to kill the enemy. If no one has proposed the intended direction to the discussion, the following question is then posed: What was unique about trench warfare as opposed to other theaters of war? Someone will eventually point out that it involved the same people fighting each other day in, day out. This observation suggests a model of soldiers interacting repeatedly over time. We then consider repeating the original trench warfare game twice, which, of course, has a unique subgame perfect equilibrium of both sides shooting to kill. After exploring why the same outcome has emerged, the argument is then extended to any finitely repeated game. Finally, we consider a game with an indefinite (or infinite) horizon which ultimately produces the cooperative outcome displayed by troops.

What is appealing about this approach is that students gain a deeper understanding as to why the prospect of future interactions is the foundation for cooperation among people. Taking such an approach can be time consuming, but if students are to truly learn a concept, rather than simply results (such as the Folk Theorem), it is important to patiently describe how to go from a question to a model to a solution.

Delivering Value

The third and last facet to my teaching method is to deliver something to students at the end of all of the analysis. If you're going to put them through a long train of logic, which you should, be sure to deliver something worthwhile at the end. The entire exercise should pass a student's internal cost-benefit analysis if we want them to willingly go along on the next thought adventure. The reward at the end could be an insightful answer to a puzzle, as with understanding cooperative behavior in the trenches of World War I. At the same time, you shouldn't be afraid to point out where game theory doesn't work, to tell students there is a phenomenon we don't understand or evidence that runs counter to theory. Thus, presenting experimental evidence of cooperation in a finitely repeated setting or how behavior in the ultimatum game runs counter to the theory can initiate a spirited in-class discussion – why doesn't the theory work? is it preferences? rationality? – and that can be the reward at the end of this process.

The deliverable may be clever reasoning. It could be a cheeky argument for why man should not believe in God or how 1960s "white flight" in response to a few black families moving into a neighborhood could occur even if both whites and blacks actually preferred racial integration. Or what is delivered at the end may be pure entertainment. After solving the Tosca game, a video clip of the scene in which Tosca stabs Scarpia can be shown. Appealing to students' senses can reinforce concepts wrestled within the associated game-theoretic model.

A similar case occurs after reviewing network effects in the context of Windows vs Mac operating systems. For the simple game presented, there are two equilibria (all consumers buy Windows and all consumers buy Mac) and the emphasis is on consumers' expectations being self-fulfilled. If all consumers believe Windows will dominate, then Windows will indeed dominate, and if instead all consumers believe Mac will dominate, then Mac will indeed dominate. It follows that companies selling products with network effects will try to figure out ways to influence consumers' beliefs. What is crucial, however, is not simply convincing a consumer that one's product is great, but also that other consumers believe one's product is great. Thus, a company wants to advertise when a consumer watching the ad knows that many other consumers are also watching it. At that point, the 1984 Apple commercial is shown which was aired during the Super Bowl – the ultimate event during which people know other people are watching. Delivering such a visual exclamation mark to the lecture may help students retain the insight that you've just delivered.

It really goes without saying (but, of course, I'm now going to say it) that in-class experiments are a valuable multidimensional tool for teaching game theory. First, experiments can be used to document a phenomenon which will then be examined. For example, have students play the ultimatum game and then summarize and present the experimental output. After reviewing the standard theory (which is sure to run counter to the more egalitarian offers made and the rejection of proposals observed in the experiments), the stage is set for an in-class discussion as to why the theory performs so poorly. Second, experiments can produce introspection among students which is conducive to them learning about strategic reasoning and how to solve a particular game; having to make decisions themselves, they are likely to discover on their own what incentives are at work, to what extent players' interests coincide or conflict and other issues relevant to behavior. An example is the repeated prisoners' dilemma; students think about signaling a desire to cooperate, recognize the temptation to cheat and witness the role of punishments. When the instructor moves on to discuss these issues, students have already begun to think about them.

Running experiments faces two constraints: money and time. The former is easy to solve as students' performance in experiments can be a (small) part of their final grade, which obviates the necessity for monetary payments. The time constraint is more challenging, especially when the class is large. Fortunately, there are experiments that can be conducted even for a class exceeding a hundred students, and some of them are collected in the Instructor's Guide to my textbook. (The payoffs have also been calibrated so that the payoff from each experiment can be given equal weight in determining a student's grade.)

Another teaching tool is to require a capstone project. Quoting from my syllabus:

> For the project, you are to use game theory to model and make predictive statements about the behavior of people for either a real-world, historical, or fictional situation. A real-world situation is one that routinely occurs in human or non-human society. A fictional situation may be drawn from a story, poem, play, television show, movie, or computer software program but it is not to be a product of your imagination. Your imagination may be used to model a situation but not in creating the situation. Most critically, the situation cannot be one that we have gone over in class. The project is meant to be original work and will be graded on: i) how creative, sophisticated, and accurate is your model; and ii) how compelling, insightful, and correct is your analysis.

In contrast to lectures, readings, problem sets, and exams, where students are given a situation to consider and a model to analyze, now they must discover the situation and develop a model for the purpose of analysis. This is a chance for students to use the framework developed in class to explore what interests them.

OPENING AND CLOSING ACTS

In concluding, let me offer a few tips on the first and last classes of the semester. Game theory is a unique subject, in terms of both its content and its potential for intellectual fun (not that the Gauss-Markov theorem isn't scintillating), and this ought to be made exceedingly clear by the end of the first class. For this purpose, I recruit two students to play the Centipede game in front of the class. With 20 one dollar bills for all to see, a dollar is placed on the table and one of the volunteers is given the chance to take it. The right to either take or leave the money alternates between them and, each time the pile of money remains, a dollar is added to it. When eventually a student grabs the money, he or she walks away with the cash. (The singularity of the class has already been conveyed since instructors don't usually dole out money.) The lecture then turns to talking about strategic reasoning by mentally walking through the decision-making process faced by these volunteers. Students now know what strategic reasoning is and what the course is about. Game theory is then presented as a mathematical tool for exploring strategic reasoning.

The second phase of the first class is to review some of the strategic situations to be analyzed over the course of the semester. My intent is to get them excited and realize the course is truly interdisciplinary; economic settings are just one of many venues to be explored. A clip may be shown from *Raiders of the Lost Ark* where Indiana Jones must decide whether to throw the idol to Satipo in the hope that Satipo will throw him the whip; and I mention that, later in the semester, we'll see where Indy went wrong. A variety of other situations are briefly mentioned, including the medieval law merchant, reciprocal altruism among vampire bats, and the tragic episode in 1964 in which Kitty Genovese was murdered. In each case, a puzzle is posed to be solved later in the semester.

The first class concludes by looking at one strategic situation in some detail: the card game Concentration. This situation is unusual in that game theory can deliver a concrete rule for playing the game. Showing how this rule leads to some unanticipated prescriptions makes the case that game theory can generate fresh insight. But the opportunity is also taken to point out what we can and cannot expect of game theory. The rare simplicity of this setting allows game theory to say exactly what someone should do, but this is presented as an exception, not the rule. Generally, you cannot turn the crank of game theory and out pops a recommended course of action. What game theory *can* deliver is qualitative insight which will help to understand behavior and, from a prescriptive perspective, identify factors and relationships relevant to making an intelligent decision. It is important that students have realistic expectations about game theory before the process of learning is initiated.

My college has a peculiar practice – known as senior option – which allows for a dramatic ending to the semester. If an instructor chooses to offer senior option, it means that graduating seniors can skip the final examination and have their final grade based on the remaining class work. Students are told at the first class that whether there is senior option will be determined at the end of the semester. The final class begins by describing a model of the strategic situation faced by the instructor and seniors which, without getting into details, has as its solution the instructor choosing not to offer senior option. The floor is then opened to possible modifications in the model as well as alternative solutions, while maintaining the same set of assumptions on payoffs. Once seniors realize that what happens at that class will influence whether or not there is senior option, they are powerfully energized. The discussion is animated as students, and not only seniors, spew forth clever ideas and argue on their behalf. If you don't have senior option, try to create a situation in which students have something at stake, so as to give them the opportunity and incentive to use all that they've learned in class. As an instructor, it is a most satisfying finality. Students are using game theory in a thoughtful and intelligent manner to solve a real problem. What more could one want?

NOTE

1. For more discussion on incorporating film and television, see Chapter 13, "Incorporating Media and Response Systems in the Economics Classroom", in this volume.

REFERENCE

Harrington, J. E., Jr. (2009), *Games, Strategies and Decision Making*, London, UK: Worth Publishers.

49 Teaching a research-inspired course on growth and development

Marla Ripoll

It is hard to find someone who would not be curious to know why we live in a world where people have very different standards of living. This is largely true of undergraduate students, regardless of their majors. Not only do people find the issue interesting, but everyone has at least one potential explanation for why some countries have been able to grow faster and provide their citizens with more food, better shelter, health, education, and public services, while in many other countries a large fraction of the population struggles, living on less than two dollars a day. Teaching growth and development has the great advantage that it is a fascinating course for most students. The challenge is to design a course that effectively teaches how to take all those potential explanations and evaluate them as rigorously as possible using the tools of economics.

At a general level, the growth and development course is concerned with the question of why there are such large differences in standards of living across countries. An alternative but related way of posing this question is to think about it on the time series dimension: How did the United States and other Western nations transform from being poor and mainly agricultural societies to being the industrialized and technological leaders of today? What sparked such transformation? How can we compare the structural transformation and growth experiences of countries in Africa, Asia, Latin America and East Europe? Answering these questions eventually requires focusing on a broad set of topics including geography and natural resources, agricultural productivity, technology creation, adoption and diffusion, the global economy and its institutions, local institutions, inequality, financial development, microcredit, fertility, health and mortality, education, the role of women, urbanization and labor markets.

Traditionally, growth has been treated as a separate field from development. Development economics has been associated with the study of households, villages, and the persistence of poverty at the local level. Growth economics is instead seen as a branch of macroeconomics that focuses on the behavior of aggregate savings, accumulation of human capital and technological progress (Aghion and Arméndariz, 2006). It appears as though these were two disconnected fields. But as macroeconomists have developed models and tools to incorporate heterogeneous units within the aggregate analysis, the disconnect begins to fade, and growth and development start to complement each other. Even at the policy level, the bottom-up approach to poverty alleviation advocated by development economists should no longer be considered in isolation from the top-down approach traditionally attributed to growth economists. It is the combination of these tools and approaches that can best guide policy action.

GENERAL GOALS

A growth and development course can be designed with at least three general goals in mind. The first goal is to increase the international profile of undergraduate students by raising awareness and by generating a deeper understanding of differences in standards of living as one of the most pressing issues of our time. We now live in a world where easier access to information has made distant people more aware of each other. Whether among villages and regions within the same country, or among people who live in various nations, awareness of the remarkable differences in standards of living quickly turns into a moral issue. Growth and development economists are now armed with ever expanding and richer data sets that provide useful descriptive statistics of the issues at hand. This first goal of the course is not limited to providing a detailed description of the relevant growth and development facts. More importantly, the course can promote a deeper understanding of these issues by helping students learn how to ask meaningful questions, and how to evaluate the feasibility of answering them with available data and theories.

The second goal is to help students master an array of tools from the field of economics that are useful in gaining an understanding of growth and development issues. These tools belong to a variety of subfields within economics: macro and microeconomic theory, applied economics, and experimental economics. One of the exciting aspects of teaching growth and development is that this is a course that can be organized around the general topic of standards of living, but tools from apparently distant subfields within economics can be used to shed light on the subject. Indeed, frontier research on different aspects of growth and development uses very different sets of tools. For example, consider the topic of financial development and growth. There are a number of macroeconomic models that analyze how financial systems influence savings, investment, innovation decisions and hence economic growth.[1] But microeconomic theorists have also contributed to the understanding of financial systems in the context of corporate governance theory. In addition, measures of financial development have been introduced in aggregate cross-country growth regressions, while applied economists have used industry and firm-level data to provide direct empirical evidence on the mechanisms linking finance and growth. There is a recent growing branch of field experiments in developing countries that seeks to evaluate the effects of microfinance on consumption, saving and entrepreneurship across different types of households (Banerjee, Duflo, Glennerster and Kinnan, 2009; Kaboski and Townsend, forthcoming). To close the circle, it is now feasible to use macroeconomic models with heterogeneous producers to evaluate the potential effects of large-scale microfinance programs. These models can be built to be consistent with the evidence provided by field experiments, but they enrich our understanding of the issues by allowing for an evaluation of the aggregate effects. As these examples suggest, an important goal in teaching growth and development is to illustrate how these various tools, although limited when used in isolation, can complement each other in advancing our knowledge.

The third teaching goal is to use the content of the growth and development course to illustrate and reflect on the challenges scientists face in understanding complex reality and in devising effective ways to change it to the benefit of humanity. Reflecting on the difficulties of creating knowledge speaks to the very heart of a liberal arts education. Understanding the sources of differences in standards of living across countries is challenging. Part of the difficulty arises from the fact that potential explanations as to why income levels are so different around the world are themselves endogenous. There is often feedback between income levels and its determinants (human capital, technology, institutions, and so on). Finding a truly exogenous variable that could be hypothetically changed in a model to evaluate the chain of mechanisms that lead to a change in income levels is almost impossible. Consider, for example, the connection between property rights protection and income levels. The idea that absence of this protection is detrimental to growth and development is reasonable. Indeed, many undergraduates would think differences in property rights protection a potential explanation for why income levels vary so much from one country to the other. But this represents an occasion to help students think about the complexity of the issue at hand by pointing out the possibility that high income countries have the resources to enforce the protection of property rights, and thus the causation may run in reverse. Indeed, frontier research on the topic attempts to resolve this causation conundrum (Acemoglu, Johnson and Robinson, 2001). In sum, a course on growth and development provides a unique opportunity to reflect on the intellectual challenges scientists face, as well as to transcend the limits of the field of economics and incorporate other fields of knowledge. History, psychology, sociology and political science are examples of fields that study the very issues economic models often take as exogenous.

PHILOSOPHY AND METHODS

The general goals proposed above are naturally associated with the philosophy that teaching should be inspired by research. This inspiration is not limited to teaching specific research findings as part of the course content. Indeed, the content can be structured to reflect the historic evolution of research and the gradual creation of knowledge. More importantly, the teaching methods in the classroom can be designed to exemplify research methodology, with assignments that give students the opportunity to try out research methods on their own.

Reading Research Papers

One approach to teaching a research-inspired growth and development class is to assign reading materials taken directly from academic journals or working paper series. Selected reading materials from the *Journal of Economic Perspectives* and the *Journal of Economic Literature* are suitable for introductory courses of predominantly non-economics majors. Most of these papers provide an overview of research findings and are written by prominent authors in the field. Reading primary source articles gives students the opportunity to learn content, obtain a perspective on how research on a specific topic has evolved, and be exposed to a process of comparing potentially conflicting research findings.

Upper-level economics majors, who have already taken intermediate micro and macroeconomics, as well as some econometrics, benefit from reading a selection of more advanced papers from the *Journal of Economic Growth*, the *Quarterly Journal of Economics*, the *Journal of Development Economics*, the *American Economic Review*, and the NBER Working Paper series, among others. In addition to content, one of the great benefits of reading these types of papers is that students learn how to structure the presentation of research findings; starting with a motivation and brief summary of the current state of knowledge, before moving to the formulation of a hypothesis, and the execution of methods to validate it. Learning how to structure a written document is a useful skill for students, regardless of whether they evolve into researchers.

For example, consider the topic of technology and industrial policy. This topic lies at the intersection between the traditional "big push" multiple equilibria model of economic development (Rosenstein-Rodan, 1943), the new growth macroeconomic models of technology creation (Romer, 1986), the models of international technology diffusion and adoption through trade and foreign direct investment (Grossman and Helpman, 1993), and the literature on industrial policy. The growth and development experience in South Korea can be chosen as an example that brings together these different elements. The main concepts and ideas from the models listed above are discussed in chapters 3, 8 and 9 of Easterly's (2001) celebrated book, all of which may be part of the mandatory section of the reading list for this topic. In addition, Westphal (1990) provides a detailed discussion of the case of South Korea, and reflects on the difficulties involved in the process of technology adoption. These readings are appropriate for students with minimal economics training.

Further readings materials for this topic may consist of longer, more specific and more advanced papers. Some of these may be part of the mandatory reading list for upper-level economics majors, but listing them under further reading on the syllabus of a lower-level class can provide guidance for more ambitious students. Readings may include some longer survey papers (for example, Harrison and Rodriguez-Clare, 2009), some recent empirical papers on technology diffusion (Comin, Easterly and Gong, 2010), some current discussions on industrial policy (Rodrik, 2008), and the original paper on the industrialization of Eastern and South-Eastern Europe by Rosenstein-Rodan (1943).

Research in an Historic Perspective

Teaching growth theories provides a great opportunity to illustrate the evolution of knowledge from a historic perspective. This approach highlights the incremental character of scientific knowledge in general, the historic circumstances that may have influenced the emergence of specific growth theories, and the ways in which these theories have influenced policy making at different points in time. An example of how to structure growth and development theory contents is contained in chapters 2, 3, 8 and 9 of Easterly's (2001) book. If one reads the four chapters consecutively, they place a good number of models in a historic perspective: Harrod (1939), Domar (1946), Solow (1956), and Romer (1986), among others. The value of this material lies in the description of the feedback between historic events, growth models and policy action, as well as in the wealth of examples provided to illustrate the models' principles.

An alternative approach to using the historic perspective in structuring a growth and development course is to focus on the evolution of research tools in the field. For instance, while earlier models of growth models tended to be quite aggregate, more recent models focus on the dynamic interaction of either different sectors of production, heterogeneous firms, or agents with different occupations. In addition, earlier applied work used econometric methods on aggregate or micro-level data, whereas more recent work constructs data from natural experiments or field experiments in order to establish causality in a more controlled setting. For instance, the presentation of microfinance and development can begin with examples of traditional theories and empirical approaches from Morduch (1999), followed by the more recent quasi-experimental approach of Kaboski and Townsend (forthcoming), and finally the field experimental design of Banerjee, Duflo, Glennerster and Kinnan (2009). This historic presentation of the tools can be used to reflect on the limitations of the tools themselves, an example being the case of recent field experiments in microfinance, which do not provide guidance on how implementing large-scale microfinance programs affects per capita income for the economy as a whole. Although it may be necessary to adjust materials and omit some more technical details, depending on the level of the course, it is possible to provide students with an understanding of how the tools have evolved, and to bring them to the very frontier of what we know. This historic overview of the tools instills admiration for the progress made, as well as curiosity for what we still do not know.

Research in the Classroom

One way of teaching almost any specific topic in a growth and development course is to proceed as if one was conducting research, with students and the teacher being "coauthors." This provides a first-hand illustration of research methodology. Specifically, one begins by introducing a number of tables and figures that illustrate the relationship between certain variables of interest. The tables and figures should be purposely designed to highlight patterns, exceptions, potential correlations and possible mechanisms that explain those correlations. In the case of the relationship between per capita income and growth, one can use world histograms of per capita income at different dates, identifying by name some of the countries at the tails, as well as those that have moved up or down the distribution. A world histogram of the average annual per capita income growth in each country since 1960 can be contrasted with tables on decade by decade growth for a sample of countries. Color maps on per capita income groups according to the World's Bank income classification can be compared with similar color-coded maps by average annual growth groups. Students can be organized into small groups in order to identify patterns, exceptions and correlations suggested by the tables and figures. The small-group activities can be reinforced by a whole class discussion of the different ideas drawn by each group.

The next step is to study available models and theories associated with the relationships illustrated on the tables. This "literature review" can be accomplished by assigning relevant articles, and complementing these with in-class presentations of specific models and theories. While the instructor explains the main building blocks of a model, and how the model works, students meeting in small groups derive the main implications of the model and discuss whether those implications are consistent with the conclusions drawn from the tables. In the case of the per capita income and growth example, models such as Solow and Romer might be included to highlight the per capita income convergence versus divergence predictions.

A second round of tables and figures can be designed to investigate the validity of the models. In the case of the Solow model, time series and cross-section data are gathered for population growth, capital-output ratios, capital per worker, and investment rates. These data/model iterations illuminate limitations of the theories, as well as the difficulties in uncovering the exact mechanisms that explain observed patterns. They also reveal motivations for studying alternative theories, or the need to construct new theories as a task for future research. In the case of per capita income and growth, one can use steady-state equations of the Solow model together with data on the United States and Tanzania in order to show that it is not possible to explain the 70-fold difference in per capita income between these two countries based on their differences in average saving rates and population growth. This development accounting exercise highlights the quantitative importance of productivity, or Solow residuals, and it motivates the study of theories where technology creation and adoption are at the core of understanding differences in standards of living. The process of teaching a topic by pretending the whole class is doing research is quite rewarding for both the students and the teacher, and it generally leads to interesting discussions. It is also a risky process because it tends to uncover the limitations of what we know, which may be disillusioning for some students. But this cost is low compared with how this process enhances students' intellectual and critical capabilities.

Student Research Projects

Upper-level undergraduate students, especially within the context of small classes, can be given the opportunity to develop their own research projects. The experience of reading articles and participating in the "collective research" process in the classroom provides students with important building blocks for developing their own research projects, as well as with some potential questions to be explored. While expectations of final project quality may vary depending on individual students' abilities and ambitions in pursuing research, all students should be required to carefully motivate their topic, formulate a specific question, review the relevant literature, advance a hypothesis, and sketch a method to validate it. The use of freely available online data from the World Bank, the OECD, UNESCO, UNCTAD, WHO, FAO, Penn World Tables, ILO, IMF, Polity IV and Free the World, among others, makes data analysis a feasible component of any research project.

COURSE STRUCTURE, CONTENTS AND OTHER TIPS

The goals and philosophy discussed above can be implemented by employing a wide array of course content. The number of topics to explore in a growth and development course is vast, so the final selection of content is necessarily incomplete. This section offers some suggestions on potential topics to include, and how to structure the course around these topics.

Topics, Videos and Other Materials

Box 49.1 contains sample topics for a growth and development course. This model course begins with an introduction that highlights per capita income differences around

BOX 49.1   EXAMPLE OF COURSE TOPICS AND VIDEO
MATERIALS

Topic 1 – Introduction: World income inequality
Countries: Peru and Tanzania
Video: Commanding Heights, Episode 3. Excerpt: The global divide

Topic 2 – Institutions, inequality and economic performance
Country: Brazil
Video: Brazil's land revolution, Bullfrog films

Topic 3 – Investment, foreign debt and foreign aid
Country: Uganda
Video: The debt police, Bullfrog films

Topic 4 – Technology and industrial policy
Country: South Korea
Video: Asia Rising, PBS People's Century. Excerpt: South Korea

Topic 5 – Trade, dependency and growth
Country: Ethiopia
Video: The coffee-go-round, Bullfrog films

Topic 6 – Agricultural development and structural transformation
Country: Malawi
Video: Malawi: A nation going hungry, Films Media Group

Topic 7 – Microcredit and poverty
Country: Bangladesh
Video: Credit when credit is due, Bullfrog films

Topic 8 – Population, fertility and health
Countries: India, Peru and Kenya
Video: Not the numbers game, Bullfrog films

Topic 9 – Education and women in development
Country: Turkey
Video: Educating Yaprak, Bullfrog films

Topic 10 – Urbanization and labor markets
Country: India
Video: India: Slum futures, Bullfrog films

the world as the object of study (Topic 1). This can be accomplished by using a variety of tables and figures, and by exploring one of the most prolific research topics in development in recent years: the relationship between institutions and economic performance (Topic 2). This immediate exposure to current research sets the tone of the course and provides a useful reference point to contrast alternative theories subsequently explored. From this point on, topics can be organized with a top-bottom approach, starting with a focus on more aggregate, economy-wide issues and then moving to a more disaggregated analysis involving sectors, communities and individual households. Economy-wide topics include aggregate investment, saving, foreign aid and debt, productivity, long-run convergence, technology diffusion and adoption, and trade and growth (Topics 3 through 5).

Agricultural productivity and the process of structural transformation provide a transition from aggregate to more disaggregated issues (Topic 6). The analysis of the agricultural sector naturally leads to the exploration of the economic lives of the poor, a large proportion of whom are rural. Relevant issues include insurance and credit markets, micro-credit programs, fertility, education, the role of women in development, and rural-urban migration (Topics 7 through 10). Although topics are organized with a top-bottom approach, it is important to provide a bottom-top perspective by discussing the extent to which policies implemented at the level of specific sectors or communities may have an economy-wide impact.

Consistent with the philosophy of teaching discussed above, each topic has its corresponding reading list from journals and working papers. Space limitations prevent including a reading list for each topic, but one is available upon request.[2] In addition to the reading list, video materials featuring specific economic issues in developing countries can be used to illustrate the different topics. Data and figures provide a description of facts in the developing world, but watching a video or documentary featuring the actual sites and people who are part of that reality can be enlightening. Box 49.1 includes suggested video materials for each topic. In presenting videos, it is important to avoid falling into a passive teaching trap. Keeping video presentation short (20 minutes) to allow for enough class time before and after ensures the video is used as a preamble and motivates meaningful discussion.

Consider again the example of technology and industrial policy. The associated video clip is about South Korea's developmental success story and can be used to illustrate the Rosenstein-Rodan (1943) or big push model of development, as well as the role of investment, education, technology adoption and industrial policy. Before showing the video, the instructor might ask students to discuss the following question: Why do you think there are so many Asian Tigers (Hong Kong, Singapore, Taiwan, South Korea, and more recently China, India, Philippines, Malaysia, and Indonesia), but only one "Latin American Tiger" (Chile) and no African Tigers? This question brings about a wide range of hypotheses, and it serves as a preamble for the potential issues the video may or may not address. In addition to this initial brainstorming, a short slide presentation of data associated with economic and social indicators for South Korea provides additional insights ahead of the video. Focusing students' attention during the video can be achieved by asking them to ponder specific questions, such as: What are the main components of South Korea's development success story? Is this "recipe" applicable to other developing countries? These questions invite individual reflection during the video, and prepare students for a group discussion thereafter. Discussion on how the video provides a potential answer to the preamble question can be conducted for the class as a whole, or using small-group activities to analyze the ways in which the different models studied within this unit shed light on the issues portrayed in the video. The discussions before and after the video, and the video itself, provide students with interesting opportunities to use the models and theories to interpret very specific situations that are part of the history or daily lives of people in different countries. In addition, most videos portray a number of non-economic aspects that are relevant in understanding economic outcomes such as the political regime, the work ethic and the culture of present sacrifices in exchange for future benefits in the case of South Korea. Videos provide an opportunity to navigate to fields outside of economics.

Finally, news and magazine articles relevant to growth and development come to light every day. Bringing these to the students' attention, and using some class time to comment on these current events as they fit under the different topics is always refreshing. To reinforce the relevancy of material covered in the course, it is helpful to comment on news and articles by explicitly linking them to a specific model, theory, data observation, video or paper that has already been examined as part of the course content.

Teaching Models

The content students are exposed to through news, articles and videos can be complemented with a more formal in-class presentation of economic models. A combination of mathematical equations with graphs facilitates the presentation of formal models. It is important that students are directly involved in deriving results to enhance their understanding of how models work. The instructor's explanation and demonstration of the building blocks of a model is reinforced when students are organized in small groups to derive some of the model equations. Alternatively, assign students the task of creating graphs to represent the mathematical equations. Students learn better when they are given the opportunity to be actively involved in understanding how models work. For example, aggregate models by Harrod (1939), Domar (1946), Solow (1956), and Romer (1986) can be summarized in a few equations and represented graphically. Once students master the Solow model, they can be actively involved in understanding Romer's model. One of the difficulties in explaining the mathematical formulation of Romer's model is the distinction between the individual production function of a particular firm, and the representation of the aggregate production function of the economy. This distinction requires introducing the idea of "learning by investing" and explaining the concept of an externality to the firm. While the instructor can guide students through the process of aggregating production functions from the firm to the economy-wide level, students must use their knowledge of the Solow model to draw dynamic graphs of Romer's model for the cases of decreasing, constant and increasing returns. In addition, students can discuss the implications of these different cases for the relationship between per capita income and growth, and the convergence or divergence of per capita income among countries. Finally, students can reflect on how the Romer model sheds light on the growth miracle of South Korea as shown in the video.

A final suggestion in presenting formal models is to show students a picture of the economist who formulated it. Briefly commenting on notable biographical details helps associate the model's equations with the face of an economist and gives additional context to the origin of the model and other ideas its author may have contributed. It is not clear why, but students tend to laugh when presented with pictures of economists!

CONCLUDING COMMENTS

Teaching growth and development is fascinating. Without doubt, the subject is relevant and its study has potentially enormous implications for humanity's well-being. It does not take much to convince students, or almost anyone, about this. The challenge in teaching this class is that, perhaps as much as content, the objective should be to teach students to recognize how complex the issues are and provide them with a method with which to start thinking about the models used to understand these complexities. Although we can expose students to the knowledge accumulated by development economists, it is as important to acknowledge what we do not know, and how we think we could gain some understanding of such unknowns. This goal can be best achieved by directly exposing students to the tools, findings and limitations of current research papers, and choosing a teaching style that simulates elements of research methodology. This philosophy of teaching growth and development has the additional advantage that the instructor is also going to learn a lot in the process.

NOTES

1. See Levine (2005) for a comprehensive review of the theoretical and empirical literature on finance and growth.
2. Reading lists are available at http://www.pitt.edu/~ripoll or can be requested via e-mail from ripoll@pitt.edu.

REFERENCES

Acemoglu, D., S. Johnson and J. Robinson (2001), "The colonial origins of comparative development: An empirical investigation", *American Economic Review*, **91** (5), 1369–401.
Aghion, P. and B. Arméndariz de Aghion (2006), "The new growth approach to poverty alleviation", in A. Banerjee, R. Bénabou and D. Mookherjee (eds), *Understanding Poverty*, New York, NY: Oxford University Press, pp. 73–84.
Banerjee, A., E. Duflo, R. Glennerster and C. Kinnan (2009), "The miracle of microfinance? Evidence from a randomized evaluation", Manuscript.
Comin, D., W. Easterly and E. Gong (2010), "Was the wealth of nations determined in 1000 BC?", *American Economic Journals: Macroeconomics*, **2**, 65–97.
Domar, E. (1946), "Capital expansion, rate of growth and employment", *Econometrica*, **14** (2), 137–47.
Easterly, W. (2001), *The Elusive Quest for Growth*, Cambridge, MA: MIT Press.
Grossman, G. and E. Helpman (1993), *Innovation and Growth in the Global Economy*, Cambridge, MA: MIT Press.
Harrison, A. and A. Rodriguez-Clare (2009), "Trade, foreign investment and industrial policy for developing countries", NBER Working Paper, 15261.
Harrod, R. (1939), "An essay in dynamic theory", *Economic Journal*, **49**, 14–33.
Kaboski, J. and R. Townsend (forthcoming), "A structural evaluation of a large-scale quasi-experimental microfinance initiative", *Econometrica*.

Levine, R. (2005), "Finance and growth: theory and evidence", in P. Aghion and S. Durlauf (eds), *Handbook of Economic Growth*, The Netherlands: Elsevier Science, pp. 865–934.

Morduch, J. (1999), "The microfinance promise", *Journal of Economic Literature*, **37**, 1569–614.

Rodrik, D. (2008), "Normalizing industrial policy", Commission on Growth and Development, Working Paper No. 3.

Romer, P. (1986), "Increasing returns and long-run growth", *Journal of Political Economy*, **94** (5), 1002–37.

Rosenstein-Rodan, P. (1943), "Problems of industrialization of Eastern and South-Eastern Europe", *Economic Journal*, **53**, 202–11.

Solow, R. (1956), "A contribution to the theory of economic growth", *Quarterly Journal of Economics*, **70** (1), 65–94.

Westphal, L. (1990), "Industrial policy in an export-propelled economy: Lessons from South Korea's experience", *Journal of Economic Perspectives*, **4**, 41–59.

50 Teaching American economic history
Price Fishback and Pamela Nickless

Our combined years of experience teaching economic history is approaching seventy and we realized as we wrote this essay that we are still learning more about teaching with each class we teach. At the beginning of a career, it may be hard to believe how much more one will know after a couple of decades of reading and researching. We teach at very different institutions, a large research-oriented public university, and a teaching-oriented undergraduate public university. Yet, the only real difference in the way we teach undergraduates is that graduate students play more of a role at the research-oriented university. Our experiences in research and teaching have led us both to have more complex views of our discipline than when we started. In some ways, that makes it easier – we can both give impromptu lectures on many topics and good ones too! Yet the easy generalization is harder and the impromptu lecture might be a little too long.

Teaching is hard work and it gets harder as you get better at it. The best teachers we have known made it look easy, but the easy result came from working hard at finding better ways to present the material in a clear and interesting fashion. Emphasis on key points and clarity in presentation helps enormously. Economic history combines telling a story about prior events with the logical analysis of why the events developed the way they did.

COURSE OBJECTIVES

When planning a course, think about the role the course plays in the curriculum. Most US Economic History courses are electives for economics majors and minors and may be electives for history majors as well. This role offers the freedom to tailor the course to the interests of your students as well as your own. Don't overlook your own interests – particularly at institutions with a substantial teaching load. Add readings to a course that complement an area you are researching. We have found that teaching the literature of a topic enhances our own understanding. It is a rare professor who has not had a revelatory experience in the classroom.

Do not be afraid to challenge undergraduate students. In studying the Great Depression, they *can* read contemporary scholars like Irving Fisher on debt deflation, the 1960s scholarship by Milton Friedman and Anna Schwartz on the Great Contraction, and the 1990s work by Barry Eichengreen on the gold standard. With some help in learning how to read modern journal articles, they can understand the central points made in the vast majority of academic articles. If the historical *New York Times* is available, send the students to read the newspaper from the period. Reporters' coverage of the banking crises in 1933 or the end of the Bretton Woods agreement is often illuminating. Seeing the article embedded in the paper gives them a richer appreciation of the other issues of the day.

Economic history courses are likely to have history students enrolled who will know that history is important but need more training using the economics of markets, the organization of firms, and public choice to understand history. They often have very naïve notions about the importance of markets in history. For example, in western North Carolina it is widely believed that the "mountain people" were isolated and self-sufficient until sometime in the early 20th century. Indeed, the notion of the self-sufficient farmer is a perennial favorite for most Americans. Yet, in downtown Asheville, there is an art installation celebrating the Buncombe Turnpike or Drovers' Trail – a road that connected northeastern Tennessee and western North Carolina with markets in South Carolina in the early 1800s. Use local history – particularly if many of the students are from the region. Most history departments teach a course in the state's history and the professor who teaches it can be a valuable resource.

Our own objectives in the undergraduate classroom fall into two broad categories. First, we use economic reasoning and methods to analyze past events, while emphasizing long run changes and recurring problems that have arisen in American history. Second, we illustrate the use of quantitative evidence to analyze past events.

ECONOMIC REASONING AND METHODS

As economists teaching in economics departments, we teach our students economic theory and application. But understanding our economic past is different from simply using historic data to test economic theory. Economic history offers a rich context for understanding modern and historical decisions in several ways. The same major issues arise in different times and places. Spikes in fuel prices occurred when the fuels were wood, whale oil, coal, uranium, natural gas, as well as with oil in modern times. Threats to financial stability and recessions have recurred throughout US history. Many of the economic issues that arise with the internet today also arose with the introduction of tele-graphs, telephones, railroads, and automobiles. The current move toward increasing glo-balization in many ways mirrors the globalization that peaked in the late 19th century. That globalization halted and then receded during World War I, the Great Depression, and World War II, a tragic result that set back the world economy a great deal.

Decisions are often influenced by the historical path to the decision. In the aftermath of World War II, the technological choices made by US manufacturers differed from those in Germany and Japan because the US had not experienced the same wholesale destruction of people, machinery, and buildings. The relative incomes of black and white families in 1900, and probably in more recent times, were strongly influenced by the fact that the vast majority of blacks had only gained their freedom at the end of the Civil War. They started into their new lives with very little property and no formal schooling in the lowest wage region of the country. The health of adults in 1980 was influenced by whether they were born during the Great Influenza epidemic in 1918 and 1919.

Economic history focuses on the causes and results of long-term changes in institu-tions. Property rights, the rule of law, individual freedoms, religion, regulation, and organizations play important roles in American history. Economic history courses are a natural spot where the subfields of economics are blended into a single analysis because the discussion of the economy in any period in economic history is influenced by the fact that there are changes in labor, the extent of concentration in industry, demography, macroeconomic policy, and regulation that all interact at that time.

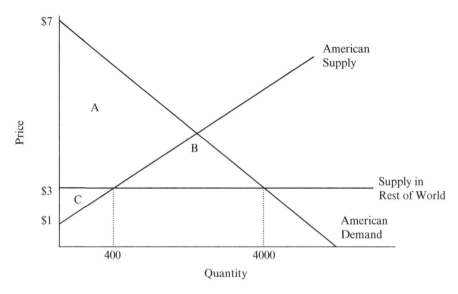

Figure 50.1   Free trade with imports

Using Graphs to Tell Stories

Economic historians like to tell stories and we use graphs to illustrate the stories and clarify analysis. There is a tendency to think that the students already know the logic of a graph, say one about tariffs, because they learned it in a previous economics course. Therefore, all that need be done is flash the finished graph in all its glory in a power-point slide, describe the results that come from the graph by quickly pointing at different parts of the graph, and then tell a story with some numbers that fits the graph. Voilà! In a short time, they all know what happened with tariffs in this episode in American history. This may work with graduate students, but undergraduates – even economics majors – will tend to dismiss the graph and the economic theory and focus on the story. In fact, it really does not work with graduate students either.

The key to an economic analysis of history is the logical application of economic concepts and the use of real-world evidence. One effective technique can be illustrated with the use of graphs to explain the possible impact of tariffs in American history. It is extremely important to work with the students in class to construct the graph, so they see the economic logic underlying it. Ask them to work in teams and draw the US supply curve, a flat foreign supply curve, and the US consumer demand curve with no tariff. Then write a series of sentences that use information in the graph, as in Figure 50.1. "Under free trade without a tariff, US consumers paid a price of $3 and bought 4,000 yards of cloth. Meanwhile, American producers produced and sold 400 yards of cloth; therefore, imports from foreign sellers were 3,600 yards (4,000 – 400)." Have them describe the area representing American consumer surplus and American producer surplus, areas A + B and C, respectively. Then have them work with you to construct Figure 50.1 on the board. If their team did something different, ask them why. The discussion often illuminates the graph for everybody.

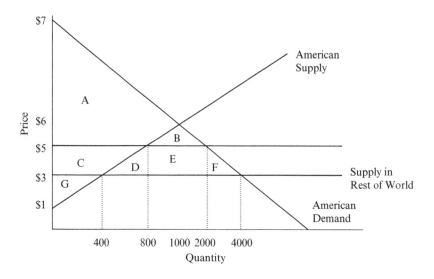

A $2 tariff on foreign imports of cloth causes the supply curve from the rest of the world to rise from $3 to $5.

- American consumers will reduce their purchases from 4,000 to 2,000 yards of cloth.
- American producers will increase their sales from 400 to 800 yards of cloth.
- Suppliers in the rest of the world will see their sales in America fall from 3,600 to 1,200 yards of cloth.
- American consumer surplus falls from area A + B + C + D + E + F to area A + B. American consumers therefore lose area C + D + E + F.
- American producer surplus rises C from area G to area C + G, and they gain G.
- Area F is a deadweight loss that measures the lost gains from trade from the reduction in purchases from 4,000 to 2,000.
- Area E represents the tariff revenue collected on the 1,200 yards of cloth that are imported.
- Area D represents the loss due to inefficient production, the amount by which the costs of American producers of raising production from 400 to 800 exceed the prices that would have been paid by consumers under free trade.

Figure 50.2   Trade with a tariff

Have them draw a new starting graph, which will eventually become Figure 50.2, and then ask them to work in teams to show how the tariff shifts the foreign supply on the graph. Some will be able to tell you how to add the tariff shift to the graph on the board, so follow their instructions. Have them write sentences about the shift: "The $2 tariff raised the foreign supply curve from a flat line at $3 to a flat line at $5." Then piece by piece ask them to write sentences about changes they see from the addition of the tariff. As one example: "A foreign tariff of $2 per unit raised the price paid in America from $3 to $5." Ask them to explain why American and foreign producers would both raise the price from $3 to $5 even though the American producer does not pay the tariff. Have them write a sentence about each change they see, and then make sure all of the key sentences get written on the board, so that they can see the complete economic analysis. Have them walk you back through the analysis by pointing out the key points to be made, summarized in Figure 50.2. The graph provides a starting point for discussions about what the partial equilibrium model would predict. Figure 50.2 shows a situation where the tariff leads to revenue collection. To see how well they understand the graph, ask them to redraw a situation with a protective tariff that leads to collection of no tariff revenue, working in teams in class or for homework. Then the discussion can expand to incorporate issues that are more dynamic.

The next step is to give them a table of prices and quantities for commodities before and after a tariff was introduced in American history, say under the Hawley-Smoot tariff of 1930 or the Tariff of Abominations of 1828. Ask them to work in teams and write sentences about what they see in the table. Does the data fit the model? Often yes, but sometimes no. Then discuss why the data might not fit. Ask them who was collecting the data and why, so that you can talk about potential biases in the data source. Discuss what factors that were omitted from the graphical presentation might have caused changes that led the data not to fit the model.

It is important to have them work in teams and ask them to write sentences about what they see, and work as a class to write good sentences on the board. The process simultaneously shows the logic, confirms the answer drawn from the theory, and improves the students' technical writing skills about graphs and tables. By working in teams of two or three, a far larger percentage of the students are engaged in thinking about the issues, and they are teaching each other.[1] Our role then is to ask different groups to describe their answers and then clean up faulty logic or misunderstandings.

The writing is time consuming but essential. The graph may be worth a thousand words, but students need to provide an executive summary that hits the key points of what they have learned from graphical analysis. We both have lecture notes from our undergraduate days with poorly labeled supply and demand graphs and no descriptions of what they mean. Notice how many books and articles just slap a graph down with very little writing about it. Often, the graph or table is just wasted space because people just skim forward and read the text. But the graph or table can be tied into the text directly by referring to key values and using them to make the point you want to make. Each sentence here and in the caption to Figure 50.2 draws the reader's eye to some change on the graph.

USE QUANTITATIVE DATA

In all our classes, we want students to understand not only economic theory but also how economists use and evaluate information. How are we measuring the economic variables we are analyzing? We want to move students beyond just reading numbers from a disembodied table. They have to *use* the data to address key questions and issues. What were people trying to measure? Often statistics from the antebellum census are used to calculate the number of slave owners, but the census directions are clear; the task was to count *slaves* not owners. Likewise, the survey questions used to measure unemployment in the 1900 and 1910 censuses differ from those asked today. How much error does this introduce into what we can infer from the data?

It is always important to think about the magnitude of an economic variable or an effect. Past values are best understood in relative terms. For example, when students learn that railroad workers earned $644 per year in 1909, they are horrified. Yet, in 1909, US railroad workers were among the best-paid workers in the world. They earned about 24 percent more annually than manufacturing workers and coal miners and 58 percent more than farm workers (Margo, 2006). Meanwhile, annual American manufacturing earnings were roughly 1.5 times those of English manufacturing workers and two to three times the earnings of manufacturing workers in Italy or Poland (Rosenbloom, 2002, pp. 138–9). After adjusting for inflation, $644 in 1909 would have bought the equivalent of $15,649 worth of goods in 2009 dollars, which is much lower than what a US railroad worker earns today.[2] But this 2009 purchasing power is higher than the average incomes in all but 50 countries in today's world. The beauty of the comparisons is that they engender discussions about why wages differed across industries and countries at the time the railroad workers were living. In fact, the importance of a high school education is highlighted when the students discover that clerical workers were earning nearly double what railroad workers earned. The comparisons with today then raise issues about why earnings are so much higher in the US now than in 1909, and why the 1909 railroad worker was faring better than people in many parts of the world today.

Many students believe that there is no good information available about the past. We cannot "know," we can only guess. We stress the vast amounts of data about the past that are currently available. Even more importantly, during our teaching careers scholars have uncovered large amounts of new data about the past buried in libraries, archives, attics, and warehouses around the world. Our understanding of many historical issues has been revolutionized by this process, not only because the data help answer the old questions, but also because the new evidence allowed people to ask and answer a broad range of questions that it did not seem possible to answer before.

Finding Quantitative Data

Have the students take a good hard look at one or more studies based on a large data collection project. Find one that combines several different sources of information. The easy accessibility of the manuscript census on websites[3] or census data sets from the Integrated Public Use Microdata Samples[4] make classroom examples easy and underscores the idea that we can know a great deal about individuals in the past. Try having students match up information from states and cities where the people in the census are living to see how various state or federal policies influenced people's lives. Many scholars now routinely post the data sets from their projects on their website. For example, Price Fishback has excel data sets at his website that provide information on all sorts of political, economic, and demographic variables at the state level between 1900 and 1930 and at the city and county levels between 1929 and 1940. The Interuniversity Consortium for Political and Social Research (ICPSR) has large numbers of data sets with individual information and policy information from the past that can be used for examples. The websites of the Federal Reserve Banks, particularly St. Louis, offer large amounts of historical data on banking, GDP, industrial production, and GDP. The Departments of Agriculture, Census, Labor, and many others have historical data sets.

One of the best sources for time series data about all aspects of the economy is the *Historical Statistics of the United States, Earliest Times to the Present: Millennial Edition*, which was published in five volumes in 2006 (Carter et al., 2006). A large community of scholars compiled the data from thousands of sources, and the scholars have written informative essays about how the data were collected and what can be said with the evidence. The typical university library allows access to the online version of the volumes, where people can typically download the essays and the data (in excel spreadsheets).

COVERING OVER TWO CENTURIES IN ONE SEMESTER

Since we usually cover all of US history in one semester, it is impossible to cover the whole history well. Therefore, we often develop the course around specific topics. Readings from a standard economic history textbook provide the context to those topics in terms of time and place. It is extremely important to have the students read this material, so that they can see where the specific topics fit. We have implemented a variety of mechanisms to encourage students to read the material: random quizzes; multiple choice tests to be completed electronically before class; written comments about the readings; and grading the quality of classroom discussion each day. Linking grades to the reading of assignments makes for better and more efficient class discussion.

One way to focus in more depth on a few topics is to require each student to write a paper that summarizes and critiques the literature on one or more of the topics you will cover. Some professors have students write short papers about each of three or four topics. We have had more success with having students write a single paper that involves writing a rough draft, making a presentation and leading a discussion of the topic with the class, and then writing a final draft on one topic. Papers are usually about ten to twenty pages, but this varies by topic. This process allows the student to go into more depth on a topic and have the experience of revising and rethinking issues after getting substantial feedback from the professor and other students. A number of students have used the final versions of their papers as examples of writing for job interviews and graduate school applications. Often, we restrict the list of topics on which students can write to about fourteen topic statements spread over seven broad areas of interest. We limit the choice of topics to make sure we know the literature well enough to provide advice to the students on what literature to read, as well as a method of controlling potential cheating on the paper.

A set schedule and structure for the writing assignment is important. During the first week, we talk about the assignment, the topics, and then discuss how the students can seek out academic articles and books using the reference list in the textbook, online bibliographical sites like EconLit and GoogleScholar, as well as the references in articles that they find. By the end of week three, in a fifteen-week semester, the student submits a one-page description of the topic, along with a reference list of articles and papers they have found. We then meet one-on-one with each student to discuss the topic, help them fine-tune it and agree on key articles and books to examine. We will let up to two or three students work on the same topic, but we want coverage across all seven broad areas because class time will be devoted to each area. The rough draft is due about the seventh week of the semester. Students at this stage can provide input on the readings for the rest of the class on the topic. Paper writers make short presentations of what they found and the class discusses the readings and the presentations. After written feedback on their paper and presentation, the students then turn in the final version of their paper about a week or two before the end of the semester.

The economic history course with a writing requirement is a natural feeding ground into senior theses and honors theses because both narratives and quantitative evidence play such an important role. Many students are engaged by studying current policy issues in a historical context. Often historical data are available on variables that they cannot access for the current period. They can also run some simple hypotheses tests in excel or more sophisticated econometric tests if they have taken an undergraduate econometrics course. It may be possible to get grants that provide some funding for students to be paid for entering data related to their research projects and even for travel to discover new data. Typically, the students negotiate with us about the topic within the framework of how it fits into our own broader research agendas. If you have graduate students working on similar topics, you can have biweekly workshops where the undergraduates and graduate students present their research and talk about problems they are facing.

FINAL WORDS

In the final analysis, what students learn depends heavily on their own motivation. Our role is to give students opportunities to learn. We can help motivate students to take advantage of these opportunities by showing our passion for the subject, having the students talk to each other and drive the discussions, working with them to understand more difficult material and striving hard for clarity. Professors who teach and research economic history obviously have a passion for it because they have made it their life's work. We have seen people with a broad range of personalities, from friendly to quiet, to sarcastic and self-deprecating, succeed with their students. The common element for all was their ability to find ways for students to share their obvious passion for their subject.

NOTES

1. For more about effective teams, see Chapter 4, "Using Cooperative Learning Exercises in Economics", in this volume.
2. An inflation-adjusted measure can be found www.measuringworth.com (accessed 19 March 2011).
3. See, for example, ancestry.com (accessed 8 June 2011).
4. IPUMS at www.ipums.org (accessed 8 June 2011).

REFERENCES

Carter, S. B., S. S. Gartner, M. R. Haines, A. L. Olmstead, R. Sutch and G. Wright (editors-in-chief) (2006), *Historical Statistics of the United States, Earliest Times to the Present: Millennial Edition*, New York: Cambridge University Press.
Douglas, Paul H. (1930), *Real Wages in the United States, 1890–1926*, New York: Houghton Mifflin.
Eichengreen, B. (1992), *Golden Fetters: The Gold Standard and the Depression, 1919–1939*, New York: Oxford University Press.
Fisher, I. (1933), "The debt-deflation theory of depressions", *Econometrica*, 1 (October), 337–57.
Friedman, M. and A. Schwartz (1963), *A Monetary History of the United States, 1867–1960*, Princeton, NJ: Princeton University Press.
Margo, R. (2006), "Table Ba4320-4334 – Annual earnings in selected industries and occupations: 1890–1926", in S. B. Carter, S. S. Gartner, M. R. Haines, A. L. Olmstead, R. Sutch and G. Wright (eds), *Historical Statistics of the United States, Earliest Times to the Present: Millennial Edition*, Vol. 2, New York: Cambridge University Press, pp. 54–5.
Rosenbloom, J. (2002), *Looking for Work, Searching for Workers: American Labor Markets During Industrialization*, New York: Cambridge University Press.

51 The economic history of European growth
Daniel Barbezat

European economic history has been a long-time staple in many economic departments. However, both history and the concentration on Europe have come under scrutiny. Undergraduate students often demand courses for which they can see direct, practical uses and have become much more interested in other parts of the world that are increasingly more and more intertwined with both the United States and Europe and whose economic histories are complicated outgrowths of long colonial periods: for example, India, China, Latin America, and Africa. Given the profound economic impacts after the financial crisis of 2008, students have become more skeptical that studying history can help them cope with an increasingly complicated world. How can studying 17th, 18th or 19th century economies help them understand their world? In addition, as the economy globalizes and students gain interest in the world beyond the US and Europe, why should European economic history still remain a staple?

A course on the economic history of Europe can be created with the intention of providing strong answers to these questions. First, Europe is a rich collection of many different cultures and languages, making it an ideal region to examine the diversity of economic experience over the past 1000 years. The various institutional histories, trade relations, religions, migration patterns, wars, demographics, etc. all have deeply rich and well-documented histories throughout Europe. Second, it was in Europe that the first economies shed the "Malthusian Trap" and increased per capita income in an unprecedented manner. Any study of long-term growth would be enriched by a discussion of the incredible expansion of incomes and the beginning of the global "Great Divergence" at the end of the 18th century; essentially, these are all stories that center on European history. Third, from the 16th through the 19th centuries, western European economies created colonies all over the world. It is becoming more and more apparent that the long-term impacts of these colonial regimes are still playing themselves out in the institutional, political and economic development of much of the world and thus provide insights into the study of developing economies. Lastly, the formation of the United States was undertaken under the influence of European nations (England, Scotland, Ireland, France, Spain, Germany, etc.), so any study of the creation of the United States (its Constitution, early commercial policy, foreign political relations, the pace and nature of its geographical expansion, etc.) must incorporate its early and changing relationships with European economies. No matter the actual design of the course, providing clear motivation will help students work through difficult material and provide the framework for them to make connections to contemporary economic outcomes.

OVERALL ORGANIZATION

Unlike teaching a core theory course, there is no clear, broadly accepted structure for a course on European economic history. One could readily imagine a course strictly organized chronologically or one that was, rather, thematically based. However, even this does not solve the issue: if organized chronologically, it is not at all clear when one would begin, or what might be included or ignored. And if structured thematically, what variations should be included on which themes? This problem, though, is actually an asset: the rich opportunity of teaching a course on European Economic history is the wide latitude one has over its structure and content.

The first step in organizing this course is identifying broad learning objectives based on the topics, concepts and theories you find most interesting and important and what you want the students to take away from the course. For example, if you want the students to leave the course with a strong understanding of the background and development (and dissolution!) of European integration, then the course should be organized very differently from one that stresses the growth and development of financial institutions, or globalization, or long-run growth. What follows is an outline of the way I have approached these decisions. The description that follows is organized around themes and examples of possible sources. Clearly, these are not the only sources or even necessarily the best. However, my aim has been to offer sources that provide a good starting point for creating a syllabus.

I believe that the best way to organize the course is through the use of chapters from books and articles rather than a single text in order to tailor the course to identified objectives.[1] Developing a syllabus which presents this organized framework clearly signals to students the overall motivation for the course. For example, my course concentrates on the development and determinants of long-run growth, emphasizing the transition from an agrarian Malthusian-type economy to the more complicated endogenous growth during the later period of increasing industrialization and international trade. The economic future of both developed and developing nations depends upon the support and maintenance of steady, per-capita long-run economic growth. By emphasizing the central phases and determinants of past growth, students come to realize that a rich source of material is available in the economic history of Europe to deepen their understanding of contemporary economic change. An essential contemporary economic question underscores the motivation for this course: How does long-run growth occur and what can be done to initiate and support it? The consequences of not participating in long-run growth have been devastating for a large part of the world's population. Framing the study of European economic history as the study of successful long-run economic growth provides a clear motivation and organization for the course. Robert Lucas (1988, p. 5) expressed this well by saying,

> Is there some action a government of India could take that would lead the Indian Economy to grow like Indonesia's or Egypt's? If so, what, exactly? If not, what is it about the "nature of India" that makes it so? The consequences for human welfare involved in questions like these are simply staggering: once one starts to think about them, it is hard to think about anything else.

The economic history of Europe is a wonderful laboratory for this inquiry since it was in this area, along with key European colonial areas (for example, United States, Canada and Australia), that per capita income began and continued to increase in an unprecedented manner. In the last several years, a large literature has developed concentrating on answering questions like "Why did Britain become such an early industrial power?" and "Why was the unprecedented growth of per capita incomes after the 18th century centered in Europe?" Capitalizing on this rich, new analysis, students can more easily see the relevance of studying European history.

The process of growth in Europe was not radically discontinuous, as the term "the industrial revolution" might suggest. In order to understand the changes that occurred during more modern growth, one must examine the economic history well before the 19th century. In fact, the structures created in the high middle ages through the 16th century created the context for the increasing changes over the age of exploration and enlightenment. One of the key aspects of teaching European economic history is to motivate the study of older, less familiar histories by linking them to the modern growth process. Since there is not a single, accepted cause of both the timing and location of modern growth, studying the markets for land, labor and marriage in the middle ages, for example, could provide the background for discussing the shift from a Malthusian-type equilibrium of early Europe to the more sophisticated, endogenous growth of the 19th and 20th centuries. It also demonstrates that the process of economic sophistication began far earlier than many students expect. The evidence, for example, of the financial integration of Europe by the beginning of the 18th century is an example of both the early complexity of European markets and the growing needs of international payments during the early "globalization" (Neal, 1990).

MALTHUSIAN ECONOMY

Teaching economic history has a strong similarity to teaching economic development, especially in courses analyzing a region over a very long period. In both types of courses, a predominantly agrarian, Malthusian-type economy is described and the process by which the economy industrializes is explained. The simplicity and power of the Malthusian model can easily seduce students into thinking that nothing at all happened until the major, industrial developments of the last 150 years and care must be taken to show the incremental change that occurred prior to that. In examining the agrarian economy, students should be aware that the development of settled agriculture had mixed welfare effects and that the unfolding of agrarian technology took centuries. A fine, short and provocative piece to demonstrate this to students is "The worst mistake in the history of mankind," by Jared Diamond (1987). This gets the students thinking about agriculture in a new way and is important since most of our students probably have not been around farms, let alone know much about the history of agrarian societies. Diamond sets up the context to introduce the Malthusian framework that provides the theoretical background to examine pre-industrial Europe. While the use of a Malthusian equilibrium is very helpful in explaining the agrarian equilibrium, it is also important to show the students that this era was also a period of incremental change.

Prior to examining the details of European agrarian development, I introduce the Malthusian equilibrium and its implications for demography, technology and growth. An excellent, noncalculus-based description of the model is Weil's text *Economic Growth* (chapter 4, Weil, 2008), as well as chapter 2 of Clark's (2007) *A Farewell to Alms*. Presenting the diagrammatic explanations demonstrates clearly the major features of the model and its implications. Adding the data about European demographic history allows the students to see just how closely the Malthusian model explains much of European demographic history.

After students have a solid understanding of the basic model, they are in a position to tackle the more formal version of the model found in Ashraf and Galor's (2008) "Malthusian population dynamics: Theory and evidence." This presentation clarifies both the assumptions under which this type of model operates and the parameters that determine its conclusions. The paper begins with a sweeping overview of very long-run population dynamics before presenting a simple overlapping-generations model. Placing the Malthusian model within an optimizing framework enables the students to work through the mechanics in a format familiar from their microeconomic theory course and has them carefully work through the model.[2] To end this section, I also assign parts of Malthus' *Essay on Population* (Malthus, 1798), and ask students to track differences between what Malthus actually said and the abstracted models that bear his name. Though this is more an economic history of thought-type assignment, it does require students to look very carefully at the arguments and models and seems to deepen their understanding of the historical context from which they arose.

AGRARIAN ECONOMY STRUCTURE AND CHANGE

After the opening, theoretical section of the course, students are ready to look at the variation and development of the agrarian economy in Europe. This section sets the stage for describing the changes in consumer behavior, trade and economic organization that slowly developed over the centuries so that students see that the transition to the modern, industrial economy was not a sudden, discrete shift; rather, students will come to realize why understanding the historical development is necessary to explain the shift to industrial economies. Because England led this development and so much has been written on England, this country provides a logical starting point of reference.

Explaining the long-run development of labor productivity and foundational changes in agrarian structure through the process of enclosures sets the necessary background to understand the British economy through the 18th century. Among the many options to guide the students through these topics are, for example, Eona Karakacili's (2004) "English agrarian labor productivity rates before the black death: A case study," and classic papers on enclosure by Jane Humphries (1990) and Donald McCloskey (1972). An excellent review of changes since 1500 is provided by Robert Allen's (1999) "Tracking the agricultural revolution in England." In order to examine the changes in worker wages over this period and into the modern period, students can read Gregory Clark's (2005) "The condition of the working class in England, 1209–2004." Transitioning analysis beyond England to greater Europe, chapter 2 in Jan de Vries' (1982) *The Economy of Europe in an Age of Crisis, 1600-1750* provides excellent detail on all the major issues for England as well as for Spain, Denmark, Italy, Eastern Europe, Western Germany, France, and the Low Countries.

SLOW, STEADY CHANGE LEADING TO ENDOGENOUS GROWTH: INSTITUTIONS, TRADE AND FINANCE

Examining agriculture and the markets for land and labor throughout Europe provides the context for students to examine the state and change of technology prior to any major industrial developments, directly challenging the misconception that the agrarian economy had *no* innovation or developing structure. Providing examples of persistent change demonstrates the importance of careful historical study, and prepares students to think about the long-run changes leading to sustained, endogenous growth. An excellent source to begin this section is Joel Mokyr's (1990) *The Lever of Riches*, especially chapters 3 and 4. Also, S. R. Epstein's (1998) "Craft guilds, apprenticeships, and technological change in preindustrial Europe" provides details on the changes brought well before any period that might be deemed the "industrial revolution" and explains the system of "putting out" that characterized the proto-industrial production of goods. In order to explain this system, see Sheilagh Ogilvie's (1996) review chapter "The theories of proto-industrialization" in *European proto-industrialization*. The book also contains specific examples of proto-industrialization throughout Europe. These are only suggestions; the objective is for students to understand that Europe was not in a period of unchanging stasis, even though we can meaningfully discuss a "Malthusian trap."

While discussing these slow and steady changes, the growing sophistication and importance of global trade and finance can be introduced. As with agriculture, these sectors were of increasing importance well before the 19th century. Robert Allen's (2009) *The Industrial Revolution in Global Context* provides an excellent guide to the expanding role of global trade. An earlier working paper, "The British industrial revolution in global perspective: how commerce created the industrial revolution and modern economic growth," demonstrates the specific ways in which British trade created the context for the rapid expansion of production in the 19th century (Allen, 2006). A compelling, if somewhat advanced, piece on the domestic impacts of trade is Kevin O'Rourke and Jeffrey Williamson's (2005), "From Malthus to Ohlin: Trade, industrialization and distribution since 1500." In addition, Ronald Findlay and Kevin O'Rourke's (2007) *Power and Plenty: Trade, War and the World Economy in the Second Millennium* is a text that combines very specific historical detail with an excellent explanation of how international markets led to domestic and international economic growth. Chapters 4 and 5 cover the period 1500–1780, but for a course that really concentrates on a theme of globalization the earlier chapters would provide very good background.

Turning to capital markets and financial development, students are typically surprised to learn of the extent of financial integration by the beginning of the 18th century. Larry Neal has done much of this work. His "How it all began: the monetary and financial architecture of Europe during the first global capital markets, 1648–1815" is an excellent overview of the political and economic changes after the Treaty of Westphalia (Neal, 2000). In addition, chapter 7 in his *The Rise of Financial Capitalism: International Capital Markets in the Age of Reason* shows the extent of early financial integration (Neal, 1990). In versions of the course which stress financial markets, one might use Charles Kindleberger's (1993) classic *A Financial History of Western Europe*, beginning with an overview of the evolution of money, bimetallism and the gold standard, before turning to banking in various western European nations and finishing with public finance and foreign investment.

The preceding course sections (Malthusian Economy, Agrarian Economy Structure and Change, and Slow, Steady Change Leading to Endogenous Growth: Institutions, Trade and Finance) provide students with a good understanding of the economic history of Europe prior to industrialization, essentially covering the period of 1000–1780. Instructors who have the luxury of teaching European economic history in two classes could use this as a natural ending point for the first course. Since it is uncommon to have two courses in European economic history, the remainder of material to be covered extends the examination through to the 19th century and includes themes of the industrialization, demographic transition, and growing income disparities that accompany the long process of endogenous growth. Traditionally, this transition has been called the "industrial revolution;" however, this term confuses students into thinking that the break was discrete and abrupt. And, as noted above, the principal challenge of the course is to demonstrate that change, though slow, was ongoing and not discrete.

UNIFIED GROWTH THEORY, THE DEMOGRAPHIC TRANSITION AND ENDOGENOUS GROWTH

After stressing incremental change, students are well prepared for the transition from a Malthusian equilibrium to an equilibrium that could be better described by endogenous growth. An excellent overview is provided by Oded Galor's (2004) "From stagnation to growth: Unified growth theory." Although the theory is difficult, the first 55 pages are an amazing historical overview of the Malthusian equilibrium and the changes in demography and growth that begin in the late 18th century. The article both serves as a review of the material covered and raises salient issues in thinking about discerning the key variables that contributed to Western Europe's industrial transition. Unified growth theories are really designed to unpack the transition from the Malthusian regime to a more modern growth regime and hence are especially well suited for describing this transition.

Since at this point in the course students are still thinking broadly in a Malthusian framework, they need to be introduced to Europe's demographic transition. Ronald Lee's (2003) "The demographic transition: Three centuries of fundamental change" provides an excellent overview. For a more provocative, Darwinian angle on this issue, you can turn again to Greg Clark's *A Farewell to Alms* and use his "Malthus and Darwin: survival of the richest." Even though it makes sense to focus on the transition, it is very important that students understand that it was not simply the demographic transition that caused the industrialization of Europe. Galor's overview makes this clear, but, as stressed in earlier sections of the course, the long process of industrialization far preceded marked changes of fertility. After discussing the history and theory of the demographic transition, one can turn to specific impacts on broader variables. For example, George Alter and Gregory Clark's (2010) "The demographic transition and human capital" shows the vital part played by the demographic transition, but also the limited ability for the transition to explain the rapid increases in per capita incomes. Because fertility is such an important issue in developing economies today, students need to understand that the economic factors that generate increasing development and industrialization also tend to lower fertility rates. A number of articles exist that cover increasing opportunity costs for women, decreased infant mortality, reductions in opportunity for child labor, increases in rearing-costs (for example, education), and alternative sources of old-age security.

In order to stress the importance of path dependency of technical change, I like to use a Romer-type endogenous growth model. A good starting point is Charles Jones' (2002) book *Introduction to Economic Growth*, focusing on chapter 5. Although I don't assign it, I do use the explanation of the "New Growth Theory" in chapter 3 of David Romer's (2005) *Advanced Macroeconomics* text. Once these have been introduced, I proceed through Michael Kremer's "Population growth and technological change: One million B.C. to 1990." (It's fun to use for the title alone!)

Now that students begin to understand that growth is occurring under a new paradigm, they begin to understand the importance of structural changes that have already been covered in the course. To assist students in applying this new understanding to Europe, an excellent overview of the issues is provided by Joel Mokyr and Hans-Joachim Voth's (2010) "Understanding growth in Europe, 1700–1870: Theory and evidence." A number of interesting themes naturally follow, including the divergence in outcomes, technology, human capital and culture, and trade and colonial expansion.

THE GREAT DIVERGENCE

At this point in the course it has been established that the process of growth led to unprecedented disparities in national incomes. This process was occurring in Europe from very early on. In order to describe the changes in long-run outcomes, I first outline the global changes in income disparities (Pritchett, 1997) and then describe the growing divergence in wages and prices in Europe (Allen, 2001). Explaining this dramatic increase in inequality has occupied much research and one major theme has been the impact of culture on development. Gregory Clark's discussion of global divergence from his *A Farewell to Alms* (chapter 16) opens the way to discussing culture and human capital, while the work of David Landes (1990 and 1999) and Joel Mokyr (1990 and 2010) deepen and extend this approach. An article that can be used as theoretical background is Mattias Doepke and Fabrizio Zilibotti, "Occupational choice and the spirit of capitalism." They present a model of the implications of the growth of the middle class as the economy shifted from agriculture and the power of the landed class to industry and the power of "shopkeepers."

Clearly, one of the accelerants of the industrial policy and the growing inequality was the uneven development of technology. Besides Joel Mokyr's (1990) *The Lever of Riches*, his contribution to the *Handbook of Economic Growth*, "Long-term economic growth and the history of technology" (Mokyr, 2004), is an excellent overview. In addition to the growing divergence in incomes and the steady rise of technological progress, this section of the course should address the increasing importance of trade, along with the impacts of European colonization on the rest of the world. European exploration and colonialism has profoundly affected the developing world. Understanding the history of this process is important in order for students to begin to fully comprehend the challenges facing developing societies, especially in Africa. While in lectures I discuss colonization more broadly, I organize this section around two strands in the literature. One is the work by Stanley Engerman and Kenneth Sokoloff (2002), as in their "Factor endowments, institutions and differential paths of growth among New World economies." They emphasize the initial endowment of the colonial lands and the subsequent institutional development that grew out of it. The other strand includes research by Daron Acemoglu, Simon Johnson and James Robinson, including "The role of institutions in growth and development," (Acemoglu et al., 2010) and "Reversal of fortune: Geography and institutions in the making of the modern world income distribution" (Acemoglu et al., 2002). These papers provide a very good structure around which to organize a section on colonialism. Concerning the growth and expansion of trade, I would return to Findlay and O'Rourke's (2007) *Power and Plenty*, this time focusing on chapters 6 and 7 which provide an introduction to any one of many themes concerning trade.

CONCLUSION

Although late 19th and 20th century Europe is fascinating, it demands a standalone course of its own. Trying to cover the long history of Europe from 1300 all the way until 2000 is simply too much. Building on the course outlined above, another could examine the growth and development of the nation states in the late 19th century, leading to World War I and the turbulent inter-war period, and the split of Europe after 1945 into the Warsaw Pact, NATO and the European Economic Community, along with the collapse of the colonial empires. But, indeed, this would be an entirely different course with a very different intention and emphasis.

The course I have outlined focuses on the earlier period, with a main objective of revealing the process of long-run economic development. In some ways, the course is a careful analysis of the transition from a Malthusian-type economy to a modern, industrial economy. In examining this transition, the importance of closely studying the history of growth demonstrates the limits of the theory and, actually, enables students to understand both the theory and the historical process better. Students should leave the course with a strong sense of why studying both Europe and economic history is useful and, I would hope, interesting.

NOTES

1.   This is not to say that very good overviews of global and European economic history are unavailable; from the broad and classic Cameron and Neal, *A Concise Economic History of the World* to the recently published Allen, *The Industrial Revolution in Global Context* or de Vries, *The Industrious Revolution*, texts are available that can provide very good overall frameworks for a course. A fun text to supplement the different sections of the course is Clark's *A Farewell to Alms*. Clark conducted some of the seminal work on early modern wages and living standards and his book on the long-run development of Europe is grounded in this scholarship. The book's anthropological data and Darwinian perspective is not without controversy, so it can serve as a stimulating text providing a counterbalance for other readings.
2.   Clearly, if students have not had intermediate microeconomics, then this article could not be used. I have found, though, that requiring microeconomic theory really extends the number of articles that can be covered and deepens the manner in which theory can be used to explain the historical processes.

REFERENCES

Acemoglu, D. and J. Robinson (2010), "The role of institutions in growth and development", *Review of Economics and Institutions*, **1**(2), 1–33.

Acemoglu, D., S. Johnson, and J. Robinson (2002), "Reversal of fortune: Geography and institutions in the making of the modern world income distribution", *Quarterly Journal of Economics*, **117**, 1231–94.

Allen, R. (1999), "Tracking the agricultural revolution in England", *Economic History Review*, **LII** (2), 209–35.

Allen, R. (2001), "The great divergence in European wages and prices from the Middle Ages to the First World War", *Explorations in Economic History*, **38**, 411–47.

Allen, R. (2006), "The British industrial revolution in global perspective: How commerce created the industrial revolution and modern economic growth", Working Paper.

Allen, R. (2009), *The Industrial Revolution in Global Context*, New York: Oxford University Press.

Alter, G. and G. Clark (2010), "The demographic transition and human capital", in S. Broadberry and K. O'Rourke (eds), *The Cambridge Economic History of Modern Europe, 1700–1870*, New York: Cambridge University Press, pp. 7–42.

Ashraf, Q. and O. Galor (2008), "Malthusian population dynamics: Theory and evidence", Working Paper 2008-6, Department of Economics, Brown University.

Cameron, R. and L. Neal (2003), *A Concise Economic History of the World: From Paleolithic Times to the Present*, Oxford: Oxford University Press.

Clark, G. (2005), "The condition of the working class in England, 1209–2004", *Journal of Political Economy*, **113** (61), 1307–40.

Clark, G. (2007), *A Farewell to Alms*, Princeton, NJ: Princeton University Press.

de Vries, J. (1982), *The Economy of Europe in an Age of Crisis, 1600–1750*, New York: Cambridge University Press.

de Vries, J. (2008), *The Industrious Revolution*, Cambridge, UK and New York: Cambridge University Press.

Diamond, J. (1987), "The worst mistake in the history of the human race", *Discover Magazine*, (May), 64–6.

Doepke, M. and F. Zilibotti (2008), "Occupational choice and the spirit of capitalism", *The Quarterly Journal of Economics*, **123** (2), 747–93.

Engerman, S. and K. Sokoloff (2002), "Factor endowments, institutions and differential paths of growth among New World economies", NBER Working Paper 9259.

Epstein, S. R. (1998), "Craft guilds, apprenticeships, and technological change in preindustrial Europe", *Journal of Economic History*, **58** (3), 684–713.

Findlay, R. and K. O'Rourke (2007), *Power and Plenty: Trade, War, and the World Economy in the Second Millennium*, Princeton, NJ: Princeton University Press.

Galor, O. (2004), "From stagnation to growth: Unified growth theory", in P. Aghion and S. Durlauf (eds), *Handbook of Economic Growth*, Amsterdam: Elsevier, pp. 172–275.

Humphries, J. (1990), "Enclosures, common rights and women: The proletarianization of families in the late eighteenth and early nineteenth centuries", *Journal of Economic History*, **50** (1), 17–42.

Jones, C. (2002), *Introduction to Economic Growth*, New York: Norton.

Karakacili, E. (2004), "English agrarian labor productivity rates before the black death: A case study", *Journal of Economic History*, **64** (2), 24–60.

Kindleberger, C. (1993), *A Financial History of the Western World*, Oxford: Oxford University Press.

Kremer, M. (1993), "Population growth and technological change: One million B.C. to 1990", *The Quarterly Journal of Economics*, **108** (3), 681–716.

Landes, D. (1990), "Why are we so rich and they so poor?", *American Economic Review*, **80** (2), 1–13.

Landes, D. (1999), *The Wealth and Poverty of Nations: Why are Some so Rich and Some so Poor*, New York: Norton.

Lee, R. (2003), "The demographic transition: Three centuries of fundamental change", *The Journal of Economic Perspectives*, **17** (4), 167–90.

Lucas, R. (1988), "On the mechanics of economic development," *Journal of Monetary Economics*, **22**, 3–42.

Malthus, Thomas (1798), *An Essay on the Principle of Population as it Affects the Future Improvement of Society with Remarks on the Speculations of Mr. Godwin, M. Condorcet, and Other Writers*, London: Printed for J. Johnson in St. Paul's Church-Yard.

McCloskey, D. N. (1972), "The enclosure of open fields: Preface to a study of its impact on the efficiency of English agriculture in the eighteenth century", *Journal of Economic History*, **32** (1), 15–35.

Mokyr, J. (1990), *The Lever of Riches*, New York: Oxford University Press.

Mokyr, J. (2004), "Long-term economic growth and the history of technology", in P. Aghion and S. Durlauf (eds), *Handbook of Economic Growth*, Amsterdam: Elsevier, pp. 1113–80.

Mokyr, J. (2010), *The Enlightened Economy: An Economic History of Britain, 1700–1850*, New Haven, CT: Yale University Press.

Mokyr, J. and H. Voth (2010), "Understanding growth in Europe, 1700–1870: Theory and evidence", in S. Broadberry and K. O'Rourke (eds), *The Cambridge Economic History of Modern Europe, 1700–1870*, New York: Cambridge University Press, pp. 7–42.

Neal, L. (1990), *The Rise of Financial Capitalism: International Capital Markets in the Age of Reason*, New York: Cambridge University Press.

Neal, L. (2000), "How it all began: The monetary and financial architecture of Europe during the first global capital markets", *Financial History Review*, 117–40.

Ogilvie, S. (1996), "The theories of proto-industrialization", in S. Ogilvie and M. Cerman (eds), *European Proto-industrialization*, New York: Cambridge University Press, pp. 1–11.

O'Rourke, K. and J. Williamson (2005), "From Malthus to Ohlin: Trade, industrialization and distribution since 1500", *Journal of Economic Growth*, **10**, 5–34.

Pritchett, L. (1997), "Divergence, big time", *The Journal of Economic Perspectives*, **11** (3), 3–17.

Romer, D. (2005), *Advanced Macroeconomics*, Boston, MA: McGraw-Hill.

Weil, D. (2008), *Economic Growth*, New York: Addison-Wesley.

52 Why and how to teach the history of economic thought: economics as historically produced knowledge[1]

Avi J. Cohen and Ross B. Emmett

Practical men, who believe themselves to be quite exempt from any intellectual influences, are usually the slaves of some defunct economist. (John Maynard Keynes, 1936, p. 383)

HISTORY OF HISTORY OF ECONOMIC THOUGHT COURSES

From World War I until the 1960s, the core undergraduate and graduate economics curricula included micro and macro theory, statistics *and one or two courses in the history of economic thought!* The history of economic thought (HET) was considered "as simply an historical extension of theory, and practitioners as simply a special kind of theorist with a long time horizon" (Goodwin, 2008). The core journals (including the *American Economic Review, Journal of Political Economy, Quarterly Journal of Economics, Economic Journal*) regularly published articles on HET. George Stigler's ([1941] 1994) doctoral dissertation was all history of economic thought: the only Nobel Prize winner with that distinction.

By the 1960s, history of economic thought courses were being removed from the core curricula to the periphery of optional courses. Economics departments were no longer training historians of economics, and had no reason to hire them. Optional HET courses withered over time with the retirement of older practitioners. Mainstream journals and societies became uninterested in, and disparaging of, HET.[2]

Mark Blaug (2001, p. 145) began his *Journal of Economic Perspectives* article, "No History of Ideas Please, We're Economists," with "It is no secret that the study of the history of economic thought is held in low esteem by mainstream economists and sometimes openly disparaged as a type of antiquarianism." Most economists today believe that, like the natural sciences, economics progresses in an evolutionary fashion, where wrong ideas are weeded out through hypothesis testing. It follows that current textbooks and refereed journals contain all accumulated truths. That leaves the study of the history of economic thought as an antiquarian interest in what Pigou called "the wrong opinions of dead men" (and they were mostly men).[3] Graduate students often have similar views, doubting the relevance of HET for their careers beyond the cachet of sounding educated by quoting Adam Smith.

Paradoxically, while many *courses* in the history of economic thought have disappeared, *research* in the field is enjoying a renaissance.[4] In the late 1960s, practitioners in exile regrouped and created a sub-field, complete with specialized journals, professional societies and conferences. The *History of Political Economy* (HOPE) launched in 1969, and was followed by the *Journal of the History of Economic Thought* (JHET), the *European Journal of the History of Economic Thought* (EJHET) and others.[5] The History of Economics Society formed in 1974, the European Society for the History of Economics in 1995 and there are now active societies with regular conferences in North America, throughout Europe, in Australia and Japan (going back to 1950).

Young scholars around the world, but especially in Europe, have revitalized the field and expanded its scope, resulting in a rich literature for use in History of Economic Thought courses. And the fact that the 2008 financial crisis took most economists by surprise has revived interest in past thinkers (for example, Keynes, Hayek, Hyman Minsky) who, to varying degrees, previously had been relegated to antiquarian status. Perhaps there were some valuable insights from defunct economists that didn't make it into the current literature, as well as other benefits from studying history![6]

Undergraduates are often very curious about economists they have only heard about in passing – Adam Smith, Karl Marx, John Maynard Keynes. If you are lucky enough to be teaching the history of economic thought, you can motivate the course by challenging the dominant misconceptions about HET and engaging your students in an active research field. You will help students learn how to think (and write) more critically and analytically about the economics they have learned in other courses and about the applicability of the history of economic thought to the current economic analysis of real-world issues.

THE EXPANDING SCOPE OF THE HISTORY OF ECONOMIC THOUGHT

Online Resources

If you are about to create or refresh an undergraduate history of economic thought course, there are valuable online resources to help you. Among them, the (left-leaning) New School for Social Research has long maintained a History of Economic Thought website[7] that includes concise descriptions of differing schools of thought in economics, essays and surveys on major themes and controversies, and web links to primary and secondary resources, societies, journals and working papers. An excellent online source of primary texts is the McMaster University Archive for the History of Economic Thought.[8] It contains hundreds of complete texts by important authors, giving your students easy and free access. The (right-leaning) Liberty Fund has an online library[9] with hundreds of original texts and useful historical timelines, including the complete works of Adam Smith and Karl Marx's *Capital*. The Economics Network of the UK's Higher Education Academy has a web page[10] cataloguing books and textbooks on the history of economic thought. *The New Palgrave Dictionary of Economics Online* (Durlauf and Blume, 2008) is an excellent first stop for information about authors and topics, written by subject experts. The online availability of old articles through JSTOR[11] has been invaluable. Finally, the recently created Center for the History of Political Economy (CHOPE) at Duke University (also the home of the journal HOPE) has a new website[12] that includes resources for historians of economics. There are links to journals, societies, online archives, blogs and, most importantly for the instructor, teaching resources, including a large set of HET course outlines and assignments from instructors all over the world. Those outlines are a good place to start when constructing a new course.

Core Content for a One-semester Course

The wealth of resources available may make developing a course on the history of economic thought seem like an overwhelming task. In this section we offer a model of the typical core content of a one-semester survey course and a brief discussion of new directions.

Begin by motivating the importance of studying the history of economics – good options include Boulding (1971), Vaughn (1993), Blaug (2001), and Heilbroner (1979).[13] The course will cover three main schools of thought. Classical political economy (or more broadly, Enlightenment political economy) consists of the works of the French Physiocrats, A. R. J. Turgot, Adam Smith, David Ricardo, T. Robert Malthus, John Stuart Mill, Jean-Baptist Say, Nassau Senior and Karl Marx. The core authors that most instructors include are Smith, Ricardo and Marx.

The marginal revolution of the 1870s heralds the rise of the neoclassical school. The core authors are the revolutionaries – William Stanley Jevons, Leon Walras, Carl Menger – as well as Alfred Marshall, who codified the developing neoclassical approach in his *Principles of Economics*, still the model for today's introductory textbooks. Possible secondary additions are precursors of the neoclassical school (Fernando Galiani, Jules Dupuit, Augustin Cournot, Hermann Gossen) and second-generation neoclassicals like Vilfredo Pareto, Francis Y. Edgeworth, Knut Wicksell, Eugen von Böhm-Bawerk, J. B. Clark, Irving Fisher and Frank Knight.

The third school is the Keynesians, although it is rare to find courses which go beyond the works of Keynes alone. Reading Keynes is an eye-opener for most students, as Keynes's own ideas, which are being rediscovered after the 2008 financial crisis and the Great Recession, differ significantly from what has been taught (beginning with the IS-LM model) over the years as "Keynesian economics."[14]

Beyond the core, there are common clusters of authors that individual instructors cover, depending on their personal interests: ancient and medieval economic thought, Mercantilism, early macro/monetary thought, American Institutionalism (including Thorstein Veblen), the Chicago School, post-Keynesianism, development economics, and Austrian economics (including Hayek). The online resources (described above) or the textbooks (described below) identify authors associated with these topics.

New Directions for the History of Economic Thought

Over the last 30 years, research in the history of economic thought has expanded far beyond this "core plus" model of a traditional HET survey course. Adding some of this new scholarship to the traditional HET survey course helps students link the relevancy of economic thought to more current economic discussions. While time constraints limit coverage of the expanded scope and methods of HET, what follows is a sampling of this new work which may also be used to motivate students.

A good place to start is the yearly book supplement to HOPE, which draws together work from a conference held each year around an emerging topic. Examples include: *History of Econometrics*; *Religious Belief and Political Economy*; *Biography and Autobiography in the History of Economics*; *Consumer Theory in the 20th Century*; *Role of Government in the History of Economic Thought*; *The Rise, Fall and Strange Persistence of the IS-LM Model*; *History of Game Theory*; *Interactions between Economics and National Security*. Each book begins with an overview of the issues and papers, providing important background for both instructors and students. A complete listing of HOPE conferences appears on the CHOPE website.

The "Retrospectives" feature in most issues of the *Journal of Economic Perspectives* explores some current area of research in the history of economic thought, and is easily accessible to undergraduates. See, for example, the history of Engel curves in the Winter 2010 issue (Chai and Moneta, 2010).

The 21st century has seen significant growth in work on more recent economics. The HISRECO (History of Recent Economics) conferences focus on the ongoing work of post-World War II economics (including living economists), using historical methods of investigation that analyze the present as history. "History of Recent Economics" is not so much about a particular historical period, as it is about using historical methods to examine ongoing economics. HISRECO papers[15] have addressed the diffusion of rational choice theory in explanations of war, neo-liberal economists' analysis of trade unions, the role of the Chicago School in constructing a medical marketplace, the history of the martingale approach in modern finance, visual imagery in post-war economics textbooks and interactions between the cold war, dynamic programming and economics.

Historians of economics are using methods of other historians of science, and turning their attention to the new competing research programs in economics, including game theory, behavioral economics, experimental economics, evolutionary economics, complex adaptive systems theory, neuroeconomics, market design theory, the subjective well-being approach, and the capability approach.[16] This HET work analyzing current economics may be especially useful for engaging students *not only* in HET courses, *but also in other economics courses*, providing context and awareness of how theories are developing in the present, just as they did in the past.

THE RELEVANCE AND VALUE OF THE HISTORY OF ECONOMIC THOUGHT TO YOUR STUDENTS

What can your students take away from a history of economic thought course? The answers to this key question provide the motivation – the *why* – for teaching the history of economic thought. Since it is increasingly common to explicitly state learning objectives on course syllabi, we decided to organize the answers as a list of possible learning objectives, grouped into categories. No survey course can accomplish all of these objectives, but the intellectual coherence of a HET course will depend on selecting a few (at least one from each category) and arranging readings (and assignments) to enable students to meet the objectives. A well-designed HET course is much more than a collection of (dead men's) ideas. It is a focused roadmap leading students to learn how to think and practice like a historian of economics, begin wrestling with big questions in the field, and become more critically aware of the origins, strengths and limitations of economics.

The specific objectives divide into four content categories: taxonomy, historical context, theoretical trajectories and critical assessment.[17] The individual objectives listed in each category overlap considerably, as this sampling was generated by a number of instructors teaching HET courses, and provides a broad perspective of how to support the four categories.[18] Imagine each learning objective following from the sentence "After completing this course, students should be able to:"

Taxonomy

Taxonomy is the first step in acquiring historical sensibilities. Students need to learn the main ideas of each author, and then the shared characteristics of the larger "school" in which the author is situated. Examples of taxonomic learning objectives include:

- Engage with primary texts to get a feel for the author's own voice, and form an opinion about the readings.
- Identify the main ideas of classical political economy, neoclassical economics and Keynesian economics.
- Identify the major themes of European economic thought prior to Adam Smith, particularly of Mercantilism.
- Identify the major ideas associated with each school or author studied, and thereby comprehend the origins of contemporary theory.

Historical Context

Once students have a sense of individual authors and schools, they can start examining the interaction between economic ideas and their historical context – how events and historical context shape the development of ideas, and how ideas affect history and events. Specific objectives that help motivate this historical context include:

- Place economic ideas in the context of the time in which they developed.
- Give examples of how events shape economic ideas, and how economic ideas shape events.
- Explain the influence of developments in natural sciences, mathematics and other social sciences on the development of economics, and vice versa.
- Illustrate how changing historical circumstances have affected the evolution of the scope and methods of economic analysis.
- Understand the diversity of economic thinking and how ideas that emerged at any point in the past were a product of a swirling array of forces, including: the actual economy, social interests at work in the economy, prevailing views on what constituted science, prevailing views on justice and fairness, dominant ideas in the natural and other social sciences, available tools/techniques and individual personality.

Theoretical Trajectories

Historical analysis can then be extended to examine how economic ideas and schools of thought develop over longer time frames. What are the characteristics of the broad trajectories of ideas, theories and schools of thought? Note that "trajectory" does *not* necessarily mean progress, just a long-run pattern of development and change. Here are some theoretical trajectories learning objectives:

- Appreciate that most modern ideas have long histories, and that there is "little new under the sun."
- Evaluate similarities and differences across the schools/paradigms/theoretical frameworks of classical political economy, neoclassical economics and Keynesian economics.
- Distinguish between the "surplus" and "exchange" interpretations of the history of classical political economy, with particular reference to the: theories of value, distribution and growth; theories of prices and markets, for both domestic and international exchanges.
- See where the economic ideas we currently study came from.
- Explain how an orthodoxy – a set of ideas that define the "field of economics" – emerges and evolves.
- Trace how the scope of what is considered an economic question, and the methods of those who explore economic questions, have evolved.
- Explain how distinctions between *orthodox* versus *heterodox* economics ideas are determined and defined.
- Explain how and why the field of economics became professionalized, and how that professionalization affected the subsequent evolution of economic ideas.
- Chronicle the ways in which economics has transformed over the past centuries from a largely verbal discipline studying human agency in commercial settings to a mathematical discipline incorporating instruments (such as statistics and laboratory practices) from the scientific toolbox.
- Understand why economists do "economics" in the way that they do today – why some possibilities were chosen and others rejected.

Critical Assessment

The ultimate objective of exposing students to the history of economic thought is to develop their ability to critically assess the strengths and weaknesses of economic ideas, both in the past and in the present. In wrestling with "big think" intellectual questions about the way in which economic knowledge is produced and develops, students should evaluate competing answers to those questions, and begin to form their own positions.[19] Examples of critical assessment learning objectives include:

- Use the ideas and history of pre-market societies to assess the assumption of self-interest as a necessary organizing principle of economic activity.
- Assess the extent to which there has been *continuity or discontinuity* in the move from classical political economy to neoclassical economics to Keynesian economics.
- Appraise the distinction between classical political economic and neoclassical economics, explaining why some scholars de-emphasize the distinction altogether, while others regard it as a fundamental shift in the character of economic theorizing.

- Use differences across schools/paradigms/theoretical frameworks to think critically about the underlying assumptions and focus of economics learned in other courses.
- Assess whether the theoretical trajectories drawn in the course represents "progress" in economics.
- Evaluate the ways in which the evolution of economic thought has provided a progressively more, or less, rich understanding of the human condition.
- Recognize that many theories are short-lived and often reflect the concerns of a particular time period, thereby developing a critical understanding of contemporary theory.
- Begin to see that the economics of intermediate micro and macro textbooks is just as much a product of a swirling array of forces as the theories of the past, and current theories too may pass.
- Assess the gains and losses from the transformation of the scope and methods of economics from a largely verbal discipline studying human agency in commercial settings to a mathematical discipline incorporating instruments (such as statistics and laboratory practices) from the scientific toolbox.
- Historically assess the merits and limitations of contemporary economics in addressing major economic and social questions.
- Assess to what extent the economics we do today is intellectually continuous with, and represents a necessary development of, the political economy of the classical authors.
- Evaluate the intellectual strengths and weaknesses of current "orthodox" economic theory in relation to alternative ways of formulating the questions and methods of economic science.

The inclusion of at least one objective from each of these categories of taxonomy, historical context, theoretical trajectories and critical assessment will provide a basis for demonstrating the relevance and value of the history of economic thought to students.

TEACHING GOALS AND TEACHING CHALLENGES

The four categories of learning objectives articulate *content and analytical goals* for teaching the history of economic thought. However, *two teaching* goals complement this approach to teaching HET – exposing students to multidisciplinary scholarship and improving their reading and writing skills. These teaching goals also generate important teaching challenges you will need to confront to make your course successful.

Multidisciplinary Scholarship

A history of economic thought course is likely to be the most multidisciplinary course in the economics curriculum. While economists place a relatively low value on multidisciplinarity, other academics can be more welcoming of such efforts, and many undergraduate institutions with a liberal arts focus will place a high value on a HET course. In small liberal arts colleges, multidisciplinarity is a core value, and in most schools those who teach a HET course may garner institutional rewards for serving non-majors.

To attract students, especially outside of economics, the history of economic thought can be integrated into courses other than a traditional survey course. In the course outlines on the CHOPE website, you will find courses with the titles "Economics in the Bloomsbury Group," "The Uses of Economics," "Contemporary Economics in Historical Perspective," "The Philosophy and Methodology of Economics," "Freedom and Markets: The Clash of Economic Ideas," "Re-Covering the Keynesian Revolution," "Seminar on the Theoretical Origins of Capitalism as a Moral System" and "Economic Science Studies." While such specialized courses are often a luxury most institutions cannot afford, recognize that their possibility provides avenues for greater student engagement than a survey course.

In teaching the history of economic thought, instructors should also be aware that the ideas of past economists are taught across the university, not just in the economics department. English departments often have courses in which readings from Smith, Ricardo, Malthus and Senior are teamed with the reading of the industrial novels of Charles Dickens and Elizabeth Gaskell and the social criticism of Robert Owen, John Ruskin, William Morris or George Bernard Shaw. Ronald Coase's work features more prominently in law schools than in economics courses, and can often be found in courses in communications theory or organizational management. Karl Marx's work (although perhaps not *Capital*) is often taught as part of courses in the humanities, social theory, philosophy, and cultural studies. Business school courses on entrepreneurship and innovation are more likely than economics courses to introduce students to Frank H. Knight, Joseph Schumpeter and Israel Kirzner. And your students are far more likely to encounter pre-Smithian approaches to economics in courses in the classics, early modern European history, or even religious studies, than in their economics courses.

Students in a history of economic thought course may have encountered economic ideas prior to entering the course, so it is important to reflect upon the range of ideas they have encountered, and the relevance of those ideas to the students' economics education. Correspondingly, what they learn in a HET course can inform and enrich what they learn in history, political science, psychology or philosophy courses. These overlaps and interactions of ideas make for a richer learning experience. Do you remember the thrill as an undergraduate when readings and ideas in disparate courses intersected?

Reading and Writing Instruction

The AEA report on "The Status and Prospects of the Economics Major" (Siegfried et. al. 1991) suggests integrating the *writing across the curriculum* approach into the teaching of economics. A history of economic thought course is ideally suited for this purpose. All of the learning objectives for a HET course are well-suited to assignments involving careful reading and writing, with a constantly rising value of writing in moving from taxonomy to historical context, to theoretical trajectories, culminating in critical analysis.[20] There is much controversy among historians of economics, so students can authentically and safely argue many different points of view in trying to figure out their own thoughts about the core issues. It is possible to structure a HET course as a set of debates, requiring the students to argue a position and address counterarguments: classical political economy versus Mercantilism; neoclassical economics versus classical (or Marx or Institutionalism); Keynes versus Chicago (or Hayek); continuity versus discontinuity in the history of economics. Such debates, especially around macroeconomic topics, have direct policy relevance to contemporary policy debates.

Cohen and Spencer (1993) report on the costs and benefits of restructuring a history of economic thought course to a writing-intensive format, and provide enough information for instructors to experiment with such a restructuring. That course was explicitly restructured around the primary objective of getting students thinking analytically and making arguments. The authors provide critical advice on how to reduce the frustration of having to mark badly written student papers. The CHOPE website also contains paper topics and other writing assignments that can serve as starting points to develop assignments for achieving specific learning objectives.

Teaching Challenges

The two biggest challenges in teaching a history of economic thought course are time constraints and selecting appropriate, accessible readings.

It is impossible to do justice to the full range of authors – from Aristotle to Keynes, let alone recent economists – in a one-semester survey course. It is *not* advisable to "cover the literature" on the grounds that students should at least "get exposed" to each author. Breadth of coverage without depth will make for a boring course. To give students a feel for the intellectual excitement of the field, use fewer authors combined with more discussion of big issues. HET courses which are smaller can be organized as seminars, with much class discussion as students wrestle with the issues. This further constrains the amount of material that can be covered, but will make for a better course. The collected course outlines on the CHOPE website provide a sense of the range of authors and topics that other instructors have found "doable."

Textbooks and reading materials provide the other major challenge, especially for first-time instructors who may be tempted to organize the course around a textbook. While textbooks have the advantage of providing structure, they can take the life out of a subject. Who, in their leisure time, chooses to read a textbook for pleasure? Textbooks are designed to give an "objective" account of a field – or at least the textbook author's account – which can drain the controversy and excitement of multiple voices from the subject. Exposing students to the richness of the history of economics, and achieving the four learning objective categories, requires the use of primary and secondary sources.

Most, though not all, courses described on the CHOPE website assign a textbook, but do so in conjunction with supplemental readings. There are many good textbooks available, but we draw the reader's attention to two in particular.

Robert Heilbroner's (1999) *The Worldly Philosophers: The Lives, Times, and Ideas of the Great Economic Thinkers* is among the best-selling economics texts of all time, along with Samuelson's *Economics*. More economists point to this book as the reason they were attracted to study the discipline than to all other books combined. Heilbroner is a brilliant storyteller, and engages the reader by placing authors in the context of their historical times. Even though the book has not been revised since 1999 (Heilbroner died in 2005), it is worth looking at. We both have used this book in our courses with great success.

Roger Backhouse, one of the pre-eminent historians of economics, also does a good job of placing authors and ideas in context in *The Ordinary Business of Life: A History of Economics from the Ancient World to the Twenty-First Century* (2004). While not as captivating as Heilbroner (who is?), Backhouse is stronger on the economic content and this book has the advantage of taking the history of economics right up to the present.

Other excellent textbooks place authors in historical context, so compare before you make a decision.

There are also published collections that conveniently collect primary and secondary readings. These include general collections of many authors' works (akin to greatest hits in the history of economic thought) like Medema and Samuels (2003), Heilbroner (1996), as well as collections of key works by particular authors such as Smith (Heilbroner, 1986) and Marx (Tucker, 1978). Many primary texts are online in the resources listed earlier, and the secondary literature appears both in the economics (and history of economics) journals and as book chapters. All textbooks contain suggestions for further reading; Blaug's (1997) annotated bibliographies at the end of each chapter are particularly good. The course outlines on the CHOPE website will acquaint you with many of these primary and secondary texts.

John Cunningham Wood edited two book series published by Croom Helm and Routledge between 1982 and 2006 entitled *Critical Assessments of Leading Economists* and *Critical Assessments of Contemporary Economists*. Each multi-volume collection assembles secondary literature that developed around particular authors – Smith, Ricardo, Malthus, Marshall, etc. Mark Blaug edited a similar 45-volume series for Edward Elgar in 1991 called *Pioneers in Economics*, with secondary literature organized by particular authors. Samuels, Biddle and Davis (2003) is an excellent collection of articles from experts analyzing the history of economic thought, the history of the discipline of economics, and the historiography of HET.

Finally, if you have *any* questions about the history of economic thought – about authors, texts, assignment ideas, controversies, current research – you should subscribe to the free SHOE (Societies for the History of Economics) listserv[21] which is supported by professional history of economic thought societies around the world, and to which most historians of economics subscribe. As members of a lively but underrepresented field of economics, historians of economics are eager to respond to questions, especially to help instructors and scholars who are furthering the cause of the history of economics.

ECONOMICS AS HISTORICALLY PRODUCED KNOWLEDGE

While the ideas of past economists do not change, our knowledge of those ideas does change through archival research, analysis and historical contextualization. Understanding how ideas develop, both in the past and the present, will make for better, more self-aware, economists and citizens.

The history of economic thought, whose subject matter admittedly includes the ideas of dead men, is actually about understanding the forces that produce economic knowledge. This chapter opened with a quote from Keynes which highlighted the impact of economic ideas on events. Of at least equal importance is the impact of events, and historical context, on ideas. While the internal development of economic ideas is a crucial part of the production of economic knowledge, a paraphrase of Keynes (1936, p. 383) describes additional insights economics students can gain from a course in the history of economic thought:

> Practical *economists*, who believe themselves to be quite exempt from any intellectual influences, are usually the slaves of the historical mix of ideas, techniques, events, institutions and incentives existing at the time they produce economic knowledge.

History matters, not only for understanding the past, but also the present, from which the future of economics, and its impact on the world, emerges.

NOTES

1. We received helpful suggestions from Bruce Caldwell, Neil de Marchi, Evelyn Forget, Craufurd Goodwin, Kevin Hoover, Tiago Mata, Teresa Tomas Rangil and other participants at the Center for the History of Political Economy Workshop at Duke University.
2. See Goodwin (2008) for the complete – and fascinating – history. The reasons for this fall from grace is a current subject of study for historians of economics. The reasons are varied, but include the economics profession's turn to the natural sciences as a disciplinary model – Philip Mirowski (1989) calls it "physics envy" – and the study of the history of those sciences had been pushed to history or history of science departments. Also, the pluralism of interwar approaches to economics gave way to the "neo-classical synthesis" – as Paul Samuelson (1955) called it – a more homogeneous, confident, emerging orthodoxy, less interested in theoretical alternatives, past or present. The 21st century splintering of that synthesis (see below) is connected to the renaissance in history of economic thought research.
3. The "dead men" quote is attributed to Pigou by Keynes (Moggridge 1992, p. xvi). For the female exceptions (or exceptional females), see Dimand, Dimand and Forget (2000).
4. See Weintraub (2002) for competing assessments of the future of the history of economics.
5. Other HET journals include: *History of Economics Review*, *History of Economic Ideas*, *The History of Economic Thought* and *Oeconomia*.
6. The 2008 financial crisis even produced an HET rap video – "Fear the Boom and Bust" – starring Keynes and Hayek (http://econstories.tv/2010/06/22/fear-the-boom-and-bust/ (accessed 4 April 2011).
7. http://www.newschool.edu/nssr/het (accessed 4 April 2011).
8. http://socserv.mcmaster.ca/econ/ugcm/3ll3/ (accessed 4 April 2011).
9. http://oll.libertyfund.org/ Accessed 4/4/2011 (accessed 4 April 2011).
10. http://www.economicsnetwork.ac.uk/books/HistoryofEconomic.htm (accessed 4 April 2011).
11. www.jstor.org (accessed 4 April 2011).
12. http://econ.duke.edu/HOPE/CENTER/home (accessed 4 April 2011).
13. See Blaug (1991b) for a collection of similar articles. Although aimed at students and others with more economic knowledge, Weintraub (1999) is an excellent introduction to different approaches to the history of economics, and is effective in getting students to start thinking like an historian. Weintraub (1999, pp. 139–40) begins with "The modern economist looks at a textbook history of nineteenth century economics and wonders what, for the twentieth century, will correspond to the chapter titles of 'Malthus', 'Ricardo', 'The Mills', 'Marx', and 'The Rise of Marginalism'. Will Monetarism survive editing? Will Game Theory rate its own section? Will Keynes be a hero or goat? Economists look to the historian and wonder how the historian decides what is important, and how we go about deciding what will go into a future history book."
14. Those ideas include fundamental uncertainty which cannot be reduced to measurable risk, the resulting volatility of expectations, and the role of money as a store of value allowing consumers and businesses not to spend in the face of uncertainty. Keynes (1937) is an excellent, accessible short summary of what he considered to be revolutionary about *The General Theory* (1936), and it ties to recent "rediscovery" of Keynes's ideas in Akerlof and Shiller (2009) and elsewhere. The original Keynesian economics is also very different from the new Keynesian economics represented by authors like Gregory Mankiw.
15. These papers can be found at http://hisreco.org/ (accessed 4 April 2011).
16. In a presidential address to the History of Economics Society, Colander (2000) announced "The Death

of Neoclassical Economics." He was describing, not the demise of modern theory, but the splintering of the post-World War II neoclassical synthesis into separable research programs. See Rizvi (2003) for an excellent account of how the Sonnenschein-Mantel-Debreu arbitrariness results caused the collapse of the postwar general equilibrium research program, opening the door for other programs.

17. We also have some skills-based learning objectives – exposure to multidisciplinary scholarship and improved reading and writing skills – discussed below under "teaching challenges".
18. Thanks to Bruce Caldwell, John Davis, Jerry Evensky, Wade Hands, Harro Maas, Tiago Mata and Anthony Waterman for allowing us to incorporate content from their course outlines.
19. Colander and McGoldrick (2009) makes for interesting reading about "big think" questions and the place of HET in the economics curriculum.
20. In other words, the value of writing rises as you move up the scale of Bloom et al.'s (1956) taxonomy.
21. SHOE@yorku.ca. Go to https://listserv.yorku.ca/archives/shoe.html and click on "Join or leave the list" (accessed 4 April 2011).

REFERENCES

Akerlof, G. A. and R. J. Shiller (2009), *Animal Spirits: How Human Psychology Drives the Economy, And Why it Matters for Global Capitalism,* Princeton, NJ: Princeton University Press.

Backhouse, R. (2004), *The Ordinary Business of Life: A History Of Economics from the Ancient World to the Twenty-First Century,* Princeton, NJ: Princeton University Press.

Blaug, M. (ed.) (1991a), *Pioneers in Economics Series,* Aldershot, UK and Brookfield, US: Edward Elgar.

Blaug, M. (ed.) (1991b), *The Historiography Of Economics (Pioneers in Economics Series, Vol. 1),* Aldershot, UK and Brookfield, US: Edward Elgar.

Blaug, M. (1997), *Economic Theory In Retrospect* (5th ed.), Cambridge, UK and New York: Cambridge University Press.

Blaug, M. (2001), "No history of ideas, please, we're economists", *Journal of Economic Perspectives,* **15** (1), (Winter), 145–64.

Bloom, B., M. Engelhart, E. Furst, W. Hill and D. Krathwohl (1956), *Taxonomy of Educational Objectives Handbook I: Cognitive Domain,* New York: David McKay.

Boulding, K. E. (1971), "After Samuelson, who needs Adam Smith?", *History of Political Economy,* **3** (2), (Fall), 225–37.

Chai, A. and A. Moneta (2010), "Engel curves", *Journal of Economic Perspectives,* **24** (1), (Winter), 225–40.

Cohen, A. J. and J. Spencer (1993), "Using writing across the curriculum in economics: Is taking the plunge worth it?", *Journal of Economic Education,* **24** (3), (Summer), 219–30.

Colander, D. (2000), "The death of Neoclassical economics", *Journal of the History of Economic Thought,* **22** (2), (June), 127–43.

Colander, D. and K. McGoldrick (eds) (2009), *Educating Economists: The Teagle Discussion On Re-evaluating the Undergraduate Economics Major,* Cheltenham, UK and Northampton, MA, US: Edward Elgar.

Dimand, R. W., M. A. Dimand and E. Forget (eds) (2000), *A Biographical Dictionary of Women Economists,* Cheltenham, UK and Northampton, MA, US: Edward Elgar.

Durlauf, S. N. and L. E. Blume (eds) (2008), *The New Palgrave Dictionary of Economics Online,* Basingstoke, UK and New York: Palgrave Macmillan.

Goodwin, C. D. (2008), "History of economic thought", in S. N. Durlauf and L. E. Blume (eds), *The New Palgrave Dictionary of Economics Online,* Basingstoke, UK and New York: Palgrave Macmillan, http://www.dictionaryofeconomics.com/article?id=pde2008_H000174, accessed 23 February 2011.

Heilbroner, R. L. (1979), "Modern economics as a chapter in the history of economic thought", *History of Political Economy,* **11** (2), (Summer), 192–8.

Heilbroner, R. L. (ed.) (1986), *The Essential Adam Smith,* New York: Norton.

Heilbroner, R. L. (ed.) (1996), *Teachings from the Worldly Philosophers,* New York: Norton.

Heilbroner, R. L. (1999), *The Worldly Philosophers: The Lives, Times, and Ideas of the Great Economic Thinkers* (7th ed.), New York: Simon & Schuster.

Keynes, J. M. (1936), *The General Theory of Employment, Interest and Money,* New York: Harcourt Brace.

Keynes, J. M. (1937), "The General Theory of Employment", *Quarterly Journal of Economics,* **51** (2), (February), 209–23.

Marshall, A. [1890–1920] (1961), *Principles of Economics* (9th Variorum ed.), London: Macmillan for the Royal Economic Society.

Medema, S. G. and W. J. Samuels (eds) (2003), *The History of Economic Thought: A Reader,* New York: Routledge.

Mirowski, P. (1989), *More Heat than Light: Economics as Social Physics, Physics as Nature's Economics,* Cambridge, UK and New York: Cambridge University Press.

Moggridge, D. E. (1992), *Maynard Keynes: An Economist's Biography,* London: Routledge.

Rizvi, S. A. T. (2003), "Postwar Neoclassical microeconomics", in W. J.Samuels, J. E. Biddle and J. B. Davis (eds) (2003), *A Companion to the History of Economic Thought,* Malden, MA: Blackwell, pp. 377–94.

Samuels, W. J., J. E. Biddle and J. B. Davis (eds) (2003), *A Companion to the History of Economic Thought,* Malden, MA: Blackwell.

Samuelson, P. A. (1955), *Economics: An Introductory Analysis* (3rd ed.), New York: McGraw Hill.

Siegfried, J. J., R. L. Bartlett, W. L. Hansen, A. C. Kelley, D. N. McCloskey and T. H. Tietenberg (1991), "The status and prospects of the economics major", *Journal of Economic Education,* **22** (3), (Summer), 197–224.

Stigler, G. J. [1941] (1994), *Production and Distribution Theories,* New Brunswick, NJ: Transaction Publishers.

Tucker R. C. (ed.) (1978), *The Marx-Engels Reader* (2nd ed.), New York: Norton.

Vaughn, K. I. (1993), "Why teach the history of economics?", *Journal of the History of Economic Thought,* **15** (2), (Spring), 174–83.

Weintraub, E. R. (1999), "How should we write the history of twentieth century economics?", *Oxford Review of Economic Policy,* **15** (4), (Winter), 139–52.

Weintraub, E. R. (ed.) (2002), *The Future of the History of Economics,* Annual Supplement to Volume 34, *History of Political Economy,* Durham, NC: Duke University Press.

Wood, J. C. (1982–7), *Critical Assessments of Leading Economists,* London: Croom Helm.

Wood, J. C. and R. N. Woods (1989–2006), *Critical Assessments of Contemporary Economists,* London: Routledge.

53 Health economics – methods for a new field

Allen C. Goodman

Health economics is a newcomer to the economics discipline and economics pedagogy. Microeconomics, macroeconomics, and econometrics have served as foundations of economics curricula for more than fifty years, and public finance, international economics, or industrial organization date back even further. Many university economics departments have only recently instituted health economics courses, and in many institutions health economics courses reside *outside* of economics departments, in schools of public health, business, or nursing.

Present-day interest in health economics comes from the importance of health and health care to the population, as well as the novel idea that economic analysis can address issues for which many health care professionals, until at least recently, denied its relevance. Methods of health economics apply to health policy, but also to health prevention and health treatment. Cost-effectiveness and cost-benefit analyses take on new importance in examining impacts of activities that often do not face market tests, including organ transplantation, immunization programs, or prevention initiatives. As recently as the 1980s, many physicians, health services professionals, and those serving the health sectors, including regulators and attorneys, argued that providers, rather than consumers, make the important decisions, or that health is a necessity, inimical to economic analysis. The burgeoning interest since then has challenged those who seek to teach health economics, and those who wish to learn it.

There are increasing numbers of health economists, but course instructors also come from applied microeconomics fields like industrial organization, labor, or urban/regional economics. While some adapt their research interests to health economics, many are generalists who wish to cover a new course. This chapter provides a presentation of the key features of teaching health economics, starting with teaching goals and objectives and following with a discussion of some underlying principles for structuring the health economics course. It finishes with effective methods in health economics teaching.

GOALS AND OBJECTIVES

It is important to "keep the economics" in health economics. Students and practitioners may dwell on what the Medicare or Medicaid programs cover, how DRGs (diagnosis-related groups) work, what limitations programs or insurers put on reimbursements, or how HMO, PPO, and POS-managed care plans differ as organizations. Instructors who ignore field-specific references can render any course irrelevant, but economists have a comparative advantage over others in applying the concepts of opportunity cost, supply and demand, and the importance of technology, which promote an understanding of the health care system, and which form the firm foundations for teaching it.

Secondly, instructors must recognize that the health economy changes constantly, and that students, scholars, and the public can observe these changes, largely due to the Internet, in ways unimaginable even fifteen years ago. In the mid-1990s, as in previous decades, discussing health insurance meant discussing Blue Cross – Blue Shield. Not any more. Students read daily about new insurance plans, new drug treatments, or the increased incidence and costs of obesity. In the health economy, last year's data are "old data." Information on health care systems around the world, or the HIV/AIDS pandemic, for example, is constantly updated by researchers and journalists. Health databases are abundant and available for downloading, often at no charge.

PHILOSOPHY

Most economists recognize that economic knowledge comes from researchers and their research. In developing *The Economics of Health and Health Care* (first published in 1993), Folland, Stano and I have sought to convince students that economic behavior is measured by researchers, that there are ongoing debates on how it is measured, and that it is important to show why these debates occur and how they might be resolved. The devotion to research findings represented a foundation of the book and has continued through its most recent (sixth) edition.

Examples of important empirical work include the path-breaking Rand Health Insurance study (Newhouse et al., 1993), which finds that health care demand is somewhat responsive to health insurance coinsurance rates, with an elasticity of -0.2. Other researchers (Jensen and Morissey, 1986) find that hospital care processes are provided with varying degrees of substitution of physicians, nurses and office staff, rather than the fixed input ratios (originating with Lee and Jones, 1933) that were used to characterize health care production, and motivate health labor force planning.

However, both the Newhouse and the Jensen-Morissey studies refer to a health economy of thirty years ago. At the time of the Rand study, "fee for service care" ruled. Now, where managed care dominates, and where employer-provided health insurance is waning, is the elasticity still -0.2? Jensen and Morissey's study predates widespread managed care and the Medicare prospective payment system that has turned hospital management upside down. In 1980, for example, nearly 70 percent of mothers experiencing regular deliveries had hospital stays of three days or more (Gillum, Graves and Wood, 1998, Table R). Contrast that to the concern about "drive-through deliveries" of the past fifteen years. Can one assume that hospital practices and substitution patterns have remained unchanged?

Other questions abound. Is health care a luxury with an income elasticity greater than +1, seen by looking across countries, or is it a necessity (income elasticity much less than +1), as measured at the individual level? Does an increase in the supply of physicians or hospitals promote increased service demand (so-called supplier-induced demand), or is the causality reversed? Do hospitals experience scale economies? And if so, at what levels are they exhausted? Students deserve nuanced discussion as to the issues, how studies are conducted, where researchers agree . . . and where they disagree.

PRINCIPLES IN STRUCTURING COURSES

Possibly the most important underlying principle in structuring an undergraduate health economics course is that incentives matter – to the consumers, providers, hospitals, bureaucrats, and regulators. Economists tend to focus on individuals, physicians, and hospitals, and courses taught in economics departments tend to follow this focus. However, many health economics courses are taught in public health settings. This may lead to a different set of topics related to what agencies do, how programs are set up, who they serve, and whether they provide services equitably. Even if instructors focus on individuals' responses to incentives, introducing the "public" component early provides important context throughout.

Most undergraduate health economics courses require at least one course in economics principles and sometimes a course in intermediate microeconomics. Despite these requirements, and because the course is often taught outside of economics departments, classroom review of key microeconomic tools sets the stage for their application. Undergraduate health economics texts (typically containing twenty or more chapters) contain too much material for a single semester. The approach here emphasizes topics that students are not likely to see in other economics courses. These include insurance, health capital, equity and need, and the US system in international perspective.

Insurance defines all health care economies. In the United States, third parties pay for well over eight of every ten dollars spent, with no other private good coming close; in other countries, the percentages are higher. Insurance is probably the most difficult topic to teach and it receives special attention in a section below.

Grossman (1972) was the first to conceptualize *health capital*, to explain patterns relating to age or income in health care utilization and expenditures. Over time, health capital applications have grown. Apart from looking at single period and time profiles of health expenditures, health capital topics have expanded to include obesity, ingestion of addictive substances, and decisions by the elderly and their families about "when to pull the plug."

With the exception of some public finance courses, most economists avoid teaching about *equity* and few look at "need". They (we) appeal to Pareto optimality and avoid interpersonal comparisons of utility. Many health economics students, particularly those with a public health bent, are interested in these issues. Yet, Pareto analyses provide little insight into issues of health care for those who do not participate actively in markets, such as children, the elderly, or the infirm. Health economics instructors who ignore inequality and problems of health care access risk rendering a health economics course irrelevant.

Many undergraduates expect to discuss health care policy at the local and at the national level. They are often unaware that close to fifty million Americans lack health insurance, and they know little about the US national health care system, especially in comparison with other systems around the world (with much media coverage either simplistic or incorrect). Many very good databases (for example, OECD 2010) allow teachers and students to examine these issues directly, discovering for example that we spend a lot (a greater percentage of GDP than anyone else), and that our output or quality (as measured by infant deaths, or population longevity for example) are arguably inferior to other countries that spend (often considerably) less.

INSURANCE – THE MOST DIFFICULT TOPIC

The primacy of insurance relates to several important questions: (1) Why do we buy insurance (demand)? (2) How do we sell insurance (supply)? (3) What determines the price? (4) What is moral hazard? and (5) Who pays for insurance? The economic analysis involves consumers' maximization of expected utility in a risky environment, assuming that insurance buyers are risk averse. Maximization of expectations will be new to many undergraduates, and most will not have learned about risk aversion. The demand and supply questions are more challenging because many courses do not require calculus methods that would simplify the analyses.

Further, most health economics students know little about health insurance. Younger undergraduates generally are healthy, and most have been carried on parents' policies. Asking them about their coverage often brings blank stares, and many do not know whether they are covered by fee-for-service or by some kind of managed care. Older students, and those students with children and/or families, are more likely to have some personal insights, although they may have limited knowledge of their own plans. Many elderly who receive Medicare benefits think that Medicare pays for everything (it does not). To complicate matters, health economics requires learning a new language including terms such as *premiums*, *copayments*, and *deductibles*.

A simple example eschews most of the jargon. Consider a club (motorcycle clubs usually get students' attention) with a hundred members – all about the same age, and with similar lifestyles. About once per year one of the members gets sick and incurs health care costs of $5,000. The illness incidence seems random with respect to gender or age. Club members donate $50 per year to a fund that will earn some interest and pay for the member's treatment if necessary. Without premiums, copayments, deductibles, or moral hazard, students have learned the concept of insurance. By paying $50 with certainty, the member has insured against the uncertainty (or risk) of having to spend $5,000. Issues such as surplus (because no one gets sick), deficit (more than one person gets sick), or adverse selection (the same member gets sick each year) follow naturally.

While not all people wish to avoid risk (they are not risk averse), those who do must determine how much insurance to buy. Begin with the observation that a small amount of insurance may bring utility if the buyer falls ill, and costs utility if the buyer stays healthy. Without specifying the price per unit of insurance, Figure 53.1 shows that for $500 of insurance, the marginal utility (if ill) at point A exceeds the foregone marginal utility (if well) at A'. Additional increments of $500 are subject to diminishing marginal benefits in terms of payments (or reimbursements) if ill, and increasing marginal costs (in terms of foregone utility), leading to a policy of size q^* that is purchased. This is the demand side.

There are few good alternatives to algebra for the supply side, which compares revenue to costs, using the equation:

$$\text{Profits} = \text{Revenue} - \text{Costs},$$
$$\text{Profits} = aq - (pq + t)$$

where a is the premium in fractional terms of payout q, p is the probability of payout, and t is a per policy processing cost. Assuming perfect competition, profits approach 0, and the competitive premium a (with zero profits) is:

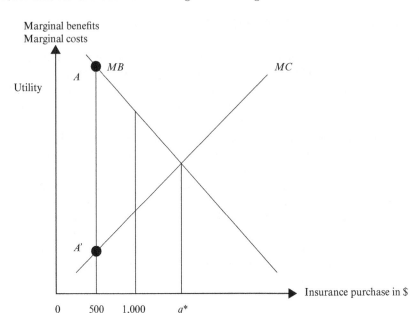

Figure 53.1   Optimal purchase of insurance

$$a = p + t/q.$$

Premium a is directly related to probability p, and if t is small relative to q, then the premium a, in fractional terms is roughly equal to probability p.

Ignoring t, one can solve for the optimal coverage q^*. Buyers will add coverage to the point that the wealth will be the same whether they are well or ill. Letting $\overline{W}$ signify initial wealth leads to:

$$\overline{W} - aq^* = \text{Wealth if well} = \text{Wealth if ill} = \overline{W} - loss - q^* - aq^*$$

or when simplified:

$$q^* = loss.$$

In the absence of processing costs t, a consumer insures fully, thus solving for the equilibrium value of q^* in Figure 53.1. With positive and possibly substantial processing (or loading) costs t, the price of insurance rises, so the best choice is to buy less of it, insuring for less than the full loss.

The previous analysis assumes that health care demand is totally price inelastic, like insulin for brittle diabetics. However, students realize that low insurance copayments may lead them to purchase other items (contact lenses or prescription shampoo, for example) that they might not otherwise have purchased. This leads to a discussion of *moral hazard*, the impact of insurance (more generally, any contractual arrangement) on economic behavior. Full insurance or fractional coinsurance induces "over-consumption" of goods that (unlike insulin) are responsive to lower prices, beyond the point at which marginal benefits equal marginal costs, a textbook example of moral hazard. Buying prescription shampoo rather than the store brand or Head and Shoulders® would seem like a social waste, but what about heart surgery procedures that a patient could not afford without insurance, or other treatments that may not increase length of life, but definitely increase quality of life?

Nyman (1999) has developed important analyses that recognize such income effects of insurance. Noting that the income transfers from the health insurance go only to those who are ill, he considers a woman who receives an insurance settlement that allows her to purchase a mastectomy, breast reconstruction surgery, and an extra two days in the hospital to recover. The conventional insurance literature (dating from Pauly, 1968) treats the entire expenditure as welfare decreasing if paid for by health insurance. Nyman shows that the part of the expenditure for the mastectomy and to correct the disfigurement that comes from an income transfer is welfare increasing. The additional hospital days purchased due to low copayments are still inefficient and welfare decreasing.

Finally, the question of "who pays" is critical in discussing insurance. Many US residents (and US politicians) believe that employers "pay" for the insurance. Careful analysis shows otherwise. Ask students to suppose that they earn $20 per hour with no health insurance. Now, suppose that the employer offers a health insurance policy that is worth at least $2 per hour to them, while costing the employer $2 per hour to provide. While employees would prefer to get their $20 per hour *plus* the health insurance, most students will agree that if workers value the insurance at more than $2 per hour, they (the workers) would accept a wage of $18 plus the $2 per hour of insurance. Who pays? The workers do, whether the employer writes the check or they write the check.[1]

INNOVATIVE TEACHING METHODS

Most professional economists come from the background of "chalk and talk," a term popularized by Becker and Watts (1996). Formal chalk and talk was supplanted by transparencies, and many instructors now use either publisher-created or instructor-designed PowerPoint presentations. There can be bad PowerPoint presentations, but the ability for economics instructors to sequence in points and to draw clear, multi-color, and precise diagrams can enhance teaching. Three practices to engage students in health economics courses beyond chalk and talk are: "News of the Day," EXCEL exercises, and empirical papers.

Many university economics students complete their undergraduate careers without ever presenting material to others. News of the Day addresses this shortcoming. It starts with a news item broadly related to health-care from the news media or (increasingly) from the Internet. I introduce students to the issue, providing background information before relating it to key economic analysis, typically in the form of a supply-demand or similar diagram, and summarize it in no more than six to seven PowerPoint slides. For example, media reports of labor negotiations that change the health care package will be accompanied by a simple market supply and demand for labor diagram that addresses "who pays."

After two to three weeks, the students begin presentations, with each presentation

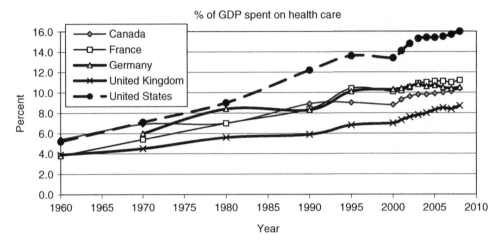

% of GDP spent on health care

Figure 53.2   Health expenditure share of GDP by country

evaluated as approximately 5 percent of the total grade, on the basis of topic, analysis, and style. Students pick presentation slots at random. They may exchange, buy, or sell the slots, with the goal simply that everyone presents by a certain date. In larger classes, each student presents once per term – in smaller classes, students may present as many as three times.

These presentations enhance communication skills as well as economic knowledge. Students' presentation quality improves over the course of the term, with better graphics and analyses. The PowerPoint presentations are then added to the class web site, and students are told that content contained in any presentation may appear on mid-term and final exams – and it does. This added layer of assessment enhances both the presentations themselves, and the student discussion that accompanies it.

EXCEL (or comparable spreadsheet) programs serve as valuable teaching aids in several ways. On occasion one is looking at small data sets like national income or health expenditures. Graphing, and looking at means, medians, and distributions are easy with EXCEL.

For example, the Organisation for Economic Development and Co-operation (OECD 2010) has created a database that is available to most students through library web sites. The data are collected at the country level for over thirty developed countries, including the United States, Canada, Mexico, most of Europe, some Asian countries, and Australia. Starting from a 1960 baseline, there is a range of health utilization, expenditure, and outcome measures. A simple exercise examines the share of GDP going to health expenditures over time. Figure 53.2 shows, for Canada, France, Germany, the United Kingdom, and the United States, that expenditures have grown everywhere, but faster in the United States. Students cannot help but see that the US share is nearly twice that of the United Kingdom. For a larger sample of 34 countries (too crowded for a single graph), EXCEL's functions calculate that the mean (median) expenditure share for countries rose from 3.8 percent (3.8 percent) in 1960 to 8.9 percent (8.7 percent) in 2008.

A second important EXCEL use involves equation solving. Economists customarily draw graphs and shift curves, showing price and/or quantity changes. Recalculating the equilibrium amounts with each shift in demand and/or supply quickly becomes a mechanical exercise, subject to calculation errors, rather than one which builds intuition. Solving the equations on a spreadsheet requires the same analytical skills, and allows the students to change the parameters and to look at the impacts.

Consider Grossman's health capital model, which views consumer's time as an input to health production. In a simple model, leisure is either traded for wages, or used to produce health through visits to a provider. A decrease in the money price of visits (inputs into health production), relative to all other market goods, makes health more attractive, but it must also lead to a decrease in work (or, in a more complex model, both work and leisure used for other goods) because of the time components of visits. Changing parameters in this exercise shows the complex interaction between the labor-leisure choice and health demand, and improves discussion.

Writing original research papers is valuable for undergraduates. One of the best data sources for empirical papers is the OECD data archive mentioned above. Students may examine countries' health expenditures as a proportion of GDP, or examine economic determinants of health outcomes such as longevity or infant deaths. They may compare health outcomes in countries with centralized health insurance systems such as the United Kingdom, with decentralized systems such as Germany or the United States. They can look at these items over time for a single country or across many countries (or both, in a panel study). Students who have taken undergraduate econometrics classes can use packages such as EViews, SAS, SPSS, or STATA, but others can use EXCEL's regression package.

The assignment comprises at least two stages over seven to eight weeks, culminating in the finished paper. The first stage requires preliminary student work. In the world of economic consultants, a buyer requires the consultant to provide a "deliverable" after a short period of time to demonstrate progress on the work. Here, after three to four weeks, the student provides the instructor with an eight-to-ten slide PowerPoint presentation, including: hypotheses (does the student expect increased income to affect expenditures positively or negatively? Will the elasticity be small or large?); a list of five journal sources; expected analyses, including diagrams or regressions; and expected findings. PowerPoint forces students to synopsize their thoughts, acting as an informal outline.

The second stage is the finished paper with full explanations of methods and results, and with the computer output as an appendix. Consistent with the premise that health economics is an empirical field, and that researchers develop, accept, and/or change theories based on empirical findings, this paper of ten to fifteen pages plus tables (and journal sources) serves as an important capstone experience for both undergraduate and graduate classes. Depending on the class size, as a third stage, students may present findings (in PowerPoint) in fifteen- to twenty-minute blocks.

CONCLUSIONS

Health economics instructors increasingly rely on careful models of people, firms, hospitals, or governments that make decisions in circumstances where insurance is important, and health outcomes are both difficult to measure and uncertain (treatments may not be effective). Health economics analyses apply to questions of policy, prevention, and treatment. Some of the tools used, including cost-effectiveness and cost-benefit analyses, have become mainstays of health effectiveness, pharmaceutical, and policy research.

Instructors new to the field might find international perspectives to be most instructive because, while insurance and health technology are universal around the world, different countries do things in different ways. How is it that other advanced countries spend much less than the US, and yet manage to insure all of their people? International students often provide enlightening home country perspectives in these discussions.

Whether beginning their teaching careers, or diversifying their teaching portfolios, health economics instructors should recognize that their venerable analytical tools will provide valuable insights into people's health and health care decisions. Because the field is so new, and so fluid, instructors can easily address topics from the news media as well as the textbook. The analyses of health economists, and the roles these analyses play in improving policies and practices, serve as foundations in the courses that we teach.

NOTE

1.   For a more complete graphical example, see Folland, Goodman, and Stano (2010), pp. 206–8.

REFERENCES

Becker, W. E. and M. Watts (1996), "Chalk and talk: A national survey on teaching undergraduate economics", *American Economic Review*, **86**, 448–53.

Folland, S., A. C. Goodman and M. Stano (2010), *The Economics of Health and Health Care* (6th ed.), Upper Saddle River, NJ: Pearson.

Gillum, B. S., E. J. Graves and E. Wood (1998), *National Hospital Discharge Survey, Annual Summary, 1995*, National Center for Health Statistics, Vital Health Statistics 13.

Grossman, M. (1972), "On the concept of health capital and the demand for health", *Journal of Political Economy*, **80**, 223–55.

Jensen, G. A. and M. A. Morrissey (1986), "The role of physicians in hospital production", *Review of Economics and Statistics*, **68**, 432–42.

Lee, R. I. and L. W. Jones (1933), *The Fundamentals of Good Medical Care*, Chicago: University of Chicago Press.

Newhouse, J. P. et al. (1993), *Free for All? Lessons from the RAND Health Experiment*, Cambridge, MA: Harvard University Press.

Nyman, J. A. (1999), "The economics of moral hazard revisited", *Journal of Health Economics*, **18**, 811–24.

Organisation for Economic Co-operation and Development (2010), "Health data", http://www.sourceoecd.org/rpsv/statistic/s37_about.htm?jnlissn=99991012, accessed 27 October 2010.

Pauly, M. V. (1968), "The economics of moral hazard: Comment", *American Economic Review*, **58**, 531–7.

54 Teaching undergraduate industrial organization economics
Elizabeth J. Jensen

> Just as eating against one's will is injurious to health, so study without a liking for it spoils the memory, and it retains nothing it takes in. (Leonardo da Vinci)

It was studying industrial organization as an undergraduate that made me decide to become an economist. I was hooked by the issues and by the mix of theory, empirical work, and policy. I have been fortunate to have had the opportunity to share my enthusiasm with hundreds of undergraduates over the years, helping many of them discover the compelling questions in industrial organization and learn approaches to answering those questions. My experiences have convinced me of the wisdom of Leonardo da Vinci's maxim: exciting students' interest will help them learn better, which will in turn make teaching a more rewarding and fulfilling experience. I hope the ideas in this chapter will help you engage your students and organize your course and class time in a useful way. However, I also hope that you will do what we all want our students to do: think critically about my advice, take what works for you and your students, and adapt as seems appropriate. Be willing to experiment, but also be sensitive to your own style and your particular students. And enjoy yourself!

BEFORE THE SEMESTER BEGINS

Just as there is not one model of oligopoly behavior, there is not one best structure for an industrial organization course. Circumstances matter. Before the semester begins, when thinking about the syllabus and the structure of the course, keep the following issues in mind.

Math background of students   Are the students who are likely to enroll in the course comfortable with algebra and with abstractions? For example, would they find a linear demand curve written as $P = a - bq$ to be considerably more intimidating than one written as $P = 100 - 2q$? Or are there gains to being more general? Is calculus a prerequisite? If so, are the students sufficiently proficient at calculus to set up and solve a problem such as finding optimal mixed strategies? If not, is doing the problem using calculus important enough to spend time, in class or in office hours, helping them understand the setup and the solution technique? While many concepts in industrial organization can be usefully analyzed with mathematics, if the students are relatively unsophisticated mathematically, then the math can easily get in the way of their understanding the economics. This should probably be one of the first issues to consider, since it will affect the textbook decision.

Level of the course   A related consideration is the level of and the prerequisites for the course. Is intermediate microeconomics a requirement? What types of outside readings would be most appropriate? While I recommend using examples from *The Wall Street Journal, The New York Times,* or other business press in any industrial organization course, I would make different decisions about antitrust case studies, industry studies, and articles in economics journals depending on the level of the course. Just as good writers keep their intended audience in mind as they write, good teachers think about the students they will teach as they design their courses.

Focus of the course   Industrial organization is a broad field; it has its roots in empirical observations about firms and industries, but the field has been enriched in recent decades by the application of more rigorous and sophisticated theoretical models. In addition, antitrust policy and regulation are interwoven with industrial organization topics. Consequently, questions arise about the desired mix of topics. Will the focus be primarily on theory? To what extent might the use of a variety of case studies be effective? How much emphasis on understanding empirical work is optimal, and within empirical work, what is a good balance between the older structure-conduct-performance work and the new empirical industrial organization? How much time, if any, is appropriate to spend on antitrust policy or regulation? One reason I particularly enjoy teaching industrial organization is that the course can differ from year to year, but this also means that I have to make more conscious choices each time than for a new iteration of microeconomic theory, for example.

Class size   Is the class small enough to permit a significant amount of in-class discussion? Can students be divided into groups to work on a problem or analyze an aspect of an antitrust case and then report and discuss with the class? Will it be possible to conduct "hands-on" activities such as games or taste tests? In the case of large lectures, what methods can be used to engage the students in the good stories industrial organization has to tell?

GOALS, OBJECTIVES, AND PHILOSOPHY

Less is more: something I have increasingly come to believe over the years. Early in my teaching career, filled with enthusiasm and knowledge from graduate school, I tried to teach much of what I had studied and in lots of detail. Gradually, I have decided that it often makes sense to do fewer things, taking more time to work through the theory, look at a case study, and talk about policy for the issues I do cover. I have realized that the vast majority of my students are not destined for Ph.D. programs in economics; those few who are will have time to master the intricacies of theoretical modeling and econometric analyses in their graduate study. Additionally, times change, with the consequence that current students' search strategies – ways they collect information, look for ideas, and try to answer questions – bear little resemblance to my own search strategies when I was a student before the age of the internet. If a student has forgotten, for example, how to solve for a reaction function when solving a Cournot model, she will probably quickly search for the term and find examples or posted lecture notes to help her. Putting these things together, I have refined my thinking about what really matters to me – about what I hope my students will be able to do years after they have graduated.

I have also become more intentional about communicating my objectives and my organizational framework to my students as I remind myself that while I have studied economics for many years and have a reasonably good idea of how various pieces fit together, my students are learning material for the first time. Education is a developmental process; learning takes time and practice, and not all students are at the same level of intellectual maturity. I may not need to look at the photo on the cover of the jigsaw puzzle for the industrial organization course, but without it, my students can sometimes feel overwhelmed by detail and, in their words, "too many models." Consequently, I tell my industrial organization students that I want them to hold onto three things: (1) a curiosity and awareness that lets them recognize interesting issues and ask questions; (2) an understanding of problem-solving techniques that allows them to think about how to answer questions; and (3) a critical eye and common sense for looking at evidence to see if hypotheses are supported. I talk about these objectives on the first day of class, but I also remind the students of them throughout the semester, helping them understand why we are asking a particular question or working through a specific model. I also work to show them connections among models and reasons for choosing one model over others to analyze a particular issue or industry. Finally, I have become more aware of the value of telling students how exciting I find economics, especially industrial organization; I believe that passion is contagious. Context also matters here, however. As a middle-aged, experienced professor, I have an authority I lacked when I was a young, new professor. So, think about the circumstances, but don't underestimate the value of sharing enthusiasm with students.

THE BEGINNING OF THE COURSE

Having said there is no one best way to structure an industrial organization course, I nonetheless thought it might be useful to share a few ideas about things that I cover and what I emphasize when teaching the material. To put things in perspective: my course is an upper-level (seniors and juniors) elective, with microeconomic theory as a prerequisite. Although single variable calculus is a prerequisite for intermediate microeconomics, I cannot expect my students to set up and solve a constrained maximization problem without considerable help. Primarily, I try to rely on algebra, using specific numerical equations, and graphical analyses. I typically incorporate theory, case studies, and applications from the business press in my course.

I begin the semester by talking about the theory of the firm, using a discussion of transactions costs to examine a firm's choice between using the market and undertaking an activity internally. Doing this allows me to demonstrate that industrial organization often builds upon neoclassical concepts studied in microeconomic theory, enriching the concepts to correspond more closely with the real world. This shows students the relevance of theory and helps them understand that looking at actual firm and industry behavior can make things both more interesting and more complicated – one of the things I point out throughout the semester. Teaching about the firm versus the market allows the instructor to combine theory, including a review of economies of scale and scope and the introduction of bounded rationality and opportunism, with examination of actual firms. Students enjoy discussing why, for example, an automobile company might purchase light bulbs for headlights but make engine blocks itself or why the soda industry has recently been moving toward vertical integration of bottlers and concentrate manufacturers. In addition, discussing the types of firms and the development of the corporation leads nicely into a discussion of the assumption of profit maximization. Questions of executive compensation and incentives invariably interest students and create opportunities for thoughtful debate, encouraging students to take an active role in class discussions.

I then spend a few classes reviewing perfect competition and monopoly. In this review, I ask students to think about industry characteristics and what they would examine in order to determine if an industry is competitive, monopolistic, or somewhere in between, connecting what they have learned with the examination of industries we will do later in the course. I also focus on the basic rule for choosing the profit-maximizing level of output and emphasize that determining marginal revenue will often be key for a firm in an oligopolistic industry. A third important objective in this discussion is to help students understand that the perfectly competitive model serves as a valuable reference point when examining other industry structures; comparing perfect competition and monopoly highlights the welfare consequences of a firm's choice of output level and price. For a course that includes consideration of policy, this is a good place to begin a discussion of antitrust policy by explaining why economists worry about market power.

FRAMING OF OLIGOPOLY DECISION-MAKING

In most industrial organization courses, the core material is oligopoly behavior. Because the recognized mutual interdependence in an oligopoly requires firms to consider their competitors' probable responses as they make their own decisions, predicting oligopolistic price and output or decisions about non-price strategies such as advertising or investment decisions is complicated. Consequently, in contrast to the cases of perfect competition, monopoly, or even monopolistic competition, there is not one standard model of oligopoly. This fact can result in students feeling overwhelmed by what seems to be a series of unrelated and sometimes highly theoretical models, but here is a place where embracing the complexity can work. When introducing oligopoly, I explain that because modeling the real world is complicated, one size does not fit all. I also stress how crucial it is to figure out what model to use for a specific industry or question. To do this, I talk about the array of factors that matter in modeling oligopoly behavior and in the process, introduce various oligopoly models and show the connection to real-world firms and industries. This is also a good place to introduce game theory and to show how a game-theoretic perspective provides a unifying framework. My list of factors includes the following:

Homogeneous or differentiated products?   Some oligopolies produce very similar products; examples include steel bars or aluminum ingots. In homogeneous oligopolies, it makes sense to talk about a market demand curve and to expect prices across firms to be uniform in equilibrium. Models of homogeneous oligopolies allow consideration of issues such as price leadership, the prisoner's dilemma, attempts at collusion, and entry decisions. In other oligopolies, such as automobiles or beer, products are differentiated and prices can vary across firms in equilibrium. Teaching about differentiated oligopolies creates opportunities for enriching models, such as the introduction of product differentiation into a Bertrand model, and considering solution techniques. In my course, I typically introduce the distinction between homogeneous and differentiated oligopolies and then begin the discussion with homogeneous models. Within that framework, I ask students to consider the following additional four questions.

Zero-sum or non-zero-sum game? Some interactions between firms in an oligopoly can be modeled as a zero-sum game. A simple example is a market share game among oligopolists facing a given market demand curve and no possibility of entry or exit. Students easily understand a story of two ice cream vendors deciding where to locate along a parade route, for example, and because zero-sum games have relatively straightforward solutions, this is a useful way to introduce the concept of a Nash equilibrium. Most oligopoly interactions, however, are best depicted as non-zero-sum games. Firms' decisions about prices and non-price strategies such as advertising typically affect total industry profits as well as the market share of each firm. For example, an intensive advertising campaign by McDonald's may both shift out the overall demand for fast-food dinners and induce some of Burger King's customers to switch to McDonald's. Consequently, I spend the majority of the time in oligopoly discussing non-zero-sum models.

Competing in quantities or competing in prices? Working through a simple Cournot duopoly model with homogeneous products and costs and comparing the equilibrium to the Bertrand equilibrium shows students how important it is to think about whether quantity or price is the decision variable for a firm in an oligopoly. Once they have seen this, I ask students to consider industries such as steel, automobiles, and passenger aircraft compared to industries such as computer software, video games, and insurance. In the first type of industry, firms have to choose their production capacity in advance and quantity cannot be changed quickly or easily. Firms in these industries choose quantity with price adjusting to clear the market, so a quantity-setting model is appropriate. In the second type of industry, firms can easily produce another unit of output, so it makes sense to think of a firm setting its price and then selling the quantity demanded at that price.

Simultaneous or sequential decision? Here again I show the students the importance of this factor using a simple duopoly model, comparing the Cournot and Stackelberg equilibria. Then we talk about types of decisions where a simultaneous model is appropriate – where the information lag is long enough that a firm must make its strategic choice without knowing its competitors' decisions. For example, PetSmart and Pet Supplies "Plus" choose prices for dog treats without knowing what price the other store has chosen that day. McDonald's and Burger King decide on new advertising campaigns without seeing each other's plans. However, in some situations, decisions are sequential: one firm acts first and then other firms decide how to respond. Sequential business decisions include entry decisions in which potential competitors must decide whether to enter a particular market and bargaining decisions such as those in which a firm negotiates with its suppliers over prices.

Collusion or competition? This question is key in considering oligopoly behavior. I emphasize that if firms can see the "big picture," they will realize that collusion is more profitable in the long run than competing with and undercutting each other. In this case, they will work to maximize joint profits, figuring out how to divide up the market. Then we talk about the many factors that affect the likelihood of collusion in the face of the temptation each firm faces to cheat on the agreement in order to increase its short-term profits. Given the goals for my course (as informed by its level, the enrolled students, and the theory/policy mix), I have chosen factors including whether the interaction is repeated a finite number of times; whether all firms have complete and perfect information or whether there are asymmetries or uncertainties; the elements that complicate or facilitate collusion among firms; and the relevant antitrust law.

Let me end this section where I began: urging you to be intentional in your choices of what to teach and to communicate those intentions to your students. Because it is easy for them to get lost in the details of models, an important part of the teacher's job is helping them step back and think critically about what questions to ask and what models to use in analyzing specific questions.

SOME IDEAS ABOUT IN-CLASS ACTIVITIES AND ASSIGNMENTS

Part II of this *Handbook* contains much useful information about aspects of teaching; what I say here builds upon some of these ideas in the context of an industrial organization course.

I like to vary the format of classes. When I teach in 50-minute blocks three times a week, that usually means taking one entire class period every other week or so for consideration of material found in the business press, an antitrust case study, or a game, experiment, or demonstration. When I teach in 75-minute blocks two times a week, I am more likely to switch sometime during a class period; I often find students' attention flagging after 40 or 45 minutes of class. The following examples were taken from a recent iteration of my course; specifics change from semester to semester. The purpose of sharing these examples is not to define how one might incorporate alternative pedagogies, but rather to engage the reader in thinking about the wide range of activities that are possible.

Current Events

Students in industrial organization are easily drawn in through discussion in the business press – "current events" or "news stories."[1] For example, after talking about the advantages of using the market versus producing internally and the factors that affect transactions costs, I asked students to read some recent newspaper columns about Apple's decision to produce the microprocessor chip for the iPad, the A4, itself and to apply what we had learned in class to this business decision. Why had the norm within the mobile device industry been to buy the primary chips from specialized microprocessor companies? Why did Apple decide to break with this practice? Why did Apple enter chip-making by acquiring a start-up company that had been working on specific kinds of chips rather than developing its own chips from scratch? How might Apple be able to benefit from economies of scope in chip-making? Such discussion questions, assigned in advance of the class, are useful both in identifying key issues for students and in structuring the discussion within class. Sometimes I write the questions and post them; sometimes I ask the students to submit two or three questions each to me via email before class and then I organize, edit, and arrange them. In both cases, students can also be paired up or assigned to small groups to tackle the questions and be responsible for presenting their answers to the class.[2] A variation on this theme requires that the students find relevant articles; this is also a way to give some participation credit to students who are shy.

Antitrust Cases

I also break from lecturing by assigning antitrust cases.[3] When we talk about market definition, my students enjoy thinking about a decades-old case decided by the Supreme Court, the *Cellophane*[4] case. Often I designate some students to be economic consultants for du Pont and some to play the role of government economists, asking them what standards should be used to define the market and what types of evidence they would look for to support their market definition. Sometimes I am the judge, asking questions, and sometimes I have a team of students ruling as judges. This fairly simple case also allows consideration of the effects of technological change and the introduction of new products upon market definition and market power. Another example of an antitrust case that works well is the lysine antitrust litigation[5, 6]; this illustrates how many factors associated with collusion come into play. Lysine is homogeneous: why does this matter? What is the role of a breakthrough in technology? Why didn't entry occur prior to 1991 when Archer-Daniels-Midland (A-D-M) entered? How did the large scale of A-D-M's entry affect the cartel? What were the logistics of coordinating the cartel activities and the enforcement mechanisms? This case also allows a discussion of the contribution economists make when calculating the "overcharge" resulting from a collusive agreement and the various advantages and disadvantages of different approaches to calculating that overcharge. Having students work in pairs or in small groups before considering the issues as a class has been an effective pedagogical technique. Students frequently comment on course evaluations that they like discussing the antitrust cases because these applications help them understand the theory more fully.

Games

Games are a third type of activity that is especially effective in an industrial organization course. Some of these are straightforward and short; a good example is a simple Bertrand model game. I provide students with information that defines a linear market demand curve and tell them that products are homogeneous and that all firms have the same constant marginal cost. For purposes of comparison, we first work out the perfectly competitive equilibrium, the monopoly equilibrium, and the Cournot equilibrium. After explaining that firms in the Bertrand model pick their price and sell whatever quantity is demanded at that price, I pick a few students, give them each an index card, and ask each to choose a price.[7] After I collect the cards, I order them from highest to lowest price and then show students how price converges to marginal cost simply by reading out the highest price and then saying something like, "Bill's price is $80. But Sara has set a price of $70. So, Bill, would you like to change your price?" and then continue throughout the chosen prices.

Other games can be more complicated and theoretical, typically requiring one 50-minute class time or the equivalent chunk of time from a longer class period. Because of the time commitment, I usually choose only one or two of these during the semester. A current favorite of mine is a demonstration of network externalities (Ruebeck et al., 2003). To introduce this game, I explain that the key characteristic of a market with network externalities is that a consumer's utility depends in part on the size of the network: the number of other consumers making the same choice with regard to technology or brand. This is easily described with examples such as Skype, Facebook, and games and game systems. A simple utility function such as $U = 20 + 2S$, where S is the number of adopters, illustrates the network externalities. The game has several rounds; the basic idea is that students must independently choose a technology whose value will depend on the total number of students who choose it. After students have individually made their choices, a count is made of choices by the class as a whole so that each student can calculate his or her utility. The game is gradually made more complicated by introducing more realistic elements. This demonstration helps students understand several issues, including network externalities, standardization, switching costs, and the role of imperfect information. While students can grasp these concepts fairly easily without much math, it is also possible to develop the mathematical model for more advanced classes.

A TEACHING CHALLENGE

Because my students struggle with the mathematical aspects of some industrial organization models, I try to present the steps clearly, while also helping them keep track of the big picture. To illustrate, consider solving a Bertrand model with product differentiation. I often use the example of ice cream, posing the puzzle of why Ben & Jerry's vanilla ice cream does not necessarily sell for the same price as Häagen-Dazs vanilla ice cream, assuming that the two firms have the same costs. I show how product differentiation can be represented in demand curves using two simple linear demand curves such as the following:

$$q_1 = 192 - 2p_1 + p_2$$
$$q_2 = 192 - 2p_2 + p_1$$

Even these simple equations help students see that the two ice creams are not perfect substitutes; a higher price for one ice cream will not result in quantity demanded of that brand equal to 0. Talking about the coefficients of the price variables helps students think about substitutability of the products and see the connection to the math.[8]

My next step in the solution process is to find each firm's reaction function and then solving the reaction functions simultaneously to identify the equilibrium. I emphasize that because *price* is the decision variable in a Bertrand model, the reaction function for each firm will be an equation that expresses its price as a function of the other firm's price. I also remind students that firms always maximize profits by setting marginal revenue equal to marginal cost. So the steps I outline for the students are:

1. Solve firm 1's demand curve for its price and find its corresponding marginal revenue curve.
2. Set marginal revenue equal to marginal cost to find an equation for firm 1's quantity.
3. Substitute for q_1 from the demand curve to get an equation that only involves prices.
4. Solve the equation for firm 1's price to get its reaction function.
5. If the demand curves are symmetric, point out the symmetry for firm 2's reaction function; if not, repeat the process to solve for firm 2's reaction function.
6. Solve the two reaction functions simultaneously to find the equilibrium.

In this case, the equilibrium price is $80: considerably higher than the marginal cost of $24. This result shows the power of product differentiation and opens discussion of this important and interesting topic.

What are the take-home lessons from this example? First, think about why you are teaching a particular model and share that context with your students. Is it something they need for further work in economics? Will it help them understand the observed behavior of firms? Tell them! Second, show them the solution process in whatever level of detail is appropriate for your students. You can do this in a lecture, in a handout, with PowerPoint, or by having students work it out in groups. Third, emphasize the economic importance of the results. Finally, give them practice with the technique on a problem set. Students are willing to work through difficult material when they understand the point of the exercise and when they have the appropriate amount of guidance.

CONCLUDING THOUGHTS

Industrial organization is a rich field, full of interesting models and good stories. As the field has evolved over the past three or four decades, it has moved from being primarily empirically oriented to relying more extensively on sophisticated theoretical models. In particular, game theory has proved useful as a framework for analyzing firm and industry behavior. Related to this incorporation of theory is a re-examination of empirical methodology: in response to criticisms of structure-conduct-performance studies, industrial organization economists have employed techniques labeled the "new empirical industrial organization" (NEIO).[9] This approach recognizes the complexity and individuality of oligopoly behavior across industries, arguing that the institutional details and specificity are so important that researchers cannot learn anything useful from broad cross-section studies. Consequently, NEIO studies attempt to understand firm behavior within a specific industry. Additionally, NEIO studies build upon the theory by specifying and estimating behavioral equations about how firms in an industry set price and quantity and using these equations to make statements about market power within the industry. This narrative shows the important interaction and feedback of empirical work and theory within industrial organization – something that is likely to continue as the field advances.

Another exciting change over recent decades has taken place within antitrust policy (Kwoka and White, 2009).[10] Industrial organization economics now guides antitrust policy throughout its various stages: selection of cases, framing of issues, use of data to evaluate likely consequences of structural changes such as mergers or of various practices by firms such as resale price maintenance. Economic reasoning is central for many antitrust cases as both lawyers and judges have become better educated about economics. The connection between the theory and evidence students learn in industrial organization courses and policymaking, and the associated opportunity to motivate students by using real-world applications, is secure.

NOTES

1. For a more detailed, formal approach to leading class discussion, see Chapter 5, "Improving Classroom Discussion in Economics Courses", in this volume.
2. For more information about developing such activities, see the Chapter 4 on cooperative learning in this volume.
3. Some readers might find Chapter 44, "An Interdisciplinary Approach to Teaching Antitrust Economics", in this volume a good complement to this discussion.
4. *United States v. E. I. du Pont de Nemours & Co.*, 351 U.S. 377 (1956).
5. *Amino Acid Lysine Antitrust Litigation*, MDL No. 1083 (Northern District of Illinois 1996).
6. See Connor (1996) for a discussion of this case.
7. Perhaps because I set up the problem by reminding students of the profits that can be made by a monopolist or by Cournot duopolists, at least one student invariably chooses a price considerably above marginal cost.
8. To solve for the equilibrium prices, assume that marginal costs are constant for each firm at $24.
9. See Einav and Levin (2010) for a summary of the evolution of empirical work in industrial organization and discussion of several current areas of inquiry.
10. See Kwoka and White (2009) for an interesting summary of the history of antitrust policy and the role of economics within policy.

REFERENCES

Connor, J. M. (1996), "Global cartels redux: The Lysine antitrust litigation", in J. E. Kwoka, Jr. and L. J. White (eds) (2009).

Einav, L. and J. Levin (2010), "Empirical industrial organization: A progress report", *Journal of Economic Perspectives*, **24** (2), 145–162.

Kwoka, J. E. Jr. and L. J. White (2009), *The Antitrust Revolution: Economics, Competition, and Policy* (5th edition), New York, NY: Oxford University Press.

Ruebeck, C., S. Stafford, N. Tynan, W. Alpert, G. Ball and B. Butkevich (2003), "Network externalities and standardization: A classroom demonstration", *Southern Economic Journal*, **69** (4), 1000–1008.

55 Teaching international finance, adapting to globalization

Stefan C. Norrbin and Onsurang Norrbin

The pace of the globalization of the world has increased dramatically in the last decade. According to the Bank for International Settlements 2010 survey, daily trading of foreign exchange is now almost $4 billion dollars.[1] In comparison, the daily trading in the 2001 survey of the Bank for International Settlements was only $1.2 billion dollars. Thus, the international arena is becoming more and more important for economists to study.

Many economics departments have divided up the International Economics sequence into an International Trade course, and an International Money and Finance course. The International Trade course deals with the issues surrounding why a country trades, whereas an International Money and Finance course deals with the aggregate payments that are exchanged between countries. Because the emphasis is on the aggregate payments, the course also serves as a good place to extend the macroeconomic policy learned in an intermediate course to show the constraints that the international environment places on policy makers.

Students often go into this course with some misconceptions about what will be covered. Most commonly, students believe they will learn how to make money in the global foreign exchange markets. Clearly, we would not be teaching if we knew how to make money! The second misconception is that this course is very mathematical or graph-intensive. There are several numerical calculations, but no high-level mathematics. Furthermore, there are many fewer graphs than, for example, in International Trade.

Traditionally this course has been taught in both Finance and Economics departments to majors as an upper-level course. However, more and more International Affairs/ Relations majors have also become interested in topics covered in this course. Therefore it is important to gauge what type of audience comprises the majority of the class. A large number of finance majors in the class would suggest an increased emphasis on international banking and hedging issues. In contrast, a predominance of upper-level economics majors allows the instructor to focus more on policy making, whereas a large international affairs contingency would make an increased focus on parity conditions, International Monetary Fund (IMF) conditionality and capital flows more appropriate.

Although the composition of the audience might differ, there are three general content categories that all students should be familiar with, namely: foreign exchange terminology, international parity conditions, and foreign exchange rate models. These three categories are found in Melvin and Norrbin (forthcoming) and also appear in one form or another in most international textbooks. This chapter will be divided into three sections covering each of the major categories. The first focuses on providing students with a basic understanding of the terminology and history of the foreign exchange environment. The second section extends the terminology by discussing parity conditions and capital flows, while the final section of the course emphasizes open economy macroeconomics.

UNDERSTANDING THE GLOBAL FINANCIAL ENVIRONMENT

In this first section of the course, it is important to remember that students in the US have very limited experience with foreign exchange markets and thus need a thorough understanding of how exchange rates work.

Foreign Exchange Markets

One way to help students become more comfortable with exchange rates is to introduce the student to how banks set buy and sell rates in the market. Fortunately *The Financial Times* reports buy and sell rates for each of the major currencies, on a daily basis.[2] Such quotes can then be used to show students how banks make money by selling using the spread. Furthermore it is a tool which allows for the introduction of discussions of risk and uncertainty when one shows how a trader will worry about holding positions and will adjust his/her rate to eliminate positions during the day. The use of buy/sell rates will also naturally allow the instructor to do a simple two-point arbitrage scenario, to show that arbitrage opportunities will disappear quickly once they appear.

Historical Context of the Global Financial Environment

For students to understand the international monetary arrangements that exist today, they need some background first. The historical context is important to be able to understand why countries make such different choices of exchange rate systems. For example, why did Ecuador choose to adopt the US dollar as its official currency, while Brazil decided to float its currency? Clearly exchange rate systems have existed throughout civilization, but most ancient systems have been based on some type of metal or other valuable commodity of different types. It is convenient to start the historical context more recently, with the gold standard of the 1800s. The gold standard offers a good introduction as to what happens if monetary policy is controlled by an exogenous phenomenon such as gold discoveries. This can easily be illustrated using a graph of inflation in the 1800s, where it is revealed that average inflation is low, but variability is high. Thus, a metal-based exchange rate system has some desirable and some undesirable features.

The gold standard also provides a good contrast to the Bretton Woods system. The Bretton Woods system is hard to distinguish from a gold standard for most students without a direct comparison. In particular, it is important for students to understand the role of an anchor currency. The mechanism of adjustment towards this anchor currency is best shown in a partial equilibrium trade flow model. This model has the feature of clearly showing the excess supply or demand as a flow concept. The gap leads to a continuous intervention as long as the imbalance exists. This provides a vivid picture of how the reserves are depleted unless something changes. Understanding that something has to be adjusted, the student can appreciate the potential for applying to the IMF for adjustment of the rate. For example, when Mexico had a fixed exchange rate regime in the early 1970s, the Central Bank in Mexico had to continuously buy Mexican pesos and sell US dollars. The longer this went on, the more depleted the

Central Bank of Mexico's reserves became, and in 1976 Mexico had to abandon the fixed exchange rate.

In addition, the trade flow model is useful for motivating why the Bretton Woods system was something that was desired at the time. Taste changes leading to fluctuating supply and demand makes the exchange rate move up and down, resulting in a high variability of the exchange rate. Such a high variability could be avoided with the Bretton Woods system.

The Current Global Financial Environment

Once the Bretton Woods system broke down, each country had to choose how to control their exchange rate. Essentially the current system includes two basic choices, to float or not. However, within these two categories there are a plethora of sub-categories. If a country chooses to fix the exchange rate, the country then has to choose the type of fixed exchange rate system and who to fix the rate with. The two categories that are particularly interesting are the currency board and "dollarization" categories.[3] The currency board choice was seen as the logical choice for developing countries after Argentina seemingly solved their inflationary problems using a currency board. Unfortunately, time revealed that the currency board approach was not as effective as was hoped, and recently developing countries have turned to "dollarization" as a possible alternative. The differences between currency board and "dollarization" approaches are difficult for students to grasp. However, using the states in the United States as an example of "dollarization" makes the concept easier for students. For example, Hawaii has adopted the US dollar as a currency, but has some say in how monetary policy is conducted in Washington. Furthermore, the seigniorage revenue, collected in Washington, is distributed back to Hawaii through the Federal government.

Discussing dollarization also provides a nice segue to a discussion about Euroland, the European Union countries that adopted the Euro as their currency. This is one of the most remarkable changes in international monetary arrangements, where several major traditional currencies are replaced for a previously non-existing currency, and deserves a detailed discussion for students to understand the importance of this event. Never before in history have some of the major currencies, such as the Deutsche Mark and the French Franc, been removed from circulation and a new currency taken their place. This type of multilateral "dollarization" is also a great opportunity to contrast unilateral "dollarization" of Ecuador with the multilateral adoption of the Euro by, for example, the Slovak Republic. This also lends itself well to discussions of central bank differences between the two cases, and extensions which compare these to the US Federal Reserve and the 50 US states.

Balance of Payments

Students seem to dread the balance of payments part of the course, because it reminds them of accounting, but it enhances student understanding of how the trade and capital flows are counted. When the press discusses the balance of payments they focus on the trade flows in such a way that it sounds like a positive balance is a winning formula, whereas a negative trade balance somehow indicates a less productive nation. Thus the first thing to point out to students is that only goods and capital flowing across a border are counted in the balance of payments. Therefore, the production of Coca-Cola in Japan does not enter the balance of payments, but a Lexus built in Japan and sold in the US is counted.

It is also important to show students that the transactions that are recorded in the balance of payments will by definition balance out due to the double-entry accounting system. Initially, it helps to have students do a few balance of payments accounting entries, so they understand how the double entry accounting works. Once the students are familiar with the textbook-type entries, it is useful to show the actual balance of payments sheets to illustrate that the entries are exactly the same as the textbook entries. The actual balance of payments schedules can be downloaded from the Bureau of Economic Analysis: US International Transactions Accounts Data.

The capital account is particularly useful to examine in more detail because students can see the large foreign central bank intervention that takes place. For example, the balance of payments accounts show that in 2009, foreign central banks bought over $450 billion of US assets. That is an enormous amount, and covers more than the entire trade deficit that year. Equally interesting is the current account line for US investment income. While it is the largest borrower in the world, the US still earns more on its ownership of foreign assets than foreigners earn on the holdings of US assets. This is very important for the current debate about the US foreign debt. The US has the largest foreign debt of any country in the world, but still collects more income on its foreign asset holdings than foreigners earn on US asset holdings. In fact, investment income earned on foreign assets exceeded investment income paid to foreign asset holders by about $122 billion in 2009. The reason for these earnings is the large holdings of assets by foreign central banks. In the last five years, foreign central banks have accumulated over $2 trillion in US assets. Foreign central banks do not have any profit incentive for these purchases, and therefore keep the assets in low-yielding liquid assets. Consequently, the US has a very low cost foreign debt as compared with any other country in the world.

HEDGING FOREIGN EXCHANGE RISK AND PARITY CONDITIONS

The second section of the course deals with the financial interdependence between countries. Countries are connected through trade flows and capital flows. The current wave of globalization is led by financial instruments that have resulted in this interdependence increasing much faster than the growth of trade flows, although the latter is more visible. The reason for this is that capital flows have connected countries to an extent that we have never seen before. Deposits and loans are made across borders and in foreign currencies. For example, an individual can now obtain a mortgage in a foreign currency to reduce the cost of borrowing relative to their domestic currency interest rate. Such cross-country markets have given rise to a large number of financial instruments to deal with foreign currency risk. This section of the course introduces the connections between countries, interest rate parity and purchasing power parity, and also some basic foreign currency hedging instruments.

Forward-looking Markets

When a company or an individual has a receivable or liability due in the future in a foreign currency, they have to consider the risk of the value changing in the future. For example, if a payment has to be made next year in foreign currency, and the cost of the currency rises, then the cost of the liability also increases.

The simplest forward-looking market is the forward market itself. It is important for students to understand how convenient it is for firms to eliminate their currency risk exposure through the forward market. The company with a liability now realizes the exact amount they will pay a year from now, and will not be surprised by the currency value changing. Furthermore, students need to understand the broader implications of this risk being adopted and hedged by banks. A comparison with an insurance company is useful to make students understand how a forward market differs from hurricane insurance. In the case of banks offering fixed forward rates, they can perfectly hedge the risk by selling the same contract in the other currency. Thus, banks do not keep any foreign exchange rate risk by selling forward contracts. Instead, they earn money by a forward spread from the buy and sell rate of the forward contracts. In contrast, an insurance firm is not able to perfectly diversify away a hurricane risk, and has to charge a risk premium. This comparison is a good way to discuss the existence of a risk premium in insurance, but a risk premium does not normally exist in the forward market because the bank can perfectly diversify the risk. The forward market discussion can easily be augmented by discussing the currency swap market that banks use. The currency forward and currency swap markets are the cornerstone of how currency risk is hedged in international financial markets.

Other forward-looking markets are also interesting. The currency futures markets provide an interesting discussion for potential speculative activity. Currency futures can be bought with a small investment, and the quick movements in currency values can cause large gains or losses in futures contracts. Illustrating the potential gains and losses by going through how one buys a contract and the potential gains/losses teaches students about the risks associated with speculating in the currency futures market, when currency rates move substantially.

In addition, a rudimentary coverage of the option market provides a good example of how options are a useful, but expensive, alternative to the forward market. If a company has a future liability in a foreign currency and buys a forward contract, such a contract has to be exercised even if the cost of the foreign currency actually falls in the future. However, if the same company chose to buy a currency option, they would not need to exercise the contract and could take advantage of the falling cost of the foreign currency in the future. Comparing the cost side, between currency forwards and options, one can see that the option not to exercise a contract is not cheap. Buying a forward contract is very cheap, whereas an option carries a high cost which has to be paid immediately.

Covered Interest Rate Parity

Once students are exposed to forward rates, they often ask how banks set such rates. If exchange rates are so difficult to forecast, then why are banks so "certain" of the forward rate? This question connects perfectly with the Covered Interest Rate Parity (CIRP) concept. Exposing the class to interest rates from two equivalent maturity bonds and the forward premium in two different countries makes the interest rate parity condition more real to students. It is also a good exercise to have students compute it to see how close one gets to the forward premium.

Students' understanding of the concept is enhanced when they are introduced to what happens if an incorrect forward rate is set. In the real world, this would not happen, but it is useful to see the arbitrage that would happen. How would interest rates, the spot rate and forward rates have to adjust to reach the arbitrage-free condition again? Once the students see how many problems an incorrect forward rate causes, one can introduce the idea that in the real world banks use the CIRP to set the forward rate, to make sure it is always correct.

Purchasing Power Parity

Once the CIRP condition has been discussed, it is natural to continue with the Purchasing Power Parity (PPP) condition. This order makes it easy to show how CIRP is a subset of PPP. It also highlights the weakness of PPP relative to CIRP. A discussion of what price index to use in the PPP condition will further emphasize the weakness of a broadly defined PPP condition.

The PPP condition provides an opportunity to discuss two important extensions to the basic foreign exchange markets, namely the real exchange rate and over/undervaluation. Both of these concepts can be easily motivated by examining the Big Mac Index. The Big Mac Index is published on a regular basis by *The Economist* and samples the cost of a Big Mac across the world, and computes the real cost using the prevailing exchange rates at the time the price was sampled. This index provides a way for students to identify with real exchange rates and PPP calculations.

International Capital Flows

The CIRP and PPP conditions motivate one-way capital flows. However, in the real world, capital flows both in and out of a country. Basic portfolio diversification is a concept economics students should become familiar with, because it is the cornerstone of financial investment. Introducing a return-risk tradeoff provides a good introduction to financial markets, and may make students curious about financial economics.

It is easiest to motivate global diversification by showing graphically the international diversification gain. Solnik (1974) presents the diversification gain in a nice and intuitive way for students of many backgrounds, including students with very limited mathematical background. Once students understand the theoretical advantage of international diversification, one can compare the actual portfolio investments with the theoretical ones. The actual US portfolio investments are far less internationally diversified than theory would predict. Thus, it is useful to have a discussion of why US portfolio diversification appears suboptimal.

OPEN ECONOMY MACROECONOMIC MODELS

The most intuitive approach to international macroeconomic models is to approach them in chronological order, to show students what constraints are relaxed and which assumptions are added to generate the new model. However, in some instances it might be better to move one of these categories up earlier in the course to generate some excitement about the topic. For example, on a Master's level course, one might prefer to move the Mundell-Fleming framework earlier to generate some discussion of current macroeconomic conditions.

Elasticity Theory

The elasticity theory follows nicely from the development of the trade flow model introduced in the section on the historical global environment. Using the trade flow model, a currency devaluation ought to resolve a persistent trade deficit situation, but the J-curve indicates that this does not happen immediately. The elasticity response is composed of a contracting phase (no elasticity response), a medium run with some elasticity response, and finally a long run with sufficient elasticity response to generate an improvement in the balance of trade. For example, a country that devalues may have an immediate worsening of the trade balance in the contracting phase. In addition, the demand elasticities may be too low to have an improvement following the contracting phase. However, once sufficient time has passed, alternative substitutes will be discovered, and the demand elasticities will be sufficient to see an improvement in the trade balance.

Absorption Approach with IMF Conditionality

The absorption approach follows naturally from the elasticity approach in that appropriate macroeconomic conditions have to exist so that a devaluation of the foreign currency has the expected effect. As the absorption approach is simple to explain, one can use this section of the course to introduce the more recent role of the IMF. In the historical global environment section of the course, the IMF was introduced as the overseer of the global exchange rate system. In this section, the IMF can be discussed as an approval agency that sets sufficient conditions to make the private lenders feel comfortable when the repayment potential of the country is in question. The IMF pays particular attention to the absorption approach because the country applying for a loan needs to have sufficient expected foreign exchange earnings to repay future loans.

Short-run Macroeconomic Policy: The Mundell-Fleming Approach

Including a Mundell-Fleming extension to the IS-LM model (here called the IS-LM-BP approach) in the International Money and Finance course, assumes that the students have a solid economics background.[4] It is preferable that students have seen the IS-LM model before in an intermediate macroeconomics class, but the basic model can quickly be reviewed so students are at the same starting point. The IS-LM-BP is a useful approach to show the desired and undesired effects of fiscal and monetary policy in an international setting. Specifically, it is relevant for students to see how fiscal policy effectiveness changes dramatically if the country is in a fixed or flexible exchange rate regime.

The IS-LM-BP approach is particularly useful for showing changes in international borrowing conditions. The BP curve shifts according to the risk premium that a particular country has. The perceived riskiness of a country's assets can cause dramatic consequences that are clear in the IS-LM-BP schedule. For example, the Asian financial crisis can easily be shown using the IS-LM-BP model. A substantial loss of confidence in the Thai economy resulted in a sharp upward shift in the BP schedule. The fixed exchange rate policy in Thailand caused a sharp inwards shift in the LM curve, and a deep recession followed. Contagion effects resulted in similar shifts in the BP schedule in neighboring countries, causing the Asian financial crisis to spread through South-East Asia.

The IS-LM-BP schedule can also be used to illustrate China's reluctance to let its exchange rate to float. The BP schedule has shifted down for China, since it is seen as a safe investment by foreign investors. Resisting a revaluation of the Yuan has resulted in a sharp buildup of reserves as monetary policy is constrained by capital flows. However, at the same time, the increase in Yuan assets may be causing too much stimulus in the long run. Therefore the model would predict that China is likely to allow the Yuan to revalue at some point.

Long-run Macroeconomic Policy: The MABP/MAER Approach

The IS-LM-BP model is convenient for showing how macroeconomic policy works in the short run when prices are fixed, but output is allowed to move. In the long run, prices will move, and macroeconomic policy will have a different effect. In the monetary approach, the simplifying assumption of long-run monetary neutrality implies that output becomes exogenous, but prices are perfectly flexible. The monetary model applies both to a flexible exchange rate framework and a fixed exchange rate framework. The flexible exchange rate framework is referred to as the Monetary Approach to the Exchange Rates (MAER) and the fixed exchange rate framework is referred to as the Monetary Approach to the Balance of Payments (MABP).

The Intuition behind the MABP and MAER

MABP is easy to motivate using the specie-flow mechanism of David Hume (1752). If specie is destroyed, then the effect would be felt in price reductions if the output remained at full employment. Specie-based currency implies a fixed exchange rate, thus the price reduction would make the goods in the country attractive to neighboring countries. In a two-country framework, this would lead to an increase in specie flowing from the neighboring country until the specie and prices are equilibrated across countries.

Extending the specie-flow mechanism to fiat money is informative for students. They can appreciate how in a perfectly fixed exchange rate system the monetary policy in the MABP becomes completely dependent on the country that the country is fixing the exchange rate with. Using the Mexican fixed exchange rate, as an example, students can see how futile it is for a Central Bank to attempt to have a fixed exchange rate and pursue its own monetary policy objectives.

The MAER approach follows conveniently from the MABP. Allowing the exchange rates to move causes the Hume specie-flow to disappear. In the simple setup, the relative price change is perfectly offset by an exchange rate adjustment. Thus, it is easy to show students that monetary policy would now be insulated. Therefore, the US would prefer to have a floating exchange rate in order to have an independent monetary policy.

Formalizing the MABP and MAER

Although it is easy to motivate the MABP and MAER using a simple specie-flow model, introducing the formal model has advantages as well. From a pedagogical viewpoint, it is useful for students to see how the model works and to see how we have to make some strong assumptions to make the model tractable. A useful model entails simplifying the money demand equation to be a Cambridge-k money demand equation. Using the PPP condition, one can derive a simple relationship between money supply, exchange rates, foreign prices and domestic output growth.[5] The money supply can be subdivided into an international reserve component and a domestic money creation component. The domestic money creation is the standard money creation that the central bank does (for example, an open market operation). The international component is the official balance in the balance of payment (for example, a foreign exchange intervention). Using the more formal model, students can see how international reserves are affected in a MABP by a change in domestic money creation or a change in foreign prices. Similarly, students learn about exchange rate movements in response to domestic output movements or domestic money creation.

Extensions of the MAER

Examining the implied exchange rate from a monetary model, one can show that the variability of the implied exchange rate is small relative to the actual exchange rates. Therefore some extensions to the MAER are relevant. Two extensions of the MAER are often mentioned in the news media. The first is the currency substitution argument that money demand might be affected through expectations, and the other extension is the overshooting theory of Dornbusch (1976).

Currency substitution causes a double effect on exchange rates, because the supply effect is augmented by a money demand effect from the reduction in use of a currency that is viewed as weak. The interesting part of the theory is that the policy prescription becomes focused on cooperation between countries. This cooperation is easily viewed in the G-7 and now G-20 meeting to coordinate policies. In the pure MAER, there would be no need for those meetings as policies are completely independent.

The overshooting theory is also interesting because of its policy prescription. The overshooting theory allows for a quick adjustment of CIRP, but a slow adjustment of PPP. With this combination, the exchange rate has to over-adjust in the short run, and then will follow the MAER approach in the long run. Again the policy prescription is interesting for students, because it provides some support for government intervention in the exchange rate market as the short-run exchange rate is excessively variable. For example, Japan has often slowed down exchange rate movements with intervention, on the basis that the foreign exchange market is overreacting to news events.

The General Equilibrium Approach

Unless the course is a pure open economy macroeconomics course, it is unlikely that there will be much time left over to be devoted to the vast literature that uses general equilibrium models to explain exchange rate movements. For Master's level students, in particular, it is useful to introduce the more recent work on general equilibrium theory to explain exchange rate movements. Stockman (1987) provides an accessible overview of the general equilibrium approach.[6] In his model, the real exchange rate reflects the marginal rate of substitution between consumption of domestic and foreign goods. An exogenous increase in the home good would then reduce the real exchange rate; in other words, there would be a real depreciation of the home currency.

Stockman's simple model provides a real exchange rate and output connection that is consistent with the real-world stylized facts. However, some other dimensions are not as easily reproduced. Therefore most of the recent work has been to extend this type of model to mimic other cross-country stylized facts. The models are becoming more and more complex, necessitating solution techniques that can find numerical solutions to the models. So far no single model has become adopted as the model to replace the MAER.

PEDAGOGICAL TECHNIQUE

This chapter has focused on the content of an international money and finance course. However, it is also important to consider specific pedagogical approaches one can use to stimulate students. The press is full of examples of international financial concerns and issues. For example, a falling dollar has caused pressure on oil prices to increase, resulting in high gas prices for US consumers. Therefore it is useful to have as many current examples as possible. Students find it stimulating to hand in (and discuss) recent press clips. It is also useful to allow students to discuss a recent event in detail as a research paper. This paper can be based on a recent article in, for example, the *Wall Street Journal*. Thus, students can discuss a recent international finance event and relate this event to the theoretical discussion in class. For example, the recent scare that some European countries may have to default on their fiscal debt has brought downward pressure on the Euro. This effect can be shown using the IS-LM-BP model that was developed in the exchange rate theory section.

Frequent homework assignments are also beneficial for students in that the concepts appear simple when the professor solves the concept on the board, but students tend to become much more confused when they have to solve a similar problem themselves. For example, a triangular arbitrage problem appears simple when the professor leads the students through the answer on the board, but students do not know where to start when they face a new version of the problem. Homework assignments are particularly useful in helping students to understand the reciprocal nature of exchange rates. When students must buy or sell currency in a homework problem, they better understand that one currency increasing in value means that the other will decrease in value. This is the most fundamental concept in international money and finance, and the hardest for students to understand. Fortunately, the increasing globalization of the world makes students more exposed to international events, such as exchange rate movements and trade deficits, making a course in international money and finance interesting and relevant to students with many different educational backgrounds.

CONCLUSIONS

The world is becoming increasingly global. In the 1970s and 1990s, this was mostly apparent in increased trade flows. However, global capital flows grew exponentially in the 1990s and 2000s. This global interdependence is being felt in numerous fields of study. For example, International Affairs students now have to learn about global capital flows as this affects every aspect of international negotiations. With an increasing emphasis on the global environment, international money and finance courses are likely to have an increasing share of students coming from a non-economic background. Therefore it is important to have the flexibility to increase the emphasis of the first two sections of the course, at the expense of the traditional open economy models. In addition, the recent "great recession" has made students more interested in international banking. Therefore increased coverage of the second section would be appropriate to make students more familiar with how global investment flows have become the cornerstone of the housing bubble in the US. As the global environment changes, the coverage of international money and finance courses will change slightly, but they should always contain the three major sections discussed in this chapter.

NOTES

1. Bank for International Settlements (2010).
2. See, for example, http://markets.ft.com/RESEARCH/markets/DataArchiveFetchReport?Type=DSP&Date=02/25/2011, where closing dollar spot rates with buy and sell spreads are shown for 25 February (accessed 25 February 2011).
3. Here we use "dollarization" as the act of adopting another country's currency than the one used in the domestic economy previously.
4. The IS-LM-BP acronym comes from Melvin and Norrbin (forthcoming). Other textbooks may have slightly different names.
5. See Melvin and Norrbin (forthcoming) for details on the derivation.
6. See also Stockman (1998) for an interesting overview of correlations.

REFERENCES

Bank for International Settlements (2010), "Triennial Central Bank survey of foreign exchange and derivatives market activity in April 2010 – preliminary results", Monetary and Economic Department, September, available at: www.bis.org/publ/rpfx10.pdf (accessed 10 June 2011).

Dornbusch, R. (1976), "Expectations and exchange rate dynamics", *Journal of Political Economy*, **84** (6), 1161–76.

Hume, D. [1752] (1985), *Essays: Moral, Political and Literary*, edited by D. Miller, Indianapolis: Liberty Fund.

Melvin, M. and S. Norrbin (forthcoming), *International Money & Finance, eighth edition*, Elsevier: Academic Press.

Solnik, B. (1974), "Why not diversify internationally rather than domestically?", *Financial Analysts Journal* (July/August), 48–54.
Stockman, A. (1987), "The equilibrium approach to exchange rates", *Federal Reserve Bank of Richmond Economic Review*, **73**, 12–31.
Stockman, A. (1998), "New evidence connecting exchange rates to business cycles", *Federal Reserve of Richmond Economic Quarterly*, **84** (2), 73–89.

56 Teaching international trade by bridging the gap between theory and practice
Raymond Robertson

International Trade is a great subject to teach undergraduates because students generally need very little, if any, persuading that the topic is relevant and important. It is nearly a cliché to say that we live in a truly globalized world. President Barak Obama's 2011 State of the Union address contained multiple references to exports and international trade agreements. Students see evidence of globalization both in their current role as consumers and when looking ahead to their roles as producers.

But international trade's ubiquitous nature creates its own problems. Students often come to class filled with information they have absorbed about international trade and, as Krugman (1993, p. 23) remarks, ". . . most of what a student is likely to read or hear about international economics is nonsense." He argues that students are frequently bombarded with statements and ideas that do not hold up well when subjected to the rigors of economic reasoning, and teaching them to identify nonsense when they hear it would do them and society a great service.

Krugman was specifically directing his comments at those teaching introductory economics (principles), and therefore he recommends that professors teaching that course prioritize the core – budget constraints and comparative advantage – over relatively recent innovations in the field. A full course in international economics or international trade offers professors the opportunity to cover not only the core but also the two subsequent waves of innovation in the field (sometimes referred to at conferences as "new" trade theory and the "new new" trade theory). Covering all three of these is probably much more important today because trade patterns have shifted dramatically since Krugman's article.

The specific topics covered in the course, as clearly relevant as they are, may only be half of the contribution that international trade makes to a student's economic education. One of the strengths of economics as a discipline is its widespread use of models that simplify the world in ways that generate powerful insights. While students are introduced to models in principles (such as the production possibilities frontier and supply and demand), international trade is exceptionally blessed with elegant models that both provide valuable insights and can help students develop their skills in using and understanding economic models.

Of course, students are often reluctant to accept an emphasis on models because they desire their courses to be as practical and applied as possible. After all, most students will not go on to graduate work in economics. Few will work in jobs that specifically use economic models. Therefore, one of the significant challenges of teaching international trade is to make the models relevant and show students why models have real-world applicability.

My underlying philosophy is based on directly addressing one of the most frequent complaints undergraduates have about economic models: they are simply not realistic. Since the students prefer a model more closely aligned with reality, presenting the material through the process of gradually relaxing assumptions of the most restrictive model motivates them and the material as the course progresses.

The sections that follow focus on three important course dimensions: audience, content, and structure. One of the strengths of international trade is that there is a solid core of material that is generally accepted. Given that this core is fairly universal, instructors have the opportunity to tailor the course towards the students who will be taking the course. The sections that follow offer one possible structure. The structure is not particularly novel – the large number of textbooks in international economics often follow a loosely similar structure – but the emphasis described here offers a suggestion of how one might give students practice in using models as well as learning key content.

KNOW YOUR AUDIENCE

There are many parallels between theater and teaching. One similarity is that it is important in both cases to know your audience. Two of the questions that may guide decisions of how to present the material may most simply be expressed as "Where are the students coming from?" and "Where are the students going?"

Undergraduate students vary considerably in terms of their principles and math preparation, the preconceptions they bring into the class and their exposure to popular ideas about international trade. The math preparation consideration is straightforward, and one can usually discern how much students remember from principles in the first day or two of class (I usually dedicate the first day for a principles review). The others, however, may be less obvious. When asking one colleague about teaching at his particular institution, he explained that he had just moved from a school in which students were extremely skeptical of markets to another in which students took markets to be basically infallible. The difference between the two schools was largely one of culture. These attitudes are also strongly affected by time. Students from Latin America might understandably have a very different attitude about trade liberalization now than they had in the early 1990s. If you do not discern where the students are coming from, it is likely that you will encounter obstacles in their learning. The obverse is also true: knowing the strengths will make teaching more efficient because you can spend less time on material or assumptions that the students bring to the class.

Where students are going should also affect how one structures the course. I had one student ask me at the beginning of a course when we were going to learn how to import and export goods (which I had not included on the syllabus), because, of course, it was a course in international trade. Knowing if students are going into business, graduate school, or policy work will inform decisions on how to allocate time in the course between the different core areas discussed below and the approach used to present the material (such as the emphasis on solving specific models numerically). It is also helpful to know what skills the students are expected to gain, if any, from the course that may be used in other classes in the department or major.

Therefore I try to spend time either before the semester or early in the semester learning about the students. This is a lot easier when classes are small, but even with larger classes, colleagues, graduate students who have taught, and even upper-division undergrads can generally provide relevant information about the students. As with driving, it is a lot easier to provide directions when you know the point of departure.

CONTENT: THE CORE OF INTERNATIONAL TRADE

The popularity of International Economics is reflected in the number of both print and online textbooks. The intersection of what these books cover might be considered to be the "core" of international trade. This core can be divided into three parts: foundations (basically neoclassical trade theory), renovations (the "new" trade theory), and implications (trade policy). The core does not necessarily cover all relevant topics. In fact, one might even add a fourth part – innovations – to cover some of the relatively recent advances in trade theory and empirics (sometimes referred to as the "new new" trade theory).

Foundations

Most courses in international trade require principles or some similar introductory course. This means that students will probably have been exposed to the ideas of gains from exchange and specialization at some point. They have also been exposed to models as economic tools and, to the extent that they are taking another course beyond principles, have not rejected the idea of using models outright. Together this means that the principles of economics course often provides a reasonable, if not excellent, foundation for international trade.

From this foundation, it is easy to present the basic theorems of international economics. International trade has an exceptionally rich theoretic foundation that traces back directly to David Hume, Adam Smith, and David Ricardo. The contributions of these classical economists are universally accepted: eyebrows would certainly rise upon hearing that a student from an international trade course was not familiar with the Ricardian model. The foundations of international trade include Heckscher-Ohlin, Rybczynski, and the Stolper-Samuelson theorems. Most textbooks also feature the Ricardo-Viner model (specific factors). In many cases, these models are grouped under all resource/technology-based trade models and called the "neoclassical model" of international trade that explains trade volumes through differences in relative output prices. Krugman (1993) argues that covering these core models is essential for today's undergraduates. An informal survey of available textbooks suggests that nearly every textbook author would agree. These theorems permeate policy discussions and provide a common foundation for our understanding of exchange between countries. They also form a common foundation for all subsequent topics in international economics and illustrate the fundamental reason for international trade (and, in fact, nearly all economic activity): mutually beneficial gains from exchange.

As mentioned above, textbooks do not vary so much in content as they do in presentation. Students bound for graduate work might find rigorous model-solving to be the most engaging presentation. Other students might balk at such an approach.

Table 56.1   US trade partners and total trade

1985		2010	
Canada	116257.4	Canada	480457.7
Japan	91413.8	China	415899.1
Mexico	32766.4	Mexico	359244.9
Germany	29289.4	Japan	164073.6
United Kingdom	26210	Germany	119420.2
Taiwan	21096.3	United Kingdom	89617.1
Korea, South	15969.6	Korea, South	80101.5
France	15577.6	France	59292.7
Italy	14299	Taiwan	56100.66
Netherlands	11350.3	Brazil	53906.68

Notes: Values are not seasonally adjusted and are in millions of current US dollars.

Source: US Census Bureau Foreign Trade Division, available at: http://www.census.gov/foreign-trade/balance/country.xls, accessed 25 May 2011.

Regardless of presentation, however, it seems reasonable to say that having a very solid foundation in the neoclassical trade models is very important for any course in international trade.

Renovations

One of the main problems students have with the neoclassical models is the one that economists raised in the 1970s: do these very restrictive models work in reality? These questions invariably surface in class and provide an excellent opportunity to introduce both testing trade theory and the innovations based on monopolistic competition, economies of scale, intra-industry trade, and global value chains.

Testing trade theory

One of the easiest topics to motivate is the famous Leontief paradox because Leontief asked the same question that most international trade students ask: how accurate are these elegant trade theories in reality? This question and the subsequent Leontief paradox therefore serve as a springboard to the discussion of "stylized facts" about trade. Like many textbooks, I often open the course with some emphasis on empirical trade patterns. In particular, I require students to go online and find trade data that describe US trade patterns in terms of both goods and partners.

Table 56.1 shows the top ten US trade partners (based on the sum of imports and exports) and trade volumes in 1985 and 2010. In 1985, three of the top ten US trade partners (in terms of total trade) might have been considered "labor abundant" countries based on GDP per capita: Mexico, Taiwan, and South Korea. In the 1970s and 1980s, this pattern motivated the emphasis on the gravity model that has become a standard model of empirical trade analysis. Since it is so often used, and is straightforward to describe, it can be used to motivate the renovations in trade theory.[1] The gravity model shows that distance and size, which are not included in the simplest forms of the classical trade models, are powerful determinants of trade and therefore have inspired some of the "new" trade theory.

New trade theory
In 2008, Paul Krugman won the Nobel Prize in economics for his role in helping to develop what has become to be known as "new" trade theory. His work, among others, helped explain trade among similar countries, trade in product variety, and economies of scale. Today nearly every current textbook features at least one chapter on economies of scale (generally distinguishing external from internal) and monopolistic competition. Not surprisingly, the newer books have been expanding this area. Like the other areas of trade theory, the "new" trade theory is easy to motivate and there are many entertaining examples of the theory at work. Two-way trade in beverages or automobiles are just two examples. It is also important to introduce students to the idea that expanding the number of possible consumption varieties increases social welfare in measurable ways. Broda and Weinstein (2006), for example, show that the welfare gains from the observed increase in import variety may be as high as 2.8 percent of GDP.

While this material is important, well-known, and increasingly taught in international economics courses, one aspect is worth emphasizing. Discussing varieties and intra-industry trade on the consumption side significantly advances our understanding of why developed countries trade more with each other rather than with developing countries and why they exchange similar products. But discussing the production side as well lays the groundwork for improving students' understanding of the trade in product parts (sometimes referred to as production fragmentation, outsourcing, or off-shoring) that increasingly characterizes world trade.

Global value chains
The organization of an industry that engages in trade in product parts is often called a *global value chain*. Global value chains play a critical role in the rise of developing country exporters. Reconsidering Table 56.1, we see that by 2010, Brazil and China became significant exporters, bringing the number of "labor abundant" countries up to half of the top ten. China and Mexico approached Canada's trade level and Brazil's exports significantly increased. Developing countries, which as a group played a relatively small role in global manufacturing trade in 1980, are becoming increasingly important. Distance and size may still be the most powerful explanatory variables for explaining trade, but Table 56.1 seems to suggest that they may be losing their importance relative to more traditional comparative advantage explanations.

These shifts have not made the "new" trade theory less relevant. Developing country trade, especially for relatively new entrants, is commonly characterized by participation in global value chains. Apparel might be the best-known example. These relatively new trade patterns pave the way for the discussion of how the insights of both classical trade theory (such as trade based on differences in factor endowments) combine with the "new" trade theory (allowing for production fragmentation) to explain today's observed trade patterns.

Implications: Trade Policy

The popular media constantly bombard undergraduates with terms like "competitiveness" and "level playing field" that contain policy implications but are difficult to define. Given the media's focus on trade restrictions, it is important to explain to future voters both the history and mechanics of various trade policy instruments.

History

One of the challenges of teaching international trade to undergraduates is that they often lack a historical perspective. Most people agree that the lessons of the Smoot-Hawley Tariff Act of 1930, the subsequent dramatic fall in tariffs, and corresponding rise in world trade since World War II are important to share with today's undergraduates. Tariffs have not disappeared, however, and students should understand how tariffs work and how their use has changed over time.

One approach I have found to be relatively successful when discussing the history of trade policy is to reduce the focus on developed countries and include trade policies of developing countries from the 1940s through the 1990s. In particular, the contrast between the East Asian countries' export focus[2] and other developing countries' (such as India and Latin America) import substitution model is often very illustrative of the effects of not only tariffs *per se* but government management of trade for development purposes.

I have found that discussing trade policy history offers an effective opportunity to present stages of economic integration. The surge of trade agreements in the 1990s and the relative stagnation of the World Trade Organization motivate the debate over whether or not these agreements are road blocks or building blocks for multilateral liberalization. Describing the conditions that the European Union imposed for membership, as well as some of the implications of forming the European Union, are also very interesting to students and help balance out the focus on developing countries mentioned above.

Trade policy instruments

Since tariffs are easy to incorporate into trade models, illustrating the welfare and distributional costs of tariffs is straightforward. But while it is important to define and present the mechanics of tariffs, it is probably even more important to discuss the fact that trade policy is far more complex than tariffs alone. For example, the North American Free Trade Agreement was over one thousand pages long, which is far more than it might take to simply codify tariff reductions.

The popularity of trade policy instruments shifts over time. In the 1980s, voluntary export restraints (VERs) and voluntary import expansions (VIEs) seemed to dominate trade policy debates. In the 1990s strategic trade policy was followed by administrative protection. Today the complexity of trade policy has grown to include Rules of Origin (ROO), dispute resolution, and temporary trade barriers (anti-dumping measures, safeguards, and countervailing duties). For many countries, especially developing countries, temporary trade barriers (TTBs) have become the instrument of choice for providing protection in the face of economic downturn or perceived injury from imports.

Innovations: The "New New" Trade Theory and Firm-Level Dynamics

Theory has historically been the strength of international economics. Data had been relatively scarce. Advances in both data collection and computing power opened up the way for empirical investigations in international trade.[3] Firm-level dynamics in response to both trade liberalization and trade shocks are now understood to be important aspects of the effects of international trade. While most of the two-good trade models (including those with varieties) focus on changes between industries, recent papers that focus on firm-level dynamics focus on changes within industries. Changes within industries are important because firms within industries are heterogeneous in terms of productivity, capital and skill intensity, and propensity to engage in international trade (in terms of both importing inputs and exporting).

The "new new" trade theory focuses on how trade, or exposure to foreign markets, affects firms and employment within industries. Melitz (2003) is one of the literature's leading examples. When there are fixed costs to exporting, the most productive firms will export. These firms tend to use more capital and employ more relatively skilled workers. When a trade shock occurs, this affects the returns from exporting within industries and therefore can affect the margin at which firms enter the export market.

Krugman (1993) raises the point that relatively new advances in trade theory (and at the time he was even referring to some of his own contributions) are not nearly as important to teach as the foundations of international trade theory. But, like the advances in international trade theory that gave us increasing returns, it seems likely that the advances in empirical trade that highlight the importance of within-industry heterogeneity will have staying power and work themselves into the canon. The basic concept of within-industry heterogeneity that is very important for trade and trade policy is significant enough for students to benefit from exposure to these ideas.

STRUCTURE: ONE POSSIBLE APPROACH

There is no "one size fits all" model for an international trade course. Instead, there is considerable leeway about the detail, rigor (generally understood to be the amount of math used when presenting the material), and depth in which different sections are presented. A unifying theme for the course often helps students stay focused on the "big picture" and keeps them from feeling lost in a sea of material. One approach that I have found to work well is to combine the strength of international trade – the elegant models – with the student's desire for practicality and realism to form the structure. Starting with the most restrictive model and then gradually relaxing its assumptions complements students' inclination for making the models more realistic, illustrates the main points (content) of international trade, and provides a "road map" for the entire course. The Ricardian model, which illustrates comparative advantage through differences in productivity, is often considered the least realistic of the main trade models because of the restrictive assumptions. I highlight fourteen assumptions at the beginning of the course and tell students that as we progress, we will relax one at a time to both make the model more realistic and to illustrate the importance of each assumption.

To illustrate this approach, consider the assumptions listed in Box 56.1. Relaxing the

---

BOX 56.1   RICARDIAN ASSUMPTIONS

1. One homogeneous factor
2. Perfect mobility between sectors
3. Imperfect mobility between countries
4. No trade policy
5. Constant returns to scale
6. Homogeneous products
7. Homogeneous firms

---

first assumption and allowing for two factors brings us to the Heckscher-Ohlin (HO) model. The HO model introduces gains and losses from trade, which is critical for understanding current policy debates. It also opens the door for discussion of how to evaluate policy decisions, such as how to weigh gains and losses and what policies might make sense from the criterion of (Pareto) optimality. I have found that the prediction that some people will lose from trade, and that these losses should be considered when making policy, helps students confront their common misperception that "neoclassical economics" is out to "get" workers.

Relaxing the perfect mobility between sectors assumption motivates the Ricardo-Viner (specific factors) model. Students find this model appealing because they often appreciate how difficult it is for a 45-year-old automotive worker to shift into Information Technology. But it also addresses the questions students have about what the "long run" is for models that work in the "long run," and what assumptions make a "short-run" model. Magee's three simple tests of the Stolper-Samuelson theorem is a great example because it shows how the difference between a short-run model and a long-run model can show up in policy (Magee, 1978).

The assumption of no mobility between countries is especially difficult for students to swallow when they live in communities affected by migration. The migration debate is one opportunity for students to see how economists disagree and how different models generate debate among economists. For example, the debate between the labor economists and the trade economists about the wage effects of immigration has been traced back to the (one-good) aggregate labor supply and aggregate labor demand model used by labor economists and the (two-good) Heckscher-Ohlin framework and the companion Rybczynski and Factor Price Insensitivity theorems.

Relaxing the last four assumptions in order shows the importance of trade policy, scale economies, gains from varieties, and within-industry variation that provide a logical structure for presenting both the "new" and "new new" trade theories described above.

PEDAGOGY: LEARNING BY DOING

Hardly anyone would argue that watching, but not practicing, sports would increase performance. Watching only helps in conjunction with practice. International trade provides ample opportunities for active learning. I have found that the following two approaches are particularly helpful for students while learning international trade.

Keeping it Real

Born after the creation of the internet, today's students are more technology-focused than ever before. Getting information online is an integral part of their daily lives. At the same time, online data related to international economics have become increasingly available. It is natural, therefore, to design activities in which students seek, find, and analyze available data. I do this in three ways.

First, at the beginning of the course I have students identify which countries and products dominate the trade patterns of the United States and another country. Doing this early in the course achieves two pedagogical goals. First, it introduces students to the "real world" aspect of international trade. Second, it inspires students to wonder "Why do countries trade?" In-class discussion helps students confirm their US findings and learn about other countries.

Second, it is extremely important to connect the models with the real world as much as possible, which is why nearly all textbooks are full of case studies. I always emphasize these case studies in class.[4] In addition, engaging students in current events is also very effective. Giving incentives for students to include a recent news article when submitting homework assignments, along with a paragraph explaining how that article is related to something discussed in class has seemed effective. Since this is so easy to do, participation is high and it successfully connects class material with current events. While this might be a good idea for any economics class, it is especially easy for international economics.

Third, students can use data they find as the basis of an independent research paper. Although students are often not yet trained in regression analysis, I remind them of the Leontief paradox, Magee's "Three Simple Tests", and the simple observation that developed countries historically have traded most amongst themselves. These are all results that are not based in regression analysis. Student research papers allow them to address topics that may not be emphasized in class, such as cartels (for example, OPEC), specific provisions of trade agreements (for example, labor provisions), or case studies of specific trading partners (for example, China and sub-Saharan Africa).

Practice Problems

The models of international trade provide an excellent opportunity to give students experience in solving economic models. Solving models achieves several pedagogical objectives. First, it helps internalize the key insights of the model. That is, if the students can see how the inner workings of the model combine to produce the main insight, it seems likely that they will leave with a deeper understanding of the insight itself.

Second, it gives students a taste of the mathematical side of economics, which has been, in my experience, one of the most significant psychological barriers keeping students from continuing in economics. When introduced gently, the simple trade models help increase students' confidence with solving economic models and reduce a barrier to further economics study. Third, it makes reading journal articles a bit less intimidating. While they generally will not understand journal-level mathematics, they at least have a sense of the process authors might be following to get a particular result.

To help students get practice with economic models, I developed a very simple set of online practice problems in java script.[5] Eight topic areas include the Ricardian model, the supply and demand model, tariffs (small and large country), quotas (small and large country), a simple migration model, and the specific factors model. The java script uses a random-number generator to create a new problem every time the page is reloaded. Students can solve the problem and enter their answers. The page will then immediately tell the student if the answer is correct and, if not, provide the correct answer. Since the problems are in java script, there is no need to communicate with a server, the application is very fast, and the problems can be accessed from anywhere, by anyone, free of charge.

CONCLUSIONS

Students will probably disperse wildly after they leave your international trade course. Having a very clear vision of what you want them to remember will help make your class more memorable. When I ask young teachers what they want the students to remember from their course, they generally reply "everything." Having one clear message, a simple sentence or even a word, that you can emphasize repeatedly throughout the course will give students something they may never forget. For some professors, this is "free trade is best." For others, it is "free trade has mixed consequences." The point is not which message to emphasize, but to have one simple and clear message. My experience has been that when students return for their fifth, tenth, or twentieth reunion, they will still remember that one message from your course. So make it count!

NOTES

1. The gravity model provides a good exercise in subsequent econometric courses as well.
2. Featured in the World Bank (1993) publication *The East Asian Miracle.*
3. In 1994 Jon Haveman and others founded the annual Empirical Investigations in International Trade (EIIT) conference that draws economists from all over the world and has spawned sister conferences in both Asia and Europe. See http://www.eiit.org/ (accessed 24 May 2011).
4. For more information about using case studies in economics, see Chapter 2, "Case Use in Economics Instruction", in this volume.
5. See http://www.macalester.edu/~robertson/courses/econ221/Practice/Infinite_Title.htm (accessed 24 May 2011).

REFERENCES

Broda, C. and D. E. Weinstein (2006), "Globalization and the gains from variety", *The Quarterly Journal of Economics,* **121** (2), (May), 541–85.

Krugman, P. (1993), "What do undergrads need to know about trade?", *American Economic Review,* **83** (2), (May), 23–6.

Magee, S. P. (1978), "Three simple tests of the Stolper-Samuelson Theorem", in P. Oppenheimer (ed.), *Issues in International Economics*, Oxford: Oriel Press, pp. 138–53.

Melitz, M. J. (2003), "The impact of trade on intra-industry reallocations and aggregate industry productivity", *Econometrica,* Econometric Society, **71** (6), (November), 1695–725.

World Bank (1993), *The East Asian Miracle: Economic Growth and Public Policy*, Oxford and New York: Oxford University Press, published for the World Bank.

57 Building human capital in the labor economics course
Barry T. Hirsch

Labor economics is a course that can engage students, is relevant to their everyday lives, and provides an ideal setting in which to apply key economic principles. Despite its importance and the interesting topics addressed – earnings, employment, education, discrimination, to name just a few – the labor economics course often fails to provide an enjoyable experience for students. Failure is not inevitable, but making the course a rewarding experience requires effort and a bit of imagination.

It is argued in this chapter that a successful course should not march through or be bound by a textbook. Nor do instructors need to reduce human behavior to some ultra-rational form not recognized by any student who has had a job. Course content ought not be determined by what is easily tested using multiple-choice, computational, and graphical questions. What I do recommend is that instructors adopt a broad organizing framework that will accommodate most course material and provide students with simple but important "take-away" concepts. Learning requires students not only to attend and listen in class, but to read, write, and question. Students understandably desire certainty and want to "know answers." Instructors can provide students with certainty about the structure and expectations of a course, but at the same time make clear that answers absent qualification are rarely good answers. Students need to embrace some degree of complexity and ambiguity, not with frustration but with curiosity and at least a little enthusiasm.

In what follows I develop these themes, first by showing how the labor economics course can be organized around a flexible demand-supply framework, second by suggesting emphasis on important but simple-to-learn "take-away" concepts, and finally by offering my views on how a course might be taught. Although there is some discussion of pedagogy, emphasis is given to course content. As may already be evident, the tone of this chapter is "personal" in that it describes how I think it best to teach a course based on my values and experience. Although the focus is on undergraduate labor economics, some if not all of the discussion can be applied to graduate courses.

AN ORGANIZING FRAMEWORK FOR LABOR ECONOMICS

In this section it is argued that the labor economics course is enhanced by adopting a unified organizing framework from which one can develop key themes and create clear-cut links to other economics courses. My preference for the labor course is that it be organized around the demand-supply (DS) framework, wage and employment determination, and allocation of labor resources. An alternative organizing framework is the principle of time use, discussed briefly at the end of this section.

Why the Demand-Supply (DS) Framework?

A succinct description of labor economics is that it is "the study of wage and employment determination in labor markets." This description has two attractive attributes. First, it is a simple definition that is also comprehensive, being sufficiently broad to encompass most topics and approaches in a labor economics course. Second, because "wages" and "employment" correspond to price and quantity outcomes determined (largely) through labor demand and supply forces, this description implicitly identifies the demand-supply approach as the core organizing framework for the course.

I recommend organizing the labor course around the DS framework for several reasons. First, the framework provides a valuable approach to understanding some of the most important determinants of wages, hours, employment, and the distribution of earnings. The competitive demand-supply model ought not be presented as "truth" – that is, as a mechanical determinant of labor outcomes. But it does provide instructors with a coherent way to frame discussion of the labor market. Regardless of whether an instructor has "tight" or "loose" priors about the competitive model (Reder, 1982), a good labor economics course requires that students develop an understanding of how labor demand and supply influence wages and employment.

A second reason to emphasize (and test) the DS framework is that it is necessary to do so. Although (nearly) all students in a labor economics course have taken a principles course, principles texts relegate labor markets to the end of the micro course and most instructors spend little or no time on the subject.[1] Absent guidance, even students with a good understanding of the DS framework as applied to product markets will have difficulty extending this framework and its principles to labor markets. Such guidance can be provided early in the labor economics course.

Of course many students will not have developed or retained a good understanding of the DS framework in micro principles. Thus, a third reason to emphasize it in the labor course is that it explicitly reinforces what students have or should have learned previously and ties this directly to what they now need to know. Making explicit the links between micro principles and labor economics establishes in students' minds the belief that what they learn in their courses is broadly applicable and that there is logic to economics and the economics curriculum.

Applying the Demand-Supply Framework to Labor Markets

In this section I identify and discuss examples of how the DS framework can be used to understand wage and employment determination, teach key economic concepts, and tie together micro principles and the labor course. Familiar concepts include shifts versus movements along D&S curves and short versus long run. Fundamental but less familiar concepts are (a) a parallel between product market economic profits/losses and the determination of equalizing (or equilibrium) wage differentials and (b) how the invisible hand narrative regarding efficient resource allocation applies in labor markets. Additional applications are briefly discussed.

It is important to provide a quick overview of demand and supply in the labor market at the start of the course. This provides students with a look at where they are headed and establishes links between what they have seen applied in product markets with what they will be using to understand labor markets. Even elementary discussion of the demand and supply axis labels will be informative. Labor "quantity" is measured on the horizontal axis, but during the course it will sometimes refer to individual work hours, sometimes to employment in a homogeneous market (say, workers in some occupation and skill level in a metropolitan area), and sometimes to aggregate employment as seen in the macro principles course. Labor "price" is shown on the vertical axis and designated by W, which reflects both wage and non-wage compensation. A wage for labor services differs from a product market purchase price. Purchase of, say, a hamburger provides the buyer with ownership rights and broad discretion in use of the burger, short of harming others. In the labor market, that is called slavery. The wage is best thought of as a contractual price for labor services. Individuals retain ownership rights to their stock of human capital, which affects the willingness of individuals and firms to invest in skill acquisition.

All students will recall that the distinction between shifts and movements along demand and supply curves largely determined their first exam grade in micro principles. Emphasizing this distinction early in the labor course may not excite students, but it will capture their attention. Instructors know this drill well. Changes in the wage represent movements along demand or supply. Shift factors for labor demand include output q, which enables the instructor to emphasize that labor demand is derived demand, and the price of other factors (not only capital but other labor, so that early in the course one introduces capital-labor and labor-labor substitution). For supply, shift factors can include wages in other markets (occupations and/or location), costs of acquiring the appropriate skills, attractiveness of the job, and population size. A homework assignment or in-class exercise can reinforce this basic theory.[2]

Perhaps the most fundamental topic tying labor economics to micro principles is determination of equilibrium wage differentials, requiring discussion of resource movement, the invisible hand, and economic efficiency.[3] Addressing the important question of "why wages differ" parallels the approach students have seen when learning about the competitive equilibrium in product markets. First, one differentiates short- and long-run time horizons, the latter being the time period over which individuals can acquire training and move to alternative markets. Long-run wage differentials in competitive labor markets (say, for occupations by metropolitan area) result from labor supply shifts that reflect the costs of acquiring skills and from the utility or disutility associated with working conditions or other attributes tied to a job and location (workplace safety, income and employment risk, location, timing of work, etc.). If individuals had identical preferences, natural abilities, and opportunities, long-run labor supply curves would be horizontal, everyone requiring the same equilibrium differential for any given job/ location. Differences in preferences, ability, and opportunities create upward-sloping supply curves. For example, some persons would be willing to acquire the skills to be an accountant for $30,000 a year even though most others will not or cannot do so at $60,000. In this way, long-run equilibrium wage differentials across individuals and jobs are determined by the interaction of labor demand and labor supply.

For students, the most engaging portion of this narrative concerns efficiency and the invisible hand. Technology and other determinants of labor demand and supply constantly change so that one is always groping toward but never arriving at long-run equilibrium. Long-run adjustments in labor markets require the acquisition of new sets of skills (whose principal cost is time) and moving to new locations. At any point in time, workers in some occupations and locations earn wages above their long-run opportunity costs; that is, above-normal returns or "economic profits" on their human capital and location investments. Others (including the unemployed) are earning below normal returns (suffering "losses"). Just as in product markets, economic "profits" and "losses" signal resource movement. Individuals, particularly the young, will train for (via decisions on college-going, area of study, occupation, etc.) and move to markets with good wage and employment opportunities. This process continues until above-normal returns are squeezed out. In occupations and locations where wage and employment opportunities are poor, there is exit among some existing workers and fewer persons train for or move to these jobs/locations. Such decisions eventually lead to normal returns on workers' human capital investments and, in some cases, the disappearance or near extinction of some occupations, industries, and job locations. This is the invisible hand at work in labor markets, automatically attracting (decreasing) human resources in those activities and locations where they are most (least) highly valued. More so than in product markets, the labor adjustment process requires time and can be accompanied by considerable social costs such as long-term unemployment and income loss.[4]

There are numerous other but less fundamental DS applications that instructors can teach. Obvious examples are use of the DS framework coupled with discussion of elasticities to examine the predicted employment effects of minimum wages and the effects of immigration on wages and employment. Although the basic analysis is simple, the small employment effects associated with minimum wages and modest effects on low-skill wages resulting from immigration require that instructors stress that each of these applications involves more than just movements along static labor demand curves. A DS application that is valuable but requires some time is payroll tax incidence and the effects of mandated benefits on wages, employment, and efficiency (Summers, 1989).

For instructors who discuss earnings inequality, a "suspect list" for rising inequality can be organized into demand, supply, and institutional factors. Leading suspects include (a) demand shifts due to skill-biased technical change – the job task SBTC associated with Autor et al. (2003); (b) slow growth in the supply of college graduates relative to demand (losing the "race" between education and technology); (c) demand shifts from increasing trade and globalization; (d) supply shifts from immigration affecting the lower tail of the wage distribution; (e) declining real minimum wages, particularly during the 1980s; and (f) declining private sector unionization, the link being that unions compress wages across and within job positions.

Although I recommend the DS model as the organizing framework for most labor economics courses, a time use/labor supply approach provides an alternative framework for courses populated primarily by economics majors, especially if intermediate micro is a prerequisite. Such a course would make heavy use of indifference curve analysis to address labor supply topics such as labor force participation, hours worked, time spent in home production and leisure, the effects of government policies and programs on labor supply, retirement decisions, household formation, and the changing roles of women and men (for example, age at first marriage, fertility, production specialization versus consumption complementarities in households, women's catch-up and subsequent overtaking of men in college-going, and the gender wage gap). My reluctance to adopt this approach is that, for most undergraduate students, mastering indifference curve analysis requires a substantial time investment in and outside the classroom, crowding out topics and analyses that are arguably more valuable. Most of the topics mentioned above can be adequately addressed absent mastery of indifference curve analysis and identification of income and substitution effects. Heavy reliance on indifference curve analysis provides an easy way to test and sort students based on ability. It may be less effective in enhancing students' knowledge and understanding of labor markets.

'TAKE-AWAY' CONCEPTS STUDENTS WILL RETAIN FROM YOUR COURSE

It is difficult to know what students take away from a course. Nonetheless, it is essential to identify key concepts that are important, easy to learn, and likely to be retained by students. Concepts in the principles course such as opportunity costs and gains from trade stick with students, even if the subtleties of comparative advantage are not fully comprehended. In this section, "take-away" concepts for labor economics students are identified. The first three are important, simple, and require little class time, while the latter two are more complex. Some of these concepts are obvious once understood, but are not so widely appreciated. The list below is intended to be illustrative and not definitive.

The Principal Cost of Human Capital is Time

Labor courses rightly emphasize the importance of human capital. I stress that acquiring skills typically involves learning-by-doing and requires time, with few available short-cuts. Information or society's stock of knowledge is a readily available non-rival good, all the more so following growth of the Internet. Although abundant information is freely available (think MIT class lectures online), understanding such information (that is, adding to one's human capital) is difficult, requiring a lot of time and hard work. One reason to stress this simple point is that it is important and likely to stick. A second is that your students are put on alert that learning and a good return on their college education requires considerable time and effort in and out of class.

The Principal Source of "Wealth" is Human Capital

Wealth is generally measured by the stock of financial assets. Asset wealth is very unequally distributed, with the top 1 percent of households holding most wealth and a large share of households having close to zero or negative wealth. The principal source of "wealth" for virtually all students and their instructors, however, will be their embedded stock of human capital. It is their knowledge, skills, motivation, and lifelong learning that will enable them (at least on average) to generate a reasonably good stream of income over their lives. The good news is that the distribution of human capital (and resulting earnings) is far more equally distributed than is asset wealth. Persons with a large amount of asset wealth cannot easily increase their human capital since they face the same time constraint as do you and your students.[5]

Jobs are Not Fixed and Worker Flows are Large

A natural inclination is to view the labor market as static, with a fixed set of jobs in number and type (occupation/industry). Such a view leads to misleading conclusions. Immigrants working in the US displace natives on a one-for-one basis. Delayed retirement by older workers decreases employment of younger workers by roughly equivalent amounts. Entry of women into the labor force in the 1970s and 1980s necessarily decreased the employment of men. Technology that largely eliminates some occupations, say telephone operators, type setters, bank tellers, and reservation agents, decreases total employment. And in months when total employment is largely unchanged, few new jobs have been created and few lost. Each of the above statements is incorrect.

I emphasize that labor markets are dynamic, with large flows of jobs destroyed and created. If wages are reasonably flexible, the number of jobs roughly expands to the size of the labor force. Entry of women into the labor market in the 1970s and immigrants in the 1990s and 2000s was associated with large increases in employment (jobs) and not wide-scale unemployment. In any given month, including one with little net change in employment, there are several hundred thousand jobs lost (destroyed) and several hundred thousand created. The most notable feature of the US job market is the degree of churning, with immense numbers of jobs destroyed in good times and new jobs created in bad times. This is Schumpeter's "creative destruction" at work.[6]

Micromotives and Macrobehavior: An Application to Discrimination

An important theme in economics, widely associated with Nobel laureate Thomas Schelling (1978), is that it is often difficult to infer individual preferences based on aggregate outcomes or to infer aggregate outcomes based on individual preferences. Schelling's famous example is neighborhood segregation. He shows that even with relatively weak preferences about the race of neighbors, complete segregation often occurs and neighborhoods can "tip" from all white to all black, or vice-versa. Absent knowledge of the choice mechanism (that is, absent an appropriate model), one is likely to infer (incorrectly) that highly segregated neighborhoods result from strong racial preferences.[7]

Gary Becker's taste theory of discrimination provides a vehicle showing the potential disconnect between micromotives and macrobehavior. His employer taste model predicts that there cannot be wage differences for similarly productive white and black workers if employers maximize profits. If there were, employers would increase (decrease) hiring of black (white) workers until there was no difference. In a competitive environment, profit maximization trumps prejudice. Although the macro outcome is the absence of market wage discrimination, it may be wrong to infer that employers do not have or act on their discriminatory tastes (micromotives). As racial wage gaps between workers become small, it is no longer costly for employers to act on their prejudice, so many will discriminate in hiring. The market equilibrium is one in which the many non-discriminating employers (relative to the pool of black workers) employ black workers at wages similar to white workers. Prejudiced employers discriminate in hiring without cost. Absent theory, one cannot readily infer micromotives based on the market outcome nor predict the macro outcome based on knowledge of micromotives.

The scenario described above is not just theoretical. Two distinct empirical literatures on discrimination appear to produce inconsistent conclusions. "Audit" studies send out "equivalent" black and white job applicants (or applicants for mortgages or apartments). The general finding is that black applicants receive fewer job offers than white applicants (offer rates are low for both groups). Such evidence offers clear-cut evidence of *hiring* discrimination. Yet a large literature on *wage* differences concludes that racial wage gaps are small (not zero) in studies with detailed controls for skill. The Becker model reconciles these seemingly inconsistent results. Incidents of discriminatory hiring may be widespread, but such discrimination need not produce large wage differentials given sufficiently large numbers of non-discriminating, profit-maximizing employers.

Applications of General versus Specific Human Capital

An easy concept for students to learn and remember is general (transferable) versus firm-specific (non-transferable) skills. The general/specific distinction is used to examine who bears the cost of training, how wages rise with experience and diverge from marginal revenue products, and the implications for hiring, labor hoarding, and layoffs in response to demand shocks. Two simple applications increase the odds that students will continue to apply this concept following graduation. Students are concerned about jobs following graduation and sometimes ask for advice. In class I advise students to avoid placing undue weight on salary offers and instead consider (a) whether skills they will acquire will be transferable and (b) the extent to which their training will lead to future wage growth and interesting employment opportunities. Students instantly understand the logic of such advice. They need to be reminded that this is an application of Becker's theory of human capital. A second application works best for classes that include older students, many of whom have tuition paid by their employer, seemingly at odds with Becker's theory wherein employers do not bear general training costs. Discussing when and why employers "pay" tuition for general training engages students and provides a nuanced application of Becker's theory (Acemoglu and Pischke, 1998).[8]

In short, there are numerous "take-away" concepts that are valuable and easy-to-learn. Instructors who look for them will find them.

MAKING THE COURSE A GOOD LEARNING EXPERIENCE

This chapter focuses more on course content than teaching methods. Many methods work just fine, if executed well. All require preparation. Several features of my labor economics course are discussed below.

Labor Market Overview

After reviewing the course syllabus, the first class period is devoted to a survey of "important features of the labor market." Among the broad headings are: employment statistics; dynamic labor markets; earnings and productivity; changes in labor force composition (gender, education, age, foreign-born); technology and sectoral job change (occupation, industry, location); non-wage compensation; earnings inequality; decline of private sector unionism; unemployment; labor regulation; and competition and globalization in product and labor markets. This overview whets students' appetite for what will follow, informs students about important course topics and labor markets features, and lets students know that we will make good use of scarce class time.

Beyond Textbooks

As a student I was often excited by something I read, but I don't recall that "something" ever being a textbook. Textbooks are arguably necessary for the undergraduate course, but instructors can design their own courses and need not march lockstep through a text. Students need to be exposed to varied and compelling narratives that can excite them about issues or the value (and limitations) of economics. My course syllabus includes timely news articles, plus engaging and accessible research articles from the *Journal of Economic Perspectives* (and elsewhere). The latter can be explored by students or used for papers. Students write brief summaries of selected articles. These articles excite students in ways difficult to predict in advance.

Class Assignments and Expectations

Learning is not a passive endeavor; student assignments and classroom interaction are essential. I frequently hand out "queries" at the beginning or end of class. Each asks a question about material we will discuss that class period or next.[9] Students receive credit if they complete a query and their completion tally for the semester contributes to their participation grade. Query topics are typically tested on exams. Queries increase attendance and are an effective learning device. Having thought about a question, students are engaged when it is discussed. Students like being rewarded for attending class and find queries a painless way to learn. Students also receive participation credit when they attend and provide a write-up for designated speakers or when they provide write-ups for articles discussed in class. Although not graded, most students are surprisingly conscientious.

Labor economics students have varying backgrounds and diverse interests and expectations. Many are not economics majors. Intermediate micro is often not a prerequisite for the labor course. Compared to economics majors, business students prefer a course emphasizing personnel economics topics. Social science majors outside economics often prefer a policy-oriented course. Fortunately, labor economics has plenty to offer each type of student. Instructors can select topics and fashion an approach that caters to students' interests, while still teaching the core principles.

What to Teach and Test?

Economists understand tradeoffs. In all courses instructors must consider the tradeoff between breadth of topics and depth of analysis. It is essential to touch on key insights for the principal topics that make up labor economics. Substantial depth for selected topics, however, is equally important. Concepts and knowledge learned deeply are the ones retained. Time is fixed, but emphasizing important concepts that are quickly learned provides students with a mix of breadth *and* depth.

What is emphasized in courses is often what is easy to test. These include concepts readily tested by multiple-choice or knowledge that can be graphically displayed and quickly graded (say labor supply income and substitution effects). Time required for grading is a legitimate concern. And sorting students by grade will differ little using time-intensive versus easy-to-grade exams. But the chief responsibility of instructors is not student sorting (although this is necessary), but to enhance students' skills, knowledge, and future ability to learn. Among the many paths to such ends, multiple-choice testing cannot rank high.[10] An effective teacher thinks carefully about what students should take away from a course, designs assignments that enhance such skills, and relies on "best-to-learn" rather than "easy-to-grade" evaluation methods.

Certainty or Ambiguity?

Students crave certainty. They like questions with clear-cut answers and teachers who extol the power of economics. But there is value in ambiguity, particularly so in labor economics where actual workplaces look so different from those emanating from frictionless market models. The competitive DS framework helps tell the "big story" and is necessary for understanding labor markets, but not sufficient. For most questions, it is essential to discuss institutions, market imperfections, and behavioral proclivities. Students can appreciate the value of the big-picture DS framework while realizing that deeper understanding requires more knowledge and imagination. Economists know that textbook models are often inadequate to handle the questions at hand. We should not keep this a secret from our students.

Although most students prefer certainty over ambiguity, an instructor providing students with a false sense of understanding does them no favor. Students need to know that some economists and many non-economists approach questions and see the world differently. I am bothered that professors in other fields often bad-mouth economics (and economists) in their classes. I am equally offended when economists disparage other disciplines. The best scholars in other fields are neither stupid nor fools. Some economists are. One can (rightly) emphasize the substantial contribution and power of the economic approach and at the same time make students aware of its limitations and the existence of different perspectives.

AFTERWORD

Economists, particularly labor economists, like evidence. In this chapter, I have discussed the content and approach taken in my courses. But does it work? Based on teaching evaluation scores and student comments, anecdotes, and (most important) knowledge demonstrated by students, I think my approach is a reasonable one. But there is no systematic evidence comparing my approach with other possible ones. My courses are typically less technical and problem-oriented than those of colleagues, but they are perceived as difficult and demanding by students. I never want to disappoint my best students. I make sure that bright and intellectually curious students enjoy and are challenged in the course. These are students that flourish on (or at least tolerate) nuance, uncertainty, puzzles, and alternative perspectives. Not all students appreciate this approach, but I think (or want to think) that most do.

While it is essential that one's best students are challenged, it is equally important that all conscientious students learn and be rewarded for their efforts. Weaker students may benefit little from approaches that provide high value added for better students. So it is important that one present, test, and reward learning of simple, core concepts in the course.[11]

Labor economists know, perhaps better than anyone, that human capital (interpreted broadly) is our greatest source of wealth and that learning begets learning. My choices on content and teaching methods are determined by my asking the question: "What material and methods best enable students to learn now and in the future?" Instructors who ask and carefully consider this question will not respond with the same set of answers I provide in this chapter, but they are likely to produce a labor economics course that has high value added for their students.

NOTES

1. Labor chapters in many principles texts are rather mechanical and disappointing, failing to provide the big picture regarding relative wage determination and the invisible hand in the labor market.
2. An overview of labor demand and supply is not routinely included in the introductory chapters of most labor texts.
3. I use the terms equilibrium, equalizing, and compensating wage differentials interchangeably. It's instructive to explain to students how each term applies.
4. When my younger son was in eighth grade, he had a career day homework assignment that asked him to identify an occupation that he might pursue. Because he knew that my work had something vaguely to do with jobs, he innocently asked: "Dad, what type of job pays well, would be a lot of fun, and does not require you to go to school forever?" Using the logic of Adam Smith, I carefully explained why no such job should exist. He regarded my answer as a thinly disguised refusal to help him with his homework.
5. Becker makes this point in his 1967 Woytinsky lecture (Becker, 1975). Of course, the very wealthy can hire employees rich in human capital.
6. A simple exercise is to go back fifty years to the 1960 Census and compare large industries and occupations then with those today. Some of the older jobs now barely exist, while some important jobs today did not exist in 1960.
7. Economics is often distinguished from other social sciences in that it not only develops models that specify the motives and behavior of individual actors (individuals, firms, etc.), but also model how the actors interact in markets and what equilibrium outcomes arise.
8. A third application informed by the general/specific distinction is to discuss why some companies choose to hire from within and create internal job ladders rather than hire externally.
9. Queries ask questions of the following type. (1) If the wage on your current job doubles, would you choose to work fewer, the same, or more hours per week? Explain? (2) If you are an employer searching for new hires, will you rely on referrals from current employees? Why or why not?
10. If an instructor must use multiple choice questions, take the time to make them good and avoid reliance on test banks. Test banks are often poorly written, provide answers that are sometimes wrong or ambiguous, and often emphasize topics for which it is easiest to write questions rather than those which are most important.
11. Lazear (2006) provides a model in which for "high cost" learners teachers announce the exact requirements in order to concentrate student effort (study to the test), insuring that something is learned. For more able students, an "amorphous" standard, say a lengthy syllabus and vagueness about what will be tested, produces superior learning.

REFERENCES

Acemoglu, D. and J. S. Pischke (1998), "Why do firms train? Theory and evidence", *Quarterly Journal of Economics*, **113** (1), 79–119.

Autor, D. H., F. Levy and R. J. Murnane (2003), "Skill content of recent technological change: An empirical exploration", *Quarterly Journal of Economics*, **118** (4), 1279–333.

Becker, G. S. (1975), *Human Capital: A Theoretical and Empirical Analysis, with Special Reference to Education* (2nd ed.), Chicago: University of Chicago Press.

Lazear, E. P. (2006), "Speeding, terrorism, and teaching to the test", *Quarterly Journal of Economics*, **121** (3), 1029–61.

Reder, M. W. (1982), "Chicago economics: Permanence and change", *Journal of Economic Literature*, **20** (1), 1–38.

Schelling, T. C. (1978), *Micromotives and Macrobehavior*, New York: W.W. Norton.

Summers, L. H. (1989), "Some simple economics of mandated benefits", *American Economic Review Papers and Proceedings*, **79** (2), 177–83.

58 The challenges and pleasures of teaching law and economics
Thomas S. Ulen

I have taught law and economics (or the economic analysis of law) for thirty years. I originally developed a course for upper-level economics students at the University of Illinois at Urbana-Champaign in 1980. Then in 1981 I began to teach the subject to law students, first at the University of California – Davis School of Law and, since 1982, at the University of Illinois College of Law. I taught economics students and law students in separate courses in the Department of Economics and the College of Law throughout much of the 1980s. Since 1989 I have taught law students exclusively. In addition to teaching at the University of Illinois College of Law, I have also taught courses on law and economics, behavioral law and economics, empirical legal studies, and other law-and-economics topics in a large number of foreign countries, such as the People's Republic of China, Argentina, Belgium, Brazil, Germany, India, Israel, the Netherlands, and Switzerland.

These varied experiences in teaching law and economics give a broad perspective on the general issues of professing this subject and the particular challenges and pleasures of teaching graduate and undergraduate economics students, domestic law students, and foreign law students (including LL.M. students, almost all of whom are foreign law graduates studying law for a year at US law schools). Additionally, my friend and co-author, Robert D. Cooter (an economist teaching at the University of California at Berkeley School of Law), and I have had the good fortune to have written a successful textbook, *Law and Economics.* That experience has taught us both a great deal about what works and what does not in presenting law and economics to students.

The chapter begins with a brief overview of the subject matter of law and economics. After laying out how we structured a text to teach what was, in essence, a new subject in the early 1980s, the chapter turns toward the particular challenges of teaching a subject that is new and, therefore, changing and developing very quickly. The next section of the chapter addresses the unique challenges of teaching economics students, law students, and foreign law students. There is a concluding section that summarizes the central points.

SOME PRELIMINARIES: AN OVERVIEW OF LAW AND ECONOMICS

Although many readers of this chapter may be familiar with law and economics, it is a useful exercise to consider, first, salient points about the material covered in the basic introductory course in law and economics. It is also helpful to consider a few points about changes that are occurring in the field and that have some impact on how the course is likely to be taught. And finally, it is beneficial to think about how to interact with students in this course and on the role of changing educational technologies.

What is Likely to be Covered in a Law and Economics Course?

The field of law and economics is sufficiently new to the economics and law-school curricula that the classroom presentation of the basic introductory course is not necessarily standardized. While there are several standard texts (such as Posner, *The Economic Analysis of Law* (8th ed. 2010), and Cooter and Ulen, *Law and Economics* (6th ed. 2011)), those who teach the subject frequently include extensive collections of supplemental materials either as a substitute or a substantial complement to one of those texts.

The breadth of subject matter that might be covered in a one-semester (or one-quarter) law-and-economics course is very large. If there is a modal set of topics covered, the list likely includes the economics of property, contract, torts, some aspects of the legal process (such as litigation and settlement), and crime and punishment. In addition to that modal core, it is also likely modal that a course on law and economics in an economics department or business school contains a section that introduces students to some basic concepts of the law (such as the elements of a civil complaint, the structure of the court system – trial, appellate, and supreme courts – and how a case proceeds through that system, the distinction between civil and criminal cases, different standards of proof and evidence and outcome in civil and criminal cases, and related topics). Similarly, in a law-and-economics class in a law school, the instructor can generally assume that the students understand the legal system. But the instructor is likely to want to include a brief introduction to microeconomic analytical tools (such as notions of efficiency, rational choice, individual preferences, market equilibrium, game theory, decision making under uncertainty, behavioral economics, and the like).

Beyond those core topics, there is a very broad (and roughly uniformly distributed) range of topics that may be covered, including government regulation generally, antitrust, taxation, business associations, public choice, international trade, environmental law, bankruptcy, and securities regulation.

Given that there is not necessarily standard subject-matter coverage in law and economics, might there be a theme or methodology that unifies these disparate topics? I would argue that one unifying theme is that legal rules, through price-like incentives, seek to guide decision makers in promoting socially efficient actions and deterring socially inefficient behaviors. For example, creating a remedy that encourages only efficient breach of contract requires the breacher either to pay the breachee the monetary benefit that she anticipated from performance or to perform the contractual promise.[1] Breach is said to be efficient if it is more efficient to breach than to perform; otherwise, performing the contractual promise is more efficient than breach.

Because this core concept of analyzing legal rules as incentives for efficient behavior can be applied in such a wide variety of different legal topics, the actual topics covered in a law-and-economics course is not as important in defining the field as may be the case in other economics courses.

Changing Course Content

The field is relatively new, and it is developing rapidly. For instance, in its early years law and economics applied the rational-choice model assiduously and to great effect in its analysis of how rational actors are likely to respond to law. So, there was a kind of standardization in the material covered because of the close ties between rational choice theory and its application to almost any legal issue.

The rise of behavioral economics in the 1990s[2] and of empirical legal studies more recently[3] have brought so much new material to the study of law that a teacher intent on informing her students about the most recent scholarly developments will be challenged to revise her course material significantly.

To take one example that illustrates the power and importance of new empirical findings, consider liquidated damages for contract breach.[4] The settled law in the US (but not in Europe) on these clauses is that in order to be enforceable the stipulated amount must be a reasonable approximation of the actual losses from nonperformance. Economic analysis has criticized this limitation as being inefficient. The criticism is that, for example, allowing the parties to stipulate to a supracompensatory amount of damages for breach might be an efficient means of protecting idiosyncratic values associated with performance or simply of signaling one party's strong belief and intent to perform. Thus, a party ought to be allowed to ask for and receive (perhaps in exchange for a higher contract price) a liquidated damages clause that guarantees her substantially more than a court (which can only award objectively verifiable damages, such as the cost of arranging a substitute performance) would award. So long as there is no coercion or fraud or other inappropriate behavior in arranging these terms, economists have argued that the parties ought to be allowed to stipulate to whatever they can mutually agree.

Recently, some new experimental evidence has suggested that having a liquidated damages clause in a contract predisposes parties to feel that breach is more acceptable and, therefore, more likely than if there is no such clause in the contract. Wilkinson-Ryan (2010) finds that this may be a move toward more efficient breaches of contract. The reason is that moral sanctions against breaching are so strong that most people do not breach a contractual promise even where it would be more efficient to breach (and pay damages) than to perform. Therefore, the presence of a liquidated damages clause, by making breach more acceptable, may overcome this moral squeamishness and make efficient breach more likely and more frequent.

The fact that this important finding came from a series of carefully designed experiments illustrates another source of pressure on the teacher. Of course, one can simply report the finding, but both economics students and law students are not likely to understand the finer points of empirical research. In this instance, they may not understand the extent to which these experiments were well-designed and, therefore, produced results worth paying attention to. So, one must take some time to explain the rudiments of experimental design.

To take an example of an important addition to the core of law and economics from behavioral economics, consider crime and punishment. This field owes much to the seminal work of Gary Becker, who hypothesized that criminals are rational actors like all the rest of us, that they compare the expected costs and benefits of crime and of legal activity, and may commit a crime if the expected costs of the crime are less than the expected benefits. This simple but remarkably powerful insight had an important policy implication: the keys to deterring crime are to increase the opportunity cost of crime (by, for instance, making legitimate work more likely and more rewarding) and by raising the expected costs of crime (by increasing the probabilities of detection, arrest, and conviction and by increasing the sanction upon conviction).

Not only did the Becker hypothesis spawn an outpouring of empirical work to test his hypotheses,[5] it also caused a flurry of scholarly inquiry into whether the assumption of rational choice was appropriate for potential criminals. Consider two of the literally hundreds of findings that have emerged from this scholarship. The first is the famous finding that the decline in all kinds of crime in the US since the early 1990s owes a great deal to the legalization of abortion by the US Supreme Court in January, 1973. Donohue and Levitt (2001) contend, on the basis of careful but highly controversial econometric work, that half of the decline in crime since 1991 is attributable to *Roe v. Wade*.[6, 7]

The second is a summary of recent literature from the behavioral sciences that contends that the ability of criminal law to deter criminal behavior is very limited.[8] Among the many factors that make it unlikely that incarceration deters is the finding that human beings adapt very quickly to changed circumstances. Just as winning millions of dollars in a lottery will result in only a temporary increase in subjective well-being, so incarceration in a seven-foot by seven-foot prison cell will result in only a temporary decrease in subjective well-being. Those of us who have never been incarcerated may find the prospect of imprisonment so horrific that it deters us from committing crime. But it is possible that those who have been to prison may remember the experience as being "Not so bad!" Not only may they not, therefore, be deterred from committing crimes in the future, but to the extent that they communicate this experience to their community, those who have never been to prison may become inured to its deterring possibility. This finding is so at odds with what economists and law-and-economics scholars have believed, taught, and thought that they had conclusively demonstrated both theoretically and empirically that one feels obliged to teach this material in the core law-and-economics course.

Keeping up with the professional literature and incorporating interesting new findings into the core content of any course is a vital part of what good teachers do. It is a particularly important part of teaching law and economics, in which scholarly developments, such as the incorporation of behavioral insights and the results of new empirical work, have been so common.

Interaction with Students and Changing Educational Technologies

How should one teach law and economics? Consider two points in this regard. The first is that because this course is most likely to be taught to students who have very little background in half of the course's subject (economists tend not to know the law, and lawyers tend not to know economics), the instructor has got a real challenge on her hands. I have already suggested that one method of dealing with this challenge is to include several lectures at the beginning of the semester or quarter to equip the students with the missing half of the necessary background.[9] In addition, I very strongly recommend that the instructor include lots of examples and discussions as part of class preparation. There are many ways in which to do this, such as requiring periodic written answers to questions, discussing actual cases, oral presentations to the class by small groups, the use of immediate, anonymous question-answering and discussion (as is done, for instance, through the i-Clicker[10]), or simply stopping the lecture periodically and having a discussion about some particular real examples of the theoretical points at issue. Law and economics is a subject that all students will learn more thoroughly through application to problems, issues, hypothetical cases, and the like.

The second point that I want to make has to do with the use of presentation software (such as Microsoft PowerPoint and Apple Keynote) in a lecture. I know that there is a significant difference of opinion on the utility of these methods of presenting lecture material.[11] There seems to me to be a sense among students today that presentation software is a very valuable enhancement of any course. My own view is that using those programs – judiciously and making sure not simply to read the slides – can be an effective complement to lectures and discussion. To take one example for illustration, it is far easier to discuss a complicated graph (of, say, the efficient determination of the social-cost-minimizing level of precaution) when it is displayed on a large overhead screen. Moreover, preparing slides on a topic has the very beneficial side effect of making the instructor organize his material better.

There is one more pedagogic point. Cooter and I have found that there is simply too much material to fit into a semester-long text on law and economics. We have hit upon the device of putting what we call "web notes" onto our book's website: these are short essays that illustrate or extend the text material. We put references to these web notes in the text so that instructors and students are aware of the online material and can refer students to that material, perhaps for the purpose of making a class presentation.

TEACHING LAW AND ECONOMICS

One of the particular sources of challenge and pleasure in teaching law and economics is that it is inherently a cross-disciplinary subject. As a result, it is taught (and appeals) to students in very different departments and circumstances. In this brief section, I comment on how to tailor the course material to economics students, US law students, and foreign law students.

Economics Students

Economics students, both undergraduate and graduate students, find law and economics interesting and challenging. The interest arises from the fact that the applicability of relatively simple economic concepts to the law is likely to be new to them, easily intelligible, and deals with important social issues. The challenge comes from the fact that all of this is not couched in the formal models that upper-level undergraduates and graduate students expect. For example, the point above about efficient remedies for breach of contract is rarely made in a formal, mathematical model, but is, rather, made through simple examples using hypothetical values.[12]

One of the most important contributions that the instructor can make in a classroom of economics students is to take the time to explain how the legal system works, in particular, the private civil law system that, in the common law countries, allows judges to make law in resolving private disputes. Economics students (like the general population of nonlawyers) typically believe that legislatures (and their agents, such as administrative agencies) and the US Supreme Court are the principal sources of law. They are astonished to learn that most law in the common law countries, including almost all of contract and tort law, has long been made by judges in the course of resolving private disputes.

More generally, economics students may find the very contingent conclusions on if and how law works efficiently and the vague but important relationship between efficiency and equity concerns to be troubling. Many law-and-economics analyses do not have the crisp and precise answers that characterize many economic problems. Rather, they depend on additional assumptions or facts that need to be ascertained. Identifying those assumptions and facts is an important part of the learning in this course.

US Law Students

Teaching law and economics to US law students presents singular pleasures and challenges. The first of the challenges is that the material in the typical course will be new to the vast majority of law students who, because they have not had any formal training in economics or the social sciences, are very much like economics undergraduates taking their first microeconomics course. Worse, many law students are afraid of what they suspect are the formal mathematical models that will form the core of the class. And even worse, many law students will have heard or been taught that law and economics is informed by a deeply conservative political agenda – for instance, to get rid of much governmental regulation. Offsetting this negative introduction to the field is the fact that law and economics has had such a significant impact on modern US legal education that nearly every first-year law student has had some exposure to law and economics in their courses on property, contract, tort, and crime. For example, the leading contracts case books begin with a selection of cases to illustrate the concept of "efficient breach of contract."

The students who surmount these dissuading impediments and take law and economics are typically in for an exhilarating educational experience. One reason for this is that the increasing amount of empirical work being done on legal issues, such as the contract and crime examples mentioned above, means that the course typically goes beyond theoretical controversies to empirical evidence supporting or questioning those theories. My experience has been that law students, by their second and third years, are tired of jurisprudential controversy and very eager to have evidence to help them resolve "on the one hand, on the other hand" theoretical controversies.

A more practical issue with respect to teaching law and economics to US law students has to do with their expectations of how they will learn the material. Almost every core course in a US law school teaches the course material by having the students read cases. Whatever one thinks of this method of teaching students the law,[13] it is perhaps not the most effective way to learn law and economics. One can, of course, use hypothetical and actual legal disputes to illustrate how the concepts of the course might be applied, particularly in advising their clients so as to avoid litigation.

Foreign Law Students

Teaching foreign law students about law and economics presents a different set of challenges and pleasures. First, the impact of law and economics has not been nearly as profound in other countries as it has been in US legal education (with the possible exceptions of the Netherlands and Israel).[14] As a result, foreign law students do not come to the study of law and economics with any preconceived notions.

Second, in almost every country except the United States, the study of law is an undergraduate major. So, foreign law students often have no training in disciplines other than the law.[15] This obviously has both advantages (instructors can focus on the law) and disadvantages (students do not bring in insights from other disciplines, such as economics, psychology, and political science). This fact underscores the importance of toning down the economic formality of the models and of providing some introductory training in nontechnical microeconomic theory when teaching these law students.

Third, foreign law students almost invariably come from the civil law tradition, not the common law tradition of North America, the United Kingdom, Australia, India, and a few other countries.[16] The distinctions between the two systems are perhaps more cosmetic than real, but there are widespread perceptions that the differences are significant, that, for example, the common law relies on judge-made law, while the civil law relies almost exclusively on legislators to make law. As a result, the careful instructor from the common law countries should make some statement early in the course to civilians (as they are called) to allay concerns that they are being taught a subject that has appeal and practical importance only to common law lawyers. The simplest reply to that concern is to point out that the concerns of law and economics about the efficiency of the legal system do not presume a particular form of that system, or a particular set of substantive or procedural laws. Rather, law and economics is meant to be a more general discussion of law. Just as economics is a subject that is independent of time and geography, so law and economics aspires to be a general discussion of the goals and consequences of law, independent of the particularities of any given legal system.

CONCLUSION

Teaching is a marvelous profession. Its pleasures and challenges are many, with a large surfeit of pleasure over challenge. I have tried to indicate how an instructor might address the concerns that arise when teaching law and economics to economics students, US law students, and foreign law students. Most fundamentally, economics students do not understand the legal system, how a private lawsuit originates and proceeds through the court system, what remedies are available, the rudiments of property, contract, tort, and other areas of the law, and much more. Law students are not familiar with microeconomic theory, empirical methods, behavioral science, and the like. The instructor must herself be comfortable in both these disciplines and make her students reasonably conversant in both. These pedagogical demands are not inconsiderable, but the rewards to both the instructor and the students of surmounting those demands and getting to the marvelous scholarship in law and economics are immense.

NOTES

1. The command to perform a contractual promise is called "specific performance." Economic analysis suggests that if specific performance is the remedy for breach, the breacher will negotiate with the breachee to pay him full compensation (including nonpecuniary benefits); if the breachee (or "innocent party") finds an amount proffered by the breacher to be more valuable than performance, he will waive his right to performance in exchange for the money offered. Otherwise, he will insist on performance.
2. See, for example, Korobkin and Ulen (2000).
3. See, for example, Lawless, Robbennolt, and Ulen (2010) and the *Journal of Empirical Legal Studies*, which began publication in 2004.
4. A "liquidated" or "stipulated damages" clause is a negotiated part of a contractual promise in which the parties specify what the breaching party will owe the innocent party if he fails to perform.
5. See the summary of this literature in Cooter and Ulen (2011), pp. 485–532.
6. *Roe v. Wade*, 410 U.S. 113 (1983).
7. Another finding of this remarkable article is that half of the 50 percent decline in crime can be attributed to a "cohort size effect" – that is, there were fewer 18-year-old young men (who commit a disproportionately large fraction of crime in any society) beginning in 1991 – and the other half to a "cohort quality effect" – that is, that the quality of the young men who *were* born after the legalization of abortion were less likely to commit crimes, all other things equal. The reason for this second effect is, the authors believe, that the availability of abortion allows women to wait to have children till their circumstances (their income, a job, the presence of a partner, their health insurance, and the like) are more conducive to attentive and supportive child-rearing.
8. See, for example, Robinson and Darley (2004).
9. *Law and Economics* contains a short chapter summarizing modern microeconomics for law students and another summarizing basic facts about the US legal system for economists.
10. See http://www.iclicker.com/dnn/ (accessed 31 May 2011). See also Chapter 13, "Incorporating Media and Response Systems in the Economics Classroom", in this volume.
11. See, for example, Tufte (2003).
12. For a more formal economic treatment of the subject matter, see Shavell (2004).
13. I do not think much of the method. First, it leads students to believe that preparing for litigation is what they will be doing as lawyers. That is simply not true: the vast majority of lawyers engage in transactional work, one of whose principal goals is to keep disputes to a minimum. The best current estimate is that 3 to 5 percent of all disputes result in litigation. And the absolute number of trials has declined significantly over the past 40 years. See Galanter (2004). Second, learning how to write a good contract by studying what went wrong with other contracts (which is what one reads about in judicial opinions about contract disputes) is like learning how to fly an airplane by studying airplane crashes. It is not a crazy way to instruct – I am told that engineers learn how to build bridges that do not fall down by studying bridges that did fall down – but there may be a better way.
14. See Garoupa and Ulen (2008). Most law students in the rest of the world complete their legal education without ever hearing of law and economics.
15. Because law is a graduate course in the US, all law students have an undergraduate degree in some subject other than law. This fact – combined with the fact that US law students are older than foreign law students – typically brings a diverse richness to classroom discussions that may be missing in other countries.
16. One very practical consideration arising from this is that the instructor cannot expect foreign law students to be familiar with the cases that US law students have learned in their earlier classes. To use common law cases as instructional material for foreign law students, one should extract the relevant facts of the case and present them as hypothetical controversies about those facts.

REFERENCES

Cooter, R. and T. Ulen (2011), *Law and Economics* (6th ed.), Boston, MA: Pearson.
Donohue, J. J. and S. D. Levitt (2001), "The impact of legalized abortion on crime", *Quarterly Journal of Economics*, **116** (2), 379–420.
Galanter, M. (2004), "The vanishing trial: An examination of trials and related matters in Federal and State courts", *Journal of Empirical Legal Studies*, **1** (3), 459–570.
Garoupa, N. and T. S. Ulen (2008), "The market for legal innovation: Law and economics in Europe and the United States", *Alabama Legal Review*, **59** (5), 1555–633.

Korobkin, R. B. and T. S. Ulen (2000), "Law and behavioral science: Removing the rationality assumption from law and economics", *California Law Review*, **88** (4), 1051–143.

Lawless, R. M., J. K. Robbennolt and Thomas S. Ulen (2010), *Empirical Methods in Law,* New York, NY: Aspen Publishers.

Posner, R. A. (2010), *Economic Analysis of Law* (8th ed.), New York, NY: Aspen Publishers.

Robinson, P. and J. Darley (2004), "Does criminal law deter?: A behavioral science investigation", *Oxford Journal of Legal Studies,* **24** (2), 173–205.

Shavell, S. (2004), *Foundations of Economic Analysis of Law,* Cambridge, MA: Belknap Press of Harvard University Press.

Tufte, E. (2003), "PowerPoint is evil: Power corrupts, PowerPoint corrupts absolutely", *Wired* (September), http://www.wired.com/wired/archive/11.09/ppt2.html (accessed 31 May 2011).

Wilkinson-Ryan, T. (2010), "Liquidated damages encourage efficient breach?: A psychological experiment", *Michigan Law Review,* **108,** 633–71.

59 Teaching managerial economics with problems instead of models[1]

Luke M. Froeb and James C. Ward

Imagine spending an entire class period taking your students through an economics article. You carefully motivate and explain the model, and then relax the model assumptions one by one to demonstrate the sensitivity of the policy conclusions to a variety of factors. You sit back, satisfied that you have given your students a thorough understanding of the problem. Then one of them raises a hand and asks "Why did you make us read this if it's wrong?"

The story illustrates a basic tension between demand for business education (students want practical knowledge) and supply (professors are trained to provide abstract theory).[2] This tension is found throughout academia, but it is perhaps most acute in a business school. Business professors have academic training and publish in the same journals as their colleagues in Arts and Sciences. They value methodology above application, but their students have more immediate concerns. They expect a return on a fairly sizable investment and consequently don't want to learn material that doesn't have tangible and obvious value.

One implication of this mismatch is that teaching economics in the usual way – with models and public policy applications – is not likely to satisfy student demand. Business students have difficulty learning abstract theory, and even those who understand it have difficulty applying its lessons to real-world problems. In addition, they have little interest in the public policy applications used to motivate and illustrate economic theory.

In this chapter, we propose a problem-solving pedagogy as a better way to teach economics to business students. The pedagogy begins with a business problem, like the fixed-cost fallacy, and then gives students just enough analytic structure to compute the costs and benefits of various solutions. Teaching students to solve problems, rather than learn models, satisfies student demand in a straightforward way because it allows students to "see" the value of the education they are receiving. It also allows students to absorb the lessons of economics without as much of the analytical "overhead" as a model-based pedagogy. This is an advantage, especially in a terminal or stand-alone economics course, like those typically taught in a business school. To see this, ask yourself which of the following ideas is more likely to stay with a business student after the class is over: the fixed-cost fallacy or that the partial derivative of profit with respect to price is independent of fixed costs.

The sections that follow describe student demand for business education and then show how the elements of a problem-solving pedagogy satisfy this demand.

WHY ECONOMISTS SHOULDN'T TEACH ECONOMICS IN THE SAME WAY AS THEY LEARNED IT

This section characterizes student demand, focusing on the peculiar features of business education that make teaching economics with a model-based pedagogy so unsuccessful.

Business Education is an Investment, and Students Want to "See" a Return

Most professors are attracted to academia by a love of learning. For them, knowledge is its own reward. But business students, both those seeking MBA degrees and those taking undergraduate business courses, have a different goal in mind. They are making a very big investment, and expect that a business education will help them perform better in a business setting, further their careers, and make more money. In fact, business schools tout the starting salaries of their graduates as an indicator of the school's ability to help students achieve these goals. Most business students have calculated the cost of each class that they take – about \$130/hour for a top ranked program – and if they don't receive obvious value from each class, they are not shy about letting the dean know.

Students Want Practical Knowledge Not Abstract Theory

The decision to pursue a professional education instead of – or after – a traditional liberal arts education reveals a preference for specialized over general knowledge and a preference for application over theory. But most importantly, business students want to be able to apply the lessons they learn to help them realize their goals of furthering their careers and making more money.

This is a pretty high bar for any class, but especially daunting for those teaching using a model-based pedagogy. Even the economics majors who take these classes have trouble applying its lessons to real-world situations. Ferraro and Taylor (2005, p. 3 and pp. 7–8) illustrate the difficulty with a simple quiz about "opportunity cost," one of the most useful ideas in economics.

Select the Best Answers to the Following Questions:

1. You won a free ticket to see an Eric Clapton concert (which has no resale value). Bob Dylan is performing on the same night and is your next-best alternative activity. Tickets to see Dylan cost \$40. On any given day, you would be willing to pay up to \$50 to see Dylan. Assume there are no other costs of seeing either performer. Based on this information, what is the opportunity cost of seeing Eric Clapton?

   A. \$0
   B. \$10
   C. \$40
   D. \$50

2. You won a free ticket to see an Eric Clapton concert (which has no resale value). Bob Dylan is performing on the same night and is your next-best alternative activity. Tickets to see Dylan cost \$40. On any given day, you would be willing to pay up to \$50 to see Dylan. Assume there are no other costs of seeing either performer. Based on this information, what

is the minimum amount (in dollars) you would have to value seeing Eric Clapton for you to choose his concert?

A. $0
B. $10
C. $40
D. $50

Of course, the right answer to both questions is B – the cost of something is what you give up to pursue it. But Ferraro and Taylor (2005) found that only 22 percent of students answered the first question correctly, and only 40 percent answered the second one correctly. Year of degree, quality of school, and other educational inputs were unrelated to a student's ability to answer these simple questions. The only significant finding was that micro theorists were better than all other groups, but macroeconomists were indistinguishable from undergraduates who never took an economics course.

Ferraro and Taylor (2005) reach the obvious conclusion (p. 11):

> If we are unable to instill in our students a deep and intuitive understanding of one of the most fundamental ideas that the discipline has to offer and the idea whose frequent application could do the most good in people's private and public lives, then we wonder what we can claim as our value-added to the college curriculum.

For business students, who are less able to realize the value of abstract theory, the problem is even worse.

Business Students Learn Concretely, Not Abstractly

Psychological research (Schroeder, 1993) suggests that students, on average, are less comfortable than their professors with abstract ideas and have less tolerance for ambiguity. Rather, students are more dependent on immediate gratification and crave structure and clarity. For them, a successful educational path is usually from practice to theory, not the more traditional route from theory to practice. For these learners, Schroeder (1993) calls for a "concrete-active" pedagogy as opposed to the more traditional "abstract-reflective" one (p. 25):

> Concrete active learners come to class seeking direct, concrete experience, moderate-to-high degrees of structure, and a linear approach. They value the practical and the immediate, and the focus of their perception is primarily on the physical world. Their instructors, on the other hand, prefer the global to the particular, [and] are stimulated by the realm of concepts, ideas, and abstractions.

The traditional model-based pedagogy falls into the abstract-reflective category, while a problem-based pedagogy is designed to fit into the concrete-active category.

Public Policy vs. Business Applications

The application of economics to public policy is often the focus of economics and is often the subject of the professor's academic research. It is natural, therefore, to use public policy applications to illustrate, motivate, and validate the usefulness of economics. However, making the link between the public policy examples taught in class and the business applications of interest to students is difficult because it requires students to move from the particular (public policy example) to the abstract (economic theory) and then back again to the particular (business decision). It is easy for students to get lost along the way. For example, suppose a student is interested in analyzing a problem with transfer prices that are set above marginal cost. If a student has not seen the link between the application (transfer pricing) and the appropriate model (successive monopoly), it might never occur to him. Making these links explicit helps business students learn which analytic tools to apply to a particular business decision, which also makes it easier for business students to see and appreciate the value of economic theory.

Students of Differing Backgrounds

Students seeking a business education come to class with a variety of educational backgrounds: some are English majors, some are engineers, and some are economics majors. Teaching economics using a traditional model-based pedagogy raises the problem of how to pitch the class: aim too low and you will bore the economics majors; aim too high and you will lose the English majors; aim at the median student and you will satisfy no one. Using a problem-solving pedagogy mitigates this problem because the business applications are new to all. In addition, with less analytical overhead, it is easier for the English majors to keep up, or to learn the material outside of class using online tools.[3] Allowing students to learn the analytics at their own pace allows the less analytically inclined students to spend more time on the tools, while the more analytical students can focus on the business applications.

Economics is Taught as a Stand-alone Course

Most professors learned economics from a traditional model-based pedagogy as part of a sequence of classes in a curriculum. Each course in the curriculum builds on the ones before it, and students often realize the value of a class only after taking the next class in the sequence. In a business curriculum, however, economics is taught as a stand-alone subject, typically in a terminal class. In this setting, professors must design courses that stand on their own. Building a course around solving business problems is one way to do this.

ELEMENTS OF A PROBLEM-SOLVING PEDAGOGY

This section outlines the elements of a problem-solving pedagogy and shows how they satisfy student demand. Much of this material is taken from Froeb and McCann (2010), but elements of the approach can be found in many managerial economics texts.

Begin with a Business Problem

Beginning with a real-world business problem puts the particular ahead of the abstract and motivates the material in a straightforward way. For teaching principles in a functional area like economics, avoid ill-defined and open-ended problems (see, for example, Lamy, 2007), because there are many potential ways of looking at an open-ended problem, and many potential analytical tools that could be used to fix it. Instead, use narrower problems whose solution requires students to use the analytical tools of interest; or, at least, tightly manage the class discussion so that you can "steer" it towards the tools of interest.

Inefficiency Implies Opportunity

The first element of a problem-solving pedagogy is to show students how to use the traditional tools of economic analysis to identify problems. To do this, turn the traditional focus of economics on its head. Instead of trying to fix inefficiencies by changing public policy, teach students to view inefficiency as an opportunity for business to make money.

Economics is valuable to business students because it gives them the tools to spot inefficiency, in other words, an asset in a lower-valued use. Business views each under-employed asset as a potential wealth-creating transaction, and the art of business is to identify these transactions and find ways to profitably consummate them. Making money is simple in principle, find an under-employed asset, buy it, and then sell it to someone who places a higher value on it.

In practice, it is rarely that simple, particularly when the inefficiency occurs within a larger organization. Companies can be thought of as collections of transactions, from buying raw materials like capital and labor to selling finished goods and services. In a successful company, these transactions move assets to higher-valued uses and thus make money for the company. But this is not always the case. Some organizational designs encourage profitable decision-making; but others do not. A poorly designed company will consummate unprofitable transactions or fail to consummate profitable ones. The next section takes up the problem of goal alignment within an organization: how to make sure that employees have enough information to make good decisions, and the incentive to do so.

Organizational Design

To solve business problems in a simple, linear way, distill each problem down to a bad decision, and then proceed in two steps: show students how to figure out what is wrong (why was the bad decision made?); and then show them how to fix it. Both steps require that you understand how people are likely to behave in different circumstances, and this motivates the use of economics. The rational actor paradigm not only helps students figure out why people behave the way they do, but also shows them how to motivate them to change.

If you assume that people act rationally, optimally and self-interestedly, then mistakes have only one of two causes: either people lack the *information* necessary to make good decisions; or they lack the *incentive* to do so. This immediately suggests a problem-solving algorithm: start by asking three questions to diagnose the cause of the problem.

1. Who is making the bad decision?;
2. Do they have enough information to make a good decision?; and
3. Do they have the incentive to do so?

Note that incentives have two pieces, a performance evaluation metric and a scheme to reward good performance.

Answers to these three questions should allow students to identify the source of the problem. If an employee is acting in a way contrary to the goals of the organization, answers to these three questions should also suggest ways to fix the problem:

1. Let someone else make the decision – someone with better information or incentives;
2. Give more information to the current decision-maker; or
3. Change the current decision-maker's incentives.

Students use benefit-cost analysis to choose from among the viable solutions.

Those of you familiar with the so-called Rochester approach to Organizational Design should recognize the similarity of this problem-solving algorithm to the "three legs" of Organizational Architecture – decision rights, performance evaluation, and reward structures – developed by Jensen and Meckling (2000) and later refined by Brickley, Smith, and Zimmerman (1997). It differs in that they decompose incentives into two pieces, performance evaluation and reward schemes, rather than lump them together, and don't consider information flows separately from the incentives. The justification for this difference is that decision makers with appropriately designed performance evaluation metrics and reward schemes already have an incentive to gather the information necessary to make a good decision. The substance is similar, but it is often useful to consider the problem of information acquisition separately from incentives.

EXAMPLES

High Transportation Costs at a Coal-burning Utility

A power-generating utility owns a large coal-burning power plant on a river and each week a dozen barges arrive loaded with coal to feed the power plant. The transportation division of the parent company is responsible for transporting coal to the power plant, and it pays a barge company to pick up the coal at a railhead and transport it down river.

Once a barge arrives at the docks, the power plant is very slow to unload the coal because they have just one crew of dockworkers and they rarely work overtime or on weekends. The barge company gives its customers three days to unload the coal, but if it takes longer, it charges late fees of $500 per day. Because very few barges are unloaded within three days, the transportation division pays very high late fees.

The immediate problem is that the late fees paid by the transportation division are bigger than the overtime fees that would cause them to disappear, but the unloaded barges also represent inefficiency, in other words, the barges have a higher valued use in transporting coal to other customers.

Imagine that you are brought in to fix the problem. Start by using our problem-solving algorithm:

1. *Who is making the bad decision?* The power plant is unloading the barges too slowly, which leads to big late fees.
2. *Does the power plant have enough information to make a good decision?* Yes. The power plant knows that leaving barges at the dock beyond three days results in extra charges.
3. *Does the power plant have the incentive to make a good decision?* No. Promptly unloading the barges would require overtime pay to the dockworkers. Since dockworkers' overtime wages are twice the normal wages, the power plant saves money by waiting until the barges can be unloaded during normal work hours.

The cause of the problem should now be obvious: the power plant division increases its own division profit by keeping the barges at the dock until they can be unloaded during regular work hours, requiring no overtime pay. The delay results in late fees falling on the transportation division.

There are two obvious solutions to this problem. The first is to change the performance evaluation metric of the power plant to include late fees. If the costs of paying overtime are less than late fees, this change will give the power plant an incentive to unload the barges within three days. If not, it won't. Either way, this change would better align the incentives of the power plant with the profitability goals of the parent company.

The other obvious solution is to move the decision rights about when to unload the coal to the division that is already paying the late fees (the transportation division). Although this solution achieves the same goal alignment, it would likely create coordination problems because the dockworkers have other responsibilities within the power plant. It is never easy for employees to serve two bosses.

Outsourcing a Washing Machine Agitator

In 1996, GE operated a washing machine plant that was trying to decide whether to outsource its plastic agitator. The firm received a bid of $0.70 per unit from a trusted supplier and compared it to internal production costs. Put yourself in the role of plant manager and make your decision on the basis of Table 59.1.

The relevant comparison should neglect the costs of depreciation and overhead because GE incurs these costs regardless of whether it decides to outsource. The relevant cost of internal production is $0.80, and the relevant cost of outsourcing is $0.70. Outsourcing is cheaper.

In this example, however, identifying the right decision was easier than implementing it for the plant manager. Six years earlier, the plant had incurred $1 million in tooling costs to make molds for the agitators. Following Generally Accepted Accounting Principles (GAAP), they were charging themselves $100,000/year, over ten years, for the tooling cost. This is called straight-line depreciation. Since it had been six years since the tooling costs were incurred, there was still $400,000 worth of undepreciated capital on the company's balance sheet. Accountants at his firm told the plant manager that if he decided to outsource the agitator, these "assets" would "become worthless," and the manager would be forced to take a charge against his division's profitability. The $400,000 charge would prevent him from reaching his performance goal, and he would

Table 59.1   Benefit-cost analysis of outsourcing

Internal production		Outsourcing	
Category	Unit Cost	Category	Unit Cost
Material	$0.60	Material	$0.50
Labor	$0.20	Labor	$0.10
Depreciation	$0.10	Tooling	$0.10
Other overhead	$0.10		

Notes: Annual unit volume is 1,000,000. Depreciation refers to straight-line depreciation of the $1,000,000 initial tooling cost, equal to $100,000 per year for ten years ($0.10 = $100,000/1,000,000).

Source: Froeb and McCann (2010, p. 29).

have to forgo his bonus. The manager rationally decided not to outsource even though outsourcing would have been a profitable move for the company.

Run this problem through our problem-solving framework to identify the source of the problem, and try to find a way to fix it.

1. *Who is making the bad decision?* The plant manager decided not to outsource, even though outsourcing would be profitable for the company.
2. *Does the plant manager have enough information to make a good decision?* Yes. In fact, he is the one who identified the profitable decision.
3. *Does the plant manager have the incentive to make a good decision?* No. Outsourcing reduces accounting profit, and because the manager's bonus is tied to plant income, he rationally decided not to outsource.

Although the problem seems simple, the solution is not. The first reaction of most students is to suggest a change in the performance evaluation metric of the plant manager so that his incentives are not tied to accounting profit, which includes the sunk-cost depreciation. Instead they would change the performance evaluation metric to a measure of accounting profit without the sunk costs.

But this solution raises another, more subtle problem. What if the same plant manager made the initial decision to incur the $1 million tooling cost? If you allow the plant manager to walk away from every investment decision that doesn't work out, you create an incentive to over-invest in capital equipment.

Once they recognize this additional problem, students often suggest moving the decision rights for investment decisions to another business unit, with incentives to increase the net present value of the capital investments that they make. Although moving decision rights to an investment center might sound like a good idea, how would the new decision-maker get the information necessary to make good investment decisions? Ultimately, they would have to rely on information from the plant manager, which leads us back to the very first problem. The plant manager has an incentive to manipulate the decisions of the business unit by selectively feeding them information about the profitability of capital investment projects.

This is a rich problem in that a professor can use it to illustrate a lot of important principles: that accounting costs do not necessarily correspond to economic costs; that there are no perfect solutions, only tradeoffs; and that sometimes the best solution is to do nothing. It never occurs to most students that their solution is perhaps more costly than the problem it is designed to solve. This example can also be used to talk about ethics. What differentiates the behavior of our plant manager from the managers at Enron, who enriched themselves at the expense of shareholders? Isn't the GE plant manager doing the same thing?

CONCLUSION

Using the traditional tools of microeconomics in tandem with the tools of organizational design shows students how to solve problems in a simple, linear way. Economics teaches students to identify profitable decisions, while organizational design shows students how to implement them. Teaching one without the other may explain why students have difficulty seeing the relevance of economics to business. Identifying profitable decisions without being able to implement them, or implementing decisions without knowing whether they are profitable, are both fruitless exercises.

A problem-solving pedagogy is but one way to teach microeconomic principles to business students. Hybrid approaches use some of the same elements to teach business students (see, for example, Baye, 2007). In addition there are different pedagogies, like Bergstrom and Miller's (1999) classroom experiments and Maital (1994)'s "executive" approach that satisfy Schroeder's call for "concrete-active" teaching. However, for the reasons outlined above, we think a problem-solving pedagogy is the best way to teach microeconomic principles to business students in a managerial economics course.

NOTES

1. We wish to acknowledge useful comments from Brian McCann.
2. The discussion in this chapter is primarily focused on business education at the MBA level, given that this course is primarily taught in such programs. However, these concepts apply to undergraduate business courses as well.
3. See, for example, the Managerial Economics module of Southwestern's MBAprimer.com, accessed 25 May 2011.

REFERENCES

Baye, Michael R. (2007), *Managerial Economics and Business Strategy* (6th edition), New York: McGraw-Hill.
Bergstrom, T. and J. Miller (1999), *Experiments with Economic Principles: Microeconomics*, Chicago: McGraw-Hill/Irwin.
Brickley, J., C. Smith, and J. Zimmerman (2007), *Managerial Economics and Organizational Architecture* (4th edition), New York: McGraw-Hill.
Ferraro, P. J. and L. O. Taylor (2005), "Do economists recognize an opportunity cost when they see one? A dismal performance from the dismal science", *Contributions to Economic Analysis & Policy,* 4 (1), Article 7, http://www.bepress.com/bejeap/contributions/vol4/iss1/art7, accessed 25 May 2011
Froeb, L. and B. McCann (2010), *Managerial Economics: A Problem-solving Approach* (2nd edition), Cincinnati, OH: Cengage.

Jensen, M. and W. Meckling (2000), *A Theory of the Firm: Governance, Residual Claims and Organizational Forms,* Cambridge, MA: Harvard University Press.

Lamy, S. L. (2007), "Challenging hegemonic paradigms and practices: Critical thinking and active learning strategies for international relations", *Political Science and Politics,* **40** (1), 112–16.

Maital, S. (1994), *Executive Economics: Ten Essential Tools for Managers,* New York: Free Press.

Schroeder, C. C. (1993), "New students – New learning styles", *Change* (September), **25** (5), Research Library Core, 21–26.

60 Using real-world applications to policy and everyday life to teach money and banking
Dean Croushore

Teaching a course in money and banking can be simultaneously challenging and easy. It is challenging because teaching the course well often requires a fair amount of institutional knowledge, which an instructor may not have acquired in graduate school. However, it is easy because the course can be geared to the coverage of current events, so economic data releases and the state of the economy help the instructor develop a new course every semester and produce an interesting lecture every day.

There are many different ways to teach a course on money and banking. At most schools, the only prerequisite is principles of economics, so the course typically covers financial markets and institutions, present value, principles of banking, basic macroeconomic concepts, institutional details of central banking, and key concepts concerning monetary policy. At some universities, students take a course in intermediate macroeconomics before they take money and banking, so students can see how monetary policy operates in the context of a detailed macroeconomic model. At other universities, especially those without finance courses, the course may be geared more to the microeconomics of financial markets, and may contain more detailed discussions of institutions and the determination of asset prices.

COURSE GOALS

Depending on which of the structures described in the preceding paragraph is relevant, an instructor will want to establish a corresponding set of goals for the course. For the most basic course, where students only have taken principles of economics as a prerequisite, and where the instructor plans to work with current economic data as a major component of the course, the goals might be something like this:

> This course takes a policy-oriented approach to analyzing the financial and monetary systems of the US economy. Our focus will be on the Federal Open Market Committee (FOMC) and the major decisions it makes about setting monetary policy. We will examine the financial system and the role of money; financial markets and instruments; financial institutions; selected elements of macroeconomics, including a discussion of international economics and the importance of exchange rates; and monetary policy, including the money supply process and the conduct of monetary policy in the United States, with an emphasis on current policy issues. We will discuss current economic events and how they affect financial markets and monetary policy. By taking this course, you will: (1) learn the fundamentals of the financial and monetary systems of the US economy; (2) understand how economic news affects financial markets and how it influences the decisions of policymakers; (3) understand how to think analytically, using economic theory to solve problems; (4) study several topics in greater depth than provided by the textbook.

Modest modification of these goals can be used to satisfy other course structures. For a course geared to macroeconomic modeling, the goals might include "studying monetary policy in the context of the AS-AD/IS-LM model from your intermediate macroeconomics course." (Alternatively, "dynamic" may be substituted for "AS-AD/IS-LM," depending on what intermediate macroeconomics textbook the students used.) For a course geared to greater detail on financial markets, goals might include "to understand the details of financial institutions and the pricing of financial securities."

Most standard money and banking textbooks will cover all the basic elements needed to meet any of these goals. For emphasis in particular areas, the instructor may need to develop additional materials to meet these goals. For example, for a course that includes the details of the pricing of financial securities, the instructor may want to develop a set of notes that pull material from more advanced finance courses, because derivative pricing is not often included in standard money and banking textbooks.

Following current events is a natural part of any money and banking course. The challenge for the instructor is to keep on top of everything that is going on. The most interesting money and banking class that I taught was in fall 2008, during the financial crisis, when we would spend as much as half of each class period discussing all the events of the previous few days, and watch how much the stock market would fall each day while we were in class. But not every semester will be as dynamic as that one, so to fulfill my second course goal (understand how economic news affects financial markets and how it influences the decisions of policymakers), I require the following:

> *Current Events Report and Memo:* Early in the semester, you will be assigned one particular macroeconomic variable to follow throughout the semester. Each variable is released monthly. When your variable is released, you are to prepare a short (two-minute maximum) oral report on your variable and show at least one graph that you have prepared yourself using Excel. In your oral report, you must be clear and concise: (1) describe the new numbers that were released and any revisions to prior data; (2) put the new data in historical perspective; (3) explain the implications of the data for our understanding of the economy and its implications for monetary policy. Your graph must use data on your variable to illustrate recent trends in your data. At the end of the semester, you are to write up your analysis of each release over the semester in a brief (three-page text maximum; extra for charts) memo that summarizes your oral reports and provides an overall evaluation of what the data mean for the analysis of the economy and for monetary policy. In your memo, you must prepare at least two explanatory graphs or tables (using Excel).

This assignment is actually one that students are at first a bit fearful of, but come to enjoy by the end of the semester and it promotes learning in a number of ways. First, it keeps all of them (and the instructor) aware of the current state of the economy in every imaginable dimension. Second, students get practice using Excel to illustrate their data, and I will give the students suggestions on how to make the graph more informative. For example, they tend to want to plot the levels of the variable, when growth rates might be much more informative. Students also tend to plot very volatile series, so I show them how to smooth a series out to see the trend more clearly. Third, they get to practice their oral presentation skills, making three presentations during the semester, and they see how to discuss a graph as a point of focus. In the case of a large class, this exercise is easily modified by splitting the class into teams, requiring each team member to present once during the semester. Strictly enforcing the two-minute time limit challenges students to be concise, while also allowing for a greater number of such presentations.

For the final goal (study several topics in greater depth than provided by the textbook), there are a number of ways to proceed. The instructor could require them to write a report on some additional readings found in the textbook, or to do research on some element of the course that they found particularly interesting. Because I emphasize monetary-policy issues in my money and banking course, I collected a set of Federal-Reserve articles and I require the students to do an extra assignment:[1]

> I will post a list on Blackboard of extra readings for each chapter, along with questions to answer about each reading and possibly data-related questions. You must pick three readings during the semester and write a one-page memo for each. Only one reading may come from each chapter. Each memo should provide a brief synopsis of the reading and answer the questions related to it. Each memo is due within one week after we complete discussion of the chapter in class.

When I first made this assignment, I worried that the students might minimize the time spent on it, doing just the bare minimum to answer the questions and to summarize the article. I found, to the contrary, that this assignment became one of their favorite parts of the course and they spent many hours on it. Many of them came to ask me questions about the details of the article or the research behind it. In the end-of-year student evaluations of the course, many indicated that this was one of the most valuable things they did, in part because it let them explore an area of interest to them and to go beyond the textbook's standard discussion. The structure of this assignment also imposes little cost on the instructor as the one-page memo is quickly graded.

TEACHING PHILOSOPHY

In teaching money and banking, I stress three ideas: (1) understanding the economy today; (2) the value of the concepts that are useful for everyday life; and (3) analytical thinking.

Making the class relevant to economic issues of the day helps the students see the importance of the theory they are covering. When they read an interview with a member of the Federal Open Market Committee (FOMC) that appeared in the *Wall Street Journal* and we discuss it in class, along with graphs showing what that FOMC member has been focusing on, the students realize that this is not some abstract theory, but that the theory affects policy decisions, which affects the interest rates they observe in the market. Tying theoretical discussions to data helps students see that, without theory to help them interpret the data, the data are not very informative.

One of the best examples of how theory can help students interpret data is the term structure of interest rates. Students, especially those interested in finance, are often intrigued by the term structure of interest rates, but often begin with very faulty ideas about it. There is a popular video on a finance web site showing how the term structure has changed over time and what it looks like in economic recessions and expansions.[2] But without understanding the expectations theory of the term structure, combined with the concept of a term premium, students' interpretations of the term structure are often incorrect. Once they learn how to decompose the data on the term structure into pieces, part reflecting the term premium and part representing the expected future path of short-term interest rates, they begin to understand why you need theory to help explain data.

In teaching money and banking, it is vital to show students how the information in the class is helpful for their everyday lives. There are many ways to do this, including how to invest efficiently, how economic growth affects their incomes, and how to calculate the optimal amount of cash to keep in their wallets. My favorite example, however, shows students how to take an abstract equation, the present-value formula, and use it to help them when they buy or lease a car. With a few assumptions, one can use the formula to approximate the monthly payment for either a car purchase or lease, and check whether the car dealer's calculations are correct, or if they have added in some fees surreptitiously. Students recognize that they will be buying or leasing cars on their own soon, if they haven't done so already, and they understand that they can't just rely on someone to tell them the truth – especially a car dealer who has an incentive to cheat them.

A course in money and banking should provide students with the ability to engage in analytical thinking. Many students take money and banking fairly early in their college years, perhaps after having only principles of economics, so they haven't been exposed to much analytical thinking or done very much problem solving. One of the best ways to teach students how to think about complicated problems is to work through present-value problems, where it is critical to set up the problem correctly, not to blindly apply a formula.

COURSE CONTENT

What concepts should be covered in a course in money and banking? As with any course, the content must depend on the course goals and prerequisites, and the course's place in the curriculum. For a course in money and banking, these can vary widely. However, there are some basic elements that I think are essential in any money and banking course. The main elements are: money and the financial system; fundamentals of banking; macroeconomic concepts; and monetary policy.

Money and the Financial System

A discussion, usually lasting three to four weeks in a 15-week semester, of money and the financial system develops the institutional building blocks for the course. Topics are likely to include the structure of the financial system in the economy, the role played by money compared with other financial assets, the present-value concept, the term structure of interest rates, real interest rates, and fundamentals of the stock market. Many students may have already had a course on the financial system and they may have learned about the role of money in the economy from their economic principles courses, so the instructor may review this information fairly quickly. Although much of this material is institutional in nature, the instructor can build on the institutional details in those sections in two ways: describing an investor's decisions in terms of return and risk, showing how a market can aggregate the decisions of individual investors, and making students think about the role of money in an economy when most payments are made with credit cards or electronic payments, and not with cash.

In this first section of the course, by far the most important concept is that of present value. It is a building block for everything done in finance and for much of the discussion of returns and interest rates that will follow. Finance majors who may be enrolled in the course often have the most difficult time with present value because they have learned what buttons to push on their financial calculators to solve a problem that fits neatly into their calculator's canned programs, but they are less skilled at solving more complicated analytical problems. Ask them to calculate the present value of $1000 received today and they will actually reach for their calculators and want to know the interest rate, instead of realizing that it must be $1000 because that is what present value means.

For many students, the course in money and banking is the only place they will encounter two concepts: the term structure of interest rates and the concept of the real interest rate. As mentioned above, the theory of the term structure is crucial for understanding data on interest rates on securities with differing times to maturity. Getting students to understand the expectations theory and the concept of a term premium is vital to developing their ability to understand data on interest rates. After going through the theory and looking at the historical patterns in the data, I then like to illustrate the combination of theory and data by showing the class how to use term spreads to predict the probability of a recession.

Students often don't realize that real interest rates, not nominal interest rates, are the key equilibrating variable in many economic models. Students may wonder why economic models are driven by a variable that is not even observable! But the theory behind the real interest rate should be clear, and they need to understand why the concept is needed, for the same reason that real GDP is the key macroeconomic aggregate, rather than the observable nominal GDP. I like to illustrate the concept of the real interest rate by examining the interaction between inflation and taxes, which shows how after-tax real returns received by investors can be very small, even when nominal interest rates are high. When students see how the after-tax real interest rate can be negative, even with inflation rates that are not much higher than they are currently, they become very concerned about the costs of inflation.

Fundamentals of Banking

The second key section of a money and banking course concerns the fundamentals of banking. This is often a difficult area for many instructors, especially those whose background is in macroeconomics and who may not know very much about the institutional details of banking. One way to handle this part of the course is to focus on theory rather than institutional details. The instructor can spend a fair amount of time discussing asymmetric-information problems, a critical theoretical concept in banking. If students gain a solid understanding of both adverse selection and moral hazard, they will be able to comprehend why bankers do what they do.

Another fundamental area of banking that students must understand is regulation and supervision. This is inherently an area that depends on institutional details, of which the instructor must be aware. Fortunately, most textbooks have good discussions of the institutional details, so rather than lecture on these details, instructors can focus on solving problems, such as working through bank balance sheets and the determination of required reserves. I like to discuss the way in which regulators analyze bank mergers, so I talk about the Herfindahl-Hirschman index and how it is determined. This provides both an opportunity to discuss regulation and also a formulaic approach to analytical problems.

Overall, unless the instructor knows a lot about the microeconomics of banking, I suggest that the instructor focus on concepts that are important in terms of their macro-economic consequences. That's why I spend more time on banks' balance sheets and the calculation of excess reserves, which helps students understand open-market operations and how they work to affect the overall quantity of money in the economy, as well as the determination of interest rates.

Macroeconomic Concepts

The third major section of a money and banking course is macroeconomics. Again, the degree to which an instructor covers this area is a function of personal preference and how the course fits into the curriculum. If the course requires intermediate macro-economics as a prerequisite, then this section of the course can be streamlined. Since most money and banking courses don't require intermediate macroeconomics, an intro-duction to aggregate supply and aggregate demand, or dynamic models of money, is useful. I don't recommend trying to develop a full-blown IS-LM analysis because it takes too much time away from other topics, such as monetary policy. It is more important that students get a basic understanding of business cycles and how monetary policy can influence the cycle. In particular, they should gain a sense of the main debate among macroeconomists about the efficacy of policy. To provide a balanced presentation, the instructor can discuss both the activist view that the government (and central bank) can and should intervene to smooth out the business cycle and the non-activist view that government action is potentially counterproductive and destabilizing.

The other key component of the macroeconomics discussion is exchange rates. Because this is a difficult topic for students to understand without substantial class time, the instructor should avoid trying to cover all the nuances. Critical issues relevant to money and banking are the effect of a change in the exchange rate on the prices of imported and exported goods, the effect of international trade and investment on exchange rates, how inflation affects the nominal exchange rate, and the concept of the real exchange rate. The instructor may wish to discuss purchasing-power-parity con-cepts, but should recognize that most models based on those concepts perform poorly in forecasting exchange rates.

Monetary Policy

The final major section of the money-and-banking course is monetary policy. The instructor may wish to introduce basic monetary policy concepts during the first week of class, and follow all the events related to monetary policy, especially FOMC decisions, throughout the semester. Even though students are not likely to understand why the Fed is taking particular actions early in the semester, by the end of the course they will come to understand the Fed's actions in context. Such an integrated discussion of policy issues whets students' appetite for this final section of the course.

There are four main areas of monetary policy that are vital to understanding how policy works: (1) the structure of the central bank; (2) how the central bank controls the money supply and interest rates; (3) the goals and accomplishments of monetary policy, and the tradeoffs that policymakers face; and (4) the debate about rules versus discretion.

A brief introduction to the structure of the central bank is crucial, though the instructor can assign much of this as background reading. If the instructor has had the good fortune to have worked within the Federal Reserve, students always enjoy hearing an insider's view. Key elements to convey are how a central bank is set up, how power is divided within the central bank, and how decisions are made. Many students (and journalists) pay too much attention to which policymakers are voting members of the FOMC, rather than understanding the generally collegial nature of the discussion. The power of the Fed chairman is substantial compared with the power of other members, yet the chairman is constrained by having to convince other members that his proposed policy is sensible. A chairman who does not lead by consensus is not likely to last very long as chairman.

Students find the discussion of how the Fed controls monetary policy to be the most challenging in the course. This was especially true from 2008 to 2011, when the Fed engaged in extraordinary policy measures. Students should gain an understanding of how the market for reserves works, so they can see how increases in the supply of reserves leads to a decline in the federal funds interest rate, and vice versa. Then the instructor can illustrate the impact of open-market operations, changes in the discount rate, changes in reserve requirements, and changes in the interest rate on bank reserves.

Of course, the analysis of the market for reserves is just a short-run analysis and it is crucial for students to get a longer-run view by learning about the goals and strategy of the central bank. To understand these, the instructor needs to give them a long-run perspective by examining time-series data on output, unemployment, and inflation. Some discussion of the history of monetary policy will help them understand successes and failures, especially the Great Inflation of the 1970s and the Great Moderation from the mid-1980s to the mid-2000s. This discussion allows the instructor to bring up the Phillips curve and tradeoffs the Fed faces in the short run, which will help students understand why policy decisions are subject to so much debate.

The last major issue in discussing monetary policy is the debate over rules versus discretion. In this section, the instructor can bring up the concept of the time inconsistency of optimal plans and get students to understand how a well-meaning central bank can make major errors despite its own good intentions. The instructor should also discuss the lags inherent in monetary policy, especially the long and variable effectiveness lag. Then the instructor can discuss rules for monetary policy, starting with suggestions by monetarists to keep the growth rate of the money supply constant. The instructor must discuss the Taylor rule, noting its popularity in recent research, in part because it is a rule, though an activist one; it also provides the opportunity to point out how difficult such a rule is to implement in real time, mainly because of the problems of measuring the output gap. Finally, the instructor might discuss inflation targeting as a strategy that is not formally a rule, but has certain desirable long-run characteristics, like those of rules for monetary policy.

In this last section on monetary policy, students are more likely to develop an understanding of how policy works if the instructor can relate the theory being discussed to current policy actions. This real-world connection is easy to develop during a crisis and its aftermath (as was the case from fall 2008 to spring 2011), when monetary policy is the center of discussion in the daily news. The course is less exciting in normal times, such as most of the 1990s, when policy just doesn't do very much. Thus, providing a historical perspective of policy during crises will help students understand how policy works in a more interesting environment.

COMMON MISPERCEPTIONS

The most common misperception of students taking money and banking is that monetary-policy decisions are obvious. Many students need to gain an appreciation for the difficulty in making monetary-policy decisions in real time. To give them some understanding of that, I like to discuss data and how data revisions can affect policy decisions. My favorite example comes from my days as an economist at the Federal Reserve Bank of Philadelphia. I remember in the late 1990s during a briefing of our bank's president before an FOMC meeting how we noted that the personal saving rate had turned negative "for the first time in history," which was a bad sign for investment. But then a year later, I looked at current data that showed the saving rate turning negative "for the first time ever." It turns out that the personal saving rate is often revised, and during the 1990s and early 2000s, the revisions generally increased the measured personal saving rate. So, one could accurately have reported for many years in a row that the savings rate had become negative for the first time ever!

Another way to show the uncertainty about monetary-policy decisions comes from looking at output gap data. At the time that a monetary-policy decision is made, a policymaker really does not have a very good idea about the level or growth rate of potential output, so does not have a very precise notion of whether expansionary policy or contractionary policy is needed. Even though a discussion of the optimal policy in the face of uncertainty is beyond the mathematical ability of most students, an instructor can still give students a sense of the difficulties faced by policymakers in formulating policy when they don't know precisely where the economy is. Most importantly, talking about this issue gives students a better idea of why there is a policy debate and why the central bank's decisions require a great deal of thought and analysis.

The other common misperception in the money and banking course comes at the micro level. Many students come into the class with preconceived notions about the evil nature of bankers or participants in financial markets. They think that greed and avarice are the common traits of those participants and they don't think they play any useful role in society. The money and banking course helps them to understand that those financial market participants play a useful role in society, even if some of them behave in what appears to be an evil way.

DIFFICULT TOPICS

The two most difficult topics to teach in a money and banking course, in my experience, are: (1) the present-value formula when there is more than one payment each year; and (2) the market for bank reserves when the Fed pays interest on reserves and when banks can borrow from the discount window at a penalty rate over the fed funds target interest rate.

In the first case, when there are multiple payments each year, the present-value formula can be modified easily, assuming students understand how the formula works when there is one payment at the end of each year. For an interest rate compounded n times per year, the same present-value formulas can still be employed, using as the discount rate a number equal to the annual rate of interest divided by n, and treating each period of length $1/n$ in place of the number of years in the formula. This procedure prevents students from having to learn more complicated formulas.

In the second case, the market for bank reserves is more difficult to handle. The Fed's decision to allow banks in good condition to borrow substantial amounts at the discount window puts a ceiling on the federal funds rate equal to the primary credit discount rate, causing the supply curve of reserves to be kinked. The Fed's payment of interest on reserves puts a lower bound on the federal funds rate in normal times, constraining the demand curve for reserves. Thus, the federal funds rate must be somewhere between the interest rate on reserves and the primary credit discount rate, in normal times. (However, during the financial crisis of 2008 and its aftermath, this constraint failed to hold, but only because of the odd institutional feature that Fannie Mae and Freddie Mac could lend in the federal funds market but were not eligible to earn interest on their reserves.) The instructor can then draw a diagram of demand and supply in the reserves market, allowing students to see how the market for bank reserves works on a daily basis.

CONCLUSION

The course in money and banking is a delight to teach. Instructors can base the course on real-world applications to policy and to everyday life. Many students find the course to be the one that helps them the most in their future careers.

My recommendations are that instructors consider the development of clear and concise learning goals for the course (a function of where the course fits in the curriculum), stress three main ideas (understanding the economy today, concepts that are useful for everyday life, and analytical thinking), and develop four main topic areas (money and the financial system, fundamentals of banking, macroeconomic concepts, and monetary policy). Instructors should realize that the difficult part of teaching this course is that the material is in a constant state of flux, depending on what happens in the economy. The financial crisis that began in 2008 led to many changes in the financial system and regulation of banks, as well as innovations in monetary policy. So instructors of money and banking must be on constant alert for changes in the material. While this may seem difficult, these constant changes actually make the course easy to teach because nearly every day's newspaper provides new course material.

NOTES

1. These articles can be found on my web site (https://facultystaff.richmond.edu/~dcrousho/docs/Readings%20from%20the%20Federal%20Reserve%20with%20RQs%2010Jan.doc) and also on the web

site of the publisher of *M&B*, Cengage Learning, Mason, OH, 2010 (http://www.cengage.com/cgi-wadsworth/course_products_wp.pl?fid=M20bI&product_isbn_issn=9780538745871) (accessed 10 April 2011).

2. http://www.smartmoney.com/investing/bonds/the-living-yield-curve-7923/ (accessed 10 April 2011).

61 Teaching political economy to undergraduate students

William Waller

In a perfect world, where students could take as many courses in economics as we would like, they would have ample opportunity to master all the tools, methods, theories, and approaches of economics. But students have a limited time to study economics over the course of their undergraduate career. Moreover, the overwhelming hegemony of mainstream neoclassical economics and the ever increasing level of mastery of theory, statistical methods, and mathematical ability required for entrance to graduate study, make the inclusion of anything beyond the standard material difficult to add to the curriculum. Yet I believe there is a responsibility for all departments to make some space in the curriculum to introduce political economy, by which I mean alternative approaches to mainstream neoclassical economics, to their students. In this chapter I describe how this can be done so our undergraduates can become economically educated citizens and potential professional economists.

Departments that include political economy in their curriculum often begin introducing it as topics in principles classes. This is accomplished by introducing some elements of heterodox thought in appropriate places within the existing introductory framework. There are three approaches to incorporating political economy into the existing introductory framework that are manageable for faculty with little training in alternative approaches. The first is simply to choose an introductory textbook that introduces some of this material. Existing textbooks have considerable variation in the amount of and method by which they include political economy including short essays on an innovative economic thinker; texts that introduce both mainstream and heterodox approaches to principles of economics; supplementary texts added to the course; and alternative texts intended to be used side-by-side with the main text.[1] Bucknell University's economics department has been particularly innovative in incorporating political economy into the principles of economics by developing their own principles text and supplements (Sackrey and Schneider, 2002).

Some departments offer a course in political economy as a survey of heterodox or alternative approaches. The goal of such courses is to introduce the origins of alternative approaches to mainstream neoclassical orthodox economic analysis. They necessarily introduce both the methodological and theoretical underpinnings of alternative approaches to economics. Ideally, students have opportunities to take more advanced courses in various approaches to political economy to deepen their knowledge. Also desirable would be stand-alone courses on alternative approaches to mainstream economics.

PHILOSOPHY FOR TEACHING POLITICAL ECONOMY AND THE RESULTING STRUCTURE

Students need grounding in the history of economic thought to understand political economy. But most students' understanding of history of thought is of the rational reconstruction approach characterization (typical of principles of economics textbooks) which takes current economic thought as scientifically warranted and traces it back as an unbroken line of progressive incremental developments beginning with the work of Adam Smith. Teaching political economy necessitates that the student be shown that the history of economic thought can also be understood as developing and changing as a result of vigorous debate among competing ideas that emerge, including disagreement over the most fundamental definitions of economic inquiry, methodology, theory, appropriate methods of analysis, underlying philosophical foundations, and the relationship of economic inquiry to other social science disciplines. As such, primary texts use is preferable to secondary sources that inevitably end up characterizing the original author's contribution to economics through the lens of the secondary text's author. Undergraduate students with a good foundation in neoclassical economics can, with guidance, read and comprehend the work of Marx, Veblen, Keynes, Hayek, Schumpeter and many other classic texts. Of course this will introduce the instructor's perspective into the discussion. But following Gunnar Myrdal's (1969, p. 72) approach – making your preferences and intellectual commitments clear rather than claiming objectivity – gives the student an opportunity to evaluate your perspective from an informed position.

Additionally, since alternatives to economic orthodoxy were generated by disagreements in the development of economic thought, for students to understand the alternatives, they need to understand the original economic theories and ideas that were in dispute. There is little point in teaching the economics of Karl Marx to students who know nothing of Classical economics. Thorstein Veblen's critique of marginalism motivated his reconstruction of economics along evolutionary lines by focusing on the evolution of social institutions. But this critique and reconstruction is meaningless unless students know the marginalist approach to economics. Similarly John Maynard Keynes's innovations are a response to the Marshallian orthodoxy of his day, so the argument of *The General Theory* makes the most sense in that context. Similar points can be made regarding all the alternative approaches. Thus students need a solid foundation in intermediate level microeconomic and macroeconomic theory and some exposure to the history of economic thought and economic history to understand the emergence and persistence of alternatives to mainstream economic thought. Obviously it is not practical for departments to require course work in all these areas, but teaching political economy before intermediate theory courses tends to be more confusing than helpful for undergraduates. They need to know mainstream theory to understand why heterodox economists proposed alternatives.

IMPORTANT CONTENT AND IDEAS: IMPROVING STUDENT UNDERSTANDING

After setting up the reason for studying political economy, students with a clear understanding of mainstream methodology can read Friedman's (1953) famous essay on "The

Methodology of Positive Economics." Friedman's essay is the source of the methodology sections of most mainstream principles texts and a significant number of intermediate and advanced texts. It is a very clear statement that economic analysis is value-free and is not normative. Since Friedman presented his essay as the work of a master practitioner of economics, rather than as an expert on philosophy or scientific methodology, presenting how he believed economic analysis created economic knowledge accurately contextualizes his contribution. Friedman's essay is also among the most critiqued and controversial essays in the history of the discipline. After reading Friedman's essay, I have students read several critical essays assessing Friedman's methodology (see Caldwell, 1984) that point to multiple understandings of an appropriate methodology for economics.

It is important for students to understand that the way economic knowledge is constructed has been contested throughout its history. Marxian, institutional, Austrian and much feminist economics are built on fundamentally different ontological, epistemological, and methodological foundations from neoclassical economics. What defines economic questions, answers to those questions, and what constitutes knowledge is contested terrain in political economy, but presented as settled matters of fact in introductory and intermediate neoclassical theory texts.

Marxian Economics

After making the point that economics is not a settled science, I introduce alternative frameworks for economic analysis using Karl Marx and Marxian economics. Since the approach stresses methodology, it makes sense to start Marx with *The German Ideology* (Tucker, 1978) which introduces historical materialism and dialectical thought. Marx makes the case that all societies are organized by a particular mode of production, each consisting of forces and relations of production that structure all social relations in that society. Distinct classes of people characterize every mode of production: one class controls the forces of production, another class uses them for production. Those who control production own the output. This creates an inherent conflict between these classes. Social analysis is inherently economic because the fundamental production relations structure all social phenomena. Individual action is simply one person's manifestation of class relations. Consequently, hypotheses and theoretical statements in Marxian economics will be at a different level of analysis than in the individual agent framework of neoclassical economics. This is a key reason that theories in one framework appear nonsensical to economists working in another framework.

The Economic and Philosophical Manuscripts of 1844 (Tucker, 1978) are assigned next because they include Marx's analysis of worker estrangement or alienation under capitalist production relations. This is a powerful analysis of the structural character of production relations and its debilitating effects on human beings and human social relations.

Economic analysis moves into the foreground with selected readings from Marx's *Capital*, vol. 1 (Tucker, 1978). Marx's analysis of capitalism is built on historical materials (class conflict), the forces that dominate Classical economics (pursuit of profit and competition) and the labor theory of value. Marx argued that capitalism is a monetary economy where the capitalist uses physical capital and liquid capital (money) and employs laborers in order to produce commodities to sell for money profits (liquid capital). The creation of surplus value in production results from workers producing sufficient output for the capitalist to cover the value of their wages plus additional output that (when sold) will realize a money amount that exceeds the production cost of the capitalist. The capitalist expropriates this surplus value as profits and the next cycle of commodity production begins. The productivity and profits of enterprise and the exploitation of workers are results of the creation of surplus value in capitalist social relations. This is the main contradiction in capitalism and the source of the fundamental class conflict that is the engine of social change in historical materialism.

Competition leads to attempts by the capitalist to intensify work effort to increase and then maintain the level of surplus value in the face of fierce competition. Competition erodes profits and firms fail. Workers are unemployed and the capital of failed firms is acquired by others, leading to successive rounds of capital accumulation (industry concentration). As capital accumulation proceeds, the relative surplus value of employed workers necessarily decreases. Crises involving firm liquidation, worker unemployment and reorganization of capital continue with increasing severity, leading to the possibility of a radical transformation of society through the replacement of the capitalist mode of production.

I always assign the section in *Capital*, vol.1 (Tucker, 1978) on commodity fetishism because it extends the consequence of workers' estrangement and alienation resulting from capitalism production relations to consumption behavior. Workers' obsession with acquiring commodities, regardless of the usefulness in their day-to-day lives and despite the economic hardship workers often endure to acquire quite superfluous and even ridiculous objects, becomes a bit more understandable to those exposed only to subjective utility theory.

I often make available a short introduction to Marxian analysis by John Gurley reprinted in Albelda, Gunn and Waller (1987) for students who struggle with reading Marx himself – this is done with some regret because students may not persist in reading the original text.

After the students have read Marx, two types of readings logically follow. One is a contemporary example of Marxist economic analysis. The other is a mainstream publication's assessment of the impact of Marx on the evolution of market economies (see, for example, Myers, 1991, and Cassidy, 1997).

Keynes and Post Keynesian Economics

An effective way to introduce Keynes and post Keynesian economics is using *The General Theory of Employment, Interest and Money* (1964). Surprisingly, this is not as hard for undergraduates as many economists would think. The key to having undergraduates read *The General Theory* is to recognize that contemporary economics undergraduates are not Keynes's intended audience, focus on selected topics that differentiate Keynes from mainstream economists, and spend time on Keynes's "Concluding Notes."

Keynes was making an argument for his contemporary Marshallian trained economist colleagues. His rhetorical strategy was to state three premises of mainstream analysis that did not hold, demonstrating why economic models of his day could not account for general downturns in economic activity generated endogenously from the Marshallian model. Nor could their model explain how the actual economy would automatically be restored to health as the mainstream model claimed. Keynes, in presenting his alternative approach, anticipates the objections of his contemporary economic colleagues – your students will not anticipate the objections. Students need to be guided to understand when each objection is addressed or Keynes's argument could become very confusing and overwhelming. Thus, the associated strategy is to guide students to focus on a few topics as they read, ones that differentiate Keynes from the mainstream. This is especially useful because many of the topics that differentiate Keynes from the mainstream are the point of departure for post Keynesian economics.

The first topic is the use of historical time by Keynes: time is not logical for Keynes; it is historical and there is a known past and an unknowable future. This leads directly to the second topic, that the economy is characterized by uncertainty because the future is unpredictable and unknowable. However, since investment decisions are based on expectations about future states of the economy, economic decisions about the future have no rational basis. Furthermore, the condition of equilibrium identified by Keynes's contemporaries is not a condition or place towards which real economies tend to move. Keynes continues to use the language of equilibrium, but his model is fundamentally about an economy in flux characterized by disequilibrium. Finally, Keynes treats money as endogenous, produced by the system in its normal operations, and thus the Keynesian approach is a monetary theory of production. Money is not neutral in Keynes's theory. As such, instructors can make the point that he is more like Marx than the Classicists and his contemporaries. If students read *The General Theory* focusing on where Keynes discusses these key concepts, they will realize that Keynes differs both from other approaches to macroeconomics and to the Keynes they encountered in their own mainstream macroeconomic training.

The final strategy for making Keynes comprehensible to undergraduates is to include reading the often-neglected Book VI because these "Concluding Notes" are not after-thoughts. This is where Keynes describes his methodological approach, the values that motivate his economics, the historical antecedents to his own theorizing. This last section of *The General Theory* shows that while Keynes's arguments were presented using the discourse conventions of Marshallian economics, Keynes's own theorizing encompassed much more. It also makes a compelling case for the careful study of the history of economic thought.

After reading Keynes, contemporary readings that address the focal topics, including historic time, uncertainty, expectations, disequilibrium and money, will enhance students' understanding of the relevance of Keynes to contemporary macroeconomic issues, as discussed in the post Keynesian literature. Readings that discuss Hyman Minsky's contribution to modern monetary theory show the importance of post Keynesian thought for understanding recent economic financial crises. There are excellent resources for this purpose, including the *Journal of Post Keynesian Economics* and the *Cambridge Journal of Economics*. The Levy Institute[2] and the Center for Full Employment and Price Stability[3] provide online access to publications accessible to undergraduate students.

Post Keynesian economics differs from mainstream macroeconomic analysis in that it takes features of Keynes's analysis that have been discarded or ignored by the mainstream and makes them central. Another distinguishing feature of post Keynesian economics is that it continues to focus on aggregate analysis – economists working in this tradition do not seek microeconomic foundations in neoclassical microeconomics.

Instead, to the degree that they are concerned with something akin to microeconomic foundations, they often employ original institutional economics as the foundation of post Keynesian analysis of individual behavior. Two excellent examples of exploiting this convergence are Todorova (2009) and Brown (2008).

Original Institutional Economics

Introducing institutional economics is complex because the frequently used phrase "institutions matter" is employed to suggest that there is no difference between modern discussions in mainstream economics that discuss social institutions. I begin with a focus on original institutional economics because the role of institutions in social and economic change is the level of the analysis and central theoretical question in this tradition. Since Thorstein Veblen's critique of neoclassical economics and approach to evolutionary and institutional analysis remains the foundation of most original institutional economics, his work remains the best way to introduce institutional economics. Veblen's total rejection of the philosophical and epistemological foundations of marginalist economics is scathing and comprehensive. His contribution to the discipline of economics is only comprehensible from the perspective of evolutionary methodology, instinct psychology, pragmatic philosophy and a cultural approach that greatly diminishes the significance of individual behavior.

Assigning four articles by Thorstein Veblen provides an introductory survey to institutional economics. "Why Economics is not an evolutionary science" makes a case for economics to be reconceptualized in evolutionary terms (Veblen, 1990, pp. 56–81). "The instinct of workmanship and the irksomeness of labor" introduces Veblen's concept of instincts as the biological motivation for behavior and the cultural meaning inscribed upon productive labor (Veblen, 1964, pp. 78–96). "Industrial and pecuniary employments" introduces the framework used in his reconstruction of the theory of the firm (Veblen, 1990, pp. 279–323). "The economic theory of women's dress" introduces his theory of consumption, based on the cultural meaning ascribed to goods and services in an economy where consumers are motivated by pecuniary emulation to engage in conspicuous consumption and conspicuous leisure (Veblen, 1964, pp. 65–77). I also include the first part of Chapter VIII of *The Theory of the Leisure Class* (Veblen, 1934, pp. 188–94) because this is where Veblen describes how institutions evolve. An alternative way to provide a survey of institutional economics grounded in Veblen is to assign *Veblen in Plain English* (McCormick, 2006). This book is an excellent introduction to Veblen's thought; however, reading primary sources exposes the student to Veblen's prose style or humor.

Of course, institutional economics is broader than Veblen. Three additional components complete the teaching of institutional economics. The rejection of the positive/normative dualism is central. All knowledge is culturally constructed, using language and symbols (which are cultural artifacts), and given meaning within a bounded discourse community. Consequently there must be explicit criteria for evaluating knowledge claims; criteria which emerge from the pragmatism of Peirce (1955) and Dewey (1929). They are expressed in two forms: instrumental value theory (discussed by Tool in Albelda et al., 1987, pp. 225–43) and the concept of reasonable value developed by Commons (1990, pp. 680–84).

As in the case of Keynes, providing readings in contemporary institutional economics on various topics expands historical grounding beyond Veblen and into modern institutional economics. *The Journal of Economic Issues* and *The Journal of Institutional Economics* are excellent sources.

The relationship between the original institutional economics and the "new" institutional economics is complex. Much of the new institutional economics is merely an extension of mainstream economics. However some of the work in the "new" institutional economics does converge with the original institutional economics.

The Uniqueness of Feminist Economics

Introducing feminist economics is complicated because it approaches many similar issues as the broader heterodox movement, but with much more methodological diversity than other alternatives to mainstream neoclassical economics. Feminist economics is more appropriately characterized as a movement rather than a single alternative framework with an alternative epistemology and different methodology. Placing it after the other approaches in the class allows the instructor to highlight this difference. What is shared by all feminist economists is their acceptance that gender is an important analytic rather than descriptive category, so gendered behavior is to be treated as a core-analytic concept in theorizing. This is in sharp contrast to a simple description of the differences between men and women's behavior in the economy, known as the descriptive or "add women and stir" approach to economics. There are feminist economists whose training and methodological inclinations emerge from their training and interest in mainstream neoclassical economics, Marxian economics, and just about every other analytic framework in the economics discipline. *Beyond Economic Man* (Ferber and Nelson, 1993) includes many essays that introduce the shared methodological concerns of feminist economics, the critiques of non-feminist economic analysis and essays that introduce feminist economics from a number of viewpoints, including some heterodox frameworks.

The introduction of gender as an analytic concept in the economics classroom at most undergraduate institutions is both important and complicated by the fact that it is usually a disproportionately male environment. Reasons for introducing feminist economics might not be intuitively obvious to this student audience, especially since gender does not fit neatly into the alternative analytic framework of the other heterodox traditions. Moreover, the non-neoclassical traditions track record of attention to women and feminist issues is not better than that of the mainstream. One way to motivate interest in feminist issues is to introduce Waring's (1990) argument on the systematic exclusion of women's contributions to economic provisioning in economic data. For the purpose of a survey class, however, the film *Who's Counting? Marilyn Waring on Sex, Lies and Global Economics* is a more time-efficient option (Nash and Waring, 1995).

As in the case of other approaches covered in a political economy course, it is important to provide contemporary examples of how feminist economics adds to our knowledge and understanding of actual economic issues. The first and most obvious approach is to select several articles from the journal *Feminist Economics*, which includes articles representing every analytic approach in the economics discipline. It also has the advantage of introducing students to the feminist economics discourse community that, like the journal, is open and diverse. Rarely do economists from different analytic traditions seriously engage one another. The shared intellectual concern for incorporating gender analytically into economic theorizing and research has caused feminist economists to be extraordinarily open and receptive to making the effort to be understood and to understand others from different analytic traditions. This makes feminist economics a vehicle for introducing students to alternative methodologies applied to a common goal.

Another approach to demonstrating the importance of gender in economic analysis is to select a book that approaches important economic topics from a feminist perspective. There are a number of good options available, including Barker and Feiner (2004) covering several economic topics, Figart, Mutari and Power (2002) on labor economics, or Benería (2003) on economic development. All are appropriate (if challenging) for undergraduates and are of reasonable length.

Other Approaches

Arguably, some variants of modern Austrian economics could be considered both sufficiently methodologically distinct and complete to be considered a break with mainstream orthodoxy. Many other so-called alternative approaches such as the "new" institutional economics, behavioral economics and experimental economics, by virtue of sharing the notions of optimization and equilibrium, might be more appropriately considered as extensions of neoclassical economics.

CONVEYING RELEVANCE

I always begin the political economy course by looking at either current or historical cases of the economics discipline in crisis. I have used Deane's analysis to explore the nature and resolution of the *methodenstreit* (1983, reprinted in Albelda et al., 1987), stagflation in the late 1970s, and of course the current financial crisis to begin a discussion of alternative visions of economics. Since historical events such as these have caused professional economists to reconsider theory and methodology, it is a logical way to raise questions with students about these same matters. It demonstrates how periodic re-examinations of economics at every level of analysis are something that the profession as a whole undertakes periodically and is not the provenance of disgruntled heterodox economists. On occasion, ideas and concepts once considered outside the mainstream are incorporated into the mainstream.

There are many examples to look at, such as the transition from classical economics to marginalism through the substitution of the utility theory of value for the labor theory of value and subsequent restructuring of economic theory that resulted. A similar transition is the combination of marginalist price theory with Hicksian IS-LM macroeconomics inspired by Keynes's critique of economics. Or alternately, the heterodox economics of Marx, Menger, Veblen, and Keynes that emerged from these historical transitions in the mainstream. Each of these examples is grounded in real economic crises and can motivate and create a context for the students to explore alternatives to mainstream economics as emerging from recurring issues of importance in economic inquiry at times of actual economic crises.

COMMON STUDENT MISPERCEPTIONS AND HOW TO ADDRESS THEM

Students' most common response to the introduction of political economy is to ask which approach is "right" or the best. Handling this question is important for two reasons. First, it is a serious question that anyone teaching this material will likely have a strong opinion. It is important that you acknowledge this and urge students to explore alternative approaches and form their own opinion. Second, an instructor's answer to this question will determine how his or her students view the presentation of the various alternatives. I try very hard to present a fair representation of readings from each tradition that make strong cases for the use of each particular approach to economic analysis. I point out that each approach evolves as part of economics discourse on different problems that each approach was intended to address. It can be incredibly helpful to work with colleagues whose preference and expertise are in approaches and traditions different from your own perspective to ensure readings and assignments are appropriate for the topics covered. If students believe the instructor is open minded, they work hard to remain open minded as well.

This approach deals with students' concerns (about the "right approach") and is the first step in presenting a case for pluralism in the economics discipline. There is an important emerging literature on economic pluralism, and resources to begin exploring this approach include Chapter 23, "Pluralism in Economics Education", in this volume and Garnett, Olsen and Starr (2010). The student-led push for greater pluralism in economics emerged from graduate students' concerns about the singular dominance of formal neoclassical theory in their education. This concern was formalized in the Post-Autistic Economics (PAE) movement.

> This student-led movement called for a more open and scientific economics, guided by a philosophically principled pluralism: [a pluralism] that regards the various "schools" of economics, including neoclassicalism, as offering different windows on economic reality, each bringing into view different subsets of economic phenomena . . . [and] rejects the idea that any school could possess final or total solutions, but accepts all possible means for understanding re-life economic problems (Fullbrook, 2003, pp. 8–9, cited in Garnett et al., 2010).

A topical pluralist exploration of alternative economic theories of the state can be found in Pressman (2006).

STRATEGIES FOR ASSIGNMENTS AND ASSESSMENT

Political economy courses present a perfect opportunity to add a large dose of critical thinking to the economics curriculum. Analytic essays give students an opportunity to demonstrate their critical thinking and written communications skills. Longer format essays that require students to look at alternative approaches in more depth than the classroom introduction provide a deeper understanding and an opportunity to develop research skills. Shorter essays allow students' concerns about the reasons for considering alternatives to mainstream economics to be foregrounded by assignments that require close reading of classic passages of texts on related concerns and comparing them.

I find it most useful to have students compare and contrast different approaches to economic analysis in papers associated with a limited range of questions associated with a topic: How do Marxists and institutionalists theorize about the firm? What are the similarities and differences? What are the differences in their emphasis and concerns regarding the role of the firm in the economy? Alternately, students can be asked to explain how economists in the differing analytic traditions would explain a contemporary economic problem and how such differences relate to the underlying methodology or concerns of each tradition. Having students select a text that contains contemporary analyses of current or past economic crises and having them write a book review modeled on those appearing in economic journals is simultaneously a good opportunity for critical thinking and analysis, a good skill for any aspiring scholar to acquire and empowering (because the text is selected by the student – albeit with some directions from the instructor). All of these formats can serve as the basis for assessing the student's work in the course.[4]

Political economy courses also require economic students, who are often learning much of their core material from textbooks, to read primary sources of varying length. Structured discussions, where students have responsibility for presenting and commenting on different parts of the texts, help create a strong incentive to keep up with the reading – especially if this participation is a formal part of their course assessment. Requiring presentations gives students an opportunity to speak about economics in public. Presenting material orally in a competent way is an important skill that is often neglected in undergraduate instruction. Individual presentations may benefit each student greatly, but they are very time consuming and the variation in presentation quality often hinders understanding by other students. Small group presentations raise the average quality and take considerably less time, although they may be harder to individually assess.

Reading journals, where students are required to choose a key passage in each reading assignment and write a one-page essay (in a notebook) analyzing the selected passage, is an excellent way of moving students through the reading, as well as teaching them what close reading actually means. However, it is not clear that the benefits of this practice outweigh the costs of the very labor-intensive process of keeping students on task by collecting the journals, commenting upon entries, and evaluating journals in a regular and timely way.

CONCLUDING COMMENTS

Teaching political economy to undergraduates provides a broader understanding of the discipline of economics than the standard economics curriculum of all neoclassical economics all the time. It provides opportunities to expand students' understanding of economic phenomena, as well as an opportunity to reinforce critical thinking and integrate writing skills into the economics curriculum. Additionally, proponents of political economy believe it will make our students better economists and better citizens.

NOTES

1. A mainstream text with some coverage of alternatives is *Economics* (8th ed.) by David Colander (2009). Texts that introduce both mainstream and alternative approaches are *Economics: A Tool for Critically Understanding Society* (9th ed.) by Tom Riddell, et al. (2010), *Economics: An Introduction to Traditional and Progressive Views* (7th ed.) by Howard Sherman et al. (2008) and *Economics: A New Introduction* by Hugh Stretton (2000). Examples of supplementary text include *The ABCs of Political Economy* by Robin Hahnel (2003) and *Capitalism and its Economics: A Critical History* by Douglas Dowd (2004). *Alternative Principles of Economics* by Stanley Bober (2000) and *Economics, An Alternative Text* by Guy Routh (1984) are alternative texts presenting the post Keynesian and original institutionalist approach to economics.
2. levyinstitute.org (accessed 15 June 2011).
3. cfeps.org (accessed 15 June 2011).
4. My own department at Hobart and William Smith Colleges considers the portfolio of papers in our required political economic core course plus the required econometrics research project in our econometrics course as equivalent to a capstone experience because it provides the students with the opportunity to demonstrate the full range of their capabilities as economists in tangible scholarly form.

REFERENCES

Albelda, R., C. Gunn and W. Waller (eds) (1987), *Alternatives to Economic Orthodoxy*, Armonk, NY: M.E. Sharpe, Inc.
Barker, D. K. and S. F. Feiner (2004), *Liberating Economics*, Ann Arbor, MI: University of Michigan Press.
Benería, L. (2003), *Gender, Development and Globalization*, New York: Routledge.
Bober, S. (2000), *Principles of Economics*, Armonk, NY: M.E. Sharpe, Inc.
Brown C., (2008), *Inequality, Consumer Credit and the Savings Puzzle*, Cheltenham, UK and Northampton, MA, US: Edward Elgar.
Caldwell, B. (1984), *Appraisal and Criticism in Economics*, Boston, MA: Allyn and Unwin.
Cassidy, J. (1997), "The return of Karl Marx", *The New Yorker*, October, (20 & 27), 248–59.
Colander, D. (2009), *Economics* (8th ed.), New York: McGraw-Hill/Irwin.
Commons, J. R. (1990), *Institutional Economics* (vol. 2.), New Brunswick, NJ and London: Transactions Press.
Dewey, J. (1929), *The Quest for Certainty*, New York: Minton, Balch & Co.
Dowd, D. (2004), *Capitalism and its Economics: A Critical History*, London: Pluto Press.
Ferber, M. A. and J. A. Nelson (1993), *Beyond Economic Man: Feminist Theory and Economics*, Chicago: University of Chicago Press.
Figart, D. M., E. Mutari and M. Power (2002), *Living Wages, Equal Wages*, New York: Routledge.
Friedman, M. (1953), "The methodology of positive economics", in *Essays in Positive Economics*, Chicago: University of Chicago Press, pp. 3–43.
Fullbrook, E. (2003), *The Crisis in Economics: The Post-Autistic Economics Movement: The First 600 Days*, London: Routledge.
Garnett, R., E. K. Olsen and M. Starr (2010), *Economic Pluralism*, New York: Routledge.
Hahnel, R. (2003), *The ABCs of Political Economy*, London: Pluto Press.
Keynes, J. M. (1964), *The General Theory of Employment, Interest, and Money*, New York: Harcourt Brace and Co.
Marx, K. and F. Engels (1967), *The German Ideology*, New York: International Publishers.
McCormick, K. (2006), *Veblen in Plain English: A Complete Introduction to Thorstein Veblen's Economics*, Youngstown, NY: Cambria Press.
Myers, H. F. (1991), "His statues topple, his shadow persists: Marx can't be ignored", *The Wall Street Journal*, **25** (November), (A4), 1.
Myrdal, Gunnar (1969), *Objectivity in Social Research*, New York: Pantheon.
Nash, T. and M. Waring (1995), *Who's Counting? Marilyn Waring on Sex, Lies and Global Economics*, Documentary Film produced by National Film Board of Canada and Studio B. Distributed by Media Services (New Zealand).
Peirce, C. S. (1955), *Philosophical Writings of Peirce*, New York: Dover.
Pressman, S. (ed.) (2006), *Alternative Theories of the State*, New York: Palgrave Macmillan.
Riddell, T., J. Shackelford, S. Stamos and G. Schneider (2010), *Economics: A Tool for Critically Understanding Society* (9th ed.), New York: Prentice Hall.
Routh, G. (1984), *Economics, An Alternative Text*, Dobbs Ferry, NY: Sheridan House.

Sackrey, C. and G. Schneider with J. Knoedler (2002), *Introduction to Political Economy* (3rd ed.), Cambridge, MA: Economic Affairs Bureau.

Sherman, H., E. K. Hunt, R. Nesiba, P. Ohara and B. Wiens-Tuers (2008), *Economics: An Introduction to Traditional and Progressive Views* (7th ed.), Armonk, NY: M.E. Sharpe.

Stretton, H. (2000), *Economics: A New Introduction*, London: Pluto Press.

Todorova, Z. (2009), *Money and Households in a Capitalist Economy: A Gendered Post Keynesian-Institutional Analysis*, Cheltenham, UK and Northampton, MA, US: Edward Elgar.

Tool, M. R. (1987), "Value and its corollaries", in R. Albelda, C. Gunn and W. Waller (eds), *Alternatives to Economic Orthodoxy*, Armonk, NY: M.E. Sharpe, Inc., pp. 225–43.

Tucker, R. C. (ed.) (1978), *The Marx-Engels Reader* (2nd ed.), New York: Norton.

Veblen, T. B. (1934), *The Theory of the Leisure Class*, New York: Modern Library.

Veblen, T. B. (1964), *Essays in Our Changing Order* (L. Ardzrooni, ed.), New York: Augustus M. Kelley.

Veblen, T. B. (1978), *The Theory of Business Enterprise*, New Brunswick, NJ and London: Transactions Press.

Veblen, T. B. (1990), *The Place of Science in Modern Civilization*, New Brunswick, NJ and London: Transactions Press.

Waring, M. (1990), *If Women Counted*, New York: HarperCollins.

62 Some reflections on teaching the economics of poverty

James P. Ziliak

From the New Deal to the War on Poverty to Welfare Reform, economists have played a central role in the measurement, design, and evaluation of anti-poverty programs in the United States. A course on the Economics of Poverty offers the unique opportunity to bring to bear theories and methods from labor economics, public economics, macroeconomics, and demography on a pressing social problem like poverty. In the process, students are exposed to the great inequality of economic status across age, gender, race, education, and family structure in a way that is unlike most other courses offered to undergraduates in economics.

Perhaps reflecting the complexity of the problem, courses on poverty are regularly offered across a variety of disciplines, including anthropology, history, political science, public policy, sociology, and social work. There are also a number of well-known books in the popular press on the topic. This means there are a plethora of pedagogical options open to the economics instructor to draw from other academic disciplines and the press in designing a course of poverty. While I have on occasion included contributions from other disciplines in my course, the overarching approach follows the neoclassical paradigm. The central objectives are to define how poverty and inequality are measured, to describe recent trends in poverty and inequality in America, and to present an economic framework for evaluating the battery of tax and transfer programs available to low-income Americans. Specifically, within the neoclassical framework of labor supply and demand, the course analyzes the effects of income transfers, income taxes, human capital, family structure, race, gender, and macroeconomic factors, such as economic growth, globalization, and technical change, on poverty and inequality. The course is designed for students who have completed Intermediate Microeconomics, but it can be readily modified for students with only a principles background by dropping some of the more technical methodological material.

MEASUREMENT

A major contribution by economists over the past century has been the proper measurement of economic inputs and outcomes, and the Economics of Poverty is a chance to showcase some of those contributions. Certainly standing near the top is the work of Mollie Orshansky, who as an applied economist and statistician at the Social Security Administration in the early 1960s, established a metric of how to measure poverty in the American family that we continue to use to this day (Fisher, 1992).

This first part of the course provides an overview of the Orshansky measure, which consists of two components – the poverty threshold, which is that level of subsistence income below which the person is poor, and resources, which is the measure of income that is compared to the family's threshold.[1] Covering the Orshansky measure serves several purposes. For starters, it opens up a dialogue with the class on the normative concepts of "wants" and "needs" in thinking about what it means to be poor. In addition, it allows for discussion of who the reference person is or should be when drawing the poverty line. The Orshansky approach is an absolute measure and thus not referenced to a specific point in the income distribution, but because most other countries in the OECD tie their poverty measure to median income, one then has the opportunity to discuss the merits and pitfalls of absolute and relative measures of poverty and why some countries may favor one over the other. Because the Census Bureau provides the official estimates of poverty in the US, the discussion of the Orshansky measure then opens up how the Census goes about collecting information on incomes on an annual basis. At times, this has led to detailed discussions on the survey design of the Current Population Survey (CPS), and more recently, the American Community Survey, the combination of which (re)introduces students to sampling techniques.

The resources component of the Orshansky measure also allows for the possibility of discussing the economic and philosophical merits of whether "well-being" is better captured by income or consumption or some other metric of material hardship. There are several critiques of the Orshansky measure that receive coverage here, including the fact that the poverty thresholds are in sore need of updating and that resources do not capture the effects of in-kind transfers or taxes (which in turn brings in current policy discussion of revising the poverty line), and that the poverty rate tells us nothing about the intensity or persistence of poverty.

The first section on poverty measurement is complemented with a thorough treatment of the measurement of inequality, including variance, coefficient of variation (CV), quintiles, Lorenz Curve, and the Gini coefficient. Depending on the background of the students, this section can be somewhat challenging. Most, if not all, have had a basic statistics course, and many have had some econometrics, but few have directly seen these measures beyond the variance and thus it is prudent not to take knowledge of these concepts for granted and a basic review is generally appreciated by the students. A method to assist the students with these concepts that has met some success is to assign a homework using CPS data and Excel. I provide the students with a random subsample of families from a March CPS and ask them to compute measures of variance, the CV, and quintiles, and then, with the quintiles, draw a Lorenz Curve. The hands-on experience seems to improve their understanding, and also expands their familiarity with a widely used spreadsheet package.

The opening section of the course concludes with a detailed accounting of trends in poverty and inequality. Prior to smart classrooms with internet access, the primary way to present trends visually was to produce graphs of time series of poverty and inequality from Census data and burn them onto overhead transparencies. Now, with access to wired classrooms, I take the students directly to the source – the Census Bureau website – where we navigate to the pages dedicated to income, poverty, and health insurance. Pedagogically this accomplishes two main goals, one is to introduce the students to our nation's major statistical agency and the other is to introduce the students to wide disparities in poverty and inequality. Too often students are presented with "representative agents," but here is an ideal opportunity to show students the great heterogeneity in outcomes over time and across race, gender, family structure, and education.

OVERVIEW OF ANTI-POVERTY PROGRAMS

A central focus of the course is the role of the social safety net in alleviating poverty and inequality. After introducing the students to the basic concepts of poverty and inequality, the second section continues with "big picture" material by providing students with a sweeping overview of anti-poverty programs. These programs are divided into social insurance, which includes Social Security, Medicare, Unemployment Insurance, Disability Insurance, and Workers Compensation, and means-tested transfers and credits, which include Temporary Assistance to Needy Families (formerly Aid to Families with Dependent Children), Medicaid, Supplemental Nutrition Assistance Program (formerly food stamps), Supplemental Security Income, Supplemental Nutrition Program for Women, Infants, and Children, Housing Assistance, and the Earned Income Tax Credit. The basic target population for each program is described, as well as the administrative home for the program within the family of federal agencies, the basic programmatic details (including the funding source and method of benefit payment), and time series changes in aggregate expenditures. Many of the students have heard of these programs in passing, but with few exceptions, most do not know this sort of detail and are frequently amazed at the size and scope of the safety net, and are astonished to learn that even with this extensive intervention, poverty and inequality remain at critically high levels.

LABOR SUPPLY AND DEMAND FRAMEWORK

The overview of the safety net provides a key gateway into the analytic portion of the course, which leans heavily on the neoclassical model of labor supply and demand. A case is made early in the course that perhaps the best elixir against poverty is strong economic growth, which in turn hinges on outcomes of the labor market. Moreover, the safety net in the United States is frequently described as a "work-based" safety net, and thus it is natural to rely on the supply and demand framework. Indeed, because eligibility for means-tested transfers is a function of labor earnings, this creates a wedge between before-transfer and after-transfer wage rates and thus distorts the consumption-leisure decision. This material synthesizes key insights from both labor and public economics.

My experience has been that most students taking my class have not had a formal course in labor economics, though more have had public economics. Intermediate microeconomics is a prerequisite, but not labor or public economics. I have also taught the course with no formal prerequisites, and in those instances the most technical material is presented in a more stripped-down fashion and de-emphasized. Regardless, because the course relies on indifference curves, along with nonlinear budget constraints, the strategy for this section of the course has always been to begin with fundamentals by providing students with a six-page handout on labor supply and demand.[7] On some occasions, this

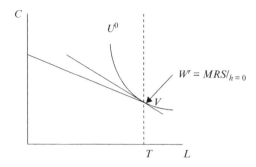

Figure 62.1   The labor supply decision

material is supplemented with readings on labor supply and demand from a textbook (for example, Borjas or Ehrenberg and Smith), though this is not essential.

Because the theory of the consumer forms the backbone of much of the discussion surrounding poverty and the safety net, the major emphasis here is placed on making sure the students understand indifference curves and can manipulate budget constraints (labor demand is covered too, but comparatively briefly). I begin with the static utility-maximizing framework where individuals maximize utility over consumption and leisure subject to linear time and budget constraints. Let $U = U(C, L)$ denote individual preferences over consumption (C) and leisure (L); the time constraint as $T = L + h$, where $T =$ total time available, and $h =$ hours of labor market work; and the budget constraint as $pC = Wh + V$, where $p =$ price of consumption (usually set $= \$1$), $W =$ hourly wage rate, and $V =$ nonlabor income (in other words, income from other sources such as government transfers, gifts from family, interest income). The slope of the indifference curve is the marginal rate of substitution of leisure for consumption (MRS), where

$$MRS = -\frac{\Delta U/\Delta L}{\Delta U/\Delta C},$$

which reflects the worker's willingness to forgo C for additional L. The slope of the budget constraint is equal to $-W$, the opportunity cost (or price) of leisure.

We can now combine worker preferences and constraints to examine the decision to work, as depicted in Figure 62.1.

At point V, where $h = 0$, the slope of the indifference curve U^0 is known as the reservation wage (W^τ). This wage is the lowest wage necessary to induce the worker into the labor market. If $W^\tau > W$, then the worker chooses to consume full leisure (in other words, $L = T$, $h = 0$). If, however, $W^\tau < W$, then the worker finds it profitable to enter the labor force. Suppose that the worker chooses to work because $W^\tau < W$. We say that the worker is in equilibrium once the $MRS = W$. Figure 62.2 shows the optimal choice of consumption (C^*) and leisure (L^*) given the wage rate W.

At this point, students who have had intermediate microeconomics generally follow along without too much struggle. There are some differences between the labor supply decision presented here and the microeconomic presentation of optimal consumption bundle choice. First, the extensive (participation) margin is rarely discussed in

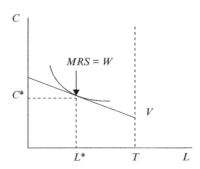

Figure 62.2   Consumer equilibrium

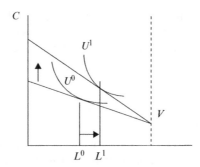

Figure 62.3   The effect of a wage increase on hours of work

intermediate micro (in that context, it is the decision to buy), whereas it receives primary attention in labor supply with treatment of the work/no-work decision. Second, in the standard two-good consumer model with X_1 on the horizontal axis and X_2 on the vertical axis, as the consumer moves horizontally toward the origin they just consume less of X_1. In labor supply, however, less of leisure implies more hours of market work because there are both time and money constraints. Thus, some students get confused with the behavioral interpretation that reducing leisure (L) leads to more work.

The real challenge comes when, once in equilibrium, we examine how the worker reacts to a change in the wage.

Figure 62.3 depicts an increase in the wage rate from W to W'. When the wage changes, we get two effects, a substitution effect because the relative prices of consumption and leisure change, and an income effect because income changes. When W increases to W', the substitution effect says that the price of leisure has increased, thus the worker should increase hours of work and decrease leisure. At the same time, when W increases, income increases, and since leisure is a normal good, more is demanded with the higher income. *Thus, a priori, a wage change has an indeterminate effect on leisure and hours of work.* If the income effect dominates (as in the figure), then leisure increases. If the substitution effect dominates, then leisure decreases. If they offset each other, then hours remain unchanged. This can stop students in their tracks. They are used to substitution and income effects working in tandem, but with the outcome of interest being hours of work, they operate in opposite directions, and quite frankly, some students never master this issue. I provide examples in class and also some homework problems, and for the vast majority this helps them grasp the concepts. For example, a typical problem might be:

> Consider the typical worker with nonlabor income of $5000, with a wage rate of $10 per hour who maximizes utility by working 2500 hours out of a total of 6000 hours per year available for work and leisure. Suppose the worker receives a 25 percent wage increase. You have the information that leisure is a normal good and that the wage elasticity of labor supply is -0.2. What happens to the optimal choice of labor supply and how many hours of work does the worker supply? Which effect dominates, substitution or income effect? Why? Support your answer with a consumption/leisure graph showing the new choice of hours.

LABOR MARKET EFFECTS OF THE SAFETY NET

Mastery of the basic labor supply model is crucial because this is where the fun in the course begins. The typical means-tested anti-poverty program in the US can be characterized by three main components: the maximum benefit guarantee (G) in the absence of other income sources; the benefit reduction rate (t), known as the 'taper rate' in the United Kingdom, which reduces the size of the benefit as labor and/or nonlabor income increases; and the "break-even" income level (Y_b), which is the income level whereby the individual no longer qualifies for income benefits. The benefit formula, B, is thus $B = G - t*(Wh + V - D)$, where D is meant to reflect any earned or unearned income that is exempted from welfare benefit taxation, e.g. most welfare programs exempt a certain fraction of labor market earnings from taxation. The break-even income level is that level of $(Wh + V)$ at which $B = 0$, or $Y_b = G/t + D$.

For simplicity, assume that $V = D = 0$ so that $B = G - t*Wh$. If we plug this into the budget constraint, we get $C = Wh + G - t*Wh$, or $C = W(1 - t)h + G$. Under the means-tested transfer program, the intercept of the budget constraint is now G, and the slope of the budget line equals $-W(1 - t)$ if the individual qualifies for benefits and $-W$ if not. Suppose that $t = 1$, or that the welfare benefit gets reduced $1 for each $1 in labor market earnings. This was the case under the former Aid to Families with Dependent Children program and continues in some states under its replacement Temporary Assistance to Needy Families. The budget constraint in the consumption-leisure diagram in this situation becomes as shown in Figure 62.4.

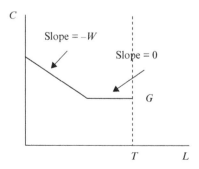

Figure 62.4   The budget constraint in the presence of means-tested transfer program

The budget constraint in Figure 62.4 is now nonlinear, and indeed nonconvex, which opens up the possibility for multiple equilibria in the interior. In other words, it is possible for the indifference curve to be tangent to the budget line on both the horizontal and downward-sloping portions at the same time. Moreover, facing the prospect of a 100 percent marginal tax rate, the option of being a labor-force nonparticipant and receiving an income of G becomes attractive to many.

This simple diagram tends to generate a tremendous amount of discussion as it lays bare the "equity versus efficiency" tradeoff facing policymakers. A high benefit reduction rate makes work less attractive and thus generates deadweight loss, while a lower rate makes work more attractive, but also makes more workers eligible for benefits, thus raising welfare expenditures and also perhaps induces some who are ineligible to reduce hours of work in order to qualify. Because each program in the safety net has different guarantees and tax rates, I spend a considerable amount of classroom time drawing diagrams to highlight the labor-supply (dis)incentive effects of the various programs. Crucially, this course is not all about theory, but the theory is used as an analytic tool to understand fundamental challenges facing policymakers in the War on Poverty – how to design a program that is simple, fair, and with minimum distortion in private markets.

The safety net is intended to ameliorate poverty, though at times perverse incentives are created that can lead to the opposite result. Thus, the course is designed as evidence-based. For each topic covered, I review what the frontier social science research has found regarding the labor supply consequences of social insurance and means-tested transfers (see, for example, Moffitt, 2003; Ziliak, 2009). In more recent years, as the literature has moved beyond labor supply, I also discuss the evidence of the programs on fertility, marriage, consumption, saving, and health.

OTHER CAUSES OF POVERTY

Because poverty is a complex phenomenon, there are other important features beside the safety net and, in my course, I attempt to address some of these causes and solutions. In this vein considerable attention is devoted to human capital. Within the neoclassical paradigm, I present Becker's model of investment prior to labor-market entry, and his model of specific versus general on-the-job training. In this context, I discuss research on returns to schooling, but also research on the anti-poverty effectiveness of early childhood investments that affect the development of both cognitive and noncognitive skills. For example, evidence from the Perry Preschool Project, an experimental preschool intervention conducted in the 1960s, suggests that the long-term gains from the program came from being not better test takers in school, but better citizens and workers (Karoly, Kilburn, and Cannon, 2005). The students seem to grasp well the notion that labor-market productivity results from multiple skills, and thus interventions may affect more than just test scores. In addition, I delve into issues of family structure, fertility, gender, and race as causes of poverty. Less time is spent on theoretical constructs in this part (except perhaps for the economics of discrimination) and more on empirical evidence from economics, demography, and other social sciences. Students tend to find this material enriching as it speaks to the human condition on a different level, and perhaps one that they are more familiar with on a personal basis than the safety net.

ENGAGING STUDENTS

The structure of my course on the Economics of Poverty is based on the classic lecture-style format. Students are encouraged to interrupt with questions at any time during the course of the lecture, though admittedly this varies widely from term to term. Even though the topic of poverty can be politically charged, by and large students have shown great respect for differing viewpoints and have refrained from the use of divisive rhetoric. As mentioned previously, students are also engaged through empirical homework using programs like Excel, as well as homework problems on how transfer and tax programs affect labor supply decisions. In some years, I have assigned term papers or group papers about some dimension of poverty and the safety net, including the effectiveness of the Earned Income Tax Credit or how to reform the Medicaid program.

A concept employed on a couple of occasions to enhance group discussion is to assign students to a series of "Council of Economic Advisers" to advise the "President" on how to reform various elements of the safety net. For example, suppose a class has 25 students enrolled and that there are five policy reforms under consideration, then there will be five Councils with five students each. The issues covered in the past have included welfare reform, health care reform, housing policy, hunger, family structure, and Social Security, among others. Each Council is assigned one issue and they are charged with writing a three to five page policy brief and to prepare a ten minute Powerpoint presentation to deliver to the "President," which in this case includes me and all the other class members. We then pepper the Council with questions regarding cost, political efficacy, unintended consequences, etc . . . much like the give and take that occurs inside the Oval Office (or at least so we hope!). In addition to fostering class discussion, the goal of the exercise is to simultaneously enhance skills related to formal speaking and the writing of issue briefs.

I have found teaching the Economics of Poverty to be an exceptionally rewarding experience as it brings to the table theory, policy, econometrics, data, and evidence. It is my hope that this enthusiasm for the subject matter serves as the best mechanism for engaging the students on an issue of such national importance.

NOTES

1. For an explanation of how the official US poverty measure is defined see http://www.census.gov/hhes/www/poverty/about/overview/measure.html (accessed 15 June 2011).
2. This is available upon request.

REFERENCES

Fisher, G. (1992), "The development of the Orshansky poverty thresholds and their subsequent history as the official U.S. poverty measure", US Census Bureau, http://www.census.gov/hhes/povmeas/publications/orshansky.html, accessed 21 April 2011.

Karoly, L. A., R. Kilburn and J. S. Cannon (2005), *Early Childhood Interventions: Proven Results, Future Promise*, Santa Monica, CA: RAND Corporation.
Moffitt, R. (2003), *Means-Tested Transfer Programs in the United States*, Chicago, IL: University of Chicago Press.
Ziliak, J. P. (2009), *Welfare Reform and its Long-Term Consequences for America's Poor*, Cambridge, UK: Cambridge University Press.

63 Public economics
Edgar O. Olsen

In almost all countries, governments play a large role in determining who consumes how much of each good, who does how much of each type of work, when they do them, and hence the levels of well-being enjoyed by the members of the society. In the United States, governments achieve these effects through thousands of expenditure programs and regulations and many taxes. The tax revenue and the expenditure of all levels of government in the US exceed 30 percent of GDP. Because government action is so important in determining economic outcomes, a substantial number of economists spend at least a part of their time studying public policies.

Public economics is the only broad field devoted entirely to public policy. Although other fields deal with particular public policies that fit naturally within their scope, such as minimum wage laws (labor economics), tariffs (international economics), and anti-trust policy (industrial organization), they focus primarily on understanding behavior in private markets. The coverage of public policies in undergraduate public economics courses is much broader. Public economics courses focus on the justifications for a wide range of government activities and the effects of major expenditure programs and taxes, with some attention to the behavior of actors in the political process.

I have taught the general undergraduate public economics course at the University of Virginia for more than thirty years. The broad goal of this course is to develop each student's ability to think clearly about public policy issues. This involves aligning their views concerning the desirability of particular government actions with their underlying preferences by helping them think through what it is that they care about beyond their own consumption of private goods and providing a more accurate picture of the effects of different government actions. Although I cover the standard topics in the leading public economics textbooks, my treatment of these topics deviates from these textbooks in many cases. In some cases, the alternatives involve more detailed analyses. In others, the deviations are more fundamental. This is most marked in the treatment of the concern that individuals have for others. In my view, this is the primary justification for many government programs, and it influences the actual and optimal design of many others.

The purpose of this chapter is to share some general thoughts about teaching the broad undergraduate public economics course that might be helpful to new teachers of this course and some ideas about dealing with particular topics that might be useful to even experienced teachers. Like others who teach courses in the United States, my coverage of particular programs is limited to expenditure programs and taxes in the US. However, the advice in this chapter is not US centric. My hope is that all readers will find a least few nuggets that are helpful in their teaching.

GENERAL ADVICE

What Material Should I Cover in the Course?

Because the field of public economics is so vast, considerable selectivity is necessary in teaching a one-semester course on this topic. The leading public economics textbooks, such as Gruber (2010) and Rosen and Gayer (2008), provide excellent overviews of the most important theoretical and empirical research in the field. In the interest of appealing to a broad audience, their technical level is modest and it might be possible to cover the entire textbook in a semester at the most selective colleges. However, I doubt that many experienced teachers at any university attempt to cover this much material. Some teachers will want to cover material at a higher technical level and assign outside reading, while others will want their students to spend some time outside of class solving problems rather than reading.

My approach is to cover a smaller number of topics in greater detail, specifically, the largest expenditure programs and taxes in the US – the social security retirement program, Medicare, Medicaid and several other welfare programs, the public school system, and the federal individual income and social security taxes. These few expenditure programs and taxes account for most government spending and revenue. Fortunately, dealing with these programs provides the opportunity to talk about how government programs influence choices between different produced goods, between all produced goods and leisure, and between present and future consumption.

The omissions and inclusions in my list illustrate important general principles for selection of topics, namely, playing to instructor expertise and student interest. I give more attention to several welfare programs such as the Earned Income Tax Credit (EITC) than to national defense on that account. Although public expenditure on these welfare programs is substantial, it is much smaller than spending on national defense. However, my knowledge of the welfare programs is so much greater that I can provide deeper insights in this area than in most others in the small amount of time devoted to them. Even though environmental protection is not one of the largest areas of government activity as measured by public expenditure, it is certainly one of the largest in terms of its effect on the allocation of resources. Furthermore, students are very interested in this topic. Its inclusion in many public economics courses reflects, in part, the view of many economists that environmental protection should be pursued primarily through taxation rather than regulation. My coverage is limited to the welfare economics of negative external effects, using pollution as the example. However, time spent discussing the cost-effectiveness of alternative approaches to environmental protection would be time well spent.

What Readings Should I Assign?

In courses required for the economics major, there is considerable unanimity concerning what material should be covered, lectures often follow textbooks closely, and the primary decision is what textbook to choose. This is far less true for courses in broad fields such as public economics.

Over time, my course has deviated so much from textbooks that it became increasingly difficult to justify asking students to buy an expensive textbook. I cover a very small fraction of their material, and my treatment of many topics deviates significantly. Nevertheless, my advice to new teachers of public economics is to assign a textbook in their early years. Some of the country's leading public economics scholars and most thoughtful teachers, such as Gruber (2010) and Rosen and Gayer (2008), have written textbooks that provide an excellent account of the state of knowledge of the field. The textbook will be especially valuable to students while new teachers are determining an approach to the course that suits them. Over time, instructors will surely want to replace or supplement assigned readings from textbooks with readings from other sources.

How should a new instructor choose a textbook? Few are likely to find the time to read several textbooks in their entirety for this purpose. A more realistic approach is to get recommendations from former teachers and current senior colleagues who have tried several alternatives and compare chapters on one justification for government action such as external effects, one area of public expenditure, and one area of taxation in several recommended or widely used textbooks.

What Should I Cover in Class?

In general, class time should be devoted to aspects of topics covered that are most important and complicated. For example, I present an indifference-curve analysis that simultaneously considers multiple features of the individual income tax (the personal exemption, standard and itemized deductions, and marginal tax rates that rise in steps with taxable income) in order to show that the current federal income tax is equivalent to a simpler income tax combined with a rather strange subsidy for the goods involved in itemized deductions. This leads to a piecewise linear budget constraint in a diagram with two privately produced goods on the axes. No undergraduate textbook contains such a complicated diagram. In general, if a more detailed analysis is available in print at all, it is embedded in a longer paper written for an audience with a very substantial background in economics and hence not explained as patiently as is appropriate for undergraduate students. By presenting more detailed analyses in lectures, instructors can deepen student understanding of the matters discussed in textbooks. This has the substantial side benefit of giving students practice in using the tools of intermediate microeconomics.

What I emphasize in class has been influenced by my perceptions of the importance of various confused arguments in popular public policy debates. I devote much more time than any textbook to addressing problematic popular arguments for government action. For example, it is often argued that we should provide a particular subsidy in kind, such as for homeownership or health insurance, because that is the first priority of the recipients. I go to unusual lengths to explain the defect of this argument. The short version is that an equally costly unrestricted cash grant would enable the recipient to achieve exactly the same outcome as would result from the subsidy in kind. If the recipient does not choose this outcome, this must not have been his or her highest priority. In this case, the recipient prefers the cash grant. Another example is the argument that we should provide subsidies for investment in small businesses because these businesses account for the bulk of new employment. Such invalid arguments dominate popular policy debates and lead to bad public policies.

What is the Appropriate Technical Level?

The appropriate technical level for teaching any course depends on its prerequisites. Microeconomic principles is the only prerequisite for the general public economics courses at some schools. At many others, intermediate microeconomics is a prerequisite. At a few colleges, all students in the course have taken calculus.

Regardless of the stated prerequisites, students need to have a good understanding of budget constraints and indifference-curve analysis because government programs affect outcomes by affecting what is possible for individual decision makers, and most programs lead to non-linear budget frontiers. Indifference curves are also the best tool for analyzing the magnitudes of gains and losses from government actions. Three lectures on this topic at the beginning of a public economics course, together with the material covered in principles provide sufficient background.

Calculus is not important for teaching undergraduate public economics. Diagrams can be used to provide rigorous theoretical analyses at the level of generality appropriate for an undergraduate course, and because the budget frontiers that result from government programs are often piecewise linear, simple calculus cannot be used to analyze the qualitative effects of many programs. If calculus were not a prerequisite for my course, I could easily replace its rare appearance in lectures with diagrams, and I would reword numerical problems involving constrained utility maximization by specifying the equation of the marginal rate of commodity substitution rather than the utility function.

How Should I Incorporate Empirical Research into the Course?

Most public economists want to integrate the results of empirical research into their course. It is important for students to understand that what economists say about public policies is not based exclusively on theoretical analyses. At best, the standard general assumptions of microeconomic theory have qualitative implications for the effect of an existing government program or proposed policy reform. Furthermore, the magnitudes of the effects are important for judging their desirability.

A perennial problem in teaching public economics is that few students have the background in econometrics to read with much comprehension the best empirical research. Only a few colleges have an introductory econometrics course as a prerequisite for their course. The traditional solution in public economics textbooks has been to cite the results of empirical studies with little or no attempt to explain their methods. Therefore, unlike the theoretical analyses, the students have little basis for assessing the credibility of the results. My solution has been to give disproportionate attention to the results of random-assignment experiments because it is easy to explain to students with little or no background in econometrics why the estimates are unbiased on average. In some cases, I use them to support the implications of theoretical analyses. For example, the results of the negative income tax (NIT) experiments indicate that this type of subsidy leads recipients to work less (Robins, 1985). In other cases where the effect is theoretically ambiguous, such as the effect of cashing out the food stamp program on food consumption, I use it to show the direction as well as the magnitude of the effect (Fraker, Martini, and Ohls, 1995).[1] In recent years, the leading textbooks have devoted chapters to the tools of empirical analysis used in public economics and made a greater effort to discuss methods underlying some of the particular empirical studies mentioned.

DEVIATIONS FROM STANDARD TEXTBOOK TREATMENT

This section presents alternatives to the standard textbook treatment of several topics that some readers might find helpful. They include a very general proof of the important result that recipients prefer lump-sum grants to any subsidy in kind with the same cost to the donor, an alternative treatment of distributional issues to replace the social welfare approach, a simple diagrammatic general equilibrium approach to public goods and external effects to replace marginal social benefit and cost curves, and thoughts about addressing defective popular arguments for government action, expanding the analyses of government expenditure programs to include the additional taxes needed to fund them, and the desirability of using indifference curves to discuss the inefficiencies that result from many government actions.

Recipient Prefers a Lump-sum Grant to any Subsidy in Kind with Same Donor Cost

Many government actions are intended to help particular subsets of the population. One of the most important insights of economics for public policy is that a recipient prefers a lump-sum grant to any subsidy in kind with the same donor cost. Most intermediate microeconomics textbooks prove this result for the special case of a per-unit subsidy for a single good. In my experience, students who have seen this proof do not appreciate the generality of the result. They often associate the term subsidy in kind with this particular type. Therefore, I prove a much more general result that accounts for all types of subsidies in kind. In courses that have intermediate microeconomics as a prerequisite, I do it in the first class. In courses with only microeconomic principles as a prerequisite, I do it directly following the theory of individual choice presented at the beginning of the course.

To provide a simplified proof, I assume that the recipient cares about two goods and has an income that is not subject to choice and that market prices are unaffected by government action. The latter can be justified by the assumption of completely elastic supply curves. I further assume that if the government directly provides a good, as in the case of public housing, its cost per unit is the same as the price per unit that private sellers would charge for it. That is, government is neither more nor less efficient than the private sector in producing the good.

In Figure 63.1, DE is the recipient's budget line in the absence of government action, B is the recipient's preferred bundle on this line, and ICC is the person's income consumption curve associated with the initial prices. A lump-sum grant or a grant that is equivalent to a lump-sum grant for this person would induce the person to choose a bundle on the ICC above B. Any subsidy in kind would induce the person to choose a bundle such as A above DE that is not on ICC. Whether the goods are provided by governments or purchased from private firms, the total cost of this bundle is $P_1 Q_1^A + P_2 Q_2^A$ and the cost to donors is $P_1 Q_1^A + P_2 Q_2^A - Y$. If an equally costly lump-sum grant replaced the subsidy in kind, the budget frontier would be the dashed line, the chosen bundle would be C, and the recipient would be better off as he judged his own well-being. The bundle A chosen

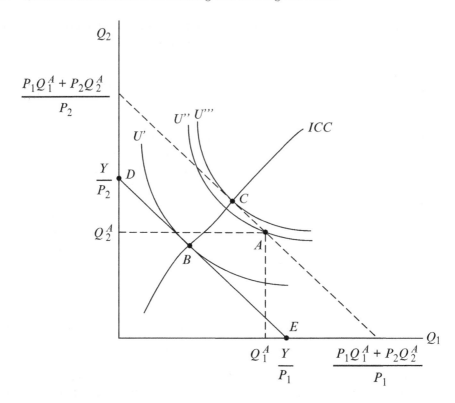

Figure 63.1 Lump-sum grant versus any subsidy in kind

under the subsidy in kind is a possible choice under the equally costly cash grant, but the recipient prefers infinitely many other bundles that become possible when the lump-sum grant replaces the subsidy in kind.

To broaden the horizons of the students concerning the wide variety of subsidies in kind and make this highly abstract proof concrete, I mention several alternative subsidies in kind that would induce the recipient to choose bundle A. For example, the government might offer the person a particular quantity of one good (in this case, Q_1^A) that can be neither supplemented nor sold for less than its market value. Public housing is a subsidy of this type. Alternatively, the government might offer this person a grant in the amount $P_1Q_1^A + P_2Q_2^A - Y$ on the condition that the recipient consumes at least Q_1^A units of the first good. HUD operated a housing voucher program of this sort. Another example is a program that offered to sell the person a voucher that could only be used to buy the first good for a charge of $Y - P_2Q_2^A$. This is a simplified description of the original food stamp program. Finally, I would draw the tangent line to the indifference curve at A to show how a per-unit subsidy for consumption of the first good combined with either a lump-sum grant or tax would induce the recipient to choose this bundle.

To explain the defects of several arguments for the superiority of lump-sum grants, instructors might also prove the theorem for the special case of a per-unit subsidy for one good. One erroneous argument is that recipients prefer lump-sum grants because they offer additional bundles. In fact, replacing a per-unit subsidy for a particular good with an equally costly lump-sum grant both adds and subtracts bundles from the budget space. The proof shows that many of the bundles added by the replacement are better than the best bundle available under the per-unit subsidy. Another erroneous argument is that the subsidy in kind offers fewer choices. Examination of the budget lines with the per-unit subsidy for one good and the lump-sum grant makes clear that this is not the case for all subsidies in kind.

Treatment of Distributional Issues

The standard model that economists use to study behavior in markets assumes that actors care only about their own consumption of private goods. This model has performed very well in explaining most market behavior. Understanding behavior in the political sphere and the justifications for government actions, however, requires a broader view of what individuals care about. Economists are very clear about this matter as it pertains to public goods such as national defense and tangible external effects such as pollution. Clarity about the implications for public policy of a concern for others is lacking in most economic analyses.

The standard textbook treatment of distributional issues involves the concept of a social welfare function. In my view, this approach is so flawed that I avoid parts of textbooks that mention it. It incorrectly imagines that we can determine which allocations are feasible and which feasible allocations are efficient by reference to individual preferences defined over each individual's own consumption of goods and then we can somehow determine which efficient allocation is best by reference to the weight that society places on the well-being of its different members. If individuals care about each other, these preferences affect which allocations are feasible and which feasible allocations are efficient. Furthermore, society does not have views about which feasible allocation is best. Different members have different views.

My dissatisfaction with the standard treatment led me to develop an alternative diagrammatic analysis dealing with tangible external effects and altruism (Olsen, 1979; Olsen, 1981). These analyses build on Samuelson's (1955) classic article and Dolbear's (1967) extension, but they avoid social welfare functions and go far beyond these papers in deriving important results. The diagrams are similar to Edgeworth box diagrams, but they allow for all feasible combinations of total amounts of goods. In dealing with altruism, I integrate the concern of each member of a society for other members into that person's utility function. With this formulation, the set of efficient allocations incorporates such feelings.

With or without tangible external effects and with and without altruism, there are infinitely many efficient allocations. Each member of society will have some most preferred feasible allocation, and this allocation is efficient. The latter result follows directly from the fundamental definition of an efficient allocation. An allocation is efficient if and only if every feasible change from it hurts someone. Obviously every feasible change from the most preferred feasible allocation of a member of society hurts that person. Different people will have different most preferred efficient allocations, and most efficient allocations will not be the preferred feasible allocation of any member of society.

In discussing distributional issues, economists have particular difficulty accepting paternalistic altruism as a justification for government action. Because paternalistic altruism is a widespread and important phenomenon, this severely handicaps their ability to contribute to the development of public policies. Since standard welfare economics is based on the acceptance of individual preferences, it requires respecting the preferences of paternalistic altruists who care about others but believe that at least some of the people that they care about undervalue some goods and overvalue others. Acceptance of paternalistic preferences does not imply support for government policies that force people to change their consumption patterns within their current resources. While it may be possible to achieve an efficient allocation by this means, this efficient allocation will not be preferred by all members of society to the allocation in the absence of government action. Achieving an efficient allocation that makes everyone better off requires imposing taxes on paternalistic altruists to provide subsidies in kind to the objects of their concern. This makes recipients better off as they judge their own well-being. Participation in the subsidies in kind that dominate the welfare system is voluntary, and hence they do not make recipients worse off as they judge their own well-being. In-kind subsidies are not limited to governments. Private charities usually provide them, based on the views of donors who believe that recipients undervalue certain goods.

It is true that the non-paternalistic altruists in the society who care about the same people prefer to give them lump-sum grants or grants as close as feasible to lump-sum. Their most preferred feasible allocations differ in this respect from the most preferred feasible allocations of paternalistic altruists. Efficient allocations that give some weight to the views of both types of altruists involve less "distortions" in recipient consumption patterns than favored by paternalistic altruists. This is not fundamentally different from the situation with public goods such as national defense. Some member of society has a most preferred feasible allocation that involves the largest amount of national defense and another has a most preferred feasible allocation that involves the smallest amount. Almost all other efficient allocations involve amounts between the two extremes.

It is impossible to argue against anyone else's most preferred feasible allocation on efficiency grounds. This does not mean that it is impossible to argue against a person's views on what government policies should be pursued. Views on that matter depend on the person's perceptions of the effects of these policies and all other policies that could be pursued, perceptions which may be wildly inaccurate. Reducing these misperceptions is arguably the most important role of economics in public policy. A person's views on what government policies should be pursued also depends on the strength of the person's feelings for a potentially enormous number of people that the person is willing to help and how, if at all, this person thinks that the decisions of others deviate from what is in their best interest.

Simple General Equilibrium Analysis of Public Goods and External Effects

The standard textbook analysis of public goods and external effects involves marginal social benefit and cost curves. This analysis gives the misleading impression that only one quantity of the public good or one level of the external effect is consistent with efficient resource allocation. It is also severely limited in its ability to deal with distributional issues. I use the diagrams developed in Samuelson (1955) and Olsen (1979) to show that there are normally infinitely many quantities of the public good or levels of the external effect consistent with efficient resource allocation and prove a wide range of other important results. For example, reducing pollution is not necessary to achieve an efficient allocation of resources, but it is necessary to achieve an efficient allocation that everyone prefers to the allocation in the absence of government action.

Dealing with Popular Arguments for Government Action

Textbook treatments of the rationales for government actions other than lump-sum transfers focus on valid arguments, that is, arguments that imply that there exists a government policy that would make everyone better off. If no such policy exists, the allocation of resources in the absence of government action is efficient, and transfers as close as feasible to lump-sum will dominate any other type of government action. Most arguments for government action in popular debates over public policy are not of this type, but popular arguments have had substantial influence on the types of government programs adopted.

Before the discussion of each major area of government activity, I ask the students to think about whether they favor government activity of the general type that we will consider, and if so, to come to class prepared to explain why. I begin the first class meeting on the topic describing the general nature of the programs under consideration. For example, the general nature of cash assistance programs such as Supplemental Security Income (SSI) and the EITC is that they provide subsidies to families with incomes below a certain level and the magnitude of the subsidy to a family does not depend on how it allocates its expenditures between produced goods. I then ask the students who favor programs of this general type to raise their hands, making clear that they are free to change their opinions in light of our discussion and analysis of the actual effects of programs. This encourages them to reveal their initial views. If no one raises his or her hand, I offer a widely used problematic argument, ask them to react to it, and raise questions that reveal its defects. I want to disabuse students of notions such as the government should subsidize homeownership because this allows recipients to pursue the American Dream. In my experience, most popular arguments for particular government actions cannot withstand critical scrutiny.

Using Indifference Curves to Talk about Gains and Losses

All gains and losses from government action ultimately accrue to individuals in their roles as buyers of goods and suppliers of inputs. Most textbooks use areas around market demand and supply curves to measure these gains and losses. The usual approach assumes that all buyers of a good pay the same price and can buy as much as they want at that price and similarly for all sellers. Most government programs lead to nonlinear budget frontiers for individuals, and thus market demand and supply curves are poorly suited to measuring gains and losses to individuals. Even in a world with linear budget constraints, the usual approach to dealing with the gains and losses due to changes in the prices of inputs facing individual providers is problematic. The standard measure of the increase in producer surplus is often interpreted as the increase in the profits of firms that presumably accrue to their residual income recipients. However, this is not generally true. In the simplest general equilibrium model where all firms in an industry are identical, an upward sloping long-run supply curve results from the increase in the prices of inputs used most heavily by this industry when its output increases and the decrease in the prices of the inputs used least heavily. At the higher and the lower output price, all firms earn zero economic profit. So the usual producer surplus measure does not measure the increase in profits. For these reasons, I use indifference curves to analyze the gains and losses from government action.

Analyzing the Combined Effect of Expenditure Programs and Taxes Needed to Fund Them

Because one of the most pernicious aspects of popular discussions of proposed expenditure programs is the failure to consider the consequences of the method used to raise money to pay for them, thereby giving citizens the idea that they can get something for nothing, I devote more time in class to such analyses than do textbooks. For example, when I analyze the work-disincentive effects of an NIT, I assume that it is funded by a positive income tax on earnings in excess of the NIT's break-even income. Similarly, my analysis of the effect of the public school system on consumption of education services and other goods assumes that the public school system is funded by lump-sum taxes.

Analyzing the Effect of Government Programs on Equilibrium Prices

Because government programs usually create budget frontiers for individuals that are not linear, it is not easy to analyze their effects on market prices using only demand and supply curves. My standard procedure for analyzing the effect of such a program is to first analyze their effect on desired consumption of various goods in an indifference curve diagram assuming no effect on market prices and then use the results to show how the relevant demand or supply curve shifts in response to this change in desired consumption at the initial market prices. For example, a negative income tax would induce all recipients to work less at the initial wage rate and market prices of produced goods. In a demand and supply curve diagram for a type of labor service provided entirely by NIT recipients, this leads to a leftward shift in the labor supply curve as a function of the market wage rate and hence an increase in the market wage rate.

CLOSING THOUGHTS

I close with two suggestions for future empirical research in public economics that will increase the significance of material that we can bring to the attention of our students, namely, more emphasis on important effects of public policies as opposed to effects that can be estimated with the greatest precision and more attention to the rationales for government policies in deciding what effects to study. I appreciate the professional norms that place high value on precision, but I am embarrassed to be unable to provide students with estimates of the effects of such large government activities as the public school system and Medicaid. The failure to think carefully about rationales for government programs has had a significant effect on the relevance of empirical research on effects of government programs. Almost all empirical studies of these effects attempt to estimate the difference between outcomes with the program and in its absence. This provides a poor basis for judging the success of a program. Almost all programs are intended to produce outcomes that differ from the outcomes of grants as close as feasible to lump-sum. These programs are not successful unless they change consumption patterns in particular directions compared with equally costly cash grants. Few studies make this comparison.

NOTE

1. The theoretical ambiguity stems from the program's housing deduction in determining adjusted income. Over a certain range of housing expenditure, the food stamp subsidy increases with increases in housing expenditure. The food stamp subsidy is a housing subsidy over that range, and many food stamp recipients are in that range.

REFERENCES

Dolbear, F. T. (1967), "On the theory of optimum externality", *American Economic Review,* **57** (1), 90–103.

Fraker, T. M., A. P. Martini and J. C. Ohls (1995), "The effect of food stamp cashout on food expenditures: An assessment of the findings from four demonstrations", *Journal of Human Resources,* **30** (4), 633–49.

Gruber, J. (2010), *Public Finance and Public Policy* (Third Edition), New York: Worth Publishers.

Olsen, E. O. (1979), "The simple analytics of external effects", *Southern Economic Journal,* **45** (3), 847–54.

Olsen, E. O. (1981), "The simple analytics of the externality argument for redistribution", in M. B. Ballabon (ed.), *Economic Perspectives: An Annual Survey of Economics, Vol. 2,* New York: Harwood Academic Publishers, pp. 155–73.

Robins, P. K. (1985), "A comparison of the labor supply findings from the four negative income tax experiments", *Journal of Human Resources,* **20** (4), 567–82.

Rosen, H. S. and T. Gayer (2008), *Public Finance* (Eighth Edition), New York: McGraw-Hill.

Samuelson, P. A. (1955), "Diagrammatic exposition of a theory of public expenditure", *Review of Economics and Statistics,* **37** (4), 350–56.

64 Sports economics as applied microeconomics
Peter von Allmen, Michael A. Leeds and Brad R. Humphreys

The Economics of Sports is a flexible applied micro course that can be tailored to all levels of undergraduate study. Advanced undergraduates can access primary sources and perform independent data analyses, while introductory-level students can learn basic economics in an interesting and relevant context.

While the economics of sports was viewed as a "novelty" elective as recently as a decade ago, the course is now widely offered at the undergraduate level in economics and sport management departments (Humphreys and Maxcy, 2007). The expansion of the course mirrors the development of sports economics as a sub-field of economics. A number of textbooks exist for students with different levels of preparation. In our experience, the economics of sport is a very popular elective course wherever it is offered.

GOALS OF THE COURSE: THE ECONOMICS OF *SPORTS* OR THE *ECONOMICS* OF SPORTS

The first decision one must make when preparing an economics of sports course is whether to emphasize sports or economics. We suspect that most instructors in Sports Management will emphasize the former, while most instructors in Economics will emphasize the latter. This decision has important consequences for how one approaches the material.

Instructors who emphasize sports will probably want to devote significant time to the importance of institutional factors across sports. For example, all professional sports leagues restrict their labor market in some way, which allows them to exercise some monopsony power over players. A sports-oriented course would devote substantial time to what makes a free agent in one sport more or less free than one in another sport. Because courses that emphasize sports over economics require knowledge of current events and institutional details, instructors who do not have a strong interest in sports would probably find them difficult to teach.

In an Economics Department, the instructor will typically look for commonalities rather than differences. In particular, the instructor can identify economic content in a variety of sports and view the course as an opportunity to teach *economics* in a context that students find relevant and interesting. From this perspective, different sports' restrictions on player movement all point toward a specific economic concept, monopsony. Such a course typically focuses on major fields in economics, using sports markets as the running example. In this approach, the institutional details of topics like free agency are covered in less detail, and class time is devoted to discussing the relevant economic models. In contrast to the sports-focused course, economics-oriented courses can be taught by instructors with substantially less knowledge of or interest in sports. The lack of background in sports can even be an advantage, as it can increase student participation and engagement when they provide the needed institutional detail. As economists, we have adopted this latter approach, which will form the basis of the remainder of this chapter.

MOTIVATING STUDENTS AND MANAGING EXPECTATIONS[1]

Economics of sports courses differ from most other economics courses in that instructors seldom have to worry about motivating their students. Topics that students find irrelevant to their everyday lives in other courses become the subject of impassioned debate when applied to sports. Students who fail to see the value of optimal tax theory eagerly analyze Arizona's efforts to raise $300 million for the construction of University of Phoenix Stadium. What might otherwise be a dry, contrived discussion of whether workers are paid their marginal revenue product becomes the basis for heated debate over how much the Yankees should pay Derek Jeter.

Students' enthusiasm also presents one of the biggest challenges facing the instructor: setting the appropriate expectations for the course. Because most students who take sports economics are sports fans, they often expect the course to consist of a roundtable discussion of current events in sport. While it would be possible to offer a current events course, such emphasis would preclude instructors from exploiting the rich economic content underlying modern sport.

Another common misperception is that sports economics is an easy course. We suspect that this perception comes from the fact that many students are familiar with the basic business of sport and assume that they already know much of its content. Additionally, because sports fans are disproportionately male, this attitude can lead to difficult gender dynamics in the class. Some males in the class might assume that their greater familiarity with sports allows them to speak with greater authority about the issues. It has frequently been our experience that the best students in the class are neither men nor ardent sports fans.

COURSE ORGANIZATION

Because we stress the *economics* of sports, we organize our courses around several sub-fields:

- Industrial Organization – sports leagues
- Public Finance – paying for facilities
- Urban Economics – economic impact of sport
- Labor Economics – pay and performance in sport

At the end of the semester, we turn to a sport-centered topic, the economics of the (ostensibly) not-for-profit sector, which largely consists of intercollegiate sports and the Olympic Games.

Because the sports industry is so dynamic, new topics continually arise. As a result, we are hesitant to get very specific about content. However, within each branch of economics several broad themes regularly appear and always require attention.

Industrial Organization

Firm objectives   One of the most important themes in industrial organization is profit maximization. Do teams maximize profits? If so, how do they do so? If not, what do they maximize instead? These questions are seldom raised in microeconomic theory and industrial organization classes. We often illustrate profit and revenue streams in the four major North American sports (football, baseball, basketball, and hockey), soccer, and other sports by using data regularly published by *Forbes* magazine.[2] While the data are not perfect, they provide useful insights into the similarities and differences among sports teams and leagues.

Monopoly power   The high-profile antitrust cases that are of interest to academic economists (for example, AT&T and Microsoft) are unfamiliar to most students. Further, given the trend toward deregulation in such areas as banking, trucking, and airlines and the large-scale mergers in banking, oil and other industries, students might not grasp the importance of the potential costs of concentrated markets. Recent antitrust lawsuits in professional sports (for example, the *American Needle* case recently before the Supreme Court) and the threat of antitrust suits in intercollegiate sports allow instructors to remind students of the costs of monopoly and the value of antitrust policy. Within the cable television industry, the inability of the National Football League Network (NFLN) and cable providers to come to an agreement over price means that Time Warner cable customers are unable to watch certain NFL games, since they are broadcast only on the NFLN.[3]

Entry barriers and the unit of analysis   In a typical discussion of firm behavior, there is little confusion over the unit of analysis. Each firm is a supplier and, depending on the number of firms in that market, competes for market share. Driving out a competitor is almost always a positive outcome for the surviving firm(s). In the sports industry, teams cannot readily exist without an organized league. While they compete on the field, individual teams would be substantially worse off if they drove out competing teams. Thus, leagues provide an interesting example of cooperative firm behavior. In some cases, we consider the team to be the unit of analysis, as each team (in most leagues) is a privately owned profit-maximizing entity. Each team sets its own ticket prices, negotiates with the local government over stadium funding; certain revenue streams, such as parking and concessions; and certain costs, such as rent and game-day operations. At the same time, each league functions as a set of teams that must cooperate to satisfy the broader market. At the most basic level, teams must coordinate their decisions about where and when to play, what rules govern the contest, and what the outcome of the game means (for example, qualifying for playoffs and so additional revenue). In addition, teams derive their monopoly power from the league, which teams must join in order to play other member teams. Monopoly power often takes the form of a guarantee that the team has sole access to its local market.[4] In such cases, it is often useful to think of the league as a cartel made up of the independent teams. While the institutional structure undeniably confers monopoly power on individual teams, the source of that power requires a discussion of the league as an economic entity.

Public Finance

A frequent challenge in economics courses is getting students to see the link between economic theory and their intuition. We find that studying public funding of stadiums is an effective way to overcome this difficulty. The value of stadiums to teams and cities allows students to study topics ranging from asset valuation to externalities to multipliers. Stadiums are assets that provide a stream of returns for decades. Students better appreciate the need to evaluate the costs of and returns to a stadium when they learn that some stadiums (for example, Three Rivers Stadium in Pittsburgh) were demolished even before the city had finished paying for them. Municipal governments often subsidize stadiums because of the indirect benefits facilities supposedly provide. These indirect benefits typically take the form of positive externalities and ripple effects of income generated by the presence of a sports team. Less well-known to students are the negative externalities that sports facilities generate, such as increased traffic, trash, and crime.

Taxation and equity   After defining horizontal and vertical equity, instructors can lead active discussions on funding. A variety of taxes have been employed to fund stadium projects, and students are eager to discuss them. Once the instructor introduces formal definitions and specific tax policies, students can translate the intuitive arguments into more formal analysis.

Urban Economics

The construction and operation of professional sports facilities are subsidized by state, local, and federal governments. The rationale for these subsidies typically involves job creation, higher wages, and urban revitalization in cities across North America. These high-profile debates provide a context for discussing important concepts in urban economics.

Many cities face a declining urban core and flight of residents to the suburbs. Sports facilities are often touted as important engines of economic growth and redevelopment, but the empirical evidence strongly suggests otherwise. Instructors can contrast the claims of subsidy proponents, which are often accompanied by promotional "economic impact studies," with empirical evidence from the scholarly literature to highlight the difference between net and gross economic impact, difficulties in forecasting economic activity, and the important role of amenities in determining the quality of life in urban areas. In addition, since most economic impact studies are based on regional input-output models, economics of sports courses provide particularly unique insights into multiplier effects, since they allow the instructor to distinguish local from nationwide multipliers, which, in turn, provides greater insight into all forms of multipliers.

Although cities often heavily underwrite sports facilities, the teams that occupy them receive most of the revenue that they generate, from signage to luxury suites. One popular revenue source is the sale of naming rights. Facilities that were once named to honor the game's pioneers or distinctive local features (for example, Chicago's Comiskey Park or Denver's Mile High Stadium) are now named for the highest bidder. As is the case with municipal spending on sports facilities, the evidence suggests that the return to buy naming rights is relatively low (Leeds, Leeds, and Pistolet, 2007). The discussion of naming rights can take place on several levels. There are numerous amusing anecdotes surrounding naming rights, such as the débâcle of Enron Field in Houston. Students can also discuss whether cities should give up an important revenue source. Finally, more econometrically sophisticated classes can use naming rights to learn about event analysis.

Labor Economics

Kahn (2000) described the sports industry as a labor market laboratory that "offers a unique opportunity for labor market research" (p. 75). The characteristics that make the sports industry a fruitful area of research make it an excellent vehicle for teaching labor economics: the variety of labor market relationships, and the availability of data.

Employment relationships   Athletes in team sports are subject to widely varying labor market rules. Players enjoying unrestricted free agency are best considered participants in a competitive labor market, but players still subject to the reserve system (under which an individual player can work only for the team that controls his/her rights) are best modeled with the monopsony model.

Participants in individual sports, such as golf or tennis, do not have their pay set in advance. It is determined by rank-order tournaments in which a given participant's marginal product is indeterminate. Thus, compensation schemes are typically non-linear.

The variation in compensation schemes across sports allows instructors to discuss the economics of incentives. For example, while large prizes often elicit optimal effort, they sometimes discourage participation, engender self-destructive behavior, or lead players to sabotage their teammates.

One of the great frustrations in teaching labor theory is the lack of worker-specific data. The plethora of data on player performance in most professional sports provides a natural and intuitive context for studying wage determination and the impact of incentive mechanisms, market institutions, such as unions, and market imperfections, such as discrimination. Many online sources of salary data in professional baseball, basketball, hockey and football exist.[5] Data on tournament winnings in individual sports, such as auto racing and golf, are also available online. Compensation data are available in cross-section form for many years, allowing students to construct panel data sets. Within the unit on labor economics, instructors can choose from a wide variety of empirical questions. Here we mention several and offer advice on how to present them.

Are professional athletes overpaid? Most professional athletes earn salaries that dwarf those earned by the average American. Median player salaries are over $800,000 in the NFL, exceed $1 million in Major League Baseball (MLB) and the National Hockey League (NHL), and top $2 million in the National Basketball Association (NBA).[6] In every sport, the distributions are strongly skewed, making average salaries much greater than the medians. It can therefore be hard for students to believe that many athletes are substantially underpaid. Until they reach free agency, players are bound to specific teams, giving those teams monopsony power, which results in wages that are below competitive levels.

Gerald Scully's (1974) seminal paper on MLB is an excellent example of an empirical test of microeconomic theory, as he estimates players' marginal revenue products (MRP) and compares those estimates to their salaries. His results indicate that the reserve clause caused players to be paid a small fraction of their MRP. Since the advent of free agency, some economists have updated and refined Scully's basic model (for example, Zimbalist, 1992), while other authors have developed entirely different approaches (for example, Krautmann, 1999). For historical and data-driven reasons, most studies focus on MLB. However, an increasing number have examined other sports. Krautmann, von Allmen, and Berri (2009) compare the impact of free agency on salaries in MLB, the NBA and the NFL. All of these papers are fairly accessible to upper-level undergraduate students; even students with a single semester of micro principles will be able to follow the logic of the arguments when presented by the instructor.

What underlies the latest labor unrest in professional sports? There has been a long decline of unionization in the US economy (down from over 20 percent in 1983 to just over 12 percent in 2009),[7] but unions in professional sports defy this trend. All players in MLB, the NBA, the NHL, and the NFL belong to player associations. As such, the leagues and player associations provide an excellent example of bilateral market power. Conflicts between leagues (i.e. the collection of owners) and player associations share a common theme with all labor–management conflicts: bargaining over economic rent. Though the player associations do not bargain over specific wages, they do bargain over wage parameters (for example, minimum salaries) as well as a wide variety of working conditions. For upper-level students in particular, professors may use this topic as an opportunity to discuss labor relations and strike activity.

Do racial and gender discrimination still play a role in professional and amateur sports? Discrimination can be a very difficult topic for students to discuss. Most students have strong opinions on whether prejudice and discrimination are active forces in the United States. Moreover, some students may feel uncomfortable voicing opinions that they feel will be at odds with those of other students. There is also a risk that students will make comments that are inconsistent with proper classroom decorum. While this is typically done without malice and so represents a "teachable moment," these moments can be very difficult, nonetheless.

Studying discrimination in professional and amateur sports allows professors to revisit some well-known moments in American history, such as the Dodgers' signing Jackie Robinson and to discuss topics that students may not have considered, such as whether referees discriminate when making calls or the extent to which pre-market or role discrimination impacts the racial distribution of players across positions.[8] Economists have conducted extensive research on discrimination in the context of sports, and upper-level students will find much of this research within their grasp. When discussing role discrimination across gender lines, students are eager to discuss what qualifies an individual to hold various front office positions. The *Racial and Gender Report Card* published by TIDES (The Institute for Diversity and Ethics in Sport) provides a wealth of data on the racial, ethnic and gender distributions of players (sometimes by position), coaches, and front office personnel.[9] Thus, while most empirical research suggests that wage discrimination in professional sports is rare and small in magnitude (see Kahn, 2000), role discrimination may still be substantial. Students might be interested to learn that, even when markets do not explicitly operate, as in intercollegiate or Olympic sports, competition on the field often presses teams, leagues, and even nations to abandon their prejudices. (For an example, see Maraniss, 2008.)

In a time of tightening state budgets, many athletic departments are once again cutting sports programs. Even national powers, such as the University of California's rugby team have been demoted to club status. Because most programs that have been cut are men's sports, the impact of Title IX has again assumed center stage. Opponents of Title IX claim that legitimate programs are being eliminated to accommodate sports that draw little interest. Backers of Title IX claim that such arguments miss the point of offering equal opportunity Thus, Title IX provides ample opportunity for discussion, as well as a challenge for the instructor to keep the students' passions in check.

Amateur Athletics

Like professional sports, intercollegiate athletics generates significant revenues, and several studies have estimated the marginal revenue product of top college football and basketball players.[10] Since many undergraduates enrolled in sports economics courses are also sports fans, a careful examination of the marginal revenue product generated by star college athletes can provide a context for discussing the nature of economic exploitation and the economic value of higher education.

TEACHING TECHNIQUES

In teaching the economics of sports, we have used a variety of teaching techniques and assignments. While some are not specific to sports-related classes, others are specifically designed for them. In this section, we discuss several possible assignments and suggest how to maximize their value and avoid pitfalls.

Class Debates

Because students are passionate about issues surrounding sports, and because of the nearly limitless supply of current-events topics related to sport, debates provide an opportunity to delve more deeply into particular topics without demanding that the students present a full-fledged research paper. At the same time, students' affiliation with or affinity to certain sports or athletes creates the risk that debates will veer off course from their intended purpose. For example, a debate might turn into a shouting match when the students identify too closely with their positions. Having a member of the women's volleyball team debate the merits of Title IX with a member of the wrestling team can create a very volatile situation and severely damage the dynamic within the class. For this reason, we suggest the following approach to debates:

1. Provide a list of topics and ask students to list the three topics they find most appealing and to designate the side that they would like to argue.

2. Create debating teams of three to four students each. Try to assign the students to their most desired topic, but assign them to the position opposite to the one they desire. This serves several purposes. It distances the students from their positions, making them less likely to respond emotionally. Further, it forces students to view the issue from an opposing point of view, humanizing the opposition and widening their perspectives.

The debates themselves are subject to several pitfalls and have to be carefully managed. To prevent long, rambling speeches, the students should be told to prepare (assuming teams of three) two statements, lasting no more than five minutes each and one rebuttal, lasting no more than three minutes. All presentations should be strictly timed.

Debates are also subject to two forms of free riding. First, some team members might not pull their weight in preparation. For that reason, the instructor should insist that every member participate and assign both a team grade and an individual grade. Second, keeping the rest of the class involved can be a challenge. One way to engage these students is to require non-participants in a given debate to write a paragraph explaining which team "won" the debate and why.

Term Papers

When undergraduates write term papers in economics courses, they face a number of challenges.[11] Among these are the lack of knowledge required to understand primary sources or even to distinguish legitimate from illegitimate sources, the lack of statistical or econometric background needed to analyze data, and unfamiliarity with disciplinary writing styles. These problems may be magnified in economics of sports classes if they attract students with widely varying course backgrounds and skills. Major term papers that include statistical analyses are best suited for upper-level courses that have statistics and intermediate theory courses as prerequisites. With appropriate preparation and guidance, however, one can have success with term papers and shorter essays for courses without such prerequisites.

Students in a class that has a prerequisite of only a one-semester course in microeconomic principles will benefit from a tightly controlled assignment, such as giving only a narrow choice of topics. For example, one might have students identify the winners and losers of a work stoppage or compare a large market team and small market team in a given sport. Although students lack the preparation to do econometric work for assignments at this level, asking them to draw and describe their own figures can solidify their understanding of basic theoretical concepts.

In upper-level courses with prerequisites in microeconomic theory, statistics and perhaps econometrics, students are able to take a much more active role in topic choice, data collection and empirical analysis. As with any upper division course, it is advisable to compel students to identify their topic early to ensure that the scope of the paper is reasonable. There is always a risk that, by the time even a conscientious student finds a topic, gathers the needed data, and learns how to analyze it, the semester is over. In sports economics, this risk is mitigated by the ready availability of free, detailed data and the ever-changing landscape of current events.

A number of issues related to writing within the discipline pose both a challenge and an opportunity for students in Sports Economics courses. Many students in elective courses have only a single course in college-level writing (for example, a first-year composition course offered through the English Department) during which they learn very little about how to write within a specific discipline. In our experience, even strong students working on honors projects struggle when discussing tables and graphs or interpreting empirical results. Even the typical structure of an economic essay and citation guidelines are likely to be a challenge for all students. The advantage of an economics of sports topic is that the wealth of readily accessible data leaves more time to focus on the writing *process*. Depending on class size, it may be feasible to establish mileposts for the students that allow them to break a large project into more manageable pieces.[12] These include annotated bibliographies, rough drafts, and peer editing sessions. It may also be possible to hold some class sessions in a computer lab to facilitate help with modeling issues.

Use of Literature and Film

In addition to receiving significant attention in the mass media, sport has been the subject of numerous short stories, novels, biographies, plays, movies, even poems. Instructors can exploit this in a number of ways. One trivial but enjoyable way to use literature is to read, or get a student to read, a short poem or monologue before class as a "warm up" for the day's lesson.[13]

Films can consume a great deal of class time, so we believe that they should be used sparingly.[14] That said, they can become a valuable part of a lesson. Showing a clip from Leni Riefenstahl's *Olympia* could supplement a discussion of the 1936 "Nazi Olympics." Excerpts from Ken Burns's documentary, *Baseball,* can add greatly to almost any aspect of the course. To avoid taking too much class time, we recommend having students view more extended clips on their own. The availability of DVDs in university libraries and of a variety of video services online and via cable makes this a viable option.

In addition to making films part of the formal class, we have also allowed students to write brief analyses of movies or novels as extra credit assignments. Here, again, it is important for the instructor to emphasize that s/he is looking for an economic interpretation of the work and not a report on "Why I liked *Slap Shot.*" We recommend providing a list of pre-approved films or books from which the students can choose.

Guest Speakers

Perhaps no other economics course can benefit as much from guest speakers as a course in sports economics. Speakers allow the instructor to provide deeper content from the perspective of a practitioner and broader content from a guest with outside expertise. For example, both students and the instructor may benefit from asking a colleague in business law to present and discuss a current case, such as the antitrust suit brought by American Needle.

One need not work in a major metropolitan area or for a Bowl Championship Series (BCS) football power to have access to excellent speakers. Minor league executives face many of the same pressures as their major league counterparts, and a small college's field hockey coach can be every bit as insightful on matters such as Title IX as a major university's football or basketball coach.

As with any aspect of the course, a successful guest speaker requires advance preparation. If at all possible, meet with the speakers in advance both to gauge how good they are at public speaking and to ensure that they know what topics you want them to cover. It is also important to prepare the class. One useful strategy for this is to have the students read some of the speaker's work (or writings about the speaker) and prepare potential questions in advance as a small group exercise.

CONCLUSION

The economics of sports course can play a valuable role in the economics curriculum by acting as a Trojan horse that attracts students who otherwise might not select an upper-level economics course. The instructor can then use the familiar and popular context of sports to teach students important economic concepts in an entertaining and engaging way. The course is also unique in economics in that it contains topics from many different fields. Because the course cuts across so many fields in economics, the instructor can introduce students to many upper-level offerings, and encourage them to enroll in additional economics classes. We have offered a number of suggestions for how to structure such a class, as well as specific teaching tips. However, the breadth of the material allows new instructors to make the material their own, focusing on the economic principles and examples that best fit their own interests and aptitudes. The more you enjoy the course, the more your students will, as well.

NOTES

1. This and other aspects of teaching a course on the economics of sports are also explored in von Allmen (2005). Von Allmen (2005) focuses primarily on the motivation for teaching such a course and the characteristics of a typical course on the economics of sports. Here, we look closely at the content of the course, teaching strategies, and challenges an instructor might confront.
2. Every year, *Forbes* publishes a "Business of . . ." for each major team sport that provides basic revenue and cost information, as well as team valuations for all teams in each league. For example, see "NHL Team Values 2010: The Business of Hockey", at http://www.forbes.com/lists/2010/31/hockey-valuations-10_land.html (accessed 6 December 2010).
3. For a more detailed description of this issue, see McCann (2010).
4. There are a few notable exceptions to this general rule such as the Los Angeles Clippers and Lakers in the NBA, the New York Giants and Jets in the NFL, and the Chicago White Sox and Cubs. The history of how an additional team came to locate in these cities can serve as interesting examples and discussion points.
5. Data are available by team and at the individual level. See for example baseball salaries "USA Today Salaries Databases: Baseball", at http://content.usatoday.com/sports/baseball/salaries/default.aspx, (accessed 6 December 2010).
6. Data on salaries are available from the *USA Today* at http://content.usatoday.com/sports/football/nfl/salaries/default.aspx.
7. Bureau of Labor Statistics (2009).
8. See Price and Wolfers (2010) for an example of research on whether referees discriminate in the NBA.
9. The Institute for Diversity and Ethics in Sport, at http://www.tidesport.org/aboutdirectors.html (accessed 14 December 2010).

10. See Brown (1993) and Brown and Jewell (2006) for empirical papers on college football and women's basketball.
11. For more information about writing, see Chapter 12, "Writing for Learning in Economics", in this volume.
12. An additional advantage of these mileposts is that they discourage plagiarism.
13. The *Baseball Almanac* is an excellent source of baseball-oriented poems, stories and anecdotes, at http://www.baseball-almanac.com (accessed 23 February 2011).
14. Incorporating films is discussed more generally in Chapter 13, "Incorporating Media and Response Systems in the Economics Classroom", in this volume.

REFERENCES

The Baseball Almanac, http://www.baseball-almanac.com/, accessed 23 February 2011.
Brown, R. W. (1993), "An estimate of the rent generated by a premium college football player", *Economic Inquiry*, **31** (4), (October), 671–84.
Brown, R. W. and T. Jewel (2006), "The marginal revenue product of a women's college basketball player", *Industrial Relations*, **45** (1), (January), 96–101.
Bureau of Labor Statistics (2009), *Union Members*, http://www.bls.gov/news.release/pdf/union2.pdf, accessed 14 December 2010.
Humphreys, B. R. and J. Maxcy (2007), "The role of sports economics in the US sport management curriculum", *Sport Management Review*, **10** (2), 177–89.
The Institute for Diversity and Ethics in Sports, "Racial and Gender Report Card", http://www.tidesport.org/racialgenderreportcard.html, accessed 14 December 2010.
Kahn, L. (2000), "The sports business as a labor market laboratory", *Journal of Economic Perspectives*, **14** (3), (Summer), 75–94.
Krautmann, A. (1999), "What's Wrong with Scully-estimates of a player's marginal revenue product", *Economic Inquiry*, **37** (2), (April), 369–81.
Krautmann, A., P. von Allmen and D. J. Berri (2009), "The underpayment of restricted players in North American sports leagues", *International Journal of Sport Finance*, **4** (3), (August), 155–69.
Leeds, E. M., M. A. Leeds and I. Pistolet (2007), "A stadium by any other name: The value of naming rights", *Journal of Sports Economics*, **8** (6), (December), 581–95.
Maraniss, D. (2008), *Rome 1960: The Olympics that Changed the World*, New York: Simon & Schuster.
McCann, M. (2010), "Seven years in, NFL network still battling cable companies", http://sportsillustrated.cnn.com/2010/writers/michael_mccann/05/26/nfl/index.html, accessed 6 December 2010.
Price, J. and J. Wolfers (2010), "Racial discrimination among NBA referees", *Quarterly Journal of Economics*, **125** (4), (November), 1859–87.
Scully, G. (1974), "Pay and performance in Major League Baseball", *American Economic Review*, **64** (6), (December), 915–30.
USA Today salaries databases: Baseball, http://content.usatoday.com/sports/baseball/salaries/default.aspx, accessed 6 December 2010.
von Allmen, P. (2005), "Teaching the economics of sports", *Journal of Sports Economics*, **6** (3), (August), 325–30.
Zimbalist, A. (1992), "Salaries and performance: Beyond the Scully model", in P. Sommers, *Diamonds are Forever: The Business of Baseball*, Washington, DC: Brookings Institution, pp. 109–33.

APPENDIX – USEFUL SUPPLEMENTAL MATERIAL[1]

Novels

Brock, Daryl (1990), *If I Never Get Back* (New York: Crown).
DeFord, Frank (1993), *Love and Infamy* (New York: Viking).
Goodman, Mark (1985), *Hurrah for the Last Man Who Dies* (New York: Atheneum).
Malamud, Bernard (1952), *The Natural* (New York: Avon Books).
Soos, Troy (1999), *Hanging Curve*[2] (New York: Kensington Books).

Biographies and Non-fiction

Asinof, Eliot (1983), *Eight Men Out* (New York: Henry Holt).
Bissinger, Buzz (1990), *Friday Night Lights* (New York: Harper Collins).
Fisher, Marshall Jon (2009), *A Terrible Splendor* (New York: Crown).
Hillenbrand, Laura (2001), *Seabiscuit* (New York: Random House).
Hillenbrand, Laura (2010), *Unbroken* (New York: Random House).
Lewis, Michael (2003), *Money Ball* (New York: W.W. Norton).
Lewis, Michael (2006), *The Blind Side* (New York: W.W. Norton).
Mandell, Richard (1971), *The Nazi Olympics* (New York: Macmillan).
Maraniss, David (2008), *Rome 1960* (New York: Simon and Shuster).
Maraniss, David (1999), *When Pride Still Mattered* (New York: Simon and Shuster).
Margolick, David (2005), *Beyond Glory* (New York: Knopf).
Ward, Geoffrey C. (2004), *Unforgivable Blackness* (New York: Knopf).

Movies

Baseball
A League of their Own (1992).
Bang the Drum Slowly (1973).
Baseball (2004).
Bull Durham (1988).
Eight Men Out (1988).
Mr. Baseball (1992).
The Bingo Long Traveling All Stars and Motor Kings (1976).
The Life and Times of Hank Greenberg (1998).
The Natural (1984).

Basketball
Blue Chips (1994).
He Got Game (1998).
Hoop Dreams (1994).

Boxing
Joe and Max (2002).
Raging Bull (1980).
The Great White Hope (1970).
Unforgivable Blackness (2004).

Football
Any Given Sunday (1999).
Horse Feathers (1932).
North Dallas Forty (1979).

Hockey
Miracle (2004).

Olympics
Chariots of Fire (1981).
Olympia (1938).

APPENDIX NOTES

1. This list is far from exhaustive, but it provides some of the most applicable and accessible sources.
2. This is the last of a series of enjoyable historical baseball novels by Troy Soos.

65 Using location, agglomeration, and policy issues to teach urban economics
Daniel P. McMillen

As virtually all policy issues have an urban twist, a course in urban economics imposes few limitations on the issues that can be covered in the classroom. At the same time, it is surprising how many students see the word "urban" in the course title and fail to recognize that it is only a modifier for "economics." The course attracts business students who want to become real estate developers, urban planners who believe that real estate developers are ruining cities, and students from a variety of backgrounds who have taken principles courses and are using the urban economics course to finish a social sciences requirement. The challenge of the course, in light of the mix of students enrolled, is to convince them that knowledge of economics is vital to understanding any issue related to urban areas.

The course organizes naturally into three primary sections. The first section of the course focuses on relationships among cities. Questions such as why do cities exist, why do some cities grow while others decline, and what is the pattern of trade between cities help satisfy the section goal of getting students to think about cities from an economic perspective. The monocentric city model is introduced next, since it is still the best tool for analyzing spatial structure within an urban area. Finally, the course ends with a set of urban policy issues to analyze. The open nature of the policy issue section of the course allows instructors to change topics frequently over time, which helps keep the material current and engaging, keeping both the students and the instructor more motivated.

This approach to the urban economics course moves from the broad to the particular by first analyzing a system of cities without regard to their internal structure, then analyzing broad spatial patterns within a city, and finally analyzing policies affecting individual households. The structure provides natural breaks for exams, while assuring that no single topic accounts for too much class time. The structure also provides flexibility. Some instructors may want to expand the first section of the course to include more economic geography, while others may want to expand the last section to include more topics. It is also possible to prepare a version of the course in which the first section is dropped nearly entirely and replaced by a large section on real estate economics. Urban economics is a flexible course, and it can be modified to suit the requirements of economics, urban planning, or real estate departments.

WHAT IS URBAN ECONOMICS?

When students come from diverse academic backgrounds, it is useful to start the course with what first seems a somewhat surprising question – what is urban economics? A superficial answer is that urban economics is simply the application of economic tools to the analysis of policy issues affecting urban areas. This definition is not very limiting since most people live in urban areas, and it has helped produce a long tradition of studies in urban economics analyzing issues related to poverty, unemployment, housing, crime, education, social programs, local government, and so on. Each of these issues often has a uniquely urban slant, and they are part of the reason why students are attracted to the course.

A less superficial answer involves a discussion of just what it is that gives these issues an urban slant. The first crucial distinction is location. Unlike most economic fields, urban economics deals explicitly with space. Since not everyone can live at the same attractive location, how do prices vary to allocate the best sites? What determines the demand for one location rather than another, and how does demand vary over time? Does the spatial concentration of crime, poverty, and unemployment pose a different set of challenges for policy makers than a situation where the problems are spread uniformly throughout the population? Are local governments constrained by competition with nearby jurisdictions from undertaking some seeming desirable policies? Why do some areas grow, while others decline?

The second distinguishing feature of urban economics is its emphasis on agglomeration economies and economies of scale. Students seldom consider the question of *why* cities exist. Their standard answer to the question – that's where the jobs are – simply moves the question back one step to asking why firms prefer to locate in urban areas. The next step in the circle – that firms prefer to locate in urban areas because that's where their workers live – simply demonstrates that there must be underlying economic forces that make urban areas attractive places for both firms and workers. In urban areas, firms are more likely to find qualified workers, can easily locate necessary supplies and specialized services, and have ready access to highway, rail, and air transportation. In turn, workers are more likely to find a job that suits them, run less risk of remaining unemployed if they lose their job, and generally receive sufficient pay to compensate for any additional costs of living in urban areas. Economies of scale produce large firms that employ many workers, transportation costs provide an incentive to locate firms and workers close together, and agglomeration economies lead to a diversity of firms and workers, all of which help to attract more firms and more people.

Many students question whether transportation costs are really lower in urban areas and ask for empirical examples of agglomeration economies. It often is possible to initiate an interesting discussion of how transportation costs have changed over time and what effects innovations in communications have had on preferences for urban locations. If agglomeration economies are so powerful, why don't all firms locate in one city? The answer is partly that land would become prohibitively costly; another answer is that traffic congestion is one of the factors that limit city size. Although transportation of bulky products over long distances is clearly cheaper now than in the past – in part because technological innovations make products lighter and less bulky – the transportation of services and ideas is still easier over short distances.

The nature of agglomeration economies is still not well developed in the literature. Most empirical studies simply include variables such as employment within an industry as the measure of localization economies, with little discussion about what the nature of the localization economies really is. Silicon Valley is a good example of labor pooling, and many cities have large medical complexes that serve as good examples of localization economies. This entire section of the course is a good place to encourage discussions among students. I rely heavily on my local knowledge of the Chicago area, and I often assign William Cronon's (1991) book, *Nature's Metropolis*, which discusses the development of Chicago's early industries.

I emphasize history in this portion of the course partly out of personal interest – I find the history of cities to be fascinating. But it is also worth emphasizing that the long run is really very long in urban areas. Old buildings are not immediately demolished, and today's transportation network often differs surprisingly little from the one that existed a century ago. Redfearn's (2009) study suggests that the location of employment concentrations in one of the seemingly most modern of American cities, Los Angeles, is explained nearly as well by the location of rail lines in the 1890s as by today's highway system. Transportation may not be as costly today as it was in the past, but the current transportation network and much of today's urban infrastructure is still dominated by past decisions. Cities that were founded because of harbors (for example, New York or San Francisco), canals or rivers (for example, Chicago and Portland), or rail lines (for example, Atlanta and Dallas) today attract firms primarily due to the advantages of agglomeration economies that arose from the concentrations of employment and population produced in part by their initial advantages in transportation.

The first section of this model urban economics course should get students used to viewing urban areas from an economic perspective. Cities don't exist now simply because they have always existed; they exist because they provide advantages over other locations for both firms and households. What are these advantages, and how have they changed over time? Many instructors will want to expand this section of the course to include new models of economic geography. Instructors emphasizing policy analysis or real estate will likely cover this material more quickly.

THE MONOCENTRIC CITY MODEL

The monocentric city model remains the standard model of intra-city spatial structure. The main predicament in presenting it to undergraduates is that they tend to view it as a vast oversimplification at the same time as they find it quite complicated. I believe that both students and instructors tend to be too dismissive of its ability to explain the spatial structure of modern urban areas. The problem may lie in the fact that the model is typically presented as a complete, logically consistent general equilibrium model of the entire city. It is more useful to think of the model as a set of tools that are useful when making less sweeping, partial equilibrium predictions. The fundamental contribution is not the full general equilibrium model; it is the bid-rent function. The bid-rent function is a powerful, useful tool that also is easy to understand.

I like to start this section of the course with a historical outline of the economic theory of land value. Adam Smith's and Karl Marx' cost-driven theories of value cannot adequately explain land prices because land does not need to be produced where it already exists. David Ricardo's (1817, chapter 2) theory of rent applies directly to land. Ricardo's theory can easily explain agricultural land prices: if there is one price for the final product (for example, corn) faced by all farmers, but the cost of producing the product is lower on more fertile land, then a farmer would earn economic rent (in other words, profit) if there were no charge for land. In equilibrium, all farmers have to be equally well (or equally badly) off in all locations, so land prices must be higher for more fertile land. When corn prices rise, the price of highly fertile land rises, and some less fertile land that was uncultivated is plowed under. If farmers rent their land – as was the case in Ricardo's world – then they are no better off even though corn prices have risen.

One advantage of leading off with Ricardo's theory of land rent is that it is a direct application of tools the students should already have learned in principles, yet it is clear that the tools are not sufficient for explaining land prices. When I taught urban economics at the University of Illinois at Chicago, I liked to point to the Sears (now Willis) Tower and indicate that it had recently sold for nearly $1 billion. Though corn could presumably be grown on the site, it is obvious that the value of the city block it occupies has nothing to do with either the cost of producing the land or the price of corn. The argument does not work as well when teaching in more remote institutions like Champaign-Urbana, an area surrounded by cornfields, but the basic point is clear. Another advantage of Ricardo's theory is that it is a clear demonstration of how equilibrium works in a land market model: land prices must vary over space in exactly the way that keeps people indifferent between all locations, for otherwise everyone would try to occupy the single plot of land that produces the highest profit. Since not everyone can occupy the same plot, the most productive areas are the most expensive.

Though many instructors may prefer to turn directly to the urban model at this point, I like to continue the agricultural theme by briefly outlining the Von Thünen (1826) model. This provides an opportunity to describe how, even in an agricultural world, land prices may be influenced by more than the fertility of the soil if farmers have to ship their produce to a market place. The modeling strategy is also interesting: whereas Ricardo implicitly assumed costless shipping, Von Thünen assumes the opposite extreme of costly shipping but uniform soil fertility. The model can be presented as simple arithmetic. All farmers produce Q bushels of corn, which they sell at a price of $\$P$ per bushel. A farmer with L acres of land has a profit of $PQ - RL - C - tQd$, where R is land rent per acre, C is the cost of other inputs (assumed to be the same everywhere), and td is the cost of shipping one bushel of corn d miles. This simple expression is all that is necessary to produce a bid-rent function: $R = (PQ - C - tQd)/L$. Despite the fact that land is equally fertile everywhere, land rent varies by exactly the amount that keeps farmers indifferent (equally miserable) at all locations.

The Von Thünen model is also an excellent point to introduce what I consider to be a fundamental insight of the bid-rent approach, the effect of substitution possibilities on land values. If L is fixed at 100, then R is just a linear function of distance from the marketplace. But if L is variable, a farmer near the marketplace can consider substituting other inputs for land to get the same amount of production from a smaller plot. A farmer farther from the marketplace can do the opposite. If prices reflect an equilibrium in which all plots are fixed at 100 acres, then all the farmers will want to move closer to the market to parcels with less than 100 acres or to more distant parcels with more than 100 acres. Land rents have to rise at both close and distant points, and the increase is larger the greater the substitution possibilities. Examples of substitution possibilities include planting corners of fields by hand (more labor), or adding fertilizer (more "other inputs"). Now note that higher land rent means that farmers will typically substitute away from land and toward other inputs, so the ratio of other inputs to land is higher closer to the market. The simplest possible arithmetical example produces smooth, convex functions for the bid rent and what will be referred to in the monocentric city model as the "capital to land ratio."

At this point, it is easy to make the model explicitly urban by moving forward to the Alonso (1964) model. Rather than assuming that farmers have to ship corn to a marketplace, assume that workers have to ship themselves to a workplace. Households care about utility rather than profit, and they are all identical, so their utility function is simply $U(L,X)$, where X is "other goods." The budget constraint is $W = RL + p_x X + td$: income or wages (W) is allocated to expenditures on land, other goods, and straight-line commuting cost. Again, the model produces a simple bid-rent function that implies that land rents are higher near the workplace. The function is "more curved", the greater are the substitution possibilities between land and other goods, and lot sizes will rise with distance to the workplace, while the consumption of other goods is higher relative to land consumption closer to the workplace. All of this can be shown graphically with standard indifference curve diagrams. I try to emphasize how much new information the model produces by the simple addition of one term to the budget constraint, td. This simple addition implies that land rents, lot sizes, and the consumption of other goods all are smooth curves, and that each of them varies depending on the values assumed for t and W.

The final step in the development of the classroom version of the monocentric city model is the transition from the Alonso to the Muth-Mills version of the model (actually an amalgamation of separate work by Muth (1969) and Mills (1972)). Rather than caring directly about land, consumers get utility from housing, which in turn is produced by combining land and capital. This addition implies that the price of housing, land rent, the consumption of other goods, and the capital to land ratio are all smooth downward-sloping functions of distance, while the consumption of housing is an upward-sloping function. Implicitly, population density is also a downward-sloping function of distance.

It is worth emphasizing that though the model predicts that the price of a unit of housing declines with distance, it is not actually clear how the overall value of housing changes. Since price declines with distance and the quantity of housing rises, the prediction for their product is ambiguous. Americans often expect that the value of housing is higher farther from the city center. Their intuition is actually based on an extension of the model: higher-income people may live farther from the city center. This observation sets the stage for the next logical step in the analysis, the comparative static predictions.

USING THE MONOCENTRIC CITY MODEL

Standard applications of the monocentric city model show how bid-rent functions change when commuting cost declines, income increases, or agricultural land rent changes. The analysis typically begins with the most straightforward of the changes, commuting cost. Emphasizing the importance of the prediction that agricultural land rent constrains city size challenges students' belief that urban sprawl cannot possibly be constrained by market forces. However, most instructors will want to spend by far the most time on the analysis of income. The basic model, somewhat surprisingly, produces an unambiguous prediction that higher income leads to a flatter bid-rent function, which in turn implies that higher-income households will live farther from the city center. Is this prediction realistic?

Students' reactions to the prediction that higher-income people live farther from the city often depends on where they are from. Students from New York and Chicago will be incredulous; those from small towns think the prediction is obvious. Astute students will ask about commuting *time*. A trivial extension of the model leads to the prediction that higher-income households will live closer to the city center if they value their time more than housing. Although useful, this prediction begs the question of why New York and Chicago are different from smaller American cities, why Europe is different from the US, and why the US today is different from the US of the early 1800s. LeRoy and Sonstelie (1983) argue that most transportation modes can be characterized by a high fixed cost at the time they are introduced, but a very low marginal cost of commuting an additional mile. Horsecars, streetcars, subways, rail, and automobiles all met this condition: if a streetcar cost 5 cents each way regardless of the distance traveled at a time when many workers earned only a dollar a day, then only comparatively wealthy people could afford the new transportation mode. But in time, as incomes rise, if everyone has the same preferences, we would expect to see an equilibrium re-established in which higher-income people live farther from the city center.

The discussion of income raises two very important points. First, it shows that income sorting does not necessarily have anything to do with zoning, school quality, racism, crime, or any of the other very real issues that many people believe are the underlying cause. If all households are identical in every conceivable way, they still will live in different locations if their incomes differ. Second, it points out the limitations of a static model. If high-income households move to distant locations, then jobs have an incentive to follow. If high-income households demand good schools and education is provided by local governments, then low-income households may want to move to distant locations to get better schools, and high-income suburbs may enact restrictive zoning provisions that keep them out if tax revenues depend on house values. The model implies that high-income households are likely to want to live near the city center, but past changes in transportation methods have made more distant locations more attractive, and this in turn leads to other changes that can prevent the expected long-run configuration from reasserting itself.

Many other sources of sorting can be analyzed using basic bid-rent functions, such as analyzing university towns as though they are monocentric cities. How do bid-rent functions differ depending on whether people walk, bike, or drive to campus? Where do single-earner households live compared with those with two earners? How does the presence of children affect a household's bid rent? Faculty tend to spend the day on campus several days per week, rarely more than five; even if students had the same income, the fact that they are more likely to want to travel back and forth to campus seven days per week tends to produce a steeper bid-rent function. The point to dispel is the widespread view that students live near campus because that is where the cheap housing is located. If wealthy people want to live near campus, they can afford to outbid the students because they are wealthy. Saying that the poor live in a location because the rich have left that neighborhood to them is the same as saying that the poor outbid the rich for the neighborhood; if the poor did *not* outbid the rich, they simply would not live in the city.

Finally, usefulness of bid-rent functions can be emphasized by showing that their basic insight carries through to the analysis of things that represent significant extensions of the monocentric city model. How do prices vary locally near a park, a toxic waste site, or along a beach? Once the framework is established, the bid-rent function is a very powerful tool.

URBAN POLICY ISSUES

The final section of the course provides the flexibility to cover a host of possible topics. Real estate, local public finance, labor economics, transportation, education, and international trade all have unique urban angles that make them fair game for an urban course. The term "urban policy issues" is a good description of this section of the course.

Many instructors begin this section with an analysis of urban housing markets. The filtering model is a simple way to introduce the notion of the unintended consequences of ambitious policies. It uses a simple supply-demand framework to show how markets for high and low quality housing are linked. After spending several weeks on the monocentric model, students find the reappearance of supply-demand diagrams to be something of a relief. A traditional analysis shows that subsidies for the construction of new homes have ripple effects leading to lower housing prices and higher housing qualities for lower-income households. The analysis can then be turned around to cover what may be the more relevant phenomenon now – severe building codes and other supply restrictions that add to the cost of new housing. The fact that such policies may raise the price of housing for low-income families and perhaps even increase the rate of homelessness illustrates unintended policy consequences: today's planning fads are tomorrow's social problems.

This point can be further emphasized through a discussion of such housing policies as old-style public housing, which can be contrasted with modern rent certificates and other demand-based policies that are meant to improve housing quality for lower-income households. Though the public housing projects of the 1940s and 1950s now have a horrible reputation, they arose out of a laudable goal of improving housing conditions for families who were often crowded into old, dilapidated housing that surprisingly frequently did not even have indoor plumbing. Large housing projects were meant to take advantage of economies of scale in housing construction to provide affordable housing for very low-income households. The projects were usually well served by public transportation, and playgrounds and even schools were built to serve the new construction. A filtering model can be used to show that directly building new housing for low-income households can lower prices for other households also. In other words, the problem was not necessarily the objectives or even the design of public housing; it was the execution. Insufficient funds were set aside for maintenance, and the spatial concentration of poverty came to be viewed as spawning a "culture of poverty." Moreover, if the long-run supply of housing is perfectly elastic, public housing ultimately simply replaces private sector housing one-for-one. These consequences now seem obvious; in the 1950s, policy makers simply wanted to do something that would help to improve conditions for low-income households.

Modern housing policies are more apt to be demand-based. Simple indifference curve diagrams establish that rent certificates provide households with sufficient flexibility to allow households to increase their utility and increase their housing consumption. To combat the spatial concentration of poverty, current planning fads encourage the dispersal of low-income households throughout both the city and suburbs. Many cities have adopted policies that require a certain portion of all new construction to be set aside for lower-income households. These policies provide access to suburban employment opportunities and the amenities of high-income residential locations. However, they also may have pitfalls. Demand-based policies may simply enrich property owners. Developers may build low-quality units to meet their quota of low-income units. However, if the insight of the monocentric city model is correct, then private markets will tend to produce sorting by income even if the rich are in no way prejudiced against the poor; if so, how can a mixing of high- and low-income households be maintained over time? Elaborate rules must be written to ensure that the low-income units are not converted. An important role of the instructor is to encourage students to identify potential problems with current policy proposals and to think about how the policies might be improved.

Environmental issues can also be introduced in the section on housing policy. It is straightforward to expand the basic monocentric model to include an industrial sector that generates pollution. This analysis is useful partly in demonstrating that upward-sloping bid-rent functions are consistent with a monocentric model: households may pay a premium to be farther from the pollution source. One solution to the problem is to impose a tax on the industry or to subsidize households. A second-best solution may involve zoning. By confining the industrial sector to a smaller area, bid-rent functions shift up for industry and shift down for households. Thus, zoning creates a discontinuity between the industrial and residential bid-rent functions – an important point to make for the monocentric model. The same reasoning applies if the sectors are relabeled as two household types, where group A is for some reason prejudiced against group B. Students quickly realize that while they may advocate taxing polluting firms, they would not advocate taxing residential group B, yet the two models are potentially formally identical.

Though these models were developed to analyze racial prejudice and discrimination, some instructors may prefer not to talk directly about race given the racial mix of students in the classroom. However, one method for discussing models of discrimination and prejudice is to return to an example of a monocentric city, a university town. Students do not appear to be offended by an assumption that professors do not like to live near students, and many university towns have quite restrictive zoning regulations that effectively confine students to an area near campus. Pointing out that professor prejudice leads to lower rents for students, while restrictive zoning benefits professors at the expense of students is a useful and relevant metaphor.

It is useful to bear in mind two meanings of the word "positive" when teaching undergraduate courses. First, students do not expect instructors to be highly critical of assigned material. It is best to assign readings you *like* and demonstrate your enthusiasm for the topic, and it is a good idea to point out the good side of any policy even as you point out potential problems. At the same time, positive economics necessarily involves critical thinking. Pointing out benefits is not the same thing as advocating a policy, and it is not inconsistent to support a policy while recognizing that it has costs.

TEACHING TECHNIQUES

Large enrollments at the University of Illinois have forced me to adopt a lecture format for my classes, with two midterm exams, several quizzes, and a final exam. Nevertheless, I try to encourage discussion whenever possible. Standard examples of urban areas that reap the benefits of agglomeration are Silicon Valley in California and the Research Triangle in North Carolina. Can you think of other examples?

Most instructors develop a similar stock of stories to illustrate important concepts in their courses. For example, Chicago owes its rapid growth to its location at the link between the Great Lakes water system and the Mississippi River system, which in turn resulted in its establishment as the rail center of the country. To illustrate the effects of growth control boundaries, I tell the story of a developer in Oregon who managed to get land annexed to Eugene by cutting down trees; to prevent him from cutting down more trees, the city annexed the land, but then it was no longer possible to prevent him from building on the land once it was part of the city.

In order to engage students more with the material, I ask students to perform a number of tasks. I sometimes ask students to describe the economic base of a city of their choice using data from County Business Patterns. Alternatively, students have gathered data on city populations in a region to test the rank-size rule. For more advanced classes, students estimate population density functions using data provided in spreadsheet form. Though I seldom assign full research papers, I use books like Cronon (1991) or Warner (1978) as the basis for a common assignment asking students to contemplate the following: How does *Nature's Metropolis* support the predictions of central place theory? Does the process of suburbanization in Boston that is described in *Streetcar Suburbs* match the predictions of the monocentric city model? I also use articles in magazines or newspapers that are examples of both good and bad economic analysis of issues relating to cities. For example, some have argued that the current system of keeping sales tax revenue in the community where the sale takes place leads to excessive competition for retail establishments; would the recent proposal to distribute sales tax revenue on the basis of population produce a more efficient outcome? Would school quality improve if the heavy reliance on local property tax funding were replaced by state support?

CONCLUSION

Urban economics first came to be viewed as a field of economics in the 1960s. The field grew rapidly as researchers such as Edwin Mills and Richard Muth developed the monocentric city model. Though their work was largely theoretical, it was motivated by the important policy issues of the day and was always accompanied by empirical testing. Recent advances in economic geography have followed a similar pattern. They were motivated in part by concerns that economic growth was concentrated in large cities and highly developed countries. New economic geography models have been developed to explain why spatial inequalities in income can persist for decades, and these models have been the subject of many empirical tests, which in turn have led to modifications of the theories. This interaction between theory and empirical modeling has always been at the heart of urban economics.

The distinguishing feature of urban economics is space. Still more generally, urban economics encompasses anything of interest to urban dwellers. Despite long commutes and the high cost of housing, cities continue to attract new migrants and they continue to account for an increasing share of employment throughout the world. One reason for the popularity of urban economics courses is that cities are important. Another reason is simply that cities are fascinating, and virtually any important economic issue affects urban areas and often takes on a different light when viewed from a spatial perspective. The attention paid to problems that are sometimes viewed as being concentrated in cities – poverty, unemployment, poor housing, crime, etc. – leads some students to enter an urban economics course with negative preconceptions of cities. By end of the course, students realize, first, that many of their preconceptions were wrong, and second, that cities are a vital and dynamic source of economic growth.

REFERENCES

Alonso, W. (1964), *Location and Land Use*, Cambridge, MA: Harvard University Press.
Cronon, W. (1991), *Nature's Metropolis: Chicago and the Great West*, New York: W.W. Norton & Company.
LeRoy, S. F. and J. Sonstelie (1983), "Paradise lost and regained: Transportation innovation, income, and residential location", *Journal of Urban Economics*, **13** (1), 67–89.
Mills, E. (1972), *Studies in the Structure of the Urban Economy*, Baltimore, MD: Johns Hopkins University Press.
Muth, R. (1969), *Cities and Housing*, Chicago, IL: University of Chicago Press.
Redfearn, C. L. (2009), "Persistence in urban form: The long-run durability of employment centers in metropolitan areas", *Regional Science and Urban Economics*, **39** (2), 224–32.
Ricardo, D. (1817), *Principles of Political Economy and Taxation*, London: John Murray.
Von Thünen, J. (1826), *The Isolated State*, Oxford: Pergamon.
Warner, Sam Bass (1978), *Streetcar Suburbs: The Process of Growth in Boston, 1870–1900*, 2nd edition, Cambridge, MA: Harvard University Press.

66 Women and men in the economy
Francine D. Blau and Anne E. Winkler

This chapter is about teaching a course on gender from an economics perspective. Such a course may have a variety of names in different institutions – Women in the Economy; Women in the Labor Market; Economics of Gender; and Work, Families and Public Policy – to name a few. We have both taught courses in this area for many years and to varying audiences – undergraduate economics majors, students from women's and gender studies, and students from a wide variety of other majors. How we teach the course has evolved over time, as the key topics of the day have changed. For instance, women used to attend college at lower rates than men but have been attending at higher rates since the 1980s; women's labor force participation rose consistently from the 1940s to 1990s, but has since plateaued; changes in technology and other factors have impacted the wage structure, leading to a widening earnings gap between less-skilled workers (both women and men) and their higher-skilled counterparts. And, looking at the family, a rising fraction of children are living in households without both biological (or adoptive) parents present – many with a single parent (typically the mother), but others with cohabiting parents, a grandparent, or other relatives. Even in married-two parent families, many more of these households are blended as parents divorce and remarry.[1] Indeed, the very notion of the family is changing; a survey conducted in 2010 finds that two-thirds of Americans define same-sex couples with children as a family, a considerable increase since 2003 (Powell et al., 2010).

This chapter also reflects the knowledge we and our close collaborator, Marianne Ferber, have gained from working on our textbook, *The Economics of Women, Men, and Work* (2010).[2] The text has encouraged us to think more deeply about how we organize the course content – the order of the topics and the emphasis placed on each – as well as how most effectively to capture the interests of a changing and diverse set of students. Each new edition reflects insights from our day-to-day teaching experience. At the same time, we find ourselves editing and rethinking our course materials after completing work on each new edition.

One goal of a course in gender is to give greater attention to women and issues of particular concern to them than is generally found in other courses, even today. But also, by its very nature, this is also a course about men. For one, assessing the status and well-being of women involves comparing their experiences and outcomes with those of men. For another, gender roles and changes in them affect both sexes. And, we have indeed seen changes in gender roles for both groups. While, as we noted, female participation rates plateaued in the 1990s, they stand at much higher levels than prevailed in the past and the gender gap in participation rates has been greatly reduced. Moreover, women are increasingly entering formerly male-dominated fields of employment, though more remains to be accomplished, particularly in the entry of women into STEM fields (in other words, science, technology, engineering and mathematics) and blue-collar occupations, and the entry of men into traditionally female occupations (Blau, Brummund and

Liu, 2010). At the same time, men are spending more time with their children, including time in routine activities such as feeding and bathing them (Bianchi, Robinson and Milkie, 2006). Nevertheless, a substantial gender gap in time spent in housework and child care remains, with women still spending nearly twice as much time performing these tasks. So, there has been some movement towards women and men holding more similar roles in the labor market and household, but inequality remains along both dimensions.

PHILOSOPHY

We both share a commitment to gender equity, by which we mean that people, regardless of whether they are female or male, should have the opportunity to reach their full potential, unconstrained by traditional gender roles. However, it is not necessary for students to share this commitment or come to subscribe to any particular point of view to benefit from the course. Basically, the course provides students with the information and tools to make their own decisions about important issues related to gender, work, and family. The course content also conveys the point that gender issues and women's well-being matter not just to women themselves but to men and to society in general. Lack of employment and opportunity for women means that a potentially valuable resource is not being put to its best use. In fact, for developing countries, women's economic status is arguably a key to economic development and growth. This point is underscored by the Millennium Development Goals set forth by the United Nations in 2000, one of which is to "promote gender equality and empower women."[3]

In teaching the course, we want students to come away with an ability to think critically. Again, our objective is not to indoctrinate them with any particular set of opinions, but rather to help them form their own judgments in a rational fashion, weighing the various inputs critically. Further, we believe that the course content is greatly enhanced when placed in broader perspective, whether by examining historical trends, drawing on international comparisons, or by pointing to important differences by race and ethnicity, and educational attainment.

A historical perspective, for instance, offers students a way to put the current situation in context and understand the relevant set of factors impacting the status of women and how they have changed over time. In the case of women's labor force participation, the rate increased from just 28 percent in 1940 to nearly 60 percent by 1990 (and has remained about the same since; see Blau, Ferber, and Winkler, 2010, chapter 4). A number of broad factors contributed to these trends: economic (the rise in the demand for clerical workers, rising wages for women in the labor market), institutional (the decline of marriage bars which previously prohibited the employment of married women in clerical work and teaching), social (changing norms), and government policy (the passage of Title VII of the Civil Rights Act).[4] These same broad factors continue to be relevant, although the specifics differ.

International comparisons are also invaluable. To what extent is the experience in the United States similar to that in other countries or relatively unique, and why? On the one hand, many of the trends we see in the United States, for example, women's rising labor force participation, are also occurring in other countries, to a greater or lesser extent. In such cases, what is happening in the United States is likely part of broader trends such as the increased educational attainment of women and the shift in industrial structure from manufacturing to services and an information-based economy. On the other hand, trends in fertility differ greatly across the globe. While fertility rates have remained at around the replacement level in the United States since the late 1980s, they have fallen drastically in most other economically advanced countries. And, despite large decreases in fertility in much of the developing world, rates remain high in Sub-Saharan Africa, though they have declined modestly (Blau, Ferber, and Winkler, 2010, chapter 12). This variation again points to the role that economic, social, institutional, and government factors play in influencing observed trends.

By studying women's situation in developing countries, in particular, students learn about the tremendous challenges women in many of these countries face – from having to carry fuel and water for long distances, to disparities in education and lack of property rights, to countries where there is a strong preference for boys over girls, placing the very survival of girls in jeopardy.

Finally, although aggregate statistics such as female labor force participation rates for the whole population or the overall gender pay gap provide valuable information, they mask the vastly different experiences of subgroups – single and married mothers, US-born women and immigrants, African-Americans and whites, and persons of Hispanic and non-Hispanic origin, for example. Consider the labor force participation rate of women, a statistic highlighted earlier. This figure masks the fact that labor force participation was historically considerably higher for immigrant and minority women than for native-born white women. In fact, it was not until the *1980s* that white women's labor force participation rates caught up with black women's (Blau, Ferber and Winkler, 2010, chapter 4). And, today, immigrant women have *lower* participation rates than native-born women (Blau, Kahn, and Papps, 2011). Apart from race and ethnicity, another divide in our society – and one that is growing – is the divide by level of educational attainment. Women's labor force participation has increased most for those with a college education; similarly, since 1980, divorce rates have declined most for this education group (Stevenson and Isen, 2010). On the other end of the spectrum, those with the least education are experiencing the greatest labor market difficulties, largely due to the decline in demand for less-skilled labor. At the same time, their rates of female headship have risen (and marriage rates have fallen) dramatically, making less educated women increasingly dependent on their own resources.

GOALS AND OBJECTIVES

First and foremost, the purpose of this course is to promote student understanding of and knowledge about women and men in the labor market and the household. As noted previously, the course serves to broaden students' horizons as they learn about the historical evolution of the current situation, and the status of women in countries very different from the United States. The course also provides an opportunity to acquaint students with many relevant policy issues, including some that are under active consideration. Although it may be helpful to draw from other disciplines from time to time, in our opinion, such a course should emphasize the contribution of economic analysis.

This leads to a second objective of the course which is to demonstrate that the principles of economics can be applied to a broad set of topics. In so doing, students have the opportunity to further develop their understanding of these concepts and their analytical ability more generally.

In fact, this course has the potential to particularly engage students and perhaps even generate future majors, especially among women who remain underrepresented in economics, as students learn to apply these tools to a myriad of decisions and issues that directly affect *them*. For instance, "Is it worth going to college?" The economic evidence provides an overwhelming "yes!" (for example, Barrow and Rouse, 2005). Or, as another example, opportunity cost becomes a more meaningful concept as students think about what they give up in attending college (tuition and book costs, foregone earnings) and further realize it is crucial in explaining a number of other important decisions, from labor force participation to marriage and childbearing.

Or consider the impact of a change in relative prices on decision making. Students may gain a deeper understanding of this concept as they consider the effect of a decrease in the price of market substitutes for work performed in the home, such as the price of purchased child care, on women's labor force participation. To reason this through, they must think about the underlying determinants of this decision, the market wage (W) and the reservation wage (W^*) and the factors that underlie each.

As another example, consider comparative advantage. In a standard principles course, this concept is taught in an international setting (for example, two countries, France and the United States, and two goods, wine and corn). Which country has a comparative advantage in the production of each good? In the course at hand, the instructor can demonstrate how this concept might be applied to understanding how time is allocated between household members, following the influential work of Becker (1991). He shows that the family can maximize its well-being through specialization of labor in the household according to comparative advantage and exchange. Again, not only does this example reinforce the concept previously learned in the principles course, but students can potentially relate it to their own household situation. They can also understand how the division of labor within the family has changed as men's and women's comparative advantage has changed over time. Finally, consider the concept of marginal thinking. This concept is reinforced as students think about the reward (return) for an extra hour of market work or time spent in home production.

Returning to an earlier point, a third goal of a course on gender is to help students learn to think critically, often with the assistance of economic concepts. Nowhere is this more evident than when analyzing policies. Consider a parental leave policy which guarantees return to the same position or its equivalent. What is the theoretical impact of a leave policy on length of leave taken, women's earnings, female labor force participation, employers' willingness to hire women, etc.? How does the policy's impact differ depending on the length of the leave or whether the leave is paid or unpaid? Students learn that policies, even those they favor, have pros and cons, costs and benefits. Further, researchers investigating the same topic do not always reach the same conclusion. This raises useful discussions about data and research methods. Questions for students might include the following: What would be the ideal research design to understand the impact of this policy? How convincing is the evidence to date? What would be the most desirable form of such a policy?

This brings us to a fourth objective of the course, which is to enhance students' understanding of the challenges of analyzing data and drawing conclusions. For one, there is the critical distinction between correlation and causation. For instance, women's education is positively correlated with their labor force participation. Is this because education *causes* an increase in their productivity and earnings, raising the opportunity cost of remaining out of the labor force, or is it that women who always intended to participate in the labor market choose to invest more in their education? Or is it a combination of both? The course content also points to the importance of alternative/multiple research methods. Consider the "unexplained" part of the gender wage gap which is potentially a measure of discrimination, but may also reflect the impact of unmeasured factors. When using regression methods, there is the issue of what measured variables are available in a given data set, and also whether to treat variables such as occupation as exogenous (in that case, including them as controls in the regression) or as a possible result of discriminatory processes (in that case, not including them). A useful discussion is how the size of the gap changes as measured human capital variables are controlled for, though even when numerous variables are included, a gap remains (Blau, Ferber and Winkler, 2010, chapter 7).

Notably, alternative empirical methods also provide evidence of discrimination, lending further support. Audit studies, in which matched pairs (individuals with the same or similar credentials) are sent out to look for jobs in the same firm, are especially useful to discuss because they make explicit what researchers mean by "controlling for productivity," especially for students without a background in regression analysis. In one such study (Neumark, Bank and van Nort, 1996), equally qualified women and men applied for positions as servers in restaurants in Philadelphia. The researchers found that, in high-end restaurants, equally qualified women had significantly lower probabilities of getting an interview, and conditional on getting an interview, being offered a server position as compared with their male counterparts. A similar approach has been taken in lab experiments. One such study (Correll, Benard and Paik, 2007) asked individuals to evaluate application forms of women with the same credentials, with one important exception: some were mothers (which could be inferred by information on the application such as PTA coordinator) and others were not. They find that mothers were perceived less favorably than non-mothers, evidence of a motherhood penalty. In contrast, when the experiment was changed to analyze perceptions about fathers versus non-fathers, the results indicate that fathers bore no penalty and even benefitted in some cases.

Finally, an added bonus of the course is that it provides an opportunity for students to learn data and numeracy skills: how to find and interpret government data, and concepts such as nominal versus real (inflation-adjusted) earnings and net present value. For instance, by examining Census Bureau data,[5] students get a first-hand look at trends in inflation-adjusted earnings for women and men. Further, for more technically inclined students, the course provides a vehicle to learn how to calculate the net present value of college. Students can obtain earnings data stratified by age and education from the Census Bureau, collect information on tuition and fees from their institution's website (the explicit cost of going to college), and then calculate the present value of this decision using a spreadsheet such as Excel. Changes in assumptions (the discount rate, expected time in the labor market, whether the student is male or female) reinforce learning about the factors that affect the decision to attend college.

ORGANIZATION AND CONTENT

Courses in gender cover a fairly standard set of topics, though the emphasis and the organization of topics may vary depending on the instructor's interests and the objectives of the specific course. A secondary consideration, within each topic area, is whether to present evidence first and then theory, or vice versa. In our experience, both are effective methods, although students often benefit from seeing evidence (data) first. This leads them to wonder "why?" and seizes their attention.

Topic-wise, a unique contribution of this course is the focus on the household as a production unit (a small factory) and the subsequent analysis of the allocation of time of household members between paid work and home production. Many students have not previously thought of the quantity and value of goods produced in the home, nor thought analytically about how time is spent. As in the case of traditional labor courses, other topics include labor supply (both the participation decision and hours worked) and the decision to acquire human capital. What differentiates this course is the emphasis on differences by gender, and often by race and ethnicity as well. Also, the gender pay gap receives considerable attention: how much is due to differences in human capital and how much is due to labor market discrimination? As we have seen, this topic provides an opportunity to discuss data, methods, and theories about how such differences are generated. The application of economic analysis to the family (marriage, cohabitation – same and opposite sex, divorce, childbearing) is also unique to this course.

Such courses also generally emphasize policy. What role can and should government play in leveling the employment "playing field" so that women and minorities have the same opportunities as white males? What policies are available or might be developed to help individuals balance paid work and family? Addressing poverty is also an important topic given that female-headed families, especially those with minority heads, face the highest rates.

As noted previously, another core component of the course is to draw on international comparisons and discuss solutions to pressing global problems, including child labor, disparities in educational attainment by gender, and distorted sex ratios in some countries. Instructors might either reserve these discussions for the latter part of the course or draw in international comparisons and discussions as each specific topic, for example, labor force participation, the gender pay gap, etc., is covered.

CHALLENGES

Teaching this course poses some challenges that are, to some extent, unique. To start with, an initial misconception among some students, notably those that end up in the course because it fulfills a requirement or because of its time slot, is that the course material is not "real" economics. There are a number of ways to dispel this notion. Consider Gross Domestic Product (GDP), which measures the value of goods and services produced within a country. Researchers in the United States and elsewhere are re-evaluating the adequacy of this concept as a measure of economic well-being (for the United States, see Abraham and Mackie, 2005). One frequent criticism is that GDP does not include non-market production (for example, child care produced at home). One important consequence of this omission is that a country's growth in GDP will be overstated if women reduce home production as they work more in the labor market, as has been the case in the United States. This example points to that fact that just because work is unpaid, this does not mean it is not valuable nor relevant from an economic standpoint.

Another way to highlight the relevance of the course to the field of economics is to point to scholars doing research on gender-related topics who have received the Nobel Prize in Economics (officially known as The Nobel Memorial Prize in Economic Sciences). For instance, Gary Becker received the Nobel Prize in 1992. His contributions run throughout the gamut of course topics: human capital theory, economics of discrimination, theory of time allocation, and the economic model of marriage, divorce, and fertility (see Becker, 1971, 1991, and 1993). As another example, in 1998 Amartya Sen received the Nobel Prize, in part for his contribution to identifying and explaining the high ratios of males to females – what he termed "missing women" – in East Asian countries such as India and China (see Sen, 1990).

Finally, students might be surprised to learn that the course topics are regularly discussed in the *Wall Street Journal*, among other business periodicals. As just one example, Sue Shellenbarger is the creator/writer of the "Work & Family" column for the *Wall Street Journal,* a column which began in 1991. Indeed, her column shows that issues of work and family cross gender, age, income, and education lines.

A second broad challenge, though not unique to this course, is that some topics tend to be difficult for students to master and require extra attention. One such topic is comparative advantage. We find that it is useful to step back and first review opportunity cost. A numerical example is also very helpful. For instance, suppose that in an hour, Dave can produce $10 worth of market goods (M) or $5 worth of home goods ($H$), while in the same time, Diane can produce $15 worth of M or $15 worth of H. In this case, for Dave, the opportunity cost of $1 worth of M is $0.5H$ (since the two goods exchange at a rate of $10 of M for $5 of H). For Diane, the opportunity cost of $1 worth of M is $1H$. Since Dave's opportunity cost of $1M$ is lower ($0.5H < $1H$), he has the comparative advantage in M production. This is a particularly helpful example for students because it shows that even when one of the members of a couple (Diane) has an absolute advantage in both M and H production, the principle of comparative advantage still implies that she should specialize to some extent.

A second difficult but important concept is marginal versus average; it is the marginal tax rate that affects the decision to work (the tax rate applied to the last hour worked), not the average rate. Students can better understand this concept when they are given an amount of taxable income, a tax rate schedule, and an assumed filing unit (for example, single or married) and are asked to calculate tax liability.

A third broad challenge in teaching the course is that the needs and interests, as well as the preparation of the "audience", may differ greatly across universities and programs. Moreover, a given class may be relatively homogeneous in students' background and interests, or may include a mix. An audience of largely economics majors might be expected to master all the relevant technical skills, including indifference curve analysis and the calculation of net present value. Depending on the instructors' preferences and the interests of the students, the emphasis on technical details may be reduced for non-majors, while the broad concepts are emphasized. For instance, take the labor force decision (if $W > W^*$ then participate). In lieu of the more formal indifference curve analysis, students can focus on the intuition behind the decision to participate: factors such as education underlie W, while factors such as spouses' income, presence of small children, and availability of market substitutes for household time underlie W^*.

A fourth broad challenge in teaching the course is addressing misconceptions that students bring to the classroom. As one example, some students may believe that the female-male pay gap calculated directly from Census Bureau data is fully the result of labor market discrimination. One way to disabuse them of this notion is to actually visit the Census website and show students that the underlying data are based on information collected for *all* full-time, full-year workers, regardless of their age, educational attainment, etc. This does not mean the measure is incorrect or that it is not useful for some purposes; it just needs to be interpreted appropriately. As a second example, some students may believe that affirmative action policies are equivalent to "quotas." The class provides an opportunity to explain that affirmative action is a series of proactive measures that include policies such as casting a wider net in job searches by placing ads in a wider range of media, etc. Indeed, actual quotas are rare in the labor market. Also, this provides a useful opportunity to examine research on the effect of affirmative action policies.

A fifth broad challenge is to teach students that while models are helpful tools in understanding the world around us, they have limitations. Again, take the neoclassical model of comparative advantage discussed above. A number of economists, including our co-author Marianne Ferber, have made useful observations in this regard (see Ferber and Birnbaum, 1977). She points out, for example, that comparative advantage likely varies over the lifecycle, but the model does not take this into account: One would expect women's comparative advantage in home production to be greater when young children are present than when they have grown up and left home. Thus, while wives' specialization in home production may maximize family well-being in the short run, this allocation of time may not be advantageous to the wife or to her family in the long-run. Another critique is that complete specialization poses particular risks for full-time homemakers, most notably in the event the relationship ends. In such a case, a homemaker may have market skills that have substantially depreciated or become obsolete.

While these criticisms have validity, the neoclassical model still provides a useful paradigm for making predictions regarding the allocation of time. Moreover, it is consistent with observed patterns. As women's earnings have increased due to their rising educational attainment and other factors, the difference in comparative advantage for wives and husbands in the household and the market has narrowed. This is consistent with women's increased labor force participation and reduction in time spent in household production.

SUGGESTED ASSIGNMENTS AND LEARNING TOOLS

A number of assignments and learning tools can enhance and extend student learning.

Discussion questions   Whether provided in the relevant textbook or created by the instructor, these help to ensure understanding of key concepts. For instance, when discussing the determinants of women's labor force participation, students might be asked to discuss how government provision of child care subsidies would affect this decision.

Data assignments   Students are asked to collect specific data from government websites such as the Bureau of Labor Statistics or the Census Bureau.[6] Such assignments enhance numeracy skills and interpretation. For instance, students might be asked to go to the Census Bureau website, find data on median earnings of female and male full-time, year-round workers, and calculate the gender earnings ratio for selected years.

Newspaper articles   Students are asked to collect articles on course-related topics and then briefly summarize and comment. This assignment offers students a chance to stay abreast of current topics and reinforces the relevance of the course content.

Short paper on a course-related topic   This provides an opportunity to demonstrate critical thinking skills on a topic not covered in class, add an enhanced international perspective, or explore additional paradigms.

Class presentations   These offer students an opportunity to learn from each other. Peer evaluations further encourage students to stay engaged.

CONCLUSION

The field of the economics of gender is ever-changing. Women and men's gender roles are shifting, albeit more slowly when it comes to housework and the most male-dominated occupations. New theories are proposed, research methods develop, and additional empirical evidence is obtained on important questions. Sometimes conclusions are reinforced; in other cases they change. Always questions remain, and more research needs to be done. In the policy arena, policies are adjusted, adopted, or abandoned with changes in the economic, political and social landscape. In teaching this course, the challenge, but also the reward, is that there is always something new to be learned by both the instructor and students.

NOTES

1. For details on these and other recent trends, as well as explanations for them, see Blau, Ferber, and Winkler (2010).
2. Other textbooks in this area include Jacobsen (2007) and Hoffman and Averett (2010).
3. Countries are to meet this goal by accomplishing several targets: increasing the ratio of girls to boys at all levels of education, increasing the share of the female labor force in the non-agricultural sector, and increasing women's share of parliamentary seats (United Nations, 2007), http://www.un.org/millennium-goals (accessed 23 May 2011).
4. For a very useful reference, see Goldin (1990).
5. www.census.gov (accessed 23 May 2011).
6. See www.bls.gov and www.census.gov, respectively (accessed 23 May 2011).

REFERENCES

Abraham, K. G. and C. Mackie (eds) (2005), *Beyond the Market: Designing Nonmarket Accounts for the United States*, Washington, DC: National Research Council.

Barrow, L. and C. E. Rouse (2005), "Does college still pay?", *The Economists' Voice*, **2** (4), Article 3.

Becker, G. S. (1971), *The Economics of Discrimination* (2nd ed.), Chicago: University of Chicago Press.

Becker, G. S. (1991), *A Treatise on the Family* (enlarged edition), Cambridge, MA: Harvard University Press.

Becker, G. S. (1993), *Human Capital: A Theoretical and Empirical Analysis, with Special Reference to Education* (3rd ed.), Chicago: University of Chicago Press.

Bianchi, S. M., J. P. Robinson and M. A. Milkie (2006), *Changing Rhythms of American Family Life*, New York: Russell Sage Foundation.

Blau, F. D., P. Brummund and A. Y. Liu (2010), "Trends in occupational segregation by gender 1980–2007: Adjusting for the impact of changes in the occupational coding system", unpublished paper, Cornell University, November.

Blau, F. D., M. A. Ferber and A. E. Winkler (2010), *The Economics of Women, Men, and Work* (6th ed.), Upper Saddle River, NJ: Pearson/Prentice Hall.

Blau, F. D., L. M. Kahn and K. L. Papps (2011), "Gender, source country characteristics, and labor market assimilation among immigrants", *Review of Economics and Statistics*, **93** (1), 43–58.

Correll, S. J., S. Benard and I. Paik (2007), "Getting a job: Is there a motherhood penalty?", *American Journal of Sociology*, **112**, 1297–338.

Ferber, M. A. and B. G. Birnbaum (1977), "The new home economics: Retrospect and prospects", *Journal of Consumer Research*, **4** (4), 19–28.

Goldin, C. (1990), *Understanding the Gender Gap: An Economic History of American Women*, Oxford: Oxford University Press.

Hoffman, S. D. and S. L. Averett (2010), *Women and the Economy: Family, Work, and Pay* (2nd ed.), Upper Saddle River, NJ: Prentice Hall.

Jacobsen, J. P. (2007), *Economics of Gender* (3rd ed.), Malden, MA: Blackwell.

Neumark, D., R. J. Bank and K. D. van Nort (1996), "Sex discrimination in hiring in the restaurant industry: An audit study", *Quarterly Journal of Economics*, **111** (3), 915–41.

Powell, B., C. Bolzendahl, C. Geist and L. C. Steelman (2010), *Counted Out: Same-Sex Relations and Americans' Definitions of Family*, New York: Russell Sage Foundation.

Sen, A. (1990), "More than 100 million women are missing", *The New York Review of Books*, **37** (20), 61–6.

Stevensen, B. and A. Isen (2010), "Women's education and family behavior: Trends in marriage, divorce and fertility", in J. Shoven (ed.) *Demography and the Economy*, Chicago: University of Chicago Press, pp. 107–40.

United Nations (2007), *The Millennium Development Goals Report 2007*, New York: UN.

PART V

INSTITUTIONAL/
ADMINISTRATIVE

Section A

Faculty Development: Mentoring, Evaluation, Documentation and Resources

67 Faculty development: mentoring, evaluation, documentation and resources

Rae Jean B. Goodman

Faculty development is one response by academic institutions to the increasing pressures of financial constraints, accountability for student learning, and highly mobile faculty. In the broadest conceptualization, faculty development focuses on the faculty member as a teacher, a scholar and a person. It includes opportunities for consultation on teaching techniques, class organization, student evaluation, student advising, career planning, grant writing, research support, committee work, wellness management, stress and time management, interpersonal skills, and numerous other topics relating to an academic career. Thus, faculty development programs can support new faculty and assist their transition into successful members of their institutions and disciplinary communities.

Graduate programs, in general, do not prepare new faculty for the life of a professor (Colander and McGoldrick, 2009; Felder, Brent and Prince, 2011). The degree to which new faculty have been exposed to academic politics, publishing strategies, grant-seeking techniques, and teaching varies widely, and faculty must learn how these apply at their own institutions. Not surprisingly, faculty success depends on performance in the realms of teaching, research, service, *and* knowing how to acquire and present convincing evidence of such outcomes. Thus, development programs can nurture faculty in their evolution as specialists in a discipline, experts in a subfield, and as contributing members of their institution.

To provide context for development programs, this chapter begins with an overview of research describing life as a new faculty member and characteristics of success. The importance of mentorship is then described, including alternative mentoring program structures, the characteristics of good mentors, and advice for developing a mentoring program. Specific mentoring programs supported by the American Economics Association are then described. Because faculty evaluation is such a critical component of faculty development, the portfolio concept is presented as a mechanism for self-reflection and evaluation of teaching and research and as a method to attain success in the promotion process. Information on faculty development opportunities outside of the institution are described in the final section, which includes economic-specific teaching resources.

THE NEW FACULTY MEMBER

Boice (1992a, pp. 111–14) offers research-based findings on the common characteristics of the typical new faculty member and contrasts those of the "quick starters." New faculty – those in their first three to four years at an academic institution – spend less time on scholarly writing than would be needed for successfully meeting promotion and tenure requirements; spend too much time preparing for teaching (typically spending approximately 30 hours a week in class preparation); equate teaching with content presentation; use particular teaching techniques to avoid student complaints; receive student evaluation values below their expectations and blame external forces; and experience a lack of collegial interaction to the point of loneliness and isolation. In contrast, Boice defines quick starters as the 5–9 percent of new faculty, who, as a result of research output, appear to be on a trajectory to be successful in the promotion and tenure process and are in the top quartile of student, peer, and self-evaluations of teaching. Quick starters are proactive in getting involved with departmental and institutional communities; balance teaching preparation and scholarly writing; allocate an appropriate amount of time to prepare class notes, and create effective collegial social networks. Boice also finds that quick starters have a positive attitude toward students at their institution; teach at a relaxed pace that permits active learning strategies; actively elicit advice about teaching from colleagues; spend less than 1.5 hours per classroom hour in preparation by the third semester of teaching; spend three hours or more per week on scholarly and grant writing, and have a greater willingness to participate in campus support programs.

Based on his research, Boice (2000) describes a 'balanced program' to help more new faculty develop the same capabilities as the quick starters. In general terms, Boice's advice can be summarized as moderating effort on teaching, developing mindful ways of writing, and socializing with compassion. Specifically, Boice advocates that new faculty limit classroom preparation to two hours for each hour in the classroom; spend 30–60 minutes each day on scholarly writing, engage in teaching and research discussions with colleagues for at least two hours per week; keep a daily record of time spent on different activities; and integrate research into teaching. Boice also stresses the need to build an institutional support system, beginning with recruiting and orienting new faculty hires and extending through the tenure process.

The department chair is the primary source of leadership for the development of new faculty. Gmelch and Miskin (2004) describe supportive roles of a department chair as modeling, motivating, mentoring and networking. In most departments, a chair is not able to provide comprehensive support for all faculty and thus must turn to others within the department, supported by faculty developers, for new faculty support structures. For example, a department chair may create a mentoring program or a classroom visiting committee to aid faculty development. Boice (1992b) and Bensimon, Ward and Snyders (2000) argue that mentoring is a primary method to ensure that new faculty have support to become quick starters and build a positive relationship with their institution.

MENTORING

Mentoring relationships can generate enhancements at all stages of one's academic career. Because it is especially beneficial in the early stages, this discussion focuses on mentoring of junior faculty members entering academe as assistant professors. However, much of what is described applies to the mentoring of undergraduates, graduate students, or mid (and even late) career faculty. Mentorship is a collaborative relationship which, in academia, includes both mentoring of a faculty member and the mentoring a faculty member does with students. The mentoring of new faculty begins in graduate school as a primary mentor helps guide dissertation research. If the dissertation advisor relationship is productive and positive, new faculty should make every effort to maintain that relationship as they move to their first job. This relationship will help the new faculty member continue to grow and develop as a professional.

Once hired into a faculty position, a faculty member needs to establish new mentoring relationships. The department or institution may have an established mentoring system which can include one-on-one mentoring, self-selection of a mentor, or mentoring by a group of colleagues. While formal mentoring is an important key to success, new faculty need not limit him/herself to the mentor, or mentors, assigned. A variety of new faculty mentorship relationships, within and across departments, allows one to tap into specific areas of expertise such as teaching or research, or perspectives from mentors with different degrees of experience at the institution. The goal of mentoring is to help the protégé (or mentee) acquire and use the professional competencies and constructive relationships for continued career success, while maintaining a balance between work and life.

The benefits of good mentoring exist for the mentor, the protégé, and institution (Wunsch, 1994; Johnson, 2007; Bland et al., 2009). Benefits for the mentor include satisfaction in transmitting knowledge of research, teaching, and the institutional environment to the protégé; motivation and creativity enhancements from interacting with the protégé; networking opportunities working with the protégé; enhanced reputation from growing talented junior colleagues; and synergistic forming of friendships and mutually supportive interactions. Although benefits may result in extrinsic rewards, many mentors are motivated by intrinsic rewards associated with the success of their protégés.

For the protégé, a good mentoring relationship yields benefits that last their entire career. There is evidence that mentoring yields higher dividends in long-term relationships (Allen et al., 2004, p. 133). Faculty with good mentoring relationships report greater satisfaction with the institution, greater commitment to an academic career, and confidence about advancing in the discipline. In institutions where productivity is measured by funded research, the interaction of a protégé with a disciplinary expert helps them to learn the necessary skills to attract and maintain research funding. Many institutions encourage mentors to enhance teaching effectiveness. The ability to discuss teaching, alternative teaching techniques, and teaching scenarios with a seasoned professional results in increased confidence in education skills (Wingard, Garman and Reznik, 2004). A comprehensive relationship with a mentor helps with the socialization process into the profession and the culture of a specific institution through an explanation of unwritten rules and guidelines. In general, career advancement, as measured by promotions and compensation, is higher for individuals involved with good mentoring relationships (Allen et al., 2004).

For the institution, an established mentoring system can be very valuable. Faculty members engaged in a mentoring program are more productive, creative, satisfied and committed to the institution. Bland et al. (2005), in a study at the University of Minnesota, found that departments rated in the top 5 percent of their discipline had formal mentoring programs.

Mentoring is especially important for under-represented groups. Driscoll et al. (2009) describe the importance of mentoring for women in science. Male-dominated disciplines, such as economics, and the accompanying low number of senior female colleagues raises the issue of cross-sex mentorships. Johnson (2007, pp. 156–8) outlines the following difficulties in cross-sex mentorships: the competitive and hierarchical structure of the male mentorship model as opposed to the collegial and egalitarian structure desired by female protégés; and the inability of male mentors to effectively model an integration of professional and personal life; the unintentional assumption of stereotypical male-female roles, leading to dependency instead of the independence of the protégé; the potential problem of romantic or sexual attraction. Johnson (2007, pp. 159–61) makes the following recommendations for mentoring women: employ an egalitarian, collaborative approach; stress the development of a mentoring network and recognize the importance of integrating professional and personal life.

Characteristics of Good Mentors and Effective Mentoring Systems

Bensimon et al. (2000, pp. 115–16) describe effective mentors as willing participants in the process who are recognized as role models at the institution, exhibiting the research, teaching and service characteristics desired by the institution. Mentors must enjoy sharing knowledge and experience, be able to guide rather than direct the protégé, appreciate the variety of approaches of different protégés, and develop a relationship based on trust, understanding and empathy.

Bland et al. (2009, pp. 29–44) point out that effective mentoring systems must be grounded in clear and concisely stated goals and purposes. Because both mentors and protégés respond to incentives it is essential that the program be supported by the faculty, department and institution. If mentoring relationships are not valued beyond the participants, they are not likely to develop and become part of the fabric of the department or institution and fall short of their true potential. Research has demonstrated that mentoring programs need institutional support to be maintained (Bland, 2009, p. 43). Further, for mentoring to be effective, organizational structures must be provided including those which promote mentor-protégé dialogues, train faculty on mentoring techniques, and act as sounding boards for difficult situations.

Mentoring relationships can generate enhancements at all stages of one's academic career. Because it is especially beneficial in early stages, this discussion focuses on mentoring of junior faculty members entering academe as assistant professors. However, much of what is said applies to the mentoring of undergraduates, graduate students, or mid (and even late) career faculty.

Models of Mentoring

There is no "correct" mentoring model for a faculty member, department or institution. What follows is a description of three basic models, including associated benefits and limitations. It is important to recognize that, in practice, mentoring may take any one or some combination of these models.

The *traditional* mentoring model (Johnson, 2007, p. 29; Bland et al., 2009, p. 22) involves one mentor and one protégé, connected for a period of time in a developmental relationship. In academic settings, the mentor is typically a senior professor engaged in the career development of a junior faculty member. The advantages for the protégé are clear as the process can help transform the new professor into a quick starter. However, there is potential for exploitation of the protégé and a perpetuation of academic systems that are out of date (such as in the case of the "old boy network"). This model is also limited in that there may be an insufficient number of trained senior faculty members to mentor junior faculty; this is especially the case with respect to under-represented groups (women and minorities). In light of these potential limitations, some institutions have developed teams of senior mentors to provide a variety of viewpoints and meet a wider range of mentoring needs.

The advantage of a *team approach* to mentoring is that the faculty receives a variety of perspectives on teaching, research and the institution's culture and no individual is expected to have all the expertise (Sorcinelli and Yun, 2007). The team can be composed entirely of senior, full professors or include tenured faculty at the associate rank and may also include faculty from other disciplines. The advantage of including a faculty member from another discipline is that he or she provides a check and balance on the degree to which a department's views incorporate a broader view of the institution. Matthews (2003), de Janasz and Sullivan (2004), and Gray and Birch (2008) provide support for the multiple-mentors model. Matthews suggests that the expanding diversity of academic work supports the need for team mentoring. De Janasz and Sullivan argue that the multiple-mentor model is more consistent with the changing academic environment, one that promotes active learning and learning-center approaches to teaching as opposed to hierarchical models such as the traditional mentoring model. Gray and Birch's team model includes several protégés as well as mentors; this model builds collegiality among the protégés and provides opportunities for junior faculty to mentor each other. No disadvantages of the team mentoring model appear in the literature.

The *peer* mentoring model connects individuals who are essentially similar in experience and rank, although not necessarily from the same discipline. Peer mentoring may develop alongside formal mentoring programs as a result of young faculty interaction at research seminars, or teaching and learning workshops. One advantage of this peer approach is that peers are likely to be willing to share information and discuss professional issues more freely. Peers are usually at similar points in their personal lives and can share insights and information concerning the balance of work and family. A successful peer mentoring process for female scholars, reported in Driscoll et al. (2009, p. 18), results in increased confidence as scholars and members of the institution. Faculty participating in peer mentoring, comparing it to prior experience with the traditional two-person mentoring approach, reported that the traditional approach left them feeling isolated and inadequate. Despite potential gains, the peer mentoring model does have potential limitations. Competition among peers may develop based on research success, funding success, or integration into the institution's culture. Junior faculty peers also have less experience and provide more limited advice on research, teaching and institutional culture.

American Economic Association Mentoring Programs

The American Economic Association (AEA) established CSWEP in 1971 "to eliminate discrimination against women, and to redress the low representation of women in the economic profession."[1] The data on women in academic positions and their presence in tenured positions and senior professorial ranks led CSWEP to establish two formal mentoring programs. The first in 1998, Creating Career Opportunities for Female

Economists (CCOFFE), aimed at increasing the probability that women economists would earn tenure at academic institutions.[2] The sessions developed by CCOFFE focused on bringing senior and junior women together to work on research projects and gain skills in proposal writing, balancing professional and personal life, and publishing. The first CCOFFE workshop was held at the AEA annual meeting in 1998 with additional workshops at regional meetings in 1999.

The second program, CSWEP Mentoring Program (CeMENT), structured very similarly to CCOFFE, commenced in 2004, supported by a National Science Foundation grant and is currently funded by the AEA. The goal of the CeMENT program is to bring senior and junior female faculty together and provide initial mentoring at a workshop held at an economics conference. There are two prongs to the program: a workshop held at the annual AEA meeting aimed at female faculty at research-focused institutions and workshops held at regional economics meetings designed for female faculty at institutions where success combines research, teaching and service. At each workshop, teams of senior and junior faculty meet to have intense discussions of participants' research in progress, with the objective of improving the work as well as making suggestions regarding publishing strategies and the direction of future research. Additional sessions provide critical information on the publishing process, work-life balance, networking, grant strategies, teaching strategies, and the promotion and tenure process (Crosen and McGoldrick, 2007). The initial assessment of this mentoring program indicates that it is very successful (Blau et al., 2010).

The Committee on the Status of Minority Groups in the Economics Profession (CSMGEP) runs a Mentoring Program (formerly called the Pipeline Project) for minority graduate students.[3] The program pairs a student with a mentor who supports the student through several critical points: the transition from course work to dissertation research and then the transition to their post-graduate career. The mentors and protégés have an annual conference in the summer which builds additional networking and support. In addition, CSMGEP runs a program to train promising undergraduates for graduate school, and a program that provides opportunities for senior graduate students and junior faculty to spend a summer at a sponsoring research institution.

EVALUATION

Effective evaluation is a critical component of faculty career advancement. Braskamp (1980 and 2000) argues that evaluation should serve both formative and summative purposes. Formative evaluation gathers information to improve an individual's performance, typically relegated to teaching, whereas summative evaluation refers to collecting data for administrative decision-making (compensation and promotion). Effective use of evaluations requires that they are perceived as unbiased, valid and reliable and that faculty must use them and be good analysts and self-evaluators.

Because teaching is the most public component of a faculty member's job, and it is arguably the most difficult to evaluate, the remainder of this section focuses on this process. Elsewhere in this volume, DeLoach examines the use of student evaluations and the pitfalls of relying on them as the primary measure of teaching and learning excellence (as is currently the practice of most institutions). Thus, the emphasis of the current discussion of teaching evaluation will focus on broadening this evaluation process.

The literature on evaluating teaching effectiveness emphasizes the need for "triangularization" or multiple measures from different sources at multiple points in time (Cashin, 1990, 1995; Chism, 2007). Hoyt and Pallett (1999) outline a multidimensional approach to assessing teaching effectiveness that incorporates student ratings, colleague ratings, evaluation of indirect contributions of faculty, and department chair ratings. The status of the faculty member also enters into the evaluation process because first year faculty are adapting to a new institution, its students and its culture, and creating new courses; non-tenured faculty are preparing for the tenure and promotion process as well as annual salary reviews; tenured faculty may be preparing for a second promotion and decisions about teaching assignments are dependent on the assessment of teaching effectiveness. To document faculty instructional efforts, Hoyt and Pallet present a sample of a faculty annual report that includes course assignment information and instructional improvement activities. The course assignment section guides the instructor to document course context, objectives, instructional strategies, instructional materials and assessment of student achievement. The instructional improvement activities section documents classroom research, collaborative improvement efforts, attendance at teaching and learning workshops and conferences, and other improvement efforts. Hoyt and Pallet point out that teaching portfolios (described below) also provide a vehicle for collecting the breadth of information needed to meet the triangularization goal.

The development of an effective evaluation system requires significant forethought, planning and engagement of both faculty and administration. As with any type of assessment, the system must be meaningful, manageable and sustainable. Cashin (1996) summarizes the important principles for establishing an effective faculty evaluation system as: extensive engagement of participants at all levels of the institution; well-defined purposes of data collection and methods of analysis prior to data collection; reliable and valid measures; use of multiple sources of data; trained evaluators and supervisors tasked with providing feedback; assurance of confidentiality; and partnering faculty development with evaluation. Seldin (1999 and 2006) presents a systematic process for evaluating faculty performance, identifying best practices and providing benchmarks for successful evaluation. He argues that faculty evaluation should emphasize methods to measure and improve teaching performance, to identify beneficial institutional service and to recognize a wide range of activities that constitute research. To sustain a faculty evaluation system, data from the evaluations must be used for formative purposes to assist with faculty growth and development, and provide summative information for administrators to use in personnel decisions. Seldin's work suggests using peer evaluations and portfolios for faculty evaluation.

Peer review serves as a critical element within any evaluation system because students are not capable of evaluating some essential elements of excellent teaching. The practice of peer review of teaching grew out of the work of Boyer (1990), Hutchings (1994, 1996), Shulman (1993), Huber (2004) and others. It connects teaching and learning, shifting the focus to student learning outcomes through a more holistic evaluation process. Reviews include an evaluation of course material, course design and content, methods of assessing student learning outcomes, and the scholarship of teaching and learning, in addition to classroom observation (Chism, 2007). Peer review can become an important component in colleges and universities, impacting hiring decisions, learning communities or teaching circles, mentoring faculty, faculty review for compensation, contract renewal and annual reviews, and determining teaching assignments, promotion and tenure, sabbatical requests, teaching award recipients, and post-tenure reviews.

Support for peer review rests on several arguments. With increasing calls for faculty accountability and the desire by faculty to enhance the value of teaching activities, teaching must become a topic that is discussed publicly and investigated through scholarly activity. Open discussion helps institutions define the characteristics and attributes of teaching excellence. Shulman (1993, 1996) and Hutchings (1994, 1996) promote the ideal of teaching as community property, leading to increased faculty discussion and collaboration, scholarship of teaching and learning, and, potentially, incorporation of a teaching demonstration into the hiring process. Feedback from peer review, that which helps teachers improve their practice, contributes to continuous quality improvement in the profession. Finally, peer review results in an acknowledgement of the complex nature of teaching and meets the triangularization criterion of multiple sources of information from different points in time (Cashin, 1990). Keig (2000) presents evidence that faculty are willing to engage in peer review involving classroom observation, videotaping of class, formative evaluation of course materials and evaluation of student work assessment.

The arguments against peer review of teaching are equally pervasive. Exposing classroom activities to observation raises issues of academic freedom and threatens, for some faculty, their autonomy in deciding what and how to teach. Agreement on who can serve as a peer and the time commitment required to perform quality peer reviews are additional concerns voiced by opponents. There is also great anxiety about the effects on department collegial relations post-review. To enhance the potential effectiveness of the peer evaluation process, these issues must be addressed before establishing the peer review system.

Chism (2007) suggests a method for establishing a peer review system and provides a sample framework for peer evaluation of teaching developed by the University of Saskatchewan. Chism presents the major design components of a peer review of teaching system and the essential roles and goals to be accomplished for a peer review system to be successful. Major design elements include a statement of the purpose of peer review, faculty involved, the structure of the review, criteria to be applied, evidence and standards to be used, reviewer instruments and the process for preparing reviewers. The roles are developed by positions of the department chair, the faculty to be reviewed and the reviewer(s). The goals of a peer review system may be formative or summative, but need to be explicitly stated. Chism also provides example rubrics for peer review of course materials, classroom observation, scholarship of teaching and leadership for teaching, and teaching portfolios. The Chism framework provides a comprehensive resource for a department or institution interested in developing a peer review of the teaching system.

DOCUMENTATION

In the previous two sections of this chapter, the focus was on mentoring and evaluation methods for faculty success in the review, promotion, and tenure processes. This complementary section focuses on how faculty can effectively present accomplishments and contributions. The emphasis in higher education on improvement in teaching and learning, and accountability for effective teaching has increased over the last twenty years (Theall, 2010, p. 87; Seldin, 1997, p. 1). As part of the response to assessing teaching effectiveness, the use of teaching portfolios has grown in institutions of higher learning. Seldin (1997) estimates that over 1000 institutions in the United States use teaching portfolios. This discussion of the teaching portfolio begins with defining a teaching portfolio and then discusses the reasons why a faculty member might construct a teaching portfolio, outlines the basic elements and guidelines of a teaching portfolio and provides a list of additional resources. The teaching portfolio construct is then extended to address evidence presentation across areas of teaching, research and service fundamental to success in the promotion and tenure process at most academic institutions through the use of an academic portfolio.

The teaching portfolio is analogous to the portfolios of artists, photographers or architects as a compilation of materials which document the teaching performance and related accomplishments of a faculty member. The portfolio provides evidence of claims made by a professor concerning the what, how and why of his/her teaching. The emphasis in a portfolio is on success. Just as photographers do not include out-of-focus or badly framed photographs in their portfolios, faculty do not include failed grant proposals or rejected research submissions in the curriculum vitae. The teaching portfolio includes examples of the best teaching done by the faculty member.

Teaching portfolios are a useful tool for faculty at all ranks. The development of a teaching portfolio will assist an untenured assistant professor analyze the intent and outcomes of teaching and learning experiences, ultimately culminating in a document used to support teaching effectiveness before promotion and tenure committees. Associate and full professors can continue to use a portfolio to document the evolution of teaching over time, share teaching experiences with younger colleagues, provide a legacy of specific course development, and to support a nomination for a teaching award, grant proposal, or position application.

A teaching portfolio typically consists of an eight to ten page teaching narrative, accompanied by appendices that provide evidence to support narrative statements. Exactly what is included in the narrative and the appendices depends a great deal on the purpose of the portfolio. Junior faculty preparing for the promotion and tenure decision may wish to include a rationale for selecting an academic career, descriptions of courses taught, course mechanics, and why he/she used particular methodologies. Course mechanics might include descriptions of student engagement activities, how different types of course assignments are used and the associated grading process, etc. Including a description of teaching methods requires the faculty member to provide a rationale for the methods selected. Other topics that might be addressed in a teaching narrative include discussions of teaching strengths and activities associated with the scholarship on teaching and learning, such as classroom research, presentations and publications. Within the narrative, effective presentation suggests that the portfolio author reference specific evidence supporting particular statements. For example, if the statement is "I teach my students to write better", then an appendix should include examples of assignments, as well as samples of student writing that demonstrate such improvement. The process of writing the narrative can also serve to improve subsequent classroom practices since faculty reflecting on his/her teaching frequently results in a truly "a-ha" moment.

Resources to help develop a teaching portfolio include Seldin (1997, chapters 1–2), Seldin, Annis and Zubizarreta, 1995), Edgerton et al. (1991), Cerbin (1994), and Murray (1997). Seldin (1997) describes the items to be included in a portfolio and provides some sample tables of content. Edgerton et al. discuss Boyer's scholarship of teaching, the use of teaching portfolios, and the content of portfolios. Murray provides concise information on the documentation of teaching strategies, items to document teaching effectiveness and the elements of a teaching improvement plan. The University of Virginia Teaching Resource Center has a resource packet on Teaching Portfolios.[4] Chism (2007) and Seldin and Miller (2009) provide rubrics and methods for evaluating teaching or academic portfolios.

An academic or professional portfolio (Froh, Gray and Lambert, 1993, and Seldin and Miller, 2009) is created to document research and service activities in addition to those described above with respect to teaching. As with the teaching portfolio, narratives play a key role. The research narrative includes descriptions of completed work, detailing emerging themes and their contribution to disciplinary literature. The faculty member also provides a description of their current research program and how it contributes to anticipated future directions of research efforts. In the case of jointly authored publications, the faculty member should state as far as possible the contributions of each author to the research. Similarly, narratives about service should describe contributions to different institutional committees and their profession, as well as mentoring activities. In developing the service narrative, faculty need to be cognizant that not all colleagues in their department or at their institution will have full knowledge of the work completed by individual committees or the faculty member's contributions to this work, so this needs to be clearly and honestly stated.

FACULTY DEVELOPMENT RESOURCES

Department chairs are the first level of support for faculty development, given their participation in hiring, annual reviews, contract renewal, and promotion and tenure decisions. Buller (2006), Gmelch and Miskin (2004), Gmelch, Allen, and Melsa (2002) and Fink (2006) describe the role of department chairs in faculty development. Yet many chairs are not specifically trained to support faculty development nor do they have the resources (time) to dedicate to such activities, hence the establishment/growth of faculty development centers. Faculty development programs and centers are available at many academic institutions and are the primary source, outside of the department, for support in evaluating and improving teaching and research efforts. Because faculty development programs rely on effective evaluation systems, communication by the department chairs, members of the promotion and tenure committee, and administration with the faculty developers is essential.

For faculty at institutions without a teaching and learning center, the following resources are available to assist faculty. A good overview is provided by Bain (2004), who describes criteria that lead to success in the classroom across a range of disciplines. Effective teaching practices and considerations, applicable to both the beginning professor and more experienced teachers, are covered by McKeachie and Svinicki (2005) and Davis (2009). These resources guide a new faculty member through the process of creating a course, text selection, syllabus writing, course policies, etc. and provide ideas for more experienced faculty to address specific common hurdles and issues. Covering more specific components of effective teaching, O'Brien, Millis and Cohen (2008) provide a thorough process for creating a learning-centered syllabus; Angelo and Cross (1993) present numerous assessment techniques, beyond quizzes and tests, to help faculty determine whether or not their students are learning the material at the depth desired. Walvoord and Anderson (2010) address the eternal problem of grading efficiently. Tomorrow's Professor is a listserv that provides "desk-top" faculty development columns 100 times a year and is sponsored by the Stanford Center for Teaching and Learning.[5] The listserv addresses topics concerning teaching and learning, research, graduate students and post-docs, academic careers, and being a member of the academy.

Faculty may also avail themselves of generalized teaching workshops and conferences. The longest running college teaching conference is the Lilly Conference on College Teaching at Miami University of Ohio.[6] Spin-offs include regional Lilly Conferences, which may be more readily accessible.[7] A week-long institute called "Boot Camp for Profs" focuses on professors at every career stage and all types of academic institutions and is extremely well attended.[8]

The American Economics Association through the Committee on Economic Education sponsors teaching workshops at the annual meeting as well as at other times during the year. Past workshops include the Teacher Training Workshop Project and the Teaching Innovations Project. The AEA Committee also sponsors an annual research in economic education conference to support their mission of improving economic education at all levels (K-graduate).[9] The AEA Committee on Economic Education webpage is the best source for finding the current activities.[10] Internet sources for teaching economics materials include the pedagogic portal, Starting Point: Teaching and Learning Economics,[11] Games Economists Play[12] and Resources for Economists.[13] Edited volumes by Becker and Watts (1998), Becker, Watts and Becker (2006), Salemi and Walstad (2011), and Simkins and Maier (2009) provide numerous teaching techniques, with explanations on implementations. Overviews of the major are provided by Siegfried et al. (1991) and, in the context of a liberal education, Colander and McGoldrick (2009)

CONCLUSION

Faculty development, whether led by a department chair, faculty development center, or self-constructed, is essential for the successful transition from graduate student to productive faculty member, enhancing an institution's teaching and research reputation. The characteristics of "quick starters" are well documented in the literature, as is the ability to assist faculty to adopt the habits of successful new faculty. Mentoring is a key component of advancing junior faculty and the multiple-mentor model receives support in research, as well as having intuitive appeal. Mentors assist faculty with evaluation and documentation of teaching and research efforts and acculturation into the institution. For mentors and protégés to be successful, the institutional and disciplinary support and resources are critical. The American Economics Association provides significant support for faculty development in teaching economics and curriculum development.

NOTES

1. http://www.aeaweb.org/committees/cswep (accessed 20 April 2011).
2. http://www.aeaweb.org/committees/cswep/annual_reports.php 1998 Annual Report (accessed 20 April 2011).
3. http://www.aeaweb.org/committees/CSMGEP/pipeline/index.php (accessed 20 April 1920).
4. http://trc.virginia.edu/home.htm (accessed 20 April 2011).
5. http://ctl.stanford.edu/dept/CTL/Tomprof/index.shtml (accessed 20 April 2011).
6. http://www.units.muohio.edu/lillycon/ (accessed 20 April 2011).
7. http://lillyconferences.com/ (accessed 20 April 2011).
8. http://profcamp.tripod.com/bootcamp09.htm (accessed 20 April 2011).
9. http://www.aeaweb.org/committees/AEACEE/Conference/index.php (accessed 20 April 2011).
10. http://www.aeaweb.org/committees/AEACEE/index.php (accessed 20 April 2011).
11. http://serc.carleton.edu/econ/index.html (accessed 20 April 2011).
12. http://www.marietta.edu/~delemeeg/games/ (accessed 20 April 2011).
13. http://www.aeaweb.org/RFE/ (accessed 20 April 2011).

REFERENCES

Allen, T. D., L. T. Eby, M. L. Poteet, E. Lentz, and L. Lima (2004), "Career success outcomes associated with mentoring for protégés: A meta-analysis", *Journal of Applied Psychology*, **89** (1), 127–36.
Angelo, T. A. and K. P. Cross (1993), *Classroom Assessment Techniques* (second edition), San Francisco, CA: Jossey-Bass.
Bain, K. (2004), *What the Best College Teachers Do*, Cambridge, MA: Harvard University Press.
Becker, W. E. and M. Watts (eds) (1998), *Teaching Economics to Undergraduates: Alternatives to Chalk and Talk*, Cheltenham, UK and Lyme, USA: Edward Elgar.
Becker, W. E., M. Watts and S. Becker (2006), *Teaching Economics: More Alternatives to Chalk and Talk*, Cheltenham, UK and Northampton, MA, USA: Edward Elgar.
Bensimon, E. M., K. Ward and K. Sanders (2000), *Department Chair's Role in Developing New Faculty into Teachers and Scholars*, Bolton, MA: Anker.
Bland, C. J., B. A. Center, D. A. Finstad, K. R. Risbey and J.G. Staples (2005), "A theoretical, practical, predictive model of faculty and department research productivity", *Academic Medicine*, **80** (3), 225–37.
Bland, C. J., A. L. Taylor, S. L. Shollen, A. M. Weber-Main and P. A. Mulcahy (2009), *Faculty Success through Mentoring: A Guide for Mentors, Mentees, and Leaders*, Lanham, MD: Rowman and Littlefield.
Blau, F. D., J. M. Currie, R. T. A. Crosen and D. Ginther, (2010), "Can mentoring help female assistant professors? Initial results from a randomized trial", *American Economic Review*, **100**, 348–52.
Boice, R. (1992a), "Quick Starters", in M. Theall (ed.), *New Directions for Teaching and Learning Effective Practices for Improving Teaching No. 48*, San Francisco: Jossey-Bass, pp. 111–21.
Boice, R. (1992b), *The New Faculty Member*, San Francisco, CA: Jossey-Bass.
Boice, R. (2000), *Advice for New Faculty Members: Nihil Nimus*, Needham Heights, MA: Allyn & Bacon.
Boyer, E. L. (1990), *Scholarship Reconsidered: Priorities of the Professoriate*, Princeton, NJ: Carnegie Foundation for the Advancement of Teaching.
Braskamp, L. A. (1980), "The role of evaluation in faculty development", *Studies in Higher Education*, **5**, 45–51.
Braskamp, L. A. (2000), "Toward a more holistic approach to assessing faculty as teachers", in K. E. Ryan (ed.), *New Directions for Teaching and Learning: No 83. Evaluating Teaching in Higher Education: A Vision for the Future*, San Francisco, CA: Jossey-Bass, pp. 19–33.
Buller, J. L. (2006), *The Essential Department Chair; A Practical Guide to College Administration*, Bolton, MA: Anker.
Cashin, W. E. (1990), "Student ratings of teaching: Recommendations for use" (IDEA Paper No. 22), Manhattan, KS: Kansas State University, Center for Faculty Evaluation and Development.

Cashin, W. E. (1995), "Student ratings of teaching: The research revisited" (IDEA Paper No. 32), Manhattan, KS: Kansas State University, Center for Faculty Evaluation and Development.

Cashin, W. E. (1996), "Developing an effective faculty evaluation system" (Idea Paper no. 33), Manhattan, KS: Kansas State University, Center for Faculty Evaluation and Development.

Cerbin, W. (1994), "The Course portfolio as a tool for continuous improvement of teaching and learning", *Journal of Excellence in College Teaching*, **5**, 95–105.

Chism, N. V. N (2007), *Peer Review of Teaching: a Sourcebook* (second edition), Boston, MA: Anker.

Colander, D. and K. McGoldrick (2009), "The Teagle Foundation Report: The Economics Major as Part of a Liberal Education", *Educating Economists: The Teagle Discussion on Re-evaluating the Undergraduate Economics Major*, Cheltenham, UK and Northampton, MA, USA: Edward Elgar, pp. 3–39.

Crosen, R. and K. McGoldrick (2007), "Scaling the wall: Helping female faculty in economics achieve tenure", in A. J. Stewart, J. E. Malley and D. LaVaque-Manty (eds), *Transforming Science and Engineering: Advancing Academic Women*, Ann Arbor, MI: University of Michigan Press.

Davis, B. G. (2009), *Tools for Teaching* (second edition), San Francisco: Jossey-Bass.

de Janasz, S. C. and S. E. Sullivan (2004), "Multiple mentoring in academe: Developing the Professional Network", *Journal of Vocational Behavior*, **64** (2), 263–83.

Driscoll, L. G., K. A. Parkas, G. A. Tilley-Lubbs, J. M. Brill and V. R. P. Bannist (2009), "Navigating the lonely sea: Peer mentoring and collaboration among aspiring women scholars", *Mentoring & Tutoring: Partnership in Learning*, **17**, 5–21.

Edgerton, R., P. Hutchings and K. Quinlan (1991), *The Teaching Portfolio: Capturing the Scholarship of Teaching*, Washington, DC: American Association of Higher Education.

Felder, R. M., R. Brent and M. J. Prince (2011), "Engineering instructional development: Programs, best practices, and recommendations", *Journal of Engineering Education*, **100** (1), 89–122.

Fink, D. (2006), "Faculty development: A medicine for what ails academe today", *The Department Chair*, **17** (1), 7–10.

Froh, C., P. J. Gray and L. M. Lambert (1993), "Representing faculty work: The professional portfolio", in R. M. Diamond and B. E. Adam (eds), *New Directions for Higher Education no 81: In Recognizing Faculty Work: Reward Systems for the Year 2000*, San Francisco, CA: Jossey-Bass, pp. 97–118.

Gmelch, W. H. and V. D. Miskin (2004), *Chairing an Academic Department* (second edition), Madison, WI: Atwood.

Gmelch, W. H., B. Allen and J. Melsa (2002), "Building a campus model for leadership development", *The Department Chair* **13** (2), 13–15.

Gray, T. and A. J. Birch (2008), "Team mentoring: an alternative way to mentor new faculty", in D. Robertson and L. B. Nilson (eds), *To Improve the Academy 26*, Somerset, NJ: Wiley, pp. 230–41.

Hoyt, D. P. and W. H. Pallett (1999), "Appraising teaching effectiveness: Beyond student ratings" (IDEA Paper Number 36), Manhattan, KS: Kansas State University, Center for Faculty Evaluation and Development.

Huber, M. T. (2004), *Balancing Acts: The Scholarship of Teaching and Learning in Academic Careers*, Sterling, VA: Stylus.

Hutchings, P. (1994), "Peer review of teaching: From idea to prototype", *AAHE Bulletin*, **47** (3), 3–7.

Hutchings, P. (1996), *Making Teaching Community Property: A Menu for Peer Collaboration and Peer Review*, Sterling, VA: Stylus.

Johnson, W. B. (2007), *On being a Mentor: A Guide for Higher Education Faculty*, Mahwah, NJ: Lawrence Erlbaum.

Keig, L. (2000), "Formative peer review of teaching: Attitudes of faculty at liberal arts colleges toward colleague assessment", *Journal of Personnel Evaluation in Education*, **14** (1), 67–87.

Matthews, P. (2003), "Academic mentoring: Enhancing the use of scarce resources", *Educational Management and Administration*, **31** (3), 313–34.

McKeachie, W. J. and M. Svinicki (2005), *McKeachie's Teaching Tips: Strategies, Research and Theory for College and University Teachers* (12th edition), Boston, MA: Houghton-Mifflin.

Murray, J. P. (1997), *Successful Faculty Development and Evaluation: The Complete Teaching Portfolio*, ASHE-ERIC Higher Education Report No. 8, Washington, DC: The George Washington University.

O'Brien, J. G., B. J. Millis and M. W. Cohen (2008), *The Course Syllabus: A Learning Centered Approach*, San Francisco, CA: Jossey-Bass.

Salemi, M. and W. B. Walstad (2011), *Teaching Innovations in Economics*, Cheltenham, UK and Northampton, MA, USA: Edward Elgar.

Seldin, P. (1993), *Successful Use of Teaching Portfolios*, Bolton, MA: Anker.

Seldin, P. (1997), *The Teaching Portfolio: A Practical Guide to Improved Performance and Promotion/Tenure Decisions* (second edition), Bolton, MA: Anker.

Seldin, P. (1999), *Changing Practices in Evaluating Teaching: A Practical Guide to Improved Faculty Performance and Promotion/Tenure Decisions*, Bolton, MA: Anker.

Seldin, P. (2006), *Evaluating Faculty Performance: A Practical Guide to Assessing Teaching, Research and Service*, San Francisco, CA: Anker.

Seldin, P. and J. E. Miller (2009), *The Academic Portfolio: A Practical Guide to Documenting Teaching, Research and Service*, San Francisco, CA: Jossey-Bass.

Seldin, P., L. Annis and J. Zubizarreta (1995), "Answers to common questions about the teaching portfolio", *Journal of Excellence in College Teaching*, **6**, 57–64.

Shulman L. S. (1993), "Teaching as community property: Putting an end to pedagogical solitude", *Change*, **25** (6), 6–7.

Shulman, L. S. (1996), "The pedagogical colloquium: focusing on teaching in the hiring process", *AAHE Bulletin*, **49**, 3–4.

Siegfried, J., R. Bartlett, W. Hansen, A. Kelley, D. McCloskey and T. Tietenberg (1991), "The status and prospects of the economic major", *The Journal of Economic Education*, **22** (3), 197–224.

Simkins, S. and M. Maier (eds) (2009), *Just in Time Teaching*, Sterling, VA: Stylus.

Sorcinelli, M. D. and J. Yun (2007) "From Mentor to Mentoring Networks: Mentoring in the New Academy", *Change*, **39** (6), 58–61.

Theall, M. (2010), "Evaluating teaching: From reliability to accountability", in *New Directions for Teaching and Learning Landmark Issues in Teaching and Learning: A Look Back at New Directions for GT&L*, No. 123, San Francisco, CA: Jossey-Bass, pp. 85–96.

Walvoord, B. E. and V. J. Anderson (2010), *Effective Grading: A Tool for Learning and Assessment in College* (second edition), San Francisco, CA: Jossey-Bass.

Wingard, D. L., K. A. Garmin and V. Reznick (2004), "Facilitating faculty success: Outcomes and cost benefits of the UCSD National Center of Leadership in academic medicine", *Academic Medicine*, **79**, S9–S11.

Wunsch, M. A. (ed.) (1994), *New Directions for Teaching and Learning, No. 57: Mentoring Revisited: Making an Impact on Individuals and Institutions*, San Francisco, CA: Jossey-Bass.

Section B

Undergraduate Education

68 The economics major in the United States[1]
John J. Siegfried

Economics is a central pillar in the social sciences at almost all American colleges and universities. About 30,000 individuals earn a bachelor's degree in economics from a US college or university each year. The program of study for these students is quite similar everywhere. In contrast to other social science disciplines, there has been widespread agreement for many decades about the appropriate curriculum for an undergraduate degree in economics in the United States (Siegfried and Wilkinson, 1982; Siegfried et al., 1991). The number of students attracted to this curriculum has waxed and waned over the past 60 years, but, over time, the proportion of American undergraduates who major in economics seems to revert to a little less than 2 percent of those who graduate. The reasons for fluctuations in interest in economics are elusive, however.

UNDERGRADUATE DEGREES IN ECONOMICS IN THE UNITED STATES

Trends in the number of four-year economics degrees awarded annually by US colleges and universities since 1969–70 (1970), as tabulated by the National Center for Education Statistics (NCES), are tracked in Figure 68.1. After doubling from the early 1950s until 1970, economics degrees declined steadily during the early 1970s. They then reversed course, rising steadily until 1990, after which they once again began to fall. This time the decline lasted five years, throughout the first half of the 1990s, when it once again reversed course and began a ten-year recovery before leveling off in about 2005. The number of bachelor's degrees awarded in economics in the US has remained fairly steady since 2005, although showing a potential upturn in 2008 and 2009.

NCES data are the official data collected by the US Department of Education. NCES data are based on a census of US colleges and universities, which is their advantage. Unfortunately, NCES data are published only with a two or (sometimes) three-year lag. They also do not recognize double majors and, as such, tabulate only about 82 percent of the bachelor's degrees awarded in economics in the US (Siegfried and Wilkinson, 1982, p. 129). While the omission of double majors does not affect trends so long as college and university registrars use consistent procedures to select which of multiple majors is reported to NCES, and so long as the propensity to double or triple major remains constant, NCES data do understate the absolute number of individuals earning a bachelor's degree in economics.

For these reasons, relying primarily on the American Economic Association's (AEA) Universal Academic Questionnaire, supplemented by an appeal to departments, the AEA began to collect economics degrees data in 1990–91 directly from departments of

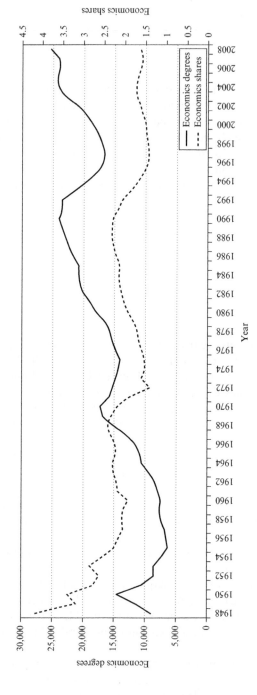

Figure 68.1   Undergraduate Bachelor's degrees awarded in the United States, 1948–2008

economics in the United States. These data include double majors, and at the time this is being written, are current through June 2009. A consistent series (of the identical institutions for each year) is reported in Table 68.1. Table 68.2 reports the same information for a sample of institutions that reported male and female graduates separately. Trends in the NCES series and the AEA data since 1991 are similar. Degrees awarded rather than declared majors or course enrollments are used to measure interest in economics because degrees are a less ambiguous measure of student commitment to studying economics.

Soon after a precipitous near-30-percent decline in the number of economics degrees awarded from 1991 to 1996, Margo and Siegfried (1996) attempted to identify the reason fewer college students were majoring in economics. Initially, they asked whether the early 1990s decline was unprecedented. They found two other dramatic post-World War II drops in the number of degrees. There was a sharp upward spike in the number of economics degrees awarded in the immediate aftermath of World War II. From a peak of 14,568 bachelor's degrees in economics awarded in the US in 1950, during the height of G.I. Bill use, the number awarded declined 56 percent during the Korean War, to 6,354 in 1955. From another peak of 17,197 degrees awarded in 1970, a consequence of the baby boom reaching college age and high rates of college attendance during the Viet Nam War, the number of bachelor's degrees awarded in economics subsequently declined 18 percent, to 14,046 in 1975. Other than the peculiar coincidence that the beginning of the three post-World War II recessions in economics degrees were spaced about 20 years apart, in 1950, 1970, and 1991, lasted about five years each, and occurred while the US was at war (Korea, Viet Nam, and Iraq Desert Storm), it is not clear what to make of the pattern.

It is no surprise that the number of economics degrees has more than tripled over the past half-century, since the total number of bachelor's degrees awarded has grown even faster, quadrupling over the period. Economics held its share of a little more than 2 percent from the mid-1950s until 1992 (see Table 68.1). Based on a statistical analysis of the share of undergraduate degrees held by economics from 1948 through 1993, Margo and Siegfried (1996) conclude that economics' share is a stationary time-series around a constant mean. The implied long-run equilibrium share was then about 2 percent. It appears to have declined modestly since those estimates were conducted. This is not surprising, since new majors are perpetually offered at large public universities, and few existing majors ever close down.

Since 1993, the number of bachelor's degrees awarded in economics has remained relatively constant, while total college and university degrees awarded have grown by 40 percent. Consequently, the share accounted for by economics has fallen, bottoming out at around 1.4 percent in 1997. Although the share accounted for by economics has since recovered modestly, to 1.6 percent in 2008, it appears that some of the downward shock that hit economics in the early 1990s may be permanent.

WHY DOES THE NUMBER OF ECONOMICS DEGREES FLUCTUATE?

There are numerous plausible explanations for fluctuations in the number of economics degrees awarded in the US. The first to come naturally to an economist's mind is the

Table 68.1 Number of baccalaureate degrees in economics awarded by US colleges and universities

Institution	n	1990–91	1991–92	1992–93	1993–94	1994–95	1995–96	1996–97	1997–98	1998–99	1999–00	2000–01	2001–02	2002–03	2003–04	2004–05	2005–06	2006–07	2007–08	2008–09
Public Institutions	142	10532	10286	9701	8684	7590	7130	7075	7316	7425	8097	8713	10015	11009	12059	12168	12270	12289	12876	13382
Ph.D.	57	8093	7921	7382	6535	5751	5443	5395	5618	5855	6297	6998	8065	8974	9778	9689	9805	9807	10342	10827
MA	34	1487	1398	1331	1209	1111	981	865	850	706	801	849	930	960	1124	1289	1278	1288	1273	1336
Bachelor's	51	952	967	988	940	728	706	815	843	864	999	866	1020	1075	1157	1190	1187	1194	1261	1219
Private Institutions	139	6339	6215	5678	5387	4907	4931	5109	5329	5724	5923	5898	6384	6564	6967	6788	6823	6627	7286	7485
Ph.D.	27	2642	2507	2358	2185	1956	1988	2147	2214	2425	2481	2498	2737	2879	3162	3214	3208	2858	3227	3284
Selective liberal arts[1]	64	2823	2799	2579	2397	2251	2300	2378	2439	2667	2767	2718	2887	2904	3004	2913	2867	2978	3272	3296
Other bachelor's	48	874	909	741	805	700	643	584	676	632	675	682	760	781	801	661	748	791	787	905
Total Sample	281	16871	16501	15379	14071	12497	12061	12184	12545	13149	14020	14611	16399	17573	19026	18956	19093	18916	20162	20867

Notes:
Pt.D. and MA indicates the highest degree in economics offered by the institution.
[1] *US News & World Report,* 1st or 2nd tier "national liberal arts colleges".
Based on data as of 24 February 2010.

Source: Author's survey for 1991 through 1999 and the American Economic Association Universal Academic Questionnaire supplemented by a survey for 2000–2009.

Table 68.2 Number of baccalaureate degrees in economics awarded by US colleges and universities (for sample divided into men and women)

Institution	n	1990–91	1991–92	1992–93	1993–94	1994–95	1995–96	1996–97	1997–98	1998–99	1999–00	2000–01	2001–02	2002–03	2003–04	2004–05	2005–06	2006–07	2007–08	2008–09
Public Institutions	119	8294 28.2%	8149 28.9%	7541 27.7%	6588 27.0%	5707 27.1%	5407 27.2%	5473 28.1%	5663 29.7%	5702 30.7%	6154 30.9%	6564 32.7%	7434 32.7%	8389 32.8%	9081 31.6%	9199 30.4%	9435 30.6%	9386 28.2%	9777 28.9%	10096 28.6%
Ph.D.	50	6382 29.2%	6241 29.8%	5721 27.9%	4356 27.3%	4243 27.8%	4064 28.1%	4125 29.7%	4273 30.6%	4363 31.6%	4629 31.7%	5139 33.9%	5815 34.2%	6704 33.5%	7251 32.7%	7216 30.9%	7505 31.5%	7424 28.6%	7795 29.6%	8116 28.8%
MA	24	1083 23.1%	1036 24.4%	956 25.3%	896 25.1%	801 25.7%	708 22.6%	622 24.3%	628 25.0%	550 26.9%	611 30.1%	646 30.7%	703 31.2%	720 32.8%	818 27.4%	918 29.2%	873 27.1%	895 27.3%	861 27.5%	900 31.1%
Bachelor's	45	829 26.8%	872 28.0%	864 29.4%	836 27.0%	663 24.1%	635 26.3%	726 22.5%	762 28.5%	789 28.8%	914 27.6%	779 26.7%	916 24.3%	965 27.9%	1012 27.2%	1065 28.5%	1057 27.2%	1067 26.2%	1121 25.3%	1080 25.4%
Private Institutions	128	5789 32.8%	5673 31.1%	5179 33.2%	4930 33.0%	4468 32.6%	4504 33.0%	4634 32.0%	4905 33.2%	5211 34.9%	5341 33.5%	5323 35.5%	5733 33.8%	5846 35.6%	6173 33.9%	5942 33.5%	5987 33.9%	5787 32.5%	6290 33.0%	6431 32.6%
Ph.D.	22	2372 29.1%	2240 27.2%	2118 31.3%	1973 31.6%	1750 31.5%	1818 29.6%	1964 28.6%	2044 30.9%	2208 33.3%	2222 31.0%	2221 34.3%	2418 32.9%	2517 33.5%	2718 33.0%	2739 32.0%	2747 33.2%	2404 30.8%	2700 32.4%	2707 31.0%
Selective liberal arts[1]	59	2571 37.3%	2538 35.5%	2341 36.3%	2167 36.3%	2032 35.9%	2058 37.8%	2110 36.5%	2195 36.4%	2378 36.9%	2466 36.5%	2428 39.4%	2559 35.8%	2569 39.4%	2670 35.9%	2565 36.8%	2516 36.1%	2609 36.0%	2824 35.2%	2853 36.7%
Other bachelor's	47	846 29.8%	895 28.7%	720 28.6%	790 27.5%	686 25.8%	628 26.9%	560 27.3%	666 29.7%	625 32.6%	653 30.3%	674 25.7%	756 29.9%	760 29.7%	785 30.4%	638 26.3%	724 29.1%	774 26.1%	766 27.2%	871 24.0%
Total Sample	247	14083 30.1%	13822 29.8%	12720 30.0%	11518 29.6%	10175 29.5%	9911 29.8%	10107 29.9%	10568 31.3%	10913 32.7%	11495 32.1%	11887 34.0%	13167 33.2%	14235 33.9%	15254 32.6%	15141 31.6%	15422 31.9%	15173 29.8%	16067 30.5%	16527 30.2%

Notes:
Percentages are degrees earned by women. Ph.D. and MA indicates the highest degree in economics offered by the institution.
[1] *US News & World Report*, 1st or 2nd tier "national liberal arts colleges".
Based on data as of 24 February 2010.

Source: Author's survey for 1991 through 1999 and the American Economic Association Universal Academic Questionnaire supplemented by a survey for 2000–2009.

economy. If students believe that an economics degree may insulate them to some extent from a (temporarily) weak labor market, they may be enticed to major in economics when unemployment is relatively high. Margo and Siegfried (1996) test this hypothesis by including the deviation between current unemployment and its natural rate in a time-series regression designed to explain the share of degrees awarded in economics. The empirical results reveal that for every 1 percentage point by which current unemployment exceeds its natural rate, the economics share of degrees (lagged by three years to adjust for the timing of major selections) rises by 1.2 percent. Thus, if the economics share was initially at 2 percent, and current unemployment was suddenly to exceed its natural rate by 3 percentage points, the economics share would rise to 2.07 percent after the three-year lag. Although this effect is statistically significant at the 0.05 level, its practical significance is trivial.

Another economics-related hypothesis pertains to expected financial returns from majoring in economics. Variation over time in employment prospects and earnings of students with different majors could alter the relative attractiveness of different majors to undergraduates. Siegfried and Raymond (1984) find that the finance, insurance, and real estate (FIRE) sector employed 38 percent of young economics graduates in 1980. Willis and Pieper (1996) report that the share of civilian employment accounted for by the FIRE sector in the United States peaked at 11.3 percent in 1988, just three years before student interest in economics waned dramatically in the early 1990s. The share fell from 11.3 percent in 1988 to 10.6 percent by 1992, and then began a modest recovery through 1997 that closely tracks the pattern of US economics degrees, allowing for a two-year recognition lag from changes in employment outcomes to changes in student choices among majors, plus another two-year lag between the timing of student major selection and degrees awarded. Unfortunately, the pattern of undergraduate economics degrees awarded does not similarly follow the trend in FIRE employment in Australia, Canada, and Germany, raising questions about the generality of this explanation (Siegfried and Round, 2001, p. 213).

The most obvious explanation for fluctuations in the number of undergraduate economics degrees is fluctuations in the number of total degrees awarded. However, over the past two decades the share of bachelor's degrees awarded in economics has not remained anywhere near constant in the United States, Australia, Canada, or Germany (Siegfried and Round, 2001). There is clearly more to economics degree cycles than simply tracing broader trends in university enrollments.

Because only about a third of US economics degrees are awarded to women, when the number of women in the overall undergraduate population grows faster than the number of men, as has been the case for the last several decades in all western countries, recently reaching about 58 percent in the United States, the share of degrees accounted for by economics can fall even if the proportions of men and women who select economics remain constant. Economics can lose share because the demographic group most likely to favor it (men) diminishes in relative importance. Unfortunately, this hypothesis does not fit the data very well. While the fraction of college and university students that is female has increased steadily for over two decades, the number of economics majors first fell precipitously (which is consistent with the hypothesis), but then reversed itself and grew in spite of the steadily growing dominance of women on American college and university campuses.

The relationship between undergraduate business education and economics is yet another potential source of fluctuations in economics degrees awarded. For students whose choice of institution dominates the choice of major and who attend an institution that does not offer a business degree, economics may be a substitute for business (Conrad, 1996). If so, generally declining interest in business would be accompanied by concurrently declining student interest in economics from those who use economics as a surrogate for business.

In contrast, for students whose choice of major dominates their choice of institution, the effect of declining interest in business on economics enrollments is more complicated. There should be no effect on aspiring economics majors enrolled at institutions not offering a business degree. Those economics majors have revealed their lack of interest in business by selecting an institution sans business offerings. Students attending institutions offering both economics and business degrees are not constrained by their preference between the two disciplines at the time they choose a college. Thus, those who prefer economics would be unaffected by reduced interest in business because they were not using economics as a surrogate for business in the first place.

The situation differs, however, if students' choice of major is constrained. Where there is a shortage of places in a business program, when the demand for business escalates, minimum entrance credentials rise and some academically weaker students who are denied access to the business program seek a place elsewhere – often in economics. During the rapidly expanding demand for business degrees in the United States from 1965 to 1985 (Willis and Pieper, 1996), many such "business wannabes" who could not gain admission to a business program enrolled in economics as a second choice. In such circumstances, strong demand for business education can increase the number (but not likely the quality) of economics majors.

Following a long period of steady sustained growth prior to 1992, the number of undergraduate business degrees declined in the United States. To the extent that those business programs that experienced declining interest replaced some of their lost enrollment by relaxing academic admission requirements, they may have attracted some students who would otherwise have majored in economics. This pattern fits well with the 12 percent decline in business degrees in the United States from 1992 through 1996. In a careful case study of the University of North Carolina (UNC), Salemi and Eubanks (1996) discover that, on average, "discouraged business majors" accounted for one-third of UNC's economics majors between 1983 and 1994, a period of strong demand for business.

There is other, more systematic evidence relating interest in business education to economics degrees. Using regression analysis to explain the proportion of an institution's student population that majors in economics, Siegfried and Wilkinson (1982) find that the presence of a competing undergraduate business major at the same university is likely to reduce the number of economics students by more than the entire average-size economics program, *ceteris paribus*. Fortunately for the typical economics program facing competition from a business degree, other things (for example, the curriculum) seldom remain the same, so that many of these economics programs survive.

Business is not the only major that may compete with economics. Herschel Kasper (2008) argues that biology is the main competitor for economics. The strong complementarity of market share between the two disciplines is persuasive. Kasper finds that for every additional three biology majors, it is likely that two come at the expense of economics, perhaps because the two disciplines attract students with similar technical and discursive aptitudes. Moreover, there are other similarities. Both economists and biologists often assume that their subjects are rationally maximizing a goal.

Systematic evidence indicates that both absolute and relative grading standards affect the number of students who major in economics (Sabot and Wakeman-Linn, 1991). For grading standards to explain economics degree cycles, however, they would have had to have been tightened up significantly at the beginning of the sharp declines in economics degrees, and then relaxed roughly five years later when the recoveries typically began. Although there is no direct evidence of grading standards over time, some departments may relax grading standards when they notice a declining number of majors (Becker, 1997, p. 1357). Curriculum requirements might also be viewed as a "price" students pay to earn a degree. However, when Siegfried and Wilkinson (1982) examine this possibility in a cross-section regression of over 500 departments, they uncover no evidence that curriculum requirements affect student choices among majors. More recently, Siegfried (1997) finds no difference in degree trends among US colleges and universities that had increased, decreased, or not changed economics major requirements.

Because economics departments were generally inundated with students from the mid-1970s through 1990, faculty had little reason to invest in adopting teaching methods that emphasize active learning. Mostly the faculty passively lectured. One might have expected the sharp decline in economics majors that began in the early 1990s to have improved the payoff to faculty investment in learning how to use more effective and more popular (with students) pedagogical techniques than traditional "chalk and talk" (Becker and Watts, 1996). Consistent with this expectation, Becker and Watts (2001) find in surveys of about 600 economics faculty that the median proportion of time full-time professors devoted to teaching increases from 50 percent in 1995 to 60 percent by 2000. The added effort devoted to teaching does not appear to have influenced instructional methods, however. The median proportion of class time devoted to traditional lecturing remains virtually constant from 1995 to 2000. Thus, there appears to be no basis for attributing the increase in economics degrees during the latter half of the 1990s to changes in pedagogical methods that were provoked by the immediately prior sharp drop in numbers.

Among the prospective explanations for the cycles in economics degrees, transmission of interest in business education and the influence of grading standards show some promise for additional investigation. Further examination of the role of labor market returns also may be fruitful. In sum, however, there is no convincing explanation for the cycles in economics degrees that have occurred over the past 60 years.

VARIATIONS IN THE PROPORTION OF WOMEN MAJORING IN ECONOMICS

Women are a steadily growing proportion of the undergraduate student population in the United States, but constitute only about one-third of economics majors (see Table 68.2, numbers in parentheses).[2] Using a sample of 195 colleges and universities, Ricks (2008) investigates variation in the gender composition of undergraduate majors across colleges and universities for the combined years of 2001–03.

She identifies four institutional characteristics that significantly (at the 0.10 level or better) affect the proportion of economics degrees awarded to women. A 10 percentage point increase in the proportion of the student body that is female (from 53 percent to 63 percent) implies an increase in the proportion of economics degrees awarded to women of about 3 percentage points (from 30 to 33 percent).

The statistically strongest predictor Ricks uncovers is the relative proportion of women faculty in economics compared to women faculty in the entire institution. As the percentage of women on the economics faculty rises relative to the percentage of women faculty at the entire institution by, say, 10 percentage points, the proportion of economics degrees awarded to women increases by about 1.5 percentage points. This result contradicts the findings of Canes and Rosen (1995), who uncover no relationship between the gender compositions of faculty and students across all of the majors at three institutions. It is consistent with the findings of Dynan and Rouse (1997), however, who find a statistically meaningful relationship between the gender composition of economics majors and the gender of their introductory economics instructor at Harvard.

Ricks also finds that the economics student population is more male dominated at larger institutions, perhaps because economics is (obviously) available at each institution in her sample, but larger universities offer more competitive majors, which may include options that are relatively more attractive to women than to men, e.g. nursing, education. As might be expected, economics departments at institutions that offer undergraduate degrees in education, a discipline that is 75 percent female nationwide, on average award degrees to 11 percentage points fewer women. Surprisingly, the presence of an engineering option seems to have no effect on the proportion of economics degrees awarded to women, even though engineering is 80 percent male nationwide.

Dynan and Rouse (1997) find evidence that quantitative ability, as measured by having taken two semesters of calculus, increases the gender gap among economics majors in the expected way. Ricks (2008), however, finds no evidence that the extent of either calculus or statistics requirements affects decisions of women to major in economics differently from the way it affects decisions of men in 2001–03.

SUMMARY

Economics degrees account for a little less than 2 percent of bachelor's degrees in the United States. Although the fraction fluctuates from time to time, it seems to revert to a relatively constant proportion of the total. The reasons for the fluctuations are not well understood, but may depend on conditions in the labor market for new graduates, the demand for business education, or the price economists charge to major in their discipline in the form of grading standards and curriculum requirements.

NOTES

1. Portions of this chapter, appropriately updated, are taken from Margo and Siegfried (1996) and Siegfried and Round (2001).

2. Data on the race/ethnicity or the citizenship status of bachelor's degrees in the United States are unavailable.

REFERENCES

Becker, W. E. (1997), "Teaching economics to undergraduates", *Journal of Economic Literature,* **35** (September), 1347–73.

Becker, W. E. and M. Watts (1996), "Chalk and talk: A national survey on teaching undergraduates", *American Economic Review, Papers and Proceedings,* **5** (May), 448–53.

Becker, W. E. and M. Watts (2001), "Teaching methods in undergraduate economics courses", *Journal of Economic Education,* **32** (3), 269–79.

Canes, B. and H. Rosen (1995), "Following in her footsteps? Faculty gender composition and women's choices of college majors", *Industrial and Labor Relations Review,* **48** (3), (April), 486–504.

Conrad, C. A. (1996), "Where have all the majors gone? Comment", *Journal of Economic Education,* **27** (Fall), 376–8.

Dynan, K. and C. Rouse (1997), "The underrepresentation of women in economics: A study of undergraduate economics students", *Journal of Economic Education,* **28** (4), (Fall), 351–68.

Kasper, H. (2008), "Sources of economics majors: More biology, less business", *Southern Economic Journal,* **75** (2), (October), 457–72.

Margo, R. A. and J. J. Siegfried (1996), "Long-run trends in economics bachelor's degrees", *Journal of Economic Education,* **27** (Fall), 326–36.

Ricks, J. A. (2008), "Explaining the variation in the proportion of women who major in economics", Undergraduate Honors Thesis, Vanderbilt University.

Sabot, R. and J. Wakeman-Linn (1991), "Grade inflation and course choice", *Journal of Economic Perspectives,* **5** (1), 159–70.

Salemi, M. and C. Eubanks (1996), "Accounting for the rise and fall in the number of economics majors with the discouraged-business-major hypothesis", *Journal of Economic Education,* **27** (Fall), 350–61.

Siegfried, J. J. (1997), "Trends in undergraduate degrees: An update", *Journal of Economic Education,* **28** (Summer), 279–82.

Siegfried, J. J. and J. Raymond (1984), "A profile of senior economics majors in the United States", *American Economic Review,* **74** (2), 19–25.

Siegfried, J. J. and D. K. Round (2001), "International trends in economics degrees during the 1990s", *Journal of Economic Education,* **32** (Summer), 203–18.

Siegfried, J. J. and J. T. Wilkinson (1982), "The undergraduate economics major in the United States: 1980", *American Economic Review, Papers and Proceedings,* **72** (2), 125–38.

Siegfried, J. J., R. Bartlett, W. L. Hansen, A. C. Kelley, D. McCloskey and T. Tietenberg (1991), "The economics major: Can and should we do better than B-?", *American Economic Review,* **81** (2), (May), 20–25.

Willis, R. A. and P. J. Pieper (1996), "The economics major: A cross-sectional view", *Journal of Economic Education,* **27** (Fall), 337–49.

69 Curricular and co-curricular aspects of the economics major at highly ranked schools

David H. Dean and Robert C. Dolan

This chapter examines current curricular and selected co-curricular aspects of the under-graduate economics major. First we describe the structure and course content of the major as outlined in the 2009 catalog descriptions of US liberal arts colleges and research universities. The discussion then focuses on two specific curricular dimensions that we regard as important developments over roughly the last two decades: (1) the capstone course; and (2) two prominent co-curricular programs that emphasize experiential learning.

STRUCTURE AND CONTENT OF THE ECONOMICS CURRICULUM

On a cursory level, the structure of the economics curriculum is straightforward and noncontroversial. Students begin with principles, proceed to a core of theory and quantitative courses, and then choose some arrangement of lower- and higher-level electives to achieve breadth and depth. Indeed, the clarity of progression in the major is regarded as unique by some economic educators.[1] Within this progression there are debatable specifics at each level. Is a two-semester principles sequence necessary? Do intermediate micro and macro theory warrant a second course in one or both areas (even if the second course is not required)? What is the appropriate number and nature of quantitative courses for *all* majors? How extensively is calculus applied, and how does a department accommodate the quantitative needs of the very small number of students who may enter graduate school?[2] At the elective level, how is the appropriate blend of breadth and depth achieved? Should the major include a "capstone experience," and if so, what constitutes such an experience?

This section contains a purely descriptive overview of the curriculum as reflected in the course offerings at 124 colleges and universities in 2009. The overview is stratified by three institutional categories. Two of these categories are Carnegie classifications: (1) research universities/very high research activity; and (2) baccalaureate colleges/arts and sciences. The third category represents economics departments at universities that also have undergraduate business schools.[3] We also apply a quality criterion in that we only consider the top-50 schools in each category.[4] However, the seeming maximum of 150 schools is reduced to a sample of 124 because these three categories are not mutually exclusive. Among the top-50 business schools, 26 are also categorized as either a top-50 research university or liberal arts school. Since this analysis examines the economics curriculum, it is worth noting that the administrative location of the economics department varies across these three institutional categories. First, seven departments of economics from the liberal arts category are affiliated with business schools or with other departments (e.g., accounting, commerce, finance, management, or general business). Second, the economics departments in six of the top 50 research universities are located within schools of business. Third, the economics department is housed within a school of business in nine of the 24 business schools ranked in the top 50, but these schools are not ranked in the top 50 research universities. Overall, the economics department is located in a school of business for 15 of the top 50 business schools (30 percent).

The rationale for stratifying the analysis is that a department's curriculum will be influenced by practical constraints and philosophical perspectives, both of which may vary by the size and focus of the institution. For example, major universities with larger faculties probably find the trade-off between breadth and depth in elective offerings less pressing. In contrast, smaller liberal arts colleges typically have neither the breadth of faculty expertise nor the critical mass of students to support a menu of electives that is both wide and deep. Similarly, a department's ability to offer dual curricula (for example, qualitative versus quantitative tracks, theory versus policy tracks) is obviously enhanced by the scale of the institution. As previously noted, there is clear evidence that the presence of an undergraduate business school can also have a discernible impact on curricular content. On a philosophical plane, economics departments that embrace the broad goal of "liberal education" may be conflicted in designing a curriculum that fosters lifetime learning skills while still assuring depth of knowledge in the discipline.[5] This conflict may be especially palpable for faculties at schools that are smaller or weaker financially.

The curriculum data for the 124 departments reflect the online course catalog descriptions for 2009. Each course listed in the catalog was categorized as a required core offering, including a capstone designation, or an elective. Whether a listed course was actually offered in the 2009 academic year is noted. The catalog descriptions were also examined to detect various features of the core, elective, and supplementary offerings of the major. To measure aspects of the core, we consider the number and sequencing of economics principles, the required quantitative courses, and the total number of core courses for the major. Calibration of the elective offerings consists of identifying the minimum number of required electives, the number of higher-level electives requiring the core, and whether advanced micro and/or macroeconomics are offered. We also consider electives that we believe reflect relatively recent economic fields (for example, European Union, behavioral, experimental, and gender). The availability of offerings such as honors programs and internships is a third dimension that can distinguish a school's elective character.

Table 69.1 describes these broad parameters of the major, stratified by the three college/university classifications.[6] These are the total number of economics courses offered, nature of the core offerings, number of required electives, and the total number of courses to complete the major. Perhaps unsurprisingly, liberal arts schools offer substantially fewer total courses on average – 33 as compared to 48 at research schools. The 24 economics departments at universities with top-ranked business schools (but which are not ranked in the top-50 research universities or liberal arts colleges) average a total of 40 courses. One important distinction to be drawn within our three classifications of schools is whether introductory content is covered in one or two semesters. Twenty-five of the 47 liberal arts colleges (53 percent) list a two-semester course versus 22 (47 percent) schools with only a one-semester course. Seventy percent of research universities require

Table 69.1   Components of the economics major

Curricular item	Top 50 liberal arts colleges (Number or Percent)	Top 50 research universities (Number or Percent)	24 of top 50 business schools (Number or Percent)
No. of total courses offered	33	48	40
Core Offerings:			
% with two principles sequence	53.2%	70.0%	95.8%
% having micro precede macro	40.0%	34.3%	52.2%
% with statistics required	100.0%	100.0%	100.0%
% with econometrics required	54.0%	64.0%	41.7%
% with calculus required	88.0%	96.0%	96.0%
No. of required core courses	5.0	6.0	5.8
No. of required electives	4.2	4.7	4.6
No. courses to complete the major	10.3	11.6	11.1

two principles courses. Moreover, 23 of the 24 (96 percent) economics departments in universities with top-50 business schools require two semesters of principles. Among the 83 schools that have a two-semester principles requirement, 34 require that micro precedes macro (41 percent). On this issue of sequencing, there is a slight difference across school classifications. Only 40 percent of the liberal arts schools and 34 percent of research universities have a required sequence, whereas more than half (52.2 percent) of the economics departments in universities with business schools require micro before macro.

Beyond principles, the economics core typically includes intermediate micro and macro theory courses, a statistics class, and perhaps an econometrics or mathematical economics course. With a couple of exceptions, the core requires two intermediate theory classes and some statistics. Only eight of the 124 schools in our sample required two or more statistics classes. Calculus, while not counted as part of the core given its general education designation, was almost a universal prerequisite in both research universities and universities with business schools. Among liberal arts schools, 45 of 50 (90 percent) require a calculus course. The calculus requirement is also often higher in the former two school classifications. Two or more calculus classes are a core requirement at 46 percent of research universities and 33 percent of universities with business schools. This contrasts sharply with liberal arts colleges/universities – only 6 percent require more than one calculus course.

One distinct trend that has arisen since performing our last curricular accounting is the rising status of econometrics in the core (Dean and Dolan, 2001). This further "quantification" of the major holds across all three school classifications. More than half of the liberal arts and research universities now require econometrics (54 percent and 60 percent, respectively). Among economics departments in universities with top-ranked business schools, 43 percent include econometrics in the core. In sum, counting all the required core courses with the exception of the *first* calculus course, the core curriculum in liberal arts schools averages roughly one less required course (5.0) than research

Table 69.2   Elective offerings of the economics major

Curricular item	Top 50 liberal arts colleges (Number or Percent)	Top 50 research universities (Number or Percent)	24 of Top 50 business schools (Number or Percent)
No. of required electives	4.2	4.7	4.6
No. High-level electives required	1.5	1.3	1.5
% with advanced micro offered	24.0%	48.0%	29.2%
% with advanced macro offered	44.0%	56.0%	29.2%
% with game theory offered	58.0%	80.0%	58.3%
% with gender offered	60.0%	40.0%	25.0%
% with behavioral offered	24.0%	32.0%	20.8%
% with experimental offered	22.0%	26.0%	25.0%
% with European Union offered	16.0%	22.0%	12.5%
% with honors offered	66.0%	80.0%	62.5%
% with internship offered	12.0%	20.0%	29.2%

universities (6.0) or universities with a business school (5.8). Beyond the core, liberal arts schools also have a slightly lower number of required electives for the major, an average of 4.2 courses. This amounts to a difference of roughly one-half of an elective compared to research universities (4.7) and those with business schools (4.6).

Adding required electives to the required core, including the possibility of a compulsory capstone experience which we consider in detail in the next section, comprises the total number of courses for the major. The total at liberal arts colleges averages 10.3 courses. This total is almost a full course less than the 11.1 required in economics departments in universities with business schools. Research universities, due to their higher number of quantitative and elective requirements, average 11.6 courses for the major.

The larger size of the faculty at research universities, coupled with the offering of advanced degrees in economics, allows for both greater breadth and depth in elective offerings. This is evidenced in Table 69.2 by the offering of advanced undergraduate coursework in micro and/or macro theory beyond the core intermediate theory class. Roughly half of the research universities offer advanced microeconomics (48 percent) and macroeconomics (56 percent) as an elective. In contrast, advanced microeconomics is offered at only about one-fourth of liberal arts schools (24 percent) and universities with business schools (29 percent); advanced macro is offered at 44 percent and 29 percent, respectively. However, the absolute size differential across cohorts has no bearing on the number of required electives that list an intermediate core theory course as a prerequisite.[7] In fact, the number of such electives is slightly greater at liberal arts schools, at 1.5 courses, than at research universities or schools offering business degrees. Similarly, institutional scale has little impact on the availability of the five courses we have defined as reflecting newer fields of economics. The highest prevalence of these field offerings exists at liberal arts colleges and research universities. Universities with business schools have the lowest percentage offering in all five fields. Game theory is the most common of the five electives, offered at 80 percent of the research universities and 58 percent of the other two institution categories. The greatest variation occurs in gender economics. This course is offered at 60 percent of the liberal arts schools as compared to 40 percent of the research universities and only 25 percent of universities with a business school. Behavioral, experimental, or economics of the European Union are listed in roughly one-fourth of the catalogs, irrespective of school classification.

The economics major can offer options beyond the basic requirements, most commonly an honors program and/or internships. An honors program is listed in 80 percent of the catalogs at research universities and roughly two-thirds of the liberal arts and universities with business schools. A for-credit internship is less prevalent but still varies notably by cohort. Almost 30 percent of the universities with business schools offer an internship for credit as compared with 20 percent of research universities and only 12 percent of liberal arts schools. The lack of such opportunities may correspond with the rise in the prevalence of capstone experiences offered.

THE CAPSTONE COURSE

This portion of the chapter focuses on the prevalence and nature of capstone experiences across cohorts. The sample size for our capstone analysis is roughly double because we now consider the top-100 schools in each category. However, as before, there is overlap between the research universities and business schools. Indeed, the top 11 business schools are located in research universities. Overall, 64 of the business schools are located in research universities or liberal arts schools.[8] Adjusting for this overlap reduced the sample to 236 observations.

A special focus on the capstone course is consistent with a clearly articulated objective stated 20 years ago in a well-known AEA report (Siegfried et al., 1991). This report claimed "a broad consensus exists among economics faculty that enabling students to think like an economist is the overarching goal of economic education" (p. 199). In support of this goal, the report specifically recommended:

> a capstone experience that synthesizes applications, encourages students to integrate economics with the rest of their college learning experience, and accords opportunities for creative writing (p. 218).

Although the virtue of a "capstone" experience seems self-evident in the title, its role in rounding out the curriculum deserves emphasis. If teaching economic thinking is the strategic goal, the specific courses are the tactics. Each course has the responsibility of assuring "proficiency" in specific areas, and a good curriculum is one in which the course contents coalesce to develop a full range of proficiencies.[9] The increments of knowledge in this process are easy to recount – definitions, concepts, abstract reasoning, modeling, prediction, empirical testing, and policy evaluation – and a student's grade point average is certainly one measure of achievement in these key areas. However, if the goal of economic education is to teach students "to think like an economist," this goal has a quality of gestalt for which a capstone experience becomes the appropriate metric.

Despite the conceptual appeal of a capstone requirement, our effort to examine the capstone offering empirically is compromised somewhat by the nature of the course. The definition of a capstone experience is, by design, fairly encompassing, but college catalogs do not typically list a course as "the capstone." For this reason, the presence

Table 69.3   Number and type of capstone experiences offered

Panel A: Percentage of schools offering the following number of capstone experiences

Number of capstone experiences	Top 100 liberal arts colleges	Top 100 research universities	36 of top 100 business schools
None	30%	72%	67%
One	23%	15%	22%
Two	30%	10%	11%
Three	16%	3%	0
Four	1%	0	0
Total	100%	100%	100%

Panel B: Percentage of schools offering the specific type of capstone experiences

Type of capstone experience			
Comprehensive Examination	13%	4%	0%
Policy Seminar	58%	11%	28%
Directed Research	40%	19%	17%
Independent Research	36%	14%	6%

of a capstone course often had to be inferred based on the fact that it was required in the senior year for completion of the major. For example, a senior seminar is a common listing. However, even a required senior seminar may lack the unifying conceptual orientation to qualify as a capstone course. In our empirical overview, we allowed the data to define themselves based on catalog copy. From this vantage point, we identified four avenues by which a school's curriculum appeared to include a capstone requirement: (1) a comprehensive examination; (2) applications to contemporary issues; (3) a directed writing assignment; and (4) an independent research project.

Table 69.3 summarizes this categorization for the 236 schools as stratified in our sample. Panel A provides a frequency distribution of the number of different types of capstone experiences for the major. An entry of zero indicates that a capstone experience is not required in the given school's economics major. Capstone experiences are required at 70 of the top 100 liberal arts schools. This ratio is almost completely reversed for the other cohorts; 72 percent of the research schools and another 24 of 36 (67 percent) of the universities with business schools do not require a capstone experience. If a school offered a capstone experience, liberal arts programs were much more likely to offer multiple types of capstone experiences. Only 10 percent of the research schools and four of 36 (11 percent) economics programs at universities with business schools had two types; three research schools offered three of the four types. In contrast, 30 percent of the liberal arts school's capstone experiences included two types and another one-sixth offered three; the capstone experience at one school contained all four types.[10]

Panel B of Table 69.3 provides the percentage of economics majors that offer a specific type of capstone. Since a capstone can be one of several types, the percentages will not sum to 100 percent. The most common type of capstone is some form of a senior seminar that is invariably current topics or policy-oriented. This senior seminar is required by 58 percent of liberal arts schools, 11 percent of research universities, and 22 percent (eight of 36) of the universities with business schools. Some schools have multiple sections of these seminars offering different topics taught by different professors in different semesters. In many instances there is a cap on the number of students enrolled in these senior seminars. Other schools appear to offer multiple topics within the senior seminar; this course might be taught by one professor or perhaps several. A reasonable assumption is that these senior seminar courses require a term paper, "major research paper," or the like. This paper may not have been explicitly described in the course description, but might be classified as "writing of directed research." Such writing does not generally entail "original" and certainly not "independent" research in that the paper is related to the topic of the seminar. They also tend to be more in the vein of dissecting or integrating economics journal articles and, while sometimes including data analysis, do not appear to require obtaining data sets.

The second most prevalent type of capstone is directed research, usually as part of a university writing requirement. This type of capstone is the most frequently offered by research universities, at 19 percent. There are also 40 liberal arts colleges and six universities with business schools that have economics majors offering directed research as at least one part of their capstone experience. An "independent research project" is mentioned as a type of a capstone experience at 36 liberal arts schools, 14 research universities, and in two of the universities with business schools. At numerous schools, the independent research project is offered as the honors portion of a senior capstone, while the non-honors majors take a more structured senior-seminar. Sometimes it is unclear whether the senior research course is required of all seniors or just those doing an honors project. A comprehensive exam is relatively rare but still present in our sample. Thirteen liberal arts schools and four research universities have some form of comprehensive exam. Some exams involve just micro and macro; others also include quantitative analysis. One school explicitly mentioned essays in micro and macro.

CO-CURRICULAR EXPERIENTIAL LEARNING

"Learning by doing" dates back to Dewey (1938). This concept has been carefully articulated since, notably by Kolb (1976, 1984) and Spencer and Van Eynde (1986), who provided one of the earliest applications of experience learning to economics. Experience learning reorders the steps commonly associated with the pedagogy in economics (in other words, abstract modeling, deductive implications, empirical hypothesis testing, relevant applications). It begins with a "concrete experience" intended to spark "reflection", which leads to recognition of more "abstract generalizations" that can be "tested in new applications" (Spencer and Van Eynde, 1986, p. 290). A number of authors have advocated the use of experiential learning in economics (for example, McGoldrick, 1998; Loomis and Cox, 2000; Walstad, 2001; Becker and Watts, 2001) and more recent research has documented its advantages, especially with regard to different types of students (Emerson and Taylor, 2004; 2007).

One can identify at least three strands of experiential method in the literature of the last decade – classroom experiments, games, and service-learning.[11] Despite the conceptual appeal of experiential learning methods, and a clear enthusiasm among those individuals who have contributed to the literature, the extent to which these applications have permeated the classroom is unclear. Indeed, Watts and Becker's (2008) most recent survey indicates only "slow growth in the use of other teaching methods" (p. 285).[12] Moreover, they suggest that acceleration of the shift toward active learning may only occur with generational turnover in the professoriate.

Against this backdrop, it is worth highlighting the Fed Challenge model and student managed investment funds (SMIF) because both experiential formats have been implemented fairly widely. In 2009, nationwide 140 schools participated in the Fed Challenge competition. Regarding SMIF, our survey of the top-50 liberal arts colleges and research universities identified 22 and 29 SMIF programs, respectively. In the majority of cases, both programs are currently extracurricular activities, although some participants receive partial or full course credit.

FED CHALLENGE

Initiated as a high school program in 1991, Fed Challenge is an intercollegiate competition administered by a limited number of Federal Reserve Banks in cooperation with the Board of Governors. Semi-final competitions are conducted at the district level and the finalists from each district compete at the Board of Governors. Teams of three to five members present economic analysis to support a Federal Open Market Committee (FOMC) policy statement regarding the federal funds rate. This competitive format is easily adapted to a course, since the class can be divided into as many teams as the class size accommodates.[13]

The Fed Challenge model is a heavily data-based experience. Students are required to analyze a wide range of macroeconomic time series covering all aspects of the household, business, government, and international sectors. These times series are readily available at FRED, a massive data depository supported by the St. Louis Federal Reserve Bank.[14] The analysis and presentation are initially data driven due to a heavy reliance on creating and interpreting charts, but the path to theory and policy is clear. Familiarity with the data supports analysis of theories of consumption and investment, estimation of Taylor rules and Okun's Law, and appreciation of historical concepts such as the "Lucas Critique" and the "Great Moderation" of inflation. In terms of policy, very accessible discussions occur in speeches that are routinely made by the Board Chairman, Governors, and Federal Reserve Bank presidents.[15] The varying opinions that are expressed in these speeches provide useful juxtaposition of normative issues on policy matters. For example, one can compare speeches by Charles Evans or Janet Yellen versus Thomas Hoenig or Charles Plosser. These district bank presidents, who served on the FOMC, have expressed very different positions on the inflation risks versus the need for sustained monetary stimulus in responding to the severe recession from 2007–09 and have been strenuously opposed to the second round of quantitative easing in 2011.

STUDENT MANAGED INVESTMENT FUNDS (SMIF)

The merits of SMIF as an experiential format for finance students are well established.[16] More recently Dolan and Stevens (2006; 2010) have provided extensive detail on the role that economics majors can have in a SMIF. This role stems from orienting a SMIF as a "top-down" versus "bottom-up" exercise. The bottom-up approach begins (and largely ends) with stock selection based on fundamental analysis of a security's intrinsic value relative to its market value. In short, stock valuation skills play a dominant role in determining the portfolio. For this reason, SMIFs were initially largely in the domain of business schools since stock valuation techniques are typically part of a finance curriculum. The top-down approach proceeds from an overview of global and national economic conditions along with an analysis of macroeconomic relationships impinging on financial markets. From this broad economic perspective, the analysis moves to a consideration of various sectors or industries. Sector weights for the portfolio reflect over-weighting those sectors offering the best position, given expectations of the broader economic environment. The last step in the top-down analysis focuses on stock selection within each sector.

If an economics department happens to have access to an undergraduate business school, the top-down approach accommodates an integration of economics and finance competencies. However, there needn't be a business school link in order to have a SMIF. Although economics students are not typically trained in valuation techniques, the top-down SMIF can still be implemented by using exchange traded funds (ETFs). An ETF is an indexed fund that trades throughout the day on an organized exchange, just like buying or selling stock. Implementation of asset allocation changes, based on an analysis of broader global and macroeconomic developments, requires buying and selling ETFs indexed to different asset classes. Students implement sector rotation strategies within the broader market index through buying and selling ETFs representing different market sectors to achieve the desired weighting. Students may overlay additional constraints on the portfolio of ETFs, such as stock capitalization (for example, "small, mid, or large cap") or investment style ("value versus growth"). A wide range of macroeconomic factors drive portfolio performance when ETFs are used. This allows economics students to make full use of macroeconomic and industry analysis.[17]

As with the Fed challenge, the students' early exposure is to a lot of real world data, but interpretation of data and events requires collective skills in micro and macro. On a macro level, the analysis focuses on forecasting key variables (for example, employment, GDP growth, inflation, and interest rates). There is also the obvious need to monitor monetary and fiscal policy. The micro applications lie in the analysis of specific industries, the profile of which would be dictated by broader economic conditions. Industry analysis would also consider factors such as the degree of competition (for example, merger activity) and possible regulatory impacts (for example, fossil fuel tax, green energy subsidies, healthcare reform).

Perhaps the most experiential aspect of a SMIF is the money – real money! Indeed, among the schools we surveyed, SMIFs at liberal arts colleges and research universities managed an average of roughly $250,000 and $625,000, respectively (although some SMIFs operate with as little as $10,000). Thus a SMIF's annual performance is clearly revealed in real dollars, and relative performance is easily benchmarked to broader market indexes. Though we lack precise data, we surmise that SMIFs are probably the oldest and most widely applied experiential learning format in economics.

CONCLUSIONS

This review of the current status of the economics curriculum warrants the following observations. The foundation theory courses that comprise the core are unchanged, but the core requirements reflect increasing quantification. Virtually all of the schools surveyed here require at least one calculus course as a prerequisite; many required more than one. This increasing quantification is also reflected in a two-semester statistics requirement or including econometrics as part of the core. These conclusions apply especially to research universities. Newer research fields (experimental, behavioral, gender) of the last couple of decades have made inroads into the undergraduate curriculum but, with the exception of game theory, not dramatically. Regarding the AEA's 1991 call for emphasis on a capstone requirement, the most substantive response has occurred at top liberal arts schools; notably less so at research universities or in economics departments affiliated with business schools. At this point, the capstone experience most commonly involves some combination of policy seminars and directed or independent research. In terms of co-curricular activities, we believe Fed Challenge and SMIF are noteworthy. The applicability of the Fed Challenge program for economics majors is straightforward and it exists at many schools. SMIF, initially in the domain of business schools, is now accessible to economics students and represents an emerging opportunity for experiential learning.

NOTES

1. Siegfried et al. (1991, p. 202) liken the economics major to a tree – with roots in principles, a trunk of core theory and branches of field-specific applications. This, they suggest, contrasts with other social science disciplines which have a "more hedge-like structure of separate and largely independent subfields."
2. In a recent survey of economics majors at 82 schools, Jones et al. (2009) find that roughly 10 percent of the majors indicate an interest in graduate school, but only 2 percent actually enter a Ph.D. program in economics.
3. Analysis of this third category is motivated by our own research, which has documented clear differences in the nature of the economics curriculum in liberal arts schools versus undergraduate institutions with business schools (Dean and Dolan, 2001). Furthermore, this category is quantitatively important since at institutions that grant undergraduate business degrees, the economics department is located in the business school about half of the time. Ignoring this cohort would exclude a large number of prominent schools that offer an economics major.
4. The Carnegie classifications identify 96 "research universities with very high research activity" and 287 "baccalaureate arts and sciences colleges." Therefore, the top-50 criterion means we consider roughly half of the research universities and slightly more than one-sixth of baccalaureate arts and sciences colleges. Rankings are based on the 2009 *US News and World Reports.*
5. The role of the economics major in "liberal education" was the subject of a 2006 study by the American Economic Association (AEA) funded by the Teagle Foundation. The edited collection of essays from this study captures the diverse perspectives of how the evolving nature of economic education, and especially graduate education, may detract from the broader goals of liberal education (Colander and McGoldrick, 2009).
6. One school, Harvey Mudd, did not list an economics department. The online course catalog for the US Naval Academy did not designate required courses and electives, so complete information is available on only 48 of the liberal arts schools.
7. Higher-level electives must specifically require one of the intermediate core theory classes and not just be labeled as a "300" or "upper-level" elective. Several of the latter courses only have principles as a prerequisite.
8. There is only one school in the liberal arts category – the authors' own University of Richmond – which has the economics department located administratively within a school of business.

9. Hansen (1986, 2001, 2009) has written extensively on calibrating economic education in terms of proficiencies. Carlson et al. (2002) provide a detailed account of how Hansen's proficiency concepts were applied to their department's curriculum revision, including specific reference to the design of their capstone course. For more information about a formal proficiencies approach, see Chapter 17, "Expected Proficiencies Approach to the Economics Major", in this volume.
10. Sewanee – University of the South appears to be the only school that requires all majors to complete a comprehensive exam and then offers majors the option of an empirical research project or a policy seminar with a directed writing assignment.
11. For more information about these techniques, see Chapter 7, "Classroom Experiments" and Chapter 6, "Experiential Education in Economics", in this volume.
12. Since 1995, the authors have surveyed more than 3,000 academic economists regarding undergraduate teaching methods at five-year intervals. This conclusion is based on the 2005 survey data.
13. The intercollegiate aspect of Fed Challenge is exciting, but the appeal of this experiential activity is not, and cannot be, based on this element. Only the New York, Boston, Richmond, and Chicago Federal Reserve banks currently support the program. Moreover, these banks have recently expressed concern about the strain on administrative resources as the popularity of the program has grown. But these facts do not diminish the virtues of the program as an experiential format. In fact, our own university is currently using the Fed challenge framework as a capstone experience. Whiting (2006) describes a similar application as part of a principles of macroeconomics course.
14. FRED contains over 34,000 times series that are downloadable in Excel format. These series are updated typically within 24 hours of a new data release (http://research.stlouisfed.org/fred2/) (accessed 2 September 2011).
15. http://www.federalreserve.gov/newsevents/speech/2010speech.htm (accessed 5 May 2011). Speeches by Federal Reserve Bank presidents not currently on the FOMC are available at individual Bank websites.
16. Block and French (1991), Lawrence (1994), Johnson et al. (1996), Kahl (1997), and Merritt (2002) represent a short list of authors describing the educational benefit of SMIF programs.
17. Websites provide most of the data and screening requirements for an ETF strategy. For example, ETF data and performance tracking capabilities appear on several websites (Morningstar, MSN Money, CNN Money, and Yahoo!Finance). Yahoo!Finance provides annual reports for all ETFs. The New York Stock Exchange, American Stock Exchange, and NASDAQ all maintain websites on ETFs to include both data and instructional information on ETF trading. Transaction costs of trading ETFs are low due to the low turnover inherent within an ETF portfolio and the infrequent trading of ETF funds consistent with implementation of a top-down strategy. Mutual funds charges range from 1.0 percent to 3.0 percent, while ETF charges are in the 0.1 percent to 1.0 percent range. There are currently over 400 different funds, with ample numbers of ETFs within any chosen category.

REFERENCES

Becker, W. and M. Watts (2001), "Teaching methods in U.S. undergraduate economics courses", *Journal of Economic Education*, **32** (3), 269–79.
Block, S. and D. French (1991), "The student managed investment fund: A special opportunity in learning", *Financial Practice and Education*, **1** (1), 35–40.
Board of Governors of the Federal Reserve, http://www.federalreserve.gov/newsevents/speech/2011speech.htm, accessed 5 May 2011.
Carlson, J., R. Cohn and D. Ramsey (2002), "Implementing Hansen's Proficiencies", *Journal of Economic Education*, Summer, **33** (2), 280–91.
Carnegie Foundation (2006), http://classifications.carnegiefoundation.org/descriptions/, accessed 5 May 2011.
Colander, D. and K. McGoldrick (2009), "The Teagle Foundation Report: The economics major as part of a liberal education", *Educating Economists: The Teagle Discussion on Re-evaluating the Undergraduate Economics Major*, Cheltenham, UK and Northampton, MA, USA: Edward Elgar, pp. 3–39.
Dean, D. and R. Dolan (2001), "Liberal arts or business: does the location of the economics department alter the major?", *The Journal of Economic Education*, **32** (1), 18–35.
Dewey, J. (1938), *Experience and Education*, New York: Collier Books.
Dolan, R. and J. Stevens (2006), "Business conditions and economic analysis: an experimental learning program for economics students", *The Journal of Economic Education*, **37** (4), 395–405.
Dolan, R. and J. Stevens (2010), "Experiential learning for undergraduates in economics and finance: A true top-down investment fund", *Journal of Financial Education*, **36** (1/2) 120–36.

Emerson, T. and B. Taylor (2004), "Comparing student achievement across experimental and lecture-oriented sections of a principles of microeconomics course", *Southern Economic Journal*, **70** (3), 672–93.

Emerson, T. and B. Taylor (2007), "Interactions between personality type and the experimental methods", *Journal of Economic Education*, **38** (1), 18–35.

Federal Reserve Bank of St. Louis, http://research.stlouisfed.org/fred2/, accessed 5 May 2011.

Hansen, W. (1986), "What knowledge is most worth knowing – for economic majors?", *American Economic Review*, **76** (2), 149–52.

Hansen, W. (2001), "Expected proficiencies for undergraduate economics majors", *Journal of Economic Education*, **32** (3), 231–42.

Hansen, W. (2009), "Reinvigorating liberal education with an expected proficiencies approach to the academic major", in D. Colander and K. McGoldrick (eds), *Educating Economists: The Teagle Discussion on Reevaluating the Undergraduate Economics Major,* Cheltenham, UK and Northampton, MA, USA: Edward Elgar, pp. 107–25.

Johnson, D., J. Alexander and G. Allen (1996), "Student managed investment funds: A comparison of alternative decision making environments", *Financial Practice and Education,* **6** (2), 97–101.

Jones, S., E. Hoest, R. Fuld, M. Dahal and D. Colander (2009), "What economics majors think of the economics major", in D. Colander and K. McGoldrick (eds), *Educating Economists: The Teagle Discussion on Reevaluating the Undergraduate Economics Major*, Cheltenham, UK and Northampton, MA, USA: Edward Elgar, pp. 191–211.

Kahl, D. (1997), "The challenges and opportunities of student-managed investment funds at metropolitan universities", *Financial Services Review* **6** (3), 197–200.

Kolb, D. (1976), *The Learning Style Inventory: Technical Manual*, Boston, MA: McBer and Co.

Kolb, D. (1984), *Experiential Learning: Experience as the Source of Learning and Development,* Englewood Cliffs, NJ: Prentice Hall.

Lawrence, E. (1994), "Financial innovation: The case of student investment funds at United States universities", *Financial Practice and Education,* **4** (1), 47–53.

Loomis, D. G. and J. E. Cox, Jr (2000), "A course in economic forecasting: Rationale and content", *Journal of Economic Education*, **31** (4), 349–57.

McGoldrick, K. (1998), "Service-learning in economics: A detailed application", *The Journal of Economic Education,* **29** (4), 365–76.

Merritt, J. (2002), "Fund managers before they graduate", *Business Week* (25 March), 106.

Siegfried, J., R. Bartlett, W. Hansen, A. Kelley, D. McCloskey and T. Tietenberg (1991), "The status and prospects of the economic major", *The Journal of Economic Education*, **22** (3), 197–224.

Spencer, R. and D. Van Eynde (1986), "Experiential learning in economics", *The Journal of Economic Education*, **17** (4), 289–94.

US News and World Reports (2009), http://colleges.usnews.rankingsandreviews.com/best-colleges, accessed 5 May 2011.

Walstad, W. (2001), "Improving assessment in university economics", *Journal of Economic Education*, Summer, **32** (3), 281–93.

Watts, M. and W. Becker (2008), "A little more than chalk and talk: Results from a third national survey of teaching methods in undergraduate economics courses", *Journal of Economic Education*, Summer, **39** (3), 273–86.

Whiting, C. (2006), "Data-base active learning in the principles of macroeconomics course: A mock FOMC meeting", *Journal of Economic Education*, Spring, **37** (2), 171–7.

Section C

The Characteristics of Economics Graduate Students

70 The characteristics of economics graduate students
Wendy A. Stock

Trends in the characteristics of economics graduate students can be described as a mix of both stability and change. According to the National Science Foundation (NSF, 2009), the number of PhDs awarded by US institutions annually in economics (and econometrics) has hovered between 850 and 1000 for 40 years. In 2007, 964 PhDs were awarded, down from a high of 1008 in 1996. The economic recession that began in 2007 undoubtedly generated an increase in the supply of potential graduate students across many disciplines (including economics), perhaps signaling that by 2013, the number of economics PhDs awarded will again rise above 1000.

The relative stability in the aggregate numbers of PhDs granted across the decades masks several dramatic changes in the demographic characteristics of economics graduate students, summarized in this chapter. The chapter also presents a point in time description of the undergraduate training and preparation characteristics of graduate students, as well as an overview of the mix of field choices, dropout decisions and time to degree for graduate students of the last decade.

DEMOGRAPHIC CHARACTERISTICS

Each year, NSF Survey of Earned Doctorates (SED) data generate a statistical profile of doctorate recipients across many disciplines. Forty years of summary characteristics of economics PhDs (from 1976–77 to 2006–07) are presented in Table 70.1, updated from Siegfried and Stock (2004).

Increasing Internationalization of the Economics PhD

As is the case in many other disciplines, graduate students in economics are increasingly internationally diverse. Forty years ago just over two-thirds of those earning PhDs in economics in the US were US citizens. Today that figure is under one-third. The globalization of the characteristics of graduate students generates both challenges and opportunities for educators. One challenge arises because as students come from more diverse educational backgrounds, graduate program admissions committees may have more difficulty reading signals of applicant preparedness and quality (Attiyeh and Attiyeh, 1997; Grodner, Grove, and Wu, 2010). This may result in increased reliance on standardized measures of applicant potential such as the Graduate Record Examinations (GRE). As discussed below, the quantitative GRE score among economics graduate students is a robust predictor of graduate school outcomes.

Challenges may also arise for US employers of economics PhDs since the increased international diversity of economics PhDs has been accompanied by an increase in the fraction of new PhDs accepting employment outside the US, rising from 16 to 24 percent between 1977 and 2007. Of course, one could argue that some of the growth in this percentage could reflect demand as well as supply factors if US employers have preferences for hiring US citizens or if employers outside the US have increased their demand for US-trained economics PhDs.

Opportunities arising from the globalization of the economics PhD come in the form of increasing interest in microeconomic theory, macroeconomic theory and international economics, fields in which higher proportions of international students specialize. Increased international diversity among graduate students also generates a globalization in the teaching of economics as many US-trained graduates take what they have learned in the US and apply it in academic jobs in their home countries.

The Gender Mix of Economics PhD Students

Parallel with the increase in the fraction of economics PhD students who are international students has been a dramatic change over the past 40 years in the percentage of PhDs awarded annually to females. As shown in Table 70.1, in 1977, just 8.7 percent of PhDs awarded in economics and econometrics went to females. Today, roughly one-third of these degrees are earned by females.

For data on graduate students in the degree pipeline (rather than recent PhD recipients), the American Economic Association's Committee on the Status of Women in the Economics Profession (CSWEP) reports on graduate students enrolled in economics PhD programs in the US. These data come primarily from the American Economic Association (AEA) Universal Academic Questionnaire, but are occasionally supplemented by CSWEP surveys (Fraumeni, 2009).

Over the past 15 years, the percentage of first-year students who are female has increased only slightly, from 30 percent in 1993 to 33.5 percent in 2009. The percentage of all-but-dissertation (ABD) students who are female also increased during the period, from 27 percent in 1993 to a similar 33.5 percent in 2009. Given that the share of undergraduate senior economics majors that is female is 28.9 percent for PhD-granting departments and 35.9 percent for liberal arts schools, the movement from undergraduate economics major to economics PhD student does not appear to be a major source of the "leaky pipeline" of progress of females into jobs as full professors or senior economists (Fraumeni, 2009). Note, however, that the aggregate percentage of graduate students in economics who are female is higher than the percentages who are female at top-10 and top-20 economics PhD programs. If the top programs are the primary source of future leaders in the economics profession, the pipeline for leadership remains "leaky" for the transition of females into the highest levels of the profession.

The Racial and Ethnic Mix of Economics PhD students

The AEA Committee on the Status of Minority Groups in the Economics Profession (CSMGEP) provides information on the racial and ethnic diversity of the economics profession. During the decade or so between 1993 and 2006, the fraction of economics PhDs earned by minorities varied between 6.6 and 11.8 percent. This translates into between 29 and 50 of the 900 or so degrees earned annually (Rouse, 2009). Roughly half of these degrees were earned by African Americans and half were earned by Hispanics. Only a very small number of economics PhDs (0–2 per year) are earned by Native American students.

The percentage of Bachelor's degrees awarded to minority students between 1995 and 2006 hovered around 12 percent. Based on these data, it appears that the pipeline of minority students from undergraduate to graduate programs in economics is more "leaky" for minority than female students. The AEA Pipeline Program is designed in part to address this gap.[1]

In terms of student demographics, faculty teaching in graduate classrooms in the US today look out over classes with a very different appearance than those of their predecessors of 40 years ago. Economics PhD students are vastly more international, somewhat more female, and slightly more African American and Hispanic than their predecessors of the 1970s.

GRADUATE SCHOOL PREPARATION

Along with the changing demographic makeup of graduate students comes a changing mix of preparation and training. Economics PhD students are less likely to hold undergraduate degrees in economics than their predecessors, but are more likely to hold Master's degrees. They are very likely to have conducted their undergraduate training outside the US.

Students' Institutions and Degrees Prior to Economics PhD Study

The internationalization of the economics PhD means that graduate students increasingly hold prior degrees from foreign institutions. Siegfried and Stock (2007) use a sample of students who entered one of 27 economics PhD programs in 2002 to investigate the undergraduate training of economics PhD students. The 27 programs produced 42 percent of the PhDs issued by US programs awarding at least one degree from 1998 to 2001, and the sample of programs is drawn from all quality tiers, but larger, higher ranked universities are overrepresented.

Siegfried and Stock (2007) report that 62 percent of the 2002 entering class of economics PhD students earned their undergraduate degrees at foreign institutions. Five percent earned degrees from British, Canadian, Irish, Australian, or New Zealand institutions, while 57 percent earned degrees from other foreign institutions. The number one undergraduate generator of eventual PhDs in economics in the world is Seoul National University, producing roughly twice as many undergraduates who eventually go on to earn economics PhDs as Harvard, the number two incubator of eventual economics PhDs in the world. Six of the top ten undergraduate alma maters of US-trained economics PhDs during the 1997–2002 period were foreign universities: Seoul National University, National Taiwan University, University of Delhi, University Commerciale "Luigi Bocconi", Yonsei University and Beijing University. Relative to the graduate classrooms of the 1970s, today's graduates are more likely to have been exposed to economics as undergraduates in South Korea, China, India, Italy and Taiwan.

Among PhD students who earned their undergraduate degrees in the US, increasing shares are alumni of top-50 liberal arts institutions. Siegfried and Stock (2007) report that the percent of economics PhDs who earned their undergraduate degrees from top-50 liberal arts institutions was 10 percent in 1970, but rose to 14 percent by 2000. About half of the eventual economics PhDs who attended US undergraduate institutions earned their undergraduate degrees from US economics PhD-granting institutions, a number that has remained relatively steady since 1970. The share of eventual economics PhDs who attended private undergraduate institutions outside the top 50 was roughly 16 percent in 2000, down from 18 percent in 1970. Among the share of economics graduate students trained as undergraduates in the US, the students increasingly come from Swarthmore, William and Mary, Miami University and similar liberal arts schools rather than from other non-PhD-granting institutions.

Students are entering economics PhD study from differing institutions than in the past; they are also coming to economics graduate programs with undergraduate degrees in economics at decreasing rates. As illustrated in Table 70.1, just over half of students awarded doctorate degrees in 2006–07 held undergraduate degrees in economics. In 1977 this figure was roughly two-thirds. Some of the decline in the proportion of students with undergraduate degrees in economics is likely accounted for by an increasing proportion of students trained in mathematics. Although they do not have comparison data for earlier periods, Stock et al. (2009) estimate that roughly 10 percent of first-year students in PhD programs in 2002 held undergraduate majors in either math or economics/math dual majors.

With respect to graduate degrees earned prior to beginning study for the economics PhD, Stock et al. (2009) report that roughly half of the entering economics PhD class of 2002 held graduate degrees at the time they began economics PhD study. The split of males and females who came to PhD programs with graduate degrees is roughly equal, but the proportion of entering international students holding graduate degrees (60 percent) is much higher than that of entering US students (14 percent).

GRE Scores

The increasing degree of mathematical rigor in economics PhD programs has been accompanied by a selection of graduate students with high levels of quantitative skill into economics graduate study. Stock et al. (2009) describe the mean GRE scores for the entering economics PhD class of 2002. The mean quantitative GRE score among entrants into a representative sample of economics PhD programs in 2002 was 772 (out of a possible 800). This places entrants into economics PhD programs at about the 85th percentile of all GRE examinees who tested between 1999 and 2001. The *median* score among the entering PhD class of 2002 was 790; 40 percent of the entrants scored a perfect 800 on the exam, and 65 percent scored 780 or higher. The mean verbal score of the entering class was 563, placing the average first-year economics PhD student at about the 75th percentile of all examinees between 1999 and 2002.[2] Because the majority of students who enter economics PhD programs are non-US citizens, it is difficult to place much weight on the verbal portion of the test. That said, although the mean verbal GRE scores are statistically different for the two groups, the gap is not particularly large. The mean verbal GRE score for non-US citizens is 543; for US citizens, it is 604.

Table 70.1 A profile of doctoral training in economics in the US: 1977, 1986/87, 1996, 2001, and 2007

	1976–77	1985–86 or 1986–87	1995–96	2000–01	2006–07
Number of doctorates awarded in economics and econometrics	838	861[a]	1008	930	964
Percent US citizens	67.3	55.7[a]	42.9	38.0	31.8
Percent female	8.7	19.3[a]	22.4	28.0	32.5
Percent with BA/BS degree in economics	63.6	59.7[a]	57.8	56.6	54.5
Number of full-time first-year graduate students (incl. Master's)	2,886	2,584[a]	2,466	2,562	2,907
Number of full- and part-time graduate students (incl. Master's)	12,063	12,830[a]	12,080	11,340	12,132
Number of full-time graduate students in economics (incl. Master's) at doctoral institutions	9,938	10,473[b]	10,991	10,755	11,438
Median years to PhD	5.7	6.3[a]	6.8	7.0	6.9
Type of support for full-time graduate students at doctoral institutions (percentage distribution)[c]					
Fellowship and traineeship	18.4	15.3[a]	18.8	19.4	16.0
Research assistant	14.5	11.9[a]	11.3	13.3	18.4
Teaching assistant	25.6	30.9[a]	28.9	31.5	29.5
Other	41.5	41.9[a]	41.0	35.8	36.1
Percent accepting employment outside U.S.	16.2	19.6[b]	30.3	26.2	23.5

Notes:
[a] 1985–86.
[b] 1986–87.
[c] Distributions do not always sum to 100 percent because some categories are not reported.

Sources: W. Lee Hansen (1991, Tables 1 and 2), Siegfried and Stock (2004, Table 1), National Science Foundation (2009), and the NSF WebCASPAR database system.

GRADUATE SCHOOL CHOICES AND OUTCOMES

Distribution of Students by Graduate School Tier

There are approximately 135 economics PhD programs in the US.[3] The distribution of graduate students in economics in the US among these programs looks a bit like a chi-squared distribution with very few degrees of freedom – the majority of graduate students are educated at a small fraction of economics PhD programs. Based on the National Research Council (NRC) rankings of graduate programs in economics (Goldberger et al., 1995), the top-10 ranked schools account for roughly 20 percent of graduate student enrollment.[4] The second quartile of students are spread among 15 different programs,

Table 70.2   Graduate student characteristics by PhD program rank

	Program Rank					Full sample
	1–6	7–15	16–30	31–48	>48[a]	
Panel A: Entering PhD class of 2002						
Number of students	103	149	142	128	64	586
GRE analytical score	**752**[c]	**737**	716	713	**667**	722
GRE verbal score	575	**547**	573	577	**517**	562
GRE quantitative score	785	782	765	771	738	772
US citizen[b]	0.32	**0.26**	**0.39**	0.34	0.38	0.33
Male[b]	0.72	0.66	0.67	**0.58**	0.67	0.66
Median age at entry to program	**24.6**	24.7	24.6	25.0	**26.5**	24.8
Hold prior graduate degree[b]	**0.38**	0.48	0.44	0.47	**0.58**	0.46
Hold undergraduate degree in economics[b]	0.73	0.69	**0.78**	0.65	**0.58**	0.70
Hold undergraduate degree in economics/math[b]	**0.10**	0.08	0.04	0.05	**0.00**	0.06
Hold undergraduate degree in math[b]	**0.08**	0.03	0.01	0.02	0.03	0.03
Type of undergraduate institution attended	**0.33**	0.21	0.24	0.21	0.25	0.24
US economics PhD-granting[b]						
US top-50 liberal arts[b]	0.08	0.05	0.07	0.05	0.02	0.06
Other US public[b]	0.02	**0.01**	0.06	**0.09**	0.08	0.05
Other US private[b]	**0.00**	0.03	0.04	0.03	**0.08**	0.03
Top-50 foreign[b]	**0.13**	0.04	0.02	**0.02**	0.02	0.04
Other foreign[b]	**0.45**	**0.66**	0.57	0.59	0.56	0.58
Panel B: Graduating PhD class of 2001–02						
Number of students	93	78	101	68	179	519
Median time to degree	**5.00**	5.42	5.08	5.25	**6.00**	5.49
US citizen[b]	**0.33**	0.47	0.45	0.49	0.44	0.43
Male[b]	0.74	0.74	0.76	0.65	0.70	0.72
Median age at degree	**30.3**	**30.7**	**30.7**	31.2	**33.1**	31.0

Notes:
[a]   Graduates from unranked institutions are included.
[b]   Proportions.
[c]   Numbers in bold are those for which the mean value for the tier is statistically higher or lower than for the rest of the sample at the 0.10 level (two-tailed tests). For variables for which we report the median, we tested the differences in means.

Sources: Panel A: Stock et al. (2009); Panel B: Siegfried and Stock (2004).

the middle quartile among 18 schools, the fourth quartile among 26 programs, the fifth quartile among the remaining programs. Put differently, the top 25 PhD programs enroll roughly 40 percent of the PhD students in the US.

Table 70.2 presents the characteristics of economics PhD students across graduate programs grouped into five "tiers" based on the method used by Hansen (1991), which employs 1993 NRC rankings for quality of graduate faculty (Goldberger et al.,

1995). The first tier of programs includes Chicago, Harvard, MIT, Princeton, Stanford and Yale; the second tier includes Columbia, Michigan, Minnesota, Northwestern, Pennsylvania, Rochester, California-Berkeley, UCLA and Wisconsin-Madison.

Panel A of Table 70.2 presents data on the entering PhD class of 2002 (Stock et al., 2009). Panel B presents data on the graduating economics PhD class of 2002 (Siegfried and Stock, 2004). Given a median time to degree of 5.5 years, Panel B could loosely be interpreted as representing the characteristics of the fastest half of the entering class into economics PhD programs in 1996 plus slower graduates from earlier entering classes.[5]

Student demographics across the tiers differ in that students in tier 1 and 2 programs appear less likely to be US citizens than students from lower-ranked programs. For the entering class of 2002, students in tier 4 programs are more likely to be female than those in higher tiers. The higher proportion of males at tier 1 and 2 programs across both cohorts of students are not statistically different from those at lower tiers. Students in higher-ranked programs are younger, on average, than those in lower-ranked programs when they enter graduate school (24.6 years for tier 1 students vs. 26.5 years for tier 5 students). Because students at higher-tier programs complete their degrees faster, this translates into a lower age at degree for those from higher-tier programs as well (a median of five years for tier 1 graduates vs. six years for tier 5 graduates).

In terms of preparation for graduate school, students enrolled in tier 1 programs average quantitative GRE scores of 785 and those in tier 2 average scores of 782, both statistically higher than the scores of their peers from other tiers. Students in tier 5 programs have significantly lower average quantitative GRE scores than those from other tiers. Students in higher-tier programs also have higher verbal GRE scores than those enrolled in tier 5 programs.

Students entering tier 1 economics PhD programs in 2002 are less likely to hold graduate degrees (for example, Master's degrees) upon their enrollment, but they are more likely to hold undergraduate degrees in mathematics or economics/math than those from lower-ranked programs. The tier 1 students are much more likely to have earned their undergraduate degrees from a US economics PhD-granting institution than their peers at lower-ranked programs. The tier 1 students who earned their undergraduate degrees from foreign institutions are more likely to have graduated from a top-50 foreign school.[6]

Financial Aid

According to Stock et al. (2009), 80 percent of the first-year economics PhD class of 2002 received some sort of financial aid during their first year of study. About half (47 percent) of the entering class of 2002 had fellowship support, almost one-third (28 percent) had teaching assistantship support and one-fifth entered their PhD programs with no financial aid. These patterns are consistent across males and females and across US citizens and non-US citizens (Stock et al., 2009). There are dramatic differences in the types of financial aid given across tiers. Ninety-three percent of the students entering tier 1 economics PhD programs in 2002 received some sort of fellowship support during their first year of study, while only 22 percent of students entering tier 5 programs received such support. Alternatively 45 percent of those entering tier 5 programs received no financial aid during their first year of study, while only 7 percent of those in the top programs received no aid.

Siegfried and Stock (2004) ask students in the graduating class of 2002 about the types of financial aid they obtained during the first five years of their graduate program, and then classify students according to their predominant source of support. They find that students who graduated in 2002 were predominantly supported by teaching assistantships during their course of study, with fewer than 10 percent of students reporting research assistantships, fellowships, or government sponsorships as their primary source of financial aid throughout the first five years of their economics PhD study. As was the case with the entering cohort of 2002, these aggregate figures mask stark differences across students in different tiers of economics PhD programs. Students graduating from tier 1 programs were much more likely to receive predominantly fellowship support than those from tier 5 programs. Alternatively those from tier 5 programs were more likely to receive teaching assistantships than those from tier 1 programs.

Professors in the top programs are much more likely to be teaching students who lack the pressures of obtaining job-related (including teaching and research assistantship) income or obtaining student loans than those teaching in tier 5 programs. As a result, tier 1 professors likely face students with fewer time constraints generated from outside the classroom than their peers at tier 5 institutions.

Fields of Specialization

Siegfried and Stock (1999, 2004) present information on the economics subfields of specialization for the graduating class of 1996–97 and 2001–02, respectively. The most popular subfields among both cohorts of graduates were macro/monetary and international economics. High proportions of students across both cohorts also specialized in industrial organization and labor economics. Relatively few students specialized in economic history, microeconomic theory, or in agricultural and natural resource economics.

The distribution of fields of specialization differs between male and female graduate students and between US citizen and non-US citizen graduate students (for the 2001–02 graduates, the only year for which such data are available). Higher proportions of students specializing in labor economics, health, education, and welfare economics, and development economics are females than in other subfields. Lower proportions of students specializing in financial economics are females than other subfields. Among the 2001–02 graduates, higher proportions of students specializing in labor economics and in agricultural and natural resources economics are US citizens than in other subfields, while lower proportions of those in micro theory, macro/monetary, and international economics are US citizens.

Attrition and Time to Degree

According to Stock et al. (2006), the two-year dropout rate in economics PhD programs is 26 percent. In other words, professors will see only 75 percent of the students they taught in the first-year core courses when the time comes to read and critique dissertation proposals. Two-year attrition rates vary across program tiers. They are higher among tiers 4 and 5 (39 and 33 percent, respectively), and lower among tiers 1 and 2 (15 and 18 percent, respectively). In a regression that controls for a wide array of program and student characteristics, Stock et al. (2006) found that only students' quantitative and verbal GRE scores and an indicator for whether the student had a research assistantship during the first year of study were student characteristics that consistently predicted lower dropout probabilities during the first two years of economics PhD study.

Among students who persist and complete the economics PhD, the median time to complete the degree is about 5.5 years from beginning the PhD program to receiving the degree (Siegfried and Stock, 2004). The NSF Survey of Earned Doctorates (SED) Table 70.1 reports slightly longer time to degree values than this, primarily because the SED number includes time spent in *any and all* post-baccalaureate programs (e.g., it includes time spent earning a terminal Master's degree in economics, an MBA, or a law degree prior to entering the PhD program). Siegfried and Stock (2004) find that students who had a child during graduate school, who took a job prior to completing the PhD, and those without financial aid during their years of PhD study took longer to earn the PhD. Those with fellowships, who wrote essay-style (rather than single-topic) dissertations, those who had undergraduate degrees from top-50 liberal arts schools or from undergraduate institutions in the UK, Ireland, Canada, Australia, or New Zealand completed their degrees more quickly.

CONCLUSION

Roughly 1000 economics PhDs are awarded by US institutions each year. The majority are earned by non-US citizens, males and non-minorities. That said, the characteristics of graduate students in US economics programs have changed substantially over the past decades, becoming a more international, female, and (at least slightly) minority demographic group.

Students' preparation for PhD study in economics is increasingly obtained abroad, with South Korean, Chinese, Indian, Italian and Taiwanese institutions generating relatively large numbers of undergraduates who eventually go on to earn economics PhDs in the US. Students are decreasingly likely to enter economics PhD programs with undergraduate degrees in economics, but rather are increasingly likely to have obtained degrees in mathematics as preparation for economics PhD study. Not surprisingly, this preparation translates into remarkably high scores on the GRE exam for economics PhD students, with the median entrant into the graduate class of 2002 earning a 790 (out of 800) on the quantitative portion of the GRE exam.

Although the existing literature tells us a lot about economics PhD production in the US, what is less clear is how the production function for US-trained PhD economists compares with that for those trained abroad. For better or worse, the economics PhD production process in the US is remarkably homogeneous across programs (Hansen, 1991). Perhaps our peers across the globe have a more diverse approach to economics PhD training. Given criticisms by Colander (2007, 2011) and others (for example, Stock and Hansen, 2004) regarding the gap between what US-trained economics PhDs learn in school and what they do in their jobs, it would be of interest to examine the graduate placement patterns of non-US economics PhD programs, as well as the degree of match between the skills and proficiencies taught in those programs and the skills required in the jobs graduates from those programs eventually take.

NOTES

1. The website: http://www.aeaweb.org/committees/CSMGEP/pipeline/index.php (accessed 12 June 2011) provides more information on the AEA Pipeline Program.
2. Source: http://www.testmasters.net/gre/Information/ScoringScale.aspx (accessed 12 June 2011), based on the Educational Testing Service (2002), "Graduate Record Examinations Guide to the Use of Scores". The latest version of this guide is available at: http://www.ets.org/Media/Tests/GRE/pdf/994994.pdf (accessed 12 June 2011).
3. Source: American Economic Association Graduate Studies in Economics Website, Alphabetical List of US Graduate Programs in Economics. http://www.vanderbilt.edu/AEA/gradstudents/Schools.htm (accessed 12 June 2011).
4. This group consists of the University of Chicago, Harvard, MIT, Stanford, Princeton, Yale, the University of California-Berkeley, the University of Pennsylvania, Northwestern University, and the University of Minnesota.
5. Differences between this median time to degree and that presented in Table 70.1 are described in the "Attrition and time to degree" section.
6. Stock et al. (2006) categorize the top-50 liberal arts colleges as identified annually by *US News and World Report*, but added Dartmouth, Miami (Ohio), Richmond, Trinity University, Tufts, and William and Mary (selective institutions with few graduate programs, but not classified as private liberal arts colleges) to the group. They classify the top-50 foreign schools as identified by Kalaitzidakis et al. (2001, Table 70.2).

REFERENCES

Attiyeh, G. and R. Attiyeh (1997), "Testing for bias in graduate school admissions", *Journal of Human Resources*, **32** (3), 524–48.

Colander, D. (2007), *The Making of an Economist Redux*, Princeton, NJ: Princeton University Press.

Colander, D. (2011), "Completion rates and time-to-degree in Economics PhD programs: Comment", *American Economic Review*, **101** (3), 188–9.

Fraumeni, B. (2009), "2009 Report of the committee on the status of women in the economics profession", http://www.cswep.org/annual_reports/2009_CSWEP_Annual_Report.pdf, accessed 15 April 2010.

Goldberger, M., B. Maher and P. Flattau (eds) (1995), *Research-Doctorate Programs in the United States: Continuity and Change*, Washington, DC: National Academy Press.

Grodner, A., W. A. Grove and S. Wu (2010), "Lost in translation? The economics PhD pipeline for US versus foreign applicants", Working Paper, http://academics.hamilton.edu/economics/swu/Grodner_Grove_Wu.pdf, accessed 15 April 2010.

Hansen, W. L. (1991), "The education and training of economics doctorates", *Journal of Economic Literature*, **29** (3), (September), 1054–87.

Kalaitzidakis, P., T. P. Mamuneas and T. Stengos (2001), "Rankings of academic journals and institutions in economics", Department of Economics, University of Cyprus, Discussion Paper 2001-10, October.

National Science Foundation, Division of Science Resources Statistics (2009), "Doctorate recipients from US universities: Summary Report 2007–08", Special Report NSF 10-309, Arlington, VA, http://www.nsf.gov/statistics/nsf10309/, accessed 9 May 2011.

Rouse, C. E. (2009), "Report on the committee on the status of minority groups in the economics profession", *American Economic Review*, **99** (2), 700–709, http://www.aeaweb.org/articles.php?doi=10.1257/aer.99.2.700, accessed 9 May 2011.

Siegfried, J. J. and W. A. Stock (1999), "The labor market for new PhD economists", *Journal of Economic Perspectives*, **13** (3), (Summer), 115–34.

Siegfried, J. J. and W. A. Stock (2004), "The labor market for new PhD economists in 2002", *American Economic Review*, **94** (2), (May), 272–85.

Siegfried, J. J. and W. A. Stock (2007), "The undergraduate origins of PhD economists", *Journal of Economic Education*, **38** (4), (Fall), 461–82.

Stock, W. A. and W. L. Hansen (2004), "Ph.D. program learning and job demands: How close is the match?", *American Economic Review*, **94** (2), (May), 266–71.

Stock, W. A., T. A. Finegan and J. J. Siegfried (2006), "Attrition in economics PhD programs", *American Economic Review*, **96** (2), (May), 458–66.

Stock, W. A., T. A. Finegan and J. J. Siegfried (2009), "Can you earn a PhD in economics in five years?", *Economics of Education Review*, **28** (5), (October), 523–37.

Section D

International Economic Education

71 Supporting economics higher education in the United Kingdom

John Sloman and Inna Pomorina

ECONOMICS HIGHER EDUCATION IN THE UK AND THE WORK OF THE ECONOMICS NETWORK

Higher education in the United Kingdom (UK) has witnessed unprecedented expansion in the past 50 years. The publication of the Report by the National Committee of Inquiry into Higher Education (HE) (1997), known as the Dearing Report[1] and the subsequent Government White Paper on lifelong learning stimulated debate into purposes, shape, structure, size and funding of higher education in the UK and laid foundations for important changes. The report also recognized the importance of teaching, learning, scholarship and research as essential parts of higher education.

Following recommendations from the report, the UK government's Higher Education Funding councils established the Learning and Teaching Support Network (LTSN), focused on promoting high quality learning and teaching in all subject disciplines. The Economics Network (EN) began life in September 1999 as part of this network. Then known as Economics LTSN, it is one of 24 Subject Centres covering all subjects taught in UK higher education. In 2004 it became part of the Higher Education Academy.

Until recently, teaching has not been a greatly valued activity in British universities: a long-term, large-scale prestige differential between teaching and research has operated both nationally (prestigious institutions tend to be research-intensive ones) and at the level of individual academics (traditionally rewarded for their research rather than teaching success). Subject Centres (SCs) have done more to change this hierarchy than any other body. They have made teaching and learning interesting to lecturers and have transformed the prestige and profile of teaching and learning within the British HE landscape. Being subject specific gives them credibility among the academic communities with which they need to engage and allows them to address specific pedagogical issues in a way that generic pedagogical training and support simply cannot.

The SCs are perceived as belonging to their subject communities: this sense of ownership is vital to their success. Over the past 11 years, the subject network has developed into a proactive as well as a highly responsive and focused organization that targets support and enhancement at the level of the individual academic and department. Subject Centres provide publications, events, funding opportunities and other resources to support university lecturers[2] and have become firmly embedded within their academic communities. This chapter will focus on the work of the Economics Network (EN) and the range of services it provides in light of current HE environment in the UK.

CHANGES IN THE HE ENVIRONMENT IN THE UK

In supporting student learning, higher education in the UK faces several key challenges, all of which are likely to become more acute over time.

- Students' expectations are increasing with higher tuition fees – rising from £3375 ($5400) per year in 2011/12 to between £6000 ($9600) and £9000 ($14,400) per year in 2012/13 – and greater input into evaluating teaching quality, including the use each year by all departments in all universities of a national student survey (the NSS);
- Government funding for teaching is being abolished in all subjects except for science, technology, engineering and mathematics (STEM). This could mean bigger classes and/or less contact time and probably more grading work;
- Rapid changes in technology create many opportunities for enhanced learning, but lecturers lag behind students in their comfort with using such technology;
- Universities face growing pressure from employers, government and funders to improve the employability of graduates;
- With a large number of international students, and to some degree a large number of international staff, HE institutions face a range of issues associated with optimizing the learning opportunities of such students and their peers. International staff also often need additional teaching support;
- Universities are attempting to be more inclusive in their policies, increasing the range of student needs and putting additional demands on both staff time and physical infrastructure.

It is in this context that the Higher Education Academy and its 24 Subject Centres seek to provide support to universities and their academic staff in their teaching role. This support is becoming ever more important as lecturers are faced with increased class sizes, increased grading loads and greater accountability to students and HE administration.

Universities in the UK have varying missions. Some are highly research intensive and take only students with the highest "A-level" grades (the standard high school qualification). Others are less research intensive and tend to take students with lower grades. Because funding follows high-quality research, it cross-subsidizes teaching in research-intensive universities, resulting in smaller classes and lower teaching loads. Such institutions also tend to make more use of graduate teaching assistants and full-time teaching fellows (on teaching-only contracts). The different types of university pose different challenges to the Subject Centres in providing support that is tailored to the needs of specific departments and academics.

The Economics Community

The economics community in UK higher education consists of over 1700 staff, teaching over 26,000 undergraduates and over 6000 postgraduates, studying over 1900 courses in economics at 96 universities. Most undergraduates in economics take it as their sole subject – a single honors degree in economics. A large minority, however, take it as half of a joint honors degree in two subjects, combining a degree in economics with any one of several subjects, such as business, politics, sociology, mathematics, statistics, geography, environmental studies, history or a modern language.

WEBSITE AND TEACHING RESOURCES

The Economics Network has four comprehensive websites:

- The main EN site[3] is designed primarily for university economics teachers and contains various publications, information about events, awards and funding opportunities, case studies of practice, learning materials, topics in pedagogy and sub-disciplines;
- Why Study Economics?[4] is designed to help prospective economics students answer questions about studying economics at university in the UK and prepare them for university life;
- Studying Economics[5] offers advice, help and information for Economics under-graduates: discusses economics course options to help them decide which ones are right for them, offers tips on writing essays, effective reading, data collection, making a presentation, revision, possible future jobs and careers;
- METAL[6] provides teachers and students with a selection of free learning resources designed to engage undergraduate students more fully and enthusiastically in mathematics for economics.

The EN's main site[7] currently receives around two and a half million hits per year. The EN's student-focused sites attract an additional half million hits per year. Among the most popular resources/online services are:

- The *Handbook for Economics Lecturers*, containing 22 chapters, including sections dedicated to lecturing, small classes, assessment, course design, and evaluations, e-learning and teaching assistants;
- An external examiners' database with 68 individuals registered. All UK universities are required to employ external examiners from other universities to conduct short site visits, checking on standards of assessment and marking;
- 170 examples of teaching practice in economics submitted by lecturers from UK, USA, Ireland, Australia and New Zealand;
- An Economics Book catalogue with more than 7000 economics textbooks, searchable and categorized by subject. A description of each book is provided, along with ISBNs and links to publishers' websites;
- An Economics Question Bank with over 1300 essay questions, multi-choice questions and problem sets. This is a password-protected site to prevent students gaining access, but any *bona fide* lecturer can apply for a free password. Lecturers can use the Question Bank to compile tests using a "shopping basket" facility;
- ExcelAssess, a library of self-marking assessment questions in Excel;
- Dedicated pages for each sub-discipline area of economics, as well as pages for many pedagogical themes, such as assessment, curriculum and content,

employability, math support, classroom experiments, student motivation, sustainability, internationalization, use of technology, etc.;
● Links to a large number of open-access data sets.

Lecturers highly value these resources, as they provide them with alternative ways of delivering the material, give a practical guide to typical problems they face in their practice and promote sharing experiences. It also gives lecturers a support network and additional confidence to try new things in their own courses.

SUPPORTING NEW LECTURERS AND GRADUATE TEACHING ASSISTANTS

Every year the Economics Network has run several dedicated annual training events for graduate teaching assistants (GTAs), and for new and early-career lecturers in both England and Scotland. By 2010, a total of 29 GTA and New Lecturer workshops had been run (most of them since 2006), with 550 participants. An average 95 percent of participants have found the workshops useful. The main aim of these events is to discuss and evaluate what makes effective teaching of economics: including lectures, seminars and small-group teaching, assessment and feedback, e-learning, module/unit design, classroom experiments and games. There is also time at the end of the workshop to reflect on key issues and to plan the next steps.

The demand for these workshops has grown significantly and there has been enthusiastic support from heads of economics departments. Because of this support, the EN has managed to secure additional funding from the Royal Economic Society and the Scottish Economic Society to run these workshops.

The workshops are seen to be more valuable by the attendees than the generic training they receive in their home institutions, as the workshops specifically address the issues they are likely to experience in teaching economics and they are able to share ideas and experience with fellow economists from other universities. The workshops are designed to complement institutional training and each participant receives a certificate which maps the workshop activities onto the UK Professional Standards Framework,[8] which specifies the broad requirements of an effective teacher in higher education. Some universities, including Bristol, Warwick and Nottingham, exempt their own GTAs and new lecturers from parts of their own training on this basis. All of the workshops involve an element of individual planning and each participant is asked what ideas they plan to apply in their practice. A special web section to support new lecturers and GTAs was developed,[9] which includes diaries, case studies and a GTA handbook chapter.

Formal evaluations conducted at each workshop provide informative feedback which has been very positive, and include comments on how they help new lecturers start their career, providing them with practical and relevant information on economics teaching and encouraging networking, sharing ideas and solutions between different GTAs from various universities. Student evaluations at the end of the academic year, during which participants implement what they have learned, reveal positive endorsement of their new approach to teaching.

A RANGE OF SUCCESSFUL CONTINUING PROFESSIONAL DEVELOPMENT ACTIVITIES

Workshops

The Economics Network had been running workshops, as part of continuing professional development activities nationally, regionally and for specific departments. The departmental workshops have been particularly successful as these can be tailored, through prior negotiation, to the needs of that particular department. Detailed discussions are held with the departmental contact and others in the department about the format and content of the workshop. Often these are informed by lecturer and student survey results (described in more detail below) for that specific department. Among the most popular topics for workshops are assessment, course design, recruitment and retention, problem-based learning and using games and experiments in teaching. Each workshop provides participants with an opportunity to share their experiences and discuss different ways of teaching or assessment.

Since 2000 the EN has held over 200 continuing professional development events, involving over 2000 participants. One key measure of success has been the high number of requests for further workshops from departments. Another measure is satisfaction expressed on feedback forms: consistently over 95 percent of participants have found the workshops useful.

Another important indicator of the need for such workshops is the rate of change in teaching/learning practices adopted by lecturers. The Economics Network's biennial lecturer surveys indicate a significant and positive trend in teaching practices adopted. In the 2009 survey, two-thirds stated that they had changed their teaching practice in the past two years, whereas only half cited such changes in the previous survey. Feedback from the participants of these events has been very positive and describes changes in their teaching practice that occurred as direct results of workshop participation.

Conferences

The Economics Network has held a biennial two-day conference on Developments in Economics Education (DEE) since 2001. This attracts some 120 participants from over 60 institutions both from the UK and abroad, with enough high-quality papers and workshops to run four concurrent sessions. For attendees, it may serve as a starting point to get involved with EN, to share ideas about teaching practice, and to network with like-minded colleagues from different universities and countries. All of the delegates from the 2007 and 2009 conferences rated keynote addresses as good or excellent and would encourage colleagues to attend.

EVIDENCE BASE: THE USE OF SURVEYS

The Economics Network conducts regular surveys to research the current state of teaching and learning in economics HE in the UK. These have provided a comprehensive evidence base to inform the planning of departments and, along with key stakeholders, to inform EN's own planning and give a voice to the community.

More than 10,000 students took part in the five EN biennial surveys, as did 741 instructors; 749 graduates responded to two alumni surveys and 36 employers completed two employer surveys. We highlight some of the more important findings below; full reports are available on the EN website.[10]

Among the most noticeable changes in the past decade, as revealed by EN's student surveys, have been: a decrease in the perceived usefulness of lectures; an increase in the use of virtual learning environments, such as Blackboard and Moodle – by 2010, more than four out of five students reported using them as part of their studies; an increased exposure to interactive forms of seminars/tutorials/classes, such as games and simulations; a greater use of group-work projects; and a big improvement in the perceived quality of teaching of math and statistcs.

Students' satisfaction with their courses has been stable during the decade surveyed, at around 75 percent. In surveys so far, the quality and enthusiasm of the teaching staff emerged as a main determinant of the quality of the student experience. Economics itself received a great deal of praise as an interesting and challenging subject, as well as offering the possibility of a good career. The students have also shown a demand for active involvement in learning. When asked to explain in what ways their experience differs from their expectations, students mention content, level of teaching, real-world relevance, and the pace of the course. In terms of the content, most comments had to do with the amount of math, since many students claimed that it was much more math-focused than they had anticipated. With respect to teaching practices, the many student comments focused on the lack of personal interaction between students and teachers, the poor quality of lecturers and the lack of contact time with lecturers.

Student surveys also asked respondents to identify the best and worst aspects of their courses. The most frequently mentioned best aspects of students' courses have been changing: along with good teaching and the choice of modules, respondents in 2002 mention pure interest in the subject, which was later supplanted by career opportunities and job prospects. In answer to the question about the aspects of the course that they did not like, a growing proportion of students over the years have felt that they liked everything about their course. Over a third of students in 2010 could not identify any aspect of their course they felt unhappy with, compared to 16.6 percent in 2006 and 26.6 percent in 2008.

Among the issues mentioned by the majority of instructors in the lecturer surveys were: students' math skills, students' motivation, plagiarism, the number of students and large-sized groups, supporting international students along with time constraints, fewer resources, use of teaching space, assessment, students' recruitment and retention. Instructors reported a lack of support and positive incentives from their departments for teaching innovation. Despite this, they are making changes to their teaching methodology, although "chalk and talk" remains dominant.

In enhancing students' learning, it is important to understand how current economics graduates are prepared for employment. EN recognizes that alumni can offer a unique perspective in evaluating the skills and knowledge developed through a degree course and those required in the workplace. Obtaining information on how degree programs could be improved was one of the main purposes of both the EN alumni surveys and the employer surveys. Many issues raised in these surveys are very similar. Both employers and economics graduates highly rated economics degrees. Nearly two-thirds of alumni would recommend students take a degree in economics. They also suggested some areas where further development would bring rewards, including enhancing general skills, such as oral and written communication, and the application of theory to real-world economic problems. Employers expressed concern with similar issues: the level of application of knowledge to problem-solving processes, communication skills and the employability skills of economics graduates.

Comparing results of different surveys over the years allows the EN to follow the changing picture of studying economics in the UK HE and to better target EN support to lecturers and departments. In some cases, students' suggestions for improvements in the way courses are run, such as smaller class sizes or more contact time, would require extra resources. In other cases, however, their suggestions could be achieved through relatively small changes in practice, such as enhancing the use of virtual learning environments, additional classroom activities or adjusting teaching styles. As a follow-up activity, the EN offers to provide workshops and advice to interested departments on the issues raised by the surveys.

DEVELOPING NETWORKS

Developing networks to build capacity and sustain interest and enhancement in student learning has been a key feature of the Economics Network's strategy. The Network has reached out not just to Key Contacts (see below) and Heads of Department, but also to enthusiasts (Associates) whose expertise can be called upon to support the economic education community through the sub-discipline-focused project, TRUE (see below).

Key Contacts

To facilitate the dissemination of ideas and practice, the Network has a key contact in every department/school (96 in total) and engages with them on a number of levels, including paper newsletters, email updates and an annual meeting that provides an opportunity to provide feedback for the EN's planning process. In 2008, a system of 17 regional network coordinators was established. Their role is to liaise with the key contacts in their area and to feed back information to the center, to help organize local events and to support the work of key contacts in their departments.

Associates

The Economics Network has 31 Associates. They all have some particular expertise in an aspect of learning and teaching in economics. They run events and attend meetings on behalf of the Network. There is an annual Associates conference to share and develop ideas for deepening the Network and its activities.

The Teaching Resources for Undergraduate Economics (TRUE) Project

Through the Network's ongoing engagement with academics, it became apparent that a major constraint on the development of modules and programs is the lack of resources available in a range of economics fields. Unlike microeconomics, macroeconomics and quantitative economics, where there is a considerable range of teaching and learning resources at the undergraduate level, lecturers in disciplinary fields have far fewer resources upon which to draw. There are two main reasons for this: there are fewer textbooks and accompanying supplementary materials available for field courses and academics are unable to access many of the excellent resources produced by colleagues in other universities as they are hidden within individual university virtual learning environments, which can only be accessed via a university password.

The Teaching Resources for Undergraduate Economics (TRUE) project covers 15 such fields, each led by a senior academic, including: Development Economics, Econometrics, Environmental Economics, European Economics, Experimental Economics, Health Economics, Heterodox Economics, International Economics, Industrial Economics, Labour Economics, Law and Economics, Economics of Money, Banking and Finance, Public-sector Economics, Regional and Local Economics, and Risk and Uncertainty. The project has focused on drawing together a number of existing resources to support lecturers in enhancing existing courses and creating new ones. A separate wiki for each field provides example syllabi, reading lists, assessment materials, seminar and workshop materials, lecture slides, handouts, case studies, videos and other innovative teaching materials. In addition to collecting, organizing, reviewing and depositing resources on the wiki, a designated lead academic for each field is tasked with launching the teaching and learning community, ultimately allowing the wiki to live beyond the initial EN support period. The Health Economic Education site[11] is a good example of this as there were over 400 submissions of materials during the first 12 months of the project. The provision of specialist wikis will, over time, improve the quality of learning resources available because they are open access and can be regularly used, updated, discussed and amended by the academics specializing in each of the fields. This resource will be of particular value to new lecturers, who have access to effective teaching materials developed by their peers.

STUDENT ENGAGEMENT AND STUDENT LEARNING

EN focuses on improving student experiences through direct surveying and engagement. In addition to the student surveys described above, since 2001 the EN has convened many student focus groups within university departments to understand economics students' experience and concerns. Not only do these provide valuable information to lecturers, they also give students an opportunity to reflect on their learning and to express their views for the benefit of other students. Specific resources have been developed for students as a result of the information gathered using these two methods.

Websites

The Economics Network launched its Why Study Economics? website[12] in 2004. The site is designed to encourage students to study economics at HE level and supports student transition from school/college to higher education. The site includes videos and diaries produced by students about specific jobs for economics graduates.

The Studying Economics website,[13] launched in September 2009, has a focus on supporting undergraduates studying economics. Although there is deliberately no specific *course* content on the site, it provides a range of other resources, including study advice, information about courses, support in writing a dissertation, career information, information on how to set up a student economics society, data and research sources, and information on work experience and employment.

The EN is in its second year of employing a full-time student to work on the above two sites. The method has proved extremely successful, allowing the Network to work more closely with students, including providing resources for students by students. The EN also has been running an annual student competition since 2005, which provides another opportunity for economics students to voice opinions on their learning experiences. In 2008/9 there were 52 entrants who addressed the question "How would you make difficult economics easier to learn?" A summary of ideas suggested by students were added to the website and were later incorporated into the lecturers' workshops.

Both websites are sponsored by the Royal Economic Society and the Studying Economics website consists of materials largely designed by students. The sites have grown rapidly in popularity, with 477,341 successful page requests for Why Study Economics? during the 2009/10 academic year and 205,205 successful page requests for the Studying Economics site.

FUNDING PROJECTS AND INITIATING CURRICULUM CHANGE

The EN sponsors small Learning and Teaching Development Projects, of up to £5000 ($8000), which focus upon the development, implementation and evaluation of innovative approaches to teaching, learning and assessment. Fifty-four have been funded since the program began in 2004/5. Among the themes covered by the projects in 2010/11 was problem-based learning, use of classroom experiments in teaching, support for international students, teaching economics through proverbs, developing academic skills, enhancing students' employability, connections in political economy, etc. Many of these Learning and Teaching Development Projects consult students about their learning experiences as part of project evaluation or provide case studies and papers for the website, conferences and workshops as the EN facilitates dissemination of outcomes across the community.

Project coordinators present their findings at an annual "Partners and Projects" workshop and have the opportunity to present at the biennial DEE conference. The "Partners and Projects" workshops often result in collaborative follow-up across different university departments. Each project is assigned a mentor, usually with prior project experience. Many of the mentors are Associates (see above). Some of the project coordinators would not be able to do pedagogic research without this funding and for some it leads to further funding opportunities and national recognition.

Externally Funded Projects

The EN has provided extensive support for the four economics projects funded under the UK government's Higher Education Funding Council for England's FDTL5 scheme (fifth round of the Fund for the Development of Teaching and Learning). The projects include:

- Beyond Dissemination Strategies: Embedding Computer-based Learning & Effective Uses of WinEcon & VLEs – working with lecturers in their institutions to customize the introductory economics software package WinEcon to their particular courses and institutional virtual learning environments (such as Blackboard);
- Bringing economic experiments into the classroom – developing, adapting, implementing and evaluating classroom experiments for the economics curriculum
- Mathematics for economics: enhancing teaching and learning (METAL) – Creating video, worksheets and assessment materials to support the teaching of mathematics to economics students;
- Developing First Year Undergraduates' Acquisition of Threshold Concepts in Economics – embedding threshold concepts in undergraduate programs to promote deep-level transformative understanding.

Support has included workshops, a dedicated part of the Economics Network's website,[14] representation on the projects' Advisory Groups and dedicated sessions at the DEE conference. It has also supported a joint dissemination project (FAME) for the four projects, including case studies from lecturers on the uses of the outputs of the four projects.

The EN is also supporting a project to analyze economics curricula across European countries at both undergraduate and postgraduate level. Findings will be shared with both UK and European economics departments.

WORKING WITH STAKEHOLDERS

During 2006/7 the Economics Network, in partnership with the Royal Economic Society (RES), commissioned a survey of key employers of economics graduates. This survey helped identify employers' requirements in terms of graduate skills which were subsequently mapped against the 2006 revised Quality Assurance Agency's (QAA) Economics Benchmark Statement.[15] The QAA is the UK's regulator of quality and standards in higher education courses and produces benchmark statements for all subjects. Findings from the employers' survey, including disparity between *the skills of students and their importance to employers*, have been used for a number of workshops, both national and departmental, and a paper was delivered jointly with the Government Economic Service (GES) at the RES annual conference in 2008.

Joint Events with Employers

The Economics Network has contributed to the annual RES employment event at the Treasury (the government's ministry of finance) for final-year economics students. At this event, it ran a session on employability and the findings of the EN's employer and alumni surveys on the skills required of graduates. It has also run work-based learning events at the Treasury for recently appointed staff on the application of core micro concepts to policy-making. In 2010, the EN ran a highly successful event in Edinburgh with fourth-year[16] undergraduates and young economists employed at the GES in Scotland. This was a joint event with the GES and the Scottish Economic Society. It consisted of presentations and workshops to consider the practical applications of economics to policy-making.

Work with Professional Bodies and Subject Associations

The Economics Network works with a variety of established organizations to support activities for students, GTAs and lecturers, and participates in activities associated with key national organizations. The EN co-runs an annual conference for prospective economics students with the Scottish Economic Society. The 2009 event had over 300 student participants (aged 16 to 18) and consisted of presentations by economists and economic journalists, study advice from a schools' examiner and the International Trade Game.[17] The Royal Economic Society and the Scottish Economic Society sponsor the EN's GTA/New lecturer program and the Royal Economics Society partially funds a student working on the EN's two student websites. The EN also has regular teaching session slots at the biennial Welsh Economics Colloquium and the annual Scottish Economic Society conference. These are research conferences, but the EN is granted a slot in each (when no other sessions are running in parallel) to examine some aspect of learning and teaching in economics. Examples include problem-based learning, the use of classroom experiments and alternative forms of assessment.

The Network Director is a member of the Conference of Heads of University Departments of Economics (CHUDE), and sits on its Steering Group. Amongst many other things, the Steering Group revised the national Economics Benchmark Statement published by the UK's university regulator, the Quality Assurance Agency (see above). The Economics Network has a standing agenda item at both the main meeting and the Steering Group meeting and this is used to inform CHUDE of Economics Network activities and engage with CHUDE in a range of development issues.

RESEARCH ON ECONOMICS LEARNING AND TEACHING

The Economics Network publishes two peer-reviewed journals, the *International Review of Economics Education* (*IREE*) and *Computers in Higher Education Economic Review* (*CHEER*). Both journals are available both electronically and in a paper version. IREE is an international peer-reviewed journal that promotes research into effective learning and teaching in economics in higher education, first published in 2003 once a year, moving to two issues per year since 2005.[18] CHEER was established in 1989 as an international peer-reviewed journal publishing articles, short notes and reviews relating to the innovative use of information technology in economics education. It was originally published by the CALECO group at Portsmouth University, then with LTSN Economics, and is now published annually by the EN. There are 274 paper copy subscribers to the IREE and 144 to CHEER. Numbers of accesses to the two journals on the EN website are particularly high; for example, 227,897 successful page accesses for CHEER during 2008/9, and 117,346 for IREE. To lower the costs, a merger IREE and CHEER has been proposed, with CHEER having a dedicated section in IREE.

CELEBRATING EXCELLENCE AND RAISING THE STATUS OF TEACHING

Since 2001 the Network has had an annual teaching awards program to recognize and reward exemplary practice from within the UK academic economics community. Awards are given under three categories: Outstanding Teaching, Student Nominated and eLearning. The Network's annual award scheme also not only engages many individuals in its nomination process (including students), but also Heads of Department, who are required to provide supporting statements for nominations. This helps to raise the profile of award winners at an institutional level. Over the past decade, there have been 43 winners and 32 commendations. Winners of an award pointed to it as one of a few that recognize the role of teaching and the only one of its kind in economics, suggesting that awards provide an incentive for them to continue to work to meet the learning needs of students and their future employers.

POSTSCRIPT

Over the past 11 years, first as the LTSN and then as the subject network of the Academy, extensive networks across all disciplines have had a major impact because they have facilitated lecturers sharing ideas and learning from the people they most respect; namely, people within their own discipline who understand the particular issues of teaching that discipline or sub-discipline. Generally academics mistrust top-down missives about how to teach – either because they see them as imposed, in which case this develops a compliance mentality, or because they emanate from educationalists who, rightly or wrongly, are perceived as not understanding how to teach students within that discipline and who use an alien conceptual framework.

The Economics Network, along with the other Subject Centres, seeks to work in the students' interests *through* academic staff. Quality enhancement is something that must ultimately be embedded at the individual level, and Subject Centres work with champions of teaching and learning in universities to achieve this. The Subject Centre structure offers significant value for money. Not only does it deliver value because it engages with hearts and minds and can effect real and valuable changes in practices rather than a tick-box compliance that is too often the response to quality assurance, but it is also cost effective. The annual budget for the Economics Network is around $720,000, considerably less than even a small Economics department in a university. However, as a result of substantial cuts being made to public expenditures in 2010, the survival of the Economics Network is in jeopardy. While it is not disputed that the Economics Network and other 23 Subject Centres have demonstrated the importance of support for teaching at the discipline level, fiscal constraints are at a critical level.

NOTES

1. http://www.leeds.ac.uk/educol/ncihe/ (accessed 28 April 2011).
2. Note that in the UK, university teachers/instructors are generally referred to as "lecturers", whether or not they are professors.
3. http://www.economicsnetwork.ac.uk (accessed 28 April 2011).
4. http://www.whystudyeconomics.ac.uk (accessed 28 April 2011).
5. http://www.studyingeconomics.ac.uk (accessed 28 April 2011).
6. http://www.metalproject.co.uk/ (accessed 28 April 2011).
7. http://www.economicsnetwork.ac.uk (accessed 28 April 2011).
8. The UK Professional Standards Framework (UKPSF) for teaching and supporting learning, launched in February 2006, is a flexible framework which uses a descriptor-based approach to professional standards. There are three standard descriptors (SDs), each of which is applicable to a number of staff roles and to different career stages of those engaged in teaching and supporting learning. The standard descriptors are underpinned by areas of professional activity, core knowledge and professional values. The framework provides a reference point for institutions and individuals, as well as supporting ongoing development within any one standard descriptor. The framework is currently under review.
9. http://www.economicsnetwork.ac.uk/themes/gta (accessed 28 April 2011).
10. http://http://www.economicsnetwork.ac.uk/projects/surveys (accessed 28 April 2011).
11. http://www.economicsnetwork.ac.uk/health (accessed 28 April 2011).
12. http://www.whystudyeconomics.ac.uk (accessed 28 April 2011).
13. http://www.studyingeconomics.ac.uk (accessed 28 April 2011).
14. http://www.economicsnetwork.ac.uk/projects/fdtl5 (accessed 28/4/11)
15. http://www.qaa.ac.uk/academicinfrastructure/benchmark/statements/Economics.asp (accessed 28 April 2011).
16. Full-time degrees in Scotland last four years. In England, Wales and Northern Ireland, they last three years.
17. see http://www.economicsnetwork.ac.uk/showcase/sloman_game (accessed 28 April 2011).
18. see http://www.economicsnetwork.ac.uk/iree (accessed 28 April 2011).

72 Economics education in Australia
Alan Duhs and Ross Guest

The Australian economy fared better than most others throughout the global financial crisis, but enrollments in economics degree courses have been less resilient. We document the decline in enrollments in economics courses that has proceeded at a varying pace over several decades and explore some reasons for this trend. One important reason is strategic: the failure to adapt the economics curriculum in response to the growing popularity of alternative business disciplines and the implications of the growing Australian trend towards mass higher education. Inertia in the curriculum caused economics to be seen as too abstract and boring, while students found new "vocationally oriented" courses in business and marketing more attractive.

ENROLLMENT TRENDS

Economics enrollment trends in Australian secondary and tertiary institutions are disappointing (Millmow 2006; 2009; 2010). Despite the fact that the world continues to report the incontestable influence of economic events, "it is evident that economics enrollments in Australia are in long-term decline" (Round and Shanahan, 2010, p. 429) and Australian economists have been unable to match their perceived practical success in Australian economic policy with similar success in responding to market forces within their own discipline. Millmow (2006) notes that economics degree enrollments have become "an issue of deep concern for Australian economists . . . [since a] marked decline in enrolments became an alarming issue in the mid 1990s" (p. 111). He also takes issue with the greater optimism of Siegfried and Round (2001), who saw signs of recovery in Australian economics degree enrollments, and argues instead that such a rebound remains less evident in Australia than in the US (p. 112). The number of Australian university economics departments has now dropped from 37 in 2000 to 27 in 2009 (Millmow 2009, p. 60; 2010).

Round and Shanahan (2010) subsequently note that economics has steadily lost market share, and go so far as to accuse the Australian economics profession of having "committed academic suicide" (p. 425). Citing Millmow's (2000) finding that "the percentage of students enrolled in economics degrees had fallen continually from 2.5 percent [in 1989] to 1.6 percent [in 1999] of all enrollments", Round and Shanahan (2010) suggest that the main damage was done in the last decades of the previous century, albeit there has been little recovery since 2000 (p. 426). Business and marketing are cognate areas in which enrollment trends have been quite different, showing strong growth (Millmow 2009; Round and Shanahan 2010, p. 427). Again drawing on Millmow, Round and Shanahan add that this trend has been sustained over a longer period as economics enrollments relative to total enrollments "fell from 1.85 percent between 1990 and 1992 to 1.21 percent between 2005 and 2007" (Round and Shanahan 2010, pp. 427 and 429).

Honors enrollments[1] have fared rather better, "The number of honours enrollments rose from 2001 to 2005, but have since declined, such that the 2007 figures are almost identical with those recorded for 2001" (Round and Shanahan, 2010, p. 428)

Against this backdrop of trends, it should be noted that the export of educational services is now a major foreign exchange earning industry for the Australian economy (RBA, 2008; Duhs and Duhs, 1997), much like the tourism industry, and this influx of foreign students reflects a heavy leaning towards degrees in business and economics. In 2007 education exports ranked as Australia's largest services export, and higher education represented 3.4 percent of total exports, while coal, the biggest single export, accounted for 9.5 percent (RBA, 2008, p. 17). Given that "International students now compose around one-third of all those graduating with an Australian economics degree" (Round and Shanahan, 2010, p. 428), the implied decline in domestic graduations is even more pronounced than is indicated by the trend figures above.

Reward Systems and Incentives

Factors explaining these disappointing economics enrollments and falling market share include growing student preference for business or international relations degrees, which are perceived to offer the prospect of higher incomes; failure by academic economists to respond to this increased competition via suitable adjustments to pedagogy and course content; and the increasingly broadly based influx of tertiary entrants, with a consequent partiality for "easier", less rigorous degrees (Round and Shanahan, 2010; Guest and Duhs, 2002). There is evidence of this at both secondary and tertiary levels (Searle, 2004).

Guest and Duhs (2002) identify shortcomings in both pedagogy and academic reward structures in the teaching of economics in Australia. In terms of pedagogy, based on surveys of graduates they argue that there are perceived deficiencies manifested as tendencies to teach an encyclopedic version of economics with excessive breadth and too little depth; to teach material that is too theoretical and devoid of real-world applications; to focus insufficiently on fundamental issues; and to under-emphasize the need for communication skills and teacher enthusiasm. In terms of reward structures, they also find – via surveys of academic economists at a range of Australian universities – that institutionalized incentives encourage time at the margin to be spent on research rather than teaching. This academic reward structure issue has in fact been a vexing question within the Australian higher education system insofar as a schism developed between the arguments of staff developers on one hand and academic economists on the other hand. Australian universities have well-funded in-house education units aimed at lifting teaching quality, and influential staff developers in those units (Ramsden, 1992, pp. 251–2) argued that providing academics with a greater financial incentive to teach well may paradoxically result in their teaching less well. This argument endorsed a "crowding-out" hypothesis, and contended that extrinsic financial rewards crowd out the intrinsic reward of internalized satisfaction attributable to successful teaching. Survey evidence makes clear, however, that when making time-allocation decisions, individual academics are well aware of the relative rewards for improved performance in research relative to teaching. Government funding decisions nonetheless seemingly reflect the influence of the staff developers.

Though still mostly State owned, Australian universities have been required since 1989 to self-fund an increasing proportion of their activities. On revenue-generating grounds, there is therefore reason to attach growing importance to tuition income and thus to perceived teaching quality and market share. Nonetheless, it is also the case that student satisfaction with teaching is only one issue with which economics schools must contend – perhaps especially in the traditional research-intensive (Group of Eight)[2] universities – since status and funding issues cause heads of economics schools also to feel increasing pressure to lift their School research profiles and rankings (University of Queensland, 2008, p.7). These rankings are not much dependent on teaching quality, and research reputation continues to dominate. Moreover, research on teaching and learning itself evidently holds little appeal, since the percentage of faculty publications appearing in major Australian economics journals on the economics of education is low to minuscule, conveying an impression that there is little perceived gain from research in such an area (Round and Shanahan, 2010).

One recent research finding which does have implications for both the quantity and quality of graduates, however, sounds a particular warning about too willingly allowing decisions about teaching quality to be based on student evaluation of teaching (SET) forms and results. Insofar as inappropriate incentive structures are institutionalized in the recognition of teaching quality, teaching staff may be induced to favor "better rewarded" approaches, rather than critical thinking approaches more needful for satisfying a university's goal of developing proclaimed graduate attributes such as "developing critical judgment and analytical abilities". Teaching evaluation (TEVAL) scores are increasingly influential in making judgments about relative teaching effectiveness, and Alauddin and Tisdell (2010, p. 14) find that "high TEVALS can be achieved at the expense of some critically important factors in teaching and learning". They find that student perceptions of how well coursework is organized, explained and presented invariably have large positive impacts at all levels (undergraduate or postgraduate), whereas the SET attribute of "emphasis on thinking rather than memorising" (THINKMEM) has no appreciable impact on TEVAL scores. Alauddin and Tisdell's (2010) empirical evidence from economics courses suggests that an instructor who works to rate highly on the THINKMEM criterion is less likely to improve his/her TEVAL score than one who focuses on attracting a favorable student response regarding coursework organization, explanation and presentation. Some tension therefore potentially exists between the goal of enhancing the quality of teaching and learning outcomes and the goal of keeping up the quantity of fee revenues, especially as the currently high value of the Australian dollar bites into the ability to attract a non-diminishing stream of overseas students.

INSTITUTIONAL STRUCTURES AND INCENTIVES

Almost all Australian universities are State owned and, despite significant reforms since 1989, the Australian tertiary education sector remains highly regulated. Governments have significant input in relation to funding, tuition levels, and accreditation. Since 1989 universities have been compelled to generate larger shares of their funding from students or outside sources, but have nonetheless not been free of government constraints in setting their tuition levels, least of all for domestic students who remain subsidized.

International students pay full fees, hence implying that competitive interest is greatest in attracting more overseas students. Some 78 percent of University of Queensland tuition income in 2007 came from international students (University of Queensland, 2008, p. 12). Increased marketing effort is accordingly put into the task of attracting international students, but this sometimes leads to complaints that international students from non-English-speaking backgrounds are allowed to underperform, as a blind eye is turned to poor written and verbal English skills, largely for revenue reasons. Foster (2011) analyzed detailed data from 12,846 students made available by the business faculties of two universities, and contends that there is evidence of "grade inflation" camouflaging the underperformance of international students. Her interpretations are not without dissent, but there are those who feel that to fail large numbers of international students is to risk having their teaching skills criticized, or risk being undermined by negative student feedback.

Awards for excellence in teaching (both within individual universities and at the national level) are now a feature of Australian university life, but the rewards in terms of career progression tend to be relatively small. The pressure to publish in top-tier journals, on the other hand, is set to become even more paramount with the first national assessment of research quality, Excellence in Research Australia (ERA), conducted in 2011. This was a trial exercise, with the first formal ERA assessment to be conducted in 2012, to be followed by similar assessments every three to four years.[3] These ERA outcomes will drive a substantial proportion of universities' block funding for research. In the preliminary 2011 assessment, the economics field of research (FOR) was rated poorly relative to other FORs – 14 out of the 36 universities that were assessed in the economics FOR received the lowest possible score of 1 out of 5 ("well below world standard"), and only two received a score of 5 ("well above world standard"). The scores for the FORs in cognate commerce and management fields were all higher on average over the assessable universities. The effect this will have on learning and teaching in economics remains to be seen. Some universities that scored a 1 may decide to shrink their economics discipline to the point where the volume of research output is too small to be ERA-assessable. This would have implications for the depth and breadth of their economics programs. Others may decide to compete by investing more resources in economics research in the hope of improving their ERA score, which would not necessarily improve their quality of teaching and learning.

Heterodox economists (discussed further below) protest that the ERA exercise undervalues their research work because it is based on the RePEc/IDEAS database, and that very different citation impact factors are indicated via Google Scholar (Earl, 2010), which reflects the impact of heterodox publications in a much more favorable light. Earl (2010) notes that there are implications here for the teaching of heterodox economics in that, in "the current ERA-obsessed climate", promotion or hiring to senior positions increasingly depends not on the actual citation impact of published work, but on having publications in "core journals". Bloch (2010) extends this critique of the ERA, and stresses that while heterodox economics research is relegated to the "other economics" classification, it is likely to be marginalized and undervalued. Accordingly, the ERA and its chosen evaluative methods have implications for faculty hiring and promotions, and thus for curricular design. Present ERA procedures effectively decrease the likelihood of heterodox economists being hired as teachers.

CURRICULUM ISSUES

Two common themes emerge in calls for curriculum renewal in undergraduate economics. These are (a) the "less is more" school and (b) the "heterodox economics" school.

The "less is more" school refers to the argument that a reduction in the breadth of curriculum content within a given economics unit will allow more active learning strategies, and lead to better learning outcomes. It offers a way of dealing with increasing diversity in Australian university classrooms (Buckridge and Guest, 2007). Relevant Australian initiatives include attention to classroom games/experiments[4] and a growing focus on "threshold concepts"[5] (TCs): the deep, transferable ideas that allow economics graduates to engage in practical problem-solving. One factor driving interest in TCs in Australia is the emerging academic standards agenda, whereby the Australian Tertiary Education Quality and Standards Agency, still in its development stage (in 2011) will be responsible for a new standards-based quality assurance framework. Minimum teaching and learning outcomes (TLOs) will be required, defined in terms of the ability to apply knowledge and skills. A university with a curriculum that emphasizes student understanding of TCs, with problem-based learning activities and assessment, would be well-placed to demonstrate that the above TLOs are being achieved. One forum for fostering such goals is the annual Australian Teaching Economics Conference.

Heterodox economics has a well-established professional tradition in Australia, if not a marked impact on the economics teaching curriculum. An annual conference of the Society of Heterodox Economists (SHE)[6] at the University of New South Wales (UNSW) was initiated in 2002 and currently attracts over 100 attendees from academia, government departments and community organizations. Papers are presented on a wide variety of issues, including the teaching of economics, the case for pluralism, and post-Keynesian themes.

Argyrous (2007) surveyed Australian economics departments and found that in 2005 there were 16 heterodox courses being taught at the introductory level across 12 universities. These courses provide a first introduction to heterodox economics, but, with just one exception, are non-compulsory, and indeed are eligible for inclusion within an economics major in only a minority of cases. An alternative major in heterodox thought was available only at Sydney and UNSW, and in many cases the available heterodox courses were in fact housed outside the Economics and Business faculty.[7]

Though not well entrenched in Australian universities (Argyrous, 2007), a pluralist approach to economics education remains strongly advocated by some (Stilwell, 2006; O'Donnell, 2004; Duhs, 2006). Pluralism[8] implies acceptance that "there is more than one approach, theory and proposed solution to every problem" (Denis, 2009, p. 12), which seems conspicuously true in the case of controversies generated by the global financial crisis and responses to it. Relatively few courses exist which contrast orthodox neoclassical, Austrian, institutionalist, evolutionary, behavioral, post-Keynesian, feminist and Marxist approaches. There is survey evidence, however, to the effect that recent graduates have viewed their economics education as only "moderately useful" to their professional lives, with no statistical difference between those working in an economics-related profession and those working in other fields (Guest and Duhs, 2002). Such findings lend support to the notion that an alternative, pluralist approach which focuses on explanations of real-world issues by drawing on alternative perspectives might have a positive impact on enrollments.

FINAL THOUGHTS

As far as economics is concerned, there are some signs of improved teaching quality, at least at some institutions, and some signs of a possible resurgence of enrollments, but in the face of increased competition from other disciplines, there remains a need for more assertive attempts to engage students and increase the reach and appeal of the subject. That likely requires further changes in incentive systems – since, as Adam Smith put it over 200 years ago, the lecturing efforts of the Dons of Oxford were not likely to improve while their rewards remained independent of their efforts.[9]

NOTES

1. Honors degrees involve a fourth year of equivalent full-time study and effectively serve as a passport to professional appointments, for example, in the Australian government bureaucracies.
2. The Group of Eight universities consists of the Universities of Sydney, Melbourne, Adelaide, Queensland, Western Australia, New South Wales, Monash and the Australian National University.
3. The ERA assessments are based primarily on the quality of a selection of research outputs and all research income over the assessment period.
4. A recent Australian example of a website promoting classroom games and experiments is the "economic games" open access website created at Griffith University, Queensland. http://www.economicgames.org/ (accessed 25 May 2011). Please also see Chapter 7, "Classroom Experiments", in this volume.
5. For more information about this pedagogic practice, see Chapter 24, "Threshold Concepts in Economics Education", in this volume.
6. Society of Heterodox Economics (SHE), http://she.web.unsw.edu.au (accessed 25 May 2011).
7. A decades-long political economy struggle at the University of Sydney eventually resulted in the creation of a separate department of political economy (Butler, Jones and Stilwell, 2009; Butler, 2010). That department was itself transferred into the Arts faculty in 2008, and continues to attract strong enrollments. Butler adds (2010) that, while over 12,000 students have completed University of Sydney political economy courses over the years, "very few students in business and commerce are able to take these courses" (p. 74) It is likewise the case that even though a 1986 Review Committee at the University of Queensland recommended the deletion of less conventional economic philosophy courses (University of Queensland, 1986, p. 19), the units were retained and enrollments stayed healthy.
8. See also Chapter 23, "Pluralism in Economics Education", and Chapter 61, "Teaching Political Economy to Undergraduate Students", in this book.
9. See Alan Duhs and Ross Guest, "Teaching tertiary economics: the real and the ideal", available at http://www.ascilite.org.au/aset_archives/confs/aset_herdsa2000/procs/duhs.html (accessed 19 August 2011) for Adam Smith's observation (quoted in George Stigler, 1982).

REFERENCES

Alauddin, M. and C. Tisdell (2010), "Quantitative impacts of teaching attributes on university TEVAL scores and their implications", *International Journal of University Teaching and Faculty*, **1** (2), 1–17.

Argyrous, G. (2007), "Alternative approaches to teaching introductory economics courses in Australian universities", *Australasian Journal of Economics Education*, **4** (1), 58–73.

Bloch, H. (2010), "Research evaluation down under: An outsider's view from the inside of the Australian approach", Centre for Research in Applied Economics, Working Paper Series, Curtin University of

Technology   (May),   http://espace.library.curtin.edu.au:80/R?func=dbin-jump-fullandlocal_base=gen01-era02andobject_id=138138, accessed 13 July 2010.

Buckridge, M. and R. Guest (2007), "A conversation about pedagogical responses to increased diversity in university classrooms", *Higher Education Research and Development*, **26** (2), 133–46.

Butler, G. (2010), "The Sydney insurrection: The battle for economics at the University of Sydney", *Challenge*, **53** (2), 54–75.

Butler, G., E. Jones and F. Stilwell (2009), *Political Economy Now: The Struggle for Alternative Economics at the University of Sydney*, Sydney: Darlington Press.

Course Experience Survey, https://www.mis.admin.UQ.edu.au/ReportalSignon/loginForm.asp, accessed 26 May 2010.

Dennis, A. (2009), "Editorial: pluralism in economics education", *The International Review of Economics Education*, **2**, 6–22.

Duhs, A. (2006), "Teaching economic philosophy: Economics, ethics and the search for the right maximand", *Australasian Journal of Economics Education*, **3** (1), 125–52.

Duhs, L.A. and E. J. Duhs (1997), "Queensland exports of tertiary education services", *Economic Analysis and Policy*, **27** (2), 159–74.

Earl, P. (2010), "Citation impact and the lack of equity for heterodox economists", http://shredecon.wordpress.com/2010/07/01/citation-impact-and-the-lack-of-equity-for-heterodox-economists/, accessed 25 May 2011.

Foster, G. (2011), "Free Ride Past Language Barrier" reported by A. Trounson in *The Australian*, 16 March.

Guest, R. and L. A. Duhs (2002), "Economics teaching in Australian universities: Rewards and outcomes", *The Economic Record*, **78** (241), 147–60.

Millmow, A. (2000), "The state we're in: University economics 1989/1999", *Economic Papers*, **19** (4), 43–52.

Millmow, A. (2006), "Trends in economics degree enrolments within Australia 1900–2004", *Australasian Journal of Economics Education*, **3** (1–2), 111–22.

Millmow, A. (2009), "The boom we didn't really have: Australian economics degree enrolments, 1990–2007", *Economic Papers*, **28** (1), (March), 56–62.

Millmow, A. (2010), "The changing sociology of the Australian academic economics profession", *Economic Papers*, **29** (1), (March), 87–95.

O'Donnell, R. (2004), "What kinds of economics graduates do we want?", *Australasian Journal of Economics Education*, **1** (1), 41–60.

Ramsden, P. (1992), *Learning to Teach in Higher Education*, London: Routledge.

Reserve Bank of Australia (RBA) (2008), "Australia's exports of education services", *Bulletin* (June), 13–17.

Round, D. and M. Shanahan (2010), "The economics degree in Australia: Down but not out", *Journal of Economic Education*, **41** (4), 425–35.

Searle, I. (2004), "Economics in schools", *Australasian Journal of Economics Education*, **1** (2), 228–31.

Siegfried, J. J. and D. K. Round (2001), "International trends in economics degrees during the 1990s", *Journal of Economic Education*, **32** (Summer), 203–18.

Stilwell, F. (2005), "Teaching political economy: Curriculum and pedagogy", *Australasian Journal of Economics Education*, **2** (1–2), 66–82.

Stilwell, F. (2006), "Four reasons for pluralism in the teaching of economics", *Australasian Journal of Economics Education*, **3** (1), 42–55.

University of Queensland (1986), "Report to the Vice Chancellor: Review of the Department of Economics, University of Queensland".

University of Queensland (2008), 2008 Review, "Report to the President of the Academic Board by the Review Committee: School of Economics".

73 Ordonomics and the current state of economic education in Germany

Ewald Mittelstaedt and Claudia Wiepcke

HUMBOLDT'S IDEA OF "BILDUNG"

Understanding economic education in Germany is aided by understanding the German concept of "Bildung," a philosophy of education which underscores much of our discussion. Because of its programmatic component, it is not directly comparable to the English expression "education" or the French expression "formation." It is more closely connected to Wilhelm von Humboldt's idea of the freedom of the individual and the dignity of the human being, which are inalienable human rights and, therefore, may not be disregarded (Humboldt, 1809). In order to educate a responsible citizen, formal curricula should neither be too "practical" nor too "specialized," as only the universal development of the character facilitates gaining access to the world. That means "Bildung" has to foster citizenship (and not only employability or societal utility) on all educational levels in a humanistic way so that the well-educated citizen can take responsibility for him/herself (individual perspective), others (group-related perspective) and the entire world (holistic perspective).

ECONOMIC EDUCATION AT THE UNIVERSITY LEVEL

Ordonomics, a composite of ordo and economics (or ordo and liberalism), is a school of economic thought highly aligned with economic education in Germany. Ordonomics evolved during and after the Second World War, when it was necessary to clear the remains of the Nazi dictatorship and to pave the way for an "open society" (Popper, 2007, p. 85).

Ordonomics is closely connected with the philosophies of neighboring academic fields, including New Political Economy, New Institutional Economics and Constitutional Economics (Müller and Tietzel, 2000) and defines economics – like Gary Becker (1965) – not primarily with respect to the subject matter, but with respect to categories of thinking which are mirrored by methodology. Ordonomics asks the fundamental question: in what way do rules have to be organized to enable the emergence and sustainability of a welfare-increasing order? Thus, the focus of ordonomics is not the study of the concrete results of transactions, but the rules of the system in which they take place. Ordonomics considers institutions and constitutions as central elements of political-economic action. It reduces insecurities over the behavior of others and facilitates well-functioning competition. Political-economic measures are to be integrated in the maintenance of order; thus, interventions by the state should be based on generally accepted rules and they should not be based on the processes which occur at the transaction level (Gerken, 2000).

As stated above, ordonomics focuses on the economic and political institutions governing modern society. It consists of only a few constitutional, regulating principles which have guided German economics slowly towards a more Western individualistic welfare economics. As the theoretical framework of the German "Wirtschaftswunder" (economic miracle), ordonomics was widely supported, and the 1950s to 1970s were the glory days for the study of economics in Germany. But ordonomics was not able to keep step with the quantitative approaches of international economics. Economics at German universities re-orientated from a core focusing on Economic Theory – Economic Policy – Public Finance towards the Anglo-Saxon triad of Microeconomics – Macroeconomics – Econometrics. The realignment brought international visibility in terms of research conducted, but also a decline in economics as a popular course of study in Germany.

In Germany, the number of students studying economic sciences and the range of economic courses offered have grown substantially, most notably in the last ten years. Whereas in the winter term of 2001/02 about 180,000 students were enrolled to study economic sciences, about 323,000 students were enrolled in the winter term of 2009/10 (Statistisches Bundesamt, 2010, p. 342). Many years ago it was only possible to choose between business administration and economics. However, there are currently 963 courses of study with the word stem "Wirtschaft" (in other words, business/economy). Among the most important are industrial engineering and management, business informatics, business and economic education, economic law, economathematics and media management (Staufenbiel and Friedenberger, 2002, pp. 48–57). Furthermore, it is only possible to study economics at public universities and more than 50 universities offer courses of study. The most renowned universities (with respect to research) in the field of economics are Humboldt-Universität zu Berlin, Rheinische Friedrich-Wilhelms-Universität Bonn and Ludwig-Maximilians-Universität München (CHE, 2008).

Over the last twenty years, economics as a course of study has been declining in popularity (especially if figures relative to the increase in management studies are considered). Only in the years between 2000 and 2003 did enrollments in economics increase. However, this is a result of the introduction of a restriction on enrollment in business administration. Students who were unable to get a university place for business administration enrolled for economics, with the intention of changing to business administration in a later semester, as is indicated by the number of graduates in both fields. The decrease in importance of economic science becomes even more apparent when looking at the ratio of business administration to economics students, which was 5:1 in the year 1995, whereas it is more than 14:1 in 2009 (see Table 73.1).

WHY THE APPARENT DECLINE IN INTEREST IN STUDYING ECONOMICS?

The reduction in the relative popularity of economics as a course of study is explained by the fact that students of related subjects show decreasing interest in an economics that has such an abstract, formal orientation. The main reason seems to be that students do

Table 73.1   Statistical data about students of economics and business administration in Germany

Year (Winter term)	Total of first-year students at German universities	First-year students – business administration	Graduates – business administration	First-year students – economics	Graduates – economics	Proportion of students of economics compared to all students (%) (first-year students)	Proportion of students of business administration compared to all students (%) (first-year students)
1995	262,407	28,232	18,405	5,955	2,242	2.27	10.76
2000	314,956	35,419	16,914	8,402	1,371	2.67	11.26
2003	377,504	36,136	17,861	10,100	1,700	2.67	9.57
2005	356,076	36,935	21,903	6,596	1,485	1.85	10.37
2006	344,967	35,389	21,875	5,411	1,689	1.56	10.26
2007	361,459	39,181	24,256	4,749	2,116	1.31	10.84
2008	396,800	48,956	24,801	5,502	2,169	1.38	12.34
2009	424,273	65,186		4,515		1.06	15.36

Source: Statistisches Bundesamt (2009 and 2010).

not believe that economics offers much with regard to business administrative occupational qualifications (Bundesagentur für Arbeit, 2010). The dilemma facing economists in Germany is that ordonomics is being pushed out of the curricula because of its lack of research applicability and status, diminishing the practical, policy orientation of economics for students. However, the ordonomics approach is very strong with respect to teaching. In contrast to this, economics, which has a formal orientation, is strong with regard to research but does not appeal to students. As a consequence, decreasing enrollments result in the cancellation of resources, which in the long run poses a risk of the cancellation or renaming of chairs (Pies, 2008).

PLACEMENT OF ECONOMIC STUDIES GRADUATES

In Germany, economics has a tradition of more than 200 years, whereas business administration is only about 110 years old. In most cases, economics as a course of study has a theoretical orientation, with the main focus on the facilitation of abstract "thinking in models and systems." Thus, students of economics are employable in various occupations, since they are able to transfer acquired knowledge to a wide range of practical problems. The top three employment placement categories, as well as the most common function of economists, are (starting with the most popular) public administration (as, for example, a consultant or statistician in government departments), the educational sector (as, for example, a general manager or lecturer) and political parties or lobby groups (as, for example, research assistants or lobbyists) (Bundesagentur für Arbeit, 2010, p. 8). The employment opportunities for students with a degree in economics vary regionally. In economic agglomerations where many big companies locate, such as the Rhein-Main area (Cologne, Düsseldorf, Frankfurt), the opportunities are excellent. But in regions that are characterized by medium-sized companies, there are fewer job opportunities. Taken as a whole, unemployment of economists in Germany is falling, from about 2,900 in 2005 to about 1,100 in 2009 (Bundesagentur für Arbeit, 2010, pp. 5 and 16).

ECONOMIC EDUCATION AT SECONDARY SCHOOL LEVEL

Despite the shift away from ordonomics at the university level, it has survived as a major approach to economic education at secondary school. At this level, the goal is to teach the principles of a "social market economy" in order to foster economic literacy (Krol, 2001). The purpose of employing ordonomics is to present important economic structures to children and young people and to enable them to identify their individual position in economic processes (Kaminski and Eggert, 2008). Here, economic education takes the categorical approach as its basis. The German educationalist Klafki (1985) developed the construct of "kategoriale Bildung" (categorical education), which is based on Kant's transcendental logic and Humboldt's educational theory. Kant (1787, p. 75) wrote: "Gedanken ohne Inhalte sind leer, Anschauungen ohne Begriffe sind blind" (thoughts without content are empty, intuitions without concepts are blind). This quotation expresses the reciprocal relativity of perception and reason. In order to understand

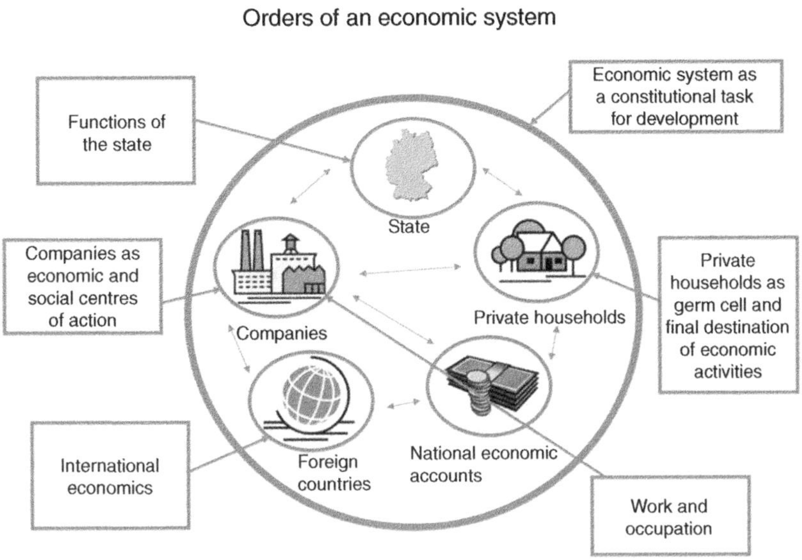

Orders of an economic system

Source: Kaminski and Eggert (2008, p. 22).

Figure 73.1 Orders of an economic system and subject matters of economics education

the world, it is necessary to form concepts. Not till then is it possible to reflect underlying assumptions.

Categorical education applied to economic education implies that it should aspire towards the extraction of basic assumptions (categories of subject matter), which are appropriate to making the complexity of economic phenomena systemically understandable (Kruber, 1994). Within each subject of secondary school education, specific structural categories are identified and used to facilitate teaching. Consequently, categories are characteristics or, rather, dimensions of an economic phenomenon. With the help of categories, it is possible to reveal universally valid structures. Thus, it is the aim of secondary economic education to enable learners to order economic structures and processes in their overall context and to understand their relevance in that context. The basic underlying processes can also be seen in neoclassical methodology, in the model of Homoeconomicus, in dilemma structures as observance patterns, as well as in the theory of action, and institutional economics.

This approach to economic education is easily related to the function of an economic system, their protagonists and sectors, as well as to the understanding of the interaction of the entire economy. Thus, it is not sufficient to teach economic episodes or to cumulate atomistic content, but the overall objective is that the economically educated individual will be able to identify his or her position within the economic order and will be able to connect specific sub-orders to each other (see Figure 73.1).

In this way, pupils learn thinking (Kaminski and Eggert, 2008, p. 16):

1. in the categories of an economic behavioral model (preferences, incentives, restrictions etc.),

2. in economic cycles and in interdependencies of the micro- and macro level (division of labor, goods and money cycle, production/consumption, saving/ investing etc.),
3. in relations of order (market, private property, economic system, function of the state etc.) and
4. in invariant characteristics of all economic action (needs, scarcity, benefit, risk etc.).

These four ways of ordering economic education processes describe basal categories employed to comprehend economic issues and to transform them into universal, or general, education insights. According to Humboldt, this is an economic geometry of thinking which enables changes and extension as an open system. The areas of application of these ways of ordering result from the institutions and rules of an economic system, which, in turn, form the range of topics of economic education.

This methodological approach to education suggests that topics and methods of economic education can be deduced from ordonomics, grounded in subject specificity and educational theory. Recently, it has been argued that educational success is not demonstrated by identifying inputs, but by assessing outputs (Wiepcke and Mittelstaedt, 2010). The paradigm shift from input to output orientation is implemented with the help of learning standards. Learning standards formulate subject-specific and interdisciplinary competencies, which are of importance for further academic and occupational education and enable learning that can interface (KMK, 2003), consistent with the mission of secondary school education. They include personality development and world orientation, which are based on central aspects of culture. Apart from that, learning standards are supposed to refer to area-specific competencies. Between 2001 and 2009 the Deutsche Gesellschaft für Ökonomische Bildung (DeGOEB – German Association of Economic Education[1]) provided learning standards for all kinds of secondary school graduation certificates. As the first versions of learning standards were not sufficient with respect to the criteria of German educational authorities (Kultusministerkonferenz), a group of economic educationalists worked out an output-oriented competency model of economic education. The model distinguishes between three sections of economic education (Retzmann et al., 2010, p. 19):

1. decision making and rationality (individual perspective);
2. cooperation (group-related perspective);
3. order and systems (holistic perspective).

So far, there is no validated German test of economic competency based on the learning standards or the competency model. Deficits in economic education at secondary school level in the majority of federal states in Germany motivated the emergence of a number of organizations supporting economic education. For example, political foundations like Konrad-Adenauer-Stiftung and Friedrich-Ebert-Stiftung, business newspapers like *Handelsblatt*, academic institutes like Institut der deutschen Wirtschaft and companies like Deutsche Bank have all contributed to the process of developing higher quality secondary school economic education. The diversity of the organizations involved suggests also a need for quality standards and more transparency concerning special interests, which has not yet happened.

CONCLUSION

Ordonomics offers an intellectual guideline and an integrative perspective on ecological, social, economic, political and general social aspects in education (Watrin, 2008). It shifts the focus from a process-oriented approach to a discourse to find rules, and enables thinking to unfold as regulative power. It has high practical relevance and clarifies the interrelations of micro and macro levels with regard to social problems.

On the basis of Humboldt's educational ideal, the authors suggest that economic educators in Germany should work to bridge the gap between the impressive success of economic research based on the quantitative approach and the apparent lack of appeal of this approach to university students. One potential solution might involve increased consideration of ordonomics, economic history, the ethics of the market economy and interdisciplinary linking with law, politics, sociology and psychology.

NOTE

1. Further information concerning the German Association of Economic Education can be accessed via www.degoeb.de (accessed 17 May 2011).

REFERENCES

Becker, Gary S. (1965), "A theory of the allocation of time", *Economic Journal*, **75**, 493–517.
Bundesagentur für Arbeit (2009/2010), "Der Arbeitsmarkt für Akademiker/Innen in Deutschland", *Arbeitsmarktberichterstattung Wirtschaftswissenschaftler/Innen*, Nürnberg.
CHE (Centrum für Hochsculentwicklung) (2008), "CHE – Forschungsranking deutscher Universitäten im Fach Volkswirtschaftslehre 2008", Working Paper No. 130, Gütersloh.
DeGOEB (Deutsche Gesellschaft für Ökonomische Bildung) (2011), *Bildungsstandards ökonomischer Bildung für den Abschluss der gymnasialen Oberstufe (2009)/mittleren Schulabschluss (2004)/Grundschulabschluss (2006)*; available at http://www.degoeb.de (accessed 15 January 2011).
Gerken, Lüder (ed.) (2000), *Walter Eucken und sein Werk: Rückblick auf den Vordenker der sozialen Marktwirtschaft*, Tübingen: Mohr Siebeck.
Humboldt, Wilhelm von (1809), "Der Königsberger und der Litauische Schulplan", in Andreas Flitner and K. Giel (eds), *Wilhelm von Humboldt*, in 5 vols, Vol. I, reprinted Darmstadt: Wissenschaftliche Buchgesellschaft, 2002.
Kaminski, Hans and K. Eggert (2008), *Konzeption für die ökonomische Bildung als Allgemeinbildung von der Primarstufe bis zur Sekundarstufe II*, Berlin: BdB.
Kant, Immanuel (1787), *Kritik der reinen Vernunft*, 2, German edition, Königsberg (English version, *Critique of Pure Reason*, trans. Werner Pluhar, Indianapolis: Hackett, 1996).
Klafki, Wolfgang (1985), *Neue Studien zur Bildungstheorie und Didaktik*, Weinheim: Belz.
KMK (Kultusministerkonferenz) (2003), *Vereinbarung über Bildungsstandards für den Mittleren Schulabschluss*, Beschluss der Kultusministerkonferenz vom 04.12.2003, Berlin.
Krol, Gerd-Jan (2001), "Ökonomische Bildung ohne Ökonomik? Zur Bildungsrelevanz des ökonomischen Denkansatzes", in *Sowi-Online-Journal*, **2** (1), available at http://www.jsse.org/2001/2001-1/pdf/krol.pdf (accessed 13 June 2011).
Kruber, Klaus-Peter (ed.) (1994), *Didaktik der ökonomischen Bildung*, Hohengehren: Schneider Verlag.
Müller, Christian and M. Tietzel (2000), "Ordnungspolitische Implikationen der Vertragstheorie", in Helmut Leipold and Ingo Pies (eds), *Ordnungstheorie und Ordnungspolitik – Konzeptionen und Entwicklungsperspektiven*, Vol. 64, Stuttgart: Lucius & Lucius, pp. 304–28.
Pies, Ingo (2008), "Mathematik und Ordnungspolitik – Kein Widerspruch", *Orientierungen zur Wirtschafts- und Gesellschaftspolitik*, **117**, 13–18.
Popper, Karl R. (2007), "After the open society", in Jeremy Shearmur and P. Turner (eds), *Selected Social and Political Writings: Karl Popper*, London: Taylor & Francis.

Retzmann, Thomas, G. Seeber, B. Remmele, and H.-C. Jongebloed (2010), *Entwicklung abschlussbezogener Bildungsstandards für die ökonomische Bildung an allen Formen der allgemein bildenden Schulen*, Essen: ZDH.
Statistisches Bundesamt (2009/2010), *Bildung und Kultur, Studierende an Hochschulen*, Fachserie 11.
Staufenbiel, Joerg E. and T. Friedenberger (2002), *Wirtschaft studieren*, Cologne: Staufenbiel Media.
Watrin, Christian (2008), "Vom Nutzen und Wert der Ordnungspolitik", *Orientierungen zur Wirtschafts- und Gesellschaftspolitik*, **117**, 2–9.
Wiepcke, Claudia and E. Mittelstaedt (2010), "Geschlechtersensible Förderung der Finanzkompetenz unter besonderer Berücksichtigung von Bildungsstandards", *Hauswirtschaft und Wissenschaft* 2/10, 60–68.

PART VI

INITIATIVES FOR TEACHING ENHANCEMENT

Section A

Private, Corporate and Government Funding for Economic Education

74 Private, corporate and government funding for economic education

William T. Alpert and Michael A. MacDowell

This chapter outlines some recent developments in support of economic education on the part of corporations, foundations, and several government agencies. It provides an explanation of the evolution of support from these various organizations and agencies. The purpose of this chapter is not to provide a how-to guide for finding support of economic education for organizations, foundations, and government agencies. Rather, this chapter provides a framework for understanding how decisions about support for economic education have changed over time and provides some samples of projects and organizations that have been successful in obtaining support.[1] However, in the current economic climate, the funding standards for economic education organizations are undergoing sweeping change. For example, economics has been broadened to include financial economics, which has become a prerequisite for support. A similar statement could be made for entrepreneurship education.

BACKGROUND

Support for economic education has ebbed and flowed over the years, often in direct relation to the economic conditions of the country. Between 1982 and 1992, support for the broadly defined topic of economic education increased 70 percent from $3.14 billion to $4.92 billion ($4.57 billion in real terms). In these years corporate contributions for economic education led the way, with 480 companies supporting economic education in 1982, collectively contributing over $2 million to the field. By 1990, support from *Fortune 500* companies had decreased to $1.2 million.[2]

As might be expected, current recessions have a major, negative and direct impact on both corporate and foundation giving. Corporate giving among the *Fortune 1000* companies topped out at $11 billion in the 2007 fiscal year – up from $10.2 million the previous fiscal year. During the 2008–09 fiscal year, however, 45 percent of the 150 companies surveyed reported that they had contributed less in the past year than in previous years. A commensurate decrease in unrestricted giving to economic education has been reported by long-serving economic education organizations.[3]

While the *Fortune 1000* companies are not the only corporate contributors, they historically represent a major source of support for economic education. Sixty-six percent of the companies that reported giving more in 2007 than in 2006 did so to health/social services and basic education. In the late 1980s and early 1990s, the Conference Board report segmented out economic education as a category of giving. Today, economic education is no longer reported separately. The latest Conference Board report, which combines both K-12 and higher education, reports that two categories – health/social services and basic education – received 28 percent of all grants given. Total giving in 2009 decreased by 3.2 percent to an estimated $303.75 billion – the sharpest decline since Giving USA began its annual report in 1956.[4] It is safe to assume that gifts and grants to economic education suffered a similar decline in support by corporations and foundations.[5]

The recession of 2008–09 has also had an anticipated impact on foundation giving. Unlike corporate giving, which tends to be more volatile as a result of business cycles, foundation giving fluctuates less severely. Foundations usually employ a "utilization rate" when determining how much to give each year. This utilization rate, the amount of earning used for grants and overhead by a foundation, is individually set by each foundation, but is often based upon the size of the foundation's portfolio as measured over the preceding 12 quarters. There are also minimal expenditure requirements established by the Inland Revenue Service (IRS). Foundations must distribute 5 percent of the value of the foundation in gifts and/or qualified operating expenses. The traditional policy of using a trailing accumulation of net assets tends to even out contributions over time. However, severe declines in financial markets have had an impact on giving that extends well beyond those declines.

FOUNDATION SUPPORT

Calvin K. Kazanjian Economics Foundation, Inc.[6]

Grant-giving foundations, as opposed to operating foundations, give solely to economic education and are rare. The Calvin K. Kazanjian Economics Foundation, Inc., formed in 1948 by Mr. Kazanjian, the founder of Peter-Paul Almond Joy, has stayed focused upon its mission of economic education.

Mr. Kazanjian's rationale for establishing the Foundation was best captured in his many writings about the importance of economic literacy among all people. He wished to "help bring greater happiness and prosperity to all through our understanding of economics."[7]

Since the Foundation's founding, the trustees have placed the majority of the approximately $20 million in gifts given over more than 60 years into materials development, including, but not limited to, the original Framework for Teaching Economics, The National Standards, the National Capstone [High School] Course in Economics, and Teaching Economics Through U.S. History. The Foundation has also underwritten several economic education teacher training efforts, including the Developmental Economic Education Programs (DEEP).[8] The Kazanjian Foundation has also given seed funding for those who teach at the college level.[9] Recently, the Foundation has moved support to enhancing the use of online teacher education in economics. The Kazanjian Foundation also supports a website which lists most school-level lesson plans which economics teachers can rate.[10]

While a secondary focus of interest, grants have been awarded for research related to economics learning and the testing of various pedagogical tools. For instance, the Kazanjian Foundation underwrote a study by Allgood, Bosshardt, van der Klanauw and Watts (2010) that examined the long-term effects of economics learning among college graduates who majored in economics, business, or neither.

The John Templeton Foundation[11]

The Templeton Foundation, with assets of $ 1.6 billion in 2008, has been a major supporter of economic studies. According to their literature ". . . for Sir John Templeton, wealth creation was no accident of history, whether for the nations of the West or for the billions of people struggling for basic necessities in the developing world."[12]

Templeton believed that human societies could experience general prosperity only when they recognized and established broad principles of freedom, competition, and personal responsibility. For him, individual freedom was the indispensable foundation of economic, social, and spiritual progress. As one of the most successful investors of modern times, Sir John understood the enormous contribution that free markets and entrepreneurship could make to material improvement. As a student of classical liberalism, from Adam Smith to Milton Friedman, he also saw that, without economic freedom, individual freedom was fragile and vulnerable.

In 2007, the Templeton Foundation awarded four major grants in economics: The first grant for $1,416,000 to Free to Choose Media for a project entitled, "The Power of the Poor: Capitalism's Moment of Truth;" the second for $2,896,284 to Free the Slaves for "The Freedom Prizes: Furthering Human Purpose by Ending Slavery;" $3,344,351 to the University of Chicago for a project entitled "Discovering the Power of Free Enterprise to Create Wealth and Alleviate Poverty through a New Applied General Equilibrium Enterprise Economics;" and $1,050,000 to Tufts University to support a project entitled "Cultural Change Institute: Freedom and Free Enterprise Research." In 2009, the Templeton Foundation extended its underwriting of Free to Choose and awarded a $4,000,000 grant to the Atlas Economic Research Foundation to support a project entitled "Discovery and Innovation in Free Enterprise Education."

Other notable Templeton Foundation grants include: a grant of $2,833,500 to support a project entitled "Project to Foster the Culture of Enterprise in an Age of Globalization" in 2006 to the Intercollegiate Studies Institute, a $628,200 grant in 2005 to the National Council on Economic Education (now The Council for Economic Education) for "Teaching Ethical Foundations in High School", and a $349,000 grant to the University of Chicago to study "Optimism, Economic Success, and Free Markets." In 2003, the Templeton Foundation awarded a $650,000 grant to the Foundation for Teaching Economics for a curriculum development project entitled "Is Capitalism Good for the Poor?"

The Ewing Marion Kauffman Foundation[13]

The Ewing Marion Kauffman Foundation of Kansas City, with assets of about $1.6 billion in 2009 is like the Templeton Foundation in size and its founder's beliefs. The Foundation is not solely tied to economic education or related fields. However, a significant portion of its funds have been allocated to entrepreneurship education. It is often difficult to distinguish between economic education and entrepreneurship education at both the high school and college levels and an exploration of funding for economic education is not within the scope of this chapter. Kauffman funds have paid for the development of materials, workshops and various research activities. For instance, the Foundation supported the groundbreaking work on entrepreneurship of Marilyn Kourilsky on teaching in elementary and secondary schools.

The Jacqueline Hume Foundation[14]

Another foundation that has been predominantly devoted to economic education is the Hume Foundation of San Francisco. In the mid-1970s the Jacqueline Hume Foundation endowed the Foundation for Teaching Economics (FTE),[15] an operating foundation with a mission to instill an economic way of thinking about national and international issues in junior and senior high schools and promoting excellence in economic education by helping teachers to become more effective educators.[16] The Foundation for Teaching Economics offers a variety of programs for teachers and students in the United States and Central Europe. FTE has developed a series of materials for junior and senior high school students which are now available online. Through specialized workshops, these materials are available to students and teachers alike. Credit courses are also offered by the FTE. The Foundation intends to spend all of the endowment over the next five years and build up its fundraising and start charging modest fees for its programs.

The Spencer Foundation[17]

The Spencer Foundation in Chicago has assisted education since its founding in 1962. While it does not focus on economic education, it does support economic connection research (research attempting to connect socio-economic status with a variety of life events, including illicit drug use, health conditions, business relationships and so on) and some classroom programs under its four primary program areas, including the Education and Social Opportunity; Organizational Learning in Schools, School Systems, Higher Education Institutions; Teaching, Learning, and Instructional Resources; and, the Purposes and Values of Education. Support has flowed relatively generously from the Foundation to several organizations and universities. Virtually all of the Spencer Foundation's recent grants have had little to do with financial or economic education, but have focused on education, educational outcomes, and educational techniques.

INDIVIDUAL SUPPORT

There are many dedicated individuals who have supported economic education themselves through organizations such as the Council for Economic Education or various councils on economic education. Eliot Snider of Cambridge, MA, supported economic education for high schools through the now defunct Leslie University National Center for Economic Education. Mr. Gus Stavros is still active in sponsoring economic education through various university centers for economic education in Florida. J. Clyde Nichols was a major contributor to economic education in the Kansas City area. S. Buford Scott continues to support economic education in his home state of Virginia and at the national level through the Council for Economic Education.

CORPORATE GIVING

As mentioned above, corporate giving to economic education has fluctuated significantly but the overall trend in corporate support of economic education, particularly unrestricted giving, is in decline. In this section of the chapter, we group corporate giving into four different categories. While somewhat arbitrary, this grouping seems to summarize the reasons behind corporate giving.

(1) *"Altruistic"* corporate giving has diminished the most. In the 1970s and early 1980s, it was hardly uncommon for companies to make general annual "unrestricted" gifts in support of the operations of economic education organizations. These companies also supported major materials development and training programs at all educational levels. For instance, leaders in the field like Exxon, Shell, AT&T, and DuPont, among others, supported expensive public television programs for teachers to use in their classrooms. They also helped underwrite many of the initial and significant economic education materials packages, including educational television programs developed by the Agency for Instructional Television, aka the Agency for Instructional Technology, including "Trade-Offs" and "Give and Take," the initial Junior Achievement Applied Economics material for the high school courses and sets of materials for the Foundation for Teaching Economics.

(2) *"Cause-related"* corporate support for economic education grew out of a sincere interest by businesses in underwriting programs which would, according to Louis V. Gerstner, Jr., who became the executive vice president of American Express in 1979, help educate the next generation of wise consumers – a phrase that has become such a cliché from financial services to life insurance that its origins have long been lost. American Express led the way in the early 1980s by introducing the concept of "cause-related giving" to non-profits organizations which supported the company's goals. For instance, American Express worked to convince high school students, many of them considered at risk of not graduating, to pursue careers in finance and established Finance Academies in New York City inner-city schools and in other major cities. The Academies were designed to help students explore entry-level positions in banks and financial intermediaries and to help train them for such positions. Some students were eventually employed by American Express.

Today's cause-related giving in economic education is more focused on personal finance and often supports materials and programs designed to help the next generation to better understand basic principles of personal economics programs. Citigroup Financial Education Curriculum, The Securities Industry and Financial Markets Association Stock Market Game, and Financial Fitness for Life, sponsored by the Bank of America, are cases in point.[18]

Special support for completion-based programs in economic education has also benefited from cause-related giving. The National Economics Challenge, which was sponsored by Goldman Sachs, is an example. The program began in 2001 and continues in an online format today, although it is no longer supported by Goldman Sachs or any other national funder. Goldman continues to provide support for a national economic knowledge contest among high school students. It funded the National Economic

Teaching Awards for Innovative Economic Education, supported for many years by the International Paper Company Foundation and before that by the Kazanjian Economics Foundation. This program, which lasted for 34 years, gave cash prizes to teachers for the best lesson plans for teaching economics at the elementary, high school, and college levels.

(3) *Coerced giving*: A related, but separate category, corporate giving, is "coerced" or mandated by the federal or state government as the result of settlements agreed upon by, or imposed upon, boards of financial intermediaries. Examples of these programs include the Connecticut Council on Economic Education and the University of Connecticut's Center for Economic Education's Green Investing program, which involved thousands of high school students, participating in Connecticut in 2008. The Bank of America's development of its "Financial Fitness for Life Program," a series of student-focused lesson plans with accompanying teachers' materials for grades 3–12 is another example of coerced giving.

(4) *Using technology*: Several technology-based companies, such as Verizon and Citi, have provided support for strategies designed to bring economic education materials to classrooms via online materials distribution and teacher training. Specifically, Verizon supports the EconEd link,[19] an innovative website that contains many lesson plans for K-12 teachers, all produced by the Council for Economic Education. These companies see a natural marriage between the content of economics, which lends itself to online presentations, and the natural interest of young people in technology, furthering their mission to increase demand for sophisticated and technologically based products among young people.

GOVERNMENT SUPPORT

Government funding for economic education and related fields is very difficult to measure over time because it frequently changes and is based on the whims of the Congress and State legislators, as well as the settlement terms of various securities infractions imposed by Federal and State courts. Furthermore, the confluence of economic education, financial literacy education, and entrepreneurial education has made the task of an accurate estimation of the annual dollar value of support virtually impossible. However, there have been several long-term government funding sources that have remained relatively steady over time. For instance, a number of states have supported economic education through their own state departments of education, state-owned universities, and by supporting state councils on economic education. The US Department of Education and the State Department have supported the Cooperative Reeducation Exchange Program (CREED) since 1995.

In addition, economic education on a national scale is occasionally supported by the Fund for the Improvement of Education Programs of National Significance, which had an appropriation of $135,461,000 in 2010 and expects to make about 285 awards, each averaging $300,000.

Other programs in support of economic education and financial literacy currently exist. For example, the Department of the Treasury's President's Advisory Council on Financial Literacy has made 15 funding recommendations in its report of December 2008. President Obama, in his Executive Order 13530 of January 29, 2010, renewed the Council under the name President's Advisory Council on Financial Capability. However, the Council no longer provides external support.

The Federal Reserve Board and each of the Federal Reserve District Banks produce education materials in print and online formats, but only under special circumstances will they provide funding.

For many years, the National Science Foundation (NSF) has supported economic education. The Economics program supports research designed to improve the under- standing of the processes and institutions of the US economy and of the world system of which it is a part. This program also strengthens both empirical and theoretical economic analysis, as well as the methods for rigorous research on economic behav- ior. Maier, McGoldrick, and Simkins (2010) summarize the substantial support of the National Science Foundation for research on effective teaching methods in the following manner:

> . . . since 1999 the National Science Foundation has awarded twenty-three grants, totaling over $5.7 million. Of that, approximately half ($2.81 million) has been awarded to nine projects sup- porting classroom or online economics experiments, with another $1.7 million divided among six projects developing economic simulations, online trading markets, and adaptations of pedagogies developed in other fields. The National Science Foundation recently awarded $1.17 million for two comprehensive projects introducing economists to a wide variety of innovative pedagogical practices – the *Teaching Innovations Project*[20] . . . and the web-based *Starting Point: Teaching and Learning Economics* pedagogic portal.[21]

For both materials creation and professional development of faculty, the NSF has been a continuing source of funds, albeit as a very small portion of their total budget. NSF has supported programs where dissertation awards have been given; however, no awards in conventional economic education programs for teaching economics at the high school level or its assessment there have been made since the 1970s.

The Bureau of Consumer Financial Protection[22] has been created by the most recent financial regulatory revision (The Dodd Frank Wall Street Reform and Consumer Protection Act). The Bureau is an independent office within the Federal Reserve and is charged with "aiding consumers in understanding and using relevant information; protecting them from abuse, deception, and fraud; ensuring that disclosures for financial products are easy to understand; conducting research; and providing financial literacy education." Only time will tell about this law and the types and levels of funding support it will provide, if any.

Since 1995, the federal government, under the Cooperative Reeducation Exchange Program (CREED), a cooperative program between the US Department of Education and the US State Department, has allocated $60 million to the Council for Economic Education. The legislation, championed by Senator Daniel K. Akaka of Hawaii, has sup- ported materials development, training, and economic education infrastructure develop- ment. The initial target of the program was the former Soviet Union. Long-serving economic educators from the US network of economic centers and state councils spent time in the former Soviet Union and Eastern Europe training those who would become those countries' economic education specialists.[23] The program has now expanded to the African and Latin American continents.

CONCLUSION

Since the late 1940s, foundations, and later, corporations, have supported economic education, often altruistically, with the goal of helping young people and others understand the benefits of the market economy and occasionally as a strategy to inform young people of particular products. Corporate support has been an essential part of economic education since the mid-1960s. Several major foundations, as well as a few smaller ones, have made a variety of major economic education programs possible and have underwritten several important research projects. Government support, either through independent agencies such as the NSF or via legislative action, has placed key support behind a myriad of domestic and international programs.

Altogether, support for economic education has certainly not seen the growth in support that has been the case in science and math education. However, on the whole, it has done well not only at the K-12 level, but at the college and adult learner level too.

While those involved in good economic education may know more about what causes business cycles and the resulting differences in the propensity to give among foundations, corporations, individuals, and government agencies, it does not make the varieties of support any easier to deduce. In the long run, we can only hope that those who have supported economic education, whether they are foundations, corporations, or government agencies, come to more fully realize that an economically literate public is the best insurance against the poor, uninformed decision-making which, it can be argued, has been mostly responsible for some of the business cycles we have endured.

NOTES

1. Most of the foundations, and particularly the corporations listed here, prefer to support institutions rather than individuals.
2. See Kaplan (1994).
3. See The Center on Philanthropy (2010).
4. Ibid.
5. Individuals contribute far more than do corporations or foundations in the United States. In fact, well over 80 percent of all contributions ($227.4 billion in 2009) were made by individuals. After gifts to religious organizations, grants to all levels of education comprise the largest category of individual giving.
6. www.kazanjian.org (accessed 12 June 2011).
7. Highlights of Calvin K. Kazanjian's thoughts on the importance of economics are found on the Foundation's website (www.kazanjian.org) (accessed 12 June 2011).
8. Note the description of the Developmental Economic Education Program (DEEP) in Chapter 1, "A History of Economic Education", in this volume.
9. The majority of the Kazanjian Foundation's spending in this area has gone to measuring the effectiveness of economic instruction at the pre-college level. Some funds have provided support for efforts to improve instruction at the college level. Some of these projects and many others are delineated in Goodman, Maier, and Moore (2003).
10. http://www.econreview.com/ (accessed 12 June 2011).
11. www.templeton.org (accessed 12 June 2011).
12. http://www.templeton.org/what-we-fund/core-funding-areas/freedom-and-free-enterprise (accessed 12 June 2011).

13. www.kauffman.org (accessed 12 June 2011).
14. No known website, but for a description see: http://www.philanthropyroundtable.org/article. asp?article=839&paper=0&cat=141 (accessed 12 June 2011).
15. www.fte.org (accessed 12 June 2011).
16. In addition to Hume, the Gillette Foundation was an early partial supporter of the Foundation for Teaching Economics, contributing $1 million to FTE.
17. www.spencer.org (accessed 12 June 2011).
18. See http://www.citi.com/citi/financialeducation/curriculum/adults.htm, www.sifma.org, and http://fffl. councilforeconed.org/, respectively (accessed 12 June 2011).
19. www.econedlink.org (accessed 12 June 2011).
20. For more information about this project, see Salemi and Walstad (2010).
21. http://serc.carleton.edu/econ/index.html (accessed 19 May 2011).
22. www.treasury.gov/initiatives/pages/cfpb.aspx (accessed 12 June 2011).
23. Some of the scholarship emanating from this support includes: Kovzik and Watts (2001); McCorkle and Watts (1996); Economic Awareness (2008); Walstad and Watts (2002); and Council on Economic Education (2009).

REFERENCES

Allgood, S., W. Bosshardt, W. van der Klaauw and M. Watts (2010), "Economic coursework and long-term behavior and experiences of college graduates in labor markets and personal finance", *Economic Inquiry*, published online, 15 April 2010, http://onlinelibrary.wiley.com/doi/10.1111/j.1465-7295.2009.00270.x/full (print edition forthcoming) (accessed 12 June 2011).

Council on Economic Education (2009), *Cross-Country Outcomes and Issues from the Cooperative Education and Exchange Program, 1995–2008*, New York: Council on Economic Education.

Economic Awareness (2008), "An American economic education in the former Soviet Bloc", *Economic Awareness*, December, 10–15.

Goodman, R., M. Maier and R. Moore (2003), "Regional workshops to improve the teaching skills of economics faculty", *American Economic Review*, **93** (1), 460–62.

Kaplan, A. (ed.) (1994), *Giving USA: The Annual Report on Philanthropy for 1993*, New York: The American Association of Fundraising.

Kovzik, A. and M. Watts (2001), "Reforming undergraduate instruction in Russia, Belarus, and Ukraine", *Journal of Economic Education*, **32** (1), 78–92.

Maier, M., K. McGoldrick and S. Simkins (2011), "Is there a Signature Pedagogy in Economics?", in N. Chick, A. Haynie, and R. Gurung (eds), *Exploring More Signature Pedagogies*, Sterling, VA: Stylus Publishing.

McCorkle, S. and M. Watts (1996), "Free riding indexes for Ukrainian economics teachers", *Journal of Economic Education*, **27** (Summer), 233–7.

Salemi, M. K. and W. B. Walstad (eds), (2010), *Teaching Innovations in Economics: Strategies and Applications for Interactive Instruction*, Cheltenham, UK and Northampton, MA, USA: Edward Elgar.

The Center on Philanthropy (2010), "Giving USA: 2010", Indiana University, pp. 1–6.

Walstad, W. B. and M. Watts (eds) (2002), *Reforming Economics and Economics Teaching in the Transition Economies: From Marx to Markets*, Cheltenham, UK and Northampton, MA, USA: Edward Elgar.

Section B

An Introduction to Economic Education Organizations in the US and Beyond

75 Near and far – an introduction to economic education organizations in the US and beyond
Franklin G. Mixon, Jr.

Much of what is referred to as "economic education" takes place beyond the college classroom. In the 20th and 21st centuries, academicians understood economic education to entail a variety of educational efforts, including publication and dissemination of research on teaching and learning, privately and publicly funded workshops and programs designed to enhance economics instruction, and the establishment and functioning of advisory councils and boards to facilitate interactions among scholars, policymakers, private enterprise and governments regarding economic education delivery, to name just a few. This chapter explores ongoing international efforts in these areas, beginning with the United States and moving into lesser-known international programs and institutions.

K-12 ECONOMIC EDUCATION IN THE US

The United States has long been a substantial contributor to economic education efforts on a wide-ranging scale. In addition to the Council for Economic Education,[1] which is based in New York City and supports economic and finance education in K-12 schools across the country, the Foundation for Economic Education (FEE), located just outside of New York City, was founded in 1946 by Leonard Read, and today provides economic education to more advanced audiences.[2] The FEE employs programs and seminars to fulfill its mission of supporting the principles of economic freedom embodied in the principles of private property, individual liberty, the rule of law, and individual choice and responsibility. Complementing this economic education program are the FEE's periodicals, which include *The Freeman: Ideas on Liberty*. Among those economists who have lectured at the FEE are F.A. Hayek, Milton Friedman, James Buchanan, George Stigler and Vernon Smith.[3] Lastly, the Foundation for Teaching Economics (FTE) is a national consortium of state-based economic education centers (or partners in economic education). In nearly two decades, FTE has provided economic education instruction to more than 16,000 high school teachers in the US, helping it to achieve the goal of "improve[ing] economic education in classrooms around [the United States] and around the world."[4]

US ECONOMIC EDUCATION FROM THE FED AND JUNIOR ACHIEVEMENT

The US Federal Reserve System has also been at the forefront of economic education and economic literacy. For instance, the Federal Reserve Bank of Richmond houses the Powell Center for Economic Literacy (PCEL), which aims "to promote economic literacy among young people."[5] In addition to producing lesson plans and economics curricula, and to hosting competitions and workshops, the PCEL launched the Infusionomics program in 2009. This program assists K-12 educators in folding the principles of economics, personal finance, and entrepreneurship into the general education curriculum at their particular schools. The Federal Reserve Bank of San Francisco maintains an economic education department on its internet site,[6] offering resources for educators, including personal finance and Federal Reserve lesson plans and games. This department also provides an Ask Dr. Econ link that provides answers to various questions about the economy. Other student activity links include the Fed Chairman Game and the Great Economists Treasure Hunt.

The Economic Education for Teachers (EET) webpage[7] provided by the Federal Reserve Bank of Minneapolis (FRBM), includes a lesson plan – the Money Curriculum Unit – that provides educators with an education guide on the history of money. EET also includes an Economic Literacy Quiz that students can take and have feedback provided in real time by the Minneapolis Fed website. The Federal Reserve Bank of Chicago provides a program for economic education that elementary education practitioners can use in the classroom. This program, known as Econ Explorers, is designed to promote economic and financial literacy through diary entries that are related to shopping/spending habits, reading/understanding children's books with economic themes, and a comic book approach to the use of money, to name a few.[8] The Chicago Fed also offers a menu of educational resources related to the US Federal Reserve System. A major component of the US Federal Reserve System's economic education effort is the Fed Challenge. In the high school version of this competition, teams of students compete while playing the role of Fed policymakers, who direct monetary policy against the backdrop of various macroeconomic conditions. Regional competitions are supported by each Fed; for example, the Federal Reserve Bank of New York hosts the competition for high schools located in the Fed's Second District.[9] In addition to building an understanding of the Fed's role and the importance of macroeconomics, the Fed Challenge is designed to promote an interest in pursuing economics both as a field of study and as a career goal/pursuit. For college students, the Fed teams with the Eastern Economic Association in offering the College Fed Challenge.[10, 11]

Junior Achievement (JA) is similar to the Fed in the depth and breadth of support it provides for economic education.[12] JA is the world's largest organization in terms of promoting financial literacy, with a history dating back to 1916, when the Eastern States Agricultural and Industrial Exposition hosted 300 business and agricultural leaders to discuss promoting activities for boys and girls.[13] Today, the JA provides various programs for young people that are designed to help them understand how to generate and manage wealth. For example, JA offers JA Banks in Action, a program that teaches high school principles of banking and finance. This program is complemented by JA's JA Economics, a program designed to familiarize high school students, through seven sessions, with the principles of macroeconomics, microeconomics, and international economics. This program may be followed by JA Exploring Economics, which "fosters lifelong skills and knowledge about how an economy works," with lessons exploring many areas of economics, such as the free-rider problem, trade restrictions, inflation, and utility, to name just a few.[14] As such, the JA provides a significant complement to the economic education programs offered through the US Federal Reserve System.

ECONOMIC EDUCATION FROM HIGHER EDUCATION ORGANIZATIONS

A number of US organizations are focused on delivery of economic education to audiences other than K-12, through a variety of means. For example, several US universities and higher education organizations support economic education through outlets for economic education scholarship.[15] The American Economic Association (AEA) maintains the Committee on Economic Education (CEE), which is "a standing committee . . . [that exists] to improve the quality of economics education at all levels: pre-college, college, adult, and general education."[16] This committee has existed since 1955, and is today extensively supported by Vanderbilt University. The Committee routinely sponsors workshops at annual meetings of the AEA. Many of the resulting essays on economic education are published in the *American Economic Review Papers and Proceedings*, which appears each May.[17] The AEA-CEE also sponsors the annual national economic education research conference.[18]

Perhaps the most prominent among university support examples is the University of Nebraska, which is home to the National Center for Research in Economic Education (NCREE). The NCREE[19] developed and maintains the Research in Economic Education Database and supports the editorial office of the *Journal of Economic Education*, the leading academic journal in the field of economic education. The Department of Economics at Idaho State University houses the editorial offices of *Perspectives on Economic Education Research*.[20] Similarly, the Department of Management and Economics at Hamline University in Minnesota is home to the editorial offices of the *International Journal of Pluralism and Economic Education*.[21] The Department of Economics and Finance at Middle Tennessee State University sponsors the *Journal for Economic Educators*.[22]

An interesting economic education venture involves the Berkeley Electronic Press (BEP), an organization developed by university professors. Among the relatively new BEP journal launches is the *Journal of Industrial Organization Education*.[23] This journal specializes in research related to undergraduate and graduate students of industrial organization. As such, it represents the first sub-field journal in economic education, and could be the gateway to new journal launches in areas such as international economics education, labor economics education, and perhaps others. Finally the Allied Academies[24] sponsors publication of the *Journal of Economics and Economic Education Research*,[25] which has been publishing research in economic education since 2000.

THE INTERNATIONALIZATION OF ECONOMIC EDUCATION ORGANIZATIONS

Arguably the most prominent international effort in the area of economic education is the Economics Network (EN) of the United Kingdom's Higher Education Academy.[26]

The EN "provides publications, events, funding opportunities and other resources to support university teachers of economics."[27] Among these are (1) the EN's Learning and Teaching Development Projects, which cover up to £5,000 in expenses for individuals in academia who seek to develop and assess new approaches to teaching practices,[28] and (2) the EN's book catalogue, password-protected question bank, and online/learning teaching materials.[29] Finally, the EN also supports two prominent academic journals in economic education – *Computers in Higher Education Economics Review* and the *International Review of Economics Education*.[30]

Although academic organizations and programs in economic education are concentrated in the United States, England and Australia,[31] there is some activity to be found in other areas of the globe. One such example is the Canadian Foundation for Economic Education (CFEE),[32] which was founded in 1974 as a non-profit organization. The CFEE seeks to improve Canadians' ability to make sound economic decisions. The CFEE has partnered with the Bank of Canada, the Canadian Bankers Association, and various ministries and departments of education throughout Canada in terms of providing curriculum development, seminars, and strategic planning/advisory services for its constituents. Additionally, the CFEE has produced print, video and CD-ROM teaching kits, and it currently maintains a database of more than 5,000 classroom teachers, resulting in the delivery of economic education to more than 300,000 students each year.

The Association of European Economics Education (AEEE) in Denmark provides an avenue for collaboration between economists and business education experts throughout Europe.[33] Additionally, according to the AEEE website, the AEEE holds biannual conferences (in various countries), "giving members opportunities to share ideas about classroom practice and observe a wide range of current developments." The organization has produced 18 of these conferences through 2010, thus the AEEE dates back to the mid-1970s.

The International Association for Citizenship, Social and Economics Education (IACSEE),[34] based at the University of Glasgow, was formed in 1994 "to bring together educational professionals, academics and members of the wider community who have an interest in how young people learn, and are taught, about society and economics and their current and future roles as citizens participating in their various educational situations, communities, nations and in our increasingly globally interconnected world." Among these activities, the IACSEE publishes *Citizenship, Social and Economics Education*, an online peer-reviewed journal that focuses on scholarly work in various educational fields, including economics. The IACSEE is primarily set up to assist teaching in schools, colleges and universities, and to engage in research on economic education.

The Economics Education and Research Consortium (EERC) in Russia, was created in 1995 to "strengthen economics education and research capabilities" within the Commonwealth of Independent States.[35] The EERC supports original policy-relevant studies, organizes training seminars and research workshops, and links academics and policymakers. According to the EERC's website, the EERC's policy research is delivered through semi-annual grant competitions, while its outreach workshops and training are provided by (1) the Focus on Policy program, launched in 2000 "to support the policy dialogue between network members and policymakers," and (2) "a yearlong cycle of summer schools, research workshops and internships at the leading academic institutes in the region."

Joining these other international organizations is the International Monetary Fund's (IMF) IMF Center, which is its Public Center for Economic Education. The IMF Center has developed resources "to help students understand the history of money, macroeconomics and the importance of international monetary cooperation, and the value of global trade."[36] To further this mission, the IMF Center hosts the Economic Forum series, which consists of panel discussions on current events. Past topic areas include poverty reduction, economic growth, financial globalization, deflation, and capitalism in modern European thought. The PCEE's online presence dates back to at least 2001.

Since 2003, the National Bank of Poland has maintained an Economic Education Portal devoted "to disseminat[ing] and broad[ing] . . . knowledge about economics and economy, and to support[ing] other educational activities of the NBP."[37] The portal, which is open access, includes facts about the Polish economy, macroeconomic analyses, online courses, teaching aids, decision quizzes and games using economics, as well as electronic publications and a dictionary of economic terms.

Maintaining an internet presence since 2006, the Network for Economic Education in Japan works "to improve economic education at schools" by utilizing a network of individuals and organizations engaged in economic education, and "by creating a 'place' for interaction and cooperation" within this academic network.[38] Among the activities organized by this network are (1) provision of information/materials on economic education (including internet-based), and (2) training programs and workshops on economic education for teachers, students and parents.

The future of global economic education efforts appears bright as well. In 2009, the Korea Economic Education Association (KEEA) was launched, creating a group of more than 100 economics professionals that will oversee the economic education efforts of 100 college students. The students have formed the Economic Education ACE Volunteers, a group that delivers economics lectures to elementary, middle, and high schools throughout the country.[39] The group has produced a textbook and manual, and it began its economic education program in May 2010. The new organization also plans to set up educational programs for low-income families, university students and social minorities.

CONCLUDING COMMENTS

That the United States' and England's presence in the field of economic education is substantial is without question. The US presence extends from its Federal Reserve System to Junior Achievement, two of the most prominent institutions in the field. The US is also home to other economic education institutions of note, such as the Council for Economic Education and the Foundation for Economic Education. England's Economics Network is also among the small group of elite institutions involved in economic education. From institutions based in these two countries come prominent resources for promoting economic literacy, as among them the Fed Challenge and the *International Review of Economics Education.*

However, the field of economic education is not simply an American or English endeavor. Organizations from around the globe have been contributing resources to the effort of educating young adults in economic science since at least 1974, with the formation of the Canadian Foundation for Economic Education. These efforts include formal education, teaching-related seminars, and publication of academic research. Prominent among these are the Economic Forum series of panel discussions produced by the IMF's Public Center for Economic Education, and *Citizenship, Social and Economics Education*, the peer-reviewed journal affiliated to the International Association for Citizenship, Social and Economics Education. As these enterprises grow and further diffuse throughout the world, as evidenced by the 2009 founding of the Korea Economic Education Association, increases in economic literacy should also occur.

NOTES

1. www.councilforeconed.org (accessed 11 April 2011).
2. This chapter offers very brief coverage of entities that focus on K-12 economic education. For a comprehensive examination, see Chapter 26, "Organizations Focused on Economic Education", in this volume.
3. http://fee.org (accessed 11 April 2011).
4. http://www.fte.org/ (accessed 11 April 2011).
5. http://www.powellcenter.org/index.asp (accessed 11 April 2011).
6. http://www.frbsf.org/education/ (accessed 11 April 2011).
7. http://www.minneapolisfed.org/community_education/teacher/ (accessed 12 April 2011).
8. http://www.chicagofed.org/webpages/education/fed_challenge/economic_education_resources.cfm (accessed 12 April 2011).
9. http://www.ny.frb.org/education/fedchal.html (accessed 12 April 2011).
10. http://www.ramapo.edu/eea/challenge/index.html (accessed 12 April 2011).
11. For a more thorough discussion of the Fed Challenge, see Chapter 69, "Curricular and Co-curricular Aspects of the Economics Major at Highly Ranked Schools", in this volume.
12. http://www.ja.org/ (accessed on 11 April 2011).
13. http://www.ja.org/about/about_history.shtml (accessed 11 April 2011).
14. http://www.ja.org/programs/programs_high_overview_obj.shtml (accessed 11 April 2011).
15. Chapter 37, "Journals and Beyond: Publishing Economics Education Research", in this volume provides a comprehensive review of the scholarly journals in economic education.
16. www.vanderbilt.edu/AEA/AEACEE/index.htm (accessed 11 April 2011).
17. For more information about the AEA and CEE support of economic education, see Chapter 25, "Economic Education in American Elementary and Secondary Schools" and Chapter 1, "A History of Economic Education" in this volume.
18. http://www.aeaweb.org/home/committees/AEACEE/Conference/index.php (accessed 11 April 2011).
19. http://cba.unl.edu/outreach/econEd/ncree/index.aspx (accessed 12 April 2011).
20. www.isu.edu/peer/ (accessed 11 April 2011).
21. www.inderscience.com/browse/index.php?journalCODE=ijpee (accessed 11 April 2011).
22. http://frank.mtsu.edu/~jee/ (accessed 11 April 2011).
23. http://www.bepress.com/jioe/ (accessed 11 April 2011).
24. www.alliedacademies.org/Public/Default.aspx (accessed 11 April 2011).
25. www.alliedacademies.org/Public/Journals/JournalDetails.aspx?jid=4 (accessed 11 April 2011).
26. For more information about this organization and its activities, see Chapter 71, "Supporting Economics Higher Education in the United Kingdom", in this volume.
27. www.economicsnetwork.ac.uk/ (accessed 11 April 2011).
28. http://www.economicsnetwork.ac.uk/projects/mini (accessed 12 April 2011).
29. For lists of previous recipients, the EN's Learning and Teaching Development Projects, see www.economicsnetwork.ac.uk/ (accessed 12 April 2011). The EN's book catalogue includes 7,000 books, with 3,000 online previews. The question bank contains more than 1,300 questions and problem sets. Lastly, the EN's online learning/teaching encompasses 600 links to online texts, assessment materials, glossaries, slides and software applications.
30. Information provided in Chapter 37 in this volume indicates that *CHEER* may be absorbed, as a special section, by *IREE*.
31. Australia is home to the University of Queensland, where the editorial office of *Australasian Journal of Economics Education* is based (see http://www.uq.edu.au/economics/AJEE/, accessed 12 April 2011). Australia is also home to the annual Australasian Teaching Economics Conference, which is being

hosted in 2011 by the University of Technology – Sydney (see http://www.finance.uts.edu.au/conferences/ATEC2011/, accessed on 12 April 2011).

32. www.cfee.org (accessed 12 April 2011).
33. www.economicseducation.eu (accessed 12 April 2011).
34. www.iacsee.org (accessed 12 April 2011).
35. www.eerc.ru (accessed 12 April 2011).
36. www.imf.org/external/np/exr/center/econed/index.htm (accessed 12 April 2011).
37. www.epractice.eu/en/cases/nbportal (accessed 12 April 2011).
38. www.econ-edu.net/ (accessed 12 April 2011).
39. www.koreatimes.co.kr/www/news/biz/2009/12/123_57565.html (accessed 12 April 2011).

Section C

Economics Teaching Workshops: Past, Present, Future

76 Economics teaching workshops: past, present, and future[1]

Joab N. Corey, James D. Gwartney and Gail M. Hoyt

A great teaching idea is like a great joke, it's best when you share it (Joab Corey)

This chapter focuses on the use of teaching workshops to further enhance the field of economic education and improve the ability of instructors to effectively teach economic concepts. For years, economic educators have relied mostly on a lecture-only format dominated by orally expressing the economic ideas, while occasionally jotting definitions, graphs, and equations on a chalk-board. Until recently, this style of teaching, dubbed "Chalk and Talk" by Becker and Watts (1996; 2001), seemed to be utilized by economic instructors to a rather greater extent than by instructors from other academic disciplines. The continual use of this lecture-only format was even listed as one of the potential causes for the reduction in enrollment in economics classes in the early 1990s (Becker and Watts, 1996; 2001). However, even more devastating than falling enrollments, relying on the abundant and repetitive use of this single method for disseminating economic knowledge, whether as a result of "convenience, custom, and inertia" or ignorance of other methods, may hinder the ability of students to internalize concepts and retain the information after the class has concluded (Becker and Watts, 2000, p. 4).

Fortunately, in recent years, economic instructors have recognized the need for change and evolved beyond the "Chalk and Talk" lecture-only style of teaching. Recently, economic teachers have helped students internalize concepts through the use of economic experiments,[2] cooperative learning,[3] music (Hall, Lawson, and Mateer, 2008), and clips from popular movies[4] and television shows (Hall, 2005; Leet and Houser; 2003; Mateer, 2005; Sexton, 2006), just to name a few. There has also been a movement to use interactive games (Delemeester and Brauer, 2000) and other hands-on, active learning lesson plans to further integrate and immerse students into the concepts that they are being taught (Becker and Watts, 1998).

While there exists a number of alternatives to the traditional lecture-dominated format of running an economics class, it may be challenging for instructors to find and properly adapt these techniques to their own class as there is no single source (either written or electronic) for theories, examples, and other teaching information.[5] Where such resources do exist, the information contained within can be hard to adapt without instructor and institution-specific guidance. This is true for both new instructors getting ready to teach their first class as well as for veteran teachers who are accustomed to lectures as their only way of conveying economic knowledge. While an extensive array of papers, books, and websites exist that contain ways to add variety to one's teaching style, these resources tend to be either too general or too specific to help a teacher adapt these techniques to their class. Teaching workshops continue to be an effective method to introduce new and ever-evolving pedagogic tools to instructors who hunger for innovative, and even entertaining, ways to motivate and educate their students.

Goodman, Maier, and Moore (2003) researched the existence, purpose, and general format of teaching workshops conducted at the time of their writing. This chapter expands their work by providing an in-depth description of a few workshops in an effort to demonstrate various styles and formats that exist so that readers can choose their most preferred format for them when attending or conducting their own teaching workshops. We conclude by using advice from current workshop leaders, providing helpful tips for setting up teaching workshops in the hope that it will further contribute to pedagogic advances being promoted in economic education.

WORKSHOPS

This section provides detailed descriptions of instructional workshops in economics, which have been and/or are currently being conducted at different institutions throughout the United States. While each teaching workshop has a similar goal of improving teaching effectiveness, their formats reflect a variety of ways in which to plan and operate these events. While an in-depth description of every workshop is beyond the scope of this chapter, we provide a representative subset of the current teaching workshops in an effort to provide an overview of format and presentation styles.[6]

Robert Morris University

The Economics Department at Robert Morris University has been conducting one of the most long-standing economics teaching workshops since 1990. Average attendance is around 80 economists who teach at the college level and Irwin/McGraw-Hill Publishing has been the primary sponsor over that entire time period. Economists are invited to this workshop by an email brochure that is sent to the Irwin/McGraw-Hill email list as well as to past workshop participants.

This two and a half day workshop offers a blend of keynote plenary speakers and concurrent sessions in which workshop participants share their ideas. Keynote speakers have included textbooks authors such as David Colander and others heavily involved in the research of economic education such as William Walstad, the current editor of the *Journal of Economic Education*. One unique feature of this workshop is the production of a proceedings volume in which papers from the concurrent sessions are compiled and distributed to participants.

Bowling Green State University

For the past 13 years, an instructional workshop has been in operation at Bowling Green State University where an average of 50 teachers attend annually. This workshop is designed for college-level instructors of economics as well as other academic disciplines, and economics graduate students. Attendees are recruited by email, targeting past participants and others. The main objective of this teaching workshop is to help teachers become better equipped at teaching critical thinking in the context of their classes.

This day-long workshop begins with a morning session featuring two to three invited economic educators presenting their innovative teaching techniques. An afternoon session consists of speakers (often identical to those in the morning session) who run interactive demonstrations using the teaching ideas presented earlier so that attendees can see how the technique works in practice. Some of the notable economists at this workshop have included Robert Frank (author of *The Economic Naturalist: In Search of Explanations for Everyday Enigmas*), who has students attempt to solve real-life mysteries through the use of economic analysis; Paul Krugman, who uses real-world news events to teach economic concepts; and Neil Brown, an expert at enhancing students' critical thinking skills.

Florida State University/University of South Florida

Florida State University, in conjunction with the University of South Florida, hosts an annual teaching conference entitled "Creative Teaching Ideas for your Basic Economics Course." This workshop is sponsored by the Stavros Center for Economic Education, which has a location at both universities and so the site of the workshop alternates between the two schools. This annual conference first held during the 2004–05 academic year, has averaged between 50 and 60 participants and is targeted at college and high school instructors, as well as graduate students. Attendees are recruited through flyers emailed to past attendees, sent to economics departments in the region, and distributed at association meetings and centers that belong to the Council for Economic Education. This workshop seeks to improve teaching effectiveness at both the high school and college level by focusing on the use of creative and exciting ways to teach economics in an effort to generate more student involvement and help students internalize key economic concepts.

Presenters include master teachers who have been recognized for their teaching excellence and who are invited to share their successful teaching techniques based on this reputation. Some notable presenters include Martha Olney, winner of several teaching awards and Mike Salemi, co-author of two books on economic education and innovative teaching ideas. This workshop is also linked to the Stavros Center for Economic Education Great Teachers Award, which is sometimes presented to outstanding teachers leading sessions at the workshop.

University of Kentucky

The University of Kentucky has held a teaching conference nearly every year since 1994 designed for college-level instructors and graduate students in economics. It averages between 60 and 65 attendees each year, about one-third of whom are their own PhD economics students. About one-half of the attendees are faculty members from nearby institutions and five to ten attendees are publisher representatives and special guests who are invited through an emailed flyer. The primary purpose of this workshop is to expose instructors to innovative ideas that they might not otherwise have the opportunity to experience.

This full-day workshop consists of a morning session of one or two keynote speakers who are experts in teaching economics or in general education and learning theory.

The afternoon consists of concurrent sessions, led by workshop participants, providing attendees with a wide variety of topics from which to choose. This workshop is known for speakers who have published articles in the area of economic education and who have authored textbooks. Some of the more notable speakers include William Becker, co-author of several economic education papers and co-editor of a volume describing innovations developed for teaching economics; Dirk Mateer, author of *Economics in the Movies* and leading expert on using pop-culture, such as music and movies, to teach economics; and Glenn Hubbard, author of a popular economics textbook.

University of North Carolina Wilmington

The University of North Carolina Wilmington has held a teaching conference in each of the last nine years. This workshop averages 50 attendees, primarily consisting of college teachers across various disciplines with some economics graduate students. Participants are invited through emails sent to past attendees and brochures mailed to all economic departments in the surrounding region. The mission of this workshop is to bring together colleagues who are passionate about teaching in the hope that they come away with new useful and innovative ideas for the classroom.

This workshop consists of four one-hour sessions lead by master teachers who are invited based on their reputation for excellence in the instruction of economics. This workshop also leaves plenty of time for discussion so that teachers can fully explore these new lessons or methods of instruction in order to fully adapt them to their respective classrooms. Some notable speakers who have led sessions include Ben Bernanke, co-author of a macroeconomics principles textbook and chairman of the Federal Reserve; Kenneth Elzinga, recipient of numerous teaching awards and co-author of a trio of murder mystery novels where an economics professor uses economic principles to solve crimes; and David Colander, co-author of a leading principles of economics textbook.

West Virginia University

West Virginia University runs a workshop designed exclusively for kindergarten through 12th grade teachers in any field, and this workshop counts for graduate credit in economics, education, or forestry. An average of 20–25 primary and secondary school teachers participate every year and they are invited through flyers sent to all school faculty senate chairs in West Virginia. The purpose of this workshop is to give teachers a foundation in the principles of economics and then help them bring these same principles to life in their own classroom in conjunction with their respective disciplines.

This instructional workshop follows a very different format from those previously mentioned as it also serves as a graduate-level class and is designed to educate kindergarten through 12th grade teachers on the basic principles of economics before helping them teach these principles in their respective classroom. This is an intensive week-long residential course that consists of traditional classes in the morning, followed by field trips to factories and logging plants to show the connection between economics and the environment in an interactive setting. The workshop also allows time for the participants to break into smaller groups consisting of teachers of a similar grade level to work on lesson plans for their own courses. At the conclusion of this course, teachers are required to submit three economic lesson plans for a grade, which are subsequently distributed to all participants. Recently, this course has been taught by Russell Sobel, winner of several teaching awards and co-author of a principles-of-economics textbook.

Worth Publishing

Worth Publishing has sponsored a large number of teaching workshops for several years. These have included meetings with textbook authors, conferences designed to train faculty in new and innovative technology for the classroom, and professional development meetings where professors meet to discuss current challenges in the classroom. The number of attendees depends on the type of meeting. For example, author meetings and technical training might include anywhere from two to 20 professors, while teaching conferences might include 40 to 100 economics instructors. Both college level and high school instructors across all disciplines are the target of these various workshops and they are invited through emails and flyers sent to academic departments. Author meetings and technology training workshops orient teachers to how new textbooks and technology can best be adapted to their classroom. Teaching conferences provide a forum for economic instructors to meet and explore new classroom practices and develop concrete innovative solutions to their current teaching challenges that can be applied to their own economics courses.

The structure of the teaching workshops usually involves general sessions where all attendees listen to an author, researcher, or master teacher, who is invited based on their reputation for excellence in their respective field. This is followed by a question and answer session and subsequent discussion about the presentation. Attendees then have the chance to choose from a series of sessions focused on specific areas of instruction and, finally, spend time in small group discussions and hands-on workshops. Notable past speakers include Jose Vazquez, winner of several teaching awards and a specialist in the development of technologies used to teach large lecture classrooms; and John Dawson, winner of an undergraduate teaching award at Appalachian State University.

South-Western Cengage Learning

South-Western, which operates as a part of Cengage Learning, is another publisher that sponsors the development of teaching workshops focused on economic education. The company will often invite instructors to presentations that include the explanation of new products, textbooks, and economic instructional techniques. These products are presented by employees of the publishing company and the instructional techniques are presented by experienced instructors who have found them to be effective.

South-Western also provides a great deal of support for teaching conferences run by universities and other institutions concerned with economic education. This support is typically in the form of monetary assistance for the event or funding speakers, provided in exchange for exposure at the event, such as a display table or advertisement in the event's program. South-Western has supported some of the workshops mentioned in this chapter, including the annual teaching workshop at the University of Kentucky and the Creative Teaching Ideas for your Basic Economics Course workshop presented by Florida State University in conjunction with the University of South Florida.

South-Western has also partnered with the Gulf Coast Economics Association to establish an annual economic teaching conference, complete with accepted papers presented by highly recognized and well-respected speakers. Recent speakers include Gregory Mankiw (author of the most widely used economic principles-level textbook) and John Taylor (winner of several teaching awards at Stanford University).

Federal Reserve

In addition to workshops hosted by universities and publishers, one can also attend instructional workshops developed by the Federal Reserve. For access to their educational information, refer to their website[7] which contains lesson plans, publications, and activities that can be used in your classroom. This site can also be used to navigate to economics education information contained at all 12 Federal Reserve banks.

STARTING YOUR OWN WORKSHOP: FUNDING AND ADVICE

Teaching workshops provide a forum for economics instructors to gather and share teaching ideas in the interest of furthering economic education and enhancing the teaching ability of fellow educators. Hosting such a workshop provides a variety of benefits that include improvement of the institution's own teachers' general instructional quality and demonstrating the institution's commitment to economic education and teaching excellence. For those interested in starting a teaching workshop, there are a number of avenues through which a college or department can obtain funding.[8] Most event organizers receive funding from publishers who pay travel expenses for presenters (who are usually authors of textbooks) or pay an exhibit fee. Several institutions have also received funding in the form of grants and donations from private organizations and foundations.[9] For example, the workshop that alternates between Florida State University and the University of South Florida is sponsored by the Stavros Center for Economics Education, which is located at both schools. The week-long instructional workshop at West Virginia University is financed through donations from private firms that also allow participants to take free factory tours as part of the program. Participant registration fees can also be useful in covering the costs of such workshops, although it is important to keep the fees low. Most of the workshops listed in this chapter have used a combination of publisher funding, private donations, and registration fees to supplement any department or college money that is used to finance these events.

Finally, we conclude with some advice to those who would like to initiate their own teaching conferences gathered from those who have successfully operated workshops. First, running a teaching workshop should be viewed as a service your institution is providing rather than an income-producing endeavor. Attempts to use high registration fees in an effort to turn a profit will likely result in a lack of attendance that will reduce the effectiveness of the workshop. If institutional financing of the workshop is problematic, consider partnering with surrounding institutions or collaborating with an already existing workshop. It is important to get support wherever it might exist, including having multiple publishing companies sponsor book exhibits. However, it is usually the case that one company will prefer to be the main sponsor.

In order to enhance the usefulness of a teaching workshop, it is important to obtain presenters who have creative (and if possible, entertaining) ideas that can be used right away in the classroom. These presenters do not have to be the most recognized names in the field, but rather those that have ideas that a fellow instructor can use to bring economic concepts to life. The more seamlessly these ideas can be integrated into any class and teaching style to enhance the quality of instruction, the more effective the conference tends to be. It is also valuable to provide materials that help instructors adapt what they learn at the workshop to their own classes. For example, the Florida State/ South Florida conference provides copies of the presentations to all of its participants and the West Virginia University teachers' course provides resources developed by the National Council for Economic Education to its attendees. Scheduling time for questions and discussion so that teachers in attendance can interact with presenters and each other will help them feel more comfortable in adopting these new techniques for their classroom. Finally, it is beneficial for a workshop to distribute an evaluation form to all participants so that these attendees can provide feedback about which parts of the workshop were most helpful. This feedback can be used to justify dedicated resources and improve the quality of future workshops and, thus, enhance the effectiveness of your event.

NOTES

1. Acknowledgements: The authors would like to thank Mary Ellen Benedict from Bowling Green State University, Patrick Litzinger from Robert Morris University, Peter Schuhmann from University of North Carolina Wilmington, Russell S. Sobel from West Virginia University, Kate Geraghty and Sarah Dorger from Worth Publishing, and John Carey from South-Western Cengage Learning for providing information about their experience with teaching workshops and economics education in general. Finally, the authors would like to thank all of our students who have likely had to suffer through some poor teaching ideas while we were in the pursuit of better ones.
2. For more information about experiments, see Chapter 7, "Classroom Experiments", in this volume.
3. For more information about cooperative learning, see Chapter 4, "Using Cooperative Learning Exercises in Economics" in this volume.
4. See also Chapter 13, "Incorporating Media and Response Systems in the Economics Classroom", in this volume.
5. While there is no single resource containing all important information for teaching strategies and techniques, the economic pedagogic portal, Starting Point: Teaching and Learning Economics, contains much of the recent information in this field. http://serc.carleton.edu/econ/index.html (Accessed 2 April 2011).
6. This chapter includes all workshops that responded to the questionnaire inquiring about their respective events. There are other workshops that were not included because representatives did not respond to the questionnaire.
7. www.federalreserveeducation.org (12 accessed June 2011).
8. Please see Goodman, Maier, and Moore (2003) for additional information regarding the funding of a teaching workshop.
9. For more information about private and public sources of funding for economic education related activities, see Chapter 74, "Private, Corporate and Government Funding for Economic Education", in this volume.

REFERENCES

Becker, W. E. and M. Watts (1996), "Chalk and talk: A national survey on teaching undergraduates economics", *American Economic Review*, **86** (May), 448–53.

Becker, W. E. and M. Watts (1998), *Teaching Economics to Undergraduates: Alternatives to Chalk and Talk*, Cheltenham, UK and Lyme, USA: Edward Elgar.

Becker, W. E. and M. Watts (2000), "Teaching economics: What it was, is and could be", in W. E. Becker and M. Watts (eds), *Teaching Economics to Undergraduates: Alternatives to Chalk and Talk*, Cheltenham, UK and Northampton, MA, USA: Edward Elgar, pp. 1–10.

Becker, W. E. and M. Watts (2001), "Teaching economics at the start of the 21st century: Still chalk-and-talk", *American Economic Review,* **96** (May), 446–51.

Becker, W. E., M. Watts and S. R. Becker (2006), *Teaching Economics: More Alternatives to Chalk and Talk,* Cheltenham, UK and Northampton, MA, USA: Edward Elgar.

Delemeester, G. and J. Brauer (2000), "Games economists play: Noncomputerized classroom games", *The Journal of Economic Education,* **31** (4) (Fall), 406.

Frank, Robert H. (2007), *The Economic Naturalist: In Search of Explanations for Everyday Enigmas*, New York, NY: Basic Books.

Goodman, R. J., M. Maier and R. L. Moore (2003), "Regional workshops to improve the teaching skills of economics faculty", *American Economic Review,* **93** (2), (May), 460–62.

Hall, J. (2005), "Homer economicus: Using the Simpsons to teach economics", *Journal of Private Enterprise,* **20** (2), (Spring), 165–76.

Hall, J., R. Lawson and D. Mateer (2008), "From ABBA to Zeppelin, Led: Using music to teach economics", *Journal of Economic Education,* **39** (1), (Winter), 107.

Leet, D. and S. Houser (2003), "Economics goes to Hollywood: Using classic films and documentaries to create an undergraduate economics course", *Journal of Economic Education,* **34** (Fall), 326–32.

Mateer, D. (2005), *Economics in the Movies,* Mason, OH: South-Western Publishing.

Sexton, R. L. (2006), "Using short movie and television clips in the economics principles class", *The Journal of Economics Education,* **37** (Fall), 406–17.

Index

Abraham, K.G. 698
absenteeism 155–6, 334
Acemoglu, D. 444, 450, 516, 540, 604
active learning/active-learning techniques
    40–43, 45, 48, 52, 58, 63, 80–81, 90, 110,
    116, 118, 121, 123, 165, 167, 191, 199, 267,
    323, 331, 395, 494, 595, 708, 711, 730, 740,
    776, 813
Adams, W. 135
Aerni, A.L. 207, 219, 220, 242
Agarwal, R. 12, 330
Agency for Instructional Television/
    Technology 18, 795
Aghion, P. 514
Akerlof, G.A. 553
Alauddin, M. 774
Albelda, R. 431, 641, 643, 645
Albouy, D.Y. 450
Alden, D. 483
Algood, S. 792
Ali, R. 161
all-but-dissertation (ABD) students 748
Allen, B. 716
Allen, D. 388
Allen, M.J. 179
Allen, R. 536, 537, 539
Allen, R.G.D. 334
Allen, T.D. 709
Allgood, S. 12, 246, 268, 286, 323
Alonso, W. 687
Alston, R.M. 316, 342
Alter, G. 538
American Colleges, Association of 11, 428, 430
American Colleges and Universities,
    Association of (AAC&U) 428, 430
    Liberal Education and America's Promise
        (LEAP) 428, 430
American economic history 525–32
    course objectives for 525–6
    economic reasoning and methods for 526–9
        using graphs 527–9
    finding and using quantitative data 529–30
    of two centuries covered in one semester
        531–2
American Economics Association (AEA) (and)
    3–14, 717–18, 805
    Ad Hoc Committee on Economics in
        Teacher Education 4–5

collection of economics degree data 723–5
Committee on Economic Education (CEE)
    see main entry
Committee on the Status of Minority
    Groups in the Economics Profession
    (CSMGEP) 712, 748
Committee on the Status of Women in
    the Economics Profession (CSWEP)
    711–12, 748
encouraging research in economics
    education 11–12
expanding college and university teacher
    training activities 12–13
First Standing Committee on Economic
    Education 4–5
mentoring programs 707, 711–12
    see also mentoring
National Task Force on Economic
    Education 4, 5–8, 259, 262, 270
    Economic Education in the Schools 6
    *Study Materials for Economic Education
        in the Schools* 6, 7
    The Test of Economic Understanding 7
other economic education activities 13–14
Pipeline Program 749
Present Standing Committee on Economic
    Education (CEE): G.L. Bach years 8
Present Standing Committee on Economic
    Education (CEE): Post-Bach era 10
Resources for Economists on the Internet
    168
studies of the undergraduate economics
    major 11
Taylor and Bowen Committees 3–4
The Teaching of Undergraduate Economics
    (1950) 285
Test of Understanding in College Economics
    (TUCE) *see main entry*
Universal Academic Questionnaire 723, 748
see also journals; United States of America
    (USA)
American Economy Television Course 6–7
American elementary and secondary schools
    259–72
    assessment of economic education in 268–70
        and National Assessment of Educational
            Progress (NAEP) 268–70
    curriculum in 260–68